SANSKRIT TEACH

All-in-One

With Transliteration

A SYSTEMATIC TEACHING AND SELF-LEARNING TOOL

Prof. Ratnakar Narale

Ratnakar
PUSTAK BHARATI
BOOKS-INDIA

Author : **Dr. Ratnakar Narale,** Ph.D (IIT), Ph.D. (Kalidas Sanskrit Univ.)
Prof. Hindi, Ryerson University, Toronto.
web : www.books-india.com * email : books.india.books@gmail.com

Title : **Sanskrit Teacher,** ***All-in-One, With Transliteration***
Teach or Learn to Read, Write, Understand, Speak and Think Sanskrit; with main emphasis on empowering the readers to understand and enjoy the precious wealth of knowledge that exists in the Sanskrit Shlokas.

In addition to the Sanskrit Script, this unique book is *Transliterated* for the English readers. This giant 700 page All-in-One book (37 Chapters + 10 large Appendices) is for all levels of Sanskrit Self Learning. It is a fine Sanskrit Tutor as well as a Complete Reference Manual for a novice as well as an expert. The book begins with basic Sanskrit Alphabet and progresses step-by-step to encompass every aspect of Sanskrit grammar and its usage that one will not find in any other book. It even has some rare topics that one may not find elsewhere. It is a treasure of new ideas, techniques, information and reference material. It is rich with examples, exercises and an important chapter of "**Answers** to all the Exercises."

Published by :
Pustak Bharati (Books-India),
Division of PC PLUS Ltd.
Web : www.books-india.com
Email : books.india.books@gmail.com

ISBN 978-1-897416-54-9
90000
9 781897 416549

ISBN 978-1-897416-54-9

Dedicated to

My Caring Wife
Sunita Narale
and my Loving Grandchildren
Samay, Sahas, Saanjh, Saaya Narale

A PRAYER
TO THE GODDESS OF LEARNING
शारदावन्दना

शारदा सदा स्मरणीया । śāradā sadā smaraṇīyā
स्वरदा वरदा स्तवनीया । svaradā varadā stavaṇīyā
भारतजननी नमनीया । bhārata jananī namanīyā
संस्कृतवाणी श्रवणीया । saṁskṛt vānī śravaṇīyā

अनुकम्पा हृदि धरणीया । anukampā hṛdi dharaṇīyā
सेवा मनसा करणीया । sevā manasā karaṇīyā
शारदा सदा स्मरणीया । śāradā sadā smaraṇīyā
स्वरदा वरदा स्तवनीया । svaradā varadā stavaṇīyā

नहि सुखशय्या शयनीया। nahi sukhaśaiyyā śayanīyā
न नीचचिन्ता चयनीया । na nīća-ćintā ćayanīyā
रज:कामना शमनीया । rajaḥ-kāmanā śamanīyā
तमोवासना दमनीया । tamo-vāsanā damanīyā

अनुकम्पा हृदि धरणीया । anukampā hṛdi dharaṇīyā
सेवा मनसा करणीया । sevā manasā karaṇīyā
शारदा सदा स्मरणीया । śāradā sadā smaraṇīyā
स्वरदा वरदा स्तवनीया । svaradā varadā stavaṇīyā

सततसुबुद्धिर्धरणीया । satata-subuddhir-dharaṇīyā
मानसशुद्धिर्वरणीया । mānasa-śuddhir-varaṇīyā
शुभा सरणिरनुसरणीया । śubhā saraṇi-ranusaraṇīyā
सत्सङ्गतिरभिलषणीया । sat-saṅgati-rabhilaṣaṇīyā
अनुकम्पा हृदि धरणीया । anukampā hṛdi dharaṇīyā
सेवा मनसा करणीया । sevā manasā karaṇīyā
शारदा सदा स्मरणीया । śāradā sadā smaraṇīyā
स्वरदा वरदा स्तवनीया । svaradā varadā stavaṇīyā

जातिकुप्रथा त्यजनीया । jāti-kuprathā tyajanīyā
बन्धुभावना भजनीया । bandhu-bhāvanā bhajanīyā
अखिलसङ्घता करणीया । akhila-saṅghatā karaṇīyā
विश्वे समता भरणीया । viśve samatā bharaṇīyā

अनुकम्पा हृदि धरणीया । anukampā hṛdi dharaṇīyā
सेवा मनसा करणीया । sevā manasā karaṇīyā
शारदा सदा स्मरणीया । śāradā sadā smaraṇīyā
स्वरदा वरदा स्तवनीया । svaradā varadā stavaṇīyā

प्रमत्तकुमतिर्दहनीया । pramatta-kumatir-dahanīyā
आगतहानिस्सहनीया । āgata-hāni-ssahanīyā
प्रजाप्रतिष्ठा वहनीया । prajā-pratiṣṭhā-vahanīyā
मया प्रतिज्ञा ग्रहणीया । mayā pratijña grahanīyā

अनुकम्पा हृदि धरणीया । anukampā hṛdi dharaṇīyā
सेवा मनसा करणीया । sevā manasā karaṇīyā
शारदा सदा स्मरणीया । śāradā sadā smaraṇīyā
स्वरदा वरदा स्तवनीया । svaradā varadā stavaṇīyā

–रत्नाकर:

INDEX

anukramaṇikā
अनुक्रमणिका ।

BOOK 2
UNDERSTAND SANSKRIT, EASY WAY

BOOK 3
SPEAK SANSKRIT

APPENDICES :

INTRODUCTION

Hari Om. The beauty and strength of this book is its new 'methodology,' which is unique in many respects. To a large extent the significant factor in the approach and structure of this book has been the input from the students regarding their needs and difficulties over number of years.

Accordingly, while putting this book together, first consideration is given to the fact that learners may not know the Devanāgarī script if they came from the countries outside India or from the provinces of India where Hindi or Marathi is not taught. Thus, for such fresh learners, the book begins with the basic Devanāgarī alphabet and covers every aspect a reader may need to learn the Devanagari script properly. Eight full lessons are devoted to teach simple characters and eight more sections to the compound characters. Section 8.2 is then designed to digest this basic purpose properly. After this, there are eight additional reading lessons to confirm that the students have learned Devanagari fully well, before they touch any grammatical topic. Further more, Sanskrit words are *English transliterated* with proper *diacritical* marks and the English meaning of each Sanskrit word is provided for the help of new readers. The readers who have learned Sanskrit, Hindi or Marathi may choose to advance to Lesson 10.

Unique is my proven scientific method of teaching Sanskrit language, even to absolutely new learners. In this new technique, purposefully, the consonants are discussed first, followed by the vowels. Within the consonants, the characters are grouped into sets based on their shapes, and not on their alphabetical order as always done. With this novel way, it is our experience that even the absolutely new learners learn to read Devanagarī Sanskrit as well as its Roman transliteration within a very short time of only few hours. Unique charts are key tools in this book. One of them you will find on the back cover of this book, in the form of the 'Chart of Sanskrit Alphabet.' Many of our students colour-copy this chart in a big size and pin it on a wall as a beautiful quick reference.

Even though the book progresses slowly, without jumping ahead on what is taught further, it covers all aspects of the Sanskrit grammar required by even the advanced learners. In addition, at after every step, the material covered up to that point is cumulatively reviewed under a novel entry called, '**what we have learned so far**.' This **cumulative learning** is one of the beautiful aspects of this book.

Another significant thing in this methodology is the care to make sure that, the material being discussed on any stage and page deals ONLY with the information covered in previous pages, a very simple principle but most uncommon. For this substantial purpose, you will notice that the 'tenses' are discussed cumulatively in eight lessons without mixing with the 'cases' prematurely. After this, the cases are discussed in eight subsequent sections, now together with the use of the tenses learned in the previous lessons. While giving examples, generally an example that appears first time in the Gita is preferred.

There are many unique techniques in this book, specially devised as easy but effective tools. Section 3.4 is a unique chart, depicting the *māheśvarāṇi sūtrāṇi.* Section 10.1 is a handy guide showing the complete chart of compound vowels (स्वरसन्धि), which is followed by full exemplification. Section 10.4 is a unique and simple one-page flowchart of Ten Golden Rules on compounding with *visarga* (विसर्गसन्धि), designed to make it easy, which otherwise with the intricate and conflicting rules, makes Sanskrit learning more difficult than it is. Section 22.2 is another unique flow chart to solve the dilemma of 'which tense to use?' from the available ten tenses and moods (लकारा:). Appendix 6 is similar important tool titled 'which verb to use?' in a particular context from the available 2000 verbs.

While discuussing the tenses in a logical order, first the fundamental aspects of person, number and gender are clarified, followed by a topic on nouns including a dictionary. After setting up such a background, the ten tenses (लकारा:) are discussed one at time, and in a cumulative manner, giving a chart of suffixes and a chart of application with each tense. Wherever possible, at least one classical example is given in addition to other examples, in order to gradually familiarize the learners to the beautiful world of *shlokas* and *suhbashitas.*

All ten (eleven) classes (गणा:) of the verbs are then individually explained with their conjugational charts with ten tenses (लकारा:) and other important details. In each case, the special verbs are specifically explained, for the reader to be aware. The study of tenses is concluded with a unique flowchart called 'which tense to use,' which walks you to the appropriate tense for any desired usage.

While teaching the cases (विभक्ति), eight very unique charts (sections 25.1-25.8) are given for the eight cases, including the Vocative, with twenty-five most common substantives. They form a very handy tool for all the learners, new and old. They form an uncommon but valuable aid for finding the root word in a given declined word, as well as for comparing the declensions within and among the Cases.

Included in this book are the Dictionary of nouns, Pictorial dictionary of popular subjects, Dictionary adverbs and a gigantic Dictionary of 2000 verb roots with their common conjugations, past participle and other derivatives, space permitting. In this book, section 34.10 is another uncommon topic on 'Parsing and Analysis' of Sanskrit sentences. The insight to this aspect of learning galvanizes the ability of a learner to look closely and carefully, an attitude necessary to develop for understanding and fathoming the Sanskrit classical literature.

The 225 pages of the helpful Appendix of this book makes it a true learners-teachers' handbook, like no other Sanskrit teaching book does. Besides the immense Dictionary of 2000 verbs, this appendix has Charts of 810 conjugations of verb √भू given in Sanskrit and English transliteration, 81 charts of case declensions of nouns, pronouns and numerical adjectives, charts of tense for 80 common verbs, a dictionary of 'which verb to use,' a handy chart of declinable and indeclinable participles, a section on breakdown, a transliteration and meaning of the 116 Sanskrit verses quoted in the book, and many other important things.

The last but quite important Appendix is the 'Answers to the Exercises.' Without this, the self learners would have been left in the dark, annoyed and helpless, wondering at each question, '**Did I Get it Right**?' and '**Did I Pronounce it Correctly**?' To me, a book is not a self-learning tool, unless the answers to the questions are provided. With this principle in mind, the book is adorned with virtually hundreds of examples, with answers in Sanskrit and its English transliteration. Therefore, please treat all 'Examples' as Exercises with answers.
A glossary of definitions could have been added in the Appendix, but as all the terms are defined at their proper places, it was deemed better to avoid the repetition. The book is filled with hundreds of examples, notes, definitions, conversational dialogues and quotes from the glorious Sanskrit literature.

It is the glorious literature written by the immortal poets that attracts the learners to the Sanskrit language. It is the profound but poetic sweetness and the melodic nature of the *Anuṣṭubha* meter of the Sanskrit language that makes its learning so very interesting. It is its unique chemical, mathematical and digital nature, well developed system of grammar, intricate compounding style and highly flexible character of composition that makes Sanskrit writings so original to study and enjoy. It is the richest word-power of Sanskrit that makes its writings extremely ornate, splendid and amazing.

Sanskrit is by far the most poetic and florid language in the world, which is exemplified in this book with a short section on it. On these strengths Sanskrit has survived for thousands of years and on the way has given birth to many wonderful cultures and numerous great languages. Naturally, therefore, explaining Sanskrit grammar with numerous examples, along with copious use of the appropriate *Shlokas*, spontaneously became natural in this book.

Sanskrit has been found by various research scholars to be very closely related to several European languages, quite possibly (being older) a parent to them. The rich Tamil language did not originate from Sanskrit, but a strong influence of Sanskrit is an unmistakable feature in Tamil language. In our Sanskrit classes, the students speaking Tamil and the European languages find it educational to associate the words and grammatical aspects of their languages with Sanskrit and to trace their correlation. In this book specific *Shlokas* and examples have been subtly selected that contain such Sanskrit words which possess a relation with these languages.

It can not be over emphasized that for learning Sanskrit, a proper understanding of its grammatical aspects is essential, before trying to speak it. Otherwise, you have to memorize model sentences, without really knowing the basics, a poor habit for the new learners. The present text is put together to deliver full benefit in return for the efforts, time and resources spent by the learners. You may learn Sanskrit in 30 days or even less, if you learn by heart 'the pet sentences' without knowing how to make them on your own, but this way you will never be able to understand a given *shloka*. Therefore, the objective of this book is to prepare you to make your own required sentences by understanding the basics. This way you will be able to understand any given *shloka* or Sanskrit text on your own.

It is important to appreciate why a particular word is used, at any particular place, in a given *shloka*, when several other words could have been equally suitable. One must take a close look at the structure of the *anuṣṭubha* meter. A short explanation is given in the next section to serve this substantial purpose. With the same objective, simplifications and meanings of verses is given in the Appendix. While this book is a 'Teach Yourself Manual,' it is also a good tool for teachers of Sanskrit language. I hope that you will follow this material step-by-step. I urge you to proceed to next page when previous page is understood. Follow the book with this technique and your success in learning Sanskrit will be assured.

I would like to thank Mr. J.C. Sharda, Mr. Sunil Narale and all others who have encouraged and helped me in the progress of this book. I must thank Dr. Penna Madhusudan, Prof. of Sanskrit, K.K. Sanskrit University, Nagpur and Dr. Pankaja Ghai, Prof. of Sanskrit, Lady Shriram College, New Delhi, for examining the MS. Thanks are due to Hindu Institute of Learning, Toronto, and the Sanskrit Bharati, Vidya Bharati and Kavikulaguru Kalidas Sanskrit University of India for being my undiminishing inspiration.

I have tried to make this book easy, unique and useful as possible. Nevertheless, I beg the readers to forgive me for any errors, omissions or imperfections that they may find. I would welcome their suggestions with a gratitude. I hope the new as well as the learned readers, will find this book interesting and useful. ॐ तत् सत् ।

-Ratnakar

The Anuṣṭubha Metre

The earliest and most important work on the Saṁskṛt prosody is the *Piṅgala-ćhanda-śāstra.* Most popular among the metres used for the *śloka*s of the Saṁskṛt epics, such as Rāmayaṇa and Mahābhārata, is the celebrated *anuṣṭubh* metre. In general a meter with 32 syllables is *anuṣṭubh* metre.

For their lyrical value and in order to maintain uniformity in this book, mostly the verses composed in the *anuṣṭubh* metre are included in this book. There are many types of the *anuṣṭubh* metre, however, the one that is used in the composition of the Saṁskṛt *śloka*s (√*ślok,* to praise in verses) is defined as follows by the author of this book, itself written in the *anuṣṭubh* metre.

संस्कृतश्लोकः

'श्लोके' षष्ठं सदा दीर्घं लघु च पञ्चमं तथा ।
अक्षरं सप्तमं दीर्घं तृतीये प्रथमे पदे ।।
चतुष्पादस्य श्रीयुक्तो वाल्मीकिकविना कृतः ।
द्वात्रिंशद्वर्णयुक्तो हि छन्दोऽनुष्टुभ् स कथ्यते ।।

रत्नाकरः

The above definition says that in a *śloka* (verse), there are four quarters (*pāda*), each with eight syllables. The fifth syllable of each quarter should be short (*laghu*), the sixth long (*dīrhga*), and the seventh alternately long and short in the odd and even quarters. e.g. a classical example (गीता : 1.1)

धर्मक्षेत्रे कुरुक्षेत्रे समवेता युयुत्सवः ।
मामकाः पाण्डवाश्चैव किमकुर्वत संजय ।।

BOOK 1

LEARN TO READ & WRITE SANSKRIT

पठन्तु संस्कृतम्। लिखन्तु संस्कृतम्।

paṭhantu saṁskṛtam, likhantu saṁskṛtam.

It is hoped that, in order to receive full benefit of this work, you will follow this material step-by-step and page by page. Make sure that you understand all examples given at each step of this learning and teaching tool. Please note that the leatners are advised to consider the 'examples' given with each lesson as an 'exercise,' to see if they can translate the examples into Sanskrit themselves, before reading the Sanskrit translation or the English transliteration provided with each example. With this reason the exercises are kept at minimum, in order to avoid repetition in the book.

DEVANAGARI ALPHABET देवनागरी वर्णमाला

अ a	आ ā (ा)	इ i (ि)	ई ī (ी)	उ u (ु)	ऊ ū (ू)	ऋ ṛ (ृ)
ए e (े)	ऐ ai (ै)	ओ o (ो)	औ au (ौ)	अं ṁ (ं)	अँ m̐ (ँ)	अः ḥ (ः)

क ka (क्)	ख kha (ख्)	ग ga (ग्)	घ gha (घ्)	ङ ṅa (ङ्)
च ća (च्)	छ ćha (छ्)	ज ja (ज्)	झ jha (झ्)	ञ ña (ञ्)
ट ṭa (ट्)	ठ ṭha (ठ्)	ड ḍa (ड्)	ढ ḍha (ढ्)	ण ṇa (ण्)
त ta (त्)	थ tha (थ्)	द da (द्)	ध dha (ध्)	न na (न्)
प pa (प्)	फ pha (फ्)	ब ba (ब्)	भ bha (भ्)	म ma (म्)
य ya (य्)	र ra (र्)	ल la (ल्)	व va (व्)	श śa (श्)
	ष ṣa (ष्)	स sa (स्)	ह ha (ह्)	
	क्ष kṣa (क्ष्)	त्र tra (त्र्)	ज्ञ gya (ज्ञ्)	

© Copyright ISBN 0-97322557-7-7 Designed by : Ratnakar Narale

० 0	१ 1	२ 2	३ 3	४ 4	५ 5	६ 6	७ 7	८ 8	९ 9

LESSON 1

Prathamaḥ abhyāsaḥ प्रथमः अभ्यासः ।

THE SANSKRIT ALPHABET

saṁskṛta-varṇamālā संस्कृतवर्णमाला ।

Vowels (*svarāḥ* स्वराः)

अ	आ	इ	ई	उ	ऊ	ऋ	ॠ	ऌ	ॡ	ए	ऐ	ओ	औ	अं	अः
a	ā	i	ī	u	ū	ṛ	ṛ́	ḷ	ḷ́	e	ai	o	au	ṁ	ḥ:

Consonants (*vyañjanāni* व्यञ्जनानि)

क	ख	ग	घ	ङ	the Gutterals
ka	kha	ga	gha	ṅa	
च	छ	ज	झ	ञ	the Palatals
ća	ćha	ja	jha	ña	
ट	ठ	ड	ढ	ण	the Cerebrals
ṭa	ṭha	ḍa	ḍha	ṇa	
त	थ	द	ध	न	the Dentals
ta	tha	da	dha	na	
प	फ	ब	भ	म	the Labials
pa	pha	ba	bha	ma	

**

य	र	ल	व	श	ष	स	ह	ळ *
ya	ra	la	va	śa	ṣa	sa	ha	ḷa

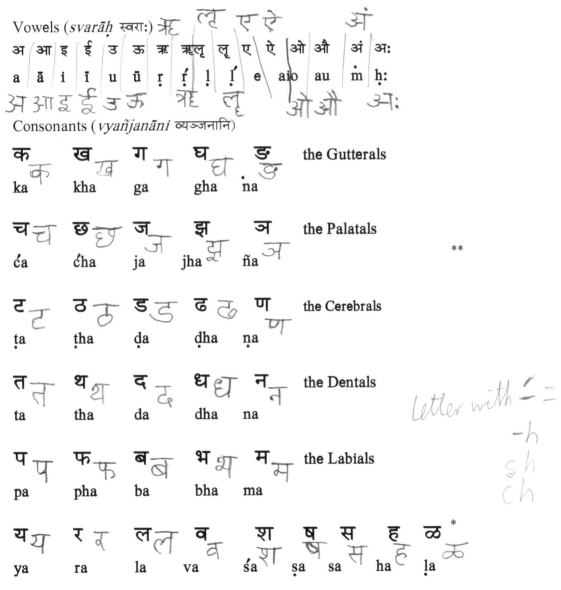

NOTES :

* Character ळ (ḷa) comes in the Vedas e.g. Rigveda 1.1 (अग्निमीळे पुरोहितम्)

** In this book, the pronunciation of Sanskrit character *'ch'* is transliterated as ć in order to distinguish it from the common English character c (which = k).

e.g. The car moves. कारयानं चलति *cāryānaṁ ćalati (cāryānaṁ calati* = कारयानं कलति or चारयानं चलति *).*

PRONUNCIATIONS:

(1) GUTTURALS : The consonants from k-class (k, kh, g, gh, ṅ) and (h) are pronounced by touching the hind part of the tongue to the THROAT (Gutter).

(2) PALATALS : The consonants from ć-class (ć, ćh, j, jh, ñ) and (i, ī, y, ś) are pronounced by touching the middle part of the tongue to the middle roof of the mouth i.e. the PALATE.

(3) CEREBRALS : The consonants from ṭ-class (ṭ, ṭh, ḍ, ḍh, ṇ) and (ṛ, ṝ, r, ṣ) are pronounced by momentarily touching tip of the tongue against roof of the mouth i.e. the CEREBRUM.

(4) DENTALS : The consonants from t-class (t, th, d, dh, n) aand (lṛ, lṝ, l, s) are pronounced by touching tip of the tongue against the base of the TEETH.

(5) LABIALS : The consonants from p-class (p, ph, b, bh, m) and (u, ū, v) are pronounced by touchning the LIPS together.

LESSON 2

dvitīyaḥ abhyāsaḥ द्वितीयः अभ्यासः ।

Learn to Pronounce Sanskrit Characters

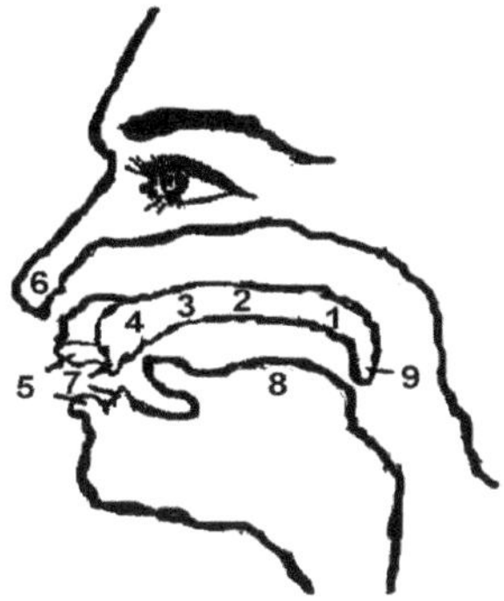

(1) Guttural	कण्ठ्य	*(kaṇṭhya)*	=	with throat
(2) Cerebral	मूर्धन्य	*(mūrdhanya)*	=	with cerebrum
(3) Palatal	तालव्य	*(tālavya)*	=	with palate
(4) Dental	दन्त्य	*(dantya)*	=	with teeth
(5) Labial	ओष्ठ्य	*(oṣṭhya)*	=	with lips
(6) Nasal	अनुनासिक	*(anunāsik)*	=	with nose

(1) THE **VOWELS :**

Vowel	Stands for	Sounds like	As in	Pronunciation
a	(अ)	A	American	Guttural
ā	(आ)	a	car	Guttural
i	(इ)	I	India	Palatal
ī	(ई)	ee	peel	Palatal
u	(उ)	u	pull	Labial
ū	(ऊ)	oo	pool	Labial

Vowel	Stands for	Sounds like	As in	Pronunciation
ṛ	(ऋ)	ri, ru	ring, crucial	Cerebral
ṛ́	(ॠ)	rī, rū		Cerebral
lṛ	(ऌ)	lri, lru		Dental
lṛ́	(ॡ)	lrī, lrū		Dental (this character is not in Paṇini)
e	(ए)	e, ay	grey, Ray	Guttural+Palatal
ai	(ऐ)	ai	aisle	Guttural+Palatal
o	(ओ)	o	go	Guttural+Labial
au	(औ)	au	gauge	Guttural+Labial

(2) THE **SEMIVOWELS** :

m̃	(अं)	ã	nasal
ḥ:	(अः)	half-h	breath

(3) THE **CONSONANTS** :

Consonant	Stands for	Sounds like	As in	Pronunciation
k	(क्)	k	kit	Guttural
kh	(ख्)	kh	khyber	Guttural
g	(ग्)	g	god	Guttural
gh	(घ्)	gh	ghost	Guttural
ṅ	(ङ्)	n	ring	Guttural
ć, c	(च्)	ch	rich	Palatal
ćh	(छ्)	chh	ć with breath	Palatal
j	(ज्)	j	jug	Palatal
jh	(झ्)	dgeh, z	hedgehop, zoo	Palatal
ñ	(ञ्)	n	hinge	Palatal

Consonant	Stands for	Sounds like	As in	Pronunciation
ṭ	(ट्)	t	cuṭ	Cerebral
ṭh	(ठ्)	th	ṭ with breath	Cerebral
ḍ	(ड्)	d	red	Cerebral
ḍh	(ढ्)	dh	adhere	Cerebral
ṇ	(ण्)	n	band	Cerebral
t	(त्)	t	(soft t)	Dental
th	(थ्)	th	thunder	Dental
d	(द्)	th	other	Dental
dh	(ध्)	dh	buddha	Dental
n	(न्)	n	no	Dental
p	(प्)	p	cup	Labial
ph	(फ्)	ph, f	photo	Labial
b	(ब्)	b	rub	Labial
bh	(भ्)	bh	abhore	Labial
m	(म्)	m	mug	Labial
y	(य्)	y	yes	Palatal
r	(र्)	r	rub	Cerebral
l	(ऌ, ल्)	l	love	Dental
v	(व्)	v, w	wave	Dental + Labial
ś	(श्)	sh	shoot	Palatal
ṣ	(ष्)	sh	should	Cerebral
s	(स्)	s	sun	Dental
h	(ह्)	h	hug	Guttural
ḷ	(ळ्)	soft l		Cerebral

LESSON 3

tṛtīyaḥ abhyāsaḥ तृतीय: अभ्यास: ।

WRITING SANSKRIT WORDS

PRACTICING SIMPLE CONSONANTS

asaṁyukta-varṇānām abhyāsaḥ असंयुक्तवर्णानाम् अभ्यास: ।

Study the order of the Sanskrit consonants given in Lesson 1, and then do the following exercises. Uniquely in this book, the characters are grouped according to their shapes, and not according to their usual aplhabetical order. For, we have observed that, with this novel way it is easy for a new learner to co-relate and remember the *Sanskrit* characters.

RULE : In order to develop a good writing style and skill, write each part of each character from left to right and from top to bottom. For example - for writing the letter व, first write the oval of ठ. Then write the vertical bar by starting it at the top and drawing it downward to bottom.

All Sanskrit **letters and words** have a line on top to group the characters into a words. Follow this rule for each letter carefully and consistently.

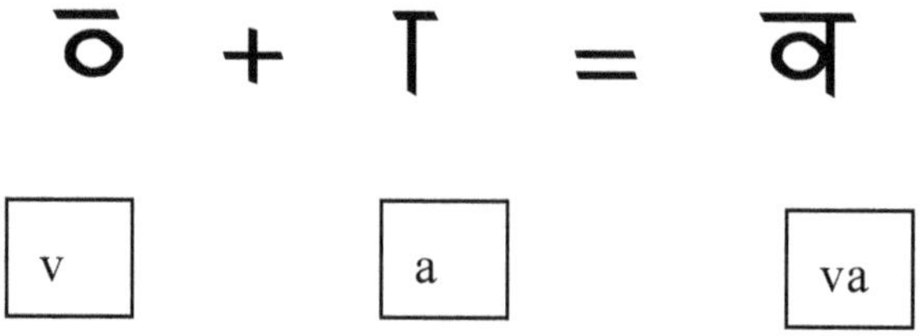

3.1 Letters : व *va (wa),* ब *ba,* क *ka*

ठ व   ब ब   ठ व क

v (w) → va (wa)   b → ba   v → va → ka

vana (forest)

baka बक (stork)

kamala (lotus)

EXERCISE 3 : Only on what we have learned so far. Write the following in Sanskrit :

1. ka, ba, ka 2. ba, va, ba 3. va, ka, ba 4. ba, va, ka 5. ka, va, ba 6. va, ba, ka

7. क, ब, व 8. कक, कब, कव 9. बब, बक, बव

10 वव, वक, वब 11 ककक, कबव, कवब 12 वबक, बकव

3.2 Letters : प *pa,* ष *ṣa,* फ *pha (fa),* ण *ṇa*

ट प   ठ ष   ट प फ   ए ण

p → pa   ṣ → ṣa   p → pa → pha, fa   ṇ → ṇa

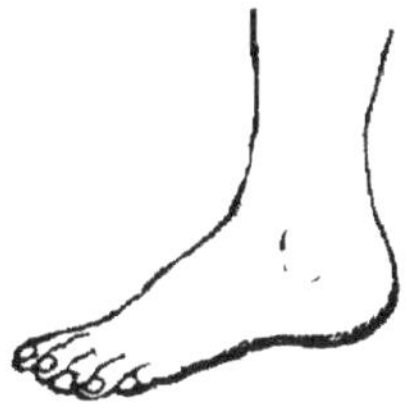

pada (foot)

viṣa (poison)

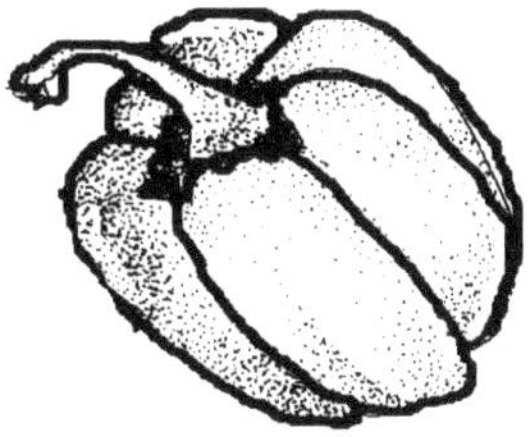

fal, phal (fruit)

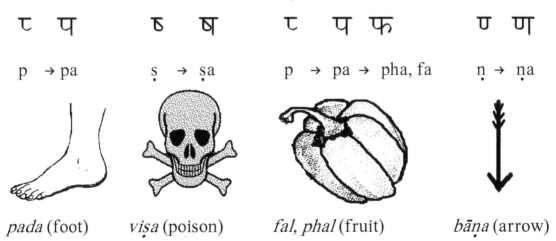

bāṇa (arrow)

EXERCISE 4 : Only on what we have learned so far. Write the following in Sanskrit :

1. pa, pha　　2. pha, ba　　3. va, pa, ka　　4. pa, ṣa, ṇa　　5. pha, ṣa, pa
6. ba, pa, pha

7. ष, प, फ　　8. क, ण, फ, व　　9. ब, ण　10. कण, बब, कप, फण, बव, कब, णण, षण, षप, बफ, कफ, पष, बक, वक, पक, बफ, वफ, पब, वण, बष, णष, पव, कव

3.3

Letters : त *ta,* न *na,* ग *ga,* म *ma,* भ *bha*

त त　　न न　　ग ग　　म म　　भ भ

t → ta　　n → na　　g → ga　　m → ma　　bh → bha

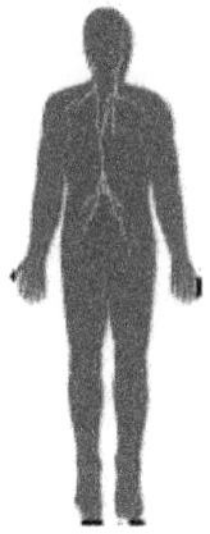

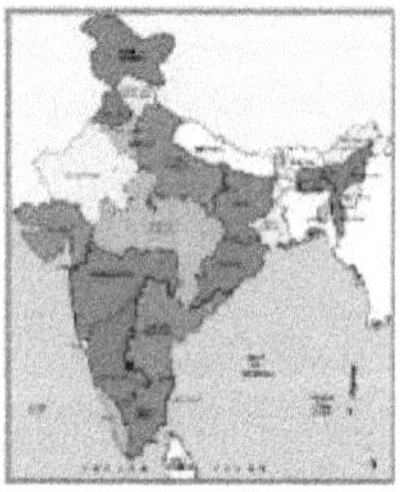

tanu (body)　*nara* (man)　*gaja* (elephant)　*mīna* (fish) *bhārata* (India)

EXERCISE 5 : Only on what we have learned so far. Write the following in Sanskrit :

(A) 1. ma, bha　2. bha, ga　3. ma, na　4. ka, ta, ga　5. va, ṣa　6. pa, na

(B) 1. त, न, भ　2. म, भ, न, त　3. ग, त, क, ब　4. मन (mind), नग (mountain), कण (particle), वन (forest), गत (gone), तम (darkness), बक (stork), मत (opinion), गगन (sky), पतन (downfall)

3.4 Letters : च *ća,* ज *ja,* ञ *ña,* ल or ल *la*

च च ज ज ञ ञ ल ल (ल)

ć (ch)→ ća (cha) j → ja ñ → ña l → la (la)

chaṭikā (sparrow)

jagat जगत् (world)

lūtā (spider)

EXERCISE 6 : Only on what we have learned so far. Write the following in Sanskrit

1. ka, ća, ṇa, pa 2. la, ma, ja, ta 3. bha, pha, ṣa 4. mana, manana 5. kaṇa, vana 6. labha, ćala 7. ज, च, ञ 8. ल, ज, च 9. ल, ल 10. जलज, चपल 11. जल, चल 10 लवण.

(WORDS : मन *mind,* मनन *meditation,* कण *particle,* वन *forest,* लभ *get,* चल *moving,* जलज *water-born,* चपल *quick,* जल *water,* लवण salt)

3.5

Letters : र *ra,* स *sa,* ख *kha,* श *śa*

र स स ख ख श श

ra s → sa kh → kha ś → śa

kara कर (hand)

sumana (flower)

khaga खग (bird)

śaśak शशक (Rabbit)

EXERCISE 7: Only on what we have learned so far. Read and write in Sanskrit :

1. ća, ja, la 2 ña, ja, ća 3. la, ća, ja 4. sa, kha, ra 5. sa, śa, kha 6. ra, sa, śa

7. च, ज, ञ, ल 8. र, स, ख, श 9. चल, जल, जन 10. कलश, चरण, रस, शर, रस, सम, फल, कमल, सरल, भरत 11. चणक, चरम, समर, कण, परम, चपल, पत, नर 12. नभ, नरक, जल, खल, शर, पर, सम, चल, शरण, सबल ।

(for meanings of the words, see Answers in Appendix 10)

3.6

Letters : घ *gha,* ध *dha,* छ *ćha*

घ् घ ध् ध छ

gh → gha dh → dha ćha

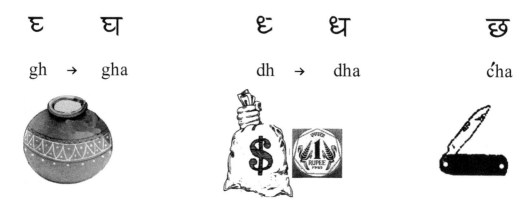

ghaṭa (pot) *dhana* (wealth) *ćhurikā* (knife)

EXERCISE 8 : Only on what we have learned so far. Read and witer in Sanskrit :

1. ća, ga, ćha 2. na, ća, ma, ćha 3. bha, ća, gha 4. घ, ध, न, ग 5. छ, च, भ, त 6. म, छ, भ, च 7. नग, घन, धन 8. मनन, गत 9. मम, वचन, कनक 10. छल, वध, धवल, मरण, वमन, खर, बल, पल, फल, मल ।

(for meanings of the words, see Answers in Appendix 10)

3.7 Letters : य *ya,* थ *tha;* क्ष *kṣa,* ज्ञ *jña*

ꣳ य   ꣳ थ

y → y a   th → tha

yajña (sacrifice)

ratha रथ (chariot)

क्ष् क्ष   ज्ञ् ज्ञ

kṣ → kṣa   jñ → jña

EXERCISE 9 : Only on what we have learned so far. Write the following in Sanskrit :

(A) 1. ćha, gha, dha 2. dha, gha 3. ya, tha 4. kṣa, jña 5. gha, jña, ya, tha 6. jña, dha, tha, gha.

(B) 1. घ, ध, छ 2. य, थ 3. क्ष, ज्ञ 4. क्षय, शर, यक्ष5. यज्ञ, रथ, धन 6. घन, यम, क्षर 7. मय धन, वध, जय, लय, यजन, छल, सधन, घन, सम, शरण; 8. भय, शयन, रण, रक्षण, कक्ष, क्षण, पक्ष, लभ, तरल, सरल, गरल; 9. चल, मत, यज्ञ, भक्षण, कर, वर, धर, भर, खर, चर, नर, हर, शर; 10. भक्ष, यक्ष, रक्ष, तक्षक, तज्ञ, कक्ष, यम, शम, क्षण, रक्षण, सज्ञ, यज्ञ, कक्ष, पक्ष, भक्ष, लक्ष, वक्ष, रक्षक, भक्षक, सयज्ञ । (for the meanings, see Answers in Appendix 10)

3.8 Letters : *ṭa, ṭha, ḍa, ṅa, ḍha, da, Jha, ha*

ट, ठ, ड, ङ, ढ, द, झ, ह

ट	ठ	ढ	द
ṭa	ṭha	ḍha	da

vaṭa वट (Banyan)	*maṭha* मठ (Ashram)	*ḍhola* (drum)	*dīpa* (lamp)

ड	ङ	झ	ह
ḍa	ṅa	jha	ha

ḍuli (ḍoli)	*aṅg* (body)	*jhaṣa* झष (fish)	*hariṇa* (deer)

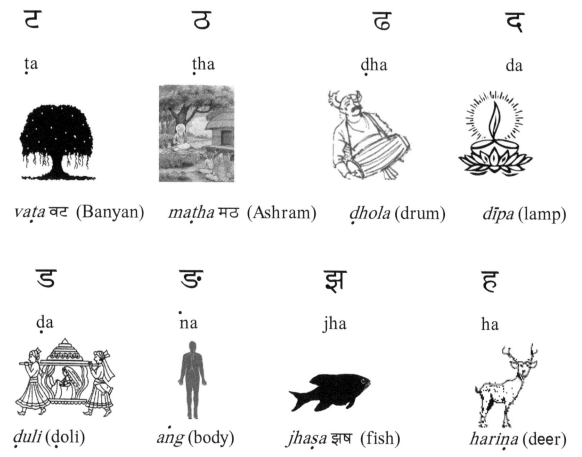

EXERCISE 10 : On what we have learned. Write the following characters in Sanskrit

1. ṭha, ṭa, ḍa, ha 2. ḍa, ṭa, ṭha 3. ṅa, ḍa, ṭha 4. ḍha, da, jha 5. da, ḍha, jha 6. ṭa, ṭha, ḍa, ḍha 7. ट, ठ, ढ, द, ड, ङ, झ, ह, झ, दल, दम, लभ, जनन 8. डयन, रम, बक, झष, हत, कर, तमस, तल, दम, शम, पवन, हर 9. झष, वर, नर, मद, पट, पटल, पद, बल, वन, सतत, खग, चल 10. भव, मन, बक, भज, वश, लक्ष, लक्षण, घन, धन, वरण, हय ।

LESSON 4

ćaturthaḥ abhyāsaḥ चतुर्थः अभ्यासः ।

STUDY OF SANSKRIT VOWELS

saṁskṛta-svarāṇām abhyāsaḥ संस्कृतस्वराभ्यासः ।

4.1 Letters : अ *a,* आ *ā,* ओ *o,* औ *au*

अ	ा	आ	अ	ो	ओ	अ	ौ	औ
a	→	ā	a	→	o	a	→	au

EXERCISE 11 : Only on what we have learned so far. Write the Sanskrit characters :

1. अ, आ, ओ, औ 2. आ, अ, औ 3. ओ, औ, ॐ

4. अक्ष आगम आगार 5. ओघ ओज 6. औदक औक्ष

(for meanings, see Answers in Appendix 10)

4.2 Letters : इ *i,* ई *ī,*

इ	ई
i	ī

EXERCISE 12 : Only on what we have learned so far. Write the following in Sanskrit :

1.a, ā 2. i, ī 3. ā, ā 4. a, ī 5. ā, ī, i 6. ā, ī

7. इ, ई, ईरण, इह, ईड, ईशः, ईक्षक, इतर, इक्षव, ईक्षण, इव ।

(for meanings, see Answers in Appendix 10)

4.3

Letters : उ *u*, ऊ *ū*, ऋ *ṛ*, ॠ *ṝ*, ऌ *lṛ*, ॡ *lṝ*

उ	ऊ	ऋ	ॠ	ऌ	ॡ
u	ū	ṛ	ṝ	lṛ	lṝ

EXERCISE 13 : Only on what we have learned so far

Write the following Sanskrit characters and words :

1. उ, ऊ, उ, ऋ, ॠ 2. उक्षण, उदर 3. उप, उपग, कृपा

4. उपपद, अवकर 5. उपमान, उपल 6. ऊत, ऊषक

(for meanings of words, see Answers in Appendix 10)

4.4

Letters : ए *e*, ऐ *ai*

ए	ऐ
e	ai

EXERCISE 14 : Only on what we have learned so far

(A) Write the following Sanskrit words :

1. ए, ऐ 2. एक, एकतर 3. एषण, ऐक्षव

4. ऐरावत, ऐल 5. एतद्, एकादश 6. ऐरावण, ऐश

(for meanings, see Answers in Appendix 10)

(B) A lphabetically arrange the words given in items 1-6 above.

LESSON 5

pañćamaḥ abhyāsaḥ पञ्चमः अभ्यासः ।

THE SANSKRIT VOWEL-SIGNS

saṁskṛta-svara-ćihnānām abhyāsaḥ संस्कृतस्वरचिह्नानाम् अभ्यासः ।

SANSKRIT VOWEL-SIGNS

Vowels :	अ	आ	इ	ई	उ	ऊ	ऋ	ॠ	ए	ऐ	ओ	औ
signs :		ा	ि	ी	ु	ू	ृ	ॄ	े	ै	ो	ौ
sound:	a	ā	i	ī	u	ū	ṛ	ṛ́	e	ai	o	au
		aa		ee		oo	ri	rī				

◌ा	◌ि	◌ी	◌ु	◌ू	◌ृ	◌ॄ	◌े	◌ै	◌ो	◌ौ
ā	i	ī	u	ū	ṛ	ṛ́	e	ai	o	au

Example :	प	पा	पि	पी	पु	पू	पृ	पॄ	पे	पै	पो	पौ
	p	pā	pi	pī	pu	pū	pṛ	pṛ́	pe	pai	po	pau

पु	पू	कु	कू	कृ	क्रु	रु	रू	छ्रु	छ्रू	तृ	हृ	दृ	शृ	तॄ	लृ	लॄ
pu	pū	ku	kū	kṛ	kru	ru	rū	ćhru	ćhrū	tṛ	hṛ	dṛ	śṛ	tṛ́	lṛ	lṛ́

EXERCISE 15 : On what we have learned. Read and write the following in Sanskrit :

1. जयी, जयति, जिगीषा 2. जिगीषु, कति 3. शृणु, कृपा 4. दीप, हृदय, पूत, पूति 5. पूजक, पूजन 6. दृति, दृढ 7. ज्ञानी, महा, सुख, दुःख, दृश्, दूषण, वृथा, पृथा, पृथिवी 8. ज्ञानयोग, महाभारतीय, संशय, नील, पौराणिक, भिक्षु, पितृणाम, गुरु, रूप, तरु, तरुण, करुण ।

(for meanings, see Answers in Appendix 10)

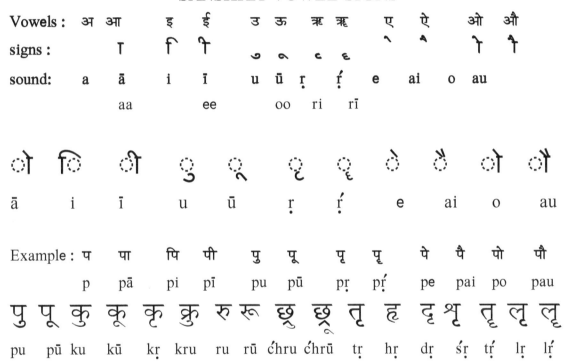

CHART OF
VOWEL-SIGNS APPLICATION

अ	आ	इ	ई	उ	ऊ	ऋ	ॠ	ए	ऐ	ओ	औ
	ा	ि	ी	ु	ू	ृ	ॄ	े	ै	ो	ौ
	ā	i	ī	u	ū	ṛ	ṛ́	e	ai	o	au
क	का	कि	की	कु	कू	कृ	कॄ	के	कै	को	कौ
क्ष	क्षा	क्षि	क्षी	क्षु	क्षू	क्षृ	क्षॄ	क्षे	क्षै	क्षो	क्षौ
ख	खा	खि	खी	खु	खू	खृ	खॄ	खे	खै	खो	खौ
ग	गा	गि	गी	गु	गू	गृ	गॄ	गे	गै	गो	गौ
घ	घा	घि	घी	घु	घू	घृ	घॄ	घे	घै	घो	घौ
ङ	ङा	ङि	ङी	ङु	ङू	–	–	ङे	ङै	ङो	ङौ
च	चा	चि	ची	चु	चू	चृ	चॄ	चे	चै	चो	चौ
छ	छा	छि	छी	छु	छू	छृ	छॄ	छे	छै	छो	छौ
ज	जा	जि	जी	जु	जू	जृ	जॄ	जे	जै	जो	जौ
ज्ञ	ज्ञा	ज्ञि	ज्ञी	ज्ञु	ज्ञू	–	–	ज्ञे	ज्ञै	ज्ञो	ज्ञौ
झ	झा	झि	झी	झु	झू	झृ	झॄ	झे	झै	झो	झौ
ञ	ञा	ञि	ञी	ञु	ञू	–	–	ञे	ञै	ञो	ञौ
ट	टा	टि	टी	टु	टू	टृ	टॄ	टे	टै	टो	टौ
ठ	ठा	ठि	ठी	ठु	ठू	ठृ	ठॄ	ठे	ठै	ठो	ठौ
ड	डा	डि	डी	डु	डू	डृ	–	डे	डै	डो	डौ
ढ	ढा	ढि	ढी	ढु	ढू	ढृ	–	ढे	ढै	ढो	ढौ
ण	णा	णि	णी	णु	णू	णृ	–	णे	णै	णो	णौ
त	ता	ति	ती	तु	तू	तृ	तॄ	ते	तै	तो	तौ
थ	था	थि	थी	थु	थू	थृ	थॄ	थे	थै	थो	थौ
द	दा	दि	दी	दु	दू	दृ	दॄ	दे	दै	दो	दौ
ध	धा	धि	धी	धु	धू	धृ	धॄ	धे	धै	धो	धौ
न	ना	नि	नी	नु	नू	नृ	नॄ	ने	नै	नो	नौ
प	पा	पि	पी	पु	पू	पृ	पॄ	पे	पै	पो	पौ
फ	फा	फि	फी	फु	फू	फृ	–	फे	फै	फो	फौ

ब	बा	बि	बी	बु	बू	बृ	बॄ	बे	बै	बो	बौ
भ	भा	भि	भी	भु	भू	भृ	भॄ	भे	भै	भो	भौ
म	मा	मि	मी	मु	मू	मृ	मॄ	मे	मै	मो	मौ
य	या	यि	यी	यु	यू	यृ	–	ये	यै	यो	यौ
र	रा	रि	री	रु	रू	–	–	रे	रै	रो	रौ
ल	ला	लि	ली	लु	लू	लृ	लॄ	ले	लै	लो	लौ
व	वा	वि	वी	वु	वू	वृ	वॄ	वे	वै	वो	वौ
श	शा	शि	शी	शु	शू	शृ	शॄ	शे	शै	शो	शौ
ष	षा	षि	षी	षु	षू	षृ	–	षे	षै	षो	षौ
स	सा	सि	सी	सु	सू	सृ	सॄ	से	सै	सो	सौ
ह	हा	हि	ही	हु	हू	हृ	–	हे	है	हो	हौ

SIGNS FOR ANUSWARA AND AVAGRAHA

अं *ṁ*, अः *ḥ*

पं पः

pam̐ paḥ

EXERCISE 16 : On what we have learned so far. Read and write the following words.

1. अम्, अः, अण्डजः (born from egg), वंशः (linage), पङ्कजं पङ्कजम् (lotus), रंगः रङ्गः (colour), दंडः दण्डः (punishment), भंगः भङ्गः (breaking), गंधः गन्धः (smell), 2. संगः सङ्गः (attachment), संशयः (doubt), हंसः (swan), कंसः (a glass), स्वतः (oneself), कंपनं कम्पनम् (shaking), खंजः खञ्जः (bald), भयंकरः भयङ्करः (terrible), चंदनं चन्दनम् (sandlewood), कंदरं कन्दरम् (cave) 3. कंठः कण्ठः (throat), पतंगः पतङ्गः (moth), भंजनं भञ्जनम् (breakage), गंधकः गन्धकः (sulphur), तरंगः तरङ्गः (wave), वदनं वदनम् (mouth), वंदनं वन्दनम् (salute), शंखः शङ्खः (conch-shell), संकलनं सङ्कलनम् (weaving), संचयः सञ्चयः (assembly), संपदा सम्पदा (wealth), मंचः मञ्चः (a stage) 4. षडंगं षडङ्गम् (of six organs), अंब अम्ब (mother), मंजनं मञ्जनम् (rubbing compound), अंबरं अम्बरम् (sky), शंकरः शङ्करः (Shiva), संचयः सञ्चयः (gathering), रंजनं रञ्जनम् (entertainment), बलवंतः बलवन्तः (powerful), भगवंतं भगवन्तम् (to god), संजयः सञ्जयः (Sanjaya), संगरः सङ्गरः (battle), संघः सङ्घः (group), संचः सञ्चः (gathering), संतः सन्तः (saint), मंद मन्दः (slow), अनंतरं अनन्तरम् (after) 5. छंदः छन्दः (meter), दंभः दम्भः (pretending), रंकः रङ्कः (poor), संगमः सङ्गमः (meeting), संकरः सङ्करः (admixture).

LESSON 6

ṣaṣṭah abhyāsaḥ षष्ठः अभ्यासः ।

THE SANSKRIT CHARACTERS

saṁskṛta-varṇāḥ संस्कृतवर्णाः ।

(see the coloured chart of Sanskrit Alphabet on the back cover)

A character (*varṇaḥ* वर्णः) that can be pronounced independently is called a VOWEL (*svaraḥ* स्वरः). यस्य वर्णस्य उच्चारणं स्वतन्त्रतया भवति सः स्वरः कथ्यते ।**

e.g. अ, इ, उ (a, i, u) ...etc.

A character that can NOT be pronounced independently (without the help of a vowel), is called a CONSONANT (*vyañjanānam* व्यञ्जनम्). ययस्य वर्णस्य उच्चारणं स्वतन्त्रं न भवति तत् व्यञ्जनम् कथ्यते । e.g. क्, ख्, ग् (k, kh, g) ...etc. Therefore,

क् + अ = क; ख्, + अ = ख k + a = ka; kh + a = kha ...etc.

** NOTE : You may understand these Sanskrit definations in your second reading of this book, when you have learned the basics.

6.1

THE VOWELS

svarāḥ स्वराः ।

(shown with red background colour in the chart on the back cover)

अहम् आत्मा इदम् ईशः उदकम् ऊर्जदायकम् ।
ऋजुकायम् ॠणान्मुक्तिः क्लृप्तम् सदा भवेत् ।
एषः ऐषम् ओ औ च स्वराः संस्कृतमार्गतः ।। (by Prof◦ BVK Sastry)

In Sanskrit, the vowels are of three types. संस्कृतस्वरा: त्रिविधा: सन्ति ।

(A) The SHORT vowels (*hrasvāḥ svarāḥ* ह्रस्वा: स्वरा:) are those which take one unit of time to pronounce them. अ, इ, उ, ऋ, ऌ (*a, i, u, ṛ, lṛ*) are the five basic short vowels.

(B) The LONG vowels (*dīrghāḥ svarāḥ* दीर्घा: स्वरा:) are those which take two units of time to pronounce them. आ, ई, ऊ, ॠ, ए, ऐ, ओ, औ, ॡ (*ā, ī, q̄, ṛ́, e, ai, o, au, lṛ́*) are the nine long vowels. Each long vowel is made up of two or more short vowels.

The Short vowels अ, इ, उ, ऋ, ऌ (*a, i, u, ṛ* and *lṛ*) and the Long vowels आ, ई, ऊ, ॠ and ॡ (*ā, ī, ū, ṛ* and *lṛ́*) are together called SIMPLE vowels (अमिश्रस्वरा:)

The four Long vowels ए, ऐ, ओ औ (*e, ai, o, au*) composed of two dis-similar vowels, are called DIPTHONGS (मिश्रस्वरा:)

EXAMPLES : Long Vowels

(1) Long vowel आ = short vowel अ + short vowel अ

(2) Long vowel ई = short vowel इ + short vowel इ

(3) Long vowel ऊ = short vowel उ + short vowel उ

(4) Long vowel ए = short vowel अ + short vowel इ

(5) Long vowel ओ = short vowel अ + short vowel उ

(C) The PLUTA vowels (*plutāḥ svarāḥ* प्लुता: स्वरा:) take at least three units of time to pronounce them. e.g. The long expressions such as vowel आ (ā) in the word राऽऽऽम ।

1.	Short vowels	अ, इ, उ, ऋ, ऌ	*a, i, u, ṛ, lṛ*
2.	Long vowels	आ, ई, ऊ, ॠ, ए, ऐ, ओ, औ, ॡ	*ā, ī, q̄, ṛ́, e, ai, o, au, lṛ́*
3.	Simple vowels	अ, आ, इ, ई, उ, ऊ, ऋ, ॠ, ऌ, ॡ	*a, ā, i, ī, u, ū, ṛ, ṛ́, lṛ, lṛ́*
4.	Dipthongs	ए, ऐ, ओ औ	*e, ai, o, au*
5.	Pluta vowels	ऽ	

एकमात्रो भवेत्-ह्रस्वो द्विमात्रो दीर्घ उच्यते ।
त्रिमात्रश्च प्लुतो ज्ञेयो व्यञ्जनं चार्धमात्रकम् ।।

ekmatro bhavet hrasvo, dvimātro dīrgha ućyate,
trimātraśća ploto jñeyo, vyañjanaṁ ćārdhamātrakam.

EXERCISE 1 : A. Read the following characters:

(1) अ, उ, इ, ऋ (2) इ, ऋ, अ (3) उ, इ, अ

(4) ऊ, आ, ई (5) औ, ए, ओ (6) ए, ऐ, ऊ, आ

B. Fill in the blanks:

(1) अ + अ = ——— (2) अ + उ = ——— (3) अ + इ = ———

6.2
THE CONSONANTS
(*vyañjanāni* व्यञ्जनानि)

In Sanskrit there are 25 class consonants (*varga-vyañjanāni* वर्गव्यञ्जनानि) and there are nine non-class (*avarga* अवर्ग-) consonants. संस्कृते पञ्चविंशतिः वर्गव्यञ्जनानि नव च अवर्गव्यञ्जनानि सन्ति ।

(1) The 25 Class Consonants (shown with a black outline in the chart on the back cover) from क् to म् are grouped phonetically into five classes (*vargāḥ* वर्गाः) consisting of five consonants each. These 25 consonants from *k* क to *m* म are also called 'Contactuals' (*sparśa-vyañjanāḥ* स्पर्श–व्यञ्जनाः । कादयः मावसानाः स्पर्शाः)

1. Class k(क) क् ख् ग् घ् ङ् k kh g gh ṅ
2. Class ć (च) च् छ् ज् झ् ञ् ć ćh j jhñ
3. Class ṭ (ट) ट् ठ् ड् ढ् ण् ṭ ṭh ḍ ḍh ṇ
4. Class t (त) त् थ् द् ध् न् t th d dh n
5. Class p (प) प् फ् ब् भ् म् p ph b bh m

(2). The next 4 characters य्, र्, ल्, व् are semi-consonsnts or semi-vowels (*antasthāḥ* यरलवाः अन्तस्थाः), shown with dark blue outline in the chart on the back cover.

(3). The remaining four characters श्, ष्, स्, ह् are the 'warm breath characters' (*uṣmāṇāḥ* उष्माणाः । शषसहाः उष्माणाः) of which the first three श्, ष्, स् are called 'sibilants' (shown with green background in the bottom row of the chart on back cover) and ह् is the aspirate (shown with purple background in the chart on the back cover).

THE PRONUNCIATIONS

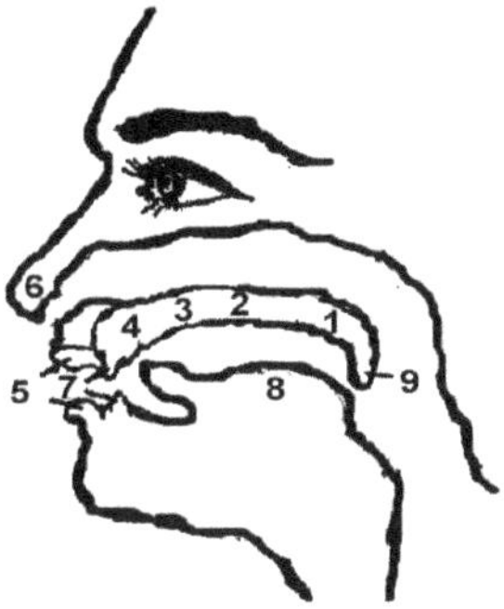

(1) Guttural कण्ठ्य *(kaṇṭhya)* = with throat; (2) Cerebral मूर्धन्य *(mūrdhanya)* = with cerebrum;
(3) Palatal तालव्य *(tālavya)* = with palate; (4) Dental दन्त्य *(dantya)* = with teeth
(5) Labial ओष्ठ्य *(oṣṭhya)* = with lips (6) Nasal अनुनासिक *(anunāsik)* = with nose.

(1) **GUTTURALS** are अ, आ, : , क्, ख्, ग्, घ्, ङ्, ह् : *(a, ā, ḥ, k, kh, g, gh, ṅ, h, ḥ).*

They are pronounced from the **throat** (See explanation of the figure in Lesson 2)

(2) **PALATALS** are इ, ई, च्, छ्, ज्, झ्, ञ्, य्, श् *i, ī, ć, ćh, j, jh, ñ, y, ś.*

They are pronounced from the **palate**

(3) **CEREBRALS** are ऋ, ॠ, ट्, ठ्, ड्, ढ्, ण्, र्, ष् *ṛ, ṝ, ṭ, ṭh, ḍ, ḍh, ṇ, r, ś, s.*

They are pronounced from the **roof of the mouth**

(4) **DENTALS** are ऌ, (ॡ), त्, थ्, द्, ध्, न्, ल्, स् *lṛ, (lṝ), t, th, d, dh, n, l.*

They are pronounced from the **teeth**

(5) **LABIALS** are उ, ऊ, प्, फ्, ब्, भ्, म्, व् *u, ū, p, ph, b, bh, m, v.*

They are pronounced from the **lips.** Character व *v* is dental-labial; ए, ऐ *e, ai* are guttural-palatal, and ओ, औ *o, au* are guttural-labials.

(6) THE **HARD** CONSONANTS (shown with green background on the back cover)

The first two consonants from each class (क्, ख्; च्, छ्; ट्, ठ्; त्, थ्; प्, फ् *k, kh, ć, ćh, ṭ, ṭh, t, th, p, ph*) and the three sibilants (श्, ष्, स् *ś, ṣ, s*) are Hard the Consonants (*kaṭhora-vyañjanāni* कठोर-व्यञ्जनानि).

(7) THE **SOFT** CONSONANTS (shown with green, blue, black and purple backgrounds on the back cover)

The rest of the consonants, namely, the last three consonants from each class (ग्, घ्, ङ्; ज्, ज्, ञ्; ड्, ढ्, ण्; द्, ध्, न्; ब्, भ्, म् *g, gh, np, j, jh, ñ, ḍ, ḍh, ṇ, d, dh, n, b, bh, m*), the semi-vowels (य्, र्, ल्, व् *y, r, l, v*) and the aspirate (ह् *h*) are Soft Consonants (*mṛdu-vyañjanāni* मृदुव्यञ्जनानि).

(8) THE **NASAL** CONSONANTS (shown with black background on the back cover)

The last character from each of the five classes ṅ, ñ, ṇ, n, m (ङ्, ञ्, ण्, न्, म्), are the Nasal Consonants (*anunāsikāni* अनुनासिकानि).

(9) THE **ANUSVĀRA** AND **THE VISARGA**

Anusvāra (˙) and *visarga* (:) are two more sounds in Sanskrit. The *anuswāra* (अनुस्वार:) is the modification of nasal consonants ङ्, ञ्, ण्, न्, म् and अं *(ṅ, ñ, ṇ, n, m, ṁ).* The the *visarga* (विसर्ग:) is the modified form of consonant स् or र् (*s* or *r*). The *anusvāra* and *visarga* are are not counted as separate characters, but they are sometimes treated as semi-vowels. Together they are called *Āyogavāhas* (*āyogavāhau* आयोगवाहौ).

6.3
THE 'SOUND-FORMULAS' FROM SHIVA
māhesvarāṇi sūtrāṇi

माहेश्वराणि सूत्राणि ।

Following 14 character strings, in the form of sounds chords, were first produced by Lord Śiva from his *damru* drum

1. अइउण् 2. ऋलृक् 3. एओङ् 4. ऐऔच् 5. हयवरट्
6. लण् 7. ञमङणनम् 8. झभज् 9. घढधष् 10. जबगडदश्
11. खफछठथचटतव् 12. कपय् 13, शषसर् 14. हल् ।

The last character of each equation string is always a consonant.

These characters are grouped into several strings (प्रत्याहारा:) according to their assigned attributes (साङ्केतिकनामानि). e.g. अण् प्रत्याहार: means the characters अ, इ, उ of the first सूत्रम् अइउण्, i.e. all characters except the last character of that *sūtra.*

प्रत्याहाराः ।

1. अक् – अ इ उ ऋ लृ (the vowels *a, i, u, ṛ, lṛ*)
2. अच् – स्वराः all the vowels (अ – औ)
3. अट् – स्वराः (अ – औ) + य, र, व ह । all vowels + consonants *y, r, v, h*
4. अण् – स्वराः + य, र ल व ह । all vowels + semi-vowels *y, r, l, v* + the aspirate *h*
5. अल् – वर्णाः all characters (अ – ह्)
6. अश् – all vowels and soft consonants (अ–औ, ग्–ङ्, ज्–ञ्, ड्–ण्, द्–न्, ब्–म्, य्–व्, ह्)
7. एङ् – vewels *e* and *o* (ए, ओ)
8. एच् – vewels *e, ai, o, au* (ए, ऐ, ओ, औ)
9. ऐच् – vewels *ai* and *au* (ऐ, औ)
10. खर् – hard consonants (क् ख् च् छ् ट् ठ् त् थ् प् फ् श् ष् स्)
11 जश् – the third consonant from each class : *g, j, ḍ, d, b* (ग्, ज्, ड्, द्, ब्)
12. झज् – the consonants *jh*, and *bh* (झ्, भ्)
13. झर् – sibilants + class consonants - nasals (क्–घ्, च्–झ्, ट्–ढ्, त्–ध् प्–भ् + श्, ष्, स्)
14. झल् – consonants other than semi-vowels and nasals क्–घ्, च्–झ्, ट्–ढ्, त्–ध्– प्–भ्, य्–ह्
15. झश् – the third and fourth class consonants (ग्, घ्, ज्, झ्, ड्, ढ्, द्, ध्, ब्, भ्)
16. झष् – the fourth consonant from each calss *gh, jh, ḍh, dh, bḥ* (घ, झ, ढ, ध, भ)
17. यण् – अन्तस्थवर्णाः (य् र् ल् व् consonants *y r l* and *v*)
18. यय् – all consonants other than *ś ṣ s h* (श् ष् स् ह् = उष्माक्षराणि)
19. यर् – all consonants other than *h* ह् (क् – स्)
20. शल् – the *ūṣma* consonants *ś, ṣ, s,* and *h* (श, ष, स, ह = ऊष्मन् → ऊष्म, ऊष्माणि)
21. हल् – व्यञ्जनानि (all consonants क् – ह्)
22. हश् – मृदुव्यञ्जनानि (soft consonants ग्–ङ्, ज्–ञ्, ड्–ण्, द्–न्, ब्–म्, य्–व्, ह्)

इत्यादयः प्रत्याहाराः । (etc. are the Syllable Making Affixes)

6.3 Māheśvarāṇī Sūtrāṇi

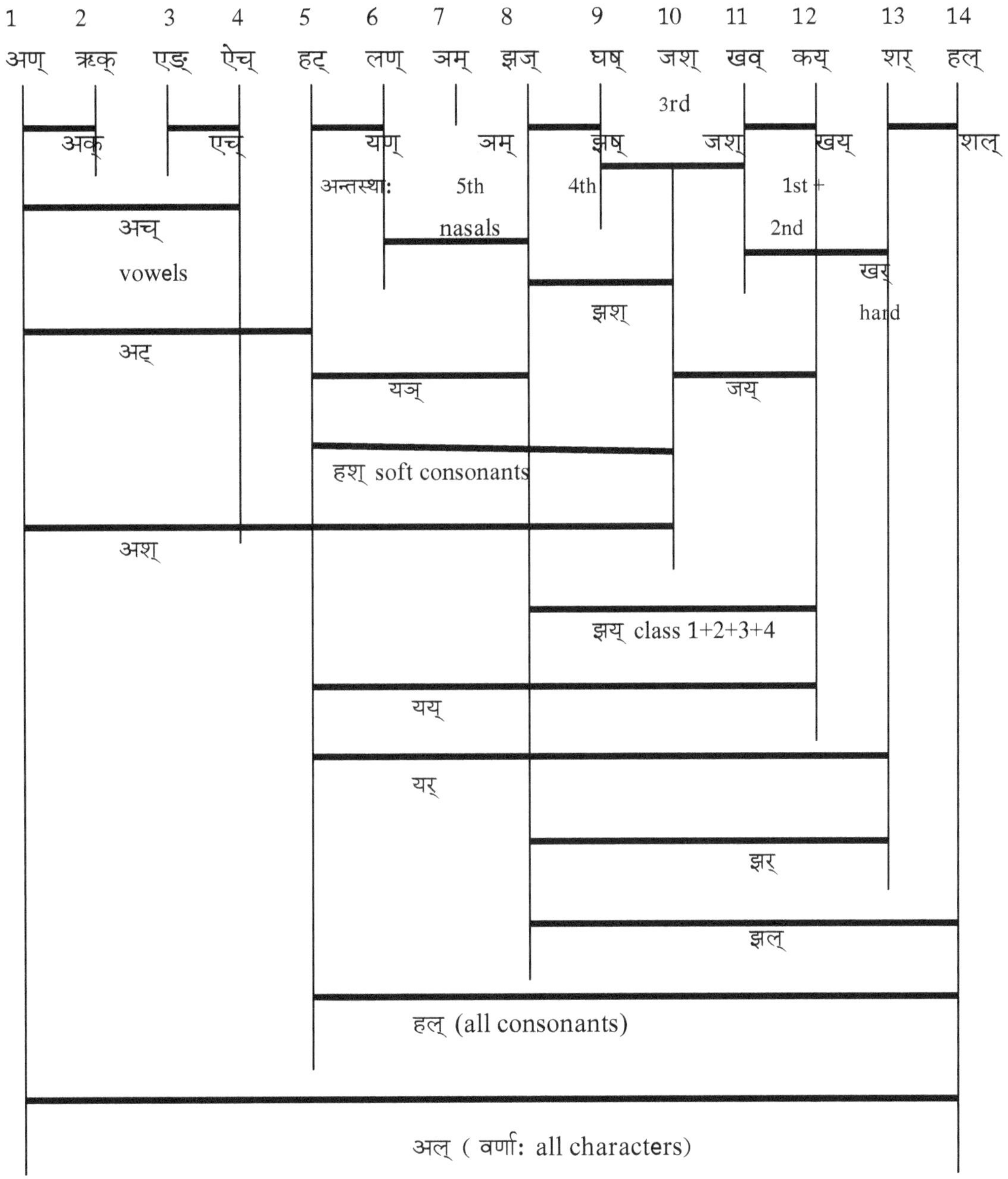

6.4 RULES FOR **PROPER** TRANSLITERATION OF

SANSKRIT CHARACTERS INTO ENGLISH, WITH DIACRITICAL MARKS

m̐ (अं), ṁ, m (म्); ma (म), ṅ (ङ्), ñ (ञ्), ṇ (ण्), n (न्), na (न)

Character *m̐* (अं) or *ṁ* (म्) is the nasal dot (अनुस्वार:) placed over a chacter in a word :

(i) **ṁ** → Within a word, when the nasal dot is followed by any consonant from p-class (p ph b bh m प फ ब भ म), then and then only that nasal dot means half character म् (m). e.g. *saṁpadā* संपदा = सम्‌पदा = सम्पदा । *guṁphana* गुंफन = गुम्‌फन = गुम्फन, *aṁbara* अंबर = अम्‌बर = अम्बर । *daṁbha* दंभ = दम्‌भ = दम्भ । *saṁmati* संमति = सम्‌मति = सम्मति ।

NOTE: संस्कृत is *sam̐skṛta* not saṁskṛta, because स् (of स्कृतम्) is not a p-class character.

(ii) **m̐** → Within a word, when the nasal dot is followed by any non-class consonant (*y r l v ś ṣ s h* य र ल व श ष स ह), **that nasal dot means *m̐* अं** (just a nasal sound, even though it is generally inaccurately transliterated as *ṁ*). e.g. संस्कृतं पठ = स्‌अंस्कृतम् पठ = *sam̐skṛtaṁ paṭha* NOT *saṁskṛtaṁ paṭha* सम्स्कृतम् पठ *nor sanskṛtam paṭha* सन्स्कृतम् पठ (NOTE: the nasal dots in *sam̐s* संस् and in *kṛtam* कृतम् both have different pronunciations, and thus must be transliterated differently (as *m̐* and *ṁ*, but NOT both as *ṁ*). Same is tru for words like मांसम् = म्‌आंसम् *mām̐sam etc.*

Similarly, संयत = sam̐yata, not सम्‌यत saṁyata; संरक्षण = sam̐rakṣaṇa, not सम्‌रक्षण saṁrakṣaṇa; संलग्न = sam̐lagna, not सम्‌लग्न saṁlagna; संवाद = sam̐vāda, not सम्‌वाद saṁvada; वंश = vam̐śa, not वम्‌श vaṁśa; मांसं = mām̐saṁ, not माम्सम् māṁsaṁ; कंस = kam̐sa, not कम्‌स kaṁsa, nor kansa; संहार = sam̐hara, not सम्‌हार saṁhāra ...etc. There is no *m* or *ṁ* in these words.

(iii) **m** → The half character *m* म् may come (1) at the end of any word that is followed by any word that is starting with a vowel, e.g. *bho Rāma māṁ tvam uddhara!* भो राम

मां त्वम् उद्धर! or (2) it may come at the end of a sentence. e.g. *bho Rāma mām̐ uddhara tvam!* भो राम माम् उद्धर त्वम्! भो राम मामुद्धर त्वम्!

(iv) The full character *ma* म (म् + अ = म *m + a = ma*) may come anywhere in a sentence. e.g. *bho Rāma mām̐ tvam uddhara!* भो राम मां त्वम् उद्धर! भो राम मां त्वमुद्धर! भो राम माम् उद्धर त्वम्! भो राम मामुद्धर त्वम्! = भो रामोद्धर त्वं माम् । भो राम त्वमुद्धर माम् ।

(v) **ṁ** → Within a sentence, when character *m* (म्) comes **at the end of any word** that is followed by a word that begins with any consonant, **only that nasal dot means *ṁ* (म्)** e.g. *aham kim karomi = ahaṁ kiṁ karomi* अहम् किम् करोमि = अहं किं करोमि ।

(vi) **m** → End of a sentence, when *m* (म्) comes at the end of a sentence, it stays as म् (m). e.g. *kim karomi aham = kiṁ karomi aham* किम् करोमि अहम् = किं करोमि अहम् ।

Anuswara = ṅ (ङ्), ñ (ञ्), ṇ (ण्), n (न्), ṁ (म्), m̐ (अं)

For transliterating the *anusvāraḥ* (अनुस्वारः) **within a word,** following six rules apply.

(refer to the characters shown in Black Background in the chart on Back Cover)

(1) When the nasal dot is followed by any character from k-class (क्, ख्, ग्, घ् k, kh, g, gh), that nasal dot is transliterated as → ṅ (ङ्) e.g. *raṅka* रङ्क, *raṅga* रङ्ग etc.

(2) When the nasal dot is followed by any character from ć-class (च्, छ्, ज्, झ् ć, ćh, j, jh), that nasal dot is transliterated as → ñ (ञ्) e.g. *pañća* पञ्च, *rañja* रञ्ज etc.

(3) When the nasal dot is followed by any character from ṭ-class (ट्, ठ्, ड्, ढ् ṭ, ṭh, ḍ, ḍh), that nasal dot is transliterated as → ṇ (ण्) e.g. *kaṇṭaka* कण्टक, *kaṇṭha* कण्ठ etc.

(4) When the nasal dot is followed by any character from t-class (त्, थ्, द्, ध् t, th, d, dh), that nasal dot is transliterated as → n (न्) *anta* अन्त, *pantha* पन्थ etc.

(5) When the nasal dot is followed by any character from p-class (प्, फ्, ब्, भ् p, ph, b, bh), that nasal dot is transliterated as → m (म्) *aṁba* अम्ब, *daṁbha* दम्भ etc.

(6) When the nasal dot is followed by any non-class character (य् र् ल् व श् ष् स ह् y, r, l, v, ś, ṣ, s), that nasal dot is transliterated as → m̐ (अं) *svam̐śaḥ* वंशः, व्अंशः ।

EXERCISE 17, the PRELIMINARY VOCABULARY :

What we learned so far. Can you Read and Write the following Sanskrit words? (pronunciations are shown for your help)

अहम् (*aham* I), आवाम् (*āvām* we two), वयम् (*vayam* we), माम् (*mām* to me), मया (*mayā* by me), मे (*me* for me), मम (*mama* my), नः (*naḥ* to us), मयि (*mayi* in me), भवान् (*bhavān* you m∘), भवती (*bhavatī* you f∘), त्वम् (*tvam* you), यूयम् (*yūyam* you pl∘), तव (*tava* your), सः (*saḥ* he), तम् (*tam* to him), तेन (*tena* by him), ते (*te* they), सा (*sā* she), ताम् (*tām* to her), यः (*yaḥ* who), कः (*kaḥ* who?), यौ (*yau* who two), कौ (*kau* who two?), ये (*ye* all who), ke (*ke* all who?), यम् (*yām* to whom), यान् (*yān* to whom all), येन (*yena* by whom), या (*yā* who f∘), याः (*yāḥ* who all f∘), याम् (*yām* to whom f∘), यया (*yayā* by whom f∘), एषः (*eṣaḥ* this), एते (*ete* these), एतम् (*etam* to this), एतान् (*etān* to these), एतेन (*etena* by this), एतैः (*etaiḥ* by these), एतेषु (*eteṣu* in these), एषा (*eṣā* this f∘), एताः (*etāḥ* these f∘), एताम् (*etām* to this f∘), एतया (*etayā* by this f∘), एतासु (*etāsu* in these f∘), एतत् (*etat* this n∘), एतद् (*etad* this n∘), एतानि (*etāni* these n∘), कः (*kaḥ* who? m∘), कौ (*kau* who two? m∘), के (*ke* who all? m∘), कम् (*kam* to whom? m∘), केन (*kena* by whom?), केषु (*keṣu* in whom?), का (*kā* who? f∘), काः (*kāḥ* who all? f∘), कया (*kayā* by whom? f∘), काभिः (*kābhiḥ* by whom all? f∘), किम् (*kim* what? n∘), कानि (*kāni* which all? n∘), अयम् (*ayam* this m∘), इमे (*ime* these m∘), इमम् (*imam* to this), अनेन (*anena* by this), एषाम् (*eṣām* of these), एषु (*eṣu* in these), इदम् (*idam* this n∘), इमानि (*imāni* these n∘), असौ (*asau* this m∘).

राम (*rāma* Rām), वन (*vana* forest), माला (*mālā* garland), कवि (*kvi* poet), वारि (*vāri* water), मति (*mati* thinking), नदी (*nadī* river), भानु (*bhānu* sun), मधु (*madhu* honey), धेनु (*dhenu* cow), वधू (*vadhū* bride), पितृ (*pitṛ* father), धातृ (*dhātṛ* bearer), मातृ (*mātṛ* mother), गो (*go* cow), नौ (*nau* boat), वाच् (*vāć* speech), राज् (*rāj* king), राट् (*rāṭ* king), जगत् (*jagat* world), आत्मन् (*ātman* soul), शशिन् (*śaśin* moon), दिक् (*dik* direction), पयस् (*payas* water), भू (*bhū* to become), अस् (*as* to be), अद् (*ad* to eat), तुद् (*tud* to hurt).

LESSON 7

saptamaḥ abhyāsaḥ सप्तमः अभ्यासः ।

COMPOUND CONSONANTS

saṁyukta-vyañjanānām abhyāsaḥ संयुक्तव्यञ्जनानाम् अभ्यासः ।

Very well, now that you have learned the chart of simple consonants and vowels, let us study compounding of the consonants and application of vowel-signs, through proper examples.

THE HALF CONSONANTS : (*halantāḥ* हलन्ताः)

The Chart shown in Lesson 1 contains the full consonants i.e. each base consonant with vowel *a* (अ) inherent in it. Let us now see the consonants without this vowel (अ) *a*. These consonants are called Half-consonants (*halantāḥ* हलन्ताः) and they are either written by attaching a small slant at the bottom of the character or by writing their half-letter shapes.

A **half-consonant** can not be pronounced by itself, unless a vowel is added to it. A vowel can be pronounced by itself. A consonant can be added to another consonant or consonants, and, at least one vowel must be added to the last consonant, to make it a complete compound character that can be pronounced.

Study the following chart of half-consonants and then do the following exercises. Please repeat the exercises, if necessary, to attain a good grasp of the material given here.

7.1

The Sanskrit Half-Consonants

EXERCISE 18 : Write the following

Half Consonants (pure consonants without a vowel)

क् क्‍	ख् ख्‍	ग् ग्‍	घ् घ्‍	ङ्
k	kh	g	gh	ṅ
च् च्‍	छ्	ज् ज्‍	झ् झ्‍	ञ् ञ्‍
ć	ćh	j	jh, z	ñ
ट्	ठ्	ड्	ढ्	ण् ण्‍
ṭ	ṭh	ḍ	ḍh	ṇ
त् त्‍	थ् थ्‍	द्	ध् ध्‍	न् न्‍
t	th	d	dh	n
प् प्‍	फ् फ्‍	ब् ब्‍	भ् भ्‍	म् म्‍
p	ph, f	b	bh	m
य् य्‍	र्	ल् ल्‍	व् व्‍	
y	r	l	v, w	
श् श्‍	ष् ष्‍	स् स्‍	ह् ह्‍	
ś	ṣ	s	h	

7.2

COMMON COMPOUND CHARACTERS

With the use of half characters such as:

क् k, ख् kh, ग् g, घ् gh, ङ् ṅ, च् ć, छ् ćh, ज् j, झ् jh, ञ् ñ, ट् ṭ, ठ् ṭh, ड् ḍ, ण् ṇ,

त् t, थ् th, ध् dh, न् n, प् p, फ् ph, ब् b, भ् bh, म् m,

य् y, र् r, ल् l, व् v, श् ś, ष् ṣ, स् s, ह् h

(क्ष kṣha, त्र tra, ज्ञ jña)

EXERCISE 19 : Read, study and write the following groups of Sanskrit Compound characters. Compare each of them with the corresponding full-character.

(1) Character k (क् क)

क k

पक्व, पक्‌व (*pakva* ripened), क्लीबम्, क्‌लीबम्, (*klībam* weakness) क्लेदः क्‌लेदः (*kledaḥ* wettness), वाक्यम्, वाक्‌यम् (*vākyam* speech), रक्तम्, रक्‌तम् (*raktam* blood), रुक्मिणी, रुक्‌मिणी (*Rukmiṇī*), क्वचित्, क्‌वचित् (*kvaćit* sometimes)

(2) Character kh (ख् ख)

ख kh

ख्याति: ख्‌याति: (*khyātiḥ* fame), आख्या आख्‌या (*ākhyā* saying), सख्यम् सख्‌यम् (*sakhyam* friendship)

(3) Characters g and gh (ग् ग ; घ् घ)

ग g; घ gh

ग्लानिः ग्‌लानिः (*glāniḥ* downfall), अग्निः अग्‌निः (*agniḥ* fire), भाग्यम् भाग्‌यम् (*bhāgyam* fortune), भग्न भग्‌न (*bhagna* broken), विघ्नम् विघ्‌नम् (*vighnam* obstacle)

(4) Characters ṅ (ङ्)

ङ् ṅ	ङ्क ṅka	ङ्क्त ṅkta	ङ्ख ṅkha	ङ्ग ṅga
ङ्घ ṅgha	ङ्म ṅma	ङ्ल ṅla	ङ्क्ष ṅkṣa	ङ्क्ष्व ṅkṣva

लङ्का लङ्‌का (*laṅkā* Sri Lanka), पङ्क्तिः पङ्‌क्तिः पङ्‌क्‌तिः (*paṅktiḥ* line, row), शङ्खः शङ्‌खः (*śaṅkhaḥ* conchshell), रङ्गः रङ्‌गः (*raṅgaḥ* colour), सङ्घः सङ्‌घः (*saṅghaḥ* group),

वाङ्मयम् वाङ्मयम् (*vāṅmayam* literature), आङ्ल आङ्ल (*āṅla* English), काङ्क्षा काङ्क्षा (*kāṅkṣā* desire), भुङ्क्ष्व (*bhuṅkṣva* please enjoy)

(5) Characters ć and ćh (च् च ; छ्)

च ć ; छ् ćh

अच्युतः अच्युतः (*aćyutaḥ* Krishna), अवाच्य अवाच्य (*avāćyaḥ* unspeakable), सुवाच्य सुवाच्य (*suvāćya* well said), उच्छ्वासः उच्छ्वासः (*uććhvāsaḥ* out breath)

(6) Characters j and ñ (ज् ज ; झ् झ ; ञ् ञ)

ज j ; झ jh ; ञ ñ

राज्यम् राज्यम् (*rājyam* kingdom), सज्ज सज्ज (*sajja* ready), उज्ज्वल उज्ज्वल (*ujjvala* bright), ज्योतिः ज्योतिः (*jyotiḥ* light), प्रोझ्य प्रोझ्य (*projhya* leaving), पञ्च पञ्च (*pañća* five), भञ्जनम् भञ्जनम् (*bhañjanam* destruction), वाञ्छा वाञ्छा (*vāñćhā* desire)

(7) Characters ṭ, ṭh (ट्, ठ्)

ट् ṭ ; ठ् ṭh

पट्टकः पट्टकः (*paṭṭakaḥ* plate), पट्टनम् पट्टनम् (*paṭṭanam* town), कण्ठ्य कण्ठ्य (*kaṇṭhya* guttural)

(8) Character ḍ, ḍh (ड्, ढ्)

ड् ḍ ; ढ् ḍh

उड्डयनम् उड्डयनम् (*uḍḍayanam* flight), उड्डित उड्डित (*uḍḍita* flown), चकृढ्वे चकृढ्वे (*ćakṛḍhve* you all had done)

(9) Character ṇ (ण्, ण)

ण ṇ

पाण्डवः पाण्डवः (*Pāṇḍvaḥ*), कण्ठः कण्ठः (*kaṇṭhaḥ* throat), कण्टकः कण्टकः (*kaṇṭakaḥ* thorn), षण्मासः षण्मासः (*ṣaṇmāsaḥ* six-months)

13

(10) Characters t, th and dh (त् त ; थ् थ ; ध् ध)

त t ; थ th ; ध dh

सत्कारः सत्कारः (*satkāraḥ* honour), दुग्धम् दुग्धम् (*dugdham* milk), रत्नाकरः रत्नाकरः (*ratnākaraḥ* ocean), उत्पातः उत्पातः (*utpātaḥ* rise), आत्मा आत्मा (*ātmā* soul), सत्यम् सत्यम् (*satyam* truth), त्यागः त्यागः

(tyāgaḥ sacrifice*)*, त्वरा त्‌वरा *(tvarā* rush*)*; तथ्यम् तथ्‌यम् *(tathyam* reality*)*; बाध्य बाध्‌य *(bādhya* binding - adj॰*)*

<u>**(11) Character n (न्, ₹)**</u>

₹ n आनन्दः आनन्‌दः *(ānandaḥ* joy*)*, अन्नम् अन्‌नम् *(annam* food*)*, जन्म जन्‌म *(janma* birth*)*, अन्य अन्‌य *(anya* other*)*, अन्वयः अन्‌वयः *(anvayaḥ* relation*)*, भिन्न भिन्‌न *(bhinna* different*)*, वन्दनम् वन्‌दनम् *(vandanam* salute*)*, बन्धनम् बन्‌धनम् *(bandhanam* bondage*)*, पान्थः पान्‌थः *(pānthaḥ* traveller*)*

<u>**(12) Characters p, ph (प् ट ; फ् फ)**</u>

ट p ; फ ph समाप्त समाप्‌त *(samāpta* ended*)*, अप्सरा अप्‌सरा *(apsarā* celestial maid*)*, स्वप्नम् स्वप्‌नम् *(svapnam* dream*)*, पाप्मन् पाप्‌मन् *(pāpman* sin*)*, रूप्यकम् रुप्‌यकम् *(rūpyakam* Rupee*)*.

<u>**(13) Characters b, bh and m (ब् ๖ ; भ् ⱶ ; म् ᴴ)**</u>

๖ b ; ⱶ bh ; ᴴ m शब्दः शब्‌दः *(śabdaḥ* word*)*, शैब्यः शैब्‌यः *(śaibyaḥ)*, सभ्य सभ्‌य *(sabhya* gentle*)*, सम्पदा सम्‌पदा *(sampadā* wealth*)*, सम्यक् सम्‌यक् *(samyak* right*)*, धृष्ट धृष्‌ट *(dhṛṣṭa* courageous*)*, अम्ल अम्‌ल *(amla* sour*)*

<u>**(14) Characters y and l (य् ᴢ ; ल् ल)**</u>

ᴢ y ; ल l शय्या! शय्‌या! *(śayyā* bed*)*, उल्का उल्‌का *(ulkā* meteor*)*, उल्लेखः उल्‌लेखः *(ullekhaḥ* reference*)*, अल्प अल्‌प *(alpa,* short*)*, कल्याणम् कल्‌याणम् *(kalyāṇam* benefit*)* वल्गना वल्‌गना *(valganā* chatter*)*

<u>**(15) Character v (व् ०)**</u>

० v व्ययः व्‌ययः *(vyayaḥ* expense*)*, व्यायामः व्‌यायामः *(vyāyāmaḥ* exercise*)*, व्योम व्‌योम *(vyoma* sky*)*, व्यूढ व्‌यूढ *(vyūḍha* arrayed*)*, व्यङ्गम् व्‌यङ्‌गम् *(vyaṅgam* deformity*)*, व्यवसायः व्‌यवसायः *(vyavasāyaḥ* business*)*

<u>**(16) Chararacter ś (श् श ४)**</u>

श ४ ś विश्वासः विश्‍वासः विश्‌वासः *(viśvāsaḥ* trust*)*, निश्चयः निश्‍चयः निश्‌चयः

(niścayaḥ firm resolution*)*, पश्चात् पश्चात् पश्चात् *(paśćāt* after*)*, काश्मीर: काश्मीर: *(kāśmīraḥ)*, अवश्यम् अवश्यम् *(avaśyam* certainly*)*, अश्मक: अश्मक: *(aśmakaḥ* stone*)*, विश्लेषणम् विश्लेषणम् *(viśleṣaṇam* analysis*)*

(17) Character ṣ (ष् ष)

ष ṣ अष्ट अष्ट *(aṣṭa* eight*)*, इष्ट इष्ट *(iṣṭa* desired*)*, कष्टम् कष्टम् *(kaṣṭam* trouble*)*, आविष्कार: आविष्कार: *(āviṣkāraḥ* discovery*)*, मनुष्य: मनुष्य: *(manuṣyaḥ* man, human*)*, पुष्पम् पुष्पम् *(puṣpam* flower*)*, उष्मा उष्मा *(uṣmā* heat*)*, ओष्ठ: ओष्ठ: *(oṣṭhaḥ* lip*)*, उष्ण: उष्ण: *(uṣṇaḥ* hot*)*, कृष्ण: कृष्ण: *(kṛṣṇaḥ)*, बाष्पम् बाष्पम् *(bāṣpam* vapour*)*, भविष्यम् भविष्यम् *(bhaviṣyam* future*)*

(18) Character s (स् स)

स s तस्कर: *(taskaraḥ* thief*)*, अस्तु अस्तु *(astu* let it be*)*, स्थिति: स्थिति: *(sthitiḥ* state, condition*)*, स्फटिक: स्फटिक: *(sphaṭikaḥ* crystal*)*, स्नायु: स्नायु: *(snāyuh,* muscle*)*, स्पष्ट स्पष्ट् *(spaṣṭa* clear*)*, अस्य अस्य *(asya* of this*)*, हास्यम् हास्यम् *(hāsyam* laughter*)*, स्मितम् स्मितम् *(smitam* a smile*)*, स्वत: स्वत: *(svataḥ* oneself*)*, स्वदेश: स्वदेश: *(svadeśaḥ* motherland*)*, स्वागतम्, स्वागतम् *(svāgatam* welcome*)*, स्कन्द: स्कन्द: *(skandaḥ)*, स्मृति: स्मृति: *(smṛtiḥ* memory, rememberance*)*

(19) Character h (ह् ह)

ह h	हृ hṛ	ह्ण hṇa	ह्न hna	ह्य hya
ह्म hma	ह्र hra	ह्ल hla	ह्व hva	

हृदयम् हृदयम् *(hṛdayam* heart*)*, बाह्य बाह्य *(bāhya* external*)*, ब्रह्म ब्रह्म *(brahma)*, आह्लाद: आह्लाद: *(āhlādaḥ* joy*)*, गृह्णाति गृह्णाति *(gṛhṇāti* he takes*)*, ह्रस्व ह्रस्व *(hrasvaḥ* short*)* चिह्नम् चिह्नम् *(ćihnam* sign*)*, वह्नि: वह्नि: *(vahniḥ* fire*)*, जिह्वा जिह्वा *(jihvā* toung*)*

(20) Characters क्ष kṣha, त्र tra, ज्ञ jña : क्षमा क्षमा *(kṣhamā* pardon); त्रि त्रि *(tri* Three); ज्ञान ज्ञान *(Jña!na* Knowledge);

LESSON 8

aṣṭamaḥ abhyāsaḥ अष्टमः अभ्यासः ।

8.1

STUDY OF SPECIAL COMPOUND CHARACTERS

RULE : When two or more consonants come in a row (without a vowel bteween them), the **last consonant is a full** consonant and **the rest are half consonants**.

(1) Characters क् + त can be written as क्त *(kta),* but there is a special single character क्त for this purpose. e.g. रक्तम् रक्तम् *(raktam* blood*),* भक्तिः भक्तिः *(bhaktiḥ* devotion*),* वक्ता वक्ता *(vaktā* speaker*),* युक्तः युक्तः *(yuktaḥ* equipped*)*

क्त क्त kta

(2) Character *da* (द्) has following common compounds

1. d + da = dda → द् + द = द्द (उद्देशः *uddeśaḥ* objective, तद्दानम् *taddānam* that charity)
2. d + dha = ddha → द् + ध = द्ध (युद्धम् *yuddham* war, बुद्धिः *buddhiḥ* thinking)
3. d + ga = dga → द् + ग = द्ग (उद्गमः *udgamaḥ* rise, भगवद्गीता *bhagavadgītā*)
4. d + gha = dgha → द् + घ = द्घ (उद्घाटनम् *udghāṭaman* inauguration)
5. d + bha = dbha → द् + भ = द्भ (सद्भावः *sadbhāvaḥ* goodness; उद्भवः *udbhavaḥ* rise)
6. d + ya = dya written as : द् + य = द्य (आद्यः *ādyaḥ* first; द्यूतम् *dyūtam,* gambling)
7. d + ma = dma written as : द् + म = द्म (पद्मम् *padmam* lotus, छद्मी *ćhadmī* cunning)
8. d + va = dva written as : द् + व = द्व (द्वन्द्वः *dvandvaḥ* dual, विद्वान् *vidvān* learned)

द्द dda   द्घ dgha   द्ध ddha   द्ग dga

द्भ dbha   द्य dya   द्म dma   द्व dva

(3) Letter *ra* (र) forms following two groups of compounds:

(A) When full-consonant र (ra) comes after any half-consonant, it is written as a slanted line (͵) attached to that half-consonant.

1. k + ra (क् + र = क्र) चक्रम् *ćakram* wheel, क्रान्तिः *krāntiḥ* revolution, क्रोधः *krodhaḥ* anger, क्रिया *kriyā* deed, क्रूरः *krūraḥ* cruel, क्रेता *kretā* buyer

2. g + ra (ग् + र = ग्र) अग्रम् *agram* tip, अग्रेसरः *agresaraḥ* leader, ग्रामम् *grāmam* village, ग्रीवा *grīvā* neck

3. d + ra (द् + र = द्र) भद्रः *bhadraḥ* gentle, सुभद्रा *subhadrā*, द्रविड *draviḍa*, द्रोहः *drohaḥ* treachery, द्रुमः *drumaḥ* tree

4. ś + ra (श् + र = श्‍ + र = श्र) श्रद्धा *śraddhā* faith, विश्रांतिः *viśrāntiḥ* rest, श्री *śrī* divine, श्रेष्ठः *śreṣṭhaḥ* superior, श्रोता *śrotā* listner, श्रुतम् *śrutam* heard

5 t + ra (त् + र = त्र) यन्त्रम् *yantram* machine, रात्रिः *rātriḥ* night, पत्रम् *patram* leaf, त्रेता *tretā* saviour, त्रिधा *tridhā* in three ways, त्रेधा *tredhā* in three ways.

क्र kra   ग्र gra   श्र śra   त्र tra

6. ṭ or ḍ + ra (ट्र, ड्र) : उष्ट्रः उष्ट्‍रः *uṣṭraḥ* camel, राष्ट्रः राष्ट्‍रः *rāṣṭraḥ* country, पौण्ड्रः पौण्ड्‍रः *pauṇḍraḥ*

7. s + ra (स् + र = स्र) सहस्रम् सहस्‍रम् *sahasram* thousand, स्रावः स्‍रावः *srāvaḥ* a flow

8. s + t + ra (स् + त् + र = स्त्र) स्त्री स्‍त्‍री *strī* woman, अस्त्रम् अस्‍त्‍रम् *astram* weapon, वस्त्रम् वस्‍त्‍रम् *vastram* cloth

ट्र tra   ड्र ḍra   स्र sra   स्त्र stra

(B) When half-consonant र् (r) comes before any consonant, it is written as (᷍)

9. र् + प = (र्प); अर्कः अर्‍कः *arkaḥ* sun, सर्गः सर्‍गः *sargaḥ* the creation, अर्चना अर्‍चना *arćanā* worship, वार्ता वार्‍ता *vārtā* news, सर्पः सर्‍पः *sarpaḥ* snake, कर्म कर्‍म *karma* deed, कार्यम् कार्‍यम् *kāryam* duty

र्क rka   र्प rpa

(4) Character *ta, na* and *ha* (त) make following common compounds

1. t + ta = tta (त्+त = त्त, त्त) उत्तमम् *uttamam* best, सत्ता *sattā* jurisdiction, सत्त्वम् *sattavam* truth. 2. n + na = nna (न् + न = न्न) खिन्न *khinn* sad

3. h + ma = hma (ह् + म = ह्म) ब्रह्मा *brahmā* the Creator, ब्रह्माण्डम् *brahmaṇḍam* world

4. h + ya = hya (ह् + य = ह्य) बाह्यः *bāhyaḥ* external, गुह्यम् *guhyam* secret

त्त tta   त्त्व ttva   न्न nna   ह्य hya

EXERCISE 20 : What we learned so far. Read and write the following Sanskrit words

1. क्रमः (order), कृष्ण (black), क्रुद्धः (angry), कृपणः (miser)
2. चञ्चलः (quick), शूच्यः (pure), पूज्यः (holy), ज्योत्स्ना (moonlight), धनञ्जयः (Arjun)
3. स्वप्नम् (dream), प्रश्नः (question), प्राधान्यम् (priority), प्रसन्नम् (pleased), धृष्टद्युम्नः (Draupadī's brother), अन्नम् (food)
4. व्याघ्रः (tiger), वज्रम् (thunderbolt), अभ्रम् (cloud), त्रिलोकः (three worlds), तृप्तः (satisfied), ध्रुवः (steady), धृतिः (courage), प्रत्येक (each), ब्रह्म (God), तीव्रम् (strong)
5. दृष्टिः (vision), वृष्टिः (rain), सृष्टिः (creation), पृथ्वी (earth), मृतात्मा (dead person), पृष्ठम् (surface)
6. वृत्तम् (news), धृतराष्ट्रः (a king's name), नृपः (king), क्रांतिः (revolution)
7. स्त्री (woman), स्त्रियः (women), स्तोत्रम् (praise), अजस्त्रम् (huge), सृजनम् (creation); पद्मनाभः (Viśṇu), पद्मा (Lakṣmī), पद्यम् (poetry), गद्यम् (prose)
8. स्थानम् (place), वयस्कः (old), स्मृतिः (memory), स्नानम् (bath), स्निग्धम् (viscous)
9. द्रौपदी, द्‌रौपदी, दुर्योधनः, दुर्‌योधनः, भार्गवः भार्‌गवः (proper nouns)
10. गर्वः (pride), सर्वः (all), पूर्वम् (earlier), स्वर्गः (heaven), अर्चना (worship), तर्कः (guess), दर्पणः (mirror)

8.2

SANSKRIT COMPOUND CHARACTERS

(WITH EXAMPLES)

sodāharaṇāḥ saṁyukta-varṇāḥ सोदाहरणाः संयुक्तवर्णाः ।

Only a Reading and Writing Exercise : Read and write the Sanskrit words.

क् क्क, क्क (वुक्कति, वुक्कति वुक्‌कति *vukkati,* he barks), क्ख (कक्खति *kakkhati* he laughs, कक्खट *kakkhaṭa* hard), क्च (त्वक्चैव *tvakćaiva* skin also), क्त (उक्त *ukta* said), क्त्य (भक्त्या *bhaktyā* with devotion), क्त्र (वक्त्रम् *vaktram,* mouth), क्त्व (उक्त्वा *uktvā* having said), क्न (शक्नोमि *śaknomi,* I am able), क्प (पृथक्पृथक् *pṛthak-pṛthak* separately), क्म (रुक्मिणी *rukmiṇī*), क्य (वाक्यम् *vākyam* speech), क्र (क्रमः *kramaḥ* order), क्ल (क्लान्त *klānta* tired), क्लृ (क्लृप्तिः *klṛptiḥ* invention), क्व (क्वचित् *kvaćit* sometimes), क्श (प्राक्शरीरविमोक्षणम् *prāk-śarīra-vimokṣaṇam* before death), क्ष (क्षमा *kṣamā,* forgiveness), क्स (ऋक्साम *ṛk-sāma* Rigveda and Sāmveda)

क्ष् क्ष्म्य (सौक्ष्म्यम् *saukṣmyam* minuteness), क्ष्य (समीक्ष्य *samīkṣya* having seen), क्ष्व (*Ikṣvāku* इक्ष्वाकुः)

ख् ख्य (सांख्यः *sāṅkhyaḥ*)

ग् ग्द (वाग्देवी *vāg-devī* Sarasvatī), ग्ध (दुग्धम् *dugdham* milk), ग्न (अग्निः *agniḥ* fire), ग्प (वाग्पटुः *vāgpaṭuḥ* elouquent), ग्भ (पृथग्भावः *pṛthag-bhāvaḥ* different nature), ग्भ्य (लिग्भ्याम् *ligbhyām* for two writers), जग्मुः (*jagmuḥ* they went), ग्य (भाग्यम् *bhāgyam* luck), ग्र (ग्रसनम् *grasanam* eating), ग्ल (ग्लानिः *glāniḥ* downfall), ग्व (पृथग्विधा *pṛthagvidhā* differently), ग्व्य (सम्यग्व्यवस्थित *samyag-vyavasthita* properly established)

घ् घ्न (विघ्नम् *vighnam* obstacle), घ्न्य (अघ्न्यः *aghnyaḥ* not to be killed), घ्य (अर्घ्य *arghya* holy), घ्र (घ्राणम् *ghrāṇam* nose), घ्व (लघ्वाशी *laghvāśī* moderate eater)

ङ् ङ्क (अङ्कः aṅkaḥ body), ङ्क्ते (भुङ्क्ते bhuṅkte he eats), ङ्क्थ (भुङ्क्थ bhuṅktha you all enjoy), ङ्ख (शङ्खः śaṅkhaḥ conch-shell), ङ्ग (गङ्गा gaṅgā), ङ्ग (सङ्गीतम् saṅgītam music), ङ्घ (सङ्घः saṅghaḥ attachment), ङ्ध्व (भुङ्ध्वे bhuṅgdhve you all enjoy), ङ्म (वाङ्मयम् vāṅgmayam literature), ङ्क्ष (काङ्क्षामि kāṅkṣāmi I desire), ङ्भ्य (प्राङ्भ्याम् prāṅgbhyām for two Easterners)

च् च्च (उच्चैः uććaiḥ, loudly), च्छ (इच्छा ićchā, desire), च्छृ (उच्छृङ्खल ućchṛṅkhala unrestrained), युद्धाच्छ्रेयः (yuddhāćchreyaḥ better than war), च्य (अच्युतः aćyutaḥ Krishna), उच्यते ućyate it is called), च्वि (ćvi existance of non-existant)

छ् छ्य (छ्यवते ćhyavate he approaches), छ्र (यच्छ्रेयः yaććhreyah that which is better), उच्छ्रित (uććhrita raised), उच्छ्वास: uććhvāsaḥ exhalation)

ज् ज्ज (सज्ज sajja ready), ज्ज्य (तज्ज्योतिः tajjyotih that light), ज्ज्ञ (तज्ज्ञात्वा tajjñātvā knowing that), ज्य (राज्यम् rājyam kingdom), ज्र (वज्रम् vajram thunderboalt), ज्व (ज्वाला jwālā flame)

ञ् ञ्च (पञ्च pañća five), ञ्छ (वाञ्छा vañćhā desire), ञ्ज (सञ्जयः sañjayaḥ), ञ्ज्य (युञ्ज्याद्योगम् yuñjādyogam should practice yoga), ञ्झ (उञ्झति uñjhati he lets it go), ञ्जम (भुञ्ज्म bhuñjma we all enjoy), ञ्ज्व (भुञ्ज्व bhuñjva we both enjoy), ञ्श्र (पश्यञ्श्रुण्वन् paśyañ-śruṇvan while seeing and hearing), ञ्श्व (स्वपञ्श्वसन् svapañśvasan sleeping and breething)

ट् ट्ट (पट्टिका paṭṭikā, plate), ष्ट्र (राष्ट्रम् rāṣṭram country), ष्ट्व (दृष्ट्वा dṛṣṭvā, seeing)

ड् ड्ड (उड्डयते uḍḍayate he flies), ड्भ्य (राड्भ्याम् rāḍbhyām for two kings), ड्य (ईड्य īdya glorified)

ढ् ढ्य (आढ्य āḍḍhya wealthy)

ण् ण्ट (कण्टकः kaṇṭakaḥ thorn), ण्ठ (वैकुण्ठम् vaikuṇṭham heaven), ण्ड (पाण्डवाः pāṇḍavāḥ), ण्ढ (षण्ढ ṣaṇḍha impotant), ण्ड्र (पौण्ड्रः pauṇḍraḥ), ण्ण (विषण्ण vṣaṇṇa dejected), ण्म (षण्मासाः ṣaṇ-māsaḥ six-months), ण्य (कार्पण्यम् kārpaṇyam pity)

त् त्क (तत्काल: *tatkālaḥ,* that time), त्कृ (अभिभवात्कृष्ण *abhibhavāt-kṛṣṇa!* O Krishna! from the rise of), त्क्र (कामात्क्रोध: *kāmātkrodhaḥ* anger from desire), त्क्ष (अन्यत्क्षत्रियस्य *anyat-kṣatriyasya* anything else for a warrior), त्च (भयात्च *bhayātca* and from the fear), त्त (सत्ता *sattā* power), त्त्य (भयात्त्यजेत् *bhayāt-tyajet* let go out of fear), त्त्र (तत्त्रयम् *tat-trayam* those three), त्त्व (तत्त्वम् *tattvam* principle), त्थ (अश्वत्थामा *aśvatthāmā*), त्न (रत्नाकर: *ratnākaraḥ* ocean), त्प (तत्परम् *tatparam* that supreme), तात्पर्यं (*tātparyam* morale), त्प्र (तत्प्राप्य *tatprāpya* having attained that), त्म (आत्मा *ātmā* soul), त्म्य (महात्म्यम् *mahātmyam* greatness), त्य (त्यक्त्वा *tyaktvā* having renounced), त्र (धर्मक्षेत्रम् *dharmakṣetram* righteous place), त्र्य (रात्र्यागमे *rātryāgame* at night), त्व (त्वम् *tvam* you), त्स (उत्साह: *utsāhah* encouragement), त्स्थ (पश्यत्स्थितान् *paśyatsthitān* he saw the standing ones), त्स्न (कृत्स्नम् *kṛtsnam* all), त्स्म (सम्मोहात्स्मृतिविभ्रम: *sammohātsmṛti-vibhramaḥ* loss of thinking as a result of delusion) त्स्य (प्रतियोत्स्यामि *pratiyotsyāmi* I will defend) त्स्व (परधर्मात्स्वनुष्ठितात् *para-dharmāt-svanuṣṭhitāt* than performed others' duty)

थ् मथ्नाति (*mathnāti* he churns), थ्य (तथ्यम् *tathyam* truth); मिथ्या *mithyā* false)

द् द्ग (उद्गार: *udgāraḥ* exclamation), द्ग्र (असद्ग्राह: *asadgrāhaḥ* misunderstanding), द्घ (उद्घाटनम् *udghāṭanam* inauguration), द्द (उद्देश: *uddeśaḥ* objective), द्द्य (महद्द्युतिकर: *mahad-dyutikaraḥ,* sun), द्द्र (अन्यद्द्रष्टुमिच्छसि *anyad-draṣṭum-icchasi* whatever else you wish to see), द्ध (युद्धम् *yuddham* war), द्ध्य (युद्ध्यस्व *yuddhyasva* please fight), द्ध्व (बुद्ध्वा *buddhvā* having known) द्ब (स्मृतिभ्रंशाद्बुद्धिनाश: *smṛti-bhraṁśād-buddhi-nāśaḥ* misunderstanding due to confusion), द्ब्र (तस्माद्ब्रह्मणि *tasmād-brahmaṇi* therefore in the brahma), द्भ (सद्भाव: *sad-bhāvaḥ* righteousness), द्भ्य (भगवद्भ्याम् *bhagavadbhyām* for two gods), द्म (पद्मम् *padmam,* lotus), द्य (पद्यम् *padyam* song), द्र (द्रुपद: *drupadaḥ*), द्व (द्वंद्वम्, द्वन्द्वम् *dvandvam* duality), द्व्य (अव्यक्ताद्व्यक्तय: *avyaktād-vyaktayaḥ,* the manifest emerged from the unmanifest)

ध् ध्न (बध्नाति *badhnāti* it binds), ध्म (दध्मौ *dadhmau* he blew), ध्य (ध्यानम् *dhyānam* meditation), ध्र (ध्रुव *dhruva* unmoving), ध्व (ध्वज: *dhvajaḥ* flag)

न् न्क (समवेतान्कुरून् *samavetān-kurūn* to the assembled Kurus), न्ग (अश्नन्गच्छन् *aśnan-gacchan* eating and going), न्त (णिजन्त *ṇijanta* causative), न्त (अन्त: *antaḥ* end), न्त्य (व्यथयन्त्येते *vyathayantyete* these do bother), न्त्र्य (आमन्त्र्य *āmantrya* having invited), न्थ (मन्थनम् *manthanam* churning), न्त्र (यन्त्रम् *yantram* machine), न्त्व (सान्त्वना *sāntvanā* consolation), न्त्स्य (भन्त्स्यति *bhantsyati* he will tie), न्द (आनन्द: *ānandaḥ* joy), न्द्र (इन्द्रियम् *indriyam* organ), न्द्व (द्वन्द्वम् *dvandvam* duality), न्द्ध (रुन्द्धाम् *runddhām* he should resist), अरुन्द्ध्वम् (*arunddhvam* you all had resisted), न्द्ध्य (रुन्द्ध्यताम् *runddhyātām* may they stop), न्ध (अन्ध *andha* blind), अरुन्ध्महि (*arundhmahi* we all had resisted), विन्ध्यन्त: (*vindhyantaḥ* lacking), अरुन्ध्वहि (*arundhvahi* we two had resisted), न्न (अन्नम् *annam* food), न्प (स्थितान्पार्थ: *sthitān-pārthaḥ* Arjuna to the seated ones), न्प्र (प्राणान्प्राणेषु *prāṇān-prāṇeṣu* breath in the breaths), न्ब (सर्वान्बन्धून् *sarvān-bandhūn* to all brothers), न्ब्र (तान्ब्रवीमि *tān-bravīmi* I tell about them), न्भ (भवान्भिष्म: *bhavān-bhīṣmaḥ* you Bhīshma), न्भ्य (खन्भ्याम् *khanbhyām* for two lame men), न्भ्र (मातुलान्भ्रातॄन् *mātulān-bhratṝn* to uncles and brothers), न्म (जन्म *janma* birth), न्य (अन्य: *anyaḥ,* other), न्र (अस्मिन्रणे *asmin-raṇe* on this battlefield), न्व (अन्वय: *anvayaḥ* following), न्व्य (भगवन्व्यक्तिम् *bhagavan-vyaktim* O Lord! Your personifiction), न्स (तान्समीक्ष्य *tān-samīkṣya* having seen them), न्स्य (बुद्धिमान्स्यात् *buddhimān-syāt* he will be wise), न्स्व (धार्तराष्ट्रान्स्वबान्धवान् *dhārtarāṣṭrān-sva-bāndha-vān,* to our brother Kauravas), न्ह (सञ्जनयन्हर्षम् *sañjanayan-harṣam,* while increasing the joy)

प् प्त (पर्याप्तम् *paryāptam* limited), प्त्व (लोलुप्त्वम् *loluptvam* eagerness), प्न (स्वप्नम् *svapnam* sleep, dream), प्म (पाप्मानम् *pāpmānam* to the wicked), प्य (अवाप्य *avāpya* having obtained), प्र (प्रति *prati* towards), प्ल (संप्लुतोदकम् *samplutodakam* full of water), प्स (अप्सु *apsu* in the water), प्स्य (अवाप्स्यसि *avāpsyasi* you will attain)

ब् ब्द (शब्दः *śabdaḥ* sound), ब्ध (लब्ध *labdha* attained), ब्ध्व (लब्ध्वा *labdhvā* having), ब्भ्य (गुब्भ्याम् *gubbhyām* for tow defenders), ब्य (शैब्यः *śaibyaḥ*), ब्र (ब्रह्म *brahma*)

भ् भ्य (अभ्यासः *abhyāsaḥ* study), भ्र (भ्रमः *bhramaḥ* delusion), भ्वादि (*bhvādi* bhū etc.)

म् म्न (धृष्टद्युम्नः *dhṛṣṭadyumnaḥ*), म्प (विकम्पः *vikampaḥ* trembling), म्फ (गुम्फित *gumphita* intertwined), म्ब (अम्बा *ambā* mother), म्भ (अम्भसि *ambhasi* in the water), म्भ्य (पुम्भ्याम् *pumbhyām* for two persons), म्म (सम्मानः *sammānaḥ* respect), म्य (रम्य *ramya* enchanting), म्र (म्रियते *mriyate* it dies)

य् य्य (त्वय्युपपद्यते *tvayyupapadyate* it befits you)

र् र्क (अर्कः *arkaḥ* sun), र्क्ष्य (सूर्क्ष्यिष्यति *sūrkṣiṣyati* he will disrespect), र्ख (मूर्ख *mūrkha* foolish) र्ग (वर्गः *vargaḥ* class), र्ग्भ्य (ऊर्ग्भ्याम् *ūrgbhyām* with two languages), र्ग्य (अस्वर्ग्य *asvargya* un-heavenly), र्घ्य (अर्घ्यम् *arghyam* of fering) र्च (अर्चना *arćanā* worship), र्च्य (अभ्यर्चः *abhyarćaḥ* salute), र्च्छ (मूर्च्छति *mūrćchati* it coagulates), र्ज (भीमार्जुनौ *bhīmārjunau* of Bhima and Arjuna), र्ज्य (वर्ज्य *varjya* without), र्ज्व (वदनैर्ज्वलद्भिः *vadanairjvaladbiḥ* with balzing mouths), र्झ (झर्झरा *jharjharā* prostitute), र्ण (वर्णः *varṇaḥ* a class), र्ण्य (आकर्ण्य *ākarṇya,* hearing), र्त (धार्तराष्ट्रः *dhārtarāṣṭraḥ* Kaurava), र्त्त (आर्त्त *ārtta* afflicted) र्त्म (वर्त्मनि *vartmani* on the path), र्त्य (मर्त्य *martya* dying), र्थ (अर्थः *arthaḥ* meaning), र्द (जनार्दनः *janārdanaḥ* Kṛṣṇa), र्ध (अर्ध *ardha* half), र्ध्न (मूर्ध्नि *mūrdhni* in the head), र्ध्न्य (मूर्ध्न्याधायात्मनः *mūrdhnyādhāyātmanaḥ* having fixed in one's head), र्ध्र (मृत्युर्ध्रुवम् *mṛtyurdhruvam* death is certain), र्ध्व (ऊर्ध्व *ūrdhva* up), र्न (निराशीर्निर्ममः *nirāsīrnirmamaḥ* indifferent and selfless), र्प (सर्पः *sarpaḥ* snake), र्ब (दुर्बुद्धिः *dur-buddhiḥ,* wicked), र्ब्र (हविर्ब्रह्माग्नौ *havirbrhmāgnau* offering in the fire of brahma), र्भ (दर्भः *darbhaḥ* grass), र्म (कर्म *karma* deed), र्म्य (धर्म्यात् *dharmyāt* than the righteous), र्य (शौर्यम् *śauryam* bravery), र्ल (चिकीर्षुर्लोकसंग्रहम् *ćikīrṣur-lokasaṅgraham* desirous of people), र्व (सर्व *sarva* all), र्व्य (बुद्धिर्व्यतितरिष्यति *buddhirvyatitariṣyati* mind will transcend), र्श (स्पर्शः *sparśaḥ* contact), र्ष (हर्षः *harṣaḥ* joy), र्ष्ण (वार्ष्णेयः *vārṣṇeyaḥ* Krishna), र्ह (अर्हः *ahraḥ* worthy), र्ज्ञ (प्रकृतेर्ज्ञानवानपि *prkrterjñānavānapi* the wise also - with his own nature)

ल् ल्क (वल्कलम् *valkalam* bark), ल्ग (वल्गना *valganā* chatter), ल्प (अल्प *alpa* short), उल्बेन (*ulbena* with umblical cord), प्रगल्भ (*pragalbha* proud), ल्म (कल्मषम् *kalmaṣam* sin), ल्य (शल्यः *śalyaḥ* thorn), ल्ल (श्रद्धावाँल्लभते *śraddhāvām̐l-labhate* the faithful person attains), ल्व (बिल्वम् *bilvam* the Bel tree)

व् व्य (व्याघ्रः *vyāghraḥ* tiger), व्र (व्रतम् *vratam* austerity)

श् श्च (आश्चर्यम् *āścaryam* wonder), श्छ (भ्रष्टश्छिन्नम् *bhraṣṭśchinnam* broken and spoiled), श्न (अश्नामि *aśnāmi* I eat), श्म (कश्मलम् *kaśmalam* delusion), श्य (पश्य *paśya* see), श्र (श्री *śrī* divine), श्व (अश्वः *aśvaḥ* horse), श्ल (अश्लील *aślīla* obscene)

ष् ष्क (निष्कामः *niṣkāmaḥ* without desire), ष्कृ (निष्कृतिः *niṣkṛtiḥ* fruitless act), ष्ट (अष्ट *aṣṭa* eight), ष्ट्य (द्वेष्ट्यकुशलम् *dveṣṭya-kuśalam* he hates non-pleasent), ष्ट्र (राष्ट्रम् *rāṣṭram* country), ष्ट्व (दृष्ट्वा *dṛṣṭvā* seeing), ष्ठ (पृष्ठम् *pṛṣṭham* surface), ष्ण (कृष्णः *kṛṣṇaḥ* black), ष्प (पुष्पम् *puṣpam* flower), ष्प्र (दुष्प्रापः *duṣprāpaḥ* difficult to attain), ष्ण्य (औष्ण्यम् *auṣṇyam* warmth), ष्म (भीष्मः *bhīṣmaḥ*), ष्य (मनुष्यः *manuṣyaḥ* man), ष्व (कुरुष्व *kuruṣva* do)

स् स्क (स्कन्दः *skandaḥ* chapter), स्ख (स्खलति *skhalati* it falls), स्ज् (भ्रस्ज् *bhrasj* to roast), स्त (अस्तम् *astam* setting), स्त्य (प्राणान्स्त्यक्त्वा *prāṇānstyaktvā* having renounced their lives), स्र (स्रंसते *sraṁsate* it falls), स्रोतः (*srotaḥ* flow), स्त्र (स्त्री *strī* woman), स्त्व (कुतस्त्वा *kutastvā* from where did you?), स्थ (स्थानम् *sthānam* place), स्न (स्नानम् *snānam* bath), स्प (स्पर्शः *sparśaḥ* contact), स्फ (विस्फोटः *visphoṭaḥ* explosion), स्म (तस्मात् *tasmāt* therefore), स्म्य (गिरामस्म्येकमक्षरम् *girām-asmyekam-akṣaram* among the syllables I am the syllable of Om), स्य (अस्य *asya* its), स्र (सहस्रम् *sahasram* thousand), स्व (स्वतः *svataḥ* oneself), स्स (हिनस्सि *hinassi* you kill)

ह् हृ (हृदयम् *hṛdayam* heart), हृष्यति (*hṛṣyati* he enjoys), ह्ण (गृह्णाति *gṛhṇāti* he takes), ह्न (वह्निः *vahni* fire), ह्म (ब्रह्मा *brahmā*), ह्य (दह्यते *dahyate* it burns), ह्र (जिह्रेति *jihreti* she blushes), ह्ल (प्रह्लादः *prahlādaḥ*), ह्व (जुह्वति *juhvati* he performs offering)

8.3

THE WORD ENDINGS

शब्दान्ताः ।

Below is how consonants and vowels are joined to form words. The last character of a word shows how the word ends. e.g. in the word राम (र् + अ + अ + म् + अ) the last letter is अ, therefore, the word राम is अकारान्त (*akārānta* = ending in character अ)

(A) अजन्त (ending in अच्, ending in a vowel)

(1) राम = र् + आ + म् + अ अकारान्त

(2) वन = व् + अ + न् + अ अकारान्त

(3) माला = म् + आ + ल् + आ आकारान्त

(4) कवि = क् + अ + व् + इ इकारान्त

(5) वारि = व् + आ + र् + इ इकारान्त

(6) मति = म् + अ + त् + इ इकारान्त

(7) नदी = न् + अ + द् + ई ईकारान्त

(8) भानु = भ् + आ + न् + उ उकारान्त

(9) मधु = म् + अ + ध् + उ उकारान्त

(10) धेनु = ध् + ए + न् + उ उकारान्त

(11) वधू = व् + अ + ध् + ऊ ऊकारान्त

(12) पितृ = प् + इ + त् + ऋ ऋकारान्त

(13) धातृ = ध् + आ + त् + ऋ ऋकारान्त

(14) मातृ = म् + आ + त् + ऋ ऋकारान्त

(B) हलन्त (ending in a consonant)

(15) वाच् = व् + आ + च् चकारान्त

(16) राज् = र् + आ + ज् जकारान्त

(17) मरुत् = म् + अ + र् + उ + त् तकारान्त

(18) जगत् = ज् + अ + ग् + अ + त् तकारान्त

(19) सुहृद् = स् + उ + ह् + ऋ + द् दकारान्त

(20) शशिन् = श् + अ + श् + इ + न् नकारान्त

(21) आत्मन् = आ + त् + म् + अ + न् नकारान्त

(22) कर्मन् = क् + अ + र् + म् + अ + न् नकारान्त

(23) दिश् = द् + इ + श् शकारान्त

(24) चन्द्रमस् = च् + अ + न् + द् +र् + अ + म् + अ + स् सकारान्त

(25) पयस् = प् + अ + य् + अ + स् सकारान्त

EXERCISE 21 : A. Fill in the blanks

(1) राम = ——— + ——— + ——— + ——— ।

(2) सीता = ——— + ——— + ——— + ——— ।

(3) पुष्प = ——— + ——— + ——— + ——— + ——— ।

(4) कृष्ण = ——— + ——— + ——— + ——— + ——— ।

(5) संस्कृत = ——— + ——— + ——— + ——— + ——— + ——— + ——— + ——— ।

(6) मनस् = ——— + ——— + ——— + ——— + ——— ।

(7) भानु = ——— + ——— + ——— + ——— ।

(8) वधू = ——— + ——— + ——— + ——— ।

(9) वेद = ——— + ——— + ——— + ——— ।

(10) वैद्य = ——— + ——— + ——— + ——— + ——— ।

(11) ब्रह्मा = ——— + ——— + ——— + ——— + ——— + ——— ।

LESSON 9

navamaḥ abhyāsaḥ नवमः अभ्यासः ।

PRACTICING RAPID READING

śīghrapaṭhanam शीघ्रपठनम् ।

9.1

THE SANSKRIT LANGUAGE

saṁskṛta-bhāṣā **संस्कृतभाषा ।**

सुरस-सुबोधा विश्वमनोज्ञा ललिता हृद्या रमणीया ।
अमृतवाणी संस्कृतभाषा नैव क्लिष्टा न च कठिना ।।1।।

Surasa-subodhā viśva-manojñā lalitā hṛdyā ramaṇīyā,
Amṛta-vāṇī saṁskṛta-bhāṣā naiva kliṣṭā na ća kaṭhinā.

(for meaning of Sanskrit verses, please see Appendix 9)

EXERCISE : ONLY FOR **READING** PRACTICE on what we have learned so far in the previous pages. I assume that you have understood all previous lessons, before proceeding to the following eight exercises.

Following eight exercises are ONLY FOR A PRACTICE IN READING simpler sentences containing easy-to-read Sanskrit compound words. Please read the exercises several times, skip the meaning at this stage, until you finish the book up to lesson 30. Attain a comfortable Sanskrit-reading skill, so that you may be able to tackle the subsequent difficult exercises.

READ THE FOLLOWING PASSAGES

संसारे अनेकाः भाषाः सन्ति ।(saṁsāre anekāḥ bhāṣāḥ santi) तासु सर्वासु संस्कृत-भाषा सर्वोत्तमा च श्रेष्ठा च अस्ति ।(tāsu sarvāsu saṁskṛta-bhāṣā sarvottamā ća śreṣṭhā ća asti) एषा अमृत-वाणी गीर्वाण-वाणी गीर्वाणभारती देव-वाणी इत्यादिभिः नामभिः ज्ञायते ।(eṣā amṛta-vāṇī, gīrvāṇa-vāṇī, gīrvāṇa-bhāratī deva-vāṇī ityādibhiḥ nāmabhiḥ jñāyate).

एषा न केवलं भारतीयानां भाषाणां जननी अस्ति (eṣā na kevalaṁ bhāratīyānaṁ bhāṣāṇāṁ jananī asti) अपितु वैदेशिकानां भाषानाम् अपि जननी अस्ति ।(apitu vaideśikānāṁ bhāṣānām api jananī asti) ऋषयः समाधिम् आस्थाय एनां साक्षात् कृतवन्तः (ṛṣayaḥ samādhim āsthāya enāṁ sākṣāt kṛtavantaḥ) अत एव एषा भाषा दोषरहिता विकारशून्या संस्कार-सम्पन्ना च अस्ति ।(ata eva eṣā bhāṣā doṣa-rahitā, vikāra-śūnyā, saṁskāra-sampannā ća asti).

अस्याः व्याकरणम् अद्भुतम् अस्ति ।(asyāḥ vyākaraṇam adbhutam asti) संस्कृतं वैज्ञानिकं सर्वाङ्गपूर्णं च अस्ति ।(saṁskṛtaṁ vaijñānikaṁ sarvāṅga-pūrṇaṁ ća asti). अस्याः शब्दरचना अभूतपूर्वा अस्ति ।(asyāḥ śabda-raćanā abhūta-pūrvā asti). अस्याः च शब्दकोषः सुविशालः अस्ति । (asyāḥ ća śabda-koṣaḥ suviśālaḥ asti). साहित्यं च सुललितम् अस्ति । (sāhityaṁ ća sulalitam asti). वाल्मीकिः व्यासः कालिदासप्रभृति महाकवयः विश्वसाहित्ये दुर्लभाः सन्ति । (vālmīkiḥ, vyāsaḥ, kālidāsaprabhṛti mahā-kavayaḥ viśva-sāhitye durlabhāḥ santi).

अस्याम् अनेकविधज्ञानम् विद्यते । (asyām aneka-vidhā-jñānaṁ vidyate). अस्यां भाषायां गणितस्य ज्योतिषस्य आयुर्वेदस्य अध्यात्मस्य च सूक्ष्म-विवेचनम् उपलभ्यते । (asyāṁ bhāṣāṁ gaṇitasya, jyotiṣasya, āyurvedasya adhyātmasya ća sūkṣma-vivećanam upalabhyate). संस्कृतं भारतीय-संस्कृतेः मूलम् अस्ति । (saṁskṛtaṁ bhāratīya-saṁskṛteḥ mūlam asti).

9.2
Rāmāyaṇam
रामायणम् ।

कविकोकिल-वाल्मीकि-विरचिता रामायण-रमणीयकथा ।
अतीव सरला मधुरा मञ्जुला नैव क्लिष्टा न च कठिना ।।2।।

Kavi-kokila-vālmīki-viraćitā, rāmāyaṇa-ramaṇīya-kathā,
Atīva saralā madhurā mañjulā, naiva kliṣṭā na ća kaṭhinā.

EXERCISE 22 : ONLY A READING EXERCISE.

रामं समुदितैः गुणैः युक्तं समीक्ष्य दशरथः तस्य यौवराज्यम् अमन्यत् । (Rāmaṁ samuditaiḥ guṇaiḥ yuktaṁ samīkṣya daśarathaḥ tasya yauvarājyam amanyat). विविधान् नागरिकान् नाना जानपदान् अपि सर्वां सभाम् आमन्त्र्य दशरथः उवाच (Vividhān nāgarikān nānā jānapadān api sarvāṁ sabhām āmantrya daśarathaḥ uvāća) श्रेष्ठः एव मम पुत्रः रामः सर्वैः गुणैः युक्तः अस्ति । अतः यौवराज्ये तम् नियोजयामि तस्मात् अनुमन्यताम् । (Śreṣṭhaḥ eva mama putraḥ rāmaḥ sarvaiḥ guṇaiḥ yuktaḥ asti. Ataḥ yauvarājye taṁ niyojayāmi tasmāt anumanyatām).

ते अपि दशरथम् ऊचुः (te api daśaratham ūćuḥ) नृपते! (Nṛpate!) श्रीरामः धर्मज्ञः सत्यसन्धः शीलवान् अनसूयकः (Śrīrāmaḥ dharmajñaḥ satyasandhaḥ śīlavān anasūyakaḥ) तस्मात् सर्वशत्रुदमनम् इमम् श्रीरामं यौवराज्ये वयम् अपि द्रष्टुम् इच्छामः (tasmāt sarvaśatrudamanam imaṁ śrīrāmaṁ yauvarājye vayam api draṣṭum ićchāmaḥ).

EXERCISE 23: Fill in the blanks.

(1) रामं समुदितैः गुणैः ——————— समीक्ष्य ।

(2) सर्वां सभाम् आमन्त्र्य ——————— उवाच ।

(3) मम पुत्रः ——————— सर्वैः गुणैः युक्तः अस्ति ।

(4) यौवराज्ये ——————— नियोजयामि ।

(5) ते अपि ——————— उचुः ।

(6) श्रीरामं यौवराज्ये ——————— अपि द्रष्टुम् इच्छामः ।

9.3

A Devotional Song

bhakti-gītam भक्तिगीतम् ।

EXERCISE 24 :

Only a Reading and Writing exercise. Read the paragrapha and write them in Sanskrit. If you want, the meaning of the verses is given in Appendix 9 at the end.

Śrīkṛṣṇa govinda hare murāre, He nātha nārāyaṇa vāsudeva,
Jihve! pibasvāmṛtametadeva, Govinda dāmodara mādhaveti.

Jihve! sadaiva bhaja sundarāṇi, Nāmāni kṛṣṇasya manoharāṇi,
Samasta bhaktārtivināśanāni, Govinda dāmodara mādhaveti.

Śrīkṛṣṇa rādhāvara gokuleśa, Gopāla govardhana nātha viṣṇo,
Jihve! pibasvāmṛtametadeva, Govinda dāmodara mādhaveti.

EXERCISE 25 :

Fill in the blanks with the Sanskrit words used in above English transliterated verses.

(1) जिह्वे सदैव ________________ सुन्दराणि । (2) ______________ कृष्णस्य मनोहराणि ।
(3) ________________ भक्तार्तिविनाशनानि । (4) श्रीकृष्ण राधावर ______________ ।
(5) गोपाल गोवर्धन ________________ विष्णो ।(6) ______________ दामोदर माधवेति ।

9.4

Mahābhāratam

महाभारतम् ।

व्यासविरचिता गणेशलिखिता महाभारते दिव्यकथा ।
कौरवपाण्डव-सङ्गर-मथिता नैव क्लिष्टा न च कठिना ।।6।।

Vyāsa-viraćitā gaṇeṣa-likhitā, mahābhārate divya-kathā,
Kaurava-pāṇḍava-saṅgara-mathitā, naiva kliṣṭā na ća kaṭhinā.

(for meaning of Sanskrit verses, please see Appendix 9)

EXERCISE 26 : READING EXERCISE.

वैशम्पायनः अब्रवीत् (Vaiśampāyanaḥ abravīt)

ते पाण्डवाः वीराः बद्धखड्गाः बद्धकेशपाशाः कालिन्दीं नदीम् अभिमुखम् कृत्वा जग्मुः (te pāṇḍavāḥ vīrāḥ baddha-khaḍgāḥ baddha-keśa-pāśaḥ kālindiṁ nadīm abhimukhaṁ kṛtvā jagmuḥ) ततः ते दक्षिणं तीरं पादाभ्याम् एव अन्वगच्छन् । (tataḥ te dakṣiṇaṁ tīraṁ padābhyām eva anvagaććhan). तदा ते पाण्डवाः (tadā te pāṇḍavāḥ) निवृत्तवनवासाः (nivṛtta-vana-vāsaḥ) स्वराष्ट्रं प्रेप्सवः (sva-rāṣṭraṁ prepsavaḥ) गिरिदुर्गेषु वनदुर्गेषु धनुष्मन्तः (giri-durgeṣu vana-durgeṣu dhanuṣmantaḥ) ते महाधनुर्धारिणः महाबलाः (te mahā-dhanurdhāriṇaḥ mahā-balāḥ) वनेषु मृगसमूहान् शरैः विन्ध्यन्तः (vaneṣu mṛgasamūhān śaraiḥ vindhyantaḥ) उत्तरेण दशार्ण देशान् (uttareṇa daṣārṇa deśān) तथा दक्षिणेन पाञ्चालान् देशान् (tathā dakṣiṇena pāñćālān deśān) अन्तरेण च (antareṇa ća) यकृल्लोमान् शूरसेनान् कृत्वा (yakṛllomān śūrasenān kṛtvā) मत्स्यस्य विषयं देशं प्रविष्टाः (matsyasya viṣayaṁ deśaṁ praviṣṭāḥ).

ततः मत्स्यस्य नगरं प्राप्य (tataḥ matsyasya nagaraṁ prāpya) धर्मराजानं द्रौपदी उवाच (dharmarājānaṁ draupadī uvāća) पश्य! एकपद्यः दृश्यन्ते । (paśya! ekapadyaḥ dṛśyante). अतः अनेन चिह्नेन व्यक्तं भवति (ataḥ anena ćihnena vyaktaṁ bhavati) यत् विराटस्य राजनगरी इतः दूरे नैव भविष्यति । (yat virāṭasya rājanagarī itaḥ dūre naiva bhaviṣyati).

EXERCISE 27 : Fill in the blanks :

(1) ते —————— वीराः बद्धखड्गाः । (2) ते —————— तीरं पदाभ्याम् एव अन्वगच्छन् ।

(3) विराटस्य राजनगरी इतः —————— नैव भविष्यति ।

9.5

The Gītā गीता ।

कुरुक्षेत्र–समरांङ्गण–गीता, विश्ववन्दिता भगवद्गीता ।
अमृतमधुरा कर्मदीपिका, नैव क्लिष्टा न च कठिना ।।7।।

Kurukṣetra-samarāṅgaṇa-gītāviśva-vanditā bhagavadgītā,
Amṛta-madhurā karma-dīpikā naiva kliṣṭā na ća kaṭhina.

EXERCISE 28 : READING EXERCISE

सञ्जयः उवाच । तं तथा कृपया आविष्टम् अश्रुपूर्णाकुलेक्षणम् विषीदन्तम् तम् इदं वाक्यम् उवाच मधुसूदनः । कुतः त्वा कश्मलम् इदम् विषमे समुपस्थितम् । अनार्यजुष्टम् अस्वर्ग्यम् अकीर्तिकरम् अर्जुन! क्लैब्यं मा स्म गमः पार्थ! न एतत् त्वयि उपपद्यते । क्षुद्रम् हृदय–दौर्बल्यं त्यक्त्वा उत्तिष्ठ परन्तप!

Sañjayaḥ uvāća. Taṁ tathā kṛpayā āviṣṭam aśru-pūrṇākulekṣaṇaṁ viṣīdan tam idaṁ vākyam uvāća madhusūdanaḥ. Kutaḥ tvā kaśmalam idaṁ viṣame sam-upasthitam. Anārya-juṣṭam asvargyam akīrtikaram arjuna! Klaibyaṁ mā sma gamaḥ pārtha! na etat tvayi upapadyate. Kṣudraṁ hṛdaya-daurbalyaṁ tyaktvā uttiṣṭha parantapa!

EXERCISE 29 : Fill in the blanks

(1) विषीदन्तम् तम् इदं वाक्यम् उवाच ———————— । (2) कुतः त्वा कश्मलम् इदम् ———————— समुपस्थितम्? (3) क्षुद्रम् हृदय-दौर्बल्यम् ———————— उत्तिष्ठ परन्तप!

9.6

I am Śiva

śivo'ham शिवोऽहम् ।

EXERCISE 30: Reade and write the verses as you see them. For meaning see Appendix 9.

Na me dveṣa-rāgau na me lobha-mohau, Mado naiva me naiva mātsarya-bhāvaḥ,
Na dharmo na ćārtho na kāmo na mokṣaḥ, Ćidānandarūpaḥ śivo'haṁ śivo'ham.

न मे द्वेषरागौ न मे लोभमोहौ । मदो नैव मे नैव मात्सर्यभाव: ।
न धर्मो न चार्थो न कामो न मोक्षः । चिदानन्दरूपः शिवोऽहं शिवोऽहम् ।।8।।

Na puṇyaṁ na pāpaṁ na saukhyaṁ na duḥkham, Na mantro na tīrthaṁ na vedā na yajñāḥ,
Ahaṁ bhojanaṁ naiva bhojyaṁ na bhoktā, Ćidānandarūpaḥ śivo'haṁ śivo'ham.

न पुण्यं न पापं न सौख्यं न दुःखम् । न मन्त्रो न तीर्थं न वेदा न यज्ञाः ।
अहं भोजनं नैव भोज्यं न भोक्ता । चिदानन्दरूपः शिवोऽहं शिवोऽहम् ।।9।।

Na me mṛtyu-śaṅkā na me jāti-bhedaḥ, Pita naiva me naiva mātā na janma,
Na bandhurna mitraṁ gururnaiva śiṣyaḥ, Ćidānandarūpaḥ śivo'haṁ śivo'ham.

न मे मृत्युशङ्का न मे जातिभेदः । पिता नैव मे नैव माता न जन्म ।
न बन्धुर्न मित्रं गुरुर्नैव शिष्यः । चिदानन्दरूपः शिवोऽहं शिवोऽहम् ।।10।।

Ahaṁ nirvikalpo nirākāra-rūpaḥ, Vibhurvyāpya sarvatra sarvendriyāṇām,
Sadā me samatvaṁ na muktirna bandhaḥ, Ćidānandarūpaḥ śivo'haṁ śivo'ham.

अहं निर्विकल्पो निराकाररूपः । विभुर्व्याप्य सर्वत्र सर्वेन्द्रियाणाम् ।
सदा मे समत्वं न मुक्तिर्न बन्धः । चिदानन्दरूपः शिवोऽहं शिवोऽहम् ।।11।।

9.7
OBEISANCE TO THE MOTHERLAND

Vande Mātaram
वन्दे मातरम्।

EXERCISE 31: Read this beautiful prayer from Bankim Chandra Chaterji's poetry.

वन्दे मातरम् । सुजलां सुफलां मलयज–शीतलाम् ।
शस्यश्यामलां मातरम् । वन्दे मातरम् ।।12।।

Vande mātaram, Sujalāṁ suphalāṁ malayaja-śītalām,
Śasya-śyāmalāṁ mātaram, vande mātaram.

शुभ्र–ज्योत्स्नां पुलकित–यामिनीम् । सुहासिनीं सुमधुर–भाषिणीम् ।
सुखदां वरदां मातरम् । वन्दे मातरम् ।।13।।

Śubhra-jyotsnāṁ pulakita-yāminīm, Suhāsinīṁ su-madhura-bhāṣiṇīm,
Sukhadāṁ varadāṁ mātaram, vande mātaram.

विद्यादायिनि नमामि त्वाम् । नमामि कमलाम् अमलाम् अतुलाम् ।
सुजलां सुफलां मातरम् । वन्दे मातरम् ।।14।।

Vidyā-dāyini! namāmi tvām, Namāmi kamalām amalām atulām,
Sujalāṁ suphalāṁ mātaram, vande mātaram.

श्यामलां सरलाम् । सुस्मितां भूषिताम् ।
धरणीं भरणीं मातरम् । वन्दे मातरम् ।।15।।

Śyāmalāṁ saralām, Susmitāṁ bhūṣitām,
Dharaṇiṁ bharaṇiṁ mātaram, vande mātaram.

9.8
THE VEDAS

The Gāyatrī Chant गायत्री-मन्त्रः ।

गीता गङ्गा च गायत्री गोविन्देति हृदि स्थिते । चतुर्गकारसंयुक्ते पुनर्जन्म न विद्यते ।।16।।
Gītā gaṅgā ća gāyatrī govindeti hṛdi sthite, ćaturgakārasaṁyukte punarjanma na vidyate.

The loftiest among all Sanskrit writings is the divine Gāyatrī Mantra.

EXERCISE 32: Read, write and compare the Sanskrit and English characters.
Oṁ bhūrbhuvaḥ svaḥ, tatsaviturvareṇyaṁ bhargo devasya dhīmahi, dhiyo yo naḥ praćodayāt.

2. ॐ एकदन्ताय विद्महे । वक्रतुण्डाय धीमहि । तन्नो दन्ती प्रचोदयात् ।।18।।

Oṁ ekadantāya vidmahe, vakratuṇḍāya dhīmahi, tanno dantī praćodayāt.

3. ॐ तत्पुरुषाय विद्महे । महादेवाय धीमहि । तन्नो रुद्रः प्रचोदयात् ।।19।।

Oṁ tatpuruṣāya vidmahe, mahādevāya dhīmahi, tanno rudraḥ praćodayāt.

4. ॐ नारायणाय विद्महे । वासुदेवाय धीमहि । तन्नो विष्णुः प्रचोदयात् ।।20।।

Oṁ nārāyaṇāya vidmahe, vāsudevāya dhīmahi, tanno viṣṇuḥ praćodayāt.

5. ॐ देव्यै ब्रह्माण्यै विद्महे । महाशक्त्यै च धीमहि । तन्नो देवी प्रचोदयात् ।।21।।

Oṁ devyai brahmāṇyai vidmahe, mahāśaktyai ća dhīmahi, tanno devī praćodayāt.

6. ॐ महालक्ष्म्यै च विद्महे । विष्णुपत्न्यै च धीमहि । तन्नो लक्ष्मीः प्रचोदयात् ।।22।।

Oṁ mahālakṣmyai ća vidmahe, viṣṇupatnyai ća dhīmahi, tanno lakṣmīḥ praćodayāt.

7. ॐ भास्कराय विद्महे । महद्द्युतिकराय धीमहि । तन्न आदित्यः प्रचोदयात् ।।23।।

Oṁ bhāskarāya vidmahe, mahaddyutikarāya dhīmahi, tanna ādityaḥ praćodayāt.

गायत्र्यास्तु परन्नास्ति शोधनं पापकर्मणाम् ।
गायन्तं त्रायते यस्माद्गायत्री सा ततः स्मृता ।।24।।

Gāyatryāstu parannāsti śodhanaṁ pāpakarmaṇām,
Gāyantaṁ tryāte yasmāt gāyatrī sā tataḥ smṛtā.

BOOK 2

Understand Sanskrit, the Easy Way

संस्कृतं बुध्यताम् ।

saṁskṛtaṁ budhyatām

This section is prepared for those who wish to understand Sanskrit language before attempting to speak it. Those who realise the importance of understanding (not necessarily memorizing) the grammar in learning a new language, will appreciate the lessons and examples given here. Please advance page by page. Make sure you understand previous page before advancing to the next. Piculiarly, in this book the material, examples and exercises on each page is based only on what we learned in the privious pages.

Sanskrit is a musical and poetic language. Most of its best writings come in poetic form. For this reason, you will see Sanskrit verses quoted all over in this book. They teach more than one can express otherwise. For your help, the simplification and meanings of all Sanskrit verses quoted in this book are given in Appendix 9. Please study the verses as best as you can. To making you able to understand Sanskrit *shlokas* on your own, is the main objective of this book.

The book is adorned with virtually hundreds of examples together with translations in Sanskrit and Roman transliteration. Therefore, **please treat all 'Examples' as Exercises,** without looking at the answers, unless you need help.

LESSON 10

daśamaḥ abhyāsaḥ दशमः अभ्यासः ।

INTRODUCTION TO SANDHI

10.1

COMPOUNDING OF VOWELS

svara-sandheḥ paricayaḥ स्वरसन्धेः परिचयः ।

RATNAKAR'S FLOWCHART FOR VOWEL SANDHI RULES

When two vowels come together, they are mathematically added into a single long vowel.

First vowel +	Second vowel	=	Result, a long vowel
1 अ, आ	+ अ, आ	=	आ
	+ इ, ई	=	ए
	+ उ, ऊ	=	ओ
	+ ऋ, ॠ	=	अर्
	+ ए, ऐ	=	ऐ
	+ ओ, औ	=	औ
2 इ, ई	+ अ, आ, उ, ऊ, ए, ऐ, ओ, औ	=	य, या, यु, यू, ये, यै, यो. यौ
	+ इ, ई	=	ई, ई
3 उ, ऊ	+ अ, आ, इ, ई, ए, ऐ, ओ, औ	=	व, वा, वि, वी, वे, वै, वो, वौ
4 ऋ	+ अ, आ, इ, उ, ऊ, ई, ए, ऐ, ओ, औ	=	अर् + अ, आ, इ, ई, उ, ऊ, ए, ऐ, ओ, औ
5 ए	+ अ, आ, इ, ई, उ, ऊ, ए, ऐ, ओ, औ	=	अय् + अ, आ, इ, ई, उ, ऊ, ए, ऐ, ओ, औ
ऐ	+ अ, आ, इ, ई, उ, ऊ, ए, ऐ, ओ, औ	=	आय् + अ, आ, इ, ई, उ, ऊ, ए, ऐ, ओ, औ
6 ओ	+ अ, आ, इ, ई, उ, ऊ, ए, ऐ, ओ, औ	=	अव् + अ, आ, इ, ई, उ, ऊ, ए, ऐ, ओ, औ
औ	+ अ, आ, इ, ई, उ, ऊ, ए, ऐ, ओ, औ	=	आव् + अ, आ, इ, ई, उ, ऊ, ए, ऐ, ओ, औ

SANSKRIT VOWEL SANDHI CHART

अ इ उ ण् ऋ ऌ क्

अ इ उ

अ आ इ ई उ ऊ ऋ

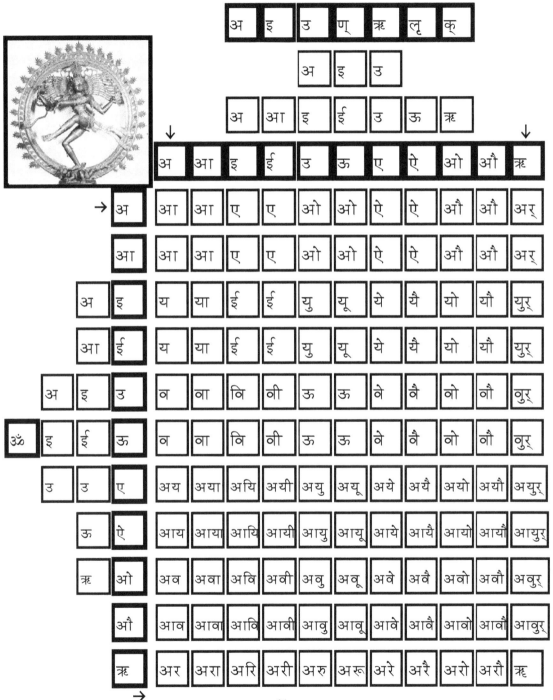

					↓										↓
					अ	आ	इ	ई	उ	ऊ	ए	ऐ	ओ	औ	ऋ
			→	अ	आ	आ	ए	ए	ओ	ओ	ऐ	ऐ	औ	औ	अर्
				आ	आ	आ	ए	ए	ओ	ओ	ऐ	ऐ	औ	औ	अर्
		अ		इ	य	या	ई	ई	यु	यू	ये	यै	यो	यौ	युर्
		आ		ई	य	या	ई	ई	यु	यू	ये	यै	यो	यौ	युर्
	अ	इ		उ	व	वा	वि	वी	ऊ	ऊ	वे	वै	वो	वौ	वुर्
ॐ	इ	ई		ऊ	व	वा	वि	वी	ऊ	ऊ	वे	वै	वो	वौ	वुर्
	उ	उ		ए	अय	अया	अयि	अयी	अयु	अयू	अये	अयै	अयो	अयौ	अयुर्
		ऊ		ऐ	आय	आया	आयि	आयी	आयु	आयू	आये	आयै	आयो	आयौ	आयुर्
		ऋ		ओ	अव	अवा	अवि	अवी	अवु	अवू	अवे	अवै	अवो	अवौ	अवुर्
				औ	आव	आवा	आवि	आवी	आवु	आवू	आवे	आवै	आवो	आवौ	आवुर्
				ऋ	अर	अरा	अरि	अरी	अरु	अरू	अरे	अरै	अरो	अरौ	ॠ

→

EXERCISE 33 : Study the following sandhis (compounds).

अ	+	अ	=	आ	वात	(अ)	+	(अ)	अयनम्	= वातायनम्
अ	+	आ	=	आ	हिम	(अ)	+	(आ)	आलयः	= हिमालयः
अ	+	इ	=	ए	देव	(अ)	+	(इ)	इन्द्रः	= देवेन्द्रः
अ	+	ई	=	ए	परम	(अ)	+	(ई)	ईश्वरः	= परमेश्वरः
अ	+	उ	=	ओ	चन्द्र	(अ)	+	(उ)	उदयः	= चन्द्रोदयः
अ	+	ऊ	=	ओ	प्र	(अ)	+	(ऊ)	ऊढः	= प्रौढः
अ	+	ऋ	=	अर्	उत्तम	(अ)	+	(ऋ)	ऋतुः	= उत्तमर्तुः
अ	+	ऌ	=	अल्	तव	(अ)	+	(ऌ)	ऌकारः	= तवल्कारः
अ	+	ए	=	ऐ	एक	(अ)	+	(ए)	एकम्	= एकैकम्
अ	+	ऐ	=	ऐ	देव	(अ)	+	(ऐ)	ऐश्वर्यम्	= देवैश्वर्यम्
अ	+	ओ	=	औ	जल	(अ)	+	(ओ)	ओघः	= जलौघः
अ	+	औ	=	औ	जन	(अ)	+	(औ)	औदार्यम्	= जनौदार्यम्

आ	+	अ	=	आ	विद्या	(आ)	+	(अ)	अर्थी	= विद्यार्थी
आ	+	आ	=	आ	विद्या	(आ)	+	(आ)	आलयम्	= विद्यालयम्
आ	+	इ	=	ए	यथा	(आ)	+	(इ)	इच्छा	= यथेच्छा
आ	+	ई	=	ए	रमा	(आ)	+	(ई)	ईशः	= रमेशः
आ	+	उ	=	ओ	महा	(आ)	+	(उ)	उत्सवः	= महोत्सवः
आ	+	ऊ	=	ओ	महा	(आ)	+	(ऊ)	ऊरुः	= महोरुः
आ	+	ऋ	=	अर्	महा	(आ)	+	(ऋ)	ऋषिः	= महर्षिः
आ	+	ए	=	ऐ	सदा	(आ)	+	(ए)	एव	= सदैव
आ	+	ऐ	=	ऐ	प्रजा	(आ)	+	(ऐ)	ऐक्यम्	= प्रजैक्यम्
आ	+	ओ	=	औ	गंगा	(आ)	+	(ओ)	ओघः	= गंगौघः
आ	+	औ	=	औ	विद्या	(आ)	+	(औ)	औत्सुक्यम्	= विद्यौत्सुक्यम्

इ	+	अ	=	य	यदि	(इ)	+	(अ)	अपि	= यद्यपि
इ	+	आ	=	या	इति	(इ)	+	(आ)	आदि	= इत्यादि
इ	+	इ	=	ई	रवि	(इ)	+	(इ)	इन्द्रः	= रवीन्द्रः
इ	+	ई	=	ई	कवि	(इ)	+	(ई)	ईश्वरः	= कविश्वरः
इ	+	उ	=	यु	अति	(इ)	+	(उ)	उत्तमम्	= अत्युत्तमम्

इ	+	ऊ	=	यू	प्रति	(इ)	+	(ऊ)	ऊहः	=	प्रत्यूहः
इ	+	ऋ	=	युर्	अति	(इ)	+	(ऋ)	ऋद्धिः	=	अत्युर्द्धिः
इ	+	ए	=	ये	प्रति	(इ)	+	(ए)	एकम्	=	प्रत्येकम्
इ	+	ऐ	=	यै	प्रति	(इ)	+	(ऐ)	ऐरावतम्	=	प्रत्यैरावतम्
इ	+	ओ	=	यो	दधि	(इ)	+	(ओ)	ओदनम्	=	दध्योदनम्
इ	+	औ	=	यौ	दधि	(इ)	+	(औ)	औषधम्	=	दध्यौषधम्
ई	+	अ	=	य	नदी	(ई)	+	(अ)	अम्बु	=	नद्यम्बु
ई	+	आ	=	या	देवी	(ई)	+	(आ)	आज्ञा	=	देव्याज्ञा
ई	+	इ	=	ई	जननी	(ई)	+	(इ)	इच्छा	=	जननीच्छा
ई	+	ई	=	ई	काली	(ई)	+	(ई)	ईश्वरी	=	कालीश्वरी
ई	+	उ	=	यु	सुधी	(ई)	+	(उ)	उपास्यः	=	सुध्युपास्यः
ई	+	ऊ	=	यू	अवी	(ई)	+	(ऊ)	ऊर्णा	=	अव्यूर्णा
ई	+	ऋ	=	युर्	महती	(ई)	+	(ऋ)	ऋक्षी	=	महर्त्यूक्षी
ई	+	ए	=	ये	गोपी	(ई)	+	(ए)	एषा	=	गोप्येषा
ई	+	ऐ	=	यै	गौरी	(ई)	+	(ऐ)	ऐश्वर्यम्	=	गौर्यैश्वर्यम्
ई	+	ओ	=	यो	नारी	(ई)	+	(ओ)	औत्कर्षम्	=	नार्योत्कर्षम्
ई	+	औ	=	यौ	वाणी	(ई)	+	(औ)	औचित्यम्	=	वाण्यौचित्यम्
उ	+	अ	=	व	मनु	(उ)	+	(अ)	अन्तरम्	=	मन्वन्तरम्
उ	+	आ	=	व	गुरु	(उ)	+	(आ)	आदेशः	=	गुर्वादेशः
उ	+	इ	=	वि	तु	(उ)	+	(इ)	इदानीम्	=	त्विदानीम्
उ	+	ई	=	वी	ऋतु	(उ)	+	(ई)	ईश्वरः	=	ऋत्वीश्वरः
उ	+	उ	=	ऊ	गुरु	(उ)	+	(उ)	उपदेशः	=	गुरूपदेशः
उ	+	ऊ	=	ऊ	चमू	(उ)	+	(ऊ)	ऊहिनी	=	चमूहिनी
उ	+	ऋ	=	वृ	मधु	(उ)	+	(ऋ)	ऋते	=	मध्वृते
उ	+	ए	=	वे	अनु	(उ)	+	(ए)	एषणम्	=	अन्वेषणम्
उ	+	ऐ	=	वै	साधु	(उ)	+	(ऐ)	ऐक्यम्	=	साध्वैक्यम्
उ	+	ओ	=	वो	गुरु	(उ)	+	(ओ)	ओजः	=	गुर्वोजः
उ	+	औ	=	वौ	मधु	(उ)	+	(औ)	औषधिः	=	मध्वौषधिः

ऊ	+	अ	=	व	शरयू	(ऊ)	+	(अ)	अम्बु	= शरय्वम्बु
ऊ	+	आ	=	वा	अमू	(ऊ)	+	(आ)	आसते	= अम्वासते
ऊ	+	इ	=	वि	बन्धू	(ऊ)	+	(इ)	इमौ	= बन्ध्विमौ
ऊ	+	ई	=	वी	वधू	(ऊ)	+	(ई)	ईक्षणम्	= वध्वीक्षणम्
ऊ	+	उ	=	ऊ	वधू	(ऊ)	+	(उ)	उत्सवः	= वधूत्सवः
ऊ	+	ऊ	=	ऊ	वधू	(ऊ)	+	(ऊ)	ऊहा	= वधूहा
ऊ	+	ऋ	=	वृ	वधू	(ऊ)	+	(ऋ)	ऋक्थम्	= वध्वृक्थम्
ऊ	+	ए	=	वे	कण्डू	(ऊ)	+	(ए)	एषणा	= कण्ड्वेषणा
ऊ	+	ऐ	=	वै	वधू	(ऊ)	+	(ऐ)	ऐश्वर्यम्	= वध्वैश्वर्यम्
ऊ	+	ओ	=	वो	वधू	(ऊ)	+	(ओ)	ओकः	= वध्वोकः
ऊ	+	औ	=	वौ	यवागू	(ऊ)	+	(औ)	औष्ण्यम्	= यवाग्वौष्ण्यम्

ऋ	+	अ	=	र	मातृ	(ऋ)	+	(अ)	अंशः	= मात्रंशः
ऋ	+	आ	=	रा	पितृ	(ऋ)	+	(आ)	आदेशः	= पित्रादेशः
ऋ	+	इ	=	रि	भ्रातृ	(ऋ)	+	(इ)	इच्छा	= भ्रात्रिच्छा
ऋ	+	ई	=	री	सवितृ	(ऋ)	+	(ई)	ईशः	= सवित्रीशः
ऋ	+	उ	=	रु	कर्तृ	(ऋ)	+	(उ)	उत्तमः	= कर्त्रुत्तमः
ऋ	+	ऊ	=	रू	नप्तृ	(ऋ)	+	(ऊ)	ऊढा	= नप्त्रूढा
ऋ	+	ऋ	=	ॠ	धातृ	(ऋ)	+	(ऋ)	ऋणम्	= धातॄणम्
ऋ	+	ए	=	रे	गन्तृ	(ऋ)	+	(ए)	एधः	= गन्त्रेधः
ऋ	+	ऐ	=	रै	नेतृ	(ऋ)	+	(ऐ)	ऐश्वर्यम्	= नेत्रैश्वर्यम्
ऋ	+	ओ	=	रो	वक्तृ	(ऋ)	+	(ओ)	ओजः	= वक्त्रोजः
ऋ	+	औ	=	रौ	भर्तृ	(ऋ)	+	(औ)	औदार्यम्	= भर्त्रौदार्यम्
लृ	+	अ	=	ल	लृ	(लृ)	+	(अ)	अनुबन्धः	= लनुबन्धः
लृ	+	आ	=	ला	लृ	(लृ)	+	(आ)	आकृतिः	= लाकृतिः

ए	+	अ	=	अय	ने	(ए)	+	(अ)	अनम्	= नयनम्
ए	+	आ	=	अया	ते	(ए)	+	(आ)	आगताः	= तयागताः
ए	+	इ	=	अयि	शे	(ए)	+	(इ)	इतः	= शयितः
ए	+	ई	=	अयी	ते	(ए)	+	(ई)	ईर्षा	= तयीर्षा
ए	+	उ	=	अयु	मे	(ए)	+	(उ)	उपदेशः	= मयुपदेशः

ए	+	ऊ	=	अयू	ये	(ए)	+	(ऊ)	ऊहन्ते	= ययूहन्ते
ए	+	ऋ	=	अयुर्	के	(ए)	+	(ऋ)	ऋच्छन्ति	= कयुर्छन्ति
ए	+	ए	=	अये	ते	(ए)	+	(ए)	एते	= तयेते
ए	+	ऐ	=	अयै	ते	(ए)	+	(ऐ)	ऐश्वर्यम्	= तयैश्वर्यम्
ए	+	ओ	=	अयो	गृहे	(ए)	+	(ओ)	ओकण:	= गृहयोकण:
ए	+	औ	=	अयौ	ते	(ए)	+	(औ)	औषधि:	= तयौषधि:

ऐ	+	अ	=	आय	गै	(ऐ)	+	(अ)	अनम्	= गायनम्
ऐ	+	आ	=	आया	तस्मै	(ऐ)	+	(आ)	आदेश:	= तस्मायादेश:
ऐ	+	इ	=	आयि	एतस्मै	(ऐ)	+	(इ)	इमानि	= एतस्मायिमानि
ऐ	+	ई	=	आयी	स्त्रियै	(ऐ)	+	(ई)	ईडा	= स्त्रियायीडा
ऐ	+	उ	=	आयु	श्रियै	(ऐ)	+	(उ)	उद्यत:	= श्रियायुद्यत:
ऐ	+	ऊ	=	आयू	कस्मै	(ऐ)	+	(ऊ)	ऊर्ज:	= कस्मायूर्ज:
ऐ	+	ऋ	=	आयुर्	यस्मै	(ऐ)	+	(ऋ)	ऋणम्	= यस्मायुर्णम्
ऐ	+	ए	=	आये	एतस्मै	(ऐ)	+	(ए)	एवम्	= एतस्मायेवम्
ऐ	+	ऐ	=	आयै	कस्मै	(ऐ)	+	(ऐ)	ऐश्वर्यम्	= कस्मायैश्वर्यम्
ऐ	+	ओ	=	आयो	कस्यै	(ऐ)	+	(ओ)	ओज:	= कस्यायोज:
ऐ	+	औ	=	आयौ	अस्यै	(ऐ)	+	(औ)	औचित्यम्	= अस्यायौचित्यम्

ओ	+	अ	=	अव	यो	(ओ)	+	(अ)	अयनम्	= यवनम्
ओ	+	आ	=	अवा	साधो	(ओ)	+	(आ)	आगच्छ	= साधवागच्छ
ओ	+	इ	=	अवि	विष्णो	(ओ)	+	(इ)	इति	= विष्णविति
ओ	+	ई	=	अवी	गो	(ओ)	+	(ई)	ईश्वर:	= गवीश्वर:
ओ	+	उ	=	अवु	नो	(ओ)	+	(उ)	उद्योग:	= नवुद्योग:
ओ	+	ऊ	=	अवू	गुरो	(ओ)	+	(ऊ)	ऊनयतु	= गुरवुनयतु
ओ	+	ऋ	=	अवुर्	विष्णो	(ओ)	+	(ऋ)	ऋच्छतु	= विष्णवुर्च्छतु
ओ	+	ए	=	अवे	गो	(ओ)	+	(ए)	एषणा	= गवेषणा
ओ	+	ऐ	=	अवै	भानो	(ओ)	+	(ऐ)	ऐशानीम्	= भानवैशानीम्
ओ	+	ओ	=	अवो	गो	(ओ)	+	(ओ)	ओकस्	= गवोकस्
ओ	+	औ	=	अवौ	मधो	(ओ)	+	(औ)	औखतु	= मधवौखतु

औ	+	अ	=	आव	पौ	(औ)	+	(अ)	अनः	=	पवनः
औ	+	आ	=	आवा	रात्रौ	(औ)	+	(आ)	आगतः	=	रात्रावागतः
औ	+	इ	=	आवि	पुत्रौ	(औ)	+	(इ)	इमौ	=	पुत्राविमौ
औ	+	ई	=	आवी	तौ	(औ)	+	(ई)	ईश्वरौ	=	तावीश्वरौ
औ	+	उ	=	आवु	गुरौ	(औ)	+	(उ)	उक्तः	=	गुरावुक्तः
औ	+	ऊ	=	आवू	रुग्णौ	(औ)	+	(ऊ)	ऊर्जयतु	=	रुग्णावूर्जयतु
औ	+	ऋ	=	आवुर्	तौ	(औ)	+	(ऋ)	ऋषी	=	तावुर्षी
औ	+	ए	=	आवे	कौ	(औ)	+	(ए)	एतौ	=	कावेतौ
औ	+	ऐ	=	आवै	द्वौ	(औ)	+	(ऐ)	ऐतिहासिकौ	=	द्वावैतिहासिकौ
औ	+	ओ	=	आवो	एतौ	(औ)	+	(ओ)	ओकसी	=	एतावोकसी
औ	+	औ	=	आवौ	नौ	(औ)	+	(औ)	औ	=	नावौ

ADVANCED VOWEL-SANDHI RULES

(1) If the dipthong ए or ओ (*e* or *o*) at the end of a word is followed by a word starting with अ (*a*), the ए or ओ remains unchanged, but vowel अ is elided (अ = ऽ). गणपतये अहम् नमामि → गणपतयेऽहं नमामि

Gaṇapataye ahaṁ namāmi → gaṇapataye'haṁ namāmi

(2) अय् and अव् of the *sandhi* (rules 5 and 6 given above), when followed by any vowel other than अ, they may optionally drop the य् and व् in them.

अहम् गणपतये इच्छामि → अहं गणपतयिच्छामि । अहं गणपत इच्छामि ।

ahaṁ gaṇapataye icchāmi → ahaṁ gaṇapatayicchāmi, ahaṁ gaṇapata icchāmi.

हे प्रभो इति वद → हे प्रभविति वद । हे प्रभ इति वद ।

he prabho iti vada → he prabhaviti vada, he prabha iti vada.

(3) ऐ and औ at the end of a word, when followed by any vowel, are changed to आय् and आव्, but they may optionally drop the य् and व् in them. तस्मै इदम् यच्छ → तस्मायिदं यच्छ । तस्मा इदं यच्छ । *tasmai idam yaccha → tasmāyidaṁ yaccha, tasmā idaṁ yaccha.*

(4) ई, ऊ, ए at the end of the dual substantives do not change when followed by a word starting with any vowel. अनादी उभौ → अनादी उभौ (Gītā 13.20)

(5) The interjections such as हे, अहो, अरि, भोः, आ do not form *sandhi* with its following word. हे अर्जुन! → हे अर्जुन! भोः इन्द्र → भोः इन्द्र

(6) The ई of अमी (the m◦ pl◦ nom◦ of pronoun अदस्) does not form *sandhi* with its following vowel. अमी इक्षन्ते सुराः → अमी इक्षन्ते सुराः ।

10.2
COMPOUNDING A CONSONANT WITH THE FOLLOWING VOWEL

vyañjana-svarayoḥ sandhiḥ व्यञ्जन-स्वरयोः सन्धिः ।

(For details on the Class Consonants, see lesson 3.2)

(1) Rule of 3rd consonant :

If a consonant from any of the five classes (k, ć, ṭ, t, p, क्, च्, ट्, त, प्), other than the nasal consonants, is followed by a vowel, this class consonant is replaced with the third consonant from that class. (This third consonant then conjugates with the vowel that comes after it). e.g.

क् + उ	=	ग् + उ	= गु	→	सम्यक्	+ उभयोः	=	सम्यगुभयोः (Gītā 5.4)
त् + अ	=	द् + अ	= द	→	तत्	+ अस्माकम्	=	तदस्माकम् (Gītā1.10)
त् + ऋ	=	द् + ऋ	= दृ	→	एतत्	+ ऋतम्	=	एतदृतम् (Gītā 10.14)
त् + ॐ	=	द् + ॐ	= दोम्	→	तस्मात्	+ ओम्	=	तस्मादोम् (Gītā 1.22)

(2) Conjugation of the word ending in n (न्) -

When a word ending in n (न्) is preceeded by any short vowel and is followed by any vowel, the ending n (न्) is doubled and becomes nn (न्न) e.g.

अनिच्छन्	+ अपि	=	अनिच्छन्नपि (Gītā 3.36)
पश्यन्	+ आत्मनि	=	पश्यन्नात्मनि ।(Gītā 6.20)
विषीदन्	+ इदम्	=	विषीदन्निदम् (Gītā 1.27)
गृह्णन्	+ उन्मिषन्	=	गृह्णन्नुन्मिषन् ।(Gītā 5.9)
युञ्जन्	+ एवम्	=	युञ्जन्नेवम् ।(Gītā 6.15)

10.3

COMPOUNDING A CONSONANT WITH THE FOLLOWING CONSONANT

vyañjanayoḥ sandhiḥ व्यञ्जनयोः सन्धिः ।

(For details on the Class Consonants, see Lesson 6.2)

(3) **Rule of 3rd consonant :**

* When a consonant, other than a nasal consonant, comes after a hard consonant from any of the five classes (namely, k, ć, ṭ, t, p, क्, च्, ट्, त्, प्), then this hard consonant is replaced by the third consonant from that same class (or optionally by the nasal consonant from that class). e.g.

क् + ब	=	ग् + ब	= ग्ब	→	पृथक् + बाला:	= पृथग्बाला: (Gītā 5.4)
क् + म	=	ङ् + म	= ङ्म	→	ईदृक् + मम	= ईदृङ्मम (Gītā 11.49)
त् + ग	=	द् + ग	= द्ग	→	यत् + गत्वा	= यद्गत्वा (Gītā 15.6)
त् + द	=	द् + द	= द्द	→	विद्यात् + दुःखं	= विद्याद्दुःखं (Gītā 6.23)
त् + ध	=	द् + ध	= द्ध	→	बुद्धियोगात् + धनञ्जय	= बुद्धियोगाद्धनञ्जय (Gita 2.49)
त् + भ	=	द् + भ	= द्भ	→	क्रोधात् + भवति	= क्रोधाद्भवति (Gītā 2.63)
त् + य	=	द् + य	= द्य	→	अपनुद्यात् + यत्	= अपनुद्याद्यत् (Gītā 2.8)
त् + र	=	द् + र	= द्र	→	यत् + राज्यम्	= यद्राज्यम् (Gītā 1.45)
त् + व	=	द् + व	= द्व	→	एतत् + विद्मः	= एतद्विद्मः (Gītā 2.6)
त् + ह	=	द् + ह	= द्ध	→	धर्म्यात् + हि	= धर्म्याद्धि (Gītā 2.31)

(4) The Rule of same order Consonant :

* When any consonant from t (त्) class (t, th, d, dh, n त्, थ्, द्, ध्, न्), is followed by any consonant from ć (च्) class (ć, ćh, j, jh, ñ च्, छ्, ज्, झ्, ञ्), then that consonant from t (त्) class is replaced by the consonant of same order from the ć (च्) class. e.g.

त् + च = च् + च = च्च	→	आश्चर्यवत् + च	=	आश्चर्यवच्च (Gītā 2.29)
त् + ज = ज् + ज = ज्ज	→	स्यात् + जनार्दन	=	स्याज्जनार्दन (Gītā 1.36)

* When a consonant from t (त्) class (t, th, d, dh, n त्, थ्, द्, ध्, न्), is followed by consonant ś (श्), then that consonant from the t (त्) class (t, th, d, dh, n त्, थ्, द्, ध्, न्), is replaced by the consonant of same order from the ć (च्) class (ć, ćh, j, jh, ñ च्, छ्, ज्, झ्, ञ्).

And the following consonant ś (श्) is optionally replaced by consonant ćh (छ्)

त् + श = च् + छ = च्छ → यत् + शोकम् = यच्छोकम् (Gītā 2.8)

त् + श्र = च् + छ्र = च्छ्र → युद्धात् + श्रेय: = युद्धाच्छ्रेय: (Gītā 2.31)

* However, When consonant t (त्) or d (द्) is followed by consonant l (ल्), then that consonant t (त्) or d (द्) is replaced by consonant l (ल्) e.g.

त् + ल = ल् + ल = ल्ल → भुवनात् + लोका: = भुवनाल्लोका: (Gita 8.16)

(5) Nasal Inflections :

* If a consonant, other than a nasal consonant, from any class (k, ć, ṭ, t, p क, च, ट, त प), is followed by a nasal consonant, then this class consonant is optionally replaced by the nasal consonant from the same class.

त् + न = न् + न = न्न → तस्मात् + न = तस्मान्न (Gītā 1.37)

त् + म = न् + म = न्म → तत् + मे = तन्मे (Gītā 1.46)

द् + म = न् + म = न्म → सुहृद् + मित्रम् = सुहृन्मित्रम् (Gītā 6.9)

(6) म् becomes a nasal dot (अनुस्वार:)

* When a word ending in letter m (म्) is followed by a word starting with any consonant, then that end-letter m (म्) becomes a nasal dot, and that is placed over the character that is before m (म्). e.g.

पाण्डवानीकम् व्यूढम् = पाण्डवानीकं व्यूढम् । (Gītā 1.2)

* But, when a word ending in letter m (म्) is at the end of the sentence, that letter m (म्) remains unchanged.

पश्यैतां पाण्डुपुत्राणामाचार्य महतीं चमूम् ।।25।। (Gītā 1.3)

पर्याप्तं त्विदमेतेषां बलं भीमाभिरक्षितम् ।।26।। (Gītā 1.10)

(7) Change of n (न्) to ṇ (ण्) at the end of a word

(a) When letter n (न्) within or at the end of a word is preceded by letter ṛ, ṝ, r or ṣ (ऋ, ॠ, र्, ष्); and

(b) between this n (न्) and the preceding ṛ, ṝ, r or ṣ (ऋ, ॠ, र्, ष्), even if any vowel, an anusvāra, a consonant from class k (क्) or a consonant from class p (प्) or letter y, r, v or h (य्, र्, व् ह्) comes,

(c) in all these cases, this n (न्) changes to ṇ (ण्). e.g.

द्रुपदपुत्रेण	→ त् + र् + ए + न	= त् + र् + ए + ण	=	त्रेण (Gītā 1.3)
शरीरिण:	→ र् + इ + न:	= र् + इ + ण:	=	रिण: (Gītā 2.18)
कर्मणा	→ र् + म् + अ + न् + आ	= र् + म् + अ + ण् + आ	=	र्मणा (Gītā 3.20)

(8) Change of s (स्) to ṣ (ष्) at the end of a word -

* If a vowel other than *a* or *ā* (अ, आ) or any consonant from the class *k* (क) or the letter *r* (र्) comes after a word ending in a case suffix such as *saḥ, sā, sām, si, su, syati, syate, syanti, syāmi, sye, sva,* etc. (स: सा, साम्, सि, सु, स्यति, स्यते, स्यन्ति, स्यामि, स्ये, स्व), then in all these cases the *s* (स्) in these suffixes changes to *ṣ* (ष्)

एष: (Gītā 3.10) एषा (Gītā 2.39) एतेषाम् (Gītā 1.10) करोषि (Gītā 9.27)

अयनेषु (Gītā 1.11) परिशुष्यति (Gītā 1.29) कथयिष्यन्ति (Gītā 2.34) विशिष्यते (Gītā 7.17)

कथयिष्यामि (Gītā 10.19) हनिष्ये (Gītā 16.14) कुरुष्व (Gītā 9.27)

10.4

CONJUGATION WITH A VISARGA (:) विसर्गसन्धिः ।

RATNAKAR'S FLOWCHART FOR VISARGA SANDHI

Before the visarga	the visarga	After the visarga	The result
1. एषः सः	:	other than अ	**visarga is deleted**
↓			
2. Any character	:	त, थ	**visarga becomes स्**
↓			
3. any other character	:	च, छ	**visarga becomes श्**
↓			
4. any chcharacter	:	ट, ठ	**visarge becomes ष्**
↓		श, ष्, स	**visarge becomes श् . स्**
5. any other character	:	any hard character	**visarga remains**
↓			
6. आ	:	any other character	**visarga is deleted**
↓			
7. अ	:	अ	**(अ + : + अ) become ओऽ**
↓			
8. अ	:	other vowel	**visarga is deleted**
↓			
9. अ	:	soft consonant	अ + **visarga become ओ**
↓			
10. other vowel	:	any character	**visarga becomes र्**

NOTE : At any place, when more than one sandhi rules appear to apply, the rule appearing first in this flowchart superceeds the rules that appear after.

EXERCISE 34 : Study the following examples for above 10 golden rules

1. एषः क्रोधः →	एष क्रोधः (Gītā 3.37)
एषः रजोगुणः →	एष रजोगुणः (Gītā 3.37)
एषः तु →	एष तु (Gītā 10.40)
सः शब्दः →	स शब्दः (Gītā 1.13)
सः कौन्तेयः →	स कौन्तेयः (Gītā 1.27)
2.सौमदत्तिः तथा →	सौमदत्तिस्तथा (Gītā 1.2)
शब्दः तुमुलः →	शब्दस्तुमुलः (Gītā 1.13)
शिष्यः ते →	शिष्यस्ते (Gītā 2.6)
3. पाण्डवाः च →	पाण्डवाश्च (Gītā 1.1)
विराटः च →	विराटश्च (Gītā 1.4)
विभ्रष्टः छिन्न →	विभ्रष्टश्छिन्न (Gītā 6.38)
4. रामः टीकते →	रामष्टीकते
रामः ठक्कुरः →	रामष्ठक्कुरः
5. चेकितानः काशिराजः →	चेकितानः काशिराजः (Gītā 1.5)
मामकाः पाण्डवाः →	मामकाः पाण्डवाः (Gītā 1.1)
योगेश्वरः कृष्णः →	योगेश्वरः कृष्णः (Gītā 18.78)
6. समवेताः युयुत्सवः →	समवेता युयुत्सवः (Gītā 1.1)
शूराः महेश्वासाः →	शूरा महेश्वासाः (Gītā 1.3)
गुणाः गुणेषु →	गुणा गुणेषु (Gītā 3.28)
7. तुमुलः अभवत् →	तुमुलोऽभवत् (Gītā 1.13)
शाश्वतः अयम् →	शाश्वतोऽयम् (Gītā 2.20)
सः अमृतत्त्वाय कल्पते →	सोऽमृतत्त्वाय कल्पते (Gītā 2.15)
8.यः एनम् →	य एनम् (Gītā 2.19)
अतः ऊर्ध्वम् →	अत ऊर्ध्वम् (Gītā 12.8)
अव्ययः ईश्वरः →	अव्यय ईश्वरः (Gītā 15.17)
9. श्रेयः भोक्तुम् →	श्रेयो भोक्तुम् (Gītā 2.5)

पार्थ: धनुर्धर: → पार्थो धनुर्धर: (Gītā 18.78)
विजय: भूति: → विजयो भूति: (Gītā 18.78)

10. मुनि: उच्यते → मुनिरुच्यते (Gītā 2.56)
दोषै: एतै: → दोषैरेतै: (Gītā 1.43)
सेनयो: उभयो: → सेनयोरुभयो: (Gītā 1.21)
स्थितधी: मुनि: → स्थितधीर्मुनि: (Gītā 2.56)
भू: मा → भूर्मा (Gītā 2.47)
उभयो: मध्ये → उभयोर्मध्ये (Gītā 1.21)

A CLASSICAL EXAMPLE, of a four way sandhi (न: *naḥ* = to us, for us, our)
स्वस्ति न इन्द्रो वृद्धश्रवा: स्वस्ति न: पूषा विश्वदेवा: ।
स्वस्ति नस्ताक्ष्र्यो अरिष्टनेमि: स्वस्ति नो बृहस्पतिर्दधातु ।।
svasti na indro vṛddhaśravāḥ svasti naḥ pūṣā viśvadevāḥ,
svasti nastākṣryo ariṣṭanemiḥsvasti no bṛhaspatirdhātu.

NOTES :

(1) The visarga before श, ष or स (*śa, ṣa or sa*), either stays or is optionally changed to श्, ष्, स् respectively.

(2) Once any *sandhi* rule is applied between two words, those two words do not conjugate again with any of the other *sandhi* rule (other than the rule of परसवर्ण-संधि: । *parasavarṇa-sandhiḥ*).

e.g. In विक्रान्त: उत्तमौजा: (Gītā 1.6), विक्रान्त: and उत्तमौजा: are conjugated into विक्रान्त उत्तमौजा: with rule 9. Now विक्रान्त उत्तमौजा: can NOT again be conjugated into विक्रान्तोत्तमौजा: using the *sandhi* rule अ + उ = ओ, with rule 10.1

Examples of परसवर्ण-संधि: parasavarṇa-sandhiḥ :
महत्पापं कर्तुम् = महत्पापङ्कर्तुम् (mahatpāpṅkartum Gītā 1.45), पदं गच्छन्ति = पदङ्गच्छन्ति (padaṅgachhanti Gītā 2.51), रूपं घोरम् = रूपङ्घोरम् (rūpaṅghoram Gītā 11.49), महतीं चमूम् = महतीञ्चमूम् (mahatiñćamūm Gītā 1.3), etc, For more examples, see section 28.13

SANDHI

EXAMPLES FROM THE CLASSICAL LITERATURE

1. एषः सूर्यस्य रश्मिः → एष सूर्यस्य रश्मिः । रश्मिरेष सूर्यस्य । सूर्यस्यैष रश्मिः । रश्मिः सूर्यस्यैषः ।
2. सूर्यस्य एकः रश्मिः सोमम् दीपयति → सूर्यस्यैको रश्मिः सोमं दीपयति । सूर्यस्य दीपयत्येको रश्मिः सोमम् । सोमं सूर्यस्यैको रश्मिर्दिपयति ।
3. गृहिभिः यज्ञाः अवश्यम् करणीयाः → गृहिभिर्यज्ञा अवश्यं करणीयाः । गृहिभिरवश्यं करणीया यज्ञाः । गृहिभिरवश्यङ्करणीया यज्ञाः । यज्ञा गृहिभिरवश्यं करणीयाः । यज्ञा गृहिभिरवश्यङ्करणीयाः ।
4. कस्मात् देशात् आगतौ विद्वांसौ पुरुषौ → कस्माद्देशादागतौ विद्वांसौ पुरुषौ । पुरुषावागतौ कस्माद्देशाद्विद्वांसौ । विद्वांसौ कस्मादागतौ देशात्पुरुषौ । विद्वांसावागतौ कस्माद्देशात्पुरुषौ ।
5. रविः प्रातः समये आगच्छति → आगच्छति प्रातस्समये रविः । रविरागच्छति प्रातस्समये ।
6. सः तस्य उदयकालः इति उच्यते → स तस्योदयकाल इत्युच्यते । उच्यते स तस्योदयकाल इति । उदयकालस्तस्य स इत्युच्यते ।
7. सः सायङ्काले अस्तम् गच्छति → स सायङ्कालेऽस्तम् गच्छति । स सायङ्कालेऽस्तङ्गच्छति । सोऽस्तङ्गच्छति सायङ्काले । सायङ्कालेऽस्तं गच्छति सः । गच्छत्यस्तं स सायङ्काले ।
8. त्वया उदधिः दृष्टः न वा → त्वयोदधिर्दृष्टो न वा । त्वया दृष्ट उदधिर्न वा । उदधिर्दृष्टस्त्वया न वा । दृष्टस्त्वयोदधिर्न वा । उदधिस्त्वया दृष्टो न वा । त्वया न वोदधिर्दृष्टः ।
9. तत् जले पतितम् आसीत् → तज्जले पतितमासीत् । तत्पतितमासीज्जले । जले पतितं तदासीत् । आसीत्तत्पतितं जले ।
10. इदानीम् उदधिं स्नानाय गच्छ → इदानीमुदधिं स्नानाय गच्छ । गच्छेदानीमुदधिं स्नानाय । गच्छेदधिमिदानीं स्नानाय ।
11. भूपतिः भूमिम् रक्षति → भूपतिर्भूमिं रक्षति । रक्षति भूपतिर्भूमिम् । भूमिं रक्षति भूपतिः ।
12. तम् ऋषिं तत्र अपश्यमानः सः राजा ताम् शकुन्तलाम् उवाच → तमृषिं तत्रापश्यमानः स राजा तां शकुन्तलामुवाच । तत्र तमृषिमपश्यमानस्ताञ्शकुन्तलां स राजोवाच । ऋषिं तमपश्यमानस्तत्र तां शकुन्तलामुवाच स राजा । स राजा तां शकुन्तलामुवाच तमृषिं तत्रापश्यमानः ।
13. तस्य यज्ञस्य अन्ते राजा दशरथः ऋषि–अशृङ्गम् अब्रवीत् → तस्य यज्ञस्यान्ते राजा दशरथ ऋष्यशृङ्गमब्रवीत् । यज्ञस्यतस्यान्ते दशरथो राजाऽब्रवीदृष्यशृङ्गम् ।
14. पश्यन् शृण्वन् स्पृशन् जिघ्रन् अश्नन् गच्छन् स्वपन् श्वसन् प्रलपन् विसृजन् गृह्णन् उन्मिशन् निमिशन् अपि (Gītā 5.8-9) → पश्यञ्शृण्वन्स्पृशञ्जिघ्रन्नश्नन्गच्छन्स्वपञ्श्वसन्प्रलपन्विसृजन्गृह्णन्नुन्मिशन्निमिशन्नपि ।

LESSON 11

ekādaśaḥ abhyāsaḥ
एकादशः अभ्यासः ।

INTRODUCTION TO THE NUMERALS

saṅkhyānām paricayaḥ
संख्यानां परिचयः ।

Devanagarī Numbers

devanāgaryāḥ aṅkāḥ
देवनागर्याः अङ्काः ।

In Sanskrit the numerals (*saṁkhaẏḥ, aṅkāḥ* संख्याः, अङ्काः) are used as adjectives (*viśeṣaṇāni* विशेषणानि) as well as substantives (*viśeṣyāni* विशेष्याणि). The numerals from 1 to 18 are adjectives, but they can be used as substantives too.

The numerals may be expressed in two ways, namely

(1) Expressive of numbers (*saṅkhyāvāćakāḥ* संख्यावाचकाः) e.g. one (*eka* एक), two (*dvi* द्वि), three (*tri* त्रि), four (*ćatur* चतुर्), five (*pañćan* पञ्चन्), six (*ṣaṣ* षष्), seven (*saptan* सप्तन्), eight (*aṣṭan* अष्टन्), nine (*navan* नवन्), ten (*daśan* दशन्), eleven (*ekādaśan* एकादशन्) ...etc.

(2) Sequence indicating (*kramavāćakāḥ* क्रमवाचकाः) e.g. 1st (*prathama* प्रथम), 2nd (*dvitīya* द्वितीय), 3rd (*tṛtīya* तृतीय), 4th (*ćaturtha* चतुर्थ), 5th (*pañćama* पञ्चम), 6th (*ṣaṣṭha* षष्ठ), 7th (*saptama* सप्तम), 8th (*aṣṭama* अष्टम), 9th (*navama* नवम), 10th (*daśama* दशम), 11th (*ekādaśa* एकादश) ...etc.

In masculine and neuter genders they end with अ (*akārānta* अकारान्त) and in feminine gender, with आ (*ākārānta* आकारान्त) or ई (*īkārānta* ईकारान्त). The suffix that converts a number into a sequence indicating numeral is called पूरणप्रत्ययः *pūraṇa-pratyahaḥ.*

Number	Numerical		Sequence		Sequence	
	m∘ n∘ f∘		m∘ n∘		f∘	
अंक	संख्यावाचक		क्रमवाचक		क्रमवाचक	
1	एक	*eka*	प्रथम	*prathama*	प्रथमा	*prathamā*
2	द्वि	*dvi*	द्वितीय	*dvitīya*	द्वितीया	*dvitīyā*
3	त्रि	*tri*	तृतीय	*tṛtīya*	तृतीया	*tṛtīyā*
4	चतुर्	*ćatur*	चतुर्थ	*ćaturtha*	चतुर्थी	*ćaturthī*
5	पञ्चन्	*pañćan*	पञ्चम	*pañćama*	पञ्चमी	*pañćamaī*
6	षष्	*ṣaṣ*	षष्ठ	*ṣaṣṭha*	षष्ठी	*ṣaṣṭhī*
7	सप्तन्	*saptan*	सप्तम	*saptama*	सप्तमी	*saptamī*
8	अष्टन्	*aṣṭan*	अष्टम	*aṣṭama*	अष्टमी	*aṣṭamī*
9	नवन्	*navan*	नवम	*navama*	नवमी	*navamī*
10	दशन्	*daśan*	दशम	*daśama*	दशमी	*daśamī*
11	एकादशन्	*ekādaśan*	एकादश	*ekādaśa*	एकादशी	*ekādaśī*
12	द्वादशन्	*dvādaśan*	द्वादश	*dvādaśa*	द्वादशी	*dvādaśī*
13	त्रयोदशन्	*trayodaśan*	त्रयोदश	*trayodaśa*	त्रयोदशी	*trayodaśī*
14	चतुर्दशन्	*ćaturdaśan*	चतुर्दश	*ćaturdaśa*	चतुर्दशी	*ćaturdaśī*
15	पञ्चदशन्	*pañćadaśan*	पञ्चदश	*pañćadaśa*	पञ्चदशी	*pañćadaśī*
16	षोडशन्	*ṣoḍaśan*	षोडश	*ṣoḍaśa*	षोडशी	*ṣoḍaśī*
17	सप्तदशन्	*saptadaśan*	सप्तदश	*saptadaṣa*	सप्तदशी	*saptadaṣī*
18	अष्टादशन्	*aṣṭādaśan*	अष्टादश	*aṣṭādaśa*	अष्टादशी	*aṣṭādaśī*
19	नवदशन्	*navadaśan*	नवदश	*navadaśa*	नवदशी	*navadaśī*

From 20 onwards तमट् suffixes (m◦ n◦ तम, f◦ तमी) may be added to a numerical value to form a sequence indicating numeral.

No.	Numerical		Sequence		Sequence	
	m◦ n◦ f◦		m◦ n◦		f◦	
अंक	संख्यावाचक		क्रमवाचक		क्रमवाचक	
20	विंशति	*vim̃śati*	विंश(विंशतितम)	*vim̃śa*	विंशी(विंशतितमी)	*vim̃śī*
21	एकविंशति	*ekvim̃śati*	एकविंश	*ekavim̃śa*	एकविंशी	*ekavim̃śī*
22	द्वाविंशति	*dvāvim̃śati*	द्वाविंश	*dvāvim̃śa*	द्वाविंशी	*dvāvim̃śī*
23	त्रयोविंशति	*trayovim̃śati*	त्रयोविंश	*trayovim̃śa*	त्रयोविंशी	*trayovim̃śī*
24	चतुर्विंशति	*chaturvim̃śati*	चतुर्विंश	*chaturvim̃śa*	चतुर्विंशी	*chaturvim̃śī*
25	पञ्चविंशति	*panćavim̃śati*	पञ्चविंश	*panćavim̃śa*	पञ्चविंशी	*panćavim̃śī*
26	षड्विंशति	*ṣaḍvim̃śati*	षड्विंश	*ṣaḍvim̃śa*	षड्विंशी	*ṣaḍvim̃śī*
27	सप्तविंशति	*saptavim̃śati*	सप्तविंश	*saptavim̃śa*	सप्तविंशी	*saptavim̃śī*
28	अष्टाविंशति	*aṣṭā!vim̃śati*	अष्टाविंश	*aṣṭā!vim̃śa*	अष्टाविंशी	*aṣṭā!vim̃śī*
29	नवविंशति	*navavim̃śati*	नवविंश	*navavim̃śa*	नवविंशी	*navavim̃śī*
30	त्रिंशत्	*trim̃śat*	त्रिंश	*trimśa*	त्रिंशी	*trim̃śī*
31	एकत्रिंशत्	*ekādaśaim̃śat*	एकत्रिंश	*ekādaśaim̃śa*	एकत्रिंशी	*ekādaśaim̃śī*
32	द्वात्रिंशत्	*dvātrim̃śat*	द्वात्रिंश	*dvātrim̃śa*	द्वात्रिंशी	*dvātrim̃śī*
33	त्रयस्त्रिंशत्	*trayastrim̃śat*	त्रयस्त्रिंश	*trayastrim̃śa*	त्रयस्त्रिंशी	*trayastrim̃śī*
34	चतुस्त्रिंशत्	*ćatustrim̃śat*	चतुस्त्रिंश	*ćatustrim̃śa*	चतुस्त्रिंशी	*ćatustrim̃śī*
35	पञ्चत्रिंशत्	*pañćarim̃śat*	पञ्चत्रिंश	*pañćarim̃śa*	पञ्चत्रिंशी	*pañćarim̃śī*
36	षट्त्रिंशत्	*ṣaṭtrim̃śat*	षट्त्रिंश	*ṣaṭtrim̃śa*	षट्त्रिंशी	*ṣaṭtrim̃śī*
37	सप्तत्रिंशत्	*saptatrim̃śat*	सप्तत्रिंश	*saptatrim̃śa*	सप्तत्रिंशी	*saptatrim̃śa*
38	अष्टात्रिंशत्	*aṣṭātrim̃śat*	अष्टात्रिंश	*aṣṭātrim̃śa*	अष्टात्रिंशी	*aṣṭātrim̃śī*
39	नवत्रिंशत्	*navatrim̃śat*	नवत्रिंश	*navatrim̃śa*	नवत्रिंशी	*navatrim̃śī*

No.	Numerical		Sequence		Sequence
	m◦ n◦ f◦		m◦ n◦		f◦
अंक	संख्यावाचक		क्रमवाचक		क्रमवाचक
40	चत्वारिंशत्	*ćatvārim̃śat*	चत्वारिंश	*ćatvārim̃śa*	चत्वारिंशी
41	एकचत्वारिंशत्	*ekaćatvārim̃śat*	एकचत्वारिंश	*ekaćatvārim̃śa*	एकचत्वारिंशी
42	द्विचत्वारिंशत्	*dvićatvārim̃śat*	द्विचत्वारिंश	*dvićatvārim̃śa*	द्विचत्वारिंशी
43	त्रिचत्वारिंशत्	*tri ćatvārim̃śat*	त्रिचत्वारिंश	*tri ćatvārim̃śa*	त्रिचत्वारिंशी
44	चतुश्चत्वारिंशत्	*catuśćatvārim̃śat*	चतुश्चत्वारिंश	*catuśćatvārim̃śa*	चतुश्चत्वारिंशी
45	पञ्चचत्वारिंशत्	*pañćaćatvārim̃śat*	पञ्चचत्वारिंश	*pañćaćatvārim̃śa*	पञ्चचत्वारिंशी
46	षट्चत्वारिंशत्	*ṣaṭćatvārim̃śat*	षट्चत्वारिंश	*ṣaṭćatvārim̃śa*	षट्चत्वारिंशी
47	सप्तचत्वारिंशत्	*saptaćatvārim̃śat*	सप्तचत्वारिंश	*saptaćatvārim̃śa*	सप्तचत्वारिंशी
48	अष्टचत्वारिंशत्	*aṣṭaćatvārim̃śat*	अष्टचत्वारिंश	*aṣṭaćatvārim̃śa*	अष्टचत्वारिंशी
49	नवचत्वारिंशत्	*navaćatvārim̃śat*	नवचत्वारिंश	*navaćatvārim̃śa*	नवचत्वारिंशी
50	पञ्चाशत्	*pañćāśat*	पञ्चाश	*pañćāśat*	पञ्चाशी
51	एकपञ्चाशत्	*ekapañćāśat*	एकपञ्चाश	*ekapañćāśa*	एकपञ्चाशी
52	द्विपञ्चाशत्	*dvipañćāśat*	द्विपञ्चाश	*dvipañćāśa*	द्विपञ्चाशी
53	त्रिपञ्चाशत्	*tripañćāśat*	त्रिपञ्चाश	*tripañćāśa*	त्रिपञ्चाशी
54	चतु:पञ्चाशत्	*ćatuḥpañćāśat*	चतु:पञ्चाश	*ćatuḥpañćāśa*	चतु:पञ्चाशी
55	पञ्चपञ्चाशत्	*pañćapañćāśat*	पञ्चपञ्चाश	*ṣaṭpañćāśa*	पञ्चपञ्चाशी
56	षट्पञ्चाशत्	*ṣaṭpañćāśat*	षट्पञ्चाश	*ṣaṭpañćāśa*	षट्पञ्चाशी
57	सप्तपञ्चाशत्	*saptapañćāśat*	सप्तपञ्चाश	*saptapañćāśa*	सप्तपञ्चाशी
58	अष्टपञ्चाशत्	*aṣṭapañćāśat*	अष्टपञ्चाश	*aṣṭapañćāśa*	अष्टपञ्चाशी
59	नवपञ्चाशत्	*navapañćāśat*	नवपञ्चाश	*navapañćāśa*	नवपञ्चाशी
60	षष्टि	*ṣaṣṭi*	षष्टितम	*ṣaṣṭi*	षष्टितमी
61	एकषष्टि	*ekaṣaṣṭi*	एकषष्ट	*ekaṣaṣṭi*	एकषष्टी
62	द्विषष्टि	*dviṣaṣṭi*	द्विषष्ट	*dviṣaṣṭi*	द्विषष्टी

No.	Numerical		Sequence		Sequence	
	m∘ n∘ f∘		m∘ n∘		f∘	
अंक	संख्यावाचक		क्रमवाचक		क्रमवाचक	
63	त्रिषष्टि	*triṣaṣṭi*	त्रिषष्ट	*triṣaṣṭa*	त्रिषष्टी	*triṣaṣṭī*
64	चतुष्षष्टि	*ćatuṣṣaṣṭi*	चतुष्षष्ट	*ćatuṣṣaṣṭa*	चतुष्षष्टी	*ćatuṣṣaṣṭī*
65	पञ्चषष्टि	*pañćaṣaṣṭi*	पञ्चषष्ट	*pañćaṣaṣṭa*	पञ्चषष्टी	*pañćaṣaṣṭī*
66	षट्षष्टि	*ṣaṭṣaṣṭi*	षट्षष्ट	*ṣaṭṣaṣṭa*	षट्षष्टी	*ṣaṭṣaṣṭī*
67	सप्तषष्टि	*saptaṣaṣṭi*	सप्तषष्ट	*saptaṣaṣṭa*	सप्तषष्टी	*saptaṣaṣṭī*
68	अष्टाषष्टि	*aṣṭāṣaṣṭi*	अष्टाषष्ट	*aṣṭāṣaṣṭa*	अष्टाषष्टी	*aṣṭāṣaṣṭī*
69	नवषष्टि	*navaṣaṣṭi*	नवषष्ट	*navaṣaṣṭa*	नवषष्टी	*navaṣaṣṭī*
70	सप्तति	*saptati*	सप्तत	*saptata*	सप्तती	*saptatī*
71	एकसप्तति	*ekasaptati*	एकसप्तत	*ekasaptata*	एकसप्तती	*ekasaptatī*
72	द्विसप्तति	*dvisaptati*	द्विसप्तत	*dvisaptata*	द्विसप्तती	*dvisaptatī*
73	त्रिसप्तति	*trisaptati*	त्रिसप्तत	*trisaptata*	त्रिसप्तती	*trisaptatī*
74	चतुस्सप्तति	*ćatussaptati*	चतुस्सप्तत	*ćatussaptata*	चतुस्सप्तती	*ćatussaptatī*
75	पञ्चसप्तति	*pañćasaptati*	पञ्चसप्तत	*pañćasaptata*	पञ्चसप्तती	*pañćasaptatī*
76	षट्सप्तति	*ṣaṭsaptati*	षट्सप्तत	*ṣaṭsaptata*	षट्सप्तती	*ṣaṭsaptatī*
77	सप्तसप्तति	*saptasaptati*	सप्तसप्तत	*saptasaptata*	सप्तसप्तती	*saptasaptatī*
78	अष्टासप्तति	*aṣṭāsaptati*	अष्टासप्तत	*aṣṭāsaptata*	अष्टासप्तती	*aṣṭāsaptatī*
79	नवसप्तति	*navasaptati*	नवसप्तत	*navasaptata*	नवसप्तती	*navasaptatī*
80	अशीति	*aśīti*	अशीतितम	*aśītitama*	अशीतितमी	*aśītitamī*
81	एकाशीति	*ekāśīti*	एकाशीत	*ekāśītitama*	एकाशीती	*ekāśītitamī*
82	द्वाशीति	*dvāśīti*	द्वाशीत	*dvāśītitama*	द्वाशीती	*dvāśītitamī*
83	त्र्यशीति	*tryaśīti*	त्र्यशीत	*tryaśīti*तम	त्र्यशीती	*tryaśītitamī*
84	चतुरशीति	*ćaturaśīti*	चतुरशीत	*ćaturaśītitama*	चतुरशीती	*ćaturaśītitamī*
85	पञ्चाशीति	*pañćāśīti*	पञ्चाशीत	*pañćāśītitama*	पञ्चाशीती	*pañćāśītitamī*

No.	Numerical	Sequence			Sequence	
	m◦ n◦ f◦	m◦ n◦			f◦	
अंक	संख्यावाचक	क्रमवाचक			क्रमवाचक	
86	षडशीति	*ṣaḍaśīti*	षडशीत	*ṣaḍaśīta*	षडशीती	*ṣaḍaśītī*
87	सप्ताशीति	*saptāśīti*	सप्ताशीत	*saptāśīta*	सप्ताशीती	*saptāśītī*
88	अष्टाशीति	*aṣṭāśīti*	अष्टाशीत	*aṣṭāśīta*	अष्टाशीती	*aṣṭāśītī*
89	नवाशीति	*navāśīti*	नवाशीत	*navāśīta*	नवाशीती	*navāśītī*
90	नवति	*navati*	नवति	*navatia*	नवति	*navatiī*
91	एकनवति	*ekanavati*	एकनवत	*ekanavata*	एकनवती	*ekanavatī*
92	द्विनवति	*dvinavati*	द्विनवत	*dvinavata*	द्विनवती	*dvinavatī*
93	त्रिनवति	*trinavati*	त्रिनवत	*trinavata*	त्रिनवती	*trinavatī*
94	चतुर्नवति	*ćaturnavati*	चतुर्नवत	*ćaturnavata*	चतुर्नवती	*ćaturnavatī*
95	पञ्चनवति	*pañćanavati*	पञ्चनवत	*pan!ćanavata*	पञ्चनवती	*pan!ćanavatī*
96	षण्णवति	*ṣaṇṇavati*	षण्णवत	*ṣaṇṇavata*	षण्णवती	*ṣaṇṇavatī*
97	सप्तनवति	*saptanavati*	सप्तनवत	*saptanavata*	सप्तनवती	*saptanavatī*
98	अष्टानवति	*aṣṭānavati*	अष्टानवत	*aṣṭānavata*	अष्टानवती	*aṣṭānavatī*
99	नवनवति	*navanavati*	नवनवत	*navanavata*	नवनवती	*navanavatī*
100	शत, एकशतम्	*śata, ekśatam*	शततम	*śatatama*	शततमी	*śatatamī*

From 100 onwards, the numbers may optionally be indicated as a single compound of one or two digit number number and the hundred value. e.g. एकशत, द्विशत, त्रिशत ..etc. But, in this case they could be confused with one hundred, two hundred, three hundred ...etc. Therefore, they may simply be written as 'hundred exceeded by one, two, three ...etc.'

e.g. एकाधिकं शतम्, द्वाधिकं शतम्, त्र्यधिकं शतं ...etc.

101 एकशत, एकाधिकशत   एकाधिकशततम   एकाधिकशततमी

102 द्विशत, द्वाधिकशत   द्वाधिकशततम   द्वाधिकशततमी

103 त्रिशत, त्र्यधिकशत   त्र्यधिकशततम   त्र्यधिकशततमी

104	चतुःशत, चतुरधिकशत	चतुःशततम	चतुःशततमी
105	पञ्चशत, पञ्चाधिकशत	पञ्चशततम	पञ्चशततमी
106	षट्शत, षडधिकशत	षट्शततम	षट्शततमी
107	सप्तशत, सप्ताधिकशत	सप्तशततम	सप्तशततमी
108	अष्टशत, अष्टाधिकशत	अष्टशततम	अष्टशततमी
109	नवशत, नवाधिकशत	नवशततम	नवशततमी
110	दशशत, दशाधिकशत	दशशततम	दशशततमी
111	एकादशशत	एकादशशततम	एकादशशततमी
112	द्वादशशत	द्वादशशततम	द्वादशशततमी
113	त्रयोदशशत	त्रयोदशशततम	त्रयोदशशततमी
114	चतुर्दशशत	चतुर्दशशततम	चतुर्दशशततमी
115	पञ्चदशशत	पञ्चदशशततम	पञ्चदशशततमी
116	षोडशदशशत	षोडशदशशततम	षोडषदशशततमी
117	सप्तदशशत	सप्तदशशततम	सप्तदशशततमी
118	अष्टदशशत	अष्टदशशततम	अष्टदशशततमी
119	नवदशशत	नवदशशततम	नवदशशततमी
120	विंशशत	विंशशततम	विंशशततमी
121	एकविंशशत	एकविंशशततम	एकविंशशततमी
↓			
130	त्रिंशशत	त्रिंशशततम	त्रिंशशततमी
140	चत्वारिंशशत	चत्वारिंशशततम	चत्वारिंशशततमी
150	पञ्चाशशत	पञ्चाशशततम	पञ्चाशशततमी
160	षष्टिशत	षष्टिशततम	षष्टिशततमी
170	सप्ततिशत	सप्ततिशततम	सप्ततिशततमी
180	अशीतिशत	अशीतिशततम	अशीतिशततमी
190	नवतिशत	नवतिशततम	नवतिशततमी

200 द्विशत	द्विशततम	द्विशततमी		
300 त्रिशत	त्रिशततम	त्रिशततमी		
400 चतु:शत	चतु:शततम	चतु:शततमी		
500 पञ्चशत	पञ्चशततम	पञ्चशततमी		
600 षट्शत	षट्शततम	षट्शततमी		
700 सप्तशत	सप्तशततम	सप्तशततमी		
800 अष्टाशत	अष्टशततम	अष्टशततमी		
900 नवशत	नवशततम	नवशततमी		
1000 दशशत, सहस्त्र Thousand	सहस्त्रतम	सहस्त्रतमी		
10,000	अयुतम्-त:	(n∘ m∘) *ayuta*		
100,000	लक्षम्-क्षा	(n∘ f∘) *lakṣa*		
1000,000	नियुतम्-त:	(n∘ m∘) *prayuta*		Million
10,000,000	कोटि:	(f∘) *koṭi*		
100,000,000	अर्बुदम्-द:	(n∘ m∘) *arbuda*		
1,000,000,000	वृन्दम्, महार्बुदम्-द:	(n∘ m∘) *vṛndam, mahārbuda*		Billion
10,000,000,000	खर्व:	(m∘) *kharvaḥ*		
100,000,000,000	निखर्व:	(m∘) *nikharvaḥ*		
1,000,000,000,000	ख्शङ्ख:	(m∘) *śaṅkhaḥ*		Trillion
10,000,000,000,000	पद्म:	(m∘) *padmaḥ*		
100,000,000,000,000	सागर:	(m∘) *sāgaraḥ*		
1,000,000,000,000,000	अत्यन्तम्	(न∘) *atyantam*		Zillion
10,000,000,000,000,000	मध्यम्	(n∘) *madhyam*		
100,000,000,000,000,000	परार्धम्	(n∘) *parārdham*		
1,000,000,000,000,000,000	प्रपरार्धम्	(n∘) *parparārdham*		
and so on ... to infinity	अनन्त:	(n∘) *anant*		Infinity

11.2

DECLENSION OF THE NUMERALS

एक (one) is always singular, द्वि (two) is always dual and three, four, five त्रि, चतुर्, पञ्च ...etc. are always plural. The declensions of the numerals in the Nominative (1st) case, in all three genders, are as below (For all other cases of numerals, see the 'Summary of Cases' in Appendix 2).

SANSKRIT NUMERALS : (1 to 10)

1	one	*ek*	एक	2	two	*dvi*	द्वि
3	three	*tri*	त्रि	4	four	*ćatur*	चतुर
5	five	*pañćan*	पञ्चन्	6	six	*saṣ*	षष्
7	seven	*satpan*	सप्तन्	8	eight	*aṣtan*	अष्टन्
9	nine	*navan*	नवन्	10	ten	*daśan*	दशन्

Nominative case		m∘		n∘		f∘	
1	१	ekaḥ	एक:	ekam	एकम्	ekā	एका
2	२	dvau	द्वौ	dve	द्वे	dve	द्वे
3	३	trayaḥ	त्रय:	trīṇi	त्रीणि	tisraḥ	तिस्त्र:
4	४	ćatvāraḥ	चत्वार:	ćatvāri	चत्वारि	ćatasraḥ	चतस्त्र:

Numbers from 5 to 10 have same case declensions in all three genders m∘ n∘ f∘

5	५	*pañća*	पंच, पञ्च	m∘ n∘ f∘
6	६	*ṣaṭ* or *ṣaḍ*	षट्, षड्	m∘ n∘ f∘
7	७	*sapta*	सप्त	m∘ n∘ f∘
8	८	*aṣṭa*	अष्ट	m∘ n∘ f∘
9	९	*nava*	नव	m∘ n∘ f∘
10	१०	*daśa*	दश	m∘ n∘ f∘

EXERCISE 35 :

(1) Say the following numbers in Sanskrit :

1 7 9 4 3 2 8 5 6

(2) Read the following Devanagari numerals :

७ ४ १ ९ ६ ५ ३ ८ २

(3) Write the following Sanskrit numerals :

चतुर्, सप्तन्, नवन्, एक, षष्, अष्टन्, पञ्चन्, द्वि, दशन्

(4) Say the following numerals in Sanskrit :

(1) 12, 53, 36, 99, 100

(2) 11, 22, 33, 44, 55, 66, 77, 88, 99

(3) 10, 20, 30, 40, 50, 60, 70, 80, 90

ANSWERS to Exercise 35 :

(1) एक, सप्तन्, नवन्, चतुर्, त्रि, द्वि, अष्टन्, पञ्चन्, षष् ।

(2) सप्तन्, चतुर्, एक, नवन्, षष्, पञ्चन्, त्रि, अष्टन्, द्वि ।

(3) 4, 7, 9, 1, 6, 8, 5, 2, 10

(4) 1. द्वादशन्, त्रिपञ्चाशत्, षट्त्रिंशत्, नवनवति, शत ।

2. एकादशन्, द्वाविंशति, त्रयस्त्रिंशत्, चतुश्चत्वारिंशत्, पञ्चपञ्चाशत्, षट्षटि, सप्तसप्तति, अष्टाशीति, नवनवति ।

3. दशन्, विंशति, त्रिंशत्, चत्वारिंशत्, पञ्चाशत्, षष्टि, सप्तति, अशीति, नवति ।

LESSON 12

dvādaśaḥ abhyāsaḥ द्वादशः अभ्यासः ।

12.1
VERBS
kriyāpadāni
क्रियापदानि ।

Whenever we say a sentence, there is always a verb in it. Without verb a sentence does not become complete. Also, wherever there is a verb, there is a doer (subject, कर्ता *kartā*) of that verb. Thus, there is no sentence without a verb and a subject.

In Sanskrit, every word comes from a verb and every verb comes from a verb root (धातु *dhātu*) which is shown by a √ sign. e.g. √*khād* √खाद् = to eat, √*dā* √दा = to give, √*kṛ* √कृ = to do, √*gam* √गम् = to go ... etc.

I give *ahaṁ dadāmi* अहं ददामि । In this sentence, 'I' am the doer (subject) of the action of giving, and 'to give' is a verb (क्रियापदम् *kriyapadam*)

Action word is called a VERB. In Sanskrit, the verb has same Person and Number as the doer (subject) of that action. REMEMBER: In Sanskrit, **the verbs do not have a Gender**.

12.2
THE TENSES AND MOODS OF THE VERBS
lakārāḥ लकाराः ।

In Sanskrit there are over 2000 verb roots (√verb), from which all Sanskrit words originate. Unlike English, in Sanskrit the Tenses are not grouped separately from the Moods of the verbs.

They are organized under a single group of ten *lakāra*s (लकारा: Tense and Mood Conjugations).

THE TEN TENSES AND MOODS OF THE VERBS

There are ten tenses and moods *lakāra*s in Sanskrit, namely

laṭ, liṭ, luṭ, lṝṭ, loṭ, leṭ,	*laṅg, liṅg, luṅg, lṛṅg*
लट्, लिट्, लुट्, लृट्, लोट्, लेट्,	लङ्, लिङ्, लुङ्, लृङ् ।

The first six *lakāra*s, ending with *ṭ* (ट्) are called *ṭit* (टित्) and the last four, ending with *ṅ* (ङ्) are *ṅit* (ङित्) *lakāra*s.

The *leṭ* (लेट्) *lakāra* is used only in the *Veda*s. In Classical Sanskrit, the *leṭ* (लेट्) *lakāra* is replaced by splitting the *liṅ lakāra* (लिङ्) into two parts, *vidhi-liṅg* (विधिलिङ्) and *āśiḥ-liṅg* (आशीर्लिङ्)

In practice, in order to congugate (रूपसंजिकरणम्) a verb, these ten names of the *lakāra*s themselves are not actually affixed to the verb roots, but in stead, the verb is treated (*pratyāhāraḥ* प्रत्याहार:) with one of the 18 terminations (*pratyayaḥ* प्रत्यया:), one for each of the ten tenses and moods (*lakārāḥ* लकारा:) 10 *lakar*s x 18 Terminations = 180 suffixes प्रत्याहारा: ।

Pāṇini (पाणिनि) has arranged these 18 conjugational affixes into a string, from *tip* (तिप्) to *mahiṅg* (महिङ्). (लस्य तिबादय आदेशा: भवन्ति ।pāṇini, 3: 4.77).

As this list starts with *ti* (ति) and ends with *ṅg* (ङ्), each affix is called *tiṅg* (तिङ्) and a conjugated root of the verb is called a *tiṅgant* (तिङन्त) or *padam* (पदम्).

The 18 terminations (9 *parasmaipadī* and 9 *ātmanepadī*) are :

tip, taḥ, jhi, sip, thaḥ, tha, mip, vaḥ, maḥ, ta, ātām, jha, thāḥ, āthām, dhvam, iṭ, vahi, mahiṅ. तिप्, त:, झि, सिप्, थ:, थ, मिप्, व:, म:, त, आताम्, झ, था:, आथाम्, ध्वम्, इट्, वहि, महिङ् । तिप्तस्झिसिप्थस्थमिब्वस्मस्ताताञ्जथासाथान्ध्वमिड्वहिमहिङ् । Pāṇini 3: 4.78

THE TEN TENSES AND MOODS

OF THE VERBS

IN CLASSICAL SANSKRIT

daśa lakārāḥ

दश लकाराः ।

The ten *lakāra*s, used in the Classical Sanskrit language are namely, *laṭ, laṅg, liṭ, luṅg, luṭ, lṛṭ, loṭ, vidhi, liṅg, lṛṅg* लट्, लङ्, लिट्, लुङ्, लुट्, लृट्, लोट्, विधि, लिङ्, लृङ् ।

With the English tenses and moods they approximately compare as :

(1)	*laṭ*	लट्	Present Tense
(2)	*laṅg*	लङ्	Past Imperfect Tense (First Praeterite)
(3)	*liṭ*	लिट्	Past Perfect Tense (Second Praeterite)
(4)	*luṅg*	लुङ्	Past Indefinite Tense (Third Praeterite or Aorist)
(5)	*luṭ*	लुट्	Future Definite Tense
(6)	*lṛṭ*	लृट्	Future Indefinite Tense
(7)	*loṭ*	लोट्	Imperative Mood
(8)	*vidhi*	विधि	Potential Mood
(9)	*liṅg*	लिङ्	Benedictive Mood
(10)	*lṛṅg*	लृङ्	Conditional Mood

NOTE :

The *leṭ* लेट् लकारः of the Vedic Sanskrit is *vidhi-liṅ* विधि (विधिलिङ्) in the Classical Sanskrit.

12.3
THE ELEVEN
CONJUGATIONAL CLASSES OF VERBS

Roots of the verbs (*dhātavaḥ* धातवः), having aims of self service (*ātmanepadī* आत्मनेपदी), service to others (*parasmaipadī* परस्मैपदी) or dual service (*ubhayapadī* उभयपदी), are arranged under a group of Eleven classes of Conjugations of Verbs (*gaṇāḥ* गणाः), namely :

(1)	भ्वादि *	*bhvādi,*	the 1st Class, of the roots like	(√*bhū*)	√भू	to become
(2)	अदादि	*adādi,*	the 2nd Class, of the roots like	(√*ad*)	√अद्	to eat
(3)	हुवादि	*huvādi,*	the 3rd Class, of the roots like	(√*hu*)	√हु	to sacrifice
(4)	दिवादि *	*divādi,*	the 4th Class, of the roots like	(√*div*)	√दिव्	to shine
(5)	स्वादि	*svādi,*	the 5th Class, of the roots like	(√*su*)	√सु	to bathe
(6)	तुदादि *	*tudādi,*	the 6th Class, of the roots like	(√*tud*)	√तुद्	to hurt
(7)	रुधादि	*rudhādi,*	the 7th Class, of the roots like	(√*rudh*)	√रुध्	to oppose
(8)	तनादि	*tanādi,*	the 8th Class, of the roots like	(√*tan*)	√तन्	to spread
(9)	क्र्यादि	*kryādi,*	the 9th Class, of the roots like	(√*krī*)	√क्री	to buy
(10)	चुरादि *	*ćurādi,*	the 10th Class, of the roots like	(√*ćur*)	√चुर्	to steal
(11)	कण्ड्वादि	*kaṇḍvādi,*	the 11th Class, of the roots like	(√*kaṇḍū*)	√कण्डू	to itch

NOTES :

(i)Some people prefer using the numerical system (1st gaṇa, 2nd gaṇa etc.) for identifying the *gaṇas*, while others prefer their nominclature (भ्वादि, अदादि etc.)

(ii) The popular first 10 classes of conjugations are divided in two GROUPS.

(iii) roots of 1st, 4th, 6th and 10th class marked with * fall under the **FIRST GROUP**

(iv) the remaining roots of the 2nd, 3rd, 5th, 7th, 8th and 9th class fall under **SECOND GROUP.**

(v) Amost all roots are monosyllables, some of them are even uniletters (e.g. √i, √ī, √u, √ṛ, √ṝ), most of them end in a consonant. Only just over a dozen are ploysyllabelic. e.g. √apās, √āndol, √bhiṣaj, √ćakās, √ćulump, √daridrā, √gaveśa, √hillol, √kumār, √kuṭumb, √lumāl, √oland, √palyul, √pampas, √prenkhol, √sabhaj, √sangrām, √viḍamb.

THE 4 DESIGNS OF VERBS (प्रक्रिया: *prakriyāḥ*)

Besides the normal *parasmaipadī* or *ātmanepadī* forms, each verb has three other designs (*prakriyāḥ* प्रक्रिया:) depending on the intension of the action.

(1) Normal (*sādhāraṇa* साधारणप्रक्रिया) (2) Causative (*ṇyanta* ण्यन्तप्रक्रिया) (3) Desiderative (*sannant* सन्नन्तप्रक्रिया) (4) Repeatetive (*yaṅgluganta* यङ्लुगन्तप्रक्रिया or *yaṅgant* यङन्तप्रक्रिया)

THE TWO AIMS OF VERBS :

(1) *Parasmaipadī* (परस्मैपदी) (2) Ātmanepadī (आत्मनेपदी), Dual - परस्मैपदी and आत्मनेपदी

THE TWO ATTRIBUTES OF VERBS :

(1) Transitive *sakarmak* (सकर्मक) (2) Intransitive *akarmak* (अकर्मक) Dual सकर्मक and अकर्मक

THE THREE VOICES OF VERBS :

(1) Active Voice *kartari prayogaḥ* (कर्तरि-प्रयोग:) (2) Passive Voice *karmaṇi prayogaḥ* (कर्मणि-प्रयोग:) (3) Abstract Voice *bhāve prayogaḥ* (भावे-प्रयोग:)

Thus, 3 presons *(puruṣāḥ* पुरुषा:) x 3 numbers *(vaćanāni* वचनानि*)* x 10 tenses *(lakārāḥ* लकारा:) x 4 designs *(prakriyāḥ* प्रतिक्रिया:) = 360 *parasmaipadī* (परस्मैपदी) and 360 *ātmanepadī* (आत्मनेपदी) single-word-actions are possible from each transitive or intransitive verb root (√).

LESSON 13

trayodaśaḥ abhyāsaḥ त्रयोदशः अभ्यासः ।

PERSON

पुरुषः *(puruṣaḥ)*

AGREEMENT OF VERB WITH THE SUBJECT

i. In a Sanskrit sentence, the verb (*kriyāpadam* क्रियापदम्) agrees with NUMBER (*vaćanam* वचनम्) and PERSON (*puruṣaḥ* पुरुषः) of the subject (*kartā* कर्ता).

ii. A single object takes a verb in SINGULAR number. Two subjects connected by the conjunction '*and,*' take a verb in the DUAL number and a group of more than two subjects takes a verb in PLURAL number.

EXAMPLE : (1) I अहम् *(aham)* (2) am अस्मि *(asmi)*

Thus, in the sentence : I am, अहम् अस्मि *(aham asmi),* the word 'I' stands for the subject. I is a noun, i.e. a person (or a thing). I is First person (me). I is Singular number (only one person). 'I' could mean a Masculine or Feminine gender.

Here the word 'am' is the verb, the act of being. The verb *asmi* अस्मि has a gender. All verbs have a TENSE. The word 'am' (*asmi* अस्मि) shows Present Tense.

In Sanskrit, there are three (1st, 2nd, 3rd) Persons : (संस्कृते पुरुषाः त्रयः सन्ति । उत्तम-पुरुषः मध्यम-पुरुषः प्रथम-पुरुषः च इति)

(1) I or We refers to FIRST PERSON (*uttama-puruśaḥ* उत्तमपुरुषः).

(2) The address 'you' refers to SECOND PERSON (*madhyama-puruśaḥ* मध्यमपुरुषः).

(3) The person (or thing) other than I and You (i.e. he, she, it, they, that, this) is the THIRD PERSON (*prathama-puruśaḥ* प्रथमपुरुषः).

1. 'I'	अहम् *aham*	first person
2. 'you'	(त्वम् *tvam*) भवान् *bhavān*	second person
3. he, she, that	सः, सा, तत् *saḥ, sā, tat*	third person

1. 'I' am अहम् अस्मि *aham asmi*
2. 'you' are (त्वम् असि *tvam asi)* भवान्-भवती अस्ति (m∘)*bhavān* (f∘) *bhavatī asti*
3. 'he, she, that' is सः सा, तत् - अस्ति *saḥ, sā, tat - asti*

NOTES : (1) Gender (m∘ he, f∘ she, n∘ that) has no effect on the verb, but the verb changes with Person, 1st∘, 2nd∘ and 3rd. (2) *ća* च = and , is = *asti* अस्ति। are = *santi* सन्ति। Two or more nouns are connected by word *ća* च । e.g. Rāma and Sītā (i) *Rāmaḥ Sītā ća* रामः सीता च । or (ii) *Rāmaḥ ća Sītā ća* रामः च सीता च ।

EXERCISE 36 : Study the following examples

1. Rāma is, *Rāmaḥ asti.* रामः अस्ति । Sītā is, *Sitā asti.* सीता अस्ति । He is, *saḥ asti.* सः अस्ति । They are, (m∘) *te santi,* (f∘) *tāḥ santi* ते सन्ति or ताः सन्ति ।
2. Rādhā is. *Rādhā asti.* राधा अस्ति । The food is there. *annam asti.* अन्नम् अस्ति ।
3. I am अहम् अस्मि *aham asmi.* I am Brahma अहं ब्रह्मास्मि *aham brahma asmi.* Thou art that तत् त्वम् असि *tat tvam asi.* Everything is that तत् सर्वम् *tat sarvam. (*सर्व = all*)*

NOTES : As can be seen above, when the English prepositional particles such as *a, an, the, there* ..etc. are customary, unnecessary, meaningless, addressless or spurious, they do not need to be translated in Sanskrit. e.g. In English we say : a boy, an egg, the toys, once up on a time there was a king etc. In Sanskrit, these prepositional particles (a, an, the, there etc.) are not attached before nouns. The number, gender case, tense etc. are already included and packed with the grammar of each word in Sanskrit. So, it is not necessary to use these prepositional articles and particles. e.g. A boy = *bālakaḥ* बालकः। The goat = *ajaḥ* अजः।

LESSON 14

ćaturdaśaḥ abhyāsaḥ चतुर्दशः अभ्यासः ।

14.1

NUMBER

vaćanam

वचनम् ।

When we say 'I am,' only one person is referred to, so 'I' is a Singular number.

In Sanskrit, the numbers are three संस्कृते वचनानि त्रीणि सन्ति । एकवचनं द्विवचनं बहुवचनं च इति

(1) One person or thing is SINGULAR NUMBER

(2) Two persons or things are DUAL NUMBER

(3) More than two persons or things are PLURAL NUMBER

Numbers		MASCULINE		NEUTER		FEMININE	
1	one	ekaḥ	एकः	ekam	एकम्	eka	एका
2	two	dvau	द्वौ	dve	द्वे	dve	द्वे
3	three	trayaḥ	त्रयः	trīṇi	त्रीणि	tisraḥ	तिस्रः
4	four	ćatvāraḥ	चत्वारः	ćatvāri	चत्वारि	ćatasraḥ	चतस्रः
5	पञ्च	pañća'	पञ्च	pañća	पञ्च	pañća	पञ्च

TABLE : PERSON AND NUMBER

Person	Singular	Dual	Plural
I, we	अहम् *aham*	आवाम् *āvām*	वयम् *vayam*
you	त्वम् *tvam*	युवाम् *yuvām*	यूयम् *yūyam*
he, she, that	सः, सा, तत् *saḥ, sā, tat*	तौ, ते, ते *tau, te, te*	ते, ताः, तानि *te, tāḥ, tāni.*

Use of the VERB to be √as √अस् in Present Tense लट्

Person	Singular	Dual	Plural
(I) am	अस्मि *asmi*	स्वः *svaḥ*	स्मः *smaḥ*
(You) are	असि *asi*	स्थः *sthaḥ*	स्थ *stha*
(He-she-that) is	अस्ति *asti*	स्तः *staḥ*	सन्ति *santi*

1. I am	अहम् अस्मि	*aham asmi*
2. We two are	आवाम् द्वौ (द्वे) स्वः	*āvāṁ dvau (dve) svaḥ*
3. We are	वयं स्मः	*vayaṁ smaḥ*
1. You are	(त्वम् असि) भवान् अस्ति	*(tvam asi) bhavān asti*
2. You two are	युवां द्वौ (द्वे) स्थः	*yuvāṁ dvau (dve) sthaḥ*
3. You (all) are	(यूयं स्थ) भवन्तः सन्ति	*(yūyaṁ stha) bhavantaḥ santi*
1. He-she-that is	सः, सा, तत् अस्ति	*saḥ, sā, tat asti*
2. They two are	तौ, ते, ते द्वौ (द्वे) स्तः	*tau, te, te dvau (dve) staḥ*
3. They all are	ते, ताः, तानि सन्ति	*te, tāḥ, tāni santi*

EXAMPLES :

(A) Singular number :

(1) Rāma is here. *Rāmaḥ atra asti.* रामः अत्र अस्ति ।

(2) The crow is black. *kākaḥ kṛṣṇaḥ asti.* काकः कृष्णः अस्ति । (crow = *kāka* काक; black = *kṛṣṇa* कृष्ण)

(3) The cuckoo is black also. *pikaḥ api kṛṣṇaḥ asti.* पिकः अपि कृष्णः अस्ति । (also = *api* अपि)

NOTES :

(1) In a sentence, if two or more subjects are connected by the conjunction 'and' (च *ća*), then the 'number' of their verb is chosen according to the number of the subjects (dual or plural).

e.g. Rāma and Sītā are here. रामः सीता च अत्र स्तः *rāmaḥ sītā ća atra staḥ. (*There are two. द्वौ/द्वे स्तः । *dvau/dve staḥ)*

Rāma, Sītā and Rītā are here. रामः सीता रीता च अत्र सन्ति *rāmaḥ sītā rītā ća atra santi.* (*atra* अत्र = here)

(2) In a sentence, when two or more subjects of a common attribute are connected by the conjunction 'and' च *ća*, the 'number' of their verb is chosen singular only.

e.g. Righteousness and purity are attained with yoga. सत्-चारित्र्यं पावित्र्यं च योगेन सिध्यते । *sat-ćaritryaṁ pāvitryaṁ ća yogena siddhyate.*

(B) Dual Number :

(4) Rāma and Sītā are here. *Rāmaḥ Sītā ća atra staḥ.* रामः सीता च अत्र स्तः ।

(5) The crow and cuckoo are black. *kākaḥ pikaḥ ća kṛṣṇau staḥ.* काकः पिकः च कृष्णौ स्तः ।

A CLASSICAL EXAMPLE : (see Appendix 8 for meaning)

(6) **काकः कृष्णः पिकः कृष्णः को भेदः पिककाकयोः ।**
वसन्तसमये प्राप्ते काकः काकः पिकः पिकः ।।28।।

kākaḥ kṛṣṇaḥ pikaḥ kṛṣṇaḥ, ko bhedaḥ pikakākayoḥ?
vasanta-samaye prāpte, kākaḥ kākaḥ pikaḥ pikaḥ.

(C) Plural Number :

(7) A crow *kākaḥ* काकः → The crows *kākāḥ* काकाः ।

(8) He *saḥ* सः → They (*te* ते)

Is *asti* अस्ति → Are (*santi* सन्ति)

(9) Rāma, Sunīl and Sītā are here. *rāmaḥ sunīlaḥ sītā ća atra santi.* रामः सुनीलः सीता च अत्र सन्ति ।

(10) The crow, cuckoo and coal are black. *kākaḥ pikaḥ aṅgāraḥ ća kṛṣṇāḥ santi.* काकः पिकः अङ्गारः च कृष्णाः सन्ति । (cuckoo = *pika* पिक; coal = *aṅgāra* अङ्गार)

(11) The crows and cuckoos are black. *kākāḥ pikāḥ ća kṛṣṇāḥ santi.* काकाः पिकाः च कृष्णाः सन्ति ।

(12) बहूनि मे व्यतीतानि जन्मानि तव चार्जुन ।। (Gītā 4.5)

bahūni me vyatitāni janmāni tava ćārjuna!

EXERCISE 37 : Person and Number :

A. Translate Sankrit into English :

(1) वयं स्मः --------------------------------------

(2) सा अस्ति --------------------------------------

(3) ते सन्ति --------------------------------------

(4) यूयं स्थ --------------------------------------

(5) त्वम् असि --------------------------------------

(6) तानि सन्ति --------------------------------------

B. Translate English into Sanskrit :

(1) We two are. --------------------------------------

(2) They (feminine) are --------------------------------------

(3) It is. --------------------------------------

4) They two (f∘) are. --------------------------------------

(5) She is. --------------------------------------

(6) They (neuter) are. --------------------------------------

(7) Rāma is. --------------------------------------

(8) Sītā is. --------------------------------------

(9) The boys are --------------------------------------

(10) The girls are. --------------------------------------

THE SANSKRIT DUAL NUMBER

Many of our students ask : In English, we have Singular and Plural, to indicate one thing or more than one thing, then for what particular reason, in Sanskrit, there is 'Dual Number' to speak of only 'two' objects?

Unlike the present day modern man made languages, Sanskrit language evolved on natural principles including its phonetics. That is why firstly the Sanskrit has no predetermined arbitrary spellings, but it is based on a systematic classification of the natural sounds that get produced in spoken utterances in the vocal cord. And this idea of systematic classification got carried into most of the Indian languages.

Another point to consider is the way the language looks at the things that occur in the nature. Yes, for a common thinking thing do occur singular. A group of more than one singular objects is called plural. So much for the common mind, but not for the inquisitive mind of Sanskrit formulators. For them, there are no singular things in nature. Every thing that appears singular has a counterpart, if you look precisely. In nature things are present in pairs, pairs of opposites to be more exact. for example, the life has death, male has female, boy and girl, man and woman, positive and negative, light and darkness, good and bad, pleasure and pain, loss and gain, victory and defeat, day and night, up and down, near and far, ahead and behind, slow and fast, rich and poor, respect and dishonor, friend and enemy, cold and hot, moving and non-moving, this and that, light and heavy, add and subtract, divide and multiply, more and less, new and old, ...etc, all are relative, solely depending on the existence of the other.

In Gita Lord Krishna says 'I am the *dvandva* (dual) *samāsa* among the all *samasas,* because even though there are several more intricate *samasas,* the *'dvandva'* is the natural one. In essence what Sanskrit is saying is that there is no one sided coin, one exists only because of the other. So there is 'Dual Number' naturally.

14.2

GENDER

liṅgam लिङ्गम् ।

In Sanskrit there are three Genders, namely, MASCULINE (m◦), FEMININE (f◦) and NEUTER (n◦). संस्कृते लिङ्गानि त्रीणि सन्ति । पुंल्लिङ्गं स्त्रीलिङ्गं नपुंसकलिङ्गं च इति ।

NOTE: Which word is masculine, feminine or neuter is to be found through a Sanskrit dictionary or from everyday usage. There is no easir way to determine it. कः शब्दः :पुंल्लिङ्गः कः शब्दः स्त्रीलिङ्गं कः च शब्दः नपुंसकलिङ्गः इति तु शब्दकोशबलात् व्यवहारबलात् वा ज्ञातव्यम् । एतां व्यवस्थां ज्ञातुं सामान्यरीतिः अन्या का अपि नास्ति ।

From the general appearance of the Sanskrit nouns and adjectives it can roughly be said that, in its nominative singular form, the word ending in अः is usually masculine, ending in म् is neuter and ending in आ, इ or ई is usually feminine, but not always.

* Remember, as said earlier, gender affects person and number only. It does not affect the tense of a verb.

EXAMPLES cum EXERCISE : See Appendix 2 for Case Declensions.

(1) I (m◦ f◦) stand. *ahaṁ tiṣṭhāmi* अहं तिष्ठामि । We stand. *vayaṁ tiṣṭhāmaḥ*. वयं तिष्ठामः ।

(2) He/she/it is standing. *saḥ tiṣṭhati. sā tiṣṭhati. tat tiṣṭhati.* सः तिष्ठति । सा तिष्ठति । तत् तिष्ठति ।

(3) He is a boy. She is a girl. It is a book. *saḥ bālaḥ asti. sā bālā asti. tat pustakam asti.* सः बालः अस्ति । सा बाला अस्ति । तत् पुस्तकम् अस्ति ।

(4) They are boys. They are girls. Those are books. *te bālāḥ santi. tāḥ bālāḥ santi. tāni pustakāni santi.* ते बालाः सन्ति । ताः बालाः सन्ति । तानि पुस्तकानि सन्ति ।

(5) He is a man. She is a woman. It is a house. *saḥ manuṣyaḥ asti. sā strī asti. tad gṛham asti.* सः मनुष्यः अस्ति । सा स्त्री अस्ति । तद् गृहम् अस्ति ।

(6) They are men. They are women. They are houses. *te manuṣyāḥ santi. tāḥ striyaḥ santi. tāni gṛhāṇi santi.* ते मनुष्याः सन्ति । ताः स्त्रियः सन्ति । तानि गृहाणि सन्ति ।

(7) One hymn. One poem. One song. *ekaḥ ślokaḥ. ekā kavitā. ekaṁ gītam.* एकः श्लोकः । एका कविता । एकं गीतम् ।

(8) Four chapters. Four poems. Four essays. *ćatvāraḥ adhyātaḥ. ćatasraḥ kavitāḥ. ćatvāri gītāni.* चत्वारः अध्यायाः । चतस्रः कविताः । चत्वारि गीतानि ।

EXERCISE 38 : (The answers are in Appendix 10)

A. Translate into Sanskrit :

(1) One boy. One girl. One House. ————

(2) Four boys. Four girls. Four houses. ————

(3) He is a man. She is a lady. That is a house. ————

(4) Those are books. They are girls. They are boys. ————

B. Translate into English : (see above for help)

(1) अहं मनुष्यः अस्मि । *ahaṁ manuṣyaḥ asmi* ————

(2) वयं स्त्रियः स्मः । *vayaṁ striyaḥ smaḥ* ————

(3) वयं चतस्रः स्त्रियः । *vayaṁ ćatasraḥ striyaḥ* ————

(4) चत्वारि गृहाणि । *ćavtāri gṛhāṇi* ————

(5) चतस्रः कविताः सन्ति । *ćatasraḥ kavitāḥ santi* ————

(6) एकः बालकः एका बाला एकं पुस्तकम् । *ekaḥ bālakaḥ ekā bālā ekaṁ pustakam* ————

(7) चत्वारः बालकाः चतस्रः बालाः चत्वारि पुस्तकानि । *ćatvāraḥ bālakāḥ, ćatasraḥ bālāḥ ćatvāri pustakāni* ————

(8) सः मनुष्यः अस्ति । सा स्त्री अस्ति । तत् गृहम् अस्ति । *saḥ manuṣyaḥ asti, sā strī asti, tat gṛham asti* ————

(9) तानि पुस्तकानि सन्ति ताः स्त्रियः सन्ति ते बालकाः सन्ति । *tāni pustakāni santi, tāḥ striyaḥ santi, te bālakāḥ santi.* ————

LESSON 15

pañćacaśaḥ abhyāsaḥ पञ्चदशः अभ्यासः ।

NOUN

nāma नाम ।

In the above discussion, the word बालकः (*bālakaḥ* a boy) is the name for a person (or thing), therefore, it is a NOUN. Noun is a person, a physical thing or an abstract thing. Each noun has a gender and number (नाम्नः लिङ्गं वचनं च भवतः). A substantive (noun, pronoun, adjective) is called आख्यात *ākhyāta.*

TABLE : Noun, gender and number

Noun	m◦	बालकः	*bālakāḥ,*	m◦ a boy
Noun	f◦	बाला	*bālā,*	f◦ a girl
Noun	n◦	पुस्तकम्	*pustakam*	n◦ a book

Gender	Singular		Dual		Plural	
Masculine noun	बालकः	*bālakaḥ*	बालकौ	*bālakau*	बालकाः	*bālakāḥ*
Feminine noun	बाला	*bālā*	बाले	*bāle*	बालाः	*bālāḥ*
Neuter noun	पुस्तकम्	*pustakam*	पुस्तके	*pustake*	पुस्तकानि	*pustakāni*

EXAMPLES cum EXERCISE 39: NUMBER

(1) One Tree. *ekaḥ vṛkṣaḥ.* एकः वृक्षः ।

(2) Two Fruits. *dve phale.* द्वे फले ।

(3) Three leaves. *trīṇi patrāṇi, trīṇi parṇāni.* त्रीणि पत्राणि, त्रीणि पर्णानि ।

(4) Four vines. *ćatasraḥ latāḥ.* चतस्रः लताः ।

(5) Five flowers. *pañća puṣpāṇi/kusumāni/sumanāni/prasūnāni.* पञ्च पुष्पाणि/कुसुमानि/सुमनानि/प्रसूनानि ।

NOTE : SANSKRIT IS A RICH LANGUAGE. IT HAS MANY WORDS FOR EACH NOUN. IN THIS BOOK, THE / SIGN INDICATES POPULAR CHOICES FOR THAT WORD.

(6) Six stones. *ṣaṭ prastarāṇi/pāṣāṇāni/śilāḥ* षट् प्रस्तराणि/पाषाणानि/शिला: ।

(7) Seven Mountains. *sapta girayaḥ/parvatāḥ/śailāḥ/nagāḥ* सप्त गिरय:/पर्वता:/शैला:/नगा: ।

(8) Eight roots. *aṣṭa mūlāni.* अष्ट मूलानि । *aṣṭau mūlāni.* अष्टौ मूलानि । One root. *ekaṁ mūlam.* एकं मूलम् । Two roots. *dve mūle.* द्वे मूले । One tree and one root. *ekaḥ vṛkṣaḥ ekaṁ ća mūlam.* एक: वृक्ष: एकं च मूलम् ।

(9) Nine rivers. *nava nadyaḥ; nava saritāḥ.* नव नद्य: नव सरिता: । One river. *ekā nadī.* एका नदी । Two rivers. *dve nadyau.* द्वे नद्यौ । A mountain and two rivers. *parvataḥ dve ća nadyau.* पर्वत: द्वे च नद्यौ ।

(10) Ten girls. *daśa bālāḥ; daśa bālikāḥ.* दश बाला: दश बालिका: । Five boys, five girls and ten flowers. *pañća bālakāḥ pañća bālikāḥ daśa ća puṣpāṇi.* पञ्च बालका: । पञ्च बालिका: । दश च पुष्पाणि ।

(11) One tree, two vines and three fruits. *ekaḥ vṛkṣaḥ dve ća late trīṇi ća phalāni.* एक: वृक्ष: द्वे च लते त्रीणि च फलानि । or एक: वृक्ष: द्वे लते त्रीणि फलानि च or एको वृक्षो द्वे लते त्रीणि च फलानि ।

EXERCISE 40 : A. Name the following nouns in Sanskrit

(1) Boy -------------- Girl ----------- (2) Man ------------- Woman ------------

(3) Book ---------------- House ----------------- Song -----------------

(4) Vine ---------------- River ---------------- Light ----------------

B. Correct the following Sanskrit sentences

(1) One boy, two girls and three houses.
एक: बालका: द्वे बाला: त्रय: च गृहाणि । एक बालक: द्वे लते त्रीणि च गृहम् ।

(2) Nine rivers. नव नदी: । नव सरिता । One river. एक: नदी । Two rivers द्वि नद्यौ ।

(3) Five flowers, six stones and seven mountains. पञ्च पुष्पा: षट् शिल: सप्त च पर्वत: ।

DICTIONARY OF COMMON SANSKRIT NOUNS

INDEX

15.1 ANIMALS, Domastic / Farm ग्राम्यप्राणिनः grāmyaprāṇinaḥ

Bitch	कुक्कुरी, शुनी, सरमा *f∘ kukkurī, śunī, sarmā (m∘) see* dog
Buffalo	महिषः, महिषी *m∘ mahiṣaḥ, f∘ mahiṣī*
Bull, Bullock	ऋषभः, बलीवर्दः, वृषः, वृषभः *m∘ ṛṣabhaḥ, balīvardaḥ, vṛṣaḥ, vṛṣabhaḥ*
Calf	गोवत्सः, तर्णकः, वत्सः *m∘ govastaḥ, tarṇakaḥ, vatsaḥ*
Camel	उष्ट्रः, क्रमेलकः, मयः; स्त्री∘ उष्ट्री, *m∘ uṣṭraḥ, kramelakaḥ, mayaḥ, f∘ uṣṭrī*
Cat	मार्जारः, बिडालः, (स्त्री∘) मार्जारी, *m∘ mārjāraḥ, biḍālaḥ, f∘ mārjārī*
Colt	अश्वशावः *m∘ aśvaśāvaḥ*
Cow	अर्जुनी, उस्रा, गौः, धेनुः, रोहिणी, शृंगिणी, सौरमेयी *f∘ arjunī, usrā, gauḥ, dhenuḥ, śṛṅgiṇī, saurameyī*
Dog	कुक्कुरः, भषकः, श्वन्, शुनकः, सारमेयः *m∘ kukkuraḥ, bhaśakaḥ, śvan, śunakaḥ, sārameyaḥ; (f∘) see* bitch
Donkey	खरः, गर्दभः, रासभः *m∘ kharaḥ, gardabhaḥ, rāsabhaḥ*
Ewe	अविला, उरणी, एडका, मेषी, लोमशा *f∘ avilā, uraṇī, eḍakā, meṣī, lomaśā*
Foal	अश्वशावः *m∘ aśvaśāvaḥ*
Goat	अजः, छगलकः, छागः, बस्तः, (स्त्री∘) अजा, छागी *m∘ ajaḥ, ćhagalakaḥ, ćāgaḥ, bastaḥ, f∘ Ajā, ćhāgī*
Hare	शशः, शशकः *m∘ śaśaḥ, śaśakaḥ*
Horse	अर्वा, आजानेयः, कर्कः, कियाहः, गन्धर्वः, घोटकः, तुरगः, तुरङ्गः, हयः, तुरङ्गमः, भूमिरक्षकः, वाजी, वाहः, वीतिः, सप्तिः, साधुवाही, सिन्धुवारः, सैन्धवः, अश्वः *m∘ arvā, ājāneyaḥ, karkaḥ, kiyāhaḥ, gandharvaḥ, ghoṭakaḥ, turagaḥ, turaṅgaḥ, hayaḥ, turaṅgamaḥ, bhūmirakṣakaḥ, vājī, vāhaḥ, vītiḥ, saptiḥ, sādhuvāhī, sindhuvāraḥ, saindhavaḥ, aśvaḥ.* (f∘ See Mare↓)
Kitten	मार्जारशावः *m∘ mārjāraśāvaḥ*
Lamb	मेशशावः *m∘ meśaśāvaḥ*
Lizard	खरटः, (स्त्री∘) गोधिका *m∘ kharaṭaḥ; f∘ godhikā*

Mare	अश्वा, तुरगी, वडवा, वाजिनी, वामी *f◦ aśvā, turagī, vaḍavā, vājinī, vāmī*
Mouse	आखुः, ऊन्दरुः, खनकः, मूषकः *m◦ ākhuḥ, undaruḥ, khanakaḥ, mūśakaḥ*
Mule	अश्वतरः, वेगसरः, वेशरः *m◦ aśvataraḥ, vegasaraḥ, veśaraḥ*
Ox	अनडुत्, भद्रः *m◦ anaḍut, bhadraḥ* (see bullock)
Pig	वराहः, शूकरः *m◦ varāhaḥ, śūkarah*
Puppy	कुक्कुरशावः *m◦ kukkuraśāvaḥ*
Rabbit	शशः, शशकः *m◦ śaśaḥ, śaśakaḥ*
Ram	अविः, उरणः, एडकः, मेढ्रः, मेषः, लोमशः *m◦ aviḥ, uraṇaḥ, eḍakaḥ, meḍhraḥ, meṣaḥ, lomaśaḥ*
Rat	बिलेशयः *m◦ bileśayaḥ* (see mouse)

15.2 ANIMALS, Wild वन्यपशवः vanya-pashavaḥ

Alligator	ग्राहः, नक्रः *m◦ grāḥ, nakraḥ*
Bat	जतुका *f◦ jatukā*
Bear	ऋक्षः, भल्लकः, भालुकः *m◦ ṛkṣaḥ, bhallakah, bhālukaḥ*
Beast	जन्तुः, पशुः, मृगः *m◦ jantuḥ, paśuḥ, mṛgaḥ*
Boa	अजगरः, वाहसः, शयुः *m◦ ajagaraḥ, vāhasaḥ, śayuḥ*
Boar	किरः, कोलः, धृष्टिः, वराहः, शूकरः *m◦ kiraḥ, kolaḥ, dhṛṣṭiḥ, varāhaḥ, śūkaraḥ*
Cobra	नागः, फणी *m◦ nāgaḥ, faṇī*
Crocodile	कुंभीरः, ग्राहः, नक्रः, मकरः *m◦ kumbhīraḥ, grāhaḥ, nakraḥ, makaraḥ*
Deer	कुरंगः, कुरंगमः, कृष्णसारः, मृगः, रुरुः, रौहिषः, वानप्रमीः, शंबरः, हरिणः *m◦ kuraṅgaḥ, kuraṅgamaḥ, kṛṣṇasāraḥ, mṛgaḥ, ruruḥ, rauhiṣaḥ, vānapramīḥ, śambaraḥ, hariṇaḥ*
Elephant	इभः, करी, कुंजरः, गजः, द्विरदः, दंती, नागः, वारणः, स्तंबेरमः, हस्ती *m◦ ibhaḥ, karī, kunjaraḥ, gajaḥ, dviradaḥ, dantī, nāgaḥ, vāraṇaḥ,*

stamberamaḥ, hastī

Fawn	कुरंगकः, मृगशावकः *m∘ kuraṅgakaḥ, mṛgaśāvakaḥ*
Fish	झषः, मत्स्यः, मीनः, विसारः *m∘ jhaṣaḥ, matsyaḥ, mīnaḥ, visāraḥ*
Fox	खिंकिरः गोमायुः, शृगालः *m∘ khiṅkiraḥ, gomāyuḥ, śṛgālaḥ*
Alligator	ग्राहः, नक्रः *m∘ grāhaḥ, nakraḥ*
Frog	दर्दूरः, भेकः, मंडुकः, लूरः *m∘ dardūraḥ, bhekaḥ, maṇḍukaḥ, lūraḥ*
Hippo	करियादः *m∘ kariyādaḥ*
Jackal	क्रोष्टुः, जंबुकः, फेरवः, शृगालः *m∘ kroṣṭruḥ, jambukaḥ, feravaḥ, śṛgālaḥ*
Leopard	चित्रकः, चित्रव्याघ्रः *m∘ ćitrakaḥ, ćitravyāghraḥ*
Lion	केसरी, मृगपतिः, सिंहः, हरिः *m∘ kesarī, mṛgapatiḥ, siṁhaḥ, hariḥ*
Mongoose	अंगुषः, नकुलः, बभ्रुः *m∘ aṅguṣaḥ, nakulaḥ, babhruḥ*
Monkey	कपिः, कीशः, प्लवंगः, बलीमुखः, मर्कटः, वानरः शाखामृगः *m∘ kapiḥ, kīśaḥ, plavaṅgaḥ, balīmukhaḥ, markaṭaḥ, vānaraḥ, śākhāmṛgaḥ*
Mosquito	मशः, मशकः *m∘ maśaḥ, maśakaḥ*
Panther	द्वीपी *m∘ dvīpī*
Porcupine	शल्यः, शल्यकः, श्वावित् *m∘ śalyaḥ, śalyakaḥ, śvāvit*
Rhino	खंडी, गंडः, गंडकः *m∘ khaṇḍī, gaṇḍaḥ, gaṇḍakaḥ*
Snake	अहिः, उरगः, उरंगमः, काकोदरः, कुंडली, चक्री, दंदशूकः, द्विजिह्वः, नागः, पन्नगः, फणी, बिलेशयः, भुजगः, भुजंगः, भुजंगमः, विषधरः, व्यालः, सरीसृपः, सर्पः *m∘ ahiḥ, uragaḥ, uraṅgamaḥ, kākodaraḥ, kuṇḍalī, ćakrī, dandaśūkaḥ, dvijihvaḥ, nāgaḥ, pannagaḥ, faṇī, bileśayaḥ, bhujagaḥ, bhujaṅgamaḥ, viṣadharaḥ, vyālaḥ, sarīsṛpaḥ, sarpaḥ*
Squirrel	काष्ठबिडालः, चमरपृच्छः, (स्त्री∘) वृक्षशायिका *m∘ kāṣṭhabiḍālaḥ, ćamarapṛććhaḥ, f∘ vṛkṣaśāyikā*
Stag	एणः *m∘ eṇaḥ*

Tiger व्याघ्रः, शार्दूलः *m∘ vyāgraḥ, śārdūlaḥ*

Turtle (m∘) कच्छपः, कमठः, कूर्मः *m∘ kaććhapaḥ, kamaṭhaḥ, kūrmaḥ*

Turtle (f∘) कमठी, कूर्मी, डुलिः *f∘ kamaṭhī, kūrmī, ḍuliḥ*

Wolf ईहामृगः, कोकः, वृकः *m∘ īhāmṛgaḥ, kokaḥ, vṛkaḥ*

Zebra रासभः *m∘ rāsabhaḥ*

15.3 INSECTS कृमयः kṛmayaḥ

Ant पिपीलिका *f∘ pipīlikā* (Anthill वल्मीकः *valmīkaḥ)*

Bedbug मत्कुणः *m∘ matkuṇaḥ*

Bee अलिः, भृंगः, भ्रमरः *m∘ aliḥ, bhṛṅgaḥ, bhramaraḥ*

Bookworm पुस्तककीटः *m∘ pustakakīṭaḥ*

Bug कीटः, कृमिः *m∘ kīṭaḥ, kṛmiḥ*

Butterfly चित्रपतंगः *m∘ ćitrapataṅgaḥ*

Centipede शतपदी *f∘ śatapadī*

Cockroach झीरुका *f∘ jhīrukā*

Crab कर्कटः, कर्कटकः *m∘ karkaṭaḥ, karkaṭakaḥ*

Cricket चीरी, झिल्लिका, भृंगारी *f∘ ćīrī, jhillikā, bhṛṅgārī*

Earthworm भूजंतुः *m∘ bhūjantuḥ*

Flea देहिका *f∘ dehikā*

Fly मक्षिका, नीला *f∘ makṣikā, nīlā*

Glow worm खद्योतः *m∘ khadyotaḥ*

Grasshopper शरभः *m∘ śarabhaḥ*

Honey bee मधुकरः, (स्त्री∘) मधुमक्षिका *m∘ madhukaraḥ, f∘ madhumakṣikā*

Hornet वरटा *f∘ varaṭā*

Insect कीटः, कृमिः, क्रिमिः *m∘ kīṭaḥ, kṛmiḥ, krimiḥ*

Locust	शिरिः *m◦ śiriḥ*
Millipede	सहस्रपदी *f◦ sahasrapadī*
Moth	शलभः *m◦ śalabhaḥ*
Oyster	शुक्तिका *f◦ śuktikā*
Scorpion	द्रोणः, वृश्चिकः *m◦ droṇaḥ, vṛścikaḥ*
Silkworm	कोशकारः, तंतुकीटः *m◦ kośakāraḥ, tantukīṭaḥ*
Snail	शंबूकः *m◦ śambūkaḥ*
Spider	ऊर्णनाभः, कोशकारः, जालिकः, तंतुनाभः, मर्कटकः, (स्त्री◦) लूता *m◦ ūrṇanābhaḥ, kośakāraḥ, jālikaḥ, tantunābhaḥ, markaṭakaḥ, f◦ lūtaḥ*
Termite	वामी *f◦ vāmī*
Worm	कीटः, कीटकः, कृमिः, क्रिमिः *m◦ kīṭaḥ, kīṭakaḥ, kṛmiḥ, krimiḥ*

15.4 BIRDS पक्षिणः pakṣiṇaḥ

Black bird	कुहूरवा, कोकिला, पिका *f◦ kuhūravā, kokilā, pikā*
Blue bird	नीलकंठः *m◦ nīlakaṇṭhaḥ*
Chicken	कुक्कुटशावः *m◦ kukkuṭaśāvaḥ*
Cockoo	कुहूरवा, कोकिला, पिका *f◦ kuhūravā, kokilā, pikā*
Cock	कुक्कुटः, ताम्रचूडः, शिखी *m◦ kukkuṭaḥ, tāmracūḍaḥ, śikhī*
Crane	बलाकः *m◦ balākaḥ*
Crow	काकः, ध्वांक्षः, मौकुलिः, वायसः *m◦ kākaḥ, dhvāṅkṣaḥ, maukuliḥ, āyasaḥ*
Dove	कपोतः, कलरवः, पारावतः *m◦ kapotaḥ, kalaravaḥ, pārāvataḥ*
Duck	कलहंसः, कादंबः, वरटः *m◦ kalahaṁsaḥ, kādambaḥ, varaṭaḥ*
Eagle	उत्कोशः, गरुडः *m◦ utkośaḥ, garuḍaḥ*
Flamingo	मरालः *m◦ marālaḥ*

Goose कलहंसः, चक्रवाकः *m◦ kalahaṁsaḥ, ćakravākaḥ*

Hawk श्येनः *m◦ śyenaḥ*

Hen कुक्कुटी *f◦ kukkuṭī*

Heron क्रौंचः, सारसः *m◦ kraunchaḥ, sārasaḥ*

Kite (स्त्री◦) आतापी, (पु◦) चिल्लः *f◦ ātāpī, m◦ ćillaḥ*

Nightangle बुल्बुलः *m◦ bulbulaḥ*

Owl उलुकः, कौशिकः, दिवान्धः, धूकः, निशाटनः, पेचकः
m◦ ulukaḥ, kauśikaḥ, divāndhaḥ, dhūkaḥ, niśāṭanaḥ, pećakaḥ

Parrot कीरः, शुकः *m◦ kīraḥ, śukaḥ*

Partridge चकोरः, तित्तिरः *m◦ ćakoraḥ, tittiraḥ*

Pigeon कपोतः, कलरवः, पारावतः *m◦ kapotaḥ, kalaravaḥ, pārāvataḥ*

Peacock केकी, मयूरः, शिखंडी, शिखी *m◦ kekī, mayūraḥ, śikhaṇḍī, śikhī*

Quail लावः, वर्तकः *m◦ lāvaḥ, vartakaḥ*

Raven काकोलः *m◦ kākolaḥ*

Rooster कुक्कुटः, ताम्रचूडः, शिखी *m◦ kukkuṭaḥ, tāmraćuḍaḥ, śīkhī*

Sparrow चटकः *m◦ ćaṭakaḥ*

Swan राजहंसः, हंसः *m◦ rājhaṁsaḥ, haṁsaḥ*

Vulture गृध्रः *m◦ gṛdhraḥ*

Woodpecker काष्ठकूटः *m◦ kāṣṭhakūṭaḥ*

15.5 THE BODY PARTS शरीराङ्गानि śarīrāṅgāni

Abdomen उदरं, कुक्षिः *m◦ udaram, kukṣiḥ*

Ankle गुल्फः, घुटिका *m◦ gulfaḥ, f◦ ghuṭikā*

Anus अपानं, गुदं, पायुः *n◦ apānam, gudam, m◦ pāyuḥ*

Arm बाहुः, भुजः, (स्त्री◦) भुजा *m◦ bāhuḥ, bhujaḥ, f◦ bhujā*

Armpit	कक्षाक्ष: *m∘ kakṣākṣaḥ*
Artery	धमनी *f∘ dhamanī*
Back	पृष्ठं *n∘ pṛṣṭham*
Bald	मुण्डं *n∘ muṇḍam*
Beard	कूर्चं, श्मश्रु *n∘ kūrcham, śmaśru*
Belly	उदरं, कुक्षिः, जठरं, तुन्दं *n∘ udaram, kukṣiḥ, jaṭharam, tundam*
Bellybutton	उदरगण्ड: *m∘ udaragaṇḍaḥ*
Blood	अस्त्रं, रक्तं, रुधिरं, लोहितं, शोणितं *n∘ asram, raktam, rudhiram, lohitam, shoṇitam*
Bloodvessel	असृग्वहा, नाडी, रक्तवाहिनी, शिरा *f∘ asṛgvahā, nāḍī, raktavāhinī, śirā*
Bosom	क्रोडं, वक्ष: *n∘ kroḍam, m∘ vakṣaḥ*
Body	अङ्गं, कलेवरं, कायः, गात्रं, तनु, देहः, वपुः, विग्रहः, शरीरं *n∘ angam, kalevaram, m∘ kāyaḥ, n∘ gātram, tanu, m∘ dehaḥ, vapuḥ, vigrahaḥ, n∘ śarīram*
Brain	गोर्दं, मस्तिष्कं *n∘ gordam, mastiṣkam*
Breath	श्वास: *m∘ śvāsaḥ* (i) in-breath श्वास: *m∘ śvāsaḥ*; (ii) out-breath उच्छ्वास: *m∘ ucćhvāsaḥ*
Breast	क्रोडं, वक्षः, (स्त्री∘) स्तन: *m∘ kroḍam, vakṣaḥ; (for female) m∘ stanaḥ*
Bun	नितम्ब: *m∘ nitambaḥ*
Cadaver	कुणप: शवः, शवं *m∘ kuṇapaḥ, śavaḥ, n∘ śavam*
Calf	पिण्डिका *f∘ pinḍikā*
Cartilage	कोमलास्थि: *f∘ komalāsthiḥ*
Cheek	करटः, कपोलः, गडः, गल्ल: *m∘ karaṭaḥ, kapolaḥ, gaḍaḥ, gallaḥ*
Chest	क्रोडं, वक्ष: *n∘ kroḍam, vakṣaḥ*
Chin	चिबुकं, हनु: *n∘ ćibukam, m∘ f∘ hanuḥ*
Corpse	कुणप: शवः, शवं *m∘ kuṇapaḥ, śavaḥ, n∘ śavam*

Ear	कर्णः, क्षोत्रं, श्रूतिः *m◦ karṇaḥ, n◦ kṣotram, f◦ śrutiḥ*
Elbow	कूर्परः, कफणिः *m◦ kūrparaḥ, f◦ kafaṇīḥ*
Eye	अक्षि, चक्षुः, नयनं, नेत्रं, लोचनं
	n◦ akṣi, ćakṣuḥ, nayanam, netram, loćanam
Eyebro	भ्रूः *m◦ bhrūḥ*
Eyelash	पक्ष्म *n◦ paksma*
Eyelid	नेत्राच्छदः *m◦ netraććhadaḥ*
Face	आननं, आस्यं, तुण्डं, मुखं, वदनं, वक्त्रं
	n◦ ānanam, āsyam, tuṇḍam, mukham, vadanam, vaktram
Far-sight	दूरदृष्टिः *f◦ dūradṛṣṭiḥ*
Feather	पक्षः, पिच्छं *m◦ pakṣaḥ, n◦ piććham*
Finger	अंगुलिः *f◦ anguliḥ*
Fist	मुष्टिः *m◦ muṣṭiḥ;* मुष्टी *f◦ muṣṭī*
Foetus	गर्भः, पिण्डः, भ्रूणः *m◦ garbhaḥ, piṇḍaḥ, bhrūṇaḥ,*
Foot	चरणं, पदं, पादः *n◦ ćaraṇam, padam, m◦ pādaḥ*
Fore-finger	तर्जनी *f◦ tarjanī*
Forehead	ललाटं *n◦ lalāṭam*
Gum	दन्तमांसं *n◦ dantamāṁsam*
Hair	कचः, कुन्तलः, केशः, चिकुरः, बालः
	m◦ kaćaḥ, kuntalaḥ, keśaḥ, ćikuraḥ, bālaḥ
Hand	करः, पाणिः, हस्तः *m◦ karaḥ, pāṇiḥ, hastaḥ*
Head	मूर्धा, मौलिः, शिरः, शीर्षं, शीर्षकं
	m◦ mūrdhā, mauliḥ, n◦ śiraḥ, śīrṣam, śīrṣakam
Heart	हृद्, हृदयं *n◦ hṛd, hṛdayam*
Heel	पार्ष्णिः *f◦ pārṣṇiḥ*
Hide	अजिनं, चर्म *n◦ ajinam, ćarma*

Hip	किटी, श्रोणी	*f∘ kiṭī, śroṇī*
Horn	विषाणं, शृङ्गं	*n∘ viṣāṇam, śṛaṅgam*
Index-finger	तर्जनी	*f∘ tarjanī*
Intestine	अन्त्रं	*n∘ antram*
Jaw,	पीचं, हनु	*n∘ pīćam, m∘ f∘ hanu*
Jaw, lower	चिबुकं, कुञ्जं	*ćbukam, kuñjam*
Jaw-tooth	दंष्ट्रा	*f∘ daṁṣtrā*
Joint	सन्धिः	*m∘ sandhiḥ*
Kidney	गुर्दः, वृक्कः	*m∘ gurdaḥ, vṛkkaḥ*
Knee	जानु	*n∘ jānu*
Knot	ग्रन्थिः	*f∘ granthiḥ*
Knuckle	अङ्गुलपर्व	*n∘ aṅguliparva*
Lap	अङ्कः, क्रोडं,	*m∘ aṅkaḥ, n∘ kroḍam*
Life	चैतन्यं, जीवनं, प्राणः	*n∘ ćaitanyam, jīvanam, m∘ prāṇaḥ*
Limb	अङ्गं, अवयवः, गात्रं	*n∘ aṅgam, m∘ avayavaḥ, n∘ gātram*
Lip	ओष्ठः	*upper-lip m∘ oṣṭhaḥ; lower-lip* अधरः *m∘ adharaḥ*
Little-finger	कनिष्ठा, कनिष्ठिका, कनीका	*f∘ kaniṣṭhā, kaniṣṭhikā, kanīkā*
Liver	कालकं, यकृतं	*n∘ kālakam, yakṛtam*
Lower-lip	अधरः	*m∘ adharaḥ*
Lungs	क्लोमं, फुप्फुसं	*n∘ klomam, fuffusam*
Marrow	मज्जा, मेदः, वपा, वसा	*f∘ majjā, m∘ medaḥ, f∘ vapā, vasā*
Meat	माँसं	*n∘ māṁsam*
Menses	रजः	*m∘ rajaḥ*
Middle-finger	मध्यमा	*f∘ madhyamā*
Moustache s	श्मश्रु	*n∘ śmaśru*
Mouth	आननं, आस्यं, तुण्डं, मुखं, लपनं, वक्त्रं, वदनं	

	m◦ ānanam, āsyam, tuṇḍam, mukham, lapanam, vaktram, vadanam
Muscle	पेशी, शिरा, स्नायुः *f◦ peśī, śirā, snāyuḥ*
Nail	नखः, नखं *m◦ nakhaḥ, n◦ nakham*
Navel	तुन्दः, नाभिः, नाभी, *m◦ tundaḥ, f◦ nābhiḥ, nābhī*
Neck	ग्रीवा *f◦ grīvā*
Nerve	मज्जा, शिरा *f◦ majjā, śirā*
Nipple	चूचुकः *m◦ ćūćukaḥ*
Nose	घोणा, घ्राणं, नसा, नासा, नासिका
	f◦ ghoṇā, n◦ ghrāṇam, f◦ nasā, nāsā, nāsikā
Nostril	नासारन्ध्रं *n◦ nāsārandhram*
Palm	करतलः, चपेटः, प्रहस्तः *m◦ kartalaḥ, ćapeṭaḥ, prahastaḥ*
Penis	मेढ्रः, लिङ्गं, शिश्नः *m◦ meḍhraḥ, n◦ liṅgam, m◦ śiśnaḥ*
Ponytail	शिखा *f◦ śikhā*
Poo	पुरीषं, मलं, विष्टा *n◦ puriṣam, malam, f◦ viṣṭā*
Pore	रन्ध्रं *n◦ randhram*
Pulse	स्पन्दनं *n◦ spandanam*
Rib	पर्शुका *f◦ parśukā*
Ring-finger	ऊर्मिका *f◦ ūrmikā*
Rump	किटी, श्रोणी *f◦ kiṭī, śroṇī*
Saliva	लाला, सृणिका *f◦ lālā, sṛṇikā*
Semen	रेतः, वीर्यं, शुक्रं *m◦ retaḥ, n◦ vīryam, śukram*
Shoulder	अंसः, स्कन्धः *m◦ aṁsaḥ, skandhaḥ*
Sight	दृष्टिः *f◦ dṛṣṭiḥ*
Skeleton	कङ्कालः, पञ्जरः *m◦ kaṅkālaḥ, pañjaraḥ*
Skin	त्वचा *f◦ tvachā*
Skull	कपालः, कपालं, कर्परः *m◦ kapālaḥ, n◦ kapālam, m◦ karparaḥ*

Snout	पोत्रं, प्रोथः	*n∘ potram, m∘ prothaḥ*
Sole	पादतलं	*n∘ pādatalam*
Soul	आत्मा	*m∘ ātmā*
Spit	शूला	*f∘ śūlā*
Stomach	अन्नाशयः, उदरं, कोष्ठः	*m∘ annāśayaḥ, n∘ udaram, m∘ koṣṭhaḥ*
Tail	पुच्छं, लाङ्गुलं	*n∘ pucćham, lāṅgulam*
Tear	अश्रु	*n∘ aśru*
Testicle	ण्डः, अण्डकोषः, मुष्कः, वृषणः	*m∘ aṇḍaḥ, aṇḍkoṣaḥ, muṣkaḥ, vṛṣaṇaḥ*
Thigh	ऊरुः, सक्थि	*m∘ ūruḥ, n∘ sakthiḥ*
Throat	कण्ठः, गलः	*m∘ kaṇṭhaḥ, galaḥ*
Thumb	अङ्गुष्ठः	*m∘ aṅguṣṭhaḥ*
Tongue	जिह्वा, रसना	*f∘ jihvā, rasanā*
Tooth	जम्भः, दन्तः, दंष्ट्रा, दशनः, रदः, रदनः	*m∘ jambhaḥ, dantaḥ, (f∘) daṁṣṭrāḥ, (m∘) daśanaḥ, radaḥ, radanaḥ*
Trunk	शुण्डः, शुण्डा	*m∘ śuṇḍaḥ, f∘ śuṇḍā*
Udder	स्तनः	*m∘ stanaḥ*
Uterus	गर्भाशयः, योनिः	*m∘ garbhāśayaḥ, f∘ yoniḥ*
Vagina	भगः, योनिः	*m∘ bhagaḥ, f∘ yoniḥ*
Vein	रक्तवाहिनी	*f∘ raktavāhinī*
Vision	दृष्टिः	*f∘ dṛṣṭiḥ*
Waist	कटिः, कटी, श्रोणिः	*m∘ kaṭiḥ, f∘ kaṭī, śroṇiḥ*
Whiskers	गुम्फः	*m∘ gumphaḥ*
Womb	गर्भः, गर्भाशयः	*m∘ garbhaḥ, garbhāśayaḥ*
Wrist	प्रकोष्ठः, मणिबंधः	*m∘ prakoṣṭhaḥ, maṇibandhaḥ*

15.6 AILMENTS and BODY CONDITIONS विकाराः vikārāḥ

Abortion गर्भपातः *m∘ garbhapātaḥ*

Acidity अम्लता, शुक्तता *f∘ amlatā, śuktatā*

Asthma श्वासरोगः *m∘ śvāsarogaḥ*

Bald मुण्डं *n∘ muṇḍam*

Belching उद्गिरणं *n∘ udgiraṇam*

Bleeding रक्तस्त्रावः *m∘ raktasrāvaḥ*

Blindness अन्धता *f∘ andhatā*

Boil गण्डः, पिटकः *m∘ gaṇḍaḥ, piṭakaḥ*

Bone अस्थि *n∘ asthi*

Cancer कर्कः, कर्कटः *m∘ karkaḥ, karkaṭaḥ*

Chill शीतः *m∘ śītaḥ*

Constipation बद्धकोष्ठः *m∘ baddhakoṣṭhaḥ*

Cough काशः, कासः, क्षवथुः *m∘ kāśaḥ, kāsaḥ, kṣavathuḥ*

Crazy भ्रांतचित्तः, वातुलः *m∘ bhrāntcittaḥ, vātulaḥ*

Diabetes मधुमेहः *m∘ madhumehaḥ*

Diarrhoea अतिसारः *m∘ atisārah*

Disease अस्वास्थ्यं, आमयः, गदः, रुजा, रोगः, विकारः, व्याधिः
n∘ asvāsthyam, m∘ āmayaḥ, gadaḥ, f∘ rujā, m∘ rogaḥ, vikāraḥ, vyādhiḥ

Dwarf खर्वः, वामनः *m∘ kharvaḥ, vāmanaḥ*

Dysentry अतिसारः *m∘ atisāraḥ*

Eczema दद्रुः, पामा *m∘ dadruḥ, f∘ pāmā*

Eyesore अक्षिशूलं *n∘ akṣiśūlam*

Frail क्षयी, भङ्गुरः *m∘ kṣayī, bhaṅguraḥ*

Giddiness घूर्णिः *f∘ ghūrṇiḥ*

Headache	शिरोवेदना *f∘ śirovedanā*
Health	अनामयं, आरोग्यं, स्वास्थ्यं *n∘ anāmayam, ārogyam, svāsthyam*
Hiccup	हिक्का, हिध्मा *f∘ hikkā, hidhmā*
Hunchback	कुब्जः, न्युब्जः *m∘ kubjaḥ, nyubjaḥ*
Hurt	अपकारः, क्षतिः *m∘ apkāraḥ, f∘ kṣatiḥ*
Indigestion	अपाकः, अजीर्णं *m∘ apākaḥ, n∘ ajīrṇam*
Jaundice	पाण्डुः, पाण्डुरोगः *m∘ pāṇḍuḥ, pāṇḍurogaḥ*
Leprosy	कुष्ठं, महारोगः, श्वित्रं *n∘ kuṣṭham, m∘ mahārogaḥ, n∘ śvitram*
Lunacy	उन्मादः *m∘ unmādaḥ*
Mad	वातुलः, हतबुद्धिः *m∘ vātulaḥ, hatabuddhiḥ*
Obese	पीनः, पीवरः *m∘ pīnaḥ, pīvaraḥ*
Pain	उद्वेगः, कष्टं, कृच्छ्रं, क्लेशः, तापः, दुःखं, पीडा, वेदना, व्यथा *m∘ udvegaḥ, n∘ kaṣṭam, kṛćhram, m∘ kleśaḥ, tāpaḥ, m∘ duḥkham,* *f∘ pīḍā, vedanā, vyathā*
Phlegem	कफः, श्लेष्म *m∘ kafaḥ, n∘ śleṣma*
Pimple	पिटिका *f∘ piṭikā*
Piles	अर्शः *m∘ arśaḥ*
Plague	महामारी *f∘ mahāmārī*
Pus	पूयं *n∘ pūyam*
Rib	पर्शुका *f∘ parśukā*
Saliva	लाला, सृणिका *f∘ lālā, sṛṇikā*
Sick	अस्वस्थः, पीडितः, रुग्णः *m∘ asvasthaḥ, pīḍitaḥ, rugṇaḥ*
Sleeplessness	निर्णिद्रता *f∘ nirṇidratā*
Sleepy	निद्रालुः, शयालुः *m∘ nidrāluḥ, śayāluḥ*
Sneeze	क्षवः, क्षुतं *m∘ kṣavaḥ, n∘ kṣutam*
Sore	ईर्मं, क्षतं, व्रणः *n∘ īrmam, kṣatam, m∘ vraṇaḥ*

Sprain	स्नायुवितानं	*n∘ snāyuvitānam*
Stool	मल:, विष्टा	*m∘ malaḥ, f∘ viṣṭā*
Sweat	घर्म:, स्वेद:	*m∘ gharmaḥ, svedaḥ*
Swelling	शूयमान:	*m∘ śūyamānaḥ*
Tears	अश्रु	*m∘ aśru*
Thirst	तृषा, तृष्णा, पिपासा	*f∘ tṛṣā, tṛṣṇā, pipāsā*
Tuberculosis	क्षय:	*m∘ kṣayaḥ*
Urine	मुत्रं, मेह:	*n∘ mutram, m∘ mehaḥ*
Vomit	वमनं	*n∘ vamanam*
Wart	किण:	*m∘ kiṇaḥ*
Wound	क्षतं, व्रण:	*n∘ kṣatam, m∘ vraṇaḥ*
Yawn	जृंभा	*f∘ jṛmbhā*

15.7 CLOTHING, DRESS etc. परिधानानि **paridhānāni**

Belt	काञ्ची, मेखला	*kāñćī, mekhalā*
Blanket	ऊर्णायु:, कम्बल:, रल्लक:	*m∘ ūrṇāyuḥ, kambalaḥ, rallakaḥ*
Button	गण्ड:	*m∘ gaṇḍaḥ*
Cap	शिरस्कं	*n∘ śiraskam*
Cloth	वसनं, वस्त्रं, वास:	*n∘ vasanam, vastram, vāsaḥ*
Coat	उत्तरीयं, कञ्चुक:, निचोल:	*n∘ uttariyam, kañćukaḥ, nićolaḥ*
Colour	रङ्ग:	*m∘ rangaḥ*
Cotton	कर्पास:, तूल:, पिचु:, पिचुल:	*m∘ karpāsaḥ, tūlaḥ, pićuḥ, pićulaḥ*
Glove	करच्छद:	*m∘ karaććhadaḥ*
Gown	कटिवस्त्रं	*n∘ kaṭivastram*
Hat	शिरस्कं, शिरस्त्राणं	*n∘ śiraskam, śirastrāṇam*

Jacket	कूर्पासकः, निचोलः	*m◦ kūrpāsakaḥ, nićolaḥ*
Lace	सूत्रजालं	*n◦ sūtrajālam*
Measurement	परिमितिः, मानं, मापनं	*f◦ parimitiḥ, n◦ mānam, māpanam*
Needle	सूचिः, सूची, सेवनी	*f◦ sūćiḥ, sūćī, sevani*
Pocket	कोषः	*m◦ koṣaḥ*
Quilt	तूलिका	*f◦ tūlikā*
Satin	चीनाञ्शुकं	*n◦ ćīnāṁśukam*
Scarf	चेलं, चेलकः	*n◦ ćlam, m◦ ćelakaḥ*
Sheet	उत्तरच्छदः, प्रच्छदः	*m◦ uttaraććhadaḥ, praććhadaḥ*
Shirt	चोलः, युतकं	*m◦ ćolaḥ, n◦ yutakam*
Silk	कौशं, कौशेयं, कौशाम्बरं, कौशिकं, क्षौमं, दुकुलं	*n◦ kauśam, kauśeyam, kauśāmbaram, kauśikam, kṣaumam, ṭukulam*
Size	आकारः, परिमाणं, मानं	*m◦ ākāraḥ, n◦ parimāṇam, mānam*
Skirt	वस्त्राञ्चलः	*m◦ vastrāñćalaḥ*
Sleeve	पिप्पलः	*m◦ pippalaḥ*
Sock	पादत्रं	*n◦ pādatram*
Style	प्रकारः	*m◦ prakāraḥ*
Thread	तन्तुः, सूत्रं	*m◦ tantuḥ, n◦ sūtram*
Towel	मार्जनवस्त्रं	*n◦ mārjanavastram*
Turban	उष्णीषं	*n◦ uṣṇīṣam*
Uniform	वेषः	*m◦ veṣaḥ*
Veil	संवरणं	*n◦ saṁvaraṇam*
Wool	ऊर्णा, लोम	*f◦ ūrṇā, n◦ loma*
Yarn	तन्तुः, सूत्रं	*m◦ tantuḥ, n◦ sūtram*

15.8 RELATIONS सम्बन्धाः sambandhāḥ

Adopted — अङ्गीकृत, परिगृहित *adj◦ aṅgīkṛta, parigṛhita*

Adopted, daughter — दत्तकपुत्री *f◦ dattakaputrī*

Adopted, son — कृतकपुत्रः, दत्तकः *m◦ kṛtakaputraḥ, dattakaḥ*

Aunt — पितृष्वसा, मातृष्वसा *f◦ pitṛṣvasā, mātṛṣvasā*

Brother — बंधुः, भ्राता, सहोदरः, सोदरः
m◦ bandhuḥ, bhrātā, sahodaraḥ, sodaraḥ

Brotherhood — बंधुता, बंधुत्वं, भ्रातृभावः, साहचर्यं, सौमात्रं
f◦ bandhutā, n◦ bandhutvam, m◦ bhrātṛbhāvaḥ,
n◦ sāhacaryam, saumātram

Brotherly — भ्रात्रीय *a◦ bhrātrīya*

Brother' son — भ्रातृव्यः, भ्रातृपुत्रः, भ्रात्रीयः *m◦ bhatṛvyaḥ, bhrātṛputraḥ, bhrātrīyaḥ*

Brother's daughter — भ्रातृकन्या, भ्रातृसुता, भ्रात्रीया *f◦ bhatṛkanyā, bhrātṛsutā, bhrātrīyā*

Brother's wife — प्रजावती, भ्रातृजाया *f◦ prajāvatī, bhrātṛjāyā*

Child — अपत्यं, अर्भकः, संततिः, सन्तानः *n◦ apatyam, arbhakam, f◦ santtiḥ,*
m◦ santānaḥ

Childless — निःसंतान *adj◦ niḥsantāna*

Country-folk — जानपदाः *m◦ jānapadāḥ*

Country-man — एकदेशस्थः, देशबंधुः, स्वदेशीयः
m◦ ekadeśasthaḥ, deśabandhuḥ, svadeśīyaḥ

Couple — युगलं, युग्मं, दम्पती, वधूवरौ
n◦ yualam, yugmam; dual◦ m◦ dampatī, vadhūvarau

Daughter — अंगजा, आत्मजा, कन्या, कुमारी, तनया, तनुजा, दुहिता, नन्दिनी, पुत्रिका, पुत्री, सुता
f◦ aṅgajā, ātmajā, kanyā, kumārī, tanayā, tanujā, duhitā,
nandinī,

putrikā, putrī, sutā

Daughter-in-law वधू:, स्नुषा *f◦ vadhūḥ, snuṣā*

Family कुटुम्बं, कुलं, गोत्रं, जाति:, वंश:

n◦ kuṭumbam, kulam, gotram, f◦ jātiḥ, m◦ vaṁśaḥ

Family man अभ्यागारिक:, उपाधि: *m◦ abhyāgārikaḥ, f◦ upādhiḥ*

Father जनक:, जनयिता, जनिता, जन्मद:, पिता, तात:

m◦ janakaḥ, janayitā, janitā, janmadaḥ, pitā, tātaḥ

Fatherhood पितृत्वं, पितृधर्म:, पितृभाव:

n◦ pitṛtvam, m◦ pitṛdharmaḥ, pitṛbhāvaḥ

Fatherless अनाथ, अपितृक, पितृहीन *adj◦ anātha, apitṛka, pitṛhīna*

Fatherly पितृतुल्यं *adv◦ pitṛtulyam*

Father-in-law श्वशुर: *m◦ śvaśuraḥ*

Father's brother पितृव्य: *m◦ pitṛvyaḥ*

Father's father पितामह: *m◦ pitamaḥ*

Father's mother पितामही *m◦ pitāmahī*

Father's sister पितृव्या, पितृस्वसा *pitṛvyā, pitṛsvasā*

Forefathers पितर:, पूर्वजा:, पूर्वा:, वृद्धा: *pl◦ pitaraḥ, pūrvajāḥ, pūrvāḥ,*
vṛddhāḥ

Friend बंधु:, मित्रं, वसस्य:, सखा, सुहृद्, हित:

m◦ bandhuḥ, n◦ mitram, m◦ vayasyaḥ, sakhā, suhṛd, hitaḥ

Grand-child पौत्र: *m◦ pautraḥ ; f◦* पौत्री *pautrī*

Grand-daughter पौत्री *f◦ pautrī*

Grand-father पितामह:; मातामह: *m◦ pitāmahaḥ; mātāmahaḥ*

Grand-son पौत्र: *m◦ pautraḥ*

Grand-son, son's son नप्ता, पुत्रसुत:, पौत्र: *m◦ naptā, putrasutaḥ, pautraḥ*

Grandee अभिजन:, कुलीन:, कुलीनजन:, महाजन:

	m◦ abhijanaḥ, kulīnaḥ, kulīnajanaḥ, mahājanaḥ
Grand-son, dauther's son	पौत्रः, दौहित्रः *m◦ pautraḥ, dauhitraḥ*
Great-gand-daughter	प्रपौत्री *f◦ prapautrī*
Great-grand-son	प्रपौत्रः *m◦ prapautraḥ*
Great-great-grand-son	परप्रपौत्रः *m◦ paraprapautraḥ*
Great-great-gand-daughter	परप्रपौत्री *f◦ paraprapautrī*
Heair	अंशहारी, उत्तराधिकारी, दायादः, रिक्थहरः, रिक्थी
	aṁśahārī, uttarādhikārī, dāyādaḥ, rikthaharaḥ, rikthī
Husband	इष्टः, उपयन्ता, कान्तः, धवः, नाथः, पतिः, परिग्रहिता, परिणेता, प्राणेशः, प्रियतमः, भर्ता, विवोढा, स्वामी, हृदयेशः
	m◦ iṣṭaḥ, upayantā, kāntaḥ, dhavaḥ, nāthaḥ, patiḥ, parigrahitā, pariṇetā, prāṇeśaḥ, priyatamaḥ, bhartā, vivoḍhā, swāmī, hṛdayeśaḥ
Husband's brother	देवरः *m◦ devaraḥ*
Husband's brother's wife	याता *f◦ yātā*
Husband and wife	जम्पती, दम्पती, जायापती, भार्यापती
	(dual◦ m◦) jampatī, dampatī, jāyāpatī, bhāryāpatī
Husband, second	दिधिषुः *m◦ didhiṣuḥ*
Husband's sister	ननांदा, याता, श्याली *f◦ nanāndā, yātā, śyālī*
Lord	ईशः, ईश्वरः, प्रभुः, स्वामी *m◦ īśaḥ, īśvaraḥ, prabhuḥ, swāmī*
Love	अनुकम्पा, अनुरागः, अभिलाषः, प्रणयः, प्रीतिः, प्रेम, भावः, रागः, वात्सल्यं, स्नेहः
	f◦ anukampā, m◦ anurāgaḥ, abhilāṣaḥ, praṇayaḥ, f◦ prītiḥ, n◦ prema, m◦ bhāvaḥ, rāgaḥ, n◦ vātsalyam, m◦ snehaḥ
Lover	दयितः *m◦ dayitaḥ*
Mistress	दयिता, रमणी *f◦ dayitā, ramaṇī*
Mother	अंबा, जननी, जनयित्री, जन्मदा, प्रसवित्री, प्रसविनी, प्रसूः

	f◦ ambā, jananī, janayitrī, janmadā, prasavitrī, prasavinī, prasūḥ
Motherhood	मातृत्वं, मातृधर्मः, मातृभावः *n◦ mātṛtvam, mātṛdharmaḥ, mātṛbhāvaḥ*
Motherless	अमातृकः, मृतमातृकः, हीनमातृकः *m◦ amātṛkaḥ, mṛtamātṛkaḥ, hīnamātṛkaḥ*
Motherly	मातृवत् *adv◦ mātṛvat*
Mother-in-law	श्वश्रूः *f◦ śvaśrūḥ*
Mother's brother	मातुलः *m◦ mātulaḥ*
Mother's brother's wife	मातुला, मातुलानी, मातुली *f◦ mātulā, mātaulānī, mātulī*
Mother's father	मातामहः *m◦ mātānahaḥ*
Mother-land	जन्मभूमिः, स्वदेशः *f◦ janmabhūmiḥ, m◦ svadeśaḥ*
Mother's mother	मातामही *f◦ mātāmahī*
Mother's sister	मातृस्वसा *f◦ mātṛsvasā*
Neighbor	प्रतिवेशी *m◦ prativeśī*
Neighborly	उपकारशीलः, प्रतिवासयोग्यः, हितः *m◦ upakāraśīlaḥ, prativāsayogyaḥ, hitaḥ*
Own, my	मदीय *adj◦ madīya*
Own, one's	आत्म, आत्मीय, निज, स्व, स्वकीय, स्वीय *adj◦ ātma, ātmīya, nija, sva, svakīya, svīya*
Own, your	त्वदीय, युष्मदीय *adj◦ tvadīya, yuṣmadīya*
Pupil	अन्तेवासी, छात्रः, शिष्यः *m◦ antevāsī, ćhātraḥ, śiṣyaḥ*
Relation	सम्बंधः *m◦ sambandhaḥ*
Relative	ज्ञातिः, बन्धुः, बान्धवः, सकुल्यः, सगोत्रः *m◦ jñātiḥ, bandhuḥ, bāndhavaḥ, sakulyaḥ, sagotraḥ*
Sister	भगिनी, स्वसा, सोदर्या *bhaginī, svasā, sodaryā*

Sister, elder	अग्रजा *f◦ agrajā*
Sister, younger	अनुजा, अवरजा *f◦ anujā, avarajā*
Sister's daughter	भागिनेयी, स्वस्रीया *f◦ bhāgineyī, svasrīyā*
Sisterhood	भगिनित्वं *n◦ bhaginitvam*
Sisterly	स्वस्रीय *adj◦ svasrīya*
Sister's husband	आवृत्तः, भगिनीपतिः *m◦ āvṛttaḥ, bhaginīpatiḥ*
Sister-in-law	ननान्दा, याता, श्याली *f◦ nanāndā, yātā, śyālī*
Sister's son	भागिनेय, स्वसृपुत्रः, स्वस्रेयः
	m◦ bhāgineyaḥ, svasṛputraḥ, svasreyaḥ
Son	अङ्गजः, आत्मजः, कुमारः, तनयः, तनुजः, दारकः, नंदनः, पुत्रः, पुत्रकः, सुतः, सुनुः
	m◦ angajaḥ, ātmajaḥ, kumāraḥ tanayaḥ, tanujaḥ,
dārakah:,	
	nandanaḥ, putraḥ, putrakaḥ, sutaḥ, sunuḥ
Sonless	अपुत्रक, निपुत्रिक *adj◦ aputrak, niputrik*
Son-in-law	जामाता *m◦ jāmātā*
Step-brother	अन्योदर्यः, विमातृजः, वैमात्रः, वैमात्रेयः
	m◦ anyodaryaḥ, vimātṛjaḥ, vaimārtaḥ, vaimātreyaḥ
Step-child	अन्योदर्यमपत्यं *n◦ anyodaryamapatyam*
Step-daughter	सपत्नीसुता *f◦ sapatnīsutā*
Step-father	मातृपतिः *m◦ mātṛpatiḥ*
Step-mother	विमाता *f◦ vimātā*
Step-sister	अन्योदर्या, विमातृजा, वैमात्री *f◦ anyodaryā, vimātṛjā, vaimātrī*
Step-son	सपत्नीसुतः *m◦ sapatnīsutaḥ*
Stranger	अनभिज्ञः, अन्यजनः, अपरिचितः, अभ्यागतः, आगन्तुकः, परः, विदेशीयः, वैदेशिकः, वैदेश्यः

	m◦ anabhigjñaḥ, anyajanaḥ, aparićitaḥ, abhyāgataḥ, āgantukaḥ, paraḥ, videśiyaḥ, vaideśikaḥ, vaideśyaḥ
Widow	अनाथा, गतभर्तृका, निर्णाथा, पतिहीना, विधवा *f◦ anāthā, gatabhartṛkā, nirṇāthā, patihīnā, vidhavā*
Widower	गतजायः, पत्नीहीनः *m◦ gatajāyaḥ, patnīhīnaḥ*
Wife	कलत्रं, कान्ता, क्षेत्रं, गृहाः, गृहिणी, गेहिनी, जाया, दयिता, दाराः, पत्नी, परिग्रहः, प्रिया, भार्या, रमणी, वधूः, वल्लभा, सहधर्मिणी, स्त्री *n◦ kalatram, f◦ kāntā, n◦ kṣetram, f◦ gṛhāḥ, gṛhiṇī, gehinī, jāyā, dayitā, m◦ dārāḥ, f◦ patnī, m◦ parigrahaḥ, f◦ priyā, bharyā, ramaṇī, vadhūḥ, vallabhā, sahadharmiṇī, strī*
Wife's brother	श्यालः *m◦ śyālaḥ*
Wife's sister	श्याली *f◦ śyālī*

15.9 HOUSEHOLD THINGS गृह्यवस्तुनि gṛhyavastuni

Bag	कोषः, स्यूतः *m◦ kośaḥ, syūtaḥ*
Basket	कण्डोली, करण्डः, मञ्जूषा *f◦ kaṇḍolī, m◦ karaṇḍah, f◦ mañjūṣā*
Bed	शय्या *f◦ śaiyyā*
Blanket	ऊर्णायुः, कम्बलः *m◦ ūrṇāyuḥ, kambalaḥ*
Bottle	कूपी *f◦ kūpī*
Bowl	कटोरं, कटोरा, भाजनं, शरावः *n◦ kaṭoram, f◦ kaṭorā, n◦ bhājanam, m◦ śarāvaḥ*
Box	पेटिका, सम्पुटः, समुद्रकः *f◦ peṭikā, m◦ samputaḥ, samudrakaḥ*
Broom	सम्मार्जनी *f◦ sammarjanī*
Brush	मार्जनी *f◦ mārjanī*
Bucket	उदञ्चनं, द्रोणी *n◦ udañćanam, f◦ droṇī*

Button	गण्ड: *m◦ gaṇḍaḥ*
Candle	दीपिका *f◦ dīpikā*
Chair	आसनं, पीठं, विष्टर: *n◦ āsanam, pīṭhaḥ, m◦ viṣṭaraḥ*
Comb	कङ्कतिका, प्रसाधनी *f◦ kaṅkatikā, prasādhanī*
Cot	खट्वा, पर्यंक: *f◦ khaṭvā, m◦ paryaṅkaḥ*
Cup	चषक: *m◦ ćaṣakaḥ*
Dictionary	अभिधानं, शब्दकोष: *m◦ abhidhānam, m◦ śabdakoṣaḥ*
Dish	शराव: *m◦ śarāvaḥ*
Fuel	ईन्धनं *n◦ īndhanam*
Furniture	उपस्कर: *m◦ upaskaraḥ*
Glass	चषक: *m◦ ćaṣakaḥ*
Glue	लेप:, संश्लेषणं *m◦ lepaḥ, n◦ saṁśleṣaṇam*
Hearth	चुल्ली *f◦ ćullī*
Key	कुञ्चिका, ताली *f◦ kuñćikā, tālī*
Knife	कृपाणी, छुरिका, छुरी *f◦ kṛpāṇī, ćhurikā, ćhurī*
Lamp	दीप:, दीपक: *m◦ dīpaḥ, dīpakaḥ*
Lock	ताल: *m◦ tālaḥ*
Mat	आस्तरणं, कट:, किलिञ्ज: *n◦ āstaraṇam, m◦ kaṭaḥ, kiliñjaḥ*
Mirror	आदर्श:, दर्पण:, मुकुर: *m◦ ādarśaḥ, darpaṇaḥ, mukuraḥ*
Needle	सूचिका, सूची, सेवनी *f◦ sūćikā, sūćī, sevanī*
Oven	कन्दु:, चुल्ली *m◦ kanduḥ, f◦ ćullī*
Paper	पत्रकं *n◦ patrakam*
Pen	कलम:, लेखनी *m◦ kalamaḥ, f◦ lekhanī*
Pillow	उपधानं, बालिशं *n◦ upadhānam, bāliśaḥ*
Plate	थालिका, स्थाली *f◦ thālikā, sthālī*
Pot	कलश:, कुंभ:, घट:, पात्रं, पिठर:, भाजनं

m◦ kalaśaḥ, kumbhaḥ, ghaṭaḥ, pātram, piṭharaḥ, n◦ bhājanam

Rolling pin वेल्लनं, वेल्लनी *n◦ vellanam, f◦ vellanī*

Rope रज्जुः, शुल्बं *f◦ rajjuḥ, n◦ śulbam*

Sack स्यूतः *m◦ syūtaḥ*

Soap फेनिलः *m◦ fenilaḥ*

Spoon चमसः *m◦ chamasaḥ*

Stove चुल्ली *f◦ cullī*

String तन्तुः, रज्जुः *m◦ tantuḥ, rajjuḥ*

Swing दोला, प्रेङ्खः, हिन्दोलः *f◦ dolā, preṅkhaḥ, m◦ hindolaḥ*

Table मञ्चः *m◦ mañcaḥ*

Thread तन्तुः *m◦ tantuḥ*

Tongs सन्दंशः *m◦ sandaṁśaḥ*

Tray आधारः *m◦ ādhāraḥ*

Umbrella छत्रं *n◦ chhatram*

Wire तारः *m◦ tāraḥ*

Wok ऋजीषं, कटाहः *n◦ ṛjīṣam, m◦ kaṭahaḥ*

15.10 TOOLS उपकरणानि upakaraṇāni

Anvil शूर्मी, स्थूणा *f◦ śūrmī, sthuṇā*

Awl आरा *f◦ ārā*

Axe कुठारः, परशुः *m◦ kuṭhāraḥ paraśuḥ*

Blade धारा *f◦ dhārā*

Chisel टङ्कः, तक्षणी, व्रश्चनः *m◦ ṭaṅkaḥ, f◦ takṣaṇī, m◦ vraścanaḥ*

Clamp कीलकः *m◦ kīlakaḥ*

Compass दिङ्निर्णययन्त्रं *n◦ diṅgnirṇayayantram*

Drill	वेधनिका *f◦ vedhanikā*	
File	पत्रपरशुः, व्रश्चनः *m◦ patraparaśuḥ, vraśćanaḥ*	
Gauge	मापकः *m◦ māpakaḥ*	
Hammer	अयोघनः, घनः, द्रुघणः, मुद्गरः *m◦ ayoghanaḥ, ghanaḥ, drughaṇaḥ, mudgaraḥ*	
Hone	शाणः *m◦ śāṇaḥ*	
Knife	कृपाणी, छुरिका, छुरी *f◦ kṛpāṇī, ćhurikā, ćhurī*	
Lever	उत्तोलनदण्डः, तुलायन्त्रं *m◦ uttolanadaṇḍaḥ n◦ tulāyantram*	
Oar	क्षेपणी *f◦ kṣepaṇī*	
Planer	तक्षणी *f◦ takṣaṇī*	
Plough	लङ्गलं, हलं *n◦ lāṅgalam, halam*	
Razor	क्षुरः *m◦ kṣuraḥ*	
Saw	करपत्रं, क्रकचं, *n◦ karapatram, krakaćam*	
Scale, length	मापकः *m◦ māpakaḥ*	
Scale, weight	तुला *f◦ tulā*	
Scissors	कर्तरिका, कर्तरी, कृपाणी, खण्डधारा, छेदनी *f◦ kartarikā, kartarī, kṛpāṇī, khaṇḍadhārā, ćhedanī*	
Sickle	दात्रं, लवित्रं *n◦ dātram, lavitram*	
Spade	अवदारणं, खनित्रं, स्तम्बघ्नः *n◦ avadāraṇam, khanitram, m◦ stambaghnaḥ*	
Syringe	शृङ्गकं *n◦ śṛangakam*	

15.11 FLOWERS पुष्पाणि puṣpāṇi

Bud	अङ्कुरः, कलिका, कुड्मलः, कौरकं, पल्लवः, मुकुलं *m◦ aṅkuraḥ, f◦ kalikā, m◦ kuḍmalaḥ, n◦ kaurakam, m◦ pallavaḥ, n◦ mukulam*
Flower	कुसुमं, पुष्पं, प्रसूनं, सुमं, सुमनं, सूनं

	n∘ kusumam, puṣpam, prasūnam, sumam, sumanam, sūnam
Fragrance	गन्धः, परिमलः, वासः, सुगन्धः, सुवासः, सौरभं
	m∘ gandhaḥ, parimalaḥ, vāsaḥ, sugandhaḥ, sauvāsaḥ, n∘ saurabham
Jasmine	अम्बष्ठा, अतिमुक्तः, कुन्दं, बकुलः, मल्लिका, माधवी, मालती, यूथिका
	f∘ ambaṣṭhā, m∘ atimuktaḥ, n∘ kundam, m∘ bakulaḥ, f∘ mallikā, mādhavī, mālatī, yūthikā
Lotus	अम्बुजं, अब्जं, अम्भोजं, अम्भोरुहं, अरविन्दं, उत्पलं, कमलं, कुशेशयं, तामरसं, नलिनं, पङ्कजं, पंकेरुहं, पद्म, पुष्करं, मरोरुहं, महोत्पलं, मृणालिनी, राजीवं, विसप्रसूनं, शतपत्रं, सरसिजं, सरसीरुहं, सहस्त्रपत्रं, सारसं
	n∘ ambujam, abjam, ambhojam, ambhoruham, aravindam, utpalam, kamalam, kuśeśayam, tāmarasam, nalinam, paṅkajam, paṅkeruham, padma, puṣkaram, maroruham, mahotpalam, f∘ mṛṇālinī, n∘ rājīvam, viprasūnam, śatapatram, sarasijam, sarasīruham, sahasrapatram, sārasam
Lotus, blue	कमलं, कुवलयं, इन्दीवरं, नीलोत्पलं
	n∘ kamalam, kuvalayam, indīvaram, nīlotpalam
Lotus, red	कमलं, कोकनदं, रक्तोत्पलं *n∘ kamalam, kokanadam, raktotpalam*
Lotus, white	कमलं, कह्वारं, कुमुदं, पुण्डरीकं, सीताभोजं
	n∘ kamalam, kahvāram, kumudam, puṇḍarīkam, sītābhojam
Marigold	गन्धपुष्पं *n∘ gandhapuṣpam*
Narium	कर्णिकारः *m∘ karṇikaraḥ*
Nectar	अमृतं, पीयूषं, मकरन्दः, मरन्दः, मधु, मुधा, रसः
	n∘ amṛtam, pīyūṣam, m∘ makarandaḥ, marandaḥ, n∘ madhu, f∘ mudhā, m∘ rasaḥ
Night Jasmine	रजनीगन्धा *f∘ rajanīgandhā*
Petal	दलं, पत्रं *n∘ dalam, patram*
Pollen	परागः, रजः, रेणुः *m∘ parāgaḥ, rajaḥ, reṇuḥ*

Rose ओड्रपुष्पं, जपा *n◦ oḍrapuṣpam, f◦ japā*

Sunflower सूर्यपुष्पं *n◦ sūryapuṣpam*

15.12 FRUITS फलानि phalani

Almond वातामफलं *n◦ vātāmaphalam*

Apple आताफलं *n◦ ātāphalam*

Banana कदली *f◦ kadalī*

Chestnut श्रृंगाटकं *n◦ śṛṅgāṭakam*

Cocoanut नारिकेलं *n◦ nārikelam*

Custard-apple सीताफलं *n◦ sītāphalam*

Date dry क्षुधाहरं *n◦ kṣudhāharam*

Fig अञ्जीरं *n◦ anjīram*

Grape द्राक्षा *f◦ drākṣā*

Guava आम्रलं *n◦ āmralam*

Lemon जम्बीरः, जभः, फलपूरः, बीजपूरः, रुचकः, मातुलङ्गकः *n◦ jambīraḥ, jabhaḥ, m◦ phalapūraḥ, bījapūraḥ, rućakaḥ, mātulangakaḥ*

Mango आम्रं, आम्रफलं *n◦ āmram, āmraphalam*

Melon खर्बूजं *n◦ kharbūjam*

Mulberry तूतं *n◦ tūtam*

Orange ऐरावतः, नारंगः *m◦ airāvataḥ, nārangaḥ*

Papaya मधुकर्कटी *f◦ madhukarkaṭī*

Peach आद्रालुः *m◦ ādrāluḥ*

Pineapple अननासं *n◦ ananāsam*

Plum बदरीफलं *n◦ badrīphalam*

Plum purple	आलुकं *n∘ ālukam*
Pomegranate	दाडिमं *n∘ dāḍimam*
Tamarind	अम्लिका *f∘ amlikā*
Walnut	अक्षोटं *n∘ akṣoṭam*
Watermelon	कालिन्दं, तारबूजं *n∘ kālindam, tārabūjam*

15.13 VEGETABLES शाकानि śākāni

Beans	माषः, शिम्बिका *m∘ māśaḥ, f∘ śimbikā*
Bittergourd	कारवेल्लं *n∘ kāravellam*
Cabbage	हरितकं *n∘ haritakam*
Carrot	गृञ्जनं *n∘ gṛñjanam*
Cauliflower	गोजिह्वा *f∘ gojihvā*
Celentro	धान्यकं *n∘ dhānyakam*
Chilli	मरिचं *n∘ maricam*
Cocoanut	नारिकेलं *n∘ nārikelam*
Cucumber	कर्कटी, चर्मटिका *f∘ karkaṭī, carmaṭikā*
Eggplant	भण्टाकी, वृत्ताङ्कः *f∘ bhaṇṭākī, m∘ vṛttāṅkaḥ*
Lemon	जम्बीरः, जभः, फलपूरः, बीजपूरः, रुचकः, मातुलङ्गकः *m∘ jambīraḥ, jabhaḥ, phalapūraḥ, bījapūraḥ, rucakaḥ, mātulangakaḥ*
Lotus, root	करहाटः, शालुः, शिफाकन्दः *m∘ karahaṭaḥ, śāluḥ, śifākandaḥ*
Okra	भिण्डकः *m∘ bhiṇḍakaḥ*
Onion	पलाण्डुः, सुकन्दकः *m∘ palāṇḍuḥ, sukandakaḥ*
Peas	कलायः *m∘ kalāyaḥ*
Potato	आलुः, गोलालुः *m∘ āluḥ, golāluḥ*

Pumpkin	कर्कारुः, कुष्माण्डः *m∘ karkāruḥ, kuṣmāṇḍaḥ*
Raddish	मूलकं, मूलिका *n∘ mūlakam, f∘ mūlikā*
Rapini	शाकं *n∘ śākam*
Salad	शदः *m∘ śadaḥ*
Spinach	पालकी *f∘ pālakī*
Sugarcane	इक्षुः, रसालः *m∘ ikṣuḥ, rasālaḥ*
Tomato	रक्तांगः *m∘ raktāṅgaḥ*
Turnip	शिखामूलं *n∘ śikhāmūlam*
Vegetable	शाकः, शाकं, हरितकं *m∘ śākaḥ, n∘ śākam, haritakam*
Yam	आरुकं, आलुकं *n∘ ārukam, ālukam*
Zuchini	जालिनी *f∘ jālinī*

15.14 PLANTS वनस्पतयः vanaspatayaḥ

Bamboo	कीचकः, वंशः, वेणुः *m∘ kīćakaḥ, vaṁśaḥ, veṇuḥ*
Banyan	अश्वत्थः, न्यग्रोधः, वटः *m∘ aśvatthaḥ, nyagrodhaḥ, vaṭaḥ*
Bark	वल्कं, वल्कलं *n∘ valkam, valkalam*
Branch	विटपः, शाखा *m∘ viṭapaḥ, f∘ śākhā*
Bud	अङ्कुरः, कलिका, कुड्मलः, कौरकं, पल्लवः, मुकुलं *m∘ aṅkuraḥ, f∘ kalikā, m∘ kuḍmalaḥ, n∘ kaurakam, m∘ pallavaḥ,* *n∘ mukulam*
Bulb	कन्दं *n∘ kandam*
Chlorophyll	हरितद्रव्यं *n∘ haritadravyam*
Climber	वल्लरी, वल्लिः, वल्ली *f∘ vallarī, valliḥ, vallī*
Farm	क्षेत्रं *n∘ kṣetram*
Flower	कुसुमं, पुष्पं, प्रसूनं, सुमं, सुमनं, सूनं

n◦ kusumam, puṣpam, prasūnam, sumam, sumanam, sūnam

Forest	अटवी, अरण्यं, काननं, वनं, विपिनं *f◦ aṭavī, n◦ araṇyam, kānanam, vanam, vipinam*
Grass	घासः, तृणं, शस्यं, शादः *m◦ ghāsaḥ, n◦ tṛṇam, śasyam, m◦ śādaḥ*
Green	हरित्, हरित *adj◦ harit, harita*
Guava	आम्रलं *n◦ āmralam*
Gum	निर्यासः *m◦ niryāsaḥ*
Juice	आसवः द्रवः, रसः *m◦ āsavaḥ, dravaḥ, rasaḥ*
Leaf	छदः, पत्रं, पर्णं, दलं *m◦ ćhadaḥ, n◦ patram, parṇam, dalam*
Lemon	जम्बीरः, जभः, फलपूरः, बीजपूरः, रुचकः, मातुलङ्गकः *m◦ jambīraḥ, jabhaḥ, phalapūraḥ, bījapūraḥ, rućakaḥ, mātulangakaḥ*
Mango	आम्रं *n◦ āmram*
Palm	तालः *m◦ tālaḥ*
Peel	वल्कं, शल्कं *n◦ valkam, śalkam*
Pine	देवदारुः *m◦ devadāruḥ*
Pollen	परागः, रजः, रेणुः *m◦ parāgaḥ, rajaḥ, reṇuḥ*
Root	पादः, मूलं *m◦ pādaḥ, n◦ mūlam*
Seed	बीजं *n◦ bījam*
Shade	छाया *f◦ ćhāyā*
Stem	काण्डं, नालं *n◦ kāṇḍam, nālam*
Stone	अष्ठिः *f◦ aṣṭhiḥ*
Tamarind	चिञ्चा *f◦ ćinćā*
Teak	अर्णं *n◦ arṇam*
Thorn	कण्टकः, शल्यं *m◦ kaṇṭakaḥ, n◦ śalyam*
Tree	तरुः, द्रुमः, पादपः, वनस्पतिः, विटपः, वृक्षः

m◦ taruḥ, drumaḥ, pādapaḥ, vanaspatiḥ, viṭapaḥ, vṛkṣaḥ

Vine लता, वल्लरी, वल्लिः, वल्ली *f◦ latā, vallarī, valliḥ, vallī*

Wood दारु, काष्ठं *n◦ dāru, kāṣṭham*

15.15 FOOD STUFF खाद्यपेयानि khādyapeyāni

Barley प्रवेटः, यवः *m◦ praveṭaḥ, yavaḥ*

Beverage पानं, पानीयं, पेयं *n◦ pānam, pānīyam, peyam*

Bread अभ्यूषः *m◦ abhyūṣaḥ*

Bread roṭi रोटिका *f◦ roṭikā*

Butter कलाटः, नवनीतं *m◦ kilāṭaḥ, n◦ navanītam*

Butter ghee आज्यं, घृतं *n◦ ājyam, ghṛtam*

Buttermilk अरिटं, कालशेयं, तक्रं *n◦ ariṭam, kālaśeyam, takram*

Black mung माषः *m◦ māṣaḥ*

Cheese दाधजं *n◦ dādhajam*

Chickpea चणकः *m◦ chaṇakaḥ*

Coffee कफघ्नी *f◦ kafaghnī*

Cook पाचकः, बल्लवः, सूदः *m◦ pāćakaḥ, ballavaḥ, sūdaḥ*

Corn शस्यं *n◦ śasyam*

Cream क्षीरजं *n◦ kṣīrajam*

Drink पानं, पानीयं, पेयं *n◦ pānam, pānīyam, peyam*

Flour क्षोदं, चूर्णं, पिष्टं *n◦ kṣodam, ćūrṇam, piṣṭam*

Food अन्नं, अशनं, आहारः, ओदनं, खादनं, खाद्यं, भक्तं, भक्षणं, भक्ष्यं, भोजनं, भोज्यं
m◦ annam, aśanam, m◦ āhāraḥ, n◦ odanam, khādanam, khādyam, bhaktam, bhakṣaṇam, bhakṣyam, bhojanam, bhojyam

Grain धान्यं, शस्यं *n◦ dhānyam, śasyam*

Honey क्षौद्रं, मधु *n◦ kṣaudram, madhu*

Ice	हिमं *n◦ himam*
Kidney beans	मुद्गः, शिंबा *m◦ mudgaḥ, f◦ śimbā*
Kitchen	पाकशाला *f◦ pākśālā*
Lentil	मसूरः, मसूरा *m◦ masūraḥ, f◦ masūrā*
Marmalade	मिष्टपाकः *m◦ miṣṭapākaḥ*
Meat	आमिषं, मांसं *n◦ āmiṣam, māṁsam*
Milk	क्षीरं, दुग्धं *n◦ kṣīram, dugdham*
Mung green	मुद्गः *m◦ mudgaḥ*
Oil	अभ्यञ्जनं, तैलं, स्नेहः *n◦ abhyañjanam, tailam, m◦ snehaḥ*
Paddy	धान्यं *n◦ dhānyam*
Pea	कलायः, रेणुकः *m◦ kalāyaḥ, reṇukaḥ*
Pigeon-peas	आढकी *f◦ āḍhakī*
Pickle	सन्धानं *f◦ sandhānam*
Pulse	वैदलं, शमीजः *n◦ vaidalam, m◦ śamījaḥ*
Rice	तन्दुलः *m◦ tandulaḥ*
Rice cooked	अन्नं, ओदनं, भक्तं *n◦ annam, odanam, bhaktam*
Salt	लवणं *n◦ lavaṇam*
Samosa	समाषः *m◦ samāṣaḥ*
Sauce	अवलेहः *m◦ avalehaḥ*
Seasum	तिलः *m◦ tilaḥ*
Sorghum	यवनालः *m◦ yavanālaḥ*
Sugar	शर्करा, सीता *f◦ śarkarā, sītā*
Sweets	मिष्टान्नं *n◦ miṣṭānnam*
Syrup	लेह्यं *n◦ lehyam*
Vinegar	शुक्तं *n◦ śuktam*
Wheat	गोधूमः *m◦ godhūmaḥ*

Water अम्बु, अम्भः, उदकं, जलं, तोयं, पयः, पानीयं, वारि, सलिलं

n∘ ambu, ambhaḥ, udakam, jalam, toyam, payaḥ, pānīyam, vāri, salilam

Wine मदिरा, मद्यं, सुरा *f∘ madirā, madyam, surā*

Yougrt दधि *n∘ dadhi*

15.16 SPICES उपस्करणानि upaskaraṇāni

Aniseed मधुरा *f∘ madhurā*

Asafoetida हिंगुः *m∘ hiṅguḥ*

Basil कुठेरकः, तुलसी, पर्णासः *m∘ kuṭherakaḥ, f∘ tulsī, m∘ parṇāsaḥ*

Betel-nut ताम्बूलं, पूगं *n∘ tāmbūlam, pūgam*

Cardamom एला *f∘ elā*

Cinnamon दारुगन्धः, दारुसिता *m∘ dārugandhaḥ, f∘ dārusitā*

Clove देवकुसुमं, लवङ्गं *n∘ devakusumam, lavaṅgam*

Coriander धान्यकं *n∘ dhānyakam*

Cumin अजाजी, कणा, जरणः, जीरकः *f∘ ajājī, kaṇā, m∘ jaraṇaḥ, jīrakaḥ*

Garlic अरिष्टं, गृञ्जनं, महाकन्दं, लशूनं, सोनहः

n∘ ariṣṭam, gṛñjanam, mahākandam, laśūnam, m∘ sonahaḥ

Ginger आर्द्रकं, गुल्ममूलं, शृंगवेरं *n∘ ārdrakam, gulmamūlam, śṛṅgaveram*

Ginger, dry शुण्ठी *f∘ śuṇṭhī*

Hot spice सौरभं *n∘ saurabham*

Linseed अतसी, उमा, क्षुमा *f∘ atasī, umā, kṣumā*

Mace जातिपत्री *f∘ jātipatrī*

Mango powder आम्रचूर्णं *n∘ āmracūrṇam*

Marjoram कठिञ्जरः, पर्णासः, फणिज्जकः *m∘ kaṭhiñjaraḥ, parṇāsaḥ, phaṇijjakaḥ*

Mint	अजगन्धः *m◦ ajagandhaḥ*
Mustard	राजिका *f◦ rājikā*
Myrobalan	आमलकः, कर्षफलः, कलिद्रुमः *m◦ āmalakaḥ, karṣafalaḥ, kalidrumaḥ*
Nutmeg	जातिफलं, पुटकं *n◦ jātiphalam, puṭakam*
Parsley	अजमोदा *f◦ ajamodā*
Poppy seeds	खसतिलः *m◦ khasatilaḥ*
Pepper	मरिचं, मरीचं *n◦ marićam, marīćam*
Pepper, black	ऊषणं, कालकं, कृष्णं, वेल्लजं *n◦ ūṣaṇam, kākalam, kṛṣṇam, vellajam*
Spice	उपस्करं *n◦ upaskaram*
Saffron	अग्निशिखं, पीतनं, लोहितचन्दनं *n◦ agniśikham, pītanam, lohitaćandanam*
Salt	लवणं *n◦ lavaṇam*
Salt, rock	सैन्धवं *n◦ saindhavam*
Sugar	शर्करा *f◦ śarkarā*
Tamarind	अम्लिका, आम्लीका, तिन्तिका, चिञ्चा *f◦ amlikā, āmlīkā, tintikā, ćinćā*
Turmeric	काञ्चनी, निशा, पीता, वरवर्णिनी, हरिद्रा *f◦ kāñćanī, niśā, pītā, varavarṇinī, haridrā*
Walnut	अक्षोटः, अक्षोटं *m◦ akṣoṭakaḥ, n◦ akṣoṭakam*
Yeast	कारोत्तरः, किण्वं, सुरामण्डं *m◦ kārottaraḥ, n◦ kiṇvam, surāmaṇḍam*

15.17 MINERALS, METALS and JEWELS खनीजानि khanījāni

Coal	अंगारः, खनिजाङ्गारः *m◦ angaraḥ, khanijāṅgāraḥ*
Coral	प्रवालः, विद्रुमः *m◦ pravālaḥ, vidrumaḥ*
Brass	आरकूटं, पित्तलं, रीती *n◦ ārakūṭam, pittalam, f◦ rītī*
Copper	उदुम्बरं, ताम्रं, ताम्रकं, द्व्यष्टं, वरिष्टं, शुल्बं

n∘ udumbaram, tāmram, tāmrakam, dvyaṣṭam, variṣṭam, śulbam

Diamond वज्रं, हीरं, हीरकः *n∘ vajram, hīram, m∘ hīrakaḥ*

Emerlad गारुत्मतं, मरकतं *n∘ gārutmatam, marakatam*

Gold अष्टापदं, कनकं, कर्बुरं, काञ्चनं, कार्तस्वरं, गांगेयं, चामीकरं, जातरूपं, जाम्बूनदं, तपनीयं, भर्म, महारजतं, रुक्मं, शातकुम्भं, शृंगिः, सुवर्णं, स्वर्णं, हेम, हाटकं,

हिरण्यं

n∘ aśṭāpadam, kanakam, karburam, kāñćanam, kārtasvaram, gāṅgeyam, ćāmīkaram, jātarūpam, jāmbūnadam, tapanīyam, bharma,

mahārajatam, rukma, śāntkumbham, śṛngī, suvarṇam, svarṇam, hema, hāṭakam, hiraṇyam

Iron अयः, आयसः, कालायसं, कृष्णायसं, पिण्डं, लोहः, लोहं, शस्त्रकं

n∘ ayaḥ, m∘ āyasaḥ, n∘ kālāyasam, kṛṣṇāyasam, piṇḍam, m∘ lohaḥ, n∘ loham, śastrakam

Jade अश्वकः *m∘ aśvakaḥ*

Jewel मणिः, रत्नं *m∘ maṇiḥ, n∘ ratnam*

Lead नागं, योगेष्टं, वप्रं, सीसं, सीसकं

n∘ nāgam, yogeṣṭam, vapram, sīsam, sīsakam

Marble मर्मरः, मर्मरोपलः, श्लक्ष्णः *m∘ marmaḥ, marmaropalaḥ, ślakṣṇaḥ*

Mercury पारदः, सूतः *m∘ pāradaḥ, sūtaḥ*

Mica अभ्रकं *n∘ abhrakam*

Mine आकरः, निधिः, रत्नाकरः *m∘ ākaraḥ, nidhiḥ, ratnākaraḥ*

Mineral खनिजं, धातुः *n∘ khanijam, m∘ dhātuḥ*

Opal पुलकः, विमलकः *m∘ pulakaḥ, vimalakaḥ*

Pearl मुक्ता, मुक्ताफलं, मौक्तिकं, शुक्तिजं

f∘ muktā, n∘ muktāphalam, mauktikam, śuktijam

Ruby पद्मरागः, माणिक्यं, शोणरत्नं, लोहितकः

m∘ padmarāgaḥ, n∘ māṇikyam, śoṇaratnam, m∘ lohitakaḥ

Sapphire इन्द्रनीलः नीलः, नीलोपलः, महानीलः

m∘ indranīlaḥ, nīlaḥ, nīlopalaḥ, mahānīlaḥ

Silver कलधौतं, खर्जूरं, दुर्वर्णं, रजतं, रूप्यं, श्वेतं

n∘ kaladhautam, kharjuram, durvarṇam, rajatam, rūpyam, śvetam

Soil मृद्, मृत्तिका *f∘ mṛd, mṛttikā*

Sulphur गन्धकः, गन्धिकः, गन्धाश्म *m∘ gandhakaḥ, gandhikaḥ, n∘ gandhāśma*

Tin त्रपु, पिच्चटं *n∘ trapu, piccaṭam*

Topaz पीताश्म *n∘ pītāśma*

Turquoise हरिताश्म *n∘ haritāśma*

Zinc दस्ता *f∘ dastā*

15.18 MUSIC सङ्गीतं Sangeetam

Ascending आरोहः *m∘ ārohaḥ*

Bell घण्टा *f∘ ghaṇṭā*

Bugle शृङ्गं *n∘ śṛṅgam*

Clarionet वंशः *m∘ vaṁśaḥ*

Conch कम्बुः, दरं, शंखः *m∘ kambuḥ, n∘ daram, m∘ śankhaḥ*

Cymbal झल्लकं, झल्लरी *n∘ jhallakam, f∘ jhallarī*

Descending अवरोहः *m∘ avarohaḥ*

Devotional song भजनं *n∘ bhajanam*

Drum डिण्डिमं, दुन्दुभिः, पटहः, भेरी

n∘ ḍinḍimam, f∘ dundubhiḥ, m∘ paṭahaḥ, f∘ bherī

Flute मुरली, वंशः, वेणुः *f∘ muralī, m∘ vaṁśaḥ, veṇuḥ*

Guitar Indian पिनाकी, वल्लकी, विपञ्ची, वीणा, सारंगी

	f◦ pinākī, vallakī, vipanćī, vīnā, sārangī
Harp	पिनाकी, वल्लकी, विपंची, वीणा, सारंगी
	f◦ pinākī, vallakī, vipanćī, vīnā, sārangī
Kettledrum	डिण्डिमा, दुन्दुभिः, भेरी *f◦ ḍinḍimā, dundubhiḥ, bherī*
Melody	रागः *m◦ rāgaḥ*
Note	स्वरः *m◦ svaraḥ*
Notation	स्वरलिपी *f◦ svaralipī*
Prayer	आरती *m◦ āratī*
Octave	सप्तकं *n◦ saptakam*
Rhythm	तालः *m◦ tālaḥ*
Song	गानं, गीतं, गीतिः *n◦ gānam, gītam, f◦ gītiḥ*
Tabor	मुरजः, मृदङ्गः *m◦ murajaḥ, mṛdangaḥ*
Tambourine	कर्णदुन्दुभिः *f◦ karṇadundubhiḥ*
Tempo	लयः *m◦ layaḥ*
Tomtom	पटहः, भेरी *m◦ paṭahaḥ, f◦ bherī*
Violin	पिनाकी, शारङ्गी *m◦ pinākī, śārangī*
Whistle	वंशी *f◦ vaṁśī*

15.19 PROFESSIONS व्यवसायाः vyavasāyāḥ

Actor	अभिनेता, नटः *m◦ abhinetā, naṭaḥ*
Actress	अभिनेत्री, नटी *f◦ abhinetrī, naṭī*
Advocate	पक्षसमर्थकः, वक्ता *m◦ pakṣasamarthakaḥ, vaktā*
Agent	प्रतिनिधिः *m◦ pratinidhiḥ*
Artizan	कलाकारः, चित्रकरः, शिल्पी *m◦ kalākāraḥ, ćitrakaraḥ, śilpī*
Artist	कलाकारः, चित्रकरः, शिल्पी *m◦ kalākāraḥ, ćitrakaraḥ, śilpī*

Assassin	घातक:, हन्ता	*m◦ ghātakaḥ, hantā*
Barber	क्षुरी, क्षौरिक:, नापित:	*m◦ kṣurī, kṣaurikaḥ, nāpitaḥ; f◦* नापिती *nāpitī*
Blacksmith	अयस्कार:, लोहकार:	*m◦ ayaskāraḥ, lohakāraḥ*
Boatman	औडुपिक:, नाविक:, पोतवाह:	*m◦ auḍupikaḥ, nāvikaḥ, potavāhaḥ*
Broker	निर्वाहक:	*m◦ nirvāhakaḥ*
Butcher	आखेटक:, मांसिक:, विशसिता, सौनिक:	*m◦ ākheṭakaḥ, māṃsikaḥ, viśasitaḥ, saunikaḥ*
Butler	गृहकर्मकर:	*m◦ gṛhakarmakaraḥ*
Carpenter	तक्षक:, त्वष्टा, स्थकार:	*m◦ takṣakaḥ, tvaṣṭā, sthakāraḥ*
Carrier	वाहक:, हर:	*m◦ vāhakaḥ, haraḥ*
Cashier	टङ्काधीश:	*m◦ ṭaṅkādhīśaḥ*
Chemist	रसज्ञ:	*m◦ rasajñaḥ*
Clerk	कायस्थ:, लिपिकार:, लेखक:	*m◦ kāyasthaḥ, lipikāraḥ, lekhakaḥ*
Conductor	अग्रणी:, परिचर:, प्रणेता, मार्गदर्शक:	*m◦ agraṇīḥ, parićaraḥ, praṇetā, mārgadarśakaḥ*
Confectioner	आपूपिक:, भक्ष्यङ्कार:	*m◦ āpūpikaḥ, bhakṣyaṅkāraḥ*
Constable	दण्डधर:	*m◦ daṇḍdharaḥ*
Contractor	पणकर्ता	*m◦ paṇakartā*
Cook	पाचक:, बल्लव:, सूपकार:, सूद:	*m◦ pāćakaḥ, ballavaḥ, sūpakāraḥ, sūdaḥ*
Dancer	नर्तक:	*m◦ nartakaḥ;* नर्तकी *f◦ nartakī*
Dentist	दन्तवैद्य:	*m◦ dantavaidyaḥ*
Doctor	वैद्य:	*m◦ vaidyaḥ*
Dramist	नाटककार:	*m◦ nāṭakakāraḥ*
Editor	संपादक:	*m◦ sampādakaḥ*
Engineer	अभियन्ता, यन्त्रकार:	*m◦ abhiyantā, yantrakāraḥ*
Examiner	परीक्षक:	*m◦ parīkṣakaḥ*

Farmer कर्षकः, कृषिकः, कृषिवलः *m∘ karṣakaḥ, kṛṣikaḥ, kṛṣivalaḥ*

Fisherman कैवतः, धीवरः *m∘ kaivataḥ, dhīvaraḥ*

Florist मालाकारः, मालिकः *m∘ mālākāraḥ, mālikaḥ*

Gardener माली *m∘ mālī*

Goldsmith कलादः, स्वर्णकारः *m∘ kalādaḥ, svarṇakāraḥ*

Guard परिचरः, रक्षकः, रक्षी *m∘ paricaraḥ, rakṣakaḥ, rakṣī*

Inspector निरीक्षकः, निरूपकः *m∘ nirīkṣakaḥ, nirūpakaḥ*

Jeweler मणिकारः, रत्नकारः *m∘ maṇikāraḥ, ratnakāraḥ*

Landlord क्षेत्री, भूस्वामी *m∘ kṣetrī, bhūsvāmī*

Lawyer विधिज्ञः *m∘ vidhijñaḥ*

Magician इन्द्रजालिकः, कुहकः, कौसृतिकः, मायाकारः, मायी
m∘ indrajālikaḥ kuhakaḥ, kausṛtikaḥ, māyākāraḥ, māyī

Manager अवेक्षकः, निर्वाहकः *m∘ avekṣakaḥ, nirvāhakaḥ*

Mason लेपकः, पलगण्डः *m∘ lepakaḥ, palagaṇḍaḥ*

Merchant आपणिकः, नैगमः, वणिक्, व्यवहारी
m∘ āpaṇikaḥ, naigamaḥ, vāṇik, vyavahārī

Messenger दूतः, वार्तायनः *m∘ dūtaḥ, vārtāyanaḥ*

Midwife साविका, सूतिका *f∘ sāvikā, sūtikā*

Milkman आभीरः, गोपः, दोहकः *m∘ ābhīraḥ, gopaḥ, dohakaḥ*

Milkmaid आभीरी, गोपिका, गोपी *f∘ ābhīrī, gopikā, gopī*

Novelist आख्यायिकाकारः *m∘ ākhyāyikākāraḥ*

Nurse परिचारिका, मातृका *f∘ paricārikā, mātṛkā*

Operator कारकः, कर्ता *m∘ kārkaḥ, kartā*

Painter चित्रकः, रञ्जकः *m∘ citrakah, rañjakaḥ*

Peon पदातिः, भृत्यः *m∘ padātiḥ, bhṛtyaḥ*

Photographer छायाचित्रकारः *m∘ chāyācitrakāraḥ*

Physician	भिषक्, वैद्यः *m∘ bhiṣak, vaidyaḥ*
Poet	कविः, सूरिः *m∘ kaviḥ, sūriḥ*
Police	रक्षकः, रक्षी, राजपुरुषः *m∘ rakṣakaḥ, rakṣī, rājpuruṣaḥ*
Politician	राजनीतिज्ञः *m∘ rājanītijñaḥ*
Postman	पत्रवाहः, पत्रहारः *m∘ patravāhaḥ, patrahāraḥ*
Priest	पण्डितः, पुरोधसाः, पुरोहितः *m∘ paṇḍitaḥ, purodhasāḥ, purohitaḥ*
Printer	मुद्रकः *m∘ mudrakaḥ*
Publisher	ख्यापकः प्रकाशकः, प्रकाशयिता *m∘ khyāpakaḥ, prakāśakaḥ, prakāśayitā*
Retailer	खण्डवणिक् *m∘ khaṇḍavaṇik*
Sailor	नाविकः, नौवाहः, पोतवाहः, समुद्रगः *m∘ nāvikaḥ, nauvāhaḥ, potavāhaḥ, samudragaḥ*
Sculptor	तक्षकः, त्वष्टा *m∘ takṣakaḥ, tvaṣṭā*
Shoe-maker	चर्मकारः *m∘ ćarmakāraḥ*
Shopkeeper	आपणिकः, क्रयविक्रयिकः, पण्यजीवः, विपणी *m∘ āpaṇikaḥ, krayavikrayikaḥ, paṇyajīvaḥ, vipaṇī*
Sorcerer	मान्त्रिकः *m∘ māntrikaḥ*
Surgeon	चिकित्सकः *m∘ ćikitsakaḥ*
Tailor	तुन्नवायः, सूचिकः, सौचिकः *m∘ tunnavāyaḥ, sūćikaḥ, saućikaḥ*
Teacher	अध्यापकः, उपदेष्टा, गुरुः, शिक्षकः *m∘ adhyapakaḥ, upadeṣṭā, guruḥ, śikṣakaḥ*
Treasurer	कोषाध्यक्षः *m∘ koṣādhyakṣaḥ*
Waiter	परिवेषकः, परिवेष्टा, सेवकः *m∘ pariveṣakaḥ, pariveṣṭā, sevakaḥ*
Washerman	रजकः *m∘ rajakaḥ*
Washerwoman	रजकी *f∘ rajakī*
Watchman	वैतालिकः, वैबोधिकः, रक्षकः *m∘ vaitālikaḥ, vaibodhikaḥ, rakṣakaḥ*
Weaver	कुविन्दः, तन्तुवापः, पटकारः *m∘ kuvindaḥ, tantuvāpaḥ, paṭakāraḥ*

15.20 BUSINESS व्यापारः vyāpāraḥ

Account	गणना, विगणनं *f◦ gaṇanā, m◦ vigaṇanam*
Accountant	गणकः, लेखकः *m◦ gaṇakaḥ, lekhakaḥ*
Advance	उपनिधिः *f◦ upanidhiḥ*
Advancement	उत्कर्षः, उन्नतिः, वर्धनं *m◦ utkarṣaḥ, f◦ unnatiḥ, n◦ vardhanam*
Advantage	लाभः, हितं *m◦ lābhaḥ, n◦ hitam*
Adventure	साहसं *n◦ sāhasam*
Adverse	प्रतिकूल *adj◦ pratikūl*
Advertise	विज्ञापनं *n◦ vijñāpanam*
Annual	वार्षिक *adj◦ vārṣik*
Annuity	वार्षिकवेतनं *n◦ vārṣikvetanam*
Annulment	लोपः *m◦ lopaḥ*
Application	याचनापत्रं *n◦ yāćanāpatram*
Arrears	ऋणशेषं *n◦ ṛṇaśeṣam*
Assistant	सहायः, सहायकः *m◦ sahāyaḥ, sahāyakaḥ*
Average	स्थूलप्रमाणं *n◦ sthūlapramāṇam*
Balance	अवशेषः, शेषः *m◦ avaśeṣaḥ, śeṣaḥ*
Balance scale	तुला *f◦ tulā*
Bank	धनागारं *n◦ dhanāgāram*
Bankruptsy	निर्धनः *m◦ nirdhanaḥ*
Broker	निर्वाहकः *m◦ nirvāhakaḥ*
Brokerage	निर्वहनद्रव्यं *n◦ nirvahanadravayam*
Business	नियोगः, यवहारः, व्यवसायः, व्यापारः *m◦ niyogaḥ, yavahāraḥ, vyavasāyaḥ, vyāpāraḥ*

Businessman नियोगी, व्यवसायी, व्यापारी *m∘ niyogī, vyavasāyī, vyāpārī*

Buyer क्रेता *m∘ kretā*

Capital मूलद्रव्यं *n∘ mūladravyam*

Cash टण्कः, नाणकं, मुद्रा *m∘ ṭaṅkaḥ, n∘ nāṇakam, f∘ mudrā*

Cell phone जङ्गमदूरवाणी *f∘ jaṅgamadūravāṇī*

Charges मूल्यं *n∘ mūlyam*

Clerk कायस्थः, लिपीकारः *m∘ kāyasthaḥ, lipīkāraḥ*

Coin टण्कः, नाणकं, मुद्रा *m∘ ṭaṅkaḥ, n∘ nāṇakam, f∘ mudrā*

Commerce क्रयविक्रयः, निगमः, वाणिज्यं *m∘ krayavikrayaḥ, nigamaḥ, n∘ vāṇijyam*

Courier दूतः, वार्ताहरः *m∘ dūtaḥ, vārtāharaḥ*

Court न्यायसभा *f∘ nyāyasabhā*

Customer क्रेता, ग्राहकः *m∘ kretā, grāhakaḥ*

Company परिषद्, श्रेणी *f∘ pariṣad, śreṇī*

Consumer विनियोजकः *m∘ viniyojakaḥ*

Customer क्रेता, ग्राहकः *m∘ kretā, grāhakaḥ*

Credit प्रतिष्ठा, विश्वासः *f∘ pratiṣṭhā, m∘ viśvāsaḥ*

Creditor उत्तमर्णः, ऋणदाता, धनिकः *m∘ uttamarṇaḥ, ṛṇadātā, dhanikaḥ*

Current प्रचलित, वर्तमान, विद्यमान *adj∘ prachalita, vartamāna, vidyamāna*

Currency प्रचलनं, प्रचलितमुद्रा *n∘ praćalanam, f∘ praćalitmudrā*

Daily दैनिक *adj∘ dainik*

Debt ऋणं *n∘ ṛṇam*

Demand अभियोगः, याचना *m∘ abhiyogaḥ, f∘ yāćnā*

Deposit निक्षेपः *m∘ nikṣepaḥ* (ii) a deposit as an advance उपनिधिः *m∘ upanidhiḥ*

Depreciation अपकर्षः, अवमानता *m∘ apakarṣaḥ, f∘ avamānatā*

Discount उद्धृतभागः *m∘ uddhṛtabhāgaḥ*

Document पत्रं, लेखः *n∘ patram, m∘ lekhaḥ*

Draft	आलेख्यं *n◦ ālekhyam*
Duty	करः, तार्यं, शुल्कः *m◦ karaḥ, n◦ tāryam, m◦ śulkaḥ*
Earnings	वेतनं *m◦ vetanam*
Economy	अर्थशास्त्रं, वित्तशास्त्रं *m◦ arthaśāstram, vittaśāstram*
Electricity	विद्युत् *f◦ vidyut*
Employee	अधिकृतः *m◦ adhikṛtah:*
Employer	अधिकारी *m◦ adhikārī*
Endowment	वृत्तिः *f◦ vṛttiḥ*
Exchange	परिवर्तनं, विनिमयः *n◦ parivartanam, m◦ vinimayaḥ*
Expense	व्ययः *m◦ vyayaḥ*
Export	निर्गमनं *n◦ nirgamanam*
Factory	कर्मशाला *f◦ karmaśalā*
Finance	धनागमः *m◦ dhanāgamaḥ*
Financier	कोशाध्यक्षः, धनाधिकारी *m◦ kośādhyakṣaḥ, dhanādhikārī*
Fixed	निश्चित *adj◦ niśċita*
Foreign	विदेशीय *adj◦ videśīya*
Fraud	कैतवं, व्याजः *n◦ kaitavam, m◦ vyājaḥ*
Freight	तार्यं *n◦ tāryam*
Fund	पुञ्जः, राशिः *m◦ puñjaḥ. rāśiḥ*
Goods	द्रव्यं, पण्यं, सामग्री *n◦ dravyam, paṇyam, f◦ sāmagrī*
Gross	स्थूल *adj◦ sthūla*
Import	आवहः *m◦ āvaḥ*
Income	आयः, धनागमः, वेतनं *m◦ āyaḥ, dhanāgamaḥ, n◦ vetanam*
Industry	उद्योगः, व्यवसायः *m◦ udyogaḥ, vyavasāyaḥ*
Inflation	आध्मानं *n◦ ādhmānam*
Insurance	योगक्षेमः, रक्षणं *m◦ yogakṣemaḥ, n◦ rakṣaṇam*

Job	कर्म *n◦ karma*
Joint	सन्धिः *f◦ sandhiḥ*
Labour	उद्यमः, श्रमः *m◦ udyamaḥ, śramaḥ*
Labourer	कर्मकरः, कर्मकारः, भृतकः *m◦ karmakaraḥ, karmakāraḥ, bhṛtakaḥ*
Land	भूः, भूमिः *f◦ bhūḥ, bhūmiḥ*
Ledger	गणनापुस्तकं *n◦ gaṇanāpustakam*
Legal	धर्म्य, न्याय्य *adj◦ dharmya, nyāyya*
Letter	पत्रं, लेखः *n◦ patram, m◦ lekhaḥ*
Loan	ऋणं *n◦ ṛṇam*
Lock	तालः *m◦ tālaḥ*
Locker	कोष्ठः, सपुटकः *m◦ koṣṭhaḥ, sapuṭakaḥ*
Loss	अपचयः, हानिः *m◦ apaćayaḥ, f◦ hāniḥ*
Management	चालनं, विनिमयः, शासनं *n◦ ćālanam, m◦ vinimayaḥ, n◦ śāsanam*
Manipulation	हस्तव्यापारः *m◦ hastvyāpāraḥ*
Market	आपणः, निगमः *m◦ āpaṇaḥ, nigamaḥ*
Merchandise	वाणिज्यं *n◦ vāṇijyam*
Merchant	आपणिकः, वाणिजः *m◦ āpaṇikaḥ, vāṇijaḥ*
Mint	टङ्कशाला *f◦ ṭaṅkśālā*
Mobile phone	जङ्गमदूरवाणी *f◦ jaṅgamadūravāṇī*
Money	अर्थः, धनं, द्रव्यं, वित्तं *m◦ arthaḥ, n◦ dhanam, dravyam, vittam*
Moneyless	धनहीन, निर्धन *adj◦ dhanahīna, nirdhana*
Monthly	मासिक *adj◦ māsik*
Net	अशेष *adj◦ aśeṣa*
Notice	निर्देशः, सूचना *m◦ nirdeśaḥ, f◦ sūćanā*
Occupation	नियोगः, वृत्तिः *m◦ niyogaḥ, f◦ vṛttiḥ*
Office	कार्यालयं *n◦ kāryālayam*

Officer	अधिकारी	*m॰ adhikārī*
Owner	स्वामी	*m॰ swāmī*
Partner	सहभागी	*m॰ sahabhāgī*
Phone	दूरवाणी	*f॰ dūravāṇī*
Price	मूल्यं	*n॰ mūlyam*
Private	आत्मीय, स्व	*adj॰ ātmīya, sva*
Profit	आय:, लाभ:, हितं	*m॰ āyaḥ, lābhaḥ, n॰ hitam*
Public	गण, जन, लोक	*adj॰ gaṇa, jana, loka*
Publication	प्रकाशनं	*n॰ prakāśanam*
Rate	गति:, मानं	*f॰ gatiḥ, n॰ mānam*
Receipt	स्वीकारपत्रं	*n॰ svīkārapatram*
Rent	कर:, भाटकं	*m॰ kraḥ, n॰ bhāṭakam*
Sale	पणनं, विक्रय:	*n॰ paṇanam, m॰ virayaḥ*
Saving	सञ्चय:, संग्रह:	*m॰ sañćayaḥ, saṃgrahaḥ*
Seal	मुद्रा	*f॰ mudrā*
Secretary	सचिव:	*m॰ saćivaḥ*
Servant	कर्मकरी, सेवक:	*m॰ karmakaraḥ, sevakaḥ*
Shop	आपण:, विपणि:	*m॰ āpaṇaḥ, vipaṇiḥ*
Sign	अभिज्ञानफलकं	*n॰ abhijñānafalakam*
Signature	स्वाक्षरं, स्वहस्ताक्षरं	*n॰ svākṣaram, svahastākṣaram*
Stamp	मुद्रा	*f॰ mudrā*
Stock	सञ्चय:, सम्भार:	*m॰ sañćayaḥ, sambhāraḥ*
Store, shop	आपण:	*m॰ āpaṇaḥ;*
Store, warehouse	निधानं, सञ्चय:, सम्भार:	*n॰ nidhānam, m॰ sañćayaḥ, sambhāraḥ*
Trade	वाणिज्यं, व्यवसाय:, व्यापार:	*n॰ vāṇijyam, m॰ vyavasāyaḥ, vyāpāraḥ*
Telephone	दूरवाणी	*f॰ dūravāṇī*

Treasury	कोषः कोषागारं, भाण्डागारं *m◦ koṣaḥ, n◦ koṣāgāram, bhāṇḍāgāram*
Warehouse	कोषः, कोषागारं, भाण्डागारं *m◦ koṣaḥ, n◦ koṣāgāram, bhāṇḍāgāram*
Wholesale	स्तूपविक्रयः *m◦ stūpavikrayaḥ*
Work	कर्म, नियोगः, व्यापारः *n◦ karma, m◦ niyogaḥ, vyāpāraḥ*

15.21 WARFARE युद्धं yuddham

Aggression	अतिक्रमणं, आक्रमणं, लङ्घनं *n◦ atikramaṇam, ākramaṇam, laṅghanam*
Aggressor	अतिक्रमकः, आक्रमकः *m◦ atikramakaḥ, ākramakaḥ*
Airforce	वायुसेना *f◦ vāyusenā*
Arm	अस्त्रं, आयुधं, शस्त्रं, शस्त्रास्त्रं *n◦ astram, āyudham, śastram, śastrāstram*
Armless	अनायुध, अभुज, अशस्त्र, निःशस्त्र *adj◦ anāyudh, abhuj, aśastra, niḥśastra*
Army	अनीकं, आनीकं, चमूः, दण्डं, दलं, पृतना, बलं, वाहिनी, सेना, सैन्यं *n◦ anīkam, ānīkam, f◦ ćamūḥ, n◦ daṇḍam, dalam, f◦ pṛtanā, n◦ balam, f◦, vāhinī, senā, n◦ sainyam*
Armament	युद्धोपकरणं *n◦ yuddhopakaraṇam*
Armour	कवचं, कञ्चुकः, तनुत्रं, तनुत्राणं, वर्म *n◦ kavaćam, kañćukam, tanutram, tanutrāṇam, varma*
Armour, head	शिरस्त्राणं *n◦ śirastrāṇam*
Armoury	शस्त्रागारं *n◦ śastrāgāram*
Arrow	इषुः, काण्डं, नाराचः, बाणः, मार्गणः, विशिखः, शरः, शीलीमुखः, सायकः *m◦ iṣuḥ, n◦ kāṇḍam, m◦ nārāćaḥ, bāṇaḥ, mārgaṇaḥ, viśikhaḥ, śaraḥ, śīlīmukhaḥ, sāyakaḥ*
Atom bomb	अण्वास्त्रं *n◦ aṇvāstram*
Attack	अभियोगः अवस्कंदः, आक्रमः, आपातः *m◦ abhiyogaḥ, avaskandaḥ, ākramaḥ, āpātaḥ*
Battle	आहवः, आजिः, द्वन्द्वं, युध्, युद्धं, प्रधनं, रणः, रणं, समरः, संख्यं, संग्रामः, समितिः

m◦ āhavaḥ, ājiḥ, n◦ dvandvam, f◦ yudh, n◦ yuddham, pradhanam, m◦ raṇaḥ, n◦ raṇam, m◦ samaraḥ, n◦, saṅkhyam, m◦ sangrāmaḥ, f◦ samitiḥ

Battle array विन्यासः, व्यूहः *m◦ vinyāsaḥ, vyūhaḥ*

Battle cry क्ष्वेडितं, सिंहनादः *n◦ kṣveḍitam, m◦ siṁhanādaḥ*

Battle field रणः, रणभूमिः, रणाङ्गणं, समरः
m◦ raṇaḥ, f◦ raṇabhūmiḥ, n◦ raṇāṅgaṇam, m◦ samaraḥ

Blockade अवरोधः, परिवेष्टनं *m◦ avarodhaḥ, n◦ pariveṣṭanam*

Bomb अग्न्यस्त्रं *n◦ agnyastram*

Bloodshed नृहत्या, रक्तपातः *f◦ nṛhatyā, m◦ raktapātaḥ*

Blow आघातः, प्रहारः *m◦ āghātaḥ, prahāraḥ*

Blunder अनवधानं, प्रमादः *n◦ anavadhānam, m◦ pramādaḥ*

Bow इष्वासः, कार्मुकं, कोदण्डं, चापं, धनुः, शरावापः, शरासनं
m◦ iśvāsaḥ, n◦ kārmukam, kodaṇḍam, ćāpam, dhanuḥ, m◦ śarāvāpaḥ, n◦ śarāsanam

Bow-man धनुर्धरः, धनुर्भृत्, धनुष्मत्, धानुष्कः, धन्वी, निषंगी
m◦ dhanurdharaḥ, dhanurbhṛt, dhanuṣmat, dhānuṣkaḥ, dhanvī, niṣaṅgī

Bow string गुणः, ज्या, मौर्वी, शिञ्ज्जिनी *m◦ guṇaḥ, f◦ jyā, maurvī, śiñjinī*

Brave धीर, पराक्रमी, विक्रांत, वीर, शूर, साहसिक
adj◦ dhīra, parākramī, vikrānt, vīra, śūra, sāhasika

Bull's eye लक्ष्यं *n◦ lakṣyam*

Bullet गुलिः, गुलिका, प्रक्षेपिणी *f◦ guliḥ, gulikā, prakṣepiṇī*

Campaign युद्धप्रवृत्तिः *f◦ yuddhapravṛttiḥ*

Cannon गुलिप्रक्षेपणी *f◦ guliprakṣepaṇī*

Cannon ball रणगुलिः *f◦ raṇaguliḥ*

Cartridge गुलिः *f∘ guliḥ*

Cavalry तुरगबलं, सादिगणः *n∘ turagbalam, m∘ sādigaṇaḥ*

Chariot रथः, स्यन्दनः *m∘ rathaḥ, syandanaḥ*

Civil-war जनप्रकोपः *m∘ janaprakopaḥ*

Cold war शीतयुद्धं *n∘ śītayuddham*

Colonel गुल्मपति, सेनाध्यक्षः *m∘ gulmapatiḥ, senādhyakṣaḥ*

Colony अधिनिवेशः *m∘ adhiniveśaḥ*

Combat आहवः, आजिः, द्वन्द्वं, युध्, युद्धं, प्रधनं, रणः, रणं, समरः, संख्यं, संग्रामः, समितिः
m∘ āhavaḥ, ājiḥ, n∘ dvandvam, f∘ yudh, n∘ yuddham, pradhanam, m∘ raṇaḥ, n∘ raṇam, m∘ samaraḥ, n∘, saṅkhyam, m∘ sangrāmaḥ, f∘ samitiḥ

Combatant भटः, योधः, योद्धा, वीरः *m∘ bhaṭaḥ, yodhaḥ, yoddhā, vīraḥ*

Combative कलहप्रियः *m∘ kalahapriyaḥ*

Command अधिकारः, अधिपत्यं, प्रभुत्वं *m∘ adhikāraḥ, n∘ adhipatyam, prabhutvam*

Commander चमूपतिः, सेनाध्यक्षः, सेनानायकः, सेनानीः
m∘ ćamūpatiḥ, senādhyakṣaḥ, senānāyakaḥ, senānīḥ

Death अन्तः, उपरमः, निधनं, मरणं, पञ्चत्वं, संस्थितिः
m∘ antaḥ, uparamaḥ, n∘ nidhanam, maraṇam, pañćatvam, f∘ saṁsthitiḥ

Defeat अभिभवः, पराजयः, पराभवः, परिभवः
m∘ abhibhavaḥ, parājayaḥ, parābhavaḥ, paribhavaḥ

Defence त्राणं, रक्षणं, रक्षा, संरक्षणं *n∘ trāṇam, rakṣaṇam, f∘ rakṣā, n∘ saṁrakṣaṇam*

Democracy प्रजातन्त्रं, लोकतन्त्रं *n. prajātantram, loktantram*

Destroyer ध्वंसकः, नाशकः *m∘ dhvaṁsakaḥ, nāśakaḥ*

Dictator एकाधिपतिः *m∘ ekādhipatiḥ*

Enemy अरातिः, अरिः, रिपुः, वैरी, शत्रुः *m∘ arātiḥ, ariḥ, ripuḥ, vairī, śatruḥ*

Expedition प्रयाणं, यात्रा *n◦ prayāṇam, f◦ yātrā*

Fight आहवः, आजिः, द्वन्द्वं, युध्, युद्धं, प्रधनं, रणः, रणं, समरः, संख्यं, संग्रामः, समितिः

m◦ āhavaḥ, ājiḥ, n◦ dvandvam, f◦ yudh, n◦ yuddham, pradhanam, m◦ raṇaḥ, n◦ raṇam, m◦ samaraḥ, n◦, saṅkhyam, m◦ sangrāmaḥ, f◦ samitiḥ

Fighter plane युद्धविमानं *n◦ yuddhavimānam*

Fist fight मुष्टियुद्धं *n◦ muṣṭiyuddham*

Foot soldier पत्तिः, पदातिः, पदिकः *m◦ pattiḥ, padātiḥ, padikaḥ*

Fort कोटः, दुर्गं *m◦ koṭaḥ, n◦ durgam*

Fortification कूटः, कोटः, दुर्गं, परिखा, प्राचीरं *m◦ kūṭaḥ, koṭaḥ, n◦ dūrgam, f◦ parikhā, n◦ prāćīram*

Freedom स्वातन्त्र्यं *n◦ svātantryam*

Gun गुलिप्रक्षेपणी, भुशुण्डी *f◦ guliprakṣepaṇī, bhuśuṇḍī*

Gunpowder आग्नेयचूर्णं *n◦ āgneyaćūrṇam*

Hand-to-hand fight बाहुयुद्धं *n◦ bāhuyuddham*

Helmet शिरस्त्राणं *n◦ śirastrāṇam*

Hostage विश्वासस्थानं *n◦ viśvāsasthānam*

Human shield मनुष्याश्रयः *m◦ manuṣyāśrayaḥ*

Indemnity प्रतिफलं, हानिपूरणं *n◦ pratiphalam, hānipūraṇam*

Marine fight नौयुद्धं *n◦ nauyuddham*

Mariner नाविकः, पोतवाहः *m◦ nāvikaḥ, potvāhaḥ*

Maritime समुद्रीय *adj◦ samudrīya*

Medal पदकं, मुद्रा *n◦ padakam, f◦ mudrā*

Melee तुमुलं, रणसंकुलं *n◦ tumulam, raṇasaṅkulam*

Mutiny द्रोहः, व्युत्थानं, संक्षोभः *m◦ drohaḥ, n◦ vyutthānam, m◦ saṅkṣobhaḥ*

Navy जलसेना, नौसेना *f◦ jalasenā, nausenā*

Non-violence अहिंसा, शान्तिः *f◦ ahimsā, śāntiḥ*

Occupation व्याप्तिः *f◦ vyāptiḥ*

Peace शांतिः *f◦ śāntiḥ*

Plan of action प्रयुक्तिः *f◦ prayuktiḥ*

Prisoner of war युद्धबन्दिः *m◦ yuddhabandiḥ*

Provision उपपादनं, परिकल्पनं *upapādanam, parikalpanam*

Recruit नवसैनिकः *m◦ navasainikaḥ*

Sacrifice त्यागः *m◦ tyāgaḥ*

Secret गुह्यं, गौप्यं, रहस्यं *n◦ guhyam, gaupyam, rahasyam*

Service सेवा *f◦ sevā*

Ship जलयानं, पोतः *n◦ jalayānam, m◦ potaḥ*

Signal सङ्केतः *m◦ saṅketaḥ*

Shot अस्त्रपातः, क्षेपः *m◦ astrapātaḥ, kṣepaḥ*

Siege परिवेष्टनं *n◦ pariveṣṭanam*

Slaughter कन्दनं, घातनं, विशंसनं, वैशंसं, संहारः
n◦ kandanam, ghātanam, viśasaṁsanam, vaiśaṁsaḥ, m◦ saṁhāhāraḥ

Strategy युद्धकौशलं, समरपाटवं *n◦ yuddhakauśalam, samarapāṭavam*

Spear कुन्तः, शूलः *m◦ kuntaḥ, śūlaḥ*

Spy अपसर्पः, गुप्तचरः, चरः *m◦ apasarpaḥ, guptacaraḥ, caraḥ*

Sword असिः, कृपाणः, खड्गः, *f◦ asiḥ, m◦ kṛpāṇaḥ, khaḍgaḥ*

Traitor राजद्रोही *m◦ rājdrohī*

Treaty सन्धानं, सन्धिः *n◦ sandhānam, f◦ sandhiḥ*

Trechery द्रोहः *m◦ drohaḥ*

Trench खातं *n◦ khātam*

Troops पदातयः, सैनिकाः, सैन्यं *m◦ padātayaḥ, sainikāḥ, n◦ sainyam*

Victor जिष्णुः, जेता, विजेता *m∘ jiṣṇuḥ, jetā, vijetā*

Victory जयः, विजयः *m∘ jayaḥ, vijayaḥ*

War आहवः, आजिः, द्वन्द्वं, युध्, युद्धं, प्रधनं, रणः, रणं, समरः, संख्यं, संग्रामः, समितिः

m∘ āhavaḥ, ājiḥ, n∘ dvandvam, f∘ yudh, n∘ yuddham, pradhanam, m∘ raṇaḥ, n∘ raṇam, m∘ samaraḥ, n∘, saṅkhyam, m∘ sangrāmaḥ, f∘ samitiḥ

Warfare युद्धं, वैरं, संप्रहारः *n∘ yuddham, vairam, m∘ samprahāraḥ*

War time युद्धकालः *n∘ yuddhakālaḥ*

World war महायुद्धं, विश्वयुद्धं *n∘ mahāyuddham, viśvayuddham*

15. 22 TIME समयः samayaḥ

COUNTING THE TIME ELEMENTS

Time समयः, कालः, वेला। *m∘ samayaḥ, kālaḥ, velā*

Second क्षणः, निमिषः, विपलम्। *m∘ kṣaṇaḥm nimiṣaḥ n∘ vipalam*

Minute पलम्, कला। *n∘ palam, f∘ kalā*

Hour घटी। *f∘ ghaṭī*

Day अहन्, दिनम्, दिवसः, वारः, वासरः, तिथिः। *n∘ ahan, dinam, m∘ divasaḥ, vāraḥ, vāsaraḥ, f∘ tithiḥ*

Night रात्रिः, रात्री, निशा। *f∘ rātriḥ, rātrī, niśā*

Dawn उषः, उषा, प्रभातम्। *n∘ uṣaḥ, f∘ uṣā, n∘ prabhātam*

Noon मध्यदिनम्, मध्याह्नः। *n∘ madhyadinam, m∘ madhyanhaḥ*

Afternoon अपराह्नः, पराह्नः, विकालः। *m∘ aparānhaḥ, parānhaḥ, vikālaḥ*

Midnight	मध्यरात्रिः, अर्धरात्रिः।*m◦madhyarātriḥ, ardharātriḥ,*
Week	सप्ताहः, सप्तदिनम्। *saptāhaḥ, n◦ saptadinam*
Year	वर्षः, वत्सरः, अब्दः, समा। *m◦ varṣaḥ, vatsaraḥ, sbdaḥ, f◦ samā*
Age	कल्पः, युगम्। *n◦ kalpam, yugam*
Day-before-yesterday	परह्यः। *adv◦ parahyaḥ*
Yesterday	ह्यः, पूर्वेद्युः। *adv◦ hyaḥ, pūrvedyuḥ*
Today	अद्य। *adv◦ adya*
Now	अधुना, इदानीम्, सम्प्रति।*adv◦ adhūnā, idānīm, samprati*
Tomorrow	श्वः, परेद्युः। *adv◦ śvaḥ, paredyuḥ*
Day-after-tomorrow	परश्वः। *adv◦ paraśvaḥ*
Always	अनीशं, सदा, सर्वदा, सततम्, निरन्तरम्। *adv◦ anīśam, sadā, sarvadā, satatam, nirantaram*
Periodically	समयतः, काले काले। *adv◦ samayataḥ, kāle kāle*
Sometime	एकदा, पुरा, प्राक्। *adv◦ ekadā, purā, prāk*
Sometimes	क्वचित्, कदाचित्। *adv◦ kvachit, kadāchit*
Maybe	कदाचित्। *adv◦ kadāchit*
Never	न कदापि, न जातु। *adv◦ na kadāpi, na jātu*
Eever	जातु, एकदा। *n◦ jātu, ekadā*

LESSON 16

ṣoḍaṣaḥ abhyāsaḥ षोडषः अभ्यासः ।

PRONOUN

sarvanāma सर्वनाम ।

Words such as I, we, you, he, she, they, that etc. are used in place of the names of those persons, therefore, they are Personal Pronouns. Pronouns such as who, which, whom - are called Relative Pronouns because they always relate or refer to some noun. The word that is used in place of a noun (*nāma* नाम) is a PRONOUN (*sarvanāma* सर्वनाम).

In Sanskrit there are 35 pronouns. namely, अदस्, अधर, अन्तर, अन्य, अन्यतर, अपर, अवर, अस्मद्, इतर, इदम्, उत्तर, उभ, उभय, एक, एतद्, किम्, डतम (कतम, यतम ...), डतर (कतर, यतर ...), तद्, त्यद्, त्व, त्वत्, दक्षिण, अन्य, अन्यतर, द्वि, नेम, पर, पूर्व, भवत्, यद्, युष्मद्, विश्व, सम, सर्व, सिम, स्व । The most commonly used pronoun forms are :

(1) I (*aham* अहम्), (2) We (*vayam* वयम्)

(3) You (*tvam* त्वम्) You, plural (*yūyam* यूयम्), Your honour m◦ (*bhavān* भवान्), Your honour f◦ (*bhavatī* भवती). Sir! (*śrīmān* श्रीमन्! महोदय!), Madam! (*śrīmatī* श्रीमति!)

(4) He, That (*saḥ* सः), They m◦ (*te* ते) (5) She That (*sā* सा), They f◦ (*tāḥ* ताः)

(6) It (*idam, etat* इदम्, एतत्), This - m◦ (*ayam, eṣaḥ* अयम्, एषः), f◦ (*iyam, eṣā* इयम्, एषा)

(7) That n◦ (*tat* तत्), Those (*tāni* तानि), These n◦ (*imāni, etāni* इमानि, एतानि), m◦ (*ime, ete* इमे, एते); f◦ (*imāḥ, etāḥ* इमाः, एताः)

(8) What? Which? (*kim?* किम्?), Which n◦ (*yat* यत्), Who m◦ (*yaḥ* यः); f◦ (*yā* या), Which - plural n◦ (*yāni* यानि), Who - plural m◦ (*ye* ये); f◦ (*yāḥ* याः)

(9) Who? m◦ (*kaḥ?* कः?), Who f◦ (*kā?* का?) (10) Whom? m◦ (*kam?* कम्?), Whom f◦ (*kām?* काम्?) (11) Whose? (m◦ *kasya?* कस्य?), (f◦ *kasya?* कस्याः?)

EXAMPLES cum EXERCISE : PRONOUNS (for declensions, see Apendix 8)

(1) I am a boy. *aham̐ bālakaḥ asmi.* (अहं बालकः अस्मि); I am a girl. *aham̐ bālikā asmi.* (अहं बालिका अस्मि)

We are boys. *vayam̐ bālakāḥ smaḥ. vayam̐ bālakāḥ.* (वयं बालकाः स्मः, वयं बालकाः); We are girls. *vayam̐ bālikāḥ smaḥ. vayam̐ bālikāḥ.* (वयं बालिकाः स्मः, वयं बालिकाः)

(2) You are a boy. *tvam̐ bālakaḥ asi.* (त्वं बालकः असि); You are girls. *yūyam̐ bālikāḥ stha.* (यूयं बालिकाः स्थ). Sir! Are you a teacher? *śrīman! bhavān adhyāpakaḥ asti vā?* (श्रीमन्! भवान् अध्यापकः अस्ति वा), Madam! Are you a teacher? *śrīmati! bhavatī adhyāpikā asti vā?.* (श्रीमति! भवती अध्यापिका अस्ति वा ।)

(3) He is a man. *saḥ manuṣyaḥ/puruṣaḥ/naraḥ asti.* (सः मनुष्यः/पुरुषः/नरः अस्ति);

That is a man. *saḥ manuṣyāh asti.* (सः मनुष्यः अस्ति); They are men. *te manuṣyāḥ santi.* (ते मनुष्याः सन्ति)

(4) She is a woman. *sā strī asti.* (सा स्त्री अस्ति); That is a woman. *sā strī asti.* (सा स्त्री अस्ति)

They are women. *tāḥ striyaḥ santi.* (ताः स्त्रियः सन्ति)

(5) It is a book. *idam̐ pustakam asti.* (इदं पुस्तकम् अस्ति)

This is a boy. *eṣaḥ bālakaḥ.* (एषः बालकः); This is a girl. *eṣā bālikā.* (एषा बालिका)

(6) That house. *tad gṛham.* (तद् गृहम्); Those houses. *tāni gṛhāṇi.* (तानि गृहाणि)

(7) These houses. *etāni gṛhāṇi.* (एतानि गृहाणि); These boys. *ete bālakāḥ.* (एते बालकाः)

These girls. *etāḥ bālikāḥ.* (एताः बालिकाः)

(8) What reason? *kim̐ kāraṇam?* (किं कारणम्?), Which house? *kim̐ gṛham?* (किं गृहम्?)

(9) Which n◦ *yat* (यत्); Who m◦ *yaḥ* (यः); f◦ *yā* (या)

(10) Who is he? m◦ *saḥ kaḥ asti?* (कः अस्ति?); Who is she? f◦ *sā kā asti?* (सा का अस्ति?)

(11) Whose book? *kasya pustakam?* कस्य पुस्तकम्?

(12) Who are they? *te ke santi?* ते के सन्ति?

(13) I am. *aham asmi.* अहम् अस्मि । He is. *saḥ asti* सः अस्ति । She is. *sā asti.* सा अस्ति । That is. *tad asti.* तद् अस्ति । They are. *te santi.* ते सन्ति or *tāḥ santi.* ताः सन्ति, or *tāni santi.* तानि सन्ति । We are. *vayam̐ smaḥ.* वयं स्मः । Books are. *pustakāni santi.* पुस्तकानि

सन्ति । Boys are, girls are. *bālakāḥ santi.* बालकाः सन्ति । *bālikāḥ santi.* बालिकाः सन्ति । Houses are. *gṛhāṇi santi.* गृहाणि सन्ति । House is. *gṛham asti.* गृहम् अस्ति ।

NOTE: The Second Person Honorific Pronouns 'you' m◦ and f◦ (भवान् m◦ and भवती f◦) are always treated as if they were Third Person Pronouns (he, she, they), instead of Second Person (you).

EXAMPLES : Honorific pronouns (m◦) *bhavān* and (f◦) *bhavatī*

(1) What do you do (m◦ singular) *tvaṁ kiṁ karoṣi?* त्वं किं करोषि ।

(2) What do you do (m◦ honorofic) *bhavān kiṁ karoti?* भवान् किं करोति ।

(3) What do you do (f◦) *tvaṁ kiṁ karoṣi?* त्वं किं करोषि ।

(4) What do you do (f◦ honorofic) *bhavatī kiṁ karoti?* भवती किं करोति ।

(5) What do you do (m◦ plural) *yūyaṁ kiṁ kurutha?* यूयं किं कुरुथ ।

(6) What do you do (m◦ honorofic, plural) *bhavantaḥ kiṁ kurvanti?* भवन्तः किं कुर्वन्ति ।

(7) What do you do (f◦ plural) *yūyaṁ kiṁ kurutha?* यूयं किं कुरुथ ।

(8) What do you all do (f◦ honorofic, plural) *bhavatyaḥ kiṁ kurvanti?* भवत्यः किं कुर्वन्ति ।

EXERCISE 41 : Fill in the blanks with pronouns. (for declensions, see Apendix 8)

(1) That book. -------------- पुस्तकम् । Which girl. -------------- बालिका ।

(2) Whose house. -------------- गृहम् ।

(3) What reason? --------------

(4) He is. -------------- अस्ति । She is. -------------- अस्ति । It is -------------- अस्ति ।

(5) You are भवान् -------------- or भवती --------------

(6) Who are they? -------------- ?

LESSON 17

saptadaśaḥ abhyāsaḥ सप्तदशः अभ्यासः ।

* THE PRESENT TENSE

laṭ lakāraḥ

लट् लकारः ।

This * sign, shown in Lessons 17, 18 and 21, indicates that these three tenses are most commonly used in Sanskrit. Therefore, you should know them well.

NOTE: Generally, distinction is not made between Present Habitual and Present Continuous tenses. अहं खादामि may mean I eat or I am eating, depending on the context. However, if you must write in the Present Continuous tense, see Lessons 28.5 to 28.8

TYPICAL SUFFIXES OF THE PRESENT TENSE:

TABLE : (All three genders - m∘, f∘ and n∘)

Person	Singular	Dual	Plural
1st p∘	**मि (mi)**	**वः (vaḥ)**	**मः (maḥ)**
2nd p∘	**सि (si)**	**थः (thaḥ)**	**थ (tha)**
3rd p∘	**ति (ti)**	**तः (taḥ)**	**अन्ति (anti)**

Verb √खाद् to eat, PRESENT TENSE (m∘f∘n∘)

Person	Singular	Plural
I eat	अहं खादामि *ahaṁ khādāmi*	वयं खादामः *vayaṁ khādāmaḥ*
you eat	त्वं खादसि *tvaṁ khādasi*	यूयं खादथ *yūyaṁ khādatha*
you eat	भवान् खादति *bhavān khādati*	भवन्तः खादन्ति *bhavantaḥ khādanti*
he/she/that eats	सः/सा/तत् खादति *saḥ/sā/tat khādati*	ते/ताः/तानि खादन्ति *te/tāḥ/tāni khādanti*

EXAMPLES cum EXERCISE : use of verbs in Present Tense

(see Appendix 6 for conjugations of the verbs)

1. I eat or I am eating. *aham̊ khādāmi. aham̊ bhojanam̊ karomi.* अहं खादामि । अहं भोजनं करोमि । We eat or we are eating. *vayam̊ khādāmaḥ. vayam̊ bhojanam̊ kurmaḥ.* वयं खादामः । वयं भोजनं कुर्मः । (√खाद् to eat, √कृ to do)
2. I eat fruit. *aham̊ phalam̊ khādāmi.* अहं फलं खादामि । I eat fruits. *aham̊ phalāni khādāmi.* अहं फलानि खादामि । We eat fruit. *vayam̊ phalam̊ khādāmaḥ.* वयं फलं खादामः । We eat fruits. *vayam̊ phalāni khādāmaḥ.* वयं फलानि खादामः । I eat three fruits. *aham̊ trīṇi phalāni khādāmi.* अहं त्रीणि फलानि खादामि । (√*khād* √खाद् to eat, *phalam* फलम् = fruit)
3. You drink. *bhavān pibati.* भवान् पिबति । *tvam̊ pibasi.* त्वं पिबसि । You drink milk. *bhavān dugdham̊ pibati.* भवान् दुग्धं पिबति । *tvam̊ dugdham̊ pibasi.* त्वं दुग्धं पिबसि । (√पा to drink)
4. We drink water. *vayam̊ jalam̊ pibāmaḥ.* वयं जलं पिबामः । (*jalam* जलम् = water)
5. She writes. *sā likhati.* सा लिखति । They write. (f॰) *tāḥ likhanti.* ताः लिखन्ति or (m॰) *te likhanti* ते लिखन्ति । (√लिख् to write)
6. I drink milk or I am drinking milk. *aham̊ dugdham̊ pibāmi.* अहं दुग्धं पिबामि । (*dugdham* दुग्धम् = milk)
7. We drink cold milk. *vayam̊ śītam̊ dugdham̊ pibāmaḥ.* वयं शीतं दुग्धं पिबामः । (*śītam* शीतम् = cold)
8. Hari reads a book. *hariḥ pustakam̊ paṭhati.* हरिः पुस्तकं पठति । (*pustakam* पुस्तकम् = book)
9. Sītā reads a book. *sītā pustakam̊ paṭhati.* सीता पुस्तकं पठति । (√*paṭha* पठ् read)

EXERCISE 42 : Fill in the blanks with verbs :

(1) I come. He comes. अहम् ———— सः ———— (2) She reads. सा ————

(3) They speak. ते ———— ताः ———— (4) She writes. सा ————

(5) You drink. त्वं ———— यूयम् ———— (6) We eat. वयं ————

EXAMPLES : Present tense (For case declensions see Appendix 2, for verb conjugations see Appendix 6)

(1) Animals live (चेतनाः/जीवाः/प्राणिनः/पशवः जीवन्ति)

(2) The cow gives milk (धेनुः/गौः दुग्धं ददाति) √दा √*dā* to drink

(3) The calf drinks milk (वत्सः दुग्धं पिबति) √पा √*pā* to tdink

(4) The ox eats grass and leaves (वृषभः तृणं पर्णानि च खादति)

(5) Buffalos and goats give milk (महिष्यः अजाः च दुग्धं ददति)

(6) Sheeps give wool (मेषाः/एडकाः/वृष्णयः/मेढ्राः/लोमशाः/ मेष्यः/एडकाः लोम ददति) (√दा √*dā* to give).

(7) The dog barks (कुक्कुरः/शुनकः/श्वानः वुक्कयति) √वुक् √vuk

(8) The cat eats mouse (बिडालः/मार्जारः उन्दरुं/मूषकं खादति)

(9) The horse runs (अश्वः/तुरङ्गः/हयः धावति) √धाव √dhav

EXERCISE 43 : Write Sanskrit nouns:

(1) Animal ------------ Cow ------------ Dog ------------

(2) Cat ------------ Mouse --------- Horse ---------

(3) Elephant ------------ Lion ------------ Monkey -------

(4) Pig ------------ Deer ------------ Fish ------------

USE OF PARTICLE *sma* स्म

WITH A PRESENT TENSE

When the particle *sma* स्म is added to a लट् Present Tense or to a Present Participle, the action is converted into Past Tense. Note that स्म could be anywhere in the sentence.

EXAMPLES cum EXERCISE

(1) Present Tense (habitual or continuous) :

I eat, I am eating. *aham̐ khādāmi* अहं खादामि । He eats, he is eating. *saḥ khādati* सः खादति । They eat, they are eating. *te khādanti.* ते खादन्ति ।

(2) Past Tense : (habitual or continuous)

I used to eat, I was eating. *aham̐ khādāmi sma.* अहं खादामि स्म ।

He used to eat (was eating) meat. *saḥ mām̐sam̐ khādati sma.* सः मांसं खादति स्म ।

They used to eat, they were eating. *te khādanti sma.* ते खादन्ति स्म ।

(3) Present Tense : (habitual or continuous)

Lion lives in the forest, a lion is living in the forest. *sim̐haḥ vane vasati* सिंहः वने वसति ।

The lions live in the forest, the lions are living in the forest. *sim̐hāḥ vane vasanti.* सिंहाः वने वसन्ति ।

(4) Past Tense : (habitual or continuous)

That lion lived in the forest, that lion was living in the forest. *saḥ sim̐haḥ vane vasati sma.* सहः सिंहः वने वसति स्म ।

Those lions lived in the forest, those lions were living in the forest. *te sim̐hāḥ vane vasanti sma.* ते सिंहाः वने वसन्ति स्म ।

WHAT WE HAVE LEARNED SO FAR

USE OF THE PRESENT TENSE

EXERCISE 44 : Following are sentences prepared in Present tense verbs. Translate the English sentences into Sanskrit. Use the Dictionaries of Nouns↑ and Verbs↓.

For your help, the √Root Verbs are shown in brackets, answers are shown in *italized transliteration* and in Devanāgarī Sanskrit. See Appendix 2 for Case Declensions↓

(1) Rāma writes a letter. *Rāmaḥ patraṁ likhati (√likh).* रामः पत्रं लिखति ।

(2) Ant walks slowly. *pipīlikā śanaiḥ ćalati (√ćal).* पिपीलिका शनैः चलति । (slowly = शनैः)

(3) She eats an apple. *sā ātāphalaṁ/sevaṁ khādti (√khā).* सा आताफलं/सेवं खादति ।

(4) They worship Krishna. *te kṛṣṇam arćanti. (√arć).* ते कृष्णम् अर्चन्ति ।

(5) Rītā throws a ball. *Rītā kandukaṁ kṣipati (√kṣip).* रीता कन्दुकं क्षिपति ।

(6) Viśāl brings a banana. *Viśālaḥ kadali-phalam ānayati (ā√nī).* विशालः कदलिफलम् आनयति ।

(7) Rānī cuts the beans. *Ranī simbāḥ kṛntati (√kṛt).* रानी सिम्बाः कृन्तति ।

(8) The bear runs. *bhallaḥ/bhālukaḥ dhāvati (√dhāv).* भल्लः/भालुकः धावति ।

(9) They are hurting the dog. *te kukkuraṁ/bhaṣakaṁ/śunakaṁ/śvānaṁ tudanti (√tud).* ते कुक्कुरं/भषकं/शुनकं/श्वानं तुदन्ति । You are hurting her. *bhavān tāṁ tudati (√tud).* भवान् तां तुदति । She hurts him. *sā taṁ dunoti (√du).* सा तं दुनोति ।

(10) He steals money. *saḥ mudrāḥ/dhanaṁ ćorayati (√ćur).* सः मुद्राः/धनं चोरयति ।

(11) The bird flies. *khagaḥ/ćaṭakaḥ/pakṣī/vihaṅgaḥ ḍayate (√ḍī).* खगः/चटकः/पक्षी/विहङ्गः डयते ।

(12) The barber does his work. *nāpitaḥ karma karoti (karma√kṛ).* नापितः कर्म करोति ।

The workers do the jobs *karmakārāḥ karmāṇi kurvanti.* कर्मकाराः कर्माणि कुर्वन्ति ।

(13) Gopāl washes hands. *Gopālaḥ hastau kṣālayati (√kṣal).* गोपालः हस्तौ क्षालयति ।

(14) Ramesh burns the grass. *Rameshaḥ ghāsaṁ/tṛṇaṁ dahati (√dah).* रमेशः घासं/तृणं दहति ।

(15) A branch fis falling. *śākhā patati (√pat).* शाखा पतति ।

(16) The email comes. *email āyāti (ā√yā).* ई-मेल आयाति ।

(17) The animals roam. *jantavaḥ/jīvāḥ/prāṇinaḥ/paśavaḥ aṭanti (√aṭ).* जन्तवः/जीवाः/प्राणिनः/पशवः अटन्ति ।

(18) You read a book. *tvaṁ pustakaṁ paṭhasi; bhavān pustakṁ paṭhati (√paṭh).* त्वं पुस्तकं पठसि । भवान् पुस्तकं पठति ।

(19) The baby cries. *bālakaḥ/śisuḥ krandati (√krand).* बालकः/शिशुः क्रन्दति ।

(20) The girl plays. *bālikā khelati/krīḍati (√khel, √krīḍ).* बालिका खेलति/क्रीडति ।

(21) Sītā cooks breads. *Sītā roṭikāḥ paćati (√pać).* सीता रोटिकाः पचति ।

(22) The bee bites. *bhramaraḥ daṁśati (√daṁś).* भ्रमरः दंशति ।

(23) We give charity. *vayaṁ dānaṁ dadmaḥ (√dā).* वयं दानं दद्मः ।

(24) The blood rushes to the heart. *rudhiraṁ hṛdayaṁ tvarate (√tvar).* रुधिरं हृदयं त्वरते ।

(25) The blood flows. *raktaṁ/rudhiraṁ/śoṇitaṁ/lohitaṁ pravahati (pra√vah).* रक्तं/रुधिरं/शोणितं/लोहितं प्रवहति ।

(26) The boat is floating. *jalayānaṁ/nauḥ/naukā tarati. (√tṝ).* जलयानं/नौः/नौका तरति ।

(27) Sonia brings the box. *Sonia peṭikāṁ/samudrakaṁ/mañjuṣāṁ ānayati (ā√nī).* सोनीया पेटिकां/समुद्रकं/मञ्जूषां आनयति ।

(28) You are buying a brecelet. *bhavān valayaṁ/kaṅkaṇaṁ krīṇāti (√kṛ).* भवान् वलयं/कंकणं क्रीणाति । You are selling a brecelet. *bhavān valayaṁ/kaṅkaṇaṁ vikrīṇāti (vi√kṛ).* भवान् वलयं/कंकणं विक्रीणाति ।

(29) Sachin is watching the sunrise. *Sachinaḥ suryodayaṁ paśyati (√dṛś).* सचिनः सूर्योदयं पश्यति ।

(30) Rādhā hears the news. *Rādhā vārtāṁ śruṇoti (√śru).* राधा वार्तां श्रुणोति ।

(31) Rājā cooks cauliflower. *Rājā gojihvāṁ paćati (√pać).* राजा गोजिह्वां पचति ।

(32) The camel is drinking water. *ūṣṭraḥ jalaṁ/udakaṁ/nīraṁ/toyaṁ pibati (√pā).* ऊष्ट्रः जलं/उदकं/नीरं/तोयं पिबति ।

(33) Mālā sews a shirt for Līlā. *Mālā Līlāyai ćolaṁ/nićulaṁ/yutakaṁ sīvyati (√siv).* माला लीलायै चोलं/निचुलं/युतकं सीव्यति ।

(35) She drives a car. *sā cārayānaṁ ćālayati (√ćāl).* सा कारयानं चालयति ।

(36) John paints the car. *Johnaḥ cārayānaṁ raṅgayati (√raṅg).* जॉनः कारयानं रङ्गयति ।

(37) Rekhā counts Rupees. *Rekhā rūpyakāṇi gaṇayati (√gaṇ).* रेखा रूप्यकाणि गणयति ।

(38) He eats chickpeas. *saḥ chaṇakān bhakṣayati (√bhakṣ).* सः चणकान् भक्षयति ।

(39) Sunītā dries the Chillies. *Sunītā marīćān śuṣkī/karoti (√śuṣ √kṛ).* सुनीता मरीचान् शुष्कीकरोति । The Chillies dry. *marīćāni śuṣyanti (√śuṣ).* मरीचानि शुष्यन्ति ।

(40) Ajīt takes the comb. *Ajītaḥ kaṅkatikāṁ/prasādhanīṁ gṛhṇāti (√grah).* अजीतः कंकतिकां/प्रसाधनीं गृह्णाति ।

(41) We cook and eat rice. *vayam odanaṁ/bhaktaṁ paćāmaḥ khādāmaḥ ća (√pać, √khād).* वयम् ओदनं/भक्तं पचामः खादामः च ।

(42) The deer dies. *hariṇaḥ mriyate (√mṛ).* हरिणः म्रियते । The tiger kills. *vyāghraḥ/śārdūlaḥ hanti (√han).* व्याघ्रः/शार्दूलः हन्ति ।

(42) Peacock dances. *mayūraḥ nṛtyati (√nṛt).* मयूरः नृत्यति ।

(43) Child sleeps. *bālakaḥ svapiti (√svap).* बालकः स्वपिति ।

(44) Devotee worships. *bhaktaḥ pūjati (√pūj).* भक्तः पूजति ।

(45) Tree falls. *vṛkṣaḥ/taruḥ/drumaḥ/pādapaḥ patati (√pat).* वृक्षः/तरुः/द्रुमः/पादपः पतति

(46) The wind blows. *anilaḥ/marut/vātaḥ/vāyuḥ/pavanaḥ vahati (√vah).* अनिलः/मरुत्/वातः/वायुः/पवनः वहति ।

(47) The corn grows. *kiṇaḥ/śasyaṁ sphuṭati (√sphuṭ).* किणः/शस्यं स्फुटति ।

(48) The flowers bloom. *puṣpāṇi/kusumāni/sumanāni vikasanti (√vikas).* पुष्पाणि/कुसुमानि/सुमनानि विकसन्ति । The cow gives milk *(√dā). dhenuḥ/gauḥ dugdhaṁ/kṣīraṁ/payaḥ dadāti.* धेनुः/गौः दुग्धं/क्षीरं/पयः ददाति ।

(49) Samīra wins the cup. *Samīraḥ ćaṣakaṁ jayati (√ji).* समीरः चषकं जयति ।

(50) Simā rides bicycle. *Sīmā dvi-ćakrikām ārohati (ā√ruh).* सीमा द्विचक्रिकाम् आरोहति ।

(51) The deer jumps. *mṛgaḥ/hariṇaḥ utpatati (ud√pat).* मृगः/हरिणः उत्पतति ।

(52) She wants gold. *sā kanakam/kāñćanam/bharma/suvarṇam/svarṇam/hema ićchati/vāñćhati/kāṅkṣati (√iććh, √vāñćh, √kāṅkṣ).* सा कनकम्/काञ्चनम्/भर्म/सुवर्णम्/स्वर्णम्/हेम इच्छति/वाञ्छति/कांक्षति ।

(53) The donkey suffers. *gardabhaḥ/kharaḥ khidyate (√khid).* गर्दभः/खरः खिद्यते ।

(54) Door closes. *dvāraṁ saṁvartate (sam√vṛt).* द्वारं संवर्तते ।

(55) Rīnā drinks (takes) a drink. *Rīnā peyaṁ pibati (√pā).* रीना पेयं पिबति ।

(56) The duck swims. *kadambaḥ tarati/plavate (√tṝ, √plu).* कदम्बः तरति/प्लवते ।

(57) The eagle soars. *garuḍaḥ uḍḍīyate (ud√dī).* गरुडः उड्डीयते ।

(58) I buy diamonds. *ahaṁ ratnāni/hīrakān krīṇāmi (√krī).* अहं रत्नानि/हीरकान् क्रीणामि ।

(59) She brings the dictionary. *sā shabda-kośam ānayati (ā√ni).* सा शब्दकोशम् आनयति ।

(60) Father teaches son. *pitā/janakaḥ/tātaḥ putram adhyāpayati (adhi√i).* पिता/जनकः/तातः पुत्रम् अध्यापयति ।

(61) Fire burns that house. *agniḥ/analaḥ/pāvakaḥ tat gṛhaṁ dahati (√dah).* अग्निः/अनलः/पावकः तत् गृहं दहति ।

(62) The fish hides the eggs. *jhaṣaḥ/matsyaḥ/mīnaḥ aṇḍāni gūhati* झषः/मत्स्यः/मीनः अण्डानि गूहति (√गुह्) ।

(63) The hen lays eggs. *kukkuṭī aṇḍāni sūyate (√sū).* कुक्कुटी अण्डानि सूयते ।

(64) The earth turns. *bhūḥ/bhūmiḥ/pṛthvī/pṛthivī/mahī/dharā/dharaṇī/medinī parivartate (pari√vṛt).* भूः/भूमिः/पृथ्वी/पृथिवी/मही/धरा/धरणी/मेदिनी परिवर्तते ।

(65) Ranī orders food. *Rānī annam/ aśanam/ khādyam/ khādanam/ bhaktam/ bhakṣaṇam/ bhakṣyam/ bhojanam/ āhāram ājñāpayati (ā√jñā).* रानी अन्नम्/ अशनम्/ खाद्यम्/ खादनम्/ भक्तम्/ भक्षणम्/ भक्ष्यम्/ भोजनम्/ आहारम् आज्ञापयति ।

(66) Elephant picks the wood. *gajaḥ kāṣṭham uddharati (ud√dhṛ).* गजः काष्ठम् उद्धरति ।

(67) Rāma says. *rāmaḥ gadati/bhaṇati/vadati (√gad √bhaṇ √vad).* रामः गदति/भणति/वदति

(68) Monīkā sends books. *Monīkā pustakāni sam-preṣayati (sam√preṣ).* मोनीका पुस्तकानि सम्प्रेषयति ।

(69) Mīnā writes letters. *Mīnā patrāṇi likhati (√likh).* मीना पत्राणि लिखति ।

(70) They go to the forest. *te vanaṁ/kānanaṁ/vipinaṁ gaććanti (√gam).* ते वनं/काननं/विपिनं गच्छन्ति ।

(71) The friend loves. *mitraṁ/bandhuḥ/suhṛd/sakhā/sakhī snihyati (√snih).* मित्रं/बन्धुः/सुहृद्/सखा/सखी स्निह्यति ।

(72) We celebrate Diwālī-festival. *vayaṁ dīpāvalī-utsavam anuṣṭhāpayāmaḥ (anu√sthā).* वयं दीपावली-उत्सवम् अनुष्ठापयामः ।

(73) The frog eats flies. *maṇḍūkaḥ/darduraḥ makṣikāḥ khādati (√khād).* मण्डूकः/दर्दुरः मक्षिकाः खादति ।

(74) The fruit ripens. *phalaṁ paćate (√pać).* फलं पचते ।

(75) Rekhā drives car. *Rekhā kārayānam ćālayati (√ćal).* रेखा कारयानं चालयति ।

(76) The goat eats leaves. *ajaḥ/ajā parṇāni atti (√ad).* अजः/अजा पर्णानि अत्ति ।

(77) Tona thinks. *Monā ćintayati (√ćint).* मोना चिन्तयति ।

(78) Sunīl deserves. *Sunilaḥ arhati (√arh).* सुनीलः अर्हति ।

(79) God exists. *Devaḥ/bhagavān/iśvaraḥ asti (√as).* देवः/भगवान्/ईश्वरः अस्ति ।

(80) The fuel burns. *indhanam/edhaḥ indhe (√indh).* इन्धनम्/एधः इन्धे ।

(81) You are jelous. *tvam īrṣyase, bhavān īrṣyate. (√īrṣ).* त्वम् ईर्ष्यसे, भवान् ईर्षते ।

(82) She is angry. *sā kupyati/krudhyati (√kup, √krudh).* सा कुप्यति/क्रुध्यति ।

(83) Farmer digs the field. *kṛṣakaḥ kṣetraṁ khanati (√khan).* कृषक: क्षेत्रं खनति ।

(84) The clouds roar/thunder. *meghāḥ garjanti (√garj).* मेघा: गर्जन्ति ।

(85) They sing Hindī songs. *te Hindī-gānāni gāyanti (√gai).* ते हिन्दी-गानानि गायन्ति ।

(86) The girl walks slowly. *bālikā śanaiḥ ćalati (√ćal).* बालिका शनै: चलति ।

(87) The hare eats green grass. *śaśakaḥ haritaṁ tṛṇaṁ/ghāsaṁ khādati (√khād).* शशक: हरितं तृणं/घासं खादति । (हरित *harita* = green)

(88) The hermit meditates. *tāpasaḥ/tapasvī/muniḥ/yatih/yogī tapati (√tap).* तापस:/तपस्वी/मुनि:/यति:/योगी तपति ।

(89) The granddaughter becomes happy. *pautrī tushyati (√tuṣ).* पौत्री तुष्यति ।

(90) The grapes wilt. *drākṣāḥ mlāyanti (√mlai).* द्राक्षा: म्लायन्ति ।

(91) The horse runs. *aśvaḥ/turaṅgaḥ/hayaḥ dhāvati (√dhāv).* अश्व:/तुरङ्ग:/हय: धावति ।

(92) The priest sings hymns. *paṇḍitaḥ ślokān gāyati (√gai).* पण्डित: श्लोकान् गायति ।

(93) The insect eats fruit. *kīṭaḥ/kṛmiḥ phalaṁ khādati (√khād).* कीट:/कृमि: फलं खादति । The leaf falls. *patraṁ/parṇaṁ patati (√pat).* पत्रं/पर्णं पतति । The leaves fall. *patrāṇi/parṇāni patanti.* पत्राणि/पर्णानि पतन्ति ।

(94) The light shines. *ālokaḥ/prakāśaḥ/bhā/ābhā/prabhā ćakāsti (√ćakās).* आलोक:/प्रकाश:/भा/आभा/प्रभा चकास्ति ।

(95) Lion hunts. *siṁhaḥ/kesarī/mṛgakesarī mṛgayate (√mṛg).* सिंह:/केसरी/मृगकेसरी मृगयते

(96) The lotus looks beautiful. *kamalaṁ/padmaṁ/aravindaṁ/paṅkajaṁ śobhate (√śobh).* कमलं/पद्मं/अरविन्दं/पङ्कजं शोभते ।

(97) The mango falls. *amraphalṁ/āmraṁ patati (√pat).* आम्रफलं/आम्रं पतति ।

(98) Monkeys jump. *kapayaḥ/markaṭāḥ/vānarāḥ plavanti (√plu).* कपय:/मर्कटा:/वानरा: प्लवन्ति ।

(99) The mouse eats seeds. *mūṣakaḥ bījāni khādati (√khād).* मूषक: बीजानि खादति ।

(100) The heart pumps blood. *hṛdayaṁ rudhiram/raktam uttulayati (ud√tul).* हृदयं रुधिरम् उत्तुलयति ।

LESSON 18

aṣṭādaśaḥ abhyāsaḥ अष्टाशः अभ्यासः ।

* THE (PAST) IMPERFECT TENSE

laṅ lakāraḥ

लङ् लकारः ।

* This is the most commonly used Past Tense in Sanskrit.

See the note in the Past Active Perticiple, Lesson 28.4

This tense is one of the three Sanskrit Past Tenses (लङ्, लिट्, लुङ्).

(1) लङ् (imperfect) represents an action not prformed today, not seen by the speaker, but is qualified by an adjective.

(2) लिट् (perfect) represents an action not prformed today, not seen by the speaker, and not qualified by an adjective.

(3) लुङ् (indfinite) represents actions prformed today or actions seen by the speaker. For details, see the unique Flow Chart of Tenses, at the end of lesson 22.

For our purpose, the IMPERFECT लङ् tense may approximately be considered almost same as the PAST INDEFINITE TENSE in English. The SUFFIXES of the Imperfect tense are : (same chart for all three genders - m∘, f∘ and n∘)

TYPICAL SUFFIXES OF THE PAST IMPERFECT (INDEFINITE लङ्) TENSE

Person	Singular	Dual	Plural
1st p∘	**अम् (am)**	**व (va)**	**म (ma)**
2nd p∘	**:**	**तम् (tam)**	**त (त)**
3rd p∘	**त् (t)**	**ताम् (tām)**	**अन्, उः (an, uḥ)**

(1) Augment अ (*a*) is added to the root before attaching any Past Imperfect suffix (shown in the chart given above). e.g. √वद् → अ + √वद् + अत् = अवदत्

(2) If the √verb is preceded by any prefix (preposition), the augment अ is inserted between the preposition and the √verb. Then, if applicable, follow the sandhi rules also.

e.g. √वद् → अवदत् । प्र√वद् → प्र + अ + वदत् → प्रावदत् ।

(3) If the √verb begins with a vowel, the augment अ forms *sandhi* with it. e.g. √इष् → अ + इच्छत् → ऐच्छत्

√खाद् to eat, PAST IMPERFECT TENSE लङ् (m∘f∘n∘)

Person	Singular	Plural
I ate	अहम् अखादम् *aham akhādam*	वयम् अखादाम । *vayam akhādāma*
You ate	त्वम् अखाद: *tvam akhādaḥ*	यूयम् अखादत । *yūyam akhādat*
He/she ate	स: सा तत् अखादत्*saḥ/sā/tat akhādat*	ते ता: तानि अखादन् । *te/tāḥ/tāni akhādan*

EXAMPLES cum EXERCISE : Past Imperfect Tense लङ् (cumulative exercise)

1. Rāma writes. *rāmaḥ likhati.* राम: लिखति (√लिख्) । Sītā goes. *sītā gacćhati.* सीता गच्छति ।

   Rāma wrote. *rāmaḥ alikhat.* राम: अलिखत् । Sītā went. *sītā agacćhat.* सीता अगच्छत् ।

2. Tree falls, tree is falling. *vṛkṣaḥ patati.* वृक्ष: पतति । (√पत्)

   A tree fell. *vṛkṣaḥ apatat.* वृक्ष: अपतत् ।

   A vine fell. *latā apatat.* लता अपतत् ।

   A flower fell. *puṣpam apatat.* पुष्पम् अपतत् ।

   Flowers fell. *puṣpāṇi apatan.* पुष्पाणि अपतन् ।

   Trees Fell. *vṛkṣāḥ apatan.* वृक्षा: अपतन् ।

   Vines fell. *latāḥ apatan.* लता: अपतन् ।

3. Bharata says. *Bharataḥ vadati.* भरत: वदति । Bharata said. *Bharataḥ avadat.* भरत: अवदत् । (√वद्) Boys went. *kumārāḥ agacćhan.* कुमारा: अगच्छन् । (√गम्)

4. He is. *saḥ asti.* सः अस्ति । He was. *saḥ āsīt.* सः आसीत् । They were. *te āsan.* ते आसन् ।

EXAMPLES cum EXERCISE : Present and Perfect Tenses: (cumulative exercise)

(1) Rāma throws a stone. *rāmaḥ prastaraṁ kṣipati,* रामः प्रस्तरं क्षिपति । Rāma is throwing a stone. *rāmaḥ prastaraṁ kṣipati,* रामः प्रस्तरं क्षिपति ।

(2) Rāma threw a stone. *rāmaḥ prastaram akṣipat.* रामः प्रस्तरम् अक्षिपत् ।

(3) I bow. *ahaṁ namāmi; ahaṁ praṇamāmi; ahaṁ praṇāmaṁ karomi.* अहं नमामि, अहं प्रणमामि, अहं प्रणामं करोमि । (√नम्, प्र√नम्)

(4) Sītā, Bharata and Rāma stayed, *sītā bharataḥ rāmaḥ ća atiṣṭhan.* सीता भरतः रामः च अतिष्ठन् । They stand up. *te/sāḥ uttiṣṭganti.* ते/साः उत्तिष्ठन्ति । (उद्√स्था)

(5) Tigers and lions ran. *vyāghrāḥ ća siṁhāḥ ća adhāvan; vyāghrāḥ siṁhāḥ ća adhāvan.* व्याघ्राः च सिंहाः च अधावन् । (√धाव्)

(6) The snake moved. *sarpaḥ aćalat.* सर्पः अचलत् । (√चल्)

(7) The boys and girls laughed. *bālakāḥ bālāḥ ća ahasan.* बालकाः बालाः च अहसन् । (√हस् ।

(8) Children cry. *bālakāḥ rudanti.* बालकाः रुदन्ति । (√रुद्)

(9) He is resting. *saḥ viśati.* (सः विशति) I sit down. *aham upaviśāmi.* अहम् उपविशामि । (√विश्, उप√विश्)

(10) They abandon. *te tyajanti.* ते त्यजन्ति । (√त्यज्)

(11) You became angry. *tvam akrudhyaḥ.* त्वम् अक्रुध्यः । (√क्रुध्)

(12) The tiger lion and elephant roam. *vyāghraḥ siṁhaḥ gajaḥ ća aṭanti.* व्याघ्राः सिंहः गजः च अटन्ति । (√अट्)

(13) I worship Kṛṣṇa. *ahaṁ kṛṣṇam archāmi.* अहं कृष्णम् अर्चामि । (√अर्च्) I go. *ahaṁ gaććāmi* अहं गच्छामि ।

(14) She wishes. *sā ićchati.* सा इच्छति । (√इष्)

(15) Trees endure. *vṛkṣāḥ kṣamante.* वृक्षाः क्षमन्ते । (√क्षम्)

EXERCISE 45: PAST IMPERFECT TENSE लङ्

A. Translate the following English verbs into Sanskrit:

(1) to throw ---------- to stay ---------- to run ----------

(2) to cry ---------- to sit down ---------- to wash ----------

B. Translate into English (see above for help).

(1) सीता अपठत् । रामः आसीत् । भरतः अपश्यत् ।

(2) सीता रामः भरतः च अपश्यन् ।

(3) वयं प्रस्तराणि क्षिपामः । सः प्रस्तरम् अक्षिपत् ।

(4) अहं कृष्णं नमामि । अहं रामं प्रणमामि । अहं सीतां वन्दे ।

(5) श्वानः बिडालः मूषकाः च अतिष्ठन् । ताः उत्तिष्ठन्ति ।

(6) धेनुः च अजा च अश्वः च अधावन् ।

(7) पुरुषाः स्त्रियः च अहसन् । बालकः अरोदत्/अरोदीत् ।

C. Translate into Sanskrit. (Answers are shown in the brackets)

(1) I was not here yesterday. (अहं ह्यः अत्र न आसम्)

(2) You all went home. (यूयं सर्वे गृहम् अगच्छन्)

(3) She did not go to school today. (सा अद्य विद्यालयं न अगच्छत्)

(4) Rāma, Lakṣamaṇa and Sītā stayed in the hermitage. (सीतारामलक्ष्मणाः आश्रमे अतिष्टन्)

(5) What did you see? (त्वं किम् अपश्यः । भवान् किम् अपश्यत्)

(6) Rāma said to Sītā. (रामः सीताम् अवदत्)

(7) They sang the hymns. (ते श्लोकान् अगायन्)

(8) We heard the songs. (वयं गानानि अशृणुम)

(9) I heard the Hindī songs. (अहं हिन्दीगानानि अशृण्वम्)

(10) She lived in Delhi. (सा दिल्याम् अवसत्)

NOTE : The Past Imperfect (लङ्) tense is characterized by the following **six key features**

(1) The action is a past tense of First Praeterite.

(2) ***Paroksa*** परोक्ष action : It includes an action that is NOT witnessed, experienced, heard from the source or seen **by the speaker of the sentence**. e.g. Sitā saw a deer. *Sītā mṛgam apaśyat* (सीता मृगम् अपश्यत्)

(3) ***Anadya*** अनद्य action : The acton performed NOT today. e.g. I stayed here yesterday. *ahaṁ śvaḥ atra eva atiṣṭham* (अहं श्वः अत्र एव अतिष्ठम्)

(4) The verb IS **qualified** by an adjective such as yesterday, day-before-yesterday, last year etc. e.g. Rāma stayed here day-before-yesterday. *Rāmaḥ paraśvaḥ atra eva atiṣṭhat* (रामः परश्वः अत्र एव अतिष्ठत्)

(5) It also denotes an action, of a **recent past, that continues during another action** and is not finished. It generally means an action that did not take place today.

CLASSICAL EXAMPLES :

(i) सञ्जयः उवाच - आचार्यम् उपसङ्गम्य राजा वचनम् अब्रवीत् । Sañjaya said - 'Having gone to Droṇa, Duryodhana said ...' (Gītā 1.2)

In this case, Duryodhana's action of speaking is preceeded by his another action of going to Droṇa. For Sañjaya, Duryodhana's action of speaking, was of recent past. So, अब्रवीत्, the Imperfect tense लङ् of the verb √ब्रू is used.

(ii) "While lamenting he said this." *viṣīdan idam abravīt.* विषीदन् इदम् अब्रवीत् । (Gītā 1.29)

NOTE : **When *ma sma* मा स्म phrase is prefixed** to a लङ् verb, the लङ् prefix अ (अट्) or आ (आट्) is dropped, and **the verb is no more a past tense. It now indicates the meaning of 'do not.'** e.g.

You became a fool. *tvaṁ mūrkhaḥ abhavaḥ* त्वं मूर्खः अभवः । Don't you be a fool. *tvaṁ mūrkhaḥ mā sma bhavaḥ* त्वं मूर्खः मा स्म भवः । See end of lesson 20, item (A).

LESSON 19

navadaśaḥ abhyāsaḥ नवदशः अभ्यासः ।

THE (PAST) PERFECT TENSE

liṭ lakāraḥ

लिट् लकारः ।

This is second of the three past tenses in Sanskrit. This tense is NOT much used in everyday conversation. Its conjugations are difficult. It is mostly found in classical writings such as Mahābhārata, Gītā and Rāmāyaṇa.

Characteristics of the The Perfect tense (लिट् लकारः)

(1) The Perfect tense (लिट् लकार) is the action concluded in absolute or remote past.

(2) It includes an action that is out of sight (*parokṣa* परोक्ष) of the person who is talking about that past event.

e.g. Gītā 1.44 अर्जुनः उवाच । उत्सन्नकुलधर्माणां मनुष्याणां नरके अनियतं वासः भवति इति अनुशुश्रुम ।।
Arjuna said, those who have lost their family traditions have to stay in the hell forever, so we had heard.

(3) (i) लङ् represents actions not prformed today, not seen by the speaker, but is qualified by an adjective. (ii) लिट् represents actions not prformed today, not seen by the speaker, and not qualified by an adjective. (iii) लुङ् represents actions prformed today, and actions seen by the speaker. See the Flow Chart of Tenses, lesson 22.

(4) The Perfect tense (लिट्) is rarely used in the first person. And even in most other cases, in classical Sanskrit, the Imperfect (लङ्) is used in place of the Perfect (लिट्).

TYPICAL SUFFIXES OF THE PERFECT TENSE (लिट्)

TABLE : (All three genders - m◦ f◦ and n◦)

Person	Singular	Dual	Plural
1p◦	**अ (a)**	**व (va)**	**म (ma)**
2p◦	**थ (tha)**	**अथुः (athuḥ)**	**अ (a)**
3p◦	**अ (a)**	**अतुः (atuḥ)**	**उः (uḥ)**

With the verb √श्रु to hear, PERFECT TENSE (m◦f◦n◦)

I heard	अहं शुश्राव	*ahaṁ śuśrāva*	वयं शुश्रुम ।	*vayaṁ śuśruma*
You heard	त्वं शुश्रोथ	*tvaṁ śuśrotha*	यूयं शुश्रुव ।	*yūyaṁ śuśruva*
He heard	सः/सा/तत् शुश्राव	*saḥ śuśrāva*	ते शुश्रुवुः ।	*te śuśrauvaḥ*

The prefix अ, added to the verbs in लङ् and लुङ् past tenses, is not necessary in the लिट् past tense.

CLASSICAL EXAMPLES : from **Rāmāyaṇa and Gītā**

(1) Lakṣmaṇaḥ had done penance. *Lakṣmaṇaḥ tapaḥ ćakāra.* लक्ष्मणः तपः चकार ।

(2) Hanūmān saw Sītā. *Hanūmān Sītāṁ dadarśa.* हनूमान् सीतां ददर्श ।

(3) Gītā 1.12 शङ्खं दध्मौ प्रतापवान् । *śaṅkhaṁ dadhmau pratāpavān.* Bhīṣma blew the conch shell

(4) Gītā 1.14 माधवः पाण्डवः च एव दिव्यौ शङ्खौ प्रदध्मतुः । *Mādhavaḥ Pāṇḍavaḥ ća eva divyau śaṅkhau pradadhmatuḥ.* Kṛṣṇa and Arjuna blew their divine conch shells.

(5) Gītā 1.18 शङ्खान् दध्मुः पृथक्पृथक् । *śaṅkhān dadhmuḥ pṛthak-pṛthak.* They blew their various conch shells.

(6) Gītā 1.25 उवाच पार्थ पश्य एतान् समवेतान् कुरून् इति । *uvāća pārtha paśya etān samavetān kurun iti.* Kṛṣṇa said, Arjuna! look at these Kurus gathered here.

(7) Gītā 2.9 न योत्स्ये इति गोविन्दमुक्त्वा तूष्णीं बभूव ह । *na yotsye iti govindam-uktvā tūṣṇīṁ babhūva ha.* Arjuna, having said to Śrī Kṛṣṇa 'I will not fight,' became quiet.

LESSON 20

viṁśaḥ abhyāsaḥ विंश: अभ्यास: ।

THE AORIST (PAST INDEFINITE) TENSE

luṅ lakāraḥ

लुङ् लकार: ।

This is the third past tense in Sanskrit.
In daily conversation this tense does NOT have much use.

Properties of the Past Indefinite tense (लुङ् लकार:)

(i) It usually indicates an action performed or (ii) happened at a remote past time, (iii) but it is sometimes used for an action performed today or at any past period.

e.g. एकदा एक: राजा आसीत् । Once upon a time there was a king. Or Gītā 18.74 संवादम् अश्रौषम् अद्भुतम् । I heard the wonderful dialogue.

COMPARISON :

(i) लङ् represents actions not prformed today, not seen by the speaker, but is qualified by an adjective.

(ii) लिट् represents actions not prformed today, not seen by the speaker, and not qualified by an adjective.

(iii) लुङ् represents actions prformed today or actions seen by the speaker and not specified by an adjective. It also includes actions witnessed, experienced or heard from someone else by the speaker.

NOTE : For details see the unique Flow Chart of Tenses, given at the end of lesson 22.

TYPICAL SUFFIXES OF THE INDEFINITE PAST TENSE (लुङ्)

TABLE : (Same for all three genders - m◦, f◦ and n◦)

Person	Singular	Dual	Plural
1st person	**सम् (sam)**	**स्व (sva)**	**स्म (sma)**
2nd per◦	**सः (saḥ)**	**स्तम् (stam)**	**स्त (sta)**
3rd person	**ईत् (īt)**	**स्ताम् (stām)**	**सुः न् (suḥ, n)**

NOTE: Prefix अ is prefixed to the verb of लुङ् Indefinite past tense (similar to the Imperfect लङ् past tense).

TABLE : √खाद् to eat, INDEFINITE PAST (m◦f◦n◦)

Person	Singular	Plural
I had been eating	अहम् अखादिषम् *aham akhādiṣam*	वयम् अखादिष्म *vayam akhādiṣma*
You had been eating	त्वम् अखादीः *tvam akhādīḥ*	यूयम् अखादिष्ट *yūyam akhādiṣṭa*
He had been eating	सः अखादीत् *saḥ akhādīt*	ते अखादिषुः *te akhādiṣuḥ*

EXAMPLES cum EXERCISE : (लुङ्)

(1) I had been. *aham abhūvam.* अहम् अभूवम् ।

We had been. *vayam abhūma.* वयम् अभूम ।

(2) You had been. *tvam abhuḥ. yūyam abhūta* त्वम् अभूः। यूयम् अभूत

(3) He/she had been. *saḥ/sā abhūt.* सः, सा अभूत् ।

They had been. *te/tāḥ abhūvan.* ते/ताः अभूवन् ।

(4) I had been working. *aham akārṣam.* अहम् अकार्षम् ।

We had been working. *vayam akārṣma.* वयम् अकार्ष्म ।

(5) You had been working. *tvam akārṣīḥ.* त्वम् अकार्षीः ।

You had been working. *yūyam akārṣṭa.* यूयम् अकार्ष्ट ।

(6) He had been working. *saḥ/sā akārṣīt.* सः अकार्षीत् ।

They had been working. *te/tāḥ akārṣuḥ.* ते/ताः अकार्षुः ।

SIMILARITY BETWEEN

INDEFINITE PAST TENSE लुङ्
AND
IMPERFECT PAST TENSE लङ्

For comparison, see Lesson 17, attachment of particle *sma* स्म ।

(A) When *mā* मा particle is attached to a लुङ् verb :

1. the लुङ् prefix अ (अट्) or आ (आट्) is dropped, now
2. the verb is no more a past tense.
3. Now it is an expression of imperative 'do not.'

(B) When *ma sma* मा स्म phrase is attached to the लङ् verb :

1. the लङ् prefix अ (अट्) or आ (आट्) is dropped, and
2. the verb is no more a past tense.
3. now it indicates the meaning of 'do not.'

EXAMPLES cum EXERCISE :

(1) You became a fool. *tvaṁ mūrkhaḥ abhavaḥ* त्वं मूर्खः अभवः (लङ् Past Imperfect tense)

(2) You had been a fool. *tvaṁ mūrkhaḥ abhūḥ* त्वं मूर्खः अभूः (लुङ् Past Indefinite tense)

(3) Don't you be a fool. *tvaṁ mūrkhaḥ mā bhūḥ* त्वं मूर्खः मा भूः (लोट् Imperative mood)

LESSON 21

ekaviṁśaḥ abhyāsaḥ एकविंशः अभ्यासः ।

* INDEFINITE FUTURE TENSE

THE SIMPLE FUTURE TENSE

lṛṭ lakāraḥ लृट् लकारः ।

This is one of the two future tenses in Sanskrit.

This is the most commonly used Future Tense in Sanskrit.

Properties of the Indefinite Future tense (लृट् लकारः)

(i) The action that will be performed at some unspecified future time, immediate or remote, or

(ii) the action that is contingent up on some future event, is the FUTURE INDEFINITE TENSE लृट्.

NOTE : This tense is also called the 'Simple Future Tense.'

TYPICAL SUFFIXES OF THE INDEFINITE FUTURE लृट्

TABLE : (All three genders - m∘, f∘ and n∘) √खाद् to eat

Person	Singular	Dual	Plural
1p∘	**स्यामि (syāmi)**	**स्यावः (syāvaḥ)**	**स्यामः (syāmaḥ)**
2p∘	**स्यसि (syasi)**	**स्यथः (syathaḥ)**	**स्यथ (syatha)**
3p∘	**स्यति (syati)**	**स्यतः (syataḥ)**	**स्यन्ति (syanti)**

Person	Singular	Plural
I will eat	अहं खादिष्यामि *aham akhādiṣyāmi*	वयं खादिष्यामः *ayaṁ khādiṣyāmaḥ*
You will eat	त्वं खादिष्यसि *tvaṁ khādiṣyasi*	यूयं खादिष्यथ *yūyaṁ khādiṣyatha*
He will eat	सः खादिष्यति *saḥ khādiṣyati*	ते खादिष्यन्ति *te khādiṣyanti.*

NOTE : लृट् represents an action that may be prformed today but not qualified by any specific adjective.

EXAMPLES cum EXERCISE : INDEFINITE FUTURE TENSE

1. The lion will eat the goat. *siṁhaḥ ajaṁ khādiṣyati.* सिंहः अजं खादिष्यति ।
2. The lion will eat the goats. *siṁhaḥ ajān khādiṣyati.* सिंहः अजान् खादिष्यति ।
3. The lions will eat the goat. *siṁhāḥ ajaṁ khādiṣyanti.* सिंहाः अजं खादिष्यन्ति ।
4. I drink milk. *ahaṁ dugdhaṁ pibāmi.* अहं दुग्धं पिबामि ।
5. I will drink milk. *ahaṁ dugdhaṁ pāsyāmi. (√pā)* अहं दुग्धं पास्यामि ।
6. We will drink milk. *vayaṁ dugdhaṁ pāsyāmaḥ.* वयं दुग्धं पास्यामः ।
7. You will drink milk. *tvam (bhavān) dugdhaṁ pāsyasi (pāsyati).* त्वं (भवान्) दुग्धं पास्यसि (पास्यति) ।
8. He will drink. *saḥ pāsyati.* सः पास्यति ।

EXAMPLES : An Exercise on 'what we have learned so far' : Exercise 46 :

(i) Present or Present continuous (लट्), (ii) Past Imperfect (लङ्) and (iii) Indefinite future (लृट्) tense.

For typical Case Declensions and Tense Conjugations,
please see the tables given in the Appendix.

1. I catch a bird. I am catching a bird. *ahaṁ khagaṁ/ćaṭakaṁ/pakṣīṁ/vihagaṁ/ vihaṅgaṁ gṛhaṇāmi (√grah).* अहं खगं/चटकं/पक्षीं/विहगं/विहङ्गं गृह्णामि (√ग्रह) ।
2. I am catching the birds. *ahaṁ khagān/ćaṭakān/pakṣīṇaḥ/ vihagān/vihaṅgān gṛhaṇāmi.* अहं खगान्/चटकान्/पक्षिणः/विहगान्/विहङ्गान् गृह्णामि ।

3. I caught a bird. *aham khagam agṛhṇām* अहं खगम् अगृह्णाम् ।

4. I will catch a bird. *aham khagam grahīṣyāmi.* अहं खगं ग्रहीष्यामि ।

5. The birds catch the fish. *pakṣiṇaḥ matsyān gṛhṇanti.* पक्षिणः मत्स्यान् गृह्णन्ति ।

6. The bird will catch a fish. *pakṣī matsyam grahīṣyati.* पक्षी मत्स्यं ग्रहीष्यति ।

7. The bird will catch the fish. *pakṣī matsyān grahīṣyati.* पक्षी मत्स्यान् ग्रहीष्यति ।

8. The birds will catch the fish. *pakṣiṇaḥ matsyān grahīṣyanti.* पक्षिणः मत्स्यान् ग्रहीष्यन्ति

9. The bird eats seeds; the bird is eating seeds. *pakṣī bījāni khādati.* पक्षी बीजानि खादति

10. The birds ate the seeds. *pakṣiṇaḥ bījāni akhādan.* पक्षिणः बीजानि अखादन् ।

11. The bird will eat the seeds. *khagaḥ/caṭakaḥ/pakṣī/vihagaḥ/vihaṅgaḥ bījāni khādiṣyati.* खगः/चटकः/पक्षी/विहगः/विहङ्गः बीजानि खादिष्यति ।

12. The Sun will shine. *sūryaḥ tapsyati.* सूर्यः तप्स्यति ।

13. The clouds will thunder (roar). *meghāḥ garjiṣyanti.* मेघाः गर्जिष्यन्ति ।

14. It will rain. *varṣā bhaviṣyati.* वर्षा भविष्यति ।

15. The light will flash. *ālokaḥ/prakāśaḥ/bhā/ābhā/prabhā sphuriṣyati.* आलोकः/प्रकाशः/भा/आभा/प्रभा स्फुरिष्यति ।

16. The boy will be agitated. *bālakaḥ kṣobhiṣyati.* बालकः क्षोभिष्यति ।

17. The peacock will dance. *mayūraḥ/kekī nartsyati.* मयूरः/केकी नर्त्स्यति ।

18. The man burns the grass; the man is burning the grass. *naraḥ tṛṇam/ghāsam dahati.* नरः तृणं/घासं दहति ।

19. The man will burn the grass. *naraḥ tṛṇam dhakṣyati.* नरः तृणं धक्ष्यति ।

20. The man burned the grass. *naraḥ tṛṇam adhākṣīt.* नरः तृणम् अधाक्षीत् ।

21. The man had burned the grass. *naraḥ ghāsam dadāha.* नरः घासं ददाह ।

22. The bee will wander about. *bhramaraḥ bhramiṣyati.* भ्रमरः भ्रमिष्यति ।

23. The honey-bee wandered about. *madhukaraḥ, bhramaraḥ* मधुकरः अभ्रमत् ।

24. The eagle will build a nest. *garuḍaḥ nīḍaṁ racayiṣyati.* गरुडः नीडं रचयिष्यति ।

25. He deserves; he is deserving. *saḥ arhati.* सः अर्हति ।

26. She will deserve. *sā arhiṣyati* सा अर्हिष्यति ।

27. I am hearing chirping of the cuckoo; I hear the cuckoo chirp. *ahaṁ kokilakūjanam ākarṇayāmi.* अहं कोकिलकूजनम् आकर्णयामि ।

28. He is getting angry. *saḥ kupyati.* सः कुप्यति ।

29. He will be angry. *saḥ kopiṣyati.* सः कोपिष्यति ।

30. The parrot is cutting a leaf; the parrot cuts a leaf. *śukaḥ parṇaṁ kṛntati.* शुकः पर्णं कृन्तति ।

31. He will cut leaves. *saḥ parṇān kartiṣyati/kartsyati.* सः पर्णान् कर्तिष्यति/कर्त्स्यति ।

32. A woodpecker will dig wood. *kāṣṭhakūṭaḥ kāṣṭhaṁ khaniṣyati.* काष्ठकूटः काष्ठं खनिष्यति ।

33. The cuckoo will sing. *kokilaḥ gāsyati.* कोकिलः गास्यति ।

34. The pigeon will eat worms. *kapotaḥ kīṭakān/kṛmīn khādiṣyati.* कपोतः कीटकान्/कृमीन् खादिष्यति ।

35. The crow will eat a mouse. *kākaḥ/vāyasaḥ mūṣakaṁ khādiṣyati.* काकः/वायसः मूषकं खादिष्यति ।

EXERCISE 47 : (A) Fill in the blanks :

(1) The swan will eat the fish. -------- मत्स्यं --------

(2) The heron will drink water. -------- जलं पास्यति ।

(3) The hens and the cock will eat seeds. -------- च -------- च बीजानि --------

(4) The earthworms will dig the earth. भूजन्तवः -------- खनिष्यन्ति ।

LESSON 22

dvāviṁśaḥ abhyāsaḥ द्वाविंशः अभ्यासः ।

THE DEFINITE FUTURE TENSE

luṭ lakāraḥ लुट् लकारः ।

This is the second future tenses in Sanskrit. This tense is NOT a very commonly used future tense.

Characteristics of the Definite Future tense (लुट् लकारः)

(1) The Definite Future tense लुट् represents actions not prformed today, but qualified by an adjective.

The Indefinite Future tense लृट् (which we studied earlier) represents actions prformed today, but not qualified by an adjective.

See the Flow Chart of Tenses at the end of this lesson.

(2) The लुट् tense denotes an action that will take place at a definite future time (including today), but neither immediate nor at remote time.

e.g. Gītā 2.52 तदा गन्तासि निर्वेदम् । Then you will attain detachment.

TYPICAL SUFFIXES OF THE DEFINITE FUTURE लुट्

TABLE : (All three genders - m◦, f◦ and n◦)

Person	Singular	Dual	Plural
1p◦	**तास्मि *(tāsmi)***	**तास्वः *(tāsvaḥ)***	**तास्मः *(tāsmaḥ)***
2p◦	**तासि *(tāsi)***	**तास्थः *(tāsthaḥ)***	**तास्थ *(tāstha)***
3p◦	**ता *(tā)***	**तारौ *(tārau)***	**तारः *(tāraḥ)***

TABLE : √खाद् to eat, INDEFINITE FUTURE (m◦f◦n◦)

I will eat	अहं खादितास्मि	वयं खादितास्मः
	ahaṁ khāditāsmi	*vayaṁ khāditāsmaḥ*
you will eat	त्वं खादितासि	यूयं खादितास्थ
	tvayaṁ khāditāsi	*yuayaṁ khāditāstha*
he will eat	सः/सा/तत् खादिता	ते/ताः/तानि खादितारः
	saḥ/sā/tat khāditā	*te/tāḥ/tāni khāditāraḥ*

NEW WORDS TO LEARN:

(1) Today (*adya* अद्य)

(2) Yesterday (*hyaḥ* ह्यः)

(3) Tomorrow (*śvaḥ* श्वः)

(4) Later (*paśćāt* पश्चात्)

(5) Day after tomorrow (*para-śvaḥ* परश्वः)

(6) Day before yesterday (*para-hyaḥ* परह्यः)

(7) Then (*tadā* तदा)

(8) When (*yadā* यदा)

(9) When? (*kadā?* कदा?)

(10) Whenever (*yadā yadā* यदा यदा)

(11) Any time (*yadā kadā* यदा कदा)

(12) Sometimes (*kadācit* कदाचित्)

(13) At this time, Now (*asmin kāle, adhunā, idānīm* अस्मिन् काले, अधुना, इदानीम्)

EXAMPLES cum EXERCISE :

(1) I will do it tomorrow. *aham etat śvaḥ kartāsmi.* अहम् एतत् श्वः कर्तास्मि ।

(2) Then he will go. *tadā saḥ gantā.* तदा सः गन्ता ।

(3) I will come when it will rain. *yadā varṣiṣyati tadā āgantāsmi.* यदा वर्षिष्यति तदा आगन्तास्मि ।

(4) We will tell you the day after tomorrow. *vayaṁ tvāṁ (bhavantaṁ) paraśvaḥ kathayitāsmaḥ.* वयं त्वां (भवन्तं) परश्वः कथयितास्मः ।

(5) You will become. *tvaṁ bhavitāsi; bhavān bhavitā; bhavatī bhavitā.* त्वं भवितासि । भवान् भविता । भवती भविता ।

EXERCISE 48 : Match the English and Sanskrit words

(1) Tomorrow	(1) अद्य
(2) Day before yesterday	(2) ह्यः
(3) When	(3) श्वः
(4) Today	(4) तदा
(5) Day after tomorrow	(5) कदा?
(6) Yesterday	(6) परश्वः
(7) Then	(7) परह्यः
(8) When?	(8) यदा

EXERCISE 49 : What we learned so far

SUMMARY of POPULAR TENSES

Present (लट्), Imperfect (लङ्) and Indefinite Future (लृट्)

Correct the Sanskrit sentences to match with English ones.

(1) I eat fruits. *ahaṁ phalaṁ khādiṣyāmi.* अहं फल खादिष्यामि ।

(2) You are looking at the peacock. *bhavān vāyasaṁ paṣyati.* भवान् वायसं पश्यति ।

(3) He wrote a letter. *sā patram alikhat/likhitavān.* सा पत्रम् अलिखत्/लिखितवान् ।

(4) She will become. *sāḥ bhavitāsmi.* सा: भवितास्मि । भवती भविष्यती ।

(5) They will bring milk. *te/tāḥ dūgdha āniṣyati.* ते/ता: दूग्ध आनिष्यति ।

(6) I am learning Sanskrit. *ahaṁ saṁskṛtaṁ paṭhiṣyāmi.* अहं संस्कृतं पठिष्यामि ।

(7) Rāma is reading the book. *Rāma pustakaṁ paṭhanti.* राम पुस्तकं पठन्ति ।

(8) The tiger will eat the goat. *vyāghrāḥ ajaṁ khādanti.* व्याघ्रा: अजं खादन्ति ।

(9) Birds will build a nest. *khagaḥ nīḍaṁ raćayiṣyati.* खग: नीडं रचयिष्यति ।

(10) The horse ran. *aśvaḥ adhāvata.* अश्व: अधावत ।

(11) We ran. *vayam adhāvam.* वयम् अधावाम् ।

(12) I know Sanskrit. *ahaṁ hindīṁ jānāmi.* अहं हिन्दीं जानामि ।

(13) They ate. *sā akhādat.* सा अखादत् ।

(14) Monkeys are eating fruits. *kapayaḥ phalaṁ khādanti.* कपय: फलं खादन्ति ।

(15) A fruit is falling from the tree. *phalam vṛkṣāt apatat.* फलं वृक्षात् अपतत् ।

(16) A leaf fell from the vine. *parṇa latāyāḥ apatat.* पर्ण लताया: अपतत् ।

(17) He is a boy. *saḥ bālakaḥ bhavati.* स: बालक: भवति ।

(18) She will go home. *sā gṛham āgamiṣyati.* सा गृहम् आगमिष्यति ।

22.2 RATNAKAR'S FLOWCHART FOR - WHICH TENSE TO USE?

(1) Has the action started? Is it a habitual action? **YES : Go to 2↓**

NO : Go to 10↓

(2) Has the action finished? **YES : Go to 4↓**

NO : Go to 3↓

(3) This action is a **Present** tense (लट्)

(4) Was it a today's event? **YES : Go to 5↓**

NO : Go to 6↓

(5) This action is a **Past Indefinite** tense (लुङ्)

(6) Was it witnessed by the speaker? **YES : Go to 5↑**

NO : Go to 7↓

(7) Is there an adjective such as 'today, yesterday, last year' ...etc. attached to the action?

YES : Go to 8↓

NO : Go to 9↓

(8) This action is a **Past Imperfect** tense (लङ्)

(9) This action is a **Past Perfect** tense (लिट्)

(10) Will this be a today's action? **YES : Go to 11↓**

NO : Go to 12↓

(11) This action is an **Indefinite Future** tense (लृट्)

(12) Is there an adjective such as today, tomorrow, next year ...etc. attached to the action?

YES : Go to 13↓

NO : Go to 11↑

(13) This action is a **Definite Future** tense (लुट्)

(14) Is the action specified with particle *mā* (मा)? Go to 5↑

Is it specified with the phrase *mā sma* (मा स्म)? Go to 8↑

LESSON 23

trayoviṁśaḥ abhyāsaḥ त्रयोविंशः अभ्यासः ।

FORMS OF THE VERBS

23.1

PARASMAIPADĪ AND ĀTMANEPADĪ VERBS

parasmaipadī ātmanepadī ća

परस्मैपदी आत्मनेपदी च ।

A Unique feature of the Sanskṛt language, *ātmanepadam* and *parasmaipadam* denotes : To whom the fruit of an action accrues? or who is the intended victim of the action?

(1) *ātmanepada* of a verb indicates that the fruit of an action accrues to the doer (*ātma* आत्म) of action, and thus the action is *ātmanepadī*, e.g. *nirīkṣe* (Gītā 1.22) 1st◦ sing◦, 'I observe for myself,' (*nirīkṣe;* निरीक्षे, उत्तमपुरुषः एकवचनं लट् भ्वादिः आत्मनेपदी ←निर्√ईक्ष्).

(2) *parasmaipada* of a verb indicates that the fruit of an action accrues to someone other (*para* पर) than the doer of that action. e.g. *bravīmi* Gītā 1.7, 1st◦ sing◦, 'I am telling you,' (*bravīmi;* ब्रवीमि, उत्तमपुरुषः एकवचनं लट् अदादिः परस्मैपदी ←√ब्रू).

This distinction, however, appears to be not observed strictly in practice. And, therefore, we have verbs which indicate accrual of the fruit of an action to the doer (i.e. *ātmanepadī*) but is sometimes optionally used in the *parasmaipadī* form, as if the action is offered to oneself, as a third person. e.g.

(i) *Saḥ naiva kiñćit karoti* (Gītā 4.20) 'he does not do anything.' सः न एव किञ्चित् करोति । (**करोति** 3rd person, singular लट् तनादिः परस्मैपदी ←√कृ).

(ii) *Saḥ yat pramāṇaṁ kurute* (Gītā 3.21) 'the standard he sets.' सः यत् प्रमाणं कुरुते । (**कुरुते,**

3rd person singular लट् तनादि: आत्मनेपदी ←√कृ).

Of course, in Sanskrit language, when there are dual verb roots, that stand for both the doer as well as the object (*ubhayapadī,* उभयपदी), this distinction of *Parasmaipadī* and *Ātmanepadī* can not always be observed meticulously.

BE CAREFUL :

In order to avoid the common errors, care must be taken not to confused in the distinction between *Parasmaipadī* and Ātmanepadī characterics of the verbs with :

(1) the passive (*karmaṇi* कर्मणि) and active (*kartari* कर्तरि) usage of the voices (*prayogāḥ* प्रयोगा:)

(2) with the intransitive (*akarmakam* अकर्मकम्) and transitive (*sakarmakam* सकर्मकम्) attributes of the verbs (क्रियापदानि)

(3) Many times Ātmanepadī is confused and translated as Middle Voice, but Ātmanepadī is not a voice. The voices are : कर्तरि, कर्मणि and भावे *kartari* (active)*, karmaṇi* (passive) and *bhāve* (abstract). They are discribed in Lesson 26.

(i) The verbs such as अटति, करोति, पचति, याचति are transitive of the *parasmaipadī* Active voice (कर्तरि: प्रयोग:)

(ii) the verbs अटते, कुरुते, ईक्षते, पचते, लभते, याचते are intransitive of the *ātmanepadī* Active voice verb (9√jñā) *jānate* जानते is transitive ātmanepadī.

(iii) and the verbs अट्यते, ईक्ष्यते, पच्यते, लभ्यते, याच्यते are transitive /intransitive *ātmanepadī* of the Passive voice (कर्मणि प्रयोग:)

In the Active voice, both Transitive and Intransitive verbs are used. But, in the Passive voice only Transitive verbs are used, and therefore, many people misunderstand *ātmanepadī* as 'passive voice.' In the *Bhāve* voice, only Intransitive verbs are used. **ātmanepadī is not a voice, it is a characterics of the verbs.**

NOTE : Which verb roots are *Parasmaipadī* and which ones are *Ātmanepadī* is to be found through a good Sanskrit Dictionary or from everyday experience. There is no other easy way to determine it. के धातवः परस्मैपदयः के धातवः आत्मनेपदयः के च धातवः उभयपदयः इति तु शब्दकोशबलात् व्यवहारबलात् वा ज्ञातव्यम् । एतां व्यवस्थां ज्ञातुं सामान्यरीतिः अन्या का अपि नास्ति ।

In earlier lessons we have learned and used several *Parasmaipadī* verbs, let us now learn some *Ātmanepadī* vebs and see some Dual verbs.

(i) The verbs like भवति, गच्छति, लिखति ending in ति are *parasmaipadī*;

(ii) The verbs रोचते, ईक्षते, वन्दते ending ते or ए are *ātmanepadī* and

(iii) The verbs करोति/कुरुते, पचति/पचते, याचति/याचते are dual (उभयपदी) verbs.

See the Dictionary of Verbs given in Appendix 5 and Conjugations given in Appendix 7.

TYPICAL SUFFIXES OF THE ĀTMANEPADĪ PRESENT TENSE (लट्)

TABLE : (All three genders - m∘, f∘ and n∘)

Person	Singular	Dual	Plural
1p∘	**ए. ई *e, ī***	**आवहे, वहे *āvahe, vahe***	**आमहे, महे *āmahe, mahe***
2p∘	**से *se***	**आथे, इथे *āthe, ithe***	**ध्वे *dhve***
3p∘	**ते *te***	**आते, इते *āte, ite***	**अते, अन्ते *ate, ante***

TABLE : √क्लृप् to be fit, PRESENT (m∘f∘n∘)

Person	Singular	Plural
I am fit	अहं कल्पे *ahaṁ kalpe*	वयं कल्पामहे *vayaṁ kalpāmahe*
You are fit	त्वं कल्पसे tvaṁ kalpase	यूयं कल्पध्वे *yūyaṁ kalpadhve*
He is fit	सः कल्पते *saḥ kalpate*	ते कल्पन्ते *te/tāḥ/tāni kalpante*

EXAMPLES cum EXERCISE : ĀTMANEPADĪ VERBS

(1) to be fit, to deserve (√क्लृप्) कल्पे/कल्पसे/कल्पते ।

(2) to see (√ईक्ष्) ईक्षे/ईक्षसे/ईक्षते; ईक्ष्ये/ईक्ष्यसे/ईक्ष्यते ।

(3) to be, to exist (√विद्) विद्ये/विद्यसे/विद्यते ।

(4) to desire (√कम्) कामये/कामयसे/कामयते ।

(5) to jump and play (√कुर्द्) कूर्दे/कूर्दसे/कूर्दते ।

(6) to happen (√घट्) घटे/घटसे/घटते ।

(7) to bargain (√पण्) पणे/पणसे/पणते ।

(8) to walk (√पद्) पद्ये/पद्यसे/पद्यते ।

(9) to begin (आ√रभ्) आरभे/आरभसे/आरभते ।

(10) to get (√लभ्) लभे/लभसे/लभते ।

(11) to increase (√वृध्) वर्धे/वर्धसे/वर्धते ।

(12) to look good (√शुभ्) शोभे/शोभसे/शोभते ।

(13) to exist (√वृत्) वर्ते/वर्तसे/वर्तते ।

(14) to say (√चक्ष्) चक्षे/चक्षे/चष्टे । pl॰ चक्ष्महे/चढ्वे/चक्षते ।

(15) to grow (√एध्) एधे/एधसे/एधते । एध्ये/एध्यसे/एध्यते ।

THE CLASSICAL EXAMPLES of Ātmanepadī usage

(1) He deserves immortality स: अमृतत्वाय कल्पते । (Gītā 2.15)

(2) He sees same everywhere. स: ईक्षते समदर्शन: (Gītā 6.29)

(3) Nonexistance does not exist. न असत: विद्यते भाव: । (Gītā 2.16)

(4) He who takes it by heart. य: मनसा आरभते । (Gītā 3.7)

(5) The faithful person attains knowledge. श्रद्धावान् लभते ज्ञानम् । (4.39)

(6) He exists in me. स: मयि वर्तते । (Gītā 6.31)

(7)जीर्यन्ते जीर्यत: केशा: दन्ता: जीर्यन्ति जीर्यत: ।
क्षीयते जीर्यते सर्वं तृष्णैवेका न जीर्यते ।।28।।

NOTE: The *Ātmanepadi* verbs can be translated into *Parasmaipadī* verbs. e.g.

(आत्म०) आरभते → (पर०) आरम्भं करोति । आरभे →आरम्भं करोमि ।

(आत्म०) वन्दते → (पर०) वन्दनां करोति । वन्दे → वन्दनां करोमि ।

(आत्म०) लभते → (पर०) प्राप्तं करोति । लभे → प्राप्तं करोमि ।

EXERCISE 50 : Fill in Sanskrit Ātmanepadī verbs.

(1) It happens. एतत् --------- (2) It looks good. एतत् ---------

(3) She attains. सा --------- (4) He jumps सः ---------

(5) I desire अहं --------- (6) He bargains. सः ---------

EXAMPLES OF DUAL VERBS :

(Dual = atmanepadī and *parasmaipadī* both)

(1) to hold (√भृ)

बिभर्मि/बिभर्षि/बिभर्ति । बिभ्रे/विभृषे/बिभृते । अहं बिभर्मि, अहं बिभ्रे ।

(2) to roam (√अट्)

अटामि/अटसि/अटति । अटे/अटसे/अटते । त्वम् अटसि, त्वम् अटसे ।

(3) to desire (√कांक्ष्)

कांक्षामि/कांक्षसि/कांक्षति । कांक्षे/कांक्षसे/कांक्षते । सः कांक्षति, सः कांक्षते ।

(4) to do (√कृ)

करोमि/करोषि/करोति । कुर्वे/कुरुषे/कुरुते । सा करोति, सः कुरुते ।

(5) to seize (√ग्रह्)

गृह्णामि/गृह्णासि/गृह्णाति । गृह्णे/गृह्णीषे/गृह्णीते । रामः गृह्णाति, रामः गृह्णिते ।

(6) to spread (√तन्)

तनोमि/तनोषि/तनोति । तन्वे/तनुषे/तनुते । सीता तनोति, सीता तनुते ।

(7) to speak (√कथ्)

कथयामि/कथयसि/कथयति । कथये/कथयसे/कथयते । इति कथयति, इति कथयते ।

23.2

THE TRANSITIVE AND INTRANSITIVE VERBS

sakarmakam akarmakaṁ ća

सकर्मकम् अकर्मकं च । सकर्मकमकर्मकञ्च ।

For Example : (i) Rāma eats. *Rāmaḥ khādati.* रामः खादति ।

(ii) Rāma sits. *Rāmaḥ upaviśati.* रामः उपविशति ।

(1) In the first sentence, when we say Rāma eats, the question arises Rāma eats 'what?' *Rāmaḥ kiṁ khādati?* रामः किं खादति? The answer may be Rāma eats rice. *Rāmaḥ odanaṁ khādati.* रामः ओदनं खादति । Therefore, 'to eat' is a TRANSITIVE VERB (action transferred to an external object).

(2) In second sentence, Rāma sits. There is no 'what' type of question, or there is no answer to such question. Thus, 'to sit' is an INTRANSITIVE VERB (action not transferred to external object, but stays <u>in</u> the subject).

लजा-सत्ता-स्थिति-जागरणं वृद्धि-क्षय-भय-जीवित-मरणम् ।
शयन-क्रीडा-रुचि-दीप्त्यर्थं धातुगणं तमकर्मकमाहुः ।।

क्रियापदम् उद्दिश्य किम्/कम्/काम् इति प्रश्नः यदा क्रियते तदा उत्तरं प्राप्तं चेत् तत् क्रियापदं सकर्मकम् ज्ञातव्यम् । क्रियापदम् उद्दिश्य किम्/कम्/काम् इति समानः प्रश्नः यदा क्रियते तदा चेत् उत्तरं न प्राप्तं तत् क्रियापदम् अकर्मकम् ज्ञातव्यम् ।

NOTE: As pointed out earlier, there is no relation between *Parasmaipadī*/Ātmanepadī and Transitive/Intransitive attributes of the verbs. However, transitive and intransitive verbs could be *parasmaipadī* or *ātmanepadī.*

सकर्मक/अकर्मक/व्यवस्थायाः परस्मैपदी/आत्मनेपदी-व्यवस्थायाः च कः अपि सम्बन्धः नास्ति । सकर्मक-क्रियापदानि अकर्मक-क्रियापदानि च परस्मैपदेषु आत्मनेपदेषु च अपि क्रियापदेषु भवन्ति ।

EXAMPLES : TRANSITIVE VERBS:

(The verbs in examples 1, 3, 5, 7, 9 are Transitive; and the verbs in examples 2, 4, 6, 8 are Intransitive)

(1) The boy throws. The boy throws what? The boy throws a ball. *bālakaḥ kandukaṁ kṣipati.* बालक: कन्दुकं क्षिपति ।

(2) The girl laughs. बाला हसति । No 'what?' type of question.

(3) Rāma writes. Rāma writes what? Rāma writes a letter. *Rāmaḥ patraṁ likhati.* राम: पत्रं लिखति ।

(4) The bird flies. पक्षी डयते । No 'what?' type of question.

(5) She flies. She flies what? She flies an airplane. *sā vāyu-yānam uḍḍīyate.* सा वायुयानम् उड्डाययति ।

(6) The stone falls. प्रस्तरं पतति । No 'what?' question.

(7) I bring. I bring what? I bring a book. *ahaṁ pustakam ānayāmi.* अहं पुस्तकम् आनयामि ।

(8) The leaf falls. पर्णं पतति । No 'what?' question.

(9) She sings. She sings what? She sings a song. *sā gītaṁ gāyati.* सा गीतं गायति ।

EXERCISE 51 : Name the verbs, transitive or intransitive?

(1) सिंह: धावति । siṁhaḥ dhāvati ————— (√धाव् √dhāv)

(2) अज: तृणं खादति । ajaḥ tṛṇaṁ khādati ————— (√खाद् √khād)

(3) बालिका रोदिति । bālikā roditi ————— (√रुद् √rud)

(4) काष्ठ: ज्वलयति । kāṣṭhaḥ jvalati ————— (√ज्वल् √jval)

(5) सा जलं पिबति । sā jalaṁ pibati ————— (√पा √pā)

(6) वृश्चिक: दंशति । vṛścikaḥ daṁśati ————— (√दंश् √daṁś)

(7) सा नृत्यति । sā nṛtyati ————— (√नृत् √nṛt)

(8) ता: पचन्ति । tāḥ paćanti ————— (√पच् √pać)

(9) स: क्लाम्यति । saḥ klāmyati ————— (√क्लम् √klam)

23.3

THE CAUSATIVE VERBS

ṇyanta/ṇijanta/prayojaka-prakriyā

ण्यन्त/णिजन्त/प्रयोजक-प्रक्रिया ।

When a verb is (caused to be) performed through someone else, the verb is causative.

Causative means 'getting the work done,' as against 'doing' the work. Generally the causative (ण्यन्त *ṇyanta*) verbs are called णिजन्त *ṇijanta* or प्रयोजक *prayojak* verbs.

Grammatically the causative verbs are णिजन्त *(ṇijanta)* verbs, because they are formed by dding णिच् *(ṇić)* suffix to the √root verbs (णिच् अन्त = णिजन्त).

e.g. *√paṭh* √पठ् to learn. *paṭhati* पठति learns. *pāṭhayati* पाठयति teaches = causes to learn.

(i) (√*paṭh*)	√पठ् + णिच् + वृद्धि:	= पाठि	teaching	
(ii)	पाठि + विकरण अ	= **पाठय**	**to teach**	अहं पाठयामि । (पाठय+आमि)
(iii)	पाठय + आमि	= पाठयामि	I teach	
	पाठय + आम:	= पाठयाम:	We teach	
	पाठय + सि	= पाठयसि	You teach	भवान् पाठयति ।
	पाठय + ति	= पाठयति	He/she teaches	स:, सा, भवान् पाठयति ।
	पाठय + न्ति	= पाठयन्ति	They teach	ते, ता:, भवन्त: पाठयन्ति ।

EXAMPLES :

(1) To listen √श्रु + णिच् + वृद्धि: = श्रावि + अ = श्रावय to cause to listen. For causative Sanskrit expressions there are no proper single-word expressions in English

language, however, most of the Indian languages do have them.

In Hindi it is सुनाना. Same is true for other Sankkrit causative verbs, viz◦

स्नापय = नहलाना । घातय = मरवाना । दापय = दिलवाना ...etc.

There are such causative single-word expressions in the Indian languages, derived from Sanskrit.

(2) To be √भू + णिच् + वृद्धिः = भावि + अ = भावय + सि = भावयसि *bhāvayasi* you cause, you are causing.

(3) To begin आ√रभ् + णिच् + वृद्धिः = आरम्भि + अ = आरम्भय + ति = आरभयति *ārabhayati* he, she, it causes to start.

(4) To kill √हन् + णिच् + वृद्धिः = घाति + अ = घातय *ghātaya* to get killed, to cause to die.

(5) To give √दा + णिच् + वृद्धिः = दापि + अ = दापय *dāpaya* to cause to give

(6) To go √या + णिच् + वृद्धिः = यापि + अ = यापय + आमि = यापयामि *yāpayāmi* I send.

(7) Please give a bath to the baby. *bālakaṁ snāpayatu.* बालकं स्नापयतु ।

(8) Having spent (caused to pass) twelve years in the forest, the Pāṇḍavas went to Virāṭa. *dvādaśa-varṣāṇi vane yāpayitvā Pāṇḍavāḥ virāṭa-nagaram agacchan (jagmuḥ).* द्वादशवर्षाणि वने यापयित्वा पाण्डवाः विराटनगरम् अगच्छन् (जग्मुः) ।

(9) I caused-to-be-listened (Hindī → सुनाया) a song yesterday. *ahaṁ hyaḥ gītam aśrāvayam.* अहं ह्यः गीतम् अश्रावयम् ।

23.4
THE DESIDERATIVE VERBS
sannanta/icchārtha-prakriyā सन्नन्त/इच्छार्थक-प्रक्रिया ।

When the verb indicates a desire of the doer of an action (subject), the verb is desiderative.

The desiderative verbs are generally called इच्छार्थक *(icchārthak)* verbs.

Grammatically they are सन्नन्त *(sannant)* verbs, because they are formed by adding सन् *(san)* suffix to the √root verbs (सन् अन्त = सन्नन्त).

NOTE : A verb receives the *san* सन् suffix, **only when the doer of that verb is the same as the doer of the desire.**

CHARACTERISTICS :

(i) When *san* सन् suffix is attached to a verb, the first letter of that verb is doubled and only *sa* स of the *san* सन् is added to this modified verb.

(ii) All कृत् suffixes given in lesson 28 (तव्यत्, अनीयर, यत्, क्त, क्तवतु, क्त्वा, णमुल, णिनि, तुमुन् ...) can form desiderative verbs.

(iii) Desiderative verbs are formed from both *parasmaipadī* and *ātmanepadī* verbs.

(iv) The two specific forms of desiderative verbs formed with सन् suffix are :

(a) ADJECTIVES formed with particle *u* उ

To read √पठ् + सन् = पिपठिष् = desire of reading

पिपठिष् + उ = पिपठिषु = One who desires to read.(adjective)

(b) FEMININE NOUNS formed with particle अ *a*

To read √पठ् + सन् = पिपठिष् = desire of reading

पिपठिष् + अ = पिपठिषा = f◦ the desire to read. (noun)

EXAMPLES :

(1) I desire to read the Gītā. *ahaṁ Gītāṁ pipaṭhiṣāmi.* अहं गीतां पिपठिषामि ।

(2) You want to read Rāmāyaṇa. *bhavān Rāmāyaṇaṁ pipaṭhiṣati.* भवान् रामायणं पिपठिषति ।

(3) She likes to read Mahābhārata. *sā Mahābhārataṁ pipaṭhiṣati.* सा महाभारतं पिपठिषति ।

23.5

THE FREQUENTATIVE VERBS

yaṅanta/yaṅluganta-prakriye यङन्त/यङ्लुगन्त-प्रक्रिये ।

When a verb indicates repetition or excess of an action, the verb is frequentative. The frequentative अतिरेकार्थक *(atirekārthak)* verbs are called यङन्त *(yaṅant)* or यङ्लुगन्त *(yaṅlugant)* verbs, because they are formed by adding यङ् *(yaṅ)* or यङ्लुक् *(yaṅ-luk)* suffixes to the √root verbs (यङ् अन्त = यङन्त । यङ्लुक + अन्त = यङ्लुगन्त).

While यङ् is used as an *ātmanepadi* suffix, and यङ्लुक् is used as a *parasmaipadī* suffix, both of these suffixes impart same meaning to the verb.

All the कृत् suffixes given in lesson 28 (तव्यत्, अनीयर, यत्, क्त, क्तवतु, क्त्वा, णमुल, णिनि, तुमुन् ..) can form the frequentive verbs.

HOW TO MAKE A यङन्त FREQUENTIVE VERB

(1) The initial letter of the verb root is doubled, (2) letter अ is added to the initial letter, (3) य is suffixed to form a यङन्त frequentive verb, (4a) to this frequentive verb, either tense suffixes are attached, after step 3. (4b) or a *kṛt* कृत् suffix is added, after the step 2.

i. to learn √पठ् → पपठ् + अ = पापठ् + य = पापठ्य to read over and over or to read a lot.

ii. पापठ्य + ए = पापठ्ये	I read over and over	
पापठ्य + से = पापठ्यसे	You read over and over	
पापठ्य + ते = पापठ्यते	He, she reads over and over	सः, सा, भवान् पापठ्यते ।
पापठ्य + अन्ते = पापठ्यन्ते	They read over and over	

iii. पापठ् + तव्यत् = पापठितव्य	Ought to read over and over
पापठ् + यत् = पापठ्य	Must be read over and over
पापठ् + अनीयर् = पापठनीय	Worth reading over and over

पापठ् + क्त्वा = पापठित्वा	Having read over and over
परि-पापठ् + य = परिपापठ्य	Having read again and again
पापठ् + इट् + क्त = पापठित	Read over and over!
पापठ् + इट् + क्तवतु = पापठितवत्	Read over and over
पापठ् + णमुल् = पापठं पापठम्	Reading over and over, again and again
पापठ् + तृच् = पापठितृ	One who reads over and over
पापठ् + ण्वुल् = पापठक	Makes read over and over
पापठ् + इट् + तुमुन् = पापठितुम्	For reading over and over
पापठ् + अ = पापठा (noun)	Reading over and over
पापठ्+शानच्=पापठ्यमान (Gerund)	While reading over and over

HOW TO MAKE A यङ्लुगन्त FREQUENTIVE VERB

(1) While adding the यङ्-लुक् suffix, the initial letter of the root verb is doubled and अ is added to the first letter of this modified verb.

(2) If it is a सेट् verb, then इ is optionally added to form a यङ्लुगन्त frequentive verb. Tense suffixs are then attached to this modified verb. (for सेट्/अनिट् verbs, see 28.6↓)

(i) To learn √पठ् → पपठ् + अ = पापठ् + इ = पापठि to read over and over or to read a lot.

(ii) पापठि + मि = पापठीमि, पापठ्मि	I read over and over	
पापठि + सि = पापठीषि, पापट्षि	You read a lot	
पापठि + ति = पापठीति, पापट्टि	He she reads a lot	सः, सा, भवान् पापठीति, पापट्टि ।
पापठि + अन्ते = पापठ्यन्ते	They read a lot	

FORMATION OF TENSES AND MOODS

From a frequentive verb (*pāpaṭhi* पापठि), all tenses, moods and participles can be formed. (लिट्) पापठाञ्चकार, (लुट्) पापठिता, (लृट्) पापठिष्यति, (लङ्) अपापठीत्, (लुङ्) अपपाठीत्, (लृङ्) अपापठिष्यत्; (लोट्) पापठितु; (तव्यत्) पापठितव्य, (अनीयर्) पापठनीय, (क्त्वा) पापठित्वा, (तुमुन्) पापठितुम्, (शतृ) पापठितवत्, (क्त) पापठित ...etc.

LESSON 24

ćaturviṁśaḥ abhyāsaḥ चतुर्विंशः अभ्यासः ।

THE ELEVEN CLASSES OF VERBS

gaṇāḥ गणाः ।

Laghu Siddhānta Kaumudi has divided the 2200 verb √roots into eleven classes (एकादशगणाः *ekādaśagaṇāḥ*). धातुएँ भ्वादि-अदादि, जुहो-दिवा-स्वा-तुदादि ।
रुधा-तना-क्र्या-चुरादि, होती हैं शेष कण्ड्वादि ।। (Gītā Kā Śabdakośa pp◦ 376)

The कण्ड्वादि *kaṇḍvādi* class is ignored by most grammarians. The remaining group of ten classes (गणाः *gaṇāḥ*) is : भ्वाद्यदादिजुहोत्यादिर्दिवादिः स्वादिरेव च ।
तुदादिश्च रुधादिश्च तनादिक्रीचुरादयः ।।30।।
bhvādyadādijuhotyādirdivādiḥ svādireva ća,
tudādiśća rudhādiśća tanādikrīćurādayaḥ

* 1st	भ्वादि	* *bhvādi*	√भू-आदि	√*bhū*	(to be)	भवामि, भवसि, भवति
2nd	अदादि	*adādi*	√अद्-आदि	√*ad*	(to eat)	अद्मि, अत्सि, अत्ति
3rd	जुहोत्यादि	*juhotyāi*	√हु-आदि	√*hu*	(to offer)	जुहोमि, जुहोषि, जुहोति
* 4th	दिवादि	* *divādi*	√दिव्-आदि	√*div*	(to shine)	दीव्यामि, दीव्यसि, दीव्यति
5th	स्वादि	*svādi*	√सु-आदि	√*su*	(to bathe)	सुनोमि, सुनोषि, सुनोति
* 6th	तुदादि	* *tudādi*	√तुद्-आदि	√*tud*	(to hurt)	तुदामि, तुदसि, तुदति
7th	रुधादि	*rudhādi*	√रुध्-आदि	√*rudh*	(to inhibit)	रुणध्मि, रुणत्सि, रुणद्धि
8th	तनादि	*tanādi*	√तन्-आदि	√*tan*	(to spread)	तनोमि, तनोषि, तनोति
9th	क्र्यादि	*kryādi*	√क्री-आदि	√*krī*	(to buy)	क्रीणामि, क्रीणासि, क्रीणाति
*10th	चुरादि	* *ćurādi*	√चुर्-आदि	√*ćur*	(to steal)	चोरयामि, चोरयसि, चोरयति

NOTES : Some people prefer using the numerical order (1st, 2nd etc) for identifying the *gaṇa*s, while others prefer their nominclature (भ्वादि, अदादि etc)

(i) The popular 10 classes of conjugations are divided in two GROUPS.

(ii) roots of 1st, 4th, 6th and 10th class marked with * fall under the **FIRST GROUP** and

(iii) the remaining roots of the 2nd, 3rd, 5th, 7th, 8th and 9th class fall under **SECOND GROUP** of conjugations.

(iv) Amost all roots are monosyllables, some of them are even uniletters (e.g. √i, √ī, √u, √ṛ, √ṝ), most of them end in a consonant. Only just over a dozen are ploysyllabelic. e.g. √apās, √āndol, √bhiṣaj, √ćakās, √ćulump, √daridrā, √gaveśa, √hillol, √kumār, √kuṭumb, √lumāl, √oland, √palyul, √pampas, √prenkhol, √sabhaj, √sangrām, √viḍamb.

THE PROCESS OF CONGUGATION

(i) The process of attaching a tense conjugation (लकार:) to an original basic verb root, to form a single worded verb, is called **Congugation**. The original basic form of the verb is called the **Verbal-root** or **Root-verb** (*dhātuḥ* धातु:) e.g. √*bhū* (√भू) to become.

(ii) A √verb undergoes modification before it takes a conjugational suffix (लकार:). The form of the √verb before it takes a suffix, is called **Verbal Base** (*aṅgam* अङ्गम्)

(iii) The initial vowel of the root verb is called the **Radical Vowel** (*maulik-svaraḥ* मौलिकस्वर:). e.g. ई of √ई; अ of √अद्

(iv) The end vowel of the √verb is **Final Vowel** (*antya-svaraḥ* अन्त्यस्वर:) e.g. ऊ of √भू

(v) The vowel between two consonants of a √verb is **Medial Vowel** *madhya-svaraḥ* मध्यस्वर: । e.g. the short vowel अ between consonants ग् and म् in √गम्; or long vowel आ in √खाद्

(vi) The vowel that is followed by a compound consonants is counted as a long vowel. e.g. NOTE : the अ in √रक्ष् (र् + अ + क् + ष्) is considered as the long vowel आ (ā).

(vII) The First Degree of modification (strengthening) of the vowel is called ***guṇaḥ*** (गुण:),

(viii) Second Degree of modification (strengthening) of the vowel is called ***vṛddhiḥ*** (वृद्धि:).

(ix) Simple vowels (short + long) of the √root take **Two-fold Strengthening** with *guṇa* and *vṛddhi* .

THE SCHEME OF TWO FOLD STRENGTHENING

Simple vowels	अ, आ	इ, ई	उ, ऊ	ऋ, ॠ	ऌ
1. guṇaḥ	अ	ए	ओ	अर्	अल्
2. vṛddhiḥ	आ	ऐ	औ	आर्	आल्

(x) The specific letter that is added to the verbal base before attachment of a tense suffix is called ***vikaraṇam*** (विकरणम्). Each class of the verbs has its own characteristic *vikaraṇam*. A *vikaraṇam* is added to the verbal base only in the Present tense (लट्), Imperfect past tense (लङ्), Imperative mood (लोट्) and the Potential mood (विधिलिङ्).

THE SCHEME OF VIKARAṆA

Class	Class-name	√root	*vikaraṇam*	Present-tense
1*	भ्वादि:	√भू	अ	भवामि
2	अदादि:	√अद्	–	अद्मि
3	जुहोत्यादि:	√हु	द्वित्व	जुहोमि
4*	दिवादि :	√दिव्	य (य्)	दीव्यामि
5	स्वादि :	√सु	नु (नो)	सुनोमि
6*	तुदादि:	√तुद्	अ	तुदामि
7	रुधादि:	√रुध्	न (न्)	रुणध्मि
8	तनादि:	√तन्	उ (ओ)	तनोमि
9	क्र्यादि:	√क्री	ना	क्रीणामि
10*	चुरादि:	√चुर्	अय	चोरयामि

NOTE : You will need this information (i-v) in the following sections :
(i) Present tense suffixes are मि व: म: सि थ: थ ति त: अन्ति । (ii) The suffixes begining with म् are मि and म: । (iii) The suffix ending in व् is व: । (iv) The suffix beginning in अ is अन्ति । (v) The अङित suffixes are मि, सि, ति, अस्, अत् and तु ।

24.1

THE FIRST CLASS

bhvādiḥ gaṇaḥ भ्वादि: गण: ।

The first and the biggest of the eleven classes of the verbs is the भ्वादि: *(bhvādi)* class. It includes 1035 of the 2000 verbs of Sanskrit language. The most typical example of this class is the verb √भू (√*bhū* to become), therefore, this class is called *bhvādiḥ gaṇaḥ* भ्वादि: गण: (भू + आदि = भ्वादि '*bhū* etc.' class).

FORMATION OF THE **VERBAL BASE** for भ्वादि: गण: ।

1. The Final vowel (e.g. ऊ in √भू) and the short Medial vowel (e.g. अ in √गम्) take *guṇa* to form a **Verbal Base**.

   e.g. √भू → भू + अ → भो; and √बुध् → बु + अ + ध् → बोध् । etc०

2. *Vikaraṇa* अ is added to this verbal base before adding any tense suffix.

   e.g. भो + अ = भव । बोध् + अ = बोध । etc.

3. This *vikaraṇa* अ becomes आ before the tense suffixes that begin with म् or व् ।

   e.g. भो + आ + मि = भवामि; भो + आ + म: = भवाम: । बोध् + आ + मि = बोधामि, बोध् + आ + म: = बोधाम: । etc.

4. This *vikaraṇa* अ is dropped before tense suffixes that begin with अ ।

   e.g. भो + अ – अ + अन्ति = भवन्ति । बोध् + अ – अ + अन्ति = बोधन्ति । etc.

Scheme of Conjugations for the First Class : Root √भू to become

(1) Present Tense : लट् (सामान्य-वर्तमाने) *Parasmaipadī*

	Singular	Dual	Plural	Meaning
1p०	भवामि (आमि)	भवाव: (आव:)	भवाम: (आम:)	I become
	bhavāmi	*bhavāvaḥ*	*bhavāmaḥ*	
2p०	भवसि (सि)	भवथ: (थ:)	भवथ (थ)	You become
	bhavasi	*bhavathaḥ*	*bhavatha*	

3p◦ भवति (ति)	भवत: (त:)	भवन्ति (अन्ति)	He becomes
bhavati	*bhavataḥ*	*bhavanti*	

(2) Past imperfect Tense : लङ् (अनद्यतन-भूते) *Parasmaipadī*

Singular	Dual	Plural	Meaning
1p◦ अभवम्	अभवाव	अभवाम	I became
abhavam	*abhavāva*	*abhavāma*	
2p◦ अभव:	अभवतम्	अभवत	You became
abhavaḥ	*abhavatam*	*abhavata*	
3p◦ अभवत्	अभवताम्	अभवन्	He became
abhavat	*abhavatām*	*abhavan*	

(3) Perfect Past Tense : लिट् (परोक्ष-भूते) *Parasmaipadī*

Singular	Dual	Plural	Meaning
1p◦ बभूव	बभूविव	बभूविम	I had become
babhūva	*babhūviva*	*babhūvima*	
2p◦ बभूविथ	बभूवथु:	बभूव	You had become
babhūvitha	*babhūvathuḥ*	*babhūva*	
3p◦ बभूव	बभूवतु:	बभूवु:	He, she, it had become
babhūva	*babhūvatuḥ*	*babhūvuḥ*	

(4) Indefinite Past Tense : लुङ् (दूरवर्ति-भूते) *Parasmaipadī*

Singular	Dual	Plural	Meaning
1p◦ अभूवम्	अभूव	अभूम	I had become
abhūvam	*abhūva*	*abhūma*	
2p◦ अभू:	अभूतम्	अभूत	You had become
abhūḥ	*abhūtam*	*abhūta*	
3p◦ अभूत्	अभूताम्	अभूवन्	He,she,it had become
abhūt	*abhūtām*	*abhūvan*	

(5) Definite Future : लुट् (सामान्य-भविष्यति) *Parasmaipadī*

	Singular	Dual	Plural	Meaning
1p॰	भवितास्मि	भवितास्वः	भवितास्मः	I will become
	bhavitāsmi	*bhavitāsvaḥ*	*bhavitāsmaḥ*	
2p॰	भवितासि	भवितास्थः	भवितास्थ	You will become
	bhavitāsi	*bhavitāsthaḥ*	*bhavitāstha*	
3p॰	भविता	भवितारौ	भवितारः	Hewill become
	bhavitā	*bhavitārau*	*bhavitāraḥ*	

(6) Indefinite Future : लृट् (अपूर्ण-भविष्यति) *Parasmaipadī*

	Singular	Dual	Plural	Meaning
1p॰	भविष्यामि	भविष्यावः	भविष्यामः	I shall become
	bhaviṣyāmi	*bhaviṣyāvaḥ*	*bhaviṣyāmaḥ*	
2p॰	भविष्यसि	भविष्यथः	भविष्यथ	You shall become
	bhaviṣyasi	*bhaviṣyathaḥ*	*bhaviṣyatha*	
3p॰	भविष्यति	भविष्यतः	भविष्यन्ति	He shall become
	bhaviṣyati	*bhaviṣyataḥ*	*bhaviṣyanti*	

(7) Conditional Mood : लृङ् (भविष्यति क्रियातिपत्तौ) *Parasmaipadī*

	Singular	Dual	Plural	Meaning
1p॰	अभविष्यम्	अभविष्याव	अभविष्याम	If I become
	abhaviṣyam	*abhaviṣyāva*	*abhaviṣyāma*	
2p॰	अभविष्यः	अभविष्यतम्	अभविष्यत	If you become
	abhaviṣyaḥ	*abhaviṣyatam*	*abhaviṣyata*	
3p॰	अभविष्यत्	अभविष्यताम्	अभविष्यन्	If he becomes
	abhaviṣyat	*abhaviṣyatām*	*abhaviṣyan*	

(8) Imperative Mood : लोट् (आज्ञार्थे; प्रश्नार्थे; विध्यादौ) *Parasmaipadī*

Singular	Dual	Plural	Meaning
1p◦ भवानि	भवाव	भवाम	Should I become?
bhavāni	*bhavāva*	*bhavāma*	
2p◦ भव	भवतम्	भवत	Please become!
bhava	*bhavatam*	*bhavata*	
3p◦ भवतु	भवताम्	भवन्तु	He should become!
bhavatu	*bhavatām*	*bhavantu*	

(9) Potential or Subjunctive Mood : विधिलिङ् (विध्यादौ) *Parasmaipadī*

1p◦ भवेयम्	भवेव	भवेम	I may become
bhaveyam	*bhaveva*	*bhavema*	
2p◦ भवे:	भवेतम्	भवेत	You may become
bhaveḥ	*bhavetam*	*bhaveta*	
3p◦ भवेत्	भवेताम्	भवेयु:	He may become
bhavet	*bhavetām*	*bhaveyuḥ*	

(10) Benedictive or Optative Mood : आशीर्लिङ् (आशिषि) *Parasmaipadī*

Singular	Dual	Plural	Meaning
1p◦ भूयासम्	भूयास्व	भूयास्म	May I become!
bhūyāsam	*bhūyāsva*	*bhūyāsma*	
2p◦ भूया:	भूयास्तम्	भूयास्त	May you become!
bhūyāḥ	*bhūyāstam*	*bhūyāsta*	
3p◦ भूयात्	भूयास्ताम्	भूयासु:	May he become!
bhūyāt	*bhūyāstām*	*bhūyāsuḥ*	

EXAMPLES Cum EXERCISE : 1st भ्वादि: class

1. I become. *aham bhavāmi.* अहं भवामि (√भू) । (Present लट्)

2. He becomes a teacher. *saḥ ācāryaḥ bhavati.* स: आचार्य: भवति ।

3. He became a doctor. *saḥ vaidyaḥ abhavat.* स: वैद्य: अभवत् । (Past tense लङ्)

4. They will become surgeons. *te śalyaćikitsakāḥ bhaviṣyanti.* ते शल्यचिकित्सकाः भविष्यन्ति । (Future लृट्)

5. She eats a mango. *sā āmraphalaṁ khādati.* सा आम्रफलं खादति (√खाद्) ।

6. You are drinking milk. *bhavān dugdhaṁ pibati.* भवान् दुग्धं पिबति (√पा) ।

7. I drank tea. *ahaṁ ćāyapeyam apibam.* अहं चायपेयम् अपिबम् ।

8. They will drink cold water. *te śītaṁ jalaṁ pāsyanti.* ते शीतं जलं पास्यन्ति । (*śita* शीत = cold)

9. We hear melodious songs. *vayaṁ madhurāṇi gānāni śṛuṇumaḥ.* वयं मधुराणि गानानि श्रुणुमः (√श्रु) ।

10. They heard songs. *te gānāni aśṛuṇvan.* ते गानानि अशृण्वन् ।

11. I will go to school. *ahaṁ pāṭhaśālāṁ gamiṣyāmi.* अहं पाठशालां गमिष्यामि (√गम्) ।

12. Kaṁsa stole Krishṇa's cows. *Kaṁsaḥ Kṛṣṇasya gāḥ aharat.* कंसः कृष्णस्य गाः अहरत् (√हृ) । (गाम्, गावौ, गाः)

13. Please hold my hand (लोट्). *kṛpayā mama hastaṁ dhara (dharatu).* कृपया मम हस्तं धर-धरतु (√धृ) ।

14. He takes away the books. *saḥ pustakāni nayati.* सः पुस्तकानि नयति (√नी) ।

15. They cooked in the evening. *te sāyam apaćan.* ते सायम् अपचन् (√पच्) । सायम् = in the evening.

THE IMPORTANT CONJUGATIONS of the भ्वादि: (1st) Class

ROOT Verb √गम् (to go)

In the Present (लट्), Imperfect past (लङ्), Imperative (लोट्) and Potential (विधि) tenses and moods (लकाराः),

(i) the म् of गम् becomes छ (paṇini 7.3.77 - √गम् √यम् √इष् इत्येतेषाम् अच् प्रत्यये परतः छकारादेशः भवति) गम् → गछ्

(ii) letter त् comes between the ग and छ् of गछ् and it then becomes च् → ग + त् + छ् =

ग + च् + छ् = गच्छ्

(iii) then the tense suffixes are added, as explained above in the scheme of conjugations. गच्छ् + आ + मि = गच्छामि ...(गच्छाव:, गच्छाम: ... गच्छन्ति)

NOTE : The root √इष् (to desire) of भ्वादि: गण: becomes इच्छ् । इष् → इ + छ् → इ + त् + छ् = इ + च् + छ् = इच्छ् → इच्छ् + अ + ति = इच्छति ।

However, in the case of √इष् of he 4th रुधादि गण: (4√इष्) becomes इष्यति and in the case of the 9th क्र्यादि गण: (9√इष्) it becomes इष्णाति । See the 4th and 9th classes below, for explanations on these conjugations.

ROOT Verb √स्था (to stay)

as well as roots पा, घ्रा, ध्मा, म्ना, दा, दृश्, ऋ, सद्, शद्, धाव ।

In the Present (लट्), Imperfect past (लङ्), Imperative (लोट्) and Potential (विधि) tenses (लकारा:), the स्था is substituted with तिष्ठ् (paṇini 7.3.78) √स्था → तिष्ठति, अतिष्ठत्, तिष्ठतु, तिष्ठेत् ।

Similarly, following substitutions take place in the cases of the roots पा → पिब (पिबति), घ्रा → जिघ्र (जिघ्रति), ध्मा → धम (धमति), म्ना → मन (मनति), दा → यच्छ (यच्छति), दृश् → पश्य (पश्यति), ऋ → ऋच्छ (ऋच्छति), सद् → सीद (सीदति), शद् → शीय (शीयते), धाव् → धौ (धावति–धावते)

ROOT √वद् (to speak)

The Past Perfect (लिट्) and Past indefinite (लुङ्) are irregular. (लिट्) उवाद्, ऊदतु:, ऊदु: । लुङ् → अवादीत्, अवादिष्टाम्, अवादिषु: ।

ROOT √श्रु (to hear)

In the Present (लट्), Imperfect past (लङ्), Imperative (लोट्) and Potential (विधि) tenses (लकारा:), **the श्रु is changed to शृ** and a syllable णो or णु is attached between the this शृ (शृ) and the tense suffix. e.g. √श्रु → शृ + णो + ति = शृणोति (he hears)

Thus the conjugations are : शृणोमि, शृणुव: (शृण्व:), शृणुम: (शृण्म:) । शृणोषि, शृणुथ:, शृणुथ ।

शृणोति, शृणुत:, शृण्वन्ति ।

ROOT √जि (to win)

When prefix वि or परा comes before root √जि, the *parasmaipadi* root √जि becomes *ātmanepadī*. (pānini 1.3.19) जयामि जयाव: जयाम: । जयसि जयथ: जयथ । जयति जयत: जयन्ति । → विजये विजयावहे विजयामहे । विजयसे विजयाथे विजयध्वे । विजयते विजयेते विजयन्ते । पराजये पराजयावहे पराजयामहे । पराजयसे पराजयाथे पराजयध्वे । पराजयते पराजयेते पराजयन्ते ।

ROOT √भ्रम् (to wander)

In the Present (लट्), Imperfect past (लङ्), Imperative (लोट्) and Potential (विधि) tenses (लकारा:), the √भ्रम् optionally takes य *vikaraṇa* between the root and the tense suffix (लकार:). Therefore, in these four tenses two forms of verbs are optionally produced.

1. लट् – भ्रमामि भ्रमाव: भ्रमाम: । भ्रमसि भ्रमथ: भ्रमथ । भ्रमति भ्रमत: भ्रमन्ति → भ्रम्यामि भ्रम्याव: भ्रम्याम: । भ्रम्यसि भ्रम्यथ: भ्रम्यथ । भ्रम्यति भ्रम्यत: भ्रम्यन्ति ।

2. लङ् – अभ्रमम् अभ्रमाव अभ्रमाम । अभ्रम: अभ्रमतम् अभ्रमत । अभ्रमत् अभ्रमताम् अभ्रमन् । → अभ्रम्यम् अभ्रम्याव अभ्रम्याम । अभ्रम्य: अभ्रम्यतम् अभ्रम्यत । अभ्रम्यत् अभ्रम्यताम् अभ्रम्यन् ।

3 लोट् – भ्रमाणि भ्रमाव भ्रमाम । भ्रम भ्रमतम् भ्रमत । भ्रमतु भ्रमताम् भ्रमन्तु । → भ्रम्याणि भ्रम्याव भ्रम्याम । भ्रम्य भ्रम्यतम् भ्रम्यत । भ्रम्यतु भ्रम्यताम् भ्रम्यन्तु ।

4 विधि॰ – भ्रमेयम् भ्रमेव भ्रमेम । भ्रमे: भ्रमेतम् भ्रमेत । भ्रमेत् भ्रमेताम् भ्रमेयु: । → भ्रम्येयम् भ्रम्येव भ्रम्येम । भ्रम्ये: भ्रम्येतम् भ्रम्येत । भ्रम्येत् भ्रम्येताम् भ्रम्येयु: ।

Same holds good for the roots √क्रम् क्लम् भ्राश् भ्लाश् त्रस् तृट् लष् । → क्रामति-क्राम्यति, क्लामति-क्लाम्यति, भ्राषते-भ्राष्यते, भ्लाशते-भ्लाश्यते, त्रसति-त्रस्यति, तृटति-तृट्यति । लषति-लष्यति लषते-लष्यते etc.

ROOT √दह् (to burn)

In the Indifinite future (लृट्), Indefinite past (लुङ्) and Conditional (लृङ्) suffixes (लकारा:), when द् is followed by ष्, this द् changes to ध् । e.g.

1. लृट् – धक्ष्यामि धक्ष्याव: धक्ष्याम: । धक्ष्यसि धक्ष्यथ: धक्ष्यथ । धक्ष्यति धक्ष्यत: धक्ष्यन्ति ।

2. लुङ् – अधाक्षम् अधाक्ष्व अधाक्ष्म । अधाक्षी: अदाग्धम् अदाग्ध । अधाक्षीत् अदाग्धाम् अधाक्षु: ।
3. लृङ् – अधक्षम् अधक्षाव अधक्षाम । अधाक्ष्य: अधक्ष्यतम् अधक्षत । अधक्ष्यत् अधक्ष्यताम् अधक्ष्यन् ।

ROOT √तॄ (to cross over)

In the Definite future (लुट्), Indifinite future (लृट्) and Indefinite past (लुङ्) tenses (लकारा:), the इ optionally changes to ई । Therefore, two types of verbs are optionally formed. e.g.

1. लुट् – तरिता तरितारौ तरितार: । → तरीता तरीतारौ तरीतार: ।
2. लृट् – तरिष्यति तरिष्यत: तरिष्यन्ति । → तरीष्यति तरीष्यत: तरीष्यन्ति ।
3. लृङ् – अतरिष्यत् अतरिष्यताम् अतरिष्यन् → अतरीष्यत् अतरीष्यताम् अतरीष्यन् ।

24.2
THE SECOND CLASS

adādiḥ gaṇaḥ अदादि: गण: ।

The second class of the verbs is अदादि *(adādi)*. The typical example of this class is root √अद् (√*ad* to eat), therefore, this class is called अदादि गण: (अद् + आदि = अदादि, *ad* अद् etc. class). There are 72 verbs in the अदादि (second) class.

The conjugations of the अदादि (2nd) class are simpler, because the अ विकरणम् added (between the root and tense suffix) in the भ्वादि: (1st) class is not added in this class.

Scheme of Conjugations for the Second Class : Root √अद् to eat

(1) Present Tense : लट् (सामान्य-वर्तमाने) *Parasmaipadī*

	Singular	Dual	Plural	Meaning
1p∘	अद्मि (मि)	अद्व: (व:)	अद्म: (म:)	I eat
	admi	*advaḥ*	*admaḥ*	
2p∘	अत्सि (सि)	अत्थ: (थ:)	अत्थ (थ)	
	atsi	*atthaḥ*	*attha*	

3p◦ अत्ति (ति)	अत्तः (तः)	अदन्ति (अन्ति)	
atti	*attaḥ*	*adanti*	

(2) Past imperfect Tense : लङ् (अनद्यतन-भूते) *Parasmaipadī*

Singular	Dual	Plural	Meaning
1p◦ आदम्	आद्व	आद्म	I ate
ādam	*ādva*	*ādma*	
2p◦ आदः	आत्तम्	आत्त	
ādaḥ	*āttam*	*ātta*	
3p◦ आदत्	आत्ताम्	आदन्	
ādat	*āttām*	*ādan*	

(3) Perfect Past Tense : लिट् (परोक्ष-भूते) *Parasmaipadī*

Singular	Dual	Plural	Meaning
1p◦ जघास	जक्षिव	जक्षिम	I had eaten
jaghās	*jakṣiva*	*jakṣima*	
2p◦ जघसिथ	जघथुः	जक्ष	
jaghasitha	*jaghathuḥ*	*jakṣa*	
3p◦ जघास	जक्षतुः	जक्षुः	
jaghāsa	*jakṣatuḥ*	*jakṣuḥ*	

(4) Indefinite Past Tense : लुङ् (दूरवर्ति-भूते) *Parasmaipadī*

1p◦ अघसम्	अघसाव	अघसाम	I had eaten
aghasam	*aghasāva*	*aghasāma*	
2p◦ अघसः	अघसतम्	अघसत	
aghasaḥ	*aghasatam*	*aghasata*	
3p◦ अघसत्	अघसताम्	अघसन्	
aghasat	*aghasatām*	*aghasan*	

(5) Definite Future : लुट् (सामान्य-भविष्यति) *Parasmaipadī*

Singular	Dual	Plural	Meaning
1p∘ अत्तास्मि	अत्तास्वः	अत्तास्मः	I will eat
attāsmi	*attāsvaḥ*	*attāsmaḥ*	
2p∘ अत्तासि	अत्तास्थः	अत्तास्थ	
attāsi	*attāsthaḥ*	*attāstha*	
3p∘ अत्ता	अत्तारौ	अत्तारः	
attā	*attārau*	*attāraḥ*	

(6) Indefinite Future : लृट् (अपूर्ण-भविष्यति) *Parasmaipadī*

Singular	Dual	Plural	Meaning
1p∘ अत्स्यामि	अत्स्यावः	अत्स्यामः	I shall eat
atsyāmi	*atsyāvaḥ*	*atsyāmaḥ*	
2p∘ अत्स्यसि	अत्स्यथः	अत्स्यथ	
atsyasi	*atsyathaḥ*	*atsyatha*	
3p∘ अत्स्यति	अत्स्यतः	अत्स्यन्ति	
atsyati	*atsyataḥ*	*atsyanti*	

(7) Conditional Mood : लृङ् (भविष्यति क्रियातिपत्तौ) *Parasmaipadī*

Singular	Dual	Plural	Meaning
1p∘ आत्स्यम्	आत्स्याव	आत्स्याम	If I eat
ātsyam	*ātsyāva*	*ātsyāma*	
2p∘ आत्स्यः	आत्स्यतम्	आत्स्यत	
ātsyaḥ	*ātsyatam*	*ātsyata*	
3p∘ आत्स्यत्	आत्स्यताम्	आत्स्यन्	
ātsyat	*ātsyatām*	*ātsyan*	

(8) Imperative Mood : लोट् (आज्ञार्थे; प्रश्नार्थे; विध्यादौ) *Parasmaipadī*

Singular	Dual	Plural	Meaning

1p◦ अदानि	अदाव	अदाम	Should I eat?
adāni	*adāva*	*adāma*	
2p◦ अद्धि	अत्तम्	अत्त	Please eat!
addhi	*attam*	*atta*	
3p◦ अत्तु	अत्ताम्	अदन्तु	He, she should eat!
attu	*attām*	*adantu*	

(9) Potential or Subjunctive Mood : विधिलिङ् (विध्यादौ) *Parasmaipadī*

Singular	Dual	Plural	Meaning
1p◦ अद्याम्	अद्याव	अद्याम	I may eat
adyām	*adyāva*	*adyāma*	
2p◦ अद्या:	अद्यातम्	अद्यात	
adyāḥ	*adyātam*	*adyāta*	
3p◦ अद्यात्	अद्याताम्	अद्यु:	
adyāt	*adyātām*	*adyuḥ*	

(10) Benedictive or Optative Mood : आशीर्लिङ् (आशिषि) *Parasmaipadī*

Singular	Dual	Plural	Meaning
1p◦ अद्यासम्	अद्यास्व	अद्यास्म	May I eat!
adyāsam	*adyāsva*	*adyāsma*	
2p◦ अद्या:	अद्यास्तम्	अद्यास्त	
adāḥ	*adyāstam*	*adyāsta*	
3p◦ अद्यात्	अद्यास्ताम्	अद्यासु:	
adyāt	*adyāstām*	*adyāsuḥ*	May he eat!

EXAMPLES cum EXERCISE : (cumulative exercise)

(1) Cruel people kill animals. *duṣṭāḥ paśūn ghnanti.* दुष्टाः पशून् घ्नन्ति (√हन्) ।

(2) Please take this money. *kṛpayā etat dhanaṁ lāhi.* कृपया एतत् धनं लाहि (√ला) ।

(3) He understands the meaning of life. *saḥ jīvanasya arthaṁ vetti.* सः जीवनस्य अर्थं

वेत्ति (√विद्) ।

(4) He is my friend. *saḥ mama mitram asti.* सः मम मित्रम् अस्ति (√अस्) ।

(5) He was my friend. *saḥ mama mitram āsīt.* सः मम मित्रम् आसीत् । They were my friends. *te mama mitrāṇi āsan.* ते मम मित्राणि आसन् ।

(6) You are saying. *bhavān bravīti.* भवान् ब्रवीति (√ब्रू) । I say. *ahaṁ bravīmi.* अहं ब्रवीमि । He-she is saying. *saḥ/ sā bravīti (āha)* सः/सा ब्रवीति (√आह) ।

(7) He said (लिट्). *saḥ uvāća.* सः उवाच । Please tell me. *māṁ brūhi.* मां ब्रूहि । He said. *saḥ uktavān (saḥ abravīt).* सः उक्तवान् (सः अब्रवीत्) ।

THE IMPORTANT VERBS : 2nd *adādi* अदादिः class :

ROOT √विद् (to know) :

As seen at the end of our Dictionary of Roots, the verb √विद् falls under five different classes, with different meaning in each class.

NOTE : In the अदादि class, the Perfect tense (लिट्) suffixes अ व म, थ अथुः अ, अ अतुः उः can also optionally be used in Present tense (लट्).

Therefore in लट् we get two forms of verbs. e.g.

(1)	वेद्मि	विद्वः	विद्मः ।	(2)	वेद	विद्व	विद्म ।
	वेत्सि	वित्थः	वित्थ ।		वेत्थ	विदथुः	विद ।
	वेत्ति	वित्तः	विदन्ति ।		वेद	विदतुः	विदुः ।

In the case of Perfect tense (लिट्), optionally

(i) the suffix आञ् or आम्, is added in the middle and

(ii) √कृ (चकार), √भू (बभूव) or √अस् (आस) is attached at the end, of the verb.

Thus we get four forms of verbs in the Perfect tense (लिट्)

1. अ अतुः उः	–	विवेद	विविदतुः	विविदुः ।
2. आञ्-चकार	–	विदाञ्चकार	विदाञ्चक्रतुः	विदाञ्चक्रुः ।
3 .आम्-बभूव	–	विदाम्बभूव	विदाम्बभूवतुः	विदाम्बभूवुः ।

4 .आम्–आस – विदामास विदामासतुः विदामासुः ।

ROOT √अस् (to be) :

Root √भू is substituted for root √अस् in the use of the following six tenses : (1) Perfect past (लिट्), (2) Definite future (लुट्), (3) Indefinite future (लृट्), (4) Indefinite past (लुङ्), (5) Conditional (लृङ्) and (6) Benedictive (आशि॰). These verb forms for the root √भू are given in the Appendix 1.

ROOT रुद् (to cry)

In the Present (लट्), Imperfect past (लङ्) and Imperative (लोट्) particle इ is added. e.g.

(लट्)	रोदिमि	रुदिवः	रुदिमः ।	(लङ्)	अरोदम्	अरुदिव	अरुदिम ।
	रोदिषि	रुदिथः	रुदिथ ।		अरोदीः	अरुदितम्	अरुदित ।
	रोदिति	रुदितः	रुदन्ति ।		अरोदीत्	अरुदिताम्	अरुदन् ।
(लोट्)	रोदानि	रोदाव	रोदाम ।				
	रुदिहि	रुदितम्	रुदित ।				
	रोदितु	रुदिताम्	रुदन्तु ।				

ROOT √इण् (to go)

In Indefinite Past tense (लुङ्), √गा comes in place of root √इण् । e.g. अगाम् अगाव अगाम । अगाः अगातम् अगात । अगात् अगाताम् अगुः ।

ROOT √ब्रू (to speak)

This is a dual (*parasmaipadī and ātmanepadī*) root.

(1) In Present tense (लट्) *parasmaipadī* form, आह् comes optionally in place of √ब्रू at five places, as shown with underlines below.

1. ब्रवीमि	ब्रूवः	ब्रूमः ।	ब्रवीमि	ब्रूवः	ब्रूमः ।
2. ब्रवीषि	ब्रूथः	ब्रूथ ।	<u>आत्थ</u>	<u>आहथुः</u>	ब्रूथ ।
3. ब्रवीति	ब्रूतः	ब्रुवन्ति ।	<u>आह</u>	<u>आहतुः</u>	<u>आहुः</u> ।

(2) Root √वच् is used in place of √ब्रू in the applications of five *parasmaipadī* and *ātmanepadi* tenses of (i) Past perfect (लिट्), (ii) Definite future (लुट्), (iii) Indefinite future (लृट्), (iv) Indefinite past (लुङ्) and (v) Conditional (लृङ्).

	PARASMAIPADI			ATMANEPADI		
(i) Past perfect (लिट्)	उवाच	ऊचतु:	ऊचु:	ऊचे	ऊचाते	ऊचिरे
(ii) Definite future (लुट्)	वक्ता	वक्तारौ	वक्तार:	वक्ता	वक्तारौ	वक्तार:
(iii) Indefinite future (लृट्)	वक्ष्यति	वक्ष्यत:	वक्ष्यन्ति	वक्ष्यते	वक्ष्येते	वक्ष्यन्ते
(iv) Indefinite past (लुङ्)	अवोचत्	अवोचताम्	अवोचन्	अवोचत	अवोचेताम्	अवोचन्त
(v) Conditional (लृङ्)	अवक्ष्यत्	अवक्ष्यताम्	अवक्ष्यन्	अवक्ष्यत	अवक्ष्येताम्	अवक्ष्यन्त

24.3
THE THIRD CLASS
juhotyādiḥ जुहोत्यादि: गण: ।

The third class of the verbs is जुहोत्यादि or हुवादि class. The typical example of this class is the verb root √हु (√*hu* to offer oblation). There are 24 verbs in the जुहोत्यादि (third) class.

(i) The अ विकरणम् that comes between the root verb and the tense suffix of the Present (लट्), Imperfect past (लङ्), Imperative (लोट्) and Potential (विधि) tenses in the भ्वादि: class, gets negated in the जुहोत्यादि: (3rd) class. हु + अ – अ = हु

(ii) And, in stead, in this (3rd) class, duplication and modification of the root takes place. e.g. हु + हु + आ + मि = जु + हु + आ + मि → जुहोमि, जुहोषि, जुहोति ।

Scheme of Conjugations for the Third Class : Root √अद् to eat

(1) Present Tense : लट् (सामान्य-वर्तमाने) *Parasmaipadī*

	Singular	Dual	Plural	Meaning
1p∘	जुहोमि (ओमि)	जुहुवः (वः)	जुहुमः (मः)	I sacrifice
	juhomi	*juhuvaḥ*	*juhumaḥ*	
2p∘	जुहोषि (सि)	जुहुथः (थः)	जुहुथ (थ)	
	juhoṣi	*juhuthaḥ*	*jihutha*	
3p∘	जुहोति (ति)	जुहुतः (तः)	जुह्वति (ति)	
	juhoti	*juhutaḥ*	*juhvati*	

(2) Past imperfect Tense : लङ् (अनद्यतन-भूते) *Parasmaipadī*

	Singular	Dual	Plural	Meaning
1p∘	अजुहवम्	अजुहुव	अजुहुम	I sacrificed
	ajuhavam	*ajuhuva*	*ajuhuma*	
2p∘	अजुहोः	अजुहुतम्	अजुहुत	
	ajuhoḥ	*ajuhutam*	*ajuhuta*	
3p∘	अजुहोत्	अजुहुताम्	अजुहवुः	
	ajuhot	*ajuhutām*	*ajuhavuḥ*	

(3) Perfect Past Tense : लिट् (परोक्ष-भूते) *Parasmaipadī*

	Singular	Dual	Plural	Meaning
1p∘	जुहाव	जुहुविव	जुहुविम	I had sacrificed
	juhāva	*juhuviva*	*juhuvima*	
2p∘	जुहुविथ	जुहुवथुः	जुहुव	
	juhuvitha	*juhuvathuḥ*	*juhuva*	
3p∘	जुहाव	जुहुवतुः	जुहुवुः	
	juhāva	*juhuvatuḥ*	*juhuvuḥ*	

(4) Indefinite Past Tense : लुङ् (दूरवर्ति-भूते) *Parasmaipadī*

Singular	Dual	Plural	Meaning
1p◦ अहौषम्	अहौष्व	अहौष्म	I had sacrificed
ahauṣam	*ahauṣva*	*ahauṣma*	
2p◦ अहौषी:	अहौष्टम्	अहौष्ट	
ahauṣīḥ	*ahauṣṭam*	*ahauṣṭa*	
3p◦ अहौषीत्	अहौष्टाम्	अहौषु:	
ahauṣīt	*ahauṣṭām*	*ahauṣuḥ*	

(5) Definite Future : लुट् (सामान्य-भविष्यति) *Parasmaipadī*

Singular	Dual	Plural	Meaning
1p◦ होतास्मि	होतास्व:	होतास्म:	I will sacrifice
hotāsmi	*hotāsvaḥ*	*hotāsmaḥ*	
2p◦ होतासि	होतास्थ:	होतास्थ	
hotāsi	*hotāsthaḥ*	*hotāstha*	
3p◦ होता	होतारौ	होतार:	
hotā	*hotārau*	*hotāraḥ*	

(6) Indefinite Future : लृट् (अपूर्ण-भविष्यति) *Parasmaipadī*

Singular	Dual	Plural	Meaning
1p◦ होष्यामि	होष्याव:	होष्याम:	I shall sacrifice
hoṣyāmi	*hoṣyāvaḥ*	*hoṣyāmaḥ*	
2p◦ होष्यसि	होष्यथ:	होष्यथ	
hoṣyasi	*hoṣyathaḥ*	*hoṣyatha*	
3p◦ होष्यति	होष्यत:	होष्यन्ति	
hoṣyati	*hoṣyataḥ*	*hoṣyanti*	

(7) Conditional Mood : लृङ् (भविष्यति क्रियातिपत्तौ) *Parasmaipadī*

Singular	Dual	Plural	Meaning
1p◦ अहोष्यम्	अहोष्याव	अहोष्याम	If I sacrifice

	ahoṣyam	*ahoṣyāva*	*ahoṣyāma*
2p॰	अहोष्य:	अहोष्यतम्	अहोष्यत
	ahoṣyaḥ	*ahoṣyatam*	*ahoṣyata*
3p॰	अहोष्यत्	अहोष्यताम्	अहोष्यन्
	ahoṣyat	*ahoṣyatām*	*ahoṣyan*

(8) Imperative Mood : लोट् (आज्ञार्थे; प्रश्नार्थे; विध्यादौ) *Parasmaipadī*

	Singular	Dual	Plural	Meaning
1p॰	जुहवानि	जुहवाव	जुहवाम	Should I sacrifice?
	juhavāni	*juhavāva*	*juhavāma*	
2p॰	जुहुधि	जुहुतम्	जुहुत	Please sacrifice!
	juhudhi	*juhutam*	*juhuta*	
3p॰	जुहोतु	जुहुताम्	जुह्वतु	He she should sacrifice!
	juhotu	*juhutām*	*juhvatu*	

(9) Potential or Subjunctive Mood : विधिलिङ् (विध्यादौ) *Parasmaipadī*

	Singular	Dual	Plural	Meaning
1p॰	जुहुयाम्	जुहुयाव	जुहुयाम	I may sacrifice
	juhuyām	*juhuyāva*	*juhuyāma*	
2p॰	जुहुया:	जुहुयातम्	जुहुयात	
	juhuyāḥ	*juhuyātam*	*juhuyāta*	
3p॰	जुहुयात्	जुहुयाताम्	जुहुयुः	
	juhuyāt	*juhuyātām*	*juhuyuḥ*	

(10) Benedictive or Optative Mood : आशीर्लिङ् (आशिषि) *Parasmaipadī*

	Singular	Dual	Plural	Meaning
1p॰	हूयासम्	हूयास्व	हूयास्म	May I sacrifice!
	hūyāsam	*hūyāsva*	*hūyāsma*	
2p॰	हूया:	हूयास्तम्	हूयास्त	

hūyāḥ	*hūyāstam*	*hūyāsta*
3p◦ हूयात्	हूयास्ताम्	हूयासुः
hūyāt	*hūyāstām*	*hūyāsuḥ*

EXAMPLES :

(1) He will be afraid. *saḥ bheṣyati.* सः भेष्यति (√भी) ।

(2) I give food. *aham annaṁ dadāmi.* अहम् अन्नं ददामि (√दा) ।

(3) You are giving money. *bhavān dhanaṁ dadāti.* भवान् धनं ददाति ।

(4) He gives an advice. *saḥ upadeśaṁ dadāti.* सः उपदेशं ददाति ।

(5) She gave an advice. *sā upadeśam adadāt.* सा उपदेशम् अददात् ।

(6) I will give an advice. *aham upadeśaṁ dāsyāmi.* अहम् उपदेशं दास्यामि ।

THE IMPORTANT ROOTS of the 3rd, जुवादि class

ROOT √दा (to give) :

(i) दा + अ – अ = दा

(ii) दा + दा + मि = द + दा + मि → ददामि, ददासि, ददाति ।

PARASMAIPADI			ATMANEPADI		
ददामि	दद्वः	दद्मः	ददे	दद्वहे	दद्महे
ददासि	दत्थः	दत्थ	दत्से	ददाथे	दद्ध्वे
ददाति	दत्तः	ददति	दत्ते	ददाते	ददते

In the *ātmanepadī* Past indefinite (लुङ्) the आ of √दा changes to इ and thus the verbs become :

अदिषि	अदिष्वहि	अदिष्महि ।
अदिथाः	अदिषाथाम्	अदिढ्वम् ।
अदित	अदिषाताम्	अदिषत ।

ROOT √धा (to bear)

(i) धा + अ – अ = धा

(ii) धा + दा + मि = द + धा + मि → दधामि, दधासि, दधाति ।

PARASMAIPADI			ATMANEPADI		
दधामि	दध्वः	दध्मः	दधे	दध्वहे	दध्महे
दधासि	धत्थः	धत्थ	धत्से	दधाथे	धद्ध्वे
दधाति	धत्तः	दधति	धत्ते	दधाते	दधते

Compare the verb forms of the root √दा and √धा

24.4
THE FOURTH CLASS
divādi gaṇaḥ दिवादिः गणः ।

The fourth class of the verbs is दिवादि *divādi* class. The typical example of this class is the verb √दिव् (√*div* to shine). There are 140 verbs in the दिवादि (fourth) class.

Like the *parasmaipadī* Present (लट्), Imperfect past (लङ्), Imperative (लोट्) and Potential (विधि) tenses of the भ्वादिः (1st) class, the दिवादिः (4th) class also has विकरणम् अ between the √verb and tense suffixes. In addition, in the दिवादिः class, य् is also prefixed to this अ । Thus,

1. *Vikaraṇa* य् and अ are added to the verbal base before adding the tense suffix. दिव् + य् + अ = दिव्य
2. This *vikaraṇa* अ becomes आ before the tense suffixes that begin with म् or व् । → दिव्य + आ + मि = दिव्यामि, दिव्यावः, दिव्यामः ।
3. The इ in the दि of दिव्यामि becomes ई because it is followed by the ङित् हलादि suffix य । Thus, दिव्यामि → दीव्यामि, दीव्यावः, दीव्यामः ।

4. *Vikaraṇa* अ is dropped before the tense suffixes that begin with अ and the इ of दिव् is changed to ई । Thus, दिव् + अ – अ + य + अन्ति = दिव्यन्ति → दीव्यन्ति ।

Scheme of Conjugations for the Fourth Class

Root √दिव् to shine, to play

(1) Present Tense : लट् (सामान्य-वर्तमाने) *Parasmaipadī*

Singular	Dual	Plural	Meaning
1p॰ दीव्यामि (आमि)	दीव्याव: (व:)	दीव्याम: (म:)	I play
dīvyāmi	*dīvyāvaḥ*	*dīvyāmaḥ*	
2p॰ दीव्यसि (सि)	दीव्यथ: (थ:)	दीव्यथ (थ)	
dīvyasi	*dīvyathaḥ*	*dīvyatha*	
3p॰ दीव्यति (ति)	दीव्यत: (त:)	दीव्यन्ति (अन्ति)	
dīvyati	*dīvyataḥ*	*dīvyanti*	

(2) Past imperfect Tense : लङ् (अनद्यतन-भूते) *Parasmaipadī*

Singular	Dual	Plural	Meaning
1p॰ अदीव्यम्	अदीव्याव	अदीव्याम	I played
adīvyam	*adīvyāva*	*adīvyāma*	
2p॰ अदीव्य:	अदीव्यतम्	अदीव्यत	
adīvyaḥ	*adīvyatam*	*adīvyata*	
3p॰ अदीव्यत्	अदीव्यताम्	अदीव्यन्	
adīvyat	*adīvyatām*	*adīvyan*	

(3) Perfect Past Tense : लिट् (परोक्ष-भूते) *Parasmaipadī*

Singular	Dual	Plural	Meaning
1p॰ दिदेव	दिदिविव	दिदिविम	I had played
dideva	*didiviva*	*didivima*	
2p॰ दिदेविथ	दिदिवथु:	दिदिव	

didevitha	*didivathuḥ*	*didiva*
3p◦ दिदेव	दिदिवतुः	दिदिवुः
dideva	*didivatuḥ*	*didivuḥ*

(4) Indefinite Past Tense : लुङ् (दूरवर्ति-भूते) *Parasmaipadī*

Singular	Dual	Plural	Meaning
1p◦ अदेविषम्	अदेविष्व	अदेविष्म	I had played
adeviṣam	*adeviṣva*	*adeviṣma*	
2p◦ अदेवीः	अदेविष्टम्	अदेविष्ट	
adevīḥ	*adeviṣṭam*	*adeviṣṭa*	
3p◦ अदेवीत्	अदेविष्टाम्	अदेविषुः	
adevīt	*adeviṣṭām*	*adeviṣuḥ*	

(5) Definite Future : लुट् (सामान्य-भविष्यति) *Parasmaipadī*

Singular	Dual	Plural	Meaning
1p◦ देवितास्मि	देवितास्वः	देवितास्मः	I will play
deviāsmi	*devitāsvaḥ*	*devitāsmaḥ*	
2p◦ देवितासि	देवितास्थः	देवितास्थ	
devitāsi	*devitāsthaḥ*	*devitāstha*	
3p◦ देविता	देवितारौ	देवितारः	
devitā	*devitārau*	*devitāraḥ*	

(6) Indefinite Future : लृट् (अपूर्ण-भविष्यति) *Parasmaipadī*

Singular	Dual	Plural	Meaning
1p◦ देविष्यामि	देविष्यावः	देविष्यामः	I shall play
deviṣyāmi	*deviṣyāvaḥ*	*deviṣyāmaḥ*	
2p◦ देविष्यसि	देविष्यथः	देविष्यथ	
deviṣyasi	*deviṣyathaḥ*	*deviṣyatha*	
3p◦ देविष्यति	देविष्यतः	देविष्यन्ति	

devișyati	*devișyataḥ*	*devișyanti*

(7) Conditional Mood : लृङ् (भविष्यति क्रियातिपत्तौ) *Parasmaipadī*

	Singular	Dual	Plural	Meaning
1p◦	अदेविष्यम्	अदेविष्याव	अदेविष्याम	If I play
	adevișyam	*adevișyāva*	*adevișyāma*	
2p◦	अदेविष्य:	अदेविष्यतम्	अदेविष्यत	
	adevișyaḥ	*adevișyatam*	*adevișyata*	
3p◦	अदेविष्यत्	अदेविष्यताम्	अदेविष्यन्	
	adevișyat	*adevișyatām*	*adevișyan*	

(8) Imperative Mood : लोट् (आज्ञार्थे; प्रश्नार्थे; विध्यादौ) *Parasmaipadī*

	Singular	Dual	Plural	Meaning
1p◦	दीव्यानि	दीव्याव	दीव्याम	Should I play?
	dīvyāni	*dīvyāva*	*dīvyāma*	
2p◦	दीव्य	दीव्यतम्	दीव्यत	Please play!
	dīvya	*dīvyatam*	*dīvyata*	
3p◦	दीव्यतु	दीव्यताम्	दीव्यन्तु	He, she should play!
	dīvyatu	*dīvyatām*	*dīvyantu*	

(9) Potential or Subjunctive Mood : विधिलिङ् (विध्यादौ) *Parasmaipadī*

	Singular	Dual	Plural	Meaning
1p◦	दीव्येयम्	दीव्येव	दीव्येम	I may play
	dīvyeyam	*dīvyeva*	*dīvyema*	
2p◦	दीव्ये:	दीव्येतम्	दीव्येत	
	dīvyeḥ	*dīvyetam*	*dīvyeta*	
3p◦	दीव्येत्	दीव्येताम्	दीव्येयु:	
	dīvyet	*dīvyetām*	*dīvyeyuḥ*	

(10) Benedictive or Optative Mood : आशीर्लिङ् (आशिषि) *Parasmaipadī*

	Singular	Dual	Plural	Meaning
1p॰	दीव्यासम्	दीव्यास्व	दीव्यास्म	May I play!
	dīvyāsam	*dīvyāsva*	*dīvyāsma*	
2p॰	दीव्याः	दीव्यास्तम्	दीव्यास्त	
	dīvyāḥ	*dīvyāstam*	*dīvyāsta*	
3p॰	दीव्यात्	दीव्यास्ताम्	दीव्यासुः	
	dīvyāt	*dīvyāstām*	*dīvyāsuḥ*	

EXAMPLES cum EXERCISE : (cumulative learning)

(1) He is never satisfied. *sah: kadāpi na tuṣyati.* सः कदापि न तुष्यति (√तुष्) ।

(2) You are wasting time. *bhavān samayaṁ nāśayati.* भवान् समयं नाशयति ।

(3) The soul neither takes birth nor dies. *ātmā na jāyate na mriyate.* आत्मा न जायते न म्रियते (√जन्, √मृ) ।

(4) Now the doubt does not exist. *ataḥ saṁśayaḥ na vidyate.* अतः संशयः न विद्यते (√विद्) ।

(5) You are fighting for truth. *bhavān satyāya yudhyate.* भनान् सत्याय युद्ध्यते (√युध्) ।

(6) Arjuna said, O Krishṇa! I shall not fight (लृट्). *Arjunaḥ uvāća, Bhoḥ Kṛṣṇa! ahaṁ na yotsye.* अर्जुनः उवाच, भोः कृष्ण! अहं न योत्स्ये ।

(7) The Lord pardons you. *devaḥ tvāṁ mṛṣyati.* देवः त्वां मृष्यति (√मृष्)

THE IMPORTANT ROOTS of the 4th दिवादिः class

ROOT √सिव् (to sew) *Parasmaipadī*

सीव्यामि	सीव्यावः	सीव्यामः
सीव्यसि	सीव्यथः	सीव्यथ
सीव्यति	सीव्यतः	सीव्यन्ति

ROOT √मन् (to know) *Atmanepadī*

मन्ये	मन्यावहे	मन्यामहे
मन्यसे	मन्येथे	मन्यध्वे
मन्यते	मन्येते	मन्यन्ते

25.5

THE FIFTH CLASS

svādiḥ gaṇaḥ स्वादिः गणः ।

The fifth class of the verbs is the स्वादिः (*svādi*) class. The most typical example of this class is the verb root √सु (√*su* to bathe). There are 35 verbs in the स्वादि (fifth) class.

The स्वादिः (5th) class takes न and उ विकरण, as well as it takes अ *guṇaḥ* (गुणः) before the अङित् suffixes of Present (लट्), Imperfect past (लङ्), Imperative (लोट्) and Potential (विधि) tenses. e.g. सु + न + उ + अ + मि = सुनोमि, सुनोषि, सुनोति । *su + na + u + a + mi = sunomi, sunoṣi, sunoti.*

Scheme of Conjugations for the Fifth Class : Root √सु (to bathe)

(1) Present Tense : लट् (सामान्य-वर्तमाने) *Parasmaipadī*

	Singular	Dual	Plural	Meaning
1p∘	सुनोमि (मि)	सुनुवः (वः)	सुनुमः (मः)	I bathe
	sunomi	*sunuvaḥ*	*sunumaḥ*	
2p∘	सुनोषि (सि)	सुनुथः (थः)	सुनुथ (थ)	
	sunoṣi	*sunuthaḥ*	*sunutha*	
3p∘	सुनोति (ति)	सुनुतः (तः)	सुन्वन्ति (अन्ति)	
	sunoti	*sunutaḥ*	*sunvanti*	

(2) Past imperfect Tense : लङ् (अनद्यतन-भूते) *Parasmaipadī*

	Singular	Dual	Plural	Meaning
1p∘	असुनवम्	असुनवाव	असुनवाम	I bathed
	asunavam	*asunavāva*	*asunavāma*	
2p∘	असुनोः	असुनुतम्	असुनुत	
	asunoḥ	*asunutam*	*asunuta*	
3p∘	असुनोत्	असुनुताम्	असुन्वन्	

asunot	*asunutām*	*asunvan*

(3) Perfect Past Tense : लिट् (परोक्ष-भूते) *Parasmaipadī*

	Singular	Dual	Plural	Meaning
1p∘	सुषाव	सुषुविव	सषुविम	I had bathed
	suṣāva	*suṣuviva*	*suṣuvima*	
2p∘	सुषुविथ	सुषुवथुः	सुषुव	
	saṣuvitha	*suṣuvathuḥ*	*suṣuva*	
3p∘	सुषाव	सुषुवतुः	सुषुवुः	
	suṣāva	*suṣuvatuḥ*	*suṣuvuḥ*	

(4) Indefinite Past Tense : लुङ् (दूरवर्ति-भूते) *Parasmaipadī*

	Singular	Dual	Plural	Meaning
1p∘	असाविषम्	असाविष्व	असाविष्म	I had bathed
	asāviṣam	*asāviṣva*	*asāviṣma*	
2p∘	असावीः	असाविष्टम्	असाविष्ट	
	asāvīḥ	*asāviṣṭam*	*asāviṣṭa*	
3p∘	असावीत्	असाविष्टाम्	असाविषुः	
	asāvīt	*asāviṣṭām*	*asāviṣuḥ*	

(5) Definite Future : लुट् (सामान्य-भविष्यति) *Parasmaipadī*

	Singular	Dual	Plural	Meaning
1p∘	सोतास्मि	सोतास्वः	सोतास्मः	I will bathe
	sotāsmi	*sotāsvaḥ*	*sotāsmaḥ*	
2p∘	सोतासि	सोतास्थः	सोतास्थ	
	sotāsi	*sotāsthaḥ*	*sotāstha*	
3p∘	सोता	सोतारौ	सोतारः	
	sotā	*sotārau*	*sotāraḥ*	

(6) Indefinite Future : लृट् (अपूर्ण-भविष्यति) *Parasmaipadī*

Singular	Dual	Plural	Meaning
1p◦ सोष्यामि	सोष्याव:	सेष्याम:	I shall bathe
soṣyāmi	*soṣyāvaḥ*	*soṣyāmaḥ*	
2p◦ सोष्यसि	सोष्यथ:	सोष्यथ	
soṣyasi	*soṣyathaḥ*	*soṣyatha*	
3p◦ सोष्यति	सोष्यत:	सोष्यन्ति	
soṣyati	*soṣyataḥ*	*soṣyanti*	

(7) Conditional Mood : लृङ् (भविष्यति क्रियातिपत्तौ) *Parasmaipadī*

Singular	Dual	Plural	Meaning
1p◦ असोष्यम्	असोष्याव	असोष्याम	If I bathe
asoṣyam	*asoṣyāva*	*asoṣyāma*	
2p◦ असोष्य:	असोष्यतम्	असोष्यत	
asoṣyaḥ	*asoṣyatam*	*asoṣyata*	
3p◦ असोष्यत्	असोष्यताम्	असोष्यन्	
asoṣyat	*asoṣyatām*	*asoṣyan*	

(8) Imperative Mood : लोट् (आज्ञार्थे; प्रश्नार्थे; विध्यादौ) *Parasmaipadī*

Singular	Dual	Plural	Meaning
1p◦ सुनवानि	सुनवाव	सुनवाम	Should I bathe?
sunavāni	*sunavāva*	*sunavāma*	
2p◦ सुनु	सुनुतम्	सुनुत	Please bathe!
sunu	*sunutam*	*sunuta*	
3p◦ सुनोतु	सुनुताम्	सुन्वन्तु	He should bathe!
sunotu	*sunutām*	*sunvantu*	

(9) Potential or Subjunctive Mood : विधिलिङ् (विध्यादौ) *Parasmaipadī*

Singular	Dual	Plural	Meaning

1p∘ सुनुयाम्	सुनुयाव	सुनुयाम	I may bathe
sunuyām	*sunuyāva*	*sunuyāma*	
2p∘ सुनुयाः	सुनुयातम्	सुनुयात	
sunuyāḥ	*sunuyātam*	*sunuyāta*	
3p∘ सुनुयात्	सुनुयाताम्	सुनुयुः	
sunuyāt	*sunuyātām*	*sunuyuḥ*	

(10) Benedictive or Optative Mood : आशीर्लिङ् (आशिषि) *Parasmaipadī*

Singular	Dual	Plural	Meaning
1p∘ सूयासम्	सूयास्व	सूयास्म	May I bathe!
sūyāsam	*sūyāsva*	*sūyāsma*	
2p∘ सूयाः	सूयास्तम्	सूयास्त	
sūyāḥ	*sūyāstam*	*sūyāsta*	
3p∘ सूयात्	सूयास्ताम्	सूयासुः	
sūyāt	*sūyāstām*	*sūyāsuḥ*	

EXAMPLES :

(1) I am taking a bath. *ahaṁ sunomi.* अहं सुनोमि (√सु) ।

(2) You take a bath. *bhavān/bhavatī sunoti.* भवान्/भवती सुनोति । She is taking a bath. *sā sunoti.* सा सुनोति ।

(3) They took bath. *te asunvan.* ते असुन्वन् ।

(4) I choose you as a friend. *ahaṁ bhavantam mitraṁ ćinomi.* अहं भवन्तम् मित्रं चिनोमि (√चि) । May we choose. *vayaṁ ćinuyāma.* वयं चिनुयाम ।

24.6

THE SIXTH CLASS

tudādiḥ gaṇaḥ तुदादिः गणः ।

The sixth class of the verbs is the तुदादिः (*tudādi*) class. The most typical example of this class is the verb root √तुद् (√*tud* to inflict). There are 157 verbs in तुदादि (sixth) class. Like the भ्वादि: (1st) class, the तुदादि: (6th) class also takes अ विकरण in the Present (लट्), Imperfect past (लङ्), Imperative (लोट्) and Potential (विधि) tenses. e.g. तुद् + अ + अ + मि = तुदामि, तुदामः, तुदामः ।

Scheme of Conjugations for the Sixth Class : Root √तुद् (to inflict, to hurt)

(1) Present Tense : लट् (सामान्य-वर्तमाने) *Parasmaipadī*

	Singular	Dual	Plural	Meaning
1p∘	तुदामि (आमि)	तुदावः (आवः)	तुदामः (आमः)	I inflict
	tudāmi	*tudāvaḥ*	*tudāmaḥ*	
2p∘	तुदसि (सि)	तुदथः (थः)	तुदथ (थ)	
	tudasi	*tudathaḥ*	*tudatha*	
3p∘	तुदति (ति)	तुदतः (तः)	तुदन्ति (अन्ति)	
	tudati	*tudataḥ*	*tudanti*	

(2) Past imperfect Tense : लङ् (अनद्यतन-भूते) *Parasmaipadī*

	Singular	Dual	Plural	Meaning
1p∘	अतुदम्	अतुदाव	अतुदाम	I inflicted
	atudam	*atudāva*	*atudāma*	
2p∘	अतुदः	अतुदतम्	अतुदत	
	atudaḥ	*atudatam*	*atudata*	
3p∘	अतुदत्	अतुदताम्	अतुदन्	
	atudat	*atudatām*	*atudan*	

(3) Perfect Past Tense : लिट् (परोक्ष-भूते) *Parasmaipadī*

	Singular	Dual	Plural	Meaning
1p∘	तुतोद	तुतुदिव	तुतुदिम	I had inflicted
	tutoda	*tutudiva*	*tutudima*	
2p∘	तुतोदिथ	तुतुदथुः	तुतुद	

	tutoditha	*tutudathuḥ*	*tutuda*
3p◦	तुतोद	तुतुदतुः	तुतुदुः
	tutoda	*tutudatuḥ*	*tutuduḥ*

(4) Indefinite Past Tense : लुङ् (दूरवर्ति-भूते) *Parasmaipadī*

	Singular	Dual	Plural	Meaning
1p◦	अतौत्सम्	अतौत्स्व	अतौत्स्म	I had inflicted
	atautsam	*atautsva*	*atautsma*	
2p◦	अतौत्सीः	अतौत्तम्	अतौत्त	
	atautsīḥ	*atauttam*	*atautta*	
3p◦	अतौत्सीत्	अतौत्ताम्	अतौत्सुः	
	atautsīt	*atauttām*	*atautsuḥ*	

(5) Definite Future : लुट् (सामान्य-भविष्यति) *Parasmaipadī*

	Singular	Dual	Plural	Meaning
1p◦	तोत्तास्मि	तोत्तास्वः	तोत्तास्मः	I will inflict
	tottāsmi	*tottāsvaḥ*	*tottāsmaḥ*	
2p◦	तोत्तासि	तोत्तास्थः	तोत्तास्थ	
	tottāsi	*tattāsthaḥ*	*tottāstha*	
3p◦	तोत्ता	तोत्तारौ	तोत्तारः	
	tottā	*tottārau*	*tottāraḥ*	

(6) Indefinite Future : लृट् (अपूर्ण-भविष्यति) *Parasmaipadī*

	Singular	Dual	Plural	Meaning
1p◦	तोत्स्यामि	तोत्स्यावः	तोत्स्यामः	I shall inflict
	totsyāmi	*totsyāvaḥ*	*totsyāmaḥ*	
2p◦	तोत्स्यसि	तोत्स्यथः	तोत्स्यथ	
	totsyasi	*totsyathaḥ*	*totsyatha*	
3p◦	तोत्स्यति	तोत्स्यतः	तोत्स्यन्ति	

totsyati	*totsyataḥ*	*totsyanti*

(7) Conditional Mood : लृङ् (भविष्यति क्रियातिपत्तौ) *Parasmaipadī*

	Singular	Dual	Plural	Meaning
1p◦	अतोत्स्यम्	अतोत्स्याव	अतोत्स्याम	If I inflict
	atotsyam	*atotsyāva*	*atotsyāma*	
2p◦	अतोत्स्यः	अतोत्स्यतम्	अतोत्स्यत	
	atotsyaḥ	*atotsyatam*	*atotsyata*	
3p◦	अतोत्स्यत्	अतोत्स्यताम्	अतोत्स्यन्	
	atotsyat	*atotsyatām*	*atotsyan*	

(8) Imperative Mood : लोट् (आज्ञार्थे; प्रश्नार्थे; विध्यादौ) *Parasmaipadī*

	Singular	Dual	Plural	Meaning
1p◦	तुदानि	तुदाव	तुदाम	Should I inflict?
	tudāni	*tudāva*	*tudāma*	
2p◦	तुद	तुदतम्	तुदत	Please inflict!
	tuda	*tudatam*	*tudata*	
3p◦	तुदतु	तुदताम्	तुदन्तु	He, she should inflict!
	tudatu	*tudatām*	*tudantu*	

(9) Potential or Subjunctive Mood : विधिलिङ् (विध्यादौ) *Parasmaipadī*

	Singular	Dual	Plural	Meaning
1p◦	तुदेयम्	तुदेव	तुदेम	I may inflict
	tudeyam	*tudeva*	*tudema*	
2p◦	तुदेः	तुदेतम्	तुदेत	
	tudeḥ	*tudetam*	*tudeta*	
3p◦	तुदेत्	तुदेताम्	तुदेयुः	
	tudet	*tudetām*	*tudeyuḥ*	

(10) Benedictive or Optative Mood : आशीर्लिङ् (आशिषि) *Parasmaipadī*

Singular	Dual	Plural	Meaning
1p॰ तुद्यासम्	तुद्यास्व	तुद्यास्म	May I inflict!
tudyāsam	*tudyāsva*	*tudyāsma*	
2p॰ तुद्याः	तुद्यास्तम्	तुद्यास्त	
tudyāḥ	*tudyāstam*	*tudyāsta*	
3p॰ तुद्यात्	तुद्यास्ताम्	तुद्यासुः	
tudyāt	*tudyāstām*	*tudyāsuḥ*	

EXAMPLES cum EXERCISE : (cumulative learning)

(1) He meets me. *saḥ mām̐ milati.* सः माम् मिलति (√मिल्) ।

(2) He met me yesterday. *saḥ mām̐ hyaḥ amilat/melitavān.* सः मां ह्यः अमिलत्/मेलितवान्

(3) Please meet me tomorrow. *kṛpayā mām̐ śvaḥ milatu.* कृपया मां श्वः मिलतु ।

(4) He attains peace. *saḥ śāntim̐ vindati (āpnaoti)* सः शान्तिं विन्दति/आप्नोति (√विद् √आप्)

(5) The Yogi attains liberation. *yogī nirvāṇam̐ ṛcchati.* योगी निर्वाणम् ऋच्छति (√ऋच्छ्) ।

(6) I want it. *aham etat icchāmi.* अहम् एतत् इच्छामि (√इष्) ।

(7) He does not want it. *saḥ etat na icchati.* सः एतत् न इच्छति ।

(8) What do you want? *bhavān kim icchati?* भवान् किम् इच्छति?

(9) Why does she want it? *sā etat kimartham icchati?* सा एतत् किमर्थम् इच्छति?

THE IMPORTANT ROOTS of the 6th, तुदादिः class

ROOT √इष् (to desire)

In the Present (लट्), Imperfect past (लङ्), Imperative (लोट्) and Potential (विधि) tenses of √इष्, prefix त् appeares befor ष् and then this ष् changes to छ् । According to the *sandhi* rule त् + छ् = च्छ् । Therefore, √इष् → इ + त् + छ् = इ + च् + छ् = इच्छ्

इच्छामि इच्छावः इच्छामः । इच्छसि इच्छथः इच्छथ । इच्छति इच्छतः इच्छन्ति ।

ROOT √मस्ज् (to purify) :

In the Present (लट्), Imperfect past (लङ्), Imperative (लोट्), Perfect past (लिट्) and Potential (विधि॰) tenses of √मस्ज्, when झलादि (any consonant other than the nasals and the semi-vowels : ङ, ञ, ण, न, म, य, र, ल, व) letter is not ahead, the स् of मस्ज् changes to द् and then this द् changes to ज् (pāṇini 8.4.53,40). Thus,

म + स् + ज् → म + द् + ज् → म + ज् + ज् + = मज्ज् and then the Present tense is मज्जामि मज्जाव: मज्जाम: । मज्जसि मज्जथ: मज्जथ । मज्जति मज्जत: मज्जन्ति ।

(1) Present (लट्)	मज्जति	मज्जत:	मज्जन्ति ।
(2) Imperfect past (लङ्)	अमज्जत्	अमज्जताम्	अमज्जन् ।
(3) Future (लृट्)	मङ्क्ष्यति	मङ्क्ष्यत:	मङ्क्ष्यन्ति ।
(4) Imperative (लोट्)	मज्जतु	मज्जताम्	मज्जन्तु ।
(5) Potential (विधि॰)	मज्जेत्	मज्जेताम्	मज्जेयु: ।

ROOT √विज् (to tremble) :

The *ātmanepadī* verb √विज् is primarily used with the prefix उद् ।

Thus, उद्√विज् = to agitate. उद्विजते उद्विजेते उद्विजन्ते ।

ROOT √मृ (to die) : The root √मृ forms :

(a) *ātmanepadī* verbs in (i) Present tense (लट्), (ii) Past imperfect (लङ्), (iii) Past indefinite (लुङ्), (v) Imperative (लोट्), (v) Benedictive (आशि॰), and (vi) Potential (विधि॰) tenses, and it forms

(b) *parasmaipadī* verbs in (vii) Past perfect (लिट्), (viii) Indefinite future (लुट्), (ix) Indefinite future (लृट्), and (x) Conditional (लृङ्) tenses.

Therefore,

(1) The *ātmanepadī* verbs from √मृ :

(i) Present tense (लट्)

म्रिये म्रियावहे म्रियामहे । म्रियसे म्रियेथे म्रियध्वे । म्रियते म्रियेते म्रियन्ते ।

(ii) Past imperfect (लङ्)

अम्रिये अम्रियावहि अम्रियामहि । अम्रियथा: अम्रियेथाम् अम्रियध्वम् । अम्रियत अम्रियेताम् अम्रियन्त ।

(iii) Past indefinite (लुङ्)

अमृषि अमृष्वहि अमृष्महि । अमृथा: अमृषाथाम् अमृढ्वम् । अमृत अमृषाताम् अमृषत ।

(iv) Imperative (लोट्)

म्रियै म्रियावहै म्रियामहै । म्रियस्व म्रियेथाम् म्रियध्वम् । म्रियताम् म्रियेताम् म्रियन्ताम् ।

(v) Benedictive (आशि॰)

मृषीय मृष्वीवहि मृषीमहि । मृषीष्ठा: मृषीयास्थां मृषीढ्वम् । मृषीष्ट मृषीयास्तां मृषीरन् ।

(vi) Potential (विधि॰)

म्रियेय म्रियावहि म्रियामहि । म्रियेथा: म्रियेयाथाम् म्रियेध्वम् । म्रियेत म्रियेयाताम् म्रियेरन् ।

(2) The *parasmaipadī* verbs fro √मृ :

(vii) Past perfect (लिट्)

ममार मम्रिव मम्रिम । ममर्थ मम्रथु: मम्र । ममार मम्रतु: मम्रु: ।

(viii) Indefinite future (लुट्)

मर्तास्मि मर्तास्व: मर्तास्म: । मर्तासि मर्तास्थ: मर्तास्थ । मर्ता मर्तारौ मर्तार: ।

(ix) Indefinite future (लृट्)

मरिष्यामि मरिष्याव: मरिष्याम: । मरिष्यसि मरिष्यथ: मरिष्यथ । मरिष्यति मरिष्यत: मरिष्यन्ति ।

(x) Conditional (लृङ्)

अमरिष्यम् अमरिष्याव अमरिष्याम । अमरिष्य: अमरिष्यतम् अमरिष्यत । अमरिष्यत् अमरिष्यताम् अमरिष्यन् ।

ROOT √मुच् (to free, to become free) :

In the Present (लट्), Imperfect past (लङ्), Imperative (लोट्) and Potential (विधि) tenses of √मुच् (as well as √सिच्, लिप्, कृत्, विद ...etc),

(i) particle न् comes in the middle of the root.

(ii) This न् becomes a nasal dot (अनुस्वार:)

(iii) and (following the rule of परसवर्ण:) it is pronounced according to the class of the following letter. e.g. मुच् → मु + न् + च् = मुंच् = मुञ्च् → मुञ्चति । सिच् → सि + न् + च् = सिंच् = सिञ्च् → सिञ्चति । लिप् → लि + न् + प् = लिंप् = लिम्प् → लिम्पति । कृत् → कृ + न् + त् = कृंत् = कृन्त् → कृन्तति । विद् → वि + न् + द् = विंद् = विन्द् → विन्दति ।

24.7
THE SEVENTH CLASS
rudhādiḥ gaṇaḥ रुधादि: गण: ।

The seventh class of the verbs is रुधादि *(rudhādi)* class. The typical example of this class is verb root √रुध् (√*rudh* to hinder). There are 25 verbs in the रुधादि (seventh) class.

In the Present (लट्), Imperfect past (लङ्), Imperative (लोट्) and Potential (विधि) tenses of √रुध् the न विकरणम् comes in. In *parasmaipadī* Indefinite Past tense (लुङ्), two kinds of verbs are formed in this class (see below).

Scheme of Conjugations for the Seventh Class : Root √रुध् to hinder

(1) Present Tense : लट् (सामान्य-वर्तमाने) *Parasmaipadī*

	Singular	Dual	Plural	Meaning
1p∘	रुणध्मि (मि)	रुन्ध्व: (व:)	रुन्ध्म: (म:)	I hinder
	ruṇadhmi	*rundhvaḥ*	*rundhmaḥ*	
2p∘	रुणत्सि (सि)	रुन्द्ध: (थ:)	रुन्द्ध (थ)	
	ruṇatsi	*runddhaḥ*	*runddha*	
3p∘	रुणद्धि (ति)	रुन्द्ध: (त:)	रुन्धन्ति (अन्ति)	
	ruṇaddhi	*runddhaḥ*	*rundhanti*	

(2) Past imperfect Tense : लङ् (अनद्यतन-भूते) *Parasmaipadī*

	Singular	Dual	Plural	Meaning
1p∘	अरुणधम्	अरुन्ध्व	अरुन्ध्म	I hindered
	aruṇadham	*arundhva*	*arundhma*	
2p∘	अरुण:	अरुन्द्धम्	अरुन्द्ध	

aruṇaḥ	*arundhatam*	*arudha*
3p◦ अरुणत्	अरुन्धाम्	अरुन्धन्
aruṇat	*arundhām*	*arundhan*

(3) Perfect Past Tense : लिट् (परोक्ष-भूते) *Parasmaipadī*

Singular	Dual	Plural	Meaning
1p◦ रुरोध	रुरुधिव	रुरुधिम	I had hindered
rurodha	*rurudhiva*	*rurudhima*	
2p◦ रुरुधिथ	रुरुधिथुः	रुरुध	
rurudhitha	*rurudhithuḥ*	*rurudha*	
3p◦ रुरोध	रुरुधतुः	रुरुधुः	
rurodha	*rurudhatuḥ*	*rurudhuḥ*	

(4) Indefinite Past Tense : लुङ् (दूरवर्ति-भूते) *Parasmaipadī*

Singular	Dual	Plural	Meaning
1p◦ अरुधम्	अरुधाव	अरुधाम	I had hindered
arudham	*arudhāva*	*arudhāma*	
2p◦ अरुधः	अरुधतम्	अरुधत	
arudhaḥ	*arudhatam*	*arudhata*	
3p◦ अरुधत्	अरुधताम्	अरुधन्	
arudhat	*arudhatām*	*arudhan*	

Optional : (पक्ष्ये)

Singular	Dual	Plural	Meaning
1p◦ अरौत्सम्	अरौत्स्व	अरौत्स्म	I had hindered
arautsam	*arautsva*	*arautsma*	
2p◦ अरोत्सीः	अरौद्धम्	अरौद्ध	
arautsīḥ	*arauddham*	*arauddha*	
3p◦ अरौत्सीत्	अरौद्धाम्	अरौत्सुः	

arautsīt *arauddhām* *arautsuḥ*

(5) Definite Future : लुट् (सामान्य-भविष्यति) *Parasmaipadī*

	Singular	Dual	Plural	Meaning
1p◦	रोद्धास्मि	रोद्धास्वः	रोद्धास्मः	I will hinder
	roddhāsmi	*roddhāsvaḥ*	*roddhāsmaḥ*	
2p◦	रोद्धासि	रोद्धास्थः	रोद्धास्थ	
	roddhāsi	*roddhāsthaḥ*	*roddhāstha*	
3p◦	रोद्धा	रोद्धारौ	रोद्धारः	
	roddhā	*roddhārau*	*roddhāraḥ*	

(6) Indefinite Future : लृट् (अपूर्ण-भविष्यति) *Parasmaipadī*

	Singular	Dual	Plural	Meaning
1p◦	रोत्स्यामि	रोत्स्यावः	रोत्स्यामः	I shall hinder
	rotsyāmi	*rotsyāvaḥ*	*rotsyāmaḥ*	
2p◦	रोत्स्यसि	रोत्स्यथः	रोत्स्यथ	
	rotsyasi	*rotsyathaḥ*	*rotsyatha*	
3p◦	रोत्स्यति	रोत्स्यतः	रोत्स्यन्ति	
	rotsyati	*rotsyataḥ*	*rotsyanti*	

(7) Conditional Mood : लृङ् (भविष्यति क्रियातिपत्तौ) *Parasmaipadī*

	Singular	Dual	Plural	Meaning
1p◦	अरोत्स्यम्	अरोत्स्याव	अरोत्स्याम	If I hinder
	arotsyam	*arotsyāva*	*arotsyāma*	
2p◦	अरोत्स्यः	अरोत्स्यतम्	अरोत्स्यत	
	arotsyaḥ	*arotsyatam*	*arotsyata*	
3p◦	अरोत्स्यत्	अरोत्स्यताम्	अरोत्स्यन्	
	arotsyat	*arotsyatām*	*arotsyan*	

(8) Imperative Mood : लोट् (आज्ञार्थे; प्रश्नार्थे; विध्यादौ) *Parasmaipadī*

	Singular	Dual	Plural	Meaning
1p॰	रुणधानि	रुणधाव	रुणधाम	Should I hinder?
	ruṇadhāni	*ruṇadhāva*	*ruṇadhāma*	
2p॰	रुन्द्धि	रुन्द्धम्	रुन्द्ध	Please hinder!
	runddhi	*runddham*	*runddha*	
3p॰	रुणद्धु	रुन्द्धाम्	रुन्द्धन्तु	He, she should hinder!
	ruṇaddhu	*runddhām*	*runddhantu*	

(9) Potential or Subjunctive Mood : विधिलिङ् (विध्यादौ) *Parasmaipadī*

	Singular	Dual	Plural	Meaning
1p॰	रुन्ध्याम्	रुन्ध्याव	रुन्ध्याम	I may hinder
	rundhyām	*rundhyāva*	*rundhyāma*	
2p॰	रुन्ध्याः	रुन्ध्यातम्	रुन्ध्यात	
	rundhyāḥ	*rundhyātam*	*rundhyāta*	
3p॰	रुन्ध्यात्	रुन्ध्याताम्	रुन्ध्युः	
	rundhyāt	*rundhyātām*	*rundhyuḥ*	

(10) Benedictive or Optative Mood : आशीर्लिङ् (आशिषि) *Parasmaipadī*

	Singular	Dual	Plural	Meaning
1p॰	रुध्यासम्	रुध्यास्व	रुध्यास्म	May I hinder!
	rudhyāsam	*rudhyāsva*	*rudhyāsma*	
2p॰	रुध्याः	रुध्यास्तम्	रुध्यास्त	
	rudhyāḥ	*rudhyāstam*	*rudhyāsta*	
3p॰	रुध्यात्	रुध्यास्ताम्	रुध्यासुः	
	rudhyāt	*rudhyāstām*	*rudhyāsuḥ*	

(1) The Lord destroys the wicked. *devaḥ duṣṭān hinasti.* देवः दुष्टान् हिनस्ति (√हिंस्) ।

(2) They shall not enjoy peace. *te śāntiṁ na bhokṣanti.* ते शांतिं न भोक्ष्यन्ति (√भुज्) ।

(3) King enjoys the kingdom. *rājā rājyaṁ bhunakti.* राजा राज्यं भुनक्ति ।

24.8

THE EIGHTTH CLASS

tanādiḥ gaṇaḥ तनादिः गणः ।

The eightth class of the verbs is तनादि (*tanādi*) class. The typical example of this class is the verb √तन् (√*tan* to spread). There are only 10 verbs in the तनादि (eighth) class. The most widely used verb is √kṛ (to do) √कृ ।

In the Present (लट्), Imperfect past (लङ्), Imperative (लोट्) and Potential (विधि) tenses of तनादिः class उ विकरणम् comes in. This उ then becomes ओ with *guṇa,* as explained in the भ्वादिः (1st) class.

1. *Vikaraṇa* उ is added to the verbal base before adding the tense suffixes. तन् + उ = तनु
2. This *vikaraṇa* उ becomes ओ before the (अङित्) suffixes of मि, सि, ति । तनु → तनो + मि = तनोमि, तनोषि, तनोति ।
3. This *vikaraṇa* उ is optionally dropped before the suffixes of वः, मः, वहि, महि etc. तनु - उ + वः = तन्वः (तनुवः), तन्मः (तनुमः) , तन्वहे (तनुवहे), तन्महे (तनुमहे) ...etc.

Scheme of Conjugations for the Eighth Class : Root √तन् to spread

(1) Present Tense : लट् (सामान्य-वर्तमाने) *Parasmaipadī*

	Singular	Dual	Plural	Meaning
1p◦	तनोमि (ओमि)	तन्वः/तनुवः (वः)	तन्मः/तनुमः (मः)	I spread
	tanomi	*tanvaḥ/tanuvaḥ*	*tanmaḥ/tanumaḥ*	
2p◦	तनोषि (सि)	तनुथः (थः)	तनुथ (थ)	
	tanoṣi	*tanuthaḥ*	*tanutha*	
3p◦	तनोति (ति)	तनुतः (तः)	तन्वन्ति (अन्ति)	
	tanoti	*tanutaḥ*	*tanvanti*	

(2) Past imperfect Tense : लङ् (अनद्यतन-भूते) *Parasmaipadī*

Singular	Dual	Plural	Meaning
1p◦ अतनवम्	अतनुव	अतनुम	I spreaded
atanavam	*atanuva*	*atanuma*	
2p◦ अतनोः	अतनुतम्	अतनुत	
atanoḥ	*atanutam*	*atanuta*	
3p◦ अतनोत्	अतनुताम्	अतन्वन्	
atanot	*atanutām*	*atanvan*	

(3) Perfect Past Tense : लिट् (परोक्ष-भूते) *Parasmaipadī*

Singular	Dual	Plural	Meaning
1p◦ ततान	तेनिव	तेनिम	I had spreaded
tatāna	*teniva*	*tenima*	
2p◦ तेनिथ	तेनथुः	तेन	
tenitha	*tenathuḥ*	*tena*	
3p◦ ततान	तेनतुः	तेनुः	
tatāna	*tenatuḥ*	*tenuḥ*	

(4) Indefinite Past Tense : लुङ् (दूरवर्ति-भूते) *Parasmaipadī*

Singular	Dual	Plural	Meaning
1p◦ अतानिषम्	अतानिष्व	अतानिष्म	I had spreaded
atāniṣam	*atāniṣva*	*atāniṣma*	
2p◦ अतानीः	अतानिष्टम्	अतानिष्ट	
atānīḥ	*atāniṣṭam*	*atāniṣṭa*	
3p◦ अतानीत्	अतानिष्टाम्	अतानिषुः	
atānīt	*atāniṣṭām*	*atāniṣuḥ*	

(5) Definite Future : लुट् (सामान्य-भविष्यति) *Parasmaipadī*

Singular	Dual	Plural	Meaning
1p◦ तनितास्मि	तनितास्वः	तनितास्मः	I will spread

tanitāsmi	*tanitāsvaḥ*	*tanitāsmaḥ*
2p◦ तनितासि	तनितास्थ:	तनितास्थ
tanitāsi	*tanitāsthaḥ*	*tanitāstha*
3p◦ तनिता	तनितारौ	तनितार:
tanitā	*tanitārau*	*tanitāraḥ*

(6) Indefinite Future : लृट् (अपूर्ण–भविष्यति) *Parasmaipadī*

Singular	Dual	Plural	Meaning
1p◦ तनिष्यामि	तनिष्याव:	तनिष्याम:	I shall spread
taniṣyāmi	*taniṣyāvaḥ*	*taniṣyāmaḥ*	
2p◦ तनिष्यसि	तनिष्यथ:	तनिष्यथ	
taniṣyasi	*taniṣyathaḥ*	*taniṣyatha*	
3p◦ तनिष्यति	तनिष्यत:	तनिष्यन्ति	
taniṣyati	*taniṣyataḥ*	*taniṣyanti*	

(7) Conditional Mood : लृङ् (भविष्यति क्रियातिपत्तौ) *Parasmaipadī*

Singular	Dual	Plural	Meaning
1p◦ अतनिष्यम्	अतनिष्याव	अतनिष्याम	If I spread
ataniṣyam	*ataniṣyāva*	*ataniṣyāma*	
2p◦ अतनिष्य:	अतनिष्यतम्	अतनिष्यत	
ataniṣyaḥ	*ataniṣyatam*	*ataniṣyata*	
3p◦ अतनिष्यत्	अतनिष्यताम्	अतनिष्यन्	
ataniṣyat	*ataniṣyatām*	*atanṣyan*	

(8) Imperative Mood : लोट् (आज्ञार्थे; प्रश्नार्थे; विध्यादौ) *Parasmaipadī*

Singular	Dual	Plural	Meaning
1p◦ तनवानि	तनवाव	तनवाम	Should I spread?
tanavāni	*tanavāva*	*tanavāma*	
2p◦ तनु	तनुतम्	तनुत	Please spread!

tanu	*tanutam*	*tanuta*	
3p◦ तनोतु	तनुताम्	तन्वन्तु	He, she should spread!
tanotu	*tanutām*	*tanvantu*	

(9) Potential or Subjunctive Mood : विधिलिङ् (विध्यादौ) *Parasmaipadī*

Singular	Dual	Plural	Meaning
1p◦ तनुयाम्	तनुयाव	तनुयाम	I may spread
tanuyām	*tanuyāva*	*tanuyāma*	
2p◦ तनुयाः	तनुयातम्	तनुयात	
tanuyāḥ	*tanuyātam*	*tanuyāta*	
3p◦ तनुयात्	तनुयाताम्	तनुयुः	
tanuyāt	*tanuyātām*	*tanuyuḥ*	

(10) Benedictive or Optative Mood : आशीर्लिङ् (आशिषि) *Parasmaipadī*

Singular	Dual	Plural	Meaning
1p◦ तन्यासम्	तन्यास्व	तन्यास्म	May I spread!
tanyāsam	*tanyāsva*	*tanyāsma*	
2p◦ तन्याः	तन्यास्तम्	तन्यास्त	
tanyāḥ	*tanyāstam*	*tanyāsta*	
3p◦ तन्यात्	तन्यास्ताम्	तन्यासुः	
tanyāt	*tanyāstām*	*tanyāsuḥ*	

EXAMPLES :

The most important verb of this class is √kṛ (√कृ to do).

The complete chart for this verb is as follows : As said above, in the Present (लट्), Imperfect past (लङ्), Imperative (लोट्) and Potential (विधि) tenses, (i) the √कृ take उ विकरणम् । (ii) when उ comes after कृ, the कृ takes *guṇa* and becomes अर् (रपरत्वम्). (iii) then उ विकरणम् is added, as shown in भ्वादिः (1st) class.

कृ = क् + ऋ → क् + ऋ + अ + उ = क् + अर् + उ = करु (iv). This *vikaraṇa* उ becomes ओ before the (अङित्) suffixes of मि, सि, ति । कृ → क् + ऋ + अ + ओ + मि = करोमि, करोषि, करोति । ...etc.

To do √kṛ √कृ

1. **लट्** (Present tense, action began but not complete e.g. I do, I am doing)

परस्मैपदी			आत्मनेपदी		
करोमि	कुर्वः	कुर्मः ।	कुर्वे	कुर्वहे	कुर्महे ।
करोषि	कुरुथः	कुरुथ ।	कुरुषे	कुर्वाथे	कुरुध्वे ।
करोति	कुरुतः	कुर्वन्ति ।	कुरुते	कुर्वाते	कुर्वते ।

2. **लङ्** (First Preterite, Imperfect Past tense, act of recent past e.g. I was doing, I did)

परस्मैपदी			आत्मनेपदी		
अकरवम्	अकुर्व	अकुर्म ।	अकुर्वि	अकुर्वहि	अकुर्महि
अकरोः	अकुरुतम्	अकुरुत ।	अकुरुथाः	अकुर्वाथाम्	अकुरुध्वम्
अकरोत्,	अकुरुताम्,	अकुर्वन् ।	अकुरुत,	अकुर्वाताम्,	अकुर्वत ।

3. **लिट्** (Second Preterite, Perfect Past tense, action of absolute past and out of sight e.g. he was, he had been)

परस्मैपदी			आत्मनेपदी		
चकार	चकृव	चकृम ।	चक्रे	चकृवहे	चकृमहे ।
चकर्थ	चक्रथुः	चक्र ।	चकृषे	चक्राथे	चकृढ्वे ।
चकार	चक्रतुः	चक्रुः ।	चक्रे	चक्राते	चक्रिरे ।

4. **लुङ्** (Third Preterite, Aorist or Indefinite Past tense, e.g. I had been, there was a king)

परस्मैपदी आत्मनेपदी

अकार्षम्	अकार्ष्व	अकार्ष्म ।	अकृषि	अकृष्वहि	अकृष्महि ।
अकार्षीः	अकार्ष्टम्	अकार्ष्ट ।	अकृथाः	अकृषाथाम्	अकृढ्वम् ।
अकार्षीत्	अकार्ष्टाम्	अकार्षुः ।	अकृत	अकृषाताम्	अकृषत ।

5. **लुट्** (Definite Future or First Future tense, the action that will happen after a fixed period, but not remote, although not immidiate. e.g. I will , I shall do it tommorrow)

परस्मैपदी			आत्मनेपदी		
कर्तास्मि	कर्तास्वः	कर्तास्मः ।	कर्ताहे	कर्तास्वहे	कर्तास्महे ।
कर्तासि	कर्तास्थः	कर्तास्थ ।	कर्तासे	कर्तासाथे	कर्ताध्वे ।
कर्ता	कर्तारौ	कर्तारः ।	कर्ता	कर्तारौ	कर्तारः ।

6. **लृट्** (Indefinite Future or Second Future tense, action is contingent up on some future event. e.g. I shall be)

परस्मैपदी			आत्मनेपदी		
करिष्यामि	करिष्यावः	करिष्यामः ।	करिष्ये	करिष्यावहे	करिष्यामहे ।
करिष्यसि	करिष्यथः	करिष्यथ ।	करिष्यसे	करिष्येथे	करिष्यध्वे ।
करिष्यति	करिष्यतः	करिष्यन्ति ।	करिष्यते	करिष्येते	करिष्यन्ते ।

(Imperative mood)

7. **लोट्** (Order, command, injunction, request, advice. It generally denotes or addresses second or third person e.g. you do, let me be, O God! help us)

परस्मैपदी			आत्मनेपदी		
करवाणि	करवाव	करवाम ।	करवै	करवावहै	करवामहै ।
कुरु	कुरुतम्	कुरुत ।	कुरुष्व	कुर्वाथाम्	कुरुध्वम् ।
करोतु	कुरुताम्	कुर्वन्तु ।	कुरुताम्	कुर्वाताम्	कुर्वताम् ।

(Subjunctive mood)

8. **विधिलिङ्** (Potential or possibility, e.g. It may happen, I may, can, would, should,

ought to do)

परस्मैपदी			आत्मनेपदी		
कुर्याम्	कुर्याव	कुर्याम ।	कुर्वीय	कुर्वीवहि	कुर्वीमहि ।
कुर्याः	कुर्यातम्	कुर्यात ।	कुर्वीथाः	कुर्वीयाथाम्	कुर्वीध्वम् ।
कुर्यात्	कुर्याताम्	कुर्युः ।	कुर्वीत	कुर्वीयाताम्	कुर्वीरन् ।

(Precative or Benedictive mood)

9. **आशीर्लिङ्** (Optative or Benedictive mood, e.g. may you succeed)

परस्मैपदी			आत्मनेपदी		
क्रियासम्	क्रियास्व	क्रियास्म ।	कृषीय	कृषीवहि	कृषीमहि ।
क्रियाः	क्रियास्तम्	क्रियास्त ।	कृषीष्ठाः	कृषीयास्थाम्	कृषीढ्वम् ।
क्रियात्	क्रियास्ताम्	क्रियासु ।	कृषीष्ठ	कृषीयास्ताम्	कृषीरन् ।

10. **लङ्** (Conditional Mood, depending upon, e.g. I should .. if)

परस्मैपदी			आत्मनेपदी		
अकरिष्यम्	अकरिष्याव	अकरिष्याम	अकरिष्ये	अकरिष्यावहि	अकरिष्यामहि
अकरिष्यः	अकरिष्यतम्	अकरिष्यत	अकरिष्यथाः	अकरिष्येथाम्	अकरिष्यध्वम्
अकरिष्यत्	अकरिष्यताम्	अकरिष्यन्	अकरिष्यत	अकरिष्येताम्	अकरिष्यन्त ।

24.9
THE NINETH CLASS

kryādiḥ gaṇaḥ

क्र्यादिः गणः ।

The nineth classe of the verbs is क्र्यादि *(kryādi)* class. The typical example of this class is the root √क्रीञ् (√*krīñ* to trade; buy or sell). There are 61 verbs in क्र्यादि (nineth) class. In the Present (लट्), Imperfect past (लङ्), Imperative (लोट्) and Potential (विधि) tenses, this class takes ना विकरणम् ।

Scheme of Conjugations for the Nineth Class : Root √क्रीञ् to trade

(1) Present Tense : लट् (सामान्य-वर्तमाने) *Parasmaipadī*

Singular	Dual	Plural	Meaning
1p◦ क्रीणामि (आमि)	क्रीणीव: (व:)	क्रीणीम: (म:)	I trade
krīṇāmi	*krīṇīvaḥ*	*krīṇīmaḥ*	
2p◦ क्रीणासि (सि)	क्रीणीथ: (थ:)	क्रीणीथ (थ)	
krīṇāsi	*krīṇīthaḥ*	*krīṇītha*	
3p◦ क्रीणाति (ति)	क्रीणीत: (त:)	क्रीणन्ति (अन्ति)	
krīṇāti	*krīṇītaḥ*	*krīṇanti*	

(2) Past imperfect Tense : लङ् (अनद्यतन-भूते) *Parasmaipadī*

Singular	Dual	Plural	Meaning
1p◦ अक्रीणाम्	अक्रीणीव	अक्रीणीम	I traded
akrīṇām	*akrīṇīva*	*akrīṇīma*	
2p◦ अक्रीणा:	अक्रीणीतम्	अक्रीणीत	
akrīṇāḥ	*akrīṇītam*	*akrīṇīta*	
3p◦ अक्रीणात्	अक्रीणीताम्	अक्रीणन्	
akrīṇāt	*akrīṇītām*	*akrīṇan*	

(3) Perfect Past Tense : लिट् (परोक्ष-भूते) *Parasmaipadī*

Singular	Dual	Plural	Meaning
1p◦ चिक्राय	चिक्रियिव	चिक्रियिम	I had traded
ćikrāya	*ćikriyiva*	*ćikriyima*	
2p◦ चिक्रयिथ	चिक्रियथु:	चिक्रिथ	
ćikrayitha	*ćikriyathuḥ*	*ćikritha*	
3p◦ चिक्राय	चिक्रियतु:	चिक्रियु:	
ćikrāya	*ćikriyatuḥ*	*ćikriyuḥ*	

(4) Indefinite Past Tense : लुङ् (दूरवर्ति-भूते) *Parasmaipadī*

Singular	Dual	Plural	Meaning
1p॰ अक्रैषम्	अक्रैष्व	अक्रैष्म	I had traded
akraiṣam	*akraiṣva*	*akraiṣma*	
2p॰ अक्रैषीः	अक्रैष्टम्	अक्रैष्ट	
akraiṣīḥ	*akraiṣṭam*	*akraiṣṭa*	
3p॰ अक्रैषीत्	अक्रैष्टाम्	अक्रैषुः	
akraiṣīt	*akraiṣṭām*	*akraiṣuḥ*	

(5) Definite Future : लुट् (सामान्य-भविष्यति) *Parasmaipadī*

Singular	Dual	Plural	Meaning
1p॰ क्रेतास्मि	क्रेतास्वः	क्रेतास्मः	I will trade
kretāsmi	*kretāsvaḥ*	*kretāsmaḥ*	
2p॰ क्रेतासि	क्रेतास्थः	क्रेतास्थ	
kretāsi	*kretāsthaḥ*	*kretāstha*	
3p॰ क्रेता	क्रेतारौ	क्रेतारः	
kretā	*kretārau*	*kretāraḥ*	

(6) Indefinite Future : लृट् (अपूर्ण-भविष्यति) *Parasmaipadī*

Singular	Dual	Plural	Meaning
1p॰ क्रेष्यामि	क्रेष्यावः	क्रेष्यामः	I shall trade
kreṣyāmi	*kreṣyāvaḥ*	*kreṣyāmaḥ*	
2p॰ क्रेष्यसि	क्रेष्यथः	क्रेष्यथ	
kreṣyasi	*kreṣyathaḥ*	*kreṣyatha*	
3p॰ क्रेष्यति	क्रेष्यतः	क्रेष्यन्ति	
kreṣyati	*kreṣyataḥ*	*kreṣyanti*	

(7) Conditional Mood : लृङ् (भविष्यति क्रियातिपत्तौ) *Parasmaipadī*

Singular	Dual	Plural	Meaning

1p◦ अक्रेष्यम्	अक्रेष्याव	अक्रेष्याम	Had I traded
akreṣyam	*akreṣyāva*	*akreṣyāma*	
2p◦ अक्रेष्य:	अक्रेष्यतम्	अक्रेष्यत	
akreṣyaḥ	*akreṣyatam*	*akreṣyata*	
3p◦ अक्रेष्यत्	अक्रेष्यताम्	अक्रेष्यन्	
akreṣyat	*akreṣyatām*	*akreṣyan*	

(8) Imperative Mood : लोट् (आज्ञार्थे; प्रश्नार्थे; विध्यादौ) *Parasmaipadī*

Singular	Dual	Plural	Meaning
1p◦ क्रीणानि	क्रीणाव	क्रीणाम	Should I trade?
krīṇāni	*krīṇāva*	*krīṇāma*	
2p◦ क्रीणीहि	क्रीणीतम्	क्रीणीत	Please tread!
krīṇīhi	*krīṇītam*	*krīṇīta*	
3p◦ क्रीणातु	क्रीणीताम्	क्रीणन्तु	He, she should tread!
krīṇātu	*krīṇītām*	*krīṇantu*	

(9) Potential or Subjunctive Mood : विधिलिङ् (विध्यादौ) *Parasmaipadī*

Singular	Dual	Plural	Meaning
1p◦ क्रीणीयाम्	क्रीणीयाव	क्रीणीयाम	I may trade
krīṇīyām	*krīṇīyāva*	*krīṇīyāma*	
2p◦ क्रीणीया:	क्रीणीयातम्	क्रीणीयात	
krīṇīyāḥ	*krīṇīyātam*	*krīṇīyāta*	
3p◦ क्रीणीयात्	क्रीणीयाताम्	क्रणीयु:	
krīṇīyāt	*krīṇīyātām*	*krīṇīyuḥ*	

(10) Benedictive or Optative Mood : आशीर्लिङ् (आशिषि) *Parasmaipadī*

Singular	Dual	Plural	Meaning
1p◦ क्रीयासम्	क्रीयास्व	क्रीयास्म	May I trade!
krīyāsam	*krīyāsva*	*krīyāsma*	

2p∘	क्रीयाः	क्रीयास्तम्	क्रीयास्त
	krīyāḥ	*krīyāstam*	*krīyāsta*
3p∘	क्रीयात्	क्रीयास्ताम्	क्रीयासुः
	krīyāt	*krīyāstām*	*krīyāsuḥ*

EXAMPLES cum EXERCISE :

(1) He buys books. *saḥ pustakāni krīṇāti.* सः पुस्तकानि क्रीणाति (√कृञ्) ।

(2) I will by the fruits. *ahaṁ phalāni kreṣyāmi.* अहं फलानि क्रेष्यामि ।

(3) She is cutting the plant. *sā vṛkṣaṁ lunāti.* सा वृक्षं लुनाति (√लु) ।

(4) He wares a blanket. *saḥ kambalaṁ gṛhṇāti.* सः कम्बलं गृह्णाति (√ग्रह) ।

(5) I am eating food. *aham annam aśnāmi.* अहम् अन्नम् अश्नामि (√अश्) ।

(6) I know him. *ahaṁ taṁ jānāmi.* अहं तं जानामि । √ज्ञा = to know.

(7) He knows you. *saḥ bhavantaṁ jānāti.* सः भवन्तं जानाति ।

(8) She knows him. *sā taṁ jānāti.* सा तं जानाति ।

(9) He knew me. *saḥ mām ajānāt.* सः माम् अजानात् ।

(10) We ought to know him. *vayaṁ taṁ jānīyāma.* वयं तं जानीयाम ।

(11) He will know you. *saḥ bhavantaṁ jñāsyati.* सः भवन्तं ज्ञास्यति ।

(12) You must know Sanskrit. *bhavān samskṛtaṁ jānātu.* भवान् संस्कृतं जानातु ।

24.10

THE TENTH CLASS

ćurādiḥ gaṇah चुरादिः गणः ।

The tenth class is चुरादि *(ćurādi)* class. The typical example is root √चुर् (√*ćur* to steal). There are 411 verbs in the चुरादि (tenth) class.

CHARACTERISTICS :

(i) If the middle vowel in a चुरादि verb has a short vowel such as इ, उ or ऋ, it takes *guṇa* (= ए, ओ, अर्) e.g. (1) चुर् + गुण = च् + उ + अ + र् = चोर् ।

(ii) If the root verb ends in इ, उ or ऋ vowel, this इ उ ऋ vowel receives *vṛddhi.* e.g. ली + वृद्धि = लै + इ = लाय् (3) यु + वृद्धि = यौ + इ = याव् (4) वृ + वृद्धि = वृ + इ = वार् ।

(iii) Then all चुरादि verbs take णिच् suffix, of which ण् and च् get dropped and only इ gets added. e.g. (1) चोर् + णिच् = चोर् + णिच् – ण् – च + इ = चोरि (2) लाय् + णिच् = लायि (3) याद् + णिच् = यादि (4) वार् + णिच् = वारि ।

(iv) This modified root verb then undergoes संज्ञा (modification) e.g. (1) चोरि = चोरय् । (2) लायि = लायय् । (3) यादि = यादय् । (4) वारि = वारय् । It forms the **verbal base.**

(v) This verbal base receives अ विकरणम् in the Present (लट्), Imperfect past (लङ्), Imperative (लोट्) and Potential (विधि) tenses. e.g. चोरय् + अ = चोरय ।

(vi) But, in Past indefinite tense (लुङ्), the root undergoes duplication and modification.

(vii) *Vikaraṇa* अ is then added before adding the tense suffix. चोरय् + अ = चोरय

(viii) This *vikaraṇa* अ becomes आ before the tense suffixes that begin with म or व । e.g. चोरय → चोरया + मि = चोरयामि, चोरयाव: चोरयाम: ।

(ix) This *vikaraṇa* अ is dropped before tense suffixes that begin with म् and व् । e.g. अ । चोरय → चोरय + अन्ति = चोरयन्ति

Scheme of Conjugations for the Tenth Class

Root √चुर् to steal

(1) Present Tense : लट् (सामान्य-वर्तमाने) *Parasmaipadī*

	Singular	Dual	Plural	Meaning
1p॰	चोरयामि (यामि)	चोरयाव: (याव:)	चोरयाम: (याम:)	I steal
	ćorayāmi	*ćorayāvaḥ*	*ćorayāmaḥ*	
2p॰	चोरयसि (यसि)	चोरयथ: (यथ:)	चोरयथ (यथ)	
	ćorayasi	*ćorayathaḥ*	*ćorayatha*	

3p∘	चोरयति (यति)	चोरयत: (यत:)	चोरयन्ति (यन्ति)
	ćorayati	*ćorayataḥ*	*ćorayanti*

(2) Past imperfect Tense : लङ् (अनद्यतन-भूते) *Parasmaipadī*

	Singular	Dual	Plural	Meaning
1p∘	अचोरयम्	अचोरयाव	अचोरयाम	I stole
	aćorayam	*aćorayāva*	*aćorayāma*	
2p∘	अचोरय:	अचोरयतम्	अचोरयत	
	aćorayaḥ	*aćorayatam*	*aćorayata*	
3p∘	अचोरयत्	अचोरयताम्	अचोरयन्	
	aćorayat	*aćorayatām*	*aćorayan*	

(3) Perfect Past Tense : लिट् (परोक्ष-भूते) *Parasmaipadī*

	Singular	Dual	Plural	Meaning
1p∘	चोरयामास	चोरयामासिव	चोरयामासिम	I had stolen
	ćorayāmāsa	*ćorayāmāsiva*	*ćorayāmāsima*	
2p∘	चोरयामासिथ	चोरयामासथु:	चोरयामास	
	ćorayāmāsitha	*ćorayāmāsathuḥ*	*ćorayāmāsa*	
3p∘	चोरयामास	चोरयामासतु:	चोरयामासु:	
	ćorayāmāsa	*ćorayāmāsatuḥ*	*ćorayāmāsuḥ*	

(4) Indefinite Past Tense : लुङ् (दूरवर्ति-भूते) *Parasmaipadī*

	Singular	Dual	Plural	Meaning
1p∘	अचूचुरम्	अचूचुराव	अचूचुराम	I had stolen
	aćūćuram	*aćūćurāva*	*aćūćurāma*	
2p∘	अचूचुर:	अचूचुरतम्	अचूचुरत	
	aćūćuraḥ	*aćūćuratam*	*aćūćurata*	
3p∘	अचूचुरत्	अचूचुरताम्	अचूचुरन्	
	aćūćurat	*aćūćuratām*	*aćūćuran*	

(5) Definite Future : लुट् (सामान्य-भविष्यति) *Parasmaipadī*

	Singular	Dual	Plural	Meaning
1p◦	चोरयितास्मि	चोरतितास्वः	चोरयितास्मः	I will steal
	ćorayitāsmi	*ćorayitāsvaḥ*	*ćorayitāsmaḥ*	
2p◦	चोरयितासि	चोरयितास्थः	चोरयितास्थ	
	ćorayitāsi	*ćorayitāsthaḥ*	*ćorayitāstha*	
3p◦	चोरयिता	चोरयितारौ	चोरयितारः	
	ćorayitā	*ćorayitārau*	*ćorayitāraḥ*	

(6) Indefinite Future : लृट् (अपूर्ण-भविष्यति) *Parasmaipadī*

	Singular	Dual	Plural	Meaning
1p◦	चोरयिष्यामि	चोरयिष्यावः	चोरयिष्यामः	I shall steal
	ćorayiṣyāmi	*ćorayiṣyāvaḥ*	*ćorayiṣyāmaḥ*	
2p◦	चोरयिष्यसि	चोरयिष्यथः	चोरयिष्यथ	
	ćorayiṣyasi	*ćorayiṣyathaḥ*	*ćorayiṣyatha*	
3p◦	चोरयिष्यति	चोरयिष्यतः	चोरयिष्यन्ति	
	ćorayiṣyati	*ćorayiṣyataḥ*	*ćorayiṣyanti*	

(7) Conditional Mood : लृङ् (भविष्यति क्रियातिपत्तौ) *Parasmaipadī*

	Singular	Dual	Plural	Meaning
1p◦	अचोरयिष्यम्	अचोरयिष्याव	अचोरयिष्याम	If I steal
	aćorayiṣyam	*aćorayiṣyāva*	*aćorayiṣyāma*	
2p◦	अचोरयिष्यः	अचोरयिष्यतम्	अचोरयिष्यत	
	aćorayiṣyaḥ	*aćorayiṣyatam*	*aćorayiṣyata*	
3p◦	अचोरयिष्यत्	अचोरयिष्यताम्	अचोरयिष्यन्	
	aćorayiṣyat	*aćorayiṣyatām*	*aćorayiṣyan*	

(8) Imperative Mood : लोट् (आज्ञार्थे; प्रश्नार्थे; विध्यादौ) *Parasmaipadī*

Singular	Dual	Plural	Meaning
1p◦ चोरयाणि	चोरयाव	चोरयाम	Should I steal?
ćorayāṇi	*ćorayāva*	*ćorayāma*	
2p◦ चोरय	चोरयतम्	चोरयत	Please steal!
ćoraya	*ćorayatam*	*ćorayata*	
3p◦ चोरयतु	चोरयताम्	चोरयन्तु	He, she should steal!
ćorayatu	*ćorayatām*	*ćorayantu*	

(9) Potential or Subjunctive Mood : विधिलिङ् (विध्यादौ) *Parasmaipadī*

Singular	Dual	Plural	Meaning
1p◦ चोरयेयम्	चोरयेव	चोरयेम	I may steal
ćorayeyam	*ćorayeva*	*ćorayema*	
2p◦ चोरये:	चोरयेतम्	चोरयेत	
ćorayeḥ	*ćorayetam*	*ćorayeta*	
3p◦ चोरयेत्	चोरयेताम्	चोरयेयु:	
ćorayet	*ćorayetām*	*ćorayeyuḥ*	

(10) Benedictive or Optative Mood : आशीर्लिङ् (आशिषि) *Parasmaipadī*

Singular	Dual	Plural	Meaning
1p◦ चौर्यासम्	चौर्यास्व	चौर्यास्म	May I steal!
ćauryāsam	*ćauryāsva*	*ćauryāsma*	
2p◦ चौर्या:	चौर्यास्तम्	चौर्यास्त	
ćauryāḥ	*ćauryāstam*	*ćauryāsta*	
3p◦ चौर्यात्	चौर्यास्ताम्	चौर्यासु:	
ćauryāt	*ćauryāstām*	*ćauryāsuḥ*	

EXAMPLES cum EXERCISE : (cumulative learning)

1. He steals money. *saḥ dhanaṁ ćorayati.* स: धनं चोरयति ।
2. He is stealing money. *saḥ dhanaṁ ćorayati.* स: धनं चोरयति (√चुर्) ।

3. I do not steal.	*aham̐ na ćorayāmi.* अहं न चोरयामि ।
Do you steal?	*api bhavān ćorayati?* अपि भवान् चोरयति ।
4. No one may steal.	*kaḥ api na ćorayet.* कः अपि न चोरयेत् ।
5. I am telling you.	*aham̐ bhavantam̐ kathayāmi.* अहं भवन्तं कथयामि ।
6. He told me a story.	*saḥ mām̐ kathām akathayat.* सः मां कथाम् अकथयत् (√कथ्) ।
7. They will tell him.	*te tam̐ kathayiṣyanti.* ते तं कथयिष्यन्ति ।
8. He is counting money.	*saḥ dhanam̐ gaṇayati.* सः धनं गणयति (√गण्) ।

24.11
THE ELEVENTH CLASS
kaṇḍvādiḥ gaṇah कण्ड्वादिः गणः ।

Even though this class contains more verbs than the 8th (तनादि) class, it is mostly ignored. The typical example of this class of the verbs is √कण्डू (√*kaṇḍū* to itch). The Roots (√) in the Eleventh (कण्ड्वादि) Class are : √असू √पम्पस् √पयस् √भिष् √लाट् √वेद् √सपर् √ह्रणी √ह्लिणी ।

Scheme of Conjugations for the Eleventh Class

Root √कण्डू to itch

(1) Present Tense : लट् (सामान्य-वर्तमाने) *Parasmaipadī*

	Singular	Dual	Plural	Meaning
1p॰	कण्डूयामि (यामि)	कण्डूयावः (यावः)	कण्डूयामः (यामः)	I itch
	kaṇḍūyāmi	*kaṇḍūyāvaḥ*	*kaṇḍūyāmaḥ*	
2p॰	कण्डूयसि (यसि)	कण्डूयथः (यथः)	कण्डूयथ (यथ)	
	kaṇḍūyasi	*kaṇḍūyathaḥ*	*kaṇḍūyatha*	
3p॰	कण्डूयति (यति)	कण्डूयतः (यतः)	कण्डूयन्ति (यन्ति)	
	kaṇḍūyati	*kaṇḍūyataḥ*	*kaṇḍūyanti*	

(2) Past imperfect Tense : लङ् (अनद्यतन-भूते) *Parasmaipadī*

1p◦	अकण्डूयम्	अकण्डूयाव	अकण्डूयाम	I itched
	akaṇḍūyam	*akaṇḍūyāva*	*akaṇḍūyāma*	
2p◦	अकण्डूय:	अकण्डूयतम्	अकण्डूयत	
	akaṇḍūyaḥ	*akaṇḍūyatam*	*akaṇḍūyata*	
3p◦	अकण्डूयत्	अकण्डूयताम्	अकण्डूयन्	
	akaṇḍūyat	*akaṇḍūyatām*	*akaṇḍūyan*	

(3) Perfect Past Tense : लिद् (परोक्ष-भूते) *Parasmaipadī*

1p◦	कण्डूयाञ्चक्रे	कण्डूयाञ्चकृवहे	कण्डूयाञ्चकृमहे	I had itched
	kaṇḍūyāñćakre	*kaṇḍūyāñćakṛvahe*	*kaṇḍūyāñćakṛmahe*	
2p◦	कण्डूयाञ्चकृषे	कण्डूयाञ्चक्राथे	कण्डूयाञ्चकृढ्वे	
	kaṇḍūyāñćakṛṣe	*kaṇḍūyāñćakrāthe*	*kaṇḍūyāñćakṛḍhve*	
3p◦	कण्डूयाञ्चक्रे	कण्डूयाञ्चक्राते	कण्डूयाञ्चक्रिरे	
	kaṇḍūyāñćakre	*kaṇḍūyāñćakrāte*	*kaṇḍūyāñćakrire*	

(4) Indefinite Past Tense : लुङ् (दूरवर्ति-भूते) *Parasmaipadī*

	Singular	Dual	Plural	Meaning
1p◦	अकण्डूयिषि	अकण्डूयिष्वहि	अकण्डूयिष्महि	I had itched
	akaṇḍūyiṣi	*akaṇḍūyiṣvahi*	*akaṇḍūyiṣmahi*	
2p◦	अकण्डूयिष्ठा:	अकण्डूयिषाथाम्	अकण्डूयिषध्वम्	
	akaṇḍūyiṣṭhāḥ	*akaṇḍūyiṣāthām*	*akaṇḍūyiṣadhvam*	
3p◦	अकण्डूयिष्ट	अकण्डूयिषाताम्	अकण्डूयिषत	
	akaṇḍūyiṣṭa	*akaṇḍūyiṣātām*	*akaṇḍūyiṣata*	

(5) Definite Future : लुद् (सामान्य-भविष्यति) *Parasmaipadī*

1p◦	कण्डूयिताहे	कण्डूयितास्वहे	कण्डूयितास्महे	I will itch
	kaṇḍūyitāhe	*kaṇḍūyitāsvahe*	*kaṇḍūyitāsmahe*	
2p◦	कण्डूयितासे	कण्डूयितासाथे	कण्डूयिताध्वे	
	kaṇḍūyitāse	*kaṇḍūyitāsāthe*	*kaṇḍūyitādhve*	

3p∘	कण्डूयिता	कण्डूयितारौ	कण्डूयितार:	
	kaṇḍūyitā	*kaṇḍūyitārau*	*kaṇḍūyitāraḥ*	

(6) Indefinite Future : लृट् (अपूर्ण-भविष्यति) *Parasmaipadī*

1p∘	कण्डूयिष्ये	कण्डूयिष्यावहे	कण्डूयिष्यामहे	I will itch
	kaṇḍūyiṣye	*kaṇḍūyiṣyāvahe*	*kaṇḍūyiṣyāmahe*	
2p∘	कण्डूयिष्यसे	कण्डूयिष्येते	कण्डूयिष्यध्वे	
	kaṇḍūyiṣyase	*kaṇḍūyiṣyete*	*kaṇḍūyiṣyadhve*	
3p∘	कण्डूयिष्यते	कण्डूयिष्येते	कण्डूयिष्यन्ते	
	kaṇḍūyiṣyate	*kaṇḍūyiṣyete*	*kaṇḍūyiṣyante*	

(7) Conditional Mood : लृङ् (भविष्यति क्रियातिपत्तौ) *Parasmaipadī*

1p∘	अकण्डूयिष्ये	अकण्डूयिष्यावहि	अकण्डूयिष्यामहि	If I itch
	akaṇḍūyiṣye	*akaṇḍūyiṣyāvahi*	*akaṇḍūyiṣyāmahi*	
2p∘	अकण्डूयिष्यथा:	अकण्डूयिष्येथाम्	अकण्डूयिध्वम्	
	akaṇḍūyiṣyathāḥ	*akaṇḍūyiṣyethām*	*akaṇḍūyiṣyadhvam*	
3p∘	अकण्डूयिष्यत्	अकण्डूयिष्येताम्	अकण्डूयिष्यन्	
	akaṇḍūyiṣyat	*akaṇḍūyiṣyetām*	*akaṇḍūyiṣyan*	

(8) Imperative Mood : लोट् (आज्ञार्थे; प्रश्नार्थे; विध्यादौ) *Parasmaipadī*

1p∘	कण्डूयै	कण्डूयावहै	कण्डूयामहै	Should I itch?
	kaṇḍūyai	*kaṇḍūyāvahai*	*kaṇḍūyāmahai*	
2p∘	कण्डूयस्व	कण्डूयेथाम्	कण्डूयध्वम्	Please itch!
	kaṇḍūyasva	*kaṇḍūyethām*	*kaṇḍūyadhvam*	
3p∘	कण्डूयताम्	कण्डूयेताम्	कण्डूयन्ताम्	He, she should itch!
	kaṇḍūyatām	*kaṇḍūyetām*	*kaṇḍūyantām*	

(9) Potential or Subjunctive Mood : विधिलिङ् (विध्यादौ) *Parasmaipadī*

1p∘	कण्डूयेय	कण्डूयेवहि	कण्डूयेमहि	I may itch

	Singular	Dual	Plural
	kaṇḍūyeya	*kaṇḍūyevahi*	*kaṇḍūyemahi*
2p∘	कण्डूयेथा:	कण्डूयेयाथाम्	कण्डूयेध्वम्
	kaṇḍūyethāḥ	*kaṇḍūyeyāthām*	*kaṇḍūyedhvam*
3p∘	कण्डूयेत	कण्डूयेयाताम्	कण्डूयेरन्
	kaṇḍūyet	*kaṇḍūyeyātām*	*kaṇḍūyeran*

(10) Benedictive or Optative Mood : आशीर्लिङ् (आशिषि) *Parasmaipadī*

	Singular	Dual	Plural	Meaning
1p∘	कण्डूयिषीय	कण्डूयिषीवहि	कण्डूयिषीमहि	May I itch!
	kaṇḍūyiṣīya	*kaṇḍūyiṣīvahi*	*kaṇḍūyiṣīmahi*	
2p∘	कण्डूयिषीष्ठा:	कण्डूयिषीयास्थाम्	कण्डूयिषीध्वम्	
	kaṇḍūyiṣīṣṭhā	*kaṇḍūyiṣīyāsthām*	*kaṇḍūyiṣīdhvam*	
3p∘	कण्डूयिषीष्ट	कण्डूयिषीयास्ताम्	कण्डूयिषीरन्	
	kaṇḍūyiṣīṣṭa	*kaṇḍūyiṣīyāstām*	*kaṇḍūyiṣīran*	

LESSON 25

pañćaviṁśaḥ abhyāsaḥ पञ्चविंशः अभ्यासः ।

THE CASES

vibhaktayaḥ विभक्तयः ।

KARAK : The relationship (*sambandhaḥ* सम्बन्धः) of the **substantives** (*sṁjñā* संज्ञाः), such as **noun** (*nāma* नाम), **pronoun** (*sarvanāma* सर्वनाम) and **adjective** (*viśaṣaṇam* विशेषणम्), with a **verb** (*kriyā* क्रिया) is called an **agent** (*kārakam* कारकम्).

कर्ता कर्म च करणं सम्प्रदानं तथैव च ।
अपादानाधिकरणमित्याहुः कारकाणि षट् ।।

(kartā, subject; karma, the object; karaṇa, the instrument; sampradāna, for whom; apādāna, from where; adhikaraṇa, at where, are the six kāraks)

VIBHAKTI : The suffix (*pratyayaḥ* प्रत्ययः) that imparts this relationship is called **Declensional Termination** or **Case suffix** (*vibhakti-pratyayaḥ* विभक्तिप्रत्ययः) of that agent कारकम् । For example,

(i) *arjunaḥ: uvāća* अर्जुनः उवाच । and

(ii) *arjunena kṛṣṇaḥ: uktaḥ:* अर्जुनेन कृष्णः उक्तः ।

In both sentences, *arjuna* अर्जुन is *kartṛ-kārakaḥ* कर्तृकारकः (the 'doer or agent' of the action). However,

(i) in the first sentence, the word *arjunaḥ* अर्जुनः, with its affix *suḥ* (सुः), of which only *visargaḥ* विसर्गः (:) remains, is in the *prathamā vibhakti* प्रथमा विभक्तिः (1st case, Nominative Case, First Declension); and

(ii) in the second sentence, the word *arjuna,* with its affix *ena* एन (अर्जुन + एन), is in the *tṛtīyā vibhakti* तृतीया विभक्तिः (3rd case, Instrumental Case, Third Declension).

The word *vibhakti* विभक्तिः means : a complete triad (singular, dual and plural) of a Case or a Tense (त्रीणि त्रीणि विभक्ति संज्ञाश्च भवन्ति सुपश्तिङश्च । (pāṇini, aṣṭādhyāyī 1:4.104)

As Pāṇini says, there are two kinds of *vibhaktis*,

(i) Case (सुप्) *vibhakti* and **(ii) Tense or Mood (तिङ्) *vibhakti*.**

By attaching a **Case suffix (सुप्प्रत्ययः)** we get a **declension (विभक्तिरूपम्)**, and

By attaching a **Tense or Mood suffix (तिङ्प्रत्ययः)** we get a **conjugation (तिङन्तरूपम्)**.

'Broadly' speaking, from Nominative to Locative are the seven cases. Vocative is not a separate case, but it is only a modified form of the Nominative Case. For the study of cases, the words are grouped into two categories :

(i) **Subtantives (nouns, pronouns and adjectives) ending in a vowel (अजन्त, स्वरान्त)**

(ii) **Subtantives ending in a consonant (हलन्त, व्यञ्जनान्त)**.

The 'original form' of the word (मूलप्रकृतिः), to which a case termination (विभक्तिप्रत्ययः) is attached, is called ***prātipādikam* प्रातिपादिकम्** ।

e.g. *brahman* ब्रह्मन् is *prātipādikaḥ* and *brahma* ब्रह्म (n॰), *brahmā* ब्रह्मा (m॰), *brāhmī* ब्राह्मी (f॰) are the Nominative singular word forms (of ब्रह्मन्) to be used in a sentence.

CHARACTERICS OF THE CASES

(1) Nominative, 1st Case (कर्तृ-कारकम्, प्रथमा-विभक्तिः)

In Active voice, the doer or subject itself; in Passive voice, the object.

(2) Accusative, 2nd Case (कर्म-कारकम्, द्वितीया-विभक्तिः)

On whom the action is performed.

Scope : to, what, to who; to where, below (अधः, अधोऽधः, अध्यधि), above (ऊर्ध्वम्), between (अन्तरा), after (अनु), along (अनु), near (निकषा, समया), towards (प्रति), in front of (अग्रे, अग्रतः, पुरः, पुरतः, समक्षम्), around (अभितः), on all sides of (परितः), on both sides of (उभयतः), verrywhere (सर्वतः), to fie on (धिक्), without (विना, ऋते, अन्तरेण), without concerning (with एनप् and विना), to go to (गति - गम्, चल्, इण्, वह्), to become, the time period (वर्षाणि, दिनानि); to sleep upon, to lie down (अधि√शी), to resort to, to reside, to dwell, to occupy (अधि√स्थ, अधि√आस्, अधि√वस्, आ√वस्, अनु√वस्, उप√वस्), following (अनु, अभि-नि√विश्) ...etc.

(3) Instrumental, 3rd Case (करण-कारकम्, तृतीया-विभक्तिः)

With or by which the (active or passive) action is done.

Scope : by, with, without (हीन, विना), because (येन), along with (सह, सार्धम्), owing to, on account of, out of-, for the reason of (प्रयोजनार्थ), by nature (स्वभाव -एन), by birth, enough, enough of (-एन अलम्), through (मध्येन, अन्तरेण, -एन), simile (सदृश), etc.

(4) Dative, 4th Case (सम्प्रदान-कारकम्, चतुर्थी-विभक्तिः)

To whom the action is directed through something.

Scope : for, to, to give to, to owe to (धारय), to send to, to promise to, to show to, to be angry with (√कृध्, √कुप्, √द्रुह्, √असू), to do for the purpose of (निमित्तम्), to desire, to long for, liking (रुचि, √स्पृह्), for some one, to go to, to be (√क्लृप्), be able (समर्थ), salutation, hail to (नमः, स्वस्ति), in the meaning of the तुमुन् infinitive, etc.

(5) Ablative, 5th Case (अपादान-कारकम्, पञ्चमी-विभक्तिः)

From where to subject is moved; or a comparison between TWO things, but not more than two things.

Scope : from, without, except (ऋते, विना), far or away (आरात्), outside, since, until, after, before (पूर्वम्), to the direction of (प्रति), to desist from (वि√रम्, नि√वृत्), to protect (√रक्ष्, त्रै), with or without motivation (अकस्मात्), in the meanings of away (पृथक्), fear

(भयम्), break (विराम), accept (√ग्रह), other (अन्य), with expressions प्रभृति, आङ्, उद्भवति, प्रभवति, प्रयच्छति, प्रमाद्यति, अधीते, जुगुप्सते, निलयते, etc.

(6) Genitive, 6th Case (सम्बन्धः, षष्ठी-विभक्तिः)

Also called Possessive Case is the relation between two things; or a comparison between more than two things i.e. superlative, but not comparative.

Scope : of, above, below, in front of, behind, beyond, away, near etc. (-स्य दूरम्, समीपम्, कृते, मध्ये, समक्षम्, अन्तरे, अन्तः), in the prepense of, for the sake of, with the subject of participles (क्त = प्रतिष्ठायाः पतनम्), words with suffix अतः, with the object of participles (पयस्य पानम्), in the use of word हेतु, in the meaning of remembering with verb √स्मृ etc.

(7) Locative, 7th Case (अधिकरण-कारकम्, सप्तमी विभक्तिः)

To locate a relationship between two things, or a quality within a group of things.

Scope : in, on, at, in side, under, upon, among, concerning, in the matter of, to express feelings for, to enter, to place, to fall, to send, to indicate time (दिने, प्रतःकाले, मध्याह्ने, सायङ्काले), in occurance of the first event after which some other event takes place, with the use of expressions मध्ये, कृते, समक्षम्, अन्तः, अन्तरा, etc.

(8) Vocative (सम्बोधनम्) To call or address someone.

Scope : bho:! O' ...etc.

RELATIONSHIPS OF THE CASES

(1st Nom◦)	the subject itself	(2nd Accu◦)	to; what?
(3rd Inst◦)	with, by	(4th Dat◦)	for, to
(5th Abl◦)	from, than	(6th Poss◦)	of
(7th loc◦)	in, on, at	(Voc◦)	the Address

Case		Singular	Dual	Plural	Sing॰	Dual	Plural
1st	Nominative	:	औ	अ:	राम:	रामौ	रामा:
2nd	Accusative	म्	औ	न्	रामम्	रामौ	रामान्
3rd	Instrumental	एन	भ्याम्	ऐ:	रामेण	रामाभ्याम्	रामै:
4th	Dative	ए	भ्याम्	भ्य:	रामाय	रामाभ्याम्	रामेभ्य:
5th	Ablative	आत्	भ्याम्	भ्य:	रामात्	रामाभ्याम्	रामेभ्य:
6th	Posssessive	स्य	अयो:	नाम्	रामस्य	रामयो:	रामाणाम्
7th	Locative	ए	अयो:	सु	रामे	रामयो:	रामेषु
--	Vocative	–	औ	आ:	राम	रामौ	रामा:

THE MOST FAMOUS CLASSICAL EXAMPLE

SHOWING THE USE OF ALL EIGHT CASES

(श्रीरामरक्षा 37)

रामो राजमणि: सदा विजयते ।	राम:	Nominative	(Rāma)	
रामं रमेशं भजे ।	रामम्	Accusative	(to Rāma)	- to, what?
रामेणाभिहिता निशाचरचमू ।	रामेण	Instrumental	(by Rāma)	- by, with
रामाय तस्मै नम:	रामाय	Dative	(for Rāma)	- for, to
रामान्नास्ति परायणं परतरम् ।	रामात्	Ablative	(than Rāma)	- from
रामस्य दासोऽस्म्यहम् ।	रामस्य	Possessive	(of Rāma)	- of
रामे चित्तलय: सदा भवतु मे ।	रामे	Locative	(in Rāma)	- in, on, at
भो राम! मामुद्धर ।।7।।	राम	Vocative	(O Rāma!)	

पाञ्चालिछन्दसि

(composed by the author of this book)

(संगीतकृष्णरामायणे 84.1)

कृष्णश्च कृष्णञ्च कृष्णेन । कृष्णाय कृष्णाच्च कृष्णस्य ।
कृष्णे च कृष्णेति रूपाणि । कृष्णस्य सर्वाणि जानीहि ।।

25.1

THE NOMINATIVE CASE

kartā-kārakam. prathamā-vibhaktiḥ कर्ता-कारकम् । प्रथमा विभक्तिः ।

The 1st Case or the First Declension of substantives, The doer or the subject itself

Rāma eats rice i.e. *Rāmaḥ odanaṁ khādati.* राम: ओदनं खादति । Rāma (राम) is the doer of the action (*kartā kārakam* कर्ता-कारकम), so Rāma is the SUBJECT (*kartā* कर्ता).

Therefore, Rāma is in the NOMINATIVE CASE (प्रथमा-विभक्तिः). *Rāmaḥ* रामः is the Singular Nominative case of the uninflected masculine substantive word *Rāma* राम ।

EXAMPLES : The subject in the THE NOMINATIVE (1st) CASE is shown in bold :

1. **Rāma** drinks milk. ***Rāmaḥ*** *dugdhaṁ pibati (√pā).* **रामः** दुग्धं पिबति । (√पा)
2. **Sītā** wrote a letter. ***Sītā*** *patram alikhat.* **सीता** पत्रम् अलिखत् । (√लिख)
3. **He** draws a picture. ***saḥ*** *ćitram likhati (√likh).* **सः** चित्रं लिखति ।
4. **You** will give money. ***bhavān*** *dhanaṁ dāsyati (√dā).* **भवान्** धनं दास्यति । (√दा)
5. **Arjuna** chatters. ***Arjunaḥ*** *prajñā-vādān bhāṣate (√bhāṣ).* **अर्जुनः** प्रज्ञावादान् भाषते । (√भाष्)
6. **विद्यार्थी सेवकः पान्थः क्षुधार्थी भयकातरः ।**
   भाण्डारी प्रतिहारी च सप्त सुप्तान्प्रबोधयेत् ।।32।।

EXERCISE 52 : (A) Find the Nominative (1st) case :

(1) I am eating a mango. अहम् आम्रं खादामि । (2) She brings a cat. सा बिडालम् आनयति ।

(3) The cow gives milk. गौः दुग्धं ददाति । (4) The dog barks. कुकुरः वुक्कति ।

(5) A parrot speaks Sanskrit. एकः शुकः संस्कृतं वदति ।

(6) शोको नाशयते धैर्यं शोको नाशयते श्रुतम् ।
शोको नाशयते सर्वं नास्ति शोकसमो रिपुः ।।33।।

(7) वृक्षाग्रवासी न च पक्षिराजः त्रिनेत्रधारी न च शूलपाणिः ।
जटाभिर्युक्तो न च सिद्धयोगी जलं च बिभ्रन्न घटो न मेघः ।।34।।

DECLENSIONS OF THE NOMINATIVE (1st) CASE

	Word ending	Gender	Word	Singular	Dual	Plural
(1)	अ	m∘	राम	रामः	रामौ	रामाः
(2)	अ	n∘	वन	वनम्	वने	वनानि
(3)	आ	f∘	माला	माला	माले	मालाः
(4)	इ	m∘	कवि	कविः	कवी	कवयः
(5)	इ	n∘	वारि	वारि	वारिणी	वारीणि
(6)	इ	f∘	मति	मतिः	मती	मतयः
(7)	ई	f∘	नदी	नदी	नद्यौ	नद्यः
(8)	उ	m∘	गुरु	गुरुः	गुरू	गुरवः
(9)	उ	n∘	मधु	मधु	मधुनी	मधूनि
(10)	उ	f∘	धेनु	धेनुः	धेनू	धेनवः
(11)	ऊ	f∘	वधू	वधू	वध्वौ	वध्वः
(12)	ऋ	m∘	पितृ	पिता	पितरौ	पितरः
(13)	ऋ	n∘	धातृ	धातृ	धातृणी	धातृणि
(14)	ऋ	f∘	मातृ	माता	मातरौ	मातरः
(15)	च्	f∘	वाच्	वाक्	वाचौ	वाचः
(16)	ज्	m∘	राज्	राट्	राजौ	राजः
(17)	त्	m∘	मरुत्	मरुत्	मरुतौ	मरुतः
(18)	त्	n∘	जगत्	जगत्	जगती	जगन्ति
(19)	द्	m∘	सुहृद्	सुहृद्	सुहृदौ	सुहृदः
(20)	इन्	m∘	शशिन्	शशी	शशिनौ	शशिनः
(21)	न्	m∘	आत्मन्	आत्मा	आत्मानौ	आत्मानः
(22)	न्	n∘	कर्मन्	कर्म	कर्मणी	कर्माणि
(23)	श्	f∘	दिश्	दिक्	दिशौ	दिशः
(24)	स्	m∘	चन्द्रमस्	चन्द्रमाः	चन्द्रमसौ	चन्द्रमसः
(25)	स्	n∘	पयस्	पयः	पयसी	पयांसि

25.2
THE ACCUSATIVE CASE

karma-kārakam. dvitīyā vibhakti

कर्म–कारकम् । द्वितीया विभक्तिः ।

The 2nd Case or the Second Declension of substantives

SIGNS: what? to, to where?; below, above, between, after, along, towards, in front of, near, around, without ...

(उपपदानि - अन्तरेण, अन्तरा, उभयतः, सर्वतः, विना, धिक्, उपर्युपरि, अभितः, परितः, समया, निकषा, अध्यधि, अधोऽधः, अधः, अनु, उप, अभि, सु, अति, प्रति, अप, अपि, अधि, हा, आङ्)

Rāma eats **rice**. *Rāmaḥ odanaṁ khādati.* रामः **ओदनम्** खादति । Rāma does the action of eating, so Rāma is the subject, so *Rāmaḥ* रामः is the Nominative (1st) case, as said earlier. To eat is a transitive verb. Rāma eats what? The answer is - rice (*odanam* ओदनम्). The rice is the **object** (कर्म–कारकम्). Therefore, rice ओदनम् is the Accusative (2nd) Case.

In intransitive actions, the object indicated by 'to' is in Accusative (2nd) case, not in the Dative (4th) case. To go is an intransitive verb. Rāma goes 'to' **town**, Rāmaḥ *grāmaṁ gaćchati* (रामः ग्रामं गच्छति), town ग्रामम् is the Accusative (2nd) case.

GENERAL RULES :

(1) To any Transitive action (e.g. I eat), if the question 'WHAT?' is asked, (e.g. eat what?), the answer to that question is in the ACCUSATIVE (2nd) CASE. e.g. Q◦ I eat what? A◦ I eat rice, *odanam* ओदनम् ।

(2) In an Intransitive action, the object indicated by 'TO or TO WHERE' is in Accusative (2nd) case.

ADVANCED RULES : NOTE : I suggest that you may study the advanced rules after you have gone through the primary study of this book at least once.

(3) In the application of the verbs with secondary prefixes अनु, अभि, अति, आ, सु, प्रति, अध: परि the Accusative (2nd) case is used with the object.

The sage lives on-in the mountain. *sādhuḥ parvatam upavasati.* साधु: पर्वतम् उपवसति (साधु: पर्वते वसति) ।

He lives in a village. *saḥ grāmam adhitiṣṭhati.* स: ग्रामम् अधितिष्ठति (स: ग्रामे तिष्ठति) ।

The Lion lives in a den. *siṁhaḥ guhām abhiniviśate.* सिंह: गुहाम् अभिनिविशते (सिंह: गुहायां निविशते) ।

I live in a house. *ahaṁ gṛham āvasāmi.* अहं गृहम् आवसामि (अहं गृहे वसामि) ।

I am running towards the lake. *ahaṁ puṣkaraṁ prati dhāvāmi.* अहं पुष्करं प्रतिधावामि ।

(4) In the use of adverbs निकषा उभयत: समया अध: अन्तरा अभित: परित: सर्वत: the Accusative (2nd) case is used for objects.

There are vines on both sides of (near, around) the house. *gṛham ubhayataḥ latāḥ santi.* गृहम् उभयत: (निकषा, अभित: परित:) लता: सन्ति ।

(5) In the use of the verb √मन् (to think) **as a simile**, the object (other than people) may optionally be used in Dative (4th) case, otherwise in Accusative (2nd) case.

He considers his house as a palace. *saḥ tasya gṛhaṁ rājamahālāya manyate (4th). saḥ tasya gṛhaṁ rājamahālaṁ manyate (2nd).* स: तस्य गृहं राजमहालाय मन्यते । स: तस्य गृहं राजमहालं मन्यते ।

(6) The verbs such as गम्, चल, इण् that indicate travel (गति:), the object is optionally in the Dative (4th) case, otherwise normally in the Accusative (2nd) case.

I am going to Now York. *ahaṁ new-yorkāya gacchāmi (4th); ahaṁ new-yorkaṁ gacchāmi (2nd);* अहं न्यू-यार्काय गच्छामि । अहं न्यू-यार्कं गच्छामि ।

EXERCISE 53 : (cumulative learning)

(A) Write Sanskrit names in Accusative case for nouns (See the previous and following tables for help)

(1) Kitchen --------	Rice --------	Bread --------
(2) Oil --------	Butter --------	Salt --------
(3) Clove --------	Cumin seeds --------	Coffee --------

(B) Write English words for the following Sanskrit nouns:

(1) ओदनम् --------	गोधूमः --------	चणकः --------
(2) शस्यम् --------	तैलम् --------	घृतम् --------
(3) तक्रम् --------	दधि --------	लवणम् --------
(4) जीरकः --------	एला --------	लवङ्गम् --------

EXAMPLES cum EXERCISE : ACCUSATIVE (2nd) CASE

(Translate into English)

The object in Accusative (2nd) case is shown in bold (Answers are given for your help)

1. **Rāma** is drinking milk. *Rāmaḥ dugdhaṁ pibati* रामः **दुग्धं** पिबति ।
2. **Sītā** wrote a letter. *Sītā patram alikhat.* सीता **पत्रम्** अलिखत् ।
3. **He** sees a zebra. *saḥ rāsabhaṁ paśyati.* सः **रासभं** पश्यति ।
4. **You** will give money. *bhavān dhanaṁ dāsyati.* भवान् **धनं** दास्यति ।
5. **I** went to Delhi. *ahaṁ Dillīm agacćham.* अहं **दिल्लीम्** अगच्छम् ।
6. **Rāma** will go to Kānpur. *Rāmaḥ **Kānpuraṁ** gamiṣyati.* रामः **कानपुरं** गमिष्यति ।

EXERCISE 54 : NOMINATIVE AND ACCUSATIVE:

Find out the Nominative and Accusative cases

(1) Rāma saw a lion.	रामः सिंहम् अपश्यत् ।
(2) She brings a parrot.	सा शुकम् आनयति ।
(3) A cow gives milk.	गौः दुग्धं ददाति ।
(4) A horse eats grass.	अश्वः घासं खादति ।
(5) A snake bites the mouse.	सर्पः मूषकं दंशति ।
(6) Character is the best jewel.	शीलं परं भूषणम् ।

THE CLASSICAL EXAMPLES :

(7) **अहिं नृपं** च **शार्दूलं कीटिं** च **बालकं** तथा ।
परश्वानं च **मूर्खं** च सप्त सुप्तान्न बोधयेत् ।35।।

(8) न **चौरहार्यं** न च **राजहार्यं** न **भ्रातृभाज्यं** न च **भारकारि** ।
व्यये कृते वर्धत एव **नित्यं विद्याधनं सर्वधनप्रधानम्** ।।36।।

(9) परोक्षे **कार्यहन्तारं** प्रत्यक्षे **प्रियवादिनम्** ।
वर्जयेत्तादृशं मित्रं विषकुम्भं पयोमुखम् ।।37।।

EXERCISE 55 : Write the Sanskrit names in the Nominative case :

(1) Vegetable ---------	Potato ---------	Onion ---------
(2) Ginger ---------	Garlic ---------	Tomato ---------
(3) Cucumber ---------	Spinach ---------	Chilli ---------

DECLENSIONS OF THE ACCUSATIVE (2nd) CASE

	Word ending	Gender	Word	Singular	Dual	Plural
(1)	अ	m∘	राम	रामम्	रामौ	रामान्
(2)	आ	n∘	वन	वनम्	वने	वनानि
(3)	आ	f∘	माला	मालाम्	माले	माला:
(4)	इ	m∘	कवि	कविम्	कवी	कवीन्
(5)	इ	n∘	वारि	वारि	वारिणी	वारीणि
(6)	इ	f∘	मति	मतिम्	मती	मती:
(7)	ई	f∘	नदी	नदीम्	नद्यौ	नदी:
(8)	उ	m∘	गुरु	गुरुम्	गुरू	गुरून्
(9)	उ	n∘	मधु	मधु	मधुनी	मधूनि
(10)	उ	f∘	धेनु	धेनुम्	धेनू	धेनू:
(11)	ऊ	f∘	वधू	वधूम्	वध्वौ	वधू:
(12)	ऋ	m∘	पितृ	पितरम्	पितरौ	पितॄन्
(13)	ऋ	n∘	धातृ	धातृ	धातृणी	धातॄणि
(14)	ऋ	f∘	मातृ	मातरम्	मातरौ	मातॄ:
(15)	च्	f∘	वाच्	वाचम्	वाचौ	वाच:
(16)	ज्	m∘	राज्	राजम्	राजौ	राज:
(17)	त्	m∘	मरुत्	मरुतम्	मरुतौ	मरुत:
(18)	त्	n∘	जगत्	जगत्	जगती	जगन्ति
(19)	द्	m∘	सुहृद्	सुहृदम्	सुहृदौ	सुहृद:
(20)	इन्	m∘	शशिन्	शशिनम्	शशिनौ	शशिन:
(21)	न्	m∘	आत्मन्	आत्मानम्	आत्मानौ	आत्मन:
(22)	न्	n∘	कर्मन्	कर्म	कर्मणी	कर्माणि
(23)	श्	f∘	दिश्	दिशम्	दिशौ	दिश:
(24)	स्	m∘	चन्द्रमस्	चन्द्रमसम्	चन्द्रमसौ	चन्द्रमस:
(25)	स्	n∘	पयस्	पय:	पयसी	पयांसि

25.3

THE INSTRUMENTAL CASE

karaṇa-kārakam. tṛtīyā vibhakti

करण-कारकम् । तृतीया विभक्तिः ।

The 3rd Case or Third Declension of substantives

SIGNS: with, by, because of, through, on account of.
(उपपदानि - अनु, सह, पृथक्, विना, नाना, सदृक्, सदृश, सदृक्ष, सन्निभः, समानः, तुल्यः, अलम्, कृतम्, दूरेण, अभ्यर्णेन, अभ्याशेन, निकटेन, अन्तिकेन)

(1) Rāma eats rice with a spoon. *Rāmaḥ ćamasena odanaṁ khādati.* रामः चमसेन ओदनं खादति ।

Rāma is doing the eating, so *Rāmaḥ* रामः is the Nominative (1st) case.

Q◦ Rāma eats what? A◦ Rice ओदनम् । So Rice ओदनम् is the Accusative (2nd) case.

To eat is a Transitive verb. Rice is eaten with (-एन) spoon. The spoon is used as an instrument (करण-कारकम् *karaṇa kārakam*) to eat the rice (the object), therefore, with a spoon चमसेन is the Instrumental (3rd) case.

(2) Rāma goes to London by airplane. *Rāmaḥ landanaṁ vāyu-yānena gaćchati.* रामः लन्दनं वायुयानेन गच्छति । Airplane (वायुयानम्), being used as an instrument, is in the Instrumental (3rd) case.

(3) I am going with Rāma. *ahaṁ Rāmeṇa saha gaććāmi.* (अहं रामेण सह गच्छामि), *Rāmeṇa* is Instrumental (3rd) case.

GENERAL RULE :

(1) The object indicated by the words 'WITH' or 'BY' is in the Instrumental (3rd) case.

EXAMPLES : - THE INSTRUMENTAL (3rd) CASE.

I eat food with a spoon. *aham annaṁ ćamasena khādāmi (√khād).* अहम् अन्नं चमसेन खादामि (√खाद्) ।

Knowledge looks beautiful with humility. *vidyā vinayena śobhate (√śobh).* विद्या विनयेन शोभते (√शोभ्) ।

Rāvaṇa was killed by Rāma. *Rāmeṇa Rāvaṇaḥ hataḥ (√hna).* रामेण रावणः हतः (√हन्) ।

ADVANCED RULES :

NOTE : It will be easier if you study the advanced rules after you have gone through the primary study of this book at least once.

(2) The object indicated by words such as सह, साकम्, सार्धम्, समानः समम्, हीन, अलम्, दूरेण, अभ्यर्णेन, अभ्याशेन, निकटेन, अन्तिकेन is in the Instrumental (3rd) case.

I go with Rāma. *ahaṁ Rāmeṇa saha gaććāmi.* अहं रामेण सह गच्छामि ।

My house is near the school. *mama gṛham vidyālayāt samīpena asti.* मम गृहं विद्यालयात् समीपेन (निकटेन, अन्तिकेन, अभ्यर्णेन, अभ्याशेन) अस्ति ।

Enough with the goodness. *sadbhāvena alam.* सद्भावेन अलम् ।

(3) In the use of a comparative suffix such as सदृश and तुल्य, the word being compared is either in the Possessive (6th) case or in Instrumental (3rd) case.

There is no king like Rāma. *Rāmasya/rāmeṇa sadṛśaḥ (tulyaḥ) kaśćit rājā nāsti.* रामेण/रामस्य सदृशः (तुल्यः) कश्चित् राजा नास्ति ।

Bhima is equal to Arjuna. *Bhīmaḥ Arjunena/ Arjunasya tulyaḥ asti.* भीमः अर्जुनेन/अर्जुनस्य तुल्यः (सदृशः सदृक्षः सदृक्, सन्निभः समानः) अस्ति ।

(4) The Accusative (2nd) or the Instrumental (3rd) case is used in the application of the expressions पृथक् (away), नाना (various) and विना (without). However, optionally the Abaltive (5th) case may also be used.

I am happy away from him. *ahaṁ tena pṛthak sukhī asmi.* अहं तेन पृथक् सुखी अस्मि ।

He has eaten various foods. *tena nānā annāni khāditāni santi.* तेन नाना अन्नानि खादितानि

सन्ति । (नाना = various)

Without humility the knowledge does not look good. *vinā vinayena vidyā na śobhate.* विना विनयेन विद्या न शोभते ।

(5) In the case of the use of Past Passive Participles (see Lesson 28 for ppp◦) in Passive Voice, normally the Instrumental (3rd) case is used for the subject, however otherwise, the Possessive (6th) case is used.

I have desired it (active voice) or it is desired by me (passive voice). *mayā/mama etat iṣṭam.* मया/मम एतत् इष्टम् ।

He has read the verse. *tena/tasya ślokaḥ paṭhita:.* तेन/तस्य श्लोक: पठित: ।

All have seen it. *etat sarvaiḥ/sarveṣāṁ dṛṣṭaḥ.* एतत् सर्वै:/सर्वेषां दृष्ट: ।

Rāma has done it. *etat Rāmeṇa/Rāmasya kṛtam.* एतत् रामेण/रामस्य कृतम् ।

It is remembered by the child. *bālakena/bālakasya etat jñātam.* बालकेन/बालकस्य एतत् ज्ञातम् ।

EXAMPLES cum EXERCISE : THE INSTRUMENTAL (3rd) CASE

The things in Instrumental (3rd) case are shown in bold.

1. I am drinking milk **with him**. *ahaṁ* ***tena saha*** *dugdhaṁ pibāmi.* अहं **तेन सह** दुग्धं पिबामि
2. I drink milk **with a cup**. *ahaṁ* ***ćaṣakena*** *dugdhaṁ pibāmi.* अहं **चषकेन** दुग्धं पिबामि ।
3. Sītā is writing letter **with a pen**. *Sītā* ***lekhanyā*** *patraṁ likhati.* सीता **लेखन्या** पत्रं लिखति ।
4. He hits ball **with a bat**. *saḥ laguḍena saha* ***kandukaṁ*** *tāḍyati.* स: **लगुडेन** कन्दुकं ताडयति ।
5. You will reply **by letter.** *bhavān* ***patreṇa*** *pratyuttaraṁ dāsyati* भवान् **पत्रेण** प्रत्युतरं दास्यति
6. I went to London **by boat**. *ahaṁ* ***jala/yānena*** *Landanam agaććham.* अहं **जलयानेन** लन्दनम् अगच्छम् ।
7. Rāma will go there **with Sītā**. *Rāmaḥ* ***Sītayā saha*** *tatra gamiṣyati.* राम: **सीतया सह** तत्र गमिष्यति ।

CLASSICAL EXAMPLES cum EXERCISE : (Instrumental case shown in **bold** letters)

8 Knowledge is beautiful **with humility**. *vidyā vinayena śobhate.* विद्या **विनयेन** शोभते ।

9. The lotus looks beautiful **because of the water**. **पयसा** कमलं विभाति । The water is beautiful **with the lotus**. **कमलेन** पयः विभाति । The lake is beautiful **because of the water**. **पयसा** सरः विभाति । The lake is beautiful **because of the lotus**. **कमलेन** सरः विभाति ।
पयसा कमलं **कमलेन** पयः । **पयसा कमलेन** विभाति सरः ।।38।।

10. The night is beautiful **with the moon. शशिना** निशा विभाति । The moon is beautiful **because of the night निशया** शशी विभाति । The sky is beautiful **because of the moon. शशिना** नभः विभाति । The sky is beautiful **because of the night. शशिना** नभः विभाति ।
शशिना च निशा **निशया** च शशी । **शशिना निशया** च विभाति नभः ।।39।।

11. The bracelet is beautiful **with the jewel. मणिना** वलयं विभाति । The jewel is beautiful **because of the bracelet वलयेन** मणिः विभाति । The hand is beautiful **with the jewel. मणिना** करः विभाति । The hand is beautiful **with the bracelet**. वलयेन करः विभाति ।
मणिना वलयं **वलयेन** मणिः । **मणिना वलयेन** विभाति करः ।।40।।

12. The assembly looks good **beacuse of you. भवता** सभा विभाति । You look good **because of the assembly सभया** भवान् विभाति । The world looks good **because of you. भवता** जगत् विभाति । The world looks good **because of the assembly. सभया** जगत् विभाति ।
सभया च भवान् **भवता** च सभा । **सभया भवता** च विभाति जगत् ।।41।।

(13) **सद्भिस्तु लीलया** प्रोक्तं शिलालिखितमक्षरम् ।
असद्भिः शपथेनापि जले लिखितमक्षरम् ।।42।।

(14) **एकेना**पि **सुपुत्रेण विद्यायुक्तेन** भासते ।
कुलं **पुरुषसिंहेन चन्द्रेणे**व हि शर्वरी ।।43।।

(15) यथा **ह्येकेन चक्रेण** न रथस्य गतिर्भवेत् ।
एवं **पुरुषकारेण विना** दैवं न सिद्ध्यति ।।44।।

EXERCISE 56 : Find the Nominative (1st), Accusative (2nd), Instrumental (3rd) cases :

(1) I caught a ball with my hand. अहं हस्तेन कन्दुकम् अगृह्णाम् ।

(2) He plays a toy with you. सः तेन सह क्रीडनकं खेलति ।

(3) She will come here by car. सा कारयानेन अत्र आगमिष्यति ।

(4) We will go with you. वयं त्वया सह गमिष्यामः ।

(5) They ate rice with milk. ते दुग्धेन सह ओदनम् अखादन् ।

(6) **चक्षुषा मनसा वाचा कर्मणा च चतुर्विधम् ।**
प्रसादयति यो लोकं तं लोकोऽनुप्रसीदति ॥45॥

EXERCISE 57 :

Find the Instrumental (3rd) cases in the following:

(1) You stitch cloth with a needle. भवान् सूचिकया वस्त्रं सीव्यति ।

(2) Rāma cuts paper with scissors. रामः कर्तरिकया पत्रकं कृन्तति ।

(3) I came with my dog. अहं मम कुकुरेण सह आगच्छम्/आगतवान् ।

(4) Knowledge grows with education. विद्यया ज्ञानं वर्धते । (√वृध् = to grow)

(5) He is blind with an eye and **lame** with a leg. सः अक्ष्णा काणः पादेन च **खञ्जः** ।

(6) Without righteousness one is like an animal. धर्मेण हीनः पशुना समानः ।

EXERCISE 58 :

Give Sanskrit words for English nouns :

(1) Spoon ---------- Boat ---------- Lake ----------

(2) Night ---------- Pot ---------- Knife ----------

(3) Scissors ---------- Needle---------- Mirror ----------

(4) Soap ---------- Towel ---------- Bed ----------

(5) Table ---------- Paper ---------- Education ----------

DECLENSIONS OF THE INSTRUMENTAL CASE

	Word ending	Gender	Word	Singular	Dual	Plural
(1)	अ	m∘	राम	रामेण	रामाभ्याम्	रामैः
(2)	अ	n∘	वन	वनेन	वनाभ्याम्	वनैः
(3)	आ	f∘	माला	मालया	मालाभ्याम्	मालाभिः
(4)	इ	m∘	कवि	कविना	कविभ्याम्	कविभिः
(5)	इ	n∘	वारि	वारिणा	वारिभ्याम्	वारिभिः
(6)	इ	f∘	मति	मत्या	मतिभ्याम्	मतिभिः
(7)	ई	f∘	नदी	नद्या	नदीभ्याम्	नदीभिः
(8)	उ	m∘	गुरु	गुरुणा	गुरुभ्याम्	गुरुभिः
(9)	उ	n∘	मधु	मधुना	मधुभ्याम्	मधुभिः
(10)	उ	f∘	धेनु	धेन्वा	धेनुभ्याम्	धेनुभिः
(11)	ऊ	f∘	वधू	वध्वा	वधूभ्याम्	वधूभिः
(12)	ऋ	m∘	पितृ	पित्रा	पितृभ्याम्	पितृभिः
(13)	ऋ	n∘	धातृ	धात्रा	धातृभ्याम्	धातृभिः
(14)	ऋ	f∘	मातृ	मात्रा	मातृभ्याम्	मातृभिः
(15)	च्	f∘	वाच्	वाचा	वाग्भ्याम्	वाग्भिः
(16)	ज्	m∘	राज्	राजा	राड्भ्याम्	राड्भिः
(17)	त्	m∘	मरुत्	मरुता	मरुद्भ्याम्	मरुद्भिः
(18)	त्	n∘	जगत्	जगता	जगद्भ्याम्	जगद्भिः
(19)	द्	m∘	सुहृद्	सुहृदा	सुहृद्भ्याम्	सुहृद्भिः
(20)	इन्	m∘	शशिन्	शशिना	शशिभ्याम्	शशिभिः
(21)	न्	m∘	आत्मन्	आत्मना	आत्मभ्याम्	आत्मभिः
(22)	न्	n∘	कर्मन्	कर्मणा	कर्मभ्याम्	कर्मभिः
(23)	श्	f∘	दिश्	दिशा	दिग्भ्याम्	दिग्भिः
(24)	स्	m∘	चन्द्रमस्	चन्द्रमसा	चन्द्रमोभ्याम्	चन्द्रमोभिः
(25)	स्	n∘	पयस्	पयसा	पयोभ्याम्	पयोभिः

25.4

THE DATIVE CASE

sampradāna-kārakam. ćaturthī vibhaktiḥ.
सम्प्रदान–कारकम् । चतुर्थी विभक्तिः ।

The 4th Case or Fourth Declension of the substantives

SIGNS: for, to, to give to, to send to, to show to, to desire (उपपदानि – अनु, प्रति, अलम्, वषट्, नमः, स्वस्ति, स्वाहा, स्वधा)

I give rice to Rāma with a spoon. *ahaṁ rāmāya ćamasena odanaṁ dadāmi.* अहं रामाय चमसेन ओदनं ददामि । I am giving, so I am the subject. I, *aham* (अहम्) is the Nominative (1st) case. I give what? I give rice. So rice is the object. Rice, *odanam* ओदनम्, is the Accusative (2nd) case.

I give with a spoon. So, with a spoon, *ćamasaena* चमसेन, is the Instrumental (3rd) case. To give is a Transitive verb (√*da, dadāti* √दा, ददाति). Rice is given to whom (कस्मै)? Rice is given to (or for) Rāma. Therefore, *Rāmāya* रामाय is DATIVE (4th) case.

GENERAL RULE :

(1) When an object is given or transferred 'To' or 'For' someone, the receiver is in DATIVE (4th) CASE.

Rāma gives a letter to Sītā. *Rāmaḥ Sītāyai patraṁ dadāti.* (रामः सीतायै पत्रं ददाति)

ADVANCED RULES : (NOTE : You may study these rules after the basic study of this book)

(2) The object attached with words such as नमः स्वस्ति, स्वाहा, स्वधा, अलम्, वषट् is in the Dative (4th) case. e.g.

i. Salute to Rāma. *Rāmāya namaḥ* रामाय नमः ।

ii. May all be well. *sarvebhyaḥ svasti* सर्वेभ्य: स्वस्ति ।

iii. The offering is for the teacher(s). *gurujanāya svadhā asti.* गुरुजनाय स्वधा अस्ति ।

Oblations to forefathers. *pitṛbhyaḥ svadhā* पितृभ्य: स्वधा ।

iv. The Offering to the Indra. *indrāya vaṣaṭ.* इन्द्राय वषट् ।

v. This is enough for these people. *etat ebhyaḥ alam.* एतत् एभ्य: अलम् ।

(3) The objects indicated by verbs √असूय्, √ईर्ष्य्, √क्रुध्, √दा, √द्रुह, √रुच्, √स्पृह् are in the Dative case.

i. Fools are hateful of the learned people *mūrkhāḥ vijñebhyaḥ asūyanti* मूर्खा: विज्ञेभ्य: असूयन्ति ।

ii. Ignorant people are jealous of the virtuous people. *mūḍhāḥ guṇibhyaḥ īrṣyanti.* मूढा: गुणिभ्य: ईर्ष्यन्ति ।

iii. Wicked people bother the good people. *duṣṭāḥ bhadrebhyaḥ druhyanti* दुष्टा: भद्रेभ्य: द्रुह्यन्ति ।

iv. Mother does not get angry with the children. *mātā putrebhyaḥ na krudhyati.* माता पुत्रेभ्य: न क्रुध्यति ।

(4) When a person inspires someone else, the person (the subject) who inspires is in the Nominative (1st) case, but the person who is being inspired is in the Dative (4th) case.

i. The teacher reads the lesson to the (for the, for the help of the) students. *śikṣakaḥ ćhātrebhyaḥ pāṭhaṁ paṭhati.* शिक्षक: छात्रेभ्य: पाठं पठति ।

(5) To say that someone likes something, the Dative case is used. Rāma likes truth. *Rāmāya satyaṁ roćate.* रामाय सत्यं रोचते ।

(6) The person to whom the √श्लाघ्, स्था, शप्, ह्नुङ् verbs are directed, is in the Dative case.

i. The servant praises the master. *sevakaḥ svāmine ślāghate.* सेवक: स्वामिने श्लाघते ।

(7) In the use of verb √धृ (√*dhṛ* - to bear), the rightful owner of the money is in Dative (4th) case.

i. You owe hundred Repees to Rāma. *bhavān Rāmaya śataṁ rūpyakāṇi dhārayati.* भवान् रामाय शतं रुप्यकाणि धारयति ।

(8) In the use of verb √स्पृह (√spṛḥ - to desire), the thing that is desired is in the Dative (4th) case.

i. All people desire wealth. *sarve dhanāya spṛhanti.* सर्वे धनाय स्पृहन्ति ।

(9) In the use of verbs √राध् and √ईक्ष्, the one about whom the enquiry is being made is in the Dative (4th) case.

i. He asks me about you. *saḥ māṁ bhavate rādhyati/īkṣate.* स: मां भवते राध्यति/ईक्षते ।

(10) The words that carry the meaning of infinitives, are in the Dative (4th) case (for details on

infinitives and examples, see Lesson 28.6).

i. For the protection of the good people and for the removal of the wicked people. *paritrāṇāya sādhūnāṁ vināśāya ća duṣkṛtām* (Gītā 4.8). परित्राणाय साधूनां विनाशाय च दुष्कृताम् ।

(11) In the use of verb √मन् (to think) as a simile, the object (other than people) may optionally be used in the Dative (4th) case, otherwise in the Accusative (2nd) case.

i. He considers his house to be a palace. *saḥ tasya gṛhaṁ rājamahālāya manyate (4th). saḥ tasya gṛhaṁ rājamahālaṁ manyate (2nd).* सः तस्य गृहं राजमहालाय मन्यते । सः तस्य गृहं राजमहालं मन्यते

(12) The verbs that indicate travel (गतिः), the object is optionally in the Dative (4th) case, otherwise in the Accusative (2nd) case.

i. I am going to Kīrti Nagar. *ahaṁ Kīrti-nagarāya gaććhāmi (4th); ahaṁ Kīrti-nagaraṁ gaććhāmi (2nd);* अहं कीर्ति-नगराय गच्छामि । अहं कीर्ति-नगरं गच्छामि ।

(13) When the words आयुष्य, भद्र, मद्र, कुशल, सुख, अर्थ, हित are used for benediction, the benefactor is optionally in the Dative (4th) case, or in the Possessive (6th) case.

i. May you live long. *tubhyaṁ (te) dīrgham āyuṣyaṁ bhūyāt (4th). tava (te) dīrgham āyuṣyaṁ bhūyāt (6th).* तुभ्यं/भवतः दीर्घम् आयुष्यं भूयात् । तव/भवतः दीर्घम् आयुष्यं भूयात् ।

ii. May the poor be happy. *akiñćanebhyaḥ madraṁ bhūyāt (4th). akiñćanānāṁ madraṁ bhūyāt* (6th). अकिञ्चनेभ्यः मद्रं भूयात् । अकिञ्चनानां मद्रं भूयात् ।

iii. May the beings be happy. *bhūtebhyaḥ bhadraṁ bhūyāt (4th). bhūtānāṁ bhadraṁ bhūyāt* (6th). भूतेभ्यः भद्रं भूयात् । भूतानां भद्रं भूयात् ।

iv. May all be happy. *sarvebhyaḥ kuśalaṁ bhūyāt (4th). sarveṣāṁ kuśalaṁ bhūyāt* (6th). सर्वेभ्यः कुशलं भूयात् । सर्वेषां कुशलं भूयात् ।

v. May the children be happy. *śiśubhyaḥ sukhaṁ bhavatu (4th). śiśunāṁ sukhaṁ bhavatu* (6th). शिशुभ्यः सुखं भवतु । शिशुनां सुखं भवतु ।

vi. May the charitable be prosperous. *dānibhyaḥ arthaḥ bhavet (4th). dāninām arthaḥ bhavet* (6th). दानिभ्यः अर्थः भवेत् । दानिनाम् अर्थः भवेत् ।

vii. May all be well. *bhūtebhyaḥ hitaṁ bhūyāt (4th). bhūtānāṁ hitaṁ bhūyāt* (6th). भूतेभ्यः हितं भूयात् । भूतानां हितं भूयात् ।

(14) Many times the Dative (4th) case is optionally used, in place of the Possessive (6th) case, (to indicate a relationship).

i. I will go to his house today. *tasmai (tasya) gṛhe aham adya gantāsmi.* तस्मै (तस्य) गृहे अहम् अद्य गन्तास्मि ।

EXAMPLES cum EXERCISE : THE DATIVE (4th) CASE

1. Obeisance **to Lord Rāma**. *Rāmāya namaḥ* रामाय नमः ।
2. I gave **him** money. *aham tasmai dhanam adadām (dattavān).* अहं तस्मै धनम् अददाम् (दत्तवान्) ।
3. Sītā sings **for you**. *Sītā te gāyati.* सीता ते गायति ।
4. He plays **for the Toronto Raptors**. *saḥ Rāptarebhyaḥ khelati.* सः टोराण्टो-राप्टरेभ्यः खेलति ।
5. You will give **me** the letter. *bhavān me patram dāsyati.* भवान् मे पत्रं दास्यति ।
6. I am going **for the meeting**. *aham sabhāyai gacchāmi.* अहं सभायै गच्छामि ।
7. Sītā! what do you like (**for yourself**)? *Sīte! te kim rocate?* सीते! ते किं रोचते?
8. Rāma! what do you desire **for you**? *Rāma! bhavān kasmai spṛhayati?* राम! भवान् कस्मै स्पृहयसि?

EXERCISE 59 : Say it in Sanskrit and find the Dative (4th) cases

(1) I gave him the ball. अहं तस्मै कन्दुकम् अददाम्/दत्तवान् ।

(2) He gave a book to (for) me. सः मे पुस्तकम् अददात्/दत्तवान् ।

(3) Duryodhana is jealous of Arjuna. दुर्योधनः अर्जुनाय ईर्ष्यति ।

(4) Milk is good for a child. बालाय क्षीरं हितम् ।

(5) Oblation to the fire. अग्नये स्वाहा ।

(6) विद्या विवादाय धनं मदाय शक्तिः परेषां परिपीडनाय ।
खलस्य साधोः विपरीतमेतत् ज्ञानाय दानाय च रक्षणाय ।।46।।

(7) रामाय रामभद्राय रामचन्द्राय वेधसे ।
रघुनाथाय नाथाय सीतायाः पतये नमः ।।47।। (Rāmarakṣā : 27)

DECLENSIONS OF THE DATIVE (4th) CASE

	Word ending	Gender	Word	Singular	Dual	Plural
(1)	अ	m∘	राम	रामाय	रामाभ्याम्	रामेभ्य:
(2)	अ	n∘	वन	वनाय	वनाभ्याम्	वनेभ्य:
(3)	आ	f∘	माला	मालायै	मालाभ्याम्	मालाभ्य:
(4)	इ	m∘	कवि	कवये	कविभ्याम्	कविभ्य:
(5)	इ	n∘	वारि	वारिणे	वारिभ्याम्	वारिभ्य:
(6)	इ	f∘	मति	मत्यै	मतिभ्याम्	मतिभ्य:
(7)	ई	f∘	नदी	नद्यै	नदीभ्याम्	नदीभ्य:
(8)	उ	m∘	गुरु	गुरवे	गुरुभ्याम्	गुरुभ्य:
(9)	उ	n∘	मधु	मधुने	मधुभ्याम्	मधुभ्य:
(10)	उ	f∘	धेनु	धेन्वै	धेनुभ्याम्	धेनुभ्य:
(11)	ऊ	f∘	वधू	वध्वै	वधूभ्याम्	वधूभ्य:
(12)	ऋ	m∘	पितृ	पित्रे	पितृभ्याम्	पितृभ्य:
(13)	ऋ	n∘	धातृ	धात्रे	धातृभ्याम्	धातृभ्य:
(14)	ऋ	f∘	मातृ	मात्रे	मातृभ्याम्	मातृभ्य:
(15)	च्	f∘	वाच्	वाचे	वाग्भ्याम्	वाग्भ्य:
(16)	ज्	m∘	राज्	राजे	राड्भ्याम्	राड्भ्य:
(17)	त्	m∘	मरुत्	मरुते	मरुद्भ्याम्	मरुद्भ्य:
(18)	त्	n∘	जगत्	जगते	जगद्भ्याम्	जगद्भ्य:
(19)	द्	m∘	सुहृद्	सुहृदे	सुहृद्भ्याम्	सुहृद्भ्य:
(20)	इन्	m∘	शशिन्	शशिने	शशिभ्याम्	शशिभ्य:
(21)	न्	m∘	आत्मन्	आत्मने	आत्मभ्याम्	आत्मभ्य:
(22)	न्	n∘	कर्मन्	कर्मणे	कर्मभ्याम्	कर्मभ्य:
(23)	श्	f∘	दिश्	दिशे	दिग्भ्याम्	दिग्भ्य:
(24)	स्	m∘	चन्द्रमस्	चन्द्रमसे	चन्द्रमोभ्याम्	चन्द्रमोभ्य:
(25)	स्	n∘	पयस्	पयसे	पयोभ्याम्	पयोभ्य:

25.5

THE ABLATIVE CASE

apādāna-kārakam. pañćamī vibhaktiḥ

अपादान-कारकम् । पञ्चमी विभक्तिः ।

The 5th Case or Fifth Declension of Substantives

SIGNS: From, than (a comparison between two objects), except, before, after, until, since, outside, without.

(उपपदानि - अप, परि, आङ्, ऋते, विना, पूर्वम्, प्राक्, अनन्तरम्, आ, प्रभृति, बहिः)

Rāma eats rice with a spoon from the dish. *Rāmaḥ odanaṁ ćamasena sthālikāyāḥ khādati.* रामः ओदनं चमसेन स्थालिकायाः खादति ।

Rāma eats, Rāma (रामः), the subject is in the Nominative (1st) case. Rice (ओदनम्) is eaten, so Rice, the object, is in the Accusative (2nd) case. Rāma eats with a spoon (चमसेन), so the Spoon is in the Instrumental (3rd) case. To eat is a transitive verb. The rice is taken out from the dish (स्थालिकायाः), therefore, the dish is in the Ablative (5th) case.

GENERAL RULES :

(1) When an object is moved from one place to another, **the place** FROM where it is moved is in ABLATIVE CASE.

A star falls from the sky. *tārā nabhāt patati.* तारा नभसः पतति ।

The ripe fruits are falling from the tree. *pakvāni phalāni vṛkṣāt patanti.* पक्वानि फलानि वृक्षात् पतन्ति ।

The student comes from school. *ćhātraḥ vidyālayāt āgaććhati.* छात्रः विद्यालयात् आगच्छति ।

My house is 100km from Banāras. *mama gṛhaṁ Vārāṇasītaḥ śata-yojanāni asti.* मम गृहं

वाराणसीतः शतयोजनानि अस्ति ।

I am here since Monday. *somavāsarataḥ aham atra asmi.* सोमवासरतः अहम् अत्र अस्मि ।

(2) When one object is compared with second object, then the second object (against which the comparison is made) is in the ABLATIVE (5th) CASE.

i. Rāma is smarter than Keśava. *Rāmaḥ keśavāt ćaturaḥ asti* रामः केशवात् चतुरः अस्ति ।

(3) The things against which verbs √गुप्, वि√रम् and प्र√मद् are directed, are in the Abaltive (5th) case.

i. The Kauravas loathed the Pāṇḍavas. *kauravāḥ pāṇḍvebhyaḥ ajugupsanta.* कौरवाः पाण्डवेभ्यः अजुगुप्सन्त ।

ii. The good people stay away from bad things. *sajjanāḥ kukarmabhyaḥ viramanti.* सज्जनाः कुकर्मभ्यः विरमन्ति ।

iii. Students should not be careless in studies. *ćhātrāḥ abhyāsāt na pramādyeyuḥ.* छात्राः अभ्यासात् न प्रमाद्येयुः ।

ADVANCED RULES : NOTE : It will be easier for you if you study the advanced rules after you have gone through the primary study of this book at least once.

(4) While using the verbs referring to fear, protection or hiding, the thing from which the fear arises or the thing against which the protection is provided, is in the Ablative (5th) case.

i. The police protects people from thieves. *nagara-rakṣiṇaḥ ćorebhyaḥ janān rakṣanti.* नगररक्षिणः चोरेभ्यः जनान् रक्षन्ति ।

ii. People are afraid of thieves. *janāḥ ćorebhyaḥ bibhyati.* जनाः चोरेभ्यः बिभ्यति । (singular बिभेति, pl॰ बिभ्यति)

iii. Thief hides from the police. *ćoraḥ nagara-rakṣakebhyaḥ vilīyate.* चोरः नगररक्षेभ्यः विलीयते ।

(5) The Ablative (5th) case is used in the application of directional expressions such as भिन्न (different), अन्य (another), आरात् (near, far), इतर (other), ऋते (without), प्रत्यक् (other side, on the West side), उदके, उत्तराहि (on the North side), दक्षिणाहि (on the South side), पूर्वं (before), पृथक् (away).

i. Shape of a banana is different than that of a mango. *āmra-phalasya ākārāt kadali-phalasya ākāraḥ bhinnaḥ asti.* आम्रफलस्य आकारात् कदलिफलस्य आकार: भिन्न: अस्ति ।

ii. The colour of a banana is different than the colour of a mango. *āmra-phala-varṇāt anyavarṇaṁ kadali-phalam.* आम्रफलवर्णात् अन्यवर्णं कदलिफलम् (अन्य: कदलिफलरङ्ग:) ।

iii. The students are standing near (or away from) the teacher. *ćhātrāḥ guroḥ ārāt tiṣṭhanti.* छात्रा: गुरो: आरात् तिष्ठन्ति ।

iv. My book is other than this one. *mama pustakam asmāt (pustakāt) itaram asti.* मम पुस्तकम् अस्मात् (पुस्तकात्) इतरम् अस्ति ।

v. Without efforts there is no success. *ṛte prayatnebhyaḥ sāphalyaṁ nāsti.* ऋते प्रयत्नेभ्य: साफल्यं नास्ति ।

vi. My school is on the other side of the market. *mama vidyālayam āpaṇāt pratyak asti.* मम विद्यालयम् आपणात् प्रत्यक् अस्ति ।

vii. His house is on the North side of my house. *tasya gṛhaṁ mama gṛhāt udakam asti.* तस्य गृहं मम गृहात् उदकम् अस्ति ।

viii. His house is before Rāma's house. *tasya gṛhaṁ Rāmasya gṛhāt pūrvam (prāk) asti.* तस्य गृहं रामस्य गृहात् पूर्वम् (प्राक्) अस्ति ।

ix. Śrīlaṅkā is on the South side of India. *Śrīlaṅkā Bhāratāt dakṣiṇāhi asti.* श्रीलङ्का भारतात् दक्षिणाहि अस्ति ।

x. India is on the North side of Śrīlaṅkā. *Bhārataṁ Śrīlaṅkāyāḥ uttarāhi asti.* भारतं श्रीलङ्काया: उत्तराहि अस्ति ।

(6) Normally the Accusative (2nd) or Instrumental (3rd) case is used in the application of the expressions पृथक् (different) and विना (without). However, optionally the Abaltive (5th) case may also be used.

i. The drinking water is different than this water. *pānīyaṁ jalam asmāt jalāt pṛthak asti.* पानीयं जलम् अस्मात् जलात् पृथक् अस्ति ।

ii. Without desire work is not completed. *icchāyāḥ vinā kāryaṁ na sidhyate.* इच्छायाः विना कार्यं न सिध्यति ।

(7) When the phrase 'up to' is used for indicating a limit, the Ablative (5th) case is used in its application.

i. Up to evening I will stay. *ā-sandhyāyāḥ ahaṁ sthāsyāmi.* आसन्ध्यायाः अहं स्थास्यामि ।

ii. Up to school I run. *ā-vidyālayāt ahaṁ dhāvāmi.* आविद्यालयात् अहं धावामि ।

iii. I bring one book from home. *aham ekaṁ pustakaṁ gṛhāt ānayāmi.* अहम् एकं पुस्तकं गृहात् आनयामि ।

iv. Vāsudeva is smarter than Gopāla. *Vāsudevaḥ Gopālat ćaturaḥ asti.* वासुदेवः गोपालात् चतुरः अस्ति ।

EXAMPLES cum EXERCISE : ABLATIVE (5th) CASE

1. Rāma came **from home**. *Rāmaḥ gṛhāt āgaćchat (āgatavān).* रामः गृहात् आगच्छत् (आगतवान्) ।
2. Rain is falling **from the sky**. *ākāśāt vṛṣṭiḥ bhavati.* आकाशात् वृष्टिः भवति–पतति (√पत्) ।
3. He goes **from here** to there. *saḥ itaḥ tatra gaćchati.* सः इतः तत्र गच्छति ।
4. You will reply **from London**. *bhavān Landanāt pratyuttaraṁ dāsyati.* भवान् लन्दनात् प्रत्युत्तरं दास्यति ।
5. Rāma is taller **than Sitā**. *Rāmaḥ Sītayāḥ uććataraḥ (prāṁśutaraḥ) asti.* रामः सीतायाः उच्चतरः (पांशुतरः) अस्ति ।

EXERCISE 60 : Say it in Sanskrit and find the words in the Ablative (5th) case

(1) He stole the ball from the box. सः पेटिकायाः कन्दुकम् अचोरयत् ।

(2) Rāma works from home. रामः गृहात् एव कार्यं करोति ।

(3) Where did you came from? भवान् कस्मात्-कुतः आगच्छत्/आगतवान्?

(4) We will go from here. वयं इतः गमिष्यामः ।

(5) May people be happy. प्रजाभ्यः स्वस्ति । जनाः सुखिनः भवन्तु ।

(6) Sītā wants flowers. सीता पुष्पेभ्यः स्पृहयति ।

(7) The Ganges originates in (from) the Himālaya. गङ्गा हिमालयात् उद्भवति ।

(8) There is no rescue without knowledge. ज्ञानात् विना न मुक्तिः ।

(9)विद्या ददाति विनयं विनयात् याति पात्रताम् ।
पात्रत्वात् धनम् आप्नोति धनात् धर्मः ततः सुखम् ।।48।।

EXERCISE 61 : Translate into Sanskrit (Answers are given in the brackets)

See Appendix 7 for Verb conjugations and Appendix 2 for Case Declensions.

1. The white flowers are falling from the trees. (वृक्षात् श्वेतानि पुष्पाणि पतन्ति)
2. The river is flowing from the mountain. (पर्वतात् नदी वहति)
3. Wicked stay away from righteousness. (दुष्टाः धर्मात् विरमन्ति)
4. The bad people are afraid of the good people. (दुर्जनाः सज्जनेभ्यः बिभ्यति)
5. The dog protects us from thieves. (कुकुरः अस्मान् चोरेभ्यः त्रायते)
6. The trees are born from the seeds. (वृक्षाः बीजेभ्यः जायन्ते)
7. Sunil saw me from the window. (सुनीलः मां वातायनात् अपश्यत्/दृष्टवान्)
8. The river Ganges originates from the Himalayas. (गङ्गानदी हिमालयात् प्रभवति)
9. The temple is on the west side of the market. (मन्दिरम् आपणात् पश्चिमम् अस्ति)
10. The baby fell from the bed. (शिशुः शयनात् अपतत्)

DECLENSIONS OF THE ABLATIVE (5th) CASE

	Word ending	Gender	Word	Singular	Dual	Plural
(1)	अ	m∘	राम	रामात्	रामाभ्याम्	रामेभ्य:
(2)	अ	n∘	वन	वनात्	वनाभ्याम्	वनेभ्य:
(3)	आ	f∘	माला	मालाया:	मालाभ्याम्	मालाभ्य:
(4)	इ	m∘	कवि	कवे:	कविभ्याम्	कविभ्य:
(5)	इ	n∘	वारि	वारिण:	वारिभ्याम्	वारिभ्य:
(6)	इ	f∘	मति	मत्या:	मतिभ्याम्	मतिभ्य:
(7)	ई	f∘	नदी	नद्या:	नदीभ्याम्	नदीभ्य:
(8)	उ	m∘	गुरु	गुरो:	गुरुभ्याम्	गुरुभ्य:
(9)	उ	n∘	मधु	मधुन:	मधुभ्याम्	मधुभ्य:
(10)	उ	f∘	धेनु	धेनो:	धेनुभ्याम्	धेनुभ्य:
(11)	ऊ	f∘	वधू	वध्वा:	वधूभ्याम्	वधूभ्य:
(12)	ऋ	m∘	पितृ	पितु:	पितृभ्याम्	पितृभ्य:
(13)	ऋ	n∘	धातृ	धातु:	धातृभ्याम्	धातृभ्य:
(14)	ऋ	f∘	मातृ	मातु:	मातृभ्याम्	मातृभ्य:
(15)	च्	f∘	वाच्	वाच:	वाग्भ्याम्	वाग्भ्य:
(16)	ज्	m∘	राज्	राज:	राड्भ्याम्	राड्भ्य:
(17)	त्	m∘	मरुत्	मरुत:	मरुद्भ्याम्	मरुद्भ्य:
(18)	त्	n∘	जगत्	जगत:	जगद्भ्याम्	जगद्भ्य:
(19)	द्	m∘	सुहृद्	सुहृद:	सुहृद्भ्याम्	सुहृद्भ्य:
(20)	इन्	m∘	शशिन्	शशिन:	शशिभ्याम्	शशिभ्य:
(21)	न्	m∘	आत्मन्	आत्मन:	आत्मभ्याम्	आत्मभ्य:
(22)	न्	n∘	कर्मन्	कर्मण:	कर्मभ्याम्	कर्मभ्य:
(23)	श्	f∘	दिश्	दिश:	दिग्भ्याम्	दिग्भ्य:
(24)	स्	m∘	चन्द्रमस्	चन्द्रमस:	चन्द्रमोभ्याम्	चन्द्रमोभ्य:
(25)	स्	n∘	पयस्	पयस:	पयोभ्याम्	पयोभ्य:

25.6

THE POSSESSIVE or GENITIVE CASE

adhikaraṇa-kārakam. ṣaṣṭhī vibhaktiḥ

अधिकरण-कारकम् । षष्ठी विभक्तिः ।

The 6th Case or Sixth Declension of the substantives

SIGNS : of, above, below, in front of, behind, beyond, in presense of, comparison of more than two, i.e. superlative.

(उपपदानि - पश्चात्, उपरि, उपरिष्टात्, परतः, पुरतः, दक्षिणतः, दक्षिणात्, उत्तरतः, उत्तरात्, अवरतः, पुरः, पुरस्तात्, अग्रे, समक्षम्, अधः, अधरात्, अवः, अवस्तात्, कृते)

Rāma eats rice with a spoon from Sītā's dish. *Rāmaḥ ćamasena Sītāyāḥ sthālikāyāḥ odanaṁ khādati.* रामः चमसेन सीतायाः स्थालिकायाः ओदनं खादति ।

Rāma eats, so Rāma (रामः), the subject, is in the Nominative (1st) case. Rice (ओदनम्) is eaten, so Rice, the object, is in the Accusative (2nd) case. Rāma eats with a spoon (चमसेन), so the Spoon is in the Instrumental (3rd) case. To eat is a Transitive verb. The rice is taken out from the dish (थालिकायाः), therefore, the Dish is in the Ablative (5th) case. The dish belongs to Sītā's (सीतायाः), therefore, Sītā is also in Possessive (6th) case.

In English, this relationship is shown by the preposition OF or by an 's also.

When we say, I am talking to Sītā's friend Rāma : it shows that,

I am (अहं) the subject, so I am in the Nominative (1st) case. Rāma is the object to whom I am talking, so Rāma (रामं) is in the Accusative (2nd) case. Friend is an adjective of Rāma. Talking (कथयामि) is the transitive verb. Sītā does not have a direct relationship with the subject in this sentence. Sītā has only indirect or external relaionship (सीतायाः), through the object Rāma. The sentence could very well be completed without Sītā's mention i.e. I am talking to Rāma. The word Sītā is not necessary to complete this sentence.

Thus, the word that is not necessary to complete the sentence, but only has an external relationship (सम्बन्धः) in the sentence, is not a कारकम् *(kārakam)*. It is merely a विभक्तिः

(vibhaktiḥ), called Possessive or Genetive (6th) case.

GENERAL RULE :

(1) When a relation (सम्बन्धः) between two things is indicated by the preposition OF, 's or MADE OF, the object indicated by 'of' is in the POSSESSIVE (6th) CASE. e.g. Brother of Rāma; Rāma's house; the dish MADE OF silver. *Rāmasya bandhuḥ; Rāmasya gṛham. rūpyakasya sthālikā.* रामस्य बन्धुः । रामस्य गृहम् । रूप्यकस्य स्थालिका ।

ADVANCED RULES : NOTE : It will be easier for you if you study the advanced rules after you have gone through the primary study of this book at least once.

(2) Things associated with the verb roots such as उप√कृ, अप√कृ, √क्षम् are in the Possessive (6th) case.

(3) Expressions such as उपरि अधः अग्रतः पुरतः पृष्ठतः उत्तरतः दक्षिणतः वामतः indicate the use of Possessive (6th) case.

उपरि –	उपरि गृहस्य ध्वजः शोभते ।	अधः –	वृक्षस्य अधः तृणं न वर्तते ।
अग्रतः –	भद्रस्य अग्रतः खलः न तिष्ठति ।	पुरतः –	बिडालस्य पुरतः मूषकः बिभेति ।
पृष्ठतः –	रामस्य पृष्ठतः लक्ष्मणः भवति ।	उत्तरतः –	जननी बालकम् उत्तरतः पश्यति ।
दक्षिणतः –	रामस्य दक्षिणतः कः अस्ति?	वामतः –	रामस्य वामतः का अस्ति?

(4) Superlative (श्रेष्ठत्वम्) and contempt (अनादरः) indicate the Possessive (6th) case.

Lion is the most powerful animal. Duryodhana was the wickedest among the wicked. पशूनां श्रेष्ठः सिंहः । दुष्टेषु दुर्योधनः । *paśunāṁ śreṣṭhaḥ siṁhaḥ. duṣṭeṣu Duryodhanaḥ.*

(5) When the verb √ज्ञा *(√jñā)* is used to show a misunderstanding of something, the 6th case is employed.

People think paper flowers to be real flowers. *janāḥ kargada-puṣpāṇi avitathānāṁ puṣpāṇāṁ jānanti.* जनाः कर्गदपुष्पाणि अवितथानां पुष्पाणां जानन्ति ।

(6) Many times 6th case is optionally used in place of 2nd, 3rd or 4th case.

i. She remembers God in the difficult times. *sā vipatkāle devaṁ/devasya smarati.* सा

विपत्काले देवं/<u>देवस्य</u> स्मरति ।

ii. Fire burns the wood. *agniḥ edhāṁsi/edhasāṁ bhasmasāt kurute.* अग्निः एधांसि/एधसां भस्मसात् कुरुते ।

iii. Wash the hands with water. *jalena/jalasya hastau kṣālayatu.* जलेन/जलस्य हस्तौ क्षालयतु ।

iv. It should be done by me. *etat mama (mayā) karaṇīyam.* एतत् मम (मया) करणीयम् ।

v. The mouse is for Gaṇeśa, the bull is for Śiva, the tiger is for Devī and the deer is for the Moon. *mūṣakaḥ Gaṇeśasya/Gaṇeśāya, vṛṣabhaḥ Śivasya/Śivāya, vyāghraḥ devyāḥ/devyai, hariṇaḥ ćandramasaḥ/ćandramase asti.* मूषकः गणेशस्य/गणेशाय, वृषभः शिवस्य/शिवाय, व्याघ्रः देव्याः/देव्यै, हरिणः चन्द्रमसः/चन्द्रमसे अस्ति ।

(7) In the use of Past Passive Participles (see Lesson 28.3 on ppp◦), normally the Instrumental (3rd) case is used for the subject; optionally the Possessive (6th) case is also used.

i. I have desired it (active voice) or it is desired by me (passive participle ppp◦).
mayā/mama etat iṣṭam. मया/मम एतत् इष्टम् ।

ii. He has read the verse. *tena/tasya ślokaḥ paṭhitaḥ.* तेन/तस्य श्लोकः पठितः ।

iii. All have seen it. *etat sarvaiḥ/sarveṣāṁ dṛṣṭaḥ.* एतत् सर्वैः/सर्वेषां दृष्टः ।

iv. Rāma has done it. *etat Rāmeṇa/Rāmasya kṛtam.* एतत् रामेण/रामस्य कृतम् ।

v. It is remembered by the me. *mayā/mama etat jñātam.* मया/मम एतत् ज्ञातम् ।

(8) In the use of a comparative suffix such as सदृश and तुल्य, the word being compared is either in Possessive (6th) case or in Instrumental (3rd) case.

There is no king like Rāma. *Rāmasya/rāmeṇa sadṛśaḥ (tulyaḥ) kaśćit rājā nāsti.* रामेण/रामस्य सदृशः (तुल्यः) कश्चित् राजा नास्ति ।

(9) When the words आयुष्य, भद्र, मद्र, कुशल, सुख, अर्थ, हित are used for benediction, the

benefactor is optionally in Dative case, normally it is in the Possessive (6th) case.

i. May you live long. *tubhyaṁ (te) dīrgham āyuṣyaṁ bhūyāt (4th). tava (te) dīrgham āyuṣyaṁ bhūyāt (6th).* तुभ्यं (ते) दीर्घम् आयुष्यं भूयात् । तव (ते) दीर्घम् आयुष्यं भूयात् ।

ii. May the poor be happy. *akiñcanebhyaḥ madraṁ bhūyāt (4th). akiñcanānāṁ madraṁ bhūyāt* (6th). अकिञ्चनेभ्यः मद्रं भूयात् । अकिञ्चनानां मद्रं भूयात् ।

iii. May the beings be happy. *bhūtebhyaḥ bhadraṁ bhūyāt (4th). bhūtānāṁ bhadraṁ bhūyāt* (6th). भूतेभ्यः भद्रं भूयात् । भूतानां भद्रं भूयात् ।

iv. May all be happy. *sarvebhyaḥ kuśalaṁ bhūyāt (4th). sarveṣāṁ kuśalaṁ bhūyāt* (6th). सर्वेभ्यः कुशलं भूयात् । सर्वेषां कुशलं भूयात् ।

v. May the children be happy. *śiśubhyaḥ sukhaṁ bhavatu (4th). śiśunāṁ sukhaṁ bhavatu* (6th). शिशुभ्यः सुखं भवतु । शिशुनां सुखं भवतु ।

vi. May the charitable be prosperous. *dānibhyaḥ arthaḥ bhavet (4th). dāniṣu arthaḥ bhavet* (6th). दानिभ्यः अर्थः भवेत् । दानिषु अर्थः भवेत् ।

vii. May all be prosperous. *bhūtebhyaḥ hitaṁ bhūyāt (4th). bhūtānāṁ hitaṁ bhūyāt* (6th). भूतेभ्यः हितं भूयात् । भूतानां हितं भूयात् ।

(10) In the use of the adverbs such as दक्षिणतः, उत्तरतः, उत्तरात्, अधस्तात्, अवरतः, परतः, उपरि, उपरिष्टात्, पश्चात्, दक्षिणात्, पुरः, अधः, अवः, पुरस्तात्, अधरात्, अवस्तात्..., the connecting word is in the possessive (6th) case.

i. India is on the North side of Śrīlaṅkā. *Śrīlaṅkāyāḥ uttarataḥ (uttarāt) Bhāratam asti.* श्रीलङ्कायाः उत्तरतः (उतरात्) भारतम् अस्ति ।

ii. He is sitting in front of (behind) me. *saḥ mama purastāt (avastāt, avarataḥ, avaḥ ...) upaviṣṭaḥ asti.* सः मम पुरस्तात् (अवस्तात्, अवरतः अवः ...) उपविष्टः अस्ति ।

For more examples, see the Ablative (5th) case.

(11) In Sanskrit, the verb 'to have' is expressed with the use of suffix 'of.'

e.g. The rich people have money. धनिकानां धनम् अस्ति *dhanikānāṁ dhanam asti.*

The students have books. छात्राणां पुस्तकानि सन्ति *ćhātrāṇām pustakāni santi*).

THE CLASSICAL EXAMPLES from Gītā (10.21-22):

1. आदित्यानाम् अहं विष्णुः ज्योतिषां रविरंशुमान् ।
मरीचिः मरुताम् अस्मि नक्षत्राणाम् अहं शशी ।।49।।

2. वेदानां सामवेदोऽस्मि देवानाम् अस्मि वासवः ।
इन्द्रियाणां मनश्चास्मि भूतानाम् अस्मि चेतना ।।50।।

EXAMPLES cum EXERCISE : POSSESSIVE (6th) CASE

1. Bharata was Rāma's Brother. *Bharataḥ Rāmasya bandhuḥ āsīt.* भरतः रामस्य बन्धुः आसीत्
2. Rāma was Daśaratha's son. *Rāmaḥ Daśarathasya putraḥ āsīt.* रामः दशरथस्य पुत्रः आसीत्
3. This is Sītā's book. *idaṁ sītāyaḥ pustakam asti.* इदं सीतायाः पुस्तकम् अस्ति ।
4. I saw a gold ring. *ahaṁ suvarṇavalayaṁ apaśyam.* अहं सुवर्णस्य सुवर्णवलयं अपश्यम् ।
5. You are sitting near them. *bhavān teṣāṁ samīpe upaviśati.* भवान् तेषां समीपे उपविशति ।
6. This is my house. *etad mama gṛham asti* एतद् मम गृहम् अस्ति ।
7. Where is our car? *asmākaṁ kār-yānaṁ kutra asti?* अस्माकं कारयानं कुत्र अस्ति?
8. He stole my Rupees. *saḥ mama rūpyakāṇi aćorayat.* सः मम रूप्यकाणि अचोरयत् ।
9. Gentleman helps everyone. *sadhuḥ sarveṣām upakaroti.* साधुः सर्वेषाम् उपकरोति ।
10. Sītā is standing on the left side of Rāma. *Ramasya vāmataḥ Sītā tiṣṭhati.* रामस्य वामतः सीता तिष्ठति ।
11. Bharata is standing on the right side of Rāma. *Ramasya dakṣiṇataḥ Bharataḥ tiṣṭhati.* रामस्य दक्षिणतः भरतः तिष्ठति ।
12. Lakṣamaṇa is standing behind Rāma. *Ramasya pṛṣṭhataḥ Lakṣamaṇaḥ tiṣṭhati.* रामस्य पृष्ठतः लक्ष्मणः तिष्ठति ।
13. There is an umbrella over Rāma. *Ramasya upari ćhatram asti.* रामस्य उपरि छत्रम् अस्ति ।

EXERCISE 62 : Find the possessive (6th) cases in the following

(1) Rāma is reading his own book. रामः स्वस्य पुस्तकं पठति ।

(2) Sītā's friend is there. सीतायाः सखी तत्र अस्ति ।

(3) He gave me my money. सः मह्यं मम धनम् अददात्-दत्तवान् ।

(4) Calcutta is in the east of India. भारतस्य पूर्वतः कोलकता अस्ति ।

(5) Mumbaī is in the west of India. भारतस्य पश्चिमतः मुम्बई अस्ति ।

(6) India is to the North of Śrīlankā. श्रीलङ्कायाः उत्तरतः भारतम् अस्ति ।

CLASSICAL EXAMPLES

(7) नरस्य आभरणं रूपं रूपस्याभरणं गुणः ।
गुणस्याभरणं ज्ञानं ज्ञानस्याभरणं क्षमा ।।51।।

(8) यस्य नास्ति स्वयं प्रज्ञा शास्त्रं तस्य करोति किम् ।
नेत्राभ्यां तु विहीनस्य दर्पणः किं करिष्यति ।।52।।

(9) आदानस्य प्रदानस्य कर्तव्यस्य च कर्मणः
क्षिप्रमक्रियमाणस्य कालः पिबति तद्रसम् ।।53।।

(10) अयं निजः परो वेति गणना लघुचेतसाम् ।
उदारचरितानां तु वसुधैव कुटुम्बकम् ।।54।।

EXAMPLES cum EXERCISE : Possessive (6th) case

(1) He is the son of my brother. *saḥ mama bhrātuḥ putraḥ asti.* सः मम भ्रातुः पुत्रः अस्ति ।

(2) Where is Rāma's younger sister? *Rāmasya anujā kutra asti?* रामस्य अनुजा कुत्र अस्ति?

(3) This is Sītā's grandfather's house. *etad Sītāyāḥ mātāmahasya gṛham asti.* एतद् सीतायाः मातामहस्य गृहम् अस्ति ।

(4) Your father's friend is coming. *tava pituḥ bandhuḥ āgacchati.* तव पितुः बन्धुः आगच्छति ।

(5) I have two brothers. *mama dvau bhrātarau staḥ.* मम द्वौ भ्रातरौ स्तः ।

EXERCISE 63 : Give Sanskrit names for the English nouns

(See Lesson 35 for the words of relationships)

(1) Family ----------- Friend ----------- Father -----------

(2) Mother ---------- Daughter ---------- Brother ---------

(3) Sister ----------- Wife ----------- Son -----------

DECLENSIONS OF THE POSSESSIVE (6th) CASE

	Word ending	Gender	Word	Singular	Dual	Plural
(1)	अ	m◦	राम	रामस्य	रामयो:	रामाणाम्
(2)	अ	n◦	वन	वनस्य	वनयो:	वनानाम्
(3)	आ	f◦	माला	मालाया:	मालयो:	मालानाम्
(4)	इ	m◦	कवि	कवे:	कव्यो:	कवीनाम्
(5)	इ	n◦	वारि	वारिण:	वारिणो:	वारीणाम्
(6)	इ	f◦	मति	मत्या:	मत्यो:	मतीनाम्
(7)	ई	f◦	नदी	नद्या:	नद्यो:	नदीनाम्
(8)	उ	m◦	गुरु	गुरो:	गुर्वो:	गुरूणाम्
(9)	उ	n◦	मधु	मधुन:	मधुनो:	मधूनाम्
(10)	उ	f◦	धेनु	धेनो:	धेन्वो:	धेनूनाम्
(11)	ऊ	f◦	वधू	वध्वा:	वध्वो:	वधूनाम्
(12)	ऋ	m◦	पितृ	पितु:	पित्रो:	पितॄणाम्
(13)	ऋ	n◦	धातृ	धातु:	धात्रो:	धातॄणाम्
(14)	ऋ	f◦	मातृ	मातु:	मात्रो:	मातॄणाम्
(15)	च्	f◦	वाच्	वाच:	वाचो:	वाचाम्
(16)	ज्	m◦	राज्	राज:	राजो:	राजाम्
(17)	त्	m◦	मरुत्	मरुत:	मरुतो:	मरुताम्
(18)	त्	n◦	जगत्	जगत:	जगतो:	जगताम्
(19)	द्	m◦	सुहृद्	सुहृद:	सुहृदो:	सुहृदाम्
(20)	इन्	m◦	शशिन्	शशिन:	शशिनो:	शशिनाम्
(21)	न्	m◦	आत्मन्	आत्मन:	आत्मनो:	आत्मनाम्
(22)	न्	n◦	कर्मन्	कर्मण:	कर्मणो:	कर्मणाम्
(23)	श्	f◦	दिश्	दिश:	दिशो:	दिशाम्
(24)	स्	m◦	चन्द्रमस्	चन्द्रमस:	चन्द्रमसो:	चन्द्रमसाम्
(25)	स्	n◦	पयस्	पयस:	पयसो:	पयसाम्

25.7

THE LOCATIVE CASE

adhikaraṇa kārakam. saptamī vibhaktiḥ

अधिकरण-कारकम् । सप्तमी विभक्तिः ।

The 7th Case or the Seventh Declension fo Substantives

SIGNS : In, on, at, in side, under, upon, among अधि ।

Rāma eats rice with spoon from Sītā's dish in the kitchen on (or at) the table. *Rāmaḥ odanaṁ ćamasena Sītāyāḥ sthālikāyāṁ pāka-gṛhe phalake khādati.* रामः ओदनं चमसेन सीतायाः स्थालिकायां पाकगृहे फलके खादति ।

Rāma eats, so *Rāmaḥ* रामः, the subject, is in the Nominative (1st) case. Rice (ओदनम्) is eaten, so Rice, the object, is in the Accusative (2nd) case. Rāma eats with a spoon (*ćamasena* चमसेन), so the Spoon is in the Instrumental (3rd) case. To eat is a Transitive verb. The rice is taken out from the dish (*thālikāyāḥ* थालिकायाः), so the dish is in the Ablative (5th) case. The dish belongs to Sītā (*sītayā* सीतायाः), so Sītā is in the Possessive (6th) case. He eats IN the kitchen (*pākagṛhe* पाकगृहे) at the table (*phalake* फलके). So, kitchen and table both are in the LOCATIVE (7th) case.

GENERAL RULE :

(1) Words that locate the object in relation to its surroundings, such as- In, On, At, Over, Above, Under ...etc. indicate the LOCATIVE (7th) CASE.

ADVANCED RULES :

(2) We have seen earlier that the expressions such as अग्रतः पुरतः पृष्ठतः उत्तरतः दक्षिणतः वामतः indicate the Possessive (6th) case. However, if these words indicate a location in relation to the subject, then these words (if they are declinable) take the suffix of the LOCATIVE (7th) case, such as, दक्षिणे on the right side, वामे on the left side. e.g.

दक्षिणे लक्ष्मणो यस्य वामे तु जनकात्मजा ।

पुरतो मारुतिर्यस्य तं वन्दे रघुनन्दनम् ।।55।। (Rāmarakṣā : 31)

(3) The words that mean near or far are normally in 2nd, 3rd or 5th case, but optionally they could be in the Locative (7th) case.

My house is far (near) from the school. *mama gṛhaṁ vidyālayāt dūre (dūram, dūreṇa, dūrāt; samīpam, samīpena, samīpāt; antikam, antikena, antikāt) asti.* मम गृहं विद्यालयात् दूरे (दूरम्, दूरेण, दूरात्; समीपम्, समीपेन, सम्पात्; अन्तिकम्, अन्तिकेन, अन्तिकात्) अस्ति ।

EXAMPLES cum EXERCISE : THE LOCATIVE (7th) CASE (cumulative learning)

1. He sat in my car. *saḥ mama yāne upāviśat/upaviṣṭavān.* सः मम यानेउपाविशत्/उपविष्टवान्
2. The bird sits on a wall. *pakṣī bhittau tiṣṭhati.* पक्षी भित्तौ तिष्ठति ।
3. Put a cap over your head. *śirasi śirastrāṇaṁ sthāpaya.* शिरसि शिरस्त्राणं स्थापय (स्थापयतु) ।
4. The cat is under the chair. *biḍālaḥ viṣṭara-tale asti.* बिडालः विष्टरतले अस्ति ।
5. Sitā is cooking rice in a pot. *Sītā pātre odanaṁ paćati.* सीता पात्रे ओदनं पचति ।
6. His heart is not in study. *tasya paṭhane ićhā/ćttaṁ nāsti.* तस्य पठने इच्छा/चित्तं नास्ति ।
7. Bad people should not be trusted. *duṣṭa-janeṣu mā viśvaset.* दुष्टजनेषु मा विश्वसेत् ।
8. The wind carries the smoke away. *vāyuḥ dhūmaṁ dūre nayati.* वायुः धूमं दूरे नयति ।
9. The smoke moves up. *dhūmaḥ upari gaććhati.* धूमः उपरि गच्छति ।
10. Rāma shot an arrow into Rāvaṇa's stomach. *Rāmaḥ Ravaṇasya udare śareṇa prāharat.* रामः रावणस्य उदरे शरेण प्राहरत् ।
11. I will eat at seven o'clock. *ahaṁ sapta-vādane khādiṣyāmi.* अहं सप्तवादने खादिष्यामि ।
12. Sītā is expert in singing. *Sītā gīta-gāyane pravīṇā asti.* सीता गीतगायने प्रवीणा अस्ति ।
13. He has a liking for Sanskrit. *tasya saṁskṛte āsaktiḥ.* तस्य संस्कृते आसक्तिः ।
14. In today's world, strength is in unity. *saṅghe śaktiḥ kalau yuge.* संघे शक्तिः कलौ युगे ।
15. Most distinguished and sweetest among all the languages is the glorious Sanskrit language. *bhāṣāsu mukhyā madhurā divyā gīrvāṇa-bhāratī.* **भाषासु मुख्या मधुरा दिव्या गीर्वाणभारती ।**

EXERCISE 64 : Find the locative (7th) case

(1) पुस्तके, पुस्तकानाम्, पुस्तकेषु ।

(2) मालायाः, मालायाम्, मालायै, मालासु ।

(3) नदी, नदीभ्यः, नदीषु, नद्यः ।

(4) कर्मणि, कर्मसु, कर्मणः ।

(5) भर्ता, भर्तृषु, भर्तृणाम् ।

(6) मातृवत् परदारेषु परद्रव्येषु लोष्ठवत् ।
आत्मवत् सर्वभूतेषु यः पश्यति स पण्डितः ।56।।

(7) कर्मण्येवाधिकारस्ते मा फलेषु कदाचन ।।57।। (Gītā 2.47)

(8) दुःखेष्वनुद्विग्नमनाः सुखेषु विगतस्पृहः ।
वीतरागभयक्रोधः स्थितधीर्मुनिरुच्यते ।।58।। (Gītā 2.56)

(9) रसोऽहमप्सु कौन्तेय प्रभाऽस्मि शशिसूर्ययोः ।
प्रणवः सर्ववेदेषु शब्दः खे पौरुषं नृषु ।।59।। (Gītā 7.8)

(10) पुण्यो गन्धः पृथिव्यां च तेजश्चास्मि विभावसौ ।
जीवनं सर्वभूतेषु तपश्चास्मि तपस्विषु ।।60।। (Gītā 7.9)

(11) तस्मात्सर्वेषु कालेषु योगयुक्तो भवार्जुन ।।61।। (Gītā 8.27)

(12) समः शत्रौ च मित्रे च तथा मानापमानयोः ।
शीतोष्णसुखदुःखेषु समः सङ्गविवर्जितः ।।62।। (Gītā 12.18)

(13) समं सर्वेषु भूतेषु तिष्ठन्तं परमेश्वरम् ।।63।। (Gītā 13.28)

EXERCISE 65 : Write Sankkrit words for English nouns

(1) Cloth ----------------- Shirt -----------------

(2) Shoe ----------------- Sari -----------------

(3) Sheet ----------------- Carpet -----------------

DECLENSIONS OF THE LOCATIVE (7th) CASE

	Word ending	Gender	Word	Singular	Dual	Plural
(1)	अ	m◦	राम	रामे	रामयोः	रामेषु
(2)	अ	n◦	वन	वने	वनयोः	वनेषु
(3)	आ	f◦	माला	मालायाम्	मालयोः	मालासु
(4)	इ	m◦	कवि	कवौ	कव्योः	कविषु
(5)	इ	n◦	वारि	वारिणि	वारिणोः	वारिषु
(6)	इ	f◦	मति	मत्याम्	मत्योः	मतिषु
(7)	ई	f◦	नदी	नद्याम्	नद्योः	नदीषु
(8)	उ	m◦	गुरु	गुरौ	गुर्वोः	गुरुषु
(9)	उ	n◦	मधु	मधुनि	मधुनोः	मधुषु
(10)	उ	f◦	धेनु	धेन्वाम्	धेन्वोः	धेनुषु
(11)	ऊ	f◦	वधू	वध्वाम्	वध्वोः	वधूषु
(12)	ऋ	m◦	पितृ	पितरि	पित्रोः	पितृषु
(13)	ऋ	n◦	धातृ	धातरि	धात्रोः	धातृषु
(14)	ऋ	f◦	मातृ	मातरि	मात्रोः	मातृषु
(15)	च्	f◦	वाच्	वाचि	वाचोः	वाक्षु
(16)	ज्	m◦	राज्	राजि	राजोः	राट्सु
(17)	त्	m◦	मरुत्	मरुति	मरुतोः	मरुत्सु
(18)	त्	n◦	जगत्	जगति	जगतोः	जगत्सु
(19)	द्	m◦	सुहृद्	सुहृदि	सुहृदोः	सुहृत्सु
(20)	इन्	m◦	शशिन्	शशिनि	शशिनोः	शशिषु
(21)	न्	m◦	आत्मन्	आत्मनि	आत्मनोः	आत्मसु
(22)	न्	n◦	कर्मन्	कर्मणि	कर्मणोः	कर्मसु
(23)	श्	f◦	दिश्	दिशि	दिशोः	दिक्षु
(24)	स्	m◦	चन्द्रमस्	चन्द्रमसि	चन्द्रमसोः	चन्द्रमःसु
(25)	स्	n◦	पयस्	पयसि	पयसोः	पयःसु

25.8

THE VOCATIVE CASE

sambodhanam सम्बोधनम् ।

ADDRESS

O' - हे, भोः, रे, अरे, अरी, अजी, अयी, हञ्जे ।

Suffixes used for addressing or calling someone, form the VOCATIVE CASE.

e.g. O Rāma! हे राम!

NOTE: Unlike European languages such as Latin, in Sanskrit there is no 8th case. Technically, the Vocative (case) is not considred a separate case, but is modified Nominative (1st) case.

EXAMPLES cum EXERCISE : VOCATIVE EXPRESSIONS

(1) O Rāma!	*hé rāma!* हे राम!
(2) O Sītā!	*hé sīte!* हे सीते!
(3) O Lord!	*hé deva! hé bhagavan* हे देव! हे भगवन्!
(4) O Sunil!	*bhoḥ sunīl!* भोः सुनील!
(5) O Mother!	*hé māta!* हे मातः!
(6) O Boys!	*hé bālakāḥ!* हे बालकाः!
(7) O Girls!	*hé bālāḥ!; hé bālikāḥ!* हे बालाः! हे बालिकाः!
(8) O Teachers!	*hé guravaḥ!* हे गुरवः!
(9) O Sir!	*hé śrīman! mahoday! mahāśay!* हे श्रीमन्! महोदय! महाशय!
(10) O Madam!	*hé śrīmati! he bhavati!* हे श्रीमति! हे भगवति! हे भवति!

DECLENSIONS OF THE VOCATIVE CASE

	Word ending	Gender	Word	Singular	Dual	Plural
(1)	अ	m◦	राम	राम	रामौ	रामाः
(2)	अ	n◦	वन	वन	वने	वनानि
(3)	आ	f◦	माला	माले	माले	मालाः
(4)	इ	m◦	कवि	कवे	कवी	कवयः
(5)	इ	n◦	वारि	वारि	वारिणी	वारीणि
(6)	इ	f◦	मति	मते	मती	मतयः
(7)	ई	f◦	नदी	नदि	नद्यौ	नद्यः
(8)	उ	m◦	गुरु	गुरो	गुरू	गुरवः
(9)	उ	n◦	मधु	मधु	मधुनी	मधूनि
(10)	उ	f◦	धेनु	धेनो	धेनू	धेनवः
(11)	ऊ	f◦	वधू	वधु	वध्वौ	वध्वः
(12)	ऋ	m◦	पितृ	पितः	पितरौ	पितरः
(13)	ऋ	n◦	धातृ	धातः	धातृणी	धातृणि
(14)	ऋ	f◦	मातृ	मातः	मातरौ	मातरः
(15)	च्	f◦	वाच्	वाक्	वाचौ	वाचः
(16)	ज्	m◦	राज्	राट्	राजौ	राजः
(17)	त्	m◦	मरुत्	मरुत्	मरुतौ	मरुतः
(18)	त्	n◦	जगत्	जगत्	जगती	जगन्ति
(19)	द्	m◦	सुहृद्	सुहृद्	सुहृदौ	सुहृदः
(20)	इन्	m◦	शशिन्	शशिन्	शशिनौ	शशिनः
(21)	न्	m◦	आत्मन्	आत्मन्	आत्मानौ	आत्मानः
(22)	न्	n◦	कर्मन्	कर्म	कर्मणी	कर्माणि
(23)	श्	f◦	दिश्	दिक्	दिशौ	दिशः
(24)	स्	m◦	चन्द्रमस्	चन्द्रमाः	चन्द्रमसौ	चन्द्रमसः
(25)	स्	n◦	पयस्	पयः	पयसी	पयांसि

LESSON 26

ṣaḍviṁśaḥ abhyāsaḥ षड्विंशः अभ्यासः ।

THE VOICES

prayogāḥ
प्रयोगाः ।

For English verbs there are two voices, active and passive.

In Sanskrit there are three voices, कर्तरि Kartari (active), कर्मणि Karmaṇi (passive) and भावे Bhāve (abstract).

26.1

THE ACTIVE VOICE

Kartari-prayogaḥ
कर्तरि-प्रयोगः ।

THE ACTIVE VOICE : The boy writes a letter. *bālakaḥ patraṁ likhati (√likh* = to write*).* बालकः पत्रं लिखति (√लिख्) । In this sentence, बालकः (*bālakaḥ* the boy) is the subject (*kartā* कर्ता); पत्रं (a letter) is the object (*karma* कर्म) and लिखति (*likhati* writes) is the verb (*kriyāpadam* क्रियापदम्).

(i) The boy writes a letter. बालकः पत्रं लिखति । *bālakaḥ patraṁ likhati.* The subject (*bālakaḥ* बालकः) and the verb (*likhati* लिखति) are both singular.

(ii) The boys write a letter. बालकाः पत्रं लिखन्ति । *bālakāḥ patraṁ likhanti.* The verb (*likhanti* लिखन्ति) became plural with the subject.

(iii) The boy writes letters. बालकः पत्राणि लिखति । *bālakaḥ patrāṇi likhati.* The object (*patrāṇi* पत्राणि) is plural but the verb (*likhati* लिखति) is singular because the subject (*bālakaḥ* बालक:) is singular.

(iv) The boys write letters. बालका: पत्राणि लिखन्ति । *bālakāḥ patrāṇi likhatni.* The verb (*likhanit* लिखन्ति) became plural with the subject (*bālakāḥ* बालका:).

In above four (i-iv) examples, when the subject is singular, the verb is singular; and when the subject is plural, the verb also becomes plural. But, when the object became plural, the verb did not change.

(v) I write a letter. अहं पत्रं लिखामि । *ahaṁ patraṁ likhāmi.* The subject (*aham* अहम्) and verb (*likhāmi* लिखामि) are 1st person.

(vi) He writes a letter. स: पत्रं लिखति । *saḥ patraṁ likhati.* The subject (*saḥ* स:) and the verb (*likhanti* लिखन्ति) both are 3rd person.

(vii) I write letters. अहं पत्राणि लिखामि । *ahaṁ patrāṇi likhāmi.* The object (*patrāṇi* पत्राणि) is plural, but verb (*likhāmi* लिखामि) is singular.

(viii) He writes letters. स: पत्राणि लिखति । *saḥ patrāṇi likhati.* The verb (*likhati* लिखति) is still following the subject.

In above four (v-viii) examples, when the subject is 1st person, the verb is also 1st person; and when the subject is 3rd person, the verb also becomes 3rd person. But, when the object became plural, the verb did not become plural.

(xi) The boy writes a letter. बालक: पत्रं लिखति । *bālakaḥ patraṁ likhati.* The verb (*likhati* लिखति) is *parasmaipadī.*

(xii) The boy gets a letter. बालक: पत्रं लभते । The verb (*labhate* लभते) is *ātmanepadī.*

From above two (xi-xii) examples, we can see that : In the Active voice, the verb could be *parasmaipadī* or *ātmanepadī.* Therefore, *Ātmanepadī* does not necessarily mean Passive voice, as many times is misunderstood.

THUS, from above twelve (i-xii) examples we can say that : **In the Aactive Voice (कर्तरिप्रयोगे)**

(1) The verb changes with the subject;

(2) It does not change with the object;

(3) The subject is always in the Nominative case;

(4) The object is always in the Accusative case;

(5) The verb in Active Voice could be *Parasmaipadī* or *Ātmanepadī.*

26.2

THE PASSIVE VOICE

karmaṇi prayogaḥ.
कर्मणि-प्रयोगः ।

(i) The letter is written by a boy. *bālakena patraṁ likhyate.* बालकेन पत्रं लिख्यते ।

In this sentence, बालकेन (*bālakena* by a boy) is the subject (कर्ता); पत्रम् (*patram* a letter) is the object (कर्म) and लिख्यते (*likhyate* is written) is the verb (क्रियापदम्).

Here, the subject (*bālakena* बालकेन) and verb (*likhyate* लिख्यते) are singular.

(ii) The letter is written by the boys. *bālakaiḥ patraṁ likhyate.* बालकैः पत्रं लिख्यते ।

The subject (*bālakaih* बालकैः) is plural but verb (*likhyate* लिख्यते) is singular.

(iii) The letters are written by a boy. *bālakena patrāṇi likhyante.* बालकेन पत्राणि लिख्यन्ते ।

The object (*patrāṇi* पत्राणि) and the verb (*likhyante* लिख्यन्ते) are plural.

In above three (i-iii) examples, when the subject is singular, the verb is singular; but when the subject is plural, the verb does not become plural. But, when the object became plural, the verb also became plural.

(iv) Letter is written by me. *mayā patraṁ likhyate.* मया पत्रं लिख्यते ।

The subject (by me मया) is 1st person singular. The object (*patraṁ* पत्रम्) is Nominative singular. The verb (*likhyate* लिख्यते) is 3rd person singular.

(v) A letter is written by us. *asmābhiḥ patraṁ likhyate.* अस्माभिः पत्रं लिख्यते ।

The subject (*asmābhiḥ* अस्माभिः) is 1st person plural. The object (*patram* पत्रम्), is Nominative singular. The verb (*likhyate* लिख्यते) is 3rd person singular.

(vi) The letters are written by me. *mayā patrāṇi likhyante.* मया पत्राणि लिख्यन्ते ।

The subject (*mayā* मया), is 1st person singular. The object, (*patrāṇi* पत्राणि), is Nominative plural. The verb, (*likhyante* लिख्यन्ते), is 3rd person plural.

(vii) The letter is written by a boy. *bālakena patraṁ likhyate.* बालकेन पत्रं लिख्यते ।

The subject (*bālakena* बालकेन) is 3rd person singular. The object (*patram* पत्रम्) is Nominative singular. The verb (*likhyate* लिख्यते) is 3rd person singular.

(viii) The letter is written by the boys. *bālakaiḥ patraṁ likhyate.* बालकैः पत्रं लिख्यते ।

The subject (*bālakaih* बालकैः) is 3rd person plural. The object (*patraṁ* पत्रम्) is Nominative singular, verb (*likhyate* लिख्यते) is 3rd person singular.

(ix) The letters are written by a boy. *bālakena patrāṇi likhyante.* बालकेन पत्राणि लिख्यन्ते ।

The subject (*bālakena* बालकेन) is 3rd person singular. The object (*patrāṇi* पत्राणि) is Nominative plural. The verb (*likhyante* लिख्यन्ते) is 3rd person plural.

In all nine (i-ix) cases above, when the object is singular, the verb is also singular; and when the object is plural, the verb is also plural. But, subject could be 1st person or 3rd person, the verb remains 3rd person, unchanged.

From above nine (i-ix) points, i**n Passive Voice (कर्मणिप्रयोगे)**

(1) In Passive voice, the number and person of the verb relate to the object, but not to the subject. कर्मणिप्रयोगे कर्मण: क्रियापदस्य च वचन-सम्बन्ध: पुरुष-सम्बन्ध: च वर्तते । कर्तु: क्रियापदस्य च वचन-सम्बन्ध: पुरुष-सम्बन्ध: च न वर्तते ।

(2) In the Passive voice, the subject (कर्ता) is always in Instrumental (3rd) case and the object (कर्म) is always in Nominative (1st) case. कर्मणि-प्रयोगे कर्ता तृतीया-विभक्तेः कर्म च प्रथमा-विभक्तेः वर्तते ।

(3) In the Passive voice, the verb is always *ātmanepadī.* कर्मणि-प्रयोगे क्रियापदं सदा आत्मनेपदी एव वर्तते ।

(4) In the Active voice, the *parasmaipadī* verbs end in ति and the *ātmanepadī* verbs end in ते । In the Passive voice, the *ātmanepadī* verbs end in य+ते । कर्तरि-प्रयोगे परस्मैपदी-क्रियाणाम् अन्ताः ति इति आत्मनेपदीनां च ते इति भवन्ति । परं कर्मणि-प्रयोगे सर्वेषां धातूनाम् अन्ताः यते (य + ते) इति एव सन्ति ।

26.3

CONVERTING THE VOICES

paryoga-parivartanam
प्रयोग-परिवर्तनम् ।

(i) Act◦ The student Rāma reads a book. Pas◦ The book is read by student Rāma.
Act◦ विद्यार्थी रामः पुस्तकं पठति । Pass◦ विद्यार्थिना रामेण पुस्तकं पठ्यते ।

(ii) Pas◦ A long letter is written by student Sītā. Act◦ Student Sītā writes a long letter.
Pas◦ विद्यार्थिन्या सीतया दीर्घं पत्रं लिख्यते । Act◦ विद्यार्थिनी सीता दीर्घं पत्रं लिखति ।

Thus, from the above (i-ii) it can be seen that :

When converting the voices, only the subject (with its adjective), the object and the verb need conversion; other parts of the sentence remain unchanged.
प्रयोग-परिवर्तन-समये कर्तुः कर्मणः क्रियापदस्य च परिवर्तनं भवति ।
अन्याः पदाः पूर्ववत् एव वर्तन्ते ।

26.4

The Bhāve voice

bhāve prayogaḥ भावे-प्रयोगः ।

(THE ABSTRACT VOICE)

1. In Active voice (कर्तरि-प्रयोगः), (i) I write essays. अहं लेखान् लिखामि *ahaṁ lekhān likhāmi,* (ii) Devotees worship the Goddess. भक्ताः देवीं पूजयन्ति *bhaktāḥ devīṁ pūjayanti,*

(i) the subjects अहम् and भक्ताः are in Nominative (1st) case, f◦ or m◦, singular or plural;

(ii) the objects लेखान् and देवीं are in Accusative (2nd) case, f◦ or m◦, singular or plural;

(iii) verbs लिखामि and पूजयन्ति are transitive, sing◦ or plu◦, *parasmai◦*, 1st or 3rd person.

2. In the Passive voice (कर्मणि-प्रयोगः), e.g. (i) The essays are written by me. मया लेखाः लिख्यन्ते *mayā lekhāḥ likhyante,* (ii) The goddess is worshipped by the devotees. भक्तैः देवी पूज्यते *bhaktaiḥ devī pūjyate,*

(i) the subjects मया and भक्तैः are in Instrumental (3rd) case

(ii) the objects लेखाः and देवी are in Nominative (1st) case, m◦ or f◦, singular or plural;

(iii) the verbs लिख्यन्ते and पूज्यते are transit◦, sing◦ or plu◦, 3rd per◦ *ātmane◦,* end in य+ते

3. In **Bhave voice** (भावे-प्रयोगः) (i) The vine grows. *latayā vardhyate,* लतया वर्ध्यते । (ii) The trees become tall. *vṛkṣaiḥ uccaiḥ bhūyate.* वृक्षैः उच्चैः भूयते ।

(i) Subjects लतया and वृक्षैः are in Instrumental (3rd) case, m◦ or f◦, singular or plural;

(ii) In both sentences, there is no object, for the verbs 'to grow' (*vardhate* वर्धते), and 'to become' (*bhūyate* भूयते) are intransitive.

(iii) Both the verbs are *ātmanepadī* (ending in ते). Thus, it can be said that :

(1) In active voice (कर्तरि-प्रयोगः), the subject (कर्ता) is in Nominative (1st) case and the verb is *parasmaipadī* or *ātmanepadī.* **In Bhave voice, the subject is in Instrumental (3rd)** case, and the verb is always *ātmanepadī* singular.

(2) **In Bhave voice, the verb is always *ātmanepadī* singular, 3rd person.**

In this voice the verb is never used in dual or plural or 1st person or 2nd person. (भावे-प्रयोगे क्रियापदं सर्वदा आत्मनेपदी एकवचनान्तं प्रथमपुरुषीयं च वर्तते । अत्र क्रियापदस्य द्विवचनान्तं बहुवचनान्तम् उत्तमपुरुषीयं मध्यमपुरुषीयं वा रूपं कदापि न भवन्ति)

(3) **In Bhave voice, the verb is always intransitive** (*akarmakam* अकर्मकम्).

(4) (i) In Active voice (कर्तरि-प्रयोग:), the person and number of the subject is same as the person and number of the verb. (ii) In Passive voice (कर्मणि-प्रयोगे), there is no such relationship between the subject and the verb. (iii) In Bhave voice (भावे-प्रयोग:) also there is no such relationship between the subject (कर्ता) and the verb (क्रियापदम्). भावे-प्रयोगे (कर्मणि-प्रयोगवत्) कर्तृ: क्रियापदस्य च सम्बन्ध: न भवति ।

NINE EXAMPLES : ACTIVE VOICE (कर्तरि-प्रयोग:)

(1) Sītā eats fruits. *Sītā phalāni khādati.* सीता फलानि खादति ।

(2) Rāma reads a book. *Rāmaḥ pustakaṁ paṭhati.* राम: पुस्तकं पठति ।

(3) I draw a picture. *ahaṁ ćitram abhilikhāmi.* अहं चित्रम् अभिलिखामि ।

(4) He goes to school. *saḥ vidyālaṁ gaććhati.* स: विद्यालयं गच्छति ।

(5) You ate the food. *tvam annam akhādaḥ.* त्वम् अन्नम् अखाद: ।

(6) She sings a song. *sā gītaṁ gāyati.* सा गीतं गायति ।

(7) The child sees the moon. *bālakaḥ ćandramasaṁ paśyati.* बालक: चन्द्रमसं पश्यति ।

(8) The child sees the toy. *bālakaḥ krīḍanakaṁ paśyati.* बालक: क्रीडनकं पश्यति ।

(9) Child sees mother. *bālakaḥ mātaraṁ paśyati* बालक: मातरं पश्यति ।

SAME NINE EXAMPLES : PASSIVE VOICE (कर्मणि-प्रयोग:)

(1) The fruits are eaten by Sītā. *Sītayā phalāni khādyante.* सीतया फलानि खाद्यन्ते ।

(2) The book is read by Rāma. *Rāmeṇa pustakaṁ paṭhyate.* रामेण पुस्तकं पठ्यते ।

(3) The picture is drawn by me. *mayā ćitraṁ likhyate.* मया चित्रं लिख्यते ।

(4) The school is attained by me. *mayā vidyalaye gamyate.* मया विद्यालय: गम्यते ।

(5) The food is eaten by you. *bhavataḥ-tvayā annaṁ khāditam.* भवत:-त्वया अन्नं खादितम् ।

(6) The song is sung by her. *tayā gītaṁ gīyate.* तया गीतं गीयते ।

(7) The moon is seen by the child. *bālakena ćandramaḥ dṛṣṭaḥ.* बालकेन चन्द्रमाः दृष्टः ।

(8) The toy is seen by the boy. *bālakena krīḍanakaṁ dṛṣṭam.* बालकेन क्रीडनकं दृष्टम् ।

(9) Mother is seen by child. *bālakena mātā dṛṣṭā.* बालकेन माता दृष्टा ।

SAME NINE EXAMPLES : BHAVE VOICE (भावे-प्रयोगः)

(1) He passes. *tena uttirṇaḥ bhūyate.* तेन उत्तिर्णः भूयते ।

(2) Plants grow. *sasyaiḥ vardhate.* सस्यैः वर्धते ।

(3) Sitā sits here. *Sītayā atra upaviṣyate.* सीतया अत्र उपविश्यते ।

(4) She stays home. *tayā gṛhe sthīyate.* तया गृहे स्थीयते ।

(5) The child laughs. *bālakena hasyate.* बालकेन हस्यते ।

(6) You grow old. *bhavatā vṛddhaḥ bhūyate.* भवता वृद्धः भूयते ।

(7) The sun shines in the sky. *sūryeṇa ākāśe tapyate.* सूर्येण आकाशे तप्यते ।

(8) The thief runs way. *ćoreṇa palāyate.* चोरेण पलायते ।

(9) Mother loves. *mātrā snihyate.* मात्रा स्निह्यते ।

EXERCISE 66: Fill in the blanks with the given verbs :
लिख्यते, दृष्टः गायामः खादामि, दृष्टा, खादितम्, पठन्ति, गीयते ।

(1) I eat a banana. अहं कदलीफलं -----
(2) They read books. ते पुस्तकानि -----
(3) We sing songs. वयं गीतानि -----
(4) The picture is drawn by me. मया चित्रं -----
(5) A mango is eaten by Sītā. सीतया आम्रं -----
(6) A poem is sung by Rāma. रामेण कविता -----
(7) A ball is seen by the girl. बालिकया कंदुकः -----
(8) A cat is seen by the boy. बालकेन मार्जारी ----

LESSON 27

saptaviṁśaḥ abhyāsaḥ सप्तविंशः अभ्यासः ।

THE MOODS

arthāḥ अर्थाः ।

RULE : The mode or the manner in which a verb is used (such as negative, interrogative, subjunctive) is called A MOOD (अर्थः)

27.1
THE NEGATIVE MOOD

nakārārthaḥ नकारार्थः ।

* In Sanskrit, the Negative mood is indicated by using such expressions as :
न, न च, नच, न वा, नो, न हि, नहि, नास्ति; मा, मा स्म, अलम्; अ, अन्, निर्, निस्, वि,
na, na ća, naća, na vā, no, na hi, nahi; nāsti, mā, mā sma, alam, a, an, nir, nis, vi ... etc.
either before or after the verb.

EXAMPLES cum EXERCISE : NEGATIVE AFFIXES (answers are given for your help)

1. It is not possible. *etat na śakyate.* एतत् न शक्यते ।
2. I won't go. *ahaṁ na gamiṣyāmi.* अहं न गमिष्यामि ।
3. Don't do it. *etat mā kuru.* एतत् मा कुरु ।
4. I never tell a lie. *ahaṁ kadāpi asatyaṁ na vadāmi.* अहं कदापि असत्यं न वदामि ।
5. This is neither mine nor his. *idaṁ na mama no tasya.* इदं न मम नो तस्य ।

6. No! this is not her either. *nahi, idaṁ na tasyāḥ api.* नहि! इदं न तस्याः अपि ।

THE CLASSICAL EXAMPLES :

7. That our army, protected by Bhiṣma, is un-limited.
अपर्याप्तं तदस्माकं बलं भीष्माभिरक्षितम् । (Gītā 1.10)

8. O Arjuna! No more of (enough with) your wisdom.
पार्थ! अलं तव ज्ञानेन ।

9. न काङ्क्षे विजयं कृष्ण न च राज्यं सुखानि च । (Gītā 1.32)

10. न हि ज्ञानेन सदृशं पवित्रम् इह विद्यते । (Gītā 4.38)

11. त्रैगुण्यविषया वेदा निस्-त्रैगुण्यो भवार्जुन । (Gītā 2.45)

12. विषया विनिवर्तन्ते निर्-आहारस्य देहिनः (Gītā 2.59)

**13. धर्मो जयति नाधर्मः सत्यं जयति नानृतम् ।
क्षमा जयति न क्रोधो देवो जयति नासुरः ।।64।।
(धर्मः जयति न अधर्मः, सत्यम् जयति न अनृतम् ।
क्षमा जयति न क्रोधः, देवः जयति न असुरः)**

EXERCISE 67 : NEGATIVE MOOD

Convert the following affirmative sentences into negative ones :

(1) The door is open. द्वारम् अपावृतम् अस्ति ।

(2) I will work with him. अहं तेन सह कर्म करिष्यामि ।

(3) Please sit in that room. कृपया तस्मिन् कक्षे उपविशतु ।

(4) This is your job. एष तव व्यापारः अस्ति ।

(5) Your advice is needed more. तव उपदेशः अधिकः अवश्यकः ।

27.2

THE INTEROGATIVE MOOD

praśnārthaḥ प्रश्नार्थः ।

In Sanskrit, a question is asked by using adverbs or pronouns such as,

वा? (or, or else); कः? का? किम्? (who?);

कुतः? कस्मात्? किमर्थम्? किंकारणम्? किन्निमित्तम्? केन हेतुना? (why?);

किम्? (what?); कदा? (when?); कुत्र? क्व? (where?);

कथम्? केन प्रकारेण? (how?);

कः? का? किम्? (which); कतर? (which one of the two); कतम्? (which one of more than two); कम्? काम्? किम्? (whom?);

कियत्? (how much?); कति? (how many?); कियतं कालम्? (how long?);

ननु? (how now?); किमु? किं पुनः? (how much more - less?), अथ किम्? (how else?) ...etc.

Sometimes *api?* अपि? is used, in the begining of the sentence, in place of *kim?* (किम्?) to ask a question.

EXAMPLES cum EXERCISE : INTEROGATIVE SENTENCES

1. Is he there? *saḥ tatra asti vā? kiṁ saḥ tatra asti? api saḥ tatra asti?* सः तत्र अस्ति वा? किं सः तत्र अस्ति? अपि सः तत्र अस्ति?
2. Are you angry? *kiṁ tvaṁ kupitaḥ/kupitā? api tvaṁ kupitaḥ/kupitā? bhavān kupitaḥ vā?* किं त्वं कुपितः/कुपिता? अपि त्वं कुपितः/कुपिता? भवान् कुपितः वा? भवती कुपिता वा?
3. Who lives here? *atra kaḥ vasati?* अत्र कः वसति?
4. Who is he? Who is she? *saḥ k:? sā ka?* सः कः? सा का?
5. What is it? *etat kim?* एतत् किम्? What is that? *tat kim?* तत् किम्?

6. What is your name? *tava nāma kim? bhavataḥ/bhavatyāḥ nāma kim? bhavataḥ/bhavatyāḥ nāmadheyaṁ kim?* तव नाम किम् । भवत:/भवत्या: नाम किम् । भवत:/भवत्या: नामधेयं किम्?

7. Why do you work so much? *tvam iyat karma kena kāraṇena karoṣi?* त्वम् इयत् कर्म केन कारणेन करोषि?

8. When will he give me the book? *saḥ māṁ pustakaṁ kada dāsyati?* स: मह्यं पुस्तकं कदा दास्यति?

9. How did it happen again? *etat punaḥ katham abhavat?* एतत् पुन: कथम् अभवत्?

10. Where will we meet again? *punaḥ kutra meliṣyāmaḥ?* पुन: कुत्र मेलिष्याम:?

11. Whom shall we ask about it? *vayaṁ etat kaṁ prakṣāmaḥ?* वयम् एतत् कं प्रक्ष्याम:?

12. Whichone is your book? *tava pustakaṁ katamam asti?* तव पुस्तकं कतमम् अस्ति?

13. How much food will she eat? *sā kiyat annaṁ khādiṣyati?* सा कियत् अन्नं खादिष्यति?

14. How many boys are here? *atra kati bālakāḥ santi?* अत्र कति बालका: सन्ति?

EXERCISE 68 : INTEROGATIVE SENTENCES

Fill in the blanks with suitable Sanskrit interrogative words.

(1) Who came to your house? तव गृहे ———————— आगच्छत्?

(2) Why was he sad? स: दु:खी ———————— आसीत्?

(3) What did Rāma say to you? राम: त्वां ———————— अब्रवीत्?

(4) When will you eat? त्वं ———————— खादिष्यसि?

(5) How does it operate? इदम् ———————— चलति?

(6) Where is Sītā's house? सीताया: गृहं ———————— अस्ति?

(7) To whom will you give a toy? त्वं क्रीडनकं ———————— दास्यसि?

(8) How long will you stay? त्वं ———————— स्थास्यसि?

(9) How much milk is there? तत्र ———————— दुग्धम् अस्ति?

(10) How many cars are there? तत्र ———————— यानानि सन्ति?

27.3

THE IMPERATIVE MOOD

loṭ lakāraḥ

लोट् लकारः ।

Command, request, invitation, solicitation, benidiction, ability and question.
आदेशार्थः निवेदनार्थः आमन्त्रणार्थः निमन्त्रणार्थः आशीर्वादार्थः सामर्थ्यार्थः प्रश्नार्थः ।

NOTE : In Sanskrit, a command, request, invitation, solicitation, benidiction, ability or even a question is indicated by attaching an Imperative लोट् suffix to the verb.

TYPICAL SUFFIXES : IMPERATIVE MOOD (लोट्)

TABLE : (All three genders - m◦, f◦ and n◦)

Person	Singular		Dual		Plural	
1st person	आनि	(āni)	आव	(āva)	आम	(āma)
2nd person	–, हि	(-, hi)	तम्	(tam)	त, तः	(ta, taḥ)
3rd person	तु	(tu)	ताम्	(tām)	अन्तु	(antu)

EXAMPLES cum EXERCISE : IMPERATIVE SENTENCES (लोट्)

A. Command:

1. Go there! *tatra gaćcha! tatra gaćchatu!* तत्र गच्छ! तत्र गच्छतु!
2. Boys! Stand up and do the reading. *bālakāḥ! uttiṣthat paṭhanaṁ ća kurut.* बालका:! उत्तिष्ठत/उत्तिष्टन्तु पठनं च कुरुत/कुर्वन्तु ।
3. Now you also read. *adhunā tvam api paṭha.* अधुना त्वम् अपि पठ । *idānīm bhavān api paṭhatu.* इदानीं भवान् अपि पठतु ।
4. Girls! come here and sit! *bālāḥ! atra āgaćchata upaviśata ća.* बाला:! अत्र आगच्छत उपविशत च ।

5. You all must answer the question! *yūyaṁ sarve praśnaṁ prativadata.* यूयं सर्वे प्रश्नं प्रतिवदत ।

6. You all must answer the questions! *yūyaṁ sarve praśnāni prativadat.* यूयं सर्वे प्रश्नानि प्रतिवदत ।

7. Come here soon! *śīghram atra āgaćcha/āgaćchatu!* शीघ्रम् अत्र आगच्छ/आगच्छतु!

B. Request :

(1) Please tell me the story. *kṛpayā mahyaṁ kathāṁ śrāvaya.* कृपया मह्यं कथां श्रावय/श्रावयतु

(2) Please have tea. *kṛpayā ćāya/pānaṁ karotu.* कृपया चायपानं कुरु/करोतु/कुरुत/कुर्वन्तु ।

(3) Please give me food. *kṛpayā mahyaṁ bhojanaṁ yaććha.* कृपया मह्यं भोजनं यच्छ/यच्छतु ।

(4) Please do it. *kṛpayā etat karotu.* कृपया एतत् कुरु/करोतु/कुरुत/कुर्वन्तु ।

C. Invitation, solicitation :

(1) Please have tea at my home. *mama sadane ćāya-pānaṁ karotu.* मम सदने चायपानं करोतु

(2) Sir! Take my car. *Bhadra! mama kāra-yānaṁ nayatu.* भद्र! मम कारयानं नयतु ।

(3) Come! We will watch TV together. *āgaćcha! āvāṁ saha eva dūradarśanaṁ paśyāva. vayaṁ sarve militvā dūradarśanaṁ paśyāma.* आगच्छ! आवां सह एव दूरदर्शनं पश्याव । आगच्छ! वयं सर्वे मिलित्वा दूरदर्शनं पश्याम ।

(4) Friends! Come to my house, it is my birthday today. *bhoḥ mitrāṇi! yūyaṁ mama gṛham āgaćchata, adya mama janma-divasaḥ asti.* भो: मित्राणि! यूयं मम गृहम् आगच्छत अद्य मम जन्मदिवस: अस्ति ।

D. Benediction :

(1) Sītā! May you live long. *Sīte! bhavatī āyuṣmatī bhavatu.* सीते! भवती आयुष्मती भवतु ।

(2) You should be healthy. *tvaṁ nīrogaḥ edhi. yūyaṁ nīrogāḥ sta.* त्वं नीरोग: एधि । यूयं नीरोगा: स्त ।

(3) They should attain success. *te siddhim adhigaćchantu. tāḥ yaśasvinyaḥ bhavantu. te*

vijayinaḥ santu. ते सिद्धिम् अधिगच्छन्तु । ताः यशस्विन्यः भवन्तु । ते विजयिनः सन्तु ।

(4) There should be progress. *pragatiḥ astu.* प्रगतिः अस्तु । उत्कर्षः अस्तु ।

(5) May you get a son. *putraṁ labhasva.* पुत्रं लभस्व ।

E. Ability :

(1) How may I help you? *ahaṁ te kiṁ śubhaṁ karvāṇi?* अहं ते किं शुभं करवाणि ।

(2) What can we offer you? *vayaṁ tubhyaṁ kiṁ dadāma?* वयं तुभ्यं किं ददाम?

(3) I can bring moon (stars) from the sky? *aham ākāśāt/nabhāt candramasam/tārāḥ ānayāni.* अहं आकाशात्/नभसः चन्द्रमसं/ताराः आनयानि ।

F. Question :

(1) Mother! Can I go out? *amb! kim ahaṁ bahiḥ gaććāni?* अम्ब! किम् अहं बहिः गच्छानि?

(2) Sir! May I come in? *bhagavan! kim ahaṁ praviśāni?* भगवन्! किम् अहं प्रविशानि?

(3) Can we wash our hands here? *kiṁ vayam asmākaṁ hastau/hastāḥ atra kṣālayāma?* किं वयम् अस्माकं हस्तौ/हस्तान् अत्र क्षालयाम? वयं हस्तान् अत्र क्षालयाम वा?

(4) May I read your book? *kim ahaṁ tava pustakaṁ paṭhāni?* किम् अहं तव पुस्तकं पठानि?

EXERCISE 69: IMPERATIVE MOOD लोट्

Fill in the blanks with imperative verbs.

(1) Rāma! Come here. राम! अत्र ———— (2) Sītā! Write a letter. सीता! पत्रं ————

(3) Please sit there. कृपया तत्र ———— (4) Please have a coffee. कृपया कॉफीपानं ——

(5) Son! Take these Rupeees. पुत्र! एतानि रूप्यकाणि —— ।

(6) May you succeed. यशस्वी ————

(7) Can I eat a mango? किम् अहम् आम्रं ————

(8) Can I ask you? किम् अहं त्वां ————

(9) Can we go there? किं वयं तत्र ————?

27.4

THE POTENTIAL MOOD

vidhi-liṅ विधिलिङ् ।

Possibility, advice, desire, appropriateness, notice. संभावना, उपदेशः इच्छा, कार्यम्, सूचना ।

कुर्यात् क्रियेत कर्तव्यं भवेत् स्यात् इति पञ्चमम् ।
एतत् स्यात् सर्ववेदेषु नियतं विधिलक्षणम् ।।65।।

A potential statement, a piece of advice, an expression of desire, a saying of appropriateness, a statement that may otherwise be expressed by an imperative mood, may fall under the POTENTIAL MOOD (विधिलिङ्म्) category.

SUFFIXES OF THE POTENTIAL विधिलिङ् । m∘ f∘ and n∘

Person	Singular		Dual		Plural	
1st person	ईयम्	(īyam)	ईव	(īva)	ईम	(īma)
2nd person	ईः	(īḥ)	ईतम्	(ītam)	ईत	(īta)
3rd person	ईत्	(īt)	ईताम्	(ītām)	ईयुः	(īyuḥ)

EXAMPLES : POTENTIAL MOOD विधिलिङ् ।

A. Potentiality or possibility :

(1) Rāma may go to India. *Rāmaḥ bhāratam gaćhet.* रामः भारतं गच्छेत् ।

(2) I may not go to school. *aham pāṭhaśālām na gaćcheyam.* अहं पाठशालां न गच्छेयम् ।

(3) She may not come to your house. *Sā tava gṛham na āgaćchet.* सा तव गृहं न आगच्छेत् ।

(4) Possibly it may snow today. *sambhavataḥ adya himavṛṣṭiḥ bhavet.* सम्भवतः अद्य हिमवृष्टिः भवेत् ।

(5) We may go to New York. *sambhavataḥ vayam New-yorkam gaćchema.* सम्भवतः वयं

न्यूयार्कं गच्छेम ।

(6) Rāma may take you too. *sambhavataḥ Rāmaḥ tvām api nayet.* सम्भवत: राम: त्वाम् अपि नयेत् ।

B. Advice :

(1) One should not sleep on the job. *kāryakāle na svapet.* कार्यकाले न स्वपेत् ।

(2) One should abstain from meat and liquor. *madhuṁ māsaṁ ća varjayet.* मधुं मासं च वर्जयेत् ।

(3) Do not lie. *asatyaṁ na brūyāt.* असत्यं न ब्रूयात् । Always speak the truth. *sadā satyaṁ brūyat.* सदा सत्यं ब्रूयात् ।

(4) The innocent person should never be punished. *nirdoṣaṁ kadāpi na daṇḍayet.* निर्दोषं कदापि न दण्डयेत् ।

(5) One should always be punctual. *sadā yathāsamayam āćaret.* सदा यथासमयम् आचरेत् ।

(6) CLASSICAL EXAMPLES :

गते शोको न कर्तव्यो भविष्यं न चिन्तयेत् ।
वर्तमानेन कालेन प्रवर्तन्ते विचक्षणा: ।।66।।

(ii) लालयेत्पञ्च वर्षाणि दशवर्षाणि ताडयेत् ।
प्राप्ते तु षोडशे वर्षे पुत्रं मित्रवदाचरेत् ।।67।।

(iii) दृष्टिपूतं न्यसेत्पादं वस्त्रपूतं पिबेज्जलम् ।
सत्यपूतां वदेद्वाचं मन: पूतं समाचरेत् ।।68।।

C. Desire :

(1) May she recover fast. *sā śīghraṁ nīrogā bhavet.* सा शीघ्रं नीरोगा भवेत् ।

(2) May everyone be righteous. *sarve dharmāćariṇaḥ bhavantu.* सर्वे धर्माचारिण: भवन्तु ।

(3) THE LOFTY VOICE OF THE VEDAS :

सर्वे भवन्तु सुखिनः सर्वे सन्तु निरामयाः ।

सर्वे भद्राणि पश्यन्तु मा कश्चिद्दुःखभाग्भवेत् ।।69।।

D. Appropriateness :

(1) Speak truth. *satyaṁ vadet.* सत्यं वदेत् ।

(2) Old people should be helped. *vṛddhānāṁ sevāṁ kuryuḥ.* वृद्धानां सेवां कुर्युः ।

(3) Self control should be observed. *saṁyamam āćaret.* संयमम् आचरेत् ।

(4) A QUOTE FROM THE NITI SHASTRA :

सद्भिरेव सहासीत सद्भिः कुर्वीत सङ्गतिम् ।

सद्भिर्विवादं मैत्रीं च नासद्भिः किञ्चिदाचरेत् ।।70।।

E. Notice :

* While talking about what is proper thing to do, Imperative (लोट्) must be used, even to impart a potential (विधिलिङ्म्) sense.

(1) One should not drink in the park. *udyāne madya-pānaṁ na karotu.* उद्याने मद्यपानं न करोतु ।

(2) People should not pick flowers in the garden. *janāḥ vāṭikāyāṁ puṣpāṇi na troṭayantu.* जनाः वाटिकायां पुष्पाणि न त्रोटयन्तु ।

(3) People should not write on the walls. *janāḥ bhitteḥ upari na likhantu.* जनाः भित्तेः उपरि न लिखन्तु ।

(4) One should not smoke in the house. *gṛhe dhūmrapānaṁ na karotu.* गृहे धूम्रपानं न करोतु

(5) Students should not talk in the library. *pustakālaye ćhātrāḥ vārtālāpaṁ na kurvantu.* पुस्तकालये छात्राः वार्तालापं न कुर्वन्तु ।

EXERCISE 70 : POTENTIAL MOOD (विधिलिङ्म्)

(A) Make plurals from the singular verbs :

(1) त्वं (यूयम्) अधर्माचरणं मा कुरु -------

(2) दुष्टतां मा कुरु ------

(3) अद्य छात्रः (छात्राः) विद्यालये कदाचित् यथासमये न आगच्छेत् ------

(4) सम्भवतः अहं (वयम्) भारते गच्छेयम् -------

(B) Translate into Sanskrit. (answers are shown in Devanagarī)

(5) Possibly it will rain today. सम्भवतः अद्य वृष्टिः भवेत् ।

(6) May you recover fast. शीघ्रं स्वास्थ्यं भवेत् । शीघ्रं स्वस्थः भवेः ।

(7) Speak the truth. सत्यं वदतु ।

(8) We all may be there tomorrow. वयं सर्वे श्वः तत्र भवेम ।

(9) Please do not be egoist. आत्म-प्रशंसकः मा भूः ।

(10) Do not befriend the fools. मूर्खैः सह मित्रं मा भूः ।

(11) May he live long. सः आयुष्मान् भवेत् ।

(12) You all may go to heaven. यूयं स्वर्गं गच्छेत ।

(13) She may go to Nagpur. सा नागपुरं गच्छेत् ।

(14) They all may drink buttermilk. ते सर्वे तक्रं पिबेयुः ।

(15) Students may study now. छात्राः अधुना अभ्यासं कुर्युः ।

(16) Rich people may give to the poor. श्रीमन्तः अकिञ्चनेभ्यः दानं यच्छेयुः ।

(17) One should listen to the teachers. गुरुजनानां वचनानि शृणोतु-शृणुतात् ।

(18) I may (should) not leave India. अहं भारतं न त्यजेयम् (त्यजानि) ।

(19) You may stay at my home. भवान् मम सदने वसेत्-वसतु ।

(20) He should cross the river by boat. सः नौकया नदीं तरेत् ।

27.5

PRECATIVE OR BENEDICTIVE MOOD

āśīrliṅ आशीर्लिङ् ।

आशीर्वाद: स्तुति: च । Optative, blessings, wish.

TYPICAL SUFFIXES

परस्मैपदी *Parasmaipadī*			आत्मनेपदी *Atmanepadī*		
यासम् *yāsam*	यास्व *yāsva*	यास्म *yāsma*	सीय *sīya*	सीवहि *sīvahi*	सीमहि *sīmahi*
या: *yāḥ*	यास्तम् *yāstam*	यास्त *yāsta*	सीष्ठा: *sīṣṭhāḥ*	सीयास्थाम् *sīyāsthām*	सीध्वम् *sīdhvam*
यात् *yāt*	यास्ताम् *yāstām*	यासु: *yāsuḥ*	सीष्ठ *sīṣṭha*	सीयास्ताम् *sīyāstām*	सीरन् *sīran*

For the benediction is a future event, the Benedictive mood is an extension of the Future tense (in passive form).

Sometimes imperative mood is used as benedictive mood. e.g. देवा: भावयन्तु व: *devāḥ bhāvayantu vaḥ.* May gods bless you both.

(1) May you always be well (may yours be well always).
सदा ते शुभं भूयात् । *sadā te śubhaṁ bhuyāt.*

(2) May your wishes come true. तव इच्छा: परिषीरन् । *tava icchāḥ pariṣīran.*

(3) May it not rain today. अद्य वृष्टि: न भूयात् । *adya vṛṣṭiḥ na bhūyāt.*

(4) May you succeed. भवत: सिद्धि: भूयात् । *bhavataḥ siddhiḥ bhuyāt.*

(5) May no one die hungry. कोऽपि क्षुधित: न म्रियेत । *ko'pi kṣudhitaḥ na mriyet.*

(6) May he give us money. स: अस्मभ्यं धनं यच्छेत् । *saḥ asmabhyaṁ dhanaṁ yacchet.*

(7) May she wish good. सा भद्रम् इच्छेत् । *sā bhadram icchet.*

(8) May he not become angry. स: न क्रुध्येत् । *saḥ na krudhyet.*

27.6

THE CONDITIONAL MOOD

lṛṅ-lakāraḥ लृङ् लकारः ।

यदि, चेत् - तर्हि *yadi, ćet - tarhi*

Possibility, advice, desire, appropriateness, notice.
सम्भावना, उपदेशः, इच्छा, उचितकार्यम्, सूचना ।

In Subjunctive (सङ्केतार्थः) construction, the word IF *yadi* यदि or *ćet* चेत is complemented with the word THEN *tarhi* तर्हि । *tarhi* तर्हि may not actually be written but it is implied.

NOTE :

When an action could not be accomplished, then in that kind of past tense लृङ् mood is used. e.g. If I was there. *yadi aham abhaviṣyam.* यदि अहम् अभविष्यम् ।

EXAMPLES : CONDITIONAL SENTENCES (लृट्)

1. If you like, give charity. *ićchasi ćet dānam kuru.* इच्छसि चेत् दानं कुरु । *yadi ićchā abhaviṣyat tarhi dānaṁ aksriṣyat.* यदि इच्छा अभविष्यत् तर्हि दानं अकरिष्यत् ।

2. If you sin, (then) sorrow will come.
yadi pātakam akariṣyaḥ tarhi paritāpaḥ bhaviṣyati.
यदि पातकम् अकरिष्यः तर्हि परितापः अभविष्यत् ।

3. If you want, I will cook.
ćet tvam aiṣiṣyaḥ tarhi aham apakṣam. चेत् त्वम् ऐषिष्यः तर्हि अहम् अपक्ष्यम् ।

4. If he will call me then only I will go.

yadi saḥ mām ahvāsyat tarhi eva aham agamiṣyam.

यदि सः माम् अह्वास्यत् तर्हि एव अहम् अगमिष्यम् ।

5. O Child! If you are a fool then cry, if you are wise then laugh.

he bālak! tvaṁ mūrkhaḥ ćet (tarhi) rudihi sujñaḥ ćet (tarhi) hasa.

हे बालक! त्वं मूर्खः चेत् (तर्हि) रुदिहि सुज्ञः चेत् (तर्हि) हस ।

THE CLASSICAL EXAMPLES :

6. यदि मामप्रतीकारमशस्त्रं शस्त्रपाणयः ।

धार्तराष्ट्रा रणे हन्युः (तर्हि) तन्मे क्षेमतरं भवेत् ।।71।। (Gītā 1.45)

7. सुखार्थी चेत् (तर्हि) त्यजेत् विद्यां विद्यार्थी चेत् (तर्हि) त्यजेत् सुखम् ।

सुखार्थिनः कुतो विद्या कुतो विद्यार्थिनः सुखम् ।।72।।

EXERCISE 71 : CONDITIONAL MOOD

Translate the following in Sanskrit. (Answers are shown in the brackets)

(1) If I call you, please come. (यदि अहं भवन्तम् आह्वासिष्यं तर्हि कृपया आगच्छतु)

(2) If he calls me, I will go (यदि सः माम् अह्वास्यत तर्हि अहम् अगमिष्यम्)

(3) If you wish, I will eat. (चेत् भवान् एषिष्यति तर्हि अहम् अखादिष्यम्)

(4) If he gives her something, she will be happy.
(यदि सः तां किमपि अदास्यत् तर्हि सा अतोक्ष्यत्)

(5) If we cleanse our vices, we will be pious.
(चेत् वयं स्वान् दुर्गुणान् अहनिष्याम तर्हि वयं पूताः अभविष्याम)

(6) If she knew him, she would not have trusted him.
(यदि सा तम् अज्ञास्यत् तर्हि सा तस्मिन् विश्वासं न अकरिष्यत्)

(7) If you had not slept in the cold, you would not have become sick.
(यदि त्वं शैत्ये न अस्वप्स्यः तर्हि रुग्णः न अभविष्यः)

LESSON 28

aṣṭāviṁśaḥ abhyāsaḥ अष्टाविंश: अभ्यास: ।

ADJECTIVES AND PARTICIPLES

viśeṣaṇāni kṛdantāni kriyāviśeṣaṇāni ća
विशेषणानि कृदन्तानि क्रियाविशेषणानि च ।

यल्लिङ्गं यद्वचनं या च विभक्तिर्विशेष्यस्य ।
तल्लिङ्गं तद्वचनं सा च विशेषणस्यापि ।।

RULES :

(1) The word that describes, qualifies or adds something to a noun (नाम, विशेष्यम्), is called an ADJECTIVE (विशेषणम्). e.g. A good boy. शोभन: बालक: ।
Adjectives have cases. They do not have tenses.

(2) The adjective that comes straight from a root verb is a PARTICIPLE (कृदन्तम्, धातुसाधित-विशेषणम्). Even though the participles appear to be verbs, they are not verbs. Therefore, **they do not have tenses; rather they have cases**. e.g.

Root verb	Past Tense	Past-participle	Nominative
(to go)	went	gone	He who has gone
√*gam* (√गम्)	*agaćchat* (अगच्छत्)	*gata* (गत)	*gataḥ* (गत:)

(3) The word that qualifies a verb (क्रिया) or an adjective, is called an ADVERB (क्रियाविशेषणम्), e.g. Eat slowly. शनै: खादतु । Very good. बहु समीचीनम् । The adverbs neither have tenses nor the cases.

28.1
ADJECTIVES
viśeṣaṇāni विशेषणानि ।

AGREEMENT OF ADJECTIVES WITH NOUNS

(1) In Sanskrit, an adjective (विशेषणम्) does not have its own gender, number or case. It follows the gender, number and case of the noun (विशेष्यम्) to which it is attached (to which it qualifies).

(2) If a pronoun (सर्वनाम) acts as an adjective, it is called a pronominal adjective (सार्वनामिक-विशेषणम्).

TABLE : ADJECTIVE (विशेषणम्) m∘ f∘ and n∘ e.g. *śobhana* शोभन good, beautiful

MASCULINE GENDER NOUNS

Singular		Plural	
अहं शोभन: बालक:	*ahaṁ śobhanaḥ bālakaḥ*	वयं शोभना: बालका:	*vayaṁ śobhanāḥ bālakāḥ*
2. त्वं शोभन: बालक:	*tvaṁ śobhanaḥ bālakaḥ*	यूयं शोभना: बालका:	*yūyaṁ śobhanāḥ bālakāḥ*
3. स: शोभन: बालक:	*saḥ śobhanaḥ bālakaḥ*	ते शोभना: बालका:	*te śobhanāḥ bālakāḥ*

FEMININE GENDER NOUNS

1. अहं शोभना बालिका	*ahaṁ śobhanā bālikā*	वयं शोभना: बालिका:	*vayaṁ śobhanāḥ bālikāḥ*
2. त्वं शोभना बालिका	*tvaṁ śobhanā bālikā*	यूयं शोभना: बालिका:	*yūyaṁ śobhanāḥ bālikāḥ*
3. सा शोभना बालिका	*sā śobhanā bālikā*	ता: शोभना: बालिका:	*tāḥ śobhanāḥ bālikāḥ*

NEUTER GENDER NOUNS

तत् शोभनं गृहम्	*tat śobhanaṁ gṛham*	तानि शोभनानि गृहाणि	*tāni śobhanāni gṛhāṇi*

EXAMPLES : USE of ADJECTIVES

(A) Masculine gender : (Singular, dual, plural)

(1) One good boy.	*śobhanaḥ bālakaḥ.*	शोभनः बालकः ।
(2) Two good boys.	*śobhanau bālakau.*	शोभनौ बालकौ ।
(3) A white horse.	*svetaḥ aśvaḥ.*	श्वेतः अश्वः ।
Two white horses.	*śvetau aśvau.*	श्वेतौ अश्वौ ।
The white horses.	*śvetāḥ aśvāḥ.*	श्वेताः अश्वाः ।
(4) An old man.	*vṛddhaḥ naraḥ.*	वृद्धः नरः ।
Two old men.	*vṛddhau narau.*	वृद्धौ नरौ ।
Old men.	*vṛddhāḥ narāḥ.*	वृद्धाः नराः ।
(5) A big mountain.	*viśālaḥ parvataḥ.*	विशालः पर्वतः ।
Big mountains.	*viśālāḥ parvatāḥ.*	विशालाः पर्वताः ।

(B) Feminine gender : (Singular, dual, plural)

(1) One good girl. Two good girls. Good girls.

śobhanā bālikā. śobhane bālike, śobhanāḥ bālikāḥ.
शोभना बालिका । शोभने बालिके । शोभनाः बालिकाः ।

(2) A white bird.	*śvetā ćaṭikā.*	श्वेता चटिका ।
Two white birds.	*svete ćaṭike.*	श्वेते चटिके ।
White birds.	*svetāḥ ćaṭikāḥ.*	श्वेताः चटिकाः ।
(3) A beautiful woman.	*sundarī strī.*	सुन्दरी स्त्री ।
Two beautiful women.	*sundaryau striyau.*	सुन्दर्यौ स्त्रियौ ।
Beautiful women.	*sundaryaḥ striyaḥ.*	सुन्दर्यः स्त्रियः ।

(C) Neuter gender : (Singular, dual, plural)

(1) A white flower. *śvetaṁ puṣpam.* श्वेतं पुष्पम् ।

Two white flowers. *śvete puṣpe.* श्वेते पुष्पे ।

White flowers. *śvetāni puṣpāṇi.* श्वेतानि पुष्पाणि ।

(2) A sweet fruit. *madhuraṁ phalam.* मधुरं फलम् ।

Two sweet fruits. *madhure phale.* मधुरे फले ।

Sweet fruits. *madhurāṇi phalāni.* मधुराणि फलानि ।

(3) A true saying. *satyaṁ vaćanam.* सत्यं वचनम् ।

True sayings. *satyāni vaćanāni.* सत्यानि वचनानि ।

(4) One boy. *ekaḥ bālakaḥ.* एक: बालक: ।

One Girl. *ekā bālikā.* एका बालिका ।

One book. *ekaṁ pustakam.* एकं पुस्तकम् ।

Three boys. *trayaḥ bālakāḥ.* त्रय: बालका: ।

Three girls. *tisraḥ bālikāḥ.* तिस्र: बालिका: ।

Three books. *triṇi pustakāni.* त्रीणि पुस्तकानि ।

(5) प्रथमे नार्जिता विद्या, द्वितीये नार्जित: अर्थ: ।
तृतीये नार्जितं पुण्यं चतुर्थे किं करिष्यति ।।73।।

EXERCISE 72 : ADJECTIVES (विशेषणानि)

A. Say in Sanskrit and find the adjectives in the following sentences:

(1) I have two brothers. मम द्वौ भ्रातरौ स्त: ।

(2) These mangos are yellow. एतानि आम्राणि पीतानि सन्ति ।

(3) We are drinking hot tea. वयम् उष्णं चायं पिबाम: ।

(4) Your car is new. तव/भवत: कारयानं नूतनम् अस्ति ।

(5) These flowers are beautiful. एतानि पुष्पाणि सुन्दराणि ।

B. Fill in the blanks with Sanskrit adjectives:

(1) Rāma's car is red. रामस्य कारयानम् ------------ अस्ति ।

(2) The clothes are new. वस्त्राणि ------------- सन्ति ।

(3) He is a smart boy. स: ------------ बालक: अस्ति ।

(4) You speak truth. त्वं/भवान् ------------ वदसि/वदति ।

(5) The town is big. नगरी ------------ अस्ति ।

NEW ADJECTIVES TO LEARN :

(A). All numerals are adjectives. See the names of the numerals in lesson 11.1

(B). The names of colours are adjectives.

(1) White	(श्वेत sveta, धवल dhavala, शुभ्र śubhra, गौर gaura)
(2) Black	(कृष्ण kṛṣṇa, श्याम śyāma, काल kāla)
(3) Red	(रक्त rakta, लोहित lohita, शोण śoṇa)
(4) Yellow	(पीत pīta, पीतल pītala)
(5) Blue	(नील nīla, श्यामल śyāmala)
(6) Green	(हरित harita)
(7) Pink	(पाटल pāṭala)
(8) Brown	(पिङ्गल piṅgala, कपिल kapila, श्याव śyāva)
(9) Purple	(धूमल dhūmala)
(10) Gold	(सुवर्ण suvarṇa), Silver (रजत rajata)

(C). The qualitative attributes are adjectives :

(1) Good (भद्र bhadra, शुद्ध śuddha, साधु sādhu; शोभन śobhana, सत् sat, निर्दोष nirdoṣa, सम्यक् samyak)

(2) Bad (कु ku, अभद्र abhadra, अशुद्ध aśuddha, सदोष sadoṣa, असम्यक् asamyak)

(3) Sweet (मधुर madhura, मिष्ट miṣṭa)

(4) Sour (अम्ल amla, शुक्त śukta)

(5) Hot (उष्ण uṣṇa, तप्त tapta; उग्र ugra, चण्ड ćaṇḍa, तीव्र tīvra)

(6) Cold (शीत sīta, हिम hima)

(7) Large (विशाल viśāla, बृहत् bṛhat, महत् mahat, विस्तीर्ण vistīrṇa)

(8) Heavy (गुरु guru, भारवत् bhāravat)

(9) Light (अल्प alpa, लघु laghu, तरल tarala)

(10) Fat (पीन pīna, पुष्ट puṣṭa, मांसल maṁsala)

(11) Thin (विरल virala, श्लक्ष्ण ślakṣaṇa, सूक्ष्म sūkṣma; कृश kṛśa)

(12) Beautiful (सुन्दर sundara, सुरूप surūpa, रम्य ramya)

(13) Ugly (कुरूप kurūpa, विकृत vikṛta)

(14) Young (कौमार kaumāra, तरुण taruṇa, बाल bāla, युवन् yuvana)

(15) Old (वृद्ध vṛddha, जरठ jaraṭha, जीर्ण jīrṇa)

(16) Open (अपावृत apāvṛta)

(17) Closed (निमीलित nimīlita, पिहित pihita)

(18) Smart, Clever (कुशाग्र kuśāgra, तीक्ष्ण tīkṣṇa, चतुर ćatura, विदग्ध vidagdha)

(19) Lazy (अलस alasa, जड jaḍa, मन्द manda)

(20) Easy (सुकर sukara, सुबोध subodha, सुगम sugama, सहज sahaja)

(21) Difficult (दुष्कर duṣkara, दुर्बोध durbodha, दुर्गम durgama, दुःसाध्य duḥsādhya, कठिन kaṭhina)

(22) Little (अल्प alpa, लघु laghu, अणु aṇu, क्षुद्र kṣudra, ह्रस्व hrasva)

(23) Much, More (अधिक adhika, भूयस् bhūyas)

(24) Big (विशाल viśāla, महत् mahat)

(25) Honest (सरल sarala, दक्षिण dakṣiṇa, साधु sādhu)

(26) Dishonest (कुटिल kuṭila, जिह्म jihma)

(27) True (ऋत ṛta, तथ्य tathya, यथार्थ yathārtha, सत्य satya)

(28) False (असत्य asatya, अनृत anṛta, मृषा mṛṣā, मिथ्या mithyā)

(29) All (अखिल akhila, सकल sakala, सर्व sarva)

(30) Happy (सुखिन् sukhin, सानन्द sānanda; तृप्त tṛpta, सन्तुष्ट santuṣṭa)

(31) Sad (अवसन्न avasanna, दुःखिन् dukhin, उद्विग्न udvigna, खिन्न khinna, म्लान mlāna, शोकाकुल śokākula, दुर्मनस् durmanas)

(32) Hard (कठिन kaṭhina; दृढ dṛḍha, घन ghana, कठोर kaṭhora, उग्र ugra)

(33) Soft (मृदु mṛdu)

(34) Wise (विज्ञ vijña, ज्ञानिन् jñānin, धीमत् dhimat, प्रज्ञ prajña, बुद्धिमत् buddhimat)

(35) Foolish (मूर्ख mūrkha, मूढ mūḍha, अज्ञ ajña, दुर्मति durmati, दुर्मेधस् durmedhas)

(36) Rich (धनिन् dhanin, धनवत् dhanavat)

(37) Poor (अकिञ्चन akiñćana, निर्धन nirdhana, दरिद्र daridra, दीन dīna)

(38) Long (चिर ćira, दीर्घ dīrgha)

(39) Short (अल्प alpa, स्वल्प svalpa, स्तोक stoka, लघु laghu, ह्रस्व hrasva)

(40) Quick (चञ्चल ćañćala, क्षिप्र kṣipra, त्वरित tvarita, शीघ्र śighra)

(41) Slow (मन्द manda)

(42) Strong (बलवत् balavat, बलिन् balin, प्रबल prabala, सबल sabala, वीर्यवत् vīryavat, शक्तिमत् śaktimat, समर्थ samartha, दृढ़ dṛḍha, क्षम kṣama)

(43) Weak (अक्षम akṣama, अशक्त aśakta, बलहीन balahīna)

(44) Tall (उच्च ućća, तुङ्ग tunga, उत्तुङ्ग uttunga)

(45) Wide (विस्तीर्ण vistīrṇa, विशाल viśāla)

(46) Narrow (संवृत saṁvṛta, निरुद्ध niruddha)

(47) Big, Large (विशाल viśāla)

28.2

THE DEGREE OF COMPARISON

tulanātmak-viśeṣaṇāni तुलनात्मकविशेषणानि ।

COMPARATIVE AND SUPERLATIVE

uttarāvasthā uttamāvasthā ća उत्तरावस्था उत्तमावस्था च ।

The adjectives can be used in three degrees for comparing nouns. They are :

(1) The Original state (मूलावस्था), when no suffix is attached.

(2) The Comparative state (उत्तरावस्था), when a comparative suffix तरप् or ईयस् is added to the adjective to suggest which one is comparatively better or worse of two nouns, and

(3) The Superlative state (उत्तमावस्था), where a तमप् or ईष्ठन् suffix is attached to an adjective to indicate which one is the best or worst within a group of more than two.

The suffixes तरप्, ईयस्, तमप् and ईष्ठन् are grouped in the *taddhita* (तद्धित) suffixes. The taddhita suffixes are discussed, with a chart of examples, in Lesson 37.

THE COMPARATIVE ADJECTIVES

Original State मूलावस्था	Comparative state उत्तरावस्था (तर) Better, more	Superlative state उत्तमावस्था (तम) Best, most
---------------	----------------------	--------------------
1. अल्प (small)	अल्पतर (smaller)	अल्पतम (smallest)
2. लघु (short)	लघुतर (shorter)	लघुतम (shortest)
3. प्रिय (dear)	प्रियतर (dearer)	प्रियतम (dearest)
4. दीर्घ (long)	दीर्घ (longer)	दीर्घतम (longest)
5. एक (one)	एकतर (one in two)	एकतम (one in many)
6. क: (which one)	कतर (which one of two)	कतम (which one of many?)

7. उद् (up, high)	उत्तर (higher)	उत्तम (highest)
8. ज्येष्ठ (great)	ज्येष्ठतर (greater)	ज्येष्ठतम (greatest)
9. श्रेष्ठ (noble)	श्रेष्ठतर (nobler)	श्रेष्ठतम (noblest)
10. गरीयस् (Most noble)	गरीयान् (singular)	गरीयांस: (plural)
11. श्रेयस् (Most noble)	श्रेयान् (singular)	श्रेयांस: (plural)

NOTE : गरीयस् and श्रेयस् are already superlative adjectives. गरीयान्, गरीयंस:, श्रेयान्, श्रेयांस: are only the Nominative (1st) case singular and Nominative plural declensions. e.g. Something is better than nothing. The half-deaf is BETTER (more noble) than all the deafs. *badhirebhyaḥ mandakarṇaḥ śreyān.* बधिरेभ्य: मन्दकर्ण: श्रेयान् ।

EXAMPLES : DEGREE OF COMPARISON

(1) Rāma is taller than Sītā. *Rāmaḥ sītāyāḥ uććataraḥ asti.* राम: सीताया: उच्चतर: अस्ति ।

(2) He is the best man. *saḥ uttamaḥ manuṣyaḥ asti.* स: उत्तम: मनुष्य: अस्ति ।

(3) This night is the longest. *eṣā rātriḥ dīrghatamā asti.* एषा रात्रि: दीर्घतमा अस्ति ।

(4) That area is the largest. *tat kṣetraṁ mahattamam asti.* तत् क्षेत्रं महत्तमम् अस्ति ।

(5) This book is unique in many. *etat pustakam ekatamam.* एतत् पुस्तकम् एकतमम् ।

(6) These flowers are the best. *etāni puṣpāṇi uttamāni santi.* एतानि पुष्पाणि उत्तमानि सन्ति ।

EXERCISE 73 : DEGREE OF COMPARISON

A. Find the comparative adjectives:

(1) नूतन, क्षुद्रतर, मृदुतम, स्थावर । (2) दृढतर, सरल, सुगम, ह्रस्वतर ।

(3) शुभ, शान्त, स्थिरतर ।

B. Find the superlative adjectives:

(1) स्थिरतर, क्षुद्रतम, पवित्र । (2) दूर, दूरतम, निकट, निकटतर ।

(3) लघुतर, दीर्घतम, महत्तम, विद्वत्तम ।

MORE ADJECTIVES TO LEARN:

(1) Whole (पूर्ण pūrṇa, सम्पूर्ण sampūrṇa, अखिल akhila)

(2) Bound (सीमित sīmita)

(3) Boundless (अगाध ragādha, अनन्त ananta, अमित amita, निःसीम niḥsīma)

(4) Steady (स्थिर sthira, स्थावर sthāvara, अटल aṭala, अचल aćala, निश्चल niśćala)

(5) Marvelous (अद्भुत adbhuta, आश्चर्यकर āśćaryakara)

(6) Blind (अन्ध andha)

(7) Deaf (बधिर badhira, अकर्ण akarṇa)

(8) Dumb (मूक mūka)

(9) Lame (पंगु pangu, खञ्ज khañja)

(10) Sick (रुग्ण rugṇa, रोगिन् rogin, अस्वस्थ asvastha)

(11) Beginningless (अनादि anādi)

(12) Beginningless and endless (सनातन sanātana)

(13) Ancient (पुरातन purātana, पुराण purāṇa)

(14) Modern (आधुनिक ādhunika, अर्वाचीन arvāćina, नव nava, नवीन navīna)

(15) Cruel (निष्ठुर niṣṭhura, निर्दय nirdaya)

(16) Loving (सस्नेह sasneha, वत्सल vatsala, प्रिय priya)

(17) Ripe (पक्व pakva, परिणत pariṇata)

(18) Raw (अपक्व apakva, आम āma)

(19) Holy (पवित्र pavitra, पुण्य puṇya, पावन pāvana)

(20) Quiet (शान्त śānta, निश्चल niśćala)

THE PARTICIPLES

dhātusādhitāni

धातुसाधितानि वा कृदन्तानि वा ।

PARTICIPLES (धातुसाधितानि, कृदन्तानि) are derived directly from the verb roots (√) by attaching primary suffixes (कृत् प्रत्यया:)

Even though the words with primary suffixes indicate a meaning of some action, they are not verbs. Therefore, they do not have tenses. They are adjectives or indeclinables. And thus, as adjectives they have gender, number and cases.
एतानि कृदन्तानि (धातुसाधितानि) यद्यपि क्रियापदस्य अर्थं बोधयन्ति तथापि एतानि क्रियापदानि न । अत: एतेषां पुरुषरूपाणि लकारा: वा न भवन्ति । एतानि विशेषणानि अव्ययानि वा । विशेषणानां लिङ्गरूपाणि विभक्तिरूपाणि च भवन्ति ।

28.3

PAST PASSIVE PARTICIPLE (ppp∘)

kta-viśeṣaṇam

क्त-विशेषणम् ।

The *kta* (क्त) suffix is added to the verbs in Passive and Abstract voices in the past tense. While adding a *kta* क्त suffix to a root verb, the *k* क is dropped and only *ta* त is attached.
NOTE : With the roots such as √री, ली, ब्ली, प्ली, धू, पू, लू, ॠ, कॄ, गॄ, जॄ, नॄ, पॄ, भॄ, वॄ, शॄ, स्तॄ and हा, suffix *ta* (त) becomes suffix *na* (न).

Use of this *kta* (क्त) suffix produces adjectives of the past tensen sometimes used as verbs.
sam-ava√i + kta (ta) = samaveta (assembed) सम्-अव√इ + क्त (त) = (सम्+अव+इ+त) समवेत

sam-ā√gam+kta (ta) = samāgata (came together) सम्–आ√गम्+ क्त (त) = समागत

√gam + kta (ta) = gata (gone) √गम् + क्त (त) = गत ।

√jṛ́ + kta (na) = jīrna (worn out) √जॄ + क्त (न) = जीर्ण ।

sam√pat + kta (na) = sampanna (rich) सम्√पत् + क्त (न) = सम्पन्न ।

(1) I go अहं गच्छामि । I 'go' is a Present tense.

(2) Rāma went रामः अगच्छत् । 'Went' is a Past tense.

(3) The man that has gone. गतः नरः । 'Gone' is an adjective (ppp◦) of the man, it is not a tense, although it acts, looks and used like a verb. नरः गतः (अस्ति) । In this case, the verb 'is' (अस्ति) is understood.

EXAMPLES :

PAST PASSIVE PARTICIPLE (ppp◦) क्त

Note that the ppp◦, as an adjective, changes according to the gender and number and case of the substantive.

(1) The book that is seen by Rāma. *Rāmeṇa dṛṣṭaṁ pustakam.* रामेण दृष्टं पुस्तकं ।

(2) The flowers seen by Sītā in the garden.
Sītayā udyāne dṛṣṭāni puṣpāṇi. सीतया उद्याने दृष्टानि पुष्पाणि ।

(3) The bird seen by him. *tena dṛṣṭā ćaṭikā.* तेन दृष्टा चटिका ।

(4) The Rāvaṇa (was) killed by Rāma. *Rāmeṇa Rāvaṇaḥ hataḥ.* रामेण रावणः हतः ।

(5) Mahābhārata (was) heard by me. *mayā Mahābhārataṁ śrutam.* मया महाभारतं श्रुतम् ।

(6) The letter written by her. *tayā likhitaṁ patram.* तया लिखितं पत्रम् ।

(7) Is my school seen by you?
tvayā mama pāṭhaśālā dṛṣṭā vā? त्वया मम पाठशाला दृष्टा वा ।

(8) I do not eat cold food. *ahaṁ śītam annaṁ na khādāmi.* अहं शीतम् अन्नं न खादामि ।

(9) अश्रद्धया हुतं दत्तं तपः तप्तं कृतं च यत् । (Gītā 17.28)

PAST PASSIVE PARTICIPLES (ppp◦)

(1) Gone (√गम् – गत)
(2) Renounced (√त्यज् – त्यक्त)
(3) Written (√लिख – लिखित)
(4) Given (√दा – दत्त)
(5) Stayed (√स्था – स्थित)
(6) Known (√ज्ञा – ज्ञात)
(7) Killed (√हन् – हत)
(8) Heard (√श्रु – श्रुत)
(9) Seen (√दृश् – दृष्ट)
(10) Done (√कृ – कृत)
(11) Protected (√रक्ष् – रक्षित)
(12) Obtained (√लभ् – लब्ध)

FOR THE COMPLETE LISTING OF PPP◦s OF ALL 2000 VERBS, SEE APPENDIX 5.

EXERCISE 74 : (ppp◦) Find the Past Passive Participles in the following word groups :

(1) गच्छामि, खादितम्, भवति, भूतम्, भक्षितम् ।

(2) पठितः, पठन्ति, रक्षितः, श्रुतम्, पतिताः ।

(3) दृष्टा, करोमि, करोति, कृतम्, कृतानि ।

(4) पृच्छसि, पृष्टः, लिख्, नीता, नीतः ।

28.4

PAST ACTIVE PARTICIPLE (Past-AP)

ktavatu-viśeṣaṇam

क्तवतु–विशेषणम् ।

A Past Active Participle is formed by attaching वत् *vat* suffix to a Past passive participle (ppp◦). e.g. गत + वत् → गतवत् । The Past-AP गतवत् becomes गतवान् in Nominative case.

Singular - (m◦) अहं गतवान् । त्वं गतवान् । सः गतवान् । अश्वः गतवान् । (f◦) चटिका गतवती ।

Plural - (m◦) वयं गतवन्तः । यूयं गतवन्तः । ते गतवन्तः । अश्वाः गतवन्तः । (f◦) चटिकाः गतवन्त्यः ।

NOTE : When we studied the Past (Imperfect) tense (लङ् लकारः) in lesson 18, we used constructions such as, अहम् अखादम्, त्वम् अखादः सः अखादत् ...etc. But, these forms are difficult. Thus, instead, the easier way is to use the क्तवतु forms e.g. अहं खादितवान्, त्वं खादितवान्, सः खादितवान्, सा खादितवती ...etc. in place of the Past tense लङ् e.g. अहम् अखादम्, त्वम् अखादः, सः/सा अखादत् ।

भूतकाले अखादम्, अखादः, अखादत् इत्यादीनि रूपाणि यद्यपि भवन्ति तेषां रूपाणि क्लिष्टानि सन्ति । किन्तु तेषां स्थाने भूतकालार्थे क्तवतु-रूपाणि सरलानि सन्ति । अतः सरलतादृष्ट्या एवं कर्तव्यम् ।

The *ktavat* (क्तवत्) suffix is used for the Active voice in the Past tense. While adding *ktavat* (क्तवत्) to a root verb, the *kta* (क्त) is dropped and only *ta* (वत्) is attached.

TABLE : √खाद् to eat, PAST ACTIVE PARTICIPLE

Verb	Singular		Plural	
1. I ate (m∘)	अहं खादितवान्	*aham khāditavān*	वयं खादितवन्तः	*vayam khāditavantaḥ*
2. You ate (m∘)	त्वं खादितवान्	*tvam khāditavān*	यूयं खादितवन्तः	*yūyam khāditavantaḥ*
3. He ate (m∘)	सः खादितवान्	*saḥ khāditavān*	ते खादितवन्तः	*te khāditavantaḥ*
4. She ate (f∘)	सा खादितवती	*sā khāditavatī*	ताः खादितवत्यः	*tāḥ khāditavatyaḥ*
5. It ate (n∘)	तत् खादितवत्	*tat khāditavat*	तानि खादितवन्ति	*tāni khāditavanti*

USAGE : Compare these three examples with the same three examples given in Lesson 18

1. Rāma wrote.	*Rāmaḥ likhitavān.*	रामः लिखितवान् ।
Sītā went.	*Sītā gatavatī.*	सीता गतवती
2. Tree fell.	*vṛkṣaḥ patitavān.*	वृक्षः <u>पतितवान्</u> ।
Vine fell.	*latā patitavatī.*	लता <u>पतितवती</u> ।
Flower fell.	*puṣpam patitavat.*	पुष्पं <u>पतितवत्</u> ।
Flowers fell.	*puṣpāṇi patitavanti.*	पुष्पाणि <u>पतितवन्ति</u> ।
Trees Fell.	*vṛkṣāḥ patitavantaḥ.*	वृक्षाः <u>पतितवन्तः</u> ।
Vines fell.	*latāḥ patitavatyaḥ.*	लताः <u>पतितवत्यः</u> ।
3. Bharata said.	*Bharataḥ uktavān.*	भरतः उक्तवान् ।
Boys went.	*kumārāḥ gatavantaḥ.*	कुमाराः गतवन्तः ।

EXAMPLES : PAST ACTIVE PARTICIPLES (क्तवतु)

Past **Passive** Participle			Past-**Active**-participle	
(1) Gone	(√गम्→ गत→	गतवत्)	गतवान्	I, you, he went
(2) Killed	(√हन्→ हत→	हतवत्)	हतवान्	I, you, he killed
(3) Left	(√त्यज्→ त्यक्त→	त्यक्तवत्)	त्यक्तवान्	I, you, he left
(4) Heard	(√श्रु→ श्रुत→	श्रुतवत्)	श्रुतवान्	I, you, he heard
(5) Written	(√लिख→	लिखितवत्)	लिखितवान्	I, you, he wrote
(6) Seen	(√दृश्→	दृष्टवत्)	दृष्टवान्	I, you, he saw
(7) Given	(√दा→	दत्तवत्)	दत्तवान्	I, you, he gave
(8) Done	(√कृ→	कृतवत्)	कृतवान्	I, you, he did
(9) Stayed	(√स्था→	स्थितवत्)	स्थितवान्	I, you, he stayed
(10) Protected	(√रक्ष्→	रक्षितवत्)	रक्षितवान्	I, you, he protected
(11) Known	(√ज्ञा→	ज्ञातवत्)	ज्ञातवान्	I, you, he knew
(12) Obtained	(√लभ्→	लब्धवत्)	लब्धवान्	I, you, he obtained
(13) Obtained	(प्र√आप्→	प्राप्तवत्)	प्राप्तवान्	I, you, he obtained
(14) Bought	(√क्री→	क्रीतवत्)	क्रीतवान्	I, you, he bought

PRESENT ACTIVE PARTICIPLES

śatṛ-śānac-viśeṣaṇāni

शतृ-शानच्-विशेषणानि ।

There are two types of Present Active Participles.

(i) The *Parasmaipadī* Participle (शतृ विशेषणम्), and

(ii) The *Ātmanepadī* Participle (शानच् विशेषणम्).

28.5

The *Parasmaipadī* Present Active Participle (PPAP)

śatṛ viśeṣaṇam (शतृ-विशेषणम्)

The *śatṛ* (शतृ) suffix *at* अत् is added to a *parasmaipadī* root to form an adjective of Present Continuous tense. e.g.

(i) *saṁ√jan + śatṛ (at अत्) + causative (ya य)= sañjanayat* (causing it to increase)
सम्√जन् + शतृ (अत्) + प्रयोजक (य) = सञ्जनयत् (Gītā 1.12)

(ii) *vi√sad + śatṛ (at) = viṣidat* (while lamenting) वि√सद् + शतृ (अत्) = विषीदत् (Gītā 1.27)

How to form a शतृ PPAP adjective from a verb?

(1) first take the desired *parasmaipadī* verb (e.g. √गम्);

(2) determine the third-person, plural, present tense of that verb (e.g. गच्छन्ति);

(3) remove the last suffix (e.g. गच्छन्ति - अन्ति = गच्छ); and then to this word,

(4) attach the अत् suffix (e.g. गच्छ् + अत्), then you get PPAP गच्छत् ।

The शतृ adjectives give a (gerund like) meaning with 'ing' attached to the verb. e.g.
गच्छत् = going, while going कुर्वत् = doing, while doing कथयत् = while saying ...etc.

In the Nominative (1st) case :

The Masculine forms of these words will be गच्छन्, गच्छन्तौ, गच्छन्तः । कुर्वन्, कुर्वन्तौ, कुर्वन्तः । कथयन्, कथयन्तौ, कथयन्तः । ... etc (like m॰ भगवत् शब्दः see Appendix 2)

The Feminine forms will be गच्छन्ती, गच्छन्त्यौ, गच्छन्त्यः । कुर्वन्ती, कुर्वन्त्यौ, कुर्वन्त्यः । कथयन्ती, कथयन्त्यौ, कथयन्त्यः । (like नदी शब्दः see Appendix 2), and

The Neuter gender forms will be गच्छत्, गच्छती, गच्छन्ति । कुर्वत्, कुर्वती, कुर्वन्ति । कथयत्, कथयती, कथयन्ति ।(like जगत् शब्दः, see Appendix 2)

EXAMPLES cum EXERCISE : PPAP (शतृ) (answers are given for your help)

1. The man goes. मनुष्यः गच्छति → गच्छन् मनुष्यः, the going man, the man that is going (गच्छन् going is a *Parasmaipadī* adjective of the m∘ noun man).

2. (m∘) A tree falls. वृक्षः पतति → <u>पतन्</u> वृक्षः *patan vṛkṣaḥ.* a falling tree.
   (m∘) Trees fall वृक्षाः पतन्ति → <u>पतन्तः</u> वृक्षाः *patantaḥ vṛkṣāḥ.* the falling trees.
   (f∘) A vine falls लता पतति→ <u>पतन्ती</u> लता *patantī latā.* a falling vine.
   (f∘) The vines fall लताः पतन्ति→ <u>पतन्त्यः</u> लताः *patantyaḥ latāḥ.* the falling vines.
   (n∘) A flower falls पुष्पं पतति → <u>पतत्</u> पुष्पम् *patat puṣpam.* a falling flower.
   (n∘) The flowers fall पुष्पाणि पतन्ति→ <u>पतन्ति</u> पुष्पाणि *patanti puṣpāṇi.* the falling flowers.

(3) A CLASSICAL EXAMPLE :
तमुवाच हृषीकेशः <u>प्रहसन्</u> इव भारत । (Gītā 2.10)

PARASMAIPADI PRESENT ACTIVE PARTICIPLES (शतृ)

(1) Going (√गम्→ गच्छत्)
(2) Killing (√हन्→ घ्नत्)
(3) Leaving (√त्यज्→ त्यजत्)
(4) Hearing (√श्रु→ श्रुण्वत्)
(5) Writing (√लिख्→ लिखत्)
(6) Seeing (√दृश्→ पश्यत्)
(7) Giving (√दा→ ददत्)
(8) Doing (√कृ→ कुर्वत्)
(9) Staying (√स्था→ तिष्ठत्)
(10) Protecting (√रक्ष्→ रक्षत्)
(11) Falling (√पत्→ पतत्)
(12) Taking (√नी→ नयत्)

EXERCISE 75 : PAP (शतृ) find Present Active Participles in the following words :

(1) गच्छत्, खादितवान्, भवति, भवत्, भक्षितवन्तः ।

(2) पठितः, पठत्, पठितवान्, रक्षितः, श्रुण्वत्, पतिताः ।

(3) दृष्टवान्, पश्यत्, करोमि, करोति, कृतवान्, कुर्वत् ।

(4) पृच्छसि, पृष्टत्, पृष्टवान्, लिख्, नीता, नयत्, नीतवन्त: ।

The Ātmanepadī Present Active Participles (ĀPAP)
śānać/kartari-viśesaṇāni शानच्/कर्तरि–विशेषणानि ।

The *śānać* (शानच्) suffixes, *māna* (मान) and *āna* (आन), are added to the *ātmanepadī* roots to form adjectives of present continuous tense, same as the शतृ suffix. e.g.

(i) *7√bhuj + śānać (āna) = bhuñjāna* (enjoying) 7√भुज् + शानच् (आन) = भुञ्जान (Gītā 15.10)

(ii) *4√yudh+ śānać (māna) = yotsyamāna* (fighter) 4√युध्+शानच् (मान) = योत्स्यमान (Gītā 1.23)

Use of these adjectives is not frequent. Their formation and use is a bit difficult, but they

are discussed here for your information. Ātmanepadī Present Active Participle शानच्

is formed by attaching मान or आन suffix to a verb.

(a) If the verb belongs to the FIRST GROUP (1st, 4th, 6th or 10th conjugation गण:), then

it takes the मान (*māna*) suffix.

(b) But, if the verb belongs to the SECOND GROUP (2nd, 3rd, 5th, 7th, 8th or 9th

conjugation), then it takes the आन (*āna*) suffix.

The शानच् adjectives give a (gerund like) meaning with 'ing' or 'er' attached to the verb.

e.g. √लभ्→ लभमान = attaining; attainer. √कृ→ कुर्वाण = working(man); worker.

28.6
ĀPAP of the FIRST GROUP
मान-शानच्-विशेषणम् ।

How to form a मान–शानच् adjective?

(1) first take the desired *ātmanepadī* verb (e.g. 1√लभ् to obtain);

(2) determine the third-person, plural, present tense of that verb (e.g. लभन्ते);

(3) remove the ending न्ते-ते suffix (e.g. लभन्ते - न्ते = लभ); and then to that word,

(4) attach the मान suffix (लभ + मान → लभमान = obtaining).

The verbs belonging to the FIRST GROUP i.e. 1st, 4th, 6th or 10th conjugation गणः, take the मान suffix. e.g.

1√लभ्→ लभन्ते→ लभमान = obtaining; 4√मन्→ मन्यते→ मन्यमान = thinking; 6√दिश्→ दिश्यते→ दिश्यमान = showing; 10√गण्→ गण्यते→ गण्यमान = counting ...etc.

All these adjectives, being अकारान्त, they decline like राम in masculine, like माला in feminine and like वन in neuter gender (see Appendix 2). e.g. लभमानः, लभमानौ, लभमानाः, लभमाना, लभमाने, लभमानाः, लभमानम्, लभमाने, लभमानानि etc.

EXAMPLES cum EXERCISE : ĀPAP (मान-शानच्)

(1) I saw him entering the house. अहं तं गृहं प्रविशमानं दृष्टवान् ।

(2) Seeing (while seeing) the child she became happy. बालकं प्रेक्षमाणा सा तुष्टवती ।

28.7

ĀPAP of the SECOND GROUP

आन-शानच्-विशेषणम् ।

To form any आन-शानच् adjective

(1) Take the desired *ātmanepadī* verb (e.g. 9√ज्ञा to know);

(2) determine the third-person, plural, present tense (जानते);

(3) remove the ending न्ते-ते suffix (e.g. जानन्ते - न्ते = जान); and then to that word,

(4) add the *ān* आन suffix (जान + आन → जानान = knowing)

The verbs belonging to the SECOND GROUP (2nd, 3rd, 5th, 7th, 8th or 9th conjugation

गण:), take आन् suffix. e.g. 2√ब्रू→ ब्रुवते→ ब्रुवाण = speaking; 3√दा→ ददते→ ददान = giving; 5√वृ→ वृण्वन्ते→ वृण्वान = choosing; 7√भुज्→ भुञ्जन्ते→ भुञ्जान = enjoying; 8√कृ→ कुर्वन्ते→ कुर्वाण doing; 9√ज्ञा→ जानन्ते→ जानान knowing ...etc.

All these participles being अकारान्त adjectives, they decline like राम in masculine, like माला in feminine and like वन in neuter gender. e.g. जानान:, जानानौ, जानाना: । जानाना, जानाने, जानाना: । जानानम्, जानाने, जानानानि । ... etc. Examples :

(1) Men doing sacrifice are rare. त्यागं कुर्वाणा: जना: दुर्लभा: ।

(2) Many are men who talk (talking) too much. अतीव ब्रुवाणा: जना: सुलभा: ।

CLASSICAL EXAMPLES : आन and मान शानच्

(3) उत्क्रामन्तं स्थितं वापि भुञ्जानं वा गुणान्वितम् । (Gītā 15.10)

(4) योत्स्यमानान् अवेक्षे अहं ये एते अत्र समागता: । (Gītā 1.23)

28.8

The Ātmanepadī Present Passive Participles (ĀPPP)

śānac-karmaṇi-viśeṣaṇāni शानच्-कर्मणि-विशेषणानि ।

Thse ĀPPP adjectives are formed from *ātmanepadī* root verbs only, and therefore, they take मान (यमान) suffix only.

To form a कर्मणि यमान-शानच् adjective

(i) First take the desired *ātmanepadī* verb (e.g. 8√कृ to do) from any group (1st or 2nd group);

(ii) take the first part of the third person plural present tense and remove the tense suffix.

(iii) then attach the यमान suffix to it (e.g. कृ (क्रि) + यमान → क्रियमाण = is being done). e.g.
प्रकृतेः क्रियमाणानि गुणैः कर्माणि सर्वशः । (Gītā 3.27)

(1)	1√लभ् →	लभ्	+ यमान	=	लभ्यमान	being obtained
(2)	2√ब्रू →	उच्	+ यमान	=	उच्यमान	being said
(3)	5√श्रु →	श्रू	+ यमान	=	श्रूयमाण	being heard
(4)	7√छिद् →	छिद्	+ यमान	=	छिद्यमान	being cut
(5)	4√नश् →	नश्	+ यमान	=	नश्यमान	being destroyed
(6)	6√दिश् →	दिश्	+ यमान	=	दिश्यमान	being shown
(7)	9√मन्थ् →	मन्थ्	+ यमान	=	मन्थ्यमान	being chruned
(8)	3√धा →	धी	+ यमान	=	धीयमान	being borne
(9)	10√वर्ण् →	वर्ण्	+ वर्ण्यमान	=	वर्ण्यमान	being defined, being described

THE POTENTIAL PARTICIPLES (pp∘)

vidyarthī-viśeṣaṇāni विध्यर्थि-विशेषणानि ।

In lesson 27 we studied the Potential Mood (विधिलिङ्). Now let us see the Potential Participles (विध्यर्थि कृदन्त-विशेषणानि).

These pp∘ participle adjectives indicate the meaning of 'something that ought to be done, should be done, proper to do, fit to be done, is worhty of, is a duty, is a precept or is a maxim.' Unfortunately, like most other Sanskrit expressions, the English language does not have single-word expressions for this purpose also.

To form these adjectives we can optionally attach either तव्य, अनीय or य suffix to the verb roots. In all three cases their meaning remains same. एकस्य धातोः एव प्रत्ययत्रयम् अपि

योजयितुं शक्नुमः एतेषां प्रत्ययानाम् अर्थः समानः एव ।

However, use of one suffix is more popular for some roots, while the other is used for some other roots. केषाञ्चित् धातूनां तव्यत-रूपाणि एव लोके प्रसिद्धानि । केषाञ्चित् धातूनाम् अनीय-रूपाणि य-रूपाणि वा एव प्रसिद्धानि । Therefore, what is most popular should be followed. अतः यत् रूपं प्रसिद्धं तत् एव योजितव्यं योजनीयं योज्यं वा ।

Use of these adjectives is quite frequent and should be understood properly. Thus, please remember that :

(1) These participles are passive (कर्मणि) and never active (कर्तरि).

(2) These can be formed from almost any verb root, transitive or intransitive.

(3) Here, the subject is always in Instrumental (3rd) case and the object in Nominative (1st) case.

(4) The gender and number of the adjective follows those of the object.

(5) Sometimes, these adjectives are used as regular non-potential adjectives or as nouns also.

(6) These are adjectives. These are not verbs.

(7) If this adjective is not connected with an object (intransitive), it will take neuter gender and singular number. मया/अस्माभिः तत्र गन्तव्यम् *mayā/asmābhiḥ tatra gantavyam.* I/we ought to go there.

Six affixes are included in this pp∘ category of *kṛtya* suffixes, namely : *tavyat* (तव्यत्), *tavya* (तव्य), *anīyar* (अनीयर्), *yat* (यत्), *kyap* (क्यप्) and *ṇyat* (ण्यत्).

These *kṛtya* suffixes are attached to:

(i) the transitive verbs (सकर्मक-धातवः) in the Passive voice (कर्मवाच्य), and

(ii) the intransitive verbs (अकर्मक-धातवः) in the Abstract voice (भाववाच्य).

28.9

The Future Passive (Potential) Participles

tavyat (तव्यत्), *anīyar* (अनीयर्) and *tavya* (तव्य) suffixes

(A) The *tavyat* (तव्यत्) and *tavya* (तव्य) suffixes :

The *tavyat* (तव्यत्) and *tavya* (तव्य) suffixes of Future passive participles produce Potential Adjectives (विध्यर्थि–विशेषणानि). e.g.

(i) √śru + tavyat (tavya) = śrotavya (fit to be heard) √श्रु + तव्यत् (तव्य) = श्रोतव्य

(ii) √śru + anīyar (anīya) = śrvaṇīya (fit to be heard) √श्रु + अनीयर (अनीय) = श्रवणीय

(B) The *yat* (यत्), *kyap* (क्यप्) and *ṇyat* (ण्यत्) suffixes :

The *yat* (यत्), *kyap* (क्यप्) and *ṇyat* (ण्यत्) suffixes produce adjectives with a sense of 'fit for' or 'ought to be' by adding y (य) to the final root.

(i) √jñā + yat (y) = jñeya (to be known) √ज्ञा + यत् (य) = ज्ञेय

(ii) √kṛ + kyap (y) = kṛtya (to be done) √कृ+ क्यप् (य) = कृत्य

(iii) a-vi√kṛ+ ṇyat (y) = avikārya (indistructible) अ–वि√कृ + ण्यत् (य) = अविकार्य

EXAMPLES cum EXERCISE : USE OF POTENTIAL ADJECTIVES

(1) Rama does not study. Rama ought to study. रामः अभ्यासं न करोति । रामेण अभ्यासः कर्तव्यः/करणीयः/कार्यः (√कृ) ।

(2) He does not drop bad habits. He should drop the bad habits. सः दुर्वर्तनानि न त्यजति । तेन दुर्वर्तनानि त्यक्तव्यानि/त्यजनीयानि/त्याज्यानि (√त्यज्) ।

(3) They do not teach Sanskrit. They should teach Sanskrit. ते संस्कृतं न शासन्ति । तैः संस्कृतं शासितव्यम्/शासनीयम्/शिष्यम् (√शास्) ।

(4) He does not give my book. He should give my book.

सः मह्यं पुस्तकं न ददाति । तेन मह्यं पुस्तकं दातव्यम्/दानीयम्/देयम् (√दा) ।

(5) He does not agree to it. He should agree it.

सः एतत् न मन्यते । तेन एतत् मन्तव्यम्/मननीयम्/मान्यम् (√मन्) ।

(6) Students should hear the instructions.

छात्रैः सूचनाः श्रोतव्याः/श्रवणीयाः/श्राव्याः (√श्रु) ।

(7) We should learn history.

अस्माभिः इतिहासः अध्येतव्यः/अध्ययनीयः/अध्येयः (अधि√इ) ।

(8) Truth must be told. सत्यं वक्तव्यम्/वचनीयम्/वाच्यम् ।

(9) One should not wear damp clothes. आर्द्रवस्त्राणि न धारणीयानि/धारितव्यानि/धार्याणि ।

(10) They should study. तैः अध्ययनं कर्तव्यम्/करणीयम्/कार्यम् ।

(11) A CLASSICAL EXAMPLE : (by Varnekar Mahodayaḥ)

लोकहितं मम करणीयम् । मनसा सततं स्मरणीयम् ।
वचसा सततं वदनीयम् । न भोगभवने रमणीयम् ।
न च सुखशयने शयनीयम् । अहर्निशं जागरणीयम् ।
न जातु दुःखं गणनीयम् । न च निजसौख्यं मननीयम् ।
कार्यक्षेत्रे त्वरणीयम् । दुःखसागरे तरणीयम् ।
विपत्तिविपिने भ्रमणीयम् । लोकहितं मम करणीयम् ।।74।।

THE POTENTIAL ADJECTIVES

(विध्यर्थि विशेषणानि)

√kṛ (to do) → pp◦ karaṇīya, kartavya, kārya = Ought to be done, fit to be done, must be done, good to be done, should be done, worth doing.

Root verb→		Potential Adjectives		
√भू	to become→	भवितव्य,	भवनीय,	भाव्य ।
√अस्	to be →	भवितव्य,	भवनीय,	भाव्य ।
√वृत्	to be →	वर्तितव्य,	वर्तनीय,	वृत्य ।
√त्यज्	to leave →	त्यक्तव्य,	त्यजनीय,	त्याज्य ।
√स्था	to stand →	स्थातव्य,	स्थानीय,	स्थेय ।
√स्मृ	to remember →	स्मर्तव्य,	स्मरणीय,	स्मार्य ।
√वन्द्	to salute →	वन्दितव्य,	वन्दनीय,	वन्द्य ।
√दा	to give →	दातव्य,	दानीय,	देय ।
√शंस्	to praise →	शंसितव्य,	शंसनीय,	शंस्य ।
√ब्रू	to speak →	वक्तव्य,	वचनीय,	वाच्य ।
√भी	to be afraid of →	भेतव्य,	भयनीय,	भेय ।
√क्षम्	to forgive →	क्षन्तव्य,	क्षमनीय,	क्षम्य ।
√मन्	to agree →	मन्तव्य,	मननीय,	मान्य ।
√आप्	to obtain →	आप्तव्य,	आपनीय,	आप्य ।
√श्रु	to hear →	श्रोतव्य,	श्रवणीय,	श्राव्य ।
√शक्	to be able →	शक्तव्य,	शकनीय,	शक्य ।
√प्रच्छ्	to ask →	प्रष्टव्य,	प्रच्छनीय,	प्रच्छय ।
√रुध्	to stop →	रोद्धव्य,	रोधनीय,	रोध्य ।
√भिद्	to break →	भेत्तव्य,	भेदनीय,	भेद्य ।

INDECLINABLE PARTICIPLES

kṛdanta-avyayāni

कृदन्त-अव्ययानि ।

The word that does not have any gender, number, person, tense or case is an INDECLINABLE word (अव्ययम्)

सदृशं त्रिषु लिङ्गेषु सर्वासु च विभक्तिषु ।
वचनेषु च सर्वेषु यन्न व्येति तदव्ययम् ।।75।।

The Two Indeclinable Past Participles (ipp∘)

ktvā, lyap

क्त्वा, ल्यप् ।

If same subject does two actions, one after other, then in that case :

In order to indicate completion of a subordinate (first) action, prior to the commencement of the main (second) action, an Indeclinable Past Participle (क्त्वा or ल्यप् = having done) is used, in stead of joining two clauses with the phrase 'and then' ततः च ।

These single-word participles (क्त्वा and ल्यप्) imply completion of the specific preceding subordinate action ('having done, or doing' पूर्वकालिक), before the following main action begins. **These participles are widely used in Saṁskrit.**

28.10

Indeclinable Past Participle (ktvā-ipp◦)

ktvā (क्त्वा) suffix

RULE 1 :

The *tvā* त्वा of the Indeclinable Past Participle *ktvā* क्त्वा may be added only to those verb-root to which any prefix, other than अ, is NOT attached.

The त्वा participle has same **nature** as the त in the Past Passive Participles (ppp◦) we studied in lesson 28.3.

√दा (*dā,* to give), दत्त (ppp◦ - *datta,* given), दत्त्वा (ipp◦ - *dattvā,* having given)
The *ktvā* suffix is used for forming a Gerund ending in suffix 'ing' that are dependent on some previous event (पूर्वकालिक-क्रिया)
√dṛś+ktvā (tvā) = dṛṣṭvā (having seen, seeing) √दृश्+ क्त्वा (त्वा) = दृष्ट्वा

RULE 2 :

The *lyp* (ल्यप्) suffix is attached only to those verb-roots that have any prefix, other than *a* (अ), is attached. The meaning and the nature of a *lyp*-participle remains same as of a *ktvā*-participle. For more details see section 28.11

CLASSICAL EXAMPLES : क्त्वा Participle :

13. सिद्ध्यसिद्ध्योः समो भूत्वा समत्वं योग उच्यते ।।77।। (Gītā 2.48)

14. योगिनः कर्म कुर्वन्ति सङ्गं त्यक्त्वा आत्मशुद्धये ।।78।।(Gītā 5.11)

28.11

Indeclinable Past Participle (lyp-ipp◦)

with *lyp* (ल्यप्) Suffix

As said earlier, the suffix य or त्य of the Indeclinable Past Participle (ल्यप् lyp-ipp◦) may be added only to that verb-root to which a prefix (other than अ *a*) is already attached.

(i) आ√दा take, आदत्त ppp◦ taken, आदाय ipp◦ having taken.

(ii) *upa-sam√gam + lyp (ya) = upa-saṅgmya* (having approached) √गम् + क्त्वा (त्वा) = गत्वा having gone. उप-सम्√गम् + ल्यप् (य) = उपसङ्गम्य having approached.

INDECLINABLE PAST PARTICIPLE क्त्वा

Verb-root		ppp◦		ipp◦-क्त्वा	
√दा	(to give)	दत्त	(given)	दत्त्वा	(having given)
√ज्ञा	(to know)	ज्ञात	(known)	ज्ञात्वा	(having known)
√भू	(to become)	भूत	(become)	भूत्वा	(having become)
√कृ	(to do)	कृत	(done)	कृत्वा	(having done)
√दृश्	(to see)	दृष्ट	(seen)	दृष्ट्वा	(having seen)
√वच्	(to speak)	उक्त	(spoken)	उक्त्वा	(having spoken)

INDECLINABLE PAST PARTICIPLE ल्यप्

Verb-root		ppp◦	ipp◦-ल्यप् – meaning	
आ√दा	(to take)	आदत्त	आदाय	having taken
वि√ज्ञा	(to know)	विज्ञात	विज्ञाय	having known
अनु√भू	(to experience)	अनुभूत	अनुभूय	having experienced

द्विधा√कृ (to duplicate)	द्विधाकृत	द्विधाकृत्य	having duplicated
अ√दृश् (to disappear)	अदृष्ट	अदृश्य	having disppeared
प्र√वच् (to tell)	प्रोक्त	प्रोच्य	having told

EXAMPLES cum EXERCISE : INDECLINABLE PAST PARTICIPLES क्त्वा, ल्यप् ।

1. Boys go to school. *bālakāḥ pāṭhaśālāṁ gaććhanti.* बालकाः पाठशालां गच्छन्ति ।
2. Boys go to school having done their study. *bālakāḥ teṣām abhyāsaṁ kṛtvā pāṭhaśālāṁ gaććhanti.* बालकाः तेषाम् अभ्यासं कृत्वा पाठशालां गच्छन्ति ।
3. We will go to New York. *vayaṁ New-Yorkaṁ gamiṣyāmaḥ.* वयं न्यू-यार्कं गमिष्यामः ।
4. Having gone to New York, we will see the University. *New-Yorkaṁ gatvā vayaṃ viśva-vidyālayaṁ drakṣyāmaḥ.* न्यू-यार्कं गत्वा वयं विश्वविद्यालयं द्रक्ष्यामः ।
5. Rāma eats a fruit. *Rāmaḥ phalaṁ khādati.* रामः खादति ।
6. Having eaten Rāma plays. *khāditvā rāmaḥ khelati.* खादित्वा रामः खेलति ।
7. He climbs a tree. *saḥ vṛkṣam ārohati.* सः वृक्षम् आरोहति ।
8. Having climbed the tree, he drops the fruits. *saḥ vṛkṣam āruhya phalāni pātayati.* सः वृक्षम् आरुह्य फलानि पातयति ।
9. Sītā comes. *Sītā āgaććhti.* सीता आगच्छति ।
10. Having sold fruit, she came. *sā phalāni vikrīya āgaććht/āgatavatī.* फलानि विक्रीय सा आगच्छत्/आगतवती ।
11. भवान् खादित्वा भ्रमति । मित्रं दृष्ट्वा अहं प्रसन्नः । तुभ्यं डालरान् दत्त्वा सः कुत्र गतवान्? सः मां रूप्यकाणि प्रदाय कुत्रचित् गतवान् । सीता जले प्रविश्य कमलम् आनयति । सा विदेशं गत्वा कीर्तिं प्राप्तवान् ...etc.

CLASSICAL EXAMPLE :

12. एवम् उक्त्वा अर्जुनः संख्ये रथोपस्थ उपाविशत् ।
विसृज्य सशरं चापं शोकसंविग्नमानसः ।76।। (Gītā 1.47)

28.12

THE INFINITIVE

tumun तुमुन् ।

Another important Indeclinable Participle, the INFINITIVE *tumun* (तुमुन्), is formed by adding the *tum* तुम् suffix directly to any verb-root.

As an infinitive. it gives the meaning of 'for doing or to do' the action indicated by the attached verb. e.g. √दा (to give) → दा + तुम् = दातुम् (for giving, to give).

THE INFINITIVES (तुमुन्)

Verb-root		ipp॰-क्त्वा		Infinitive (तुमुन्)	
√दा	(to give)	दत्त्वा	having given	दातुम्	for giving
√जि	(to win)	जित्वा	having won	जेतुम्	for winning
√ज्ञा	(to know)	ज्ञात्वा	having known	ज्ञातुम्	for knowing
*√भू	(to be)	भूत्वा	having been	भवितुम्	for being
√कृ	(to do)	कृत्वा	having done	कर्तुम्	for doing
√दृश्	(to see)	दृष्ट्वा	having seen	द्रष्टुम्	for seeing
√वच्	(to say)	उक्त्वा	having said	वक्तुम्	for saying
√नम्	(to salute)	नत्वा	having saluted	नन्तुम्	for saluting
√रभ्	(to begin)	रब्ध्वा	having begun	रब्धुम्	for begining
*√डी	(to fly)	डयित्वा	having flown	डयितुम्	for flying
√ध्यै	(to meditate)	ध्यात्वा	(having meditated)	ध्यातुम्	for meditating
√स्था	(to stand)	स्थित्वा	(having stood)	स्थातुम्	for standing
√मन्	(to think)	मत्वा	(having thought)	मन्तुम्	for thinking
√श्रु	(to hear)	श्रुत्वा	(having heard)	श्रोतुम्	for hearing
*√चुर्	(to steal)	चोरयित्वा	(having stolen)	चोरयितुम्	for stealing
*√गण्	(to count)	गणयित्वा	(having counted)	गणयितुम्	for counting

√छिद्	(to cut)	छित्त्वा	(having cut)	छेत्तुम्	for cutting
√क्षिप्	(to throw)	क्षिप्त्वा	(having thrown)	क्षेप्तुम्	for throwing
√स्पृष्	(to touch)	स्पृष्ट्वा	(having touched)	स्पर्ष्टुम्	for touching

The * sign indicates that, these are '*seṭ*' सेट् verbs. For *seṭ* सेट् and *anit* अनिट् verbs, see 28.7

EXAMPLES cum EXERCISE : THE INFINITIVES (तुमुन्)

1. I go to school. *ahaṁ pāṭhaśālāṁ gaććhāmi.* अहं पाठशालां गच्छामि ।
2. I go to school for learning (to learn). *ahaṁ pāṭhaśālāṁ paṭhituṁ/adhyetuṁ gaććhāmi.* अहं पाठशालां पठितुं/अध्येतुं गच्छामि ।
3. Rāma wants to speak (desires for speaking). *Rāmaḥ vaktum iććhati.* रामः वक्तुम् इच्छति ।
4. Sītā came here to hear Rāmāyaṇa. *Sītā Rāmāyaṇaṁ śrotum āgatavatī.* सीता रामायणं श्रोतुम् आगतवती ।
5. The child is going to garden to pick fruits. *bālakaḥ phalāni ćetum udyānaṁ gaććhati.* बालकः फलानि चेतुम् उद्यानं गच्छति ।
6. There are police to protect the city. *nagaraṁ saṁrakṣituṁ saṁrakṣakāḥ santi.* नगरं संरक्षितुं संरक्षकाः सन्ति ।
7. I went to the pump to buy gas. *ahaṁ śilā-tailaṁ kretum uttolana-yantr-sthānaṁ gatavān.* अहं शिलातैलं क्रेतुम् उत्तोलनयन्त्रस्थानं गतवान् ।
8. He brought a knife to cut mangos, wait for eating them. *saḥ āmraphalāni kartitum ćhurikām ānītavān, tāni bhoktum pratikṣāṁ karotu.* सः आम्रफलानि कर्तितुं छुरिकाम् आनीतवान् तानि भोक्तुं प्रतीक्षां करोतु ।
9. A CLASSICAL EXAMPLE :

   श्रोतुं कर्णौ वक्तुमास्यं सुहास्यं घ्रातुं घ्राणं पादयुग्मं विहर्तुम् ।
   द्रष्टुं नेत्रे हस्तयुग्मं च दातुं ध्यातुं चित्तं येन सृष्टं स पातु ।।79।।

NOTE : The Dative (4th) case may alternatively be used in place of the use of infinitives.

10. Rāma wants to speak (desires for speaking). *Rāmaḥ vaktum iććhati. Rāmaḥ vaćanāya iććhati.* रामः वक्तुम् इच्छति । रामः वचनाय इच्छति ।
11. The police are here to protect (for the protection of) the city.

nagaraṁ saṁrakṣituṁ rakṣakāḥ santi. nagara-saṁrakṣaṇāya rakṣakāḥ santi. नगरं संरक्षितुं रक्षकाः सन्ति । नगरसंरक्षणाय रक्षकाः सन्ति ।

USE OF TUMUN
in place of
POTENTIAL PARTICIPLE ipp◦

A *tumun* infinitive could be used in place of any of the three ipp◦ Indeclinable Potential Participles of अनीयर्, तव्यत्, य ।

e.g. You should not lament.

(i) tumun◦ न त्वं शोचितुम् अर्हसि । (Gītā 2.30) . =

(ii) ipp◦ त्वया शोकः न करणीयः । त्वया शोकः न कर्तव्यः । त्वया शोकः न कार्यः ।

EXERCISE 76 : Tumun

Match the English words with the corresponding Sanskrit participles.
खादित्वा, स्मर्तुम्, विक्रीय, प्राप्य, उक्त्वा, प्रष्टुम्, खादितुम्, वक्तुम्, स्मृत्वा, ज्ञातुम्, छेत्तुम्, क्रीत्वा ।

(1) I go home to eat. Having eaten I go school.

(2) Having said so he kept quiet. He wants to say no more.

(3) Having sold his old house and having bought a new one, he is happy.

(4) I came here for asking you something.

(5) Having remembered you, I am writing the letter.

(6) Having obtained the degree, I got the job.

(7) You will not be able to cut this.

(8) He is not able to remember it.

(9) They are able to know that.

28.13

सेट् and अनिट् क्रियाः ।

seṭ and *aniṭ* verbs

(i) The verb root (धातुः) that first takes an इट् *(iṭ)* suffix, while accepting a तुमुन् *(tumun)*, तव्यत् *(tavyat)*, लृट् (*lṛṭ* Indefinite future), लुट् (*luṭ* Definite future) or लृङ् (*lṛṅ* Indefinite future) suffix, is called a *seṭ* सेट् धातुः verb (स + इट् = सेट्, with *iṭ* = *seṭ*).

(ii) The root that does not take such इट् *(iṭ)* suffix, is called an अनिट् धातुः (*aniṭ* verb). Most of the roots that end in a vowel are अनिट् (*aniṭ* verbs). e.g.

(1) **सेट् धातुः (verb with *'iṭ'*)**

तुमुन्	√*bhū* to become √भू + इट् (इ) + तुम् = भवितुम् ।
तव्यत्	√भू + इ + तव्य = भवितव्य *bhavitavya*
लृट्	√भू भविष्यति, भविष्यतः, भविष्यन्ति ।
लुङ्	√भू भविता, भवितारौ, भवितारः ।
लृङ्	√भू अभविष्यत्, अभविष्यताम्, अभविष्यन् ।

(2) **अनिट् धातुः (*aniṭ* verb) :**

तुमुन्	√*dā* to give √दा + तुम = दातुम् *dātum*
तव्यत्	√दा + तव्य = दातव्य *dātavya*
लृट्	√दा दास्यति, दास्यतः, दास्यन्ति ।
लुङ्	√दा दाता, दातारौ, दातारः ।
लृङ्	√दा अदास्यत्, अदास्यताम्, अदास्यन् ।

There are 102 अनिट् verbs :

अद्, आप्, कृष्, क्रुध्, क्रुश्, क्षिप्, क्षुद्, क्षुध्, खिद्, गम्, घस्, छिद्, छुप्, तप्, तिप्, तुद्, तुष्, तृप्, त्यज्, त्विष्, निज्, दंश्, दह, दिश्, दिह, दुष्, दृप्, दृश्, दुह, नम्, नह, निज्, नुद्, पच्, पद्, पिष्, पुष्, प्रच्छ्, बन्ध्, बुध्, भज्, भञ्ज्, भिद्, भुज्, भृश्, भ्रस्ज्, मन्, मस्ज्, मिह, मुच्, यज्, यभ्, यम्, युज्, युध्, रञ्ज्, रभ्, रम्, राध्, रिच्, रिश्, रुज्, रुश्, रुह, लभ्, लिप्, लिश्, लिह, लुप्, वच्, वप्, वस्, वह, विच्, विज्, विद् (4,6,7), विनद्, विश्, विष्, व्यध्, शक्लृ, शद्, शप्, शिष्, शुष्, श्लिष्, सञ्ज्, सद्, साध्, सिच्, सिध्, सृज्, सृप्, स्कन्द्, स्पृश्, स्वञ्ज्, स्वप्, स्विद्, हन्, हृद् ।

WHAT WE LEARNED ABOUT THE PARTICIPLES

The Primary Derivatives कृदन्तानि

Root Verb √भू

	PPP॰	PAP॰	PPAP॰	APPP॰	FPPP॰	FPPP॰	FPPP॰	IPP॰	IPP॰	INF॰
	क्त	क्तवतु	शतृ	शानच्	अनीयर्	तव्यत्	तव्य	क्त्वा	ल्यप्	तुमुन्
1. Regular Actions	भूत	भूतवत्	भवत्	भूयमान	भवनीय	भवितव्य	भव्य	भूत्वा	संभूय	भवितुम्
2. Causatives	भावित	भावयितवत्	भावयत्	भावयमान	भावनीय	भावयितव्य	भाव्य	भावयित्वा	संभाव्य	बुभूषितुम्
3. Desideratives	बुभूषित	बुभूषितवत्	बुभूषत्	बुभूषमान	बुभीषणीय	बुभूषितव्य	बुभूतव्य	बुभूषित्वा	संबुभूष्य	बोभवितुम्
4. Frequentative										
(i) यङन्त	बोभूयित	बोभूयितवत्	बोभूयत्	बोभूयमान	बोभूयनीय	बोभूयितव्य	बोभूय्य	बोभूयित्वा	संबोभूय्य	बोभोयितुम्
(ii) यङ्लुगन्त	बोभुवित	बोभुषितवत्	बोभुवत्	बोभुवमान	बोभवनीय	बोभवितव्य	बोभव्य	बोभूत्वा	संबोभूय	बोभवितुम्

The Derivatives : भव, भवदीय, भवन, भवानी, भवित्र, भविष्णु, भविष्य, भाव, भावक, भावना, भाविक, भावुक, भुवन, भूति, भूमि, भूष्णू, प्रभव, प्रभाव, प्रभु, प्रभुत्व, प्रभू, विभु, विभुति, ...etc.

---

* PRONUNCIATION GUIDE FOR PARASAVARNA-SANDHI (परसवर्ण-संधिः) *

महत्पापं कर्तुम् = महत्पापङ्कर्तुम् (mahatpāpṅkartum Gītā 1.45), पदं गच्छन्ति = पदङ्गच्छन्ति (padaṅgachhanti Gītā 2.51), रूपं घोरम् = रूपङ्घोरम् (rūpaṅghoram Gītā 11.49), महतीं चमूम् = महतीञ्चमूम् (mahatiñćamūm Gītā 1.3), द्यूतं छलयताम् = द्यूतञ्छलयताम् (dyutañćhalayatām Gītā 10.36), मनुष्याणां जनार्दन = मनुष्याणाञ्जनार्दन (manuṣyāṇāñjanārdana Gītā 1.44), संज्ञार्थं तान् = संज्ञार्थन्तान् (saṁjñārtantān Gītā 1.7), व्यूढं दुर्योधनः = व्यूढन्दुर्योधनः (vyūḍhanduryodhanaḥ Gītā 1.2), देवदत्तं धनञ्जयः = देवदत्तन्धनञ्जयः (devadattandhanañjayaḥ Gītā 1.15), काङ्क्षितं नः = काङ्क्षितन्नः (kāṅkṣitannaḥ Gītā 1.33), एतां पाण्डुपुत्राणाम् = पश्यैताम्पाण्डुपुत्राणाम् (etāmpāṇḍu॰ Gītā 1.3), पुष्पं फलम् = पुष्पम्फलम् (puṣpamphalam Gītā 9.26), एतेषां बलम् = एतेषाम्बलम् (eteṣambalam Gītā 1.10), बलं भीष्माभिरक्षितम् = बलम्भीष्माभिरक्षितम् (balambhīma॰ Gītā 1.10), क्लैब्यं मा = क्लैब्यम्मा (klaibyammā Gītā 2.3), अहं योद्धुकामान् = अहं योद्धुकामान् (m̐=अं aham̐ yoddhukāmān Gītā 1.22), ऋद्धं राज्यम् = ऋद्धं राज्यम् (ṛddham̐ rājyam Gītā 2.8), नायं लोकः = नायं लोकः (nāyam̐ lokaḥ Gītā 4.31), अनियतं वासः = अनियतं वासः (aniyatam̐ vāsaḥ Gītā 1.44), अशस्त्रं शस्त्रपाणयः = अशस्त्रं शस्त्रपाणयः (aśastram̐ śastra॰ Gītā 1.46), रथं स्थापय = रथं स्थापय (ratham̐ sthāpaya Gītā 1.21),

28.14

CREATING EXISTANCE OF A NON-EXISTENT THING

ćvi suffix च्वि-प्रत्ययः ।

Another cool and unique single-word idea in Sanskrit is bringing (or coming) into existence a non-existing or imaginary thing, by attaching the *ćvi* (च्वि) suffix to a noun or to an adjective.

How the *ćvi*-nouns or adjectives are formed

(1) Take the desired (non-existent) noun (or adjective) to be *ćvi*-ed

(2) If the (non-existent) noun ends in अ *(a), (ā)* आ or *(i)* इ, modify it to *(ī)* ई; but, if it ends in *(u)* उ, modify it to *(ū)* ऊ

(3) If the (non-existent) noun comes (by itself) into existence, attach भू *(bhū)* suffix to the noun modified in step 2. But, if the noun is to be brought into existence (by someone), attach कृ *(kṛ)* suffix.

(4) Now attach the gender, number, case and other suffixes to this *ćvi*-ed (च्विरूपितम्) noun (or adjective).

EXAMPLES :

(1) A non-existent m∘ noun mountain पर्वत ending in अ ।

पर्वत → पर्वती, the च्वि रूपम् will be पर्वती + कृ = पर्वतीकृ । दुर्जनाः परदोषान् पर्वतीकुर्वन्ति । The bad people make a mountain out of others' faults.

(2) A non-existent f∘ adjective श्वेता (white) ending in आ ।

श्वेता → श्वेती, the च्वि रूपम् will be श्वेती + भू = श्वेतीभू । चन्द्रमसा निशा श्वेतीभवति । The dark night becomes white with moon.

(3) A non-existent adjective शुचि (pure) ending in इ ।

शुचि → शुची, the च्वि रूपम् will be शुची + कृ = शुचीकरोति । गङ्गास्नानं नरं शुचीकरोति । A bath in river the Gangā purifies a person.

(4) A non-existent adjective लघु (short) ending in उ ।

लघु → लघू, the च्वि रूपम् will be लघू + भू = लघूभू । तव दर्शनेन मम दुःखं लघूभवति । With your presence my sorrow becomes less painful.

Without the *ćvi* (च्वि), above four sentences will read :

(1) दुर्जनाः परदोषान् पर्वतीकुर्वन्ति → दुर्जनाः परान् दोषान् पर्वतं/पर्वतान् कुर्वन्ति ।

(2) चन्द्रमसा निशा श्वेतीभवति → चन्द्रमसा निशा श्वेता भवति ।

(3) गङ्गास्नानं नरं शुचीकरोति → गङ्गास्नानं नरं शुचिं करोति ।

(4) तव दर्शनेन मम दुःखं लघूभवति → तव दर्शनेन मम दुःखं लघु भवति ।

APPLICATION of TENSES and MOODS to *ćvi* च्वि

Full power of the *ćvi* च्वि can be seen by applying various tense and mood suffixes to above four *ćvi*-nouns and *ćvi*-adjectives for example :

(1) पर्वतीकरोमि, पर्वतीकरोषि, पर्वतीकरोति, पर्वतीकुर्वन्ति, पर्वतीकुर्वन्, पर्वतीकर्तुम्, पर्वतीकर्तव्यम्, पर्वतीकृतम् । पर्वतीभवामि, पर्वतीभवसि, पर्वतीभवति, पर्वतीभवितुम्, पर्वतीभवितव्यम्, पर्वतीभूतम् ।

(2) श्वेतीकरोमि, श्वेतीकरोषि, श्वेतीकरोति, श्वेतीकुर्वन्ति, श्वेतीकुर्वन्, श्वेतीकर्तुम्, श्वेतीकर्तव्यम्, श्वेतीकृतम् । श्वेतीभवामि, श्वेतीभवसि, श्वेतीभवति, श्वेतीभवितुम्, श्वेतीभवितव्यम्, श्वेतीभूतम् ।

(3) शुचीकरोमि, शुचीकरोषि, शुचीकरोति, शुचीकुर्वन्ति, शुचीकुर्वन्, शुचीकर्तुम्, शुचीकर्तव्यम्, शुचीकृतम् । शुचीभवामि, शुचीभवसि, शुचीभवति, शुचीभवितुम्, शुचीभवितव्यम्, शुचीभूतम् ।

(4) लघूकरोमि, लघूकरोषि, लघूकरोति, लघूकुर्वन्ति, लघूकुर्वन्, लघूकर्तुम्, लघूकर्तव्यम्, लघूकृतम् । लघूभवामि, लघूभवसि, लघूभवति, लघूभवितुम्, लघूभवितव्यम्, लघूभूतम् ।

28.15

SATI -SAPTAMI

सति-सप्तमी ।

In a sentence the action performed by the subject is indicated by choosing a right verb or sometimes by using a participle. However, in order to indicate that a subordinate action has occured, is occuring or will occur, **before the main action takes place**, use of 'sati saptamī' (सति सप्तमी) in one clause of the sentence is employed.

In the clause of sati saptami construction, the pair of a substantive and its related adjective, are **both kept in the Locative case** (सप्तमी विभक्तिः), and therefore this consruction is called *sati saptamī.*

The subject (doer) of the subordinate action i.e. sati saptamī, and the subject (doer) of the main action **must be different**.

We can remove the sati saptami and re-construct the sentence having the same meaning.

EXAMPLES :

1. रामे भूमिं पालयति जनानां दुःखं कुतः भवेत् । In Rāma's ruling of the earth, where from the people will have misery? * Without sati-saptami : यावत् रामः भूमिं पालयति, तावत् जनानां दुःखं कुतः भवेत् । As long as Rāma is ruling the earth, where from the people will have misery?
2. मनसि परितुष्टे को धनी को दरिद्रः । Being at peace in mind, what is richness and what is poverty? * Without sati-saptami : यावत् मनः परितुष्टः भवति तावत् कः धनी कः च दरिद्रः । When mind is satisfied, then who is rich and who is poor?
3. चित्रकुटं गते रामे पुत्रशोकातुरस्तथा । राजा दशरथः स्वर्गं जगाम विलपन्सुतम् ।। (रामायणं)

LESSON 29

navaviṁśaḥ abhyāsaḥ नवविंशः अभ्यासः ।

ADVERBS AND CONJUNCTIONS

kriyāviśeṣaṇāni yaugicśabdāḥ ća क्रियाविशेषणानि यौगिकशब्दाः च ।

29.1

ADVERBS

kriyāviśeṣaṇāni क्रियाविशेषणानि ।

An Adverb does not take any gender, number, person, tense or case. It does not change with the verb it qualifies, thus, it is an INDECLINABLE word (*avyayam* अव्ययम्)

NOTE : Adverbs are not the only indeclinable words, there are many other words that are indeclinables and are used adverbially, such as :

(1) There are nouns of which one conjugation or the **Nominative Case** declension is used as an indeclinable word. e.g. अस्तम् (*astam* setting, decline), अस्ति (*asti* existence), नास्ति (*nāsti* non-existence), नमः (*namaḥ* salutation), भुवर् (*bhuvar* sky), संवत् (*saṁvat* a year), स्वर् (*svar* heaven), स्वस्ति (*svasti* greeting), सुखम् (*sukham* happily), etc.

(2) There are **Adjectives** of which the Accusative Neuter is indeclinable. e.g. नित्यम् (*nityam* regularly), बहु (*bahu* very), भूयः (*bhūyaḥ* again), सत्यम् (*satyam* truly), दुःखम् (*dukham* sadly), etc.

(3) There are **Pronouns** of which Accusative Neuter is indeclinable. e.g. किम् (*kim* what), तत् (*tat* that), यावत् (*yāvat* as long), तावत् (*tāvat* so long), etc.

(4) There are other substantive **Nouns** of which the Accusative neuter is indeclinable. e.g. स्वयम् (*svayam* oneself), दुःखम् (*duḥkham* with difficulty), etc.

(5) There are nouns and adjectives of which **Instrumental Case** is indeclinable, अशेषेण (*aśeṣeṇa* fully), उच्चैः (*uććaiḥ* loudly), चिरेण (*ćireṇa* quickly), तेन (*tena* thus), पुरा (*purā* anciently, formerly), etc.

(6) There are words of which the **Dative Case** is indeclinable. e.g. अप्रदाय (*apradāya* without sharing), आस्थाय (*āsthāya* for staying), विज्ञाय (*vijñāya* for knowing), etc.

(7) There are nouns and pronouns of which the **Ablative Case** is indeclinable. e.g. तस्मात् (*tasmāt* therefore), बलात् (*balāt* forcibly), समन्तात् (*samantāt* around), etc.

(8) There are words of which the **Locative Case** is indeclinable. e.g. अग्रे (*agre* at first), अन्तरे (*antare* inside), ऋते (*ṛte* without), स्थाने (*sthāne* justly), etc.

(9) There are words of which a **Derivative** is indeclinable : e.g.

Affirmative : एव (*eva* only); Negative : न (*na* not), मा (*mā* don't), मा स्म (*mā sma* do not);

Interrogative : कच्चित् (*kaććit* does it), नु (*nu* is it possibe);

Comparative : इव (*iva* as if), एवम् (*evam* thus), तथैव (*tathaiva* as well);

Degree : अतीव (*atīva* very), सर्वथा (*sarvathā* by all means);

Mode : आशु (*āśu* soon), तूष्णीम् (*tūṣṇīm* quietly), नाना (*nānā* various), पुनर् (*punar* again), पृथक् (*pṛthak* differently);

Time : अद्य (*adya* today), जातु (*jātu* ever), प्राक् (*prāk* before), प्रेत्य (*pretya* in the next life), मुहुः (*muhuḥ* frequently);

Place : इह (*iha* here), तत्र (*tatra* there);

Doubt : उत (*uta* whether); Emphasis : अपि (*api* also), हि (*hi* indeed, because) etc.

EXAMPLES cum EXERCISE : USE of ADVERBS (क्रियाविशेषणानि)

1. Rāma works quickly. *Rāmaḥ kāryaṁ śīghreṇa karoti.* रामः कार्यं शीघ्रेण करोति ।

2. Sītā works quickly. *Sītā kāryaṁ śīghreṇa karoti.* सीता कार्यं शीघ्रेण करोति ।

3. We work quickly. *vayaṁ kāryaṁ śīghreṇa kurmaḥ.* वयं कार्यं शीघ्रेण कुर्मः

4. They worked quickly. *te/tāḥ kāryaṁ śīghreṇa kurvantaḥ/akurvan.* ते/ताः कार्यं शीघ्रेण कृतवन्तः, अकुर्वन् ।

5. He always helps. *saḥ sadā sahāyyaṁ karoti.* सः सदा सहाय्यं करोति ।

6. Please move backward. *kṛpayā pṛṣṭhataḥ saratu.* कृपया पृष्ठतः सरतु ।

7. I will come before him. *ahaṁ tasmāt pūrvam āgamiṣyāmi.* अहं तस्मात् पूर्वम् आगमिष्यामि ।

8. He wants money now. *saḥ dhanam idānīm icchati.* सः धनम् इदानीम् इच्छति ।

9. Kindly give me ten Rupees. *kṛpayā mahyaṁ daśa-rūpyakāṇi dadātu.* कृपया मह्यं दश रूप्यकाणि ददातु ।

10. Otherwise I am going. *anyathā ahaṁ gacchāmi.* अन्यथा अहं गच्छामि ।

11. Where is your friend? *tava-bhavataḥ mitraṁ kutra asti?* तव-भवतः मित्रं कुत्र अस्ति?

EXERCISE 77 : ADVERBS

Fill in the blanks with Sanskrit adverbs

(1) Why did you tell him? त्वं तं ---------- उक्तवान्?

(2) How is your brother now? तव बन्धुः ---------- अस्ति?

(3) I see it clearly. अहं तत् ---------- पश्यामि ।

(4) You are very tired. त्वं ---------- क्लान्तः असि ।

(5) Enough with (of) talking. ---------- कथनेन ।

DICTIONARY Of ADVERBS

kriyāviśeṣaṇa-kośaḥ क्रियाविशेषणकोशः ।

A little (किंचित् kiñćit, मनाक् manāk)

Above (ūrdhvam, upari ऊर्ध्वम्, उपरि)

Abruptly (एकपदे ekapade, सहसा sahasā, अकस्मात् akasmāt)

Absolutely (सर्वथा sarvathā, सर्वशः sarvaśaḥ, केवलम् kevalam, एकान्ततः ekāntataḥ)

Absurdly (अविचारेण avićāreṇa, अनुपपन्नम् anupapannam)

After (अनन्तरम् anantaram, परम् param, पश्चात् paśćāt)

Afterwards (अनन्तरम् anantaram, परम् param)

Again (भूयः bhūyaḥ, पुनः punaḥ, पुनर् punar)

Again and again (मुहुर्मुहुः muhurmuhuḥ, वारंवारम् vāraṁvāraṁ)

Against (प्रत्युत pratyuta, pratikūlam, viruddham प्रतिकूलम्, विरुद्धम्)

All (akhilam, sarvam अखिलम्, सर्वम्)

All around (परितः paritaḥ)

Almost (प्रायः prāyaḥ, भूयिष्ठ bhūyiṣṭha, कल्प kalpa)

Already (पूर्वम् pūrvam, पुरा purā, प्राक् prāk)

Also (अपि api, च ća, पुनश्च punaśća, अपिच apića)

Alternately (पर्यायेण paryāyeṇa)

Always (सदा sadā, सर्वदा sarvadā, सततम् satatam, अभीक्ष्णम् abhīkṣanam)

All around (समन्ततः samantataḥ सर्वतः sarvataḥ)

All at once (एकपदे ekapade)

Among (अन्तरम् antaram, अन्तरे antare)

Anyhow (यथाकथम् yathākatham)

Anything (ईषदपि īṣadapi, स्तोकमपि stokamapi)

Anywhere (कुत्रापि kutrāpi)

Apart (पृथक् pṛthak)

Around (परितः paritaḥ, सर्वतः sarvataḥ, समन्ततः samantataḥ)

As (यथा yathā, यद्वत् yadvat; इव iva)

As far as (यावत् yāvat)

As much as (यावत् yāvat)

As though, as if (इव iva)

At all (किमपि kimapi, मनागपि manāgapi)

At any time (कर्हिचित् karhićit)

At night (दोषा doṣā, नक्तम् naktam)

At once (युगपत् yugpat, सपदि sapadi, सद्यः sadyaḥ)

At one time (एकदा ekadā, सहसा sahasā)

At present (अद्यत्वे adyatve)

At random (अकस्मात् akasmāt, यदृच्छया yadṛććhayā, निःसन्धानम् niḥsandhānam, अविचार्य avićārya, सहसा sahasā, असम्बद्धम् asambaddham, अनियतम् aniyatam, उच्छृंखलम् ućcharṅkhalam, अव्यवस्थया avyavasthayā, अक्रमेण akrameṇa)

At the same time (सद्यम् sadyam)

At this time (एतर्हि etarhi, सम्प्रति samprati)

At what time (कर्हि karhi)

Away (अलम् alam, दूरम् dūram)

Backwards (परा parā, प्रति prati; पृष्ठतः pṛṣṭhataḥ)

Badly (युक् yuk, युत् yut)

Because (hi, yataḥ, yena hetoḥ, yat हि, यतः, तेन हेतोः, यत्)

Before, in front (सम्मुखम् sammukham, समक्षम् samakṣam, साक्षात् sākṣāt)

Before, time-place (अर्वाक् arvāk)

Behind (pṛṣṭhataḥ पृष्ठतः)

Below (अधः adhaḥ. अधस्तात् adhastāt)

Besides (अन्यच्च anyaćća)

Beyond (atītya, parataḥ अतीत्य, परतः)

But (किंतु kintu, परन्तु parantu; मात्रम् mātram, न वरम् na varam)

But how (किन्नु kinnu)

By day (दिवा divā)

By evening (दोषा doṣā)

By night (रात्रौ rātrau)

By that (तेन tena)

Ceaselessly (अनिशम् aniśam, सततम् satatam)

Certainly (अद्धा addhā, खलु khalu, नूनम् nūnam; नाम nāma, असंशयम् asaṁśayam, ध्रुवम् dhruvam)

Clearly (व्यक्तम् vyaktam, स्पष्टम् spaṣṭam, स्फुटम् sphuṭam)

Close by (अनितः anitaḥ)

Consequently (ततः tataḥ)

Constantly (अजस्रम् ajasram)

Daily (प्रतिदिनम् pratidinam)
Day after tomorrow (परश्वः paraśvaḥ)
Day before yesterday (परह्यः parahyaḥ)
Deeply (दूरम् dūram)
Dishonestly (तिर्यक् tiryak)
Don't (मा mā, मा स्म mā sma)
Downward (अधस्तात् adhastāt, अर्वाक् avāk)
Elsewhere (अन्यत्र anyatra)
Enough (अलम् alam, कृतम् kṛtam)
Entirely (कृत्स्नशः kṛtsnaśaḥ, निखिलेन nikhilena)
Equally (समम् samam, तुल्यम् tulyam)
Eternally (नित्यम् nityam, सदा sadā, निरन्तरम् nirantaram)
Ever (कदाचन kadācana, कर्हिचित् karhicit, कदाचित् kadācit, कदापि kadāpi)
Every day (प्रतिदिनम् pratidinam)
Every time (यदा यदा yadā yadā)
Everywhere (यत्र तत्र yatra tatra, सर्वत्र sarvatra)
Evidently (नाम nām, प्रत्यक्षम् pratyakṣam, स्फुटम् sphuṭam, व्यक्तम् vyaktam)
Excellently (उत्तमम् uttamam, सुष्ठु suṣṭhu)
Except (माकिम् mākim, माकिर् mākir)
Extensively (प्रतान् pratān, प्रताम् pratām)
Falsely (अनृतम् anṛtam, असत्यम् asatyam, मिथ्या mithyā, मृषा mṛṣā)
Far (आरात् ārāt, दूरम् dūram, दूरे dūre)
Forcibly (बलात् balāt, प्रसह्य prasahya)
Formerly (पुरा purā, पूर्वतरम् pūrvataram, प्राक् prāk)
Forthwith (द्राक् drāk)
Fortunately (दिष्ट्या diṣṭyā, दैवात् daivāt, सौभाग्येन saubhāgyena)
Forward (अग्रतः agrataḥ, अग्रे agre, पुरतः purataḥ)
Frequently (पुनः पुनः, punaḥpunaḥ, मुहुर्मुहुः muhurmuhuḥ, भूयोभूयः bhūyobhūyaḥ, वारंवारम् vāramvāram)
Fully (कृत्स्नशः kṛtsnaśaḥ, अशेषेण aśeṣeṇa, अशेषतः aśeṣataḥ, साकल्येन sākalyena)
Further (अपरम् aparam, दूरतरम् dūrataram)
Gladly (समुपजोषम् samupajoṣam)
Good (बाढम् bāḍham, सम्यक् samyak, सुष्ठु suṣṭhu)

Happily (सुखेन sukhena, यथासुखम् yathāsukham)

Hastily (सहसा sahasā; क्षिप्रम् kṣipram, आशु āśu, झटिति jhaṭiti, द्रुतम् drutam, सत्वरम् satvaram)

Hence (इत: itaḥ, अस्मात् asmāt, स्थानात् sthānāt)

Here (अत्र atra, इह iha)

Here after (अत: ataḥ, इत: परम् itaḥ param, अत: परम् ataḥ param, परत: parataḥ, अनन्तरम् anantaram)

Here before (इत: पूर्वम् itaḥ pūrvam, अत: पूर्वम् ataḥ pūrvam, प्राक् prāk)

Here and there (इतस्तत: itastataḥ)

Highly (दूरम् dūram)

How (कथम katham, केन प्रकारेण kena prakāreṇa)

How else (अथ किम् atha kim)

How many (कति kati, कतिकृत्व: katikṛtvaḥ)

How much (कियत् kiyat)

How much more (किमुत kimuta)

How now (ननु nanu)

However (यथातथा yathātathā, येनकेन प्रकारेण yenakena prakāreṇa)

However (तु tu, किंतु kintu, अपि तु api tu, तथापि tathāpi, परन्तु parantu)

Idly (वृथा vṛthā)

If (यदि yadi, चेत् ćet)

If not (नोचेत् noćet, अन्यथा anyathā, यदि-न yadi-na)

If-then (यदि-तर्हि yadi-tarhi)

Ignorantly (अज्ञानत: ajñānataḥ)

Immediately (द्राक् drāk, द्राङ् drāṅ, मंक्षु maṅkṣu)

Improperly (अनुचितम् anućitam, अयुक्तम्, ayuktam, असम्यक् asamyak, अस्थाने asthāne)

In (antare, madhye अन्तरे, मध्ये)

In a short time (aćireṇa, aćirāt अचिरेण, अचिरात्, नचिरात् naćirāt)

In as much as (yat, tataḥ, yasmāt यत्, यत: यस्मात्)

In detail (vistareṇa विस्तरेण)

In front of (अग्रत: agrataḥ, puraḥ, putataḥ पुर:, पुरत: अग्रे agre, पुरस्तात् purastāt)

In order (क्रमेण krameṇa, क्रमश: kramaśaḥ)

In heaven (अमुत्र amutra)

In short (alpaśaḥ अल्पशः)

In the evening (सायम् sāyam)

In the morning (उषा uṣā, प्रगे prage, प्रातर् prātar)

In the noon (पराह्णे parāhṇe)

In the afterworld (प्रेत्य pretya)

In this world (इह iha, अरत्र aratra)

Indeed (अद्धा addhā, किल kil, खलु khalu, नाम nām, नूनम् nūnam, वस्तुतः vastutaḥ, वै vai, हि hi)

Indirectly (भंग्युक्त्या bhaṅgyuktyā, वक्रोक्त्या vakroktyā, तिर्यक् tiryak, असरलम् asaralam)

Incessantly (अनिशम् aniśam, अविरतम् aviratam)

Into (अन्तर् antar)

Lately (अचिरम् aćiram)

Later (उत्तरम् uttaram, पश्चात् paśćāt)

Like this (ईदृश् īdṛś, इत्थम् ittham, एतादृश् etādṛś)

Like that (तादृश् tādṛś)

Like what? (कीदृश् kīdṛś)

Luckily (दिष्ट्या diṣṭyā)

Manifestly (साक्षात् sākṣāt)

Moreover (अन्यच्च anyaćća, किञ्च kiñća, अपरम् aparam, अपि तु api tu)

Mostly (प्रायः prāyaḥ, प्रायेण prāyeṇa, प्रायशः prāyaśaḥ)

Most probably (नूनम् nūnam)

Much (बहु bahu, भृशम् bhṛśam, अत्यन्तम् atyantam, गाढम् gāḍham)

Mutually (अन्योन्य anyonya, मिथः mithaḥ, परस्परम् parasparam)

Near (निकषा nikaṣā, समीपे samipe)

No, not (न na, नहि nahi, नो no)

Not at all (न किमपि na kimapi)

Not so (न किम् na kim)

Now (अधुना adhunā, इदानीम् idānīm, सम्प्रति samprati, साम्प्रतम् sāmpratam)

Now a days (अद्यत्वे adyatve)

Nowhere (न क्वचित् na kiñćit)

Often (बहुधा bahudhā, वारंवारम् vāraṁvāram, अभीक्ष्णम् abhīkṣṇam)

On, Over (upari उपरि)

On both sides (उभयतः ubhayataḥ)

On both days (उभयद्युः ubhayadyuḥ, उभयेद्युः ubhayedyuḥ)

On the contrary (प्रत्युत pratyuta)

On the next day (अपरेद्यु: aparedyuḥ)

Once (एकधा ekadhā, सकृत् sakṛt)

Only (एव eva, केवलम् kevalam, मात्र mātra)

Openly (आवि: āviḥ, सुस्पष्टम् suspaṣṭam, व्यक्तम् vyaktam)

Or (अथवा athavā, किंवा kimvā, यद्वा yadvā, वा vā, अन्यथा anyathā)

Out (bahiḥ बहि:)

Outwardly (बाह्यत: bāhyataḥ, बहि: bahiḥ)

Perhaps (कदाचित् kadāćit, किंस्वित् kimsvit, नुवा nuvā, स्यात् syāt)

Possibly (किल kila, कदाचित् kadāćit)

Privately (उपांशु upāṁśu)

Probably (नूनम् nūnam)

Properly (युक्तम् yuktam, उचितम् ućitam, सम्यक् samyak, धर्मेण dharmeṇa, यथार्हम् yathārham)

Quickly (अरम् aram, आशु āśu, शीघ्रेण śīghreṇa, झटिति jhaṭiti, तूर्णम् tūrṇam, क्षिप्रम् kṣipram)

Quietly (शान्तम् śāntam, शान्त्या śāntyā, निराकुलम् nirākulam, अव्याकुलम् avyākulam, अक्षुब्धम् akṣubdham, स्वास्थ्येन svāsthena, अनुग्रम् anugram, अचण्डम् aćaṇḍam, तूष्णीम् tūṣṇīm, नि:शब्दम् niḥśabdam)

Rarely (क्वचित् kvaćit, कृच्छ्रेण kṛ́chreṇa, कष्टेन kaṣṭena, विरल virala)

Repeatedly (अभीक्ष्णम् abhīkṣṇam, वारंवारम् vāramvāram, भूयोभूय:, पुन:पुन: punaḥpunaḥ)

Rightly (अञ्जसा añjasā, यथातथा yathātathā, समीचीनम् samīćīnam, सम्यक् samyak)

Separately (पृथक् pṛthak)

Shortly (अचिरात् aćirāt, अचिरेण aćireṇa, सपदि sapadi, झटिति jhaṭiti, शीघ्रम् śīghram)

Silently (तूष्णीम् tūṣṇīm, निभृतम् nibhṛtam)

Similarly (तथैव tathaiva, तद्वत् tadvat)

Simultaneously (युगपत् yugapat)

Slightly (ईषत् īṣat)

Slowly (शनै: शनै: śanaiḥ śanaiḥ, मन्दं मन्दम् mandam mandam)

So (इति iti, इत्थम् ittham, तथा tathā, तद्वत् tadvat, एवम् evam)

So be it (आम् ām, ओम् om, तथास्तु tathāstu)

So far as (तावत् tāvat)

So much (ईदृक् īdṛk, तादृक् tādṛk)

So that (यथा yathā, येन yena)

Somehow (कथमपि kathamapi, कथञ्चित् kathañćit)

Sometimes (कदाचित् kadāćit, क्वचित् kvaćit)

Somewhat (ईषत् īṣat, किंचित् kiñćit, स्तोकम् stokam)

Somewhere (कुत्रचित् kutraćit, क्वचित् kvaćit, क्वापि kvāpi)

Speedily (आशु āśu, द्राक् drāk, भाजक् bhājak, संक्षु saṅkṣu, तूर्णम् tūrṇam)

Spontaneously (स्वयम् svayam)

Suddenly (अकस्मात् akasmāt, एकपदे ekapade)

Sufficiently (पर्याप्तम् paryāptam, यथेष्टम् yatheṣṭam)

Surely (निश्चित् niśćit, नूनम् nūnam, खलु khalu, अवश्यम् avaśyam, निश्चितम् niśćitam)

Then (ततः tataḥ, तत् tat, तदा tadā, तदानीम् tadānīm)

Thence (ततः tataḥ, तस्मात् tasmāt)

There (तत्र tatra)

Therefore (अतः ataḥ, ततः tataḥ, तस्मात् tasmāt)

Thus (इत्थम् ittham, एवम् evam)

To and fro (इतस्ततः itastataḥ)

Today (अद्य adya)

Together (एकत्र ekatra)

Tomorrow (श्वः śvaḥ)

Truly (अद्धा addhā, इद्धा iddhā, ऋधक् ṛdhak, ऋतम् ṛtam, सत्यम् satyam, वस्तुतः vastutaḥ, तत्त्वतः tattvataḥ)

Under (adhaḥ, adhastāt अधः अधस्तात्)

Universally (सर्वतः sarvataḥ, विश्वतः viśvataḥ)

Usefully (अमुधा amudhā, सफलम् saphalam)

Uselessly (वृथा vṛyhā, व्यर्थम् vyartham, मुधा mudhā, निष्फलम् niṣphalam, मोघम् mogham)

Vainly (मुधा mudhā, वृथा vṛthā)

Variously (नाम nāma, नानाविधम् nānāvidham)

Verily (खलु khalu, नाम nāma, सत्यम् satyam, वै vai)

Very (अतीव atīva, सुतराम् sutarām, भृशम् bhṛśam)

Well (सुष्ठु suṣṭhu, सम्यक् samyak, बाढम् bāḍham; भवतु bhavatu, अस्तु astu)

What? (किम् kim)

What a pity (किंकिल kiṅkila)

What else (अथ किम् atha kim, ननु nanu, आः āḥ)

What more (किमन्यत् kimanyat, किंबहुना kimbahunā)

When (यदा yadā)

When? (कदा kadā, कर्हि karhi, yadā, yadā yadā, yadā kadāćit यदा, यदा यदा, यदा कदाचित्)

Whence (कुतः kutaḥ, कस्मात् kasmāt, यतः yataḥ, यस्मात् yasmāt)

Where (यत्र yatra)

Where? (कुत्र kutra, क्व kva)

Wherever (यत्र यत्र, यत्र कुत्रापि yatra yatra, yatra kutrāpi)

Wherefore (यतम् yatam, येन yena)

Whether (kataraḥ, katarā, kiṁsvit, katarat, कतरः कतरा, किंस्वित्, कतरत्)

Which (yaḥ, yā, yat यः या, यत्)

Which? (kaḥ? kā? kim? कः? का? किम्?)

Which of the two? (katar? yatar? कतर? यतर?)

Which of the many? (katam? yatam? कतम? यतम?)

Wholly (समग्रम् samagram, सर्वतः sarvataḥ, सर्वशः sarvaśaḥ)

Why? (किम् kim, कुतः kutaḥ, किमर्थम् kimartham, किन्निमित्तम् kinnimittam)

Widely (विपुलम् vipulam)

With (सह saha, सहितम् sahitam, साकम् sākam, सार्धम् sārdham)

Willingly (स्वेच्छया sveććhayā, कामतः kāmataḥ)

Within (अन्तर् antar, मध्ये madhye)

Without (अन्तरेण antareṇa, विना vinā, ऋते ṛte)

Yes (अथकिम् athakim, आम् ām, बाढम् bāḍham)

Yesterday (ह्यः hyaḥ, पूर्वेद्युः pūrvedyuḥ)

EXAMPLES cum EXERCISE : USING WORDS ADVERBIALLY

(1) Where is your house? *bhavataḥ gṛhaṁ kutra asti?* भवत: गृहं कुत्र अस्ति?

Where is Rāma? *Rāmaḥ kutra asti?* राम: कुत्र अस्ति?

Where are they? *te/tāḥ kutra santi?* ते/ता: कुत्र सन्ति?

(2) Stay quiet, he is here. *tūṣṇīṁ tiṣṭhatu saḥ atra asti.* तूष्णीं तिष्ठतु स: अत्र एव अस्ति ।

(3) Happiness is where peace is. *yatra śāntiḥ, tatra sukham.* यत्र शान्ति: तत्र सुखम् ।

Where there is a will there is a way. *yatra icćhā, tatra mārgaḥ.* यत्र इच्छा तत्र मार्ग: ।

(4) Somehow he got a job. *katham-api tena vyavasāyaḥ prāptaḥ.* कथमपि तेन व्यवसाय: प्राप्त: । Please say it again. *punaḥ vadtu.* पुन: वदतु ।

(5) How can you not know this? *etat kathaṁ na jānāti bhavān?* एतत् कथं न जानाति भवान्?

(6) Be kind to the poor. *dīnaṁ prati dayāṁ karotu.* दीनं प्रति दयां करोतु ।

(7) I drink milk, nothing else. *ahaṁ kevalaṁ dugdhaṁ pibāmi, anyat kim-api na.* अहं केवलं दुग्धं पिबामि अन्यत् किमपि न ।

(8) Knowledge indeed comes slowly. *jñānaṁ khalu śanaiḥ śanaiḥ prāpyate.* ज्ञानं खलु शनै: शनै: प्राप्यते ।

(9) Do not tell a lie, otherwise you will be punished. *mithyā mā vadatu, no ćet daṇḍaṁ prāpsyasi.* मिथ्या मा वदतु नो चेत् दण्डं प्राप्स्यसि ।

(10) From here my house is near. *itaḥ mama gṛhaṁ samīpe asti.* इत: मम गृहं समीपे अस्ति । How about your? *bhavataḥ.* भवत:?

(11) The sun rises in the morning. *sūryaḥ prage udayati.* सूर्य: प्रगे उदयति ।

(12) As long as the moon and the sun are there. *yāvat ćandra-divākarau.* यावत् चन्द्रदिवाकरौ ।

(13) Long ago there was a righteous king named Rāma. *purā Rāmaḥ nāma sāttvikaḥ*

rājā āsīt. पुरा रामः नाम सात्त्विकः राजा आसीत् ।

(14) He is cunning like a fox. *saḥ śṛgālaḥ iva dhūrtaḥ asti.* सः शृगालः इव धूर्तः अस्ति ।

(15) The sky is high. *nabhaḥ uccaiḥ asti.* नभः उच्चैः अस्ति । The lion roars loudly. *siṁhaḥ uccaiḥ garjati.* सिंहः उच्चैः गर्जति ।

(17) What is the use of pouring oil into the lamp that has been extinguished? *nirvāṇa-dīpe kimu tailam?* निर्वाणदीपे किमु तैलम्?

(18) Who is clever, you or he? *kaḥ caturaḥ bhavān vā saḥ vā?* कः चतुरः भवान् वा सः वा? कः चतुरः त्वम् अथवा सः?

(19) No pains no gains. *yatnaṁ vinā na lābhaḥ.* यत्नं विना न लाभः ।

(20) You are certainly a gentleman. *nūnaṁ/avaśyaṁ/niścayena bhavān satpuruṣaḥ.* नूनं/अवश्यं/निश्चयेन भवान् सत्पुरुषः ।

(21) Although he is rich, he is not happy. *yadyapi saḥ dhanī saḥ sukhī nāsti.* यद्यपि सः धनी अस्ति सः सुखी नास्ति ।

(22) Do not do anything suddenly. *sahasā ikm-api mā karotu.* सहसा किमपि मा करोतु ।

(23) Animals do not enter the mouth of a sleeping lion indeed. *na hi suptasya siṁhasya praviśanti mukhe mṛgāḥ.* न हि सुप्तस्य सिंहस्य प्रविशन्ति मुखे मृगाः ।

PARADGIMES :

(24) अंग (vocative expression) → अंग प्रिय! प्रियं रामं भज । O Dear! Worship dear Rāma.

(25) अकस्मात् (suddenly) → ह्यः वृष्टिः अकस्मात् आगता । Yesterday it rained suddenly.

(26) अग्रतः (in front of) → गुरोः अग्रतः उपविशतु । Please sit in front of the teacher.

(27) अचिरम्, अचिरात्, अचिरेण, नचिरात्, नचिरेण (quickly, soon) → श्रद्धावान् अचिरेण शान्तिम् अधिगच्छति । Faithful person attains peace quickly.

(28) अतः, अतएव (therefore) → अतः समत्वं योगः उच्यते । Therefore, the equanimity is called yoga..

(29) अथ किम् (what else, yes, exactly, of course, certainly, quite so) → एतत् अहम् एव कृतवान् अथ किम् । Of course I have done it.

(30) अधुना, इदानीम् (now) → अधुना गृहम् रिक्तं भाति । Now the house looks empty.

(31) अधः (down) → दुर्जनः अधः गच्छति । The wicked person goes down.

(32) अन्तरा (between) → नेत्रयोः अन्तरा नासिका अस्ति । The nose is between two eyes.

(33) अन्येद्यु, अपरेद्यु (other day) → अन्येद्युः एतत् भविष्यति । It will happen some other day.

(34) अपि (does it, do you) → अपि जानाति सः कः । Do you know who is he.

(35) अपि च (further) → अपि च वदतु भवान् । Please tell me further.

(36) अलम् (enough) → अर्जुन! अलं तव पाण्डित्येन । O Arjuna! enough with your wisdom.

(37) आहोस्वित् (or) → सः विजितः आहोस्वित् पराजितः । Did he win or loose.

(38) इत्थम् (in this manner) → इत्थं सः पलायितः । In this manner he escaped.

(39) उपरि/ऊर्ध्वं गच्छन्ति सत्त्वस्थाः (up) → The righteous people rise above.

(40) उभयतः (on both sides) → वनम् उभयतः नद्यौ स्तः । Rivers are on both sides of the forest.

(41) ऋते, विना (without) → भवतः ऋते मनः अस्वस्थम् । Without you mind is disturbed .

(42) एकदा (once) → एकदा एकः राजा आसीत् । Once up on a time there was a king.

(43) एवम् (like this) → एवं कथम् अभवत् । How did it happen like this.

(44) कथमपि (somehow) → सः कथमपि गृहं गतवान् । Somehow he reached home.

(45) अकच्चित् (hopefully, did it) → कच्चित् एतत् श्रुतं पार्थ । O Arjuna! Did you hear it.

(46) किमुत, किं पुनः (what more) → किमुत सः कथयिष्यति । What more can he say.

(47) किल (probably) → अर्जुनः किल विजेष्यति कर्णम् । Arjuna will probably defeate Karṇa.

(48) केवलम् (only, just) → पयःपानं भुजङ्गानाम् केवलं विषवर्धनम् । Feeding milk to snakes is just growing poison.

(49) खलु (actually, quite) → न खलु सः क्रुद्धः । He is not quite angey.

(50) चिरम् (long) → चिरं जीवतु भवान् । May you live long.

(51) जातु (ever) → न जातु दुःखं गणनीयम् । Suffering should never be counted.

(52) ततः (then) → ततः सः उक्तवान् । Then he said.

(53) ततस्ततः (after that) → ततः सः उक्तवान् । ततस्ततः? Then he spoke. Then after that?

(54) तावत्, यावत् (so long, as long) → यावत् चन्द्रदिवाकरौ तावत् संस्कृतम् । As long moon and sun are there, so long Sanskrit will be there.

(55) तूष्णीम् (quietly) → तूष्णीम् तिष्ठतु भवान् । You please stay quietly.

(56) ननु (or, is it) → ननु खादितवान् सर्वे मोदकान् सः । He ate all sweets or what.

(57) नितराम्, सुतराम् (totally) → सः नितरां मूर्खः । He is totally a fool.

(58) नूनम् (actually, certainly) → अद्यापि नूनं ते प्रामाणिकाः । Even today they are honest.

(59) परश्वः (day after tomorrow) → रविवासरः परश्वः वर्तते । Sunday is day after tomorrow.

(60) परितः (around) → गृहं परितः वृक्षाः सन्ति । There are trees around the house.

(61) पुनः, भूयः, असकृत् (again) → शुभः अवसरः पुनः आगमिष्यति । Good time will come again.

(62) पुरा (before) → आसीत् पुरा रामः नाम राजा । In old days there was a king called Rāma.

(63) पृथक् (different) → रामः कृष्णात् पृथक् नास्ति । Rāma is not different from Kṛṇa.

(64) प्रातः (in the morning) → हरिः प्रातः स्मरणीयः । Rāma should be remembered in the morning.

(65) प्रायः, प्रायेण (mostly, usually) → द्राक्षाः प्रायः मधुराः । The grapes are usually sweet.

(66) मुहुर्मुहुः (again and again) → अहं तं मुहुःमुहुः स्मरामि । I remember him again and again.

(67) यतः (because) → अहं तत्र न गन्तुम् शक्नोमि यतः रुग्णः अस्मि । I can not go there because I am sick.

(68) युगपत् (together) → कष्टानि युगपत् एव आगच्छन्ति । The difficulties come all together.

(69) वरम् (better) → वरं प्राण: गच्छेत न कीर्ति: । Better the life goes, not the good name.

(70) सद्य: (the same day, immidiately, quickly) → सत्कर्मण: फलं सद्य: एव न प्राप्यते । Fruit of good deeds do not come immidiately.

(71) सम्यक् (properly) → सम्यक् विचिन्त्य करणीयम् । One should act after thinking properly.

(72) सहसा (suddenly) → सहसा क्रोधं मा करोतु भवान् । Do not get angry suddenly.

(73) स्थाने (righttly) → स्थाने तव दर्शनेन वयं तुष्याम: । Rightly we are delighted seeing you.

(74) हन्त (ok, alright) → हन्त! ते कथयिष्यामि । All right! I will tell you.

SOME CLASSICAL EXAMPLES :

(75) न कश्चित् अपि जानाति किं कस्य श्व: भविष्यति ।
अत: श्व: करणीयानि कुर्यात् अद्य एव बुद्धिमान् ।।80।।

(76) दिवा पश्यति न उलुक: काक: नक्तम् न पश्यति ।
विद्याविहीन: मूढ: तु दिवा नक्तम् न पश्यति ।।81।।

(77) यथा परोपकारेषु नित्यं जागर्ति सज्जन: ।
तथा परापकारेषु नित्यं जागर्ति दुर्जन: ।।82।।

(78) Thus ends the study of adverbs. इति क्रियाविशेषणानाम् अभ्यास: समाप्यते ।

EXERCISE 78 : Find the adverbial usages :

(for the simplification and meaning of the verses please see Appendix 9)

(1) यथा देश: तथा भाषा यथा राजा तथा प्रजा ।
यथा भूमि: तथा तोयं यथा बीजं तथा अंकुर: (भविष्यति) ।।83।।

(2) स्वभावो न उपदेशेन शक्यते कर्तुमन्यथा ।
सुतप्तम् अपि पानीयं पुनर्गच्छति शीतताम् ।।84।।

(3) क्षणश: कणश: च एव विद्याम् अर्थं च साधयेत् ।
क्षणत्यागे कुत: विद्या कणत्यागे कुत: धनम् ।।85।।

29.2

CONJUNCTIONS

yaugika-śabdāh यौगिकशब्दाः ।

Words like - and, or, but, for, if, that, where, either, neither, nor, still, till, only, else, after, before ...etc. make a connection or conjunction (*yogaḥ* योगः) between two parts of a sentence and, therefore, they are called CONJUNCTIONS (यौगिक-शब्दाः *yaugika-śabdāḥ*)

EXAMPLES cum EXERCISE : We have learned some of these words, let us learn new ones now.

1. Rāma AND Sunīl are brothers. *Rāmaḥ Sunīlaḥ ća bandhū staḥ.* रामः सुनीलः च बन्धू स्तः
2. Bring mango AND a knife. *āmram evaṁ ćhurikām ānayatu.* आम्रम् एवं छुरिकाम् आनयतु ।
3. He works day AND night. *saḥ divā naktaṁ ća kāryaṁ karoti.* सः दिवा नक्तं च कार्यं करोति
4. He AS WELL AS Neil were there. *saḥ tathaiva Neilaḥ tatra āstām.* सः तथैव नीलः तत्र आस्ताम् ।
5. Give me a mango OR a banana. *mahyam āmraṁ kadalīṁ vā dadātu.* मह्यं आम्रं कदलीं वा ददातु ।
6. Speak in Sanskrit OR English. *Saṁskṛtena athavā Englisha-bhāṣayā vadatu.* संस्कृतेन अथवा इंग्लिशभाषया वदतु ।
7. EITHER speak Sanskrit, OR speak English. *Saṁskṛtena vā Englisha-bhāṣayā vā vadatu.* संस्कृतेन वा इंग्लिश-भाषया वा वदतु ।
8. It is NEITHER good, NOR beautiful. *etat na śobhanaṁ na ća sundaram. etat na śobhanaṁ na vā sundaram.* एतत् न शोभनं न च सुन्दरम् । एतत् न शोभनं न वा सुन्दरम् ।
9. WHETHER he does it OR NOT, I will do it. *saḥ etat akariṣyat vā na akariṣyat, ahaṁ etat kariṣyāmi eva.* स एतत्करोतु न करिष्यत् वा न अकरिष्यत् अहम् एतत् करिष्यामि एव ।
10. I do not know WHETHER he is here OR there. *ahaṁ na jānāmi saḥ (api) atra asti*

tatra ut. aham̐ na jānāmi yat saḥ atra asti tatra vā. अहं न जानामि सः (अपि) अत्र अस्ति तत्र उत । अहं न जानामि यत् सः अत्र अस्ति तत्र वा ।

11. Sit down OR ELSE leave. *upaviśatu anyathā gaććhatu.* उपविशतु अन्यथा गच्छतु ।
12. Give me money if you have, OTHERWISE I am going. *yadi asti mahyam̐ dhanam̐ dadātu anyathā aham̐ gaććhāmi.* मह्यं धनं ददातु अन्यथा अहं गच्छामि । *dhanam asti ćet dadātu no ćet aham̐ gaććhāmi.* धनं अस्ति चेत् ददातु नो चेत् अहं गच्छामि ।
13. He told me THAT Sītā was not there. *saḥ mām uktavān yat Sītā tatra nāsti iti.* सः माम् उक्तवान् यत् सीता तत्र नास्ति इति ।
14. He is rich BUT he is not charitable. *saḥ dhanī asti kintu dānī nāsti.* सः धनी अस्ति किन्तु सः दानी नास्ति । Not only I told him, BUT I wrote him too. *na kevalam aham̐ tam uktavān aham̐ tam̐ likhitavān api.* न केवलम् अहं तम् उक्तवान् अहं तं लिखितवान् अपि ।
15. Run FROM 'a' TO 'b.' A-*taḥ* B-*patyantam̐ dhāvatu.* अ तः ब पर्यन्तम् धावतु ।
16. She is slow BUT will win. *sā mandagatiḥ param̐ jeṣyati.* सा मन्दगतिः परं जेष्यति ।
17. I have eaten, BUT I am still hungry. *aham̐ khāditavān tathāpi kṣudhitaḥ asmi.* अहं खादितवान् तथापि क्षुधितः अस्मि ।
18. Even though he is in pain, YET he is quiet. *yadyapi saḥ dukhitaḥ asti tathāpi saḥ śāntaḥ asti.* यद्यपि सः दुःखितः अस्ति तथापि सः शान्तः अस्ति ।
19. ALTHOUGH he did not ask, I gave him money. *yadyapi saḥ na yāćitavān, aham̐ tasmai ḍālarān/rūpyakāṇi/mudrāḥ dattavān.* यद्यपि सः न याचितवान् अहं तस्मै डालरान्/रूप्यकाणि/मुद्राः दत्तवान् ।
20. IN SPITE OF what I said, (s)he did not do that. *yadyapi aham uktavān, saḥ tat na kṛtavān (sā tat na kṛtavatī).* यद्यपि अहम् उक्तवान्, सः तत् न कृतवान् (सा तत् न कृतवती) ।
21. Notice was posted IN ORDER THAT everyone might be aware. *sūćanā-patram̐ sthāpitam āsīt yena sarve api sāvadhānāḥ syuḥ.* सूचनापत्रं स्थापितम् आसीत् येन सर्वे अपि सावधानाः स्युः ।
22. AS SOON AS the bell rang, I went inside. *yāvat ghaṇṭā nāditavatī, tāvat aham*

abhyantare gatavān/gatavati. यावत् घण्टा नादितवती तावत् अहम् अभ्यन्तरे गतवान्/गतवती ।

23. He is walking AS THOUGH he is lame. *saḥ paṅguḥ iva ćalati.* सः पंगुः इव चलति ।

24. He was alright, EXCEPT that he was tired. *saḥ svasthaḥ paraṁ klāntaḥ āsīt.* सः स्वस्थः परं क्लान्तः आसीत् ।

25. Something certainly fell down, FOR I heard the noise. *kim-api niśćitaṁ patitaṁ yataḥ ahaṁ śabdaṁ/dhvaniṁ śrutavān.* किमपि निश्चितं पतितं यतः अहं शब्दं/ध्वनिं श्रुतवान् ।

26. He sat down BECAUSE he was tired. *saḥ upāviśat yatah saḥ klāntaḥ āsīt.* सः उपाविशत् यतः सः क्लान्तः आसीत् ।

27. WHEN I was young, I used to work very hard. *yadā ahaṁ taruṇaḥ āsam tadā ahaṁ praćuraṁ karma karomi sma.* यदा अहं तरुणः आसं तदा अहं प्रचुरं कर्म करोमि स्म ।

28. His watch is WHERE he had kept it. *tasya ghaṭikā tatra eva asti yatra tena sthāpitā āsīt.* तस्य घटिका तत्र एव अस्ति यत्र तेन स्थापिता आसीत् ।

29. Let us give charity, WHILE we have money. *yāvat dhanam asti tāvat dānaṁ kuryāma.* यावत् धनम् अस्ति तावत् दानं कुर्याम ।

30. WHENEVER I see him, he becomes happy. *yadā yadā hi ahaṁ taṁ paśyāmi saḥ ānanditaḥ bhavati.* यदा यदा हि अहं तं पश्यामि सः आनन्दितः भवति । WHEREVER the rain falls, the water goes to the ocean. *yatra yatra eva vṛṣṭiḥ bhavati, tataḥ tataḥ jalaṁ sāgaraṁ prati eva gaććhati.* यत्र यत्र एव वृष्टिः भवति ततः ततः जलं सागरं प्रति एव गच्छति ।

31. Rāma is taller THAN Hari. *Rāmaḥ hareḥ apekṣayā unnataḥ.* रामः हरेः अपेक्षया उन्नतः ।

32. He said yes, THEREFORE I went there. *saḥ ām uktavān tasmāt ahaṁ tatra gatavān.* सः आम् उक्तवान् तस्मात् अहं तत्र गतवान् ।

EXERCISE 79 : Fill in the blanks with suitable Sanskrit conjunctions.

(1) Mangos AND Bananas are fruits. आम्राणि ——————— कदलीफलानि फलानि सन्ति ।

(2) Give me paper AND a pencil. मह्यं पत्रं लेखनीं/वार्तिकां ——————— देहि/ददातु ।

(3) He buys and sells books. स: पुस्तकानि क्रीणाति ———— विक्रीणाति ———

(4) Give me a pen AS WELL AS paper. मह्यं लेखनीं ——— पत्रकं देहि ।

(5) Pay the fine OR go to jail. दण्डधनं ददातु ——— कारागृहं गच्छतु ।

(6) Come by bus OR car. बसयानेन कारयानेन ——— आगच्छतु ।

(7) It is NEITHER bad, NOR good. एतत् ——— अभद्रं ——— भद्रम् अस्ति ।

(8) He said THAT it is difficult. स: उक्तवान् ——— एतत् कठिनम् अस्ति ।

(9) Eat it OR ELSE stay hungry. एतत् खादतु ——— क्षुधित: तिष्ठतु ।

(10) Take an umbrella, OTHERWISE you will get wet. छत्रं नयतु ——— भवान् क्लेदिष्यति ।

(11) I told her BUT she did not listen. अहं तम् उक्तवान् ——— स: न श्रुतवान् ।

(12) It is thin BUT strong. एतत् श्लक्ष्णं ——— दृढम् अस्ति ।

(13) He does not like it, YET he is quiet. एतत् तस्मै न रोचते ——— स: किमपि न वदति ।

(14) ALTHOUGH he did ask, I did not give it to him. ——— स: याचितवान् अहं तस्मै न दत्तवान् ।

(15) THOUGH he did pay, he did not take the thing. —— स: रूप्यकाणि दत्तवान् स: वस्तुं न नीतवान् ।

(16) The milk was boiled IN ORDER THAT it may not get spoiled.
दुग्धम् उष्णीकृतम् आसीत् ——— तत् न नश्येत् ।

(17) AS SOON AS the door opened, the dog got out. ——— द्वारम् अपावृतं ——— कुकुर: बहिर्गतवान् ।

(18) He walked slowly AS THOUGH he was a turtle. स: शनै:शनै: कूर्म: —— चलति स्म ।

(19) I do not trust you, FOR you are stupid. अहं त्वयि विश्वासं न करोमि ——— त्वं मूर्ख: असि ।

(20) I did not go there, BECAUSE I forgot. अहं तत्र न गतवान् ——— अहं विस्मृतवान् ।

(21) WHEN your letter came, I was already gone. ——— भवत: पत्रम् आगतम् अहं गतवान् आसम् ।

(22) My office is THERE, WHERE your old house was.
मम कार्यालय: ——— अस्ति ——— तव पुरातनं गृहम् आसीत् ।

(23) WHILE he was sick, I was there. ——— स: रुग्ण: आसीत् ——— अहं ——— ——— आसम् ।

(24) WHENEVER I win, he becomes happy. ——— ——— अहं जयामि स: आनन्दित: भवति ।

(25) WHEREVER God is worshipped, only Krishna gets worshipped.
——— ——— ईश्वर: पूज्यते केवलं कृष्ण: एव पूजित: भवति ।

(26) Grapes were sweet, THEREFORE, I ate them. द्राक्षा: मधुरा: आसन् ——— अहं ता: खादितवान् ।

LESSON 30

trimśaḥ abhyāsaḥ त्रिंशः अभ्यासः ।

THE PREPOSITIONS

aupasargika-śabdāḥ औपसर्गिकशब्दाः ।

The Prepositional Prefixes

upasargāḥ उपसर्गाः ।

The preposition (उपसर्गः *upasargaḥ*) is an indeclinable word (*avyayam* अव्ययम्), prefixed to a verb (*kriyāpadam* क्रियापदम्) or its derivative (*sādhita-śabdaḥ* साधित-शब्दः). It can be seen that the 22 prepositional prefixes listed by Pāṇini and Varadāćārya do intensify, modify, alter, change or make no change in the sense of the root verb.

उपसर्गेण धात्वर्थो बलादन्यत्र नीयते । प्रहाराहारसंहारविहारपरिहारवत् ।।
धात्वर्थं बाधते कश्चित्कश्चित्तमनुवर्तते । तमेव विशिनष्ट्यन्यः उपसर्गगतिस्त्रिधा ।।

(1) *ati* (अति) over, beyond. (i) क्रमः a step, pace → अतिक्रमः aransgression. (ii) रिक्त empty → अतिरिक्त remaining; supreme.

(2) *adhi* (अधि) power, right. (i) कारः causer → अधिकारः the right, power. (ii) क्षिपः casting away → अधिक्षेपः censure.

(3) *anu* (अनु) along, after, behind; each, every. (i) कम्पः shaking, a tremor → अनुकम्पा compassion. (ii) √कृ to do → अनुकृतिः imitation.

(4) *antar* (अन्तर्) with interval, within, inner. (i) यामः restraint, control → अन्तर्यामः inner control. (ii) धानम् a seat → अन्तर्धानम् disappearance.

(5) *apa* (अप) away, away from. (i) शकुनम् a good omen → अपशकुनम् a bad omen. (ii) कारः

doer, causer → अपकारः Harm.

(6) *api* (अपि) also; over, near, near to; indeed, also. (i) अयनम् entrance → अप्ययनम् junction, union. (ii) हितम् benefit → अपिहितम् openly, visibly.

(7) *abhi* (अभि) towards, near. (i) मुखम् mouth, face → अभिमुखम् In front of. (ii) मानः pride → अभिमानः ego, self-pride.

(8) *ava* (अव) away, off, down. (i) √स्था to stay → अवस्था condition, state. (ii) गुणः quality, character → अवगुणः a bad quality

(9) *ā* (आ) up to, towards, from, around; a little. (i) गमनम् going → आगमनम् coming. (ii) जन्म birth → आजन्म from the birth.

(10) prefixes *ut, ud* (उत्, उद्) over, superior, higher; facing. (i) √स्था to stay → उत्थानम् Getting up, rising. (ii) भवः Existence → उद्भवः Birth.

(11) *upa* (उप) secondary; towards, near to, by the side of. (i) √विश् to enter → उपविश to sit. (ii) √स्था to stay → उपस्थम् the middle part.

(12) *dur, dus,* (दुर्, दुस्) hard to do, difficult. (i) √लभ् to get, obtain → दुर्लभम् difficult to attain. (ii) बुद्धिः mind → दुर्बुद्धिः malignity, evil mind.

(13) *ni* (नि) in, into; great; opposed to, without. (i) बन्धः A bond, tie → निबन्धः an essay. (ii) दानम् a gift, giving → निदानम् a cause, diagnosis.

(14) *nir* (निर्) out of, away from, without, ◦less, un◦ (i) मलम् dirt → निर्मलम् a clean thing.

(15) *nis* (निस्) out of, away from, without, ◦less, un◦ (ii) √चल् to move → निश्चलम् steady.

(16) *parā* (परा) away, back, opposed to. (i) क्रमः a step, pace → पराक्रमः bravery. (ii) भवः existence → पराभवः Defeat.

(17) *pari* (परि) about, around. (i) भाषा language → परिभाषा definition. (ii) नाम name → परिणामः effect, result.

(18) *pra* (प्र) good, opposite, excess, progress. (i) कृतिः action, doing → प्रकृतिः nature. (ii) वदनम् mouth → प्रवदनम् announcement.

(19) *prati* (प्रति) towards, back, in return, in opposition; each. (i) √ज्ञा to know → प्रतिज्ञा vow.

(ii) दिनम् day → प्रतिदिनम् every day.

(20) *vi* (वि) reverse of, apart, separate from. (i) कृतिः action, doing → विकृतिः disorder. (ii) क्रमः a step, pace → विक्रमः bravery.

(21) *sam* (सम्) together with, full, excellent. (i) बन्धः A bond, tie → सम्बन्धः relationship. (ii) योगः union → संयोगः bondage.

(22) *su* (सु) very, good, well, easily; thorough. (i) रूपम् Form → सुरूपम् beauty. (ii) कृतम् done → सुकृतम् done well.

NOTE : For the affixes that are suffixed to root verbs and substantives, see Lesson 37.

EXERCISE 80 : Find the prefixes in the following words :

(1) अतिसारः, अधिक्षेपः, अनुक्रमणम्, अनुचराः ।

(2) अन्तर्यामी, अपहारः, उपहारः, अपकारः, उपकारः ।

(3) अपिधानम्, अभिरुचिः, अभिरामः, अवमानः ।

(4) अवतारः, अवसादः, आकाशः, आकारः, उद्यमः, उत्सर्गः ।

(5) उद्गमः, उपस्थानम्, उपगमः, दुराचारः, दुस्सहः ।

(6) निकेतम्, निश्चयः, निर्दोषः ।

(7) पराजयः, प्रतिकारः, प्रतिबिम्बम् ।

(8) विक्रयः, विशेषः, विकारः ।

(9) संस्कारः, सङ्गमः, सुभाषितम्, सुकृतम् ।

More Examples : उपसर्गयुक्ताः शब्दाः ।

(1) अति (beyond, over) → अतिशय, अतिक्रमः

(2) अधि (over, above) → अधिकारः, अधिपतिः, अधिवासः

(3) अनु (after, behind, following) → अनुकम्पा, अनुक्रमः, अनुरक्त, अनुक्रमणम्, अनुकृतिः

(4) अप (away, away from; wrong; harm) → अपमानः, अपशकुनः, अपहरणम्

(5) अपि (near to, over) → अपिधानम्, अप्यय:

(6) अभि (near, towards) → अभिनन्दनम्, अभिमान:, अभ्यास:

(7) अव (away, down, off, disrespect) → अवगुण:, अवतार:, अवमान:, अवस्था, अवज्ञा

(8) आ (up to, towards, all around) → आकार:, आजन्म, आमरणम्

(9) उत्, उद् (upon, up to) → उद्भव:, उद्गम:, उद्धार:, उद्यम:, उत्सर्ग:

(10) उप (towards, near to, by the side of) → उपकार:, उपचार:, उपदेश:

(11) दुर् (bad, difficult, hard to be done) → दुर्गम, दुर्बुद्धि:, दुर्बोध:, दुर्मुख, दुर्लभ

(12) दुस् (improper, bad) → दुष्कर, दुष्कृत्यम्, दुष्परिणाम:, दुस्सह

(13) नि (in, into; insult, without, opposed to) → निग्रह:, नियम:, नियुक्त, निचय:, निदेश:

(14) निर् (away, without, out) → निर्गत, निरीक्षणम्, निर्देश:

(15) निस् (without) → निषेध:, निष्पाप, निश्चल, निश्चित्

(16) परा (away, back, opposed to, reject, despise) → पराक्रम:, पराजय:, पराभव:

(17) परि (about, around) → परिक्रमा, परिग्रह:, परित्याग:, परिवर्तनम्

(18) प्र (more, opposite) → प्रकाश:, प्रकृति:, प्रणाम:, प्रबुद्ध, प्रमाणम्, प्रयोग:, प्रवेश:, प्रज्ञा

(19) प्रति (towards, back, in return, opposite) → प्रतिकूल, प्रत्यक्ष, प्रतिज्ञा, प्रतिकार:

(20) वि (opposite, apart) → विचलित, विजय:

(21) सम् (together, full, be united, perfection) → संग्रह:, समक्ष, संयोग:, संस्कृति:

(22) सु (good, well, thorough) → सुकृतम्, सुगम, सुबोध, सुहृद्

EXERCISE 81 : Identify the prefixes in the following words:

सुशिक्षित: प्रहार: संहार: विहार: आहार: उद्योग: आभास: अपघात: सन्तोष: प्रचार: अनुचर: पराक्रमम् प्रबलम् प्रख्यात: दुश्चरित्रम् विशेषम् उत्कर्ष: अभिलाषा उत्कण्ठा उत्तमम् अटला अधोगति: विमल अमृतम् प्रत्युपकार: उपसर्ग: अतीव अतीत: आघात: दुर्दैवम् दुर्गति: दुरुपयोग: दुस्तरम् परित्राणम् परिच्छेद: विक्षेप: विपरीतम् व्यवस्थिता वियोग: आचरणम् अभेद्यम् आजीवनम् अहिंसा समाचरत् अनुभव: प्रतिजानामि प्रतिगच्छति उपसङ्गम्य प्राप्स्यसि अवाप्स्यसि विरमति विसरति परिहार: अनुवर्तते उपपदम् विस्मृति: ।

LESSON 31

ektrimśaḥ abhyāsaḥ एकत्रिंशः अभ्यासः ।

COMPOUND WORDS

sāmāsāḥ समासाः ।

When TWO or MORE related words compounded together with a **logical defination** to form a single MEANINGFUL word, forms a *sāmāsik-śabdaḥ* (सामासिकशब्दः compound word). अनेकपदानाम् तार्किकम् एकीभवनं समासः ।

On the other hand, when TWO words are joined together purely with grammatical rules, to form a single word, it is called a *sandhi* (सन्धिः) betweeb two words.

The word *samāsa* comes from ←ind◦ *sam* (सम् equal, even) + par◦ 4√*as* (√अस् to be, unite, aggregate, combine, join, connect, compound). समसनं समासः ।

Eight main *samāsas* are briefly explained below, with examples from the Gītā.

A *samāsa* can be formed in five ways. कृत्तद्धितसमासैकशेषसनाद्यन्तधातवः पञ्च वृत्तयः ।

(1) By adding suffix to a verbal root;

(2) By attaching suffix to a noun stem;

(3) By joining simpler noun stems into a single word;

(4) By merging two or more nouns with a single stem;

(5) By adding desiderative or other affixes to roots.

NOTE : Before forming a *samasa* between two (or more) words, the words being compounded should generally be first rendered in their original forms, removing the case, gender, number or any other suffixes attached to them. The case, gender, number or any other suffixes are added to the compound word, after forming a *samasa.*

SAMASA CLASSIFICATION

(A) विशेष-समासः (तत्पुरुष-बहुव्रीहि-द्वंद्व-अव्ययीभावादिसंज्ञायुक्तः विशेष-समासः)

(i) तत्पुरुष-समासः (प्रायः उत्तरपदप्रधानः तत्पुरुष-समासः)

(a) सामान्य-समासः (सामान्यरूपेण पदयोः मध्ये विभक्तेः सम्बन्धः)

(1) प्रथमा-तत्पुरुष-समासः (सर्वे आरम्भाः, सर्वारम्भाः Gītā 12.16)

(2) द्वितीया-तत्पुरुष-समासः (मद्भावम् आगताः, मद्भावमागताः Gītā 4.10)

(3) तृतीया-तत्पुरुष-समासः (योगेन युक्तः, योगयुक्तः Gītā 5.6)

(4) चतुर्थी-तत्पुरुष-समासः (मोक्षाय परायणः, मोक्षपरायणः Gītā 5.28)

(5) पंचमी-तत्पुरुष-समासः (योगात् भ्रष्टः, योगभ्रष्टः Gītā 6.41)

(6) षष्ठीत-त्पुरुष-समासः (धर्मयुक्त-कर्मणां क्षेत्रम्, धर्मक्षेत्रम् Gītā 1.1)

(7) सप्तमी-तत्पुरुष-समासः (योगे स्थः, योगस्थः Gītā 2.48)

(b) कर्मधारय-समासः (समानाधिकरणः तत्पुरुषः कर्मधारय-समासः)

(1) विशेषण-पूर्वपद-कर्मधारय-समासः (महान् इष्वासाः, महेष्वासाः Gītā 1.4)

(2) विशेषणोत्तरपद-कर्मधारय-समासः (रथेषु उत्तमम्, रथोत्तमम् Gītā 1.24)

(3) विशेषणोभयपद-कर्मधारय-समासः (आगमाः अपायिनः, आगमापायिनः Gītā 2.14)

(4) उपमान-पूर्वपद-कर्मधारय-समासः (सिंहस्य इव नादम्, सिंहनादम् Gītā 1.12)

(5) उपमानोत्तरपद-कर्मधारय-समासः (नरः पुङ्गवः इव, नरपुङ्गवः Gītā 1.5)

(6) अवधारणा-पूर्वपद-कर्मधारय-समासः (ज्ञानम् एव असि, ज्ञानासिना Gītā 4.42)

(7) सम्भावना-पूर्वपद-कर्मधारय-समासः (संसार इव सागरः, संसारसागरात् Gītā 12.7)

(8) मध्यमपद-लोप-कर्मधारय-समासः (सत्त्वेन आत्मनः संशुद्धिः, सत्त्वसंशुद्धिः Gītā16.1)

(9) मयूरव्यंसकादि-कर्मधारय-समासः (निवृत्तो निरुद्धो वा वातो यस्मात्, निवात Gītā 6.19)

(c) द्विगु-समासः (सांख्यवाचकेन सुबन्तेन समस्यमानः द्विगु-समासः)

(1) समाहार-द्विगु-समासः (त्रयाणां विधानां समाहारः, त्रिविध Gītā 16.21)

(2) तद्धितर्थ-द्विगु-समासः (त्रिगुणेषु उत्पन्नानां विषयाः, त्रैगुण्यविषयाः Gītā 2.45)

(3) उत्तरपद-द्विगु-समासः (लोकानां त्रयम्, लोकत्रयम् Gītā 11.20)

(d) नञ्-तत्पुरुष-समासः (न धर्मः, अधर्मः Gītā 1.40)

(ii) बहुव्रीहि-समासः (अन्यपदप्रधानः बहुव्रीहि समासः)

(a) सामान्य-बहुव्रीहि-समासः (सामान्यरूपेण पदयोः मध्ये विभक्तेः सम्बन्धः)

(1) द्वितीया-बहुव्रीहि-समासः (दुःखं च सुखंच समं यं सः, समदुःखसुखम् Gītā 2.15)

(2) तृतीया-बहुव्रीहि-समासः (जितानि इन्द्रियाणि येन सः, जितेन्द्रियः Gītā 5.7)

(3) चतुर्थी-बहुव्रीहि-समासः (मया आश्रयः दत्तः यस्मै सः, मद्व्यपाश्रयः Gītā 18.56)

(4) पञ्चमी-बहुव्रीहि-समासः (गतः रसः यस्मात् तत्, गतरसम् Gītā 17.10)

(5) षष्ठी-बहुव्रीहि-समासः (महान् आत्मा यस्य सः, महात्मा Gītā 7.19)

(6) सप्तमी-बहुव्रीहि-समासः (नास्ति श्रद्धा यस्मिन् तत्, श्रद्धाविरहितम् Gītā 17.13)

(b) विशेष-बहुव्रीहि-समासः (विशेषरूपेण पदयोः मध्ये सम्बन्धः)

(1) व्यधिकरण-बहुव्रीहि-समासः (पाणिषु शस्त्राणि यस्याम् ते, शस्त्रपाणयः Gītā 1.46)

(2) संख्योत्तरपद-बहुव्रीहि-समासः (मनः षष्ठं येषाम् तानि, मनःषष्ठानि Gītā 15.7)

(3) संख्योभयपद-बहुव्रीहि-समासः (द्वे वा त्रिणि वा यस्य, द्वित्राणि)

(4) सह-बहुव्रीहि-समासः (गद्गदेन सह, सगद्गदम् Gītā 11.35)

(5) नञ्-बहुव्रीहि-समासः (न भवति च्युतः यः, अच्युत Gītā 1.21)

(iii) द्वंद्व-समास (उभयपदप्रधानः द्वंद्व-समासः)

(a) इतरेतर-द्वंद्व-समासः (पदयोः वा पदानां वा समाहारः)

(1) द्विपद-द्वंद्व-समासः (सुघोषः च मणिपुष्पकः च, सुघोषमणिपुष्पकौ Gītā 1.16)

(2) बहुपद-द्वंद्व-समासः (पणवाः आनकाः गोमुखाः च, पणवानकगोमुखाः Gītā 1.13)

(b) समाहार-द्वंद्व-समासः (संज्ञानां वा परिभाषाणां वा समाहारः)

(1) समाहार-द्वंद्व-समासः (गुणानां च कर्मणां च समाहारः तेषु, गुणकर्मसु Gītā 13.14)

(1) नित्यसमाहार-द्वंद्व-समासः (पाणीनां पादानां समाहारः, पाणिपादम् Gītā 13.14)

(iv) अव्ययीभाव-तत्पुरुष-समासः (अव्ययेन सुबन्तेन समस्यमानः अव्ययीभाव-समासः)

(1) अव्ययपूर्वपद-तत्पुरुष-समासः (भागम् यथा, यथाभागम्, Gītā 1.11)

(2) अव्ययोत्तरपद-अव्ययीभाव-समासः (सहस्त्रं वारम्, सहस्त्रकृत्वः Gītā 11.39)

(B) केवल-समासः (तत्पुरुष-बहुव्रीहि-द्वंद्व-अव्ययीभावादिसंज्ञाविनिमुक्तः केवल-समासः ।)

(1) अलुक-समासः (युधि स्थिरः, युधिष्ठिरः, Gītā 1.16)

(2) प्रादि-समासः (प्रभावः Gītā 11.43)

(7) उपपद-समासः (उपपदं नाम काचन संज्ञा, मम यजी, मद्याजी Gītā 9.34)

SAMASA - GENERAL RULES

परस्परान्वितयोः सुबन्तयोः समासः भवति । प्रायः तिङ्तानां समासः न भवति ।

1. **Tatpuruṣa samāsa** (tat◦ तत्पुरुष–समासः), the Determinative or Dependent Compound : In this *samāsa*, the last component-word is primary (प्रधानः) and the other words are secondary (गौणाः). Therefore, the case, number and gender of the last word dictate the case, number and gender of the entire composite word. (परस्य यल्लिङ्गं तद्भवति द्वंद्वस्य तत्पुरुषस्य च - pāṇini, *aṣṭādhyāyī* 2: 4.26).

e.g. *dharmakṣetre* धर्मक्षेत्रे n◦ loc◦ sing◦ *dharmasya kṣetre* धर्मस्य क्षेत्रे on sacred land. (Gītā 1.1)
dharma-mayam धर्ममयम् (the sacred, righteous) pos◦ sing◦ ←m◦ *dharma* धर्म (righteousness) *kṣetre* क्षेत्रे (on the land) loc◦ sing◦ ←n◦ *kṣetr* (the field).

(i) Generally, the compound words of which last component is a Past Passive Participle, such as *gata, mṛta, atíta, sthita, rata, āsakta, prāpta, mukta, stha, ja, tulya, pūrva,* etc., come under *tatpuruṣa-samāsa.*

(ii) The *karmadhāraya* and *dvigu samāsas* are subdivisions of the *tatpuruṣa-samāsa.*

2. **Bahuvrīhi samāsa** (bah◦ बहुव्रीहि–समासः), the Attributive or Relative Compound : In this *samāsa*, any one component is not primary. The whole compound word is an epithet (adjective) of an element outside of the compound itself. (अन्यपदप्रधानः बहुव्रीहिः । अन्यपदार्थे बहुव्रीहिः । pāṇini, 2: 2: 24).

Bhīmārjaunasamāḥ भीमार्जुनसमाः nom◦ pl◦ ←adj◦ *bhīmārjaunasama, bhīmasya arjaunasya vā samaḥ yaḥ saḥ* भीमार्जुनसम, भीमस्य अर्जुनस्य वा समः यः सः । (he who is equal to *bhīma* or *arjauna*). The adjective in this *samāsa* is an epithet of some third person, (other than *bhīma* and *arjauna*), who is not mentioned in the *samāsa.*

3. **Dvandva samāsa** (dvan◦ द्वन्द्व-समासः), the Dual or Aggregative Compound : In this *samāsa*, all component words have equal importance and they are connected together with an ind◦ copulative conjunction *ća* च (and). Though this *samāsa* is a simple aggregation of individual nouns, the case, number and gender of the whole *samāsa* is usually attached to the last element only (similar to tat◦), keeping the rest in stem form. (परवत्-लिङ्गं द्वन्द्व-तत्पुरुषयोः pāṇini, 2: 4.26) This *samasa* must always consist of words which, if uncompounded, will have same case-declensions. e.g. *paṇavānakagomukhā:* पणवानकगोमुखाः (Gītā 1.13) ←*paṇavāḥ ća ānakāḥ ća gomukhāḥ ća* पणवाः च आनकाः च गोमुखाः च *(paṇavas and anakas and gomukhas)* ←m◦ *paṇava* पणव (cymbal) + m◦ *ānaka* आनक (drum) + *gomukha* गोमुख (horn).

(i) As there are always two or more individual word elements in this *samāsa*, it is usually in dual or plural form. However, when it denotes a single collective noun, it is in singular neuter gender.

(ii) When more than two singular words are aggregated together, only the last element is pluraled and the compound word then assumes the gender of the last element. e.g. *harṣāmarṣabhayodvegaiḥ,* हर्षामर्षभयोद्वेगैः Instrumental case, (*harṣeṇa ća āmarṣeṇa ća bhayena ća udvegena ća* हर्षेण च आमर्षेण च भयेन च उद्वेगेन च). However, in a plural *dvanva* word, each individual element could be plural too, but not necessarily..
e.g. *kaṭvamlalavaṇātyuṣṇatīkṣṇarūkṣavidāhinaḥ* कट्वम्ललवणात्युष्णतीक्ष्णरूक्षविदाहिनः । *kaṭvaḥ ća amlāḥ ća lavaṇāḥ ća atyuṣṇāḥ ća tīkṣṇāḥ ća rūkṣāḥ ća vidāhinaḥ ća* कट्वः च अम्लाः च लवणाः च अति-उष्णाः च तीक्ष्णाः च रूक्षाः च विदाहिनः च । (Gītā 17.9)

(iii) When words are aggregated, the इकारान्त, ईकारान्त word should be kept first, the rest anywhere. eg. हरि: and चन्द्र: हरिश्चन्द्र, not चन्द्रहरि: । When there are many इकारान्त words, at least one इकारान्त word kept first, the rest anywhere. e.g. राम: हरि: गुरु: हरिगुरुरामा: । Generally, the words starting with any vowel, and ending with vowel अ should be kept first. eg. इन्दु: इन्द्र: वायु: अग्नि:, इन्द्र: इन्दु: अग्नि: वायु: = इन्द्विन्द्रग्निवायव: । The word that has less characters should come first. हरि: केशव:, हरिकेशवौ । Normally, the **feminine name** should come first then masculine name. e.g. सीतारामौ, राधाकृष्णौ ।

4. **Dvigu samāsa** (द्विगु-समास:), the Numeral or Collective Compound (dvigu◦) : In this *samāsa*, the first element is a numerical adjective (संख्या-विशेषणम्) and the entire compound word is a singular collective noun. (द्विगुरेकवचनम् । pāṇini, *aṣṭādhyāyī* 2: 4.1)

e.g. *navadvāra* नवद्वार (the aggregate of nine gates) ←num◦ adj◦ *nava* (nine) + m◦ *dvāra* (gate) Gītā 5.13. Note: This *samāsa* is always in singular number collective noun.

5. **Karmadhāraya samāsa** (कर्मधारय-समास:), Appositional Compound (kar◦) : In this *samāsa*, usually there are two component words and they are always in Nominative (1st) case. The first element is a usually an adjective (विशेषणम्) and the second word is a substantive (विशेष्यम्). Sometimes there are three words, where the middle word physically does not exist but is only understood. eg. *svabhāva* स्वभाव (the inherent nature) ←adj◦ *sva* स्व (inherent) + substantive *bhāva* भाव (nature)

6. **prādi samāsa** (प्रादि-समास:) : If the first word is an adjective-prefix indicating such meanings as- much, extreme, more, improper, opposite, etc. (प्र-, अति-, उद्-, अधि, अनु, अव-, नि:-, वि, परि-, e.g. प्रगत, अत्यन्त, उद्गत, अधिक, अनुचित, अवक्रुष्ट, निर्गत, विपरीत, परिक्लान्त) then the *samasa* is known It is also used to express an opposite

circumstance, e.g. prefix adj∘ *vi* वि (opposite) + substantive *sama* सम (normal circumstance) (Gītā 2.2)

As said earlier, the *dvigu samāsa* and the *karmadhāraya samāsa* are subdivisions of the *tatpuruṣa-samāsa* (द्विगुकर्मधारयौ तत्पुरुषभेदौ).

7. **Avyayībhāva samāsa** (अव्ययीभाव-समासः) Adverbial Compound : In this *samāsa*, the first word is indeclinable, it is the primary term, and the whole compound word is an indeclinable adverb. (अनव्ययम् अव्ययं भवति). Sometimes, however, the first word is a noun-stem and the last word is indeclinable. e.g. in∘ *yathābhāgam* यथाभागम् (as appointed) ←in∘ *yathā* यथा (as) + m∘ *bhāgam* भागम् (appointment).

Note: (नञ्-समासः) A word with the negative prefix *nañ* नञ् is not an *ayayibhāva.* It forms negative-tat∘ *samāsa* (e.g. *aparyāpta*) or negative-bah∘ *samāsa* (e.g. *aćyuta*).

8. **Aluk samāsa** (अलुक्समासः) In this *samāsa*, the case-affixes (विभक्तिप्रत्ययाः) of the member words are not dropped, they remain intact in the compound word.

e.g. *yudhisṭhiraḥ* युधिष्ठिरः ←*yudhi* युधि + *sthiraḥ* स्थिरः ←locative of noun *yudh* (in the battle) + nom∘ adj∘ *shtiraḥ* (stable). युधिष्ठिरः ←युधि + स्थिरः ←युध् सप्तमी + वि∘ स्थिरः

THUS, (mostly) पूर्वपदार्थप्रधानोऽव्ययीभावः उत्तरपदार्थप्रधानस्तत्पुरुषः ।
अन्यपदार्थप्रधानो बहुव्रीहिः उभयपदार्थप्रधानो द्वंद्वः ।।86।।

(i) In an Avayībhāva samāsa (अव्ययीभाव समासः), its first member is dominant; in a Tatpuruṣa samāsa (तत्पुरुषसमासः), its last member is dominant.

(ii) In Bahuvrīhi samāsa (बहुव्रीहिसमासः) no single word is dominating. It points to a thing different from the individual meanings of any of its component members.

(iii) In a Dvandva samāsa (द्वंद्वसमासः), all words are equally dominating, and the meanings of all its members are have same importance.

WHAT WE LEARNED SO FAR

EXERCISE 82 :

Following sentences are in various tenses, moods and cases. Translate the English sentences into Sanskrit.

Compare tem with the corresponding 100 sentences given in Exercise 44. √Root Verbs are shown in brackets. For your help, Answers are given in *italic transliteration* and in Devanāgarī (देवनागरी) Sanskrit.

(1) Rāma writes letters. *Rāmḥ patrāṇi likhati (√likh).* रामः पत्राणि लिखति ।

Rāma wrote letters. *Rāmḥ patrāṇi alikhat/likhitavān.* रामः पत्राणि अलिखत्/लिखितवान्

(2) The ants are walking. *pipīlikāḥ ćalanti (√ćal).* पिपीलिकाः चलन्ति (चलन्त्यः सन्ति) ।

(3) She will eat apples. *sā ātāphalāni/sevāni khādiṣyati (√khā).* सा आताफलानि/सेवानि खादिष्यति ।

(4) They worshiped Krishna. *te kṛṣṇam ārćan/arćitavantaḥ. (√arć).* ते कृष्णम् आर्चन्/अर्चितवन्तः ।

(5) Rītā was throwing a ball. *Rītā kandukaṁ kṣipati sma (√kṣip).* रीता कन्दुकं क्षिपति स्म ।

(6) The cart is brought by Viśāl. *Viśālena yānam ānītaṁ (ā√nī).* विशालेन यानम् आनीतम् ।

(7) Yes, Rānī will cut the beans. *ām! Ranī simbāḥ kartiṣyati.* आम्! रानी सिम्बाः कर्तिष्यति ।

(8) The bears run <u>freely</u> in the forest. *bhallāḥ/bhallukāḥ vane svairaṁ dhāvanti*

(√dhāv). भल्लाः/भल्लुकाः वने स्वैरं धावन्ति । (स्वैरम् = freely)

(9) They must not kill the dog. *taiḥ kukkuraḥ/bhaṣakaḥ/śunakaḥ/śvānaḥ na hantavyaḥ (√han).* तैः कुक्कुरः/भषकः/शुनकः/श्वान न हन्तव्यः ।

(10) He may steal the money. *kadāćit saḥ mudrāḥ/dhanaṁ ćorayet (√ćur).* कदाचित् सः मुद्राः/धनं चोरयेत् ।

(11) The black bird flew to the nest. *kṛṣṇaḥ khagaḥ/ćaṭakaḥ/pakṣī/vihaṅgaḥ nīḍam aḍayata (√ḍī).* कृष्णः खगः/चटकः/पक्षी/विहङ्गः नीडम् अडयत ।

(12) The barber works in his shop. *nāpitaḥ tasya āpaṇe/kartanālaye kāryam karoti (karma√kṛ).* नापितः तस्य आपणे/कर्तनालये कार्यं करोति ।

(13) Gopāl will come here to wash his hands. *Gopālḥ tasya hastau kṣālayitum atra āgamiṣyati (√kṣal).* गोपालः तस्य हस्तौ क्षालयितुम् अत्र आगमिष्यति ।

(14) Ramesh should burn the dry grass in the fields. *Rameshaḥ kṣetreṣu śuṣkaṁ ghāsaṁ dahet (√dah).* रमेशः क्षेत्रेषु शुष्कं घासं दहेत् ।

(15) The dry branch should not fall on your head. *śuṣkā śākhā bhavataḥ śirasi na patet (√pat).* शुष्का शाखा भवतः शिरसि न पतेत् ।

(16) When the time comes you will not stay here. *yadā samayaḥ āgamiṣyati/bhaviṣyati bhavān atra na sthāsyati (ā√gam, √bhū).* यदा समयः आगमिष्यति/भविष्यति भवान् अत्र न स्थास्यति ।

(17) The animals should roam freely. *jantavaḥ/jīvāḥ/prāṇinaḥ/paśavaḥ svećchayā/yathā-ićchā-tathā aṭantu (√aṭ).* जन्तवः/जीवाः/प्राणिनः/पशवः स्वेच्छया (यथा इच्छा तथा) अटन्तु ।

(18) You all should read that book. *bhavantaḥ tat pustakaṁ paṭhantu (√paṭh).* भवन्तः तत् पुस्तकं पठन्तु ।

(19) The baby will cry. *bālakaḥ/śisuḥ krandiṣyati (√krand).* बालकः/शिशुः क्रन्दिष्यति ।

(20) The girl played. *bālikā/bālā akhelat/akrīḍat (√khel, √krīḍ).* बालिका/बाला अखेलत्/अक्रीडत् । The girls played. *bālikāḥ/bālāḥ akhelan/akrīḍan (√khel, ̸krīḍ).* बालिकाः/बालाः अखेलन्/अक्रीडन् ।

(21) Sītā is not cooking bread/breads. *Sītā roṭikāṁ/roṭikāḥ na paćati (√pać).* सीता रोटिकां/रोटिकाः न पचति ।

(22) Honey-bee bites. *madhu-makṣikā daṁśayate (√daṁś).* मधुमक्षिका दंशयते । Honey-bee will bite. *madhu-makṣikā daṁśayiṣyate (√daṁś).* मधुमक्षिका दंशयिष्यते ।

(23) We should give charity. *vayaṁ dānaṁ kuryāma (√dā).* वयं दानं कुर्याम ।

(24) Blood rushes to the heart. *rudhiraṁ hṛdayam prati dhāvati (√dhāv).* रुधिरं हृदयं प्रति धावति ।

(25) The blood flows in the veins. *raktaṁ/rudhiraṁ/śoṇitaṁ/lohitaṁ nāḍīṣu pravahati (pra√vah).* रक्तं/रुधिरं/शोणितं/लोहितं नाडीषु प्रवहति ।

(26) Two boats are floating on the water. *dve jalayāne/nāvaṁ/nauke jale tarataḥ. (√tṝ).* द्वे जलयाने/नावौ/नौके जले तरतः ।

(27) Does Sonia bring the box? *Sonia peṭikāṁ/samudrakaṁ/mañjuṣām ānayati vā? (ā√ni).* सोनीया पेटिकाम्/समुद्रकम्/मञ्जूषाम् आनयति वा ।

(28) Are you buying a brecelet from the market? *api/kiṁ bhavān āpaṇāt valayaṁ/kaṅkaṇaṁ krīṇāti? (√kṛ)* अपि/किं भवान् वलयं/कङ्कणम् आपणात् क्रीणाति?

(29) Ramesh is going to the building belonging to Govind. *Rameshaḥ*

Govindasya bhavanaṁ gaćchati (√gam). रमेश: गोविन्दस्य भवनं गच्छति ।

(30) Rādhā makes butter from milk. *Rādhā dhgdhāt navanītaṁ/ghṛtaṁ sādhayati (√sādh).* राधा दुग्धात् नवनीतं/घृतं साधयति ।

(31) Rājā cooked Cauliflower yesterday and tomorrow he may cook Okras. *Rājā hyaḥ gojihvam apaćat śvaḥ ća saḥ bhiṇḍakān paćet (√pać).* राजा ह्य: गोजिह्वाम् अपचत् श्व: च स: भिण्डकान् पचेत् ।

(32) The camels are drinking water from the pond. *ūṣṭrāḥ jalaṁ/udakaṁ/nīraṁ/toyaṁ jalāśayāt pibatni (√pā).* ऊष्ट्रा: जलं/उदकं/नीरं/तोयं जलाशयात् पिबन्ति ।

(33) When I went to Mālā's home, she was sewing a shirt for her mother. *Yadā ahaṁ Mālāyaḥ gṛhaṁ gatavān tadā sā tasyāḥ matre ekaṁ ćolaṁ/nićulaṁ/yutakaṁ sīvyati sma (√siv).* यदा अहं मालाया: गृहं गतवान् तदा सा तस्या: मात्रे एकं चोलं/निचुलं/युतकं सीव्यति स्म ।

(35) One day she drove a car from Bombay (Mumbāpurī, Mumbaī) to Nagpur. *ekadā sā Mumbāpurītaḥ Nagpuraṁ paryantaṁ cārayānam aćālayat (√ćāl).* एकदा सा मुम्बापुरीत: नागपुर-पर्यन्तं कारयानम् अचालयत् ।

(36) That car is painted by John. *tat car-yānaṁ Johnena raṅgaliptam asti (raṅga√lip).* तत् कारयानं जॉनेन रङ्गलिप्तम् अस्ति ।

(37) Rekhā counted Rupees/Dollars quickly. *Rekhā rūpyakāṇi śīghram agaṇayat/gaṇitavatī (√gaṇ).* रेखा रूप्यकाणि/डालरान् शीघ्रम् अगणयत्/गणितवती ।

(38) She will eat chick-peas with a roṭī. *saḥ roṭyā saha chaṇakān bhakṣayiṣyati/khādiṣyati (√bhakṣ).* स: रोट्या सह चणकान् भक्षयिष्यति/खादिष्यति ।

(39) Sunītā will dry Chillies in the sun. *Sunītā marīćān ātape śuṣkī-kariṣyati*

(śuṣki√kṛ). सुनीता मरीचान् आतपे शुष्कीकरिष्यति । Chillies will dry in the sun. *marīćāni ātape śokṣyanti (√śuṣ).* मरीचानि आतपे शोक्ष्यन्ति ।

(40) Ajīt gives a comb to Rādhā. *Ajītaḥ prasādhanīṁ/kaṅkatikāṁ Rādhāyai dadāti (√dā).* अजीतः कङ्कतिकां/प्रसाधनीं राधायै ददाति ।

(41) We cooked rice but did not eat it. *vayam odanam apaćāma paraṁ na akhādama/khaditavantaḥ (√pać, √khād).* वयम् ओदनम्/भक्तम् अपचाम परं न अखादम/खादितवन्तः ।

(42) The crow is dead. *kākaḥ/vāyasaḥ mṛtaḥ asti (√mṛ).* काकः/वायसः मृतः अस्ति । The dead crow. *mṛtaḥ kākaḥ/vāyasaḥ (√mṛ).* मृतः काकः/वायसः ।

(42) The dancing peacock sings. *nṛtyan mayūraḥ gāyati (√nṛt; √gā).* नृत्यन् मयूरः गायति ।

(43) Child sleeps with his mother. *bālakaḥ tasya matrā saha svapiti (√svap).* बालकः तस्य मात्रा सह स्वपिति ।

(44) The devotees worship Krishna. *bhaktāḥ kṛṣṇaṁ pūjyanti (√pūj).* भक्ताः कृष्णं पूयन्ति । The devotees were worshiping Krishna. *bhaktāḥ kṛṣṇaṁ pūjyanti sma (√pūj).* भक्ताः कृष्णं पूयन्ति स्म ।

(45) The trees in the forest do not fall with wind. *vaneṣu vṛkṣāḥ/taravaḥ/drumāḥ/pādapāḥ vāyunā na patatni (√pat).* वनेषु वृक्षाः/तरवः/द्रुमाः/पादपाः वायुना न पतन्ति ।

(46) The wind blows the leaves. *anilaḥ/marut/vātaḥ/vāyuḥ/pavanaḥ parṇāni vahati (√vah).* अनिलः/मरुत्/वातः/वायुः/पवनः पर्णानि वहति ।

(47) The corn grows in the fields of the farmers. *kiṇaḥ/śasyaṁ kṛṣakānāṁ kṣetreṣu sphuṭati (√sphuṭ).* किणः/शस्यं कृषकानां क्षेत्रेषु स्फुटति ।

(48) The red and yellow flowers bloom in that garden. *tasmin udyāne raktāni pītāni ćа puṣpāṇi vikasanti (√vikas).* तस्मिन् उद्याने रक्तानि पीतानि च पुष्पाणि विकसन्ति । All cows give white milk *(√dā). sarvāḥ dhenavaḥ/gāvaḥ śvetam dugdhaṁ/kṣiraṁ/payaḥ dadati.* सर्वाः धेनवः/गावः श्वेतं दुग्धं/क्षीरं/पयः ददति ।

(49) Rādhā did not win the cup. *Rādhā ćaṣakaṁ na ajayat/vijitavatī (vi√ji).* राधा चषकं न अजयत्/विजितवती ।

(50) Simā was riding Sītā's bicycle. *Sīmā Sītāyāḥ dvi-ćakrikām ārohati sma (ā√ruh).* सीमा सीतायाः द्विचक्रिकाम् आरोहति स्म ।

(51) The deers jump while running. *mṛgāḥ/hariṇāḥ dhāvantaḥ utpatatni (ud√pat).* मृगाः/हरिणाः धावन्तः उत्पतन्ति ।

(52) She wants gold for her mother. *sā tasyāḥ mātre kanakam/kāñćanam/bharma/suvarṇam/svarṇam/hema ićchati/ vāñćhati/ kāṅkṣati (√iććh, √vāñćh, √kāṅkṣ).* सा तस्याः मात्रे कनकम्/ काञ्चनम्/ भर्म/ सुवर्णम्/ स्वर्णम्/ हेम इच्छति/वाञ्छति/कांक्षति ।

(53) Cows suffer in the hot sun. *gāvaḥ/dhenavaḥ uṣṇe ātape khidyante (√khid).* गावः/धेनवः उष्णे आतपे खिद्यन्ते ।

(54) The doors will close at seven O'Clock. *dvārāṇi sapta vādane saṁvartsyante (sam√vṛt).* द्वाराणि सप्तवादने संवर्त्स्यन्ते ।

(55) Rīnā drinks tea in the morning and evening. *Rīnā uṣā/prage sāyaṁ ća ćāyapānaṁ karoti (√pā).* रीना उषा/प्रगे सायं च चायपानं करोति ।

(56) The ducks and swans swim in the lake. *kadambāḥ haṁsāḥ ća taḍāge/sarovare taranti/plavante (√tṛ́, √plu).* कदम्बाः हंसाः च तडागे/सरोवरे तरन्ति/प्लवन्ते ।

(57) Eagles soar in the sky to look for mice on the ground. *bhūmau mūṣakān draṣṭuṁ garuḍāḥ ākāśe uḍḍīyante (ud√dī).* भूमौ मूषकान् द्रष्टुं गरुडाः आकाशे उड्डीयन्ते ।

(58) I will buy diamonds for you. *aham tubhyaṁ ratnāni/hīrakān kreṣyāmi (√krī).* अहं तुभ्यं रत्नानि/हीरकान् क्रेष्यामि । I bought diamonds for you all. *ahaṁ yuṣmabhyam ratnāni/hīrakāḥ akrīṇām/krītavān (√krī).* अहं युष्मभ्यं रत्नानि/हीरकाः अक्रीणाम्/क्रीतवान् ।

(59) She brings Sanskrit dictionary from the library. *sā pustakālayāt Saṁskṛta-shabda-kośam ānayati (ā√ni).* सा पुस्तकालयात् संस्कृतशब्दकोशम् आनयति ।

(60) A father should teach Sanskrit to his son. *pitā/janakaḥ/tātaḥ putraṁ Saṁskṛtam adhyāpayet (adhi√i).* पिता/जनकः/तातः पुत्रं संस्कृतम् अध्यापयेत् ।

(61) Fire burnt a house on the farm. *agniḥ/analaḥ/pāvakaḥ kṣetre ekaṁ gṛham adahat/dagdhavān (√dah).* अग्निः/अनलः/पावकः क्षेत्रे एकं गृहम् अदहत्/दग्धवान् ।

(62) Having seen a fish the boy cried. *jhaṣaṁ/matsyaṁ/mīnaṁ dṛṣṭvā bālakaḥ arodīt/ruditavān (√dṛś, √rud)* झषं/मत्स्यं/मीनं दृष्ट्वा बालकः अरोदीत्/रुदितवान् ।

(63) The hen lays eggs. *kukkuṭī aṇḍāni sūyate (√sū).* कुक्कुटी अण्डानि सूयते ।

(64) The earth turns day and night. *bhūḥ/bhūmiḥ/pṛthvī/pṛthivī/mahī/dharā/dharaṇī/medinī ahorātraṁ parivartate (pari√vṛt).* भूः/भूमिः/पृथ्वी/पृथिवी/मही/धरा/धरणी/मेदिनी अहोरात्रं परिवर्तते ।

(65) Ranī orders food. *Rānī annam/aśanam/khādyam/khādanam/bhaktam/bhakṣaṇam/bhakṣyam/bhojanam/āhāram ājñāpayati (ā√jñā).* रानी अन्नम्/अशनम्/खाद्यम्/खादनम्/भक्तम्/भक्षणम्/भक्ष्यम्/भोजनम्/आहारम् आज्ञापयति ।

(66) The elephant picked the wood for cutting. *gajaḥ kāṣṭham chettum*

auddharat/udhṛtavān (√ćhid, ud√dhṛ). गजः छेत्तुं काष्ठम् औद्धरत्/उद्धृतवान् ।

(67) Rāma said. *Rāmaḥ abhaṇat/agadat/uvāća = bhaṇitavān/uktavān (√vać, √bhaṇ, √gad, √brū).* रामः अभणत्/अगदत्/उवाच = भणितवान्/गदितवान्/उक्तवान् ।

(68) Monīkā wanted to send the books. *Monīkā pustakāni sampreṣayitum iććhati sma (sam√preṣ).* मोनीका पुस्तकानि सम्प्रेषयितुम् इच्छति स्म ।

(69) Mīnā writes letters in Hindī. *Mīnā hindyāṁ patrāṇi likhati (√likh).* मीना हिन्द्यां पत्राणि लिखति ।

(70) They went to forest for hunting. *te mṛgayārthaṁ vane/kānane/vipine agaććan/gatavantaḥ (mṛgayā√kṛ).* ते मृगयार्थं वने/कानने/विपिने अगच्छन्/गतवन्तः

(71) The friend loves friend. *mitraṁ/bandhuḥ/suhṛd/sakhā/sakhī mitraṁ/bandhuṁ/suhṛdaṁ/sakhāyaṁ/sakhīṁ snihyati (√snih).* मित्रं/बन्धुः/सुहृद्/सखा/सखी मित्रं/बन्धुं/सुहृदं/सखायं/सखीं स्निह्यति ।

(72) We will go to Mathurā for Diwālī-festival. *vayaṁ dīpāvalī-utsavāya Mathurāṁ gaććhāmaḥ (√gam).* वयं दीपावली-उत्सवाय मथुरां गच्छामः ।

(73) The frog catches the flies with his tongue. *maṇḍūkaḥ/darduraḥ jihvayā makṣikāḥ gṛhṇāti (√grah).* मण्डूकः/दर्दुरः जिह्वया मक्षिकाः गृह्णाति ।

(74) The fruits are ripe. *phalāni paripakvāṇi santi (pari√pać).* फलानि परिपक्वानि सन्ति ।

(75) The garlic stinks. *laśunaṁ durgandhaṁ janayati (√jan).* लशुनं दुर्गन्धं जनयति

(76) The goats eat almost anything. *ajāḥ īṣadapi/stokamapi adanti/khādanti (√ad).* अजाः ईषदपि/स्तोकमपि अदन्ति/खादन्ति ।

(77) Tūlikā thinks very properly. *Tūlikā atīva suṣṭhu/samyak/bāḍhaṁ ćintayati (√ćint).* तूलिका अतीव सुष्ठु/सम्यक्/बाढं चिन्तयति ।

(78) Sunīl deserves a prize. *Sunīlaḥ pāritoṣakam arhati (√arh).* सुनीलः पारितोषकम् अर्हति ।

(79) God exists everywhere. *Devaḥ/bhagavān/iśvaraḥ sarvatra asti (√as).* देवः/भगवान्/ईश्वरः सर्वत्र अस्ति ।

(80) Oil is a fuel. *tailam indhanam/edhaḥ asti (√as).* तैलम् इन्धनम्/एधः अस्ति ।

(81) Are you jealous of me. *bhavān mām īrṣyati vā (√īrṣ).* भवान् माम् ईर्ष्यति वा?

(82) She is getting angry with you. *sā tubhyaṁ kupyati/krudhyati (√kup, √krudh).* सा तुभ्यं कुप्यति/क्रुध्यति ।

(83) She digs the field and sows the seeds. *sā kṣetraṁ khanati bijāni ća vapati (√khan, √vap).* सा क्षेत्रं खनति बीजानि च वपति ।

(84) The clouds that thunder do not rain. *ye meghāḥ garjanti te na varṣanti (√garj, √varṣ).* ये मेघाः गर्जन्ति ते न वर्षन्ति ।

(85) Having listened the tape, he sings songs. *dhvani/mudrikāṁ śrutvā saḥ gItāni gāyati (√gai).* ध्वनिमुद्रिकां श्रुत्वा सः गीतानि गायति ।

(86) She is walking alone. *sā ekākinī ćalantī asti (√ćal).* सा एकाकिनी चलन्ती अस्ति

(87) The hare will eat grass and leaves. *śaśakaḥ tṛṇaṁ/ghāsaṁ parṇāni ća khādiṣyati (√khād).* शशकः तृणं/घासं पर्णानि च खादिष्यति ।

(88) The hermit worships Goddess Kālī. *tāpasaḥ/tapasvī/muniḥ/yatiḥ kālyai devyai arćati (√tap).* तापसः/तपस्वी/मुनिः/यतिः काल्यै देव्यै अर्चति ।

(89) Having seen a toy the granddaughter became happy. *krīḍanakaṁ dṛṣṭvā pautrī ahṛṣyat/hṛṣṭavatī (√tuṣ).* क्रीडनकं दृष्ट्वा पौत्री अहृष्यत्/हृष्टवती ।

(90) Those grapes were sweeter than the plums. *tāḥ drākṣāḥ badarebhyaḥ*

miṣṭāḥ āsan (√as). ताः द्राक्षाः बदरेभ्यः मिष्टाः आसन् ।

(91) The horse is taller than the cow. *aśvaḥ/turaṅgaḥ/hayaḥ goḥ/dhenoḥ uććataraḥ asti (√as).* अश्वः/तुरङ्गः/हयः गोः/धेनोः उच्चतरः अस्ति ।

(92) The devotee sings hymns for Lord Rāma. *bhaktaḥ Rāmāya/devāya ślokāḥ gāyati (√gai).* भक्तः रामाय/देवाय श्लोकाः गायति ।

(93) The insects ate all the fruits. *kīṭāḥ/kṛmayaḥ sarvāṇi phalāni akhādan/khāditavantaḥ (√khād).* कीटाः/कृमयः फलानि अखादन्/खादितवन्तः ।

(94) The sun shines in the world. *sūryasya ālokaḥ/prakāśaḥ/bhā/ābhā/prabhā sarvasmin viśve ćakāsti/prakāśyate (√ćakās, pra√kāś).* सूर्यस्य आलोकः/प्रकाशः/भा/आभा/प्रभा सर्वस्मिन् विश्वे चकास्ति/प्रकाश्यते ।

(95) The lion hunts animals. *siṁhaḥ mṛgayate (√mṛg).* सिंहः/केसरी मृगयते ।

(96) The lotus looks beautiful in the water. *kamalaṁ/padmaṁ/aravindaṁ/paṅkajaṁ jale śobhate (√śobh).* कमलं/पद्मं/अरविन्दं/पङ्कजं जले शोभते ।

(97) The ripe mango falls. *pakvam amraphalṁ patati (√pat).* पक्वम् आम्रफलं पतति

(98) The monkey jumps from tree to tree. *kapiḥ/markaṭaḥ/vānaraḥ vṛkṣāt vṛkṣaṁ plavate (√plu).* कपिः/मर्कटः/वानरः वृक्षात् वृक्षं प्लवते ।

(99) The mouse is eaten by a cat. *mūṣakaḥ biḍālena khaditaḥ (√khād).* मूषकः बिडालेन खादितः । The cat ate the mouse. *biḍālaḥ mūṣakam akhadat/khāditavān (√khād).* बिडालः मूषकम् अखादत्/खादितवान् ।

(100) The heart pumps the blood in the body. *dehe hṛdayaṁ rudhiraṁ/raktam uttulayati (ud√tul).* देहे हृदयं रुधिरम् उत्तुलयति ।

NUMERALS FROM 0 to 99

	0	1	2	3	4	5	6	7	8	9
0	૦	૧	૨	૩	૪	૫	૬	૭	૮	૯
1	૧૦	૧૧	૧૨	૧૩	૧૪	૧૫	૧૬	૧૭	૧૮	૧૯
2	૨૦	૨૧	૨૨	૨૩	૨૪	૨૫	૨૬	૨૭	૨૮	૨૯
3	૩૦	૩૧	૩૨	૩૩	૩૪	૩૫	૩૬	૩૭	૩૮	૩૯
4	૪૦	૪૧	૪૨	૪૩	૪૪	૪૫	૪૬	૪૭	૪૮	૪૯
5	૫૦	૫૧	૫૨	૫૩	૫૪	૫૫	૫૬	૫૭	૫૮	૫૯
6	૬૦	૬૧	૬૨	૬૩	૬૪	૬૫	૬૬	૬૭	૬૮	૬૯
7	૭૦	૭૧	૭૨	૭૩	૭૪	૭૫	૭૬	૭૭	૭૮	૭૯
8	૮૦	૮૧	૮૨	૮૩	૮૪	૮૫	૮૬	૮૭	૮૮	૮૯
9	૯૦	૯૧	૯૨	૯૩	૯૪	૯૫	૯૬	૯૭	૯૮	૯૯

BOOK 3
LEARN TO UNDERSTAND, THINK AND THEN SPEAK SANSKRIT

संस्कृतेन चिन्तयन्तु। संस्कृतेन वदन्तु।

sam̐skṛtena ćintayantu, sam̐skṛtena vadantu.

Now that you have learned to read and wtite Sanskrit and you have understood the basic nature of the Sanskrit grammar, let us learn how to speak Sanskrit by taking a closer look at conversations. First we will see the basic conversatinos between two people, followed by the prose constructions. Then we will see some poetic compositions.

Remember, Sanskrit is a poetic language. To prepare you to understand the Sanskrit poetry is the main objective of this book. Thus, taking a close look at its poetic writings is necessary in order to appreciate the beauty, richness and uniqueness of the Sanskrit language, the supreme among all world languages, extant and non-extant.

The learners are again reminded to use All the 'Examples' as Exercises, to see if they can translate the english sentences into Sanskrit by themselves, before reading the Sanskrit translation or English transliration.

BOOKS-INDIA.COM

पुस्तक भारती

Since 1980

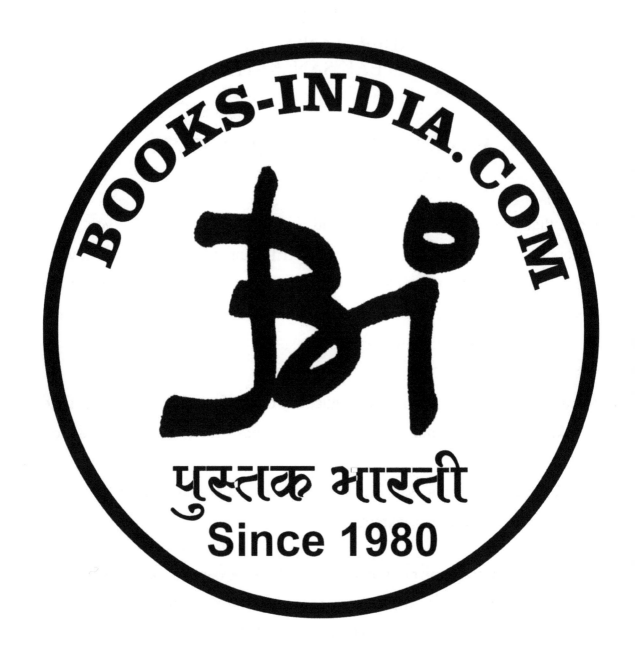

LESSON 32

dvātriṁśaḥ abhyāsaḥ द्वात्रिंशः अभ्यासः ।

LET US SPEAK SANSKRIT

saṁskṛtena vadānaḥ

संस्कृतेन वदामः ।

पठन्तु संस्कृतम् । वदन्तु संस्कृतम् ।

लसतु संस्कृतम् । जयतु संस्कृतम् ।

paṭhantu saṁskṛtam, vadantu saṁskṛtam,

lasatu saṁskṛtam, jayatu saṁskṛtam.

CONVERSATIONS

vārtālāpāḥ

वार्तालापाः ।

1. Hello! नमस्ते! नमस्कारः! स्वस्ति! जयराम! सीताराम! साईराम! हरि ओम्! *namaste! namaskāraḥ! jayarāma! sītārām! sāīrām! hari om!*
2. Good monring. सुप्रभातम् । *suprabhātam!*
3. Good night शुभरात्रिः *śubha-rātriḥ!*
4. How are you? भवान् कथम् अस्ति? त्वं कथमसि? *bhavān katham asti? tvaṁ kathamasi?*
5. Is everything ok? सर्वं कुशलं वा? *sarvaṁ kuśalaṁ vā?* Yes. *ām* आम् ।

6. Sir! How are you? आर्य! भवान् कथमस्ति? *ārya! bhāvān kathamasti?*

7. Madam! How are you? आर्ये! भवती कथमस्ति? *ārye bhavatī kathamasti?*

8. Are you well (m∘)? *kuśalī vā?* (f∘) *kuśalinī vā* कुशली वा? कुशलिनी वा?

9. Welcome. *svāgatam* स्वागतम् ।

10. You are welcome (m∘f∘). स्वागतं ते/भवतः/भवत्याः । *svāgataṁ (m∘f∘) te; (m∘) bhavataḥ, (f∘) bhavatyāḥ.*

11, Please come in. कृपया अभ्यन्तरम् आगच्छतु । अन्तः आस्यताम् । *kṛpayā abhyantaram āgaćchatu. antaḥ āsyatām.*

12. Have a seat. उपविशतु । *upaviśatu.*

13. Where should I sit? कुत्र उपविशानि? *kutra upaviśāni?*

14. Sit wherever you wish. यत्र इच्छसि तत्र उपविश, यत्र भवान् इच्छति तत्र उपविशतु । *yatra ićchasi tatra upaviśa. yatra bhavān ićchati tatra upaviśatu.*

15. Who is he (this person)? एषः कः? *eśaḥ kaḥ?* अत्रभवान् कः? *atrabhavān kaḥ?*

16. Who is she (this lady)? एषा का? *eśā kā?* अत्रभवती का? *atrabhavatī kā?*

17. What is the news? कः समाचारः? का वार्ता? किं वृत्तम्? *kaḥ samāćāraḥ? kā vātrā? kiṁ vṛttam?*

18. I hope you are well. (m∘f∘) अपि नाम भवान्/भवती कुशली/कुशलिनी अस्ति । *api nāma bhavān/bhavatī kuśalī/kuśalinī asti.*

19. Is everything ok at home? गृहे सर्वं कुशलं वा । *gṛhe sarvaṁ kuśalaṁ vā?*

20. Are you not well? (m∘f∘) अपि भवान्/भवती न स्वस्थः/स्वस्था? *api bhavān/bhavatī na svasthaḥ/svasthā?*

21. Yes. I am alright. आम् । अहं कुशली/कुशलिनी । मम सर्वं सम्यक् अस्ति । *ām. ahaṁ kuśalī/kuśalinī. mama sarvaṁ samyak asti.*

22. Thank you very much. बहुशः धन्यवादाः । *bahuśaḥ dhanyavādāḥ.*

23. Best wishes for the New Year. नववर्षस्य शुभेच्छाः । *nava-varṣasya śubhećchāḥ.*

24. See! I brought something special for you. पश्य! मया भवते/त्वदर्थं किमपि विशेषम् आनीतम् । अहं ते किमपि विशिष्टम् आनीतवान् । *paśya mayā bhavate/tvadarthaṁ kimapi ānītam. ahaṁ te kim/api viśiṣṭam ānītavān.*

25. Is it really? एवम्? *evam?* एवम् वा? *evaṁ vā?*

26. Very good. साधु साधु । *sādhu sādhu!*

27. It is really nice, Sir! Madam!. इदं शोभनं खलु श्रीमन्! श्रीमति! *idaṁ śobhanaṁ khalu, śrīman! śrīmati!.*

28. I am grateful. (m॰f॰) अहम् उपकृतः/उपकृता अस्मि । *aham upakṛtaḥ/upakṛtā asmi.*

29. Congratulations. अभिनन्दनम् । *abhinandanam.*

30. Friend! What is your name? (m॰f॰) मित्र! तव/भवतः/भवत्याः नाम किम्? *mitra! tava/bhavataḥ/bhavatyāḥ nāma kim?*

31. Sir! what is your name? आर्य/महोदय/भगवन्! भवतः शुभनाम/नामधेयं किम्? *ārya/mahodaya/bhagavan! bhavataḥ śubhanāma/nāmadheyaṁ kim?*

32. Madam! What is your name? आर्ये/महोदये/भगवति! भवत्याः शुभनाम/नामधेयं किम्? *ārye/mahaedye/bhagavati! bhavatyāḥ śubhanāma/nāmadheyaṁ kim?*

33. My name is Rāma. मम नाम रामः अस्ति । *mama nāma Rāmaḥ asti.*

34. My name is Sītā. मम नाम सीता अस्ति । *mama nāma Sītā asti.*

35. Where do you live? क्व निवससि त्वम् । क्व निवसति भवान्/भवती । कुत्र विद्यते तव (भवतः भवत्याः) निवासः? *kva nivasasi tvam? kva nivasati bhavān? kutra vidyate tava (bhavataḥ/bhavatyāḥ) nivasaḥ?*

36. I live near Modern High School. अहं नूतनविद्यालयस्य निकटे/समीपे निवसामि । *ahaṁ nūtana-vidyālayasya nikaṭe/samīpe nivasāmi.*

37. I live in Kingston. अहं किंग्स्टन-नगरे निवसामि । *ahaṁ Kingston nagare nivasāmi.*

38. I live in Downtown. अहम् अधःपुरे निवसामि । *aham adhaḥpure nivasāmi.*

39. How far is it from here? इतः कियत् दूरम् अस्ति? *itaḥ kiyat dūram asti?*

40. Not far away. नाति दूरम् । समीपे एव । *nāti dūram. samīpe eva.*

41. It may be about 4 miles from here. इतः प्रायेण क्रोशद्वयं स्यात् । *itaḥ prāyeṇa krośa-dvayaṁ syāt.*

42. By car it takes only ten minutes. कारयानेन मात्रं दशक्षणानां मार्गः । *cāra-yānena mātraṁ daśa-kṣaṇānāṁ mārgaḥ.*

43. What do you do? त्वं किम् उद्योगं करोषि? भवान्/भवती किम् उद्योगं करोति? *tvaṁ kim udyogaṁ karoṣi? bhavān/bhavatī kim udyogaṁ karoti?*

44. I am a teacher in a high school. अहं महाविद्यालये अध्यापकः/अध्यापिका अस्मि । *ahaṁ mahāvidyālaye adhyāpakaḥ/adhyāpikā asmi.*

45. What do you teach there? भवान्/भवती तत्र किम् अध्यापयति? *bhavān/bhavatī tatra kim adhyāpayati?*

46. I teach Hindī there. तत्र अहं हिन्दीम् अध्यापयामि । *tarta ahaṁ Hindīm adhyāpayāmi?*

47. Don't you teach Sanskrit also? किं भवान् संस्कृतम् अपि न अध्यापयति? *kiṁ bhavān saṁskṛtam api na adhyāpayati?*

48. No! I don't teach Sanskrit there, but at my home I teach Sanskrit to some students. नहि । अहं तत्र संस्कृतं न अध्यापयामि परं मम गृहे एव कतिपयछात्रान् संस्कृतम् अध्यापयामि । *nahi! ahaṁ tatra saṁskṛtaṁ na adhyāpayāmi, paraṁ mama gṛhe eva katipaya-ćhātrān saṁskṛtam adhyāpayāmi.*

49. Do you like teaching Sanskrit? भवते/भवत्यै संस्कृताध्यापनं रोचते वा? *bhavate/bhavatyai saṁskṛta-adhyāpanaṁ roćate vā?*

50. Yes. I like Sanskrit very much. आम् । मह्यं संस्कृतम् अतीव रोचते । *ām! mahyaṁ saṁskṛtam atīva roćate.*

51. Why so? किमर्थम् इति? *kimartham iti?*

52. Because, of all languages, Sanskrit language is the most poetic, sweetest and the best. यतः सर्वासु भाषासु संस्कृतभाषा काव्यमयी मधुरा मुख्या च अस्ति । *yataḥ sarvāsu bhāṣāsu*

saṁskṛta-bhāṣā kāvya-mayī, madhurā mukhyā ća asti.

53. What do you want? तव/भवतः/भवत्याः किम् आवश्यकम्? *tava/bhavataḥ/bhavatyāḥ kim āvaśyakam?*
54. What does he/she want? तस्य/तस्याः किम् आवश्यकम्? *tasya/tasyāḥ kim āvaśyakam?*
55. What is he doing? सः किं करोति? सः किं कुर्वन् अस्ति? *saḥ kiṁ karoti? saḥ kiṁ kurvan asti?*
56. What for? किं कारणम्? केन हेतुना? किमर्थं? *kiṁ kāraṇam? kena hetunā? kimartham?*
57. What did you say? (m∘f∘) त्वं/भवान्/भवती किम् उक्तवान्/उक्तवती? *tvaṁ/bhavān/bhavatī kim uktavān/uktavatī?*
58. What do you mean? (m∘f∘) तव/भवतः/भवत्याः कथनस्य आशयः कः अस्ति? *tava/bhavataḥ/bhavatyāḥ kathanasya āśayaḥ kaḥ asti?*
59. What do you desire? त्वं किं चिकीर्षसि? भवान्/भवती किं चिकीर्षति? *bhavān/bhavatī kiṁ ćikīrṣati?*
60. What should you do? भवान्/भवती किं कर्तुम् अर्हति? *bhavān/bhavatī kiṁ kartum arhati?* भवता/भवत्या किं करणीयम्? *bhavatā/bhavatyā kiṁ karaṇīyam?* भवान्/भवती किं कुर्यात्? *bhavān/bhavatī kiṁ kutyāt?*
61. What will you do? भवान्/भवती किं करिष्यति? *bhavān/bhavatī kiṁ kariṣyati?*
62. What happened? किं जातम्? किम् अभवत्? *kiṁ jātam? kim abhavat?*
63. Nothing. न किमपि । *na kimapi.*
64. What more? किंबहुना? *kiṁbahunā?*
65. Why are you quiet? (m∘f∘) त्वं/भवान्/भवती तूष्णीं किमर्थं? *tvaṁ/bhavān/bhavatī tūṣṇīṁ kimartham?*
66. Why don't you keep quiet? भवान् तूष्णीं किमर्थं न तिष्ठति? *bhavān tūṣṇīṁ kimarthaṁ na tiṣṭhati?*
67. Why don't you speak? भवान् किंकारणं न वदति? *bhavān kiṅkāraṇaṁ na vadati?*

68. Why did you not answer? त्वया/भवता/भवत्या प्रत्युत्तरं केन हेतुना न दत्तम्? *tvayā/bhavatā/bhavatyā pratyuttaraṁ kena hetunā na dattam?*

69. Why should I go there? अहं तत्र किन्निमित्तं गच्छेयम्? *mayā tatra kinnimittaṁ gaccheyam?* मया तत्र किंकारणं गन्तव्यम्? *mayā tatra kiṅkāraṇaṁ gantavyam?*

70. Why should he/she not go there? तेन/तया तत्र किं हेतुना न गन्तव्यम्/गमनीयम्/गम्यम्? *tena/tayā tatra kiṁ hetunā na gantavyaṁ/gamanīyaṁ/gamyam?*

71. Why may it happen? एतत् कस्मात्/कथं भवेत्? *etat kasmāt/kathaṁ bhavet?*

72. Why may it not happen? एतत् कस्मान्न भवेत्? एतत् कुतः न भवेत्? *etat kasmānna bhavet? etat kutaḥ na bhavet?*

73. When will he/she come? सः/सा कदा आगमिष्यति? *saḥ/sā kadā āgamiṣyati?*

74. When you will give him permission, then only he/she will come here.
यदा भवान्/भवती तस्मै अनुमतिं दास्यति तदा एव सः/सा अत्र आगमिष्यति । *yadā bhavān/bhavatī tasmai anumatiṁ dāsyati tadā eva saḥ/sā atra āgamiṣyati.*

75. Whenever he comes, I become very happy. यदा यदा हि सः आगच्छति, अहम् अतीव हृष्यामि । *yadā yadā hi saḥ āgacchati, aham atīva hṛṣyāmi.*

76. Where are you? त्वं कुत्र असि? भवान्/भवती कुत्र अस्ति? *tvaṁ kutra asi? bhavān/bhavatī kutra asti?*

77. Where are you coming from? भवान्/भवती कुतः आगच्छति? *bhavān/bhavatī kutaḥ āgacchati?*

78. Wherever there is light there is shadow. यत्र कुत्रापि प्रकाशः अस्ति तत्रैव छाया अपि भवति । *yatra kutrāpi prakāśaḥ asti tatraiva chāyā api bhavati.*

79. Whenever you come, we feel happy. यदा कदाचित् भवान्/भवती आगच्छति वयं हृष्यामः । *yadā kadācit bhavān/bhavatī āgacchati vayaṁ hṛṣyāmaḥ.*

80. What should we do to protect our health? अस्माकं स्वास्थ्यस्य रक्षायै वयं किं कुर्याम? *asmākaṁ svāsthyasya rakṣāyai vayaṁ kiṁ kuryāma?*

81. One should exercise regularly. नियमतः व्यायामं कुर्यात् । *niyamataḥ vyāyāmaṁ kuryāt.*

82. Should the old people also exercise? किं वृद्धाः अपि व्यायामं कुर्युः? *kiṁ vṛddhāḥ api vyāyāmaṁ kuryuḥ?*

83. Yes, as possible they should exercise too. आम्, ते अपि यथाशक्ति व्यायायमं कुर्युः । *ām! te api yathā-śaktiḥ vyāyāmaṁ kuryuḥ?*

84. One should eat healthy food. स्वास्थ्यवर्धकानि खाद्यानि खादेयुः *svāsthya-vardhakāni khādyāni khādeyuḥ.*

85. And one should not eat too much, or again and again. अधिकं च मुहुर्मुहुः वा न खादेयुः । *adhikaṁ ća muhurmuhuḥ vā na khādeyuḥ.*

86. Shall I go to the market? किम् अहम् आपणं गच्छानि? *kim aham āpaṇaṁ gaććāni?* They should go. ते गच्छन्तु । *te gaććhantu.*

87. Stay in the house! *gṛhe tiṣṭha/tiṣṭhatu.* गृहे तिष्ठ/तिष्ठतु ।

88. Do you remember that he was here yesterday? किं भवान्/भवती स्मरति यत् सः ह्यः अत्र आसीत्? *kiṁ bhavān/bhavatī smarati yat saḥ hyaḥ atra āsīt.*

89. Do this right now! एतत् अधुना/इदानीम् एव कुरु/करोतु । *etat adhunā/idānīm eva kuru/karotu.*

90. Be happy! सुखी/सुखिनी भवतु । *sukhī/sukhinī bhavatu.*

91. Do not talk unnecessarily! व्यर्थं मा वदतु । *vyarthaṁ mā vadatu.*

92. Excuse me. *kṣamyatām.* क्षम्यताम् ।

93. Do not make noise! कोलाहलं मा करोतु । *kolāhalaṁ mā karotu.*

94. Stand properly! सम्यक् तिष्ठतु । *samyak tiṣṭhatu.*

95. Don't worry! चिन्ता मास्तु । *ćintā māstu.*

96. I do not want what you want. तत् अहं न इच्छामि यत् भवान्/भवती इच्छति । *tat ahaṁ na ićchāmi yat bhavān/bhavatī ićchati.*

97. Does any of you know her name? किं युष्मासु कोऽपि तस्याः नाम जानाति? *kiṁ*

yuṣmāsu ko'pi tasyāḥ nāma jānāti?

98. She lives somewhere else. सा अन्यत्र कुत्रापि निवसति । *sā anyatra kutrāpi nivasati.*

99. Go if you want to go. गन्तुम् इच्छति चेत् गच्छतु । *gantum iććhati ćet gaććhatu.*

100. He is really a gentleman. सः नूनं भद्रपुरुषः । *saḥ nūnaṁ bhadra-puruṣaḥ.*

101. I have seen you somewhere. अहं भवन्तं/भवतीं कुत्रचित् दृष्टवान्/दृष्टवती । *ahaṁ bhavantaṁ/bhavatīṁ kutraćit dṛṣṭavān/dṛṣṭavatī.*

102. Do not waste time! समयनाशं मा करोतु । समयं मा नाशयतु । *samaya-nāśaṁ mā karotu! samayaṁ mā nāśayatu!*

103. Don't try to be smart! चातुर्यं मा करोतु । *ćāturyaṁ mā karotu.*

104. Don't tease! उपहासं मा करोतु । *upahāsaṁ mā karotu.*

105. Don't shout! चीत्कारं मा करोतु । *ćītkāraṁ mā karotu.*

106. Don't be shy सङ्कोचं मा करोतु । *saṁkoćaṁ mā karotu.*

107. Don't be stubborn. हठं मा करोतु । *haṭhaṁ mā karotu.*

108. Please don't mind! मनसि मा करोतु । *manasi mā karotu.*

109. Have no doubt! सन्देहं मा धारयतु । *sandehaṁ mā dhārayatu.*

110. Help me! मम सहाय्यं कुरु/करोतु । मम सहायः/सहाया भव/भवतु । *mama sahāyyaṁ kuru/karotu. mama sahāyaḥ/sahāyā bhava/bhavatu.*

111. It was good luck. सौभाग्यम् आसीत् । *saubhāgyam āsīt.*

112. Good idea! साधु विचारः । *sādhu vićāraḥ.*

113. Well done! साधु कृतम् । *sādhu kṛtam.*

114. Nice day! रमणीयं दिनम् । *ramaṇīyaṁ dinam.*

115. It depends. सापेक्षम् इदम् । *sāpekṣam idam.*

116. See you पुनर् दर्शनाय । *punar darśanāya.*

117. Alright, OK, Well. अस्तु । *astu.* सम्यक्! *samyak!*

118. How surprising. *aho āśćaryam.* अहो आश्चर्यम् ।

119. where is my book? *mama pustakaṁ kutra asti?* मम पुस्तकं कुत्र अस्ति?

120. It is where your glasses are, please look. यत्र भवत:/भवत्या: उपनेत्रम् अस्ति तत्र एव तद् अस्ति, पश्यतु । *yatra bhavataḥ/bhavatyāḥ upanetram asti tatra eva tad asti, paśyatu.*

121. You keep things at one place and search elsewhere. *tvam ekatra ekaṁ sthāpayasi anyatra ća anveṣaṇaṁ karoṣi.* त्वम् एकत्र एकं स्थापयसि अन्यत्र च अन्वेषणं करोषि ।

122. Found it. *prāptam.* प्राप्तम् । Good! *samīćīnam.* समीचीनम् ।

EXERCISE 83 : Fill in the blanks with the words given below

कृपया, शीघ्रम्, कथम्, चल, मम, इत: दर्शय, तिष्ठ, कृतज्ञ: उपकृत: धैर्यम्, वद, कुरु, इदम्, किमर्थम्, व्यापारे, विलम्बम्, बहुश: तस्य, मा, तम्, शुभेच्छा: ।

1. How is she? अधुना सा ---------- अस्ति? 2. What is his name? ---------- नामधेयं किम्?

3.Please come. ---------- आस्यताम् । 4. I am thankful to you. अहं ---------- अस्मि ।

5.Best wishes for success. साफल्याय हार्दिका: ----------

6.May you be healthy soon. आरोग्यं ---------- भूयात् ।

7. Don't make a noise. कोलाहलं ---------- कुरु-करोतु ।

8. Be quite! तूष्णीं ---------- 9.Have patience! ---------- धारय-धारयतु ।

10. Walk properly! सम्यक्---------- 11. Come this way! ---------- आगच्छतु ।

12. Show me the way. मां मार्गं ---------- 13. Speak loudly (slowly). उच्चै: (मन्दम्) ----

14. Please hold my hand. कृपया ---------- हस्तं धर ।

15. Do you go to school? त्वं पाठशालां गच्छसि ---------- ?

16. Don't get angry! (mad!) कोपं मा ----------

17. Don't interfere in my work! मम ---------- हस्तक्षेपं मा कुरु-करोतु ।

18. Do not drink this milk! ---------- दुग्धं मा पिब-पिबतु ।

19. Don't bother him! ---------- मा बाधस्व ।

20. Don't delay ---------- मा कुरु-करोतु

LESSON 33

trayastriṁśaḥ abhyāsaḥ त्रयस्त्रिंश: अभ्यास: ।

CORRECTING MISTAKES

śuddhikaraṇam शुद्धीकरणम् ।

EXERCISE 84 : From what we learned so far. Study the following incorrect sentences given on the LEFT side and try to correct them on your own. For help answers are given on the RIGHT side in the brackets and charts of cases and tenses are given in Appendix.

(1) Children drink milk. बालका: दुग्धं पिबति । (बालका: दुग्धं पिबन्ति) * Child eats a fruit. बालक: फलं खादती । (बालक: फलं खादति) * Child eats fruits. बालका: फलानि खादन्ती । (बालक: फलानि खादति) * Children eat fruits. बालका: फलानी खादन्ति । (बालका: फलानि खादन्ति)

(2) He is my brother. स: मम भ्रातृ अस्ति । (स: मम भ्राता अस्ति) * She is my sister. सा मम भगिनी: अस्ति । (सा मम भगिनी अस्ति) * How many brothers do you have? किती तव भ्रातर:? (कति ते भ्रातर:?) * I have two brothers. द्वौ मे भ्रातरा: (द्वौ मे भ्रातरौ) * Who is your elder brother? क: ते ज्येष्ठ भ्राता? (क: ते ज्येष्ठ: भ्राता?) * My elder brother is Rāma. रामा मे ज्येष्ठ: भ्राता । (राम: मे ज्येष्ठ: भ्राता) * What does he do? स: किं करोति? (क: तस्य व्यवसाय:?) * He is a Sanskrit teacher. स: संस्कृत टीचर: अस्ति । (स: संस्कृताध्यापक: अस्ति) * Good! शुभ! (शोभनम्!)

(3) I am doing work. अहं कर्मं करोमि । (अहं कर्म करोमि) * I am doing works. अहं कर्मा: कुर्म: । (अहं कर्माणि करोमि) * We are doing work वयं कर्म कूर्म: । (वयं कर्म कुर्म:) * You are doing work त्वं/भवान्/भवति कर्मं करोषि । (त्वं/भवान्/भवती कर्म करोषि/करोति) *They are doing work. ते/ता कर्म कुर्वन्ति । (ते/ता: कर्म कुर्वन्ति)

(4) What is your name? भवानस्य नाम किम्? (भवत: नाम किम्?) * What are their names?

भवता: नामानी किम्? (तेषां/तासां नामानि कानि?) * What is her name? तस्य नाम किम्? (तस्या: नाम किम्?)

(5) Please come here. कृपया आत्र गच्छ । (कृपया अत्र आगच्छ/आगच्छतु)

(6) Give me the book. पुस्तकं मां देहि । (पुस्तकं मह्यं देहि/ददातु)

(7) This work is done by me. एतत् कर्मम् अहं कृतम् । (एतत् कर्म मया कृतम्) * I did this work. एतत् कर्म मया कृतम् । (एतत् कर्म अहं कृतवान्) * Let it be. मास्तु । (अस्तु)

(8) This is my house. एतत् मम गृह: । (एतत् मम गृहम्) * This is my brother. एतत् मम बन्धु: अस्ति । (एष: मम बन्धु: अस्ति) * This is my watch. एष: मम घटिका अस्ति । (एषा मम घटिका अस्ति) * My houses. मम गृहानि । (मम गृहाणि)

(9) I write with my right hand. अहं मम वामहस्तेन लिखामि । (अहं मम दक्षिणहस्तेन लिखामि)

(10) I saw him in the market. अहं स: आपणे दृष्टवान् । (अहं तम् आपणे दृष्टवान् । अहं तम् आपणे अपश्यम्) * I went to the library to bring books. अहं पुस्तकम् आनेतुं पुस्तकालय गतवान् । (अहं पुस्तकानि आनेतुं पुस्तकालयम् अगच्छम्/गतवान्)

(11) One cat from this house went to that house last night. गत रात्रौ अस्य गृहात् एक बिडाल: तत् गृहात् प्राविशत्/प्रविष्टवान् । (गतरात्रौ अस्मात् गृहात् एक: बिडाल: तत् गृहं प्राविशत्/प्रविष्टवान्)

(12) She gave a gift to my sister. सा मम भगिन्यै उपहारं दत्तम् । (सा मम भगिन्यै उपहारम् अददात्/दत्तवती । तया मम भगिन्यै उपहारं दत्तम्)

(13) When did he have his breakfast? स: अल्पाहार: कदा कृतवान्? (स: अल्पाहारं कदा अकरोत्/कृतवान्? तेन अल्पाहार: कदा कृत:?)

(14) I want to go to the market. अहम् आपणे गन्तुम् इच्छामि । (अहम् आपणं गन्तुम् इच्छामि) * You want to go to the market. त्वम् आपणं गन्तुम् इच्छति । (त्वम् आपणं गन्तुम् इच्छसि । भवान्/भवती आपणं गन्तुम् इच्छति)

(15) I came here to learn Sanskrit. अहम् अत्र संस्कृत पठितुम आगतवान् । (अहम् अत्र संस्कृतं पठितुम् आगतवान्)

(16) I can do this work. अहं यत् कार्य कर्तुं शक्नोमि । (अहम् एतत् कार्यं कर्तुं शक्नोमि) * Can you do this work? अपि भवान् एतत् कार्य कर्तुं शक्नोषि । (अपि भवान् एतत् कार्यं कर्तुं शक्नोति)

(17) I will study after going home. अहं गृहे गन्तुं पठामि । (अहं गृहं गत्वा पठिष्यामि) * After eating I will go to the park for playing ball. अहं खादित्वा कन्दुकं खेलितुम् उद्यानं गच्छामि । (अहं खादित्वा कन्दुकेन खेलितुम् उद्यानं गमिष्यामि)

(18) I was looking for you. अहं भवन्तं अन्वेषयामि स्म । (अहं भवन्तम् अन्वेषयामि स्म) * I am looking for you. अहं त्वामेव अन्वेषयामि स्म । (अहं त्वामेव अन्वेषयामि)

(19) It is somewhere here. एतत् अत्र कुत्र अस्ति । (एतत् अत्र एव कुत्रापि अस्ति) * Let me look for it. अहं तत् अन्वेषयामि । (अहं तत् अन्वेषयानि) * Can I look for it? किम् अहं तस्मै अन्वेषयानि । (किम् अहं तत् अन्वेषयानि?)

(20) See you tomorrow. पुन: दर्शनं श्व: (पुनर्-दर्शनाय श्व:) * We will meet again. वयं पुन: मिलाम: । (वयं पुन: मेलिष्याम:)

(21) How did it happen? किम् एवं भवति? (किमर्थम् एवं जातम्/संवृत्तम्? कथम् एवम् अभवत्? केन कारणेन एवम् अघटत्?) * What is the reason for it? किम् अस्ति कारणम् एतस्मै? (अस्य कारणं किम्?)

(22) Why so late? कथं समय:? (किमर्थम् एतावान् विलम्ब:?)

(23) I do not like it. तत अहं न इच्छामि । (एतत् मह्यं न रोचते) * I do not want that. तत अहं न इच्छामि । (तत् अहं न इच्छामि) * Why did you not say it before? प्रथमं किमर्थं न कथवान्? (पूर्वं किमर्थं न उक्तवान्?) * Now keep quiet. अद्य तुष्णीम् । (अधुना तूष्णीं तिष्ठतु)

(24) Do'nt worry. चिन्ता न कुरु । (चिन्ता मास्तु) * Have no fear. भयतां मास्तु । (भीति: मास्तु) * There is no reason for fear. तत्र भयाय कारणं नास्ति । (भयस्य कारणं नास्ति) * You worry unnecessarily. भवान् वृथा चिन्ता करोति । (भवान् वृथा चिन्तां करोषि । भवान् वृथा चिन्तयति)

(25) Will we meet tomorrow in the evening? श्व: सायं मिलाम: किम्? (श्व: सायं मेलिष्याम: किम्?)

(26) You should not do so. भवान् इदं मा करोतु । (भवता एवं न कर्तव्यम्) * Should you do so? त्वया एवं कर्तव्यम् अस्ति? (किं भवता एवं कर्तव्यम् अस्ति? भवान् एवं कर्तुम् अर्हति किम्?

(27) See how time passed. पश्यतु! समय: किमर्थं व्यतित: (पश्यतु! समय: कथम् अतीत:) * I have

a doubt in my mind. मम मने सन्देहः जातः । (मम मनसि सन्देहः जातः) * He will not do anything in this life. अस्मिन् जन्मे सः किमपि न करिष्यति । (अस्मिन् जन्मनि सः किमपि न करिष्यति)

(28) When did you come? कदा भवान् आगतः? (भवान् कदा आगतवान्?)

(29) Who brought the book? कः पुस्तकम् आनीतम्? (केन पुस्तकम् आनीतम्? कः पुस्तकम् आनीतवान्?) * Who brought the books? केन पुस्तकानि आनीतम्? (केन/कैः पुस्तकानि आनीतानि?) * Who brought the ball? केन कन्दुकम् आनीतः? (केन कन्दुकः आनीतः?) * Who brought the watch? केन घटिका आनीतः? (केन घटिका आनीता?)

(30) Whose book is this? केन पुस्तकम् इदम्? (कस्य पुस्तकम् इदम्?) * Whose horse is this? कस्य अश्वम् इदम्? (कस्य अश्वः अयम्?) * Whose watch is this? कस्या घटिका इयम्? (कस्याः घटिका इयम्?)

(31) His name is Rāma. यस्य नाम राम अस्ति । (अस्य नाम रामः अस्ति) * Her name is Sītā. अस्याः नाम सीताः अस्ति । (अस्याः नाम सीता अस्ति)

(32) Tell me his/its name. तस्य नामं कथयतु । (तस्य नाम कथयतु) * Tell me her name. तस्य नाम कथयतु । (तस्याः नाम कथयतु)

(33) Gandhī was a great soul. गान्धी महानात्मा आसीत् । गान्धी माहात्मा आसीत् । गान्धी सत्जनः आसीत् । (गान्धी महात्मा आसीत् । गान्धी नहोदयः सज्जनः आसीत्)

(34) Flowers bloom on the vine. लतां पुष्पाणि विकसन्ति । (लतायां पुष्पाणि विकसन्ति) * Flowers bloom on the vines. लताषु पुष्पाणि विकसन्ति । (लतासु पुष्पाणि विकसन्ति)

(35) I am looking at the moon. अहं चन्द्रमां पश्यामि । (अहं चन्द्रमसं पश्यामि) * She looks at the moon. सा चन्द्रमसां पश्यति । (सा चन्द्रमसं पश्यति)

(36) I am doing. अहं करामि । (अहं करोमि) * I was doing. अहं करोमि आसीत् । (अहं करोमि स्म)

(37) This is my watch. अयं मे घटिका अस्ति । (इयं मे घटिका अस्ति) * This is my house. इयं मे गृहम् अस्ति । (इदं मे गृहम् अस्ति) * This is my ball. इदं मे कन्दुकः अस्ति । (अयं मे कन्दुकः अस्ति)

(38) These are my houses. एते मम गृहानि सन्ति । (एतानि मे गृहाणि सन्ति) * These are my friends. एषाः मे मित्राः सन्ति । (एतानि मे मित्राणि सन्ति) * These are my watches. इमे मे घटिकाः सन्ति । (इमाः मे घटिकाः सन्ति)

(39) Sītā is a teacher. सीता अध्यापिकः अस्ति । (सीता अध्यापिका अस्ति) * Sītā is lucky. सीता भाग्यवान् अस्ति । (सीता भाग्यवती अस्ति) * A river flows in the town. नगरे एकः नदीः वहति । (नगरे एका नदी वहति)

(40) Cows give milk for their calves. धेनवः वत्सेभ्यः क्षीर ददन्ति । (धेनवः वत्सेभ्यः क्षीरं ददति) * Children go to school. बालकः पाठशाला गच्छन्ति । (बालकाः पाठशालां गच्छन्ति) * People go to other countries for earning money. जनाः धनाय देशान्तरं गच्छति । (जनाः धनाय देशान्तरं गच्छन्ति).

(41) We will never be afraid of the enemy. वयम् शतृभ्यः कदापि न भेष्यामः । (वयं शत्रुभ्यः कदापि न भेष्यामः ।)

(42) What did he say you yesterday? सः श्वः भवन्तं किम् अब्रवीत । (सः ह्यः भवन्तं किम् अब्रवीत्)

(43) Where do you all study? भवान् कुत्र अधीयते । (भवन्तः कुत्र अधीयते ।)

(44) What are the things we will know today? अधुना वयं किं किं बोधिष्यामः । (अद्य वयं किं किं बोधिष्यामः ।)

(45) Students are running fast on the playground. छात्राः क्रीडाङ्गणे वेगे धावन्ति/धावन् अस्ति । (छात्राः क्रीडाङ्गणे वेगेन धावन्ति/धावन्तः सन्ति)

(46) The police protect people from the thieves. नगररक्षकः जनान् चोरैः त्रायन्ते । (नगररक्षकाः जनान् चोरेभ्यः त्रायन्ते)

(48) He will excuse you this time. सः अधुना भवान् क्षमिष्यते । (सः अधुना भवन्तं क्षमिष्यते)

LESSON 34

ćatustriṁśaḥ abhyāsaḥ चतुस्त्रिंशः अभ्यासः ।

PROSE READING

gadya-paṭhanam गद्यपठनम् ।

SHORT STORIES

laghu-kathāḥ लघुकथाः ।

34.1

MOTHER AND THE BABY PARROT

śukī śāvahaḥ ća शुकी शावकः च ।

मनसि एकस्य चित्रस्य कल्पनां कुरुत । *manasi ekasya ćitrasya kalpanāṁ kurut.* Imagine a picture in mind.

कुत्रचित् कस्मिंश्चित् नगरे, *kutraćit kasminśćit nagare* Somewhere in some town, एकः शुकशावकः पञ्जरे बद्धः तिष्ठति । *ekāḥ śuka-śāvakaḥ puñjare baddhaḥ tiṣṭhati.* A baby parrot is sitting trapped in a bird cage. तस्य माता शुकी पञ्जरात् बहिः निकटे वृक्षशाखायां स्थिता अस्ति । *tasya mātā, śukī, pañjarāt bahiḥ nikaṭe vṛkṣa-śākhāyāṁ sthitā asti.* His mother, Shukī, is sitting outside the cage, on a branch of a nearby tree. सा स्व-शावकं बद्धं दृष्ट्वा नेत्राभ्याम् अश्रूणि मुञ्चन्ती भाषते- *sā sva-śāvakaṁ baddhaṁ dṛṣṭvā, netrābhyām aśruṇi muńćanti bhāṣate-* Seeing her baby trapped in the cage, she is talking with tears flowing from her eyes,

वत्स! उक्तं खलु मया (*vatsa! uktaṁ khalu mayā.* O Child! I had indeed told you) नीडात् न

निर्गन्तव्यं (*nīḍāt na nirgantavyaṁ* the nest is not to be left), कोऽपि त्वां गृह्णियात् -इति (*ko'pi vtāṁ gṛhṇiyāt¯iti.* someone may catch you -so). मम वाक्यम् अनादृत्य (*mama vākyam anādṛtya.* Having not listened to what I said) त्वं क्रीडितुं लतां गतः (*tvaṁ krīḍituṁ latāṁ gataḥ.* you went to play on the flower-vines).

ततः शुकशावकः मातरम् आह (*tataḥ śuka-śāvakaḥ mātaram āha-* Then the baby parrot said to his mother) मातः! (*māt!* O Mother!) मातुः वाक्यम् अनुल्लंघनीयम् इति जानामि अहम् (*mātuḥ vākyam anullaṅghanīyam iti jānāmi aham.* I know that Mother's word is not to be disobeyed) अथापि, (*athāpi,* However) क्रीडासक्तेन (*krīḍā-saktena* with the attraction of playing) चापल्यात् मया तत् न आलोचितम् (*ćāpalyāt mayā tat na āloćitam.* in the rush it was not obeyed by me).

शुकी आह- (*śukī āha,* Shukī said-) जात! (*jāt!* Whatever!) एवं गते त्वयि कथं त्वत् एकपुत्रया मया आयुः शेषः नेयः? (*evaṁ gate tvai kathaṁ tvat eka-putrayā mayā āyuḥ śeṣaḥ neyaḥ?* You, the only child, gone like this, how may I spend my life?)

शुकशावकः मातरम् अपृच्छत्- (*śuka-śāvakaḥ mātaram apṛćchat-* The baby parrot asked his mother-) "अम्ब! किम् एवं वदति भवान्? (*amb! kim evaṁ vadati bhavān?* O Mother! Why are you saying this?) किं मम मुक्तिः न स्यात् अस्मात् पञ्जरात्? (*kiṁ mama muktiḥ na syāt asmāt pañjarāt?* Why, will I not be free from this cage?)"

शुकी अकथयत्- (*śukī akathayat-* Shukī said-) दृढतराः पञ्जरस्य शलाकाः (*dṛḍhatarāḥ pañjarasya śalākāḥ* . the bars of the cage are very strong). कथं ते मुक्तिः भविष्यति? (*kathaṁ te muktiḥ bhaviṣyati?* How will you become free?) ...

34.2
UNNECESSARY ADVICE
nirarthakaḥ upadeśaḥ निरर्थकः उपदेशः ।

मनसि अन्यस्य चित्रस्य कल्पनां कुरुत । *manasi anyasya ćitrasya kalpanāṁ kurut.* Imagine another picture in your mind.

कुत्रापि वने वर्षाकाले वृक्षात्-वृक्षं विटपात्-विटपं प्लवमानः वानरः क्वापि वृक्षे क्रीडति स्म । *kutrāpi vane varṣā-kāle vṛkṣāt-vṛkṣaṁ viṭapāt-viṭapaṁ plavamānaḥ vānaraḥ vṛkṣe krīḍti sma.* In a forest in the rainy season, a monkey, jumping from tree to tree and branch to branch, was playing on a tree. तस्य वृक्षस्य शाखायाम् एकः नीडः आसीत् । (*tasya vṛkṣasya śākhāyām ekāḥ nīḍaḥ āsīt.* In the branches of that tree there was a bird nest). तत्र नीडे कश्चन चटकः पत्न्या सह वसति स्म । (*tatra nīḍe kaśćana ćaṭakaḥ patnyā saha vasati sma.* There, in the nest some bird was living with his wife).

वानराः प्रायेण नरैः तुल्यरूपाः । *vānarāḥ prāyeṇa naraiḥ tulya-rūpāḥ.* The monkeys are mostly like people. अथापि, (*athāpi* However) नराः इव गृहाणि खगाः इव नीडानि वा कर्तुं न शक्नुवन्ति (*narāḥ iva gṛhāṇi khagāḥ iva nīḍāni vā kartuṁ na śaknuvanti.* they cannot build houses like people or nests like the birds). सदैव एव ते वृक्षेषु निवसन्ति (*sadaiva eva te vṛkṣeṣu nivasanti.* They always live in the trees). कन्दैः फलैः च उदरं पूरयन्ति (*kandaiḥ phalaiḥ ća udaraṁ pūrayanti.* They fill their bellies with tubers and fruits). वानराः स्वभावतः एव चपलाः कोपनाः च । (*vānarāḥ svabhāvataḥ eva ćapalāḥ kopanāḥ ća.* Monkeys are by nature fickle and irascible).

एकदा वर्षासु सः वानरः शैत्येन बाधितः दन्तवीणां वादयन् वृक्षम् अनारुह्य मूलम् उपविष्टवान् (*ekadā varṣāsu saḥ vānaraḥ śaityena bādhitaḥ danta-vīṇāṁ vādayan vṛkṣam anāruhya mūlam upaviṣṭavān.* Once, wet with the rains and frozen with the cold, that monkey came down to the root of the tree and sat with his teeth chattering). बहिः सर्वत्र शीतलं वातावरणम् आसीत् (*bahiḥ sarvatra śītalaṁ vātāvaraṇam āsīt,* Outside, it was cold everywhere). नीडे तु

औष्ण्यम् आसीत् (*nīḍe tu auṣṇyam āsīt.* but in the nest it was warm). तं शैत्येन कम्पमानं वानरं दन्तवीणां वादयन्तं दृष्ट्वा सा चटका उक्तवती- (*taṁ śaityena kampamānaṁ vānaraṁ danta-vīṇāṁ vādayantaṁ dṛṣṭvā sā ćaṭakā uktavatī.* Mrs. Bird said to that monkey who was trembling with cold and was chattering his teeth-)

नीडं कुर्मो वयं चापि चञ्चुमात्रैर्हृतैस्तृणैः । पाणिपादादिसंयुक्ता यूयं किमिति सीदथ ।।87।।

nīḍaṁ kurmo vayaṁ ćāpi ćañćumātrairhṛtaistṛṇaiḥ, pāṇi-pādādi-saṁyuktā yūyaṁ kimiti sīdatha.

Even we build a nest, by carrying grass only with our beaks,
Equipped with arms and limbs, how can you freeze like this?

तत् श्रुत्वा सः वानरः उक्तवान् (*tat śrutvā saḥ vānaraḥ uktavān,* Hearing it, the monkey said) "रे दुष्टे! (*re duṣṭe!* O Wicked!) अलं जल्पेन । (*alaṁ jalpena!* Enough of the talk). किमर्थं मौनं न तिष्ठसि (*kimarthaṁ maunaṁ na tiṣṭhasi?* Why don't you shut up?). मम विषये किंकारणं चिन्तयसि ("*mama viṣaye kiṅkāraṇaṁ ćintayasi.* Why do you worry about me?")

परन्तु चटका मौनं न स्थितवती । (*parantu ćaṭakā maunaṁ na sthitavatī.* But Mrs. Bird did not keep quiet). पुनः सा तथा एव उपदेशम् आरब्धवती (*punaḥ sā tathā eva upadeṣam ārabdhavatī.* Again she started the same advice). तत् आकर्ण्य कुपितः मर्कटः आह– (*tat ākarṇya kupitaḥ markaṭaḥ āha-* Hearing that the agitated monkey said-) सूचिमुखि! (*sūći-mukhi!* O Needlemouth!) दुराचारे! (*durāćāre!* O Corrupt One!) किं प्रलपसि? (*kiṁ pralapayasi?* Why are you talking nonsense?) इति वदन् (*iti vadan,* Saying this) वृक्षम् आरुह्य (*vṛkṣam āruhya,* climbing the tree) सः चटकयोः नीडं खण्डशः कृतवान् क्षिप्तवान् च (*saḥ ćaṭakayoḥ nīḍaṁ khaṇḍaśaḥ kṛtavān kṣiptavān ća.* he broke the birds' nest into pieces and threw it away). मूर्खम् प्रति एवं व्यर्थेन उपदेशेन चटकयोः नीडः अपि नष्टः अभवत् । *mūrkhaṁ prati evaṁ vyarthena upadeśena ćaṭakayoḥ nīḍaḥ api naṣṭaḥ abhavat.* Thus by giving unnecessary advice to a fool, their nest also got destroyed.

मूर्खम् प्रति उपदेशं न कुर्यात् । *mūrkham prati upadeśaṁ na kuryāt*

One should not advise fools.

34.3

INHERENT NATURE

jāti-svabhāvaḥ जातिस्वभावः ।

मनसि एकस्य दृश्यस्य कल्पनां कुरुत । Imagine a scene in your mind.

एकस्मिन् वने सिंहदम्पती वसतः स्म । कालान्तरे सिंही पुत्रद्वयं प्रसूतवती । सिंहः प्रतिदिनं मृगान् मारयित्वा मांसम् आनीय पत्नीपुत्रेभ्यः ददाति स्म । एकदा सिंहः मृगयायै वने अटति स्म । तत्र सः एकं शृगालशिशुं दृष्टवान् । करुणया तं शिशुं गुहाम् आनीय सः पत्न्यै दत्तवान् । सा अपि तं शिशुं मारयितुं न इष्टवती । अतः तं शृगालं वात्सल्येन स्वपुत्रवत् पालितवती । स्वपुत्राभ्यां यथा सा आहारादिकं ददाति तथा शृगालशिशवे अपि ददाति स्म । अतः ते त्रयः शिशवः परस्परं भेदं न जानन्ति स्म । ते परस्परं खेलन्ति स्म । एवमेव ते प्रवृद्धाः ।

In a forest, a lion couple was living. In due course, the lioness gave birth to two cubs. The lion used to kill animals and bring the meat for wife and children. One day, while he was roaming in the forest to hunt animals, he saw a baby fox. Overwhelmed with pity, he brought the cub to the den and gave it to his wife. The lioness also did not desire to kill the cub. Therefore, she raised the baby fox lovingly, as if it was her own son. As she was feeding her cubs, so she fed the baby fox too. Thus those three cubs did not know any difference between them. They were always playing together. That is how they grew.

कदाचित् ते त्रयः अपि शिशवः अरण्ये खेलन्ति स्म । तत्र एकः गजः आगतः । गजं दृष्ट्वा सिंहपुत्रौ आक्रमणं कर्तुं सिद्धौ । तदा शृगालपुत्रः आह– "बन्धू! एषः गजः अस्माकं कुलशत्रुः । तस्य पुरतः न गन्तव्यम् ।" इति उक्त्वा ततः गृहं पलायनं कृतवान् । तं दृष्ट्वा निरुत्साहेन सिंहपुत्रौ अपि गृहम् आगतवन्तौ । अनन्तरं तौ पितरम् उक्तवन्तौ – "आवयोः अग्रजः कातरः अस्ति । सः गजं दृष्ट्वा भीत्या पलायनं कृतवान्" इति । सिंहः तत् श्रुत्वा कुपितः अभवत् । "युवयोः सिंहकुलस्य एव अपमानं तेन कृतम्" इति सः पुत्रौ निन्दितवान् ।

One day those three cubs were playing in the forest. There came an elephant. Seeing the elephant, the lion cubs got ready to charge. But the fox cub said- "Brothers! this elephant is an enemy of our race. Therefore, we ought to go in front of him." Saying so, he ran to the den. Seeing him gone, the two lion cubs became nervous and came home. Thereafter, the two lion cubs told their father, "Our brother is timid. He ran away with fear having seen the elephant." Hearing this, the lion became angry. He scolded his cubs, "He has insulted your lion race."

सिंही शृगालपुत्रम् एकान्ते उक्तवती – "वत्स! पुन: कदापि त्वं तव भ्रात्रो: उत्साहभङ्गं मा कुरु" इति ।
The lioness privately said to the fox cub, "Son! Do not put off your brothers ever again."
तदा कुपित: शृगालशिशु: उक्तवान्– "मात:! किम् अहं शौर्येण, रूपेण वा ताभ्यां हीन: अस्मि? किमर्थं तौ माम् उपहसत:?" इति । सिंही मनसि एव हसित्वा तम् उक्तवती – Then the agitated fox cub said- "O Mother! Am I less brave or beautiful than those two? Why did they ridicule me?" Laughing in her mind, the lioness said -

"शूरोऽसि कृतविद्योऽसि दर्शनीयोऽसि पुत्रक ।
यस्मिन् कुले त्वमुत्पन्नो गजस्तत्र न हन्यते" ।।88।।

"You are brave, you are well trained, you are beautiful, Son Dear!
The race into which you are born, the elephant is not hunted there."

त्वं शूर: असि । तेन विद्याभ्यास: अपि कृत: अस्ति । त्वं सुन्दर: अपि असि । तथापि त्वं वस्तुत: शृगालपुत्र: असि । अहं करुणया त्वां मम पुत्रम् इव पालितवती । परन्तु युष्माकं शृगालकुले जाता: गजं मारितुं शक्ता: न भवन्ति । त्वं शृगालपुत्र: असि इति यदि मम पुत्रौ जानीत: तर्हि त्वां तौ मारयत: एव । अत: तत् पूर्वम् एव त्वं गत्वा स्वजातीयै: शृगालै: सह वासं कुरु" इति ।

You are gallant. Education is also done by you. You are handsome too. Even then, in reality, you are a son of a fox. With pity I raised you like my own child. But those who are born into your fox race are not able to kill an elephant. If my children ever know that you are a son of a fox, they will kill you. Therefore, before that happens, go away and live with your own fox race. तत् श्रुत्वा शृगालपुत्र: जातिस्वभावेन अपरिहार्येण भयेन तत: तूष्णीं गतवान् । Hearing that, and driven by his inherent fear, the fox cub quietly went away from there.

SHORT ESSAYS

laghu-nibandhāḥ लघुनिबन्धाः ।

34.4

THE HORSE

aśvaḥ अश्वः ।

अर्वा, आजानेयः, कर्कः, कियाहः, गन्धर्वः, घोटकः, तुरगः, तुरङ्गः, हयः, तुरङ्गमः, भूमिरक्षकः, वाजी, वाहः, वीतिः, सप्तिः, साधुवाही, सिन्धुवारः, सैन्धवः, इत्यादिभिः, अभिधानैः अश्वः अभिज्ञायते ।

The horse is known by such names as *arvā, ājāneyaḥ, karkaḥ, kiyāhaḥ, gandharvaḥ, ghoṭakaḥ, turagaḥ, turaṅgaḥ, hayaḥ, turaṅgamaḥ, bhūmirakṣakaḥ, vājī, vāhaḥ, vītiḥ, saptiḥ, sādhuvāhī, sindhuvāraḥ, saindhavaḥ ityādibhiḥ abhidhānaihiḥ aśvaḥ abhijñāyate.*

अश्वः विनीतः पशुः । *aśvaḥ vinītaḥ paśuḥ* The horse is a disciplined animal. सः गौः इव उपयुक्तः पशुः भवति । *saḥ gauḥ iva upayuktaḥ bhavati.* He is a useful animal like a cow. गोः अश्वस्य च कः भेद? *goḥ aśvasya ća kaḥ bhedaḥ?* What is the difference between a cow and a horse? अश्वस्य शृंगे न स्तः । *aśvasya śṛṅge na staḥ.* The horse does not have two horns. तस्य ग्रीवायां रोमराजिः वर्तते । *tasya grīvāyāṁ roma-rājiḥ vartate.* His neck has a hairy mane. गोः शफः द्वेधा दलितः अस्ति न तु अश्वस्य । *goḥ śaphaḥ dvedhā dalitaḥ asti, na tu aśvasya.* A cow's hoof is divided into two halves, but not the horse's. अतः अश्वः शीघ्रतरं धावति । *ataḥ aśvaḥ śīghrataraṁ dhāvati.* Therefore, the horse runs faster. सः सबलः च । *saḥ sabalaḥ ća.* He is strong too.

अश्वः चतुरः पशुः । *aśvaḥ ćaturaḥ paśuḥ.* The horse is a smart animal. लोकाः तम् आरोहन्ति । *lokāḥ tam ārohanti.* People ride him. ते हयपृष्ठे उपविश्य प्रवसन्ति । *te haya-pṛṣṭhe upaviṣya pravasanti.* They travel sitting on horseback. सः मनुजानां विश्वस्तं मित्रं खलु । *saḥ manujānāṁ viśvastaṁ mitraṁ khalu.* He is indeed a friend of human beings. प्राचीनकाले

नृपाः अश्वान् युद्धेषु उपयुञ्जते स्म । *prācina-kāle nṛpāḥ aśvān yuddheṣu upayuñjate sma.* In olden days kings used horses in the battles.

कश्चित् कविः अश्वप्रशंसायाम् एवं निवेदयति- *kaścit kaviḥ aśva-praśaṁsāyām evaṁ nivedayati-* Some poet says in praise of the horse-

अश्वाः यस्य जयः तस्य यस्य अश्वाः तस्य मेदिनी ।
अश्वाः यस्य यशः तस्य यस्य अश्वाः तस्य काञ्चनम् ।।89।।

aśvāḥ yasya jayaḥ tasya, yasya aśvāḥ tasya medinī,
aśvāḥ yasya yaśaḥ tasya, yasya aśvāḥ tasya kāñcanam.

(Victory is his, who has horses, Who has horses, on land he has hold;
Success is his, who has horses, Who has horses, his is gold.)

34.5

THE SUN

sūryaḥ सूर्यः ।

सूरसूर्यार्यमादित्यः द्वादशात्मादिवाकरः ।
भास्कराहस्करब्रध्नः प्रभाकरविभाकरः ।
भास्वद्विवस्वत्सप्ताश्वः हरिदश्वोष्णरश्मयः ।
विकर्तनार्कमार्तण्डः मिहिरारुणपूषणः ।
द्युमणिस्तरणिर्मित्रः चित्रभानुर्विरोचनः ।
विभावसुर्ग्रहपतिः त्विषां पतिरहर्पतिः ।
भानुर्हंसः सहस्रांशुः तपनः सविता रविः ।।90।।

सूरः, सूर्यः, अर्यमा, आदित्यः, द्वादशात्मा, दिवाकरः, भास्करः, अहस्करः, ब्रध्नः, प्रभाकरः, विभाकरः, भास्वत्, विवस्वत्, सप्ताश्वः, हरिदश्वः, उष्णरश्मयः, विकर्तनः, अर्कः, मार्तण्डः, मिहिरः, अरुणः, पूषणः, द्युमणिः, तरणिः, मित्रः, चित्रभानुः, विरोचनः, विभावसुः, ग्रहपतिः, त्विषपतिः, अहर्पतिः, भानुः, हंसः, सहस्रांशुः, तपनः, सविता, रविः ...इत्यादिभिः नामधेयैः अमरकोषे सूर्यः अभिज्ञायते ।

In the Amarakosha, the Sun is referred by such names as, Sūraḥ (Remover of the diseases), Sūryaḥ (The One with twelve names), Aryamā (The Most excellent one, the Dear friend), Āditya (Son of Aditi), Dvādaśātmā (The Twelvefold soul), Divākaraḥ (The Day maker), Bhāskaraḥ (The Light maker), Ahaskaraḥ (The Day maker), Bradhnaḥ (The Producer), Prabhākaraḥ (The Brightness maker), Vibhākaraḥ (The Glow maker), Bhāsvat (The Glittering one), Vivasvat (Manu Vaivasvat), Saptāśvaḥ (The One with seven horses), Haridaśvaḥ (The One on the green horse), Uṣṇaraśmayaḥ (The One with blazing rays), Vikartanaḥ (The One with special cutting power), Arkaḥ (The Ray of light), Martaṇḍaḥ (That Came from an egg that is not live), Mihiraḥ (The One that sprays rains), Aruṇaḥ (The Red coloured one), Pūṣaṇaḥ (The Growth causer), Dyumaṇi (The Jewel in the sky), Taraṇiḥ (The One that crosses from one to other end), Mitraḥ (The Friend) Ćtrabhānuḥ (The Bright rays), Viroćanaḥ (The One that is specially pleasing), Vibhāvasuḥ (The Brightest jewel), Grahapatiḥ (The King of planets), Tviṣapatiḥ (The King of illuminations), Aharpatiḥ (The King of the day time) Bhānuḥ (The One with rays), Ham̐saḥ (The Shining one), Sahasrām̐śuḥ (The one with thousands of rays), Tapanaḥ (The Heat giver), Savitā (The Originator), Raviḥ (The Silence breaker, the Slumber ender, the Day starter) ...etc.

सूर्यः गगनस्य अलङ्कारः । सूर्यः प्राच्यां दिशि उदयते । सम्प्रति तस्य प्रकाशः रक्तः कोमलः च वर्तते । उदयमानः सूर्यः अन्धकारं नाशयति प्राणिनः प्रबोधयति कुसुमानि च विकासयति । क्रमेण उद्गच्छन् यदा सूर्यः मध्यम् आरोहति तदा मध्याह्नः भवति । मध्याह्ने सूर्यस्य प्रकाशः कठोरः भवति । अतः सूर्यः क्रमेण पश्चिमां दिशम् अवतरति । अन्ते च सूर्यः पश्चिमदिशि अस्तं गच्छति ।

The Sun is an adornment of the sky. The Sun rises in the East. At this time its light is red and soft. The rising sun destroys the darkness, wakes the animals up and makes the flowers bloom. Gradually the Sun reaches the center of the sky and it is then noon. At noon the sun-light is hard. From here, the Sun gradually comes down in the West. And eventuaally the Sun sets in the West.

सूर्यः स्वयं प्रकाशते । सूर्यस्य भासा सकला सृष्टिः प्रकाशते । सूर्यः जगते उष्णतां यच्छति । सूर्येण

तुल्यः अन्यत् किमपि तेजस्वि न वर्तते । सूर्यः प्रत्यक्ष देवता । सः देवैः असुरैः च नमस्कृतः । तस्मात् वाल्मीकिरामायणे कथितम् अस्ति–

The Sun shines by itself. The entire universe is brightened by the light of the Sun. The Sun gives warmth to the world. There is nothing as brilliant as the sun. The Sun is God Himself. He is worshipped by the Gods as well as demons. Therefore, in the Rāmāyaṇa of Vālmīki, it is said-

रश्मिमन्तं समुद्यन्तं देवासुरनमस्कृतम् ।
पूजयस्व विवस्वं तं भास्करं भुवनेश्वरम् ।।91।।

raśmimantaṁ samudyantaṁ devāsuranamaskṛtam,
pūjayasva vivasvantaṁ bhāskaraṁ bhuvaneśvaram.

Full of rays, up high in the sky, worshipped by the Gods and demons as well,
Worship that Vaivasvat, the light maker, the Lord of the universe all.

34.6

KNOWLEDGE

vidyā विद्या ।

कस्यापि वस्तुनः सम्यक् ज्ञानं विद्या इति कथ्यते । Proper understanding of anything is called knowledge. दर्शनस्य विज्ञानस्य साहित्यस्य च अध्ययनम् अपि विद्या । The study of any system of philosophy, science or literature is also knowledge. यद्यपि विश्वम् इदं नाना धनैः परिपूर्णम् अस्ति, परं विद्या तेषु प्रधानतमम् अस्ति । Even though the world is full of different treasures, knowledge is the most superior to them all. यतः एतत् धनम् ईदृशम् अद्वितीयम् अस्ति यत्– because it is such a unique thing which- व्ययतः वृद्धिम् आयाति क्षयम् आयाति च सञ्चयात् । grows as you use it, and diminishes as you conserve it. उक्तञ्च– It has been said that-

न चोरहार्यं न च राजहार्यं न भ्रातृभाज्यं न च भारकारि ।
व्यये कृते वर्धत एव नित्यं विद्याधनं सर्वधनप्रधानम् ।।92।।

na ćorahāryaṁ na ća rāja-hāryaṁ, na bhrātṛ-bhājyaṁ na ća bhāra-kāri,

vyaye kṛte vardha eva nityaṁ, vidyā-dhanaṁ sarva-dhana-pradhānam.

A thief can steal it not, a king will seize it never,
A brother can claim it not, nor is it a burden at all;
As much as it is used, it grows and grows for ever,
The wealth of knowledge is superior to all.

विद्या मनुष्यस्य आन्तरिकाः सत्-प्रवृत्तीः विकासयति । Knowledge expands the good qualities of the man. विद्यां प्राप्य मनुष्यः विवेकशीलः भूत्वा कर्तव्य-अकर्तव्य-विवेचनाय प्रभवति । Having gained knowledge, the man is able to discern between what should be done and what should not be done. उक्तञ्च- *uktañća* it is said that-

विद्या नाम नरस्य रूपमधिकं प्रच्छन्नगुप्तं धनम् ।
विद्या भोगकरी यशसुखकरी विद्या गुरूणां गुरुः ।।93।।

vidyā nāma narasya rūpam-adhikaṁ praććhanna-guptaṁ dhanam,

vidya bhoga-karī yaśaḥ sukha-karī, vidyā gurūṇāṁ guruḥ.

Knowledge is the beauty of a person;
It is a treasure hidden and mysterious,
Knowledge gives joy, success and pleasure;
It is most superior among the things precious.

विद्यावान् मनुष्यः विनयशीलः भवेत् । यतः विनयस्य प्रभावेण मनुष्यः योग्यताम् अधिगच्छति । A knowledgable person should be humble, for with the strength of humility one attains propriety. विद्या विनयेन शोभते । The knowledge looks beautiful with humility.

सरस्वती विद्यायाः देवता । Sarasvatī is the Goddess of knowledge. तस्याः एकस्मिन् हस्ते वीणा शोभते अपरकरे च पुस्तकं वर्तते । In her one hand is a Viṇā and in the other hand is a book. एतौ तस्याः आभूषणे । These two are her ornaments. सर्वे देवाः तां वन्दन्ते । All the Gods worship her. तस्मात् वयम् अपि तां नमस्कुर्याम । Thus, we should worship her.

34.7
GOOD SAYINGS
subhāṣitāni सुभाषितानि ।

सुभाषितम् इत्युक्ते शोभनं भाषितम् अथवा शोभना उक्तिः । Subhāṣita means beautifully said or beautiful saying. संस्कृतभाषा सर्वासु भाषासु पद्यमयी भाषा । Among all languages Sanskrit language is the most poetic language. संस्कृते सुभाषितानि अनेकानि सन्ति । In Sanskrit there are many Subhāṣitas. एतानि सुभाषितानि मधुराणि गेयानि च वर्तन्ते । These verses are sweet and singable. सुभाषितेषु अल्पैः शब्दैः महान्तम् अर्थम् अभिव्यक्तिं नयन्ति कवयः । Poets put deep meaning in the verses with a few words only. उत्कृष्ट-निबन्ध-लेखनार्थं तथा वक्तृत्व-कलायां नैपुण्य-सम्पादनार्थं सुभाषितानि अतीव उपयुक्तानि भवन्ति । For writing superb essays as well as for attaining excellence in the art of eloquent speech, the Subhāṣitas are very useful.

भाषासु मुख्या मधुरा दिव्या गीर्वाणभारती ।
तस्माद्धि मधुरं काव्यं तस्मादपि सुभाषितम् ।।94।।

Among all languages Sanskrit language is the best and sweetest language. Within that too even sweeter is the poetry and within that, the most sweet is a Subhāṣita.

पृथिव्यां त्रीणि रत्नानि जलमन्नं सुभाषितम् ।
मूढैः पाषाणखण्डेषु रत्नसंज्ञा विधीयते ।।95।।

There are three jewels on the earth - water, food and *subhāṣita*; but the stones are jewels for the ignorant people.

काव्यशास्त्रविनोदेन कालो गच्छति धीमताम् ।
व्यसनेन तु मूर्खाणां निद्रया कलहेन वा ।।96।।

Wise people spend their time with the amusement in the science of poetry; but the fools with devotion to addiction, slumber and fighting. प्रश्नः अस्ति- The qustion is :

कं पृच्छामः सुराः स्वर्गे निवसामो वयं भुवि ।
किं वा काव्यरसः स्वादु किं वा स्वादीयसी सुधा ।।97।।

Whom shall we ask, if the necter of poetry or the *amṛta* is sweeter? The Gods (who drink the juice called *amṛta*) live in the heavens and we (who drink the nectar of poetry) live on the earth. उत्तरं स्यात्– The answer may be :

द्राक्षा म्लानमुखी जाता शर्करा च अश्मतां गता ।
सुभाषितस्य अग्रे सुधा भीता दिवं गता ।।98।।

Sour with the sweetness of the *Subhāṣita,* the grapes have gone sour and wilted, the sugar became tasteless and froze and the *amṛta* got scared and ran away to the heavens.

कविः करोति काव्यानि रसं जानाति पण्डितः ।
तरुः सृजति पुष्पाणि वायुः वहति सौरभम् ।।99।।

The poet makes poetry, and its sweetness is relished by the wise; (just as,) while the trees grow blossoms, the fragrance is carried away by the wind.

संसारवृक्षस्य द्वे फले हि अमृतोपमे ।
सुभाषितरसस्वादः संलापः सज्जनैः सह ।।100।।

The tree of the worldly-life has two sweet fruits, the first is *subhāṣita* and the other is dialogue with the wise people.

34.8
WORDS OF WISDOM
sadupadeśāḥ
सदुपदेशाः ।

अविचार्य न वक्तव्यं वक्तव्यं सुविचारितम् ।
किञ्च तत्रैव वक्तव्यं यत्रोक्तं सफलं भवेत् ।।101।।

उपकारोऽपि नीचानामपकारो हि जायते ।

पयः पानं भुजङ्गानां केवलं विषवर्धनम् ।।102।।

क्षमाशस्त्रं करे यस्य दुर्जनः किं करिष्यति ।

अतृणे पतितो वह्निः स्वयमेवोपशाम्यति ।।103।।

यदशक्यं न तच्छक्यं तच्छक्यं शक्यमेव तत् ।

न जले शकटं याति न च नौर्गच्छति स्थले ।।104।।

अकृत्वा परसन्तापमगत्वा खलमन्दिरम् ।

अनुत्सृज्य सतां वर्त्म यत्स्वल्पमपि तद्बहु ।।105।।

कुसुमं वर्णसम्पन्नं गन्धहीनं न शोभते ।

न शोभते क्रियाहीनं मधुरं वचनं तथा ।।106।।

उद्यमेन हि सिध्यन्ति कार्याणि न मनोरथैः ।

न हि सुप्तस्य सिंहस्य प्रविशन्ति मुखे मृगाः ।।107।।

उद्यमः साहसं धैर्यं बुद्धिः शक्तिः पराक्रमः ।

षडेते यत्र वर्तन्ते तत्र दैवं प्रसीदति ।।108।।

गच्छन्पिपीलिका याति योजनानां शतान्यपि ।

अगच्छन् वैनतेयोऽपि पदमेकं न गच्छति ।।109।।

स्वगृहे पूज्यते मूर्खः स्वग्रामे पूज्यते प्रभुः ।

स्वदेशे पूज्यते राजा विद्वान्सर्वत्र पूज्यते ।।110।।

सर्पदुर्जनयोर्मध्ये वरं सर्पो न दुर्जनः ।

सर्पो दंशति कालेन दुर्जनस्तु पदे पदे ।।111।।

रविश्चन्द्रो घना वृक्षाः नदी गावश्च सज्जनाः ।

एते परोपकाराय भुवि दैवेन निर्मिताः ।112।।

छायामन्यस्य कुर्वन्ति तिष्ठन्ति स्वयमातपे ।

फलान्यपि परार्थाय वृक्षाः सत्पुरुषा इव ।।113।।

यो ध्रुवाणि परित्यज्य अध्रुवं परिसेवते ।

ध्रुवाणि तस्य नश्यन्ति अध्रुवं नष्टमेव च ।।114।।

यस्मिन्देशे न सन्मानो न वृत्तिर्न च बान्धवाः ।

न च विद्यागमोप्यस्ति वासं तत्र न कारयेत् ।।115।।

न देवो विद्यते काष्ठे न पाषाणे न मृन्मये ।

भावे हि विद्यते देवस्तस्माद्भावो हि कारणम् ।।116।।

34.9

RIGHTEOUS SAYINGS

suvaćanāni

सुवचनानि ।

(1) **सत्यमेव जयते नानृतम्** । *satyameva jayate nānṛtam.* (सत्यम् एव जयते, न अनृतम्) Only the truth wins, not the false.

(2) **परोपकारार्थम् इदं शरीरम्** । *paropakārārtham idaṁ śarīram.* The body is for service to others.

(3) **लोभः पापस्य कारणम्** । *lobhaḥ pāpasya kāraṇam.* Greed is the root of sins.

(4) **जननी जन्मभूमिश्च स्वर्गादपि गरीयसी** । *jananī janmabhūmiśća svargādapi garīyasī.* (जननी जन्म-भूमिः च स्वर्गात् अपि गरीयसी) The Mother and the Mother-earth are superior to heaven.

(5) **शीलं परं भूषणम्** । *śīlaṁ paraṁ bhūṣaṇam.* Character is the best adornment.

(6) **अति सर्वत्र वर्जयेत्** । *ati sarvatra varjayet.* Too much should always be avoided.

(7) **न गृहं गृहिणीहीनं गृहिणी गृहम् उच्यते** । *na gṛhaṁ gṛhiṇī-hīnaṁ, gṛhiṇī gṛhaṁ ućyate.* It is not a home without a lady, with a lady a house is called a home.

(8) **दीर्घसूत्री विनश्यति** । *dīrghasūtrī vinaśyati.* The procastinator perishes.

(9) **अक्रोधेन जयेत् क्रोधम्** । *akrodhena jayet krodham.* Violence should be defeated with peace.

(10) **अहिंसा परमो धर्मः** । *ahiṁsā paramo dharmaḥ.* Non-violence is the greatest righteousness.

(11) **अकरणान्मन्दकरणं श्रेयः** । *akaraṇānmandakaraṇaṁ śreyaḥ.* (अकरणात् मन्दकरणं श्रेयः) । Better late than never.

(12) **अनर्थः संघचारिणः** । *anarthaḥ saṅgha-ćāriṇaḥ.* Calamities occur in groups.

(13) **मूर्खस्य नास्त्यौषधम् ।** *mūrkhasya nāsi-auṣadham.* (मूर्खस्य नास्ति औषधम्) You can not cure fools. Brains are not injected.

(14) **वरमद्य कपोतो न श्वो मयूरः ।** *varamadya kapoto na śvo mayūraḥ.* (वरम् अद्य कपोतः न श्वः मयूरः) A pigeon today is better than a peacock tomorrow.

(15) **कोऽतिभारः समर्थानां किं दूरं व्यवसायिनाम् ।**
को विदेशः सविद्यानां कः परः प्रियवादिनाम् ॥120॥

(कः अति-भारः समर्थानाम्? किं दूरं व्यवसायिनाम्? कः विदेशः स-विद्यानाम्? कः परः प्रिय-वादिनाम्?)

For able people what is too difficult? (Nothing). For industrious people what is inaccessible? (None). For the learned people where is there foreign land? (Nowhere). For agreeable people who is a foreigner? (Nobody).

(16) **तावद्भयस्य भेतव्यं यावद्भयमनागतम् ।**
आगतं तु भयं वीक्ष्य नरः कुर्याद्यथोचितम् ॥121॥

(तावत् भयस्य भेतव्यं यावत् भयम् अनागतम् । आगतं तु भयं वीक्ष्य नरः कुर्यात् यथा उचितम् ॥)

One should fear, as long as there is no calamity. But, seeing the calamity a person should act appropriately)

(17) **त्यजेदेकं कुलस्यार्थे ग्रामस्यार्थे कुलं त्यजेत् ।**
ग्रामं जनपदस्यार्थे आत्मार्थे पृथिवीं त्यजेत् ॥122॥

(त्यजेत् एकं कुलस्य अर्थे, ग्रामस्य अर्थे कुलं त्यजेत् । ग्रामं जनपदस्य अर्थे, आत्मार्थे पृथिवीं त्यजेत् ॥)

One person may be sacrificed for the sake of the family, a family may be sacrificed for the sake of the town, a town may be sacrificed for the sake of the country and for the sake of soul, the earth may be left.

(18) **अक्रोधेन जयेत्क्रुद्धमसाधुं साधुना जयेत् ।**
जयेत्कदर्यं दानेन जयेत्सत्येन चानृतम् ॥123॥

(अक्रोधेन जयेत् क्रुद्धम्, असाधुं साधना जयेत् । जयेत् कदर्यं दानेन, जयेत् सत्येन च अनृतम् ॥)

Violence should be won with non-violence; the unrighteous should be won being righteous, a miser should be won over with charity; the false should be won with truth)

LESSON 35

pañćatrimśaḥ abhyāsaḥ पञ्चत्रिंश: अभ्यास: ।

GENERAL KNOWLEDGE

sāmānya-jñānam
सामान्यज्ञानम् ।

35.1

NAMES OF THE DAYS OF THE WEEK

saptāhasya dinānaṁ nāmāni
सप्ताहस्य दिनानां नामानि ।

The names of the seven days of the week are :

(1) Sunday	*Ravivāraḥ*	*Ravivāsaraḥ*	रविवार:	रविवासर:
(2) Monday	*Somavāraḥ*	*Somavāsaraḥ*	सोमवार:	सोमवासर:
(3) Tuesday	*Maṅgalvāraḥ*	*Maṅgalvāsaraḥ*	मंगलवार:	मंगलवासर:
(4) Wednesday	*Budhavāraḥ*	*Budhavāsaraḥ*	बुधवार:	बुधवासर:
(5) Thursday	*Guruvāraḥ*	*Guruvāsaraḥ*	गुरुवार:	गुरुवासर:
(6) Friday	*Śukravāraḥ*	*Śukravāsaraḥ*	शुक्रवार:	शुक्रवासर:
(7) Saturday	*Śanivāraḥ*	*Śanivāsaraḥ*	शनिवार:	शनिवासर:

There are 30 days in a month. मासे त्रिंशत् दिनानि सन्ति । There are two bi-weekly periods in each month, namely Kṛṣṇa-pakṣaḥ and Śukla-pakṣaḥ. प्रतिमासे द्वौ पक्षौ भवत: नामनी कृष्णपक्ष: शुक्लपक्ष: च इति । In each biweekly period there are 15 days. प्रतिपक्षे पञ्चदश

तिथयः भवन्ति । Their names- तासां नामानि–

(1) प्रतिपदा (2) द्वितीया (3) तृतीया (4) चतुर्थी (5) पञ्चमी (6) षष्ठी (7) सप्तमी (8) अष्टमी (9) नवमी (10) दशमी (11) एकादशी (12) द्वादशी (13) त्रयोदशी (14) चतुर्दशी (15) अमावस्या अथवा पौर्णिमा ।

35.2

NAMES OF THE MONTHS OF THE YEAR

वर्षस्य मासानां नामानि ।

The names of the twelve months are:

(1) March-April	*Caitraḥ*	चैत्रः
(2) April-May	*Vaiśākhaḥ*	वैशाखः
(3) May-June	*Jyeṣṭhaḥ*	ज्येष्ठः
(4) June-July	*Āṣāḍhaḥ*	आषाढः
(5) July-August	*Śrāvaṇaḥ*	श्रावणः
(6) Aug.-Sept.	*Bhādrapadaḥ*	भाद्रपदः
(7) Sept.- Oct.	*Āśvinaḥ*	आश्विनः
(8) Oct.-Nov.	*Kārtikaḥ*	कार्तिकः
(9) Nov.-Dec.	*Mārgaśīrṣaḥ*	मार्गशीर्ष
(10) Dec.-Jan.	*Pauṣaḥ*	पौषः
(11) Jan.-Feb.	*Māghaḥ*	माघः
(12) Feb.-March	*Phālgunaḥ*	फाल्गुनः

The names of the six seasons are:

(1) Spring	*Vasantaḥ*	वसन्तः
(2) Summer	*Grīṣmaḥ*	ग्रीष्मः

(3) Rainy-season	*Varṣā*	वर्षा
(4) Autumn	*Sharad*	शरद्
(5) Winter (Nov-Jan)	*Hemantaḥ*	हेमन्तः
(6) Winter(Jan-Mar)	*Śiśiraḥ*	शिशिरः

35.3
THE MEASUREMENTS

parimāṇāni

परिमाणानि ।

Length	आयामः, द्राघिमन्, दैर्घ्यम् ।
Width	विस्तारः, व्यासः, विशालता, परिणाहः ।
Height	आरोहः, उन्नयः, उच्छ्रयः, उच्चता, तुङ्गता ।
Thickness	घनता, संहति, सान्द्रता; पिण्डत्वम्, वेधः ।
Weight	गुरुत्वम्, तोलः, भारः, मानम्; प्रभावः ।
Wetness	आर्द्रता, तेमः, क्लेदः ।
Dryness	शुष्कता, शोषः, निर्जलत्वम् ।
Distance	अन्तरम्, दूरता, असान्निध्यम् ।
Nearness	सामीप्यम्, आसन्नता, नैकट्यम् ।
Smoothness	श्लक्ष्णता, अक्षोभः
Roughness	पारुष्यम्, वैषम्यम्; उग्रता ।
Roundness	वृत्तता, गोलत्वम्, वर्तुलता, पीनता ।
Straightness	ऋजुता, सारल्यम् ।
Obliqueness	वक्रता, अनृजुता ।

35.4

THE NAMES OF THE DIRECTIONS

diśaḥ दिशः ।

East	पूर्वदिश्, पूर्वा, प्राची, ऐन्द्री ।
West	पश्चिमा, प्रतीची, वारुणी ।
North	उत्तरा, उदीची, कौबेरी ।
South	दक्षिणा, अवाची, याम्या ।
South-east	दक्षिणपूर्वा, आग्नेयी ।
South-west	दक्षिणपश्चिमा, नैर्ऋती ।
North-east	उत्तरपूर्वा, पूर्वोत्तरा, प्रागुत्तरा, ऐशानी ।
North-west	उत्तरपश्चिमा, वायवी ।
Right	दक्षिण, वामेतर, अपसव्य, सव्येतर ।
Left	वाम, सव्य, दक्षिणेतर ।
Above	उपरि, ऊर्ध्वम्, उच्चैः ।
Below	अधः, तले ।
Down	अधस्तात् ।
In front of	पुरस्तात्, अग्रतः, अग्रे, मूर्ध्नि, शिरसि ।
In between	अभ्यन्तरे, मध्ये
In	अन्तरे, मध्ये ।
Out	बहिः ।
Toward	प्रति, अभिमुखम् ।
Up	ऊर्ध्वम्, उच्चैः ।

35.5

TIME

samayaḥ **समयः ।**

Names of the time elements :

Second	क्षणः, निमिषः, विपलम् ।
Minute	पलम्, कला ।
Hour	घण्टाः ।
Day	अहन्, दिनम्, दिवसः, वारः, वासरः, तिथिः ।
Night	रात्रिः, रात्री, निशा ।
Dawn	उषः, उषा, प्रभातम् ।
Noon	मध्यदिनम्, मध्याह्नः ।
Afternoon	अपराह्नः, पराह्नः, विकालः ।
Midnight	मध्यरात्रः, अर्धरात्रः, रात्रिमध्यम्, निशीथः ।
Week	सप्ताहः, सप्तदिनम् ।
Year	वर्षः, वत्सरः, अब्दः, समा ।
Age	कल्पः, युगम् ।
Time	समयः, कालः, वेला ।
Day-before-yesterday	परह्यः ।
Yesterday	ह्यः, पूर्वेद्युः ।
Today	अद्य ।
Now	अधुना, इदानीम्, सम्प्रति ।
Tomorrow	श्वः, परेद्युः ।
Day-after-tomorrow	परश्वः ।

Always	सदा, सर्वदा, सततम्, सन्तत, निरन्तरम् ।
Periodically	समयतः, काले काले ।
Sometime	एकदा, पुरा, प्राक् ।
Sometimes	क्वचित्, कदाचित्, कदा कदा, काले काले ।
Maybe	कदाचित् ।
Never	न कदापि, न कदाचन, न जातु ।
Eever	जातु, एकदा ।
* What time is it now?	कः समयः? इदानीं कः समयः सञ्जातः?

kaḥ samayaḥ? idānīṁ kaḥ samayaḥ sañjātaḥ?

EXAMPLES cum EXERCISE : TIME

1. It is one O' clock. *eka-vādanam.* एकवादनम् ।
2. It is 5 minutes past 1 O' clock.
   pañćādhika-eka-vādanam, pañćādhikaika-vādanam पञ्चाधिक–एकवादमन्, पञ्चाधिकैकवादनम् ।
3. It is 5 to 3.
   pañća-nyūna-tri-vādanam. पञ्चन्यूनत्रिवादनम् ।
4. It is four-thirty.
   sārdha-ćatur-vādanam, triṁśādhika-ćatur-vādanam. सार्धचतुर्वादनम्, त्रिंशाधिकचतुर्वादनम् ।
5. It is 7 o'clock.
   sapta-vādanam. सप्तवादनम् ।
6. It is 12 o'clock.
   dvādaśa-vādanam. द्वादशवादनम् ।
7. 4. It is quarter to five.
   pādona-pañća-vādanam. पादोनपञ्चवादनम् ।

35.6 RELATIONSHIPS

sambandhāḥ सम्बन्धाः ।

Bride नववधूः, वधूः, पाणिगृहीता, नवोढा

Brother बन्धुः भ्राता, सोदरः, सहोदरः, सोदर्यः, सहजः, सगर्भः

Brother elder अग्रजः

Brother younger अनुजः

Brother's daughter (niece) भ्रातृकन्या, भ्रातृसुता, भ्रात्रीया

Brother's son (nephew) भ्रातृव्यः, भ्रात्रीयः, भ्रातृपुत्रः

Brother's wife (sister-in-law) भ्रातृजाया, भ्रातृपत्नी, प्रजावती

Brotherhood भ्रातृभावः, सौभ्रात्रम्, साहचर्यम्, समाजः, संसर्गः

Child अपत्यम्; बालः, बालकः, अर्भकः, दारकः, वत्सः, वत्सा, जातः, जाता, शिशुः, सन्तानः, सन्ततिः

Daughter कन्या, सुता, दुहिता, पुत्रका, पुत्री, तनया, आत्मजा, सुनुः, सुनूः, स्वजा, अङ्गजा, जाता, दारिका

Daughter-in-law स्नुषा, पुत्रवधूः, सुतस्त्री

Daughter's daughter (grand-daughter) दौहित्री, पुत्रिकासुता

Daughter's son (grandson) दौहित्रः, पुत्रिकासुतः, पुत्रिकापुत्रः

Family परिवारः, कुलम्, वंशः

Father पिता, जनकः, जन्मदः, तातः

Father-in-law श्वसुरः

Father's brother (uncle) पितृव्यः, पितृभ्राता, तातगुः

Father's brother's daughter (cousin sister) पितृव्यपुत्री

Father's brother's son (cousin) पितृव्यपुत्रः

Father's brother's wife (aunt) पितृव्या

Father's father (grandfather) पितामहः, पितृपिता

Father's mother (grandmother) पितामही, पितृमाता, पितृप्रसूः

Father's sister (aunt) पितृस्वसा

Father's sister's daughter (cousin sister) पितृष्वसेयी

Father's sister's son (cousin) पितृष्वसेयः

Friend मित्रम्, बन्धुः, बान्धवः, सुहृद्, सखा, सखी, स्नेही, हितः, विभावः; सहायः, सहकारी, सहभोगी, सहभागी, सहवर्ती, समदुःखसुखः, प्रतियोगी, सङ्गी, अनुरागी, पथकः

Husband पतिः, स्वामी, वरः, वल्लभः, भर्ता, वोढाः, कान्तः, दयितः, नायः, धवः

Husband's brother (brother-in-law) देवरः

Husband's sister (sister-in-law) ननान्दा, ननन्दा, नन्दा, पतिस्वसा

Lover (boy-friend) प्रियः, प्रणयी, कान्तः, रमणः, रमकः, रमः, वल्लभः, अनुरागी

Mother माता, जननी, अम्बा, जनी, प्रसूः

Mother and father (parents) पितरौ, मातापितरौ, मातरपितरौ

Mother-in-law श्वश्रूः

Mother's brother (uncle) मातुलः, मातृभ्राता, मातगुः

Mother's brother's daughter (niece) मातुलपुत्री

Mother's brother's son (nephew) मातुलपुत्रः

Mother's brother's wife (aunt) मातुली, मातुलानी

Mother's father (grandfather) मातामहः, मतृपिता

Mother's mother (grandmother) मातामही, मातृमाता

Mother's sister (aunt) मातृस्वसा

Mother's sister's daughter (niece) मातृष्वसेयी

Mother's sister's son (nephew) मातृष्वसेयः

Neighbor (fellow) प्रतिवासी, प्रतिवासिनी, समीपवर्ती, निकटस्थः, समीपस्थः, समीपस्थायी,

समीपवासी, समन्तः, अदूरस्थः

Parents (mother and father) पितरौ, मातापितरौ, मातरपितरौ

Relative सम्बन्धी, सगोत्रः, सकुल्यः, बन्धुः, बान्धवः, ज्ञातिः

Sister स्वसा, भगिनी

Sister, elder अग्रजा

Sister, younger अनुजा

Sister's daughter स्वस्त्रीया, भगिनेया

Sister's son (nephew) भगिनेयः, स्वस्त्रीयः, स्वसृसुतः

Sister's husband देवृ (देवा)

Some one, some body कोपि, अमुकः, यःकश्चन, कश्चित्

Son पुत्रः, पुत्रकः, सुतः, सुनुः, तनयः, नन्दनः, आत्मजः, स्वजः, अङ्गजः, तनुजः, दारकः, उद्वहः

Son-in-law जामाता, दुहितुः पति, दुहितुभर्ता

Son's daughter (grand-daughter) पौत्री, पुत्रसुता, पुत्रात्मजा, दौहित्री

Son's son (gradnson) पौत्रः, पुत्रसुतः, पुत्रात्मजः, सुतात्मजः, पुत्रात्मजः, पुत्रकसुतः, नप्ता, पुत्रपुत्रः

Stranger आगन्तुकः, अभ्यागतः, वैदेशिकः, अपरिचितः, परः, परपुरुषः, पारक्यः, अनभ्यस्तः, अज्ञातः, अनभिज्ञः ।

Step brother वैमात्रः, वैमात्रेयः, विमातृजः, अन्योदर्यः

Step daughter सपत्नीसुता

Step father मातुःपतिः

Step mother विमातृ, सपत्नीमाता

Step Sister वैमात्री, वैमात्रैयी, विमातृजा, अन्योदर्या

Step son सपत्नीसुतः

Wife पत्नी, भार्या, स्त्री, जाया, वधूः, गृहिणी, दायिता, कान्ता, वल्लभा, वनिता; दारा (m॰)

Wife's brother (brother-in-law) श्यालः

Wife's sister (sister-in-law) श्याली, श्यालिका, स्यालकी, पत्नीस्वसा, जायाभगिनी

LESSON 36

ṣaṭtriṃśaḥ abhyāsaḥ षट्त्रिंश: अभ्यास: ।

ANTONYMS

viloma-śabdāḥ विलोमशब्दा: ।

अमृतम्	X	विषम्	निर्भय	X	सभय	सजीव	X	निर्जीव
असत्	X	सत्	निस्तेज	X	सतेज	सज्जन:	X	दुर्जन:
उष्ण	X	शीत	निन्दा	X	स्तुति:	सत्यम्	X	असत्यम्
कुकर्म	X	सुकर्म	परकीय	X	स्वकीय	सन्तोष:	X	असन्तोष:
कुटिल	X	सरल	पूर्णता	X	शून्यता	सन्धि:	X	विग्रह:
कुमति:	X	सुमति:	प्रीति:	X	वैरम्	सफल	X	असफल
कुमार्ग:	X	सन्मार्ग:	यश:	X	अपयश:	सम्पद्	X	विपद्
जंगम	X	स्थावर	युक्त	X	विहीन	संयुक्त	X	वियुक्त
तरल	X	शुष्क	विमुख	X	सम्मुख	संयोग:	X	वियोग:
दु:खद	X	सुखद	विस्तिर्ण	X	सङ्कीर्ण	सक्षम	X	अक्षम
दुर्गन्ध:	X	सुगन्ध:	वृद्धि:	X	ह्रास:	साधर्म्यम्	X	वैधर्म्यम्
दुर्गम	X	सुगम	व्यक्त	X	अव्यक्त	सामान्य	X	विशेष
दुर्बल	X	सबल	शांति:	X	अशांति:	सुन्दर	X	विकृत
दुर्बुद्धि:	X	सुबुद्धि:	शूर:	X	कापुरुष:	सुर:	X	असुर:
दुर्बोध	X	सुबोध	श्याम	X	श्वेत	स्मरणं	X	विस्मरणं
दुर्भाग्यं	X	सौभाग्यं	श्रद्धा	X	अश्रद्धा	स्वामी	X	सेवक:
दुष्कर	X	सुकर	श्रीगणेश:	X	इतिश्री	हर्ष:	X	शोक:
दुष्कर्म	X	सत्कर्म	सखा	X	शत्रु:	हिंसा	X	अहिंसा
निराकार	X	साकार	संग:	X	असंग:	क्षुद्र	X	महान्
निराधार	X	साधार	सगुण	X	निर्गुण	ज्ञानम्	X	अज्ञानम्

LESSON 37

saptatrimśaḥ abhyāsaḥ सप्तत्रिंशः अभ्यासः ।

1. WORDS WITH SUFFIXES

pratyayānta-śabdāḥ प्रत्ययान्तशब्दाः ।

In Sanskṛt, words (*śabdāḥ* शब्दाः) and their forms (*rūpāṇi* रूपाणि) are derived in two ways. (1) By attaching suffixes to the roots (*dhātavaḥ* धातवः), and (2) by attaching suffixes to the words. The suffixes are the syllables (*śabdāṁśāḥ* शब्दांशाः) or marks (*ćihnāni* चिह्नानि) that, are added to modify the meaning of the words.

Besides the case suffixes (*vibhakti-pratyayāḥ* विभक्ति-प्रत्ययाः) and the tense and mood suffixes (*tiṅganta-pratyayāḥ* तिङन्त-प्रत्ययाः) described in Lessons 17-27, there are two other types of suffixes, as described in the Lesson on participles, in this Lesson and in the next Lesson.

(1) The suffixes that are attached to the verb roots to form nouns, adjectives and indeclinable words, are known as Primary suffixes (*kṛt- pratyayāḥ* कृत्-प्रत्ययाः).

(2) The suffixes that are attached to words to form derivative nouns, pronouns, adjectives and indeclinable words, are known as Secondary suffixes (*taddhita-pratyayāḥ* तद्धित-प्रत्ययाः), given in the next Lesson.

A word that is formed with a primary suffix, is called a Participle (*kṛdantahm* कृदन्तम्); and the word that is formed with a secondary suffix, is called a Derivative Word (*taddhita-śabdaḥ* तद्धित-शब्दः).

WE MUST ALWAYS REMEMBER THAT :

(1) *tahddhita* (तद्धित) suffixes are never attached to verb roots.

(2) the *kṛt* (कृत्) suffixrs are not attached to the words.

(3) The declensions (*vibhakti-rūpāṇi* विभक्ति-रूपाणि) of the nouns, pronouns and adjectives are formed by attaching Case suffixes (*sup-pratyayāḥ* सुप्-प्रत्यया:). Thus, the case suffixes are never attached to verbs; and

(4) the conjugations of Tense-and-Moods (*tiṅgant-lakarāḥ* तिङन्त-लकारा:) of the verbs (*kriyāpadāni* क्रियापदानि) are formed by attaching the Tense-and-Mood suffixes (*tiṅg-pratyayāḥ* तिङ्-प्रत्यया: See Lesson17-27). Thus, the tense suffixes are never attached to nouns or adjectives.

37.1
WORDS WITH PRIMARY SUFFIXES
कृत्-प्रत्ययान्ता: शब्दा: ।

The primary suffixes are attached only to the root verbs. (कृत्-प्रत्ययानां प्रयोग: धातुभि: सह एव भवति)

While the prefixes are attached before the root verbs and their derivatives, as prepositions, the suffixes are added after the verbs, as postpositions. For prefixes that are attached to the verb roots, see Lesson 30, on Prepositiopns.

PRIMARY SUFFIXES :

(A) *kvin, kañ* and *ksa* क्विन्, कञ् and क्स suffixes : When the pronouns such as त्यद्, तद्, यद्, एतद्, इदम्, युष्मद्, अस्मद्, भवत्, किम्, समान, अन्य are prefixed to the √roots, attachment of the क्विन्, कञ् and क्स suffixes give adjectives indicating similitude.

Prefix+√root	+ *kvin* क्विन्	+ *kañ* कञ्	+ *ksa* क्स	Meaning
त्यद् √दृश्	त्यादृक्	त्यादृशः	त्यादृक्ष	like that
तद् √दृश्	तादृक्	तादृशः	तादृक्ष	like that
यद् √दृश्	यादृक्	यादृशः	यादृक्ष	as
एतद् √दृश्	एतादृक्	एतादृशः	एतादृक्ष	like this
इदम् √दृश्	ईदृक्	ईदृशः	ईदृक्ष	like this
युष्मद् √दृश्	युष्मादृक्	युष्मादृशः	युष्मादृक्ष	like you
भवत् √दृश्	भवादृक्	भवादृशः	भवादृक्ष	like you
अस्मद् √दृश्	अस्मादृक्	अस्मादृशः	अस्मादृक्ष	like me
किम् √दृश्	कीदृक्	कीदृशः	कीदृक्ष	like what
समान √दृश्	सदृक्	सदृशः	सदृक्ष	similar
अन्य √दृश्	अन्यादृक्	अन्यादृशः	अन्यादृक्ष	like other

* These adjectives decline in seven cases, in three genders and in three numbers, similar to other regular adjectives.

(B) *lyuṭ* ल्युट्

lyuṭ ल्युट् suffix अन (*an*) is added to a √root to form a neuter abstract noun. e.g.

to tolerate	√सह्	+	ल्युट् (अन)	=	सहनम्	tolerance
to read	√पठ्	+	ल्युट् (अन)	=	पठनम्	reading
to sleep	√शी	+	ल्युट् (अन)	=	शयनम्	sleep
to give	√दा	+	ल्युट् (अन)	=	दानम्	giving
to listen	√श्रु	+	ल्युट् (अन)	=	श्रवणम्	listening
to do	√कृ	+	ल्युट् (अन)	=	करणम्	doing
to become	√भू	+	ल्युट् (अन)	=	भवनम्	becoming

(C) *ṇini* णिनि (इन्) suffix

If there is a substantive prefixed to the √root verb, *ṇini* णिनि (इन्) suffix is attached to produce an adjective suggesting one's nature. e.g.

noun	+	√root	+	णिनि	=	adjective	m∘	f∘	n∘
ब्रह्मन्	+	√चर्	+	णिनि	=	ब्रह्मचारिन्	ब्रह्मचारी	ब्रह्मचारिणी	ब्रह्मचारि
सुख	+	√दा	+	णिनि	=	सुखदायिन्	सुखदायी	सुखदायिनी	सुखदायि
चिर	+	√स्था	+	णिनि	=	चिरस्थायिन्	चिरस्थायी	चिरस्थयिनी	चिरस्थायि

(D) *dhiṇun* धिणुन् (इन्) suffix

If a substantive is NOT prefixed to the √root verb, then by attaching the *dhiṇun* धिणुन् (इन्) suffix, an adjective suggesting one's nature is produced.

√root	+	इन्	=	adjective	m∘	f∘	n∘
√युज्	+	इन्	=	योगिन्	योगी,	योगिनी,	योगि
√श्रम्	+	इन्	=	श्रमिन्	श्रमी,	श्रमिनी,	श्रमि
√भज्	+	इन्	=	भागिन्	भागी,	भागिनी,	भागि

(E) *ṇamul* णमुल् suffix

When a subject performs two actions, then to indicate completion of the first (subordinate) action prior to the last (main) action, an Indeclinable Past Participle ipp∘ (क्त्वा) is used instead of a verb (see 28.6). This participle (क्त्वा) implies completion of the preceding action ('having done, or doing' पूर्वकालिक) before the following action begins.

If the action indicated by ipp∘ is repeatitive, then णमुल् suffix indicates the repitition or excess of that action.

√श्रु + क्वा = श्रुत्वा श्रुत्वा having heard over and over

√श्रु + णमुल् = श्रावं श्रावम् having heard over and over

(F) *tṛṇ* and *tṛć* तृण् and तृच् suffixes

When *tṛṇ* or *tṛć* तृण् or तृच् suffix is attached to a verb √root, it produces an adjective meaning 'having the habit that is indicated by the verb' or 'one performing the verb in the best manner.'

√भू + तृण् (तृ) = भवितृ *bhavitṛ* One who becomes

√भू + तृच् (तृ) = भवितृ *bhavitṛ* One who becomes

Both these suffixes produce same word, but they are different in sound. In Vedic Sanskrit, where the pronunciation is an important factor, use of each of these two suffixes makes a significant difference. However, in the Classical sanskrit, this difference is not measurable.

√हन् + (तृ) = हन्तृ One who kills, killer

√जि + (तृ) = जेतृ One who wins, winner

NOTE : The adjective produced by तृ suffix in the Nominative case is same as the verb produced by लृट् (indefinite future) tense, third person, singular.

(G) *ṇvul* ण्वुल् (वु) suffix

When attached to a verb, it produces an adjective meaning 'doer' of that verb.

√कृ	+ ण्वुल् (अक)	=	कारक, कारिका, कारकम्	the doer
√स्था	+ ण्वुल् (अक)	=	स्थायक, स्थायिका, स्थायकम्	the stayer
√सेव्	+ ण्वुल् (अक)	=	सेवक, सेविका, सेवकम्	the server
√गै	+ ण्वुल् (अक)	=	गायक, गायिका, गायकम्	the singer

Kṛt Suffixes and their Substitutes

कृत्-प्रत्ययाः तेषां च आदेशाः ।

क्विन्, क्विप्, ण्वि, विच्	= the whole suffix disappears
अच्, अण्, अप्, क, खच्, खञ्, खल्, खश्, ट, टक्, ड, ण, श	= अ
क्वुन्, ण्वुच्, ण्वुल्, वुञ्, वुन्, ष्वुन्	= अक
युच्, ल्यु, ल्युट्	= अन
झच्, झिच्	= अन्त्
णमुल्	= अम्
टाप्, डाप्, चाप्	= आ
षानक्	= आक्
फिञ्, फक्, ष्फ	= आयन्
णिच्, णिङ्	= इ
ठक्, ठञ्, ठन्	= इक
इनि, णिनि, घिनुण्	= इन्
घ	= इय्
इष्णुच्, खिष्णुच्	= इष्णु
ङीप्, ङीष्, ङीन्	= ई
ख	= ईन्
छ	= ईय्
उण्, डु	= उ
उकञ्	= उक
ऊङ्	= ऊ
ढक्, ढञ्	= एय्
कन्, कप्	= क
क्त	= त
क्तवतु = तवत्	क्तिच्, क्तिन् = ति
क्त्वा = त्वा	नङ्, नन् = न
क्वनिप् = वन्	क्वरप् = वर
क्यप्, यक्, यञ्, यत्, ण्य, ण्यत्, ल्यप्, ष्यञ्	= य

37.2

WORDS WITH SECONDARY SUFFIXES

taddhita-śabdāh तद्धित-शब्दाः ।

The Secondary Suffixes तद्धित-प्रत्ययाः ।

Nouns or adjectives can be derived from primitive nouns, pronouns, adjectives and indeclinables, to imply a particular relation to a thing, action or notion that belongs (*tat-dhit* तत्-हित्) to that primitive subject itself.

The secondary suffix, that forms such a noun or adjective from a primitive subject, is called a derivative affix (तद्धित-प्रत्ययः).

Remember, that *thddhita* suffixes are never atteched to verb roots. They are only attached to subtantives (प्रातिपादिकाः) to form derivative nouns, pronouns, adjectives and indeclinable words.

For convenience, the *taddhita* suffixes can be grouped into three sections :

(A) Suffixes showing relationship of possession,

(B) suffixes forming adverbs, and

(C) miscellaneous secondary suffixes.

(A) Taddhita suffixes showing possession (मत्वर्थीय-आदेशाः)

When attached, these affixes form adjectives possessing the sense or the quality that is possessed by the noun to which they are attached. e.g.

NOTE : The words in the brackets show actual substitutes.

(1) Taddhita suffix *itać* (इतच्)

n◦ puṣpa + *itać (it)* = adj◦ puṣpita (Gītā 2.42)

* पुष्प + इतच् (इत) = पुष्पित । पुष्प = n◦ flower, पुष्पित = adj◦ flowery, decorated, ornamented, embellished, showey.

(2) Taddhita suffixes *ini* (इनि), *ṭhañ* (ठञ्) and *ṭhak* (ठक्)

* *jñāna + ini (in) = adj◦ jnānin* (Gītā 7.16)
  ज्ञान + इनि (इन्) = ज्ञानिन् । ज्ञान = n◦ knowledge; ज्ञानिन् (ज्ञानी) = adj◦ One who possesses knowledge, wise, learned, experienced.
* *sattva + ṭhañ (ika) = sāttvika* (Gītā 1.14) सत्त्व + ठञ् (इक) = सात्त्विक (righteous),
* *ātman + ṭhak (ika) = ātmika* (Gītā 2.41) आत्मन् + ठक् (इक) = आत्मिक (own)

(3) Taddhita suffix *yap* (यप्)

* *triguṇa + yap (ya) = traiguṇya* (Gītā 2.45) त्रिगुण + यप् (य) = त्रैगुण्य (belonging to the three *gunas*); त्रिगुण = Collective noun◦ Three Guṇas; त्रैगुण्य = adj◦ that which possesses the three guṇas.

(4) Taddhita suffix *vin* (विन्)

* *medhā + vin (vin) = medhāvin* (Gītā 18.10)
  मेधा + विन् (विन्) = मेधाविन् । मेधा = n◦ Intellect, intelligence; मेधाविन् (मेधावी) adj◦ Intelligent, brilliant, clever, smart, wise, astute

(B) Taddhita suffixes yield Adverbs (क्रियाविशेषणकारकाः)

These suffixes produce adverbs when they are attached attached to adjectives.

(1) Taddhita suffix *ena* (एन)

* *aćira + ena (ena) = aćireṇa* (Gītā 4.39) अचिर + एन (एन) = अचिरेण । अचिर = adj◦ short, quick; अचिरेण = adv◦ shortly, quickly, fast, soon.
* *naćira + ena (ena) = naćireṇa* (Gītā 5.6) नचिर + एन (एन) = नचिरेण adv◦ shortly, quickly.

(2) Taddhita suffix *tas* (तस्)

* *parmukha + taḥ = pramukhataḥ* (Gītā 1.25)

प्रमुख + तस् (तः) = प्रमुखतः । प्रमुख = adj◦ facing; प्रमुखतः = प्रमुखे = adv◦ In front of, before, opposite to.

(3) Taddhita suffix *nā* (ना)

* *nā + nā (nā) = nānā* (various) (Gītā 1.9) ना + ना (ना) = नाना

ना = adj◦ Not that; नाना = adv◦ ind◦ in different ways, differently, variously.

* *vi + nā (nā) = vinā* (without) (Gītā 10.39) वि + ना = विना

(4) Taddhita suffix *vatup* (वतुप्)

Similitude of a noun or verb with another object.

* *āścarya + vatup (vat) = āścaryavat* (Gītā 2.29) आश्चर्य + वतुप् (वत्) = आश्चर्यवत् । आश्चर्य = n◦ Wonder; आश्चर्यवत् = adv◦ like a wonder, wondrously, wonderingly.

(5) Taddhita suffix *śas* (शस्)

* *sarva + śas (śaḥ) = sarvaśaḥ* (Gītā 1.18) सर्व + शस् (शः) = सर्वशः । सर्व = pron◦ all; सर्वशः = adv◦ ind◦ all together.

(C) Miscellaneous Taddhita suffixes (सङ्कीर्ण-प्रत्ययाः)

(1) Suffixes *a, i, eya, ya* (अ, इ, एय, य) = offspring of

Usually letter *a* (अ) is added to the first chararcter of the word and then the Taddhita suffix is added. e.g.

* *pāṇḍu + a = a + pāṇḍu + a = pāṇḍava* (Gītā 1.1) पाण्डु + अ = पाण्डव, पाण्डोः अपत्यम् । पाण्डु = n◦ King Pāṇḍu; पाण्डव = n◦ King Pāṇḍu's son.

* *somadatta + i = saumadatti* (Gītā 1.8) सोमदत्त + इ = सौमदत्ति, सोमदत्तस्य अपत्यम् ।

* *kunti + eya = kaunteya* (Gītā 1.8) कुन्ती + एय = कौन्तेय, कुन्त्याः अपत्यम्

* *diti + ya = daitya* (Gītā 10.30) दिति + य = दैत्य, दितेः अपत्यम्

(2) Taddhita suffixes *aṇ* (अण्), *tva* (त्व), *ṇyañ* (ण्यञ्), *yak* (यक्), *tal* (तल्), and *imanić*

(इमनिच्)

All these suffixes form abstract nouns.

(i) The suffixes *aṇ* (अण्), *tva* (त्व), *ṇyañ* (ण्यञ्), *yak* (यक्) form neuter nouns,

(ii) *tal* (तल्) forms feminine nouns, and

(iii) *imaniś* (इमनिच्) forms masculine nouns.

* *muni + aṇ (a) = mauna* (Gītā 10.38) मुनि + अण् (अ) = मौन = मुनेः भावः

* मुनि = adj◦ The person who is holy, ascetic, saintly; मौन (मौनम्) = n◦. The attitude of silence, silence, taciturnity

* *śatru + tva (tva) = śatrutva* (Gītā 6.6) शत्रु + त्व (त्व) = शत्रुत्व

* *durbala + ṇyañ (ya) = daurbalya* (Gītā 2.3) दुर्बल + ण्यञ् (य) = दौर्बल्य

* *rājan + yak (ya) = rājya* (Gītā 1.32) राजन् + यक् (य) = राज्य

* *deva + tal (tā) = devatā* (Gītā 4.12) देव + तल् (ता) = देवता

* *mahat + imaniś (iman) = mahiman* (Gītā 11.41) महत् + इमनिच् (इमन्) = महिमन्

(3) Taddhita suffixes of comparison *īyasun* (ईयसुन्), *tarap* (तरप्), *tamap* (तमप्), *iṣṭhan* (इष्ठन्)

(a) Suffix *tarap* (तरप्) is comparison between two objects, *īyasun* (ईयसुन्) is comparison between two qualities;

(b) *tamap* (तमप्) suggests comparison between more than two objects, and

(c) *iṣṭhan* (इष्ठन्) is used optionally in place of *tamap.*

* *guru + īyasun (īyas) = garīyas* (Gītā 1.32) गुरु + ईयसुन् (ईयस्) = गरीयस् । गुरु = adj◦ big, good, great; गुरु + ईयस्, गरीयस् = comparative adj◦ better, greater.

* *kṣema + tarap (tara) = kṣematara* (Gītā 1.46) क्षेम + तरप् (तर) = क्षेमतर

* *dvija + ud + tamap (tama) = dvijottama* (Gītā 1.7) द्विज + उद् + तमप् (तम) = द्विजोत्तम

* *śrī + iṣṭhan (iṣṭha) = śreṣṭha* (Gītā 3.21) श्री + इष्ठन् (इष्ठ) = श्रेष्ठ

* गुरु + इष्ठन् (इष्ठ) = गरिष्ठ = biggest, best, greatest.

(4) Taddhita suffixes *matup* (मतुप्) and *maya* (मय)

Suffixes *matup* (मतुप्) and *mayad* (मयद्) suggest inclusion of one thing into another. e.g.

* *dhī + matup (mat) = dhīmat* (Gītā 1.3) धी + मतुप् (मत्) = धीमत् । धी = Intellect, intelligence; धीमत् (धीमान्) = adj∘ Intelliogent, having intelligence.

* *mat + mayad (maya) = manmaya* (Gītā 4.10) मत् + मयद् (मय) = मन्मय

NOTE: Sometimes the *matup* (मत्) suffix undergoes a change (वत्व) and becomes a *vat* (वत्) suffix, and declines like the word भगवत् । e.g.

* *Bhaga + matup (vat) =* bhagavat (divine) (Gītā 10.14)

  भग + (मतुप्) वत् = भगवत् See Appendix 2 for all Case declensions↓

(5) Taddhita suffixes *gha* (घ) and *ćh* (छ) indicating relationship

* *kṣatra + gha (iya) = kṣatriya* (Gītā 3.31) क्षत्र + घ (इय) = क्षत्रिय

* *asmad + ćh (īya) = asmadīya* (Gītā 11.26) अस्मद् + छ (ईय) = अस्मदीय

* अस्मद् = pron∘ I, we; अस्मदीय = pronominal∘ Our

(6) Other Taddhita suffixes- *āmaha* (आमह), *tyul* (ट्युल्), *tal* (तल्), *tyap* (त्यप्), and *śālać* (शालच्)

* *pitṛ + āmaha (āmaha) = pitāmaha* (Gītā 1.12) पितृ + आमह (आमह) = पितामह

* *sadā + ṭyul (tana) = sanātana* (Gītā 1.40) सदा + ट्युल् (तन) = सनातन

* *sama + tal (tā) = samatā* (Gītā 10.5) सम + तल् (ता) = समता

* *ni + tyap (tya) = nitya* (Gītā 2.15) नि + त्यप् (त्य) = नित्य

* *vi + śālać (śāla) = viśāla* (Gītā 9.29) वि + शालच् (शाल) = विशाल

NOTE : The *taddhita* words may also be prepared from other taddhita words. e.g. भरत → भारत → भारतीय; पण्डा → पण्डित → पाण्डित्य । पण्डा → पाण्डु → पाण्डुपुत्र, पाण्डव → पाण्डवीय ।

SOME COMMONLY USED TADDHITA WORDS

अस्मदीय (Belonging to us अस्मद्)
आस्तिक (Existance of in God अस्ति)
ऐतिहासिक (About history इतिहास)
कौन्तेय (Son of Kuntī कुन्ती)
कौरव (Descendent of Kuru कुरु)
गुरुत्व (Quality of greatness गुरु)
जनता (A group of people जन)
जलमय (Flooded with water जल)
जागतिक (Belonging to world जगत्)
जानकी (Daughter of Janaka जनक)
तामसिक (of the Tamasa तमस्)
दैत्य (Descendent of Diti दिति)
दैनिक (daily day दिन)
धनवान् (Possessing wealth धन)
धार्मिक (Belonging to Dharma धर्म)
धीमान् (Possessing intellect धी)
नाविक (Rider of a boat नौ)
नास्तिक (Non-existence of God नास्ति)
न्याय्य (Abiding law न्याय)
पशुता (Nature of an animal पशु)
पाण्डव (Son of Pāṇḍu पाण्डु)
पार्थ (Son of Pṛthā पृथा)
पौराणिक (Relating to Purāṇa पुराण)
प्राणिन् (Possessing life प्राण)
बलवान् (Possessing strength बल)
बुद्धिमान् (Possessing intellect बुद्धि)
भवदीय (Belonging to you भवत्)
भारतीय (Of linage of Bharata भरत)

भौतिक (About the beings भूत)
मदीय (Belonging to me मत्)
महिमा (Quality of greatness महिमन्)
माधुर्य (Quality of being sweet मधुर)
मासिक (Once a month मास)
मूर्खत्व (Nature of a fool मूर्ख)
मृदुता (Quality of softness मृदु)
यौवन (Quality of a youth यून)
राघव (Descendent of Raghu रघु)
राजसिक (Belonging to Rajasa रजस्)
राष्ट्रिय (Belonging to the nation राष्ट्र)
रूपवती (f∘ Possessing beauty रूप)
रूपवान् (m∘ Possessing beauty रूप)
लघुत्व (Quality of shortness लघु)
वार्षिक (Once a year वर्ष)
वासुदेव (Son of Vasudeva वसुदेव)
विद्यावान् (Possessing knowledge विद्या)
वैदिक (Belonging to Veda वेद)
शक्तिमान् (Possessing power शक्ति)
शारीरिक (Pertaining to body शरीर)
शौर्य (Nature of a brave person शूर)
श्रीमती (f∘ Possessing divinity श्री)
श्रीमान् (m∘ Possessing divinity श्री)
सात्त्विक (Belonging to Sattva सत्त्व)
सुन्दरता (Bing beautiful सुन्दर)
स्वकीय (Belonging to oneself स्व)
ज्ञानवान् (Possessing knowledge ज्ञान)
ज्ञानिन् (Possessing knowledge ज्ञान)

The Feminine Suffixes (स्त्री प्रत्ययाः)

In Saṁskrit some words are feminine by nature (e.g. yudh, saṁjñā, bheri, pṛthivī, ćamū), however, the masculine words can also be converted into femine words using such suffixes as, *ā* (आ), *ī* (ई), ū (ऊ) and ti (ति). e.g.

(i) m∘ dhīmat + *ṭāp* (ā) = *dhīmatā* धीमत् + टाप् (आ) धीमता ।

(ii) m∘ brahman + *ñIp* (ī) = *brahmī* ब्रह्मन् + ङीप् (ई) ब्राह्मी ।

(iii) m∘ bandh + *ūṅ* (ū) = *vadhū* बन्ध् + ऊङ् (ऊ) वधूः ।

(iv) m∘ sanga + *ktin* (ti) = *saṅgati* सङ्ग + क्तिन् (ति) सङ्गतिः ।

MASCULINE TO FEMININE GENDER CONVERSION

लिङ्गपरिवर्तनम् ।

EXAMPLES

पुंल्लिङ्गस्य च शब्दस्य स्त्रीलिङ्गे कीदृशं भवेत् । रूपं चेति मयाऽधस्तात्तव बोधाय लिख्यते ।।
पतिः पत्नी नरो नारी देवो देवी नदो नदी । गौरो गौरी गुरुर्गुर्वी हंसो हंसी शुकः शुकी ।।
सिंहः सिंही पिता माता राक्षसो राक्षसी तथा । भागिनेयो भागिनेयी राजा राज्ञी मृगो मृगी ।।
रजको रजकी चैव ब्रह्मणो ब्रह्मणी तथा । पुत्रः पुत्री प्रपौत्रश्च प्रपौत्री च यमो यमी ।।
पौत्रः पौत्री प्रभुः प्रभ्वी सारसः सारसी तथा । मानवो मानवी श्रीमान्श्रीमती व परः परा ।।
सुन्दराः सुन्दरी धाता धात्री चैव चरः चरी । मातुलो मातुलानी च भ्राता च भगिनी तथा ।।
दशमो दशमी चेति महीयांश्च महीयसी । नर्तको नर्तकी पापी पापिनीश्वर ईश्वरी ।।
गुणवान्गुणवती च श्यामः श्यामा नृपो नृपा । बुद्धिहीनो बुद्धिहीना मानुषश्चाथ मानुषी ।।
दौहित्रस्त्वथ दौहित्री हरिणो हरिणी तथा । व्याघ्रो व्याघ्री च वैश्यश्च वैश्या मूषकश्च मूषिका ।।
एकः एका द्वितीयश्च द्वितीयेदृश ईदृशी । दशमो दशमी चैव पञ्चमः पञ्चमी तथा ।।
षष्ठः षष्ठी द्वादशश्च द्वादशी च कृपः कृपी । प्रथमः प्रथमा सौम्यः सौम्या गजो गजेति च ।।

37.3

USING NOUNS AS VERB ROOTS

नामधातुः ।

So far we have used only the verb roots to make tenses. However, popular nouns or adjectives can also be used as a root verbal base (नामधातुः) to form a verb indicating 'to be, to be like or to act like.' **These verbs are formed by adding य *(y)* to a noun or adjective and then attaching a *parasmaipadi* or an *ātmanepadi* tense suffix.** Normally these verbs are used in present tense.

CLASSICAL EXAMPLES :

(1) गुणैरुत्तङ्गतां याति नोच्चैरासन्संस्थितः ।
प्रासादशिखरस्थोऽपि काकः किं गरुडायते ।।

(गुणैः उत्तङ्गतां याति न-उच्चैः आसन्-संस्थितः प्रासाद-शिखर-स्थः अपि काकः किं गरुडायते ।)

Sitting up high not necessarily means excellence in virtues. Does a crow seated on top of a palace become an eagle?

noun गरुडः (eagle) + य *(y)* + present tense suffix ते *(te)* = गरुडायते *(garudāyate)* to become an eagle.

(2) सज्जनमुखे दोषाः गुणायन्ते, दुर्जनमुखे तु गुणाः दोषायन्ते ।

(3) आवेष्टितं महासर्पैः चन्दनं न विषायते ।

(4) पूर्णकुम्भः न करोति शब्दं परम् अर्धघटः शब्दायते ।

(5) जनन्या प्रेम्णा दत्तं पयोऽपि अमृतायते ।

(6) वृद्धस्य शरीरं जीर्यते परं तृष्णा तस्य न मन्दायते ।

37.4

THE AMAZING SANSKRIT CREATIONS

Due to the unique fluidity and very scientific digital nature of its grammar, amazing possibilities are inherent in Sanskrit language which provide originality and creativity to its writers like no other world language does.

A large number of Sanskrit creations are so marvelously embellished that they rather fall under a special Sanskrit classification of *varna-chitras* (character graphics) than common poetics. For example :

(1) The following *śloka* looks as if it is saying, "when Hanūmāna killed Rāma, the monkeys started dancing with joy and the demons cheered." But the real meaning is : *When the garden (of Ravana) was destroyed by hanūmān, the monkeys started dancing with joy and the demons cried, "the garden is destroyed, the garden is destroyed."*

हनूमति हतारामे वानरा हर्षनिर्भराः ।
रुदन्ति राक्षसाः सर्वे हा हारामो हतो हतः ।।

Hanūmati hatārāme vānarā harṣanirbharā,
rudanti rākṣasāḥ sarve hā hārāmo hato hataḥ.

(2) And what is most amazing, as well as interesting of all, is the work of poet Sūrya, *Rāmakṛṣṇa-Kāyam,* written in Anuśṭubha meter. Each stanza of this entire voluminous poetic work when read forward describes Rama's story from the Rāmāyaṇa and when the same read backward reads Krishna's story from the Bhāgavata. It exhibits the flexibility and richness of Sanskrit language. In which other world language can this be achieved?

Of course, None!

Given below, for example, is just the first *ślóka* from *Ramakrishṇa-Kāvyam* of poet Surya's great work :

तं भूसुतामुक्तिमुदारहासं वन्दे यतो भव्यभवं दयाश्रीः ।
श्रीयादवं भव्यभतोयदेवं संहारदामुक्तिमुतासुभूतम् ।।

Taṁ bhūsutāmuktimudārahāsaṁ vande yato bhavyabhavaṁ dayāśrīḥ,
Śrīyādavaṁ bhavyabhatoyadevaṁ saṁhāradāmuktimutāsubhūtam.

Read forward : *"I pay my homage to Him who rescued Sīta, whose laughter is captivating, whose incarnation is grand, and from whom mercy and splendour arise everywhere."*

Read backwards : "*I bow before that Srikrishna, the descendent of Yādava family; who is a divinity of the sun as well as the moon; who destroyed Pūtanā who only gave destruction; and who is the soul of all this universe."*

(3) Another amazing feat is this śloka in which each word is an adjective of Lord Śiva. But, when the first letter from each word is deleted, it becomes an adj◦ of Lord Viśṇu.

गवीशपत्रो नगजार्तिहारी कुमारतातः शशिखण्डमौलिः ।
लङ्केशसंपूजितपादपद्मः पायादनादिः परमेश्वरो नः ।।

gavīśapatro nagajātirhārī kumāratātaḥ śaśikhaṇḍamauliḥ,
laṅkeśasaṁpūjitapādapadmaḥ pāyādanādiḥ parameśvaro naḥ.

It means : May he protect us whose carrier is the bull, he who is the remover of the sorrow of Goddess Pārvatī, he who is the father of Skanda, he whom the Rāvaṇa worshipped, he who is beginingless, he who is the greatest Lord.

When first letter of each word removed, we get : May he protect us whose carrie is Garuḍa the eagle, he who is the remover of the sorrow of the Gajendra the puraṇic elephent, he who is the father of Cupid, he who is the bearer of the crown of peacock peathers, he who is worshipped by the Brahma and Śiva, he who is the husband of goddess Lakṣmī.

(4) Then an amazing example of a poetic composition with *anuprāsa* (recurring letters) :

कल्पान्तः क्रूरकेलिः क्रतुकदनकरः कुन्दकर्पूरकान्तिः ।
क्रीडन्कैलासकूटे कलितकुमुदिनीकामुकः कान्तकायः ।
कङ्कालक्रीडनोत्कः कलितकलिकलः कालकालीकलपत्रः ।
कालिन्दीकालकण्ठः कलयतु कुशलं कोऽपि कापालिको नः ।।

kalpāntaḥ krūrakeliḥ kratukadanakaraḥ kundakarpūrakāntiḥ krīḍaṅkailāsakūṭe kalitakumudinīkāmukaḥ kāntakāyaḥ,
kaṅkālakrīḍanotkaḥ kalitakalikalaḥ kālakālīkalapatraḥ kālindīkālakaṇṭhaḥ kalayatu kuśalaṁ ko'pi kapāliko naḥ.

May he protect us who does *tāṇḍava* dance at the dissolution of the universe, he who performed the play of destruction of the *yajña* of Dakṣa, who has the bright colour like the spotless wildflowers and the camphor, he who dances at the top of Kaliāsa mountain, he who is very charming, he who plays with bones and skeletons, he who has a sweet voice, he whose wife is Kalī, he who bares the garland of snake around his neck, he who bares a necklace of skulls.

(5) In the following example of power and flexibility of Sanskrit language, poet is able to ask four questions, answer them and arrange questions and answers in the anuṣṭubh

meter, with the use of only 32 syllables.

कं सञ्जघान कृष्णः का शीतलवाहिनी गङ्गा ।
के दारपोषणरताः कं बलवन्तं न बाधते शीतम् ।।

kaṁ sañjaghāna kṛṣṇa? kā śītalavāhinī gaṅgā?
ke dārapoṣaṇaratā? kaṁ balavantaṁ na bādhate śītam?

(The answers to each question is obtained by joining first two syllables of each question)

(6) In the following interesting example, again with only 32 syllables, the poet is able to make graphic but insightful observation :

साक्षरा विपरिता चेद्राक्षसा एव केवलम् ।
सरसो विपरितोऽपि सरसत्वं न मुञ्चति ।।
(साक्षराः विपरिता चेत् राक्षसाः एव केवलम् ।
सरसः विपरितः अपि सरसत्वं न मुञ्चति ।)

sākṣarā viparitā ćedrākṣasā eva kevalam,
saraso viparito'pi sarasatvaṁ na muñćati.

(The 'educated,' if reversed, turn only into 'demons,' but the 'wise' remains same even in adverse state)

(7) And, then one of my own little riddles :

मेघमार्गे हयो याति भूम्यां तिष्ठति घोटकः ।
धावन्पवनवेगेन पदमेकं न गच्छति ।।

nagha mārge hayo yāti bhūmyāṁ tiṣṭhati ghoṭakaḥ,
dhāvanpavanavegena padamekaṁ na gaćchati.

(The answer is : Kite आतापी, पतङ्गः)

APPENDIX

THE CHARTS OF CONJUGATIONS

e.g. the verb root √*bhū* (√भू to become, to be)

(A)

ACTIVE VOICE PARASMAIPADI

1A. THE 360 PARASMAIPADI ACTIONS (10 Parasmaipadi Tenses)
from the verb √bhū (भू)

(A) REGULAR (साधारण) ACTIONS

(1) Present Tense : लट् (सामान्य-वर्तमाने) *Parasmaipadī* - e.g. I become

	Singular	Dual	Plural
1p◦	भवामि *bhavāmi*	भवाव: *bhavāvaḥ*	भवाम: *bhavāmaḥ*
2p◦	भवसि *bhvasi*	भवथ: *bhavathaḥ*	भवथ *bhavatha*
3p◦	भवति *bhavati*	भवत: *bhavataḥ*	भवन्ति *bhavanti*

(2) Past Imperfect Tense : लङ् (अनद्यतन-भूते) *Parasmaipadī* - e.g. I became

1p◦	अभवम् *abhavam*	अभवाव *abhavāva*	अभवाम *abhavāma*
2p◦	अभव: *abhavaḥ*	अभवतम् *abhavatam*	अभवत *abhavata*
3p◦	अभवत् *abhavat*	अभवताम् *abhavatām*	अभवन् *abhavan*

(3) Perfect Past Tense : लिट् (परोक्ष-भूते) *Parasmaipadī* - e.g. I had become

1p◦	बभूव *babhūva*	बभूविव *babhūviva*	बभूविम *babhūvima*
2p◦	बभूविथ *babhūvitha*	बभूवथु: *babhūvathuḥ*	बभूव *babhūva*
3p◦	बभूव *babhūva*	बभूवतु: *babhūvatuḥ*	बभूवु: *babhūvuḥ*

(4) Indefinite Past Tense : लुङ् (दूरवर्ति-भूते) *Parasmaipadī* - e.g. I had become

1p∘ अभूवम् *abhūvam*	अभूव *abhūva*	अभूम *abhūma*
2p∘ अभूः *abhūḥ*	अभूतम् *abhūtam*	अभूत *abhūta*
3p∘ अभूत् *abhūt*	अभूताम् *abhūtām*	अभूवन् *abhūvan*

(5) Definite Future : लुट् (सामान्य-भविष्यति) *Parasmaipadī* - e.g. I will become

Singular	Dual	Plural
1p∘ भवितास्मि *bhavitāsmi*	भवितास्वः *bhavitāsvaḥ*	भवितास्मः *bhavitāsmaḥ*
2p∘ भवितासि *bhavitāsi*	भवितास्थः *bhavitāsthaḥ*	भवितास्थ *bhavitāstha*
3p∘ भविता *bhavitā*	भवितारौ *bhavitārau*	भवितारः *bhavitāraḥ*

(6) Indefinite Future : लृट् (अपूर्ण-भविष्यति) *Parasmaipadī* - e.g. I shall become

1p∘ भविष्यामि *bhaviṣyāmi*	भविष्यावः *bhaviṣyāvaḥ*	भविष्यामः *bhaviṣyāmaḥ*
2p∘ भविष्यसि *bhaviṣyasi*	भविष्यथः *bhaviṣyathaḥ*	भविष्यथ *bhaviṣyatha*
3p∘ भविष्यति *bhaviṣyati*	भविष्यतः *bhaviṣyataḥ*	भविष्यन्ति *bhaviṣyanti*

(7) Conditional Mood : लृङ् (भविष्यति क्रियातिपत्तौ) *Parasmaipadī* - e.g. If I become

1p∘ अभविष्यम् *abhaviṣyam*	अभविष्याव *abhaviṣyāva*	अभविष्याम *abhaviṣyāma*
2p∘ अभविष्यः *abhaviṣyaḥ*	अभविष्यतम् *abhaviṣyatam*	अभविष्यत *abhaviṣyata*
3p∘ अभविष्यत् *abhaviṣyat*	अभविष्यताम् *abhaviṣyatām*	अभविष्यन् *abhaviṣyan*

(8) Imperative Mood : लोट् (आज्ञार्थे; प्रश्नार्थे; विध्यादौ) Parasmai∘ - e.g. May I become?

1p∘ भवानि *bhavāni*	भवाव *bhavāva*	भवाम *bhavāma*
2p∘ भव *bhava*	भवतम् *bhavatam*	भवत *bhavata*
3p∘ भवतु *bhavatu*	भवताम् *bhavatām*	भवन्तु *bhavantu*

(9) Potential or Subjunctive Mood : विधिलिङ् (विध्यादौ) *Parasmaipadī* - e.g. I may become

1p∘ भवेयम *bhaveyama*	भवेव *bhaveva*	भवेम *bhavema*
2p∘ भवेः *bhaveḥ*	भवेतम् *bhavetam*	भवेत *bhaveta*
3p∘ भवेत् *bhavet*	भवेताम् *bhavetām*	भवेयुः *bhaveyuḥ*

(10) Benedictive or Optative Mood : आशीर्लिङ् (आशिषि) *Parasmaipadī* - e.g. May I become!

1p∘ भूयासम *bhūyāsama*	भूयास्व *bhūyāsva*	भूयास्म *bhūyāsma*
2p∘ भूयाः *bhūyāḥ*	भूयास्तम् *bhūyāstam*	भूयास्त *bhūyāsta*

3p◦ भूयात् *bhūyāt*	भूयास्ताम् *bhūyāstām*	भूयासुः *bhūyāsuḥ*

(B) THE CAUSATIVE (ण्यन्त) ACTIONS

ACTIVE VOICE - PARASMAIPADI

(1) Present Tense : लट् (सामान्य-वर्तमाने) *Parasmaipadī*, Causative - e.g. I am made

Singular	Dual	Plural
1p◦ भावयामि *bhāvayāmi*	भावयावः *bhāvayāvaḥ*	भावयामः *bhāvayāmaḥ*
2p◦ भावयसि *bhāvayasi*	भावयथः *bhāvayathaḥ*	भावयथ *bhāvayatha*
3p◦ भावयति *bhāvayati*	भावयतः *bhāvayataḥ*	भावयन्ति *bhāvayanti*

(2) Past Imperfect : लङ् (अनद्यतन-भूते) *Parasmaipadī*, Causative - e.g. I was made

1p◦ अभावयम् *abhāvayam*	अभावयाव *abhāvayāva*	अभावयाम *abhāvayāma*
2p◦ अभावयः *abhāvayaḥ*	अभावयतम् *abhāvayatam*	अभावयत *abhāvayata*
3p◦ अभावयत् *abhāvayat*	अभावयताम् *abhāvayatām*	अभावयन् *abhāvayan*

(3) Perfect Past : लिट् (परोक्ष-भूते) *Parasmaipadī*, Causative - e.g. I was made

1p◦ भावयाञ्चकार *bhāvayāñćakāra*	भावयाञ्चकृव *bhāvayāñćakṛva*	भावयाञ्चकृम *bhāvayāñćakṛma*
भावयाम्बभूवम् *bhāvayāmbabhūvam*	भावयाम्बभूव *bhāvayāmbabhūva*	भावयाम्बभूम *bhāvayāmbabhūma*
भावयामास *bhāvayāmāsa*	भावयामासिव *bhāvayāmāsiva*	भावयामासिम *bhāvayāmāsima*
2p◦ भावयाञ्चकर्थ *bhāvayāñćakartha*	भावयाञ्चक्रथुः *bhāvayāñćakrathuḥ*	भावयाञ्चक्र *bhāvayāñćakra*
भावयाम्बभूथ *bhāvayāmbabhūtha*	भावयाम्बभूवथुः *bhāvayāmbabhūvathuḥ*	भावयाम्बभूव *bhāvayāmbabhūva*
भावयामासिथ *bhāvayāmāsitha*	भावयामासथुः *bhāvayāmāsathuḥ*	भावयामास *bhāvayāmāsa*
3p◦ भावयाञ्चकार *bhāvayāñćakāra*	भावयाञ्चक्रतुः *bhāvayāñćakratuḥ*	भावयाञ्चक्रुः *bhāvayāñćakruḥ*

भावयाम्बभूव bhāvayāmbabhūva | भावयाम्बभूवतुः bhāvayāmbabhūvatuḥ | भावयाम्बभूवुः bhāvayāmbabhūvuḥ

भावयामास bhāvayāmāsa | भावयामासतुः bhāvayāmāsatuḥ | भावयामासुः bhāvayāmāsuḥ

(4) Indefinite Past : लुङ् (दूरवर्ति-भूते) *Parasmaipadī*, Causative - e.g. I had been made

Singular	Dual	Plural
1p◦ अभावयिष्यम् *abhāvayiṣyam*	अभावयिष्याव *abhāvayiṣyāva*	अभावयिष्याम *abhāvayiṣyāma*
2p◦ अभावयिष्यः *abhāvayiṣyaḥ*	अभावयिष्यतम् *abhāvayiṣyatam*	अभावयिष्यत *abhāvayiṣyata*
3p◦ अभावयिष्यत् *abhāvayiṣyat*	अभावयिष्यताम् *abhāvayiṣyatām*	अभावयिष्यन् *abhāvayiṣyan*

(5) Definite Future : लुट् (सामान्य-भविष्यति) *Parasmaipadī*, Causative - e.g. I will be made

1p◦ भावयितास्मि *bhāvayitāsmi*	भावयितास्वः *bhāvayitāsvaḥ*	भावयितास्मः *bhāvayitāsmaḥ*
2p◦ भावयितासि *bhāvayitāsi*	भावयितास्थः *bhāvayitāsthaḥ*	भावयितास्थ *bhāvayitāstha*
3p◦ भावयिता *bhāvayitā*	भावयितारौ *bhāvayitārau*	भावयितारः *bhāvayitāraḥ*

(6) Indefinite Future : लृट् (अपूर्ण-भविष्यति) *Parasmaipadī*, Causative - e.g. I shall be made

1p◦ भावयिष्यामि *bhāvayiṣyāmi*	भावयिष्यावः *bhāvayiṣyāvaḥ*	भावयिष्यामः *bhāvayiṣyāmaḥ*
2p◦ भावयिष्यसि *bhāvayiṣyasi*	भावयिष्यथः *bhāvayiṣyathaḥ*	भावयिष्यथ *bhāvayiṣyatha*
3p◦ भावयिष्यति *bhāvayiṣyati*	भावयिष्यतः *bhāvayiṣyataḥ*	भावयिष्यन्ति *bhāvayiṣyanti*

(7) Conditional Mood : लृङ् (भविष्यति क्रियातिपत्तौ) *Parasmaipadī*, Causative - e.g. If I am made

1p◦ अभावयिष्यम् *abhāvayiṣyam*	अभावयिष्याव *abhāvayiṣyāva*	अभावयिष्याम *abhāvayiṣyāma*
2p◦ अभावयिष्यः *abhāvayiṣyaḥ*	अभावयिष्यतम् *abhāvayiṣyatam*	अभावयिष्यत *abhāvayiṣyata*
3p◦ अभावयिष्यत् *abhāvayiṣyat*	अभावयिष्यताम् *abhāvayiṣyatām*	अभावयिष्यन् *abhāvayiṣyan*

(8) Imperative Mood : लोट् (आज्ञार्थे; प्रश्नार्थे; विध्यादौ) *Parasmaipadī*, Causative - May I be made?

1p◦ भावयानि *bhāvayāni*	भावयाव *bhāvayāva*	भावयाम *bhāvayāma*
2p◦ भावय *bhāvaya*	भावयतम् *bhāvayatam*	भावयत *bhāvayata*
3p◦ भावयतु *bhāvayatu*	भावयताम् *bhāvayatām*	भावयन्तु *bhāvayantu*

(9) Potential or Subjunctive Mood विधिलिङ् (विध्यादौ) *Parasmaipadī* Causative - I may be made

1p◦ भावयेयम् *bhāvayeyam*	भावयेव *bhāvayeva*	भावयेम *bhāvayema*
2p◦ भावये: *bhāvayeḥ*	भावयेतम् *bhāvayetam*	भावयेत *bhāvayeta*
3p◦ भावयेत् *bhāvayet*	भावयेताम् *bhāvayetām*	भावयेयु: *bhāvayeyuḥ*

(10) Benedictive or Optative Mood आशीर्लिङ् (आशिषि) *Parasmai◦* Causative May I be made!

Singular	Dual	Plural
1p◦ भाव्यासम् *bhāvyāsam*	भाव्यास्व *bhāvyāsva*	भाव्यास्म *bhāvyāsma*
2p◦ भाव्या: *bhāvyāḥ*	भाव्यास्तम् *bhāvyāstam*	भाव्यास्त *bhāvyāsta*
3p◦ भाव्यात् *bhāvyāt*	भाव्यास्ताम् *bhāvyāstām*	भाव्यासु: *bhāvyāsuḥ*

(C) THE DESIDERATIVE (सन्नन्त) ACTIONS

ACTIVE VOICE - PARASMAIPADI

(1) Present Tense : लट् (सामान्य-वर्तमाने) *Parasmaipadī*, Desiderative - e.g. I want to become

Singular	Dual	Plural
1p◦ बुभूषामि *bubhūṣāmi*	बुभूषाव: *bubhūṣāvaḥ*	बुभूषाम: *bubhūṣāmaḥ*
2p◦ बुभूषसि *bubhūṣasi*	बुभूषथ: *bubhūṣathaḥ*	बुभूषथ *bubhūṣatha*
3p◦ बुभूषति *bubhūṣati*	बुभूषत: *bubhūṣataḥ*	बुभूषन्ति *bubhūṣanti*

(2) Past Imperfect : लङ् (अनद्यतन-भूते) Parasmai◦ Desiderative - e.g. I wanted to became

1p◦ अबुभूषम् *abubhūṣam*	अबुभूषाव *abubhūṣāva*	अबुभूषाम *abubhūṣāma*
2p◦ अबुभूष: *abubhūṣaḥ*	अबुभूषतम् *abubhūṣatam*	अबुभूषत *abubhūṣata*
3p◦ अबुभूषत् *abubhūṣat*	अबुभूषताम् *abubhūṣatām*	अबुभूषन् *abubhūṣan*

(3) Perfect Past : लिट् (परोक्ष-भूते) *Parasmaipadī*, Desiderative - e.g. I had wanted to become

1p◦ बुभूषाञ्चकार *bubhūṣāñćakāra*	बुभूषाञ्चकृव *bubhūṣāñćakṛva*	बुभूषाञ्चकृम *bubhūṣāñćakṛma*
बुभूषाम्बभूवम् *bubhūṣāmbabhūvam*	बुभूषाम्बभूव *bubhūṣāmbabhūva*	बुभूषाम्बभूम *bubhūṣāmbabhūma*
बुभूषामास *bubhūṣāmāsa*	बुभूषामासिव *bubhūṣāmāsiva*	बुभूषामासिम *bubhūṣāmāsima*

2p◦ बुभूषाञ्चकर्थ *bubhūṣāñćakartha*	बुभूषाञ्चक्रथु: *bubhūṣāñćakrathuḥ*	बुभूषाञ्चक्र *bubhūṣāñćakra*
बुभूषाम्बभूथ *bubhūṣāmbabhūth*	बुभूषाम्बभूवथु: *bubhūṣāmbabhūvathuḥ*	बुभूषाम्बभूव *bubhūṣāmbabhūva*
बुभूषामासिथ *bubhūṣāmāsitha*	बुभूषामासथु: *bubhūṣāmāsathuḥ*	बुभूषामास *bubhūṣāmāsa*
3p◦ बुभूषाञ्चकार *bubhūṣāñćakāra*	बुभूषाञ्चक्रतु: *bubhūṣāñćakratuḥ*	बुभूषाञ्चक्रु: *bubhūṣāñćakruḥ*
बुभूषाम्बभूव *bubhūṣāmbabhūva*	बुभूषाम्बभूवतु: *bubhūṣāmbabhūvatuḥ*	बुभूषाम्बभूवु: *bubhūṣāmbabhūvuḥ*
बुभूषामास *bubhūṣāmāsa*	बुभूषामासतु: *bubhūṣāmāsatuḥ*	बुभूषामासु: *bubhūṣāmāsuḥ*

(4) Indefinite Past : लुङ् (दूरवर्ति-भूते) Parasmai◦ Desiderative - e.g. I had wanted to become

Singular	Dual	Plural
1p◦ अबुभूषिषम् *abubhūṣiṣam*	अबुभूषिष्व *abubhūṣiṣva*	अबुभूषिष्म *abubhūṣiṣma*
2p◦ अबुभूषी: *abubhūṣīḥ*	अबुभूषिष्टम् *abubhūṣiṣṭam*	अबुभूषिष्ट *abubhūṣiṣṭa*
3p◦ अबुभूषीत् *abubhūṣīt*	अबुभूषिष्टाम् *abubhūṣiṣṭām*	अबुभूषिषु: *abubhūṣiṣuḥ*

5. Definite Future लुट् (सामान्य-भविष्यति) Parasmai◦ Desiderative eg. I would want to become

1p◦ बुभूषितास्मि *bubhūṣitāsmi*	बुभूषितास्व: *bubhūṣitāsvaḥ*	बुभूषितास्म: *bubhūṣitāsmaḥ*
2p◦ बुभूषितासि *bubhūṣitāsi*	बुभूषितास्थ: *bubhūṣitāsthaḥ*	बुभूषितास्थ *bubhūṣitāstha*
3p◦ बुभूषिता *bubhūṣitā*	बुभूषितारौ *bubhūṣitārau*	बुभुषितार: *bubhūṣitāraḥ*

6. Indefinite Future लृट् (अपूर्ण-भविष्यति) Parasmai◦ Desiderative - e.g. I shall want to become

1p◦ बुभूषिष्यामि *bubhūṣiṣyāmi*	बुभूषिष्याव: *bubhūṣiṣyāvaḥ*	बुभूषिष्याम: *bubhūṣiṣyāmaḥ*
2p◦ बुभूषिष्यसि *bubhūṣiṣyasi*	बुभूषिष्यथ: *bubhūṣiṣyathaḥ*	बुभूषिष्यथ *bubhūṣiṣyatha*
3p◦ बुभूषिष्यति *bubhūṣiṣyati*	बुभूषिष्यत: *bubhūṣiṣyataḥ*	बुभूषिष्यन्ति *bubhūṣiṣyanti*

(7) Conditional Mood लृङ् (भविष्यति क्रियातिपत्तौ) *Parasmaipadī* Desiderative If I want to become

1p◦ अबुभूषिष्यम् *abubhūṣiṣyam*	अबुभूषिष्याव *abubhūṣiṣyāva*	अबुभूषिष्याम *abubhūṣiṣyāma*
2p◦ अबुभूषिष्य: *abubhūṣiṣyaḥ*	अबुभूषिष्यतम् *abubhūṣiṣyatam*	अबुभूषिष्यत *abubhūṣiṣyata*

3p◦ अबुभूषिष्यत् *abubhūṣiṣyat* अबुभूषिष्यताम् *abubhūṣiṣyatām* अबुभूषिष्यन् *abubhūṣiṣyan*

(8) Imperative Mood लोट् (आज्ञार्थे; प्रश्नार्थे; विध्यादौ) *Parasmaipadī* Desi◦ I should want to become!

1p◦ बुभूषाणि *baubhūṣāṇi*	बुभूषाव *bubhūṣāva*	बुभूषाम *bubhūṣāma*
2p◦ बुभूष *bubhūṣa*	बुभूषतम् *bubhūṣatam*	बुभूषत *bubhūṣata*
3p◦ बुभूषतु *bubhūṣatu*	बुभूषताम् *bubhūṣatām*	बुभूषन्तु *bubhūṣantu*

(9) Potential or Subjunctive Mood विधिलिङ् (विध्यादौ) *Parasmaipadī* Desi◦ I may want to become!

Singular	Dual	Plural
1p◦ बुभूषेयम् *bubhūṣeyam*	बुभूषेव *bubhūṣeva*	बुभूषेम *bubhūṣema*
2p◦ बुभूषेः *bubhūṣeḥ*	बुभूषेतम् *bubhūṣetam*	बुभूषेत *bubhūṣeta*
3p◦ बुभूषेत् *bubhūṣet*	बुभूषेताम् *bubhūṣetām*	बुभूषेयुः *bubhūṣeyuḥ*

(10) Benedictive or Optative Mood आशीर्लिङ् (आशिषि) *Parasmaipadī* Desiderative May I become!

1p◦ बुभूष्यासम् *bubhūṣyāsam*	बुभूष्यास्व *bubhūṣyāsva*	बुभूष्यास्म *bubhūṣyāsma*
2p◦ बुभूष्याः *bubhūṣyāḥ*	बुभूष्यास्तम् *bubhūṣyāstam*	बुभूष्यास्त *bubhūṣyāsta*
3p◦ बुभूष्यात् *bubhūṣyāt*	बुभूष्यास्ताम् *bubhūṣyāstām*	बुभूष्यासुः *bubhūṣyāsuḥ*

(D) THE REPEATETIVE or FREQUENTATIVE (यङ्लुगन्त) ACTIONS

ACTIVE VOICE - PARASMAIPADI

(1) Present Tense : लट् (सामान्य-वर्तमाने) *Parasmaipadī*, Frequentative - e.g. I become more

Singular	Dual	Plural
1p◦ बोभवीमि-बोभोमि *bobhavīmi-bobhomi*	बोभूवः *bobhūvaḥ*	बोभूमः *bobhūmaḥ*
2p◦ बोभवीषि-बोभोषि *bobhaviṣi-bobhoṣi*	बोभूथः *bobhūthaḥ*	बोभूथ *bobhūtha*
3p◦ बोभवीति-बोभोति *bobhavīti-bobhoti*	बोभूतः *bobhūtaḥ*	बोभुवति *bobhuvati*

(2) Past Imperfect : लङ् (अनद्यतन-भूते) *Parasmaipadī*, Frequentative - e.g. I became more

1p◦	अबोभवम् *abobhavam*	अबोभूव *abobhūva*	अबोभूम *abobhūma*
2p◦	अबोभवी: *abobhavīh*	अबोभूतम् *abobhūtam*	अबोभूत *abobhūta*
3p◦	अबोभवीत् *abobhavīt*	अबोभूताम् *abobhūtām*	अबोभूवु: *abobhūvuḥ*

(3) Perfect Past : लिट् (परोक्ष-भूते) *Parasmaipadī*, Frequentative - e.g. I had become more

	Singular	Dual	Plural
1p◦	बोभवाञ्चकार *bobhavāñćakāra*	बोभवाञ्चकृव *bobhavāñćakṛva*	बोभवाञ्चकृम *bobhavāñćakṛma*
	बोभवाम्बभूवम् *bobhavāmbabhūvam*	बोभवाम्बभूव *bobhavāmbabhūva*	बोभवाम्बभूम *bobhavāmbabhūma*
	बोभवामास *bobhavāmāsa*	बोभवामासिव *bobhavāmāsiva*	बोभवामासिम *bobhavāmāsima*
2p◦	बोभुवाञ्चकर्थ *bobhūvāñćakartha*	बोभुवाञ्चक्रथु: *bobhūvāñćakṛthuḥ*	बोभुवाञ्चक्र *bobhūvāñćakra*
	बोभुवाम्बभूथ *bobhuvāmbabhūtha*	बोभुवाम्बभूवथु: *bobhuvāmbabhūvathuḥ*	बोभुवाम्बभूव *bobhuvāmbabhūva*
	बोभुवामासिथ *bobhuvāmāsitha*	बोभुवामासथु: *bobhuvāmāsathuḥ*	बोभुवामास *bobhuvāmāsa*
3p◦	बोभुवाञ्चकार *bobhuvāñćakāra*	बोभुवाञ्चक्रतु: *bobhuvāñćakratuḥ*	बोभुवाञ्चक्रु: *bobhuvāñćakruḥ*
	बोभुवाम्बभूव *bobhuvāmbabhūva*	बोभुवाम्बभूवतु: *bobhuvāmbabhūvatuḥ*	बोभुवाम्बभूवु: *bobhuvāmbabhūvuḥ*
	बोभुवामास *bobhuvāmāsa*	बोभुवामासतु: *bobhuvāmāsatuḥ*	बोभुवामासु: *bobhuvāmāsuḥ*

(4) Indefinite Past : लुङ् (दूरवर्ति-भूते) *Parasmaipadī*, Frequentative - e.g. I had become more

1p◦	अबोभूवम् *abobhūvam*	अबोभूव *abobhūva*	अबोभूम *abobhūma*
2p◦	अबोभूवी: *abobhūṿīh*	अबोभूतम् *abobhūtam*	अबोभूत *abobhūta*
3p◦	अबोभूवीत् *abobhūvīt*	अबोभूताम् *abobhūtām*	अबोभवु: *abobhavuḥ*

(5) Definite Future : लुट् (सामान्य-भविष्यति) *Parasmaipadī*, Frequentative - I will become more

1p◦	बोभवितास्मि *bobhavitāsmi*	बोभवितास्व: *bobhavitāsvaḥ*	बोभवितास्म: *bobhavitāsmaḥ*
2p◦	बोभवितासि *bobhavitāsi*	बोभवितास्थ: *bobhavitāsthaḥ*	बोभवितास्थ *bobhavitāstha*
3p◦	बोभविता *bobhavitā*	बोभवितारौ *bobhavitārau*	बोभवितार: *bobhavitāraḥ*

(6) Indefinite Future : लृट् (अपूर्ण-भविष्यति) *Parasmaipadī*, Frequentative - I will become more

	Singular	Dual	Plural
1p◦	बोभविष्यामि *bobhaviṣyāmi*	बोभविष्याव: *bobhaviṣyāvaḥ*	बोभविष्याम: *bobhaviṣyāmaḥ*
2p◦	बोभविष्यसि *bobhaviṣyasi*	बोभविष्यथ: *bobhaviṣyathaḥ*	बोभविष्यथ *bobhaviṣyatha*
3p◦	बोभविष्यति *bobhaviṣyati*	बोभविष्यत: *bobhaviṣyataḥ*	बोभविष्यन्ति *bobhaviṣyanti*

(7) Conditional Mood लृङ् (भविष्यति क्रियातिपत्तौ) *Parasmaipadī* Frequentative If I become more

1p◦	अबोभविष्यम् *abobhaviṣyam*	अबोभविष्याव *abobhaviṣyāva*	अबोभविष्याम *abobhaviṣyāma*
2p◦	अबोभविष्य: *abobhaviṣyaḥ*	अबोभुविष्यतम् *abobhaviṣyatam*	अबोभविष्यत *abobhaviṣyata*
3p◦	अबोभविष्यत् *abobhaviṣyat*	अबोभविष्यताम् *abobhaviṣyatām*	अबोभविष्यन् *abobhaviṣyan*

(8) Imperative Mood लोट् (आज्ञार्थे; प्रश्नार्थे; विध्यादौ) *Parasmai*◦ Frequ◦ I should become more!

1p◦	बोभवानि *bobhavāni*	बोभवाव *bobhavāva*	बोभवाम *bobhavāma*
2p◦	बोभोहि *bobhohi*	बोभूतम् *bobhūtam*	बोभूत *bobhūta*
3p◦	बोभवीतु *bobhvītu*	बोभूताम् *bobhūtām*	बोभुवतु *bobhuvatu*

(9) Potential or Subjunctive Mood विधिलिङ् (विध्यादौ) *Parasmaipadī* Frequ◦ I may become more

1p◦	बोभूयाम् *bobhūyām*	बोभूयाव *bobhūyāva*	बोभूयाम *bobhūyāma*
2p◦	बोभूया: *bobhūyāḥ*	बोभूयातम् *bobhūyātam*	बोभूयात *bobhūyāta*
3p◦	बोभूयात् *bobhūyāt*	बोभूयाताम् *bobhūyātām*	बोभूयु: *bobhūyuḥ*

(10) Benedictive or Optative Mood आशीर्लिङ् (आशिषि) *Parasmaipadī* Freq◦ May I become more!

1p◦	बोभूयासम् *bobhūyāsam*	बोभूयास्व *bobhūyāsva*	बोभूयास्म *bobhūyāsma*
2p◦	बोभूया: *bobhūyāḥ*	बोभूयास्तम् *bobhūyāstam*	बोभूयास्त *bobhūyāsta*
3p◦	बोभूयात् *bobhūyāt*	बोभूयास्ताम् *bobhūyāstām*	बोभूयासु: *bobhūyāsuḥ*

(2)

ACTIVE VOICE ATMANEPADI

(1B) THE 360 ĀTMANEPADI SINGLE-WORD ACTIONS (10 Atmanepadi Tenses)

e.g. from the verb √bhū (भू)

(E) REGULAR (साधारण) ACTIONS

(1) Present Tense : लट् (सामान्य-वर्तमाने) Ātmanepadī - e.g. I become

Singular	Dual	Plural
1p॰ भवे *bhave*	भवावहे *bhavāvahe*	भवामहे *bhavāmahe*
2p॰ भवसे *bhavase*	भवेथे *bhavethe*	भवध्वे *bhavadhve*
3p॰ भवते *bhavate*	भवेते *bhavete*	भवन्ते *bhavante*

(2) Past Imperfect Tense : लङ् (अनद्यतन-भूते) Ātmanepadī - e.g. I became

1p॰ अभवे *abhave*	अभवावहि *abhavāvahi*	अभवामहि *abhavāmahi*
2p॰ अभवथा: *abhavathāḥ*	अभवेथाम् *abhavethām*	अभवध्वम् *abhavadhvam*
3p॰ अभवत *abhavata*	अभवेताम् *abhavetām*	अभवन्त *abhavanta*

(3) Perfect Past Tense : लिट् (परोक्ष-भूते) Ātmanepadī - e.g. I had become

1p॰ बभूवे *babhūve*	बभूविवहे *babhūvivahe*	बभूविमहे *babhūvimahe*
2p॰ बभूविषे *babhūviṣe*	बभूवाथे *babhūvāthe*	बभूविध्वे *babhūvidhve*
3p॰ बभूवे *babhūve*	बभूवाते *babhūvāte*	बभूविरे *babhūvire*

(4) Indefinite Past Tense : लुङ् (दूरवर्ति-भूते) Ātmanepadī - e.g. I had become

1p॰ अभविषि *abhaviṣi*	अभविष्वहि *abhaviṣvahi*	अभविष्महि *abhaviṣmahi*
2p॰ अभविष्ठा: *abhaviṣṭāḥ*	अभविषाथाम् *abhaviṣāthām*	अभविध्वम् *abhavidhvam*
3p॰ अभाविष्ट *abhāviṣṭa*	अभविषाताम् *abhaviṣātām*	अभविषत *abhaviṣata*

(5) Definite Future : लुट् (सामान्य-भविष्यति) Ātmanepadī - e.g. I will become

1p॰ भविताहे *bhavitāhe*	भवितास्वहे *bhavitāsvahe*	भवितास्महे *bhavitāsmahe*
2p॰ भवितासे *bhavitāse*	भवितासाथे *bhavitāsāthe*	भविताध्वे *bhavitādhve*

3p◦ भविता *bhavitā*	भवितारौ *bhavitārau*	भवितार: *bhavitāraḥ*

(6) Indefinite Future : लृट् (अपूर्ण-भविष्यति) Ātmanepadī - e.g. I shall become

1p◦ भविष्ये *bhaviṣye*	भविष्यावहे *bhaviṣyāvahe*	भविष्यामहे *bhaviṣyāmahe*
2p◦ भविष्यसे *bhaviṣyase*	भविष्येथे *bhaviṣyethe*	भविष्यध्वे *bhaviṣyadhve*
3p◦ भविष्यते *bhaviṣyate*	भविष्येते *bhaviṣyete*	भविष्यन्ते *bhaviṣyante*

(7) Conditional Mood : लृङ् (भविष्यति क्रियातिपत्तौ) Ātmanepadī - e.g. If I become

Singular	Dual	Plural
1p◦ अभविष्ये *abhaviṣye*	अभविष्यावहि *abhaviṣyāvahi*	अभविष्यामहि *abhaviṣyāmahi*
2p◦ अभविष्यथा: *abhaviṣyathāḥ*	अभविष्येथाम् *abhaviṣyethām*	अभविष्यध्वम् *abhaviṣyadhvam*
3p◦ अभविष्यत *abhaviṣyata*	अभविष्येताम् *abhaviṣyetām*	अभविष्यन्त *abhaviṣyanta*

(8) Imperative Mood : लोट् (आज्ञार्थे; प्रश्नार्थे; विध्यादौ) Ātmanepadī - e.g. May I become?

1p◦ भवै *bhavai*	भवावहै *bhavāvahai*	भवामहै *bhavāmahai*
2p◦ भवस्व *bhavasva*	भवेथाम् *bhavethām*	भवध्वम् *bhavadhvam*
3p◦ भवताम् *bhavatām*	भवेताम् *bhavetām*	भवन्ताम् *bhavantām*

(9) Potential or Subjunctive Mood : विधिलिङ् (विध्यादौ) Ātmanepadī - e.g. I may become

1p◦ भवेय *bhaveya*	भवेवहि *bhavevahi*	भवेमहि *bhavemahi*
2p◦ भवेथा: *bhavethāḥ*	भवेयाथाम् *bhaveyāthām*	भवेध्वम् *bhavedhvam*
3p◦ भवेत *bhaveta*	भवेताम् *bhavetām*	भवेरन् *bhaveran*

(10) Benedictive or Optative Mood : आशीर्लिङ् (आशिषि) Ātmanepadī - e.g. May I become!

1p◦ भविषीय *bhaviṣīya*	भविषीवहि *bhaviṣīvahi*	भविषीमहि *bhaviṣīmahi*
2p◦ भविषीष्ठा: *bhaviṣīṣṭhāḥ*	भविषीयास्थाम् *bhaviṣīyāsthām*	भविषीध्वम् *bhaviṣīdhvam*
3p◦ भविषीष्ट *bhaviṣīṣṭa*	भविषीयास्ताम् *bhaviṣīyāstām*	भविषीरन् *bhaviṣīran*

(F) THE CAUSATIVE (ण्यन्त) ACTIONS

ACTIVE VOICE - ĀTMANEPADI

(1) Present Tense : लट् (सामान्य-वर्तमाने) Ātmanepadī, Causative - e.g. I am made

Singular	Dual	Plural

1p◦ भावये *bhāvaye*	भावयावहे *bhāvayāvahe*	भावयामहे *bhāvayāmahe*
2p◦ भावयसे *bhāvayase*	भावयेथे *bhāvayethe*	भावयध्वे *bhāvayadhve*
3p◦ भावयते *bhāvayate*	भावयेते *bhāvayete*	भावयन्ते *bhāvayante*

(2) Past imperfect Tense : लङ् (अनद्यतन-भूते) Ātmanepadī, Causative - e.g. I was made

Singular	Dual	Plural
1p◦ अभावये *abhāvaye*	अभावयावहि *abhāvayāvahi*	अभावयामहि *abhāvayāmahi*
2p◦ अभावयथा: *abhāvayathāḥ*	अभावयेताम् *abhāvayetām*	अभावयध्वम् *abhāvayadhvam*
3p◦ अभावयत *abhāvayata*	अभावयेताम् *abhāvayetām*	अभावयन्त *abhāvayanta*

(3) Perfect Past Tense : लिट् (परोक्ष-भूते) Ātmanepadī, Causative - e.g. I was made

1p◦ भावयाञ्चक्रे *bhāvayāñćakre*	भावयाञ्चकृवहे *bhāvayāñćakṛvahe*	भावयाञ्चकृमहे *bhāvayāñćakṛmahe*
2p◦ भावयाञ्चकृषे *bhāvayāñćakṛṣe*	भावयाञ्चक्राथे *bhāvayāñćakrāthe*	भावयाञ्चकृढ्वे *bhāvayāñćakṛḍhve*
3p◦ भावयाञ्चक्रे *bhāvayāñćakre*	भावयाञ्चक्राते *bhāvayāñćakrāte*	भावयाञ्चक्रिरे *bhāvayāñćakrire*

(4) Indefinite Past Tense : लुङ् (दूरवर्ति-भूते) Ātmanepadī, Causative - e.g. I had been made

1p◦ अबीभवे *abībhave*	अबीभवावहि *abībhavāvahi*	अबीभवामहि *abībhavāmahi*
2p◦ अबीभवथा: *abībhavathāḥ*	अबीभवेथाम् *abībhavethām*	अबीभवध्वम् *abībhavadhvam*
3p◦ अबीभवत *abibhavata*	अबिभवेताम् *abibhavetām*	अबिभन्त *abibhavanta*

(5) Definite Future : लुट् (सामान्य-भविष्यति) Ātmanepadī, Causative - e.g. I will be made

1p◦ भावयिताहे *bhāvayitāhe*	भावयितास्वहे *bhāvayiitāsvahe*	भावयितास्महे *bhāvayiitāsmahe*
2p◦ भावयितासे *bhāvayitāse*	भावयितासाथे *bhāvayitāsāthe*	भावयिताध्वे *bhāvayitādhve*
3p◦ भावयिता *bhāvayitā*	भावयितारौ *bhāvayitārau*	भावयितार: *bhāvayitāraḥ*

(6) Indefinite Future : लृट् (अपूर्ण-भविष्यति) Ātmanepadī, Causative - e.g. I shall be made

1p◦ भावयिष्ये *bhāvayiṣye*	भावयिष्यावहे *bhāvayiṣyāvahe*	भावयिष्यामहे *bhāvayiṣyāmahe*
2p◦ भावयिष्यसे *bhāvayiṣyase*	भावयिष्येथे *bhāvayiṣyethe*	भावयिष्यध्वे *bhāvayiṣyadhve*
3p◦ भावयिष्यते *bhāvayiṣyate*	भावयिष्येते *bhāvayiṣyete*	भावयिष्यन्ते *bhāvayiṣyante*

(7) Conditional Mood : लृङ् (भविष्यति क्रियातिपत्तौ) Ātmanepadī, Causative, e.g. I had been made

1p∘ अभावयिष्ये	अभावयिष्यावहि	अभावयिष्यामहि
abhāvayiṣye	*abhāvayiṣyāvahi*	*abhāvayiṣyāmahi*
2p∘ अभावयिष्यथा:	अभावयिष्येथाम्	अभावयिष्यध्वम्
abhāvayiṣyathāḥ	*abhāvayiṣyethām*	*abhāvayiṣyadhvam*
3p∘ अभावयिष्यत	अभावयिष्येताम्	अभावयिष्यन्त
abhāvayiṣyata	*abhāvayiṣyetām*	*abhāvayiṣyanta*

(8) Imperative Mood : लोट् (आज्ञार्थे; प्रश्नार्थे; विध्यादौ) Ātmanepadī, Causative - May I be made?

Singular	Dual	Plural
1p∘ भावयै *bhāvayai*	भावयावहै *bhāvayāvahai*	भावयामहै *bhāvayāmahai*
2p∘ भावयस्व *bhāvayasva*	भावयेयाथाम् *bhāvayeyāthām*	भावयध्वम् *bhāvayadhvam*
3p∘ भावयताम् *bhāvayatām*	भावयेताम् *bhāvayetām*	भावयन्ताम् *bhāvayantām*

(9) Potential or Subjunctive Mood विधिलिङ् (विध्यादौ) Ātmanepadī, Causative, I may be made

1p∘ भावयेय *bhāvayeya*	भावयेवहि *bhāvayevahi*	भावयेमहि *bhāvayemahi*
2p∘ भावयेथा: *bhāvayethāḥ*	भावयेथाम् *bhāvayethām*	भावयेध्वम् *bhāvayedhvam*
3p∘ भावयेत *bhāvayeta*	भावयेयाताम् *bhāvayeyātām*	भावयेरन् *bhāvayeran*

(10) Benedictive or Optative Mood आशीर्लिङ् (आशिषि) Ātmanepadī, Causative, May I be made!

1p∘ भावयिषीय *bhāvayiṣīya*	भावयिषीवहि *bhāvayiṣīvahi*	भावयिषीमहि *bhāvayiṣīmahi*
2p∘ भावयिषीष्ठा:	भावयिषीयास्थाम्	भावयिषीध्वम्
bhāvayiṣīṣṭhāḥ	*bhāvayiṣīyāsthām*	*bhāvayiṣīdhvam*
3p∘ भावयिषीष्ट	भावयिषीयास्ताम्	भावयिषीरन्
bhāvayiṣīṣṭa	*bhāvayiṣīyāstām*	*bhāvayiṣīran*

(G) THE DESIDERATIVE (सन्नन्त) ACTIONS

ACTIVE VOICE - ĀTMANEPADI

(1) Present Tense : लट् (सामान्य-वर्तमाने) Ātmanepadī, Desiderative - e.g. I want to become

	Singular	Dual	Plural
1p∘	बुभूषे *bubhūṣe*	बुभूषावहे *bubhūṣāvahe*	बुभूषामहे *bubhūṣāmahe*
2p∘	बुभूषसे *bubhūṣase*	बुभूषेथे *bubhūṣethe*	बुभूषध्वे *bubhūṣadhve*
3p∘	बुभूषते *bubhūṣate*	बुभूषेते *bubhūṣete*	बुभूषन्ते *bubhūṣante*

(2) Past Imperfect : लङ् (अनद्यतन-भूते) Ātmanepadī, Desiderative - e.g. I wanted to became

	Singular	Dual	Plural
1p∘	अबुभूषे *abubhūṣe*	अबुभूषावहि *abubhūṣāvahi*	अबुभूषामहि *abubhūṣāmahi*
2p∘	अबुभूषथाः *abubhūṣathāḥ*	अबुभूषेथाम् *abubhūṣethām*	अबुभूषध्वम् *abubhūṣadhvam*
3p∘	अबुभूषत *abubhūṣata*	अबुभूषेताम् *abubhūṣetām*	अबुभूषन्त *abubhūṣanta*

(3) Perfect Past Tense : लिट् (परोक्ष-भूते) Ātmanepadī, Desiderative - I had wanted to become

1p∘	बुभूषाञ्चक्रे *bubhūṣāñćakre*	बुभूषाञ्चकृवहे *bubhūṣāñćakṛvahe*	बुभूषाञ्चकृमहे *bubhūṣāñćakṛmahe*
2p∘	बुभूषाञ्चकृषे *bubhūṣāñćakṛṣe*	बुभूषाञ्चक्राथे *bubhūṣāñćakrāthe*	बुभूषाञ्चकृढ्वे *bubhūṣāñćakṛḍhve*
3p∘	बुभूषाञ्चक्रे *bubhūṣāñćakre*	बुभूषाञ्चक्राते *bubhūṣāñćakrāte*	बुभूषाञ्चक्रिरे *bubhūṣāñćakrire*

(4) Indefinite Past Tense लुङ् (दूरवर्ति-भूते) Ātmanepadī, Desiderative - I had wanted to become

1p∘	अबुभूषिषि *abubhūṣiṣi*	अबुभूषिष्वहि *abubhūṣiṣvahi*	अबुभूषिष्महि *abubhūṣiṣmahi*
2p∘	अबुभूषिष्ठाः *abubhūṣiṣṭhāḥ*	अबुभूषिषाथाम् *abubhūṣiṣāthām*	अबुभूषिढ्वम् *abubhūṣiḍhvam*
3p∘	अबुभूषिष्ठ *abubhūṣiṣṭha*	अबुभूषिषाताम् *abubhūṣiṣātām*	अबुभूषिषत *abubhūṣiṣata*

(5) Definite Future : लुट् (सामान्य-भविष्यति) Ātmanepadī, Desiderative, I will want to become

1p∘	बुभूषिताहे *bubhūṣitāhe*	बुभूषितास्वहे *bubhūṣitāsvahe*	बुभूषितास्महे *bubhūṣitāsmahe*
2p∘	बुभूषितासे *bubhūṣitāse*	बुभूषितासाथे *bubhūṣitāsāthe*	बुभूषिताध्वे *bubhūṣitādhve*

3p◦ बुभूषिता *bubhūṣitā* बुभूषितारौ *bubhūṣitārau* बुभूषितार: *bubhūṣitāraḥ*

(6) Indefinite Future : लृट् (अपूर्ण–भविष्यति) Ātmanepadī, Desiderative, I shall want to become

1p◦ बुभूषिष्ये *bubhūṣiṣye* बुभूषिष्यावहे *bubhūṣiṣyāvahe* बुभूषिष्यामहे *bubhūṣiṣyāmahe*

2p◦ बुभूषिष्यसे *bubhūṣiṣyase* बुभूषिष्येथे *bubhūṣiṣyethe* बुभूषिष्यध्वे *bubhūṣiṣyadhve*

3p◦ बुभूषिष्यते *bubhūṣiṣyate* बुभूषिष्येते *bubhūṣiṣyete* बुभूषिष्यन्ते *bubhūṣiṣyante*

(7) Conditional Mood लृङ् (भविष्यति क्रियातिपत्तौ) Ātmanepadī, Desiderative, If I want to become

1p◦	अबुभूषिष्ये *abubhūṣiṣye*	अबुभूषिष्यावहि *abubhūṣiṣyāvahi*	अबुभूषिष्यामहि *abubhūṣiṣyāmahi*
2p◦	अबुभूषिष्यथा: *abubhūṣiṣyathāḥ*	अबुभूषिष्येथाम् *abubhūṣiṣyethām*	अबुभूषिष्यध्वम् *abubhūṣiṣyadhvam*
3p◦	अबुभूषिष्यत *abubhūṣiṣyata*	अबुभूषिष्येताम् *abubhūṣiṣyetām*	अबुभूषिष्यन्त *abubhūṣiṣyanta*

(8) Imperative Mood लोट् (आज्ञार्थे; प्रश्नार्थे; विध्यादौ) Ātmanepadī Desi◦ I should want to become

	Singular	Dual	Plural
1p◦	बुभूषै *baubhūṣai*	बुभूषावहै *bubhūṣāvahai*	बुभूषामहै *bubhūṣāmahai*
2p◦	बुभूषस्व *bubhūṣasva*	बुभूषेथाम् *bubhūṣethām*	बुभूषध्वम् *bubhūṣadhvam*
3p◦	बुभूषताम् *bubhūṣatām*	बुभूषेताम् *bubhūṣetām*	बुभूषन्ताम् *bubhūṣantām*

(9) Potential or Subjunctive Mood विधिलिङ् (विध्यादौ) Ātmanepadī Desi◦ I may want to become

1p◦	बुभूषेय *bubhūṣeya*	बुभूषेवहि *bubhūṣevahi*	बुभूषेमहि *bubhūṣemahi*
2p◦	बुभूषेथा: *bubhūṣethāḥ*	बुभूषेयाथाम् *bubhūṣeyāthām*	बुभूषेध्वम् *bubhūṣedhvam*
3p◦	बुभूषेत *bubhūṣeta*	बुभूषेयाताम् *bubhūṣeyātām*	बुभूषेरन् *bubhūṣeran*

(10) Benedictive or Optative Mood : आशीर्लिङ् (आशिषि) Ātmanepadī, Desi◦ May I become!

1p◦	बुभूषिषीय *bubhūṣiṣīya*	बुभूषिषीवहि *bubhūṣiṣīvahi*	बुभूषिषीमहि *bubhūṣiṣīmahi*
2p◦	बुभूषिषीष्ठा: *bubhūṣiṣīṣṭhāḥ*	बुभूषिषीयास्थाम् *bubhūṣiṣīyāsthām*	बुभूषिषीध्वम् *bubhūṣiṣīdhvam*
3p◦	बुभूषिषीष्ट *bubhūṣiṣīṣṭa*	बुभूषिषीयास्ताम् *bubhūṣiṣīyāstām*	बुभूषिषीरन् *bubhūṣiṣīran*

(H) THE REPEATETIVE or FREQUENTATIVE (यङन्त) ACTIONS

ACTIVE VOICE - ĀTMANEPADI

(1) Present Tense : लट् (सामान्य-वर्तमाने) Ātmanepadī, Frequentative - e.g. I become more

Singular	Dual	Plural
1p∘ बोभूय *bobhūye*	बोभूयावहे *bobhūyāvahe*	बोभूयामहे *bobhūyāmahe*
2p∘ बोभूयसे *bobhūyase*	बोभूयेथे *bobhūyethe*	बोभूयध्वे *bobhūyadhve*
3p∘ बोभूयते *bobhūyate*	बोभूयेते *bobhūyete*	बोभूयन्ते *bobhūyante*

(2) Past imperfect Tense : लङ् (अनद्यतन-भूते) Ātmanepadī, Frequentative - e.g. I became more

1p∘ अबोभूये *abobhūye*	अबोभूयावहि *abobhūyāvahi*	अबोभूयामहि *abobhūyāmahi*
2p∘ अबोभूयथा: *abobhūyathāḥ*	अबोभूयेथाम् *abobhūyethām*	अबोभूयध्वम् *abobhūyadhvam*
3p∘ अबोभूयत *abobhūyata*	अबोभूयेताम् *abobhūyetām*	अबोभूयन्त *abobhūyanta*

(3) Perfect Past Tense : लिट् (परोक्ष-भूते) Ātmanepadī, Frequentative - e.g. I had become more

Singular	Dual	Plural
1p∘ बोभूयाञ्चक्रे *bobhavāñćakre*	बोभवाञ्चकृवहे *bobhavāñćakṛvahe*	बोभवाञ्चकृमहे *bobhavāñćakṛmahe*
2p∘ बोभुवाञ्चकृषे *bobhūvāñćakṛṣe*	बोभुवाञ्चक्राथे *bobhūvāñćakrāthe*	बोभुवाञ्चकृढ्वे *bobhūvāñćakṛḍhve*
3p∘ बोभुवाञ्चक्रे *bobhuvāñćakre*	बोभुवाञ्चक्राते *bobhuvāñćakrāte*	बोभुवाञ्चक्रिरे *bobhuvāñćakrire*

(4) Indefinite Past Tense : लुङ् (दूरवर्ति-भूते) Ātmanepadī, Frequentative e.g. I had become more

1p∘ अबोभूयिषि *abobhūyiṣi*	अबोभूयिष्वहि *abobhūyiṣvahi*	अबोभूयिष्महि *abobhūyiṣmahi*
2p∘ अबोभूयिष्ठा: *abobhūyiṣṭhāḥ*	अबोभूयिषाथाम् *abobhūyiṣāthām*	अबोभूयिध्वम् *abobhūyidhvam*
3p∘ अबोभूयिष्ट *abobhūyiṣṭa*	अबोभूयिषाताम् *abobhūyiṣātām*	अबोभूयिषत *abobhūyiṣat*

(5) Definite Future : लुट् (सामान्य-भविष्यति) Ātmanepadī, Frequentative - e.g. I will become more

1p∘ बोभूयिताहे *bobhūyitāhe*	बोभूयितास्वहे *bobhūyitāsvahe*	बोभूयितास्महे *bobhūyitāsmahe*

2p◦	बोभूयितासे *bobhūyitāse*	बोभूयितासाथे *bobhūyitāsāthe*	बोभूयिताध्वे *bobhūyitādhve*
3p◦	बोभूयिता *bobuhūyitā*	बोभूहितारौ *bobhūyitārau*	बोभूयितार: *bobhūyitāraḥ*

(6) Indefinite Future : लृट् (अपूर्ण-भविष्यति) Ātmanepadī, Frequentative, e.g. I will become more

1p◦	बोभूयिष्ये *bobhūyiṣye*	बोभूयिष्यावहे *bobhūyiṣyāsvahe*	बोभूयिष्यामहे *bobhūyiṣyāsmahe*
2p◦	बोभूयिष्यसे *bobhūyiṣyase*	बोभूयिष्येथे *bobhūyiṣyethe*	बोभूयिष्यध्वे *bobhūyiṣyadhve*
3p◦	बोभूयिष्यते *bobhūyiṣyate*	बोभूयिष्येते *bobhūyiṣyete*	बोभूयिष्यन्ते *bobhūyiṣyante*

(7) Conditional Mood : लृङ् (भविष्यति क्रियातिपत्तौ) Ātmanepadī, Frequentative, If I become more

1p◦	अबोभूयिष्ये *abobhūyiṣye*	अबोभूयिष्यावहि *abobhūyiṣyāvahi*	अबोभूयिष्यामहि *abobhūyiṣyāmahi*
2p◦	अबोभूयिष्यथा: *abobhūyiṣyathāḥ*	अबोभूयिष्येथाम् *abobhūyiṣyethām*	अबोभूयिष्यध्वम् *abobhūyiṣyadhvam*
3p◦	अबोभूयिष्यत *abobhūyiṣyata*	अबोभूयिष्येताम् *abobhūyiṣyetām*	अबोभूयिष्यन्त *abobhūyiṣyant*

(8) Imperative Mood लोट् (आज्ञार्थे; प्रश्नार्थे; विध्यादौ) Ātmanepadī, Frequ◦ I should become more!

	Singular	Dual	Plural
1p◦	बोभूयै *bobhūyai*	बोभूयावहै *bobhūyāvahai*	बोभूयामहै *bobhūyāmahai*
2p◦	बोभूयस्व *bobhūyasva*	बोभूयेथाम् *bobhūyethām*	बोभूयध्वम् *bobhūyadhvam*
3p◦	बोभूयताम् *bobhūyatām*	बोभूयेताम् *bobhūyetām*	बोभूयन्ताम् *bobhūyantām*

(9) Potential or Subjunctive Mood विधिलिङ् (विध्यादौ) Ātmanepadī, Freq◦ I may become more

1p◦	बोभूयेय *bobhūyeya*	बोभूयेवहि *bobhūyevahi*	बोभूयेमहि *bobhūyemahi*
2p◦	बोभूयेथा: *bobhūyethāḥ*	बोभूयेयाथाम् *bobhūyeyāthām*	बोभूयेध्वम् *bobhūyedhvam*
3p◦	बोभूयेत *bobhūyeta*	बोभूयेयाताम् *bobhūyeyātām*	बोभूयेरन् *bobhūyeran*

(10) Benedictive or Optative Mood आशीर्लिङ् (आशिषि) Ātmane◦ Frequ◦ I should become more!

1p◦	बोभूयिषीय *bobhūyiṣīya*	बोभूयिषीवहि *bobhūyiṣīvahi*	बोभूयिषीमहि *bobhūyiṣīmahi*
2p◦	बोभूयिषीष्ठा: *bobhūyiṣīṣṭhāḥ*	बोभूयिषीयास्थाम् *bobhūyiṣīyāsthām*	बोभूयिषीढ्वम् *bobhūyiṣīḍhvam*
3p◦	बोभूयिषीष्ट *bobhūyiṣīṣṭa*	बोभूयिषीयास्ताम् *bobhūyiṣīyāstām*	बोभूयिषीरन् *bobhūyiṣīran*

(B)

THE PASSIVE VOICE

360 ĀTMANEPADI PASSIVE VERBS

(I) REGULAR ACTIONS

PASSIVE VOICE - ĀTMANEPADI

(1) Present Tense : लट् (सामान्य-वर्तमाने) Passive Voice - e.g. I become

	Singular	Dual	Plural
1p◦	भूये *bhūye*	भूयावहे *bhūyāvahe*	भूयामहे *bhūyāmahe*
2p◦	भूयसे *bhūyase*	भूयेथे *bhūyethe*	भूयध्वे *bhūyadhve*
3p◦	भूयते *bhūyate*	भूयेते *bhūyete*	भूयन्ते *bhūyante*

(2) Past Imperfect Tense : लङ् (अनद्यतन-भूते) Passive Voice - e.g. I became

	Singular	Dual	Plural
1p◦	अभूये *abhūye*	अभूयावहि *abhūyāvahi*	अभूयामहि *abhūyāmahi*
2p◦	अभूयथा: *abhūyathāḥ*	अभूयेथाम् *abhūyethām*	अभूयध्वम् *abhūyadhvam*
3p◦	अभूयत *abhūyata*	अभूयेताम् *abhūyetām*	अभूयन्त *abhūyanta*

(3) Perfect Past Tense : लिट् (परोक्ष-भूते) Passive Voice - e.g. I had become

1p◦	बभूवे *babhūve*	बभूविवहे *babhūvivahe*	बभूविमहे *babhūvimahe*
2p◦	बभूविषे *babhūviṣe*	बभूवाथे *babhūvāthe*	बभूविध्वे *babhūvidhve*
3p◦	बभूवे *babhūve*	बभूवाते *babhūvāte*	बभूविरे *babhūvire*

(4) Indefinite Past Tense : लुङ् (दूरवर्ति-भूते) Passive Voice - e.g. I had become

1p◦	अभविषि *abhaviṣi*	अभविष्वहि *abhaviṣvahi*	अभविष्महि *abhaviṣmahi*
2p◦	अभविष्ठा: *abhaviṣṭāḥ*	अभविषाथाम् *abhaviṣāthām*	अभविध्वम् *abhavidhvam*
3p◦	अभावि *abhāvi*	अभविषाताम् *abhaviṣātām*	अभविषत *abhaviṣata*

(5) Definite Future : लुट् (सामान्य-भविष्यति) Passive Voice - e.g. I will become

1p◦	भविताहे *bhavitāhe*	भवितास्वहे *bhavitāsvahe*	भवितास्महे *bhavitāsmahe*

2p◦ भवितासे *bhavitāse*	भवितासाथे *bhavitāsāthe*	भविताध्वे *bhavitādhve*
3p◦ भविता *bhavitā*	भवितारौ *bhavitārau*	भवितार: *bhavitāraḥ*

(6) Indefinite Future : लृट् (अपूर्ण-भविष्यति) Passive Voice - e.g. I shall become

1p◦ भविष्ये *bhaviṣye*	भविष्यावहे *bhaviṣyāvahe*	भविष्यामहे *bhaviṣyāmahe*
2p◦ भविष्यसे *bhaviṣyase*	भविष्येथे *bhaviṣyethe*	भविष्यध्वे *bhaviṣyadhve*
3p◦ भविष्यते *bhaviṣyate*	भविष्येते *bhaviṣyete*	भविष्यन्ते *bhaviṣyante*

(7) Conditional Mood : लृङ् (भविष्यति क्रियातिपत्तौ) Passive Voice - e.g. If I become

1p◦ अभविष्ये *abhaviṣye*	अभविष्यावहि *abhaviṣyāvahi*	अभविष्यामहि *abhaviṣyāmahi*
2p◦ अभविष्यथा: *abhaviṣyathāḥ*	अभविष्येथाम् *abhaviṣyethām*	अभविष्यध्वम् *abhaviṣyadhvam*
3p◦ अभविष्यत *abhaviṣyata*	अभविष्येताम् *abhaviṣyetām*	अभविष्यन्त *abhaviṣyanta*

(8) Imperative Mood : लोट् (आज्ञार्थे; प्रश्नार्थे; विध्यादौ) Passive Voice - e.g. May I become?

Singular	Dual	Plural
1p◦ भूयै *bhūyai*	भूयावहै *bhūyāvahai*	भूयामहै *bhūyāmahai*
2p◦ भूयस्व *bhūyasva*	भूयेथाम् *bhūyethām*	भूयध्वम् *bhūyadhvam*
3p◦ भूयताम् *bhūyatām*	भूयेताम् *bhūyetām*	भूयन्ताम् *bhūyantām*

(9) Potential or Subjunctive Mood : विधिलिङ् (विध्यादौ) Passive Voice - e.g. I may become

1p◦ भूयेय *bhūyeya*	भूयेवहि *bhūyevahi*	भूयेमहि *bhūyemahi*
2p◦ भूयेथा: *bhūyethāḥ*	भूयेयाथाम् *bhūyeyāthām*	भूयेध्वम् *bhūyedhvam*
3p◦ भूयेत *bhūyeta*	भूयेताम् *bhūyetām*	भूयेरन् *bhūyeran*

(10) Benedictive or Optative Mood : आशीर्लिङ् (आशिषि) Passive Voice - e.g. May I become!

1p◦ भविषीय *bhaviṣīya*	भविषीवहि *bhaviṣīvahi*	भविषीमहि *bhaviṣīmahi*
2p◦ भविषीष्ठा: *bhaviṣīṣṭhā*	भविषीयास्थाम् *bhaviṣīyāsthām*	भविषीध्वम् *bhaviṣīdhvam*
3p◦ भविषीष्ट *bhaviṣīṣṭa*	भविषीयास्ताम् *bhaviṣīyāstām*	भविषीरन् *bhaviṣīran*

Thus, the table continues for the Passive Voice, for Causative actions, desiderative actions and frequentive actions, as shown above for the Active voice.

APPENDIX - 2

CHARTS of CASES

TYPICAL DECLENSIONS OF THE SEVEN CASES

(1) MASCULINE NOUN ENDING IN *(a)* **अ (राम)** Rāma (Gītā 10.31)

CASE–विभक्ति	Singular	Dual	Plural
(1st) Nominative -	रामः	रामौ	रामाः
(2nd) Accusative (to, what?)	रामम्	रामौ	रामान्
(3rd) Instrumental (with, by)	रामेण	रामाभ्याम्	रामैः
(4th) Dative (for, to)	रामाय	रामाभ्याम्	रामेभ्यः
(5th) Ablative (from. than)	रामात्	रामाभ्याम्	रामेभ्यः
(6th) Possessive (of)	रामस्य	रामयोः	रामाणाम्
(7th) Locative (in, on)	रामे	रामयोः	रामेषु
Vocative (address)	राम	रामौ	रामाः

(2) NEUTER NOUN ENDING IN *(a)* **अ (वन)** forest

(1st) Nominative -	वनम्	वने	वनानि
(2nd) Accusative (to, what?)	वनम्	वने	वनानि
(3rd) Instrumental (with, by)	वनेन	वनाभ्याम्	वनैः
(4th) Dative (for, to)	वनाय	वनाभ्याम्	वनेभ्यः
(5th) Ablative (from. than)	वनात्	वनाभ्याम्	वनेभ्यः
(6th) Possessive (of)	वनस्य	वनयोः	वनानाम्
(7th) Locative (in, on)	वने	वनयोः	वनेषु
Vocative (address)	वन	वने	वनानि

(3) MASCULINE NOUN ENDING IN *(ā)* **आ (सोमपा)** Nectar drinker (Gītā 9.20)

(1st) Nominative -	सोमपाः	सोमपौ	सोमपाः

(2nd) Accusative (to, what?)	सोमपाम्	सोमपौ	सोमपः
(3rd) Instrumental (with, by)	सोमपा	सोमपाभ्याम्	सोमपाभिः
(4th) Dative (for, to)	सोमपे	सोमपाभ्याम्	गोपाभ्यः
(5th) Ablative (from. than)	गोपः	गोपाभ्याम्	सोमपाभ्यः
(6th) Possessive (of)	सोमपः	सोमपोः	सोमपाम्
(7th) Locative (in, on)	सोमपि	सोमपोः	सोमपासु
Vocative (address)	सोमपाः	सोमपौ	सोमपाः

(4) FEMININE NOUN ENDING IN *(ā)* **आ (माला)** necklace

CASE–विभक्ति	Singular	Dual	Plural
(1st) Nominative -	माला	माले	मालाः
(2nd) Accusative (to, what?)	मालाम्	माले	मालाः
(3rd) Instrumental (with, by)	मालया	मालाभ्याम्	मालाभिः
(4th) Dative (for, to)	मालायै	मालाभ्याम्	मालाभ्यः
(5th) Ablative (from. than)	मालायाः	मालाभ्याम्	मालाभ्यः
(6th) Possessive (of)	मालायाः	मालयोः	मालानाम्
(7th) Locative (in, on)	मालायाम्	मालयोः	मालासु
Vocative (address)	माले	माले	मालाः

(5) MASCULINE NOUN ENDING IN *(i)* **इ (कवि)** poet (Gītā 10.39)

(1st) Nominative -	कविः	कवी	कवयः
(2nd) Accusative (to, what?)	कविम्	कवी	कवीन्
(3rd) Instrumental (with, by)	कविना	कविभ्याम्	कविभिः
(4th) Dative (for, to)	कवये	कविभ्याम्	कविभ्यः
(5th) Ablative (from. than)	कवेः	कविभ्याम्	कविभ्यः
(6th) Possessive (of)	कवेः	कव्योः	कवीनाम्

(7th) Locative (in, on)	कवौ	कव्योः	कविषु
Vocative (address)	कवे	कवी	कवयः

(6) **NEUTER NOUN ENDING IN** *(i)* **इ (वारि)** water

CASE-विभक्ति	Singular	Dual	Plural
(1st) Nominative -	वारि	वारिणी	वारीणि
(2nd) Accusative (to, what?)	वारि	वारिणी	वारीणि
(3rd) Instrumental (with, by)	वारिणा	वारिभ्याम्	वारिभिः
(4th) Dative (for, to)	वारिणे	वारिभ्याम्	वारिभ्यः
(5th) Ablative (from. than)	वारिणः	वारिभ्याम्	वारिभ्यः
(6th) Possessive (of)	वारिणः	वारिणोः	वारीणाम्
(7th) Locative (in, on)	वारिणि	वारिणोः	वारिषु
Vocative (address)	वारे, वारि	वारिणी	वारीणि

(7) **FEMININE NOUN ENDING IN** *(i)* **इ (मति)** mind (Gītā 6.36)

(1st) Nominative -	मतिः	मती	मतयः
(2nd) Accusative (to, what?)	मतिम्	मती	मतीः
(3rd) Instrumental (with, by)	मत्या	मतिभ्याम्	मतिभिः
(4th) Dative (for, to)	मत्यै , मतये	मतिभ्याम्	मतिभ्यः
(5th) Ablative (from, than)	मत्याः, मतेः	मतिभ्याम्	मतिभ्यः
(6th) Possessive (of)	मत्याः, मतेः	मत्योः	मतीनाम्
(7th) Locative (in, on)	मत्याम्, मतौ	मत्योः	मतिषु
Vocative (address)	मते	मती	मतयः

(8) **MASCULINE NOUN ENDING IN** *(ī)* **ई (सुधी)** pundit

(1st) Nominative -	सुधीः	सुधियौ	सुधियः
(2nd) Accusative (to, what?)	सुधियम्	सुधियौ	सुधियः

(3rd) Instrumental (with, by)	सुधिया	सुधिभ्याम्	सुधिभि:
(4th) Dative (for, to)	सुधियै	सुधिभ्याम्	सुधिभ्य:
(5th) Ablative (from. than)	सुधिय:	सुधिभ्याम्	सुधिभ्य:
(6th) Possessive (of)	सुधिय:	सुधियो:	सुधियाम्
(7th) Locative (in, on)	सुधियि	सुधियो:	सुधीषु
Vocative (address)	सुधी:	सुधियौ	सुधिय:

(9) FEMININE NOUN ENDING IN *(ī)* **ई (नदी)** river (Gītā 11.28)

CASE–विभक्ति	Singular	Dual	Plural
(1st) Nominative -	नदी	नद्यौ	नद्य:
(2nd) Accusative (to, what?)	नदीम्	नद्यौ	नदी:
(3rd) Instrumental (with, by)	नद्या	नदीभ्याम्	नदीभि:
(4th) Dative (for, to)	नद्यै	नदीभ्याम्	नदीभ्य:
(5th) Ablative (from. than)	नद्या:	नदीभ्याम्	नदीभ्य:
(6th) Possessive (of)	नद्या:	नद्यो:	नदीनाम्
(7th) Locative (in, on)	नद्याम्	नद्यो:	नदीषु
Vocative (address)	नदि	नद्यौ	नद्य:

(10) MASCULINE NOUN ENDING IN *(u)* **उ (गुरु)** teacher (Gītā 2.5)

(1st) Nominative -	गुरु:	गुरू	गुरव:
(2nd) Accusative (to, what?)	गुरुम्	गुरू	गुरून्
(3rd) Instrumental (with, by)	गुरुणा	गुरुभ्याम्	गुरुभि:
(4th) Dative (for, to)	गुरवे	गुरुभ्याम्	गुरुभ्य:
(5th) Ablative (from. than)	गुरो:	गुरुभ्याम्	गुरुभ्य:
(6th) Possessive (of)	गुरो:	गुर्वो:	गुरूणाम्
(7th) Locative (in, on)	गुरौ	गुर्वो:	गुरुषु

Vocative (address)	गुरो	गुरू	गुरवः

(11) **NEUTER NOUN ENDING IN** *(u)* **उ (मधु)** honey

CASE-विभक्ति	Singular	Dual	Plural
(1st) Nominative -	मधु	मधुनी	मधूनि
(2nd) Accusative (to, what?)	मधु	मधुनी	मधूनि
(3rd) Instrumental (with, by)	मधुना	मधुभ्याम्	मधुभिः
(4th) Dative (for, to)	मधुने	मधुभ्याम्	मधुभ्यः
(5th) Ablative (from. than)	मधुनः	मधुभ्याम्	मधुभ्यः
(6th) Possessive (of)	मधुनः	मधुनोः	मधूनाम्
(7th) Locative (in, on)	मधुनि	मधुनोः	मधुषु
Vocative (address)	मधो-मधु	मधुनी	मधूनि

(12) **FEMININE NOUN ENDING IN** *(u)* **उ (धेनु)** cow (Gītā 10.28)

(1st) Nominative -	धेनुः	धेनू	धेनवः
(2nd) Accusative (to, what?)	धेनुम्	धेनू	धेनूः
(3rd) Instrumental (with, by)	धेन्वा	धेनुभ्याम्	धेनुभिः
(4th) Dative (for, to)	धेन्वै	धेनुभ्याम्	धेनुभ्यः
(5th) Ablative (from. than)	धेनोः	धेनुभ्याम्	धेनुभ्यः
(6th) Possessive (of)	धेनोः	धेन्वोः	धेनूनाम्
(7th) Locative (in, on)	धेन्वाम्	धेन्वोः	धेनुषु
Vocative (address)	धेनो	धेनू	धनवः

(13) **MASCULINE NOUN ENDING IN** *(ū)* **ऊ (स्वभू)** brahmā

(1st) Nominative -	स्वभूः	स्वभुवौ	स्वभुवः
(2nd) Accusative (to, what?)	स्वभुवम्	स्वभुवौ	स्वभुवः
(3rd) Instrumental (with, by)	स्वभुवा	स्वभुभ्याम्	स्वभुभिः

(4th) Dative (for, to)	स्वभुवे	स्वभुभ्याम्	स्वभुभ्य:
(5th) Ablative (from. than)	स्वभुव:	स्वभुभ्याम्	स्वभुभ्य:
(6th) Possessive (of)	स्वभुव:	स्वभुवो:	स्वभुवाम्
(7th) Locative (in, on)	स्वभुवि	स्वभुवो:	स्वभुषु
Vocative (address)	स्वभू:	स्वभुवौ	स्वभुव:

(14) FEMININE NOUN ENDING IN *(ū)* **ऊ (वधू)** bride

CASE–विभक्ति	Singular	Dual	Plural
(1st) Nominative -	वधू:	वध्वौ	वध्व:
(2nd) Accusative (to, what?)	वधूम्	वध्वौ	वधू:
(3rd) Instrumental (with, by)	वध्वा	वधूभ्याम्	वधूभि:
(4th) Dative (for, to)	वध्वै	वधूभ्याम्	वधूभ्य:
(5th) Ablative (from. than)	वध्वा:	वधूभ्याम्	वधूभ्य:
(6th) Possessive (of)	वध्वा:	वध्वो:	वधूनाम्
(7th) Locative (in, on)	वध्वाम्	वध्वो:	वधूषु
Vocative (address)	वधु	वध्वौ	वध्व:

(15) MASCULINE NOUN ENDING IN *(ṛ)* **ऋ (पितृ)** father (Gītā 1.26)

(1st) Nominative -	पिता	पितरौ	पितर:
(2nd) Accusative (to, what?)	पितरम्	पितरौ	पितॄन्
(3rd) Instrumental (with, by)	पित्रा	पितृभ्याम्	पितृभि:
(4th) Dative (for, to)	पित्रे	पितृभ्याम्	पितृभ्य:
(5th) Ablative (from. than)	पितु:	पितृभ्याम्	पितृभ्य:
(6th) Possessive (of)	पितु:	पित्रो:	पितॄणाम्
(7th) Locative (in, on)	पितरि	पित्रो:	पितृषु
Vocative (address)	पित:	पितरौ	पितर:

(16) MASCULINE ADJ◦ ENDING IN *(ṛ)* ऋ (कर्तृ) doer (Gītā 3.24)

CASE–विभक्ति	Singular	Dual	Plural
(1st) Nominative -	कर्ता	कर्तारौ	कर्तारः
(2nd) Accusative (to, what?)	कर्तारम्	कर्तारौ	कर्तॄन्
(3rd) Instrumental (with, by)	कर्त्रा	कर्तृभ्याम्	कर्तृभिः
(4th) Dative (for, to)	कर्त्रे	कर्तृभ्याम्	कर्तृभ्यः
(5th) Ablative (from. than)	कर्तुः	कतृभ्याम्	कर्तृभ्यः
(6th) Possessive (of)	कर्तुः	कर्त्रोः	कर्तॄणाम्
(7th) Locative (in, on)	कर्तरि	कर्त्रोः	कर्तृषु
Vocative (address)	कर्तः	कर्तारौ	कर्तारः

(17) NEUTER NOUN ENDING IN *(ṛ)* ऋ (धातृ) supporter (Gītā 9.17)

CASE–विभक्ति	Singular	Dual	Plural
(1st) Nominative -	धातृ	धातृणी	धातॄणि
(2nd) Accusative (to, what?)	धातृ	धातृणी	धातॄणि
(3rd) Instrumental (with, by)	धात्रा	धातृभ्याम्	धातृभिः
(4th) Dative (for, to)	धात्रे	धातृभ्याम्	धातृभ्यः
(5th) Ablative (from. than)	धातुः	धातृभ्याम्	धातृभ्यः
(6th) Possessive (of)	धातुः	धात्रोः	धातॄणाम्
(7th) Locative (in, on)	धातरि	धात्रोः	धातृषु
Vocative (address)	धातृ–धातः	धातृणी	धातॄणि

(18) FEMININE NOUN ENDING IN *(ṛ)* ऋ (मातृ) mother (Gītā 9.17)

CASE–विभक्ति	Singular	Dual	Plural
(1st) Nominative -	माता	मातरौ	मातरः
(2nd) Accusative (to, what?)	मातरम्	मातरौ	मातॄः
(3rd) Instrumental (with, by)	मात्रा	मातृभ्याम्	मातृभिः
(4th) Dative (for, to)	मात्रे	मातृभ्याम्	मातृभ्यः

(5th) Ablative (from. than)	मातु:	मातृभ्याम्	मातृभ्य:
(6th) Possessive (of)	मातु:	मात्रो:	मातृणाम्
(7th) Locative (in, on)	मातरि	मात्रो:	मातृषु
Vocative (address)	मात:	मातरौ	मातर:

(19) MASCULINE AND FEMININE NOUN ENDING IN *(ai)* ऐ (रै) wealth

CASE–विभक्ति	Singular	Dual	Plural
(1st) Nominative -	रा:	रायौ	राय:
(2nd) Accusative (to, what?)	रायम्	रायौ	राय:
(3rd) Instrumental (with, by)	राया	राभ्याम्	राभि:
(4th) Dative (for, to)	राये	राभ्याम्	राभ्य:
(5th) Ablative (from. than)	राय:	राभ्याम्	राभ्य:
(6th) Possessive (of)	राय:	रायो:	रायाम्
(7th) Locative (in, on)	रायि	रायो:	रासु
Vocative (address)	रा:	रायौ	राय:

(20) MASCULINE AND FEMININE NOUN ENDING IN *(o)* ओ (गो) cow, bull (Gītā 5.18)

(1st) Nominative -	गौ:	गावौ	गाव:
(2nd) Accusative (to, what?)	गाम्	गावौ	गाव:
(3rd) Instrumental (with, by)	गवा	गोभ्याम्	गोभि:
(4th) Dative (for, to)	गवे	गोभ्याम्	गोभ्य:
(5th) Ablative (from. than)	गो:	गोभ्याम्	गोभ्य:
(6th) Possessive (of)	गो:	गवो:	गवाम्
(7th) Locative (in, on)	गवि	गवो:	गोषु
Vocative (address)	गौ:	गावौ	गाव:

(21) MASCULINE NOUN ENDING IN *(au)* औ (ग्लौ) moon

(1st) Nominative -	ग्लौः	ग्लावौ	ग्लावः
(2nd) Accusative (to, what?)	ग्लावम्	ग्लावौ	ग्लावः
(3rd) Instrumental (with, by)	ग्लावा	ग्लौभ्याम्	गौभिः
(4th) Dative (for, to)	ग्लावे	ग्लौभ्याम्	गौभ्यः
(5th) Ablative (from. than)	ग्लावः	ग्लौभ्याम्	गौभ्यः
(6th) Possessive (of)	ग्लावः	ग्लावोः	ग्लावाम्
(7th) Locative (in, on)	ग्लावि	ग्लावोः	ग्लौषु
Vocative (address)	ग्लौः	ग्लावौ	ग्लावः

(22) FEMININE NOUN ENDING IN *(au)* **औ (नौ)** boat (Gītā 2.67)

CASE-विभक्ति	Singular	Dual	Plural
(1st) Nominative -	नौः	नावौ	नावः
(2nd) Accusative (to, what?)	नावम्	नावौ	नावः
(3rd) Instrumental (with, by)	नावा	नौभ्याम्	नौभिः
(4th) Dative (for, to)	नावे	नौभ्याम्	नौभ्यः
(5th) Ablative (from. than)	नावः	नौभ्याम्	नौभ्यः
(6th) Possessive (of)	नावः	नावोः	नावाम्
(7th) Locative (in, on)	नावि	नावोः	नौषु
Vocative (address)	नौः	नावौ	नावः

(23) MASCULINE NOUN ENDING IN *(k)* **क् (शक्)** an able man

(1st) Nominative -	शक्	शकौ	शकः
(2nd) Accusative (to, what?)	शकम्	शकौ	शकः
(3rd) Instrumental (with, by)	शका	शग्भ्याम्	शग्भिः
(4th) Dative (for, to)	शके	शग्भ्याम्	शग्भ्यः
(5th) Ablative (from. than)	शकः	शग्भ्याम्	शग्भ्यः

(6th) Possessive (of)	शकः	शकोः	शकाम्
(7th) Locative (in, on)	शकि	शकोः	शक्षु
Vocative (address)	शक्	शकौ	शकः

(24) MASCULINE NOUN ENDING IN *(kh)* ख् (लिख्) a writer

CASE–विभक्ति	Singular	Dual	Plural
(1st) Nominative -	लिक्	लिखौ	लिखः
(2nd) Accusative (to, what?)	लिखम्	लिखौ	लिखः
(3rd) Instrumental (with, by)	लिखा	लिग्भ्याम्	लिग्भिः
(4th) Dative (for, to)	लिखे	लिग्भ्याम्	लिग्भ्यः
(5th) Ablative (from. than)	लिखः	लिग्भ्याम्	लिग्भ्यः
(6th) Possessive (of)	लिखः	लिखोः	लिखाम्
(7th) Locative (in, on)	लिखि	लिखोः	लिक्षु
Vocative (address)	लिक्	लिखौ	लिखः

(25) NEUTER NOUN ENDING IN *(kh)* ख् (लिख्) a printer

(1st) Nominative -	लिख्	लिखी	लिङ्खि
(2nd) Accusative (to, what?)	लिख्	लिखी	लिङ्खि
(3rd) Instrumental (with, by)	लिखा	लिग्भ्याम्	लिग्भिः
(4th) Dative (for, to)	लिखे	लिग्भ्याम्	लिग्भ्यः
(5th) Ablative (from. than)	लिखः	लिग्भ्याम्	लिग्भ्यः
(6th) Possessive (of)	लिखः	लिखोः	लिखाम्
(7th) Locative (in, on)	लिखि	लिखोः	लिक्षु
Vocative (address)	लिख्	लिखी	लिङ्खि

(26) FEMININE NOUN ENDING IN *(ć)* च् (वाच्) speech (Gītā 2.42)

MASCULINE NOUN ENDING IN *(ć)* च् (सत्यवाच्) truth speeker

(1st) Nominative -	(सत्य)वाक्	वाचौ	वाच:
(2nd) Accusative (to, what?)	वाचम्	वाचौ	वाच:
(3rd) Instrumental (with, by)	वाचा	वाग्भ्याम्	वाग्भि:
(4th) Dative (for, to)	वाचे	वाग्भ्याम्	वाग्भ्य:
(5th) Ablative (from. than)	वाच:	वाग्भ्याम्	वाग्भ्य:
(6th) Possessive (of)	वाच:	वाचो:	वाचाम्
(7th) Locative (in, on)	वाचि	वाचो:	वाक्षु
Vocative (address)	वाक्-वाग्	वाचौ	वाच:

(27) MASCULINE NOUN ENDING IN *(j)* ज् (राज्) king

MASCULINE NOUN ENDING IN *(j)* ज् (वणिज्) merchant

CASE-विभक्ति	Singular	Dual	Plural
(1st) Nominative -	राट्-ड्	राजौ	राज:
(1st) Nominative -	वणिक्-ग्	वणिजौ	वणिज:
(2nd) Accusative (to, what?)	राजम्	राजौ	राज:
(3rd) Instrumental (with, by)	राजा	राड्भ्याम्	राड्भि:
(4th) Dative (for, to)	राजे	राड्भ्याम्	राड्भ्य:
(5th) Ablative (from. than)	राज:	राड्भ्याम्	राड्भ्य:
(6th) Possessive (of)	राज:	राजो:	राजाम्
(7th) Locative (in, on)	राजि	राजो:	राट्सु
Vocative (address)	राट्-राड्	राजौ	राज:

(28) NEUTER NOUN ENDING IN *(j)* ज् (ऊर्ज्) power

(1st) Nominative -	ऊर्क्-र्ग्	ऊर्जौ	ऊर्ज:
(2nd) Accusative (to, what?)	ऊर्क्-र्ग्	ऊर्जौ	ऊर्ज:
(3rd) Instrumental (with, by)	ऊर्जा	ऊग्र्भ्याम्	ऊर्ग्भि:

(4th) Dative (for, to)	ऊर्जे	ऊर्ग्भ्याम्	ऊर्ग्भ्यः
(5th) Ablative (from. than)	ऊर्जः	ऊर्ग्भ्याम्	ऊर्ग्भ्यः
(6th) Possessive (of)	ऊर्जः	ऊर्जोः	ऊर्जाम्
(7th) Locative (in, on)	ऊर्जि	ऊर्जोः	ऊर्क्षु
Vocative (address)	ऊर्क्-र्ग्	ऊर्जौ	ऊर्जः

(29) FEMININE NOUN ENDING IN ***(j)*** **ज् (स्रज्)** necklace

(1st) Nominative -	स्रक्-ग्	स्रजौ	स्रजः
(2nd) Accusative (to, what?)	स्रक्-ग्	स्रजौ	स्रजः
(3rd) Instrumental (with, by)	स्रजा	स्रग्भ्याम्	स्रग्भिः
(4th) Dative (for, to)	स्रजे	स्रग्भ्याम्	स्रग्भ्यः
(5th) Ablative (from. than)	स्रजः	स्रग्भ्याम्	स्रग्भ्यः
(6th) Possessive (of)	स्रजः	स्रजोः	स्रजाम्
(7th) Locative (in, on)	स्रजि	स्रजोः	स्रक्षु
Vocative (address)	स्रक्	स्रजौ	स्रजः

(30) MASCULINE NOUN ENDING IN ***(ñc)*** **ञ्च् (प्राञ्च्)** East

CASE-विभक्ति	Singular	Dual	Plural
(1st) Nominative -	प्राङ्	प्राञ्चौ	प्राञ्चः
(2nd) Accusative (to, what?)	प्राञ्चम्	प्राञ्चौ	प्राञ्चः
(3rd) Instrumental (with, by)	प्राचा	प्राङ्भ्याम्	प्राङ्भिः
(4th) Dative (for, to)	प्राचे	प्राङ्भ्याम्	प्राङ्भ्यः
(5th) Ablative (from. than)	प्राचः	प्राङ्भ्याम्	प्राङ्भ्यः
(6th) Possessive (of)	प्राचः	प्राञ्चोः	प्राञ्चाम्
(7th) Locative (in, on)	प्राचि	प्राञ्चोः	प्राङ्क्षु
Vocative (address)	प्राङ्	प्राञ्चौ	प्राञ्चः

(31) MASCULINE NOUN ENDING IN *(ñj)* ञ्ज् (खञ्ज्) lame

(1st) Nominative -	खन्	खञ्जौ	खञ्जः
(2nd) Accusative (to, what?)	खञ्जम्	खञ्जौ	खञ्जः
(3rd) Instrumental (with, by)	खञ्जा	खन्भ्याम्	खन्भिः
(4th) Dative (for, to)	खञ्जे	खन्भ्याम्	खन्भ्यः
(5th) Ablative (from. than)	खञ्जः	खन्भ्याम्	खन्भ्यः
(6th) Possessive (of)	खञ्जः	खञ्जोः	खञ्जाम्
(7th) Locative (in, on)	खञ्जि	खञ्जोः	खन्सु
Vocative (address)	खन्	खञ्जौ	खञ्जः

(32) MASCULINE NOUN ENDING IN *(t)* त् (मरुत्) wind (Gītā 10.21)

(1st) Nominative -	मरुत्	मरुतौ	मरुतः
(2nd) Accusative (to, what?)	मरुतम्	मरुतौ	मरुतः
(3rd) Instrumental (with, by)	मरुता	मरुद्भ्याम्	मरुद्भिः
(4th) Dative (for, to)	मरुते	मरुद्भ्याम्	मरुद्भ्यः
(5th) Ablative (from. than)	मरुतः	मरुद्भ्याम्	मरुद्भ्यः
(6th) Possessive (of)	मरुतः	मरुतोः	मरुताम्
(7th) Locative (in, on)	मरुति	मरुतोः	मरुत्सु
Vocative (address)	मरुत्	मरुतौ	मरुतः

(33) MASCULINE ADJECTIVE ENDING IN *(t)* त् (भगवत्) divine (Gītā 10.14)

CASE-विभक्ति	Singular	Dual	Plural
(1st) Nominative -	भगवान्	भगवन्तौ	भगवन्तः
(2nd) Accusative (to, what?)	भगवन्तम्	भगवन्तौ	भगवतः
(3rd) Instrumental (with, by)	भगवता	भगवद्भ्याम्	भगवद्भिः
(4th) Dative (for, to)	भगवते	भगवद्भ्याम्	भगवद्भ्यः

(5th) Ablative (from. than)	भगवतः	भगवद्भ्याम्	भगवद्भ्यः
(6th) Possessive (of)	भगवतः	भगवतोः	भगवताम्
(7th) Locative (in, on)	भगवति	भगवतोः	भगवत्सु
Vocative (address)	भगवन्	भगवन्तौ	भगवन्तः

(34) MASCULINE PRONOUN ENDING IN *(t)* त् (भवत्) you (Gītā 1.8)

(1st) Nominative -	भवान्	भवन्तौ	भवन्तः
(2nd) Accusative (to, what?)	भवन्तम्	भवन्तौ	भवतः
(3rd) Instrumental (with, by)	भवता	भवद्भ्याम्	भवद्भिः
(4th) Dative (for, to)	भवते	भवद्भ्याम्	भवद्भ्यः
(5th) Ablative (from. than)	भवतः	भवद्भ्याम्	भवद्भ्यः
(6th) Possessive (of)	भवतः	भवतोः	भवताम्
(7th) Locative (in, on)	भवति	भवतोः	भवत्सु
Vocative (address)	भवन्	भवन्तौ	भवन्तः

(35) MASCULINE PARTICIPLE ENDING IN *(t)* त् (कुर्वत्) while doing, doer (Gītā 4.21)

CASE-विभक्ति	Singular	Dual	Plural
(1st) Nominative -	कुर्वन्	कुर्वन्तौ	कुर्वन्तः
(2nd) Accusative (to, what?)	कुर्वन्तम्	कुर्वन्तौ	कुर्वतः
(3rd) Instrumental (with, by)	कुर्वता	कुर्वद्भ्याम्	कुर्वद्भिः
(4th) Dative (for, to)	कुर्वते	कुर्वद्भ्याम्	कुर्वद्भ्यः
(5th) Ablative (from. than)	कुर्वतः	कुर्वद्भ्याम्	कुर्वद्भ्यः
(6th) Possessive (of)	कुर्वतः	कुर्वतोः	कुर्वताम्
(7th) Locative (in, on)	कुर्वति	कुर्वतोः	कुर्वत्सु
Vocative (address)	कुर्वन्	कुर्वन्तौ	कुर्वन्तः

(36) NEUTER NOUN ENDING IN *(t)* त् (जगत्) world (Gītā 7.6)

(1st) Nominative -	जगत्	जगती	जगन्ति
(2nd) Accusative (to, what?)	जगत्	जगती	जगन्ति
(3rd) Instrumental (with, by)	जगता	जगद्भ्याम्	जगद्भिः
(4th) Dative (for, to)	जगते	जगद्भ्याम्	जगद्भ्यः
(5th) Ablative (from. than)	जगतः	जगद्भ्याम्	जगद्भ्यः
(6th) Possessive (of)	जगतः	जगतोः	जगताम्
(7th) Locative (in, on)	जगति	जगतोः	जगत्सु
Vocative (address)	जगत्	जगती	जगन्ति

(37) NEUTER ADJECTIVE ENDING IN *(t)* त् (महत्) great (Gītā 1.14)

(1st) Nominative -	महत्	महती	महान्ति
(2nd) Accusative (to, what?)	महत्	महती	महान्ति
(3rd) Instrumental (with, by)	महता	महद्भ्याम्	महद्भिः
(4th) Dative (for, to)	महते	महद्भ्याम्	महद्भ्यः
(5th) Ablative (from. than)	महतः	महद्भ्याम्	महद्भ्यः
(6th) Possessive (of)	महतः	महतोः	महताम्
(7th) Locative (in, on)	महति	महतोः	महत्सु
Vocative (address)	महत्	महती	महान्ति

(38) FEMININE ADJECTIVE ENDING IN *(t)* त् (सरित्) river

(1st) Nominative -	सरित्	सरितौ	सरितः
(2nd) Accusative (to, what?)	सरितम्	सरितौ	सरितः
(3rd) Instrumental (with, by)	सरिता	सरिद्भ्याम्	सरिद्भिः
(4th) Dative (for, to)	सरिते	सरिद्भ्याम्	सरिद्भ्यः
(5th) Ablative (from. than)	सरितः	सरिद्भ्याम्	सरिद्भ्यः
(6th) Possessive (of)	सरितः	सरितोः	सरिताम्

(7th) Locative (in, on)	सरिति	सरितोः	सरित्सु
Vocative (address)	सरित्	सरितौ	सरितः

(39) MASCULINE NOUN ENDING IN *(d)* द् (सुहृद्) friend (Gītā 1.26)

CASE–विभक्ति	Singular	Dual	Plural
(1st) Nominative -	सुहृद्	सुहृदौ	सुहृदः
(2nd) Accusative (to, what?)	सुहृदम्	सुहृदौ	सुहृदः
(3rd) Instrumental (with, by)	सुहृदा	सुहृद्भ्याम्	सुहृद्भिः
(4th) Dative (for, to)	सुहृदे	सुहृद्भ्याम्	सुहृद्भ्यः
(5th) Ablative (from. than)	सुहृदः	सुहृद्भ्याम्	सुहृद्भ्यः
(6th) Possessive (of)	सुहृदः	सुहृदोः	सुहृदाम्
(7th) Locative (in, on)	सुहृदि	सुहृदोः	सुहृत्सु
Vocative (address)	सुहृद्	सुहृदौ	सुहृदः

(40) NEUTER NOUN ENDING IN *(d)* द् (हृद्) heart (Gītā 8.12)

CASE–विभक्ति	Singular	Dual	Plural
(1st) Nominative -	हृत्	हृदी	हृन्दि
(2nd) Accusative (to, what?)	हृत्	हृदी	हृन्दि
(3rd) Instrumental (with, by)	हृदा	हृद्भ्याम्	हृद्भिः
(4th) Dative (for, to)	हृदे	हृद्भ्याम्	हृद्भ्यः
(5th) Ablative (from. than)	हृदः	हृद्भ्याम्	हृद्भ्यः
(6th) Possessive (of)	हृदः	हृदोः	हृदाम्
(7th) Locative (in, on)	हृदि	हृदोः	हृत्सु
Vocative (address)	हृद्	हृदौ	हृदः

(41) FEMININE NOUN ENDING IN *(dh)* ध् (क्षुध्) hunger

(1st) Nominative -	क्षुत्-क्षुद्	क्षुधौ	क्षुधः

(2nd) Accusative (to, what?)	क्षुधम्	क्षुधौ	क्षुधः
(3rd) Instrumental (with, by)	क्षुधा	क्षुद्भ्याम्	क्षुद्भिः
(4th) Dative (for, to)	क्षुधे	क्षुद्भ्याम्	क्षुद्भ्यः
(5th) Ablative (from. than)	क्षुधः	क्षुद्भ्याम्	क्षुद्भ्यः
(6th) Possessive (of)	क्षुधः	क्षुधोः	क्षुधाम्
(7th) Locative (in, on)	क्षुधि	क्षुधोः	क्षुत्सु
Vocative (address)	क्षुत्-क्षुद्	क्षुधौ	क्षुधः

(42) MASCULINE NOUN ENDING IN *(in)* इन् (शशिन्) moon (Gītā 10.21)

CASE-विभक्ति	Singular	Dual	Plural
(1st) Nominative -	शशी	शशिनौ	शशिनः
(2nd) Accusative (to, what?)	शशिनम्	शशिनौ	शशिनः
(3rd) Instrumental (with, by)	शशिना	शशिभ्याम्	शशिभिः
(4th) Dative (for, to)	शशिने	शशिभ्याम्	शशिभ्यः
(5th) Ablative (from. than)	शशिनः	शशिभ्याम्	शशिभ्यः
(6th) Possessive (of)	शशिनः	शशिनोः	शशिनाम्
(7th) Locative (in, on)	शशिनि	शशिनोः	शशिषु
Vocative (address)	शशिन्	शशिनौ	शशिनः

(43) NEUTER ADJECTIVE ENDING IN *(in)* इन् (भाविन्) future

(1st) Nominative	भावि	भाविनी	भावीनि
(2nd) Accusative (to, what?)	भावि	भाविनी	भावीनि
(3rd) Instrumental (with, by)	भाविना	भाविभ्याम्	भाविभिः
(4th) Dative (for, to)	भाविने	भाविभ्याम्	भाविभ्यः
(5th) Ablative (from. than)	भाविनः	भाविभ्याम्	भाविभ्यः
(6th) Possessive (of)	भाविनः	भाविनोः	भाविनाम्

(7th) Locative (in, on)	भाविनि	भाविनो:	भाविषु
Vocative (address)	भावि	भाविनी	भावीनि

(44) MASCULINE NOUN ENDING IN *(an)* **न् (आत्मन्)** soul (Gītā 6.5)

(1st) Nominative -	आत्मा	आत्मानौ	आत्मान:
(2nd) Accusative (to, what?)	आत्मानम्	आत्मानौ	आत्मन:
(3rd) Instrumental (with, by)	आत्मना	आत्मभ्याम्	आत्मभि:
(4th) Dative (for, to)	आत्मने	आत्मभ्याम्	आत्मभ्य:
(5th) Ablative (from. than)	आत्मन:	आत्मभ्याम्	आत्मभ्य:
(6th) Possessive (of)	आत्मन:	आत्मनो:	आत्मनाम्
(7th) Locative (in, on)	आत्मनि	आत्मनो:	आत्मसु
Vocative (address)	आत्मन्	आत्मानौ	आत्मान:

(45) NEUTER NOUN ENDING IN *(an)* **न् (कर्मन्)** deed (Gītā 2.49)

CASE–विभक्ति	Singular	Dual	Plural
(1st) Nominative -	कर्म	कर्मणी	कर्माणि
(2nd) Accusative (to, what?)	कर्म	कर्मणी	कर्माणि
(3rd) Instrumental (with, by)	कर्मणा	कर्मभ्याम्	कर्मभि:
(4th) Dative (for, to)	कर्मणे	कर्मभ्याम्	कर्मभ्य:
(5th) Ablative (from. than)	कर्मण:	कर्मभ्याम्	कर्मभ्य:
(6th) Possessive (of)	कर्मण:	कर्मणो:	कर्मणाम्
(7th) Locative (in, on)	कर्मणि	कर्मणो:	कर्मसु
Vocative (address)	कर्म	कर्मणी	कर्माणि

(46) FEMININE NOUN ENDING IN *(an)* **न् (सीमन्)** limit

(1st) Nominative -	सीमा	सीमानौ	सीमान:
(2nd) Accusative (to, what?)	सीमानम्	सीमानौ	सीम्न:

(3rd) Instrumental (with, by)	सीम्ना	सीमभ्याम्	सीमभिः
(4th) Dative (for, to)	सीम्ने	सीमभ्याम्	सीमभ्यः
(5th) Ablative (from. than)	सीम्नः	सीमभ्याम्	सीमभ्यः
(6th) Possessive (of)	सीम्नः	सीम्नोः	सीम्नाम्
(7th) Locative (in, on)	सीम्नि, सीमनि	सीम्नोः	सीमसु
Vocative (address)	सीमन्	सीमानौ	सीमनः

(47) MASCULINE AND FEMININE NOUN ENDING IN *(p)* प् (गुप्) defender

FEMININE NOUNS ENDING IN *(p)* प् (आप्) water

				Plural only (Gītā 2.23)
(1st) Nominative -	गुप्-भ्	गुपौ	गुपः	आपः
(2nd) Accusative (to, what?)	गुपम्	गुपौ	गुपः	अपः
(3rd) Instrumental (with, by)	गुपा	गुब्भ्याम्	गुब्भिः	अद्भिः
(4th) Dative (for, to)	गुपे	गुब्भ्याम्	गुब्भ्यः	अद्भ्यः
(5th) Ablative (from. than)	गुपः	गुब्भ्याम्	गुब्भ्यः	अद्भ्यः
(6th) Possessive (of)	गुपः	गुपोः	गुपाम्	अपाम्
(7th) Locative (in, on)	गुपि	गुपोः	गुप्सु	अप्सु
Vocative (address)	गुप्-भ्	गुपौ	गुपः	आपः

(48) MASCULINE AND FEMININE NOUN ENDING IN *(bh)* भ् (लभ्) finder

(1st) Nominative -	लभ्	लभौ	लभः
(2nd) Accusative (to, what?)	लभम्	लभौ	लभः
(3rd) Instrumental (with, by)	लभा	लग्भ्याम्	लग्भिः
(4th) Dative (for, to)	लभे	लग्भ्याम्	लग्भ्यः
(5th) Ablative (from. than)	लभः	लग्भ्याम्	लग्भ्यः
(6th) Possessive (of)	लभः	लभोः	लभाम्
(7th) Locative (in, on)	लभि	लभोः	लप्सु

Vocative (address)	लभ्	लभौ	लभः

(49) MASCULINE NOUN ENDING IN *(r)* र् (चर्) mover (Gītā 13.15)

CASE–विभक्ति	Singular	Dual	Plural
(1st) Nominative -	चर्	चरौ	चरः
(2nd) Accusative (to, what?)	चरम्	चरौ	चरः
(3rd) Instrumental (with, by)	चरा	चर्भ्याम्	चर्भिः
(4th) Dative (for, to)	चरे	चर्भ्याम्	चर्भ्यः
(5th) Ablative (from. than)	चरः	चर्भ्याम्	चर्भ्यः
(6th) Possessive (of)	चरः	चरोः	चराम्
(7th) Locative (in, on)	चरि	चरोः	चर्षु
Vocative (address)	चर्	चरौ	चरः

(50) NEUTER NOUN ENDING IN *(r)* र् (वार्) water

(1st) Nominative -	वाः	वारी	वारि
(2nd) Accusative (to, what?)	वाः	वारी	वारि
(3rd) Instrumental (with, by)	वारा	वार्भ्याम्	वार्भिः
(4th) Dative (for, to)	वारे	वार्भ्याम्	वार्भ्यः
(5th) Ablative (from. than)	वारः	वार्भ्याम्	वार्भ्यः
(6th) Possessive (of)	वारः	वारोः	वाराम्
(7th) Locative (in, on)	वारि	वारोः	वार्षु
Vocative (address)	वाः	वारी	वारि

(51) FEMININE NOUN ENDING IN *(r)* र् (गिर्) speech (Gītā 10.25)

FEMININE NOUN ENDING IN *(r)* र् (पुर्) city, town

(1st) Nominative -	गीः	गिरौ	गिरः
(1st) Nominative -	पूः	पुरौ	पुरः

(2nd) Accusative (to, what?)	गिरम्	गिरौ	गिर:
(3rd) Instrumental (with, by)	गिरा	गीर्भ्याम्	गीर्भि:
(4th) Dative (for, to)	गिरे	गीर्भ्याम्	गीर्भ्य:
(5th) Ablative (from. than)	गिर:	गीर्भ्याम्	गीर्भ्य:
(6th) Possessive (of)	गिर:	गिरो:	गिराम्
(7th) Locative (in, on)	गिरि	गिरो:	गीर्षु
Vocative (address)	गी:	गिरौ	गिर:

(52) FEMININE NOUN ENDING IN *(v)* **व् (दिव्)** sky (Gītā 9.20)

CASE–विभक्ति	Singular	Dual	Plural
(1st) Nominative -	द्यौ:	दिवौ	दिव:
(2nd) Accusative (to, what?)	दिवम्	दिवौ	दिव:
(3rd) Instrumental (with, by)	दिवा	द्युग्भ्याम्	द्युग्भि:
(4th) Dative (for, to)	दिवे	द्युग्भ्याम्	द्युग्भ्य:
(5th) Ablative (from. than)	दिव:	द्युग्भ्याम्	द्युग्भ्य:
(6th) Possessive (of)	दिव:	दिवो:	दिवाम्
(7th) Locative (in, on)	दिवि	दिवो:	द्युषु
Vocative (address)	द्यौ:	दिवौ	दिव:

(53) MASCULINE NOUN ENDING IN *(ś)* **श् (नश्)** ruin

MASCULINE NOUN ENDING IN *(ś)* **श् (विश्)** merchant (Gītā 18.41)

(1st) Nominative -	नक्-ग्	नशौ	नश:
(1st) Nominative -	विश्	विशौ	विश:
(2nd) Accusative (to, what?)	नशम्	नशौ	नश:
(3rd) Instrumental (with, by)	नशा	नग्भ्याम्	नग्भि:
(4th) Dative (for, to)	नशे	नग्भ्याम्	नग्भ्य:

(5th) Ablative (from. than)	नश:	नग्भ्याम्	नग्भ्य:
(6th) Possessive (of)	नश:	नशो:	नशाम्
(7th) Locative (in, on)	नशि	नशो:	नक्षु
Vocative (address)	नक्-ग्	नशौ	नश:

(54) FEMININE NOUN ENDING IN *(ś)* श् (दिश्) direction (Gītā 6.13)

(1st) Nominative -	दिक्-दिग्	दिशौ	दिश:
(2nd) Accusative (to, what?)	दिशम्	दिशौ	दिश:
(3rd) Instrumental (with, by)	दिशा	दिग्भ्याम्	दिग्भि:
(4th) Dative (for, to)	दिशे	दिग्भ्याम्	दिग्भ्य:
(5th) Ablative (from. than)	दिश:	दिग्भ्याम्	दिग्भ्य:
(6th) Possessive (of)	दिश:	दिशो:	दिशाम्
(7th) Locative (in, on)	दिशि	दिशो:	दिक्षु
Vocative (address)	दिक्-दिग्	दिशौ	दिश:

(55) m∘ NOUN ENDING IN *(ṣ)* ष् (चिकीर्ष्) a desirer

(1st) Nominative -	चिकी:	चिकीर्षौ	चिकीर्ष:
(2nd) Accusative (to, what?)	चिकीर्षम्	चिकीर्षौ	चिकीर्ष:
(3rd) Instrumental (with, by)	चिकीर्षा	चिकीर्भ्याम्	चिकीर्भि:
(4th) Dative (for, to)	चिकीर्षे	चिकीर्भ्याम्	चिकीर्भ्य:
(5th) Ablative (from. than)	चिकीर्ष:	चिकीर्भ्याम्	चिकीर्भ्य:
(6th) Possessive (of)	चिकीर्ष:	चिकीर्षो:	चिकीर्षाम्
(7th) Locative (in, on)	चिकीर्ष:	चिकीर्षो:	चिकीर्षु
Vocative (address)	चिकी:	चिकीर्षौ	चिकीर्ष:

(56) NEUTER NOUN ENDING IN *(ṣ)* ष् (धनुष्) bow (Gītā 1.20)

(1st) Nominative -	धनु:	धनुषी	धनूंषि

(2nd) Accusative (to, what?)	धनुः	धनुषी	धनूंषि
(3rd) Instrumental (with, by)	धनुषा	धनुर्भ्याम्	धनुर्भिः
(4th) Dative (for, to)	धनुषे	धनुर्भ्याम्	धनुर्भ्यः
(5th) Ablative (from. than)	धनुषः	धनुर्भ्याम्	धनुर्भ्यः
(6th) Possessive (of)	धनुषः	धनुषोः	धनुषाम्
(7th) Locative (in, on)	धनुषि	धनुषोः	धनुःषु
Vocative (address)	धनुः	धनुषी	धनूंषि

(57) FEMININE NOUN END॰ IN *(ṣ)* ष् (आशिष्) blessing

CASE–विभक्ति	Singular	Dual	Plural
(1st) Nominative -	आशीः	आशिषौ	आशिषः
(2nd) Accusative (to, what?)	आशिषम्	आशिषौ	आशिषः
(3rd) Instrumental (with, by)	आशिषा	आशीर्भ्याम्	आशीर्भिः
(4th) Dative (for, to)	आशिषे	आशीर्भ्याम्	आशीर्भ्यः
(5th) Ablative (from. than)	आशिषः	आशीर्भ्याम्	आशीर्भ्यः
(6th) Possessive (of)	आशिषः	आशिषोः	आशिषाम्
(7th) Locative (in, on)	आशिषि	आशिषोः	आशीःषु
Vocative (address)	आशीः	आशिषौ	आशिषः

(58) MASCULINE NOUN ENDING IN *(s)* स् (चन्द्रमस्) moon (Gītā 15.12)

(1st) Nominative -	चन्द्रमाः	चन्द्रमसौ	चन्द्रमसः
(2nd) Accusative (to, what?)	चन्द्रमसम्	चन्द्रमसौ	चन्द्रमसः
(3rd) Instrumental (with, by)	चन्द्रमसा	चन्द्रमोभ्याम्	चन्द्रमोभिः
(4th) Dative (for, to)	चन्द्रमसे	चन्द्रमोभ्याम्	चन्द्रमोभ्यः
(5th) Ablative (from. than)	चन्द्रमसः	चन्द्रमोभ्याम्	चन्द्रमोभ्यः
(6th) Possessive (of)	चन्द्रमसः	चन्द्रमसोः	चन्द्रमसाम्

(7th) Locative (in, on)	चन्द्रमसि	चन्द्रमसोः	चन्द्रमःसु
Vocative (address)	चन्द्रमः	चन्द्रमसौ	चन्द्रमसः

(59) MASCULINE ADJECTIVE ENDING IN *(s)* स् (श्रेयस्) better (Gītā 3.35)

(1st) Nominative -	श्रेयान्	श्रेयांसौ	श्रेयांसः
(2nd) Accusative (to, what?)	श्रेयांसम्	श्रेयांसौ	श्रेयसः
(3rd) Instrumental (with, by)	श्रेयसा	श्रेयोभ्याम्	श्रेयोभिः
(4th) Dative (for, to)	श्रेयसे	श्रेयोभ्याम्	श्रेयोभ्यः
(5th) Ablative (from. than)	श्रेयसः	श्रेयोभ्याम्	श्रेयोभ्यः
(6th) Possessive (of)	श्रेयसः	श्रेयसोः	श्रेयसाम्
(7th) Locative (in, on)	श्रेयसि	श्रेयसोः	श्रेयःसु
Vocative (address)	श्रेयान्	श्रेयांसौ	श्रेयांसः

(60) NEUTER ADJECTIVE ENDING IN *(s)* स् (श्रेयस्) better (Gītā 1.31)

(1st) Nominative -	श्रेयः	श्रेयसी	श्रेयांसि
(2nd) Accusative (to, what?)	श्रेयः	श्रेयसी	श्रेयांसि
(3rd) Instrumental (with, by)	श्रेयसा	श्रेयोभ्याम्	श्रेयोभिः
(4th) Dative (for, to)	श्रेयसे	श्रेयोभ्याम्	श्रेयोभ्यः
(5th) Ablative (from. than)	श्रेयसः	श्रेयोभ्याम्	श्रेयोभ्यः
(6th) Possessive (of)	श्रेयसः	श्रेयसोः	श्रेयसाम्
(7th) Locative (in, on)	श्रेयसि	श्रेयसोः	श्रेयःसु
Vocative (address)	श्रेयः	श्रेयसी	श्रेयांसि

(61) NEUTER NOUN ENDING IN *(s)* स् (पयस्) water, milk

(1st) Nominative -	पयः	पयसी	पयांसि
(2nd) Accusative (to, what?)	पयः	पयसी	पयांसि
(3rd) Instrumental (with, by)	पयसा	पयोभ्याम्	पयोभिः

(4th) Dative (for, to)	पयसे	पयोभ्याम्	पयोभ्य:
(5th) Ablative (from. than)	पयस:	पयोभ्याम्	पयोभ्य:
(6th) Possessive (of)	पयस:	पयसो:	पयसाम्
(7th) Locative (in, on)	पयसि	पयसो:	पय:सु
Vocative (address)	पय:	पयसी	पयांसि

(62) MASCULINE ADJECTIVE ENDING IN *(s)* स् (गरीयस्) superior (Gītā 11.43)

CASE–विभक्ति	Singular	Dual	Plural
(1st) Nominative -	गरीयान्	गरीयांसौ	गरीयांस:
(2nd) Accusative (to, what?)	गरीयांसम्	गरीयांसौ	गरीयस:
(3rd) Instrumental (with, by)	गरीयसा	गरीयोभ्याम्	गरीयोभि:
(4th) Dative (for, to)	गरीयसे	गरीयोभ्याम्	गरीयोभ्य:
(5th) Ablative (from. than)	गरीय:	गरीयोभ्याम्	गरीयोभ्य:
(6th) Possessive (of)	गरीय:	गरीयसो:	गरीयसाम्
(7th) Locative (in, on)	गरीयसि	गरीयसो:	गरीयसु
Vocative (address)	गरीयन्	गरीयांसौ	गरीयांस:

NEUTER ADJECTIVE ENDING IN *(s)* स् (गरीयस्) superior (Gītā 2.6)

(1st) Nominative -	गरीय:	गरीयांसौ	गरीयांसि
(2nd) Accusative (to, what?)	गरीय:	गरीयांसौ	गरीयांसि

Remaining same as masculine forms

FEMININE ADJECTIVE ENDING IN *(s)* स् (गरीयस्) superior

(1st) Nominative -	गरीयसी	गरीयांस्यौ	गरीयस्य:

Remaining same as masculine forms

(63) MASCULINE NOUN ENDING IN *(ṁs)* ंस् (पुंस्) man (Gītā 2.71)

(1st) Nominative -	पुमान्	पुमांसौ	पुमांस:
(2nd) Accusative (to, what?)	पुमांसम्	पुमांसौ	पुंस:

(3rd) Instrumental (with, by)	पुंसा	पुम्भ्याम्	पुम्भिः
(4th) Dative (for, to)	पुंसे	पुम्भ्याम्	पुम्भ्यः
(5th) Ablative (from. than)	पुंसः	पुम्भ्याम्	पुम्भ्यः
(6th) Possessive (of)	पुंसः	पुंसोः	पुंसाम्
(7th) Locative (in, on)	पुंसि	पुंसोः	पुंसु
Vocative (address)	पुमान्	पुमांसौ	पुमांसः

(64) MASCULINE NOUN ENDING IN *(h)* ह् (मुह्) charmer

(1st) Nominative -	मुक्-ग्	मुहौ	मुहः
(2nd) Accusative (to, what?)	मुहम्	मुहौ	मुहः
(3rd) Instrumental (with, by)	मुहा	मुग्भ्याम्	मुग्भिः
(4th) Dative (for, to)	मुहे	मुग्भ्याम्	मुग्भ्यः
(5th) Ablative (from. than)	मुहः	मुग्भ्याम्	मुग्भ्यः
(6th) Possessive (of)	मुहः	मुहोः	मुहाम्
(7th) Locative (in, on)	मुहि	मुहोः	मुक्षु, मुट्सु
Vocative (address)	मुक्-ग्	मुहौ	मुहः

(65) FEMINENE NOUN ENDING IN *(h)* ह् (उपानह्) shoe

(1st) Nominative -	उपानत्-द्	उपानहौ	उपानहः
(2nd) Accusative (to, what)	उपानहम्	उपानहौ	उपानहः
(3rd) Instrumental (with, by)	उपानहा	उपानद्भ्याम्	उपानद्भिः
(4th) Dative (for, to)	उपानहे	उपानद्भ्याम्	उपानद्भ्यः
(5th) Ablative (from. than)	उपानहः	उपानद्भ्याम्	उपानद्भ्यः
(6th) Possessive (of)	उपानहः	उपानहोः	उपानहाम्
(7th) Locative (in, on)	उपानहि	उपानहोः	उपानत्सु
Vocative (address)	उपानत्-द्	उपानहौ	उपानहः

DECLENSIONS OF THE IRREGULAR WORDS

(66) MASCULINE NOUN ENDING IN *(i)* इ (सखि) friend (Gītā 4.3)

(1st) Nominative -	सखा	सखायौ	सखाय:
(2nd) Accusative (to, what?)	सखायम्	सखायौ	सखीन्
(3rd) Instrumental (with, by)	सख्या	सखिभ्याम्	सखिभि:
(4th) Dative (for, to)	सख्ये	सखिभ्याम्	सखिभ्य:
(5th) Ablative (from. than)	सख्यु:	सखिभ्याम्	सखिभ्य:
(6th) Possessive (of)	सख्यु:	सख्यो:	सखीनाम्
(7th) Locative (in, on)	सख्यौ	सख्यो:	सखिषु
Vocative (address)	सखे	सखायौ	सखाय:

(67) MASCULINE NOUN ENDING IN *(i)* इ (पति) husband (Gītā 1.18)

(3rd) Instrumental (with, by)	पत्या	पतिभ्याम्	पतिभि:
(4th) Dative (for, to)	पत्ये	पतिभ्याम्	पतिभ्य:
(5th) Ablative (from. than)	पत्यु:	पतिभ्याम्	पतिभ्य:
(6th) Possessive (of)	पत्यु:	पत्यो:	पतीनाम्
(7th) Locative (in, on)	पत्यौ	पत्यो:	पतिषु

(68) NEUTER NOUN ENDING IN *(i)* इ (अक्षि) eye (Gītā 13.14)

(3rd) Instrumental (with, by)	अक्ष्णा	अक्षिभ्याम्	अक्षिभि:
(4th) Dative (for, to)	अक्ष्णे	अक्षिभ्याम्	अक्षिभ्य:
(5th) Ablative (from. than)	अक्ष्ण:	अक्षिभ्याम्	अक्षिभ्य:
(6th) Possessive (of)	अक्ष्ण:	अक्ष्णो:	अक्ष्णाम्
(7th) Locative (in, on)	अक्ष्णि, अक्षणि	अक्ष्णो:	अक्षिषु

(69) FEMININE NOUN ENDING IN *(ī)* ई (स्त्री) woman (Gītā 1.41)

(2nd) Accusative (to, what?)	स्त्रियम्, स्त्रीम्	स्त्रियौ	स्त्रीयः

(70) FEMININE NOUN ENDING IN *(ī)* ई (श्री) wealth (Gītā 10.34)

(1st) Nominative -	श्रीः	श्रियौ	श्रियः
(2nd) Accusative (to, what?)	श्रियम्	श्रियौ	श्रियः
(3rd) Instrumental (with, by)	श्रिया	श्रीभ्याम्	श्रीभिः
(4th) Dative (for, to)	श्रियै, श्रिये	श्रीभ्याम्	श्रीभ्यः
(5th) Ablative (from. than)	श्रियाः, श्रियः	श्रिभ्याम्	श्रीभ्यः
(6th) Possessive (of)	श्रियाः, श्रियः	श्रियोः	श्रियाम्, श्रीणाम्
(7th) Locative (in, on)	श्रियाम्, श्रियि	श्रियोः	श्रीषु
Vocative (address)	श्रीः	श्रियौ	श्रियः

(71) FEMININE NOUN ENDING IN *(ū)* ऊ (भू) earth (Gītā 2.47)

(2nd) Accusative (to, what?)	भूवम्	भुवौ	भुवः
(4th) Dative (for, to)	भुवै, भुवे	भूभ्याम्	भूभ्यः
(5th) Ablative (from. than)	भुवाः, भुवः	भूभ्याम्	भूभ्यः
(6th) Possessive (of)	भुवाः, भुवः	भुवोः	भुवाम्, भूनाम्
(7th) Locative (in, on)	भुवाम्, भुवि	भुवोः	भूषु

(72) MASCULINE NOUN ENDING IN *(s)* स् (विद्वस्) learned (Gītā 3.25)

(1st) Nominative -	विद्वान्	विद्वांसौ	विद्वांसः
(2nd) Accusative (to, what?)	विद्वांसम्	विद्वांसौ	विदुषः
(3rd) Instrumental (with, by)	विदुषा	विद्वद्भ्याम्	विद्वद्भिः
(4th) Dative (for, to)	विदुषे	विद्वद्भ्याम्	विद्वद्भ्यः
(5th) Ablative (from. than)	विदुषः	विद्वद्भ्याम्	विद्वद्भ्यः
(6th) Possessive (of)	विदुषः	विदुषोः	विदुषाम्
(7th) Locative (in, on)	विदुषि	विदुषोः	विद्वत्सु

Vocative (address)	विद्वान्	विद्वांसौ	विद्वांसः

(73) MASCULINE NOUN ENDING IN *(in)* इन् (पथिन्) way (Gītā 6.38)

(1st) Nominative -	पन्थाः	पन्थानौ	पन्थानः
(2nd) Accusative (to, what?)	पन्थानम्	पन्थानौ	पथः
(3rd) Instrumental (with, by)	पथा	पथिभ्याम्	पथिभिः
(4th) Dative (for, to)	पथे	पथिभ्याम्	पथिभ्यः
(5th) Ablative (from. than)	पथः	पथिभ्याम्	पथिभ्यः
(6th) Possessive (of)	पथः	पथोः	पथाम्
(7th) Locative (in, on)	पथिः	पथोः	पथिषु
Vocative (address)	पन्थाः	पन्थानौ	पन्थानः

(74) FEMININE NOUN ENDING IN *(ā)* आ (जरा) old age (Gītā 2.13)

(1st) Nominative -	जरा	जरे, जरसौ	जराः, जरसः
(2nd) Accusative (to, what?)	जराम्, जरसम्	जरे, जरसौ	जराः, जरसः
(3rd) Instrumental (with, by)	जरया, जरसा	जराभ्याम्	जराभिः
(4th) Dative (for, to)	जरायै, जरसे	जराभ्याम्	जराभ्यः
(5th) Ablative (from. than)	जरयाः, जरसः	जराभ्याम्	जराभ्यः
(6th) Possessive (of)	जरायाः, जरसः	जरयोः, जरसोः	जराणाम्, जरसाम्
(7th) Locative (in, on)	जरायाम्, जरसि	जरयोः, जरसोः	जरासु
Vocative (address)	जरे	जरे, जरसौ	जराः, जरसः

(75) FEMININE NOUN ENDING IN *(ā)* आ (निशा) night (Gītā 2.69)

(1st) Nominative -	निशा	निशे	निशाः
(2nd) Accusative (to, what?)	निशाम्	निशे	निशाः, निशः
(3rd) Instrumental (with, by)	निशया, निशा	निशाभ्याम्, निज्भ्याम्, निड्भ्याम्	निशाभिः, निज्भिः, निड्भिः
(4th) Dative (for, to)	निशायै, निशे	निशाभ्याम्, निज्भ्याम्, निड्भ्याम्	निशाभ्यः, निज्भ्यः निड्भ्यः
(5th) Ablative (from. than)	निशायाः, निशः	निशाभ्याम्, निज्भ्याम्, निड्भ्याम्	निशाभ्यः, निज्भ्यः

निड्भ्य

(6th) Possessive (of)	नशायाः, निशः	निशायोः, निशोः	निशानाम्, निशाम्
(7th) Locative (in, on)	निशायाम्, निशि	निशायोः, निशोः	निशासु, निच्सु, निड्सु, निटत्सु
Vocative (address)	निशा	निशे	निशाः

(76) FEMININE NOUN ENDING IN ***(ā)*** **आ (नासिका)** nose (Gītā 6.13)

(2nd) Accusative (to, what?)	नास्का	नासिके	नासिकाः, नसः
(3rd) Instrumental (with, by)	नासिकया, नसा	नासिकाभ्याम्, नोभ्याम्	नासिकाभिः, नोभिः
(7th) Locative (in, on)	नास्कायाम्, नसि	नासिकयोः, नसोः	नासिकासु, नःसु, नस्सु

(77) MASCULINE NOUN ENDING IN ***(a)*** **अ (पाद)** foot (Gītā 13.13)

(2nd) Accusative (to, what?)	पादम्	पादौ	पादान्, पदः
(3rd) Instrumental (with, by)	पादेन, पदा	पादाभ्याम्, पद्भ्याम्	पादैः, पद्भिः
(7th) Locative (in, on)	पादे, पदि	पादयोः, पदोः	पदेषु, पत्सु

(78) NEUTER NOUN ENDING IN ***(a)*** **अ (हृदय)** heart (Gītā 1.19)

(2nd) Accusative (to, what?)	हृदयम्	हृदये	हृदयानि, हृन्दि
(3rd) Instrumental (with, by)	हृदयेन	हृदयाभ्याम्, हृद्भ्याम्	हृदयैः, हृद्भिः
(7th) Locative (in, on)	हृदये, हृदि	हृदयोः, हृदोः	हृदयेषु, हृत्सु

(79) NEUTER NOUN ENDING IN ***(a)*** **अ (उदक)** water (Gītā 1.42)

(2nd) Accusative (to, what?)	उदकम्	उदके	उदकानि, उदानि
(3rd) Instrumental (with, by)	उदकेन, उद्ना	उदकाभ्याम्, उद्भ्याम्	उदकैः, उदभिः
(7th) Locative (in, on)	उदके, उद्नि, उदनि	उदकयोः, उदोः	उदकेषु, उदसु

(80) MASCULINE NOUN ENDING IN ***(a)*** **अ (मास)** month (Gītā 10.35)

(2nd) Accusative (to, what?)	मासम्	मासौ	मासान्, मासः
(3rd) Instrumental (with, by)	मासेन, मासा	मासाभ्याम्, माभ्याम्	मासैः, माभिः
(7th) Locative (in, on)	मासे, मासि	मासयोः, मासोः	मासेषु, माःसु, मास्सु

APPENDIX - 3

DECLENSIONS OF THE PRONOUNS

NOTE : Personal pronoun अस्मद् refers to a first person (m◦f◦n◦), युष्मद् to the second person (m◦f◦n◦) and तद् refers to a third person, genfer specific.

(81) FIRST PERSON, I (अस्मद्) **2nd PERSON, You (युष्मद्)**

(1st)	अहम्	आवाम्	वयम्	त्वम्	युवाम्	यूयं
(2nd)	माम्,मा	आवाम् , नौ	अस्मान्, न:	त्वाम्, त्वा	युवाम्, वां	युष्मान्,व:
(3rd)	मया	आवाभ्याम्	अस्माभि:	त्वया	युवाभ्यां	युष्माभि:
(4th)	मह्यम्, मे	आवाभ्याम्, नौ	अस्मभ्य:, न:	तुभ्यम्, ते	युवाभ्या, वां	युष्मभ्य:,व:
(5th)	मत्	आवाभ्याम्	अस्मत्	त्वत्	युवाभ्यां	युष्मत्
(6th)	मम,मे	आवयो:, नौ	अस्माकम्, न:	तव, ते	युवयो:, वां	युष्माकं,व:
(7th)	मयि	आवयो:	अस्मासु	त्वयि	युवयो:	युष्मासु

Pronouns derived from अस्मद् with छ, अण् and खञ् suffixes :

छ	m◦ (my)	मदीय	m◦ (our)	अस्मदीय	f◦ (my)	मदीया	f◦ (our)	अस्मदीया
अण्	m◦ (my)	मामक	m◦ (our)	आस्मक	f◦ (my)	मामिका	f◦ (our)	आस्माकी
खञ्	m◦ (my)	मामकीन	m◦ (our)	आस्माकीन	f◦ (my)	मामकीना	f◦ (our)	आस्माकीना

Pronouns derived from युष्मद् with छ, अण् and खञ् suffixes :

छ	m◦ (your)	त्वदीय	m◦ (pl◦)	युष्मदीय	f◦ (your)	त्वदीया	f◦ (pl◦)	युष्मदीया
अण्	m◦ (your)	तावक	m◦ (pl◦)	यौष्माक	f◦ (your)	तावकी	f◦ (pl◦)	यौष्माकी
खञ्	m◦ (your)	तावकीन	m◦ (pl◦)	यौष्माकीण	f◦ (your)	तावकीना	f◦ (pl◦)	यौष्माकीणा

(82) THIRD PERSON, He she,it - away **(तद्)**

MASCULINE, he FEMININE, she

(1st)	स:	तौ	ते	सा	ते	ता:

(2nd)	तम्	तौ	तान्	ताम्	ते	ता:
(3rd)	तेन	ताभ्याम्	तै:	तया	ताभ्याम्	ताभि:
(4th)	तस्मै	ताभ्याम्	तेभ्य:	तस्यै	ताभ्याम्	ताभ्य:
(5th)	तस्मात्	ताभ्याम्	तेभ्य:	तस्या:	ताभ्याम्	ताभ्य:
(6th)	तस्य	तयो:	तेषाम्	तस्या:	तयो:	तासाम्
(7th)	तस्मिन्	तयो:	तेषु	तस्याम्	तयो:	तासु

NEUTER GENDER, it

(1st) तत्-तद् ते तानि

(2nd) तत्-तद् ते तानि The rest is same as MASCULINE↑

(83) WHO, WHICH (यद्)

	MASCULINE			FEMININE		
(1st)	य:	यौ	ये	या	ये	या:
(2nd)	यम्	यौ	यान्	याम्	ये	या:
(3rd)	येन	याभ्याम्	यै:	यया	याभ्याम्	याभि:
(4th)	यस्मै	याभ्याम्	येभ्य:	यस्यै	याभ्याम्	याभ्य:
(5th)	यस्मात्	याभ्याम्	येभ्य:	यस्या:	याभ्याम्	याभ्य:
(6th)	यस्य	ययो:	येषाम्	यस्या:	ययो:	यासाम्
(7th)	यस्मिन्	ययो:	येषु	यस्याम्	ययो:	यासु

NEUTER GENDER

(1st) यत्-यद् ये यानि

(2nd) यत्-यद् ये यानि The rest is same as MASCULINE↑

NOTE : Pronoun इदम् refers to a thing at hand, एतद् to the one still nearer, अदस् refers to a thing at a distance, and तद् to the the third person one that is absent.

इस्मस्तु सन्निकृष्टं समीपतरवर्ति चैतरो रूपम् ।
अदस्तु विप्रकृष्टं तदिति परोक्षे विजानियात् ।।

(84) THIS - near **(इदम्)**

	MASCULINE			FEMININE		
(1st)	अयम्	इमौ	इमे	इयम्	इमे	इमा:
(2nd)	इमम्	इमौ	इमान्	इमाम्	इमे	इमा:
(3rd)	अनेन	आभ्याम्	एभि:	अनया	आभ्याम्	आभि:
(4th)	अस्मै	आभ्याम्	एभ्य:	अस्यै	आभ्याम्	आभ्य:
(5th)	अस्मात्	आभ्याम्	एभ्य:	अस्या:	आभ्याम्	आभ्य:
(6th)	अस्य	अनयो:	एषाम्	अस्या:	अनयो:	आसाम्
(7th)	अस्मिन्	अनयो:	एषु	अस्याम्	अनयो:	आसु

NEUTER GENDER

(1st)	इदम्	इमे	इमानि
(2nd)	इदम्	इमे	इमानि The rest is same as MASCULINE↑

(85) **THIS** - close **(एतद्)**

	MASCULINE			FEMININE		
(1st)	एष:	एतौ	एते	एषा	एते	एता:
(2nd)	एतम्	एतौ	एतान्	एताम्	एते	एता:
(3rd)	एतेन	एताभ्याम्	एतै:	एतया	एताभ्याम्	एताभि:
(4th)	एतस्मै	एताभ्याम्	एतेभ्य:	एतस्यै	एताभ्याम्	एताभ्य:
(5th)	एतस्मात्	एताभ्याम्	एतेभ्य:	एतस्या:	एताभ्याम्	एताभ्य:
(6th)	एतस्य	एतयो:	एतेषाम्	एतस्या:	एतयो:	एतासां
(7th)	एतस्मिन्	एतयो:	एतेषु	एतस्याम्	एतयो:	एतासु

NEUTER GENDER

(1st)	एतत्	एते	एतानि
(2nd)	एतत्	एते	एतानि The rest is same as MASCULINE↑

(86) THAT - far (अदस्)

	MASCULINE			FEMININE		
(1st)	असौ	अमू	अमी	असौ	अमू	अमूः
(2nd)	अमूम्	अमू	अमून्	अमूम्	अमू	अमूः
(3rd)	अमुना	अमूभ्याम्	अमीभिः	अमुया	अमूभ्याम्	अमूभिः
(4th)	अमुष्मै	अमूभ्याम्	अमीभ्यः	अमुष्यै	अमूभ्याम्	अमूभ्यः
(5th)	अमुष्मात्	अमूभ्याम्	अमीभ्यः	अमुष्याः	अमूभ्याम्	अमूभ्यः
(6th)	अमुष्य	अमुयोः	अमीषाम्	अमुष्याः	अमुयोः	अमूषाम्
(7th)	अमुष्मिन्	अमुयोः	अमीषु	अमुष्याम्	अमुयोः	अमुषु

NEUTER GENDER

(1st)	अदः	अमू	अमूनि
(2nd)	अदः	अमू	अमूनि The rest is same as MASCULINE↑

(87) MASCULINE PRONOUN सर्व (all)

CASE-विभक्ति	Singular	Dual	Plural
(1st) Nominative -	सर्वः	सर्वौ	सर्वे
(2nd) Accusative (to, what?)	सर्वम्	सर्वौ	सर्वान्
(3rd) Instrumental (with, by)	सर्वेण	सर्वाभ्याम्	सर्वैः
(4th) Dative (for, to)	सर्वस्मै	सर्वाभ्याम्	सर्वेभ्यः
(5th) Ablative (from. than)	सर्वस्मात्	सर्वाभ्याम्	सर्वेभ्यः
(6th) Possessive (of)	सर्वस्य	सर्वयोः	सर्वेषाम्
(7th) Locative (in, on)	सर्वस्मिन्	सर्वयोः	सर्वेषु
Vocative	सर्व	सर्वौ	सर्वे

NEUTER PRONOUN सर्व

(1st)	सर्वम्	सर्वे	सर्वाणि
(2nd)	सर्वम्	सर्वे	सर्वाणि The rest is same as MASCULINE↑

FEMININE PRONOUN सर्व

(1st) Nominative -	सर्वा	सर्वे	सर्वाः
(2nd) Accusative (to, what?)	सर्वाम्	सर्वे	सर्वाः
(3rd) Instrumental (with, by)	सर्वया	सर्वाभ्याम्	सर्वाभिः
(4th) Dative (for, to)	सर्वस्यै	सर्वाभ्याम्	सर्वाभ्यः
(5th) Ablative (from. than)	सर्वस्याः	सर्वाभ्याम्	सर्वाभ्यः
(6th) Possessive (of)	सर्वस्याः	सर्वयोः	सर्वासाम्
(7th) Locative (in, on)	सर्वस्याम्	सर्वयोः	सर्वासु
Vocative	सर्वे	सर्वे	सर्वाः

(88) MASCULINE PRONOUN किम् (what, who?)

CASE-विभक्ति	Singular	Dual	Plural
(1st) Nominative -	कः	कौ	के
(2nd) Accusative (to, what?)	कम्	कौ	कान्
(3rd) Instrumental (with, by)	केन	काभ्याम्	कैः
(4th) Dative (for, to)	कस्मै	काभ्याम्	केभ्यः
(5th) Ablative (from. than)	कस्मात्	काभ्याम्	केभ्यः
(6th) Possessive (of)	कस्य	कयोः	केषाम्
(7th) Locative (in, on)	कस्मिन्	कयोः	केषु

NEUTER PRONOUN किम्

(1st) किम् के कानि

(2nd) किम् के कानि The rest is same as MASCULINE↑

FEMININE PRONOUN किम्

(1st) Nominative -	का	के	काः
(2nd) Accusative (to, what?)	काम्	के	काः

(3rd) Instrumental (with, by)	कया	काभ्याम्	काभि:
(4th) Dative (for, to)	कस्यै	काभ्याम्	काभ्य:
(5th) Ablative (from. than)	कस्या:	काभ्याम्	काभ्य:
(6th) Possessive (of)	कस्या:	कयो:	कासाम्
(7th) Locative (in, on)	कस्याम्	कयो:	कासु

(89) MASCULINE PRONOUN कश्चित् (someone)

(1st) Nominative -	कश्चित्	कौचित्	केचित्
(2nd) Accusative (to, what?)	कञ्चित्	कौचित्	कांश्चित्
(3rd) Instrumental (with, by)	केनचित्	काभ्याञ्चित्	कैश्चित्
(4th) Dative (for, to)	कस्मैचित्	काभ्याञ्चित्	केभ्यश्चित्
(5th) Ablative (from. than)	कस्माश्चित्	काभ्याञ्चित्	केभ्यश्चित्
(6th) Possessive (of)	कस्यचित्	कयोश्चित्	केषाञ्चित्
(7th) Locative (in, on)	कस्मिंश्चित्	कयोश्चित्	केषुचित्

NEUTER PRONOUN कश्चित्

(1st) किञ्चित् केचित् कानिचित्

(2nd) किञ्चित् कचिेत् कानिचित् The rest is same as MASCULINE↑

FEMININE PRONOUN काचित्

(1st) Nominative -	काचित्	केचित्	काश्चित्
(2nd) Accusative (to, what?)	काञ्चित्	केचित्	काशित्
(3rd) Instrumental (with, by)	कयाचित्	काभ्यांचित्	काभिश्चित्
(4th) Dative (for, to)	कस्यैचित्	काभ्यांचित्	काभ्याश्चित्
(5th) Ablative (from. than)	कस्याश्चित्	काभ्यांचित्	काभ्याश्चित्
(6th) Possessive (of)	कस्याश्चित्	कयोश्चित्	कासाञ्चित्
(7th) Locative (in, on)	कस्यांञ्चित्	कयोश्चित्	कासुचित्

APPENDIX - 4

DECLENSIONS OF THE NUMERICAL ADJECTIVES

(90) ONE (एक)

Always Singular

CASE	Masculine	Neuter	Feminine
(1st)	एक:	एकम्	एका
(2nd)	एकम्	एकम्	एकाम्
(3rd)	एकेन	एकेन	एकया
(4th)	एकस्मै	एकस्मै	एकस्यै
(5th)	एकस्मात्	एकस्मात्	एकस्या:
(6th)	एकस्य	एकस्य	एकस्या:
(7th)	एकस्मिन्	एकस्मिन्	एकस्याम्
(Voc)	एक	एके	एक

(91) TWO (द्वि)

Always Dual

CASE	Masculine	Neuter	Feminine
(1st)	द्वौ	द्वे	द्वे
(2nd)	द्वौ	द्वे	द्वे
(3rd)	द्वाभ्याम्	द्वाभ्याम्	द्वाभ्याम्
(4th)	द्वाभ्याम्	द्वाभ्याम्	द्वाभ्याम्
(5th)	द्वाभ्याम्	द्वाभ्याम्	द्वाभ्याम्
(6th)	द्वयो:	द्वयो:	द्वयो:
(7th)	द्वयो:	द्वयो:	द्वयो:
(Voc)	द्वौ	द्वे	द्वे

(92) THREE (त्रि)

Always Plural

CASE	Masculine	Neuter	Feminine
(1st)	त्रय:	त्रीणि	तिस्र:
(2nd)	त्रीन्	त्रीणि	तिस्र:
(3rd)	त्रिभि:	त्रिभि:	तिसृभि:
(4th)	त्रिभ्य:	त्रिभ्य:	तिसृभ्य:
(5th)	त्रिभ्य:	त्रिभ्य:	तिसृभ्य:
(6th)	त्रयाणाम्	त्रयाणाम्	तिसृणाम्
(7th)	त्रिषु	त्रिषु	तिसृषु
(Voc)	त्रय:	त्रीणि	तिस्र:

(93) FOUR (चतुर्)

Always Plural

CASE	Masculine	Neuter	Feminine
(1st)	चत्वार:	चत्वारि	चतस्र:
(2nd)	चतुर:	चत्वारि	चतस्र:
(3rd)	चतुर्भि:	चतुर्भि:	चतसृभि:
(4th)	चतुर्भ्य:	चतुर्भ्य:	चतसृभ्य:
(5th)	चतुर्भ्य:	चतुर्भ्य:	चतसृभ्य:
(6th)	चतुर्णाम्	चतुर्णाम्	चतसृणाम्
(7th)	चतुर्षु	चतुर्षु	चतसृषु
(Voc)	चत्वार:	चत्वारि	चतस्र:

(94) FIVE	SIX	SEVEN	EIGHT	NINE
पञ्चन्	षष्	सप्तन्	अष्टन्	नवन्

Same in all three genders; always plural.

5.	6.	7.	8.	9.
पञ्च	षट्-षड्	सप्त	अष्ट-अष्टौ	नव
पञ्च	षट्-षड्	सप्त	अष्ट-अष्टौ	नव
पञ्चभिः	षड्भिः	सप्तभिः	अष्टभिः	नवभिः
पञ्चभ्यः	षड्भ्यः	सप्तभ्यः	अष्टभ्यः	नवभ्यः
पञ्चभ्यः	षड्भ्यः	सप्तभ्यः	अष्टभ्यः	नवभ्यः
पञ्चानाम्	षण्णाम्	सप्तानाम्	अष्टानाम्	नवानाम्
पञ्चसु	षट्सु	सप्तसु	अष्टसु	नवसु
पञ्च	षट्-षड्	सप्त	अष्ट-अष्टौ	नव

NOTES:

(i) Numerals from दशन् to नवदशन् decline same as नवन् ।

(ii) एकोनविंशति, ऊनविंशति and विंशति are feminine words and they decline like the word मति given in (7) above.

EXAMPLES :

ईश्वरः एकः अस्ति हस्तौ पादौ च द्वौ भवतः । महादेवाः त्रयः कथ्यन्ते वेदाः चत्वारः सन्ति ।
पाण्डवाः पञ्च आसन् ऋतवः षट् भवन्ति । सप्ताहे सप्त वासराः लूतायाः अष्ट पादाः वै ।
ग्रहाः तु नव ज्ञाताः रावणस्य मुखानि दश ॥

SPECIAL NUMERICAL EXPRESSIONS : (बहुव्रीहि adjectives)

1. One or two एको वा द्वौ, एकद्वाः । 2. Two or three द्वौ वा त्रयो, द्वित्राः ।

3. Three or four त्रयो वा चत्वारः, त्रिचतुराः । 4. Four or five चत्वारो वा पञ्च, चतुःपञ्चः ।

5. Five or six पञ्च वा षट्, पञ्चषाः । 6. Group of two, a pair द्वय, युगल, युग्म ।

7. Two opposites, opposite pair द्वंद्व, दम्पती । 8. Group of three त्रय, त्रिक ।

9. Group of four चतुष्टय, चतुष्टक ।

10. Group of five पञ्चतय, पञ्चक ।

11. Group of six षष्टक ।

12. Group of seven सप्तक ।

13. Group of eight अष्टक ।

14. Group of nine नवक ।

15. Group of ten दशक ।

16. Group of hundred शतक ।

(95) NEUTER COMPARATIVE एकतर One among two

CASE–विभक्ति	Singular	Dual	Plural
(1st) Nominative -	एकतरम्	एकतरे	एकतराणि
(2nd) Accusative (to)	एकतरम्	एकतरे	एकतराणि
(3rd) Instrumental (with)	एकतरेण	एकतराभ्याम्	एकतरैः
(4th) Dative (for, to)	एकतरस्मै	एकतराभ्याम्	एकतरेभ्यः
(5th) Ablative (from)	एकतरस्मात्	एकतराभ्याम्	एकतरेभ्यः
(6th) Possessive (of)	एकतरस्य	एकतरयोः	एकतरेषाम्
(7th) Locative (in, on)	एकतरस्मिन्	एकतरयोः	एकतरेषु
Vocative (address)	एकतर	एकतरे	एकतराणि

(96) NEUTER SUPERLATIVE एकतम One among many

(1st) Nominative -	एकतमम्	एकतमे	एकतमानि
(2nd) Accusative (to)	एकतमम्	एकतमे	एकतमानि
(3rd) Instrumental (with)	एकतमेन	एकतमाभ्याम्	एकतमैः
(4th) Dative (for, to)	एकतमस्मै	एकतमाभ्याम्	एकतमेभ्यः
(5th) Ablative (from)	एकतमस्मात्	एकतमाभ्याम्	एकतमेभ्यः
(6th) Possessive (of)	एकतमस्य	एकतमयोः	एकतमेषाम्
(7th) Locative (in, on)	एकतमस्मिन्	एकतमयोः	एकतमेषु
Vocative (address)	एकतर	एकतरे	एकतराणि

EXPRESSIONS OF COMPARISON

ADJECTIVE	COMPARATIVE	m∘	f∘	n∘	SUPERLATIVE
1. बहुः	भूयस्	भूयान्	भूयसी	भूयः	भूयिष्ठः
2. महान्	महीयस्	महीयान्	महीयसी	महीयः	महिष्ठः
3. लघुः	लघीयस्	लघीय ान्	लघीय सी	लघीयः	लघिष्ठः
4. गुरुः	गरीयस्	गरीयान्	गरीयसी	गरीयः	गरिंष्ठः
5. ह्रस्वः	ह्रसीयस्	ह्रसीयान्	ह्रसीयसी	ह्रसीयः	ह्रसिष्ठः
6. दीर्घः	द्राघीयस्	द्राघीय ान्	द्राघीय सी	द्राघीय :	द्राघिष्ठः
7. अल्पः	अल्पीयस्	अल्पीयान्	अल्पीयसी	अल्पीयः	अल्पिष्ठः
अल्पः	कनीयस्	कनीय ान्	कनीय सी	कनीय :	कनिष्ठः
8. वरः	वरीयस्	वरीयान्	वरीयसी	वरीयः	वरिष्ठः
9. कृश	क्रशीयस्	क्रशीय	क्रशीयसी	क्रशीयः	क्रशिष्ठः
10. दृढ	द्रढीयस्	द्रढीयान्	द्रढीयसी	द्रढीयः	द्रढिष्ठः
11. प्रिय	प्रेयस्	प्रेयान्	प्रेयसी	प्रेयः	प्रेष्ठः
12. श्रेय	श्रेयस्	श्रेयान्	श्रेयसी	श्रेयः	श्रेष्ठः
13. वृद्ध	वर्षीयस्	वर्षीयान्	वर्षीयसी	वर्षीयः	वर्षिष्ठः
14. क्षिप्र	क्षेपीयस्	क्षेपीयान्	क्षेपीय सी	क्षेपीय :	क्षेपिष्ठः
15. क्षुद्र	क्षोदीयस्	क्षोदीयान्	क्षोदीयसी	क्षोदीयः	क्षोदिष्ठ
16. मृदु	म्रदीयस्	म्रदीयान्	म्रदीयसी	म्रदीयः	म्रदिष्ठ
17. दूर	दवीयस्	दवीयान्	दवीयसी	दवीयः	दविष्ठ
18. मतिमत्	मतीयस्	मतीयान्	मतीयसी	मतीयः	मतिष्ठः
10. मेधाविन्	मेधीयस्	मेधीयान्	मेधीयसी	मेधीयः	मेधिष्ठः
20. बहुल	बंहीयस्	बंहीयान्	बंहीयसी	बंहीयः	बंहिष्ठः

APPENDIX - 5

THE DICTIONARY OF THE 2000 SANSKRIT VERBS

THE ELEVEN CLASSES OF THE VERBS ROOTS

बृहद्धातुपाठः ।

With just some exceptions, almost all verbs are monosyllables,
most of them ending in a consonant (हलन्त), some of them even uni-letters.

NOTE : * = ppp॰ adjective (क्त विशेषणम्), followed by other participles

(लट् = present॰, लृट् = indefinite future, लङ् = imperfect past॰ लोट् = imperative॰. विधि॰ = potential)

(अ) (a)

अक् *1√ak* (to walk in circular motion like a snake) अकति अकिष्यति आकत् अकतु अकेत् *अकित अकनीय

अक्ष् *5√akṣ* (to occupy, pervade; to collect) अक्षणोति अक्षिष्यति अक्ष्णोतु आक्षणोत् अक्ष्णुयात् *अष्ट अक्षि अक्षणा

अग् *1√ag* (to walk in zigzag way like a snake, to curl, wind) अगति अगिष्यति आगत् अगतु अगेत् *अगित

अघ् *10√agh* (to sin, err, act improperly) अघयति-ते अघयिष्यति-ते आघयत्-त अघयतु-ताम् अघयेत्-त *अघित

अङ्क् *1√aṅk* (to aim, mark, stamp; to walk crooked) अङ्कते अङ्किष्यते आङ्कत अङ्कताम् अङ्केत *अङ्कित अङ्कनीय

अङ्क् *10√aṅk* (to count, mark, aim) अङ्कयति-ते अङ्कयिष्यति-ते आङ्कयत्-त अङ्कयतु-ताम् अङ्कयेत्-त *अङ्कित अङ्क

अङ्ख् *10√aṅkh* (to crawl, walk on knees) अङ्खयति-ते अङ्खयिष्यति-ते आङ्खयत्-त अङ्खयतु-ताम् अङ्खयेत्-त *अङ्खित

अङ्ग् *1√aṅg* (to wander, stamp, count) अङ्गति अङ्गिष्यति आङ्गत् अङ्गतु अङ्गेत् *अङ्गित अङ्गनीय अङ्गित्वा अङ्गितुम्

अङ्ग् *10√aṅg* (to circle, to mark, count) अङ्गयति-ते अङ्गयिष्यति-ते आङ्गयत्-त अङ्गयतु-ताम् अङ्गयेत्-त *अङ्गित

अङ्घ् *1√aṅgh* (to walk, start, rush, scold, blame) अङ्घते अङ्घिष्यते आङ्घत अङ्घताम् अङ्घेत *अङ्घित अङ्घित्वा

अच् *1√ać* (to request, honor, move) अचते अचिष्यति-ते आचत्-त अचतु-ताम् अचेत्-त *अक्त अचित्वा अचितुम्

अज् *1√aj* (to drive, go, lead, throw, cast) अजति अजिष्यति आजत् अजतु अजेत् *अजित अजनीय अजितव्य

अञ्च् *1√añć* (to worship, beg, bend) अञ्चति-ते अञ्चिष्यति-ते आञ्चत्-त अञ्चतु-ताम् अञ्चेत्-त *अञ्चित, अक्त

अञ्च् *10√añć* (to respect, worship) अञ्चयति-ते अञ्चयिष्यति-ते आञ्चयत्-त आञ्चयतु-ताम् आञ्चयेत् *अञ्चित

अञ्ज् *7√añj* (to anoint, make, show, represent) अनक्ति अङ्क्ष्यति-अञ्जिष्यति आनक् अनक्तु अञ्ज्यात् *अक्त-अङ्क

अञ्ज् *10√añj* (to say, speak) अञ्जयति-ते अञ्जयिष्यति-ते आञ्जयत्-त अञ्जयातु-ताम् अञ्जयेत् *अञ्जित अञ्जितुम्

अट् *1√aṭ* (to roam about, wander) अटति अटिष्यति आट अटतु अटेत् अट्यते *अटित अटनीय अटित्वा अटितुम्

अट्ट् *1√aṭ* (to go beyond, transgress, diminish, lessen, kill) अट्टते अट्टिष्यते आट्टत अट्टताम् अट्टेत *अट्टित

अट्ट् *10√aṭ* (to despise, dishonor, reduce) अट्टयति-ते अट्टयिष्यति-ते आट्टयत्-त अट्टयतु-ताम् अट्टयेत्-त *अट्टित

अठ् *1√aṭh* (to go) अठति-ते अठिष्यते आठत अठताम् अठेत *अठित अठत् अठनीय अठितव्य अठित्वा अठितुम्

अड् *1√aḍ* (to work, trade, try, attempt, exert) अडति अडिष्यति अडत् अडतु अडेत् *अडित अडनीय अडितव्य अड्

5√aḍ (to spread, pervade, attain) अड्णोति अडिष्यति आड्नोत् अड्नोतु अड्नुयात् *अडित अडत् अडितुम्

अड्ड् *1√aḍ* (to attack, to meditate, argue, infer, discern) अड्डति अड्डिष्यति आडत् अड्डतु अड्डेत् *अड्डित

अण् *1√aṇ* (to sound, breathe) अणति अणिष्यति आणत् अणतु अणेत् *आण अणनीय अणितव्य अणित्वा अणितुम्

अण् *4√aṇ* (to live, breathe) अण्यते अणिष्यते आण्यत अण्यताम् अण्येत आणयत् *आण अणत् प्राण प्राणिन्

अण्ड् *1√aṇṭh* (go) अण्डते अण्डिष्यते आण्डत अण्डताम् अण्डेत *अण्डित अण्डनीय अण्डितव्य अण्डित्वा अण्डितुम्

अत् *1√at* (to wander, walk constantly) अतति अतिष्यति आतत् अततु अतेत् *अतित अतनीय अतित्वा अतितुम्

अथ् *10√at* (to be weak) अथयति-ते अथयिष्यति-ते आथयत्-त अथयतु अथयेत् *अथित अथयित्वा अथयितुम्

अद् *2√ad* (to eat) अत्ति अत्स्यति आदत् अत्तु अद्यात् अद्यते *जग्ध-अन्न अदनीय अत्तव्य आद्य जग्ध्वा अन्नवान् अत्तुम्

अन् *2√an* (to breathe, live) अनिति अनिष्यति आनीत-आनत् अनितु अन्यात् *अनित अनत् अनित्वा अनितुम् आनन

अन् *4√an* (to live, to take birth, move, go about) अन्यते अनिष्यते आन्यत अन्यताम् अन्येत *अनित अनितव्य

अन्त् *1√ant* (to tie, fasten, get) अन्तति अन्तिष्यति आन्तत् अन्ततु अन्तेत् *अन्त अन्तत् अन्तनीय अन्तित्वा अन्तितुम्

अन्द् *1√and* (to bind, fasten) अन्दति अन्दिष्यति आन्दत् अन्दतु अन्देत् *अन्दित अन्दत् अन्दनीय अन्नवत्

अन्ध् *10√andh* (be become make - blind) अन्धयति-ते अन्धयिष्यति-ते आन्धयत्-त अन्धयतु-तां अन्धयेत्-त *अन्धित

अपास् *4√apās* (to cast, fling, reject, discard) अपास्यति अपासिष्यति अपास्यत् अपास्यतु अपास्येत् * अपास्त

अभ्र् *1√abhr* (to go, wander about) अभ्रति अभ्रिष्यति आभ्रत् अभ्रतु अभ्रेत् *अभ्रित अभ्रणीय अभ्रितव्य अभ्रित्वा

अम् *1√am* (to sound, go, serve, honor, eat) अमति अमिष्यति आमत् अमतु अमेत् *अमित-आन्त अमनीय अमितव्य

अम् *10√am* (to hurt, attack, afflict) आमयति-आमयते आमयिष्यति-ते आमयत्-त आमयतु-ताम् आमयेत्-त *अमित

अम्ब् *1√amb* (to go; sound) अम्बति-ते अम्बिष्यते आम्बत अम्बताम् अम्बेत *अम्बित अम्बनीय अम्बितव्य अम्बितुम्

अम्भ् *1√ambh* (to sound) अम्भते अम्भिष्यते आम्भत अम्भताम् अम्भेत *अब्ध अब्धवत् अम्भनीय अब्ध्वा

अय् *1√ay* (to go) अयते अयिष्यते आयत अयताम् अयेत अय्यते *अयित अयनीय अयितव्य अयित्वा अयितुम् अयमान

अर्क् *10√ark* (to praise, heat, warm) अर्कयति-ते अर्कयिष्यति-ते आर्कयत्-त अर्कयतु-ताम् अर्कयेत्-त *अर्कित

अर्घ् *1√argh* (to be valuable, be worth, cost) अर्घति अर्घिष्यति आर्घत् अर्घतु अर्घेत् *अर्घित अर्घनीय अर्घितव्य

अर्च् *1√arć* (to worship, adore, salute) अर्चति अर्चिष्यति आर्चत् अर्चतु अर्चेत् *अर्चित अर्चित्वा अर्चितुम् अर्चा

अर्च् *10√arć* (to honor, sing praises) अर्चयति-ते अर्चयिष्यति-ते आर्चयत्-त अर्चयतु-ताम् अर्चयेत्-त *अर्चित

अर्ज् *1√arj* (to earn, gain) अर्जति अर्जिष्यति आर्जत् अर्जतु अर्जेत् *अर्जित अर्जनीय अर्जितव्य अर्जित्वा अर्जितुम्

अर्ज् *10√arj* (to procure, make, prepare) अर्जयति-ते अर्जयिष्यति-ते आर्जयत्-त अर्जयतु-ताम् अर्जयेत्-त *अर्जित

अर्थ् *10√arth* (to want, beg, request) अर्थयते अर्थयिष्यते आर्थयत अर्थयताम् अर्थयेत *अर्थित अर्थयित्वा अर्थयितुम्

अर्द् *1√ard* (to demand, go) अर्दति अर्दिष्यति आर्दत् अर्दतु अर्देत् *अर्दित अर्दत् अर्दनीय अर्दित्वा अर्दितुम् अर्द्यमान

अर्द् *10√ard* (to kill, afflict, torment) अर्दयति-अर्दयिष्यते आर्दयत्-त अर्दयतु-ताम् अर्दयेत्-त *अर्दित-अर्ण अर्दयत्

अर्ब् *1√arb* (to kill, go one side) अर्बति अर्बिष्यति आर्बत् अर्बतु अर्बेत् *अर्बित अर्बत् अर्बनीय अर्बितव्य अर्बित्वा

अर्व् *1√arv* (to inflict, to go towards) अर्वति अर्विष्यति आर्वत् अर्वतु अर्वेत् *अर्वित अर्वणीय अर्वितव्य अर्वित्वा

अर्ह् *1√arh* (to be fit, deserve; worship) अर्हति अर्हिष्यति आर्हत् अर्हतु अर्हेत् *अर्हित अर्हनीय अर्हितव्य अर्हित्वा

अर्ह् *10√arh* (to deserve, be suitable) अर्हयति-ते अर्हयिष्यति-ते आर्हयत्-त अर्हयतु-ताम् अर्हयेत्-त *अर्हित अर्ह्य

अल् *1√al* (to save, adorn, prevent) अलति-ते अलिष्यति आलत् अलतु अलेत् *अलित अलनीय अलितव्य अलित्वा

अव् *1√av* (to please, protect, defend, do good) अवति अविष्यति आवत् अवतु अवेत् *अवित अवनीय अवित्वा

अंश् *10√aṁś* (to divide, apportion) अंशयति अंशयिष्यति-ते आंशयत्-त अंशयतु-ताम् अंशयेत्-त *अंशित

अश् *5√aś* (to occupy, penetrate, pervade, fill) अश्नुते अशिष्यते अश्नुवीत अश्नुताम् आश्नुत अश्यते *अशित-अष्ट अशनीय अशितव्य-अष्टव्य आश्य अशित्वा-अष्ट्वा अशितुम्-आष्टुम् अश्यमान अशन अश्व अक्ष अक्षर अक्षि

अश् *9√aś* (to eat, consume, enjoy) अश्नाति अशिष्यति अश्नात् अश्नातु अश्नियात् *अशित-अष्ट अशनीय अशितुम्

अष् *1√aṣ* (to shine, go, move, receive, take) अषति-ते अषिष्यति-ते आषित्-त अषतु-ताम् अषेत्-त *अषित-अहेष्ट

अंस् *10√aṁs* (to divide, apportion) अंसयति-ते अंसयिष्यति-ते आंसयत्-त अंसयतु-ताम् अंसयेत्-त *अंसित

अस् *1√as* (to go, take) असति-ते असिष्यति-ते आसित्-त असतु-ताम् असेत्-त *असित असनीय असितव्य असितुम्

अस् *2√as* (to be, exist, live) अस्ति भविष्यति आसीत् अस्तु स्यात् *भूत भवनीय भवितव्य भाव्य भूत्वा भवितुम् भूति

अस् *4√as* (to throw) अस्यति असिष्यति आस्यत् अस्यतु अस्येत् *असित असनीय असितव्य आस्य असित्वा-अस्त्वा असितुम् अस्यमान अस्तित्व उपास्ति आस आसक असित-देवल व्यास निरासन समस्या असुर असि अस्त्र इष्वास

असू *11√asū* (to be jealous) असूयति असूयिष्यति आसूयत् असूयतु असूयेत् असूयाञ्चकार असूयिता *असूयित

अंह् *1√aṁh* (to reach, approach, start, set out) अंहते अंहिष्यते आहत अंहताम् अंहेत *अंहित-ओढ अंहनीय

अंह् *10√aṁh* (to send, speak) अंहयति-ते अंहयिष्यति-ते आंहयत्-त अंहयतु-ताम् अंहयेत्-त *अंहित अंहयितुम्

अह् *1√ah* (to say, compose) only 5 forms आत्थ आहथुः आह आहतुः आहुः the rest from the root 2√ब्रू ↓

अह् *5√ah* (to pervade) अह्नोति अहिष्यति आह्नोत् अह्नोतु अह्नुयात् this verb belongs to the vaidic Sanskrit.

(आ) (ā)

आञ्छ् *1√āñćh* (to stretch, lengthen) आञ्छति आञ्छिष्यति आञ्छत् आञ्छतु आञ्छेत् *आञ्छित आच्छनीय

आन्दोल् *10√āndol* (to swing) आन्दोलयति-ते आन्दोलयिष्यति-ते आन्दोलयत्-त आन्दोलयतु-ताम् आन्दोलयेत्-त

*आन्दोलित आन्दोलयत् आन्दोलयनीय आन्दोलयितव्य आन्दोलयित्वा आन्दोलयितुम् आन्दोलयमान आन्दोलन

आप् *1√āp* (to obtain, attain, pervade, catch) आपति आप्स्यति आपत् आपतु आपेत् *आप्त आप्त्वा आप्तुम्

आप् *5√āp* (to obtain, attain, reach, pervade, catch) आप्नोति आप्स्यति आप्नोत् आप्नोतु आप्नुयात् *आप्त आपनीय-ईप्सनीय आप्तव्य-ईप्सितव्य आप्य-ईप्स्य आप्तव्य-ईप्सितव्य आप्त्वा-ईप्सित्वा आप्तुम्-ईप्सितुम् आप्ति-ईप्सा

आप् *10√āp* (to get) आपयति-ते आपयिष्यति-ते आपयत्-त आपयतु-ताम् आपयेत्-त *आपित आपयित्वा आपयितुम्

आंस् *10√āṁs* (to march) आसादयति आसादयिष्यति आसादयत् आसादयतु आसादयेत् *आसादित आसादयितुम्

आस् *2√ās* (to sit, stay, rest, live, be, exist) आस्ते आसिष्यते आस्त आस्ताम् आसीत् *आसित आसितवान् आसनीय आसितव्य आस्य आसित्वा आसितुम् आसयितुम् आसीन आस आसक आसन कैलास उपास उपासना समास अध्यास

<u>(इ) (i)</u>

इ *1√i* (to go, enter, reach, attain, get, obtain, come, come to) अयति एष्यति ऐत् एतु ऐषीत् *इत एतुम्

इ *2√i* (to learn) एति-अधीते एष्यति-अध्येष्यते ऐत्-अध्यैत एतु-अधीताम् इयात्-अधीयीत *इत इत्वा एतुम् ईयमान

इक् *2√i* (to remember, have down pat, learn) अध्येति अध्येष्यति अध्यैत् अध्येतु अधीयात् *अधीत अध्येतव्य

इख् *1√ikh* (to go) एखति एखिष्यति ऐखत् एखतु एखेत् *इङ्खित इङ्खत् इङ्खनीय इङ्खित्वा इङ्खितुम् इङ्खयमान

इङ्ख् *1√iṅkh* (to come) इङ्खति इङ्खिष्यति ऐङ्खत् इङ्खतु इङ्खेत् *इङ्खित इङ्खत् इङ्खनीय इङ्खित्वा इङ्खितुम् इङ्खयमान

इङ् *2√iṅ* (to read, study, go) अधीते अध्येष्यते अध्यैत अधीताम् अधीयीत *अधीत अध्येतुम् अध्यापक अध्याय

इङ् *4√iṅ* (to go) ईयते एष्यते ऐयत ईयताम् ईयेत *ईत अयनीय एतव्य एय ईत्वा एतुम् ईयमान अयन परायण

इङ्ग् *1√iṅg* (to shake, move, be agitated) इङ्गति इङ्गिष्यति ऐङ्गत् इङ्गतु इङ्गेत् *इङ्गित इङ्गत् इङ्गनीय इङ्गित्वा

इट् *1√iṭ* (to go, go to, go towards) एटति एटिष्यति ऐटत् एटतु एटेत् *इटित इटनीय इटितव्य इटित्वा इटितुम्

इण् *2√iṇ* (to go, go to go towards, come to, come near) एति एष्यति ऐत एतु इयात् अगात् *इत एतव्य एतुम्

इन्द् *1√ind* (to be powerful) इन्दति इन्दिष्यति ऐन्दत् इन्दतु इन्देत् *इन्दित इन्दत् इन्दनीय इन्दितव्य इन्दित्वा इन्दितुम्

इन्ध् *7√indh* (to shine, kindle, light, set on fire) इन्धे इन्धिष्यते ऐन्ध इन्धाम् इन्धीत *इद्ध इन्धनीय इन्धितुम् इन्धन

इन्व् *1√inv* (to pervade) इन्वति इन्विष्यति ऐन्वत् इन्वतु इन्वेत् *इन्वित इन्वनीय इन्वितव्य इन्वित्वा इन्वितुम्

इल् *6√il* (to be quiet, sleep; throw, cast) इलति एलिष्यति ऐलत् इलतु इलेत् *इलित एलितव्य एलित्वा एलितुम्

इल् *10√il* (to encourage, inspire) एलयति-ते इलयिष्यति ऐलयत् एलयतु एलयेत् *एलित एलनीय एलयितव्य

इष् *4√iṣ* (to go) इष्यति एषिष्यति ऐष्यत् इष्यतु इष्येत् *इषित-इष्ट एषणीय एषितव्य एष्य एषित्वा एषितुम् एषण अन्वेषण

इष् *6√iṣ* (to desire, like, want) इच्छति एषिष्यति ऐच्छत् इच्छतु इच्छेत् *इष्ट एधनीय एधितव्य एषित्वा-इष्ट्वा एष्टुम्

इष् *9√iṣ* (to repeat) इष्णाति एषिष्यति ऐष्णात् इष्णातु ऐष्ण्यात् *इष्ट एषितव्य-इष्टव्य एषित्वा-इष्ट्वा एषितुम्-एष्टुम्

<u>(ई) (ī)</u>

ई *2√ī* (to go, depart, shine, pervade, want, desire, wish) एति एष्यति अयेत् एतु ईयात् *ईत ईत्वा एतुम्

ई *4√ī* (to go) ईयते एष्यते ऐयत ईयताम् ईयेत *ईत

ईक्ष् *1√īkṣ* (to see, stare, know, think) ईक्षते ईक्षिष्यते ऐक्षत ईक्षताम् ईक्षेत *ईक्षित ईक्षणीय ईक्ष्य ईक्षितुम् ईक्षण ईक्षा
ईङ् *4√īṅ* (to go, enter) ईयते एष्यते ऐयत ईयताम् ईयेत *ईत एतव्य अयनीय एय एतुम् ईत्वा ईयमान अयन
ईङ्ख् *1√īṅ* (to swing) ईङ्खति ईङ्खिष्यति ऐङ्खत् ईङ्खतु ईङ्खेत् *ईङ्खित-ईत ईङ्खत् ईङ्खनीय ईङ्खित्वा ईङ्खितुम् ईङ्खमान
ईज् *1√īj* (to blame, go, blemish, censure) ईजते ईजिष्यते ऐजत ईजताम् ईजेत *ईजित ईजनीय ईजित्वा ईजितुम्
ईञ्ज् *1√īj* (to blame, go, blemish, censure) ईञ्जते ईञ्जिष्यते ऐञ्जत ईञ्जताम् ईञ्जेत *ईञ्जित ईञ्जनीय ईञ्जितुम्
ईट् *1√īṭ* (go) एटति एटिष्यति ऐटत् एटतु-एटतात् एटेत् *इटित-एटित एटत् एटनीय एटितव्य एटित्वा एटितुम् एटयमान
ईड् *2√īḍ* (to praise) ईट्टे-ईडे ईडिष्यते ऐट्ट ईट्टाम्-ईडाम् ईडीत ईड्यते *ईडित ईड्य ईडनीय ईडितव्य ईडित्वा ईडितुम्
ईड् *10√īḍ* (to praise) ईडयति-ते ईडयिष्यति-ते ऐडयत्-त ईडयतु-ताम् ईडयेत्-त *ईडित ईडयितव्य ईडयित्वा इडयितुम्
ईर् *2√īr* (to go, tremble) ईर्ते ईरिष्यते ऐर्त ईर्ताम् ईरीत *ईरित ईरणीय ईरितव्य ईर्य ईरित्वा ईरितुम् समीरण स्वैरिन्
ईर् *10√īr* (to set in motion, go, shake) ईरयति-ते ईरयिष्यति-ते ऐरयत्-त ईरयतु-ताम् ईरयेत्-त ईर्यते *ईरित ईरयितुम्
ईर्क्ष्य् *1√īrksy* (to envy, be jealous) ईर्क्ष्यति ईर्क्षिष्यति ऐर्क्ष्यीत् ईर्क्ष्यतु ईर्क्ष्येत् *ईर्क्षित ईर्क्ष्यणीय ईर्क्ष्य ईर्क्ष्यमाण
ईर्ष्य् *1√īrṣy* (to be jealous) ईर्ष्यति ईर्ष्यिष्यति ऐर्ष्यत् ईर्ष्यतु ईर्ष्येत् ईर्ष्याञ्चकार *ईर्ष्यित ईर्ष्यणीय ईर्ष्य ईर्ष्यमाण ईर्ष्या
ईश् *2√īś* (to rule, prosper, be able) ईष्टे ईशिष्यते ऐष्ट ईष्टाम् ईशीत *ईशित-ईष्ट ईशितव्य ईशित्वा ईशितुम् ईशः
ईष् *1√īṣ* (to fly away, see, give, kill) ईषति ईषिष्यति ऐषत् ईषतु ईषेत् *ईष्ट ईष्यत् ईषणीय ईषितव्य ईष्य ईषित्वा
ईह् *1√īh* (to want, wish, desire, long for) ईहते ईहिष्यते ऐहत ईहताम् ईहेत *ईढ ईहितुम् ईहणीय समीह्य ईहमान

(उ) (u)

उ *1√u* (to proclaim) अवते ओष्यते आवत अवताम् आवत *उत अवितुम्
उ *5√u* (to ask, demand, claim) उनोति ओष्यति उनोत् उनोतु ऊयात् *उत
उक्ष् *1√ukṣ* (to sprinkle, moisten, remove, let go) उक्षति उक्षिष्यति औक्षत् उक्षतु उक्षेत् *उक्षित उक्षितुम् उक्षण
उक्ष् *6√ukṣ* (to sprinkle, pour down up on, emit) उक्षति उक्षिष्यति औक्षत् उक्षतु उक्षेत् *उक्षित उक्षणीय उक्षितव्य
उख् *1√ukh* (to go, move) ओखति ओखिष्यति औखत् ओखतु ओखेत् *उखित ओखत् ओखनीय ओखित्वा ओखितुम्
उङ्क् *1√uṅk* (to go) उङ्कति उङ्किष्यति औङ्कत् उङ्कतु उङ्केत् *उङ्कित उङ्कत् उङ्कनीय उङ्कितव्य उङ्कित्वा उङ्कितुम्
उङ्ख् *1√uṅkh* (to go) उङ्खति उङ्खिष्यति औङ्खत् उङ्खतु उङ्खेत् *उङ्खित उङ्खत् उङ्खनीय उङ्खितव्य उङ्खित्वा उङ्खितुम्
उच् *4√uć* (to be pleased, be useful) उच्यति ओचिष्यति औच्यत् उच्यतु उच्येत् *उचित ओचनीय ओचित्वा ओचितुम्
उच्छ् *1√uććh* (to end, tie, let go) उच्छति उच्छिष्यति औच्छत् उच्छतु उच्छेत् *उच्छित उच्छनीय उच्छितव्य उच्छित्वा
उच्छ् *6√uććh* (to end, finish off, tie, let go) उच्छति उच्छिष्यति औच्छत् उच्छतु उच्छेत् *उच्छित-उच्छन्न उच्छितुम्
उछ् *6√ućh* (to end, finish, stop) उच्छति उच्छिष्यति औच्छत् उच्छतु उच्छेत् *उच्छित-उच्छन्न उच्छनीय उच्छितुम्
उञ्छ् *1,6√uñćh* (to pick grains) उञ्छति उञ्छिष्यति औञ्छत् उञ्छतु उञ्छेत् *उञ्छित उञ्छनीय उञ्छित्वा
उझ् *6√ujh* (to forsake) उझति उझिष्यति औझत् उझतु उझेत् *उझित उझत् उझनीय उझितव्य उझित्वा उझितुम्

उज्झ् *6√uñjh* (to let go, drive away) उज्झति उज्झिष्यति औज्झत् उज्झतु उज्झेत् *उज्झित उज्झनीय उज्झितुम्

उठ् *1√uṭh* (to hit, strike down, go) ओठति ओठिष्यति औठत् ओठतु ओठेत् *उठित उठनीय उठितव्य उठितुम्

उड् *1√uḍ* (to collect) ओडति ओडिष्यति औडत् ओडतु ओडेत् *उडित उडत् उडनीय उदितव्य उडित्वा उडितुम्

उन्द् *7√und* (to wet, bathe, water) उनत्ति उन्दिष्यति औनत् उनत्तु उन्द्यात् *उन्दित उन्दनीय उन्दितव्य उन्द्य उन्दितुम्

उब्ज् *6√ubj* (to press down, bring under control, streighten) उब्जति उब्जिष्यति औब्जित् उब्जतु उब्जेत् *उब्जित

उभ् *6√ubh* (to join two, complete, cover) उभति ओभिष्यति औभत् उभतु ऊभेत् *उब्ध उभनीय उब्ध्वा उब्धुम्

उम्भ् *6√umbh* (to join two, confine) उम्भति उम्भिष्यति औम्भित् उम्भतु ऊम्भेत् *उब्ध उम्भनीय

उर् *1√ur* (to go) ओरति ओरिष्यति औरत् ओरतु ओरेत् *उरित उरणीय उरितव्य उरित्वा उरितुम् उर

उर्द् *1√urd* (to play, taste, grant, give, measure) ऊर्दते ऊर्दिष्यते और्ददत ऊर्दताम् ऊर्देत *ऊर्दित ऊर्दनीय ऊर्दित्वा

उर्व् *1√urv* (to hurt, hit, kill) ऊर्वति ऊर्विष्यति और्वत् ऊर्वतु ऊर्वेत् *ऊर्ण-ऊर्वित ऊर्वणीय ऊर्वितव्य ऊर्वितुम्

उल् *1√ul* (to give) ओलति ओलिष्यति औलत् ओलतु ओलेत् *उलित उलनीय उलितव्य उलित्वा उलितुम् उलुक

उष् *1√uṣ* (to burn, punish, be sick) ऊषति-ओषति ओ-ऊषिष्यति औषत् ऊषतु ऊषेत् *ऊषित-उष्ट ऊष्मा ऊषण

उह् *1√uh* (to destroy, hurt) ओहति-ऊहते ओहिष्यति-ऊहिष्यते औहत्-त ऊहतु-ताम् ऊहेत्-त उह्यते *उहित ओह्य

(ऊ) (ū)

ऊन् *10√ūn* (to reduce, lessen) ऊनयति-ते ऊनयिष्यति-ते औनयत्-त ऊनयतु-ताम् ऊनयेत्-त *ऊनित ऊनयितुम्

ऊय् *1√ūy* (to knit, sew) ऊयते ऊयिष्यते औयत ऊयताम् ऊयेत *ऊत-ऊयित ऊयनीय ऊयितव्य ऊय्य ऊयित्वा ऊयमान

ऊर्ज् *10√ūrj* (to live, be strong) ऊर्जयति-ते ऊर्जयिष्यति-ते और्जयत्-त ऊर्जयतु-ताम् ऊर्जयेत्-त *ऊर्जित

ऊर्णु *2√ūrṇu* (to cover) ऊर्णौति-ऊर्णोति-ऊर्णुत ऊर्णविष्यति-ते और्णोत्-त ऊर्णौतु-ऊर्णोतु-ताम् ऊर्णुयात्-त *ऊर्णुत

ऊर्द् *1√ūrd* (to play, play, taste, grant, give) ऊर्दते ऊर्दिष्यते और्दत ऊर्दताम् ऊर्देत *ऊर्दित उर्दितव्य ऊर्दितुम्

ऊष् *1√ūṣ* (to fall sick) ऊषति ऊषिष्यति औषत् ऊषतु ऊषेत् *ऊषित-ऊष्ट ऊपित्वा-ऊष्ट्वा ऊषितुम्-ऊष्टुम्

ऊह् *1√ūh* (to argue, mark, understand, know, expect) ऊहते उहिष्यते ऊहताम् औहत ऊहेत ऊह्यते *ऊढ समूह्य

(ऋ) (ṛ)

ऋ *1√ṛ* (to get, attain, reach, display) ऋच्छति अरिष्यति आर्च्छत् ऋच्छतु ऋच्छेत् आर अर्ता *ऋत ऋतु ऋण अरुण

ऋ *3√ṛ* (to get, go, reach, meet, sow, keep, give, shake) इयर्ति अरिष्यति ऐयः इयर्तु इयृयात् आरत् *ऋत-ऋण-ईर्ण

ऋ *5√ṛ* (to get, attack, hurt, inspire, encourage) ऋणोति अरिष्यति आर्णोत् ऋणोतु ऋणुयात् आर्षीत *ऋत

ऋच् *6√ṛć* (to praise, cover) ऋचति अर्चिष्यति आर्चत् ऋचतु ऋचेत् *ऋचित अर्चनीय अर्चित्वा अर्चितुम् ऋचा अर्चना

ऋच्छ् *6√ṛćch* (to go, be hard) ऋच्छति ऋच्छिष्यति आर्च्छत् ऋच्छतु ऋच्छेत् *ऋच्छित ऋच्छनीय ऋच्छितव्य ऋच्छितुम्

ऋज् *1√ṛj* (to attain, acquire, go, be firm) अर्जते अर्जिष्यते आर्जत अर्जताम् अर्जेत *ऋजित-ऋष्ट अर्जनीय अर्जित्वा

ऋञ्ज् *1√ṛñj* (to spring forward, strive, decorate, roast) ऋञ्जते ऋञ्जिष्यते अऋञ्जत ऋञ्जताम् ऋञ्जेत *ऋञ्जित

ऋण् *8√ṛṇ* (to go) ऋणोति-ते अर्णोति-ऋणुते अर्णिष्यति-ते आर्णुत ऋणुताम् ऋण्वीत *अर्ण अर्णनीय अर्णितुम् वर्ण सुवर्ण

ऋत् *10√ṛt* (to reproach, censure, pity, rival) ऋतियते अर्तीयत ऋतीयताम् ऋतीयेत * ऋतित अर्तित्वा अर्तितुम्

ऋध् *4√ṛdh* (to grow, prosper) ऋध्यति अर्धिष्यति आर्ध्यत् ऋध्यतु ऋध्येत् *ऋत्-ऋद्ध-अर्धित अर्धनीय अर्धितव्य ऋद्ध्वा

ऋध् *5√ṛdh* (to please) ऋध्नोति अर्धिष्यति आर्ध्नोत् ऋध्नोतु ऋध्नुयात् *ऋद्ध अर्धनीय ऋध्य ऋद्ध्वा अर्धितुम् समृद्धि

ऋफ् *6√ṛph* (to give, hit, kill, injure, criticize, fight) ऋफति अर्फिष्यति आर्फत् ऋफतु ऋफेत् आर्फीत् *ऋफित

ऋम्फ् *6√ṛmpf* (to criticize, rebuke) ऋम्फति ऋम्फिष्यति आर्म्फत् ऋम्फतु ऋम्फेत् आर्म्फीत् *ऋम्फित

ऋश् *6√ṛś* (to think, ponder, go, kill) ऋशति अर्शिष्यति आर्शत् ऋशतु ऋशेत् *ऋशित-ऋष्ट

ऋष् *6√ṛṣ* (to go,) ऋषति अर्षिष्यति आर्षत् ऋषतु ऋषेत् *ऋष्ट अर्षणीय अर्षितव्य अर्ष्य अर्षित्वा अर्षितुम् ऋषि आर्ष

ॠ *9√ṝ* (to go) ऋषति-ऋणाति अरिष्यति-अरीष्यति आर्णात् ऋणातु ऋणीयात *अर अरणीय अरितव्य अर्य ईर्त्वा अरितुम्

(ए) (e)

एज् *1√ej* (to tremble, shake, move, stir) एजति-ते एजिष्यति-ते ऐजत्-त एजतु-ताम् एजेत्-त *एजित एजनीय

एठ् *1√eṭh* (to tease annoy resist oppose face) एठते एठिष्यते ऐठत एठताम् एठेत *एठित एठनीय एठितव्य एठित्वा

एध् *1√edh* (to grow, increase, prosper, live in comfort) एधते एधिष्यते ऐधताम् ऐधत एधताम् एधेत *एधित

एष् *1√eṣ* (to hasten, go, approach, request) एषते एषिष्यते ऐषत एषताम् एषेत *एषित एषणीय एषित्वा एषितुम्

(ओ) (o)

ओख् *1√okh* (to be fit, able, dry; to refuse, prevent, adorn) ओखति ओखिष्यति औखत् ओखतु ओखेत् *ओखित

ओण् *1√oṇ* (to remove, take or drag along) ओणति ओणिष्यति औणत् ओणतु ओणेत् *ओणित ओणित्वा ओणितुम्

ओलण्ड् *10√olaṇḍ* (to bounce) ओलण्डयति-ते ओलण्डयिष्यति-ते ओलण्डयत्-त ओलण्डयतु-ताम् ओलण्डयेत्-त

(क) (k)

कक् *1√kak* (to want, wish, be proud, be unsteady) ककते ककिष्यते अककत ककताम् ककेत *ककित ककितुम्

कक्क् *1√kakk* (to laugh at, deride) कक्कति कक्किष्यति अकक्कत् कक्कतु कक्केत् *कक्कित कक्कितुम्

कक्ख् *1√kakkh* (to laugh at, deride) कक्खति कक्खिष्यति अकक्खत् कक्खतु कक्खेत् *कक्खित कक्खितुम्

कख् *1√kakh* (to laugh) कखति कखिष्यति अकखत् कखतु कखेत् *कखित कखनीय कखित्वा कखितुम्

कग् *1√kag* (to hide) कगति कगिष्यति अकगत् कगतु कगेत् *कगित कगनीय कगितव्य कगित्वा कगितुम्

कङ्क् *1√kaṅk* (to go) कङ्कते कङ्किष्यते अकङ्कत कङ्कताम् कङ्केत *कङ्कित कङ्कनीय कङ्कितव्य कङ्कित्वा कङ्कितुम्

कच् *1√kać* (to shout, shine, bind, fasten) कचति-ते कचिष्यते अकचत कचताम् कचेत *कचित कचनीय कचित्वा

कञ्च् *1√kañć* (to shine, bind, tie) कञ्चते कञ्चिष्यते अकञ्चत कञ्चताम् कञ्चेत *कञ्चित कञ्चनीय कञ्चित्वा

कट् *1√kaṭ* (to rain, go, cover, screen, surround, encompass) कटति कटिष्यति अकटत् कटतु कटेत् *कटित

कठ् *1√kaṭh* (to live in distress) कठति कठिष्यति अकठत् कठतु कठेत् *कठित कठनीय कठितव्य कठित्वा कठितुम्

कड् *1√kaḍ* (to un-husk, be pleased, be proud) कडति कडिष्यति अकडत् कडतु कडेत् *कडित कडनीय कडितव्य
कड् *6√kaḍ* (to protect, detach, tear, break) कडति कडिष्यति अकडत् कडतु कडेत् *कडित कडत् कडित्वा कडन
कड् *10√kaḍ* (to protect, husk, detach, tear) कडयति-ते कडयिष्यति-ते अकडयत्-त कडयतु-ताम् कडयेत्-त *कडित
कड्ड् *1√kaḍḍ* (to be firm, hard, harsh, severe) कड्डति कड्डिष्यति अकड्डत् कड्डतु कड्डेत् *कड्डित कड्डनीय कड्डितुम्
कण् *1√kaṇ* (to moan, cry, go, become small) कणति कणिष्यति अकणत् कणतु कणेत् *कणित कणनीय कणितव्य
कण् *10√kaṇ* (to wink, sigh, sound) काणयति-ते काणयिष्यति-ते अकाणयत्-त काणयतु-ताम् काणयेत्-त * काणित
कण्ट् *1√kaṇṭ* (to go, move) कण्टति कण्टिष्यति अकण्टत् कण्टतु कण्टेत् *कण्टित कण्टनीय कण्टितव्य कण्टित्वा
कण्ट् *10√kaṇṭ* (to go, move) कण्टयति-ते कण्टयिष्यति-ते अकण्टयत्-त कण्टयतु-ताम् कण्टयेत्-त *कण्टित कण्टनीय
कण्ठ् *1√kaṇṭh* (to lament, grieve for) कण्ठते कण्ठिष्यते अकण्ठत कण्ठताम् कण्ठेत *कण्ठित कण्ठनीय कण्ठित्वा
कण्ठ् *10√kaṇṭh* (to remorse, long for) कण्ठयति-ते कण्डयिष्यति-ते अकण्ठयत्-त कण्ठयतु-तां कण्ठयेत्-त * कण्ठित
कण्ड् *1√kaṇḍ* (to boast, be proud, satisfied) कण्डति-ते कण्डिष्यते अकण्डत कण्डताम् कण्डेत *कण्डित कण्डितुम्
कण्ड् *10√kaṇḍ* (to defend, unhusk) कण्डयति-ते कण्डयिष्यति-ते अकण्डयत्-त कण्डयतु-ताम् कण्डयेत्-त *कण्डित
कण्डू *11√kaṇḍū* (to itch, scratch, rub slowly) कण्डूयति-ते कण्डूयिष्यति-ते अकण्डूयत्-त कण्डूयतु-ताम् कण्डूयेत्-त
कत्थ् *1√katth* (to boast, praise, rebuke) कत्थते कत्थिष्यते अकत्थत कत्थताम् कत्थेत *कत्थित कत्थनीय कत्थित्वा
कत्र् *10√katr* (to loosen, slacken, remove) कत्रयति-ते कत्रयिष्यति-ते अकत्रयत्-त कत्रयतु-ताम् कत्रयेत्-त *कत्रित
कथ् *10√kath* (to tell, narrate, communicate) कथयति-ते कथयिष्यति-ते अकथयत्-त कथयतु-ताम् कथयेत्-त
कद् *1√kad* (to cry, grieve, be confounded, be confused) कद्यते कद्यिष्यते अकद्यत कद्यताम् कद्येत *कत्त
कन् *1√kan* (to enjoy, love, wish, be contented) कनति कनिष्यति अकनत् कनतु कनेत् *कान्त कननीय कनित्वा
कन्द् *1√kand* (to cry, lament, be perplexed) कन्दति कन्दिष्यति अकन्दत् कन्दतु कन्देत् *कन्दित कन्दनीय
कप् *1√kap* (to shake, move) कपते कपिष्यते अकपत कपताम् कपेत *कपित-कप्त कपनीय कपितव्य कपित्वा
कब् *1√kab* (to color, praise) कबति-ते कबिष्यते अकबत कबताम् कबेत *कबित कबनीय कबितव्य कबित्वा कबितुम्
कम् *1√kam* (to desire, be enamored) कामयते कामयिष्यते अकामयत कामयताम् कामयेत *कान्त-कमित काम्य
कम्प् *1√kamp* (to tremble, move about) कम्पते कम्पिष्यते अकम्पत कम्पताम् कम्पेत *कम्पित कम्पनीय कम्प
कम्ब् *1√kamb* (to go, move) कम्बति कम्बिष्यति अकम्बत् कम्बतु कम्बेत् *कम्बित कम्बनीय कम्बितव्य कम्बित्वा
कर्क् *1√kark* (to laugh) कर्कति कर्किष्यति अकर्कत् कर्कतु कर्केत् *कर्कित कर्कणीय कर्कितव्य कर्कित्वा कर्कितुम्
कर्ज् *1√karj* (to bother, pain, make uneasy, distress) कर्जति कर्जिष्यति अकर्जत् कर्जतु कर्जेत् *कर्जित कर्जनीय
कर्ण् *10√karṇ* (to pierce; with preposition ā : to hear) कर्णयति-ते कर्णयिष्यते अकर्णयत् कर्णयतु कर्णयेत् *कर्णित
कर्त् *10√kart* (to be loose, slacken, remove) कर्तयति-ते कर्तयिष्यति-ते अकर्तयत्-त कर्तयतु-ताम् कर्तयेत्-त *कर्तित
कर्द् *1√kard* (to rebuke, rumble, caw like a crow) कर्दति कर्दिष्यति अकर्दत् कर्दतु कर्देत् *कर्दित कर्दनीय कर्दित्वा

कर्व् *1√karv* (to move, approach) कर्वति कर्विष्यति अकर्वत् कर्वतु कर्वेत् *कर्वित कर्वणीय कर्वितव्य कर्वित्वा

कल् *1√kal* (to sound, count) कलते कलिष्यते अकलत कलेत् *कलित कलनीय कलितव्य कलित्वा कलितुम्

कल् *10√kal* (to hold, bare, carry, have, put on) कलयति-ते कलयिष्यति-ते अकलयत्-त कलयतु-ताम् कलयेत्-त

कल्ल् *1√kall* (to shout) कल्लते कल्लिष्यते अकल्लत *कल्लित कल्लनीय कल्लितव्य कल्लित्वा कल्लितुम्

कव् *1 √kav* (to describe, compose, paint, picture) कवते कविष्यते अकवत कवताम् कवेत *कवित कवनीय

कश् *1√kaś* (to sound) कशति कशिष्यति अकशत् कशतु कशेत् *कशित-कष्ट कशनीय कशितव्य कशित्वा कशितुम्

कश् *2√kaś* (to punish, go) कष्टे कशिष्यते अकष्ट कष्टाम् कशीत *कशित-कष्ट कशनीय कशितव्य कशित्वा कशितुम्

कष् *1√kaṣ* (to scratch, scrape, rub,) कषति कषिष्यति अकषत् कषतु कषेत् *कषित-कष्ट कषणीय कषितव्य कषित्वा

कंस् *2√kas* (to go, destroy) कंस्ते कंसिष्यते अकंस्त कंस्ताम् कंसीत *कंसित कंसनीय कंसितव्य कंसित्वा कंसितुम्

कस् *1√kas* (to go, move, approach) कसति कसिष्यति अकसत् कसतु कसेत् *कसित कसनीय कसितव्य कसित्वा

काङ्क्ष् *1√kāṅkṣ* (to desire, wish, want) काङ्क्षति काङ्क्षिष्यति अकाङ्क्षत् काङ्क्षतु काङ्क्षेत् *काङ्क्षित काङ्क्षितुम् काङ्क्षा

काञ्च् *1√kāñć* (to glitter, bind) काञ्चते काञ्चिष्यते अकाञ्चत काञ्चताम् काञ्चेत *काञ्चित काञ्चनीय काञ्चित्वा

काश् *1√kāś* (to look beautiful) काशते काशिष्यते अकाशत काशताम् काशेत *काशित प्रकाशित काशनीय काशितव्य

काश् *4√kāś* (to appear, shine) काश्यते काशिष्यते अकाश्यत काश्यताम् काश्येत *काशित-काष्ट काशित्वा प्रकाश्य

कास् *1√kās* (to cough, make sound) कासते कासिष्यते अकासत कसताम् कासेत *कासित कासनीय कासितव्य

कि *3√ki* (to know, have knowledge of) चिकेति चिकिष्यति अचिकेत् चिकेतु चिकियात् *चिकित चिकितुम्

किट् *1√kiṭ* (to fear, terrify, dread, approach) केटति केटिष्यति अकेटत् केटतु केटेत् *केटित केटनीय केटित्वा

कित् *1√kit* (to live; with *prefix* चि = examine, operate on) केतति-चिकित्सति चिकित्सिष्यति अचिकित्सत् चिकित्सतु चिकित्सेत् *चिकित्सित चिकित्सनीय चिकित्सितव्य चिकित्सित्वा चिकित्सितुम् चिकित्सक चिकित्सा

कित् *3√kit* (to know) चिकेति चिकित्स्यति अचिकेत् चिकेतु चिकियात् अकेतीत् *चिकित चिकित्वा चिकितुम्

कित् *10√kit* (to dwell) केतयति केतयिष्यति अकेतयत् केतयतु केतयेत् अचिकियत् *केतित केतयित्वा केतयितुम्

किर् *2√kir* (to scatter, spread out, distribute) कीर्ते करिष्यते अकीर्त कीर्ताम् कीरीत *कीर्ण किरात, किराताशिन्

किल् *6√kil* (to freeze, become white, play, sport) किलति किलति किलिष्यति अकिलत् किलतु किलेत् *किलित

कीट् *10√kīṭ* (to tinge, color, fasten) कीटयति-ते कीटयिष्यति-ते अकीटयत्-त कीटयतु-ताम् कीटयेत्-त *कीटित

कील् *1√kīl* (to pin, stake, bind) कीलति कीलिष्यति अकीलत् कीलतु कीलेत् *कीलित कीलनीय कीलित्वा कीलितुम्

कु *1√ku* (to make sound, moan, groan, cry) कवते कोष्यते अकवत् कवताम् कवेत अकोष्ट *कवित

कु *2√ku* (to make sound, hum, coo, tut, cluck) कौति कोष्यति अकौत् कौतु कुयात् कूयते *कूत कु कुतन्त्रिन्

कु *6√ku* (to groan) कुवते कोष्यते अकवत कुवताम् कुवेत *कुत कुवनीय कुवितव्य कुत्वा कवितुम् कुवन

कुच् *1√kuć* (to shout, shrink, contract, lessen, bend) कोचति कोचिष्यति अकोचत् कोचतु कोचेत् *कुचित सङ्कोच

कुच् *6√kuć* (to shrink, stop, impede) कुचति कुचिष्यति अकुचत् कुचतु कुचेत् *कुचित कुचनीय कुचित्वा कोचितुम्

कुज् *1√kuj* (to steal) कोजति कोजिष्यति अकोजत् कोजतु कोजेत् *कोजित कोजनीय कोजितव्य कोजित्वा कोजितुम्

कुञ्च् *1√kuñć* (to bow) कुञ्चति कुञ्चिष्यति अकुञ्चत् कुञ्चतु कुञ्चेत् *कुञ्चित कुञ्चितव्य कुञ्चित्वा कुञ्चितुम्

कुञ्ज् *10√kuñj* (to murmur) कुञ्जति-ते कुञ्जयिष्यति-ते अकुञ्जयत्-त कुञ्जयतु-ताम् कुञ्जयेत्-त *कुञ्जित

कुट् *4√kuṭ* (to divide, break to pieces, split, speak unclear) कुट्यति कुटिष्यति अकुट्यत् कुट्यतु कुट्येत्

कुट् *6√kuṭ* (to cheat, be cunning, crooked, curved) कुटति कुटिष्यति अकुटत् कुटतु कुटेत् *कुटित कुटितुम्

कुट् *10√kuṭ* (to cut) कोटयते कोटयिष्यति अकोटयत्-त कोटयतु-ताम् कोटयेत् *कुटित कुटयित्वा कुटयितुम्

कुटुम्ब् *10√kuṭumb* (to bear) कुटुम्बयते कुटुम्बयिष्यते अकुटुम्बयत कुटुम्बयताम् कुटुम्बयेत *कुटुम्बित कुटुम्ब

कुट्ट् *10√kuṭṭ* (to divide, cut, grind, blame) कुट्टयति-ते कुट्टयिष्यति-ते अकुट्टयत्-त कुट्टयतु-ताम् कुट्टयेत्-त *कुट्टित

कुड् *6√kuḍ* (to trifle, play or act as a child) कुडति कुडिष्यत अकुडत् कुडतु कुडेत् *कुडित कुडितव्य कुडितुम्

कुण् *6√kuṇ* (to aid, make sound) कुणति कुणिष्यति अकुणत् कुणतु कुणेत् *कुणित कुणनीय कुणितव्य कुणितुम्

कुण् *10√kuṇ* (to summon, order) कुणयति-ते कुणयिष्यति-ते अकुणयत्-त कुणयतु-ताम् कुणयेत्-त *कुणित

कुण्ठ् *1√kuṇṭh* (to be dulled, blunted, idle, stupid) कुण्ठति-ते कुण्ठिष्यते अकुण्ठत कुण्ठताम् कुण्ठेत *कुण्ठित

कुण्ठ् *10√kuṇṭh* (to hide, cover) कुण्ठयति-ते कुण्ठयिष्यति-ते अकुण्ठयत्-त कुण्ठयतु-ताम् कुण्ठयेत्-त *कुण्ठित

कुण्ड् *1√kuṇḍ* (to burn, eat, mutilate) कुण्डति-ते कुण्डिष्यति-ते अकुण्डयत्-त कुण्डयतु-ताम् कुण्डयेत्-त *कुण्डित

कुण्ड् *10√kuṇḍ* (to rescue, protect) कुण्डयति-ते कुण्डयिष्यति-ते अकुण्डयत्-त कुण्डयतु-ताम् कुण्डयेत *कुण्डित

कुत्स् *10√kuts* (to castigate, condemn, censure) कुत्सयते कुत्सयिष्यते अकुत्सयत कुत्सयताम् कुत्सयेत *कुत्सित

कुथ् *4√kuth* (to whimper, stink, become putrid) कुथ्यति कोथिष्यति अकुथ्यत् कुथ्यतु कुथ्येत् *कोथित कोथनीय

कुन्थ् *1√kunth* (to molest, hurt, suffer pain, cling to) कुन्थति कुन्थिष्यति अकुन्थत् कुन्थतु कुन्थेत् *कुन्थित

कुन्थ् *9√kunth* (to hurt, cause trouble) कुथ्नाति कुन्थिष्यति अकुन्थात् कुथ्नातु कुथ्नीयात् *कुन्थित कुन्थनीय कुन्थितुम्

कुन्द्र् *10√kundr* (to lie) कुन्द्रयति-ते कुन्द्रयिष्यति-ते अकुन्द्रयत्-त कुन्द्रयतु-ताम् कुन्द्रयेत्-त *कुन्द्रित कुन्द्रयितुम्

कुप् *4√kup* (to agitate) कुप्यति कोपिष्यति अकुप्यत् कुप्यतु कुप्येत् *कुपित कोपनीय कोपितव्य कुपित्वा कोपितुम् कोप

कुप् *10√kup* (to speak, shine) कोपयति-ते कोपयिष्यति-ते अकोपयत्-त कोपयतु-ताम् कोपयेत्-त *कोपित

कुमार् *10√kumār* (to play as a child) कुमारयति कुमारिष्ययति अकुमारयत् कुमारयतु कुमारयेत् *कुमारित

कुम्ब् *1√kumb* (to cover) कुम्बति कुम्बिष्यति अकुम्बित् कुम्बतु कुम्बेत् *कुम्बित कुम्बितव्य कुम्बित्वा कुम्बितुम्

कुम्ब् *10√kumb* (to cover) कुम्बयति-ते कुम्बयिष्यति-ते अकुम्बयत्-त कुम्बयतु-ताम् कुम्बयेत्-त *कुम्बित

कुम्भ् *10√kumbh* (to cover) कुम्भयति-ते कुम्भिष्यति-ते अकुम्भयत्-त कुम्भयतु-ताम् कुम्भयेत्-त *कुम्भित-कुब्ध

कुर् *6√kur* (to resound) कुरति कोरिष्यति अकोरत् कुरतु कुरेत् *कुरित कुरणीय कुरितव्य कुरित्वा कुरितुम्

कुर्द् *1√kurd* (to play) कूर्दते कूर्दिष्यते अकूर्दत कूर्दताम् कूर्देत *कूर्दित कूर्दयत् कूर्दनीय कूर्दित्वा कूर्दितुम् कूर्दयमान

कुल् *1√kul* (to connect, accumulate, be related, be kinsman) कोलति कोलिष्यति अकोलत् कोलतु कोलेत्

कुंश् *10√kuṁś* (to speak, shine) कुंशयति-ते कुंशयिष्यति-ते अकुंशयत्-त कुंशयतु-ताम् कुंशयेत्-त *कुंशित

कुष् *9√kuṣ* (to tear, pull out, test, examine, shine) कुष्णाति कोषिष्यति अकुष्णात् कुष्णातु कुष्णीयात् *कुष्ट

कुंस् *1√kuṁs* (to speak) कुंसति कुंसिष्यति अकुंसत् कुंसतु कुंसेत् *कुंसित कुंसनीय कुंसितव्य कुंसित्वा कुंसितुम

कुंस् *10√kuṁs* (to speak, shine) कुंसयति-ते कुंसयिष्यति-ते अकुंसयत्-त कुंसयतु-ताम् कुंसयेत्-त *कुंसित

कुस् *4√kus* (to hug, embrace, surround) कुस्यति कोसिष्यति अकुस्यत् कुस्यतु कुस्येत् *कुसित कुसनीय कुसितुम्

कुस्म् *10√kusm* (to laugh improperly) कुस्म्यते कुस्मयिष्यते अकुस्मयत कुस्मयताम् कुस्मयेत *कुस्मित

कुह् *10√kuh* (to surprise, cheat, deceive) कुहयति-ते कुहयिष्यति-ते अकुहयत्-त कुहयतु-ताम् कुहयेत्-त *कूढ

कू *6√kū* (to design, cry out in distress) कवते-कुवते कविष्यति अकूवत कवताम् कवेत *कवित कू कूच कूचिका

कू *9√kū* (to wail) कुनाति-कुनीते-कूनाति-कूनीते कविष्यति-ते अकूनात्-नीत कूनातु-कूनीताम् कूनीयात्-कुनीत *कून

कूज् *1√kūj* (to chirp, hum, coo, moan, groan) कूजति कूजिष्यति अकूजत् कूजतु कूजेत् *कूजित कूजनीय कूजित्वा

कूट् *10√kūṭ* (to hide, censure, invite, call, burn, counsel) कूटयति-ते कूटयिष्यति अकूटयत् कूटयतु कूटयेत् *कूटित

कूड् *6√kūḍ* (to graze, become firm or solid or fat) कूडति कूडिष्यति अकूडत् कूडतु कूडेत् *कूडित कूडितुम्

कूण् *1√kūṇ* (to shrink, converse, speak) कूणति कूणिष्यति अकूणत् कूणतु कूणेत् *कूणित कूणनीय कूणित्वा कूणितुम्

कूण् *10√kūṇ* (to talk) कूणयति-ते कूणयिष्यति-ते अकूणयत्-त कूणयतु-ताम् कूणयेत्-त *कूणित कूणितव्य कूणितुम्

कूप् *10√kūp* (to be weak) कूपयति-ते कूपयिष्यति-ते अकूपयत्-त कूपयतु-ताम् कूपयेत्-त *कूपित कूपित्वा कूपितुम्

कूर्द् *1√kūrd* (to leap, jump, frolic) कूर्दति-ते कूर्दिष्यति-ते अकूर्दत्-त कूर्दतु-ताम् कूर्देत्-त *कुर्दित कुर्दित्वा कुर्दितुम्

कूल् *1√kūj* (to cover, screen, protect, enclose) कूलति कूलिष्यति अकूलत् कूलतु कूलेत् *कूलित कूलितुम् कूलित्वा

कृ *5√kṛ* (to ravish, hurt kill) कृणोति-कुणुते करिष्यति-ते अकृणोत्-अकृणुत कृणोतु-ताम् कृणुयात्-कृण्वीत *कृत

कृ *6√kṛ* (to scatter) किरति करिष्यति अकिरत् किरतु किरेत् *कीर्ण करणीय करितव्य कीर्त्वा करितुम् अवकर उपस्कर

कृ *8√kṛ* (to do) करोति-कुरुते करिष्यति-ते अकरोत्-अकुरुत करोतु-कुरुताम् कुर्यात्-कुर्वीत *कृत कुर्वत् कृतवत् करणीय कर्तव्य कार्य कृत्वा कर्तुम् कुर्वाण क्रियमाण कर्मकृत् सुकृत् तस्कर भास्कर भयङ्कर कर्मकार अन्धकार संस्कार चिकीर्षा

कृ *9√kṛ* (to ravish) कृणाति-कुणीते करिष्यति-ते अकृणात्-अकृणीत कृणातु-कृणीताम् कृणीयात्-कृणीत कीर्यते *कृत

कृड् *6√kṛḍ* (to become dense or solid) कृडति कृडिष्यति अकृडत् कृडतु कृडेत् *कृडित कृडनीय कृडितव्य कृडितुम्

कृत् *6√kṛt* (to cut) कृन्तति कर्तिष्यति-कर्त्स्यति अकर्तत् कृन्ततु कृन्तेत् *कृत्त कर्तनीय कर्तितव्य कर्तित्वा कर्तितुम् कर्तन

कृत् *7√kṛt* (to spin, surround, encompass, attire) कृणत्ति कर्तिष्यति-कर्त्स्यति अकृणत् कृणतु कृन्त्यात् *कृत्त

कृप् *1√kṛp* (to imagine, to be able : उभयपदी in लुङ्, लुट्, लृट् and लृङ्) कल्पते कल्पिष्यते अकल्पत कल्पताम् कल्पेत क्लृप्यते *क्लृप्त क्लृप्तवत् कल्पनीय कल्पितव्य कल्प्य कल्पित्वा कल्पितुम् कल्पमान कल्प कल्पना क्लृप्ति कृपा कृपालु कृपाचार्य कृपण कृपाण कल्पना विकल्प प्रकल्प

कृप् *10√kṛp* (to be weak; to think, imagine) कृपयति-ते कृपयिष्यति-ते अकृपयत्-त कृपयतु-ताम् कृपयेत्-त कल्पयति-ते क्ल्पयिष्यति-ते अकल्पयत्-त कल्पयतु-ताम् कल्पयेत्-त कल्प्यते *कृप्त-कल्पित कल्पयितुम् कल्पन

कृश् *4√kṛś* (to be lean, emaciated, to wane) कृश्यति कर्शिष्यति अकृश्यत् कृश्यतु कृश्येत् *कृशित-कृष्ट कर्षितुम्

कृष् *1√kṛṣ* (to drag, pull, draw towards, attract) कर्षति कर्क्ष्यति अकर्षत् कर्षतु कर्षेत् *कृष्ट-कर्षित आकर्षण

कृष् *6√kṛṣ* (to plough, make furrows, cultivate) कृषति-ते क्रक्ष्यति-ते अकृषत्-त कृषतु-ताम् कृषेत्-त *कृष्ट कृषि

कॄ *6√kṝ* (to disperse, throw, cast, pour out) किरति करिष्याति-करीष्यति अकिरत् किरतु किरेत् कीर्यते *कीर्ण कीर्त्वा

कॄ *9√kṝ* (to injure; know, inform) कृणाति-कृणीते करीष्यति-ते अकृणात्-अकृणीत कृणातु-कृणीताम् कृणीयात्-कृणीत

कॄत् *10√kṝt* (to announce, declare, tell) कीर्तयति-ते कीर्तयिष्यति-ते कीर्तयेत्-त कीर्तयतु-ताम् कीर्तयेत्-त *कीर्तित

क्लृप् *1√klṛp* (to be fit, accomplish, produce) कल्पते कल्पिष्यते अकल्पत कल्पताम् कल्पेत *क्लृप्त-कल्पित

कृप् *10√kṛp* (to imagine, picture) कल्पयति-ते कल्पयिष्यति-ते अकल्पयत्-त कल्पयतु-ताम् कल्पयेत्-त *कल्पित

केत् *10√ket* (to invite, listen, call) केलयति-ते केतयिष्यति अकेतयत केतयताम् केतयेत् *केतित केतनीय केतयितव्य

केप् *1√kep* (to shake, tremble) केपते केप्स्यते अकेप्त केपताम् केपेत *केप्त केपनीय केपितव्य केप्त्वा केप्तुम्

केल् *1√kel* (to play, sport be frolicsome) केलति केलिष्यति अकेलत केलताम् केलेत् *केलित केलनीय केलितव्य

केव् *1√kev* (to render service) केवते केविष्यते अकेवत केवताम् केवेत *केवित केवनीय केवितव्य केवित्वा केवितुम्

कै *1√kai* (to clatter, sound) कायति कास्यति अकायत् कायतु कायेत् अकासीत् *कायित-कान कातव्य कीत्वा कातुम्

क्नथ् *1√knath* (to hurt, injure, kill) क्नथति क्नथिष्यति अक्नथत् क्नथतु क्नथेत् *क्नथित क्नथित्वा क्नथितुम्

क्नथ् *10√knath* (to hurt, injure, kill) क्नथयति-ते क्नथयिष्यति-ते अक्नथयत्-त क्नथयतु-ताम् क्नथयेत्-त *क्नथित

क्नस् *4, 10√knas* (to be crooked, speak, shine) क्नस्यति क्नसिष्यति अक्नस्यत् क्नस्यतु क्नस्येत् *क्नस्त क्नस्त्वा

क्नू *9√knū* (to make noise) क्नूनाति-क्नूनीते क्नविष्यति अक्नूनात् क्नूनातु क्नूनीयात् अक्नावीत्-अक्नविष्ट *क्नूत

क्नूय् *1√knūy* (to become wet, stink, make sound) क्नूयते क्नूयिष्यते अक्नूयत क्नूयताम् क्नूयेत *क्नूत

क्मर् *1√kmar* (to warp) क्मरति क्मरिष्यति अक्मरत् क्मरतु क्मरेत् *क्मरित क्मरणीय क्मरित्वा क्मरितुम् क्मरमाण

क्रथ् *1√krath* (to injure, hurt, kill) क्रथति क्रथिष्यति अक्रथत्-अक्राथत् क्रथतु क्रथेत् *क्रथित क्रथितुम्

क्रथ् *10√krath* (to delight, be enjoy) क्रथयति-ते क्रथयिष्यति-ते अक्रथयत्-त क्रथयतु-ताम् क्रथयेत्-त *क्रथित

क्रन्द् *1√krand* (to cry, shade tears, be sad) क्रन्दते क्रन्दिष्यति अक्रन्दत् क्रन्दतु क्रन्देत् क्रन्दते *क्रन्दित क्रन्दन

क्रन्द् *10√krand* (to cry out continuously, roar, rave) क्रन्दयति-ते क्रन्दयिष्यति अक्रन्दयत क्रन्दयताम् क्रन्दयेत

क्रप् *1√krap* (to pity, lament, moan, long for, desire) क्रपते क्रपिष्यते अक्रपत क्रपताम् क्रपेत *क्रप्त क्रपनीय कृपा

क्रम् *1√kram* (to climb, walk, step, leap, jump) क्रामति-ते क्रमिष्यति-ते अक्रामत्-त क्राम(म्य)तु-ताम् क्रामेत्-त *क्रान्त

क्रम् *4√kram* (to stride, march, stomp) क्राम्यति क्रमिष्यति अक्राम्यत् क्राम्यतु क्राम्येत् *क्रान्त् क्रान्ति क्रान्तिकारिन्

क्री *9√krī* (to buy) क्रीणाति-क्रिणीते क्रेष्यति-ते अक्रीणात्-अक्रणीत क्रीणातु-क्रीणीताम् क्रीणीयात्-क्रीणीत क्रीयते *क्रीत क्रयणीय क्रेतव्य क्रेय विक्रीय क्रीत्वा क्रेतुम् क्रय क्रयण विक्रय क्रयविक्रय विक्रेतृ

क्रीड् *1√krīḍ* (to play, amuse oneself) क्रीडति क्रीडिष्यति अक्रीडत् क्रीडतु क्रीडेत् *क्रीडित क्रीडनीय क्रीडितुम् क्रीडा

क्रुञ्च् *1√kruñć* (to dishonor, be crooked) क्रुञ्चति क्रुञ्चिष्यति अक्रुञ्चत् क्रुञ्चतु क्रुञ्चेत् अक्रुञ्चीत् *क्रुञ्चित

क्रुड् *6√kruḍ* (to dive) क्रुडति क्रुडिष्यति अक्रुडत् क्रुडतु क्रुडेत् *क्रुडित क्रुडनीय क्रुडितव्य क्रुडित्वा क्रुडितुम् क्रोडः

क्रुड् *9√kruḍ* (to slay) क्रुड्नाति क्रुड्निष्यति अक्रुड्नात् क्रुड्नातु क्रुड्नीयात् *क्रुडित क्रुडनीय क्रुडितव्य क्रुडित्वा क्रुडितुम्

क्रुध् *4√krudh* (to be angry) क्रुध्यति क्रुत्स्यति अक्रुधत् क्रुध्यतु क्रुध्येत् *क्रुद्ध क्रोधनीय क्रोद्धव्य क्रोध्य क्रुद्ध्वा क्रोद्धुम् क्रोध

क्रुन्थ् *9√krunth* (to embrace, be distracted) क्रुथ्नाति क्रुथ्नाति क्रुन्थिष्यति अक्रुन्थात् क्रुथ्नातु क्रुथ्नीयात् क्रश्यते *क्रुन्थित

क्रुश् *1√kruś* (to cry, weep, lament, moan, yell) क्रोशति क्रोक्ष्यति अक्रोशत् क्रोशतु क्रोशेत् *क्रुष्ट क्रोष्टुम् आक्रोश

क्रेव् *1√krev* (to serve, wait) क्रेवते क्रेविष्यते अक्रेवत क्रेवताम् क्रेवेत *क्रेवित क्रेवनीय क्रेवितव्य क्रेवित्वा क्रेवितुम्

क्रोड् *1√kroḍ* (to gamble) क्रोडति क्रोडिष्यति अक्रोडत् क्रोडतु क्रोडेत् *क्रोडित क्रोडनीय क्रोडितव्य क्रोडित्वा क्रोडितुम्

क्लथ् *1√klath* (to revolve, turn round and round, hurt) क्लथति क्लथिष्यति अक्लथत् क्लथतु क्लथेत् *क्लथित

क्लथ् *9√klath* (to revolve) क्लथ्नाति क्लथ्निष्यति अक्लन्थात् क्लथ्नातु क्लथ्नीयात् *क्लथित क्लथितव्य क्लथितुम्

क्लद् *4√klad* (to confuse, delude, be confused) क्लद्यते क्लदिष्यते अक्लद्यत क्लद्यताम् क्लद्येत *क्लिन्न

क्लन्द् *1√kland* (to lament, be confused) क्लन्दति क्लन्दिष्यति अक्लन्दत् क्लन्दतु क्लन्देत् *क्लन्दित क्लन्दनीय

क्लप् *10√klap* (to worship) क्लपयति-ते क्लपयिष्यति-ते अक्लपयत्-त क्लपयतु-ताम् क्लपयेत्-त *क्लपित

क्लब् *4√klab* (to fear, be afraid) क्लब्यते क्लबिष्यते अक्लब्यत क्लब्यताम् क्लब्येत *क्लबित क्लबितव्य क्लबितुम्

क्लम् *4√klam* (to be fatigued, depressed) क्लाम्यति क्लमिष्यति अक्लाम्यत् क्लाम्यतु क्लाम्येत् *क्लिष्ट-क्लमित

क्लिद् *4√klid* (to become wet, damp, moist) क्लिद्यति क्लेदिष्यति अक्लिद्यत् क्लिद्यतु क्लिद्येत् *क्लिन्न क्लेद्य

क्लिन्द् *1√klind* (to lament) क्लिन्दते क्लिन्दिष्यते अक्लिन्दत क्लिन्दताम् क्लिन्देत *क्लिन्दित क्लिन्द्य क्लिन्दित्वा

क्लिश् *4√kliś* (to be distressed, afflicted) क्लिश्यते क्लेशिष्यते अक्लिश्यत क्लिश्यताम् क्लिश्येत क्लिश्यते *क्लिष्ट-क्लिशित क्लिश्यत् क्लेशनीय क्लेशितव्य क्लिश्य क्लिष्ट्वा क्लेशितुम् क्लेश क्लिष्टि

क्लिश् *9√kliś* (to vex, torment, molest) क्लिश्नाति क्लेशिष्यति अक्लिश्नात् क्लिश्नातु क्लिश्नीयात् *क्लिष्ट

क्लीब् *1√klīb* (to be weak, shy, impotant) क्लीबते क्लीबिष्यते क्लीबताम् क्लीबेत * क्लीबित क्लीब क्लैब्य

क्लु *1√klu* (to move, go) क्लवते क्लविष्यते अक्लवत क्लवताम् क्लवेत *क्लवित क्लवनीय क्लवितव्य क्लवित्वा

क्लेश् *1√kleś* (to impede, hinder, strike) क्लेशते क्लेशिष्यते अक्लेशत क्लेशताम् क्लेशेत *क्लेशित क्लेशनीय

क्वण् *1√kwaṇ* (to clank, jingle, tinkle) क्वणति क्वणिष्यति अक्वणत् क्वणतु क्वणेत् *क्वाण क्वणनीय क्वणित्वा

क्वथ् *1√kwath* (to boil, decoct, digest) क्वथति क्वथिष्यति अक्वथत् क्वथतु क्वथेत् *क्वथित क्वथनीय क्वथित्वा

<u>(क्ष) (kṣ)</u>

क्षज् *1√kṣaj* (to live in pain or distress) क्षञ्जते क्षञ्जिष्यते अक्षञ्जत क्षञ्जतु क्ष्ञ्जेत *क्षञ्जित क्षञ्जित्वा क्षञ्जन

क्षज् *10√kṣaj* (to live in pain) क्षजयति-ते क्षजयिष्यति-ते अक्षजयत्-त क्षजयतु-ताम् क्षजयेत्-त *क्षजित

क्षञ्ज् *1√kṣañj* (to live in pain) क्षञ्जते क्षञ्जिष्यते अक्षञ्जत क्षञ्जताम् क्षञ्जेत *क्षञ्जित क्षञ्जनीय क्षञ्जितव्य

क्षञ्ज् *10√kṣañj* (to suffer) क्षञ्जयति-ते क्षञ्जयिष्यति-ते अक्षञ्जयत्-त क्षञ्जयतु-ताम् क्षञ्जयेत्-त *क्षञ्जित

क्षण् *8√kṣaṇ* (to wound) क्षणोति-क्षणुते क्षणिष्यति-ते अक्षणोत्-अक्षणुत क्षणोतु-क्षणुताम् क्षणुयात्-क्षण्वीत *क्षत

क्षद् *1√kṣad* (to divide, cut, kill, consume, cover, protect) क्षदते क्षदिष्यते अक्षदत क्षदताम् क्षदेत *क्षण्ण क्षदनीय

क्षप् *1√kṣap* (to be obstinate, to fast) क्षपति-ते क्षपिष्यते अक्षपत क्षपताम् क्षपेत *क्षपित क्षपनीय क्षपितव्य

क्षम्प् *10√kṣamp* (to throw, pardon) क्षम्पयति-ते क्षपयिष्यति-ते अक्षम्पयत्-त क्षम्पयतु-ताम् क्षम्पयेत्-त *क्षम्पित

क्षम् *1√kṣam* (to bare, pardon, forgive, permit) क्षमते क्षमिष्यते अक्षमत क्षमताम् क्षमेत *क्षान्त-क्षमित क्षम्य क्षमा

क्षम् *4√kṣam* (to endure, tolerate) क्षाम्यति क्षमिष्यति अक्षाम्यत् क्षाम्यतु क्षाम्येत् *क्षत क्षमणीय क्षमितव्य क्षमितुम्

क्षर् *1√kṣar* (to peish, wane, flow, glide, emit) क्षरति-ते क्षरिष्यति-ते अक्षरत्-त क्षरतु-ताम् क्षरेत्-त *क्षरित क्षरणीय

क्षल् *10√kṣal* (to wash, cleanse; *+ preffix pra*) प्र-क्षालयति-ते क्षालयिष्यति अक्षालयत् क्षालयतु क्षालयेत् *क्षालित

क्षि *1√kṣi* (to wane, reduce, decay, to govern, rule) क्षयति क्षेष्यति अक्षयत् क्षयतु क्षयेत् *क्षीण क्षयनीय क्षय

क्षि *2√kṣi* (to possess) क्षेति क्षेष्यति अक्षेत् क्षेतु क्षीयात् अक्षैषीत् क्षीयते *क्षीण

क्षि *5√kṣi* (to hurt, kill) क्षिणोति क्षेष्यति अक्षिणोत् क्षिणोतु क्षिणुयात् अक्षैषीत् *क्षिण

क्षि *6√kṣi* (to stay) क्षियति क्षेष्यति अक्षियत् क्षियतु क्षियेत् अक्षैषीत् *क्षिण-क्षित क्षेतव्य क्षित्वा क्षेतुम्

क्षि *9√kṣi* (to kill) क्षिणाति क्षेष्यति अक्षीणात् क्षिणातु क्षिणीयात् अक्षैषीत् *क्षित क्षेतम् क्षेतव्य क्षित्वा

क्षिण् *5√kṣiṇ* (to weaken, hurt, injure) क्षिणोति अक्षिणोत् क्षिणोतु क्षिणुयात् *क्षित

क्षिण् *6√kṣiṇ* (to weaken) क्षिणुते क्षेणिष्यते अक्षिणत क्षिणताम् क्षिणेत

क्षिण् *8√kṣiṇ* (to smite) (क्षे)क्षिणोति-क्षेणुते क्षेणिष्यति-ते अक्षिणोत्-अक्षिणुत क्षिणोतु-क्षिणुताम् क्षिणुयात्-क्षिण्वीत *क्षित

क्षिद् *1√kṣid* (to moisten, dampen, make wet) क्षिदति क्षेदिष्यते अक्षिदत क्षिदताम् क्षिदेत *क्षिदित-क्षिन्न क्षिदनीय

क्षिप् *4√kṣip* (to throw, cast, send, discharge, let go) क्षिप्यते क्षिपिष्यते अक्षिप्यत क्षिप्यताम् क्षिप्येत क्षिप्यते *क्षिप्त

क्षिप् *6√kṣip* (to drop) क्षिपति-ते क्षेप्स्यति-ते अक्षिपत्-त क्षिपतु-ताम् क्षिपेत्-त *क्षिप्त क्षेपणीय क्षिप्त्वा क्षिप्तुम् क्षेपण

क्षिप् *10√kṣip* (to throw, cast away) क्षिपयति-ते क्षेपयिष्यति-ते अक्षेपयत्-त क्षिपयतु-ताम् क्षिपयेत्-त *क्षिपित

क्षिव् *1√kṣiv* (to push away) क्षेवति क्षेविष्यति अक्षेवत् क्षेवतु क्षेवेत् अक्षीविष्ट *क्षिवित क्षिवितव्य क्षिवित्वा क्षिवितुम्

क्षिव् *4√kṣiv* (to spit out, vomit) क्षीव्यति क्षेविष्यति अक्षिव्यत् क्षिव्यतु क्षिव्येत् *क्षिवित क्षिवितव्य क्षिवित्वा क्षिवितुम्

क्षी *1√kṣī* (to decay, wear out) क्षयति-ते क्षयिष्यति अक्षयत्-त क्षयतु-ताम् क्षयेत्-त *क्षीत क्षीत्वा क्षयितुम्

क्षी *4√kṣī* (to weaken) क्षीयते क्षयिष्यते अक्षीयत क्षीयतु क्षीयेत *क्षीत

क्षी *5√kṣī* (to destroy, hurt, injure) क्षिणोति क्षेष्यति अक्षीणोत् क्षीणोतु क्षीणुयात् *क्षीत

क्षी *6√kṣī* (to go, live, stay) क्षीयते क्षेष्यति अक्षीयत क्षीयताम् क्षीयेत् *क्षीत

क्षी *9√kṣī* (to kill) क्षीणाति क्षेष्यति अक्षीणात् क्षीणातु क्षीणीयात् *क्षीण-क्षीत क्षयणीय क्षेतव्य क्षीत्वा क्षेतुम्

क्षीज् *1√kṣīj* (to whisper, sound indistinctly, murmer) क्षीजति, क्षीजिष्यति अक्षीजदत् क्षीजतु क्षीजेत् *क्षीजित

क्षीब् *1√kṣīv* (to be intoxicated) क्षीबते क्षेबिष्यते अक्षिबत क्षिबताम् क्षिबेत *क्षिबित क्षिबनीय क्षिबितव्य क्षिबितुम्

क्षीब् *4√kṣīv* (to be intoxicated) क्षीब्यते क्षेबिष्यते अक्षिब्यत क्षिब्यताम् क्षिब्येत *क्षिबित क्षिबयत् क्षिबयित्वा

क्षीव् *1√kṣīv* (to be intoxicated) क्षीवते क्षीविष्यते अक्षीवत क्षीवताम् क्षीवेत *क्षीवित क्षीवनीय क्षीवितव्य

क्षीव् *4√kṣīv* (to spit) क्षीव्यते क्षेविष्यते अक्षिव्यत क्षिव्यताम् क्षिव्येत *क्षीवित क्षीवित्वा क्षीवितुम् क्षीव

क्षु *2√kṣu* (to sneeze, cough) क्षौति क्षविष्यति अक्षौत् क्षौतु क्षुयात् अक्षावीत् *क्षुत क्षवणीय क्षुत्वा क्षवितुम्

क्षुद् *7√kṣud* (to crush under feet, trample up on) क्षुणत्ति क्षोत्स्यति अक्षुणत् क्षुणतु क्षुन्द्यात् क्षुद्यते *क्षुत्त क्षेदनीय

क्षुध् *4√kṣudh* (to be hungry, starve) क्षुध्यति क्षोत्स्यति अक्षुध्यत् क्षुध्यतु क्षुध्येत् *क्षुधित क्षोधनीय क्षुद्ध्वा क्षोद्धुम् क्षुधा

क्षुप् *6√kṣup* (to be startled, be taken aback) क्षुपति क्षुपिष्यति अक्षुपत् क्षुपतु क्षुपेत् *क्षुप्त क्षुप्तव्य क्षुप्तुम् क्षुप

क्षुभ् *1√kṣubh* (to be agitated, disturbed; to tremble) क्षोभते क्षोभिष्यते अक्षोभत क्षोभताम् क्षोभेत *क्षुब्ध क्षोभनीय

क्षुभ् *4√kṣubh* (to tremble, be unsteady) क्षुभ्यति क्षोभिष्यति अक्षुभ्यत् क्षुभ्यतु क्षुभ्येत् *क्षुब्ध-क्षुभित क्षोभनीय

क्षुभ् *9√kṣubh* (to tremble, stir up, exite, pertrub) क्षुभ्नाति क्षोभिष्यति अक्षुभ्नात् क्षुभ्नातु क्षुभ्यात् *क्षुब्ध

क्षुर् *6√kṣur* (to scratch, cut, make lines, make furrows) क्षुरति क्षुरिष्यति अक्षुरत् क्षुरतु क्षुरेत् *क्षुरित क्षुरणीय

क्षै *1√kṣai* (to taper off, waste away, wane, decay, wear) क्षायति क्षास्यति अक्षायत् क्षायतु क्षायेत् क्षायते *क्षाम

क्षोट् *10√kṣoṭ* (to send, throw) क्षोटयति क्षोटयिष्यति अक्षोटयत् क्षोटयतु क्षोटयेत् *क्षोटित क्षोटयित्वा क्षोटयितुम्

क्ष्णु *2√kṣṇu* (to whet, sharpen) क्ष्णौति क्ष्णविष्यति अक्ष्णौत् क्ष्णौतु क्ष्णुयात् अक्ष्णावीत् *क्ष्णुत क्ष्णवित्वा क्ष्णवितुम्

क्ष्माय् *1√kṣmāy* (to tremble, shake) क्ष्मायते क्ष्मायिष्यते क्ष्मायताम् क्ष्मायेत *क्ष्मात क्ष्मायनीय क्ष्मायित्वा क्ष्मायितुम्

क्ष्मील् *1√kṣmil* (to wink, close the eyelids) क्ष्मीलति क्ष्मीलिष्यति अक्ष्मेलत् क्ष्मीलतु क्ष्मिलेत *क्ष्मिलित क्ष्मीलनीय

क्ष्विड् *1√kṣviḍ* (to hum, murmer) क्ष्वेडति-ते क्ष्वेडिष्यते अक्ष्वेडत्-त क्ष्वेडतु-ताम् क्ष्वेडेत्-त अक्ष्वेडिष्ट *क्ष्विण्ण

क्ष्विद् *1√kṣvid* (to milk) क्ष्वेदति-ते क्ष्वेदिष्यति-ते अक्ष्विदत्-त क्ष्वेदतु-ताम् क्ष्वेदेत्-त अक्ष्वेदिष्ट *क्ष्विण्ण-क्ष्वेदित

क्ष्विद् *4√kṣvid* (to milk, become wet) क्ष्वेद्यति क्ष्वेदिष्यति अक्ष्वदत् क्ष्वेद्यतु क्ष्वेद्येत् अक्ष्वेदिष्ट *क्ष्विण्ण

क्ष्वेल् *1√kṣvel* (to play, leap, jump) क्ष्वेलति क्ष्वेलिष्यति अक्ष्वेलत् क्ष्वेलतु क्ष्वेलेत् *क्ष्वेलित क्ष्वेलनीय क्ष्वेलित्वा

(ख) (kh)

खक्ख् *1√khakkh* (to laugh, ridicule, deride) खक्खति खक्खिष्यति अखक्कत् खक्कतु खक्केत् *खक्कित

खच् *1√khać* (to purify) खचति खचिष्यति अखचत् खचतु खचेत् *खचित खचनीय खचितव्य खचित्वा खचितुम्

खच् *9√khać* (to re-appear, come forth, be reborn) खच्ञाति खचिष्यति अखच्ञात् खच्ञातु खच्ञीयात् *खचित

खच् *10√khać* (to tie, bind, inlay, set) खचयति-ते खचयिष्यति-ते अखचयत्-त खचयतु-ताम् खचयेत्-त *खचित

खज् *1√khaj* (to churn, agitate) खजति खजिष्यति अखजत् खजतु खजेत् *खजित खजनीय खजित्वा खजितुम्

खञ्ज् *1√khañj* (to limp, walk lame) खञ्जति खञ्जिष्यति अखञ्जत् खञ्जतु खञ्जेत् *खञ्जित खञ्जनीय खञ्जित्वा

खद् *1√khaṭ* (to like, desire, wish) खटति खटिष्यति अखटत्-अखाटत् खटतु खटेत् *खटित खटनीय खटितव्य

खद्द् *10√khaṭṭ* (to encircle, envelop) खद्टयति-ते खट्टयिष्यति-ते अखट्टयत्-त खट्टयतु-ताम् खट्टयेत्-त *खट्टित

खड् *10√khaḍ* (to cut, break,sever, crack) खाडयति-ते खाडयिष्यति अखाडयत् खाडयतु खाडयेत् *खाडित

खण्ड् *1√khaṇḍ* (to break) खण्डते खण्डिष्यते अखण्डत खण्डताम् खण्डेत खण्ड्यते *खण्डित खण्डनीय खण्डितव्य

खण्ड् *10√khaṇḍ* (to break, cut to pieces, tear) खण्डयति-ते खण्डयिष्यति अखण्डयत् खण्डयतु खण्डयेत् *खण्डित

खद् *1√khad* (to injure, strike, hurt, be steady, firm) खदति खदिष्यति अखदत् खदतु खदेत् *खत्त खदनीय

खन् *1√khan* (to dig up, delve, excavate) खनति-ते खनिष्यति अखनत् खनतु खनेत् *खात खननीय खनितव्य खनन

खर्ज् *1√kharj* (to hurt, make uneasy) खर्जति खर्जिष्यति अखर्जत् खर्जतु खर्जेत् *खर्जित खर्जनीय खर्जित्वा

खर्द् *1√khard* (to bite, sting) खर्दति खर्दिष्यति अखर्दत् खर्दतु खर्देत् *खर्दित खर्दत् खर्दनीय खर्दित्वा खर्दितुम्

खर्ब् *1√kharb* (to stiffen) खर्बति खर्बिष्यति अखर्बत् खर्बतु खर्बेत् *खर्बित खर्बनीय खर्बितव्य खर्बित्वा खर्बितुम्

खर्व् *1√kharv* (to go) खर्वति खर्विष्यति अखर्वत् खर्वतु खर्वेत् *खर्वित खर्वणीय खर्वितव्य खर्वित्वा खर्वितुम्

खल् *1√khal* (to gather, collect, move, shake) खलति खलिष्यति अखलत् खलतु खलेत् *खलित खलनीय खलित्वा

खल्ल् *1√khall* (to be relaxed) खल्लते खल्लिष्यते अखल्लत् खल्लतु खल्लेत् *खल्लित खल्लनीय खल्लित्वा

खव् *9√khav* (to enrich, cause prosperity, purify) खव्नाति खविष्यति अखव्नात् खव्नातु खव्नीयात् *खवित

खष् *1√khaṣ* (to hurt, injure) खषति खषिष्यति अखषत् खषतु खषेत् *खषित-खष्ट खषनीय खषित्वा खषितुम्

खाद् *1√khād* (to eat, consume, feed) खादति खादिष्यति अखादत् खादतु खादेत् *खादित खादनीय खाद्य खादित्वा

खिट् *1√khiṭ* (to fear, dread, surprise, be terrified, freightened) खेटति खेटिष्यति अखेटत् खेटतु खेटेत् *खेटित

खिद् *4 √khid* (to suffer pain or misery) खिद्यते खेत्स्यते अखिद्यत खिद्यताम् खिद्येत खिद्यते *खिन्न खिद्य खेतुम् खेद

खिद् *6 √khid* (to cause pain) खिन्दति खेत्स्यति अखिनदत् खिन्दतु खिन्देत *खिन्न खेदनीय खेतव्य खेद्य खित्वा खेत्तुम्

खिद् *7 √khid* (to strike, assult, press down, afflict) खिन्ते खेत्स्यते अखिन्त खिन्ताम् खिन्दीत *खिन्न खेदनीय

खिल् *6√khil* (to pick, pick grains) खिलति खेलिष्यति अखिलत् खिलतु खिलेत् *खिलित खिलनीय खिलितुम्

खु *1√khu* (to make sound) खवते खोष्यते अखवत् खवतु खवेत् अखोष्ट *खवित खवनीय खवितव्य खवितुम्

खुच् *1√khuć* (to steal) खोचति खोचिष्यति अखोचत् खोचतु खोचेत् *खोचित खोचनीय खोचितव्य खोचित्वा खोचितुम्

खुज् *1√khuj* (to rob, steal) खोजति खोजिष्यति अखोजत् खोजतु खोजेत् *खोजित खोजनीय खोजितव्य खोजित्वा

खुड् *10√khuḍ* (to rip, cut up, divide in pieces) खोडयति-ते खोडयिष्यति अखोडयत् खोडयतु खोडयेत् *खोडित

खुण्ड *1√khuṇḍ* (to break, cut) खुण्डते खुण्डिष्यते अखुण्डत खुण्डताम् खुण्डेत अचुखुण्डत् *खुण्डित खुडितव्य

खुर् *1√khur* (to cut) खुरति खुरिष्यति अखुरत् खुरतु खुरेत् अखोरीत् *खुरित खुरणीय खुरित्वा खुरितुम् खर प्रखर

खुर् *6√khur* (to shine, be rich) खुरति खुरिष्यति अखुरत् खुरतु खुरेत् *खुरित खुरणीय खुरित्वा खुरितुम्

खुर्द *1√khurd* (to play) खूर्दते खूर्दिष्यते अखूर्दत खूर्दताम् खूर्देत *खूर्दित खूर्दयत् खूर्दनीय खूर्दित्वा खूर्दितुम्

खूर्द *1√khūrd* (to play) खूर्दते खूर्दिष्यते अखूर्दत खूर्दताम् खूर्देत *खूर्दित खूर्दितव्य खूर्दित्वा खूर्दनीय

खे *1√khe* (to play) खेलति खेलिष्यति अखेलत् खेलतु खेलेत् अखेलीत् *खेलित खेलनीय खेलितुम् खेलन

खेट् *10√kheṭ* (to eat, consume) खेटयति खेटयिष्यति-ते अखेटयत्-त खेटयतु-ताम् खेटयेत्-त *खेटित खेटयितुम्

खेल् *1√khel* (to play, sport) खेलति खेलिष्यति अखेलत् खेलतु खेलेत् खेल्यते *खेलित खेलनीय खेलित्वा खेलितुम्
खेव् *1√khev* (to serve, wait up on) खेवते खेविष्यते अखेवत खेवताम् खेवेत अखेविष्ट *खेवित खेवितुम् खेवन
खै *1√khai* (to eat, cause harm) खायति ख्यास्यति अखासत् खायतु खायेत् *खात खातव्य खीत्वा खातुम् खीयमान
खोट् *10√khoṭ* (to eat) खोटयति-ते खोटयिष्यति-ते अखोटयत्-त खोटयतु-ताम् खोटयेत्-त अचुखोटत्-त *खोटित
खोड् *1√khoḍ* (to be hindered) खोडति खोडिष्यति अखोडत् खोडतु खोडेत् *खोडित खोडनीय खोडित्वा खोडितुम्
खोर् *1√khor* (to be obstructed) खोरति खोरिष्यति अखोरत् खोरतु खोरेत् *खोरित खोरणीय खोरित्वा खोरितुम्
खोल् *1√khol* (to limp) खोलति खोलिष्यति अखोलत् खोलतु खोलेत् *खोलित खोलनीय खोलित्वा खोलितुम्
ख्या *2√khyā* (to be famous or known, to tell, declare) ख्याति ख्यास्यति अख्यात् ख्यातु ख्यायात् *ख्यात ख्यानीय

(ग) (g)

गज् *1√gaj* (to roar, sound, be drunk) गजति गजिष्यति अगाजत् गजतु गजेत् *गजित गजनीय गजित्वा गजितुम्
गज् *10√ gaj* (to make sound) गाजयति गाजयिष्यति अगाजयत् गाजयतु गाजयेत् *गाजित गाजनीय गाजयित्वा
गञ्ज् *1√gañj* (to resound) गञ्जति गञ्जिष्यति अगञ्जत् गञ्जतु गञ्जेत् *गञ्जित गञ्जनीय गञ्जित्वा गञ्जितुम्
गड् *1√gaḍ* (to pull, distill, draw out, run) गडति गडिष्यति अगडत् गडतु गडेत् *गडित गडनीय गडित्वा गडितुम्
गण् *10√gaṇ* (to count, calculate, compute, enumerate) गणयति-ते गणयिष्यति अगणयत् गणयतु गणयेत् *गणित
गण्ड् *1√gaṇḍ* (to be sour) गण्डति जगण्ड गण्डिष्यति अगण्डत् गण्डतु गण्डेत् *गण्डित गण्डनीय गण्डित्वा गण्डितुम्
गद् *1√gad* (to speak, say, relate) गदति गदिष्यति अगदत् गदतु गदेत् निगद्यते *गदित गदनीय गदित्वा गदितुम्
गद् *10√gad* (to thunder) गदयति-ते गदयिष्यति-ते अगदयत्-त गदयतु-ताम् गदयेत्-त गद्यते *गदित गदयितव्य गद्य
गन्द् *10√gand* (to hurt, put to shame) गन्दयते गन्दयिष्यते अगन्दयत गन्दयताम् गन्दयेत *गन्दित गन्दितव्य
गध् *4√gadh* (to be mixed) गध्यति गधिष्यति अगध्यत् गध्यतु गध्येत् *गद्ध गधनीय गधितव्य गद्धा गद्धुम्
गध् *10√gadh* (to beg, move, adorn, hurt) गधयति-ते गधयिष्यति-ते अगधयत्-त गधयतु-ताम् गधयेत्-त *गद्ध
गन्ध् *10√gandh* (to ask, go) गन्धयते गन्धयिष्यते अगन्धयत गन्धयताम् गन्धयेत अजगन्धत *गन्धित सुगन्धित
गम् *1√gam* (to go, move, depart, arrive, approach) गच्छति गमिष्यति अगच्छत् गच्छतु गच्छेत् गम्यते *गत गमनीय गन्तव्य गम्य गत्वा गच्छत् गन्तुम् गम्यमान गम्यते संगम्य गतवत् ग गम गामी गमन गति खग पन्नग विहग
गर्ज् *1√garj* (to roar, growl) गर्जति गर्जिष्यति अगर्जत् गर्जतु गर्जेत् *गर्जित गर्जनीय गर्जितव्य गर्जित्वा गर्जितुम्
गर्ज् *10√garj* (to thunder) गर्जयति-ते गर्जयिष्यति-ते अगर्जयत्-त गर्जयतु-ताम् गर्जयेत्-त *गर्जित गर्जयितुम् गर्जना
गर्द् *1,10√gard* (to sound, roar) गर्दति-गर्दयति-ते गर्दिष्यति अगर्दत् गर्दतु गर्देत् *गर्दित गर्दनीय गर्दित्वा गर्दितुम्
गर्ध् *10√gardh* (to like) गर्धयति-ते गर्धयिष्यति-ते अगर्धयत्-त गर्धयतु-ताम् गर्धयेत्-त अजगर्धत्-त *गर्धित गर्ध
गर्व् *1√garv* (to be proud or haughty) गर्वति गर्विष्यति अगर्वत् गर्वतु गर्वेत् *गर्वित गर्वणीय गर्वित्वा गर्वितुम् गर्व
गर्व् *10√garv* (to possess ego, show pride) गर्वयते गर्वयिष्यते अगर्वयत गर्वयताम् गर्वयेत *गर्वित गर्वयितुम्
गर्ह् *1√garh* (to ridicule, reproach) गर्हते गर्हिष्यते अगर्हत गर्हताम् गर्हेत *गर्हित गर्हणीय गर्ह्य गर्हित्वा गर्हितुम्

गर्ह् *10√garh* (to ridicule) गर्हयति-ते गर्हयिष्यति-ते अगर्हयत्-त गर्हयतु-ताम् गर्हयेत्-त गर्हयाञ्चकार *गर्हित गर्हा

गल् *1√gal* (to drop, trocle, drip, ooze) गलति गलिष्यति अगलत् गलतु गलेत् *गलित गलनीय गलित्वा गलितुम्

गल् *10√gal* (to filter, strain, flow, liquify, dissolve) गालयते गालयिष्यते अगालयत गालयताम् गालयेत *गालित

गल्भ् *1√galbh* (to dare, be bold or confident) गल्भते गल्भिष्यते अगल्भत गल्भताम् गल्भेत *गल्भित गल्भनीय

गल्ह् *1√galh* (to blame, censure) गल्हते गल्हिष्यते अगल्हत गल्हताम् गल्हेत *गल्हित गल्हनीय गल्हित्वा गल्हितुम्

गवेष् *10√gaveṣ* (to search, seek, inquire, hunt for) गवेषयति गवेषयिष्यति अगवेषयत् गवेषयतु गवेषयेत् *गवेषित

गह् *10√gah* (to be dense, thick, impervious) गहयति-ते गहयिष्यति-ते अगहयत्-त गहयतु-ताम् गहयेत्-त *गाढ

गा *1√gā* (to go, see) गाते गास्यते अगात् गातु गायेत् अगास्त *गात गानीय गातव्य गात्वा गातुम् गान

गा *2√gā* (to go, see) गाति गास्यति अगात् गातु गायात् *गात गानीय गातव्य गात्वा गातुम्

गा *3√gā* (to praise, sing, praise in song) जिगाति गास्यति अगासत् गायतु गायात् अगासीत् *गात गानीय गातुम्

गा *4√gā* (to sing) गायति गास्यति अगायत् गायतु गायेत् *गात गानीय गातव्य गात्वा गातुम्

गाध् *1√gādh* (to pause, stand, stay, remain, seek) गाधते गाधिष्यते अगाधत गाधताम् गाधेत *गाधित गाधनीय

गाह् *1√gāh* (to plunge, dive, immerse, bathe) गाहते गाहिष्यते अगाहत गाहताम् गाहेत गाह्यते *गाढ गाहनीय गाढ्वा

गिल् *6√gil* (to swallow, gulp) गिलति गेलिष्यति अगिलत गिलतु गिलेत् *गिलित गीर्णवान् गिलनीय गिलितुम्

गु *1√gu* (to sound, hum, speak indistinctly, whisper) गवते गोष्यते अगवत गवताम् गवेत अगोष्ट *गून

गु *6√gu* (to excrete, pass by stool) गुवति गुष्यति अगुषत् गुवतु गुवेत् *गून गुवत् गुवनीय गुवितव्य गुत्वा गुतुम्

गुज् *1,6√gu* (to make sound) गुजति गुजिष्यति अगुजत् गुजतु गुजेत् *गुजित गुजनीय गुजितव्य गुजित्वा *गुजित

गुञ्ज् *1√guñj* (to murmer, hum) गुञ्जति गुञ्जिष्यति अगुञ्जत् गुञ्जतु गुञ्जेत् गुञ्जते *गुञ्जित गुञ्जनीय गुञ्जित्वा

गुड् *6√guḍ* (to save, preserve, defend) गुडति गुडिष्यति अगुडत् गुडतु गुडेत् *गुडित गुडितव्य गुडित्वा गुडितुम्

गुण् *10√guṇ* (to multiply, advise, invite) गुणयति-ते गुणयिष्यति-ते अगुणयत्-त गुणयतु-ताम् गुणयेत्-त *गुणित

गुण्ठ् *10√guṇṭh* (to surround, encircle, envelop) गुण्ठयति गुण्ठयिष्यति अगुण्ठयत् गुण्ठयतु गुण्ठयेत् *गुण्ठित

गुण्ड् *10√guṇḍ* (to cover, pound, make powder) गुण्डयति गुण्डयिष्यति अगुण्डयत् गुण्डयतु गुण्डयेत् *गुण्डित

गुद् *1√gud* (to play) गोदते गोदिष्यते अगोदत गोदताम् गोदेत *गुदित गुदनीय गुदितव्य गुदित्वा गुदितुम्

गुद्र् *10√gudr* (to tie) गुद्रयति-ते गुद्रयिष्यति-ते अगुद्रयत्-त गुद्रयतु-ताम् गुद्रयेत्-त *गुद्रित गुद्रयितव्य गुद्रयित्वा

गुध् *1√gudh* (to play, sport) गोधते गोधिष्यते अगोधत गोधताम् गोधेत अगोधिष्ट गुध्यते *गोधित-गुद्ध गोधितुम्

गुध् *4√gudh* (to wrap up, envelop, clothe) गुध्यति गोधिष्यति अगुध्यत् गुध्यतु गुध्येत् अगोधीत् *गुधित-गुद्ध

गुध् *9√gudh* (to be angry, hinder, stop) गुध्नाति गोधिष्यति अगुध्नात् गुध्नातु गुध्नीयात् अगोधीत् *गुद्ध

गुप् *1 √gup* (to protect) गोपते-जुगुप्सते गोपिष्यते-जुगुप्सिष्यते अगुपत- अजुगुप्सत गुपताम्-जुगुप्सताम् गुपेत-जुगुप्सेत जुगुप्स्यते *जुगुप्सित-गुपित गोपनीय गोपितव्य गोप्य गोप्त्वा गोप्तुम् जुगुप्स्य जुगुप्सितुम् जुगुप्सा

गुप् *4√gup* (to chide) गुप्यति गोपिष्यति अगुप्यत् गुप्यतु गुप्येत् *गुप्त गुप्त्वा गुप्तुम् गुप्तक गुप्ति गोप

गुप् *10√gup* (to chide) गोपायति गोपायिष्यति अगोपायत् गोपायतु गोपायेत् जुगोप गोपिता गुप्यात् गुप्यते *गोपित

गुफ् *6√guph* (to twine, string, weave, wind round) गुफति गुफिष्यति अगुफत् गुफतु गुफेत् गुफ्यते *गुफित

गुम्फ् *6√gumph* (to weave) गुम्फति गुम्फिष्यति अगुम्फत् गुम्फतु गुम्फेत् *गुम्फित गुम्फनीय गुम्फितव्य गुम्फितुम्

गुर् *1√gur* (to extend) गुरते गूरिष्यते अगूरत गूरताम् गूरेत *गूर्ण

गुर् *4√gur* (to injure, hurt, go) गुर्यते गूरयिष्यते अगूर्यत गूर्यताम् गूर्येत गूर्यते अगुरिष्ट *गुर्ण

गुर् *6√gur* (to greet, try, endeavor, make an effort or exertion) गुरते गुरिष्यते अगुरत गुरताम् गुरेत *गूर्ण

गुर् *10√gur* (to do business) गुरयते गूरयिष्यते अगूरयत गूरयताम् गूरयेत अजूगुरत *गुरित गुरयितुम्

गुर्द् *1√gurd* (to play) गूर्दते गूर्दते गूर्दिष्यते अगूर्दत गूर्दताम् गूर्दते *गूर्दित गूर्दत् गूर्दनीय गूर्दित्वा गूर्दितुम्

गुर्द् *10√gurd* (to sport) गूर्दयति-ते गूर्दयिष्यति-ते अगूर्दयत्-त गूर्दयतु-ताम् गूर्दयेत्-त *गूर्दित गूर्दितव्य गूर्दितुम्

गुर्व् *1√gurv* (to endavor, elevate) गुर्वति गुर्विष्यति अगुर्वत् गुर्वतु गुर्वेत् *गुर्वित गुर्वणीय गुर्वितव्य गुर्वित्वा गुर्वितुम्

गुह् *1√guh* (to conceal, hide, cover, keep secret) गूहति-ते गूहिष्यति अगूहत् गूहतु गूहेत् *गूढ गोढुम् गुह्य गूह्य गूहा

गू *6√gū* (to pass stool) गवति गविष्यति अगवत् गवत गवेत् *गूत गवितुम् गवित्वा गव:

गूर् *4√gūr* (to go) गूर्यते गूरिष्यते अगूर्यत गूर्यताम् गूर्येत *गूर्ण

गूर् *10√gūr* (to struggle) गूरयते गूरयिष्यते अगूरयत गूरयताम् गूरयेत *गूरित गूरयित्वा गूरयितुम्

गूर्द् *1√gūrd* (to sport) गु-गूर्दते गूर्दिष्यते अगूर्दत गूर्दताम् गुर्देत *गूर्दित गूर्दनीय गूर्दित्वा गूर्दितुम्

गूर्द् *10√gūrd* (to sport) गूर्दयति-ते गूर्दयिष्यति-ते अगूर्दयत्-त गूर्दयतु-ताम् गूर्दयेत्-त *गूर्दित गूर्दयित्वा गूर्दयितुम्

गूर्ध् *10√gūrdh* (to extole) गूर्धयति गीर्धयिष्यति-ते अगूर्धयत्-त गूर्धयतु-ताम् गूर्धयेत्-त *गूर्धित गूर्धयित्वा गूर्धयितुम्

गृ *1√gṛ* (to sprinkle, moisten, wet, grant) गरति गरिष्यति अगरत् गरतु गरेत् अगार्षीत् *गरित गरणीय गरितुम्-गरीतुं

गृ *10√gṛ* (to know properly) गारयते गारयिष्यते अगारयत गारयताम् गारयेत *गारित गारणीय गारयित्वा गारयितुम्

गृज् *1√gṛj* (to blare) गर्जति गर्जिष्यति अगर्जत् गर्जतु गर्जेत् *गर्जित गर्जनीय गर्जितव्य गर्जित्वा गर्जितुम् गर्जना

गृञ्ज् *1√gṛñj* (to clamor) गृञ्जति गृञ्जिष्यति अगृञ्जत् गृञ्जतु गृञ्जेत् *गृञ्जित गृञ्जनीय गृञ्जित्वा गृञ्जितुम्

गृध् *4√gṛdh* (to covet, desire, strive, long for, be greedy) गृध्यति गर्धिष्यति अगृध्यत् गृध्यतु गृध्येत् *गृद्ध गृद्ध्वा

गृह् *1√gṛh* (to accept) गर्हते गर्हिष्यते-घर्क्ष्यते अगर्हत गर्हताम् गर्हेत *गर्हित-गृढ विगृह्य गर्हित्वा-गृढ्वा गर्हितुम्-गर्ढुम्

गृह् *10√gṛh* (to accept, bear) गृह्यते गृहयिष्यते अगृह्यत गृह्यताम् गृह्येत अजगृहत *गृहित-गृढ ग्रहणीय ग्रहितव्य

गॄ *6√gṝ* (to swallow) गिरति गरिष्यति अगिरत् गिरतु गिरेत् *गीर्ण गिरत् गरणीय गीर्त्वा गरितुम् ग्रीवा उद्गार गरिमा गर्भ

गॄ *9√gṝ* (to praise, utter, utter praises) गृणाति गरिष्यति-गरीष्यति अगृणात् गृणातु गृणीयात् आगारीत गीर्यते *गीर्ण

गेप् *1√gep* (to shake, tremble, be unstable) गेपते गेपिष्यते अगेपत गेपताम् गेपेत *गेप्त गेप्तव्य गेप्त्वा गेप्तुम्

गेव् *1√gev* (to serve, wait up on) गेवते गेविष्यते अगेवत गेवताम् गेवेत अगेविष्ट *गेवित गेवनीय गेवित्वा गेवितुम्

गेष् *1√geṣ* (to search, do research) गेषते गेषिष्यते अगेषत गेषताम् गेषेत *गेषित गेषणीय गेषित्वा गेषितुम् गेषणा

गै *1√gai* (to sing) गायति गास्यति अगायत् गायतु गायेत् गीयते *गीत गानीय गातव्य गातुम् गेय गान गीता
गोष्ट् *1√goṣṭ* (to collect) गोष्टते गोष्टिष्यते अगोष्टत गोष्टताम् गोष्टेत *गोष्टित गोष्टनीय गोष्टितव्य गोष्टित्वा गोष्टितुम्
गोम् *10√gom* (to smear) गोमयति गोमयिष्यति अगोमयत् गोमयतु गोमयेत् *गोमयित गोमयितव्य गाम्य गोमयितुम् गोमन
ग्रथ् *1√grath* (to bend) ग्रथते ग्रथिष्यते अग्रथत ग्रथताम् ग्रथेत अग्रथीत *ग्रथित ग्रथनीय ग्रथितव्य ग्रथित्वा ग्रथितुम् ग्रन्थ
ग्रध् *1√gradh* (to be wicked) ग्रधते ग्रधिष्यते अग्रधत ग्रधताम् ग्रधेत *ग्रधित ग्रधनीय ग्रधितव्य ग्रधित्वा ग्रधितुम्
ग्रन्थ् *1√granth* (to bend, form, make, produce) ग्रन्थते ग्रन्थिष्यते अग्रन्थत ग्रन्थताम् ग्रन्थेत *ग्रथित ग्रन्थनीय
ग्रन्थ् *9√granth* (to compose, write, thread) ग्रथ्नाति ग्रथिष्यति अग्रथ्नात् ग्रथ्नातु ग्रथ्नीयात् *ग्रन्थित ग्रन्थ
ग्रन्थ् *10√granth* (to string together) ग्रन्थयति-ते ग्रन्थयिष्यति-ते अग्रन्थयत्-त ग्रन्थयतु-ताम् ग्रन्थयेत्-त *ग्रन्थित
ग्रभ् *1√grabh* (take) गृभ्णाति-गृभ्णीते ग्रभीष्यति-ते अगृभ्णात्-अगृभ्णीत गभ्णातु-गृभ्णीता गृभ्णीयात्-गृभ्णीत*गृभित-ग्रब्ध
ग्रस् *1√gras* (to sulrp, swallow, devour, eat up, consume) ग्रसते ग्रसिष्यते अग्रसत ग्रसताम् ग्रसेत *ग्रस्त ग्रसनीय
ग्रस् *10√gras* (to take, eat, gulp) ग्रासयति-ते ग्रासयिष्यति-ते अग्रासयत्-त ग्रासयतु-ताम् ग्रासयेत्-त ग्रस्यते *ग्रासित
ग्रह् *9√grah* (to take) गृह्णाति-गृह्णीते ग्रहीष्यति-ते अगृह्णात्-अगृह्णीत गृह्णातु-गृह्णीताम् गृह्णीयात्-गृह्णीत गृह्यते *गृहित गृह्णत् ग्रहणीय ग्रहीतव्य ग्राह्य गृहीत्वा ग्रहीतुम् ग्रह ग्रहण ग्राहिन् गृह आग्रह निग्रह
ग्रुच् *1√gruć* (to steal) ग्रोचति ग्रोचिष्यति अग्रोचत् ग्रोचतु ग्रोचेत् *ग्रोचित-ग्रुक्त ग्रोचनीय ग्रोचितव्य ग्रोचित्वा ग्रुक्त्वा
ग्लस् *1√glas* (to devour, eat, gulp) ग्लसते ग्लसिष्यते अग्लसत ग्लसताम् ग्लसेत अग्लसिष्ट *ग्लस्त ग्लसनीय
ग्लह् *1√glah* (to move, steal, rob, deprive, take) ग्लहति-ते ग्लहिष्यति-ते अग्लत्-त ग्लहतु-ताम् ग्लहेत्-त *ग्लहित
ग्लह् *10√glah* (to gamble) ग्लाहयति-ते ग्लाहयिष्यति-ते अग्लाहयत्-त ग्लाहयतु-ताम् ग्लाहयेत्-त *ग्लाहित
ग्ला *4√glā* (to be weary) ग्लायति ग्लायिष्यति अग्लायत् ग्लायतु ग्लायेत् *ग्लात ग्लानीय ग्लातव्य ग्लात्वा ग्लातुम्
ग्लुच् *1√gluć* (to steal, rob) ग्लोचति ग्लोचिष्यति अग्लोचत् ग्लोचतु ग्लोचेत् *ग्लुक्त ग्लोचनीय ग्लोचित्वा-ग्लुक्त्वा
ग्लुञ्च् *1√gluñć* (to steal) ग्लुञ्चति ग्लुञ्चिष्यति अग्लुञ्चत् ग्लुञ्चतु ग्लुञ्चेत् *ग्लुङ्क्त ग्लुञ्चनीय ग्लुञ्चित्वा ग्लुञ्चितुम्
ग्लेप् *1√glep* (to shiver, be poor, miserable) ग्लेपते ग्लेपिष्यते अग्लेपत ग्लेपताम् ग्लेपेत *ग्लिप्त ग्लिप्त्वा ग्लिप्तुम्
ग्लेव् *1√glev* (to worship, serve) ग्लेवते ग्लेविष्यते अग्लेवत ग्लेवताम् ग्लेवेत *ग्लेवित ग्लेवनीय ग्लेवित्वा ग्लेवितुम्
ग्लेष् *1√gleṣ* (to search for, seek, find out) ग्लेषते ग्लेषिष्यते अग्लेषत ग्लेषताम् ग्लेषेत अग्लेषिष्ट *ग्लेषित-ग्लिष्ट
ग्लै *1√glai* (to fall, fade) ग्लायति ग्लास्यति अग्लायत् ग्लायतु ग्लायेत् *ग्लान ग्लातव्य ग्लानीय ग्लानि ग्लौ ग्लानि

(घ) (gh)

घङ्घ् *1√ghaṅgh* (to flow, stream, loose luster,) घङ्घते घङ्घिष्यते अघङ्घत घङ्घताम् घङ्घेत *घङ्घित घङ्घितुम्
घंष् *1√ghaṁṣ* (to stream) घंषते घंषिष्यते अघंषत घंषताम् घंषेत *घंषित-घष्ट घंषणीय घंषितव्य घंषित्वा घंषितुम्
घग्घ् *1√ghaggh* (to laugh, laugh at) घग्घते घग्घिष्यते अघग्घत घग्घताम् घग्घेत *घग्घित घग्घनीय घग्घितव्य
घघ् *1√ghagh* (to laugh) घघति-ते घघिष्यति अघघत्-अघाघत् घघतु घघेत् *घघित घघनीय घघित्वा घघितुम्
घट् *1√ghaṭ* (to happen, take place) घटते घटिष्यते अघटत घटताम् घटेत *घटित घटनीय घटित्वा घटितुम् घटना

घट् *10√ghaṭ* (to speak, unite, join, shine) घाटयति-ते घाटयिष्यति-ते अघाटयत्-त घाटयतु-ताम् घाटयेत्-त *घाटित

घट्ट् *1√ghaṭṭ* (to rub, touch, move, smoothen, rebuke) घट्टयते घट्टयिष्यते अघट्टयत घट्टयताम् घट्टयेत *घट्टित

घट्ट् *10√ghaṭṭ* (to shake, stir, disturb) घट्टयति-ते घट्टयिष्यति-ते अघट्टयत्-त घट्टयतु-ताम् घट्टयेत्-त *घट्टित

घण् *6√ghaṇ* (to shine, glitter) घणोति-घणुते घणिष्यति-ते अघणत्-त घणतु-ताम् घणेत्-त अघणिष्ट *घणित

घण्ट् *10√ghaṇṭ* (to ring, make sound) घण्टयति-ते घण्टयिष्यति-ते अघण्टयत्-त घण्टयतु-ताम् घण्टयेत्-त *घण्टित

घम्ब् *1√ghamb* (to move) घम्बति घम्बिष्यति अघम्बत् घम्बतु घम्बेत् *घम्बित घम्बनीय घम्बित्वा घम्बितुम्

घर्व् *1√gharv* (to go) घर्वति घर्विष्यति अघर्वत् घर्वतु घर्वेत् *घर्वित घर्वणीय घर्वितव्य घर्वित्वा घर्वितुम्

घस् *1√ghas* (to eat more) घसति-घस्ति घस्यति अघसत् घसतु घसेत् *घस्त घस्तव्य घस्तव्य घस्त्वा घस्तुम् घस्मर

घिण्ण् *1√ghiṇṇ* (to take) घिण्णते घिण्णिष्यति अघिण्णत घिण्णताम् घिण्णेत *घिण्णित घिण्णनीय घिण्णितव्य घिण्णित्वा

घु *1√ghu* (to murmur, hum, chatter, garble, make indistinct sound) घवते घोष्यते अघवत घवताम् घवेत *घुत

घुट् *1√ghuṭ* (to move back, come back, return) घोटते घोटिष्यते अघोटत घोटताम् घोटेत *घुटित घोटनीय घोटितुम्

घुट् *6√ghuṭ* (to fight back, retaliate, protect) घुटति घुटिष्यति अघुटत् घुटतु घुटेत् *घुटित घुटनीय घुटित्वा घुटितुम्

घुड् *6√ghuḍ* (to prevent, defend) घुडति घुडिष्यति अघुडत् घुडतु घुडेत् *घुडित घुडनीय घुडित्वा घुडितुम्

घुण् *1√ghuṇ* (to take, receive) घुणते घुणिष्यति अघुणत घुणताम् घुणेत *घुणित घुणनीय घुणितव्य घुणित्वा घुणितुम्

घुण् *6√ghuṇ* (to return, stagger, reel, whirl) घुणति घुणिष्यति अघुणत् घुणतु घुणेत् *घुणित घुणनीय घुणित्वा

घुण्ण् *1√ghuṇṇ* (to receive) घुण्णते घुण्णिष्यते अघुण्णत घुण्णताम् घुण्णेत *घुण्णित घुण्णनीय घुण्णितव्य घुण्णित्वा

घुर् *1,6√ghur* (to snore) घुरति घोरिष्यति अघुरत् घुरतु घुरेत् अघूरिष्ट-अघूर्णीत् *घूरित घूरणीय घूरितव्य घूरित्वा घूरितुम्

घुर् *4√ghur* (to hurt, grow old, get old, age) घूर्यते घूर्यत् घूरिष्यते अघूर्यत घूर्यताम् घूर्येत अघूरिष्ट *घूर्ण

घुष् *1√ghuṣ* (to make noise) घोषति घोषिष्यति अघोषत् घोषतु घोषेत् घोष्यते *घोषित घोषणीय घोषितुम् घोष घोषणा

घुष् *10√ghuṣ* (to make noise) घोषयति-ते घोषयिष्यति अघोषयत् घोषयतु घोषयेत् *घोषित घोषयित्वा घोषयितुम्

धूप् *10√dhūp* (to be hot) धूपयति-ते धूपयिष्यति-ते अधूपयत्-त धूपयतु-ताम् धूपयेत्-त *धूपित or धूप्त

घूर् *4√ghūr* (to become old) घूर्यते घूरिष्यते अघूर्यत घूर्यताम् घूर्येत *घूरित घूरणीय घूरितव्य घूरित्वा घूरितुम् घोर

घूर्ण् *1√ghūrṇ* (to wander, go around) घूर्णते घूर्णिष्यते अघूर्णत घूर्णताम् घर्णेत अघूरिष्ट *घूर्णित घूर्णितव्य घूर्णितुम्

घूर्ण् *6√ghūrṇ* (to waver) घूर्णति घूर्णिष्यति अघूर्णत् घूर्णतु घुर्णेत् अघूर्णीत् *घूर्णित-घूर्ण घूर्णितव्य घूर्णितुम्

घृ *1√ghṛ* (to give water, irrigate, drip, reel, whirl) घरति घरिष्यति अघरत् घरतु घरेत् अघार्षीत् *घृत

घृ *3√ghṛ* (to shine, drip) जिघर्ति घरिष्यति जिघर्तु जिघृयात् *घृत घर्तव्य घर्त्वा घर्तुम् घृणा घृणि घृत

घृ *10√ghṛ* (to give water, irrigate, drip, reel, whirl) घारयति घारयिष्यति अघर्षयत् घर्षयतु घर्षयेत् *घारित

घृण् *8√ghṛṇ* (to shine) घृणोति-घर्णोति-घृणते-घर्णुते घर्णिष्यति अघृणोत् घृणोतु घृणुयात् अघर्णिष्ट *घृत

घृण्ण् *1√ghṛṇṇ* (to take) घृण्णते घृण्णिष्यते अघृण्णत घृण्णताम् घृण्णेत *घृण्णित घृण्णनीय घृण्णितव्य घृण्णित्वा

घृष् *1√ghṛṣ* (to rub, crash, pound, grind) घर्षति-ते घर्षिष्यति अघर्षत् घर्षतु घर्षेत् *घृष्ट-घर्षित घर्षणीय

घ्रा *1√ghrā* (to smell, smell at, kiss) जिघ्रति घ्रास्यति अजिघ्रत् जिघ्रतु जिघ्रेत् *घ्रात-घ्राण घ्राणीय घ्रातव्य घ्रेय घ्रात्वा

(ङ) (ṅ)

ङु *1√ṅu* (to sound) ङवते ङविष्यते अङवत ङवतु ङवेत *ङवित ङवितुम्

(च) (ć)

चक् *1√ćak* (to cheat, be satisfied) चकति-ते चकिष्यते अचकत चकताम् चकेत *चकित चकनीय चाक्य चकित्वा

चकास् *2√ćakās* (to glitter, shine, be bright) चकास्ति चकात्स्यति अचकात् चकातु चकास्यात् *चकासित चकास्य

चक्क् *10√ćakk* (to inflict pain or trouble, be unhappy) चक्कयति-ते चक्कयिष्यति अचक्कयत् चक्कयतु चक्कयेत्

चक्ष् *2√ćakṣ* (to see, recognize, perceive) चष्टे ख्यास्यते अचष्ट चष्टाम् चक्षीत *ख्यात-क्शात आख्या व्याख्या चक्षु

चञ्च् *1√ćañć* (to droop, move, wave, shake, leap, jump) चञ्चति चञ्चिष्यति अचञ्चत् चञ्चतु चञ्चेत् *चञ्चित

चट् *1√ćaṭ* (to rain, break, fall off, separate) चटति चटिष्यति अचटत् चटतु चटेत् *चटित चटनीय चटित्वा चटितुम्

चट् *10√ćaṭ* (to hit, break, pierce, injure) चाटयति-ते चाटयिष्यति-ते अचाटयत्-त चाटयतु-ताम् चाटयेत्-त *चाटित

चण् *1√ćaṇ* (to go, give, sound, go, injure, hurt, kill) चणति चणिष्यति अचणत् चणतु चणेत् *चणित चणनीय चण्ड्

1√ćaṇḍ (to agitate, be angry) चण्डते चण्डिष्यते अचण्डत चण्डताम् चण्डेत *चण्डित चण्डनीय चण्डितव्य चण्ड्

10√ćaṇḍ (to disturb) चण्डयति-ते चण्डयिष्यति-ते अचण्डयत्-त चण्डयतु-ताम् चण्डयेत्-त *चण्डित चण्डी

चत् *1√ćat* (to demand) चतति-ते चतिष्यति अचतत् चततु चतेत् *चतित चतनीय चतितव्य चतित्वा चतितुम्

चद् *1√ćad* (to beg, ask, request) चदति चदिष्यति अचदत् चदतु चदेत् *चदित चदनीय चदितव्य चदित्वा चदितुम्

चन् *1√ćan* (to injure, make sound) चनति चनिष्यति अचनत्-अचानत् चनतु चनेत् *चनित चननीय चनितव्य चनित्वा

चन् *10√ćan* (to believe) चानयति-ते चानयिष्यति-ते अचानयत्-त चानयतु-ताम् चानयेत्-त *चानित चनयितुम्

चन्द् *1√ćand* (to shine, be pleased) चन्दति चन्दिष्यति अचन्दत् चन्दतु चन्देत् *चन्दित चन्दनीय चन्दित्वा चन्दितुम्

चप् *1√ćap* (to encourage, console, soothe) चपति चपयिष्यति अचपत् चपतु चपेत् *चप्त-चपित चपनीय

चप् *10√ćap* (to grind, kneed, pound; cheat) चपयति-ते चपयिष्यति-ते अचपयत्-त चपयतु-ताम् चपयेत्-त *चपित

चम् *1√ćam* (to sip, drink, eat) आ-चमति चमिष्यति अचमत् चमतु चमेत् आ-चम्यते *चान्त चाम्य चान्त्वा चमितुम्

चम् *5√ćam* (to eat) चम्नोति चमिष्यति अचम्नोत् चम्नोतु चम्नुयात् *चान्त चान्तव्य चान्त्वा चान्तुम् चान्त्वा-चमित्वा

चम्प् *10√ćamp* (to go, move) चम्पयति-ते चम्पयिष्यति-ते अचम्पयत्-त चम्पयतु-ताम् चम्पयेत्-त *चम्पित

चम्ब् *1√ćamb* (to move, go) चम्बति चम्बिष्यति अचम्बत् चम्बतु चम्बेत् *चम्बित चम्बितव्य चम्बितुम्

चय् *1√ćay* (to go, go towards) चयते चयिष्यते अचयत चयताम् चयेत *चयित चयनीय चयितव्य चयित्वा चयितुम्

चर् *1√ćar* (to move) चरति-ते चरिष्यते अचरत् चरतु चरेत् *चरित चरणीय चरितव्य चरितुम् चर चरित्र चराचर चरिष्णु

चर् *10√ćar* (to doubt) वि-चारयति-ते चारयिष्यति-ते अचारयत्-त चारयतु-ताम् चारयेत्-त *वि-चारित विचार

चर्च् *1√ćarć* (to talk, hurt, injure, hit) चर्चति चर्चिष्यति अचर्चत् चर्चतु चर्चेत् *चर्चित चर्चितव्य चर्चितुम्

चर्च् *6√ćarć* (to talk, rebuke, abuse, condemn, menace) चर्चति चर्चिष्यति अचर्चत् चर्चतु चर्चेत् *चर्चित चर्चा

चर्च् *10√ćarć* (to read carefully, do study) चर्चयति-ते चर्चयिष्यति-ते अचर्चयत्-त चर्चयतु-ताम् चर्चयेत्-त *चर्चित

चर्ब् *1√ćarb* (to eat, chew; go, move) चर्बति चर्बिष्यति अचर्बत् चर्बतु चर्बेत् *चर्बित चर्बितव्य चर्बित्वा चर्बितुम्

चर्व् *1√ćarv* (to chew, chop, eat, bite) चर्वति चर्विष्यति अचर्वत् चर्वतु चर्वेत् *चर्वित चर्वितव्य चर्वित्वा चर्वितुम्

चल् *1√ćal* (to move, shake, throb, palpitate, stir) चलति चलिष्यति अचलत् चलतु चलेत् अचालीत् *चलित

चल् *6√ćal* (to frolic, sport, play) चलति चीलष्यति अचलत् चलतु चलेत् चल्यते *चलित चलनीय चलित्वा चलितुम्

चल् *10√ćal* (to foster) चालयति-ते चालयिष्यति-ते अचालयत्-त चालयतु-ताम् चालयेत्-त *चालित चालयितुम्

चष् *1√ćaṣ* (to eat, injure, hurt, kill) चषति-ते चषिष्यति-ते अचषत्-त चषतु-ताम् चषेत्-त *चष्ट चषितव्य चषितुम्

चह् *1√ćah* (to cheat, deceive, be proud or haughty) चहति चहिष्यते अचहत चहताम् चहेत चह्यते *चहित-चाढ

चह् *10√ćah* (to be evil) चहयति-ते चहयिष्यति-ते अचहयत्-त चहयतु-ताम् चहयेत्-त *चहित-चाढ चहनीय चहयितुम्

चाय् *1√ćāy* (to discern, see, observe) चायति-ते चायिष्यति अचायत् चायतु चायेत् अचायीत्-अचायिष्ट *चायित

चि *5√ći* (to gather) चिनोति-चिनुते चेष्यति-ते अचिनोत्-अचिनुत चिनोतु-चिनुताम् चिनुयात्-चिन्वीत *चित चयनीय

चि *10√ći* (to gather) चयति-चपयति-चययति-ते चप-चययिष्यति-ते अचपयत्-त चपयतु-ताम् चपयेत्-त चीयते *चित

चिक्क् *10√ćikk* (to harass) चिक्कयति-ते चिक्कयिष्यति-ते अचिक्कयत्-त चिक्कयतु-ताम् चिक्कयेत्-त *चिक्कित

चिट् *1√ćiṭ* (to send forth someone) चेटति चेटिष्यति अचेटत् चेटतु चेटेत् *चेटित चेटनीय चेटितव्य चेटित्वा चेटितुम्

चिट् *10√ćiṭ* (to dispatch) चेटयति-ते चेटयिष्यति-ते अचेटयत्-त चेटयतु-ताम् चेटयेत्-त अचेटीत् *चेटित चेटितुम्

चित् *1√ćit* (to perceive, notice, observe, aim, intend) चेतति चेतिष्यति अचेतत् चेततु चेतेत *चित्त चेतनीय

चित् *10√ćit* (to be aware) चेतयते चेतयिष्यते अचेतयत चेतयताम् चेतयेत चेतयाञ्चक्रे चेतयिता चेतयिषीष्ट चेत्यते

चित्र् *10√ćit* (to draw, sketch) चित्रयति-ते चित्रयिष्यति-ते अचित्रयत्-त चित्रयतु-ताम् चित्रयेत्-त *चित्रित चित्रणीय चित्र

चिन्त् *10√ćint* (to think, reflect) चिन्तयति-ते चिन्तयिष्यति-ते अचिन्तयत्-त चिन्तयत्-ताम् चिन्तयेत्-त *चिन्तित

चिल् *6√ćil* (to wear, put on clothes) चेलति चेलिष्यति अचेलत् चेलतु चेलेत् *चेलित चेलितव्य चेलितमि्

चिल्ल् *1√ćill* (to be loose, slack, flaccid, act wantonly) चिल्लति चिल्लिष्यति अचिल्लत् चिल्लतु *चिल्लित

चिह्न् *10√ćihn* (to aim, mark, stamp) चिह्नयति-ते चिह्नयिष्यति-ते अचिह्नयत्-त चिह्नयत्-ताम् चिह्नयेत्-त *चिह्नित

चीक् *1√ćik* (to suffer, endure, bear; touch) चीकति चीकिष्यति अचीकत् चीकतु चीकेत् *चीकित चीकितुम्

चीक् *10√ćik* (to suffer) चीकयति-ते चीकयिष्यति-ते अचीकयत्-त चीकयतु-ताम् चीकयेत्-त *चीकित चीकयितव्य

चीभ् *1√ćibh* (to brag, swagger, coax, wheedle, flatter) चीभते चीभिष्यति अचीभत् चीभतु चीभेत् *चीब्ध

चीव् *1√ćiv* (to wear cover, take, receive, seize) चीवति-ते अचीवत् चीवतु चीवेत् *चीवित चीवनीय चीवित्वा

चीव् *10√ćiv* (to speak, shine) चीवयति-ते चीवयिष्यति-ते अचीवयत्-त चीवयतु-ताम् चीवयेत्-त *चीवित

चुक्क् *10√ćukk* (to inflict or suffer pain) चुक्कयति-ते चुक्कयिष्यति अचुक्कयत् चुक्कयतु चुक्कयेत् *चुक्कित

चुच्य् *1√ćućy* (to bathe) चुच्यति चेच्यिष्यति अचुच्यत् चुच्यतु चुच्येत् *चुच्यित चुच्यनीय चुच्यितव्य चुच्यित्वा

चुट् *6√ćuṭ* (to cut off, divide) चुटति चुटिष्यति अचुटत् चुटतु चुटेत् *चुटित चुटनीय चुटितव्य चुटित्वा चुटितुम्

चुट् *10√ćuṭ* (to become diminished, wane) चोटयति चोटयिष्यति-ते अचोटयत्-त चोटयतु-ताम् चोटयेत्-त

चुट्ट् *10√ćuṭṭ* (to go short, become small) चुट्टयति-ते चुट्टयिष्यति-ते अचुट्टयत्-त चुट्टयतु-ताम् चुट्टयेत्-त *चुट्टित

चुड् *6√ćuḍ* (to conceal, hide) चुडति चुडिष्यति अचुडत् चुडतु चुडेत् *चुडित चुडनीय चुडितव्य चुडितुम्

चुड्ड् *1√ćuḍḍ* (to do, act, dally) चुड्डति चुड्डिष्यति अचुड्डत् चुड्डतु चुड्डेत् *चुड्डित चुड्डनीय चुड्डितव्य चुड्डित्वा चुड्डितुम्

चुण् *6√ćuṇ* (to cut off) चुणति चुणिष्यति अचुणत चुणतु चुणेत् *चुणित चुणितव्य चुणित्वा चुणितुम्

चुण्ट् *1√ćuṇṭ* (to cut) चुण्टति चुण्टिष्यति अचुण्टत् चुण्टतु चुण्टेत् *चुण्टित चुण्टनीय चुण्टितव्य चुण्टित्वा चुण्टितुम्

चुण्ट् *10√ćuṇṭ* (to cut, become small) चुण्टयति चुण्टयिष्यति अचुण्टयत् चुण्टयतु चुण्टयेत् *चुण्टित चुण्टितुम्

चुण्ड् *1√ćuṇḍ* (to go short) चुण्डति चुण्डिष्यति अचुण्डत् चुण्डतु चुण्डेत् *चुण्डित चुण्डनीय चुण्डितव्य चुण्डित्वा

चुत् *1√ćut* (to ooze, leak, trickle) चोतति चोतिष्यति अचोतत् चोततु चोतेत् *चोतित चोतनीय चोतितव्य चोतित्वा

चुद् *1√ćud* (to impel, inspire, excite, enjoin, solicit) चोदति चोदिष्यति अचोदत् चोदतु चोदेत् *चोदित चोदनीय

चुद् *10√ćud* (to send, suggest, instigate, inspire) चोदयति-ते चोदयिष्यति-ते अचोदयत्-त चोदयतु-ताम् चोदयेत्-त

चुप् *1√ćup* (to stir, crawl, move slowly) चोपति चोपिष्यति अचोपत् चोपतु चोपेत् *चोपित चोप्य चोपित्वा

चुम्ब् *1√ćumb* (to kiss, touch softly) चुम्बति चुम्बिष्यति अचुम्बत् चुम्बतु चुम्बेत् *चुम्बित चुम्बनीय चुम्बितुम् चुम्बन

चुम्ब् *10√ćumb* (to strike) चुम्बयति-ते चुम्बयिष्यति-ते अचुम्बयत्-त चुम्बयतु-ताम् चुम्बयेत्-त *चुम्बित चुम्बितुम्

चुर् *10√ćur* (to steal, rob; take, have, possess) चोरयति-ते चोरयिष्यति-ते अचोरयत्-त चोरयत्-ताम् चोरयेत्-त चोरयते *चोरित चोरयत् चोरणीय चोरितव्य चोर्य चोरयित्वा चोरयितुम् चोर्यमाण चौर चोर चोरण-चोरणा

चुल् *10√ćul* (to grow) चोलयति-ते चोलिप्थति-ते अचोलयत्-त चोलयतु-ताम् चोलयेत्-त *चोलित चोलित्वा चोलितुम्

चुलुम्प् *1√ćulump* (to swing) चुलुम्पति चुलुम्पिष्यति अचुलुम्पत् चुलुम्पतु चुलुम्पेत् *चुलुम्पित चुलुम्पितुम्

चुल्ल् *1√ćull* (to play, sport, conjecture) चुल्लति चुल्लिष्यति अचुल्लत् चुल्लतु चुल्लेत् *चुल्लित चुल्लितुम्

चूण् *10√ćūṇ* (to contract, close, shrink) चूणयति-ते चूणयिष्यति-ते अचूणयत्-त चूणयतु-ताम् चूणयेत्-त *चूणित

चूर् *4√ćūr* (to burn) चूर्यते चूरिष्यते अचूर्यत चूर्यताम् चूर्येत अचूरिष्ट *चूरित चूरणीय चूरितव्य चूरित्वा चूरितुम्

चूर्ण् *10√ćūrṇ* (to pound, pulverize) चूर्णयति-ते चुर्णयिष्यति-ते अचुर्णयत्-त चुर्णयत्-ताम् चुर्णयेत्-त *चूर्णित चूर्ण

चूष् *1√ćūṣ* (to suck, drink) चूषति चूषिष्यति अचूषत् चूषतु चूषेत् *चूषित-चूष्ट चूषत् चूषितव्य चूषितुम् चूषण चूषा

चृत् *6√ćṛt* (to bind, hurt) चृतति चर्तिष्यति अचृतत् चृततु चृतेत् *चृत चर्तनीय चर्तितव्य चर्त्य चर्तित्वा चर्तितुम्

चृत् *10√ćṛt* (to kindle, light) चर्तयति-ते चर्तयिष्यति-ते अचर्तयत्-त चर्तयतु-ताम् चर्तयेत्-त *चर्तित चर्तयितुम्

चेल् *1√ćel* (to walk, go, move, be disturbed, shake) चेलति चेलिष्यति अचेलत् चेलतु चेलेत् *चेलित चेलनीय

चेष्ट् *1√ćeṣṭ* (to try, make effort, endeavor, struggle) चेष्टते चेष्टिष्यते अचेष्टत चेष्टताम् चेष्टेत *चेष्टित चेष्टा

च्यु *1√ćyu* (to ooze, flow, come out, trickle, drop) च्यवति-ते च्यविष्यते अच्यवत च्यवताम् च्यवेत *च्युत च्यवनीय
च्यु *10√ćyu* (to tolerate, endure) च्यावयति-ते च्यावयिष्यते अच्यावयत्-त च्यावयतु-ताम् च्यावयेत्-त *च्यावित
च्युत् *1√ćyut* (to drip, stream forth, fall) च्योतति च्योतिष्यति अच्योतत् च्योततु च्योतेत *च्युतित च्योतनीय च्योतित्वा
च्युस् *10√ćyus* (to laugh, hurt) च्योसयति-ते च्योसयिष्यति-ते अच्योसयत्-त च्योसयतु-ताम् चोसयेत्-त *त *च्योसित

(छ) (ćh)

छद् *1√ćhad* (to hide, veil, cover, conceal, spread, eat) छदति छदिष्यति अछदत् छदतु छदेत् छाद्यते *छत्त-छादित
छद् *10√ćhad* (to hide) आ+छादयति-ते आच्छादति-ते छादयिष्यति-ते अछादयत्-त छादयत्-ताम् छादयेत्-त *छादित
छन्द् *10√ćhand* (to please, gratify; persuade) छन्दयति-ते छन्दयिष्यति अछन्दयत् छन्दयतु छन्दयेत् *छन्दित
छम् *1√ćham* (to eat, consume) छमति छमिष्यति अछमत् छमतु छमेत् *छान्त छमनीय छमितव्य छमित्वा छमितुम्
छम्प् *1√ćhamp* (to go, move) छम्पति छम्पिष्यति अछम्पत् छम्पतु छम्पेत् *छम्पित छम्पनीय छम्पितव्य छम्पित्वा
छम्प् *10√ćhamp* (to move) छम्पयति-ते छम्पयिष्यति-ते अछम्पयत्-त छम्पयतु-ताम् छम्पयेत्-त *छम्पित
छर्द् *10√ćhard* (to vomit, throw up) छर्दयति-ते छर्दयिष्यति अछर्दयत् छर्दयतु छर्दयेत् *छर्दित छर्दयितुम्
छष् *1√ćhaṣ* (to injure, hurt, kill) छषति-ते छषिष्यति अछषत् छषतु छषेत् *छषित-छष्ट छषनीय छषितव्य छषितुम्
छा *1√ćhā* (to cut up, chop, mow, reap) छाति छायिष्यति अछायत् छायतु छायेत् *छात-छित छात्वा छातुम्
छिद् *7√ćhid* (to cut off, lop off) छिनत्ति-छिन्ते छेत्स्यति-ते अछिनत्-त छिनत्तु-ताम् छिन्द्यात्-त *छिन्न छेदनीय छेत्तुम्
छिद्र् *10√ćhid* (to bore) छिद्रयति-ते छिद्रयिष्यति-ते अछिद्रयत्-त छिद्रयतु-ताम् छिद्रयेत्-त *छिद्रित छिद्रयितुम् छिद्र
छुट् *6√ćhuṭ* (to cut, clip off) छुटति छुटिष्यति अछुटत् छुटतु छुटेत् *छुटित छुटनीय छुटितव्य छुटित्वा छुटितुम् छोटिका
छुट् *10√ćhuṭ* (to cut) छोटयति-ते छोटयिष्यति-ते अछोटयत्-त छोटयतु-ताम् छोटयेत्-त *छुटित छोटयित्वा छोटयितुम्
छुड् *6√ćhuḍ* (to hide, screen, cover) छुडति छुडिष्यति अछुडत् छुडतु छुडेत् *छुडित छुडितव्य छुडितुम्
छुप् *6√ćhup* (to touch, make contact) छुपति छोप्स्यति अछुपत् छुपतु छुपेत् अच्छौप्सीत *छुपित-छुप्त
छुर् *6√ćhur* (to cut, divide, engrave, smear, coat) छुरति छुरिष्यति अछुरत् छुरतु छुरेत् चुछोर छुर्यते *छुर्ण छुरितुम्
छृ *7√ćhṛ* (to shine, glitter, play, sport) छृणत्ति-छृन्ते छर्दिष्यति-ते छत्स्र्यति-ते अछर्दत् छदर्तु छर्देत् *छृत
छृद् *10√ćhṛd* (to spew, vomit, pour out) छर्दयति-ते छर्दयिष्यति-ते अछर्दयत्-त छर्दयतु-ताम् छर्दयेत्-त *छर्दित
छृद् *7√ćhṛd* (to spew) छृणाति छर्दिष्यति अच्छृणत् छृणत्तु छृन्द्यात् *च्छृण्ण छर्दनीय छर्दितव्य छर्दयित्वा छर्दयितुम्
छृष् *10√ćhṛṣ* (to request, beg, ask) छर्षयति-ते छर्षयिष्यति-ते अछर्षयत्-त छर्षयतु-ताम् छर्षयेत्-त *छर्षित-छृष्ट
छेद् *10√ćhed* (to divide, severe, cut) छेदयति-ते छेदयिष्यति-ते अछेदयत्-त छेदयतु-ताम् छेदयेत्-त *छिन्न
छो *4√ćho* (to cut, chop, mow, reap) छ्यति छास्यति अच्छ्यत् छ्यतु छ्येत् अच्छासीत् *छात-छित छात्वा-छित्वा
छ्यु *1√ćhyu* (to approach, go, move) छ्यवते छ्योष्यते-छ्यविष्यते अछ्यवत छ्यवताम् छ्यवेत *छ्यवित

(ज) (j)

जंस् *10√jaṁs* (to protect) जंसयति जंसयिष्यति-ते अजंसयत्-त जंसयतु-ताम् जंसयेत्-त *जंसित जंसयितुम् जंसनीय

जक्ष् *2√jakṣ* (to eat, eat up, consume, destroy) जष्टे जक्षिष्यते अजष्ट जष्टाम् जक्षीत *जक्षित जक्षणीय जक्ष्य

जज् *1√jaj* (to fight, battle) जजति जजिष्यति अजाजत्-अजजत् जजतु जजेत् *जजित जजनीय जजित्वा जजितुम्

जञ्ज् *1√jañj* (to fight) जञ्जति जञ्जिष्यति अञ्जजत् जञ्जतु जञ्जेत् *जञ्जित जञ्जनीय जञ्जितव्य जञ्जित्वा

जञ्झ् *1√jañjh* (to bang, make a dashing sound) जञ्झति जञ्झिष्यति अजञ्झत् जञ्झतु जञ्झेत् *जञ्झित

जट् *1√jaṭ* (to tangle) जटति जटिष्यति अजाटत्-अजटत् जटतु जटेत् *जटित जटनीय जटितव्य जटित्वा जटितुम्

जड् *1√jaḍ* (to join) जडति जडिष्यति अजाडत्-अजडत् जडतु जडेत् *जडित जडनीय जडित्वा जडितुम्

जन् *3√jan* (to give birth, beget) जजन्ति जनिष्यति अजजत् जजन्तु जिजायात् अजनीत्-अजानीत् *जात

जन् *4√jan* (to be born, produced, give birth, beget) जायते जनिष्यते अजायत जायताम् जायेत् जन्यते *जात-जनित जायमान जननीय जनितव्य जन्य जनित्वा जनितुम् जन्म जन जनक जाया जठर अज द्विज बीज जन्तु जाति प्रजन प्रजा

जप् *1√jap* (to repeat internally, utter in low voice) जपति जपिष्यति अजपत् जपतु जपेत् *जपित-जप्त जाप्य जप

जभ् *1√jabh* (to copulate, yawn, gape, snap) जम्भते जम्भिष्यते अजम्भत जम्भताम् जम्भेत *जब्ध जम्भनीय जम्भित्वा

जम् *1√jam* (to eat) जमति जमिष्यति अजमत् जमतु जमेत् *जान्त जमनीय जाम्य जमित्वा-जान्त्वा जमितुम्

जम्भ् *1√jambh* (to yawn) जम्भते जम्भिष्यते अजम्भत् जम्भतु जम्भेत् *जम्भित-जब्ध जम्भनीय जम्भा

जम्भ् *10√jambh* (to destroy) जम्भयति-ते जम्भयिष्यति-ते अजम्भयत्-त जम्भयतु-ताम् जम्भयेत्-त *जम्भित-जब्ध

जर्च् *1√jarć* (to say, speak, blame, reprove, censure, threaten) जर्चति जर्चिष्यति अजर्चत् जर्चतु जर्चेत् *जर्चित

जर्च् *6√jarć* (to say, menace) जर्चति जर्चिष्यति अजर्चत् जर्चतु जर्चेत् *जर्चित जर्चितव्य जर्चित्वा जर्चितुम्

जर्छ् *1√jarćh* (to say) जर्छति जर्छिष्यति अजर्छत् जर्छतु जर्छेत् *जर्छित जर्छनीय जर्छितव्य जर्छित्वा जर्छितुम्

जर्छ् *6√jarćh* (to say) जर्छति जर्छिष्यति अजर्छत् जर्छतु जर्छेत् *जर्छित जर्छनीय जर्छितव्य जर्छित्वा जर्छितुम्

जर्ज् *1√jarj* (to slap) जर्जति जर्जिष्यति अजर्जत् जर्जतु जर्जेत् *जर्जित जर्जितव्य जर्जित्वा जर्जितुम्

जर्ज् *6√jarj* (to criticize) जर्जति जर्त्स्यति अजर्जत् जर्जतु जर्जेत् *जर्जित जर्जितव्य जर्जित्वा जर्जितुम्

जर्झ् *6√jarjh* (to say, blame, threaten) जर्झति जर्झिष्यति अजर्झत् जर्झतु जर्झेत् *जर्झित जर्झितव्य जर्झितुम्

जर्त्स् *6√jarts* (to abuse, criticize) जर्त्सति जर्त्सिष्यति अजर्त्सत् जर्त्सतु जर्त्सेत् *जर्त्सित जर्त्सितव्य जर्त्सितुम्

जल् *1√jal* (to be bright, wealthy, rich; to encircle, entangle) जलति जलिष्यति अजलत् जलतु जलेत् *जलित

जल् *10√jal* (to cover, screen) जालयति-ते जालयिष्यति-ते अजालयत्-त जालयतु-ताम् जालयेत्-त *जालित

जल्प् *1√jalp* (to talk, murmur chatter, babble, prattle)जल्पति जल्पिष्यति अजल्पत् जल्पतु जल्पेत् *जल्पित जल्प

जष् *1√jaṣ* (to injure, hurt, kill) जषति जषिष्यति अजषत् जषतु जषेत् अजषीत् *जषित-जष्ट जष्टव्य जष्ट्वा

जंस् *10√jaṁs* (to protect, save) जंसयति-ते जंसयिष्यति-ते अजंसयत्-त जंसयतु-ताम् जंसयेत्-त *जंसित

जस् *4√jas* (to liberate, set free, release) जस्यति जसिष्यति अजस्यत् जस्यतु जस्येत् *जसित जसनीय जसितुम्

जस् *10√jas* (to hate, hurt, disregard) जासयति-ते जासयिष्यति-ते अजासयत्-त जासयतु-ताम् जासयेत्-त *जासित

जागृ *2√jāgṛ* (to stay awake) जागर्ति जागरिष्यति अजागः जागर्तु जागृयात् *जागरित जागरणीय जागरितुम् जागरुक

जि *1√ji* (to win, conquer, defeat, vanquish, control) जयति जेष्यति अजयत् जयतु जयेत् जीयते *जीत-विजित-पराजित जयत् जयनीय जेतव्य जय्य जित्वा विजित्य जीयमान जापयितुम् जिगीषा जिष्णु जय पराजय जयी जयिनी जेय

जि *10√ji* (to win) जापयति-ते जापयिष्यति-ते अजापयत्-त जापयतु-ताम् जापयेत्-त *जापित जापयित्वा जापयितुम्

जिन्व् *1√jinv* (to please) जिन्वति जिन्विष्यति अजिन्वत् जिन्वतु जिन्वेत् *जिन्वित जिन्वितव्य जिन्वित्वा जिन्वितुम्

जिन्व् *10√jinv* (to speak, confer) जिन्वयति-ते जिन्वयिष्यति-ते अजिन्वयत्-त जिन्वयतु-ताम् जिन्वयेत्-त *जिन्वित

जिम् *1√jim* (to eat, consume) जेमति जेमिष्यति अजेमत् जेमतु जेमेत् *जेमित जेमनीय जेमितव्य जेमित्वा जेमितुम्

जिरि *5√jiri* (to hurt, kill) जिरिणोति जेरिष्यति अजिरिणोत् जिरिणोतु जिरिणुयात् *जिरित जिरितव्य जिरितुम्

जिष् *1√jiṣ* (to spray, sprinkle) जेषति जेषिष्यति अजेषत् जेषतु जेषेत् अजैषीत् *जेषित-जिष्ट जेषितव्य जेषितुम्

जीव् *1√jīv* (to live, be alive, come to life, revive) जीवति जीविष्यति अजीवत् जीवतु जीवेत् *जीवित जीव्य जीव

जु *1√ju* (to walk fast) जवति जविष्यति अजवत् जवतु जवेत् अजवीत् *जवित जवनीय जवितव्य जवित्वा जवितुम्

जु *9√ju* (to be swift) जुनाति-जुनीते जविष्यति-ते अजुनात्-नीत जुनातु-जुनीताम् जुनीयात्-जुनीत *ववित-जुन

जुङ्ग् *1√juṅg* (to sacrifice, abandon, set aside, exclude) जुङ्गति जुङ्गिष्यति अजुङ्गत् जुङ्गतु जुङ्गेत् *जुङ्गित जुङ्गित्वा

जुट् *6√juṭ* (to bind, tie together) जुटति जुटिष्यति अजुटत् जुटतु जुटेत् *जुटित जुटनीय जुटितव्य जुटित्वा जुटितुम्

जुड् *6√juḍ* (to send) जुडति जोडिष्यति अजोडत् जुडतु जुडेत् *जुडित जुडत् जुडनीय जुडितव्य जुडित्वा जुडितुम्

जुड् *10√juḍ* (to throw, cast; grind) जुडयति जोडयिष्यति अजुडयत्-त जुडयतु-ताम् जुडयेत्-त *जुडित जुडितुम्

जुत् *1√jut* (to shine, give out light) जोतते जोतिष्यते अजोतत जोतताम् जोतेत अजोतिष्ट जोत्यते *जुतित

जुन् *6√jun* (to move) जुनति जुनिष्यति अजुनत् जुनोतु जुनेत् *जुनित जुनितव्य जुनित्वा जुनितुम्

जुर् *1,6√jur* (to consume) जुर्वति जुर्विष्यति अजुर्वत् जर्वतु जुर्वेत् *जूर्ण जुरितुम् जुरणीय जुर्य

जुर् *4√jur* (to decay, become or grow old, perish) जुर्यते जूरिष्यते अजूर्यत जूर्यताम् जूर्येत *जूर्ण

जुल् *10√jul* (to grind, reduce to powder) जुलयति-ते जुलयिष्यति-ते अजुलयत्-त जुलयतु-ताम् जुलयेत्-त *जुलित

जुष् *1√juṣ* (to be pleased, be satisfied) जोषति जोषिष्यते अजोषत् जोषतु जोषेत् जोष्यते *जोषित-जुष्ट जुष्टव्य जुष्ट्वा

जुष् *6√juṣ* (to cheer up, inspire) जूषते जोषिष्यते अजुषत जुषताम् जुषेत *जुष्ट जोषणीय जोषितव्य जोषित्वा जोषितुम्

जुष् *10√juṣ* (to be pleased) जोषयति जाषयिष्यते अजोषयत् जोषयतु जोषयेत् अजूषीत् *जुष्ट-जोषित

जुष् *10√juṣ* (to examine) जोषयति-ते जोषयिष्यति-ते अजोषयत्-त जोषयतु-ताम् जोषयेत्-त *जोषित-जुष्ट

जूर् *6√jūr* (to become old, decay, wear out) जुरति जुरिष्यति अजुरत् जुरतु जुर्येत् *जूर्ण जुरा

जूष् *1√jūṣ* (to hurt, injure, hit, kill) जूषति जूषिष्यति अजूषत् जूषतु जूषेत् अजूषीत् *जूष्ट

जृभ् *1√jṛbh* (to yawn, gape; open, expand) जृभते *जृभित-जृब्ध जृम्भितव्य जृब्ध्वा जृब्धुम्

जृम्भ् *1√jṛmbh* (to yawn) जृम्भते जृभिष्यते अजृम्भत जृम्भताम् जृम्भेत जम्भ्यते *जृम्भित-जृब्ध

जॄ *1√jṝ* (to grow old, ware out, decay) जरति जरिष्यति अजरत् जरतु जरेत् *जीर्ण जरणीय जीर्णवत् जरितव्य

जॄ *4√jṝ* (to grow old) जीर्यते जरिष्यति-जरीष्यति अजीर्यत् जीर्यतु जीर्येत् जीर्यते *जीर्ण जीर्णवत् जरणीय जरितुम् जरा

जॄ *9√jṝ* (to grow old) जृणाति जरिष्यति-जरीष्यति अजृणात् जृणातु जृणीयात् *जीर्ण जीर्णवत् जरणीय जरितव्य जरितुम्

जॄ *10√jṝ* (to grow old) जारयति-ते जारयिष्यति-ते अजारयत्-त जारयतु-ताम् जारयेत्-त *जीर्ण-जारित जरित्वा-जरीत्वा

जेष् *1√jeṣ* (to go, move) जेषते जेषिष्यते अजेषत जेषताम् जेषेत *जेषित-जेष्ट जेषणीय जेषित्वा जेषितुम्

जेह् *1√jeh* (to try, reach, go towards, exert, gasp, pant) जेहते जेहिष्यते अजेहत जेहताम् जेहेत *जेहित

जै *1√jai* (to wane, perish, decline, decay) जायति जायिष्यति अजायत् जायतु जायेत् *जायित

ज्ञप् *10√jñap* (to know, tell, praise) ज्ञपयति-ते ज्ञपयिष्यति-ते अज्ञपयत्-त ज्ञपयतु-ताम् ज्ञपयेत्-त *ज्ञपित-ज्ञप्त ज्ञप्ति

ज्ञा *9√jñā* (to know) जानाति-जानीते ज्ञास्यति-ते अजानात्-अजानीत जानातु-जानीताम् जानीयात्-जानीत ज्ञायते-ज्ञाप्यते *ज्ञात-ज्ञापित-ज्ञप्त ज्ञानीय-ज्ञापनीय ज्ञातव्य-ज्ञाप्तव्य ज्ञेय-ज्ञाप्य ज्ञात्वा-ज्ञापयित्वा ज्ञातुम्-ज्ञापयितुम् ज्ञान ज्ञानिन् प्रज्ञा संज्ञा

ज्ञा *10√jñā* (to direct, request) आ+ज्ञापयति-ते ज्ञापयिष्यति-ते अज्ञापयत्-त ज्ञापयतु-ताम् ज्ञापयत्-त *ज्ञापित ज्ञापयत्

ज्या *9√jyā* (to grow old) जिनाति ज्यास्यति अजिनात् जिनातु जिनीयात् *जीन ज्यानीय ज्यातव्य ज्येय जीत्वा ज्यातुम्

ज्यु *1√jyu* (to live, approach, go near) ज्यवते ज्यविष्यते अज्यवत ज्यवताम् ज्यवेत *ज्युत-ज्यवित ज्यवनीय

ज्युत् *1√jyut* (to shine, light) ज्योतति-ते ज्योतिष्यति-ते अज्योतत्-त ज्योततु-ताम् ज्योतेत्-त *ज्योतित

ज्यो *1√jyo* (to give advise, instruct) ज्यवते ज्योष्यते अज्यवत ज्यवताम् ज्यवेत *जीत ज्यवनीय

ज्रि *1√jri* (to press, supress, press deown) ज्रयति ज्रेष्यति अज्रयत् ज्रयतु ज्रयेत् अज्रैषीत् *ज्रयित ज्रयनीय ज्रयितुम्

ज्रि *10√jri* (to grow old) ज्राययति ज्राययिष्यति-ते अज्राययत्-त ज्राययतु-ताम् ज्राययेत्-त *ज्रायित

ज्वर् *1√jwar* (to be sick, feverish) ज्वरति ज्वरिष्यति अज्वरत् ज्वरतु ज्वरेत् *ज्वरित ज्वरणीय ज्वर्यमाण ज्वरितुम् ज्वर

ज्वल् *1√jwal* (to blaze, glow) ज्वलति ज्वलिष्यति अज्वलत् ज्वलतु ज्वलेत् ज्वल्यते *ज्वलित ज्वलितुम् ज्वलन ज्वाला

ज्वल् *10√jwal* (to blaze) ज्वलयति-ते ज्वलयिष्यति-ते अज्वलयत्-त ज्वलयतु-ताम् ज्वलयेत्-त *ज्वालित-ज्वलित

(झ) (jh)

झट् *1√jhaṭ* (to become tangled, matted, interlocked) झटति झटिष्यति अझटत् झटतु झटेत् *झटित झटनीय झटित्वा

झम् *1√jham* (to eat, consume) झमति झमिष्यति अझमत् झमतु झमेत् *झान्त झाम्य झमनीय झमितव्य झमित्वा झमितुम्

झर्च् *6√jharć* (to speak, blame, censure, threaten) झर्चति झर्चिष्यति अझर्चत् झर्चतु झर्चेत् *झर्चित

झर्झ् *1,6√jharjh* (to hit, shout at) झर्झति झर्झिष्यति अझर्झत् झर्झतु झर्झेत् *झर्झित झर्झनीय झर्झितव्य झर्झित्वा

झष् *1√jhaṣ* (to put on, wear, kill) झषति-ते झषिष्यति अझषत् झषतु झषेत् *झषित-झष्ट झषणीय झषितव्य झष

झॄ *4√jhṛ* (to grow old) झीर्यति झरिष्यति-झरीष्यति अझीर्यत् झीर्यतु झीर्येत् झीर्यते *झीर्ण झीर्णवत् झरणीय झरितुम्

झॄ *9√jhṛ* (to grow old, age) झृणाति झरिष्यति-झरीष्यति अझृणात् झृणातु झृणीयात् *झीर्ण

झ्यु *1√jhyu* (to move) झ्यवति झ्यविष्यते अझ्यवत झ्यवताम् झ्यवेत *झ्यवित झ्यवनीय झ्यवितुम्

(ट) (t)

टङ्क् *10√ṭaṅk* (to cover, wrap, cover, tie, bind) टङ्कयति टङ्कयिष्यति अटङ्कयत् टङ्कयतु टङ्कयेत् *टङ्कित टङ्कितुम्

टल् *1√ṭal* (to be uneasy, confused, uneasy) टलति टलिष्यति अटलत् टलतु टलेत् *टलित टालनीय टलितव्य टलित्वा

टिक् *1√ṭik* (to go, move) टेकते टेकिष्यते अटेकत टेकताम् टेकेत *टेकित टेकनीय टेकितव्य टेकित्वा टेकितुम्

टिप् *10√ṭip* (to inspire, direct, throw, cast) टेपयति-ते टेपयिष्यति-ते अटेपयत्-त टेपयतु-ताम् टेपयेत्-त *टेपित-टिप्त

टीक् *1√ṭīk* (to go, resort to) टीकते टीकिष्यते अटीकत टीकताम् टीकेत *टीकित टीकनीय टीकित्वा टीकितुम् टीका

ट्वल् *1√ṭval* (to be uneasy, become disturbed) ट्वलति ट्वलिष्यति अट्वलत् ट्वलतु ट्वलेत् *ट्वलित ट्वलितुम्

<u>(ड) (ḍ)</u>

डप् *10√ḍap* (to collect, amass, heap together) डापयते डापयिष्यते अडापयत डापयताम् डापयेत *डापित

डम् *1√ḍam* (to sound) डमति डमिष्यति अडमत् डमतु डमेत् *डमित डमनीय डमितव्य डमित्वा डमितुम्

डम्प् *10√ḍamp* (to see, order, throw) डम्पयति-ते डम्पयिष्यति-ते अडम्पयत्-त डम्पयतु-ताम् डम्पयेत्-त *डम्पित

डम्ब् *10√ḍamb* (to send, confer, inspire) डम्बयति-ते डम्बयिष्यति-ते अडम्बयत्-त डम्बयतु-ताम् डम्बयेत्-त *डम्बित

डम्भ् *10√ḍambh* (to collect) डम्भयति-ते डम्भयिष्यति-ते अडम्भयत्-त डम्भयतु-ताम् डम्भयेत्-त *डम्भित

डिप् *4√ḍip* (to criticize, throw, cast) डिप्यति डेपिष्यति अडिप्यत् डिप्यतु डिप्येत् *डिप्त डेपयितुम्

डिप् *6√ḍip* (to gather, direct) डिपति डिपिष्यति अडिपत् डिपतु डिपेत् *डिपित डिपितव्य डिपित्वा डिपितुम्

डिप् *10√ḍip* (to gather, heap, collect) डेपयते डेपयिष्यते अडेपयत डेपयताम् डेपयेत *डेपित

डिम्प् *10√ḍimp* (to collect) डिम्पयति-ते डिम्पयिष्यति-ते अडिम्पयत्-त डिम्पयतु-ताम् डिम्पयेत्-त *डिम्पित

डिम्भ् *10√ḍimbh* (to inspire) डिम्भयति-ते डिम्भयिष्यति-ते अडिम्भयत्-त डिम्भयतु-ताम् डिम्भयेत्-त *डिम्भित

डी *1√ḍī* (to fly, fly away, go) डयते डयिष्यते अडयत डीयताम् डीयेत *डीन-डयित डयनीय डयित्वा डयितुम डयन

डी *4√ḍī* (to fly, fly away) उत्+डीयते उड्डयिष्यते अडीयत डीयताम् डीयेत डीयते *डीन डयितुम् उड्डयन

डुल् *10√ḍul* (to throw) डोलयति-ते डोलयिष्यति-ते अडोलयत्-त डोलयतु-ताम् डोलयेत्-त *डोलित डोलयितुम्

ड्वल् *10√ḍval* (to mix) ड्वालयति-ते ड्वालयिष्यति-ते अड्वालयत्-त ड्वालयतु-ताम् ड्वालयेत्-त *ड्वालित

<u>(ढ) (ḍh)</u>

ढुण्ढ् *1√ḍhuṇḍh* (to search) ढुण्ढति ढुण्ढिष्यति अढुण्ढत् ढुण्ढतु ढुण्ढेत् *ढुण्ढित ढुण्ढितव्य ढुण्ढित्वा ढुण्ढितुम्

ढौक् *1√ḍhauk* (to approach, bring near, present, offer) ढौकते ढौकिष्यते अढौकत ढौकताम् ढौकेत *ढौकित

<u>(ण) (ṇ)</u>

णय् *1√ṇay* (go) णयते णयिष्यते अणयत णयताम् णयेत *णयित णयनीय णयितव्य णयित्वा णयितुम् णयमान

<u>(त) (t)</u>

तक् *1√tak* (to fly, dart, rush; scoff at, laugh at) तकति तकिष्यति अतकत् तकतु तकेत् *तकित तकनीय तकित्वा

तक् *2√tak* (to laugh, bare, endure) तक्ति तक्ष्यति अताक् तक्तु तक्यात् अतकीत्-अताकीत् *तक्त तक तकाट तक्र

तक्ष् *1√takṣ* (to chop, cut, pare, chisel, slice, split) तक्षति तक्षिष्यति तक्षतु अतक्षत् तक्षेत् *तष्ट तष्टव्य-तक्षितव्य

तक्ष् *5√takṣ* (to chop, carve, chisel, make) तक्ष्णोति तक्षिष्यति अतक्ष्णोत् तक्ष्णोतु अक्ष्णुयात् *तष्ट तष्ट्वा तष्टुम्

तङ्क् *1√taṅk* (to tolerate, endure, bare) तङ्कति तङ्किष्यति अतङ्कत् तङ्कतु तङ्केत् *तङ्कित तङ्कनीय तङ्कित्वा तङ्कितुम्

तङ्ग् *1√taṅg* (to shiver, tremble, stumble) तङ्गति तङ्गिष्यति अतङ्गत् तङ्गतु तङ्गेत् *तङ्गित तङ्गनीय तङ्गित्वा तङ्गितुम्

तञ्च् *1√tañć* (to shrink, contract) तञ्चति तञ्चिष्यति अतञ्चत् तञ्चतु तञ्चेत् *तक्त तञ्चनीय तञ्चित्वा तञ्चितुम्

तञ्च् *7√tañć* (to shrink) तनक्ति तञ्चिष्यति-तङ्क्ष्यति अतनक् तनक्तु तञ्च्यात् *तञ्चित-तक्त तञ्चनीय तञ्चितुम्

तञ्ज् *7√tañj* (to shine, give out lighrt) तनक्ति तञ्जिष्यति-तङ्क्ष्यति अतनक् तनक्तु तञ्ज्यात् *तङ्क तञ्जिता

तट् *1√taṭ* (to rise, be raised, elevated; groan) तटति तटिष्यति अतटत्-अताटत् तटतु तटेत् *तटित तटनीय तटित्वा

तट् *10√taṭ* (to strike, beat) ताटयति-ते ताटयिष्यति-ते अताटयत्-त ताटयतु-ताम् ताटयेत्-त *ताटित

तड् *10√taḍ* (to clink, dash against, beat, strike) ताडयति-ते ताडयिष्यति अताडयत् ताडयतु ताडयेत् *ताडित

तण्ड् *1√taṇḍ* (to hit) तण्डते तण्डिष्यते अतण्डत तण्डताम् तण्डेत *तण्डित तण्डनीय तण्डितव्य तण्डित्वा तण्डितुम्

तन् *1√tan* (to stretch, spread, cover) तनति तनिष्यति अतनत् तनतु तनेत् *तत तानितुम्

तन् *8√tan* (to spread) तनोति-तनुते तनिष्यति-ते अतनोत्-अतनुत तनोतु-तनुताम् तनुयात्-तन्वीत तन्यते *तत तन्वत् तननीय तनितव्य वितन्य तान्य तनित्वा-तत्वा तानयित्वा तनितुम् तानयमान तनन तनु तन्तु तन्ति सन्तति सन्तान तनय

तन् *10√tan* (to believe, confide, assist, aid) तानयति-ते तानयिष्यति-ते अतानयत्-त तानयतु-ताम् तानयेत्-त *तानित

तन्त्र् *10√tantr* (to govern, control, rule, maintain, support) तन्त्रयते तन्त्रयिष्यते अतन्त्रयत तन्त्रताम् तन्त्रयेत *तन्त्रित तन्त्रणीत तन्त्रयितव्य तन्त्र्य तन्त्रयित्वा तन्त्रयितुम् तन्त्रयमाण तन्त्रणा तन्त्र तन्त्रिन् तन्त्रक स्वतन्त्र स्वातन्त्र्य तान्त्रिक

तप् *1√tap* (to blaze, heat, make warm) तपति तप्स्यति अतपत् तपतु तपेत् *तप्त तपनीय तप्तव्य तप्त्वा तप्तुम् ताप

तप् *4√tap* (to mortify the body, do penance, suffer pain) तप्यते तप्स्यते अतप्यत तप्यताम् तप्येत *तप्त तप्तुम्

तप् *10√tap* (to burn, give out heat, make warm) तापयति-ते तापयिष्यति-ते अतापयत्-त तापयतु-ताम् तापयेत्-त

तम् *4√tam* (to choke, faint, be fatigued, fained) ताम्यति तामिश्यति अताम्यत् ताम्यतु ताम्येत् *तान्त तान्त्वा-तनित्वा

तय् *1√tay* (to protect, guard, go, move) तयते तयिष्यते अतयत तयताम् तयेत *तयित तयनीय तयितव्य तयित्वा

तर्क् *10√tark* (to guess, suspect, infer, think) तर्कयति तर्कयिष्यति अतर्कयत् तर्कयतु तर्कयेत् तर्क्यते *तर्कित तर्कः

तर्ज् *1√tarj* (to threaten, terrify) तर्जति तर्जिष्यति अतर्जत् तर्जतु तर्जेत् *तर्जित तर्जनीय तर्जितव्य तर्जित्वा तर्जितुम्

तर्ज् *10√tarj* (to scare) तर्जयते तर्जयिष्यते अतर्जयत तर्जयताम् तर्जयेत् तर्ज्यते *तर्जित तर्जितव्य तर्जित्वा तर्जितुम्

तर्द् *1√tard* (to strike, injure, cut through) तर्दति तर्दिष्यति अतर्दत् तर्दतु तर्देत् *तर्दित तर्दनीय तर्दित्वा तर्दितुम्

तर्व् *1√tarv* (to move) तर्वति तर्विष्यति अतर्वत् तर्वतु तर्वेत् तर्व्यते *तर्वित तर्वणीय तर्वितव्य तर्वित्वा तर्वितुम्

तल् *1√tal* (to be complete, full, fixed) तलति-ते तलिष्यति-ते तलतु-ताम् तलेत्-त *तलित तलितुम् तलनीय

तल् *10√tal* (to be full, be fixed) तालयति-ते तालयिष्यति-ते अतालयत्-त तालयतु-ताम् तालयेत्-त *तालित

तंस् *1√taṁs* (to shake, pour, beg, request) तंसति-ते तंसिष्यति-ते अतंसत्-त तंसतु-ताम् तंसेत्-त *तंसित-तंस्त

तंस् *10√taṁs* (to decorate) तंसयति-ते तंसयिष्यति-ते अतंसयत्-त तंसयतु-ताम् तंसयेत्-त तंस्यते *तंसित-तंस्त

तस् *4√tas* (to toss, reject, cast, fade away) तस्यति तसिष्यति अतस्यत् तस्यतु तस्येत् *तसित-तस्त तसनीय तसितुम्

ताय् *1√tāy* (to grow, spread, extend, protect, preserve) तायते तायिष्यते तायताम् तायेत *तीत तीतवान् तायित्वा

तिक् *1√tik* (to go or move) तेकते तेकिष्यति अतेकत तेकताम् तेकेत *तेकित तेकनीय तेकित्वा तेकितुम्

तिक् *5√tik* (to attack, assail, assult, wound, challenge) तिक्नोति तिकिष्यति अतिक्नोत् तिक्नोतु तिक्नुयात् *तिक्त

तिग् *5√tig* (to go, move, leave) तिग्नोति तिगिष्यति अतिग्नोत् तिग्नोतु तिग्नुयात् अतेगीत् *तिक्त

तिघ् *5√tigh* (to hurt) तिघ्नोति तेघिष्यति तिघ्नोत् तिघ्नोतु तिघ्नुयात् *तिघित-तिघ्न विघ्नितव्य तिघ्नित्वा तिघ्नितुम्

तिज् *1√tij* (to endure, bear) तेजते, अतेजत् तेजताम् तेजेत * तेजित तिजित्वा (desiderative सन्)तितिक्षते तितिक्षिष्यते अतितिक्षत तितिक्षताम् तितिक्षेत *तितिक्षित तितिक्षितुम् तितिक्षा तीतक्षु

तिज् *10√tij* (to sharpen, instigate, stir up) तेजयति-ते तेजयिष्यति-ते अतेजयत्-त तेजयतु-ताम् तेजयेत्-त *तिक्त

तिप् *1√tip* (to drop, distill, ooze, leak) तेपते तेपिष्यते अतेपत तेपताम् तेपेत *तेपित तेपनीय तेपित्वा तेपतुम् तेपमान

तिम् *1√tim* (to moisten, make damp, make wet) तेमति तेमिष्यति अतेमत् तेमतु तेमेत् *तिमित तिमितव्य तिमितुम्

तिम् *4√tim* (to become wet, become quiet, tranquil, calm) तिम्यति तेम्ष्यति अतिम्यत् तिम्यतु तिम्येत् *तिमित

तिल् *1√til* (to go, move) तेलति तेलिष्यति अतेलत तेलतु तेलेत् *तेलित तेलनीय तेलितव्य तेलित्वा तेलितुम्

तिल् *6√til* (to go, move) तिलति तिलिष्यति अतिलत् तिलतु तिलेत् *तिलित तिलनीय तिलितव्य तिलितुम्

तिल् *10√til* (to be unctuous, greasy, anoint, smear with oil) तेलयति-ते तेलयिष्यति अतेलयत् तेलयतु तेलयेत्

तीक् *1√tīk* (to go) तीकते तीकिष्यते अतीकत तीकताम् तीकेत *तीकित तीकनीय तीकित्वा तीकितुम्

तीम् *4√tīm* (to become wet, moist) तीम्यति तीमिष्यति अतीम्यत् तीम्यतु तीम्येत् *तीमित

तीर् *10√tīr* (to cross over, get through) तीरयति-ते तीरयिष्यति-ते अतीरयत्-त तीरयतु-ताम् तीरयेत्-त *तीरित

तीव् *1√tīv* (to fatten, be large) तीवति तीविष्यति अतीवत् तीवतु तीवेत् *तीवित तीवितव्य तीवित्वा तीवितुम्

तु *2√tu* (to thrive, be strong, have power, authority) तौति तविष्यति अतौत् तौतु तुयात् *तुत

तुज् *1√tuj* (to violate, injure) तोजति तोजिष्यति अतोजत् तोजतु तोजेत् *तोजित तोजनीय तोजितव्य तोजित्वा

तुञ्ज् *1√tuñj* (to reach, convey, live, emit, incite) तुञ्जति तुञ्जिष्यति अतुञ्जत् तुञ्जतु तुञ्जेत् *तुञ्जित तुञ्जनीय

तुञ्ज् *10√tuñj* (to energize) तुञ्जयति-ते तुञ्जयिष्यति-ते अतुञ्जयत्-त तुञ्जयतु-ताम् तुञ्जयेत्-त *तुञ्जित तुञ्जयितुम्

तुट् *6√tuṭ* (to quarrel, dispute, injure) तुटति तुटिष्यति अतुटत् तुटतु तुटेत् अतुटीत् *तुटित तुटितव्य तुटितुम्

तुड् *1√tuḍ* (to break, split, rend) तुडते तुडष्यते अतुडत तुडताम् तुडेत *तुडित तुडत् तुडनीय तुडित्वा तुडितुम्

तुड् *6√tuḍ* (to break, cut) तुडति तुडिष्यति अतुडत् तुडतु तुडेत् *तुडित तुडनीय तुडितव्य तुडित्वा तुडितुम्

तुड्ड् *1√tuḍḍ* (to disregard) तुड्डति तुड्डिष्यति अतुड्डत् तुड्डतु तुड्डेत् *तुड्डित तुड्डितव्य तुड्डित्वा तुड्डितुम्

तुण् *6√tuṇ* (to cheat, deceive) तुणति तुणिष्यति अतुणत् तुणतु तुणेत् *तुणित तुणनीय तुणितव्य तुणित्वा तुणितुम्

तुण्ड् *1√tuṇḍ* (to break, press out) तुण्डते तुण्डिष्यते अतुण्डत तुण्डताम् तुण्डेत *तुण्डित तुण्डनीय तुण्डितव्य तुण्डित्वा

तुत्थ् *10√tutth* (to praise, screen, spread) तुत्थयति-ते तुत्थयिष्यति-ते अतुत्थयत्-त तुत्थयतु-ताम् तुत्थयेत्-त *तुत्थित

तुद् *6√tud* (to thrust, strike, wound, hit, goad, afflict) तुदति-ते तोत्स्यति अतुदत् तुदतु तुदेत् तुतोद तोत्ता अतौत्सीत-अतुत्त तुद्यते *तुत्त तोदनीय तोत्तव्य तोद्य तुत्त्वा तोत्तुम् तुद्यमान ततुत्सा तोदक

तुन्द् *1√tund* (to search) तुन्दति तुन्दिष्यति अतुन्दत् तुन्दतु तुन्देत् *तुन्दित तुन्दनीय तुन्दितव्य तुन्दित्वा तुन्दितुम्

तुप् *1√tup* (to violate, injure) तोपति तोपिष्यति अतोपत् तोपतु तोपेत् अतोपीत् *तुप्त-तुपित-तोपित

तुप् *6√tup* (to violate) तुपति तुपिष्यति अतुपत् तुपतु तुपेत् *तुप्त तुप्तव्य तुप्त्वा तुप्तुम्

तुफ् *1√tuph* (to violate) तोफति तोफिष्यति अतोफत् तोफतु तोफेत् *तोफित तोफितव्य तोफित्वा तोफितुम्

तुफ् *6√tuph* (to violate) तुफति तुफिष्यति अतुफत् तुफतु तुफेत् *तुफित तुफितव्य तुफित्वा तुफितुम्

तुभ् *1√tubh* (to hurt) तोभते तोभिष्यते अतोभत तोभताम् तोभेत अतोभीत् *तोभित-तुब्ध तुब्धव्य तुब्ध्वा तब्धुम्

तुभ् *4√tubh* (to violate) तुभ्यति तुभिष्यति अतुभ्यत् तुभ्यतु तुभ्येत् अतोभीत् *तुब्ध तुभ्य तोभनीय तुभ्यते

तुभ् *9√tubh* (to violate) तुभ्नाति तुभिष्यति अतुभ्नात् तुभ्नातु तुभ्नीयात् *तुब्ध

तुम्प् *1√tump* (to hurt) तुम्पति तुम्पिष्यति अतुम्पत् तुम्पतु तुम्पेत् *तुम्पित तुम्पितव्य तुम्पित्वा तुम्पितुम्

तुम्प् *6√tump* (to hurt) तुम्पति तुम्पिष्यति अतुम्पत् तुम्पतु तुम्पेत् *तुम्पित तुम्पनीय तुम्पितव्य तुम्पितुम्

तुम्फ् *1√tumph* (to hurt) तुम्फति तुम्फिष्यति अतुम्फत् तुम्फतु तुम्फेत् *तुम्फित तुम्फितव्य तुम्फित्वा तुम्फितुम्

तुम्फ् *6√tumph* (to hurt) तुम्फति तुम्फिष्यति अतुम्फत् तम्फतु तुम्फेत् *तुम्फित तुम्फितव्य तुम्फित्वा तुम्फितुम्

तुम्ब् *1,10√tumb* (to hurt, trouble) तुम्बति-तुम्बयति-ते तुम्बिष्यति अतुम्बत् तुम्बतु तुम्बेत् *तुम्बित तुम्बितुम्

तुर् *3√tur* (to rush, run) तुतोर्ति तोरिष्यति अतोरीत् तुरतु तुरेत् *तुर्ण

तुर् *6√tur* (to rush) तुरति तुरिष्यति अतुरत् तुरतु तुरेत् *तुर्ण तुर्य

तुर्व् *1√turv* (to remove) तूर्वति तूर्विष्यति अतूर्वत् तूर्वतु तूर्वेत् *तूर्ण तूर्वित्वा तूर्वितुम्

तुल् *1√tul* (to weigh, measure) तूलति-तोलति तुलिष्यति अतूलत् तूलतु तूलेत् *तूलित तुलनीय तुल्य तूलितुम् तूलित्वा

तुल् *10√tul* (to weigh, weigh in mind, compare) तोलयति-ते तोलयिष्यति-ते अतोलयत्-त तोलयतु-ताम् तोलयेत्-त

तुश् *1√tuś* (to drip, trickle, be pressed out) तोशते ताशिष्यते अतोशत तोशताम् ताशेत *तुशित-तुष्ट

तुष् *4√tuṣ* (to be content, satisfied) तुष्यति तोक्ष्यति अतुष्यत् तुष्यतु तुष्येत् *तुष्ट तोषणीय तोषित्वा तोष्टव्य तोष्टुम्

तुस् *1√tus* (to sound) तोसति तोसिष्यति अतोसत् तोसतु तोसेत् *तुस्त तुस्य तोसनीय

तुह् *1√tuh* (to hurt, harm, injure, slaughter, murder) तोहति तोहिष्यति अतुहत् तोहतु तोहेत् *तूढ तुहनीय तूढ्वा

तूड् *1√tūḍ* (to disrespect, contemn) तूडति तूडिष्यति अतूडत् तूडतु तूडेत् *तूडित तूडितव्य तूडितुम्

तूण् *10√tūṇ* (to complete, fill, fill up) तूणयते तूणयिष्यते अतूणयत तूणयताम् तूणयेत *तूणित तूणितव्य तूणितुम्

तूर् *4√tūr* (to rush, make haste, go quickly) तूर्यते तूरिष्यते अतूर्यत तूर्यताम् तूर्येत *तूर्ण

तूल् *1√tūl* (to weigh, ascertain, measure) तूलति तूलिष्यति अतूलत् तूलतु तूलत् *तूलित तूलितव्य तूलितुम्

तूल् *10√tūl* (to fill) तूलयति-ते तूलयिष्यति-ते अतूलयत्-त तूलयतु-ताम् तूलयेत्-त *तूलित तूलनीय तूलित्वा

तूष् *1√tūṣ* (to be pleased, pleased) तूषति तूषिष्यति अतूषत् तूषतु तूषेत् *तूष्ट-तुष्ट तुष्टव्य तुष्ट्वा तुष्टुम्

तृक्ष् *1√tṛkṣ* (to go) तृक्षति तृक्षिष्यति अतृक्षत् तृक्षतु तृक्षेत् *तृक्षित-तृष्ट

तृण् *8√tṛṇ* (to eat grass, graze) तृणोति-तर्णोति or तृणते-तर्णुते तर्णिष्यति अतृणोत् तृणोतु तृणुयात् *तृत

तृद् *1√tṛd* (to split) तर्दति तर्दिष्यति अतर्दत् तर्दतु तर्देत् *तर्दित तर्दनीय तर्दितव्य तर्दित्वा तर्दितुम्

तृद् *7√tṛd* (to split, cleave, pierce) तृणत्ति-तृन्ते तर्दिष्यति-तर्त्स्यति-तर्दिष्यते-तर्त्स्यते अतृन्त तृन्ताम् तृन्दीत *तृण्ण

तृप् *1√tṛp* (to kindle) तर्पति तर्पिष्यति अतृपत् तृपतु तृपेत् तृप्यते *तर्पित तर्पणीय तर्पितव्य तर्पित्वा तर्पितुम् तृप्त्वा

तृप् *4√tṛp* (to be satisfied) तृप्यति तर्पिष्यति-तर्पस्यति-त्रप्स्यति अतर्प्यत तर्प्यतु तर्प्येत *तृप्त-तर्पित तर्पणीय तर्पितुम्

तृप् *5√tṛp* (to be pleased, satisfied, contented) तृप्नोति तर्पिष्यति अतृप्नोत् तृप्नोतु तृप्नुयात् *तृप्त तृप्त्वा-तर्पित्वा

तृप् *6√tṛp* (to be pleased) तृपति तर्पिष्यति अतृपत् तृपतु तृपेत् *तृप्त तर्पणीय तर्पितव्य तर्पित्वा तर्पितुम् तर्पण

तृप् *10√tṛp* (to kindle) तर्पयति-ते तर्पयिष्यति-ते अतर्पयत्-त तर्पयपतु-ताम् तर्पयेत्-त *तर्पित तर्पयित्वा तर्पयितुम्

तृम्प् *6√tṛmp* (to be pleased) तृम्पति तर्पिष्यति अतृपत् तृपतु तृपेत् *तर्पित तर्पणीय तर्पितव्य तर्पित्वा तर्पितुम्

तृम्फ् *6√tṛmph* (to be pleased) तृम्फति तृम्फिष्यति अतृम्फत् तृम्फतु तम्फेत् *तृम्फित तृम्फितव्य तृम्फितुम्

तृष् *4√tṛṣ* (to be thirsty) तृष्यति तर्षिष्यति अतृष्यत् तृष्यतु तृष्येत् *तृषित-तुष्ट तर्षणीय तर्षितव्य तर्षित्वा-तृषित्वा तृष्णा

तृंह् *6√tṛm̐h* (to strike) तृंहति तृंहिष्यति-तङ्क्ष्यति अतृंहत्-अताङ्क्षत् तृंहतु तृंहेत् *तृंहित-तृढ

तृह् *6√tṛh* (to strike) तृहति तर्हिष्यति-तर्क्ष्यति अतर्हत् तर्हतु तर्हेत् *तृढ तृहत् तर्हणीय तर्हितव्य तृहित्वा-तृढ्वा तर्हितुम्

तृह् *7√tṛh* (to strike) तृणेढि तर्हिष्यति अतृणेट्-ड् तृणेढु तृह्यात् *तृढ तर्हितवत् तर्हणीय तर्हितव्य तर्ह्य तर्हित्वा तर्हितुम्

तॄ *1√tṝ* (to swim across) तरति तरीष्यति-तरिष्यति अतरत् तरतु तरेत् *तीर्ण तरितव्य तरणीय तीर्त्वा तरणी तारण तरुण

तेज् *1√tej* (to obey, protect) तेजति तेजिष्यति अतेजत् तेजतु तेजेत् *तेजित तेजनीय तेजितव्य तेजित्वा तेजितुम्

तेप् *1√tep* (to flow, sprinkle, ooze, shake, tremblee) तेपते तेप्ष्यते अतेपत तेपताम् तेपेत * तेप्त तेप्तव्य तेपनीय

तेव् *1√tev* (to play, sport, weep, lament) तेवते तेविष्यते अतेवत तेवताम् तेवेत *तेवित तेवनीय तेवित्वा तेवितुम्

तोड् *1√toḍ* (to breal, disrespect) तोडति तोडिष्यति अतोडत् तोडतु तोडेत् *तोडित तोडितव्य तोडित्वा तोडितुम्

त्यज् *1√tyaj* (to forsake, leave) त्यजति त्यक्षति अत्यजत् त्यजतु त्यजेत् त्यज्यते *त्यक्त त्याज्य त्यक्त्वा त्यक्तुम् त्याग

त्रङ्क् *1√traṅk* (to go) त्रङ्कते त्रङ्किष्यते अत्रङ्कत त्रङ्कताम् त्रङ्केत *त्रङ्कित त्रङ्कनीय त्रङ्कितव्य त्रङ्क्य त्रङ्कित्वा त्रङ्कितुम्

त्रङ्ख् *1√traṅkh* (to go) त्रङ्खति त्रङ्खिष्यति अत्रङ्खत् त्रङ्खतु त्रङ्खेत् *त्रङ्खित त्रङ्ख्य त्रङ्खित्वा

त्रङ्ग् *1√traṅg* (to move) त्रङ्गति त्रङ्गिष्यति अत्रङ्गत् त्रङ्गतु त्रङ्गेत् *त्रङ्गित त्रङ्गित्वा

त्रन्द् *1√trand* (to try) त्रन्दति-ते त्रन्दिष्यति अत्रन्दत् त्रन्दतु त्रन्देत् *त्रन्दित त्रन्दनीय त्रन्दितव्य त्रन्दित्वा त्रन्दितुम्

त्रप् *1√trap* (to be ashamed, embarrassed) त्रपते त्रपिष्यते अत्रपत त्रपताम् त्रपेत त्रप्यते *त्रप्त त्रप्त्वा-त्रपित्वा

त्रंस् *1√tram̐s* (to speak) त्रंसति त्रंसिष्यति अत्रंसत् त्रंसतु त्रंसेत् *त्रंसित-त्रंस्त

त्रंस् *10√tram̐s* (to speak) त्रंसयति-ते त्रंसयिष्यति-ते अत्रंसयत्-त त्रंसयतु-ताम् त्रंसयेत्-त *त्रंसित-त्रंस्त

त्रस् *1√tras* (to be terrified, shaken) त्रसति-ते त्रसिष्यति-ते अत्रसत्-त त्रसतु-ताम् त्रसेत्-त त्रस्यते *त्रस्त

त्रस् *4√tras* (to fear) त्रस्यति त्रसिष्यति अत्रस्यत् त्रस्यतु त्रस्येत् *त्रस्त त्रसनीय त्रसितव्य त्रसित्वा त्रसितुम् त्रस्यमान त्रास

त्रस् *10√tras* (to oppose) त्रासयति-ते त्रासयिष्यति-ते अत्रासयत्-त त्रासयतु-ताम् त्रासयेत्-त *त्रासित

त्रिङ्ख् *1√triṅkh* (to go) त्रिङ्खति त्रिङ्खिष्यति अत्रिङ्खत् त्रिङ्खतु त्रिङ्खेत् *त्रिङ्खित

त्रा *2√trā* (to rescue) त्राति त्रास्यति अत्रात् त्रातु त्रायात् *त्रात त्राण त्राता गोत्र मन्त्र कलत्र

त्रा *4√trā* (to rescue) त्रायते त्रायिष्यते अत्रायत त्रायताम् त्रायेत *त्रात त्रातृ

त्रु *4√tru* (to tear) त्रुट्यति त्रुटिष्यति अत्रुट्यत् तुट्यतु त्रुट्येत् *त्रुटित त्रुट्यते त्रुट्य त्रोटनीय

त्रु *6√tru* (to tear) त्रुटति त्रुटिष्यति अत्रुटते त्रुटतु त्रुटेत् *त्रुटित

त्रुट् *6√truṭ* (to cut) त्रुट्यति-त्रुटति त्रुटिष्यति अत्रुटत्-अत्रुट्यत् त्रुटतु त्रुटेत्-त्रुट्येत् *त्रुटित त्रुटनूय त्रुटितव्य त्रुटित्वा त्रुटितुम्

त्रुट् *10√truṭ* (to cut) त्रोटयते त्रोटिष्यते अत्रोटयत त्रोटयताम् त्रोटयेत *त्रोटित त्रोटनीय त्रोटयितव्य त्रोटयित्वा त्रोटयितुम्

त्रुप् *1√trup* (to hurt) त्रुपति त्रुपिष्यति अत्रुपत् त्रुपतु त्रुपेत् *त्रुप्त

त्रुफ् *1√truph* (to hurt) त्रुफति त्रुफिष्यति अत्रुफत् त्रुफतु त्रुफेत् *त्रुफित त्रुफितव्य त्रुफित्वा त्रुफितुम्

त्रुम्फ् *1√trumph* (to hurt) त्रुम्फति त्रुम्फिष्यति अत्रुम्फत् त्रुम्फतु त्रुम्फेत् *त्रुम्फित त्रुम्फितव्य त्रुम्फित्वा त्रुम्फितुम्

त्रै *1√trai* (to protect, rescue) त्रायते त्रास्यते अत्रायत त्रायताम् त्रायेत् त्रायते *त्रात-त्राण त्रातव्य त्रात्वा त्रातुम् त्रातृ मन्त्र

त्रौक् *1√trauk* (to go) त्रौकते त्रौकिष्यते अत्रौकत त्रौकताम् त्रौकेत *त्रौकित त्रौकनीय त्रौकितव्य त्रौकित्वा त्रौकितुम्

त्वक्ष् *1√tvakṣ* (to hew, make thin, peel) त्वक्षति त्वक्षिष्यति अत्वक्षत् त्वक्षतु त्वक्षेत् अत्वक्षीत् त्वक्ष्यते *त्वष्ट

त्वङ्ग् *1√tvaṅg* (to leap, gallop, move, go) त्वङ्गति त्वङ्गिष्यति अत्वङ्गत् त्वङ्गतु त्वङ्गेत् *त्वङ्गित त्वङ्गनीय त्वङ्गित्वा

त्वच् *6√tvać* (to cover) त्वचति त्वचिष्यति अत्वचत् त्वचतु त्वचेत अत्वचीत्-अत्वाचीत् *त्वक्त त्वचा

त्वञ्च् *6√tvañć* (to go) त्वञ्चति त्वञ्चिष्यति अत्वञ्चत् त्वञ्चतु त्वञ्चेत् *त्वञ्चित त्वञ्चनीय त्वञ्चित्वा त्वञ्चितुम्

त्वर् *1√tvar* (to hasten, haste, hurry, rush) त्वरते त्वरिष्यते अत्वरत त्वरताम् त्वरेत *त्वरित-तूर्ण त्वरमाण त्वरा सत्वर

त्विष् *1√tviṣ* (to brighten, shine, glitter, blaze, sparkle) त्वेषति-ते त्वेक्ष्यति अत्वषत् त्वेषतु त्वेषेत त्विष्यते *त्विष्ट

त्सर् *1√tsar* (to creep, approach slowly, approach stealthily) त्सरति त्सरिष्यति अत्सरत् त्सरतु त्सरेत् *त्सरित

(थ) (th)

थर्व् *1√tharv* (to go, move) थर्वति थर्विष्यति अथर्वत् थर्वतु थर्वत् *थर्वित थर्वनीय थर्वितव्य थर्वित्वा थर्वियुम्

थुड् *6√thuḍ* (to hide, cover) थुडति थुडिष्यति अथुडत् थुडतु थुडेत् *थुडित थुडनीय थुडितव्य थुडित्वा थुडितुम्

थुर्व् *1√thurv* (to injure, hurt, violate) थूर्वति थूर्विष्यति अथूर्वत् थूर्वतु थूर्वेत् *थूर्ण थूवितव्य थूर्वित्वा थूर्वितुम्

(द) (d)

दक्ष् *1√dakṣ* (to be smart, able, competent) दक्षते दक्षिष्यते अदक्षत दक्षताम् दक्षेत *दष्ट दक्ष दक्षिण दक्षिणा

दघ् *4√dagh* (to reach, attain, go away) दघ्यति दघिष्यति अदघ्यत् दघ्यतु दघ्येत् *दघित

दघ् *5√dagh* (to hurt, go, leap) दघ्नोति दघिष्यति अदघ्नोत् दघ्नोतु दघ्नुयात् *दघित-दघ्न

दङ्घ् *1√dangh* (to abandon, leave; protect, cherish) दङ्घति दङ्घिष्यति अदङ्घत् दङ्घतु दङ्घेत् *दङ्घित

दण्ड् *10√daṇḍ* (to punish, fine, chastise) दण्डयति दण्डयिष्यति अदण्डयत् दण्डयतु दण्डयेत् **दण्डित दण्ड

दद् *1√dad* (to give, offer, present) ददते ददिष्यते अददत ददताम् ददेत *ददित ददित्वा ददितुम्

दध् *1√dadh* (to have, hold, possess) दधते दधिष्यते अदधत दधिष्यते *धत्त-दधित दधनीय दाध्य दधित्वा दधितुम्

दध् *5√dadh* (to hurt, protect) दध्नोति दधिष्यति अदध्नोत दध्नोतु दध्नुयात् *धत्त

दम् *4√dam* (to be quie, tamed, calm, tranquil) दाम्यति दमिष्यति अदाम्यत् दाम्यतु दाम्येत् ददाम दम्यते *दमित-दान्त दमयत् दमनीय दमितव्य दम्य दमित्वा-दान्त्वा दमितुम् दम दमन दमक दमयितृ दमयन्ती दम्पती

दम्भ् *5√dambh* (to deceive) दभ्नोति दम्भिष्यति अदभ्नोत् दभ्नोतु दभ्नुयात् *दब्ध दब्ध्वा दम्भितुम् दम्भ

दम्भ् *10√dambh* (to send, collect) दम्भयति-ते दम्भयिष्यति-ते अदम्भयत्-त दम्भयतु-ताम् दम्भयेत्-त *दम्भित

दय् *1√day* (to be merciful, passionate, have sympathy) दयते दयिष्यते अदयत दयताम् दयेत *दयित दयनीय

दरिद्रा *2√daridrā* (to be poor) दरिद्राति दरिद्रिष्यति अदरिद्रात् दरिद्रातु दरिद्रियात् *दरिद्रित दरिद्रणीय दरिद्रितुम् दरिद्र

दल् *1√dal* (to burst open, split, cleave, crack) दलति दलिष्यति अदलत् दलतु दलेत् *दलित दलनीय दलितुम्

दल् *10√dal* (to tear) दालयति दालयिष्यति-ते अदालयत्-त दालयतु-ताम् दालयेत्-त *दालित

दंश् *1√daṁś* (to sting) दशति दङ्क्ष्यति अदशत् दशतु दशेत् *दष्ट दष्टवान् दष्ट्वा दंशनीय दंष्टुम् दंशमान दशन

दंश् *10√daṁś* (to bite, destroy, overpower) दंशयति-ते दंशयिष्यति-ते अदंशयत्-त दंशयतु-ताम् दंशयेत्-त *दष्ट

दंस् *10√daṁś* (to bite) दंसयति-ते दंसयिष्यति-ते अदंसयत्-त दंसयतु-ताम् दंसयेत्-त *दंसित-दंस्त

दस् *4√das* (to rob, throw, toss, perish) दस्यति दसिष्यति अदस्यत् दस्यतु दस्येत् *दसित-दस्त दसनीय दसितुम्

दह् *1√dah* (to burn, scorch, consume) दहति धक्ष्यति अदहत् दहतु दहेत् *दग्ध दहनीय दग्ध्वा दग्धुम् दहन दाहक

दा *1√dā* (to give, grant, bestow, yield) यच्छति दास्यति अयच्छत् यच्छतु यच्छेत् *दत्त दानीय देय दत्त्वा दान दातृ

दा *2√dā* (to cut) दाति-दत्ते दास्यति अदात दातु दायात् दीयते *दात दानीय देय दात्वा दातुम्

दा *3√dā* (to give) ददाति-दत्ते दास्यति-ते अददात्-अदित ददातु-दत्ताम् दद्यात्-ददीत *दत्त दानीय दातुम् दारु सुदामा

दा *4√dā* (to bind) दायति दायिष्यति अदायत् दायतु दायेत् दीयते *दात दातव्य दात्वा दातुम्

दान् *1√dān* (to divide, cut) दी+दांसते दांसिष्यते अदांसत् दांसताम् दांसेत् *दांसित दांसनीय दांसितव्य दांसितुम्

दाय् *1√dāy* (to give) दायते दायिष्यते अदायत दायताम् दायेत *दायित दायनीय दायितव्य दायित्वा दायितुम्

दाश् *1√dāś* (to make offering) दाशति-ते दाशिष्यते अदाशत दाशताम् दाशेत *दाशित दाशितव्य दाशित्वा दाशितुम्

दाश् *2√dāś* (to make offering) दाष्टे दाश्स्यिति अदाष्ट दाष्टाम् दाशीत *दाशित-दाष्ट दाशितुम् दाश दाश्य

दाश् *1,10√dāś* (to offer, give, grant) दाशयति-ते दाशयिष्यति-ते अदाशयत्-त दाशयतु-ताम् दाशयेत्-त *दाशित

दाश् *5√dāś* (to hurt, injure) दाश्नोति दाशिष्यति अदाश्नोत् दाश्नोतु दाश्नुयात् *दाशित-दाष्ट

दास् *1√dās* (to give, grant, offer) दासति दासिष्यति अदासत् दासतु दासेत् *दासित दास्य दासितुम् दास दासी

दिन्व् *1√dinv* (to be glad, happy, pleased, to please) दिन्वति दिन्विष्यति अदिन्वत् दिन्वतु दिन्वेत् *दिन्वित दिन्वनीय

दिम्प् *10√dimp* (to order, accumulate) दिम्पयते दिम्पयिष्यति-ते अदिम्पयत्-त दिम्पयतु-ताम् दिम्पयेत्-त *दिम्पित
दिव् *1√div* (to shine, throw, play) देवति देविष्यति अदेवत् देवतु देवेत् दीव्यते *द्यूत-द्यून
दिव् *4√div* (to play) दीव्यति देविष्यति अदीव्यत् दीव्यतु दीव्येत् *द्यूत देवनीय देवितव्य देव्य देवित्वा-द्यूत्वा द्यौ देव
दिव् *10√div* (to rub) देवयते देवयिष्यते अदेवयत देवयताम् देवयेत देव्यते *द्यूत देवितुम्
दिश् *6√diś* (to point out, show) दिशति-ते देक्ष्यति-ते अदिशत्-त दिशतु-ताम् दिशेत-त *दिष्ट देशनीय देष्टुम् सन्देश
दिह् *2√dih* (to smear) दोग्धि-दिग्धे धेक्ष्यति-ते अधेक्-अदिग्ध देग्धु-दिग्धाम् दिह्यात्-दिहीत *दिग्ध-दीढ
दी *3√dī* (to shine, please, appear good, be admired) दिधेति दास्यति अदिधेत् दिधेतु दिधियात् *दीत-दीन
दी *4√dī* (to perish, die, waste) दीयति-ते दास्यते अदीयत दीयताम् दीयेत *दीन दापनीय देय प्रदाय दत्त्वा दातुम्
दीक्ष् *1√dīkṣ* (to anoint, consecrate, initiate, be shaved) दीक्षते दीक्षिष्यते अदीक्षत दीक्षताम् दीक्षेत *दीक्षित
दीधी *2√dīdhī* (to appear, seem; shine) दीधीते दीधिष्यते अदीधीत दीधीताम् दीधीत *दीधित दीध्यनीय दीधयितुम्
दीप् *4√dīp* (to shine, blaze) दीप्यते दीपिष्यते अदीप्यत दीप्यताम् दीप्येत अदीपिष्ट *दीप्त दीप्तव्य दीप्त्वा दीप्तुम्
दु *1√du* (to move, burn, cause pain) दवति दोष्यति अदवत् दवतु दवेत् *दूत-दून दवितुम्
दु *5√du* (to consume, burn, torture) दुनोति दोष्यति अदुनोत् दुनोतु दुनुयात् दुदाव दूयते अदौषीत् *दूत-दून
दुःख् *10√duḥkh* (to pain, afflict) दुःखयति-ते दुःखयिष्यति-ते अदुःखयत्-त दुःखयतु-ताम् दुःखयेत्-त *दुःखित
दुर्व् *1√durv* (to hurt) दूर्वति दूर्विष्यति अदूर्वत् दूर्वतु दूर्वेत् *दूर्ण दूवितव्य दूर्वित्वा दूर्वितुम्
दुल् *10√dul* (to swing, oscillate, move about) दोलयति-ते दोलयिष्यति-ते अदोलयत्-त दोलयतु-ताम् दोलयेत्-त
दुष् *4√duṣ* (to spoil, be bad, corrupted) दुष्यति दोक्ष्यति अदुष्यत् दुष्यतु दुष्यात् *दुष्ट दोषनीय दोषयित्वा दोषयितुम्
दुह् *1√duh* (to hurt, pain, distress) दोहति-दुग्धे धोक्ष्यति-ते अधोक्-अदुग्ध दोग्धु-दुग्धाम् दुह्यात्-दुहीत दुह्यते *दुग्ध दुहत् दुहन्ती दोहनीय दोग्धव्य दुह्य दोह्य दुग्ध्वा दोग्धुम् दोदुह्यमान दोहन दोहक दोही दुधुक्षा दुधुक्षु गोधुक् कामधुक्
दुह् *2√duh* (to milk, squeeze out, extract) दोग्धि-दुग्धे धोक्ष्यति-ते अधोक्-अदुग्ध दोग्धु-दुग्धाम् दुह्यात्-दुहीत *दुग्ध
दू *4√dū* (to pain, be afflicted, suffer pain, be sorry) दूयते दविष्यते अदूयत दूयताम् दूयेत अदविष्ट दूयते *दून
दृ *1,6√dṛ* (to honor, respect, worship, revere) आ+द्रियते दरिष्यते अद्रियत द्रियताम् द्रियेत *दृत दरणीय दृत्वा दर्तुम्
दृ *5√dṛ* (to hurt) दृणोति दरिष्यति अदृणोत् दृणोतु दृणुयात् *दृण दृणनीय दृणितव्य दृणितुम् दीर्यते
दृ *10√dṛ* (to tear, fear) दरयति-ते दरयिष्यति-ते अदरयत्-त दरयतु-ताम् दरयेत्-त *दीर्ण
दृप् *1√dṛp* (to kindle) दर्पति दर्पिष्यति अदर्पत् दर्पतु दर्पेत् दृप्यते *दर्पित दर्पणीय दर्पितव्य दर्पितुम् दर्प
दृप् *4√dṛp* (to be proud) दृप्यति दर्पिष्यति अदृप्यत् दृप्यतु दृप्येत् *दृप्त दर्पणीय दर्पितव्य दृप्त्वा दर्पितुम् दर्प दर्पण
दृप् *6√dṛp* (to torture) दृपति दर्पिष्यति अदर्पत् दर्पतु दर्पेत् *दर्पित दर्पणीय दर्पितव्य दर्पित्वा दर्पितुम् दर्प
दृप् *10√dṛp* (to be arrogant) दर्पयति-ते दर्पयिष्यति-ते अदर्पयत्-त दर्पयतु-ताम् दर्पयेत्-त *दर्पित दर्पयित्वा दर्पयितुम्
दृभ् *1√dṛbh* (to fasten, bind, tie) दर्भति दर्भिष्यति अदर्भत् दर्भतु दर्भेत् *दृब्ध द्रब्धुम् सन्दर्भ
दृभ् *6√dṛbh* (to tie, string) दृभति दर्भिष्यति अदर्भत् दर्भतु दर्भेत् अदभीत् *दृब्ध

दृभ् *10√dṛbh* (to relate) दर्भयति-ते दर्भयिष्यति-ते अदर्भयत्-त दर्भयतु-ताम् दर्भयेत्-त *दृब्ध

दृम्फ् *6√dṛmph* (to afflict) दृम्फति दृम्फिष्यति अदृम्फत् दृम्फतु दृम्फेत् *दृम्फित दृम्फितव्य दृम्फित्वा दृम्फितुम्

दृम्भ् *10√dṛmbh* (to relate to) दर्भयति-ते दर्भयिष्यति-ते अदर्भयत्-त दर्भयतु-ताम् दर्भयेत्-त *दृब्ध

दृश् *1√dṛś* (to see) पश्यति द्रक्ष्यति अपश्यत् पश्यतु पश्येत् दृश्यते *दृष्ट-दर्शित दर्शनीय दृष्ट्वा दृश्य द्रष्टुम् दर्शन दृष्टि

दृंह् *1√dṛm̃h* (to make firm, strengthen, fasten, fortify) दृंहति-ते दृंहिष्यति-ते अदृंहत्-त दृंहतु-ताम् दृंहेत्-त *दृढ

दृह् *1√dṛh* (to grow, increase, be fixed, firm, tie firmly) दर्हति दर्हिष्यति अदर्हत् दर्हतु दर्हेत् अदर्हीत् *दृढ

दृह् *4√dṛh* (to hate, be a traitor) दृह्यति द्रोहिष्यति अदृह्यत् द्रुह्यतु दृह्येत् *दृढ द्रोहणीय द्रोह्य दृढ्वा द्रोढुम् द्रोह द्राहिन्

दॄ *1√dṝ* (to fear, be afraid) दरति दरिष्यति अदरत् दरतु दरेत् अदारीत् दीर्यते *दीर्ण दरणीय दरितुम्

दॄ *9√dṝ* (to rip, tear, break) दृणाति दरिष्यति-दरीष्यति अदृणात् दृणातु दृणीयात् अदारीत् *दीर्ण दरणीय दरितुम्

दे *1√de* (to protect, cherish) दयते दास्यते अदायत दायताम् दायेत *दित दातव्य दित्वा देय दातुम् दयमान *दात

देव् *1√dev* (to shine, sport, play, gamble, throw, lament) देवते, देविष्यते अदेवत देवताम् देवेत *देवित देवनीय

दै *1√dai* (to purify, sanctify, cleanse) दायति दास्यति अदायत् दायतु दायेत् अदासीत् *दात

दो *4√do* (to cut, divide, reap) द्यति दास्यति अद्यत् द्यतु द्येत् दीयते *दात-दीत दानीय देय दातव्य दात्वा-दत्वा दातुम्

द्यु *2√dyu* (to attack, encounter, assail, advance) द्यौति द्योष्यति अद्यौत द्योतु द्युयात *द्युत द्यवनीय द्योतव्य द्योतुम्

द्युत् *1√dyut* (to shine, be brilliant) द्योतते द्योतिष्यते अद्योतत द्योतताम् द्योतेत *द्युतित-द्योतित द्योत्य द्योतमान खद्योत

द्यै *1√dyai* (to abhore, look down up on) द्यायति द्यास्यति अद्यायत् द्यायतु द्यायेत् *द्यान द्यातुम्

द्रम् *1√dram* (to go about) द्रमति द्रमिष्यति अद्रमत् द्रमतु द्रमेत् *द्रमित द्रमत् द्रमनीय द्रमित्वा द्रमितुम् द्रम्यमान

द्रा *2√drā* (to sleep; fly, run away, run) नि+द्राति द्रास्यति द्रात् द्रातु द्रयात् *द्राण द्राणीय द्रेय द्रात्वा द्रातुम् निद्रा तन्द्रा

द्राख् *1√drākh* (to dry out, prohibit, prevent, be able) द्राखति द्राखिष्यति अद्राखत् द्राखतु द्राखेत् *द्राखित द्राखित्वा

द्राघ् *1√drāgh* (to increase, stretch, exert, be fatigued) द्राघति-ते द्राघिष्यते अद्राघत द्राघताम् द्राघेत *द्राघित द्राघ्य

द्राङ्क्ष् *1√drāṅkṣ* (to want, desire) द्राङ्क्षति द्राङ्क्षिष्यति अद्राङ्क्षत् द्राङ्क्षतु द्राङ्क्षेत् *द्राङ्क्षित द्राङ्क्षितुम्

द्राड् *1√drāḍ* (to divide, cut, split) द्राडते द्राडिष्यते अद्राडत द्राडताम् द्राडेत *द्राड द्राडनीय द्राडितव्य द्राडित्वा

द्राह् *1√drāh* (to wake) द्राहते द्रहिष्यते अद्राहत द्राहताम् द्राहेत *द्राढ द्राहणीय द्राहितव्य द्राहित्वा द्राहितुम्

द्रु *1√dru* (to melt, flow, run away, fly, rush) द्रवति द्रोष्यति अद्रवत् द्रवतु द्रवेत् *द्रुत द्रवणीय द्रव उपद्रव

द्रु *5√dru* (to injure) द्रुणोति दरिष्यति अद्रुणोत् द्रुणोतु द्रुणुयात् द्रूयते *द्रुण द्रवितुम्

द्रुड् *1√druḍ* (to sink, perish) द्रोडति द्रोडिष्यति अद्रोडत् द्रोडतु द्रोडेत् *द्रुडित द्रुडितव्य द्रुडित्वा द्रुडितुम्

द्रुड् *6√druḍ* (to sink) द्रुडति द्रुडिष्यति अद्रुडत् द्रुडतु द्रुडेत् *द्रुडित द्रुडनीय द्रुडितव्य द्रुडित्वा द्रुडितुम्

द्रुण् *6√druṇ* (to bend, make crooked) द्रुणति द्रोणिष्यति अद्रोणत् द्रोणतु द्रोणेत् *द्रुणित द्रुणितव्य द्रुणित्वा द्रुणितुम्

द्रुह् *4√druh* (to be hostile, be a traitor, tu turn against) द्रुह्यति द्रोहिष्यति-ध्रोक्ष्यति अद्रूह्यत् द्रुह्यतु द्रुह्येत् *द्रुग्ध-द्रूढ

द्रू *5√drū* (to injure) द्रूणोति दरिष्यति अद्रूणोत् द्रूणोतु द्रूणुयात् *द्रूण

द्रू *9√drū* (to injure) द्रूणाति-द्रूणिते द्रविष्यति अदूनात् द्रूनातु द्रूणीयात् *द्रण

द्रेक् *1√drek* (to grow, increase, sound, show) द्रेकते द्रेकिष्यते अद्रेकत द्रेकताम् द्रेकेत *द्रेकित द्रेकनीय द्रेकित्वा

द्रै *1√drai* (to sleep, lie down, rest) द्रायति द्रास्यति अद्रायत् द्रायतु द्रायेत् अद्रासीत् *द्रात

द्विष् *2√dviṣ* (to dislike, hate) द्वेष्टि-द्विष्टे द्वेक्ष्यति-ते अद्वेद्-अद्विष्ट द्वेष्टु-द्विष्टाम् द्विष्यात्-द्विषीत *द्विष्ट द्वेष्य द्वेष्टुम् द्वेष

द्वृ *1√dvṛ* (to hinder, disregard) द्वरति द्वरिष्यति अद्वरत् द्वरतु द्वरेत् *द्वरित

(ध) (dh)

धक्क् *10√dhakk* (to destroy) धक्कयति-ते धक्कयिष्यति-ते अधक्कयत् धक्कयतु धक्कयेत् *धक्कित धक्कितुम्

धण् *1√dhaṇ* (to sound) धणति धणिष्यति अधणत् धणतु धणेत् *धणित धणनीय धणितव्य धणित्वा धणितुम्

धन् *1√dhan* (to run, scurry) धनति धनिष्यति अधानत्-अधनत् धनतु धनेत् *धनित धननीय धनितव्य धनित्वा धनितुम्

धन्व् *1√dhanv* (to go, run, scurry) धन्वति धन्विष्यति अध्वनत् धन्वतु धन्वेत् *धन्वित धन्वनीय धन्वितव्य धन्वितुम्

धम् *1√dham* (to make sound) धमति धमिष्यति अधमत् धमतु धमेत् *धमित धमनीय धमितव्य धमित्वा धमितुम्

धव् *1√dhav* (to flow) धवते धविष्यते अधवत धवताम् धवेत *धौत धाव्य धवितुम्

धा *3√dhā* (to put) दधाति-धत्ते धास्यति-ते अदधात्-अधत्त दधातु-अत्ताम् दध्यात्-अधत्त *हित हित्वा धातुम् धान्य श्रद्धा

धाख् *1√dhākh* (to dry) धाखति धाखिष्यति अधालाखत् धाखतु धाखेत् *धाखित धाखनीय धाखित्वा धाखितुम्

धाव् *1√dhāv* (to run, glide, flow, stream) धावते-ति धाविष्यति अधावत् धावतु धावेत् *धावित-धौत धावनीय

धि *5√dhi* (to nourish, hold, get, have, catch, possess) धिनोति धेष्यति अधिनोत् धिनोतु धिनुयात् *धित

धि *6√dhi* (to have) धियति धेष्यति अधियत् धियतु धियेत् अधैषीत् *धित धीयात्

धिक्ष् *1√dhikṣ* (to kindle, live, be harassed) धिक्षते धिक्षिष्यते अधिक्षत धिक्षताम् धिक्षेत *धिक्षित

धिन्व् *1√dhinv* (to be pleased) धिन्वति धिन्विष्यति अधिन्वत् धिन्वतु धिन्वेत् *धिन्वित धिन्वनीय धिन्वित्वा धिन्वितुम्

धिष् *3√dhiṣ* (to sound) दिधेष्टि *धिष्ट this verb is used in the vaidic Sanskrit.

धी *4√dhī* (to propitiate, bear) धीयते धेष्यते अधीयत धीयताम् धीयेत *धीन धयनीय धेतव्य धेय धीत्वा धेतुम्

धु *5√dhu* (to tremble, shake, be unstable) धुनोति-धुनुते धाष्यति-ते अधुनोत् धुनोतु धुनुयात् धूयते *धुत

धुक्ष् *1√dhukṣ* (to kindle) धुक्षते धुक्षिष्यते अधुक्षत धुक्षताम् धुक्षेत अधुक्षिष्ट *धुक्षित

धुर्व् *1√dhūrv* (to injure) धूर्वति धूर्विष्यति अधूर्वत् धूर्वतु धूर्वेत् *धूर्ण धूर्वितव्य धूर्वित्वा धूर्वितुम्

धू *1√dhū* (to shake, tremble) धवति-ते धविष्यति-ते अधवत्-त धवतु-ताम् धवेत्-त *धूत-धून

धू *5√dhū* (to shake, move, tremble) धुनोति-धूनुते धोष्यति-धविष्यते अधूनोत-अधीनुत् धुनोतु-धूनुताम् धूनुयात्-धून्वीत धूयते *धून धवनीय धोतव्य धूत्वा धोतुम् धूयमान धवन

धू *6√dhū* (to shake, tremble) धूवति धुविष्यति अधुवत् धुवतु धुवेत् *धूत धूतवान् धुवनीय धुवितव्य धुवितुम्

धू *9√dhū* (to shake) धुनाति-धुनीते धविष्यति-ते अधुनात्-नीत धुनातु-धुनीताम् धुनीयात्-धुनीत *धुन धवनीय धवितुम्

धू *10√dhū* (to shake) धूनयति-ते धुनयिष्यति-ते अधूनयत्-त धूनयतु-ताम् धूनयेत्-त *धून विधूनन

धूप् *1√dhūp* (to warm up) धूपायति धूपायिष्यति अधूपायत् धूपायतु धूपायेत् धूपाय्यते *धूप्त

धूप् *10√dhūp* (to warm up) धूपयति-ते धूपयिष्यतिते अधूपयत्-त धूपयतु-ताम् धूपयेत्-त *धूपित धूपयित्वा धूपयितुम्

धूर् *4√dhūr* (to go, move about) धूर्यते धूरिष्यते अधूर्यत धूर्यताम् धूर्येत *धूर्ण धूरितुम् धूर्य

धूर्व् *1√dhurv* (to injure) धूर्वति धूर्विष्यति अधूर्वत् धूर्वतु धूर्वेत् *धूर्ण

धूश् *10√dhūś* (to adorn, decorate) धूशयति-ते धूशयिष्यति-ते अधूशयत्-त धूशयतु-ताम् धूशयेत्-त *धूष्ट

धूष् *10√dhūṣ* (to adorn) धूषयति-ते धूषयिष्यति-ते अधूषयत्-त धूषयतु-ताम् धूषयेत्-त *धूषित-धूष्ट

धूस् *10√dhūs* (to adorn) धूसयति-ते धूसयिष्यति-ते अधूसयत्-त धूसयतु-ताम् धूसयेत्-त *धूसित

धृ *1√dhṛ* (to bear) धरति-ते धरिष्यति-ते अधरत्-त धरतु-ताम् धरेत्-त *धृत धरणीय धार्य धृत्वा धरण धर्म आधार

धृ *6√dhṛ* (to stay, wait, stop) ध्रियते धरिष्यते अध्रियत ध्रियताम् ध्रियेत अधृत ध्रियते *धृत

धृ *9√dhṛ* (to stay) धृणाति धरिष्यति अधृणात् धृणातु धृणीयात् *धृत धर्तुम्

धृ *10√dhṛ* (to bear, hold, carry) धारयति-ते धारयिष्यति-ते अधारयत्-त धारयतु-ताम् धारयेत्-त धार्यते *धृत-धारित

धृज् *1√dhṛj* (to go) धर्जति धर्जिष्यति अधर्जत् धर्जतु धर्जेत् *धर्जित धर्जनीय धर्जितव्य धर्जित्वा धर्जितुम्

धृञ्ज् *1√dhṛñj* (to go) धृञ्जति धृञ्जिष्यति अधृञ्जत् धृञ्जतु धृञ्जेत् *धृञ्जित धृञ्जनीय धृञ्जितव्य धृञ्जित्वा धृञ्जितुम्

धृष् *1√dhṛṣ* (to dare, come together, become compact) धर्षति धर्षिष्यति अधर्षत् धर्षतु धर्षेत् *धर्षित-धृष्ट

धृष् *5√dhṛṣ* (to be proud) धृष्णोति धर्षिष्यति अधृष्णोत् धृष्णोतु धृष्णुयात् *धृष्ट धर्षणीय धर्षितव्य धृष्ट्वा धर्षितुम धर्षण

धृष् *10√dhṛṣ* (to attack) धर्षयति-ते धर्षयिष्यते अधर्षयत धर्षयताम् धर्षयेत धर्षयाञ्चकार धर्षयिता *धर्षित-धृष्ट

धॄ *9√dhṝ* (to grow old, age) धृणाति धरिष्यति अधृणात् धृणातु धृणीयात् अधारीत *धूर्ण

धे *1√dhe* (to suck, drink) धयति धास्यति अधयत् धयतु धयेत् धीयते *धीत धातुम् धातव्य प्रधाय सुधा धेनु सन्धि

धेक् *10√dhek* (to see) धेकयति-ते धेकयिष्यति-ते अधेकयत्-त धेकयतु-ताम् धेकयेत्-त *धेकित

धेट् *1√dheṭ* (to drink) धयति धास्यति अधात् धयतु धयेत् *धीत धयनीय धयित्वा धयितुम् स्तनन्धय

धोर् *1√dhor* (to go quickly, walk properly) धोरति धोरिष्यति अधोरीत् दुधोर धोरतु धोरेत् *धोरित धोरितुम्

ध्मा *1√dhmā* (to blow, exhale) धमति ध्मास्यति अधमत् धमतु धमेत् *ध्मात ध्मानीय ध्मेय ध्मात्वा ध्मायमान धमनि

ध्माङ्क्ष् *1√dhmāṅkṣ* (to crow, caw) ध्माङ्क्षति ध्माङ्क्षिष्यति अध्माङ्क्षत् ध्माङ्क्षतु ध्माङ्क्षेत् *ध्माङ्क्षित

ध्या *4√dhyā* (to think) ध्यायति ध्यायिष्यति अध्यायत् ध्यायतु ध्यायेत् *ध्यात

ध्यै *1√dhyai* (to meditate) ध्यायति ध्यास्यति अध्यायत् ध्यायतु ध्यायेत् ध्यायते *ध्यात ध्यानीय ध्यात्वा ध्यातुम् ध्यान

ध्रज् *1√dhraj* (to sweep) ध्रजति ध्रजिष्यति अध्राजत्-अध्रजत् ध्रजतु ध्रजेत् *ध्रजित ध्रजनीय ध्रजितव्य ध्रजित्वा ध्रजितुम्

ध्रञ्ज् *1√dhrañj* (to) ध्रञ्जति ध्रञ्जिष्यति अध्रञ्जत् ध्रञ्जतु ध्रञ्जेत् *ध्रञ्जित ध्रञ्जनीय ध्रञ्जितव्य ध्रञ्जित्वा ध्रञ्जितुम्

ध्रण् *1√dhraṇ* (to sound) ध्रणति ध्रणिष्यति अध्राणत्-अध्रणत् ध्रणतु ध्रणेत् *ध्राण ध्रणनीय ध्रणितव्य ध्रणित्वा ध्रणितुम्

ध्रल् *9√dhral* (to glean) ध्रलति ध्रलिष्यति अध्रल्नात् ध्रल्नातु ध्रल्नीयात् *ध्रलित ध्रलितुम् ध्रलित्वा

ध्रस् *10√dhras* (to throw, toss up) उद्+ध्रासयति-ते ध्रासयिष्यति-ते अध्रासयत्-त ध्रासयतु-ताम् ध्रासयेत्-त *ध्रासित

ध्रा *1√dhrā* (to go) ध्राति ध्रायिष्यति अध्रायत् ध्रायतु ध्रायेत् *ध्रात धात्वा धातुम्

ध्राक्ष् *1√dhrākṣ* (to wish) ध्राक्षति ध्राक्षिष्यति अध्राक्षत् ध्राक्षतु ध्राक्षेत् *ध्राक्षित ध्राक्षनीय ध्राक्षित्वा ध्राक्षितुम्

ध्राख् *1√dhrākh* (to dry) ध्राखति ध्राखिष्यति अध्राखत् ध्राखतु ध्राखेत् *ध्राखित ध्राखनीय ध्राखित्वा ध्राखितुम्

ध्राघ् *1√dhrāgh* (to be able) ध्राघते ध्राघिष्यते अध्राघत ध्राघतान् ध्राघत *ध्राघित

ध्राड् *1√dhrāḍ* (to divide, split, tear) ध्राडते ध्राडिष्यते अध्राडत ध्राडतु ध्राडेत् *ध्राडित ध्राडनीय ध्राडितव्य

ध्रिज् *1√dhrij* (to go, move, move about) ध्रेजति ध्रेजिष्यति अध्रेजत् ध्रेजतु ध्रेजेत् *ध्रेजित

ध्राङ्क्ष् *1√dhrāṅkṣ* (to caw) ध्राङ्क्षति ध्राङ्क्षिष्यति अध्रकाङ्क्षत् ध्राङ्क्षतु ध्राङ्क्षेत् *ध्राङ्क्षित ध्राङ्क्षितुम्

ध्रु *1√dhru* (to be steady) ध्रवति ध्रोष्यति अध्रवत् ध्रवतु ध्रवेत् *ध्रुण

ध्रु *6√dhru* (to be steady) ध्रुवति ध्रुष्यति अध्रुषत् ध्रुवतु ध्रुवेत् *ध्रुण

ध्रुव् *6√dhruv* (to be steady) ध्रुवति ध्रुविष्यति अध्रुवत् ध्रुवतु ध्रुवेत्

ध्रै *1√dhrai* (to be satisfied) ध्रायति ध्रायिष्यति अध्रायत् ध्रायतु ध्रायेत् *ध्रात

ध्रेक् *1√dhrek* (to sound, rejoice) ध्रेकते ध्रेकिष्यते अध्रेकत ध्रेकताम् ध्रेकेत *ध्रेकित ध्रेकनीय ध्रेकित्वा ध्रेकितुम्

ध्वज् *1√dhvaj* (to move) ध्वजति ध्वजिष्यति अध्वाजत्-अध्वजत् ध्वजतु ध्वजेत् *ध्वजित ध्वजनीय ध्वजितव्य ध्वजित्वा

ध्वञ्ज् *1√dhvañj* (to go) ध्वञ्जति ध्वञ्जिष्यति अध्वञ्जत् ध्वञ्जतु ध्वञ्जेत् *ध्वञ्जित ध्वञ्जनीय ध्वञ्जित्वा ध्वञ्जितुम्

ध्वण् *1√dhvaṇ* (to sound) ध्वणति ध्वणिष्यति अध्वणत् ध्वणतु ध्वणेत् *ध्वाण ध्वणनीय ध्वणितव्य ध्वणित्वा

ध्वन् *1√dhvan* (to sound) ध्वनति ध्वनिष्यति अध्वनत् ध्वनतु ध्वनेत् *ध्वनित-ध्वान्त ध्वननीय ध्वनितव्य ध्वनितुम् ध्वनि

ध्वन् *10√dhvan* (to sound) ध्वनयति-ते ध्वनयिष्यति-ते अध्वनयत्-त ध्वनयतु-ताम् ध्वनयेत्-त *ध्वनित ध्वन्य ध्वानि

ध्वंस् *1√dhvaṁs* (to vanish, be destroyed ruined) ध्वंसते ध्वंसिष्यते अध्वंसत ध्वंसताम् ध्वंसेत ध्वस्यते *ध्वस्त

ध्वाङ्क्ष् *1√dhvāṅkṣ* (to resound, crow, caw) ध्वाङ्क्षति ध्वाङ्क्षिष्यति अध्वकाङ्क्षत् ध्वाङ्क्षतु ध्वाङ्क्षेत् *ध्वाङ्क्षित

ध्वृ *1√dhvṛ* (to bend) ध्वरति ध्वरिष्यति अध्वरत् अध्वार्षित् ध्वरतु ध्वरेत् *ध्वरित

(न) (n)

नक्क् *10√nakk* (to destroy) नक्कयति-ते नक्कयिष्यति अनक्कयत् नक्कयतु नक्कयेत् *नक्कित नक्कितव्य नक्कितुम्

नक्ष् *1√nakṣ* (to attain, come near, approach) नक्षति नक्षिष्यति अनक्षत् नक्षतु नक्षेत् *नक्षित नक्षितव्य नक्षितुम्

नख् *1√nakh* (to go, move) नखति नखिष्यति अनाखत्-अनखत् नखतु नखेत् *नखित नखत् नखनीय नखित्वा नखितुम्

नङ्ख *1√nakh* (to go, move) नङ्खति-ते नङ्खिष्यति नङ्खतु नङ्खेत *नङ्खित नङ्खत् नङ्खनीय नङ्खितव्य नङ्खित्वा नङ्खितुम्

नज् *1√naj* (to be shy, ashamed, bashful) नजते नजिष्यते अनजत जनताम् नजेत *नजित नजनीय नजितव्य

नट् *1√naṭ* (to dance, act, gesticulate) नटति नटिष्यति अनाटत्-अनटत् नटतु नटेत् *नटित नटनीय नटितव्य नटित्वा

नट् *10√naṭ* (to speak, drop, fall) नाटयति-ते नाटयिष्यति-ते अनाटयत्-त नाटयतु-ताम् नाटयेत्-त *नाटित

नण्ट् *10√naṇṭ* (to speak, drop, fall) नण्टयति-ते नण्टयिष्यति-ते अनण्टयत्-त नण्टयतु-ताम् नण्टयेत्-त *नण्टित

नद् *1√nad* (to echo, resound) नदति नदिष्यति अनदत् नदतु नदेत् नद्यते *नत्त नत्तवत् नदनीय नदितव्य नाद

नद् *10√nad* (to speak) नादयति-ते नादयिष्यति-ते अनादयत्-त नादयतु-ताम् नादयेत्-त नन्द्यते *नादित

नन्द् *1√nand* (to rejoice) नन्दति नन्दिष्यति अनन्दत् नन्दतु नन्देत् *नन्दित नन्दनीय नन्दित्वा नन्दितुम् नन्द नन्दिन्

नभ् *1√nabh* (not to be) नभते नभिष्यते अनभत नभताम् नभेत *नभित-नब्ध नभनीय नभितव्य नभित्वा नभितुम्

नभ् *4√nabh* (to violate) नभ्यति नभिष्यति अनभ्यत् नभ्यतु नभ्येत् *नब्ध नब्धुम् नब्धव्य

नभ् *9√nabh* (to violate) नभ्नाति नभिष्यति अनभ्नात् नभ्नातु नभ्नीयात् *नब्ध नब्धव्य नब्ध्वा नब्धुम्

नम् *1√nam* (to greet, bow) नमति नंस्यति अनमत् नमतु नमेत् *नत नतनीय नतितव्य प्रणम्य नतित्वा नमन प्रणाम

नय् *1√nay* (to go, protect) नयते नयिष्यते अनयत नयताम् नयेत *नयित नयनीय नयितव्य नयित्वा नयितुम्

नर्द् *1√nard* (to roar, bellow) नर्दति नर्दिष्यति अनर्दत् नर्दतु नर्देत् *नर्दित नर्दत् नर्दनीय नर्दित्वा नर्दितुम् नर्द्यमान

नर्ब् *1√narb* (to go, move) नर्बति नर्बिष्यति अनर्बत् नर्बतु नर्बेत् *नर्बित नर्बत् नर्बनीय नर्बित्वा नर्बितुम् नर्बदा

नल् *1√nal* (to smell) नलति नलिष्यति अनलत्-अनालत् नलतु नलेत् *नलित नलनीय नलितव्य नलित्वा नलितुम् नल

नल् *10√nal* (to smell) नालयति-ते नालयिष्यति-ते अनालयत्-त नालयतु-ताम् नालयेत्-त *नालित नलनीय नलितव्य

नश् *4√naś* (to ruin, be lost) नश्यति नशिष्यति अनश्यत् नशतु नश्येत् *नष्ट नाशनीय नष्टव्य नष्ट्वा नष्टुम् नाश नश्वर

नस् *1√nas* (to approach) नसते नसिष्यते अनसत नसताम् नसेत *नसित-नस्त नसनीय नसितव्य नसित्वा नसितुम्

नह् *4√nah* (to tie, bind, grid) नह्यति-ते नत्स्यति अनह्यत् नह्यतु नह्येत *नद्ध नाहनीय नद्धव्य नाह्य नद्ध्वा नद्धुम् नह्यमान

नाथ् *1√nāth* (to beg) नाथते नाथिष्यते अनाथत् नाथताम् नाथेत *नाथित नाथनीय नाथितव्य नाथित्वा नाथितुम् नाथमान

नाध् *1√nādh* (to beg) नाधते नाधिष्यते अनाधत नाधताम् नाधेत *नाधित-नद्ध नाधनीय नाधितव्य नाधितुम्

नास् *1√nās* (to sound) नासते नासिष्यते अनासत नासताम् नासेत *नासित नासितव्य नासित्वा नासितुम्

निक्ष् *1√nikṣ* (to pierce, kiss) निक्षति निक्षिष्यति अनिक्षत् निक्षतु निक्षेत् *निक्षित निक्षितव्य निक्षित्वा निक्षितुम्

निज् *3√nij* (to wash, cleanse) नेनेक्ति-क्ते नेक्ष्यति अनेनक् नेनेक्तु नेनिज्यात् *निक्त नेजनीय नेक्तव्य नेज्य निक्त्वा नेक्तुम्

निञ्ज् *2√niñj* (to purify, cleanse, clean) निङ्क्ते निञ्जिष्यते अनिङ्क्त निङ्क्ताम् निञ्जीत *निञ्जित निञ्जित्वा निञ्जितुम्

निद् *1√nid* (to approach, be near; blame, criticize) नेदति-नेदते नेदिष्यति-ते अनेदत्-त नेदतु-ताम् निद्यात्-त *निन्न

निन्द् *1√nind* (to revile, find fault, reproach, condemn) निन्दति निन्दिष्यति अनिन्दत् निन्दतु निन्देत् निनिन्द निन्दिता निन्द्यते *निन्दित निन्दत् निन्दनीय निन्दितव्य निद्य निन्दित्वा निन्दितुम् निन्द्यमान निन्दन निन्दा निन्दक निन्दिन्

निन्व् *1√ninv* (to water) निन्वति निन्विष्यति अनिन्वत् निन्वतु निन्वेत् *निन्वित निन्वनीय निन्वित्वा निन्वितुम्

निल् *6√nil* (to fatten) निलति नेलिष्यति अनेलत् नेलतु नेलेत् *नेलित नेलनीय नेलितव्य नेल्य नेलित्वा नेलितुम्

निश् *1√niś* (to concentrate) नेशति नेशिष्यति अनेशत् नेशतु नेशेत् *नेशित नेशत् नेशनीय नेशितव्य नेशितुम्

निष् *1√niṣ* (to moisten, wet) नेषति नेषिष्यति अनेषत् नेषतु नेषेत् *निष्ट

निष्क् *10√nisk* (to balance, weigh, measure) निष्कयते निष्कयिष्यते अनिष्कयत निष्कयताम् निष्कयेत *निष्कित
निंस् *2√nims* (to kiss, touch closely, salute) निंस्ते निंसिष्यते अनिंस्त निंस्ताम् निंसीत *निंसित-निंस्त निंसितुम्
नी *1√nī* (to take, carry, conduct) नयति-ते नेष्यति-ते अनयत्-त नयतु-ताम् नयेत्-त *नीत नेतुम् नयनीय नेतव्य नेय
नील् *1√nīl* (to color) नीलति नीलिष्यति अनीलत् नीलतु नीलेत् *नीलित नीलनीय नीलितव्य नीलित्वा निलितुम्
नीव् *1√nīv* (to be steady) नीवति नीविष्यति अनीवत् नीवतु नीवेत् *नीवित नीवनीय नीवितव्य नीवित्वा निवितुम्
नु *2√nu* (to praise, extol, commend) नौति नविष्यति अनौत् नौतु नुयात् *नुत नवितव्य नुत्वा नवितुम् प्रणव
नुड् *6√nuḍ* (to hurt, injure) नुडति नुडिष्यति अनुडत् नुडतु नुडेत् *नुडित नुडनीय नुडितव्य नुडितुम्
नुद् *6√nud* (to push) नुदति-ते नोत्स्यति-ते अनुदत्-ते नुदतु-ताम् नुदेत्-त *नुत्त-नुन्न नोदनीय नोत्तव्य नुत्वा नोत्तुम् विनोद
नू *6√nū* (to praise) नुवति नुविष्यति अनुवत् नुवतु नुवेत् *नुत-नूत नूतवान् नुवनीय नुवितव्य नुवितुम्
नृत् *4√nṛt* (to dance) नृत्यति नर्तिष्यति-नर्त्स्यति अनृत्यत् नृत्यतु नृत्येत् नृत्यते *नृत्त नर्तनीय नर्तित्वा नर्तितुम् नृत्य
नॄ *9√nṝ* (to carry away, take away) नृणाति नरिष्यति अनृणात् नृणातु नृणीयात् *नीर्ण
नेद् *1√ned* (to censure, bring near, go) नेदति नेदिष्यति अनेदत् नेदतु नेदेत् *नेदित
नेष् *1√neṣ* (to go, move) नेषते नेषिष्यते अनेषत नेषताम् नेषेत *नेष्ट-नेषित नेषणीय नेषितव्य नेषित्वा नेषित्वा नेषितुम्
न्यज् *7√nyaj* (to besmear, anoint) न्यनक्ति न्यङ्क्ष्यति अन्यक् न्यक्तु न्यञ्ज्यात् *न्यक्त न्यजनीय न्यक्त्वा न्यक्तुम्
न्युच् *4√nyuć* (to assent, agree to, rejoice, delight, be pleased) न्योच्यति न्योचिष्यति अन्योच्यत् न्योच्यतु न्योच्येत्
न्युब्ज् *6√nyubj* (to drop, throw, press, bend, droop) न्युब्जति न्युब्जिष्यति अन्युब्जत् न्युब्जतु न्युब्जेत्

(प) (p)

पक्ष् *1√pakṣ* (to take, hold, seize, accept, side with) पक्षति पक्षिष्यति अपक्षत् पक्षतु पक्षेत् *पक्षित
पक्ष् *10√pakṣ* (to take, take a side) पक्षयति-ते पक्षयिष्यति अपक्षयत्-त पक्षयतु-ताम् पक्षयेत्-त *पक्षित पक्षयितुम्
पच् *1√pać* (to cook roast bake digest) पचति-ते पक्ष्यति-ते अपचत्-त पचतु-ताम् पचेत्-त *पक्व पक्ववान् पक्त्वा
पञ्च् *1√pañć* (to reveal) पञ्चते पञ्चिष्यते अपञ्चत पञ्चताम् पञ्चेत *पङ्क पञ्चनीय पञ्चित्वा पञ्चितुम्
पञ्च् *10√pañć* (to nerrate) पञ्चयति-ते पञ्चियिष्यति-ते अपञ्चयत्-त पञ्चयतु-ताम् पञ्चयेत्-त *पङ्क
पट् *1√paṭ* (to fall, go) पटति पटिष्यति अपाटत्-अपटत् पटतु पटेत् *पटित पटनीय पटितव्य पटित्वा पटितुम् पेटु
पट् *10√paṭ* (to envelop, speak, split, cut, break) पटयति-ते पटयिष्यति-ते अपटयत्-त पटयतु-ताम् पटयेत्-त *पटित
पठ् *1√paṭh* (to study, read, read aloud, recite, reherse) पठति पठिष्यति अपठत् पठतु पठेत् *पठित पठनीय पाठ
पण् *1√paṇ* (to bargain, deal, barter, purchase, buy, bet) पणते पणिष्यते अपणत पणताम् पणेत *पणित पणनीय
पण् *10√paṇ* (to sell, bargain, stake) पणयति-ते पणयिष्यति अपणयत् पणयतु-ताम् पणयेत्-त पण्यते *पणित
पण्ड् *1√paṇḍ* (to go, go wise) पण्डते पण्डिष्यते अपण्डत पण्डताम् पण्डेत *पण्डित पण्डनीय पण्डितव्य पण्डित्वा
पण्ड् *10√paṇḍ* (to collect, pile up) पण्डयति-ते पण्डयिष्यति-ते अपण्डयत्-त पण्डयतु-ताम् पण्डयेत्-त *पण्डित

पत् *1√pat* (to fall, descend, drop, alight) पतति पतिष्यति अपतत् पततु पतेत् *पतित पतनीय पतितव्य पतितुम् पत्र

पत् *4√pat* (to rule, master, govern, control, possess) पत्यते पत्स्यते अपत्यत पत्यताम् पत्येत *पतित पतित्वा

पत् *10√pat* (to be master of - intransitive; fly, fall) पतयति-ते पतयिष्यति-ते अपतयत्-त पतयतु-ताम् पतयेत्-त

पथ् *1√path* (to go) पथति पथिष्यति अपथत् पथतु पथेत् *पथित पथनीय पथितव्य पथित्वा पथितुम् पथ पथक पथिक

पथ् *10√path* (to send, throw, cast) पथयति-ते पथयिष्यति अपथयत् पथयतु पथयेत् *पन्थ पन्थनीय पन्थयितुम् पन्थन

पद् *4√pad* (to go, roam, attain, study) पद्यते पत्स्यते अपद्यत पद्यताम् पद्येत *पन्न पदनीय सम्पाद्य पत्तुम् पद पादुका

पद् *10√pad* (to go, move) पदयते पदयिष्यते अपदयत पदयताम् पदयेत पद्यते *पदित पदयितव्य पदयित्वा पदयितुम्

पन् *10√pan* (to admire) पनयति-ते पनयिष्यति-ते अपनयत्-त पनयतु-ताम् पनयेत्-त *पनित

पन्थ् *10√panth* (to go) पन्थयति-ते पन्थयिष्यति-ते अपन्थयत्-त पन्थयतु-ताम् पन्थयेत्-त *पन्थित पन्थयित्वा पन्थयितुम्

पम्पस् *11√pampas* (to go) पम्पस्यति-ते पम्पस्यिष्यति-ते अपम्पस्यत्-त पम्पस्यतु-ताम् पम्पस्येत्-त *पम्पसित

पय् *1√pay* (to go, move about) पयते पयिष्यते अपयत पयताम् पयेत *पयित पयनीय पयितव्य पयित्वा पयितुम्

पयस् *11√payas* (to spread) पयस्यति-ते पयस्यिष्यति-ते अपयस्यत्-त पयस्यतु-ताम् पयस्येत्-त *पयसित

पर्ण् *10√parṇ* (to make green) पर्णयति-ते पर्णयिष्यति-ते अपर्णयत्-त पर्अयतु-ताम् पर्णयेत्-त *पर्णित पर्णयितुम् पर्ण

पर्द् *1√pard* (to fart, pass wind) पर्दते पर्दिष्यते अपर्दत पर्दताम् पर्देत *पर्दित पर्दनीय पर्दितव्य पर्द्य पर्दित्वा पर्दितुम्

पर्प् *1√parp* (to move) पर्पति पर्पिष्यति अपर्पत् पर्पतु पर्पेत् *पर्पित पर्पणीय पर्पितव्य पर्पित्वा पर्पितुम्

पर्ब् *1√parb* (to go) पर्बति पर्बिष्यति अपर्बत् पर्बताम् पर्बेत *पर्बित पर्बणीय पर्बितव्य पर्बितुम्

पर्व् *1√parv* (to complete, fill) पर्वति पर्विष्यति अपर्वत् पर्वतु पर्वेत् *पर्वित पर्वितव्य पर्वित्वा पर्वितुम् पर्व

पल् *1√pal* (to go) पलति पलिष्यति अपलत्-अपालत् पलतु पलेत् *पलित पलनीय पलितव्य पलित्वा पलितुम्

पल्यूल् *10√palyūl* (to sanctify) पल्यूलयति पल्यूलयिष्यति अपल्यूलयत्-त पल्यूलयतु-ताम् पल्यूलयेत्-त *पल्यूलित

पल्ल् *1√pall* (to go) पल्लति पल्लिष्यति अपल्लत् पल्लतु पल्लेत् *पल्लित पल्लनीय पल्लितव्य पल्लित्वा पल्लितुम्

पश् *10√paś* (to bind, tie) पाशयति-ते पाशयिष्यति-ते अपाशयत्-त पाशयतु-ताम् पाशयेत्-त *पाशित पाशितवत् पाश

पष् *10√paṣ* (to go) पषयति पषयिष्यति-ते अपषयत्-त पषयतु-ताम् पषयेत्-त *पषित-पष्ट पषयितुम्

पा *1√pā* (to drink) पिबति पास्यति अपिबत् पिबतु पिबेत् *पीत पानीय पेय पातव्य पीत्वा पातुम् पान पिपासा पयस्

पा *2√pā* (to rescue) पाति पास्यति अपात् पातु पायात् *पात पातव्य पात्वा पातुम् पिता पति पुमान् पिपासा पिपासु

पार् *10√pār* (to finish, end, complete) पारयति-ते पारयिष्यति-ते अपारयत्-त पारयतु-ताम् पारयेत्-त *पारित

पाल् *10√pāl* (to protect) पालयति-ते पलयिष्यति अपालयत् पालयतु पालयेत् *पालित पालितव्य पालयित्वा पालियितुम्

पि *6√pi* (to shake, move, go, depart) पियति पेष्यति अपियत् पियतु पियेत् अपैषीत् *पित

पिंस् *1 √piṁs* (to speak, shine) पिंसति पिसिष्यति अपिंसत् पिंसतु पिंसेत् *पिंसित-पिंस्त

पिंस् *10√piṁs* (to speak, shine) पिंसयति पिसयिष्यति अपिंसयत् पिंसयतु पिंसयेत् *पिंसित

पिच्च् *10√picć* (to cut, divide) पिच्चयति-ते पिच्चयिष्यति-ते अपिच्चयत्-त पिच्चयतु-ताम् पिच्चयेत्-त *पिच्चित

पिच्छ् *6√picćh* (to afflict, torment, trouble, hinder, obstruct) पिच्छति पिच्छिष्यति अपिच्छत् पिच्छतु पिच्छेत्

पिच्छ् *10√picćh* (to cut, divide) पिच्छयति-ते पिच्छयिष्यति अपिच्छयत् पिच्छयतु पिच्छयेत् *पिच्छित

पिञ्ज् *2√piñj* (to dye, touch, decorate) पिङ्क्ते पिञ्जिष्यते अपिङ्क्त पिङ्क्ताम् पिञ्जित * पिङ्क्त-पिञ्जित

पिञ्ज् *10√piñj* (to give) पिञ्जयति पिञ्जयिष्यति अपिञ्जयत् पिञ्जयतु पिञ्जयेत् *पिञ्जित

पिट् *1√piṭ* (to gather, collect, heap together) पेटति पेटिष्यति अपेटत् पेटतु पेटेत् *पेटित पेटनीय पेटितव्य पेटित्वा

पिठ् *1√piṭh* (to hurt, injure, suffer, feel pain) पेठति पेठिष्यति अपेठत् पेठतु पेठेत् *पेठित पेठनीय पेठितव्य

पिण्ड् *1√piṇḍ* (to join, unite, roll together) पिण्डते पिण्डिष्यते अपिण्डत पिण्डताम् पिण्डेत *पिण्डित पिण्डनीय

पिण्ड् *10√piṇḍ* (to join, unite) पिण्डयते पिण्डयिष्यते अपिण्डयत पिण्डयताम् पिण्डयेत *पिण्डित पिण्डयित्वा

पिन्व् *1√pinv* (to water) पीन्वति पीन्विष्यति अपीन्वत् पीन्वतु पीन्वेत् *पीन्वित पीन्वितव्य पीन्वित्वा पीन्वितुम्

पिल् *1√pil* (to obstruct) पिलति पिलिष्यति अपिलत् पिलतु पिलेत् *पिलित पिलनीय पिलितव्य पिलित्वा पिलितुम्

पिल् *10√pil* (to throw, cast away) पेलयति-ते पेलयिष्यति-ते अपिलयत्-त पिलयतु-ताम् पिलयेत्-त *पिलित

पिश् *6√piś* (to shape, form, be organized, divide, share) पिशति पेशिष्यति अपिशत पिशतु पिशेत् *पेशित-पिष्ट

पिष् *7√piṣ* (to grind, make powder) पिनष्टि पेक्ष्यति अपिनट् पिनष्टु पिंष्यात् *पिष्ट पेषणीय पेष्टव्य पिष्ट्वा पेष्टुम्

पिस् *1√pis* (to give; take) पेसति पेसिष्यति अपेसत् पेसतु पेसेत् *पेसित-पिस्त

पिस् *10√pis* (to go, dwell) पेसयति-ते पेसयिष्यति-ते अपेसयत्-त पेसयतु-ताम् पेसयेत्-त *पिसित पिसयितुम्

पी *4√pī* (to drink) पीयते पेष्यते अपीयत पीयताम् पीयेत *पीन पयनीय पेतव्य पेय पेतुम्

पीड् *10√pīḍ* (to trouble, torment, harm, molest) पीडयति-ते पीडयिष्यति अपीडयत् पीडयतु पीडयेत् *पीडित पीडा

पीय् *1√pīy* (to abuse) पीयति पीयिष्यति अपीयत् पीयतु पीयेत् *पीयित पीयनीय पीयितव्य पीयित्वा पीयितुम्

पील् *1√pīl* (to check, obstruct, hinder) पीलति पीलिष्यति अपीलत् पीलतु पीलेत *पीलित पीलत् पीलनीय

पीव् *1√pīv* (to fatten, become large) पीवति पीविष्यति अपीवत् पीवतु पीवेत् अपीवीत् *पीवित

पुंस् *10√puṁs* (to grind, punish) पुंसयति-ते पुंसयिष्यति-ते अपुंसयत्-त पुंसयतु-ताम् पुंसयेत्-त *पुंसित-पुंस्त

पुच्छ् *1√puććh* (to measure) पुच्छति पुच्छिष्यति अपुच्छत् पुच्छतु पुच्छेत् अपुच्छीत् *पुच्छित

पुट् *1√puṭ* (to grind, rub) पोटति पोटिष्यति अपोटत् पोटतु पोटेत् *पोटित पोटनीय पोटितव्य पोटित्वा पोटितुम्

पुट् *6√puṭ* (to embrace, clasp, intertwine) पुटति-ते पुटिष्यति-ते अपुटत्-त पुटतु-ताम् पुटेत्-त *पुटित पुटनीय

पुट् *10√puṭ* (to join, fasten, grind, speak, shine) पुटयति-ते पुटियिष्यति अपुटयत्-त पुटयतु-ताम् पुटयेत् *पुटित

पुट्ट् *10√puṭṭ* (to shrink, become small, diminish) पुट्टयति-ते पुट्टयिष्यति अपुट्टयत्-त पुट्टयतु-ताम् पुट्टयेत् *पुट्टित

पुड् *6√puḍ* (to leave, quit, abandon) पुडति पुडिष्यति अपुडत् पुडतु पुडेत् *पुडित पुडनीय पुडितव्य पुडितुम्

पुण् *6√puṇ* (to be virtuous) पुणति पुणिष्यति अपुणत् पुणतु पुणेत् *पुणित पुणनीय पुणितव्य पुणित्वा पुणितुम् पुण्य

पुण्ट् *10√puṇṭ* (to spark, shine) पुण्टयति-ते पुण्टियिष्यति अपुण्टयत्-त पुण्टयतु-ताम् पुण्टयेत् *पुण्टित

पुण्ड् *1√puṇḍ* (to grind, reduce to powder) पुण्डति पुण्डिष्यति अपुण्डत् पुण्डतु पुण्डेत् *पुण्डित पुण्डनीय पुण्डितुम्

पुथ् *4√puth* (to crush, annihilate, overpower, drown) पुन्थति पुन्थिष्यति अपुन्थत् पुन्थतु पुन्थयेत् *पुत्थित पुन्थनीय

पुथ् *10√puth* (to speak, shine) पोथयति-ते पोथयिष्यति-ते अपोथयत्-त पोथयतु-ताम् पोथयेत्-त *पोथित

पुन्थ् *1√punth* (to hurt) पुन्थति पुन्थिष्यति अपुन्थित् पुन्थतु पुन्थेत् *पुन्थित पुन्थनीय पुन्थितव्य पुन्थित्वा पुन्थितुम्

पुर् *6√pur* (to go ahead, go forward) पुरति पुरिष्यति अपुरत् पुरतु पुरेत् *पूर्त-पूर्ण पुरणीय पुरित्वा पुरितुम्

पूर्व् *1√purv* (to fill, dwell, invite) पूर्वति पूर्विष्यति अपूर्वत् पूर्वतु पूर्वेत् *पूर्ण पूर्वितव्य पूर्वित्वा पूर्वितुम् सम्पूर्ण

पूर्व् *10√purv* (to dwell, invite) पूर्वयति-ते पूर्वयिष्यति-ते अपूर्वयत्-त पूर्वयतु-ताम् पूर्वयेत्-त *पूर्वित

पुल् *1√pul* (to grow, draw, pull out) पोलति पोलयिष्यति अपोलत् पोलतु पोलेत् *पोलित पोलनीय पोलितव्य पुलिन

पुल् *10√pul* (to grow) पोलयति-ते पोलयिष्यति-ते अपोलयत्-त पोलयतु-ताम् पोलयेत्-त *पोलित

पुष् *1√puṣ* (to nourish) पोषति पोषिष्यति अपोषत् पोषतु पोषेत् पुष्यते *पोषित-पुष्ट पोषणीय पाषित्वा पुष्यमाण पोषण

पुष् *4√puṣ* (to thrive) पुष्यति पोक्ष्यति अपुष्यत् पुष्यतु पुष्येत् *पुष्ट पोषणीय पोष्टव्य पुष्य पुष्ट्वा पोष्टुम् पुष्टि पोषण

पुष् *9√puṣ* (to thrive, nurture, foster, nourish, support) पुष्णाति पोषिष्यति अपुष्णात् पुष्णातु पुष्णीयात् *पुष्ट

पुष् *10√puṣ* (to nourish, bear) पोषयति-ते पोषयिष्यति-ते अपोषयत्-त पोषयतु-ताम् पोषयेत्-त पोष्यते *पोषित-पुष्ट

पुष्प् *4√puṣp* (to blossom, bloom, open, blow, expand) पुष्प्यति पुष्पिष्यति अपुष्प्यत् पुष्प्यतु पुष्प्येत् *पुष्पित पुष्प

पुस् *10√pus* (to rub, decrease, lessen) पोसयति-ते पोसयिष्यति अपोसयत् पोसयतु पोसयेत्

पुस्त् *10√pust* (to tie, bind) पुस्तयति-ते पुस्तयिष्यति अपुस्तयत् पुस्तयतु पुस्तयेत् *पुस्तित

पू *1√pū* (to cleanse) पवते पविष्यते अपवत पवताम् पवेत *पूत पवनीय पव्य पूत्वा-पवित्वा पवितुम् पवन पावन पूति

पू *4√pū* (to cleanse) पूयते पूयिष्यते अपूयत पूयताम् पूयेत पूयते *पूत-पवित पवनीय पवितव्य पवित्वा-पूत्वा पवितुम्

पू *9√pū* (to cleanse) पुनाति-पुनीते पविष्यति-ते अपुनात्-अपुनीत पुनातु-पुनीताम् पुनीयात्-पुनीत पूयते *पूत-पून पुनत् पूनवत् पवनीय पवितव्य पव्य पूत्वा पवितुम् पवन पान पावन पावक पवि पवित्र पूति पुत्र

पूज् *10√pūj* (to worship, revere, adore) पूजयति-ते पूजयिष्यति-ते अपूजयत्-त पूजयतु-ताम् पूजयेत्-त *पूजित पूजा

पूण् *10√pūṇ* (to gather, collect, amass) पूणयति-ते पूणयिष्यति-ते अपूणयत्-त पूणयतु-ताम् पूणयेत्-त *पूणित

पूय् *1√pūy* (to stink, putrefy, rot) पूयते पूयिष्यते अपूयत पूयताम् पूयेत *पूत पूयनीय पूयितव्य पूय्य पूयित्वा

पूर् *4√pūr* (to fill, please, satisfy) पूर्यते पूरिष्यते अपूर्यत पूर्यताम् पूर्येत पूर्यते *पूर्ण-पूरित पूरितव्य पूरितुम्

पूर् *10√pūr* (to fill) पूरयति-ते पूरयिष्यति-ते अपूरयत्-त पूरतु-ताम् पूरयेत्-त *पूरित पूरणीय पूर्य पूरयितुम् पूर्यमाण

पूर्ण् *10√pūrṇ* (to assemble, fill) पूर्णयति-ते पूर्णयिष्यति-ते अपूर्णयत्-त पूर्णयतु-ताम् पूर्णयेत्-त *पूर्णित पूर्णयित्वा

पूर्व् *10√pūrv* (to live, dwell) पूर्वयति-पूर्वति पूर्वयिष्यति-ते अपूर्वयत्-त पूर्वयतु-ताम् पूर्वयेत्-त *पूर्वत पूर्वयितुम्

पूल् *1√pūl* (to heap up) पूलति पूलिष्यति अपूलत् पूलतु पूलेत् अपूलीत् *पूलित पूलितव्य पूलित्वा पूलितुम्

पूल् *10√pūl* (to heap, collect, gather) पूलयति-ते पूलयिष्यति-ते अपूलयत्-त पूलयतु-ताम् पूलयेत्-त *पूलित

पूष् *1√pūṣ* (to grow, increase, nourish) पूषति पूषिष्यति अपूषत् पूषतु पूषेत् *पूष्ट पूषणीय पूष्ट्वा

पृ *3√pṛ* (to protect) पिपर्ति परिष्यति अपिपः पिपर्तु पिपूर्यात् पपार परिता पूर्यते पार्यते *पृत पृत्वा पर्तुम्

पृ *5√pṛ* (to be pleased) पृणोति परिष्यति अप्रणोत् पृणोतु पृणुयात् *पृत पृण्वत् परणीय पर्तव्य समृत्य पार्य पर्तुम्

पृ *6√pṛ* (to be pleased, be busy, active) प्रियते परिष्यते अप्रियत् प्रियताम् प्रियेत *पृत-परित परिणीय पर्तव्य पर्तुम्

पृ *10√pṛ* (to raise, support) पारयति-ते पारयिष्यति-ते अपारयत्-त पारयतु-ताम् पारयोत्-त *पारित

पृच् *1√pṛć* (to touch, hang, restrain) पर्चति-ते पर्चिष्यति-ते अपर्चत्-त पर्चतु-ताम् पर्चेत्-त *पृक्ण

पृच् *2√pṛć* (to mix, mingle, come in contact with something) पृक्ते पर्चिष्यते अपृक्त पर्चिषिष्ट *पृक्ण पृचीत

पृच् *7√pṛć* (to merge) पृणक्ति पर्चिष्यति अपृणक् पृणक्तु पृञ्च्यात् *पृक्त पर्चनीय पर्चितव्य पर्चित्वा पर्चितुम् सम्पृक्त

पृच् *10√pṛć* (to join, satisfy) पर्चयति-ते पर्चयिष्यति-ते अपर्चयत्-त पर्चयतु-ताम् पर्चयेत्-त *पृक्ण

पृञ्ज् *2√pṛñj* (to come in contact) पृङ्क्ते पृञ्जिष्यते अपृङ्क्त पृङ्क्ताम् पृञ्जीत *पृञ्जित पृञ्जनीय पृञ्जित्वा पृञ्जितुम्

पृड् *6√pṛḍ* (to make happy) पृडति पर्डिष्यति अपर्डत् पर्डतु पर्डेत् अपर्डीत *पृडित पृडितव्य पृडित्वा पृडितुम्

पृण् *6√pṛṇ* (to make happy, delight) पृणति पर्णिष्यति अपर्णत् पुणतु पृणेत् अपर्णीत *पृणितव्य पृणित्वा पृणितुम्

पृथ् *10√pṛth* (to send, direct, extend, cast, throw) पर्थयति-ते पर्थयिष्यति-ते अपर्थयत्-त पर्थयतु-ताम् पर्थयेत्-त

पृष् *1√pṛṣ* (to sprinkle, give, vex, pain, weary, injure) पर्षति पर्षिष्यति अपर्षत् पर्षतु पर्षेत् *पृष्ट

पॄ *1√pṝ* (to fill) परति परिष्यति अपरत् परतु परेत् *पूर्ण

पॄ *3√pṝ* (to fill) पिपर्ति परिष्यति अपिपः पिपर्तु पिपूर्यात *पूर्ण परणीय परितव्य पार्य आपूर्य पूर्त्वा परितुम् पुर पर्व

पॄ *9√pṝ* (to fill) पृणाति परिष्यति अपृणात् पृणातु पृणीयात् *पूर्ण पृणत् परणीय परितव्य पूर्य पूर्त्वा परितुम् परण

पॄ *10√pṝ* (to fill) पारयति पारयिष्यति-ते अपारयत्-त पारयतु-ताम् पारयेत्-त *पूर्ण-पारित

पेल् *1√pel* (to go, shake, tremble) पेलति पेलिष्यति अपेलत् पेलतु पेलेत् *पेलित पेलनीय पेलितव्य पेलित्वा

पेल् *10√pel* (to go) पेलयति पेलयिष्यति-ते अपेलयत्-त पेलयतु-ताम् पेलयेत्-त *पेलित

पेव् *1√pev* (to serve) पेवते पेविष्यते अपेवत पेवताम् पेवेत *पेवित पेवनीय पेवितव्य पेवित्वा पेवितुम् पेवमान

पेष् *1√peṣ* (to make effort, resolve up on) पेषते पेषिष्यते अपेषत पेषताम् पेषेत *पेषित पेषणीय पेषित्वा पेषितुम्

पेस् *1√pes* (to go, move) पेसति पेसिष्यति अपेसत् पेसतु पेसेत् *पेसित

पै *1√pai* (to dry, wither) पायति पास्यति अपायत् पायतु पायेत् पायते *पात-पायित-पान पातव्य पानीय पाय्य पात्वा

पैण् *1√paiṇ* (to inspire, motivate) पैणति पैणिष्यति अपैणत् पैणतु पैणेत् *पैणित पैणनीय पैणितव्य पैणित्वा पैणितुम्

प्याय् *1√pyāy* (to grow, swell, become big) प्यायते प्यायिष्यते प्यायताम् प्यायेत *पीन-पीत

प्यै *1√pyai* (to grow, increase, grow fat) आ+प्यायते प्यास्यते अप्यायत प्यायतु प्यायेत प्यायते *प्यान

प्रच्छ् *6√praććh* (to ask, question) पृच्छति प्रक्ष्यति अपृच्छत् पृच्छतु पृच्छेत् *पृष्ट प्रच्छनीय पृष्ट्वा पृष्टुम् पृच्छा प्रश्न

प्रथ् *1√prath* (to spread, grow) प्रथते प्रथिष्यते अप्रथत प्रथताम् प्रथेत *प्रथित प्रथनीय प्रथा पृथा पृथिवी प्रथम प्रथु

प्रथ् *10√prath* (to shine) प्रथयति-ते प्रथयिष्यति-ते अप्रथयत्-त प्रथयतु-ताम् प्रथयेत्-त *प्रथित प्रथयित्वा प्रथयितुम्

प्रस् *1√pras* (to spread, make) प्रसते प्रसिष्यते अप्रसत प्रसतु प्रसेत *प्रसित प्रसनीय प्रसितव्य प्रसितुम्

प्रस् *4√pras* (to spread) प्रस्यते अप्रस्यत प्रस्यताम् प्रस्येत *प्रस्त

प्रा *2√prā* (to complete, fill) प्राति प्रास्यति अप्रात् प्रातु प्रायात् *पूर्त-प्रीत

प्री *4√prī* (to please, gladden, delight) प्रीयते प्रेष्यते अप्रीयत प्रीयताम् प्रीयेत *प्रीत प्रयणीय प्रेतव्य प्रीत्वा प्रेतुम्

प्री *9√prī* (to please) प्रीणाति-पीणीते प्रेष्यति अप्रीणात् प्रीणातु प्रीणीयात् प्रीण्यते *प्रीण-पीत प्रीति प्रिय प्रेमन् प्रेमिन्

प्री *10√prī* (to please) प्रीणयति प्रीणयिष्यति अप्रणयत् प्रीणयतु प्रीणयेत् *प्रीणित प्रीणनीय प्रीणयितव्य प्रीणयितुम्

प्रु *1√pru* (to flow) प्रवते प्रोष्यते अप्रवत् प्रवतु प्रवेत् अप्रोष्ट *प्रवित

प्रुट् *1√pruṭ* (to rub, grind) प्रोटति प्रोटिष्यति अप्रोटत् प्रोटतु प्रोटेत् *प्रोटित प्रोटनीय प्रोटितव्य प्रोटित्वा प्रोटितुम्

प्रुष् *1√pruṣ* (to burn, put fire to) प्रोषति प्रोषिष्यति अप्रोषत् प्रोषतु प्रोषेत् *प्रुष्ट प्रोषणीय प्रोषितव्य प्रोषित्वा प्रोषितुम्

प्रुष् *9√pruṣ* (to moisten, get wet) प्रुष्णाति प्रोषिष्यति अप्रुष्णात् प्रुष्णातु प्रुष्णीयात् *प्रुष्ट प्रोषणीय प्रोषितव्य प्रोशितुम्

प्रेक्ष् *1√prekṣ* (to behold, see, watch, look, perceive) प्रेक्षते प्रेक्षिष्यते अप्रेक्षत प्रेक्षतु प्रेक्षेत् *प्रेक्षित

प्रेङ्ख् *1√preṅkh* (to vibrate, shake, tremble, go too and fro) प्रेङ्खति प्रेङ्खिष्यति अप्रेङ्खत् प्रेङ्खतु प्रेङ्खेत् *प्रेङ्खित

प्रेङ्खोल् *10√preṅkhol* (to swing, oscillate) प्रेङ्खोलयति-ते प्रेङ्खोलयिष्यति-ते अप्रेङ्खोलयत्-त प्रेङ्खोलयतु-ताम् प्रेङ्खोलयेत्-त *प्रेङ्खोलित प्रेङ्खोलयत् प्रेङ्खोलनीय प्रेङ्खोलयितव्य प्रेङ्खोलयित्वा प्रेङ्खोलयितुम्

प्रेष् *1√preṣ* (to move, send) प्रेषते प्रेषिष्यते अप्रेषत प्रेषताम् प्रेषेत *प्रेष्ट-प्रेषित प्रेषणीय प्रेषित्वा प्रेषितुम्

प्रेष् *4√preṣ* (to move, send) प्रेष्यति प्रेषिष्यति अप्रेष्यत् प्रेष्यतु प्रेष्येत् *प्रेष्ट

प्रोक्ष् *6√prokṣ* (to consecrate, sprinkle up on) प्रोक्षति प्रोक्षिष्यति अप्रोक्षत् प्रोक्षतु प्रोक्षेत् *प्रोक्षित

प्रोथ् *1√proth* (to be equal) प्रोथति-ते प्रोथिष्यति अप्रोथत् प्रोथतु प्रोथेत् *प्रोथित प्रोथनीय प्रोथित्वा प्रोथितुम् प्रोथमान

प्लक्ष् *1√plakṣ* (to eat, consume) प्लक्षति प्लक्षिष्यति अप्लाक्षत् प्लक्षतु प्लक्षेत् *प्लाक्षित

प्लिह् *1√plih* (to go) प्लेहते प्लेहिष्यते अप्लेहत प्लेहताम् प्लेहेत् *प्लिहिति-प्लीढ

प्ली *9√plī* (to go, move) प्लिनाति-प्लीनाति प्लेष्यति अप्लीनात् प्लीनातु प्लीनीयात् *प्लीन

प्लु *1√plu* (to float, swing, swim) प्लवते प्लोष्यते अप्लवत प्लवताम् प्लवेत प्लुयते *प्लुत

प्लुष् *1√pluṣ* (to burn, scorch) प्लोषति प्लोषिष्यति अप्लुषत् प्लुषतु प्लुषेत् प्लुष्यते *प्लुष्ट

प्लुष् *4√pluṣ* (to burn) प्लुष्यति ष्लोषिष्यति अप्लुष्यत् प्लुष्यतु प्लुष्येत *प्लुष्ट

प्लुष् *9√pluṣ* (to spray, sprinkle, wet, fill, anoint) प्लुष्णाति प्लविष्यति अप्लुनात् प्लुनातु प्लुनीयात् *प्लुष्ट

प्लुस् *4√plus* (to burn, shake) प्लुस्यति प्लोसिष्यति अप्लुष्यत् प्लुष्यतु प्लुष्येत *प्लुस्त

प्लेव् *4√plev* (to serve, attend, wait up on) प्लेवते प्लेविष्यते अप्लेव्यत प्लेव्यताम् प्लेव्येत

प्सा *2√psā* (to devour, eat) प्साति प्सास्यति अप्सात् प्सातु प्सायात् *प्सात

(फ) (ph)

फक्क् *1√phakk* (to go slowly, have preconceived opinion) फक्कति फक्किष्यति अफक्कत् फक्कतु फक्केत्

फण् *1√phaṇ* (to move about, spring) फणति फणिष्यति अफणत् फणतु फणेत् *फणित-फाण्ट फणनीय फणितव्य

फल् *1√phal* (to bare fruit, yield or produce) फलति फलिष्यति अफलत् फलतु फलेत् *फलित-फूल्ल फलितव्य

फुल्ल् *1√phull* (to bloom) फुल्लति फुल्लिष्यति अफुल्लत् अफुल्लत् फुल्लतु फुल्लेत् *फुल्लित फुल्लनीय फुल्लितव्य

फेल् *1√phel* (to move, go) फेलति फेलिष्यति अफेलत् फेलतु फेलेत् *फेलित फेलनीय फेलितव्य फेलित्वा फेलितुम्

(ब) (b)

बंह् *1√bam̐h* (to make firm) बंहते बंहिष्यते अबंहत बंहताम् बंहेत *बंहित-बाढ

बठ् *1√baṭh* (to grow, increase) बठति बठिष्यति अबठत् बठतु बठेत् *बठित बठितव्य बठितुम्

बण् *1√baṇ* (to speak) बणति बणिष्यति अबाणत्-अबणत् बणतु बणेत् *बाण बणनीय बणितव्य बणित्वा बणितुम्

बद् *1√bad* (to be steady) बदति बदिष्यति अबादत्-अबदत् बदतु बदेत् *बदित-बत्त बदनीय

बध् *1√badh* (to abhor) बिभित्सते बिभत्सिष्यते अबीभत्सत बीभत्सताम् बीभत्सेत *बिभत्सित बीभत्सित्वा बीभत्सा

बध् *10√badh* (to bind, tie) बाधयति बाधयिष्यति अबाधयत् बाधयतु बाधयेत् बाध्यते *बद्ध-बाधित बाध्य

बन्ध् *9√bandh* (to tie) बध्नाति भन्त्स्यति अबध्नात् बध्नातु बध्नीयात् *बद्ध बन्धनीय बन्धव्य बद्धा बन्धुम् बन्धन बन्धु

बन्ध् *10√bandh* (to bind) बन्धयति-ते बन्धयिष्यति-ते अबन्धयत्-त बन्धयतु-ताम् बन्धयेत्-त *बन्धित-बद्ध बन्धयितुम्

बर्ब् *1√barb* (to go) बर्बति बर्बिष्यति अबर्बत् बर्बतु बर्बेत् *बर्बित बर्बितव्य बर्बित्वा बर्बितुम्

बर्ह् *1√barh* (to speak, give, cover, spread) बर्हते बर्हिष्यते अबर्हत बर्हताम् बर्हेत *बर्हित

बर्ह् *10√barh* (to hurt, injure, destroy) बर्हयति-ते बर्हयिष्यति-ते अबर्हयत्-त बर्हयतु-ताम् बर्हयेत्-त *बर्हित

बल् *1√bal* (to give, hurt) बलति-ते बलिष्यति-ते अबलत्-त बलतु-ताम् बलेत्-त *बलित वलित्वा बलवत् बाल बाला

बल् *10√bal* (to support, live, describe) बलयति-ते बलयिष्यति-ते अबलयत्-त बलयतु-ताम् बलयेत्-त *बलित

बल्ह *1 √balh* (to superior) बल्हते बल्हिष्यते अबल्हत बल्हताम् बल्हेत *बल्हित

बल्ह *10√balh* (to speak) बल्हयति-ते बल्हयिष्यति-ते अबल्हयत्-त बल्हयतु-ताम् बल्हयेत्-त *बल्हित

बस् *9√bas* (to hurt) बस्नाति बसिष्यति अबस्नात् बस्नातु बस्नीयात् *बस्त

बस्त् *10√bast* (to go, hurt, kill) बस्तयते बस्तयिष्यते अबस्तयत बस्तयताम् बस्तयेत *बस्तित

बाड् *1√bāḍ* (to bathe) बाडते बाडिष्यते अबाडत बाडतु बाडेत् *बाडित बाडनीय बाडितव्य बाडित्वा बाडितुम्

बाध् *1√bādh* (to oppress) बाधते बाधिष्यते अबाधत बाधताम् बाधेत *बाधित बाधनीय बाधित्वा बाधितुम् बाध्य

बाह् *1√bāh* (to attempt) बाहते बाहिष्यते अबाहत बाहताम् बाहेत *बाढ

बिद् *1√bit* (to swear, curse, rebuke) बेटति बेटिष्यति अबेटत् बेटतु बेटेत् *बेटित बेटनीय बेटितव्य बेटित्वा बेटितुम्

बिन्द् *1√bind* (to divide, split, dissect) बिन्दति बिन्दिष्यति अबिन्दत् बिन्दतु बिन्देत् *बिन्दित बिन्दनीय बिन्दितुम्

बिल् *6√bil* (to cut, split, cleave, divide) बेलति बेलिष्यति अबेलत् बेलतु बेलेत् *बेलित

बिल् *10√bil* (to cut) बेलयति बेलिष्यति अबेलयत्-त बेलयतु-ताम् बेलयेत्-त *बेलित

बिस् *4√bis* (to instigate) बिश्यति बेशिष्यति अबिश्यत् बिश्यतु बिश्येत्

बुक्क् *1√bukk* (to bark, speak, talk) बुक्कति बुक्किष्यति अबुक्कित् बुक्कतु बुक्केत् *बुक्कित

बुक्क् *10√bukk* (to bark) बुक्कयति-ते बुक्कयिष्यति-ते अबुक्कयत्-त बुक्कयतु-ताम् बुक्कयेत्-त *बुक्कित

बुङ्ग् *1√buṅg* (to renounce, abandon) बुङ्गति बुङ्गिष्यति अबुङ्गत् बुङ्गतु बुङ्गेत् *बुङ्क

बुड् *1√buḍ* (to hide, cover, conceal) बुडति बुडिष्यति अबुडत् बुडतु बुडेत् *बुडित

बुद् *1√bud* (to perceive, discern, understand, know) बोदति-ते बोदिष्यति-ते अबोदत्-त बोदतु-ताम् बोदेत्-त *बुद्ध

बुध् *1√budh* (to understand, know, comprehend) बोधति-ते बोधिष्यति-ते अबोधत्-त बोधतु-ताम् बोधेत्-त *बुधित-बोधित बोधितव्य बोधनीत बोध्य बुध्यमान बोधितुम् बुधित्वा-बोधित्वा बोध बोधन बोधक बोधयत् बोधिता

बुध् *4√budh* (to understand) बुध्यते भोत्स्यते अबुध्यत बुध्यताम् बुध्येत *बुद्ध बोधनीय बोधितव्य बोध्य बुद्ध्वा बोद्धुम्

बुन्द् *1√bund* (to understand, descry, reflect) बुन्दति बुन्दिष्यति अबुन्दित् बुन्दतु बुन्देत् *बुन्द्य-बुन्न बुन्द्यमान बुन्नवान्

बुन्ध् *1√bundh* (to perceive, discern, see) बुन्धति बुन्धिष्यति अबुन्धित् बुन्धतु बुन्धेत् *बुन्धित बुन्धनीय बुन्धित्वा

बुल् *10√bul* (to submerge, sink, plunge) बोलयति-ते बोलयिष्यति-ते अबोलयत्-त बोलयतु-ताम् बोलयेत्-त *बोलित

बुस् *4√bus* (to let go, renounce) बुस्यति बुसिष्यति अबुस्यत् बुस्यतु बुस्येत् *बुस्त

बुस्त् *10√bust* (to respect) बुस्तयति बुस्तयिष्यति बुस्तयति-ते बुस्तयिष्यति अबुस्तयत् बुस्तयतु बुस्तयेत् *बुस्तित

बृंह् *1√bṛm̃h* (to grow) बृंहति बृंहिष्यति अबृंहत् बृंहतु बृहेत् *बृंहित बृंहितव्य बृंहणीय बृंह्य बृंहित्वा बृंहितुम् परिबृढ

बृंह् *10√bṛm̃h* (to grow) बृंहयति-ते बृंहयिष्यति-ते अबृंहयत्-त बृंहयतु-ताम् बृंहयेत्-त *बृंहित-बृढ

बृह् *1√bṛh* (to expand, grow, expand, be nourished) बर्हति बर्हिष्यति अबर्हत् बर्हतु बर्हेत् *बृढ

बृह् *6√bṛh* (to increase) बृहति बर्हिष्यति अबर्हत् बर्हतु बर्हेत् *बृढ बर्हित्वा बर्हितुम्

बेह् *1√beh* (to make an attempt) बेहते बेहिष्यते अबेहत बेहताम् बेहेत *बेहित

ब्रू *2√brū* (to speak) ब्रवीति-आह-ब्रूते वक्ष्यति-ते अब्रवीत्-अब्रूत ब्रवीतु-ब्रूताम् ब्रूयात्-ब्रूवीत उच्यते *उक्त-वाचित ब्रुवत्-उक्तवत् वचनीय वक्तव्य उक्त्वा वक्तुम् वाच्य प्रोच्य सुवाच्य वाक्य ब्रुवाण-उच्यमान-वाच्यमान वाक्-वाच वाक्पटु अवाच्य अनुवाच् उक्ति निरुक्त वच वचन वाचन वाचा वाचाल वाग्मिन् वागीश वाग्देवी विवक्षु वक्तृ वक्त्र वचन प्रवचन

ब्रूस् *10√brūs* (to kill) ब्रूसयति-ते ब्रूसयिष्यति-ते अब्रूसयत्-त ब्रूसयतु-ताम् ब्रूसयेत्-त *ब्रूसित

ब्ली *9√blī* (to choose) ब्लिनाति-ब्लीनाति ब्लेष्यति अब्लीनात् ब्लीनातु ब्लीनीयात् *ब्लीन

(भ) (bh)

भक्ष् *10√bhakṣ* (to eat, devour) भक्षयति-ते भक्षयिष्यति-ते अभक्षयत्-त भक्षयतु-ताम् भक्षयेत्-त *भक्षित भक्ष भक्षण

भज् *1√bhaj* (to divide; adore) भजति-ते भक्ष्यति-ते अभजत्-त भजतु-ताम् भजेत्-त *भक्त भजनीय भजन विभक्ति

भज् *10√bhaj* (to roast, cook, give) भाजयति-ते भाजयिष्यति-ते अभाजयत्-त भाजयतु-ताम् भाजयेत्-त *भाजित

भञ्ज् *7√bhañj* (to break) भनक्ति भङ्क्ष्यति अभनक् भनक्तु भञ्जात् *भग्न भञ्जनीय भङ्क्तव्य भङ्क्त्वा भङ्क्तुम् भङ्ग

भञ्ज् *10√bhañj* (to speak) भञ्जयति-ते भञ्जयिष्यति-ते अभञ्जयत्-त भञ्जयतु-ताम् भञ्जयेत्-त *भञ्जित

भट् *1√bhaṭ* (to foster, maintain) भटति भटिष्यति अभटत् भटतु भटेत् *भटित भटनीय भटितव्य भटित्वा भटितुम् भट

भट् *10√bhaṭ* (to converse, speak, yap) भटयति-ते भटयिष्यति-ते अभटयत्-त भटयतु-ताम् भटयेत्-त *भटित

भण् *1√bhaṇ* (to say, speak, describe) भणति भणिष्यति अभणत् भणतु भणेत् *भणित-भाण भणनीय भणितव्य

भण्ड् *1√bhaṇḍ* (to quarrel, mock, chide) भण्डते भण्डिष्यते अभण्डत भण्डताम् भण्डेत *भण्डित भण्डित्वा भण्डितुम्

भण्ड् *10√bhaṇḍ* (to cheat) भण्डयति-ते भण्डयिष्यति अभण्डयत् भण्डयतु भण्डयेत् *भण्डित

भन् *1√bhan* (to worship; cry, shout, resound) भनति भनिष्यति अभनत् भनतु भनेत् *भनित भननीय भनितव्य

भन्द् *1√bhand* (to tell a good news, be fortunate, honor) भन्दते भन्दिष्यते अभन्दत भन्दताम् भन्देत *भन्दित भन्द्य

भन्द् *10√bhand* (to do an auspicious act) भन्दयति-ते भन्दयिष्यति-ते अभन्दयत्-त भन्दयतु-ताम् भन्दयेत्-त *भन्दित

भर्त्स् *10√bharts* (to deride, revile, reproach) भर्त्सयते भर्त्सयिष्यते अभर्त्सयत भर्त्सयताम् भर्त्सयेत्-त *भर्त्सित

भर्व् *1√bharv* (to violate) भर्वति भर्विष्यति अभर्वत् भर्वतु भर्वेत् *भर्वित भर्वितव्य भर्वित्वा भर्वितुम्

भल् *1√bhal* (to describe, expound, explain) भलते भलिष्यते अभलत भलताम् *भलित भलनीय भलितुम्

भल् *10√bhal* (to see, behold) नि-भालयते भालयिष्यते अभालयत भालयताम् भालयेत *भालित

भल्ल् *1√bhall* (to narrate, tell; hurt, give) भल्लते भल्लिष्यते अभल्लत भल्लताम् *भल्लित भल्लनीय भल्लितुम्

भष् *1√bhaṣ* (to bark, growl, rail at) भषति भषिष्यति अभषत् भषतु भषेत् *भषित-भष्ट भषितुम्

भा *2√bhā* (to appear, shine, be splendid) भाति भास्यति अभात् भातु भायात् भायते *भात भानीय भेय भात्वा भातुम्

भाज् *10√bhāj* (to divide, distribute) भाजयति-ते भाजयिष्यति-ते अभाजयत्-त भाजयतु-ताम् भाजयेत्-त *भाजित

भाम् *1√bhām* (to get angry) भामते भामयिष्यति अबभामत् भामतु भामेत् *भामित भामितव्य भामित्वा भामितुम्

भाम् *10√bhām* (to get angry) भामयते भामयिष्यति-ते अभामयत्-त भामयतु-ताम् भामयेत्-त *भामित

भाष् *1√bhāṣ* (to speak, say, utter) भाषते भाषिष्यते अभाषत भाषताम् भाषेत *भाषित भाषणीय भाषितव्य भाषा भाषण

भास् *1√bhās* (to shine; appear) भासते भासिष्यते अभासत भासताम् भासेत भास्यते *भासित भासितव्य भासितुम् भास

भिक्ष् *1√bhikṣ* (to beg, ask for) भिक्षते भिक्षिष्यते अभिक्षत भिक्षताम् भिक्षेत *भिक्षित भिक्षितुम् भिक्षा भिक्षु भिक्षुक

भिद् *1√bhid* (to divide, cut into parts) भिन्दति भिन्दिष्यति अभिन्दत् भिन्दतु भिन्देत् भिद्यते *भिन्न

भिद् *7√bhid* (to break, split) भिनत्ति-भिन्ते भेत्स्यति-ते अभिनत्-अभिन्त भिनत्तु-भिन्ताम् भिन्द्यात्-भिन्दीत *भिन्न भेदनीय

भिन्द् *1√bhind* (to break) भिन्दति भिन्दिष्यति अभिन्दत् भिन्दतु भिन्दत् भिन्द्यते *भग्न

भिल् *6√bhil* (to cut) भिलति भेलिष्यति अभेलत् भेलतु भेलेत् *भिलित भिलितव्य भिलित्वा भिलितुम्

भिषज् *11√bhiṣaj* (to prevent or treat a diseases) भिषज्यति भिषज्यिष्यति अभिषज्यत् भिषज्यतु भिषज्येत् *भिषजित

भी *3√bhī* (to fear, dread, be afraid of) बिभेति भेष्यति अबिभेत् बिभेतु बिभीयात् *भीत भेय भेतव्य भेतुम् भय भीति

भुज् *6√bhuj* (to crooked) भुजति भोक्ष्यति अभुजत् भुजतु भुजेत् भुज्यते *भुग्न भोजनीय भोक्तव्य भुक्त्वा भोक्तुम्

भुज् *7√bhuj* (to eat, enjoy) भुनक्ति-भुङ्क्ते भोक्ष्यति-ते अभुनक्-अभुङ्क्त भुनक्तु-भुङ्क्ताम् भुञ्ज्यात्-भुञ्जीत भुज्यते *भुक्त भुक्तवत् भोजनीय भोक्तव्य भोज्य भुक्त्वा भोक्तुम् भुज्यमान भोज भोजन भोजक भोग उपभोग

भुण्ड् *1√bhuṇḍ* (to maintain) भुण्डते भुण्डिष्यते अभुण्डत भुण्डताम् भुण्डेत *भुण्डित भुण्डनीय भुण्डितव्य भुण्डितुम्

भुरण् *11√bhuraṇ* (to bear) भुरण्ड्यते भुरण्ड्यिष्यते अभुरण्ड्यत भुरण्ड्यताम् भुरण्ड्येत *भुरण्डित

भू *1√bhū* (to become, be) भवति-ते भविष्यति-ते अभवत्-त भवतु-ताम् भवेत्-त बभूव भविता भूयते *भूत भवत् भूतवत् भवनीय भूत्वा भाव्य भवितुम् भव भवन भुवन

भू *10√bhū* (to get) भावयति-ते भावयिष्यति-ते अभावयत्-त भावयतु-ताम् भावयेत्-त भाव्यते *भावित भावयितुम् भाव

भूष् *1√bhūṣ* (to decorate, adorn) भूषति भूषिष्यति अभूषत् भूषतु भूषेत् *भूषित भूषितव्य भूषित्वा भूषणीय भूषण

भूष् *1√bhūṣ* (to decorate) भूषयति-ते भूषयति-ते अभुषत्-त भूषतु-ताम् भूषेत्-त *भूषित भूषणिय भूषितुम् भूषण भूषा

भूष् *10√bhūṣ* (to decorate, adorn) भूषयति-ते भूषयिष्यति-ते अभूषयत्-त भूषयतु-ताम् भूषयेत्-त *भूषित

भृ *1√bhṛ* (to foster, support, fill) भरति-ते भरिष्यति-ते अभरत्-त भरतु-ताम् भरेत-त भ्रियते *भृत भरत् भरणीय भर्तव्य भृत्वा भर्तुम् भरमाण भरण भर्म भृत्य भरत भर्ता भार भार्या

भृ *3√bhṛ* (to fill, pervade) बिभर्ति-बिभृते भरिष्यति-ते अबिभः-अबिभृत बिभर्तु-बिभृताम् बिभृयात्-बिभ्रीत *भृत भार्य

भृज् *1√bhṛj* (to roast) भर्जते भर्जिष्यते अभर्जत भर्जताम् भर्जेत *भृक्त भर्जनीय भृज्य भर्जितव्य भृक्त्वा-भर्जित्वा

भृञ्ज् *1√bhṛñj* (to roast, fry) भृञ्जति-ते भृञ्जिष्यति अभृञ्जत् भृञ्जतु भृञ्जेत् *भृङ्क्त

भृड् *6√bhṛḍ* (to dip) भृडति भृडिष्यति अभृडत् भृडतु भृडेत् *भृडित

भृंश् *10√bhṛṁś* (to fall down, say) भृंशयति भृंशयिष्यति अभृंशयत् भृंशयतु भृंशयेत् *भृंशित-भृंष्ट

भृश् *4√bhṛś* (to fall down) भृश्यति भर्शिष्यति अभृश्यत् भृश्यतु भृश्येत् *भ्रष्ट भ्रंशनीय भ्रंशितव्य भ्रष्ट्वा भ्रंशितुम् भ्रंश

भॄ *9√bhṝ* (to support, maintain, nourish; to blame, censure) भृणाति भरिष्यति अभृणात् भृणातु भृणीयात् *भूर्ण भेष्

1√bheṣ (to fear, dread, be afraid) भेषति-ते भेषिष्यति-ते अभेषत्-त भेषतु-ताम् भेषेत्-त *भेष्ट

भ्यस् *1√bhyas* (to fear) भ्यसते भ्यसिष्यते अभ्यसत भ्यसताम् भ्यसेत *भ्यसित-भ्यस्त

भ्रक्ष् *1√bhrakṣ* (to eat) भ्रक्षति-ते भ्रक्षिष्यति-ते भ्रक्षिष्यति-ते अभ्रक्षत्-त भ्रक्षतु-ताम् भ्रक्षेत्-त *भ्रक्षित

भ्रण् *1√bhraṇ* (to talk) भ्रणति भ्रणिष्यति अभ्रणत्-अभ्राणत् भ्रणतु भ्रणेत् *भ्राण भ्रणनीय भ्रणितव्य भ्रणित्वा भ्रणितुम्

भ्रम् *1√bhram* (to roam) भ्रमति-म्यति भ्रमिष्यति अभ्रमत् भ्रमतु भ्रमेत् *भ्रान्त भ्रमणीय भ्रमितव्य भ्रमित्वा भ्रमितुम् भ्रान्ति

भ्रम् *4√bhram* (to roam) भ्राम्यति भ्रमिष्यति अभ्राम्यत् भ्राम्यतु भ्राम्येत् भ्रम्यते *भ्रान्त भ्रमित्वा-भ्रन्त्वा

भ्रंश् *1√bhṛṁś* (to fall, tumble) भ्रंशते भ्रंशिष्यते अभ्रंशत भ्रंशताम् भ्रंशेत भ्रश्यते *भ्रष्ट

भ्रंश् *4√bhṛṁś* (to fall) भ्रश्यति भ्रंशिश्यति अभ्रंश्यत् भ्रंश्यतु भ्रंश्येत् *भ्रष्ट भ्रंशित्वा-भ्रष्ट्वा

भ्रश् *1√bhraś* (to fall) भ्रशते भ्रशिष्यते अभ्रषत भ्रशताम् भ्रशेत *भ्रशित-भ्रष्ट

भ्रंस् *1√bhṛṁs* (to vanish) भ्रंसते भ्रंसिश्यते अभ्रंसत भ्रंसताम् भ्रंसेत *भ्रष्ट भ्रंसितुम् भ्रष्ट्वा भ्रंश

भ्रस्ज् *6√bhrasj* (to roast, parch, broil, fry) भृज्जति-ते भ्रक्ष्यति अभृज्जत् भृज्जतु भृज्जेत् भृज्यते *भ्रष्ट भ्रष्ट्वा भ्रष्टुम्

भ्राज् *1√bhrāj* (to flash, gleam, glitter, shine) भ्राजते भ्राजिष्यते अभ्राजत भ्राजताम् भ्राजेत *भ्राजित भ्राजित्वा भ्राता

भ्राश् *1√bhrāś* (to glitter) भ्राशते भ्राशिष्यते अभ्राशत भ्राशताम् भ्राशेत् *भ्राशित

भ्राश् *4√bhrāś* (to glitter) भ्राश्यते भ्राशिष्यते अभ्राश्यत भ्राश्यताम् भ्राश्येत *भ्राशित

भ्री *9√bhrī* (to fear) भ्रिणाति भ्रेष्यति अभ्रीणात् भ्रीणातु भ्रीणीयात् *भ्रीण-भ्रीत भ्रयणीय भ्रेतव्य भ्रीत्वा भ्रेतुम्

भ्रुच् *1√bhruć* (to go) भ्रोचति भ्रोचिष्यति अभ्रोचत् भ्रोचतु भ्रोचेत् *भ्रोचित भ्रोचनीय भ्रोचित्वा भ्रोचितुम्

भ्रूड् *6√bhrḍ* (to cover) भ्रुडति भ्रूडिष्यति अभ्रुडत् भ्रुडतु भ्रुडेत् *भ्रुडित भ्रुडितव्य भ्रुडित्वा भ्रुडितुम्

भ्रूण् *10√bhrūṇ* (to expect) भ्रूणयते भ्रूणयिष्यते अभ्रूणयत भ्रूणयताम् भ्रूणयेत *भ्रूणित भ्रूणनीय भ्रूणयित्वा भ्रूणयितुम्

भ्रेज् *1√bhrej* (to shine) भ्रेजते भ्रेजिष्यते अभ्रेजत भ्रेजताम् भ्रेजेत *भ्रेजित भ्रेजनीय भ्रेजितव्य भ्रेजित्वा भ्रेजितुम्

भ्रेष् *1√bhreṣ* (to dangle) भ्रेषति-ते भ्रेषिष्यते अभ्रेषत भ्रेषताम् भ्रेषेत *भ्रेष्ट भ्रेषनीय भ्रेषितव्य भ्रेषित्वा भ्रेषितुम्

भ्लक्ष् *1√bhlakṣ* (to eat) भ्लक्षति-ते भ्लक्षिष्यति-ते भ्लक्षिष्यति-ते अभ्लक्षत्-त भ्लक्षतु-ताम् भ्लक्षेत्-त *भ्लक्षित

भ्लाश् *1√bhlāś* (to glitter) भ्लाशते भ्लाशिष्यते अभ्लाशत भ्लाशताम् भ्लाशेत *भ्लाशित-भ्लाष्ट

भ्लाश् *4√bhlāś* (to glitter) भ्लाश्यते भ्लाशिष्यते अभ्लाश्यत भ्लाश्यताम् भ्लाश्येत *भ्लाशित-भ्लाष्ट

भ्लेष् *1√bhleṣ* (to be scared) भ्लेषति-ते भ्लेषिष्यति-ते अभ्लेषत्-त भ्लेषतु-ताम् भ्लेषेत्-त *भ्लेषित-भ्लेष्ट

(म) (m)

मंह् *10√mañh* (to grow, increase) मंहयति-ते मंहयिष्यति-ते अमंहयत्-त मंफयतु-ताम् मंहयेत्-त *मंहित-माढ

मक्क् *1√makk* (to go) मक्कते मक्किष्यते अमक्कत मक्कताम् मक्केत *मक्कित मक्कितव्य मक्कित्वा मक्कितुम्

मक्ष् *1√makṣ* (to collect) मक्षति मक्षिष्यति अमक्षत् मक्षतु मक्षेत् *मक्षित-मष्ट

मख् *1√makh* (to crawl) मखति मखिष्यति अमाखत्-अमखत् मखतु मखेत् *मखित मखत् मखनीय मखित्वा मखितुम्

मगध् *11√magadh* (to wind, encircle) मगध्यति-ते मगध्यिष्यति-ते अमगध्यत्-त मगध्यतु-ताम् मगध्येत्-त *मगध

मङ्क् *1√maṅk* (to beautify, decorate, adorn) मङ्कते मङ्किष्यते अमङ्कत मङ्कताम् मङ्केत *मङ्कित

मङ्ख् *1√maṅkh* (to go) मङ्खति-ते मङ्खिष्यति अमङ्खत् मङ्खतु मङ्खेत् *मङ्खित मङ्खत् मङ्खनीय मङ्खितव्य मङ्खित्वा मङ्खितुम्

मङ्ग् *1√maṅg* (to go) मङ्गति-ते मङ्गिष्यति अमङ्गत् मङ्गतु मङ्गेत् *मङ्गित मङ्गत् मङ्गनीय मङ्गितव्य मङ्गित्वा मङ्गितुम्

मङ्घ् *1√maṅgh* (to decorate, begin, cheat, move) मङ्घति-ते मङ्घिष्यति-ते अमङ्घत्-त मङ्घतु-ताम् मङ्घेत्-त *मङ्घित

मच् *1√mać* (to boast, deceive, grind, be wicked) मचते मचिष्यते अमचत मचताम् मचेत *मचित मचनीय मचितुम्

मज्ज् *1√majj* (to sink, go down) मज्जति-ते मज्जिष्यति-ते अमज्जत्-त मज्जतु-ताम् मज्जेत्-त *मज्जित

मञ्च् *1√mañć* (to hold, bear, worship) मञ्चते मञ्चिष्यते अमञ्चत मञ्चताम् मञ्चेत *मञ्चित मञ्चनीय मञ्चित्वा

मञ्ज् *10√mañj* (to clean, wipe off) मञ्जयति-ते मञ्जयिष्यति-ते अमञ्जयत्-त मञ्जयतु-ताम् मञ्जयेत्-त *मञ्जित

मट् *1√maṭ* (to live, inhibit, grind) मटति मटिष्यति अमटत् मटतु मटेत् *मटित मटनीय मटितव्य मटित्वा मटितुम्

मठ् *1√maṭh* (to stay) मठति मठिष्यति अमठत्-अमाठत् मठतु मठेत् *मठित मठनीय मठितव्य मठित्वा मठितुम्

मण् *1√maṇ* (to chatter, murmur) मणति मणिष्यति अमणत्-अमाणत् मणतु मणेत् *माण मणनीय मणितव्य मणित्वा

मण्ठ् *1√maṇṭh* (to long for, think sadly) मण्ठते मण्ठिष्यते अमण्ठत मण्ठताम् मण्ठेत *मण्ठित मण्ठनीय मण्ठित्वा

मण्ड् *1√maṇḍ* (to decorate, adorn) मण्डते मण्डिष्यते अमण्डत मण्डताम् मण्डेत *मण्डित मण्डनीय मण्डित्वा मण्डितुम्

मण्ड् *10√maṇḍ* (to adorn, rejoice, distribute) मण्डयति-ते मण्डयिष्यति अमण्डयत् मण्डयतु मण्डयेत् *मण्डित

मथ् *1√math* (to churn) मथति मथिष्यति अमथत् मथतु मथयेत् *मथित मथनीय मथितव्य मथित्वा मथितुम् मथन प्रमथ

मद् *1√mad* (to be proud, crazy, make noise) मदति मदिष्यति अमदत् मदतु मदेत् *मत्त मदनीय मत्त्वा मत्तुम् मत्सर

मद् *4√mad* (to intoxicate, be drunk, pleased) माद्यति मदिष्यति अमाद्यत माद्यतु माद्येत् *मत्त मत्तव्य मद मदन

मद् *10√mad* (to please, gratify) मादयते मादयिष्यते अमादयत मादयताम् मादयेत *मत्त-मादित मादयित्वा मादयितुम्

मन् *1√man* (to be proud, worship) मनति मनिष्यति अमनत् मनतु मनेत् *मनित मननीय मनितव्य मनित्वा मनितुम्

मन् *4√man* (to think, believe, imagine) मन्यते मंस्यते अमन्यत मन्यताम् मन्येत मन्यते मेने मन्ता *मत मननीय मन्तव्य मान्य मत्वा अनुमत्य मन्तुम् मनन मनस् मनु मुनि मौन मेनका मनोगत मनोज मनोहर मन्यु मनुष्य

मन् *8√man* (to think, suppose, conceive, fancy, consider, regard) मनुते मनिष्यते अमनुत मनुताम् मन्वीत

मन् *10√man* (to be proud) मानयति-ते मानयिष्यति-ते अमानयत्-त मानयतु-ताम् मानयेत्-त *मानित माननीय

मन्त्र् *10√mantr* (to advise, counsel) मन्त्रयते मन्त्रयिष्यते अमन्त्रयत मन्त्रयताम् मन्त्रयेत मन्त्र्यते *मन्त्रित मन्त्रणीत मन्त्रयितव्य मन्त्र्य मन्त्रयित्वा मन्त्रयितुम् मन्त्रयमाण मन्त्रण मन्त्रणा मन्त्र मन्त्रिन् मन्त्रोदक मन्त्रकृत् बीजमन्त्र मान्त्रिक

मन्थ् *1√manth* (to churn, disturb, torture) मन्थति मन्थिष्यति अमथ्नात् मथ्नातु मथ्नीयात् अमन्थीत् *मन्थित

मन्थ् *9√manth* (to churn, make by churning) मथ्नाति मन्थिष्यति अमन्थात् मथ्नातु मथ्नीयात् *मथित मन्थनीय मन्थन

मन्द् *1√mand* (to slow down, sleep, be drunk) मन्दते मन्दिष्यते अमन्दत मन्दताम् मन्देत *मन्दित मन्दनीय मन्दित्वा

मभ्र् *1√mabhr* (to go) मभ्रति मभ्रिष्यति अमभ्रत् अमभ्रत् मभ्रतु मभ्रेत् *मभ्रित मभ्रणीय मभ्रितव्य मभ्रित्वा मभ्रमाण

मय् *1√may* (to move, go) मयते मयिष्यते अमयत मयताम् मयेत *मयित मयनीय मयितव्य मयित्वा मयितुम् मयमान

मर्क् *1√mark* (to go) मर्कति मर्किष्यति अमर्कत् मर्कतु मर्केत् अमर्कीत् *मर्कित मर्कितव्य मर्कित्वा मर्कितुम्

मर्च् *10√marć* (to cleanse, take, injure, threaten, endanger) मर्चयति-ते मर्चयिष्यति अमर्चयत् मर्चयतु मर्चयेत्

मर्ब् *1√marb* (to go) मर्बति मर्बिष्यति अमर्बत् मर्बतु मर्बेत् अमर्बीत् *मर्बित मर्बितव्य मर्बित्वा मर्बितुम्

मर्व् *1√marv* (to fill) मर्वति मर्विष्यति अमर्वत् मर्वतु मर्वेत् अमर्वीत् *मर्वित मर्वितव्य मर्वित्वा मर्वितुम्

मल् *1√mal* (to occupy) मलते मलिष्यते अमलत मलताम् मलेत *मलित मलनीय मलितव्य मलितुम्

मल् *10√mal* (to occupy) मलयते मलयिष्यते अमलयत मलयताम् मलयेत *मलित मलयनीय मलयित्वा मलयितुम्

मल्ल् *1√mall* (to take, hold, possess) मल्लते मल्लिष्यते अमल्लत मल्लताम् मल्लेत *मल्लित मल्लनीय मल्लितुम्

मव् *1√mav* (to tie, fasten, bind) मवति मविष्यति अमवत्-अमावत् मवतु मवेत् अमवीत्-अमावीत् *मवित

मव्य् *1√mavy* (to tie, bind) मव्यति मव्यिष्यति अमव्यत् मव्यतु मव्येत् अमव्यीत् *मव्यित

मश् *1√maś* (to hum, buzz, sound) मशति मशिष्यति अमशत् मशतु मशेत् *मष्ट मष्टव्य मष्ट्वा मष्टुम्

मष् *1√maṣ* (to destroy, hurt, kill) मषति मषिष्यति अमषत् मषतु मषेत् *मष्ट मष्टव्य मष्ट्वा मष्टुम्

मस् *4√mas* (to alter; weigh, measure, mete) मस्यति मसिष्यति अमस्यत् मस्यतु मस्येत् *मसित-मस्त मसितुम्

मस्क् *1√mask* (to go) मस्कति-ते मष्किष्यते अमष्कत मष्कताम् मष्केत *मष्कित मष्कनीय मष्कित्वा मष्कितुम्

मस्ज् *6√masj* (to sink, plunge, dip) मज्जति मङ्क्ष्यति अमज्जत् मज्जतु मज्जेत *मग्न मज्जनीय मङ्क्त्वा मङ्क्तुम्

मह् *1√mah* (to honor, respect, regard) महति महिष्यति अमहत् महतु महेत् *माढ महनीय मह्यमान महितुम् मघवन्

मह् *10√mah* (to honor) महयति-ते महयिष्यति-ते अमहयत्-त महयतु-ताम् महयेत्-त मह्यते *महित-माढ

मा *2√mā* (to measure) माति मास्यति अमात् मातु मायात् *मित मानीय मातव्य मेय मात्वा मातुम् उपमा मात्रा

मा *3√mā* (to sound; measure) मिमिते मास्यते अमिमीत मिमीताम् मिमीत *मित मानीय मातव्य मातुम चन्द्रमा व्योम

मा *4√mā* (to exchange, balance) मायते मास्यते अमायत मायताम् मायेत *मित मानीय मातव्य मित्वा मातुम् मायमान

माङ्क्ष् *1√māṅkṣ* (to desire, desire, long for) माङ्क्षति माङ्क्षिष्यति अमाङ्क्षत् माङ्क्षतु माङ्क्षेत् *माङ्क्षित

मान् *1√mān* (to think) मीमांसते मीमांसिष्यते अमीमांसत् मीमांसताम् मीमांसेत् मीमांसते *मीमांसित मीमांसनीय मीमांसा

मान् *10√mān* (to worship) मानयते मानयिष्यते अमानयत मानयताम् मानयेत मान्यते *मानित माननीय मान्य अपमान

मान्थ् *1√mānth* (to worship) मान्थति मान्थिष्यति अमान्थत् मान्थतु मान्थेत् *मान्थित मान्थनीय मान्थितव्य मान्थित्वा

मार्ग् *1√mārg* (to search, seek for, look out for, hunt after) मार्गति मार्गिष्यति अमार्गत् मार्गतु मार्गेत् *मार्गित

मार्ग् *10√mārg* (to search) मार्गयति-ते मार्गयिष्यति अमार्गयत् मार्गयतु मार्गयेत् *मार्गित मार्गयितव्य मार्ग पन्था

मार्ज् *10√mārj* (to cleanse) मार्जयति-ते मार्जयिष्यति अमार्जयत् मार्जयतु मार्जयेत् मार्ज्यते *मार्जित

माह् *1√māh* (to measure) माहति-ते माहिष्यति अमाहत् माहतु माहेत् *माढ माहनीय माह्यमान माह्य

मि *5√mi* (to throw, scatter) मिनोति-मिनुते मास्यति-ते अमिनोत्-अमिनुत मिनुयाताम् मिनुयात्-मिन्वीत *मित-मिन मित्सत् मित्सनीय मातव्य मेय मित्वा मातुम् माप मान जामाता प्रमेय

मिच्छ् *6√miććh* (to hinder, obstruct) मिच्छति मिच्छिष्यति अमिच्छत् मिच्छतु मिच्छेत् *मिच्छ मिच्छनीय मिच्छितव्य

मिञ्ज् *10√miñj* (to talk, speak) मिञ्जयति-ते मिञ्जयिष्यति-ते अमिञ्जयत्-त मिञ्जयतु-ताम् मिञ्जयेत्-त *मिञ्जित

मिथ् *1√mith* (to associate with) मेथति-ते मेथिष्यति-ते अमेथत्-त मेथतु-ताम् मेथेत्-त *मिथित

मिद् *1√mid* (to melt, feel love) मेदति-ते मेदिष्यति-ते अमेदत्-त मेदतु-ताम् मेदेत्-त *मिन्न मेदत् मेदित्वा मेदितुम्

मिद् *4√mid* (to melt, be soft) मेद्यति मेदिष्यति अमेद्यत् मेद्यताम् मेद्येत अमिदत् *मिन्न मेदितव्य

मिद् *10√mid* (to melt) मेदयति-ते मेदयिष्यति-ते अमेदयत्-त मेदयतु-ताम् मेदयेत्-त *मिन्न मेदयत् मेदयित्वा मेदितुम्

मिन्द् *10√mind* (to be unctuous, soft) मिन्दयति-ते मिदयिष्यति-ते अमिन्दयत्-त मिन्दयतु-ताम् मिन्दयेत्-त *मिन्दित

मिन्ध् *1√mindh* (to sprinkle water, honor) मिन्धति मिन्धिष्यति अमिन्धत् मिन्धतु मिन्धेत् *मिन्धित

मिन्व् *1√minv* (to soak, make wet, moisten, water) मिन्वति मिन्विष्यति अमिन्वत् मिन्वतु मिन्वेत् *मिन्वित मिन्वितव्य

मिल् *1,6√mil* (to meet, join) मिलति-ते मिलिष्यति अमिलत् मिलतु मिलेत *मिलित मिलनीय मिलितव्य मिलित्वा मिलन

मिश् *1√miś* (to shout, make sound, be angry) मेशति मेशिष्यति अमेशत् मेशतु मेशेत् *मेशित

मिश्र् *10√miśr* (to mix, mingle, blend, add) मिश्रयति-ते मिश्रयिष्यति-ते अमिश्रयत्-त मिश्रयतु-ताम् मिश्रेत्-त *मिश्रित

मिष् *1√miṣ* (to wink, gaze, stare) मिषति-मेषति मेषिष्यति अमेषत् मेषतु मेषेत् *मिष्ट

मिष् *6√miṣ* (to wink) मिषति मेषिष्यति अमेषत् मिषतु मिषेत् *मिषित-मिष्ट मेषणीय मेषितव्य मिषित्वा मेष्य मेषितुम्

मिह् *1√mih* (to urinate, water, sprinkle, ejaculate) मेहति मेक्ष्यति अमेहत् मेहतु मेहेत् *मीढ मेढव्य मेहनीय मीढ्वा

मी *4√mī* (to die, perish) मीयते मेष्यते अमीयत मीयताम् मीयेत *मीन मयनीय मेतव्य मीत्वा मेतुम्

मी *9√mī* (to damage) मिनाति-मिनीते मास्यति-ते अमीनात्-अमीनीत मीनातु-मीनीताम् मीनीयात्-मीनीत *मीत मातुम्

मी *10√mī* (to damage) माययति-ते माययिष्यति-ते अमाययत्-त माययतु-ताम् माययेत्-त *मायित

मीम् *1√mīm* (to sound, move) मीमति मीमीष्यति अमीमत् मीमतु मीमेत् * मीमित मीमनीय मीम्य मीमित्वा मीमितुम्

मील् *1√mīm* (to wilt, wink, close) मीलति मीलिष्यति अमीलत् मीलतु मीलेत् *मीलित मीलत् मीलनीय मीलित्वा

मीव् *1√mīv* (to fatten, go, move) मीवति मीविष्यति अमीवत् मीवतु मीवेत् *मीवित मीवितव्य मीवित्वा मीवितुम्

मुच् *1√muć* (to deceive, cheat) मोचते मोचिष्यते अमोचत मोचताम मोचेत *मुक्त मोचनीय मुक्त्वा

मुच् *6√muć* (to release) मुञ्चति अमुञ्चत् मुञ्चतु मुञ्चेत् *मुक्त मुञ्चत् मोचनीय मोक्तव्य मुक्त्वा मोक्तुम् मोचन मुक्ति

मुच् *10√muć* (to free) मोचयति मोचयिष्यति अमोचयत् मोचयतु मोचयेत *मोचित मोचयितव्य मोचयित्वा मोचयितुम्

मुज् *1√muj* (to clean) मोजति मोजिष्यति अमोजत् मोजतु मोजेत् *मोजित मोजनीय मोजितव्य मोजित्वा मोजितुम्

मुज् *10√muj* (to clean) मोजयति-ते मोजयिष्यति-ते अमोजयत्-त मोजयतु-ताम् मोजयेत्-त *माजित मोजयितुम्

मुञ्च् *1√muñć* (to be cunning) मुञ्चते मुञ्चिष्यते अमुञ्चत मुञ्चताम् मुञ्चेत *मुञ्चित मुञ्चनीय मुञ्चित्वा मुञ्चितुम्

मुञ्ज् *1√muñj* (to clean) मुञ्जति मुञ्जिष्यति अमुञ्जत् मुञ्जतु मुञ्जेत् *मुञ्जित मुञ्जनीय मुञ्जितव्य मुञ्जित्वा

मुञ्ज् *10√muñj* (to clean) मुञ्जयति-ते मुञ्जयिष्यति-ते अमुञ्जयत्-त मुञ्जयतु-ताम् मुञ्जयेत्-त *मुञ्जित

मुट् *1,6√muṭ* (to crush, make powder) मोटति मुटिष्यति अमुटत् मुटतु मुटेत् *मुटित मुटनीय मुटितव्य मुटित्वा मुटितुम्

मुट् *10√muṭ* (to pound) मोटयति-ते मोटयिष्यति-ते अमोटयत्-त मोटयतु-ताम् मोटयेत्-त *मुटित मुटित्वा मुटितुम्

मुड् *1√muḍ* (to grind, crush) मुडति मोडिष्यति अमोडत् मोडितु मोडेत् *मुडित मुडनीय मुडितव्य मुडित्वा मुडितुम्

मुण् *6√muṇ* (to vow, promise) मुणति मुणिष्यति अमुणत् मुणतु मुणेत् *मुणित मुणनीय मुणितव्य मुणित्वा मुणितुम्

मुण्ट् *1√muṇṭ* (to crush, grind) मुण्टति मुण्टिष्यति अमुण्टत् मुण्टतु मुण्टेत् *मुण्टित मुण्टनीय मुण्टितव्य मुण्टित्वा

मुण्ठ् *1√muṇṭh* (to run away) मुण्ठते मुण्ठिष्यते अमुण्ठत मुण्टताम् मुण्ठेत *मुण्ठित मुण्ठनीय मुण्ठित्वा मुण्ठितुम्

मुण्ड् *1,6√muṇḍ* (to shave) मुण्डति मुण्डिष्यति अमुण्डत् मुण्डताम् मुण्डेत *मुण्डित मुण्डनीय मुण्डितव्य मुण्डित्वा

मुन्थ् *1√munth* (to move) मुन्थति मुन्थिष्यति अमुन्थत् मुन्थतु मुन्थेत् *मुन्थित मुन्थितव्य मुन्थित्वा मुन्थितुम्

मुद् *1√mud* (to be merry, be glad, rejoice) मोदते मोदिष्यते अमोदत मोदताम् मोदेत *मुदित-मुत्त मोदनीय मोदित्वा

मुद् *10√mud* (to be happy) मोदयति-ते मोदयिष्यति-ते अमोदयत्-त मोदयतु-ताम् मोदयेत्-त मुद्यते *मुदित-मुत्त

मुर् *6√mur* (to encircle, entwine, surround) मुरति मोरिष्यति अमुरत् मुरतु मुरेत् *मुरित-मूर्ण मुरणीय

मुर्च्छ् *1√murćh* (to faint, swoon) मूर्च्छति मूर्च्छिष्यति अमूर्च्छत् मूर्च्छतु मूर्च्छेत् *मूर्च्छित मूर्छा

मुर्व् *1√murv* (to tie, bind) मूर्वति मूर्विष्यति अमूर्वत् मूर्वतु मूर्वेत् *मूर्ण मूवितव्य मूर्वित्वा मूर्वितुम्

मुल् *1,10√mul* (to plant) मूलति मूलिष्यति अमूलत् मूलतु मूलेत् *मूलित मूलनीय मूलितव्य मूल्य मूलितुम् मूलित्वा

मुष् *9√muṣ* (steal, filch, plunder) मुष्णाति मोषिष्यति अमुष्णात् मुष्णातु मुष्णीयात् *मुषित-मुष्ट मोषितव्य मोषणीय

मुस् *4√mus* (to split, divide, cleave) मुस्यति मोसिष्यति अमुस्यत् मुस्यतु मुस्येत् *मुसित मुसनीय मुसितव्य मुसितुम्

मुस्त् *10√must* (to pile up, collect) मुस्तयति-ते मुस्तयिष्यति-ते अमुस्तयत्-त मुस्तयतु-ताम् मुस्तयेत्-त *मुसित

मुह् *4√muh* (to delude) मुह्यति मोहिष्यति अमुह्यत् मुह्यतु मुह्येत् *मुग्ध-मूढ मोहनीय मोह्य मुग्ध्वा मोढुम् मोह मोहनी मूर्ख

मू *1√mū* (to tie, bind, fasten, anchor) मवते मविष्यते अमवत मवताम् मवेत *मूत मवनीय मूतव्य मूत्वा मूतुम्

मूत्र *10√mūtr* (to urinate) मूत्रयति-ते मूत्रयिष्यति-ते अमूत्रयत्-त मूत्रयतु-ताम् मूत्रयेत्-त *मूत्रित मूत्रितव्य मूत्रितुम् मूत्र

मूर्च् *1√mūrć* (to thicken) मूर्चति मूर्चिष्यति अमूर्चत् मूर्चतु मूर्चेत् *मूर्चित मूर्चितव्य मूर्चित्वा मूर्चितुम्

मूर्छ् *1√mūrćh* (to faint) मूर्च्छति मूर्च्छिष्यति अमूर्च्छत् मूर्च्छतु मूर्च्छेत् *मूर्च्छित-मूर्त मूर्च्छनीय मूर्च्छित्वा मूर्च्छितुम्

मूल् *1√mūl* (to root, grow roots) मूलति-ते मूलिष्यति-ते अमूलत्-त मूलतु-ताम् मूलेत्-त *मूलित मूल निर्मूल

मूल् *10√mūl* (to root) मूलयति-ते मूलयिष्यति-ते अमूलयत्-त मूलयतु-ताम् मूलयेत्-त *मूलित मूलितव्य मूलितुम्

मूष् *1√mūṣ* (to rob, steal, plunder) मूषति मूषिष्यति अमूषत् मूषतु मूषेत् *मूष्ट मूषणीय मूष्ट्वा मूष्ट्वा मूष्टुम्

मृ *1√mṛ* (to die) मरति-ते मरिष्यति-ते अमरत्-त मरतु-ताम् मरेत्-त म्रियते *मृत

मृ *6√mṛ* (to die, perish, depart) म्रियते मरिष्यति अम्रियत म्रियताम् म्रियेत *मृत मरणीय मर्तव्य मर्त्य मर्तुम् मरण मृत्यु

मृक्ष् *1√mṛkṣ* (to heap, accumulate, collect, heap together; rub) मृक्षति मृक्षिष्यति अमृक्षत् मृक्षतु मृक्षेत् *मृक्षित

मृग् *10√mṛg* (to hunt) मृगयते मृगयिष्यते अमृगयत मृगयताम् मृगयेत मृगयते *मृगित मृगयित्वा मृगयितुम् मृग मृगया

मृज् *1√mṛj* (to sound) मार्जति मार्क्ष्यति अमार्जत् मार्जतु मार्जेत् मृज्यते *मार्जित-मृष्ट

मृज् *2√mṛj* (to purify) मार्ष्टि मार्जिष्यति-मार्क्ष्यति अमार्ट्-अमार्क्षत् मार्ष्टु मृज्यात् *मृष्ट मार्जनीय मार्जित्वा-मृष्ट्वा मार्जार

मृज् *10√mṛj* (to cleanse, wipe off) मार्जयति-ते मार्जयिष्यति अमार्जयत् मार्जयसु मार्जयेत् मार्ज्यते *मार्जित-मृष्ट

मृड् *6√mṛḍ* (to make happy, be gracious) मृडति मर्डिष्यति अमृड्नात् मृड्नातु मृड्नीयात् *मृडित मर्डनीय मर्डितुम्

मृड् *9√mṛḍ* (to forgive, pardon, be happy) मृड्नाति मृड्निष्यति अमृड्नात् मृड्नातु मृड्नीयात् *मृडित

मृण् *6√mṛṇ* (to kill, slaughter, murder) मृणति मर्णिष्यति अमर्णत् मृणतु मृणेत् अमर्णीत् *मृणित

मृद् *9√mṛd* (to squeeze, rub, press) मृद्नाति मर्दिष्यति अमृद्नात् मृद्नातु मृद्नीयात् *मृदित-मृत्त मर्दनीय मर्दन

मृध् *1√mṛdh* (to wet, neglect) मर्धति-ते मर्धिष्यति-ते अमर्धत्-त मर्धतु-ताम् मर्धेत्-त *मृद्ध

मृश् *4√mṛś* (to tolerate, bear, excuse) मृष्यति मर्षिष्यति अमृष्यत् मृष्यतु मृष्येत् *मृष्ट मर्षणीय मृषित्वा मर्षितुम्

मृश् *6√mṛś* (to touch, feel) मृशति म्रक्ष्यति-मर्क्ष्यति अम्राक्षत्-अमार्क्षत् *मृष्ट मर्क्ष्यत् मर्शनीय म्रष्टव्य-मर्ष्टव्य समृश्य मृष्ट्वा मृष्टुम्-म्रष्टुम् मृश्यमान मर्शन मर्शिन् म्रष्टृ-मर्ष्टृ विमर्श परामर्श

मृष् *1√mṛṣ* (to bear, endure) मर्षति-ते मर्षिष्यति अमर्षत् मर्षयु मर्षेत् मर्ष्यते *मृष्ट मर्षणीय मृष्टव्य मृष्ट्वा मृष्टुम्

मृष् *4√mṛṣ* (to bear, suffer, put up with) मृष्यति मर्षिष्यति अमृष्यत् मर्ष्यतु मृष्येत् *मृष्ट मर्षणीय मर्षितुम् मृषा

मृष् *10√mṛṣ* (to bear) मर्षयति-ते मर्षयिष्यति-ते अमर्षयत्-त मर्षयतु-ताम् मर्षयेत्-त *मर्षित-मृष्ट मर्षित्वा मर्षयितुम् मृष

मृ *9√mṝ* (to kill, slay) मृणाति मरिष्यति अमृणात् मृणातु मृणीयात् अमारीत् *मूर्ण मूर्णवत् मरणीय मृण्वा

मे *1√me* (to exchange, barter) मयते मास्यते अमायत मायताम् मायेत *मित मातव्य मित्वा मेय मातुम् मयमान

मेट् *1√meṭ* (to be mad, angry) मेटति मेटिष्यति अमेटत् मेटति मेटिष्यति अमेटत् मेटतु मेटेत् *मेटित मेटनीय मेटित्वा

मेड् *1√meḍ* (to be mad) मेडति मेडिष्यति अमेडत् मेडतु मेडेत् *मेडित मेडितव्य मेडित्वा मेडितुम्

मेथ् *1√meth* (to embrace, hold, hug, meet) मेथति-ते मेथिष्यति-ते अमेथत्-त मेथतु-ताम् मेथेत्-त *मेथित

मेद् *1√med* (to know) मेदति-ते मेदिष्यति-ते अमेदत्-त मेदतु-ताम् मेदेत्-त *मेदित

मेद् *4√med* (to be fat) मेद्यति मेदिष्यति अमेद्यत् मेद्यतु मेद्येत् *मेदित मेदितुम् मेदस्

मेध् *1√medh* (to meet) मेधति-ते मेधिष्यति-ते अमेधत् मेधतु-ताम् मेधेत्-त *मेधित

मेप् *1√mep* (to go, move) मेपते मेपिष्यते अमेपत मेपताम् मेपेत *मेपित

मेव् *1√mev* (to worship, attend up on, serve) मेवते मेविष्यते अमेवत मेवताम् मेवेत *मेवित मेवनीय मेवित्वा मेवा

मोक्ष् *1√mokṣ* (to release, liberate) मोक्षति मोक्षिष्यति अमोक्षत् मोक्षतु मोक्षेत् *मोचित-मुक्त मोक्ष मुमुक्षा

मोक्ष् *10√mokṣ* (to release) मोक्षयति-ते मोक्षयिष्यति-ते अमोक्षयत्-त मोक्षयतु-ताम् मोक्षयेत्-त *मोक्षित मोक्षयितुम्

म्ना *1√mnā* (to repeat, remember) मेनति म्नास्यति अमनत् मनतु मनेत् म्नायते *म्नात म्नातव्य म्नातुम् निम्न द्युम्न

म्रक्ष् *1√mrakṣ* (to heap, collect, gather) म्रक्षति म्रक्षिष्यति अम्रक्षत् म्रक्षतु म्रक्षेत् *म्रक्षित

म्रक्ष् *10√mrakṣ* (to heap) म्रक्षयति-ते म्रक्षयिष्यति-ते अम्रक्षयत्-त म्रक्षयतु-ताम् म्रक्षयेत्-त *म्रक्षित

म्रद् *1√mrad* (to pound, grind, trample up on) म्रदते म्रदिष्यते म्रदतु म्रदेत् *म्रदित-म्रत्त म्रदनीय मृदु

म्रुच् *1√mruć* (to go, move) म्रोचति म्रोचिष्यति अम्रोचत् म्रोचतु म्रोचेत् *म्रोचित म्रोचनीय म्रोचित्वा म्रोचितुम्

म्रुञ्च् *1√mruć* (to move) म्रुञ्चति म्रुञ्चिष्यति अम्रुञ्चत् म्रुञ्चतु म्रुञ्चेत् *म्रुञ्चित म्रुञ्चनीय म्रुञ्चित्वा म्रुञ्चितुम्

म्रेट् *1√mreṭ* (to be mad, crazy) म्रेटति म्रेटिष्यति अम्रेटत् म्रेटतु म्रेटेत् *म्रेटित म्रेटनीय म्रेटितव्य म्रेटित्वा म्रेटितुम्

म्रेड् *1√mreḍ* (to gratify, oblige) म्रेडति म्रेडिष्यति अम्रेडत् म्रेडतु म्रेडेत् *म्रेडित म्रेडनीय म्रेडितव्य म्रेडित्वा म्रेडितुम्

म्लक्ष् *10√mlakṣ* (to divide, cut) म्लक्षयति-ते म्लक्षयिष्यति-ते अम्लक्षयत्-त म्लक्षयतु-ताम् म्लक्षयेत्-त *म्लक्षित

म्लव् *1√mlav* (to worship) म्लवते म्लविष्यते अम्लवत म्लवताम् म्लवेत *म्लवित

म्ला *1√mlā* (to relax) म्लायति-ते म्लायिष्यति-ते अम्लायत्-त म्लायतु-ताम् म्लायेत्-त म्लायते *म्लात-म्लान

म्लुच् *1√mluć* (to set) म्लोचति म्लोचिष्यति अम्लोचत् म्लोचतु म्लोचेत् *म्लोचित म्लोचनीय म्लोचित्वा म्लोचितुम्

म्लेच्छ् *1√mleććh* (to talk wildly) म्लेच्छति म्लेच्छिष्यति अम्लेच्छत् म्लेच्छतु म्लेच्छेत् *म्लिष्ट म्लेच्छनीय म्लेच्छित्वा

म्लेच्छ् *10√mleććh* (to talk wildly) म्लेच्छयति-ते म्लेच्छयिष्यति-ते अम्लेच्छयत्-त म्लेच्छयतु-ताम् म्लेच्छयेत्-त

म्लेछ् *1√mlećh* (to talk wildly) म्लेछति म्लेछिष्यति अम्लेछत् म्लेछतु म्लेछेत् *म्लेछित-म्लिष्ट

म्लेट् *1√mleṭ* (to be crazy) म्लेटति म्लेटिष्यति अम्लेटत् म्लेटतु म्लेटेत् *म्लेटित म्लेटनीय म्लेटितव्य म्लेटित्वा म्लेटितुम्

म्लेव् *1√mlv* (serve) म्लेवते म्लेविष्यते अम्लेवत म्लेवताम् म्लेवेत *म्लेवित म्लेवनीय म्लेवितव्य म्लेवित्वा म्लेवमान

म्लै *1√mlai* (to droop, wilt, fade) म्लायति म्लास्यति अम्लायत् म्लायतु म्लायेत् *म्लान म्लायनीय

(य) (y)

यक्ष् *1√yakṣ* (to stir, move) यक्षति यक्षिष्यति अयक्षत् यक्षतु यक्षेत् *यक्षित-यष्ट

यक्ष् *10√yakṣ* (to worship) यक्षयते यक्षयिष्यते अयक्षयत यक्षयताम् यक्षयेत *यक्षित

यछ् *1√yac̓h* (to reach) यच्छति-ते यच्छिष्यति-ते अयच्छत्-त यच्छतु-ताम् यच्छेत्-त *यष्ट

यज् *1√yajñ* (to offer) यजति-ते यक्ष्यति-ते अयजत्-त यजतु-ताम् यजेत्-त *इष्ट यजनीय यष्टव्य यष्टुम् यजमान यज्ञ

यत् *1√yat* (to strive, endeavor, attempt) यतते यतिष्यते अयतत यतताम् यतेत *यत्त यतनीय यतित्वा यतितुम् यत्न

यत् *10√yat* (to injure) यातयति-ते यातयिष्यति-ते अयातयत्-त यातयतु-ताम् यातयेता-त यत्यते *यात-यातित

यन्त्र् *1√yantr* (to regulate) यन्त्रति-ते यन्त्रिष्यति-ते अयन्त्रत्-त यन्त्रतु-ताम् यन्त्रेत्-त *यन्त्रित यन्त्रणीय यन्त्र यन्त्रणा

यन्त्र् *10√yantr* (to regulate) यन्त्रयति-ते यन्त्रयति-ते यन्त्रयिष्यति-ते अयन्त्रयत्-त यन्त्रयतु-ताम् यन्त्रयेत्-त *यन्त्रित

यभ् *1√yabh* (to indulge, cohabit) यभति यप्स्यति अयभत् यभतु यभेत् यभ्यते *यब्ध

यम् *1√yam* (to control, restrain) यच्छति यंस्यति अयच्छत् यच्छतु यच्छेत् *यत यतवान् यमनीय यम्य यति नियम

यम् *10√yam* (to surround) यमयति-ते यमयिष्यति-ते अयमयत्-त यमयतु-ताम् यमयेत्-त यम्यते *यत

यस् *1√yas* (to strive, labor) यसति यसिष्यति अययत् यसतु यसेत् यस्यते *यस्त

यस् *4√yas* (to strive, endeavor, labor) यस्यति यसिष्यति अयस्यत् यस्यतु यस्येत् *यसित यसनीय यसितव्य यसितुम्

या *2√yā* (to go) याति यास्यति अयात् यातु यायात् *यात यानीय येय यात्वा यातुम् अनुयायिन् याम यात्रा ययाति

याच् *1√yāc̓* (to beg) याचति-ते याचिष्यति-ते अयाचत्-त याचतु-ताम् याचेत्-त *याचित याचित्वा याचितुम् याचना

याप् *1√yāp* (to spend) यापयति-ते यापयिष्यति-ते अयापयत्-त यापयतु-ताम् यापयेत्-त याप्यते *यापयित

यु *2√yu* (to join, unite, combine) यौति यविष्यति अयौत् यौतु युयात् *युत यवनीय युत्वा यवितुम् यवन योनि यूथ

यु *3√yu* (to detach, separate) युयोति यविष्यति अयुयोत् युयोतु युयुयात् *युत

यु *9√yu* (to join, bind, fasten) युनाति-युनिते योष्यति-ते अयौषीत्-त युनातु-युनीताम् युनीयात्-युनीत *युत यवनीय

यु *10√yu* (to censure) यावयते यावयिष्यते अयावयत यावयताम् यावयेत *यावित

युङ् *1√yuṅg* (to renounce) युङ्गति युङ्गिष्यति अयुङ्गत् युङ्गतु युङ्गेत् *युङ्गित युङ्त् युङ्गनीय युङ्गितव्य युङ्गित्वा युङ्गितुम्

युच्छ् *1√yuc̓c̓* (to err) युच्छति युच्छिष्यति अयुच्छत् युच्छतु युच्छेत् *युच्छित-युष्ट

युज् *1√yuj* (to discipline, to unite, join, connect) योजति योजिष्यति अयोजत् योजतु योजेत् युज्यते *युक्त युक्त्वा

युज् *4√yuj* (to concentrate or focus the mind) युज्यते योक्ष्यते अयुज्यत् युज्यताम् युज्येत *युक्त योजनीय योक्तव्य

युज् *7√yuj* (to unite) योक्ष्यते अयुङ्क्त युङ्क्ताम् युञ्जीत *युक्त योजनीय योक्तव्य प्रयुज्य युक्त्वा योक्तुम् योग योगिन्

युज् *10√yuj* (to unite) योजयति-ते योजयिष्यति-ते अयोजयत्-त योजयतु-ताम् योजयेत्-त *योजित

युत् *1√yut* (to shine) योतते योतिष्यते अयोतत योतताम् योतेत *युत-योतित योतत् योतनीय योतितव्य योतित्वा योतितुम्

युध् *4√yudh* (to fight, struggle, wage war, battle) युध्यते योत्स्यते अयुध्यत युध्यताम् युध्येत युध्यते *युद्ध योद्धव्य योध्य युद्ध्वा योद्धुम् योत्स्यमान युयुत्सा युयुत्सु युधिष्ठिर युयुधान दुर्योधन आयुध युद्ध योद्धा युद्धावसान युद्धभूमि

युप् *4√yudh* (to obstruct, efface, blot out) युप्यति योपिष्यति अयुप्यत् युप्यतु युप्येत् *युप्त

यूष् *1√yūṣ* (to injure) यूषति योषिष्यति अयोषत् योषतु योषेत् *यूषित-यूष्ट

येष् *1√yeṣ* (to attempt, try, strive) येषति-ते येषिष्यति-ते अयेषत्-त येषतु-ताम् येषेत्-त *येषित

यौट् *1√yauṭ* (to connect, loin) यौटति यौटिष्यति अयौटत् यौटतु यौटेत् *यौटित यौटनीय यौटितव्य यौटित्वा यौटितुम्

यौड् *1√yauḍ* (to join together) यौडति यौडिष्यति अयौडत् यौडतु यौडेत् *यौडित यौडनीय यौडितव्य यौडित्वा

(र) (r)

रक् *10√rak* (to taste, get, obtain) राकयति-ते राकयिष्यति-ते अराकयत्-त राकयतु-ताम् राकयेत्-त *राकित

रक्ष् *1√rakṣ* (to protect, guard, watch) रक्षति रक्षिष्यति अरक्षत् रक्षतु रक्षेत् *रक्षित रक्षणीय रक्षित्वा रक्षण रक्षा

रख् *1√rakh* (to go) रखति रखिष्यति अरखत्-अराखत् रखतु रखेत् *रखित रखत् रखनीय रखितव्य रखित्वा रखितुम्

रग् *1√rag* (to doubt, distrust) रगति रगिष्यति अरगत् रगतु रगेत् *रगित रगनीय रगितव्य रगित्वा रगितुम् रगन

रङ्ख् *1√raṅkh* (to move) रङ्खति-ते रङ्खिष्यति अरङ्खत् रङ्खतु रङ्खेत *रङ्खित रङ्खत् रङ्खनीय रङ्खितव्य रङ्खित्वा रङ्खितुम्

रङ्ग् *1√raṅg* (to go, dye, colour) रङ्गति रङ्गिष्यति अरङ्गत् रङ्गतु रङ्गेत् *रङ्गित रङ्गनीय रङ्गितव्य रङ्गित्वा रङ्गितुम् रङ्ग

रङ्घ् *1,10√raṅgh* (to move) रङ्घति-ते रङ्घयति-ते रङ्घिष्यति अरङ्घत् रङ्घतु रङ्घेत *रङ्घित रङ्घनीय रङ्घित्वा रङ्घितुम् रङ्घन

रच् *10√rać* (to arrange, plan) रचयति-ते रचयिष्यति अरचयत् रचयतु रचयेत रच्यते *रचित रचनीय रचयितुम् रचना

रज् *4√raj* (to color) रज्यति रजिष्यति अरज्यत् रज्यतु रज्येत् *रक्त रक्तुम् रक्त रङ्ग

रञ्ज् *1√rañj* (to be colored) रजति-ते रङ्क्ष्यति अराङ्क्षत् अरजत् रजेत् *रक्त रक्त्वा रक्तव्य रजनीय रञ्जन रजनी

रञ्ज् *4√rañj* (to be red, be colored) रज्यति-ते रञ्जिष्यति-ते अरज्यत्-त रज्यतु-ताम् रज्येत्-त *रक्त रज्यनीय रक्तुम्

रट् *1√raṭ* (to howl, shout) रटति रटिष्यति अरटत्-अराटत् रटतु रटेत् *रटित रटनीय रटितव्य रटित्वा रटितुम् रट रटन

रठ् *1√raṭh* (to speak) रठति रठिष्यति अरठत्-अराठत् रठतु रठेत् *रठित रठितव्य रठित्वा रठितुम्

रण् *1√raṇ* (to rattle, tinkle, jingle) रणति रणिष्यति अरणत् रणतु रणेत् *राण रणत् रणनीय रणितव्य रणित्वा रण

रद् *1√rad* (to uproot) रदति रदिष्यति अरदत्-अरादत् रदतु रदेत् *रद्द रदत् रदनीय रदितव्य रदित्वा रदितुम् रद्यमान

रध् *4√radh* (to torment) रध्यति-ते रधिष्यति-रत्स्यति अरध्यत् रध्यतु रध्येत् *रद्ध-रन्ध रन्धनीय रान्ध्य रद्धव्य रद्ध्वा रद्धुम्

रन्ध् *4√randh* (to torment) रन्ध्यति रन्धिष्यति-रन्स्यति अरन्ध्यत् रन्ध्यतु रन्ध्येत् *रन्ध

रन्ध् *10√randh* (to torment) रन्धयति रन्धयिष्यति अरन्धयत् रन्धयतु रन्धयेत् अरन्धत् *रन्धित

रप् *1√rap* (to chatter, prattle, babble) रपति रपिष्यति अरापत्-अरपत् रपतु रपेत् *रप्त रपनीय रपितव्य रप्त्वा रप्तुम्

रफ् *1√raph* (to go) रफति रफिष्यति अरफत् रफतु रफेत् *रफित रफितव्य रफित्वा रफितुम्

रम्फ् *1√ramph* (to go) रम्फिति रम्फिष्यति अरम्फत् रम्फतु रम्फेत् *रम्फित रम्फितव्य रम्फित्वा रम्फितुम्

रम्ब् *1√ramb* (to hang down) रम्बते रम्बिष्यते अरम्बत रम्बताम् रम्बेत *रम्बित रम्बितव्य रम्बित्वा रम्बितुम् हेरम्ब

रभ् *1√rabh* (to start, begin) आ+रभते रम्भिष्यते रप्स्यते अरभत रभताम् रभेत *रब्ध आरभ्य रिप्सितुम् रब्ध्वा आरम्भ

रम् *1√ram* (rejoice)रमते रंस्यते अरमत रमताम् रमेत विरमति विरंस्यति व्यरमत् विरमतु विरमेत् *रत रमणीय रन्तव्य राम

रम्भ् *1√rambh* (to sound) आ+रम्भते रम्भिष्यते अरम्भत रम्भताम् रम्भेत *रब्ध रम्भितव्य रम्भित्वा रम्भितुम्

रय् *1√ray* (to roam) रयते रयिष्यते अरयत रयताम् रयेत *रयित रयनीय रयितव्य रयित्वा रयितुम् रयमाण

रस् *1√ras* (to shout, scream, yell, cry) रसति रसिष्यति अरसत् रसतु रसेत् *रसित रसनीय रसित्वा रसितुम् रस रसना

रस् *10√ras* (to taste) रसयति-ते रसयिष्यति अरसयत् रसयतु रसयेत् *रसित रसनीय रसयितव्य रसयित्वा रसयितुम्

रंह् *1√raṁh* (to go with speed, hasten, flow) रंहति रहिष्यति अरंहत् रंहतु रंहेत् *रंहित-राढ

रह् *1√rah* (to desert, leave, forsake) रहति रहिष्यति अरहत् रहतु रहेत् *रहित रहणीय रहित्वा रह्यमान रहितुम्

रह् *10√rah* (to renounce, quit) रहयति रहयिष्यति अरहयत् रहयतु रहयेत् *रहित रहणीय रहयितव्य रह्य रहयितुम्

रा *2√rā* (to bestow, grant, give) राति रास्यति अरात् रातु रायात् *रात-रापित राणीय रेय रात्वा रातुम् रात्रि सुर धीर

रा *4√rā* (to bark) रायते रायिष्यते अरायत रायताम् रायेत *रात

राख् *1√rākh* (to prevent, ward off; suffice, be dry) राखति राखिष्यति अराखत् राखतु राखेत् *राखित राखित्वा

राघ् *1√rāgh* (to be able) राघते राघिष्यते अराघत राघताम् राघेत *राघित राघनीय राघित्वा राघितुम्

राज् *2√rāj* (to rule, glitter, be eminent) राजति-ते राजिष्यति-ते अराजत्-त राजतु-ताम् राजेत्-त *राजित राज्य राजन्

राध् *4√rādh* (to conciliate, propitiate) आ+राध्यति रात्स्यति अराध्यत् राध्यतु राध्येत् राध्यते *राद्ध राधनीय राध्य

राध् *5√rādh* (to accomplish, complete, perform, achieve) राध्नोति रात्स्यति अराध्नोत् राध्नोतु अराध्नुयात् *राद्ध

रास् *1√rās* (to chirp, bark, howl, yell) रासते रासिष्यते अरासत रासताम् रासेत *रास्त

रि *5√ri* (to hurt, kill, slaughter, murder) रिणोति रेष्यति अरिणोत् रिणोतु रिणुयात् अरैषीत् *रीण

रि *6√ri* (to move, go) रियति रेष्यति अरियत् रियतु रियेत् अरैषीत् *रीण-रीत रित्वा रेतुम्

रि *9√ri* (to expel, drive out) रिणाति रेष्यति अरिणात् रिणातु रिणीयात् *रीण

रिख् *1√rikh* (to go) रेखति रेखिष्यति अरेखत् रेखतु रेखेत् *रिखित रिखितव्य रिखितुम्

रिङ्ख् *1√riṅkh* (to crawl) रिङ्खति रिङ्खिष्यति अरिङ्खत् रिङ्खतु रिङ्खत् *रिङ्खित रिङ्खितव्य रिङ्खितुम्

रिङ्ग् *1√riṅg* (to crawl) रिङ्गति रिङ्गिष्यति अरिङ्गत् रिङ्गतु रिङ्गत् *रिङ्गित रिङ्गित्वा रिङ्गितुमे

रिच् *1√riĉ* (to leave, empty, evacuate, clear, purge) रेचति रेचिष्यति अरेचत् रोचतु रेचेत् *रिक्त

रिच् *7√riĉ* (to leave) रिणक्ति-रिङ्क्ते रेक्ष्यति-ते अरिणक्-अरिङ्क्त रिणक्तु-रिङ्क्ताम् रिञ्च्यात्-रिञ्चीत *रिक्त रेचनीय रेक्तुम् रिक्त

रिच् *10√riĉ* (to leave) रेचयति-ते रेचयिष्यति-ते अरेचयत्-त रेचयतु-ताम् रेचयेत्-त *रेचित

रिज् *1√rij* (to fry, parch, roast) रेजते रेजिष्यते अरेजत रेजताम् रेजेत् *रिक्त उद्रेक

रिणि *1√riṇi* (to go) रिण्वति रिण्विष्यति अरिण्वत् रिण्वतु रिण्वेत् अरिण्वीत् *रिण्वित

रिफ् *6√riph* (to scold, revile, blame) रिफति रेफिष्यति अरेफत् रेफतु रेफेत् *रेफित

रिभ् *1√ribh* (to crackle, creak, murmur, chatter) रेभति-ते रेभिष्यति-ते अरेभत्-त रेभतु-ताम् रेभेत्-त *रीब्ध

रिम्फ् *1√rimph* (to hurt) रिम्फति रेफिष्यति अरेफत् रेफतु रेफेत् *रिम्फित रिम्फितव्य रिम्फितुम्

रिम्फ् *6√rimph* (to hurt) रिम्फति रेम्फिष्यति अरिम्फत् रिम्फतु रिम्फेत् *रिम्फित रिम्फित्वा रिम्फितुम

रिश् *6√riś* (to tear, rend, eat, hurt) रिशति रेक्ष्यति अरेक्षत् रिक्षतु रिक्षेत् *रिष्ट अरिष्ट

रिष् *1,6√riṣ* (to cause harm, do damage, do unwanted thing) रेषति रेषिष्यति-रेक्ष्यति अरिषत् रिषतु रिषेत् *रिष्ट

रिष् *4√riṣ* (to hurt, injure, kill, destroy) रिष्यति रेषिष्यति अरिष्यत् रिष्यतु रिष्येत् अरिषत् *रिष्ट रिष्टव्य रिष्ट्वा-रेषित्वा

रिह् *2√rih* (to hurt) रेहति रेक्ष्यति अरेहत् रेहतु रेहेत *रीढ रीढव्य रीढ्वा रीढुम् रीढा

री *4√rī* (to drip, distill, trickle) रीयते-रेष्यते राष्यते अरीयत रीयताम् रीयेत *रीण रापणीय रेय रातुम्

री *9√rī* (to howl) रीणाति रेष्यति अरीणात् रीणातु रीणीयात् *रीण रीणनीय रीणव्य रीण्वा रीणुम्

रीष् *1√rīṣ* (to take) रीषति-ते रीषिष्यति अरीषत् रीषतु रीषत् *रीष्ट रीष्टव्य रीष्ट्वा रीष्टुम्

रु *1√ru* (to get killed) रवते रविष्यते अरवत रवताम् रवेत अरविष्ट रूयते *रुत रुत्वा रुत्तुम्

रु *2√ru* (to cry) रवीति-रौति रविष्यति अरौत् रौतु रुयात् *रुत रवणीय रवितव्य रुत्वा रवितुम् रव आरव संराव रवि मयूर

रुच् *1√ruć* (to like, be pleased) रोचते रोचिष्यते अरोचत रोचताम् रोचेत *रुचित रोचनीय रोचितव्य रुचित्वा रोचितुम्

रुज् *6√ruj* (to destroy, break) रुजति रोक्ष्यति अरुजत् रुजतु रुजेत् *रुग्ण रुग्णवान् रोग

रुज् *10√ruj* (to ravish, hurt) रोजयति रोजयिष्यति अरोजयत्-त रोजयतु-ताम् रोजयेत्-त *रोजित

रुट् *1√ruṭ* (to strike down, resist, oppose) रोटति रोटिष्यति अरोटत् रोटतु रोटेत् *रोटित रोटनीय रोटितव्य रोटित्वा

रुट् *10√ruṭ* (to resist) रोटयति-ते रोटयिष्यति-ते अरोटयत्-त रोटयतु-ताम् रोटयेत्-त *रोटित

रुठ् *1√ruṭh* (to torment) रोठति-ते रोठिष्यति अरोठत् रोठतु रोठेत् *रोठित रोठनीय रोठितव्य रोठित्वा रोठितुम्

रुण्ट् *1√ruṇṭ* (to steal) रुण्टति रुण्टिष्यति अरुण्टत् रुण्टतु रुण्टेत् *रुण्टित रुण्टनीय रुण्टितव्य रुण्टित्वा रुण्टितुम्

रुण्ठ् *1√ruṇṭh* (to be lame) रुण्ठति रुण्ठिष्यति अरुण्ठत् रुण्ठतु रुण्ठेत् *रुण्ठित रुण्ठितव्य रुण्ठित्वा रुण्ठितुम्

रुण्ड् *1√ruṇḍ* (to steal) रुण्डति रुण्डिष्यति अरुण्डत् रुण्डताम् रुण्डेत *रुण्ण रुण्डनीय रुण्डितव्य रुण्डित्वा रुण्डितुम्

रुद् *2√rud* (to weep, cry, mourn) रोदिति रोदिष्यति अरोदीत् रोदितु रुद्यात् *रुदित रुदत् रोदनीय रुदित्वा रोदितुम् रुद्र

रुध् *1√rudh* (to grow) रोधति रोधिष्यति अरोधत् रोधतु रोधेत् *रुद्ध न्यग्रोध

रुध् *4√rudh* (to obey) रुध्यते रोत्स्यते अरुध्यत रुध्यताम् रुध्येत *रुद्ध

रुध् *7√rudh* (to stop) रुणद्धि-रुन्द्धे रोत्स्यति-ते अरुणत्-अरुन्ध रुणद्धु-रुन्धाम् रुन्ध्यात्-अरुन्ध रुध्यते *रुद्ध रुन्धत् रोधनीय रोद्धव्य रुद्ध्वा उपरुध्य रोद्धुम् रोधन विरोध अनुरोध विरुद्ध

रुप् *4√rup* (to be annoyed) रुप्यति-ते रोपिष्यति अरुप्यत् रुप्यतु रुप्येत् *रुप्त

रुंश् *1√ruṁś* (to shine) रुंशति रुंशिष्यति अरुंशत् रुंशतु रुंशेत् *रुंशित-रुष्ट

रुंश् *10√rum̃ś*(to shine) रुंशयति-ते रुंशयिष्यति-ते अरुंशयत्-त रुंशयतु-ताम् रुंशयेत्-त *रुंशित-रुष्ट

रुश् *6√ruś*(to wound, vex) रुशति रोक्ष्यति अरुष्यत् रुष्यतु रुष्येत् *रुष्ट रुष्यत् रोषणीय रुषित्वा रुष्ट्वा रोष्टुम् रोष

रुष् *1,6√ruṣ* (to be angry, hurt) रुषति रुक्ष्यति अरुशत् रुषतु रुषेत् *रुष्ट-रुषित रोषितव्य

रुष् *4√ruṣ* (to be angry, vexed) रुष्यति रोषिष्यति अरुष्यत् रुष्यतु रुष्येत् रुष्यते *रुष्ट-रुषित रुष्ट्वा-रोषित्वा

रुष् *10√ruṣ* (to be angry) रोषयिष्यति-ते अरोषयत्-त रोषयतु-ताम् रोषयेत्-त *रुष्ट रोषनीय रोषयित्वा रोषयितुम्

रुह् *1√ruh* (to ascend, climb, rise) रोहति रोक्ष्यति अरोहत् रोहतु रोहेत् *रूढ रोढव्य रुह्य रोढुम् रुढ्वा आरोहण आरुरुक्षा

रूक्ष् *10√rūkṣ* (to be harsh) रुक्ष्ययति-ते रुक्षयिष्यति-ते अरूक्षयत्-त रूक्षयतु-ताम् रूक्षयेत्-त *रूक्षित रूक्षयितुम् रूक्ष

रूप् *1√rūp* (to adorn, fashion) रूपति रूपिष्यति अरूपत् रूपतु रूपेत् *रूपित-रूप्त रूप्य रूपिन्

रूप् *10√rūp* (to mark, give shape, appoint) रूपयति-ते रूपयिष्यति-ते अरूपयत्-त रूपयतु-ताम् रूपयेत्-त *रूपित

रूष् *1√rūṣ* (to beautify, adorn) रूषति रूषिष्यति अरूषत् रूषतु रूष्यात् *रूषित-रूष्ट

रूष् *10√rūṣ* (to tremble, hurt) रूषयति-ते रूषयिष्यति-ते अरूषयत्-त रूषयतु-ताम् रूषयेत्-त *रूषित-रूष्ट

रेक् *1√rek* (to doubt, suspect) रेकते रेकिष्यते अरेकत रेकताम् रेकेत *रेकित रेकनीय रेक्तव्य रेकित्वा रेकितुम् रेकमान

रेज् *1√rej* (to shine, shake, tremble) रेजते रेजिष्यते अरेजत रेजताम् रेजेत *रेजित

रेट् *1√reṭ* (to memorize, request) रेटति-ते रेटिष्यति अरेत् रेटतु रेटेत् *रेटित रेनीय रेटितव्य रेटित्वा रेटितुम्

रेप् *1√rep* (to go, move, sound) रेपते रेपिष्यते अरेपत रेपताम् रेपेत *रेपित-रेप्त

रेब् *1√reb* (to jump, leap, go) रेबते रेबिष्यते अरेबत रेबताम् रेबेत *रिब्द रेबनीय रेबित्वा रेबितुम्

रेभ् *1√rebh* (to sound, make noise) रेभते रेभिष्यते अरेभत रेभताम् रेभेत *रीब्ध रेपनीय रेप्तव्य रेप्य रेभित्वा रेभितुम्

रेव् *1√rev* (to hop, leap, jump) रेवते रेविष्यते अरेवत रेवताम् रेवेत *रेवित रेवणीय रेवितव्य रेवित्वा रेवमाण रेवा

रेष् *1√reṣ* (to bellow, neigh, howl, yell) रेषते रेषिष्यते अरेषत रेषताम् रेषेत *रेषित

रै *1√rai* (to make sound, bark) रायति रास्यति अरयत् रायतु रायेत् *रात रातव्य रात्वा रातुम्

रोड् *1√roḍ* (to go mad, despise) रोडति रोडिष्यति अरोडत् रोडतु रोडेत् *रोडित रोडितव्य रोडित्वा रोडितुम्

रौट् *1√rauṭ* (to despise, abhore, hate) रौटति रौटिष्यति अरौटत् रौटतु रौटेत् *रौटित रौटनीय रौटितव्य रौटित्वा रौटितुम्

रौड् *1√rauḍ* (to despise) रौडति रौडति रौडिष्यति अरौडत् रौडतु रौडेत् *रौडित रौडनीय रौडितव्य रौडित्वा रौडितुम्

<u>(ल) (l)</u>

लक् *10√lak* (to get; taste) लकयति-ते लकयिष्यति-ते अलकयत्-त लकयतु-ताम् लकयेत्-त *लकित

लक्ष् *1√lakṣ* (to mark, aim, perceive, observe) लक्षति-ते लक्षिष्यति अलक्षत् लक्षतु लक्षेत् लक्ष्यते *लक्षित लक्षणीय लक्षित्वा लक्षितुम् लक्ष लक्ष्य लक्षण लक्ष्मण

लक्ष् *10√lakṣ* (to see, notice, find) लक्षयते लक्षयिष्यते अलक्षयत लक्षयताम् लक्षयेत *लक्षित

लख् *1√lakh* (to go) लखति लखिष्यति अलखत्-अलाखत् लखतु लखेत् *लखित लखत् लखनीय लखित्वा लखितुम्

लग् *1√lag* (to touch) लगति लगिष्यति अलगत् लगतु लगेत् *लग्न-लगित लगनीय लगितुम् लगितव्य रगित्वा लगितुम्

लग् *10√lag* (to touch) लागयति-ते लागयिष्यति-ते अलागयत्-त लागयतु-ताम् लागयेत्-त *लागित

लङ्ख् *1√laṅkh* (to go) लङ्खति लङ्खिष्यति अलङ्खत् लङ्खतु लङ्खेत् *लङ्खित लङ्खनीय लङ्खित्वा लङ्खितुम् लङ्खन

लङ्ग् *1√laṅg* (to go lame) लङ्गति लङ्गति लङ्गिष्यति अलङ्गत् लङ्गतु लङ्गेत् *लङ्गित लङ्गनीय लङ्गित्वा लङ्गितुम्

लङ्घ् *1√laṅgh* (to leap) लङ्घते लङ्घिष्यते अलङ्घत लङ्घताम् लङ्घेत *लङ्घित लङ्घनीय लङ्घितव्य लङ्घित्वा लङ्घितुम् लङ्घन

लङ्घ् *10√laṅgh* (to pass over, go beyond) लङ्घयति-ते लङ्घयिष्यति-ते अलङ्घयत्-त लङ्घयतु-ताम् लङ्घयेत्-त *लङ्घित

लच्छ् *1√lac̍c̍h* (to mark) लच्छति लच्छिष्यति अलच्छत् लच्छतु लच्छेत् *लच्छित लच्छनीय लच्छित्वा लच्छितुम्

लज् *1√laj* (to blame) लजति लजिष्यति अलजत्-अलाजत् लजतु लजेत् *लजित लजनीय लजितव्य लजित्वा लजितुम्

लज् *6√laj* (to be ashamed) लजति-ते लजिष्यति-ते अलजत्-त लजतु-ताम् लजेत्-त *लजित-लग्न

लज् *10√laj* (to cover, conceal) लजयति-ते लजयिष्यति-ते अलजयत्-त लजयतु-ताम् लजयेत्-त *लजित

लज्ज् *6√lajj* (to blush) लज्जते लज्जिष्यते अलज्जत लज्जताम् लज्जेत *लज्जित लज्जनीय लज्जित्वा लज्जितुम् लज्जा

लञ्ज् *1√lañj* (to blame) लञ्जति लञ्जिष्यति अलञ्जत् लञ्जतु लञ्जेत् *लज्जित लज्जनीय

लञ्ज् *10√lañj* (to blame) लञ्जयति-ते लञ्जयिष्यति-ते अलञ्जयत्-त लञ्जयतु-ताम् लञ्जयेत्-त *लञ्जित

लट् *1√laṭ* (to prattle, be a baby) लटति लटिष्यति अलटत्-अलाटत् लटतु लटेत् *लटित लटनीय लटितव्य लटित्वा

लड् *1√laḍ* (to play, dally) लडति लडिष्यति अलाडत्-अलडत् लडतु लडेत् *लडित लडनीय लडितव्य लडित्वा लडितुम्

लड् *10√laḍ* (to tease, fondle, caress) लाडयति-ते लाडयिष्यति-ते अलाडयत्-त लाडयतु-ताम् लाडयेत्-त *लाडित

लण्ड् *10√lanḍ* (to speak) लण्डयति-ते लण्डयिष्यति-ते अलण्डयत्-त लण्डयतु-ताम् लण्डयेत्-त

लप् *1√lap* (to prate, whisper) लपति लपिष्यति अलपत् लपतु लपेत् लप्यते *लप्त लपनीय लपितव्य लपित्वा

लभ् *1√labh* (to obtain, get, attain, gain) लभते लप्स्यते अलभत लभताम् लभेत *लब्ध लधुम् लब्ध्वा लाभ दुर्लभ

लम्ब् *1√lamb* (to hang, dangle) लम्बते लम्बिष्यते अलम्बत लम्बताम् लम्बेत *लम्बित लम्बनीय लम्बितव्य लम्बितुम्

लय् *1√lay* (to return, go, go down) लयते लयिष्यते अलयत लयताम् लयेत *लयित

लर्ब् *1√larb* (to go) लर्बति लर्बिष्यति अलर्बत् लर्बतु लर्वेत् *लर्बित लर्बितव्य लर्बित्वा लर्बितुम्

लल् *1√lal* (to play) ललति-ते ललिष्यति-ते अललत्-त ललतु-ताम् ललेत्-त *ललित ललिता

लल् *10√lal* (to sport, frolic) लालयते लालयिष्यते अलालयत लालयताम् लालयेत *लालित

लश् *10√laś* (to learn or practice an art) लशयति-ते लशयिष्यति-ते अलशयत्-त लशयतु-ताम् लशयेत्-त *लशित

लष् *1√laṣ* (to want, desire) लषति-ते लषिष्यति-ते अलयत्-त लषतु-ताम् लषेत्-त *लषित-लष्ट अभिलाषा लशुन

लष् *4√laṣ* (to want) लष्यति लषिष्यति अलष्यत् लष्यतु लष्येत् लष्यते *लष्ट-लषित लष्टव्य लष्ट्वा

लष् *10√laṣ* (to want) लषयति-ते लषयिष्यति-ते अलषयत्-त लषयतु-ताम् लषयेत्-त *लषित-लष्ट

लंस् *1√laṁs* (to embrace) लसति लंसिष्यति-ते अलंसत् लंसतु लंसेत् *लंसित-लस्त

लस् *1√las* (to learn exercise an art, look good) वि+लसति लसिष्यति अलसत् लसतु लसेत् *लसित-लस्त

लस् *10√las* (to learn, be good) लासयति-ते लासयिष्यति-ते अलासयत्-त लासयतु-ताम् लासयेत्-त *लसित-लस्त

लस्ज् *1√lasj* (to be ashamed) लस्जते लज्जिष्यते अलज्जत लज्जताम् लज्जेत लज्ज्यते *लग्न-लज्जित लज्जितुम्

ला *2√lā* (to grasp) लाति लास्यति अलात् लातु लायात् *लात लानीय लेय लात्वा लातुम् व्याल बहुल लाल कृपालु

लाख् *2√lākh* (to dry up) लाखति लाखिष्यति अलाखत् लाखतु लाखेत् *लाखित लाखनीय लाखित्वा लखितुम्

लाघ् *1√lāgh* (to be competent) लाघते लाघिष्यते अलाघत लाघताम् लाघेत *लाघित लाघनीय लाघित्वा लाघितुम्

लाज् *1√lāñj* (to blemish) लाजति लाजिष्यति अलाजत् लाजतु लाजेत् *लाजित लाजनीय लाजित्वा लाजितुम्

लाञ्ज् *1√lāñj* (to blemish) लाञ्जति लाञ्जिष्यति अलाञ्जत् लाञ्जतु लाञ्जेत् *लाञ्जित लाञ्जनीय लाञ्जित्वा

लाञ्छ् *1√lāñćh* (to blemish) लाञ्छति लाञ्छिष्यति अलाञ्छत् लाञ्छतु लाञ्छेत् *लाञ्छित लाञ्छनीय लाञ्छित्वा

लाट् *11√lāṭ* (to live) लाट्यति-ते लाटियिष्यति-ते अलाट्यत्-त लाट्यतु-ताम् लाट्येत्-त *लाटित

लाड् *10√lāḍ* (to fondle, caress) लाडयति-ते लाडयिष्यति-ते अलाडयत्-त लाडयतु-ताम् लाडयेत्-त *लाडित

लिख् *6√likh* (to write, draw) लिखति लेखिष्यति अलिखत् लिखतु लिखेत् *लिखित लेखनीय लिखित्वा लेखितुम् लेख

लिङ्ग् *1√liṅg* (to paint) आ+लिङ्गति आ-लिङ्गिष्यति आलिङ्गत् आ-लिङ्गतु आ-लिङ्गेत *आ-लिङ्गित आलिङ्गन

लिङ्ग् *10√liṅg* (to draw, sketch, write) लिङ्गयति-ते लिङ्गयिष्यति अलिङ्गयत्-त लिङ्गयतु-ताम् लिङ्गयेत्-त

लिङ्ख् *1√liṅkh* (to move) लिङ्खति लिङ्खिष्यति अलिङ्खत् लिङ्खतु लिङ्खेत् *लिङ्खित

लिप् *6√lip* (to besmear) लिम्पति-ते लेप्स्यति अलिम्पत् लिम्पतु लिम्पेत् *लिप्त लेपनीय लिप्तव्य लिप्त्वा लिप्तुम्

लिश् *4√liś* (to tear) लिश्यते लेक्ष्यते अलिश्यत लिश्यताम् लिश्येत *लिष्ट

लिश् *6√liś* (to go) लिशति लेक्ष्यति अलिशत् लिषतु लिषेत् *लिष्ट

लिह् *2√lih* (to lick) लेढि-लीढे लेक्ष्यति-ते अलेट्-अलीढ लेढु-लीढाम् लिह्यात्-लिहीत *लीढ-लेहित लेढुम् लेहन लेह्य

ली *1√lī* (to dissolve, melt) लयते लेष्यते-लास्यते अलीयत लीयताम् लीयेत *लीन लयनीय लेय लीत्वा लेतुम्

ली *4√lī* (to cling, adhere) लीयते लेष्यते अलीयत लीयताम् लीयेत *लीन

ली *9√lī* (to join) लिनाति लेष्यति अलिनात् लिनातु लिनीयात् *लीन

ली *10√lī* (to speak) लाययति-ते लीनयिष्यति-ते अलीनयत्-त लीनयतु-ताम् लीनयेत्-त *लीन-लायित

लुञ्च् *1√luñć* (to uproot) लुञ्चति लुञ्चिष्यति अलुञ्चत् लुञ्चतु लुञ्चेत् *लुञ्चित लुञ्चितव्य लुञ्चित्वा लुञ्चितुम्

लुञ्ज् *1√luñj* (to kill) लुञ्जति लुञ्जिष्यति अलुञ्जत् लुञ्जतु लुञ्जेत् *लुञ्जित लुञ्जितव्य लुञ्जित्वा लुञ्जितुम्

लुञ्ज् *10√luñj* (to kill) लुञ्जयति-ते लुञ्जयिष्यति-ते अलुञ्जयत्-त लुञ्जयतु-ताम् लुञ्जयेत्-त *लुञ्जित

लुट् *1√luṭ* (to repel) लोटति लोटिष्यति अलोटत् लोटतु लोटेत् *लोटित लोटनीय लोटितव्य लोटित्वा लोटितुम्

लुट् *4√luṭ* (to roll) लुट्यति लोटिष्यति अलुट्यत् लुट्यतु लुट्येत् अलुटीत् *लुटित लुटितव्य लुटित्वा लुटितुम्

लुट् *6√luṭ* (to plunder) लुटति लुटिष्यति अलुटत् लुटतु लुटेत् लुट्यते *लुटित लुटितव्य लुटित्वा लुटितुम्

लुट् *10√luṭ* (to wallow) लोटयति-ते लोटयिष्यति-ते अलोटयत्-त लोटयतु-ताम् लोटयेत्-त *लोटित

लुठ् *1√luṭh* (to wallow) लोठते लोठिष्यते अलोठत लोठताम् लोठेत *लुठित लुठितव्य लुठित्वा लुठितुम्

लुठ् *6√luṭh* (to rob) लुठति लुठिष्यति अलुठत् लुठतु लुठेत् लुठ्यते *लुठित लुठितव्य लुठित्वा लुठितुम्

लुड् *1√luḍ* (to stir) लोडति लोडिष्यति अलोडत् लोडतु लोडेत् लुड्यते *लुडित लुडितव्य लुडित्वा लुडितुम्

लुड् *6√luḍ* (to adhere) लुडति लुडिष्यति अलुडत् लुडतु लुडेत् *लुडित लुडितव्य लुडित्वा लुडितुम्

लुण्ट् *1√luṇṭ* (to rob) लुण्टति-ते लुण्टिष्यति अलुण्टत् लुण्टतु लुण्टेत् *लुण्टित लुण्टनीय लुण्टितव्य लुण्टित्वा लुण्टितुम्

लुण्ट् *10√luṇṭ* (to rob) लुण्टयति-ते लुण्टयिष्यति अलुण्टयत्-त लुण्टयतु-ताम् लुण्टयेत् *लुण्टित लुण्टित्वा लुण्टितुम्

लुण्ठ् *1√luṇṭh* (to go) लुण्ठति लुण्ठिष्यति अलुण्ठत् लुण्ठतु लुण्ठेत् *लुण्ठित लुण्ठनीय लुण्ठितव्य लुण्ठित्वा लुण्ठितुम्

लुण्ठ् *10√luṇṭh* (to steal, rob, plunder, cheat) लुण्ठयति लुण्ठयिष्यति अलुण्ठयत् लुण्ठयतु लुण्ठयेत् *लुण्ठित

लुण्ड् *10√luṇḍ* (to pillage) लुण्डयति-ते लुण्डयति-ते लुण्डियिष्यति अलुण्डयत्-त लुण्डयतु-ताम् लुण्डयेत् *लुण्डित

लुथ् *1√luth* (to strike) लुन्थति लुन्थिष्यति अलुन्थत् लुन्थतु लुन्थेत् *लुन्थित लुन्थनीय लुन्थितव्य लुन्थित्वा लुन्थितुम्

लुप् *1√lup* (to vanish, confound) लुप्यति लोपिष्यति अलुप्यत् लुप्यतु लुप्येत् *लुप्त लोपनीय लुप्वा

लुप् *6√lup* (to cut) लुम्पति-ते लोप्स्यति-ते अलुम्पत्-त लुम्पतु-ताम् लुम्पेत्-त *लुप्त

लुभ् *4√lubh* (to covet, bewilder) लुभ्यति लोभिष्यति अलुभ्यत् लुभ्यतु लुभ्येत् *लुब्ध लुभ्यत् लुब्ध्वा लुभित्वा लब्धुम्

लुभ् *6√lubh* (bewilder, confound) लुभ्यति लोभिष्यति अलुभ्यत् लुभ्यतु लुभ्येत् *लुब्ध-लुभित लुभित्वा लोभितुम् लोभ

लुम्ब् *1√lubmb* (to torment, harass) लुम्बति लुम्बिष्यति अलुम्बत् लुम्बतु लुम्बेत् *लुम्बित

लुम्ब् *10√lubmb* (to vanish, get ruined) लुम्बयति-ते लुम्बयिष्यति-ते अलुम्बयत्-त लुम्बयतु-ताम् लुम्बयेत्-त *लुम्बित

लुल् *1√lul* (to roll over) लोलति लोलिष्यति अलोलत् लोलतु लोलेत् *लोलित लोलितव्य लोलित्वा लोलितुम्

लुह् *1√luh* (to covet, desire, long for) लोहति लोहिष्यति अलोहत् लोहतु लोहेत् *लोहित-लूढ लूढ्वा

लू *9√lū* (to cut) लुनाति-लुनीते लविष्यति अलुनात् लुनातु लुनीयात् लूयते *लून

लूष् *1√lūṣ* (to adorn, decorate) लूषति लूषिष्यति अलूषत् लूषतु लूषेत् *लूष्ट

लूष् *10√lūṣ* (to plunder, hurt) लूषयति-ते लूषयिष्यति-ते अलूषयत्-त लूषयतु-ताम् लूषयेत्-त *लूषित

लेप् *10√lep* (to go) लेपति-ते लेपयिष्यति-ते अलेपयत्-त लेपयतु-ताम् लेपयेत्-त *लेपित

लैण् *1√laiṇ* (to send, dispatch, embrace, go, approach) लैणति, लैणिष्यति अलैणत् लैणतु लैणेत् *लैणित लैणनीय

लोक् *1√lok* (to see) लोकते लोकिष्यते अलोकत लोकताम् लोकेत *लोकित लोकनीय लोकित्वा लोकितुम् *लोकित

लोक् *10√lok* (to seek) आ+लोकयति-ते लोकयिष्यति-ते अलोकयत्-त लोकयतु-ताम् लोकयेत्-त *आ+लोकित

लोच् *1√loć* (to see, view, percieve, observe) लोचते लोचिष्यते अलोचत लोचताम् लोचेत *लोचित लोचनीय

लोच् *10√loć* (to speak, shine) आ+लोचयति-ते लोचयिष्यति-ते अलोचयत्-त लोचयतु-ताम् लोचयेत्-त *आ+लोचित

लोट् *1√loṭ* (to deceive) लोटति लोटिष्यति अलोटत् लोटतु लोटेत् *लोटित लोटनीय लोटितव्य लोटित्वा लोटितुम्

लोड् *1√loḍ* (to go crazy) लोडति लोडिष्यति अलोडत् लोडतु लोडेत् *लोडित लोडनीय लोडितव्य लोडित्वा लोडितुम्

लोष्ट् *1√loṣṭ* (to pile) लोष्टते लोष्टिष्यते अलोष्टत लोष्टताम् लोष्टेत *लोष्टित लोष्टनीय लोष्टितव्य लोष्टित्वा लोष्टितुम्

लौड् *1√lauḍ* (to be foolish) लौडति लौडिष्यति अलौडत् लौडतु लौडेत *लौडित लौडितव्य लौडित्वा लौडितुम्

ल्पी *9√lpī* (to meet) ल्पिनाति ल्पेष्यति अप्लीनात् प्लीनातु प्लीनीयात् *प्लीत

ल्यी *9√lyī* (to meet) ल्यिनाति ल्येष्यति अल्यीनात् ल्यीनातु ल्यीनीयात् *ल्यीत

ल्वी *9√lvī* (to move) ल्विनाति ल्वेष्यति अल्वीनात् ल्वीनातु ल्वीनीयात् *ल्वीत

(व) (v)

वक्क् *1√vakk* (to move) वक्कते वक्किष्यते अवक्कत वक्कतु वक्केत *वक्कित वक्कितव्य वक्कित्वा वक्कितुम्

वक्ष् *1√vakṣ* (to increase, grow, be powerful) वक्षति वक्षिष्यति अवक्षत् वक्षतु वक्षेत् *वक्षित-वष्ट

वख् *1√vakh* (to go crookedly) वखति वखिष्यति अवखत्-अवाखत् वखतु वखेत् *वखित वखनीय वखित्वा वखितुम्

वङ्क् *1√vaṅk* (to go , move crookedly) वङ्कते वङ्किष्यते वङ्कताम् वङ्केत *वङ्कित वङ्कनीय वङ्कितव्य वङ्कित्वा

वङ्ख् *1√vaṅkh* (to go) वङ्खति वङ्खिष्यति अवङ्खत् वङ्खतु वङ्खेत *वङ्खित वङ्खत् वङ्खनीय वङ्खितव्य वङ्खित्वा वङ्खितुम्

वङ्ग् *1√vaṅg* (to limp) वङ्गति वङ्गिष्यति अवङ्गत् वङ्गतु वङ्गेत *वङ्गित वङ्गत् वङ्गनीय वङ्गितव्य वङ्गित्वा वङ्गितुम्

वङ्घ् *1√vaṅgh* (to blame; go swiftly) वङ्घते वङ्घिष्यते वङ्घताम् वङ्घेत *वङ्घित वङ्घनीय वङ्घितव्य वङ्घित्वा

वच् *2√vać* (to speak) वक्ति वक्ष्यति अवक्-ग् वक्तु वच्यात् उच्यते *उक्त वचनीय वक्तव्य वाच्य उक्त्वा वक्तुम् उक्ति

वच् *10√vać* (to speak) वाचयति-ते वाचयिष्यति-ते अवाचयत्-त वाचयतु-ताम् वाचयेत्-त *वाचित वाचयितुम् वाचन

वज् *1√vaj* (to roam) वजति वजिष्यति अवजत्-अवाजत् वजतु वजेत् *वजित वजनीय वजितव्य वजित्वा वजितुम्

वज् *10√vaj* (to prepare, trim) वाजयति-ते वाजयिष्यति-ते अवाजयत्-त वाजयतु-ताम् वाजयेत्-त *वाजित

वञ्च् *1√vañć* (to deprive of) वञ्चति वञ्चिष्यति अवञ्चत् वञ्चतु वञ्चेत् *वञ्चित वञ्चितव्य वञ्चित्वा वञ्चितुम्

वञ्च् *10√vañć* (to cheat) वञ्चयते वञ्चयिष्यति अवञ्चयत् वञ्चयताम् वञ्चयेत *वञ्चित वञ्चितव्य वञ्चितुम्

वट् *1√vaṭ* (to surround) वटति वटिष्यति अवटत्-अवाटत् वटतु वटेत् *वटित वटनीय वटितव्य वटित्वा वटितुम् वट

वट् *10√vaṭ* (to distribute) वटयति-ते वटयिष्यति अवटयत् वटयतु वटयेत् *वटित वटयितव्य वटयित्वा वटयितुम्

वठ् *1√vaṭh* (to be strong) वठति वठिष्यति अवठत्-अवाठत् वठतु वठेत् *वठित वठनीय वठितव्य वठित्वा वठितुम्

वण् *1√vaṇ* (to sound) वणति वणिष्यति अवणत्-अवाणत् वणतु वणेत् *वाण वणनीय वणितव्य वणित्वा वणितुम्

वण्ट् *1√vaṇṭ* (to divide) वण्टति वण्टिष्यति अवण्टत् वण्टतु वण्टेत् *वण्टित वण्टनीय वण्टितव्य वण्टित्वा वण्टितुम्

वण्ट् *10√vaṇṭ* (to divide) वण्टयति वण्टियिष्यति अवण्टयत् वण्टयतु वण्टयेत् *वण्टित वण्टितव्य वण्टित्वा वण्टितुम्

वण्ठ् *1√vaṇṭh* (to go alone) वण्ठते वण्ठिष्यते अवण्ठत वण्ठताम् वण्ठेत *वण्ठित वण्ठनीय वण्ठितव्य वण्ठित्वा

वण्ड् *1√vaṇḍ* (to apportion) वण्डते वण्डिष्यते अवण्डत वण्डताम् वण्डेत *वण्डित वण्डनीय वण्डितव्य वण्डित्वा

वण्ड् *10√vaṇḍ* (to apportion) वण्डयति वण्डयिष्यति अवण्डयत् वण्डयतु वण्डयेत् *वण्डित वण्डितव्य वण्डितुम्

वद् *1√vad* (to speak) वदति वदिष्यति अवदत् वदतु वदेत् उद्यते *उदित वदनीय उदित्वा वदितव्य वद्य वक्तुम् वदन वाद

वद् *10√vad* (to speak) वादयति-ते वादयिष्यति-ते अवादयत्-त वादयतु-ताम् वादयेत्-त *वादित वादनीय वाद्य वादन

वध् *1√vadh* (to slay, kill, slaughter, murder) वधति वधिष्यति अवधत वधतु वधेत् *वधित-हत हत्वा हन्तुम्

वन् *1√van* (to honor, respect) वनति वनिष्यति अवनत् वनतु वनेत् *वनित वननीय वनितव्य वनित्वा वनितुम् वनिता

वन् *8√van* (to request, beg) वनुते वनिष्यते अवनुत वनुताम् वन्वीत *वत वननीय वनितव्य वनित्वा-वत्वा वनितुम्

वन् *10√van* (to favour) वनयति-ते वनयिष्यति-ते अवनयत्-त वनयतु-ताम् वनयेत्-त *वनित वनितव्य वनितुम्

वन्द् *1√vand* (to salute, pay homage) वन्दते वन्दिष्यते अवन्दत वन्दताम् वन्देत *वन्दित वन्दनीय वन्दित्वा वन्दितुम्

वप् *1√vap* (to sow, scatter, cast) वपति-ते वप्स्यति-ते अवपत्-त वपतु-ताम् वपेत्-त उप्यते *उप्त-वपित वपत् वप्तुम्

वभ्र् *1√vabhr* (to roam) वभ्रति वभ्रिष्यति अवभ्रत् वभ्रतु वभ्रेत् *वभ्रित वभ्रणीय वभ्रितव्य वभ्रित्वा वभ्रितुम् वभ्रमाण

वम् *1√vam* (to vomit) वमति वमिष्यति अवमत् वमतु वमेत् *वान्त-वमित वमितव्य वमितुम् वान्त्वा वान्तवान् वामन

वय् *1√vay* (to move) वयते वयिष्यते अवयत वयताम् वयेत *वयित वयनीय वयितव्य वयित्वा वयितुम् वयमान

वर् *10√var* (to choose, ask for, seek) वरयति-ते वरयिष्यति-ते अवरयत्-त वरयतु-ताम् वरयेत्-त *वरित वर वरण

वर्च् *1√varć* (to glitter, shine) वर्चते वर्चिष्यते अवर्चत वर्चताम् वर्चेत *वर्चित वर्चनीय वर्चितव्य वर्चित्वा वर्चितुम्

वर्ण् *10√varṇ* (to define, describe, relate, write) वर्णयति-ते वर्णयिष्यति-ते अवर्णयत्-त वर्णयतु-ताम् वर्णयेत्-त *वर्णित

वर्ध् *10√vardh* (to divide) वर्धयति-ते वर्धयिष्यति-ते अवर्धयत्-त वर्धयतु-ताम् वर्धयेत्-त *वृद्ध

वर्फ् *1√varṣ* (to move) वर्फते वर्फिष्यते अवर्फत वर्फताम् वर्फेत *वर्फित वर्फितव्व वर्फितुम्

वर्ष् *1√varṣ* (to love, be smooth, wet) वर्षते वर्षिष्यते अवर्षत वर्षताम् वर्षेत *वर्षित

वर्ह् *1√varh* (to speak, spread, cover, hurt) वर्हते वर्हिष्यते अवर्हत वर्हताम् वर्हेत *वर्हित

वल् *1√val* (to turn, turn round, approach) वलते वलिष्यते अवलत वलताम् वलेत *वलित वलनीय वलितुम्

वल्क् *10√valk* (to speak, see) वल्कयति-ते वल्कयिष्यति-ते अवल्कयत् वल्कयतु-ताम् वल्कयेत्-त *वल्कित

वल्ग् *1√valg* (to leap) वल्गति वल्गिष्यति अवल्गत् वल्गतु वल्गेत् *वल्गित वल्गत् वल्गनीय वल्गित्वा वल्गितुम्

वल्भ् *1√valbh* (to consume, eat, devour) वल्भते वल्भिष्यते अवल्भत वल्भताम् वल्भेत *वल्भित वल्भनीय

वल्ल् *1√vall* (to cover, be covered) वल्लते वल्लिष्यते अवल्लत वल्लताम् वल्लेत *वल्लित वल्लनीय वल्लितुम्

वल्ह् *1,10√valh* (to be excellent, to speak) वल्हते वल्हिष्यते अवल्हत वल्हताम् वल्हेत *वल्हित

वश् *2√vaś* (to long for, wish) वष्टि वशिष्यति अवट् वष्टु उश्यात् *उशित-वष्ट वशनीय वशितुम् वश वशिन् उशना

वष् *1√vaṣ* (to injure) वषति वषिष्यति अवषत् वषतु वषेत् *वष्ट

वष्क् *1√vaṣk* (to move) वष्कते वष्किष्यते अवष्कत् वष्कतु वष्केत् *वष्कित

वस् *1√vas* (to stay, reside) वसति वत्स्यति अवसत् वसतु वसेत् उष्यते *वसित वसितुम्-वस्तुम् वसितव्य उषित्वा वास

वस् *2√vas* (to clothe, cover, clad) वस्ते वसिष्यते अवस्त वस्ताम् वसीत *उषित वसनीय वसितव्य वसन वास वस्ति

वस् *4√vas* (to stop, resist) वस्यति वसिष्यति अवस्यत् वस्यतु वस्येत् *उषित वसनीय वसितव्य वसित्वा वसितुम्

वस् *10√vas* (to love; dwell) वसयति-ते वसयिष्यति-ते अवसयत्-त वसयतु-ताम् वसयेत्-त *वसित

वस्क् *1√vask* (to move, move about) मस्कति-ते वष्किष्यते वष्कताम् वष्केत *वष्कित वष्कनीय वष्कित्वा वष्कितुम्

वस्त् *10√vast* (to solicit, beg, ask for) वस्तयति-ते वस्तयिष्यति-ते अवस्तयत्-त वस्तयतु वस्तयेत् *वस्कित

वंह् *1√vaṁh* (to carry) वंहति वङ्क्ष्यति अवाङ्क्षत् वङ्क्ष्यतु वङ्क्ष्येत् *ऊढ

वंह् *10√vaṁh* (to illuminate) वंहयति वंहयिष्यति-ते अवंहयत्-त वंहयतु-ताम् वंहयेत्-त *ऊढ

वह् *1√vah* (to carry) वहति-ते वक्ष्यति-ते अवहत्-त वहतु-ताम् वहेत्-त उह्यते *ऊढ ऊढ्वा वोढुम् वह्य वहन वाहन वाह

वा *2√vā* (to blow, go, move) वाति वास्यति अवात् वातु वायात् *वात-वान वानीय वातव्य वात्वा वातुम् वाम वायु

वा *4√vā* (to dry up, be dried up) वायते वास्यते अवायत वायताम् वायेत वायते *वित वात्वा वातुम्

वा *10√vā* (to move) वाययति-ते वाययिष्यति-ते अवाययत्-त वाययतु-ताम् वाययेत्-त *वायित

वाङ्क्ष् *1√vāṅkṣ* (to wish, desire) वाङ्क्षति वाङ्क्षिष्यति अवाङ्क्षत् वाङ्क्षतु वाङ्क्षेत् *वाङ्क्षित

वाञ्छ् *1√vāñćh* (to wish, desire) वाञ्छति वाञ्छिष्यति अवाञ्छत् वाच्छतु वाञ्छेत् *वाञ्छित वाञ्छनीय वाञ्छित्वा

वाड् *1√vāḍ* (to bathe) वाडते वाडिष्यते अवाडत वाडताम् वाडेत *वाडित वाडनीय वाडितव्य वाडित्वा वाडितुम्

वात् *10√vāt* (to flow, blow air) वातयति-ते वातयिष्यति-ते अवातयत्-त वातयतु-ताम् वातयेत्-त *वातित

वाश् *4√vāś* (to bellow, roar, howl, sound) वाश्यते वाशिष्यते अवाशिष्ट वाश्यताम् वाश्येत *वाशित

वास् *10√vās* (to smell) वासयति-ते वासयिष्यति-ते अवासयत्-त वासयतु-ताम् वासयेत्-त वास्यते *वासित वासयितुम्

वाह् *1√vāh* (to endavor) वाहते वाहिष्यते अवाहत वाहताम् वाहेत *वाढ

विच् *6√vić* (to cheat) विचति विचिष्यति अविचत् विचतु विचेत् *विचित विचित्वा व्यचितुम्

विच् *7√vić* (to sift) विनक्ति-विङ्क्ते वेक्ष्यति अविचत् विनक्तु विञ्च्यात् *विक्त

विच्छ् *6√viććh* (to speak) विच्छति विच्छिष्यति अविच्छत् विच्छतु विच्छेत् *विच्छित

विच्छ् *10√viććh* (to speak) विच्छयति विच्छयिष्यति अविच्छयत् विच्छतु विच्छेत् *विच्छयित विच्छयनीय

विज् *3√vij* (to separate) वेवेक्ति वेविक्ते वेक्ष्यति-ते अविजत् *विक्त

विज् *6√vij* (to irritate, agitate) उद्+विजते विजिष्यते अविजत विजताम् विजेत *विग्न वेजनीय विजित्वा विजितुम्

विज् *7√vij* (to tremble) विनक्ति विजिष्यति अविनक् विनक्तु विज्यात् *विज्न वेजनीय विजितव्य वेज्य विजित्वा विजितुम्

विट् *1√viṭ* (to curse, snare, rail at) वेटति वेटिष्यति अवेटत् वेटतु वेटेत् *वेटित वेटनीय वेटितव्य वेटित्वा वेटितुम्

विड् *1√viḍ* (to revile, cry foul) वेडति वेडिष्यति अवेडत् वेडतु वेडेत् *वेडित वेडनीय वेडितव्य वेडित्वा वेडितुम्

विडम्ब् *1√viḍamb* (to mock) विडम्बयति-ते विडम्बिष्यति-ते अविडम्बत्-त विडम्बतु-ताम् विडम्बेत्-त *विडम्बित

वित्त् *10√vitt* (to give away, give as alms) वित्तयति-ते वित्तयिष्यति-ते अवित्तयत्-त वित्तयतु-ताम् वित्तयेत्-त *वित्तित

विथ् *1√vith* (to request, ask, beg) वेथते वेथिष्यते अवेथत वेथताम् वेथेत *विप्त वेथनीय वेथित्वा वेथितुम् वेथमान

विद् *2√vid* (to know) वेत्ति-वेद वेदिष्यति अवेत् विदाङ्करोतु-वेत्तु विद्यात् विद्यते *विन्न वेदनीय वेद्य वेदितुम् वेद वैदिक

विद् *4√vid* (to be) विद्यते वेत्स्यते अविद्यत विद्यताम् विद्येत विद्यते *वित्त-विन्न वेदनीय वेत्तव्य वेद्य वेत्तुम् विद्यमान वेदना

विद् *6√vid* (to attain) विन्दति-ते वेत्स्यति-ते वेदिष्यति-ते अविन्दत्-त विन्दतु-ताम् विन्देत्-त विद्यते *वित्त-विन्न

विद् *7√vid* (to think) विन्ते वेत्स्यते अविन्त विन्ताम् विन्दीत विद्यते *विद्ध वेदनीय वेदितव्य वेद्य विदित्वा-वित्त्वा वेत्तुम्

विद् *10√vid* (to say) वेदयते वेदयिष्यते अवेदयत वेदयताम् वेदयेत वेद्यते *वेद वेदयितव्य वेद्य वेदयित्वा वेदयितुम्

विध् *6√vidh* (to state) विधति वेधिष्यति अवेधत् विधतु विधेत् *विद्ध

विन्ध् *6√vindh* (to lack) विन्धते विन्धिष्यति अविन्धत् विन्धतु विन्धेत् *विनद्ध

विल् *6√vil* (to cover, hide) विलति वेलिष्यति अवेलत् वेलतु वेलेत् *विलित विलितव्य विलित्वा विलितुम्

विल् *10√vil* (to cut, slit) विलयति-ते विलयिष्यति-ते अविलयत्-त विलयतु-ताम् विलयेत्-त *विलित विलितव्य विलितुम्

विश् *6√viś* (to enter) विशति वेक्ष्यति अविशत् विशतु विशेत् *विष्ट वेशनीय वेशितव्य वेष्टव्य वेष्टुम् प्रवेश विटप

विष् *3√viṣ* (to detach) विवेष्टि-ष्टे वेक्ष्यति-ते अविषत्-त विषतु-ताम् विषेत्-त *विष्ट वेष्य विष्ट्वा वेष्टुम् विष्णु विष वेष

विष् *9√viṣ* (to separate) विष्णाति वेक्ष्यति अविष्णात् विष्णातु विष्णीयात् *विष्ट वेशनीय वेशितव्य विष्ट्वा वेशितुम्

विष्क् *10√viṣk* (to hurt, kill) विष्कयति-ते विष्कयिष्यति-ते अविष्कयत्-त विष्कयतु-ताम् विष्कयेत्-त *विष्कित

विष्ल् *5√viṣl* (to pervade, occupy, spread) वेवेष्टि वक्ष्यति अववेट् वेवेष्टु वेविष्यात् *विष्लित विष्लितव्य विष्लितुम्

विस् *4√vis* (to abandon) विस्यति वेसिष्यति अविस्यत् विस्यतु विस्येत *विस्त

वी *2√vī* (to pervade, throw, eat) वेति वेष्यति अवेत् वेतु वीयात् *वीत वयनीय वेतव्य वीत्वा वेतुम् वीणा वेणु वेतन

वीज् *1√vīj* (to go) उद्-वीजते विजिष्यते अविजत विजताम् विजेत् वीज्यते *विग्न

वीज् *10√vīj* (to cool by fanning, fan) वीजयति-ते वीजयिष्यति अवीजयत् वीजयतु वीजयेत् *वीजित वेजन

वीभ् *1√vībh* (to brag) वीभते विभिष्यते अविभत विभताम् विभेत *वीब्ध

वीर् *10√vīr* (to be brave) वीरयते वीरयिष्यति-ते अवीरयत्-त वीरयतु-ताम् वीरयेत्-त *वीरित वीरयितुम् वीर वीर्य

वुक्क् *1√vukk* (to bark) वुक्कति वुक्किष्यति अवुक्कत् वुक्कतु वुक्केत् *वुक्कित वुक्कनीय वुक्कित्वा वुक्कितुम्

वुङ्ग् *1√vuṅg* (to forsake, give up) वुङ्गति वुङ्गिष्यति अवुङ्गत् वुङ्गतु वुङ्गेत् *वुङ्गित वुङ्गितव्य वुङ्गित्वा वुङ्गितुम्

वुण्ट् *10√vuṇṭ* (to hurt, kill) वुण्टयेते-ते वुण्टयिष्यति-ते अवुण्टयत्-त वुण्टयतु-ताम् वुण्टयेत्-त *वुण्टित

वृ *10√vṛ* (to cover, hide) वारयतिते वारयिष्यति-ते अवारयत्-त वारयतु-ताम् वारयेत्-त *वारित वारणीय वारयितुम् वार

वृ *5√vṛ* (to cover) वृणोति-वृणुते वरिष्यति-ते अवृणोत्-अवृणुत वृणातु-वृणुताम् वृणुयात्-वृण्वीत व्रीयते *वृणित वृण्वत् वरणीय वरितव्य वर्य वृत्वा वरितुम्-वरीतुम् वरण वरेण्य वर्मन् वराक वर्ण वरुण वारण वर्ग वारि वृक वृक्ष

वृ *9√vṛ* (to choose, select) वृणीते वरिष्यते अवृणीत वृणीताम् वृणीत व्रीयते *वृत

वृ *10√vṛ* (to hide) वारयति-ते वारयिष्यति-ते अवारयत्-त वारयतु-ताम् वारयेत्-त वार्यते *वारित वारणीय वारयितुम्

वृक् *1√vṛk* (to hold) वर्कते वर्किष्यते अवर्कत वर्कताम् वर्केत *वर्कित

वृक्ष् *1√vṛkṣ* (to cover) वृक्षते वृक्षिष्यते अवृक्षत् वृक्षताम् वृक्षेत *वृक्षति

वृच् *7√vṛć* (to choose) वृणक्ति वर्चिष्यति अवृणक् वृणक्तु वृञ्ज्यात् *वर्चित

वृज् *2√vṛj* (to exclude, avoid, shun, leave) वृक्ते वर्जिष्यते अवृक्त वृक्ताम् वृजीत वर्ज्यते *वृक्त

वृज् *7√vṛj* (to shun) वृणक्ति वर्जिष्यति अवृणक् वृणक्तु वृञ्ज्यात् *वर्जित वर्जनीय वृज्य वर्जित्वा वर्जितुम् वृजिन

वृज् *10√vṛj* (to shun) वर्जयति-ते वर्जयिष्यति-ते अवर्जयत्-त वर्जयतु-ताम् वर्जयेत्-त *वर्जित वर्जयित्वा वर्जयितुम

वृञ्ज् *2√vṛñj* (to avoid) वृङ्क्ते वर्जिष्यते अवृक्त वृक्ताम् वृजीत *वर्जित वर्जनीय वर्जितव्य वृज्य वर्जित्वा वर्ज्य वृजिन

वृड् *6√vṛḍ* (to hide) वृडति वृडिष्यति अवृडत् वृडतु वृडेत् *वृडित वृडितव्य वृडित्वा वृडितुम्

वृण् *6√vṛṇ* (to please) वृणति वर्णिष्यति अवर्णत् वृणतु वृणेत् *वृत

वृण् *8√vṛṇ* (to please) वृणोति-वृणुते वर्णिष्यति अवृणोत् वृणोतु वृणुयात् *वृत

वृत् *1√vṛt* (to be) वर्तते वर्तिष्यते अवर्तत वर्तताम् वर्तेत वृत्यते *वृत्त वर्तितव्य वर्तितुम् वर्तित्वा-वृत्वा वर्तमान वर्तन

वृत् *4√vṛt* (to choose) वृत्यते वर्त्तिष्यते अवृत्यत वृत्यताम् वृत्येत *वृत्त वर्तिष्यति वृत्य वर्तित्वा-वृत्वा वर्तितुम् वृत्तवान

वृत् *10√vṛt* (to speak) वर्तयते-ते वर्तयिष्यति-ते अवर्तयत्-त वर्तयतु-ताम् वर्तयेत्-त *वर्तित

वृध् *1√vṛdh* (to grow, increase) वर्धते वर्धिष्यते अवर्धत वर्धताम् वर्धेत *वृद्ध वर्धनीय वर्धितव्य वर्धितुम् वर्धित्वा

वृध् *10√vṛdh* (to shine) वर्धयति-ते वर्धयिष्यति-ते अवर्धयत्-त वर्धयतु-ताम् वर्धयेत्-त वृध्यते *वृद्ध

वृश् *4√vṛś* (to select, choose) वृश्यति वर्शिष्यति अवृश्यत् वृश्यतु वृश्येत् *वृष्ट वृष्टव्य वृष्ट्वा

वृष् *1√vṛṣ* (to rain) वर्षति वर्षिष्यति अवर्षत् वर्षतु वर्षेत् वृष्यते *वृष्ट

वृष् *10√vṛṣ* (to rain) वर्षयते वर्षयिष्यते अवर्षयत वर्षयताम् वर्षयेत *वृष्ट

वृह् *6√vṛṣ* (to tear) वृहति वर्हिष्यति-वर्क्ष्यति अवर्हत् वर्हतु वर्हेत् *वृढ वृहत् वर्हणीय वर्हितव्य वर्हित्वा-वृढ्वा वर्हितुम्

वॄ *9√vṝ* (to select, choose) वृणीते वरिष्यते अवृणीत वृणीताम् वृणीत *वूर्ण वूर्णवत् वरणीय

वे *1√ve* (to knit) वयति-ते वास्यति अवयत् वयतु वयेत् ऊयते *उत उत्वा वानीय वातव्य वेय वातुम् उतवान् प्रोत

वेण् *1√veṇ* (to know, play) वेणति-ते वेणिष्यति अवेणत् वेणतु वेणेत् *वेणित वेणनीय वेणित्वा वेणितुम् वेणि वीणा

वेथ् *1√veth* (to request) वेथते वेथिष्यते अवेथत वेथताम् वेथेत *वेथित वेथितव्य वेथित्वा वेथितुम्

वेद् *11√ved* (to dream) वेद्यति-ते वेद्यिष्यति-ते अवेद्यत्-त वेद्यतु-ताम् वेद्येत्-त *वेदित

वेन् *1√ven* (to recognize) वेनति-ते वेनिष्यति-ते अवेनत् वेनतु वेनेत् *वेनित वेननीय वेनितव्य वेनित्वा वेनितुम्

वेप् *1√vep* (to shake, tremble, quiver) वेपते वेपिष्यते अवेपत वेपताम् वेपेत *वेप्त वेपनीय वेप्तव्य वेपतुम् वेपमान

वेल् *1√vel* (to walk, be wanton) वेलति वेलिष्यति अवेलत् वेलतु वेलेत् *वेलित वेलनीय वेलितव्य वेलित्वा वेलितुम्

वेल् *10√vel* (to count the time) वेलयति-ते वेलयिष्यति-ते अवेलयत्-त वेलयतु-ताम् वेलयेत्-त *वेलित वेल्यमान

वेल्ल् *1√vell* (to tremble) वेल्लति वेल्लिष्यति अवेल्लत् वेल्लतु वेल्लेत् *वेल्लित वेल्लितव्य वेल्लित्वा वेल्लितुम्

वेवी *2√vevī* (to be pregnant) वेवीते वेविष्यते अवेवीत वेवीताम् वेवीत *वेवित वेवितव्य वेवित्वा वेवितुम्

वेष्ट् *1√veṣṭ* (to surround) वेष्टते वेष्टिष्यते अवेष्टत वेष्टताम् वेष्टेत *वेष्टित वेष्टनीय वेष्टितव्य वेष्टित्वा वेष्टितुम्

वेह् *1√veh* (to try) वेहते वेहिष्यते अवेहत वेहताम् वेहेत *वेढ

वेह्ल् *1√vehl* (to go) वेह्लते वेह्लिष्यते अवेह्लत वेह्लताम् वेह्लेत *वेह्लित वेह्लितव्य वेह्लित्वा वेह्लितुम्

वै *1√vai* (to dry, be dried, languid, exhausted) वायति वास्यति अवासत् वायतु वायेत् *वान वात्वा वातुम वात

व्यच् *6√vyać* (to cheat, deceive) विचति व्यचिष्यति अविचत् विचतु विचेत् *विचित विचनीय विचित्वा विचितुम्

व्यज् *1√vyaj* (to fan, circulate air) व्यजति-ते व्यजिष्यति-ते अव्यजत्-त व्यजतु-ताम् व्यजेत्-त *व्यग्न

व्यथ् *1√vyath* (be pained, sorry, sad) व्यथते व्यथिष्यते अव्यथत व्यथताम् व्यथेत व्यथ्यते *व्यथित व्यथितुम् व्यथा

व्यध् *4√vyadh* (to shoot strike stab) विध्यति व्यत्स्यति अविध्यत् विध्यतु विध्येत् *विद्ध व्यधनीय विद्ध्वा व्यद्धुम् व्याध

व्यप् *10√vyap* (to destroy, diminish) व्यपयति-त व्यपयिष्यति-ते अव्यपयत्-त व्यपयतु-ताम् व्यपयेत्-त *व्याप्त

व्यय् *1√vyay* (to go) व्ययति-ते व्ययिष्यति-ते अव्ययत्-त व्ययतु-ताम् व्ययेत्-त *व्ययित व्ययित्वा व्ययितुम् व्यय अव्यय

व्यय् *10√vyay* (to spend, bestow) व्यययति व्यययिष्यति व्यययिष्यति-ते अव्यययत्-त व्यययतु-ताम् व्यययेत्-त *व्ययित

व्यंस् *1√vyaṁs* (to divide, distribute; foil, ward off; deceive) व्यंसति व्यंसिष्यति अव्यंसत् व्यंसतु व्यंसेत् *व्यंसित

व्युष् *4√vyuṣ* (to burn) व्युष्यति व्युषिष्यति अव्युष्यत् व्युष्यतु व्युष्येत् *व्युष्ट व्युष्टव्य व्युष्ट्वा व्युष्टुम्

व्ये *1√vye* (to cover, sew) व्ययति-ते व्यास्यति-ते अव्यासीत्-अव्यास्त *वीत वीत्वा व्यातुम्

व्रज् *1√vraj* (to approach, proceed, walk, go) व्रजति व्रजिष्यति अव्रजत् व्रजतु व्रजेत् *व्रजित व्रजनीय व्रजित्वा

व्रज् *10√vraj* (to go, prepare, decorate) व्राजयति-ते व्राजयिष्यति-ते अव्राजयत्-त व्राजयतु-ताम् व्राजयेत्-त व्रज्यते

व्रण् *1√vraṇ* (to sound) व्रणति व्रणिष्यति अव्रणत्-अव्राणत् व्रणतु व्रणेत् *व्राण वणनीय व्रणितव्य व्रणित्वा व्रणितुम्

व्रण् *10√vraṇ* (to strike, hurt, wound) व्रणयति-ते व्रणयिष्यतिते अव्रणयत्-त व्रणयतु-ताम् व्रणयेत्-त *व्रणित

व्रश्च् *6√vraṣć* (to bite) वृश्चति व्रश्चिष्यति-व्रक्ष्यति अवृश्यत् वृश्यतु-व्रश्यतु वृश्येत्-व्रश्येत् *वृक्ण व्रश्चनीय व्रष्टुम्

व्री *4√vrī* (to select, choose, be chosen) व्रीयते व्रेष्यते अव्रीयत व्रीयताम् वीयेत *व्रीण

व्री *9√vrī* (to select, choose) व्रीणाति व्रेष्यति अव्रीणात् व्रीणातु व्रीणीयात् *व्रीण-व्रीत व्रयणीय व्रेतव्य व्रीत्वा व्रेतुम्

व्रीड् *1√vrīḍ* (to be abashed) व्रीडते व्रीडिष्यते अव्रीडत् व्रीडतु व्रीडेत् *व्रीडित व्रीडनीय व्रीडितव्य व्रीडित्वा व्रीडितुम्

व्रीड् *4√vrīḍ* (to be ashamed) व्रीड्यति व्रीडिष्यति अव्रीड्यत् व्रीड्यतु व्रीड्येत् *व्रीडित व्रीडितव्य व्रीडित्वा व्रीडितुम्

व्रीड् *10√vrīḍ* (to be abashed, ashamed) व्रीडयति-ते व्रीडयिष्यति-ते अव्रीडयत्-त व्रीडयतु-ताम् व्रीडयेत्-त *व्रीडित

व्रुड् *1,6√vruḍ* (to sink, go down, gather, collect) व्रुडति व्रुडिष्यति अव्रुडत् व्रुडतु व्रुडेत् *व्रुडित व्रुडनीय व्रुडितव्य

व्ली *9√vlī* (to support, hold, maintain) व्लिनाति व्लेष्यति अव्लीनात् व्लीनातु व्लीनीयात् *व्लीन

व्लेक्ष् *10√vlekṣ* (to see) व्लेक्षयति-ते व्लेक्षयिष्यति-ते अव्लेक्षयत्-त व्लेक्षयतु-ताम् व्लेक्षयेत्-त *व्लेक्षित

(श) (śa)

शक् *5√śak* (to be able, competent) शक्नोति शक्ष्यति अशक्नोत् शक्नोतु शक्नुयात् शक्यते *शक्त शक्तवान् शकत् शकनीय शक्तव्य शक्य शक्त्वा-शकित्वा शक्तुम् शक्ति सशक्त शकट शाक शक्र शकृत शक शकुन शकुनि शकुन्तला

शङ्क् *1√śaṅk* (to doubt, hesitate) शङ्कते शङ्किष्यते अशङ्कत शङ्कताम् शङ्केत *शङ्कित शङ्कनीय शङ्कित्वा शङ्का

शच् *1√śać* (to talk, say, tell, speak) शचते शचिष्यते अशचत शचताम् शचेत *शचित शचनीय शचितव्य शचित्वा

शञ्च् *1√śañć* (to go, move) शञ्चते शञ्चिष्यते अशञ्चत शञ्चताम् शञ्चेत *शङ्क-शञ्चित

शट् *1√śaṭ* (to cut, divide, separate) शटति शटिष्यति अशटत् शटतु शटेत् *शटित शटनीय शटितव्य शटित्वा शटितुम्

शठ् *1√śaṭh* (to defraud, cheat) शठति शठिष्यति अशठत् शठतु शठेत् *शठित शठनीय शठितव्य शठित्वा शठितुम्

शठ् *10√śaṭh* (to be lazy) शठयति-ते शठयिष्यति-ते अशठयत्-त शठयतु-ताम् शठयेत्-त *शाठित शठयितव्य शठ

शण् *1√śaṇ* (to give, give charity) शणति शणिष्यति अशणत् शणतु शणेत् *शणित शणनीय शणितव्य शणित्वा

शण्ड् *1√śaṇḍ* (to be hurtful) शण्डते शण्डिष्यते अशण्डत शण्डताम् शण्डेत *शण्डित शण्डनीय शण्डितव्य शण्डित्वा

शद् *1√śad* (to decay, wither, sink) शीयते शत्स्यति अशीयत् शीयताम् शीयेत *शन्न शत्तव्य शाद्य शत्त्वा शत्तुम्

शप् *1√śap* (to curse, exercrate, swear, take oath, promise) शपति-ते शप्स्यति अशप्यत् शप्यतु शप्येत् *शप्त

शप् *4√śap* (to curse) शप्यति-ते शप्स्यति-ते अशप्सत्-अशप्त शप्यतु-ताम् शप्येत्-त *शप्त शप्यत् शपनीय शप्तुम्

शब्द् *10√śabd* (to sound, pronounce) शब्दयति-ते शब्दयिष्यति-ते अशब्दयत्-त शब्दयतु-ताम् शब्दयेत्-त *शब्दित

शम् *1√śam* (to see, show) शमति शमिष्यति अशमत् शमतु शमेत् *शमित शमनीय शमितव्य शमित्वा शमितुम्

शम् *4√śam* (to be calm, tranquil) शाम्यति शमिष्यति अशमत् शम्यतु शम्येत् *शान्त-शमित शमनीय शान्त्वा शमितुम्

शम् *10√śam* (to extinguish, inspect, display, see, show) शमयते शमयिष्यते अशमयत शमयताम् शमयेत *शान्त

शम्ब् *1√śamb* (to go) शम्बति-ते शम्बिष्यति-ते अशम्बत्-त शम्बतु-ताम् शम्बेत्-त *शम्बित शम्बित्वा शम्बितुम्

शम्ब् *10√śamb* (to collect) शम्बयति-ते शम्बयिष्यति शम्बयति-ते शम्बयिष्यति-ते अशम्बयत्-त शम्बयतु-ताम् शम्बयेत्

शर्ब् *1√śarb* (to go, injure) शर्बति शर्बिष्यति अशर्बत् शर्बतु शर्बेत् *शर्बित शर्बितव्य शर्बित्वा शर्बितुम्

शर्व् *1√śarv* (to hurt) शर्वति शर्विष्यति अशर्वत् शर्वतु शर्वेत् *शर्वित शर्वणिय शर्वित्वा शर्वितुम्

शल् *1√śal* (to shake, agitate) शलते शलिष्यते अशलत शलताम् शलेत *शलित शलनीय शल्य शलितुम्

शल् *10√śal* (to praise) शालयति-ते शालयिष्यति-ते अशालयत्-त शालयतु-ताम् शालयेत्-त *शालित

शल्भ् *1√śalbh* (to praise) शल्भते शल्भिष्यते अशल्भत शल्भताम् शल्भेत *शल्भित शल्भितव्य शल्भित्वा शल्भितुम्

शल्ल् *1√śall* (to go) शल्लते शल्लिष्यति अशल्लत शल्लताम् शल्लेत *शल्लित शल्लितव्य शल्लित्वा शल्लितुम्

शव् *1√śav* (to transform, alter) शवति शविष्यति अशवत्-अशावत् शवतु शवेत् *शवित शवितव्य शवित्वा शवितुम्

शंस् *1√śaṁs* (to praise, extol) शंसति शंसिष्यति अशंसत् शंसतु शंसेत् *शस्त शंसनीय शंसित्वा शंस्यमान प्रशंसा

शश् *1√śaś* (to leap, bound, jump) शशति शशिष्यति अशषत्-अशाषत् शशतु शशेत् *शष्ट

शष् *1√śaṣ* (to injure) शषति शक्ष्यति अशषत् शषतु शषेत् *शष्ट शषणीय शष्ट्वव्य शष्ट्वा शष्टुम्

शस् *1√śas* (to wound, cut up) शसति शसिष्यति अशसत्-अशासत् शसतु शसेत् *शस्त

शा *3√śā* (to sharpen) शशाति शशिष्यति अशशात् शशातु शश्यात् *शस्त

शाख् *1√śākh* (to pervade, encompass) शाखति शाखिष्यति अशाखत् शाखतु शाखेत् *शाखित शाखनीय शाखित्वा

शाड् *1√śāḍ* (to praise) शाडते शाडिष्यते अशाडत शाडताम् शाडेत *शाडित शाडनीय शाडितव्य शाडित्वा शाडितुम्

शान् *1√śān* (to sharpen) शीशांसति-ते शीशांसिष्यति अशीशांसत् शीशांसताम् शीसांसेत् *शीसांसित शीसांसितुम्
शार् *10√śār* (to weaken) शीरयति-ते शारयिष्यति-ते शारयतु-ताम् शारयेत्-त *शारित
शाल् *1√śāl* (to praise, flatter; boast, vaunt) शालते शालिष्यते अशालत शालताम् शालतु *शालित
शास् *2√śās* (to govern) शास्ति-ते शासिष्यति-ते अशात्-त शास्तु-ताम् शिष्यात्-त *शासित-शिष्ट शासित्वा शासन
शि *5√śi* (to sharpen) शिनोति-शिनुते शेष्यति-शेष्यते अशिनोत्-अशिनुत शिनोतु-शिनुताम् शिनुयात्-शिन्वीत *शित-शिन
शिक्ष् *1√śikṣ* (to learn) शिक्षते शिक्षिष्यते अशिक्षित शिक्षताम् शिक्षेत *शिक्षित शिक्षणीय शिक्षमाण शिक्षा शिक्षण
शिङ्ख् *1√śinkh* (to go) शिङ्खति शिङ्खिष्यति अशिङ्खत् शिङ्खति शिङ्खिष्यति अशिङ्खत् शिङ्खतु शिङ्खेत *शिङ्खित शिङ्खत्
शिङ्घ् *1√śingh* (to smell) शिङ्घति शिङ्घिष्यति अशिङ्घत् शिङ्घतु शिङ्घेत *शिङ्घित शिङ्घत् शिङ्घनीय शिङ्घितव्य शिङ्घित्वा
शिञ्ज् *1√śiñj* (to jingle) शिञ्जते शिञ्जिष्यते अशिञ्जत शिञ्जताम् शिञ्जेत *शिञ्जित-शिङ्क्त
शिञ्ज् *2√śiñj* (to jingle) शिङ्क्ते शिञ्जिष्यते अशिङ्क्त शिङ्क्ताम् शिञ्जीत *शिञ्जित शिञ्जनीय शिञ्जित्वा शिञ्जितुम्
शिञ्ज् *10√śiñj* (to tinkle) शिञ्जयते शिञ्जयिष्यति-ते अशिञ्जयत्-त शिञ्जयतु-ताम् शिञ्जयेत्-त *शिञ्जित
शिट् *1√śiṭ* (to despise, disregard, slight) शेटति शेटिष्यति अशेटत् शेटतु शेटेत् *शेटित शेटनीय शेटितव्य शेटित्वा
शिल् *1,6√śil* (to pick left over grains) शिलति शेलिष्यति अशिलत् शिलतु शिलेत् *शिलित शेलनीय शिलितुम्
शिष् *1√śiṣ* (to injure) शषति शेशिष्यति अशेषत् शेषतु शिषेत् *शिष्ट
शिष् *7√śiṣ* (to leave remainder) शिनष्टि शेक्ष्यति अशिनट्-ड् शिनष्ट शिंष्यात् *शिष्ट शेषणीय शिष्ट्वा शेष्टुम् शेष
शिष् *10√śiṣ* (to spare, keep) शेषयति-ते शेषयिष्यति-ते अशेषयत्-त शेषयतु-ताम् शेषयेत्-त *शिष्ट
शी *2√śī* (to sleep) शेते शयिष्यते अशेत शेताम् शयीत *शयित शयनीय शेय शयित्वा शयितुम् संशय शयन शय्या
शी *4√śī* (to fall) शीयते शीयिष्यति अशीयत् शीयतु शीयेत् शय्यते *शयित
शीक् *1√śīk* (to moisten, spray water) शीकते शीकिष्यते अशीकित शीकताम् शीकेत *शीकित शीकित्वा शीकितुम्
शीक् *10√śīk* (to moisten) शीकयति-ते शीकयिष्यति-ते अशीकयत्-त शीकयतु-ताम् शीकयेत्-त *शीकित
शीभ् *1√śībh* (to boast) शीभते शीभिष्यते अशीभत शीभताम् शीभेत *शीब्ध शीभनीय शीब्धवत्
शील् *1√śīl* (to meditate) शीलति शीलिष्यति अशीलत् शीलतु शीलेत *शीलित शीलितव्य शीलित्वा शीलितुम्
शील् *10√śīl* (to study) परि+शीलयति-ते शीलयिष्यति अशीलयत्-त शीलयतु-ताम् शीलयेत्-त *शीलित शीलयितुम्
शुक् *1√śuk* (to go) शोकति शोकिष्यति अशोकत् शोकतु शोकेत् *शुक्त शुकनीय शुक्तव्य शुक्त्वा शुक्तुम्
शुच् *1√śuć* (to lament, grieve) शोचति शोचिष्यति अशोचत् शोचतु शोचेत् *शुक्त शोचनीय शोचित्वा शोचितुम् शोक
शुच् *4√śuć* (to lament) शुच्यति-ते शोचिष्यति-ते अशुच्यत्-त शुच्यतु-ताम् शुच्येत्-त *शुक्त शोचनीय शोचितुम् शुचि
शुच्य् *1√śućy* (to cleanse) शुच्यति शुच्यिष्यति अशुचत् शुच्यतु शुच्येत् *शुच्य शुच्यनीय शुच्यितुम् शुच्यमान शुच्च्य
शुठ् *1√śuṭh* (to resist, impede, hinder) शोठति शोठिष्यति अशोठत् शोठतु शोठेत् *शुठित शुठितव्य शुठितुम्
शुठ् *10√śuṭh* (to be lazy, dull, idle) शोठयति-ते शोठयिष्यति-ते अशोठयत्-त शोठयतु-ताम् शोठयेत्-त *शुठित

शुण्ठ् *1√śuṇṭh* (to purify) शुण्ठति शुण्ठिष्यति अशुण्ठत् शुण्ठतु शुण्ठेत् *शुण्ठित शुण्ठितव्य शुण्ठित्वा शुण्ठितुम्

शुण्ठ् *10√śuṇṭh* (to purify) शुण्ठयति-ते शुण्ठयिष्यति अशुण्ठयत् शुण्ठयतु शुण्ठयेत् *शुण्ठित शुण्ठयित्वा शुण्ठयितुम्

शुध् *4√śudh* (be purified, become pure) शुध्यति शोत्स्यति अशुध्यत् शुध्यतु शुध्येत् शुध्यते *शुद्ध

शुन् *6√śun* (to go) शुनति शोनिष्यति अशुनत् शुनतु शुनेत् *शुनित शुननीय शुनितव्य शुनित्वा शुनितुम्

शुन्ध् *1√śundh* (to be clean) शुन्धति-ते शुन्धिष्यति-ते अशुन्धत् शुन्धतु शुध्यात् *शुधित-शुद्ध शुधनीय शुधित्वा

शुन्ध् *10√śundh* (to become cleaned) शुन्धयति-ते शुन्धयिष्यति-ते अशुन्धयत्-त शुन्धयतु-ताम् शुन्धयेत्-त *शुन्धित

शुभ् *1√śubh* (to look good) शोभते शोभिष्यते अशोभत शोभताम् शोभेत *शोभित शोभनीय शुभ शोभन शोभना शोभा

शुभ् *6√śubh* (to shine, look beautiful) शुभति शोभिष्यति अशोभत् शोभतु शोभेत् शुभ्यते *शोभित-शुब्ध

शुम्भ् *1√śumbh* (to talk, speak, sound) शुम्भति शुम्भिष्यति अशुम्भत् शुम्भतु शुम्भेत् *शुम्भित-शुब्ध

शुर् *4√śur* (to be firm, fixed, steady, brave) शुर्यते शुरिष्यते अशुर्यत शुर्यताम् शुर्येत *शूरित

शुर् *10√śur* (to be brave) शुरयते शुरयिष्यते अशूरयत शूरयताम् शूरयेत *शूरित

शुल्क् *10√śulk* (to gain, pay,) शुल्कयति-ते शुल्कयिष्यति-ते अशुल्कयत्-त शुल्कयतु-ताम् शुल्कयेत्-त *शुल्कित

शुल्व् *10√śulv* (to give, create) शुल्वयति-ते शुल्वयिष्यति अशुल्वत् शुल्वलयतु-ताम् शुल्वयेत्-त *शुल्वित

शुष् *4√śuṣ* (to dry) शूष्यति शोक्ष्यति अशुष्यत् शुष्यतु शुष्येत् *शुष्क-पुष्ट शोषणीय शोष्टव्य शोष्य शुष्ट्वा शोष्टुम् शोष

शूर् *4√śūr* (to be firm, fixed, steady, brave) शूर्यते शूरिष्यते अशूर्यत शूर्यताम् शूर्येत शूर्यते *शूरित-शूर्ण

शूर् *10√śūr* (to be brave, hero) शूरयति-ते शूरयिष्यति-ते अशूरयत्-त शूरयतु-ताम् शूरयेत्-त *शूरित

शूर्प् *10√śūrp* (to weigh, measure) शूर्पयति-ते शूर्पयिष्यति-ते अशुर्पयत्-त शूर्पयतु-ताम् शूर्पयेत्-त *शूर्पित

शूल् *1√śūl* (to be sick, ill; to impale, pierce) शूलति शुलिष्यति अशूलत् शूलतु शूलेत् *शूलित शूलितुम् शूलित्वा

शूष् *1√śūṣ* (to produce, beget, bring forth) शूषति शुषिष्यति अशूषत् शूषतु शूषेत् *शूष्ट

शृध् *1√śṛdh* (to fart) शर्धति-ते शर्त्स्यति-शर्धिष्यति-ते अशृधत् शृधतु-ताम् शृधेत्-त *शृद्ध

शृध् *10√śṛdh* (to fart) शर्धयति-ते शर्धयिष्यति-ते अशर्धयत्-त शर्धयतु-ताम् शर्धयेत्-त *शृद्ध

शॄ *9√śṝ* (to smash into pieces) शृणाति शरिष्यति अशृणात् शृणातु शृणीयात् शीर्यते *शीर्ण शीर्णवत् शरणीय शीर्य

शेल् *1√śel* (to tremble; crush) शेलति शेलिष्यति अशेलत् शेलतु शेलेत् *शेलित शेलनीय शेलितव्य शेलित्वा

शेव् *1√śev* (to tremble) शेवते शेविष्यते अशेवत शेवताम् शेवेत *शेवित शेवनीय शेवितव्य शेव्य शेवित्वा शेवमान

शै *1√śai* (to cook) शायति शास्यति अशायत् शायतु शायेत् शायते *शान

शो *4√śo* (to sharpen)श्यति शास्यति अश्यत् श्यतु श्येत् *शात-शित शानीय शातव्य शेय शात्वा-शित्वा शातुम् संशित

शोण् *1√śoṇ* (to become red) शोणति शोणिष्यति अशोणत् शोणतु शोणेत् *शोणित शोणनीय शोणितव्य शोणित्वा

शौट् *1√śauṭ* (to be proud or haughty) शौटति शौटिष्यति अशौटत् शौटतु शौटेत् *शौटित शौटनीय शौटितव्य शौटित्वा

शौड् *1√śauḍ* (to be proud, have ego) शौडति शौडिष्यति अशौडत् शौडतु शौडेत् *शौडित शौडितव्य शौडितुम

श्चुत् *1√ścut* (to trickle, exude, ooze) श्च्योतति श्चोतिष्यति अश्च्योतत् श्चोततु श्चोतेत् *श्चोतित श्चोतितुम्
श्नथ् *1√śnath* (to pierce) श्नथति श्नथिष्यति अश्नथत् श्नथतु श्नथेत् *श्नथित श्नथितव्य श्नथित्वा श्नथितुम्
श्मील् *1√śmil* (to wink, twinkle) श्मीलति श्मीलिष्यति अश्मीलत् श्मीलतु श्मिलेत् *श्मीलित श्मीलनीय श्मीलित्वा
श्या *4√śyā* (to coagulate) श्यायति श्यायिष्यति अश्यायत् श्यायतु श्यायेत् *श्यात
श्यै *1√śyai* (to be congested) श्यायते श्यास्यते अश्यायत श्यायताम् श्यायेत *शीत-शीन
श्रङ्क् *1√śraṅk* (to creep, crawl) श्रङ्कति-ते श्रङ्किष्यते अश्रङ्कत श्रङ्कताम् श्रङ्केत *श्रङ्कित श्रङ्कनीय श्रङ्कित्वा श्रङ्कितुम्
श्रङ्ग् *1√śraṅg* (to go, move) श्रङ्गते श्रङ्गिष्यते अश्रङ्गत श्रङ्गताम् श्रङ्गेत *श्रङ्गित श्रङ्गनीय श्रङ्गितव्य श्रङ्गित्वा श्रङ्गितुम्
श्रण् *1√śraṇ* (to give) श्रणति श्रणिष्यति अश्रणत्-अश्राणत् श्रणतु श्रणेत् *श्रणित श्रणनीय श्रणितव्य श्रणित्वा श्रणितुम्
श्रण् *10√śraṇ* (to give) श्रणयति-ते श्रणयिष्यति-ते अश्रणयत्-त श्रणयतु श्रणयेत् *श्रणित श्रणितव्य श्रणित्वा श्रणितुम्
श्रथ् *1√śrath* (to hurt, be wicked) श्रन्थते, श्रन्थिष्यते अश्रन्थत श्रन्थताम् श्रन्थेत *श्रन्थित श्रन्थनीय श्रन्थित्वा श्रन्थितुम्
श्रथ् *9√śrath* (to hurt) श्रथ्नाति श्रन्थिष्यति अश्रन्थात् श्रथ्नातु श्रथ्नीयात् *श्रथित श्रन्थनीय श्रन्थितुम् श्रन्थन
श्रथ् *10√śrath* (to release, free) श्रथयति-ते श्रथयिष्यति-ते अश्रथयत्-त श्रथयतु-ताम् श्रथेत्-त *श्रथित
श्रन् *1√śran* (to give) श्रनति श्रनिष्यति अश्रानत्-अश्रनत् श्रनतु श्रनेत् *श्रन्त श्रननीय श्रन्तव्य श्रनित्वा श्रन्तुम्
श्रन्थ् *1√śranth* (to be relaxed, loose) श्रन्थति-ते श्रन्थयति अश्रन्थत् श्रन्थतु श्रन्थेत् *श्रन्थित श्रन्थनीय श्रन्थित्वा श्रन्थितुम्
श्रन्थ् *9√śranth* (to liberate, loosen) श्रथ्नाति श्रन्थिष्यति अश्रन्थात् श्रथ्नातु श्रथ्नीयात् *श्रथित श्रन्थनीय श्रन्थितुम् श्रन्थन
श्रन्थ् *10√śranth* (to knot) श्रन्थयति-ते श्रन्थयिष्यति-ते अश्रन्थयत्-त श्रन्थयतु-ताम् श्रन्थयेत्-त *श्रन्थित
श्रम् *4√śram* (to struggle, labor, toil) श्राम्यति श्रमिष्यति अश्रम्यत् श्राम्यतु श्राम्येत् श्रम्यते *श्रान्त श्रान्त्वा-श्रमित्वा
श्रम्भ् *1√śrambh* (to be unaware) श्रम्भते श्रम्भिष्यते अश्रम्भत श्रम्भताम् श्रम्भेत *श्रब्ध
श्रा *1√śā* (to cook, boil, ripen) श्राति श्रास्यति अश्रात् श्रातु श्रायात् *श्राण-श्रात-शृत
श्राम् *10√śrām* (to advise) श्रमयति-ते श्रमयिष्यति-ते अश्रमयत् श्रमयतु-ताम् श्रमयेत्-त *श्रमित श्रमित्वा श्रमितुम्
श्रि *1√śri* (to attain) श्रयति-ते श्रयिष्यति-ते अश्रयत्-त श्रयतु-श्रयताम् श्रयेत्-त *श्रित श्रित्वा श्रयितुम् आश्रित्य श्रय आश्रय
श्रिष् *1√śri* (to burn) श्रेषति श्रेषिष्यति अश्रेषत् श्रेष्यतु श्रेष्येत् *श्रिष्ट
श्री *9√śrī* (to cook, prepare) श्रिणाति-श्रीणीते श्रेष्यति-ते अश्रीणात्-अश्रीणीत श्रीणातु-श्रीणीताम् श्रीणीयात्-श्रीणीत *श्रीत
श्रु *1√śru* (to hear, listen to) श्रुणोति श्रोष्यति अश्रुणोत् शृणोतु शृणुयात् *श्रुत श्रवणीय श्राव्य श्रुत्वा श्रोतुम् श्रवण श्रोत्र
श्रै *1√śrai* (to perspire; cook, boil) श्रायति श्रास्यति अश्रायत् श्रायतु श्रायेत् श्रायते *श्राण
श्रोण् *1√śro* (to deposit) श्रोणति श्रोणिष्यति अश्रोणत् श्रोणतु श्रोणेत् *श्रोणित श्रोणनीय श्रोण्तव्य श्रोणित्वा श्रोणितुम्
श्लङ्क् *1√ślaṅk* (to go) श्लङ्कते श्लङ्किष्यते अश्लङ्कत श्लङ्कताम् श्लङ्केत *श्लङ्कित श्लङ्कनीय श्लङ्कित्वा श्लङ्कितुम्
श्लङ्ग् *1√ślaṅg* (to go) श्लङ्गते श्लङ्गिष्यते अश्लङ्गत श्लङ्गताम् श्लङ्गेत *श्लङ्गित श्लङ्गनीय श्लङ्गित्वा श्लङ्गितुम्
श्लथ् *10√ślath* (to weaken, loosen) श्लथयति-ते श्लथयिष्यति-ते अश्लयत्-त श्लथयतु-ताम् श्लथयेत्-त *श्लथित

श्ला *4√ślā* (to dissolve) श्लायति श्लायिष्यति अश्लायत् श्लायतु श्लायेत् *श्लात

श्लाख् *1√ślākh* (to pervade) श्लाखति श्लाखिष्यति अश्लाखत् श्लाखतु श्लाखेत् *श्लाखित श्लाखनीय श्लाखित्वा

श्लाघ् *1√ślāgh* (to extol) श्लाघते श्लाघिष्यते अश्लाघत श्लाघताम् श्लाघेत *श्लाघित श्लाघनीय श्लाघ्य श्लाघित्वा

श्लिष् *1√śliṣ* (to burn) श्लेषति श्लेषिष्यति अश्लेषत् श्लेषतु श्लेषेत् श्लिष्यते *श्लिष्ट श्लिष्ट्वा श्लिष्टुम्

श्लिष् *4√śliṣ* (to hug, embrace, stick, cling) श्लिष्यति श्लेक्ष्यति अश्लिष्यत् श्लिष्यतु श्लिष्येत् *श्लिष्ट श्लेषणीय

श्लेष् *10√śleṣ* (to unite, join, attach) श्लेषयति-ते श्लेषयिष्यति-ते अश्लेषयत्-त श्लेषयतु-ताम् श्लेषयेत्-त *श्लेषित

श्लोक् *1√ślok* (to praise or compose in verses) श्लोकते-श्लोक्यते-श्लोकयति-ते श्लोकिष्यते अश्लोकत श्लोकताम् श्लोकेत *श्लोकित श्लोकनीय श्लोकितव्य श्लोक्य श्लोकित्वा श्लोकितुम् श्लोकमान श्लोक

श्लोण् *1√śloṇ* (to pile up) श्लोणति श्लोणिष्यति अश्लोणत् श्लोणतु श्लोणेत् *श्लोणित श्लोणनीय श्लोणितव्य

श्वङ्क् *1√śvaṅk* (to depart) श्वङ्कते श्वङ्किष्यते अश्वङ्कत श्वङ्कताम् श्वङ्केत *श्वङ्कित श्वङ्कनीय श्वङ्कितव्य श्वङ्कित्वा

श्वच् *1√śvać* (to be split, cleft, ripped) श्वचते श्चचिष्यते अश्वचत श्वचताम् श्वचेत *श्वचित श्वचनीय श्वचितुम्

श्वञ्च् *1√śvañć* (to spread) श्वञ्चते श्वञ्चिष्यते अश्वञ्चत श्वञ्चताम् श्वञ्चेत *श्वञ्चित

श्वठ् *10√śvaṭh* (to arrange) श्वठयति-ते श्वठयिष्यति-ते अश्वठयत्-त श्वठयतु-ताम् श्वठयेत्-त *श्वठित श्वठयितुम्

श्वण्ठ् *10√śvaṇṭh* (to set up) श्वण्ठयति-ते श्वण्ठयिष्यति-ते अश्वण्ठयत्-त श्वण्ठयतु-ताम् श्वण्ठयेत्-त *श्वण्ठित

श्वभ्र् *10√śvabhr* (to hack) श्वभ्रयति-ते श्वभ्रयिष्यति-ते अश्वभ्रयत्-त श्वभ्रयतु-ताम् श्वभ्रयेत्-त *श्वभ्रित

श्वर्त् *10√śvart* (to go) श्वर्तयति-ते श्वर्तयिष्यति-ते अश्वर्तयत्-त श्वर्तयतु-ताम् श्वर्तयेत्-त * श्वर्तित

श्वल् *1√śval* (to run, go quickly, scurry) श्वलति श्वलिष्यति अश्वलत् श्वलतु श्वलेत् *श्वलित श्वलनीय श्वलित्वा

श्वल्क् *10√śvalk* (to tell) श्वल्कयति-ते श्वल्कयिष्यति-ते अश्वल्कयत्-त श्वल्कयतु-ताम् श्वल्कयेत्-त *श्वल्कित

श्वल्ल् *1√śvall* (to run, see) श्वल्लति श्वल्लिष्यति-ते अश्वल्लत् श्वल्लतु श्वल्लेत् *श्वल्लित श्वल्लनीय श्वल्लित्वा

श्वस् *2√śvas* (to breath) श्वसिति श्वसिष्यति अश्वसत् श्वसितु श्वस्यात् *श्वसीत-श्वस्त श्वसनीय श्वसितुम् निःश्वास

श्वि *1√śvi* (to swell, grow, increase) श्वयति श्वयिष्यति अश्वयत् श्वयतु श्वयेत् *शून श्वयितुम् श्वेय श्वयित्वा

श्वित् *1√śvit* (to brighten) श्वेतते श्वेतिष्यते अश्वेतत श्वेतताम् श्वेतेत *श्वेतित श्वेतनीय श्वेतयितव्य श्वेता

श्विन्द् *1√śvind* (to be pale) श्विन्दते श्विन्दिष्यते अश्विन्दत श्विन्दताम् श्विन्देत *श्विन्दित श्विन्दनीय श्विन्दितुम्

(ष) (ṣ)

षस्ज् *1ṣasj* (go) सज्जति-सज्जते सज्जिष्यते असज्जत् सज्जतु सज्जेत् *सक्त सज्जनीय सज्जित्वा-सक्त्वा सज्जितुम्

षिल् *1,6√śil* (to pick left over grains) षिलति षेलिष्यति अषिलत् षिलतु षिलेत् *षिलित षेलनीय षिलितुम्

ष्टिव् *4√ṣṭiv* (to spit, spew, sputter) ष्टीव्यति ष्टेविष्यति अष्टीव्यत् ष्टीवतु ष्टीव्येत् *ष्ट्यूत ष्ट्यूत्वा ष्टेवित्वा

ष्टै *1√ṣṭai* (to make sound, to spread) स्त्यायति स्त्यास्यति अस्त्यायत् स्त्यायतु स्त्यायेत् *स्त्यान

ष्ठिव् *1√ṣṭhiv* (to spit, spew, sputter) ष्ठीवति ष्ठेविष्यति अष्ठीवत् ष्ठीवतु ष्ठीवेत् *ष्ठ्यूत ष्ठ्यूत्वा ष्ठेवित्वा

ष्णै *1√ṣṇai* (to collect, gather, look good) स्नायति स्नास्यति अस्नायत् स्नायतु स्नायेत् *स्नात स्नात्वा स्नातुम्

ष्वक्क् *1√ṣvakk* (to go, move) ष्वक्कते ष्वक्किष्यते अष्वक्कत ष्वक्कताम् ष्वक्केत *ष्वक्कित
ष्वष्क् *1√ṣvaṣk* (to go) ष्वष्कते ष्वष्किष्यते अष्वष्कत ष्वष्कताम् ष्वष्केत *ष्वष्कित ष्वष्कनीय ष्वष्कित्वा ष्वष्कितुम्
ष्वस्क् *1√ṣvask* (to go) ष्वस्कते ष्वस्किष्यते अष्वस्कत ष्वस्कताम् ष्वस्कैत *ष्वस्कित

<u>(स) (s)</u>

सग् *1√sag* (to cover) सगति सगिष्यति असगत् सगतु सगेत् *सगित
सघ् *5√sagh* (to kill) सघ्नोति सघिष्यति असघत् सघ्नोतु सघ्नुयात् *सघित-सघ्न
सङ्ग्राम् *10√saṅgrām* (to battle) सङ्ग्रामयति-ते सङ्ग्रामयिष्यति-ते असङ्ग्रामयत् सङ्ग्रामयतु-ताम् सङ्ग्रामयेत्-त
सच् *1√sać* (to accompany) सचति-ते सचिष्यते असचत सचताम् सचैत *सचित सचनीय सचितव्य सचित्वा सचितुम्
सच् *3√sać* (to accompany, follow, pursue, go, love, like, aid) सिषक्ति सचिष्यति असिषेक् सिषक्तु सिषच्यात्
सञ्ज् *1√sañj* (to attach, adhere, cling, stick to) सजति सङ्क्ष्यति असजत् सजतु सजेत् सज्यते *सक्त सक्त्वा
सट् *1√saṭ* (to form a part of) सटति सटिष्यति असटत्-असाटत् सटतु सटेत् *सटित सटनीय सटितव्य सटित्वा सटितुम्
सट्ट् *10√saṭṭ* (to give, take) सट्टयति-ते सट्टयिष्यति-ते असट्टयत्-त सट्टयतु-ताम् सट्टयेत्-त *सट्टित
सठ् *10√saṭh* (to finish, complete) सठयति सठयिष्यति-ते असठयत्-त सठयतु-ताम् सठयेत्-त *सठित
सत्र् *10√satr* (to have relation, have offspring) सत्रयते सत्रयिष्यते असत्रयत सत्रय-ताम् सत्रयेत *सत्रित सत्र
सद् *1,6√sad* (to sit, sink, plunge, droop) सीदति सत्स्यति असीदत् सीदतु सीदेत् *सन्न सत्तव्य सत्त्वा सत्तुम् विषण्ण
सन् *1√san* (to love) सनति सनिष्यति असनत् सनतु सनेत् *सनित सननीय सनितव्य सनित्वा सनितुम् सनित्वा-सात्वा
सन् *8√san* (to love) सनोति-सनुते सनिष्यति-ते असनोत्-असनुत सनोतु-सनुताम् सनुयात्-सन्वीत *सात
सप् *1√sap* (to obey, honor) सपति सपिष्यति असपत सपतु सपेत् *सप्त
सपर् *11√sapar* (to worship) सपर्यति-ते सपर्यिष्यति-ते असपर्यत्-त सपर्यतु-ताम् सपर्येत्-त *सपरित
सभाज् *10√sabhāj* (to greet) सभाजयति-ते सभाजयिष्यति-ते असभाजयत्-त सभाजयतु-ताम् सभाजयेत्-त *सभाजित
सम् *1√sam* (to be equanimous) समति समिष्यति असमत् समतु समेत् *समित समनीय समितव्य समित्वा समितुम् सम
सम् *10√sam* (to be agitated, confused) समयति-ते समयिष्यति-ते असमयत्-त समयतु-ताम् समयेत्-त *समित
सम्ब् *1√samb* (to go) सम्बति सम्बिष्यति असम्बत् सम्बतु सम्बेत् *सम्बित सम्बनीय सम्बितव्य सम्बित्वा सम्बितुम्
सम्ब् *10√samb* (to go) सम्बयति-ते सम्बयिष्यति-ते असम्बयत्-त सम्बयतु-ताम् सम्बयेत्-त *सम्बित
सय् *1√say* (to go) सयति सयिष्यते असयत् सयतु सयेत् *सयित सयितव्य सयित्वा सयितुम्
सर्ज् *1√sarj* (to obtain, acquire, gain) सर्जति सर्जिष्यति असर्जत् सर्जतु सर्जेत् *सर्जित सर्जनीय सर्जितव्य सर्जित्वा
सर्ब् *1√sarb* (to go, move) सर्बति सर्बिष्यति असर्बत् सर्बतु सर्बेत् *सर्बित सर्बनीय सर्बितव्य सर्जित्वा सर्जितुम्
सल् *1√sal* (to go, move) सलति सलिष्यति असलत् सलतु सलेत् *सलित सलनीय सलितव्य सलित्वा सलितुम्
सस् *2√sas* (to sleep) सस्ति ससिष्यति अससत् सस्तु ससेत् *सस्त

सस्च् *1√sasć* (to be ready) सस्चति सस्चिष्यति असस्चत् सस्चतु सस्चेत् *सस्चित-सक्त

सस्ज् *1√sasj* (to be ready) सस्जति सस्जिष्यति असस्जत् सस्जतु सस्जेत् *सस्जित-सक्त

सह् *1√sah* (to endure) सहते सहिष्यते असहत सहताम् सहेत सह्यते *सोढ सह्य सोढ्वा-सहित्वा सहितुम् सोढुम् सहिष्णु

सह् *4√sah* (to be contented) सह्यति सहिष्यति असह्यत् सह्यतु सह्येत् *सोढ सोढ्वा सहितुम् सोढुम्

सह् *10√sah* (to bare) साहयति-ते साहयिष्यति असाहयत्-त साहयतु-ताम् साहयेत्-त *सोढ सोढयित्वा सोढयितुम्

सा *6√sā* (to bind) स्याति सायिष्यति असायत सायतु सायेत् *सायित सायितव्य सायित्वा सायितुम्

साट् *10√saṭ* (to publish, manifest) सटयति-ते सटयिष्यति-ते असटयत्-त सटयतु-ताम् सटयेत्-त *सटित

सात् *10√sat* (to be happy) सतयति-ते सतयिष्यति-ते असतयत्-त सतयतु-ताम् सतयेत्-त *सतित

साध् *4√sādh* (to be completed, succeeded) साध्नोति सात्स्यति असाध्नोत् साध्नोतु साध्नुयात् साध्यते *सिद्ध साध्य

साध् *5√sādh* (to accomplish) साध्नोति सात्स्यति असाध्नोत् साध्नोतु असाध्नुयात् *साद्ध

सान्त्व् *10√sāntva* (to pacify) सान्त्वयति-ते सान्त्वयिष्यति असान्त्वयत् सान्त्वयतु सान्त्वयेत् *सान्त्वित सान्त्वक सान्त्वन

साम् *10√sām* (to appease, soothe) सामयति सामयिष्यति असामयत्-त सामयतु-ताम् सामयेत्-त *सामित सामयितुम्

सार् *10√sār* (to be weak) सारयति सारयिष्यति असारयत्-त सारयतु-ताम् सारयेत्-त *सारित सामयित्वा सारणा संसार

सि *5√si* (to bind, tie) सिनोति-सिनुते सेष्यति-सेष्यते असिनोत्-असिनुत सिनोतु-सिनुताम् सिनुयात्-सिन्वीत *सित-सिन

सि *9√si* (to ensnare, net) सिनाति-सिनीते सेष्यति-ते असिनात्-असिनीत सिनातु-सिनीताम् सिनीयात्-सिनीत *सीत

सिक् *6√sik* (to water the plants) सेकते सेकिष्यति असेकत् सेकतु सेकेत् *सिक्त

सिञ्च् *6√siñć* (to pour) सिञ्चति-ते सेक्ष्यति असिञ्चत् सिञ्चतु सिञ्चेत् *सिक्त सेचनीय सेक्तव्य सिक्त्वा सेक्तुम्

सिट् *1√siṭ* (to hate, despise, disregard) सेटति सेटिष्यति असेटत् सेटतु सेटेत् *सेटित सेटनीय सेटितव्य सेटित्वा

सिध् *1√sidh* (to govern, go) सेधति सोधिष्यति असेधत् सेधतु सेधेत् *सिद्ध-सिधित सेधनीय सिधित्वा सेधनीय सेधितुम्

सिध् *4√sidh* (be successful, fulfilled) सिध्यति सेत्स्यति असिध्यत् सिध्यतु सिध्येत् *सिद्ध सेधनीय सिद्ध्वा सेद्धुम् सिद्धि

सिन्व् *4√sinv* (to be wet) सिन्व्यति सिन्विष्यति सिन्वयत् सिन्वयतु सिन्वयेत् *सिन्वित सिन्वितव्य सिन्वित्वा सिन्वितुम्

सिल् *6√sil* (to pick the left over grains) सिलति सेलिष्यति असेलत् सेलतु सेलेत् *सेलित सेलनीय सेलितव्य

सिव् *4√siv* (to sew, darn) सिव्यति सेविष्यति असीव्यत् सीव्यतु सीव्येत् *सेवित सेवनीय सेव्य सेवितुम् सेवन सूचि सूत्र

सीक् *1√sīk* (to water, sprinkle water) सीकते सीकिष्यते असीकत सीकतु सीकेत *सीक्त

सीक् *10√sīk* (to water) सीकयति-ते सीकयिष्यति असीकयत्-त सीकयतु-ताम् सीकयेत्-त *सीक्त

सु *1√su* (to give birth) सवति सविष्यति असवत् सवतु सवेत् सूयते *सुत सवनीय सोतव्य सव्य सुत्वा सोतुम् प्रसव

सु *2√su* (to produce, generate, be able) सौति सोष्यति असौत् सौतु सुयात् *सुत सवनीय सोतव्य सव्य सुत्वा सोतुम्

सु *5√su* (to sprinkle) सुनोति-सुनुते सोष्यति-ते असुनोत्-असुनुत सुनोतु-सुनुताम् सुनुयात्-सुन्वीत *सुत सुन्वत् सोम सुरा

सुख् *10√sukh* (to please) सुखयति-ते सुखयिष्यति-ते असुखयत्-त सुखयतु-ताम् सुखयेत्-त *सुखित सुखयितुम् सुख

सुट्ट् *10√suṭṭ* (to despise) सुट्टयति-ते सुट्टयिष्यति-ते असुट्टयत्-त सुट्टयतु-ताम् सुट्टयेत्-त *सुट्टित सुट्टित्वा सुट्टितुम्

सुभ् *1√subh* (to hurt) सुभति सुभिष्यति असुभत् सुभतु सुभेत् *सुब्ध

सुह् *1√suh* (to be heppy, satisfied) सुह्यति सुह्यिष्यति असुह्यत् सुह्यतु सुह्येत् *सूढ

सू *2√sū* (to deliver) सूते सविष्यते असूत सूताम् सुवीत *सूत

सू *4√sū* (to producer) सूयते सविष्यते-सोष्यते असूयत सूयताम् सूयेत *सून सवनीय सवितव्य सवित्वा-सूत्वा सवितुम्

सू *6√sū* (to impel) सुवति सविष्यति असूवत् सूवतु सूवेत् *सूत सवनीय सोतव्य सव्य सवितुम् सविता सूर्य सूर

सूच् *10√sūć* (to notify, manifest) सूचयति सूचयिष्यति असूचयत् सूचयतु सूचयेत् *सूचित सूचयितुम् सूचना

सूत्र् *10√sūtr* (to string, thread) सूत्रयति-ते सूत्रयिष्यति असूत्रयत् सूत्रयतु सूत्रयेत् *सूत्रित सूत्र

सूद् *1√sūd* (to thrash, strike, kill) सूदते सूदिष्यते असूदत सूदताम् सूदेत *सूदित सूदनीय सूदितव्य सूदित्वा सूदितुम्

सूद् *10√sūd* (to thrash) सूदयति-ते सूदयिष्यति-ते असूदयत्-त सूदयतु-ताम् सूदयेत्-त *सूदित सूदितव्य सूदितुम्

सूर् *4√sūr* (to be firm or to make firm) सूर्यते सूरिष्यते असूर्यत सूर्यताम् सूर्येत *सूर्ण

सूर्क्ष् *1√sūrkṣ* (to disrespect) सूर्क्षति सूर्क्षिष्यति असूर्क्षत् सूर्क्षतु सूर्क्षेत् *सूर्क्षित

सूर्क्ष्य् *1√sūrkṣy* (to disrespect) सूर्क्ष्यति सूर्क्ष्यिष्यति असूर्क्ष्यीत् सूर्क्ष्यतु सूर्क्ष्यात् *सूर्क्ष्यित सूर्क्ष्यणीय सूर्क्ष्य सूर्क्ष्यमाण

सूष् *1√sūṣ* (to deliver) सूषति सूषिष्यति असूषत् सूषतु सूषेत् *सूष्ट

सृ *1√sṛ* (to go) सरति सरिष्यति असरत् सरतु सरेत् स्रियते *सृत सरणीय सृत्वा सार्य्य सर्तुम् उपसृत्य प्रसार सूर्य पुरःसर

सृ *3√sṛ* (to go, move, proceed, approach) ससर्ति सरिष्यति असरत् सिसर्तु सिसृयात् *सृत

सृ *10√sṛ* (to go) सारयति-ते सारयिष्यति-ते असारयत्-त सारयतु-ताम् सारयेत्-त *सारित

सृज् *4√sṛj* (to produce) सृज्यते स्रक्ष्यते असृज्यत सृज्यताम् सृज्येत सृज्यते *सृष्ट सर्जनीय स्रज्वा-सृष्ट्वा स्रष्टुम् विसृज्य

सृज् *6√sṛj* (to produce) सृजति स्रक्ष्यति असृजत् सृजतु सृजेत् *सृष्ट सर्जनीय स्रष्टव्य विसृज्य सृष्ट्वा स्रष्टुम् सृष्टि सृष्टि

सृप् *1√sṛp* (to crawl) सर्पति सर्पिष्यति असृपत् सर्पतु सर्पेत *स्रप्त सर्प्तव्य सृप्त्वा सर्प सर्पण

सृभ् *1√sṛbh* (to kill) सर्भति सर्भिष्यति असर्भत् सर्भतु सर्भेत् *सर्भित-सृब्ध सर्भित्वा-सृब्ध्वा

सृम्भ् *1√sṛmbh* (to kill) सृम्भति सृम्भिष्यति असृम्भत् सृम्भतु सृम्भेत् *स्रब्ध स्रब्ध्वा

सॄ *9√sṝ* (to kill, hurt, injure) सृणाति वरिष्यति अवृणीत् वृणातु वृणीयात् *सीर्ण

सेक् *1√sek* (to go) सेकति-ते सेकिष्यते असेकत सेकताम् सेकेत *सेकित सेकनीय सेकितव्य सेक्य सेकित्वा सेकितुम्

सेल् *1√sel* (to move) सेलति-ते सेलिष्यति असेलत् सेलतु सेलेत् *सेलित सेलनीय सेलितव्य सेलित्वा तेलितुम्

सेव् *1√sev* (to serve) सेवते सेविष्यते असेवत सेवताम् सेवेत *सेवित सेवनीय सेवित्वा-सेवयित्वा सेवितुम सेवा

सै *1√sai* (to decline, waste away, perish) सायति सास्यति असायत् सायतु सायेत् *सायित

सो *4√so* (to finish, complete, bring to an end) स्यति सास्यति अस्यत् स्यतु स्येत् *सित सानीय सेय सात्वा सातुम्

स्कन्द् *1√skand* (to jump, ascend) स्कन्दति स्कन्त्स्यति स्कन्दतु स्कन्देत् स्कन्द्यात् *स्कन्न स्कन्तुम् स्कन्दनीय

स्कन्ध् *10√skandh* (to collect) स्कन्धयति-ते स्कन्धयिष्यति-ते अस्कन्धयत्-त स्कन्धयतु-ताम् स्कन्धयेत्-त *स्कन्धित

स्कम्भ् *1√skambh* (to resist) स्कम्भते स्कम्भिष्यते अस्कम्भत स्कम्भताम् स्कम्भेत *स्कम्भित-स्कब्ध स्कम्भितुम् सम्भित्वा

स्कम्भ् *5√skambh* (to hinder) स्कम्भ्नोति स्कम्भिष्यति अस्कम्भ्नोत् स्कम्भ्नोतु स्कम्भ्नुयात् *स्कब्ध

स्कम्भ् *9√skambh* (to prop) स्कभ्नाति स्कभिष्यति अस्कभ्नात् स्कभ्नातु स्कभ्नीयात् *स्कब्ध

स्कम्भ् *10√skambh* (to resist) स्कम्भयति-ते स्कम्भयिष्यति-ते अस्कम्भयत्-त स्कम्भयतु-ताम् स्कम्भयेत्-त *स्कब्ध

स्कु *2√sku* (to leap, jump, bound, rise, lift, bounce) स्कौति स्कविष्यति अस्कौत् स्कौतु स्कुयात्

स्कु *5√sku* (to leap) स्कुनोति स्कविष्यति अस्कुनोत् स्कुनोतु स्कुनुयात् *स्कुन

स्कु *9√sku* (to leap) स्कुनोति-स्कुनुते स्कोष्यति-ते अस्कुनोत्-अस्कुनुत स्कुनोतु-स्कुनुताम् स्कुनुयात्-स्कुन्वीत *स्कुन

स्कुद् *1√skud* (to jump) स्कुन्दते स्कुन्दिष्यते अस्कुन्दत स्कुन्दताम् स्कुदेत *स्कुन्दित स्कुन्दनीय स्कुन्दित्वा स्कुन्दितुम्

स्कुम्भ् *5√skumbh* (to stop) स्कुम्भ्नोति स्कुम्भिष्यति अस्कुम्भनोत् स्कुम्भनोतु स्कुम्भनुयात् *स्कुब्ध

स्कुम्भ् *9√skumbh* (to stop) स्कुभ्नाति स्कुभिष्यति अस्कुभ्नात् स्कुभ्नातु स्कुभ्नीयात् *स्कुब्ध

स्खद् *1√skhad* (to cut) स्खदते स्खदिष्यते अस्खदत स्खदताम् स्खदेत *स्खदित-स्खत्त स्खदनीय स्खदितव्य स्खादित्वा

स्खद् *4√skhad* (to cut) स्खद्यते स्खदिष्यते अस्खद्यत स्खद्यताम् स्खद्येत *स्खदित स्खदितव्य स्खदित्वा स्खदितुम्

स्खल् *1√skhal* (to fall, slip, trip, tumble, stumble) स्खलति स्खलिष्यति अस्खलत् स्खलतु स्खलेत् *स्खलित

स्खुड् *1√skhuḍ* (to cover) स्खुडति स्खुडिष्यति अस्खुडत् स्खुडतु स्खुडेत् *स्खुडित स्खुडितव्य स्खुडित्वा स्खुडितुम्

स्तक् *1√stak* (to save) स्तकति स्तकिष्यति अस्तकत् स्तकतु स्तकते *स्तकित-स्तक्त

स्तग् *1√stag* (to hide) स्तगति स्तगिष्यति अस्तगत् स्तगतु स्तगेत् *स्तगित-स्तक्त

स्तन् *1√stan* (to moan, groan) स्तनति स्तनिष्यति अस्तनत् स्तनतु स्तनेत् *स्तनित स्तननीय स्तनितव्य स्तनित्वा

स्तन् *10√stan* (to thunder) स्तनयति-ते स्तनयिष्यति अस्तनयत्-त स्तनयतु-ताम् स्तनयेत्-त *स्तनित स्तनयितव्य स्तन

स्तम् *1√stam* (to be afraid) स्तमति स्तमिष्यति अस्तमत् स्तमतु स्तमेत् *स्तमित स्तमनीय स्तमितव्य स्तमित्वा स्तमितुम्

स्तभ् *9√stabh* (to make steady) स्तभ्नाति स्तभिष्यति अस्तभ्नात् स्तभ्नातु स्तभ्नीयात् *स्तब्ध

स्तम्भ् *1√stambh* (to prop, stop) स्तम्भते स्तम्भिष्यते अस्तम्भत स्तम्भताम् स्तम्भेत *स्तब्ध-स्तम्भित संस्तभ्य

स्तम्भ् *5√stambh* (to support) स्तभ्नोति स्तम्भिष्यति अस्तम्भ्नोत् स्तम्भ्नोतु स्यम्भ्नुयात् *स्तब्ध

स्तम्भ् *9√stambh* (to prop) स्तभ्नाति स्तम्भिष्यति अस्तभ्नात् स्तभ्नातु स्तभ्नीयात् *स्तब्ध

स्तिघ् *5√stigh* (to mount) स्तिघ्नोति स्तिघिष्यति अस्तिघ्नात् स्तिघ्नोतु स्तिघ्नुयात् *स्तिघ्न

स्तिप् *1√stip* (to leak) स्तेपते स्तेपिष्यते अस्तेपत् स्तेपतु स्तेपेत् *स्तिप्त

स्तिम् *4√stim* (to be wet) स्तिम्यति स्तेम्ष्यति अस्तिम्यत् स्तिम्यतु स्तिम्येत् *स्तिमित स्तिमितव्य स्तिमित्वा स्तिमितुम्

स्तीम् *4√stim* (to be wet) स्तीम्यति स्तीमिष्यति अस्तीम्यत् स्तिम्यतु स्तिम्येत् *स्तीमित स्तीमितव्य स्तीमित्वा स्तीमितुम्

स्तु *2√stu* (to praise, laud) स्तवीति-स्तौति स्तुते-स्तुवीते स्तोष्यति-ते अस्तौत्-अस्तुत स्तौतु-स्तुताम् स्तुयात्-स्तुवीत स्तूयते *स्तुत स्तुवत् स्तवनीय स्तोतव्य स्तुत्य स्तुत्वा स्तोतुम् स्तव स्तवन स्तुति संस्तुति प्रस्ताव स्तोम स्तोत्र स्तोतृ

स्तुच् *1√stuć* (to be favorable) स्तोचते स्तोचिष्यते अस्तोचत स्तोचताम् स्तोचेत *स्तोचित स्तोचनीय स्तोचित्वा

स्तुभ् *1√stubh* (to criticise) स्तोभते स्तोभिष्यते अस्तोभत स्तोभताम् स्तोभेत *स्तुब्ध स्तुब्ध्वा-स्तुभित्वा-स्तोभित्वा

स्तुम्भ् *5√stumbh* (to stop) स्तुभ्नोति स्तुम्भिष्यति अस्तुभ्नोत् स्तुभ्नोतु स्तुभ्नुयात् *स्तुब्ध

स्तुम्भ् *9√stumbh* (to stop) स्तुम्भ्नाति स्तुम्भिष्यति अस्तुम्भ्नात् स्तुम्भ्नातु स्तुम्भ्नीयात् *स्तुब्ध

स्तूप् *4√stūp* (to heap) स्तूप्यति स्तुपिष्यति अस्तुप्यत् स्तुप्यतु स्तप्येत् *स्तप्त

स्तूप् *10√stūp* (to heap) स्तूपयति-ते स्तूपयिष्यति-ते अस्तूपयत्-त स्तूपयतु-ताम् स्तूपयेत्-त *स्तूपित-स्तूप्त

स्तृ *5√stṛ* (to spread) स्तृणोति-स्तृणुते स्तरिष्यति-ते अस्तृणोत्-अस्तृणुत स्तृणोतु-स्तृणुताम् स्तृणुयात्-स्तृण्वीत स्तीर्यते *स्तृत स्तृण्वत् स्तरणीय स्तर्तव्य स्तार्य सतृत्वा स्तर्तुम् स्तर्यमाण स्तरण स्तर विस्तर विस्तार

स्तृ *9√stṛ* (to spread) स्तृणाति-स्तृणिते स्तरिष्यति-ते अस्तृणात्-अस्तृणीत स्तृणातु-स्तृणीताम् स्तृणीयात्-स्तृणीत *स्तीर्ण

स्तृक्ष् *1√stṛkṣ* (to go) स्तृक्षति स्तृक्षिष्यति अस्तृक्षत् स्तृक्षतु स्तृक्षेत् *स्तृक्षित

स्तृह् *6√stṛh* (to injure) स्तृहति स्तर्क्ष्यति-स्तर्हिष्यति अस्तृक्षत्-अस्तर्हत् *स्तृढ

स्तॄ *9√stṝ* (to cover) स्तृणाति-स्तृणीते स्तरिष्यति अस्तृणात् स्तृणातु स्तृणीयात् *स्तीर्ण

स्तेन् *10√sten* (to steal) स्तेनयति-ते स्तेनयिष्यति-ते अस्तेनयत्-त स्तेनयतु-ताम् स्तेनयेत्-त *स्तेनित स्तेनयितुम स्तेनन

स्तेप् *1√step* (to flow) स्तेपते स्तेपिष्यते अस्तेपत स्तेपताम् स्तेपेत *स्तेपित-स्तप्त

स्तै *1√stai* (to encircle) स्तायति स्तास्यति अस्तायत् स्तायतु स्तायेत् *स्तात-स्तान

स्तोम् *10√stom* (to brag) स्तोमयति-ते स्तोमयिष्यति-ते अतोस्तोमयत्-त स्तोमयतु-ताम् स्तोमयेत्-त *स्तोमित

स्त्या *4√styā* (to stiffen) स्त्यायते स्त्यास्यते अस्त्यायत स्त्यायताम् स्त्यायेत *स्त्यात

स्त्यै *1√stai* (to gather) स्त्यायति स्त्यास्यति अस्त्यायत् स्त्यायतु स्त्यायेत् *स्त्यान

स्थग् *1√sthag* (to hide, halt) स्थगति स्थगिष्यति अस्थगत् स्थगतु स्थगेत् *स्थगित स्थगितव्य स्थगित्वा स्थगितुम्

स्थल् *1√sthal* (to be stable) स्थलति स्थलिष्यति अस्थलत् स्थलतु स्थलेत् *स्थलित स्थलित्वा स्थलितुम् स्थाली स्थल

स्था *1√sthā* (to stay, abide) तिष्ठति स्थास्यति अतिष्ठत् तिष्ठतु तिष्ठेत् स्थियते *स्थित स्थातव्य स्थानीय स्थेय स्थातुम्

स्थुड् *1√sthuḍ* (to cover) स्थुडति स्थुडिष्यति अस्थुडत् स्थुडतु स्थुडेत् *स्थुडित कृस्थुनीय स्थुडितव्य स्थुडितुम्

स्थूल् *10√sthūl* (to grow) स्थूलयति-ते स्थूलयिष्यति-ते अस्थूलयत्-त स्थूलयतु-ताम् स्थूलयेत्-त *स्थूलित स्थूलयितुम्

स्नस् *1√snas* (to prosper) स्नसति स्नसिष्यति अस्नसत् स्नसतु स्नसेत् *स्नस्त

स्नस् *4√snas* (to prosper) स्नस्यति स्नसिष्यति अस्नस्यत् स्नस्यतु स्नस्येत् *स्नस्त

स्ना *2√snā* (to bathe) स्नाति स्नास्यति अस्नात् स्नातु स्नायात् *स्नात स्नान् स्नानीय स्नेय स्नात्वा स्नातुम् स्नान स्नायु

स्निह् *4√snih* (be loving) स्निह्यति स्नेहिष्यति अस्निह्यत् स्निह्यतु स्निहेत् *स्निग्ध स्नेहनीय स्नेग्धव्य स्नेहित्वा-स्नीढ्वा स्नेह

स्निह् *10√snih* (to be loving) स्नेहयति स्नेहयिष्यति अस्नेहयत् स्नेहयतु स्नेहयेत् स्निह्यते *स्निग्ध

स्नु *2√snu* (to distil) स्नौति स्नविष्यति अस्नौत् स्नौतु स्नुयात् *स्नुत स्नवनीय स्नुत्वा स्नवितुम्

स्नुस् *4√snus* (to disappear, eat, swallow) स्नुस्यति स्नुसिष्यति अस्नुस्यत् स्नुस्यतु स्नुस्येत् *स्नुस्त

स्नूह् *4√snūh* (to vomit) स्नुह्यति स्नोक्ष्यति-स्नोहिष्यति अस्नुह्यत् स्नुह्यतु स्नुह्येत् *स्नूग्ध-सूढ
स्नै *1√snai* (to wrap) स्नायति स्नास्यति अस्नायत् स्नायतु स्नायेत् *स्नायित-स्नात
स्पन्द् *1√spand* (to palpitate) स्पन्दते स्पन्दिष्यते अस्पन्दत स्पन्दताम् स्पन्देत *स्पन्दित स्पन्दनीय स्पन्दित्वा स्पन्दितुम्
स्पर्ध् *1√spardh* (to contend) स्पर्धते स्पर्धिष्यते अस्पर्धत स्पर्धताम् स्पर्धेत *स्पर्धित स्पर्धनीय स्पर्धित्वा स्पर्धितुम्
स्पर्श् *10√sparś* (to touch) स्पर्शयते स्पर्शयिष्यते अस्पर्शयत स्पर्शयताम् स्पर्शयेत *स्पर्शित-स्पृष्ट
स्पर्ष् *1√sparṣ* (to be moist) स्पर्षते स्पर्षिष्यते अस्पर्षत स्पर्षताम् स्पर्षेत *स्पृष्ट
स्पश् *1√spaś* (to obstruct, gather, touch) स्पशति-ते स्पशिष्यति अस्पशत् स्पशतु स्पशेत् *स्पष्ट-स्पशित
स्पश् *10√spaś* (to take, join, touch) स्पाशयते स्पाशयिष्यते अस्पाशयत् स्पाशयतु स्पाशयेत् *स्पष्ट-स्पाशित
स्पृ *5√spṛ* (to win) स्पृणोति स्पर्क्ष्यति अस्पणोत् स्पृणोतु स्पृणोतु स्पृणुयात् *स्पृत स्पृण्वत् स्परणीय स्पर्तव्य स्पार्य स्पर्तुम्
स्पृध् *1√spṛdh* (to contend) स्पर्धते स्पर्धिष्यते अस्पर्धत स्पर्धताम् स्पर्धेत *स्पर्धित स्पर्धनीय स्पर्धित्वा स्पर्धितुम्
स्पृश् *6√spṛś* (to touch) स्पृशति स्प्रक्ष्यति अस्पृशत् स्पृशतु स्पृशेत् *स्पृष्ट स्पर्शनीय स्प्रष्टव्य स्प्रष्ट्वा स्प्रष्टुम् स्पर्श
स्पृह् *10√spṛh* (to desire) स्पृहयति स्पृहयिष्यति अपस्पृहयत् स्पृहयतु स्पृहयेत् *स्पृहित स्पृहयितव्य स्पृहयितुम् स्पृहा
स्फट् *1√sphaṭ* (to split) स्फटति स्फटिष्यति अस्फटत्-अस्फाटत् स्फटतु स्फटेत् *स्फटित स्फटनीय स्फटितव्य स्फटित्वा
स्फण्ट् *1√sphaṇṭ* (to burst) स्फण्टति स्फण्टिष्यति अस्फण्टत् स्फण्टतु स्फण्टेत् *स्फण्टित स्फण्टनीय स्फण्टित्वा स्फण्टितुम्
स्फण्ट् *10√sphaṇṭ* (to burst) स्फण्टयति-ते स्फण्टयिष्यति-ते अस्फण्टयत्-त स्फण्टयतु-ताम् स्फण्टयेत्-त *स्फण्टित
स्फण्ड् *10√sphṇḍ* (to deride) स्फण्डयति-ते स्फण्डिष्यति-ते अस्फण्डयत्-त स्फण्डयतु-ताम् स्फण्डयेत्-त *स्फण्डित
स्फर् *6√sphar* (to throb) स्फरति स्फरिष्यति अस्फरत् स्फरतु स्फरेत् *स्फरित स्फरितव्य स्फरित्वा स्फरितुम्
स्फल् *6√sphal* (to quiver) स्फलति स्फलिष्यति अस्फलत् स्फलतु स्फलेत् *स्फलित स्फलितव्य स्फलित्वा स्फलितुम्
स्फाय् *1√sphāy* (to fatten) स्फायते स्फायिष्यते स्फायताम् स्फायेत *स्फीत स्फीतवान् स्फायित्वा स्फायित्वा स्फायितुम्
स्फिट् *10√sphiṭ* (to insult) स्फिटयति-ते स्फिटयिष्यति-ते अस्फिटयत्-त स्फिटयतु-ताम् स्फिटयेत्-त
स्फिट्ट् *10√sphiṭṭ* (to hurt) स्फिट्टयति-ते स्फिट्टयिष्यति-ते अस्फिट्टयत्-त स्फिट्टयतु-ताम् स्फिट्टयेत्-त
स्फुट् *1√sphuṭ* (to blast) स्फोटति-ते स्फोटिष्यते अस्फोटत स्फोटताम् स्फोटेत *स्फुटित स्फोटनीय स्फोटित्वा स्फोटितुम्
स्फुट् *6√sphuṭ* (to appear, sprout, bloom) स्फुटति स्फुटिष्यति अस्फुटत् स्फुटतु स्फुटेत् *स्फुटित स्फुटितव्य स्फुटितुम्
स्फुट् *10√sphuṭ* (to blast) स्फोटयति-ते स्फोटयिष्यति-ते अस्फोटयत्-त स्फोटयतु-ताम् स्फोटयेत्-त *स्फुटित स्फुटित्वा
स्फुट्ट् *10√sphuṭṭ* (to abhor) स्फुट्टयति-ते स्फुट्टयिष्यति-ते अस्फुट्टयत्-त स्फुट्टयतु-ताम् स्फुट्टयेत्-त *स्फुट्टित स्फुट्टित्वा
स्फुड् *6√sphuḍ* (to cover) स्फुडति स्फुडिष्यति अस्फुडत् स्फुडतु स्फुडेत् *स्फुडित स्फुडनीय स्फुडितव्य स्फुडितुम्
स्फुड् *10√sphuḍ* (to cover) स्फुडयति-ते स्फुडयिष्यति-ते अस्फुडयत् स्फुडयतु स्फुडयेत् *स्फुडित स्फुडयितुम्
स्फुण्ट् *1√sphuṇṭ* (to despise) स्फुण्टति स्फुण्टिष्यति अस्फुण्टत् स्फुण्टतु स्फुण्टेत् *स्फुण्टित स्फुण्टनीय स्फुण्टित्वा
स्फुण्ट् *10√sphuṇṭ* (to hate) स्फुण्टयति-ते स्फुण्टियिष्यति-ते अस्फुण्टयत्-त स्फुण्टयतु-ताम् स्फुण्टयेत्-त *स्फुण्टित

स्फुण्ठ् *1√sphunṭh* (to expand) स्फुण्ठति स्फुठिष्यति अस्फुठत् स्फुण्ठतु स्फुण्ठेत् *स्फुण्ठित स्फुण्ठनीय स्फुण्ठित्वा

स्फुण्ठ् *10√sphunṭh* (to jest) स्फुण्ठयति-ते स्फुण्ठयिष्यति-ते अस्फुण्ठयत्-त स्फुण्ठयतु-ताम् स्फुण्ठयेत्-त *स्फुण्ठित

स्फुण्ड् *1√sphunḍ* (to burgeon) स्फुण्डते स्फुण्डिष्यते अपुस्फुडत स्फुण्डताम् स्फुडेत *स्फुण्डित स्फुण्डनीय स्फुण्डितुम्

स्फुण्ड् *10√sphunḍ* (to jest) स्फुण्डयति-ते स्फुण्डयिष्यति-ते अस्फुण्डयत्-त स्फुण्डयतु-ताम् स्फुण्डयेत्-त *स्फुण्डित

स्फुर् *6√sphur* (to throb) स्फुरति स्फुरिष्यति अस्फुरत् स्फुरतु स्फुरेत् *स्फुरित स्फुरणीय स्फुर्त्वा स्फुरितुम स्फुरण स्फुर्ति

स्फुर्च्छ् *1√sphrććh* (to spread) स्फूर्च्छति स्फूर्च्छिष्यति अस्फूर्छत् स्फूर्च्छतु स्फूर्च्छेत् *स्फूर्च्छित स्फूर्च्छनीय स्फूर्च्छित्वा

स्फुर्ज् *1√sphrj* (to thunder) स्फूर्जति स्फूर्जिष्यति अस्फूर्जत् स्फूर्जतु स्फूर्जेत् *स्फूर्ण स्फूर्जनीय स्फूर्जितव्य स्फूर्जित्वा

स्फुल् *6√sphul* (to jerk) स्फुलति स्फुलिष्यति अस्फुलत् स्फुलतु स्फुलेत् *स्फुलित स्फुलनीय स्फुलित्वा स्फुलितुम्

स्मि *1√smi* (to smile) स्मयते स्मेष्यते अस्मयत स्मयताम् स्मयेत *स्मित स्मयनीय स्मेतव्य स्मित्वा विस्मित्य स्मेष्यमाण

स्मि *10√smi* (to smile) स्माययति-ते स्माययिष्यति-ते अस्माययत्-त स्माययतु-ताम् स्माययेत्-त *स्मायित स्मायितुम्

स्मिट् *10√smiṭ* (to abhor) स्मेटयति-ते स्मेटयिष्यति-ते अस्मिटयत्-त स्मेटयतु स्मेटयेत् *स्मेटित स्मेटनीय स्मेटयितुम्

स्मील् *1√smil* (to wink) स्मीलति स्मीलिष्यति अस्मीलत् स्मीलतु स्मिलेत *स्मिलित स्मीलत् स्मीलनीय स्मीलित्वा

स्मृ *1√smṛ* (to remember) स्मरति स्मरिष्यति अस्मरत् स्मरतु स्मरेत् *स्मृत स्मरणीय स्मर्तव्य स्मार्य स्मृत्वा स्मृति स्मर्तृ

स्मृ *5√smṛ* (to remember) स्मृणोति स्मरिष्यति अस्मृणोत् स्मृणोतु स्मृणुयात् *स्मृत स्मरणीत स्मार्य स्मर्तव्य स्मर्तुम्

स्यन्द् *1√syand* (to run, carry) स्यन्दते स्यन्दिष्यते-स्यन्स्यते अस्यन्दत स्यन्दताम् स्यन्देत *स्यन्दित स्यन्दनीय स्यन्दितव्य

स्यम् *1√syam* (to sound) स्यमति स्यमिष्यति अस्यमत् स्यमतु स्यमेत् *स्यमित स्यमनीय स्यमितव्य स्यमित्वा स्यमितुम्

स्यम् *10√syam* (to think) स्यमयति-ते स्यमयिष्यति-ते अस्यमयत्-त स्यमयतु-ताम् स्यमयेत्-त *स्यमित स्यमितुम्

स्रङ्क् *1√sraṅk* (to be dry) स्रङ्कति-ते स्रङ्किष्यते अस्रङ्केकत स्रङ्कताम् स्रङ्केत *स्रङ्कित स्रङ्कनीय स्रङ्कित्वा स्रङ्कितुम्

स्रंस् *1√sraṁs* (to fall) स्रंसते स्रंसिष्यते अस्रंसत स्रंसताम् स्रंसेत स्रस्यते *स्रस्त स्रंसनीय स्रंसितव्य स्रस्त्वा स्रंसितुम्

स्रंह् *1√sraṁh* (to trust) स्रंहते स्रंहिष्यते अस्रंहत स्रंहताम् स्रंहेत *स्रंहित स्रंहनीय स्रंहितव्य स्रंहित्वा स्रंहितुम्

स्रम्भ् *1√srambh* (to believe) स्रम्भते स्रम्भिष्यते अस्रम्भत स्रम्भताम् स्रम्भेत *स्रम्भित स्रम्भितव्य स्रम्भित्वा स्रम्भितुम्

स्रिध् *1√sridh* (to blunder) स्रिधति स्रिधिष्यति अस्रिधत् स्रिधतु स्रिधेत् *स्रिद्ध

स्रिभ् *1√sribh* (to injure) स्रेभति स्रेभिष्यति अस्रेभत् स्रेभताम् स्रेभेत *स्रिब्ध

स्रिम्भ् *1√srimbh* (to injure) स्रिम्भति स्रिम्भिष्यति अस्रिम्भत् स्रिम्भतु स्रिभेत् *स्रिम्भित स्रिम्भित्वा स्रिम्भितुम्

स्रिव् *4√sriv* (to go) स्रिव्यति स्रेविष्यति अस्रिव्यत् स्रिव्यतु स्रिव्येत् *स्रुत स्रेवणीय स्रेवितव्य स्रेवित्वा स्रेवितुम्

स्रु *1√sru* (to leak) स्रवति स्रोष्यति अस्रवत् स्रवतु स्रवेत् *स्रुत स्रवणीय स्रोतव्य स्रुत्वा स्राव्य स्रोतुम् स्रवण स्राव

स्रेक् *1√srek* (to go) स्रेकति-ते स्रेकिष्यते अस्रेकत स्रेकताम् स्रेकेत *स्रेकित स्रेकनीय स्रेकितव्य स्रेकित्वा स्रेकितुम्

स्रै *1√srai* (to boil over) स्रायति स्रास्यति अस्रायत् स्रायतु स्रायेत् *स्रात

स्वङ्क् *1√svaṅk* (to go) स्वङ्कति स्वङ्किष्यति अस्वङ्कत् स्वङ्कतु स्वङ्केत् *स्वङ्कित स्वङ्कितव्य स्वङ्कित्वा स्वङ्कितुम्

स्वङ्ग् *1√svaṅg* (to go) स्वङ्गति स्वङ्गिष्यति अस्वङ्गत् स्वङ्गतु स्वङ्गेत् *स्वङ्गित-स्वङ्क

स्वञ्ज् *1√svañj* (to embrace) स्वजते स्वङ्क्षते अस्वजत स्वजताम् स्वजेत *स्वक्त स्वङ्क्तुम् स्वञ्जनीय स्वङ्क्त्वा

स्वठ् *10√svaṭh* (to perform rites) स्वठयति-ते स्वठयिष्यति-ते अस्वठयत्-त स्वठयतु-ताम् स्वठयेत्-त *स्वठित

स्वद् *1√svad* (to relish) स्वदते-स्वद्यते स्वदिष्यते अस्वदत स्वदताम् स्वदेत *स्वत्त स्वदत् स्वदनीय

स्वद् *10√svad* (to sweeten) स्वादयति-ते स्वादयिष्यति अस्वादयत् स्वादयतु स्वादयेत् *स्वादित स्वादयितुम् स्वाद

स्वन् *1√svan* (to sound) स्वनति स्वनिष्यति अस्वनत् स्वनतु स्वनेत् *स्वान्त-स्वनित स्वननीय स्वनितव्य स्वनित्वा

स्वप् *2√svap* (to sleep) स्वपिति स्वप्स्यति अस्वपीत् स्वपितु स्वप्यात् *सुप्त स्वपनीय स्वप्तव्य सुप्त्वा स्वप्तुम् स्वप्न

स्वर् *10√svar* (to reprove) स्वरयति-ते स्वरयिष्यति-ते अस्वरयत्-त स्वरयतु-ताम् स्वरयेत्-त *स्वरित

स्वर्द् *1√svard* (to please) स्वर्दते स्वर्दिष्यते अस्वर्दत स्वर्दताम् स्वर्देत *स्वर्दित स्वर्दितव्य स्वर्दित्वा स्वर्दितुम्

स्वल् *1√sval* (to move) स्वलति स्वेलिष्यति अस्वलत् स्वलतु स्वलेत् *स्वलित स्वलनीय स्वलितव्य स्वलित्वा स्वलितुम्

स्वस्क् *1√svask* (to go) स्वस्कते स्वस्किष्यते अस्वस्कत स्वस्कताम् स्वस्केत *स्वस्कित स्वस्कितव्य स्वस्कितुम्

स्वाद् *1√svād* (to taste) स्वादते स्वादिष्यते अस्वादत स्वादताम् स्वादेत *स्वादित स्वादनीय स्वाद्य स्वादितव्य स्वादित्वा

स्विद् *1√svid* (to smoothen, renounce) स्वेदति स्वेदिष्यति अस्वेदत् स्वेदतु स्वेदेत् स्विद्यते *स्विन्न

स्विद् *4√svid* (to sweat) स्विद्यति स्वेत्स्यति अस्विद्यत् स्विद्यतु स्विद्येत् *स्विन्न स्वेदनीय स्वेद्य स्वेत्तव्य स्वित्त्वा

स्वुर्च्छ् *1√svurććh* (to spread, extend; forget) स्वुर्च्छति स्वुर्च्छिष्यति अस्वुर्च्छत् स्वुर्च्छतु स्वुर्च्छेत् *स्वुच्छित

स्वृ *1√svṛ* (to sound) स्वरति स्वरिष्यति अस्वरत् स्वरतु स्वरेत् *स्वृत स्वरणीय स्वरितव्य-स्वर्तव्य स्वरितुम्-स्वर्तुम् स्वर

स्वॄ *9√svṝ* (to hurt) स्वृणाति स्वरिष्यति अस्वृणात् स्वृणातु स्वृणीयात् *स्वूर्ण

स्वेक् *1√svek* (to go) स्वेकते स्वेकिष्यते अस्वेकत स्वेकताम् स्वेकेत *स्वेकित स्वेकितव्य स्वेकित्वा स्वेकितुम्

(ह) (h)

हट् *1√haṭ* (to be shining) हटति हटिष्यति अहटत्-अहाटत् हटतु हटेत् *हटित हटनीय हटितव्य हटित्वा हटितुम्

हठ् *1√haṭh* (to nail) हठति हठिष्यति अहठत्-अहाठत् हठतु हठेत् *हठित हठनीय हठित्वा हठितुम्

हद् *1√had* (to void excrement, feces, stool) हदते हत्स्यते अहदत हदताम् हदेत *हत्त

हन् *2√han* (to smite, strike, kill) हन्ति-आहते हनिष्यति-अहनिष्यते अहन्-आहत हन्तु-अहताम् हन्यात्-आघ्नीत हन्यते *हत हनत् हननीय हन्तव्य प्रहत्य हत्वा हन्तुम् हन्यमान हनन वध वधक घात अपघात विघ्न कृतघ्न हेति हत्या कलह

हम्म् *1√hamm* (to go) हम्मति हम्मिष्यति अहम्मत् हम्मतु हम्मेत् *हम्मित हम्मितव्य हम्मित्वा हम्मितुम्

हय् *1√hay* (to go) हयति हयिष्यति अहयत् हयतु हयेत् *हयित हयनीय हयितव्य हयित्वा हयितुम् हय

हर् *4√har* (to be gratified) हर्यति हरिष्यति अहर्यरत् हर्यतु हर्येत् *हरित

हर्य् *1√hary* (to get tired) हर्यति हर्यिष्यति अहर्यत् जहर्य हर्यतु हर्येत् *हर्यित

हल् *1√hal* (to plough) हलति हलिष्यति अहलत् हलतु हलेत् *हलित हलितव्य हलित्वा हलितुम्

हल्ल् *1√hall* (to thrive) हल्लति हल्लिष्यति अहल्लत् हल्लतु हल्लेत् *हल्लित हल्लितव्य हल्लित्वा हल्लितुम्

हस् *1√has* (to laugh) हसति हसिष्यति अहसत् हसतु हसेत् हस्यते *हसित हसितव्य हसित्वा हसितुम्

हा *3√hā* (to go) जिहीते हास्यति अजिहीत् जिहीताम् जिहीत हीयते *हान हानीय हातव्य हात्वा विहाय हातुम् हानि

हाक् *3√hāk* (to give up, resign) जहाति हास्यति अजहात जहातु जह्यात् *हीन हीनवान् हानीय हेत विहाय हातुम् हीन

हि *5√hi* (to impel) हिनोति हेष्यति अहिनोत् हिनोतु हिनुयात् *हित हयनीय हेतव्य हेय हित्वा हेतुम् हय हेतु संहिता

हिंस् *7√hiṁs* (to be violent) हिनस्ति हिंसिष्यति अहिनत् हिनस्तु हिंस्यात् *हिंसित हिंसत् हिंसनीय हिंसित्वा हिंसितुम्

हिंस् *10√hiṁs* (to be violent) हिंसयति-ते हिंसयिष्यति अहिंसयत्-त हिंसयतु-ताम् हिंसयेत्-त *हिंसित हिंसयितुम् हिंसा

हिक्क् *1√hikk* (to garble) हिक्कति-ते हिक्किष्यति अहिक्कत् क्कितु हिक्केत् *हिक्कित हिक्कित्वा हिक्कितुम् हिक्का

हिक्क् *10√hikk* (to garble) हिक्कयति-ते हिक्कयिष्यति-ते अहिक्कयत्-त हिक्कयतु-ताम् हिक्कयेत्-त *हिक्कित

हिड् *1√hiḍ* (to be hostile) हेडते हेडिष्यते अहेडत हेडताम् हेडेत *हेडित हेडितव्य हेडित्वा हेडितुम्

हिण्ड् *1√hiṇḍ* (to wander) हिण्डते हिण्डिष्यते अहिण्डत हिण्डताम् हिण्डेत *हिण्ण हिण्डनीय हिण्डितव्य हिण्डित्वा

हिन्व् *1√hil* (to place) हिन्वति हिन्विष्यति अहिन्वत् हिन्वतु हिन्वेत् *हिन्वित हिन्वनीय हिन्वित्वा हिन्वितुम्

हिल् *6√hil* (to play) हिलति हेलिष्यति अहिलत् हिलतु हिलेत् *हिलित हिलितव्य हिलित्वा हिलितुम्

हिल्लोल् *10√hilllol* (to swing) हिल्लोलयति हिल्लोलयिष्यति अहिल्लोलयत्-त हिल्लोलयतु-ताम् हिल्लोलयेत्-त

हु *3√hu* (to offer oblation, perform yajña) जुहोति होष्यति अजहोत् जुहोतु जुहुयात् हूयते *हूत जुह्वत् होष्यत् हवनीय हव्य होतव्य हुत्वा होतुम् आहुत्य होतुम् हूयमान हविस् हविष्य होतॄ होतृ होत्र अग्निहोत्र होम हवन

हुड् *1√huḍ* (to go) होडते होडिष्यते अहोडत होडताम् होडेत *हुडित हुडितव्य हुडित्वा हुडितुम्

हुड् *6√huḍ* (to pile up) हुडति हुडिष्यति अहुडत् हुडतु हुडेत् *हुडित हुडनीय हुडितव्य हुडित्वा हुडितुम्

हुण्ड् *1√huṇḍ* (to collect, gather; to select, choose) हुण्डते हुण्डिष्यते अहुण्डत हुण्डताम् हुण्डेत *हुण्ण हुण्डनीय

हुल् *1√hul* (to hide) होलति होलिष्यति अहोलत् होलतु होलेत *हुलित हुलितव्य हुलित्वा हुलितुम्

हूड् *1√hūḍ* (to go) हूडते हूडिष्यते अहूडत हूडताम् हूडेत *हूडित हूडितव्य हूडित्वा हूडितुम्

हूर्च्छ् *1√hurććh* (to twist) हूर्च्छति हूर्च्छिष्यति अहूर्च्छत् हूर्च्छतु हूर्च्छेत् *हूर्च्छित हूर्च्छनीय हूर्च्छित्वा हूर्च्छितुम्

हृ *1√hṛ* (to take, carry away) हरति-ते हरिष्यति अहरत् हरतु हरेत् *हृत हरणीय हर्तव्य हार्य हृत्वा हर्तुम् प्रहार व्याहर

हृ *3√hṛ* (to force, molest, rape) जिहर्ति हरिष्यति जिहर्तु जिहृयात् *हृत

हृणी *11√hṛṇī* (to shy) हृणयति हृणयिष्यति अहृणयत् हृणयतु हृणयेत् *हृणित हृणितव्य हृणित्वा हृणितुम्

हृष् *1√hṛṣ* (to be joyful) हर्षति हर्षिष्यति अहर्षत् हृर्षतु हर्षेत् *हृष्ट हर्षणीय हृष्ट्वा-हर्षित्वा हृष्टुम् हर्ष सहर्ष

हृष् *4√hṛṣ* (to be joyful) हृष्यति हर्षिष्यति अहृष्यत् हृष्यतु हृष्येत् हृष्यते *हृष्ट हर्षणीय हृष्टव्य हृष्ट्वा हृष्टुम्

हेठ् *1√heṭh* (to sabotage, be cruel) हेठते हेठिष्यते अहेठत हेठताम् हेठेत *हेठित हेठनीय हेठितव्य हेठित्वा हेठितुम्

हेड् *1√heḍ* (to neglect) हेडति-हेडते हेडिष्यते अहेडत हेडताम् हेडेत *हेडित हेडनीय हेडितव्य हेडित्वा हेडितुम्

हेल् *1√hel* (to disregard) हेलते हेलिष्यति अहेलत् हेलतु हेलत् *हेलित हेलितव्य हेलित्वा हेलितुम्

हेष् *1√heṣ* (to neigh) हेषते हेषिष्यते अहेषित हेषताम् हेषेत *हेष्ट-हेषित हेषा

होड् *1√hoḍ* (to disregard) होडति-ते होडिष्यते अहोडत होडताम् होडेत *होडित होडनीय होडितव्य होडित्वा होडितुम्
ह्नु *2√hnu* (to deprive, hide) ह्नुते ह्नोष्यते अह्नुत ह्नुताम् ह्नुवीत *ह्नुत अपह्नुति निह्नव
ह्मल् *1√hmal* (to shake) ह्मलति ह्मलिष्यति अह्मलत् ह्मलतु ह्मलेत् *ह्मलित ह्मलितव्य ह्मलित्वा ह्मलितुम्
ह्रग् *1√hrag* (to conceal) ह्रगति ह्रगिष्यति अह्रगत् ह्रगतु ह्रगेत् *ह्रगित ह्रगितव्य ह्रगित्वा ह्रगितुम्
ह्रप् *10√hrap* (to speak) ह्रपयति-ते ह्रपयिष्यति-ते अह्रपयत्-त ह्रपयतु-ताम् ह्रपयेत्-त *ह्रपित
ह्रस् *1√hras* (to diminish) ह्रसति ह्रसिष्यति अह्रसत् ह्रसतु ह्रसेत् *ह्रसित-ह्रस्त ह्रसितव्य ह्रसित्वा ह्रसितुम्
ह्राद् *1√hrād* (be glad, cheerful) ह्रादते ह्रादिष्यते अह्रादत् ह्रादताम् ह्रादेत *ह्रादित ह्रादनीय ह्रादित्वा ह्रादितुम् ह्रादमान
ह्रिणी *11√hriṇī* (to blush) ह्रिणीयते ह्रिणीयिष्यते अह्रिणीयत ह्रिणीताम् ह्रिणीयेत *ह्रिणीत ह्रिणीतव्य ह्रिणीत्वा ह्रिणीतुम्
ह्री *3√hrī* (to blush) जिह्रेति ह्रेष्यति अजिह्रेत् जिह्रेतु जिह्रीयात् *ह्रीण-ह्रीत ह्रयणीय ह्रेतव्य ह्रेय ह्रित्वा ह्रेतुम् ह्रयण ह्री ह्रेतृ
ह्रीच्छ् *1√hrīććh* (to be ashamed of, be modest, be blushed) ह्रीच्छति ह्रीच्छिष्यति अह्रीच्छत् ह्रीच्छतु ह्रीच्छेत्
हुड् *1√hruḍ* (to contract) ह्रोडते ह्रोडिष्यते अह्रोडत् ह्रोडतु ह्रोडेत् *ह्रोडित ह्रोडितव्य ह्रोडित्वा ह्रोडितुम्
हूड् *1√hrūḍ* (to contract) ह्रूडति ह्रूडिष्यति अह्रूडत् ह्रूडतु ह्रूडेत् *ह्रूडित ह्रूडितव्य ह्रूडित्वा ह्रूडितुम्
ह्रेप् *1√hrep* (to go) ह्रेपते ह्रेपिष्यते अह्रेपत ह्रेपताम् ह्रेपेत *ह्रेपित ह्रेपितव्य ह्रेपित्वा ह्रेपितुम्
ह्रेष् *1√hreṣ* (to neigh) ह्रेषते ह्रेषिष्यते अह्रेषत ह्रेषताम् ह्रेषेत *ह्रेषित ह्रेषा
ह्रौड् *1√hrauḍ* (to go) ह्रौडते ह्रोडिष्यते अह्रोडित ह्रोडताम् ह्रोडेत *ह्रौडित ह्रौडितव्य ह्रौडित्वा ह्रौडितुम्
ह्लग् *10√hlag* (to hide) ह्लगयति ह्लगयिष्यति अह्लगयत् ह्लगयतु ह्लगयेत *ह्लगित ह्लगितव्य ह्लगित्वा ह्लगितुम्
ह्लप् *10√hlap* (to speak) ह्लपयति-ते ह्लपयिष्यति-ते अह्लपयत्-त ह्लपयतु-ताम् ह्लपयेत्-त *ह्लपित
ह्लस् *1√hlas* (to sound) ह्लसति ह्लसिष्यति अह्लसत् ह्लसतु ह्लसेत् ह्लसित *ह्लस्त
ह्लाद् *1√hlād* (be glad, cheerful) ह्लादते ह्लादिष्यते अह्लादत ह्लादताम् ह्लादेत *ह्लादित-ह्लन्न ह्लादितुम् उह्लास आह्लाद
ह्वग् *1√hvag* (to cover) ह्वगति ह्वगिष्यति अह्वगत् ह्वगतु ह्वगेत् *ह्वगित ह्वगितव्य ह्वगित्वा ह्वगितुम्
ह्वल् *1√hval* (to walk) ह्वलति ह्वलिष्यति अह्वालत् ह्वलतु ह्वलेत् *ह्वलित ह्वलितव्य ह्वलित्वा ह्वलितुम्
ह्वृ *1√hvṛ* (to be crooked) ह्वरति ह्वरिष्यति अह्वरत् ह्वरतु ह्वरेत् *ह्वरित ह्वरणीय ह्वरितव्य ह्वरित्वा ह्वरितुम् गह्वर
ह्वे *1√hve* (to call) आ+ह्वयति-ते ह्वास्यति-ते अह्वयत्-त ह्वयतु-ताम् ह्वयेत्-त *हुत ह्वानीय ह्वातव्य आहूय हूत्वा आहव

सत्तायां **विद्यते** ज्ञाने **वेत्ति** **विन्ते** विचारणे । **विन्दति** **विन्दते** प्राप्तौ रूपभेदो **विदेः** स्मृतः ।।
(सत्तायाम्-विद्यते, ज्ञाने-वेत्ति, विन्ते-विचारणे, विन्दति-विन्दते-प्राप्तौ (इति) रूपभेदः विदेः स्मृतः ।)

Thus, are stated different forms of the root √विद् : (विदेः)

(1) class 4 - सत्ता (to be) विद्यते (exists)
(2) class 2 - ज्ञानं (knowledge) वेत्ति (knows)
(3) class 7 - विचारणं (thinking) विन्ते (thinks)
(4) class 6 - प्राप्तिः (attainment) विन्दति-विन्दते (gets)
(5) class 10 - सचेतन् (to know) वेदयते (be aware)
स्मृतः (are known)

APPENDIX - 6

WHICH VERB TO USE?

RATNAKAR'S ENGLISH-TO-SANSKRIT CONVERTION GUIDE FOR COMMON VERBS

(a)

abandon त्यज् रह् हा उज्झ् मुच् वि-सृज् उत्-सृज्

abide स्था वस् वृत् स्था; प्रति-ईक्ष्, सह्, तिज्, पाल्

absolve मुच् वि-मुच् उद्-धृ क्षम्

abstain नि-वृत् परि-वृज् वि-वृज् परि-वृज्

abuse व्यय् भर्त्स् विनि-युज् प्र-युज् अधि-क्षिप आ-क्षिप्

accept ग्रह् वृ प्रति-ग्रह् प्रति-पद आ-दा स्वी-कृ प्रति-इष्

access अभि-गम् उप-गम् आ-गम्

accompany व्रज् अनु-इ सम्-युज् सह-चर् अनु-सृ

accomplish साध् सिध् सम्-आप् अनु-स्था सम्-पद्

accuse अधि-क्षिप् अभि-युज् अभि-शप् अप-वद्

achieve लभ् सम्-आप् प्र-आप् सम्-पद् निर्-वृत्

acknowledge ग्रह् प्रति-पद् अंगी-कृ स्वी-कृ

acquire लभ् अर्ज् अश् अव्-आप् प्रति-पद्

acquaint बुध् ज्ञा अभि-अस् अभि-ज्ञा वि-ज्ञा नि-विद्

act चेष्ट् आ-चर् वि-आव्-हृ कृ नट्

admire स्तु श्लाघ् प्र-शंस् वि-स्माय् दृश् ईक्ष्

adore आ-राध् नमस्-कृ सम्-भाव् पूज् अर्च सभाज्

adorn भूष् मण्ड् अलम्-कृ प्र-साध् सम्-कृ परिष्कृ

advance गम् व्रज् प्र-चल् प्र-स्था आनी प्रणी पुरस्कृ

advise उप-दिश् नि-विद् अनु-शास् अनु-मन् आ-लोच्

afflict क्लिश् दु व्यथ् पीड् बाध् परि-तप् आयस्

agitate क्षुभ् प्र-मथ् उद्-विज् वि-लुड् धू प्र-मन्थ् वि-ह्वल्

agree मन् सन्धा सम्-मन् सम्-विद्-कृ

allow ग्रह् अनु-ज्ञा अनु-मन् अनु-मुद् सह् अनु-दा

amuse रम् नन्द् क्रीड् वि-नुद् वि-लस् क्रीड् खेल्

be angry सम्-तप् कुप् क्रुध् रोष् आ-मृष्

announce नि-विद् आ-ख्या प्र-काश् वि-घुष् वि-ज्ञा

annoy बाध् पीड् व्यथ् क्लिश् उद्-विज् तप् अर्द् बाध्

answer प्रति-पद् प्रति-भाष् प्रति-वच् सम्-आ-धा उत्-तृ

apologize याच् प्र-अर्थ् व्यप्आ-दिश् स्वी-कृ प्रति-वद्

appear दृश् भा प्रादुर्-आविर्-भू अव-तृ प्र-काश् उत्-चर्

apply ऋ न्यस् नि-विश् नि-धा सम्-युज् न्यस् ऋ प्रार्थ

approach सम्-गम् अभि-गम् इ-या उप-स्था

arise उत्-पद् उत-इ सम्-उत्-था उद्-गम् सम्-भू उद्-भू आविर्-भू प्रादुः-भू उत्-चर् जन् उप-जन् सम्-जन्

arrange रच् घट् वि-ऊह् सम्-विध् विनि-अस् क्रम् ग्रन्थ्

arrest ग्रह् बन्ध् धृ स्तम्भ् नि-उध् आ-सिध् स्तम्भ् नि-वृ

arrive आ-गम् अभि-गम् प्र-पद् उप-स्था प्र-आप् आ-या

ask याच् अर्थ् प्रच्छ् भिक्ष् जि-ज्ञा अनु-युज्

ascertain ज्ञा विद् धृ निस्-चि वि-अव-सो स्थिरी-कृ

aspire स्पृह् आ-अभि-कांक्ष् अभि-लष् अभि-रुच् ईप्स्

assemble सम्-मिल् सम्-आ-गम् अभि-उद्-चि सम्-नि-पत् एकी-भू मिल् सम्-आ-वृ समूही-भू सम्-नि-पत्

attack आ-क्रम् अव-स्कन्द् आ-पत् प्रति-युध् आ-सद् आ-युध् अभि-द्रु उप-द्रु अभि-धाव् अभि-प्र-या

attain या लभ् गम् इ ऋ अश् प्र-आप् प्रति-पद् अधि-गम्

attend स्म्-आ-गम् उप-स्था सम्-नि-धा उप-आस् वि-लस्

attract आ-कृष् आ-वृज् वि-लुभ् प्र-लुभ् वि-मुह्

avail उप-कृ अनु-ग्रह् प्र-युज् अनु-लभ्

avenge प्रति-कृ प्रति-हिंस् दण्ड्

avert सम्-हृ प्रति-हृ अप-नुद् विमुखी-कृ अप-वृत्

await प्रति-ईक्ष् उप-ईक्ष् उत्-दृश्

(b)

bathe सु स्ना मस्ज् अव-गाह् आ-प्लु अभिषेकम्-कृ

be अस् आस् भू वृत् विद् जन् स्था

bear धा धृ भृ वह् सह् तिज् मृष्; प्र-सु जन् फल्

be born जन् उद्-भू सम्-भू उत्-पद् प्र-सु जन्

become भू सम्-भू वृत् सम्-पद् गम् प्र-आप्

begin प्र-आ-रभ् उप-क्रम् प्र-वृत् प्र-कृ प्र-स्तु

behold निः-ईक्ष् अभि-दृश् सम्-प्रेक्ष् लोक् लक्ष्

believe वि-श्वस् प्रति-इ श्रद्धाम्-कृ मन्

bind बन्ध् ग्रन्थ् वेष्ट् सम्-यम् नि-यम् नि-यन्त्र

bite दंश् चर्व् खाद् अर्द् पीड् वञ्च् अव-क्षिप्

boast गर्व दृप् श्लाघ् वि-कत्थ् वि-क्लृप्

bother क्लिश् पीड् बाध् उद्-विज् व्यथ् उद्-विज्

bow नम् प्र-नम् अभि-वद् अभि-वन्द् क्षम् अभि-उप-इ

break भञ्ज् खण्ड् चूर्ण् मृद् भिद् स्फुट् रुज् क्षुद् दल् व्यध् छिद्र् पिष् हन् वि-दृ उत्-लङ्घ् अति-चर् वि-घट्

breathe जीव् वृत् अस् प्राण् उद्-श्वस् प्र-वा

bring ला आ-नी आ-हृ उप-आ-हृ प्र-आप् आ-गम् आ-कृष् आ-वह् उप-पद्

build प्र-क्लृप् वि-रच् सम्-आ-श्रि निर्-मा वि-धा स्थ-आप् निर्-मा नि-चि कृ

burn दह् प्लुष् ज्वल् तप् दीप् उष्

(c)

call चक्ष् ह्वे शब्द् आ-ह्वे अभि-धा ब्रू ख्या सम्-बुध्

carry नी हृ वह् भृ साध् लभ् वशी-कृ तॄ गम् साध्

cast क्षिर् मुच् सृज् पत् वि-गण् आ-कल् सम्-धा

catch धृ ग्रह् बन्ध् परा-मृश् अव-लम्ब् आ-कृष् आ-हृ प्र-लुभ् लभ् प्र-आप्

cause जन् कृ अस् भू उत्-पद् साध्

celebrate अनु-नी प्र-शंस् स्तु श्लाघ् वि-ख्या कीर्ति-कृ

challenge ह्वे धृष् स्पर्ध् अभि-युज् नि-षिध् आ-ह्वे स्वीकृ

cheat वञ्च् छल् शठ् महि प्र-तॄ सम्-धा अभि-धा

cherish धृ भज् ध्यै उप-आस् नि-विश् लल् पुष् पाल् सम्-वृध् भज् दय् लल्

choose वृ ग्रह् रुच् इष् नि-युज् नि-रूप् अभि-लष् प्र-वृ

churn मथ् मन्थ् खज् सम्-आ-लुड्

circle परि-क्रम् परि-भ्रम् परदक्षिणी-कृ परि-वेष्ट् परि-वृ

claim याच् ब्रू वच् प्र-अर्थ अधि-कृ अभि-मन् प्रति-पद्

close अपि-धा पि-धा नि-मिल आ-मिल् निर्-वृत् सम्-आप् सम्-वृत् निष्-पद् वि-रम् वि-गम्

collapse अव-सद् सम-हृ क्षय-गम् लय-गम् सम्-नि-पत् सम्-कुच् सम्-हृ शृ सम्-हन् सम्-क्षिप्

collect उह् चि अव-गम् सम्-आ-धा सम्-मिल् सम्-आ-गम् सम्-ग्रह् सम्-आ-हृ सम्-भृ सम्-आ-हृ

combine मिश्र् मिल् सम्-गम् एकी-भू एकी-कृ सम्-भू सम्-युज् सम्-धा सम्-शिलष्

come आ-गम् आ-या आ-इ आ-व्रज् आ-पद् उप-स्था सम्-वृत् ए इ पै-आप्

command शास् ईश् प्र-भू नि-ग्रह् सम्-यम् नि-यम् अव्-लोक् नि-युज् अधि-स्था आ-ज्ञा आ-दिश् निर्-दिश्

commence आ-रभ् प्र-आ-रभ् उप-क्रम् अनु-स्था प्र-स्तु प्र-वृत् प्र-कृ

commend शंस् श्लाघ् स्तु प्र-शंस् सम्-ऋ

communicate कथ् वद् वच् ब्रू दा प्रति-पद् आ-चक्ष् वि-वृ आ-ख्या नि-विद् सम्-युज् सम्-चर् वि-अव-हृ प्र-काश् सम-वद्

complete साध् पूर् सम्-पद् अव-सो सम्-आप् सम्-पॄ

compose रच् ग्रन्थ घट् क्लृप् निर्-मा नि-बन्ध् सम्-ग्रन्थ् वि-नि-अस् सम्-धा वि-रच् वि-न्यस् क्लृप्

conceal गुह् गुप् अन्तर्-इ अन्तर्-धा पि-धा सम्-वृ अप-ह्नु छद् आ-च्छद् स्थग् गोपनं-कृ रहस्
conclude साध् ऊह् तर्क् निर-नी निस्-चि अव-धृ अव-सो निष्-पद् उप-शम् निस्-पत् सम्-पद् सम्-आप् निर्-वृ
congratulate अभि-नन्द् आ-मन्त्र् मङ्गलम्-वद्
consent मन् ग्रह् अनु-ज्ञा अनु-मन् सम्-मन् अनु-ज्ञा
consider वि-चर् वि-मृश् वि-चिन्त् सम्-इक्ष् अव-धृ
console सान्त्व् आ-श्वस् अभि-उप-पद्
constrict सम्-कुञ्च् आ-कुञ्च् सम्-हृ सम्-वृ सम्-नि-कृष्
construct रच् घट् कृ प्र-क्लृप् वि-धा निर्-मा जन् नि-चि
consult चिन्त् वि-चर् सम्-वद् सम्-मन्त्र् वि-मृश सम्-भाष्
contradict वि-रुध् नि-षिध् वि-षिध् प्रति-कूल् वि-वद्
control यम् दम् शास् वश् ईश् अधि-कृ नि-यन्त्र् नि-यम् नि-ग्रह् वि-नि-ग्रह् नि-रुध् सम्-यम्
cook पच् श्रा सिध् कृ सम्-धा सिद्धी-कृ
count गण् स्म्-कल् सम्-गण् अङ्क् मन्
cover छद् सतृ सतृ आ-वेष्ट् आ-छद् पि-धा नि-गुह्
criticise निन्द् अप-कृ अव-क्षिप् अप-वद् वि-तण्ड्
cross तृ लङ्घ् अति-इ अति-क्रम् आ-क्रम् तृ पारम्-गम्
crush चूर्ण मन्थ् क्षुद् सम्-पीड् वि-ध्वंस् वि-नश् उत-छिद् सम्-मृद् पिष् पृष् चूर्ण् पुथ् दम्
cry रुद् शुच् परि-देव् वि-लप् क्रन्द् रुद् मुच् रु नद् रस्
cultivate कृष् सम्-वृध् उप-चि अनु-शील् सेव् भज् वृध्
cut कृत् लू छिद् दो दा छो भिद् खन् तक्ष् खण्ड् खुर् व्रश्च्

(d)

debate वि-वद् वि-चर् सम्-भाष् वि-तर्क् प्र-लप् वि-तण्ड्
decide निस्-चि वि-निस्-चि निर्-नी वि-अव-सो
decorate भूष् मण्ड् प्र-साध् परि-कृ अलम्-कृ परिष्-कृ
defeat परा-भू परा-जि वि-जि अभि-भू वशी-कृ मृश्
defend रक्ष् पा पाल् त्रै गुप् अव् अभि-सम्-रक्ष् नि-वृ
deliver सू प्र-सू मुच् मोक्ष् नि-स्तृ नि-क्षिप् न्यस् प्र-दा
depart नि-वृत् वि-रह् प्र-स्था अप-गम् चल् प्रे त्यज्
depend वश् अव-लम्ब् आ-श्रि सम्-श्रि लस्
deposit न्यस् ऋ आ-धा नि-धा स्था पण् आधी-कृ
descend अव-तृ अव-रुह् अव-पत्
describe कृत् कथ् वच् ख्या वर्ण् लिख् निर्-दिश् नि-रूप् वि-वृ कृत् निर्-वच् वि-ब्रू
deserve उप-पद् प्र-भू अर्ह्
desire इष् कम् वाञ्छ् स्पृह् ईह् याच् आ-काङ्क्ष् अभि-अर्थ् अभि-लष् लुभ् अभि-रुच् आप् गृध् वश् अर्थ्
despise तिरस्-कृ अभि-भू परि-भू अव-ज्ञा अव-मन् गर्ह् निन्द् गुप् उप-ईक्ष् अव-ध्यै बाध् कदर्थी-कृ तुच्छी-कृ
destroy नश् ध्वंस् क्षि क्षै हन् वि-नश् वि-ध्वंस् निर्-दल् नि-सूद् प्र-वि-ली सम्-हृ उत्-छिद् लुप् मृ सूद् शद् क्षण्
die मृ गम् हा या ग्लै त्यज् क्षि वि-पत् उप-रम् अव-सद्
discover आविष्-कृ नि-दृश् वि-वृ प्र-काश् ज्ञा लभ् आप्
discuss वि-चर् आ-लोच् आ-लप् सम्-लप् वि-तर्क वि-मृश् नि-रूप् सम्-ईक्ष् अनु-सम्-धा वि-चर् वि-भू मथ्
disobey भञ्ज् लङ्घ् उत्-लङ्घ् अति-क्रम् अति-चर् अव-ज्ञा वि-रुध्
disrespect अव-मन् उप-ईक्ष् अव-ज्ञा परि-भू तिरस्-कृ
distort वि-कृ वि-रूप् व्यङ्गी-कृ आ-कुञ्च्
divide भिद् दल् वि-युज् वि-श्लिष् वि-च्छिद् वि-भज् पृथक्-कृ स्फुट् वि-दल् द्विधा-भू
do कृ साध् अनु-स्था आ-चर प्रति-पद् नि-धा वि-धा चेष्ट् घट् वृत् उत्-पद् सेव्
drink पा शुष् सेव्
drive चर् चल् गम् वह् नुद् प्रेर् कृष् नी प्र-चुद्
drop स्रु पत् स्यन्द् च्यु मुच् त्यज् अपास् नि-वृत्
dry शुष् नि-रस् शुष्की-कृ

(e)

eat अद् भक्ष् भुज् घस् जक्ष् प्सा गृ ग्रस् खाद् अश् चर्व
employ सेव् अधि-कृ नि-युज् प्र-युज् वि-धा धृ व्या-पृ
encourage प्रेर् उद्-तिज् प्र-उत्-सह प्र-वृत् आ-श्वस्
engage उप-रम् व्या-पृ प्र-युज् प्र-वृत् आ-स्था सेव्
enjoy नन्द् रम् सेव् भुज् अश् आ-स्वाद् अनु-भू
enter इ विश् गाह् आ-गम् नि-धा अभि-या गाह्
entertain रम् नन्द् क्रीड् अर्च् पूज् धृ ग्रह् वि-नुद् वि-लस् सत्-कृ सम्-भू सेव् तृष्
escape मुच् मोक्ष् लङ्घ् गम् त्यज् परि-हृ वि-मुच्
establish स्था स्तम्भ् स्म्-स्तम्भ् प्रति-पद् सम-स्था प्रति-स्था अधि-स्था स्थिरी-कृ रुह्
evacuate रिच् वि-सृज् वि-हा परि-त्यज् शून्यी-कृ
evolve उत-भिद् वि-स्तृ वि-वृ प्र-सृ
examine परि-ईक्ष् सम्-ईक्ष् सम-दृश् अव-ईक्ष् नि-रूप् अनु-सम्-धा वि-मृश वि-चर्
exhibit प्र-काश् प्र-दृश् अव्-इष्-कृ प्रकटी-कृ
exist अस् भू विद् वृत् जन् स्था उत्-पद् जीव् प्राण् आस्
experience अनु-भू भुज् अश् प्र-आप् दृश् ईक्ष्
explain वर्ण् कथ् प्र-वद् वि-वृ वि-आ-ख्या वि-आ-चक्ष् नि-रूप् प्र-काश् स्पष्टि-कृ

(f)

face अभि-इ अभि-वृत् सम्मुखी-भू
fade म्लै ग्लै नश् ध्वंस् जृ क्षि वि-लुप् वि-शृ
fail परा-जि अन्-उत्-तृ हा त्यज्
fall स्रंस् च्यु पत् गल् भ्रंश् ह्रस् प्र-ली नि-पत् अव-तृ आ-क्रम्
falter स्खल् कम्प् वेप् प्र-माद्
fear भी शङ्क् तर्क् त्रस् उद्-विज् व्यथ् त्रस्
feed अद् अश् भुज् पुष् पा पाल् भृ सम्-तृप् सम्-वृध्
fight युध् वि-ग्रह् वि-वद् वि-प्र-वद्
flow गल् क्षर् सृ री द्रु स्नु गम् चल् स्रंस् वह् प्र-वह् अनु-सृ प्र-सृ
fly डी त्यज् वृज् मुच् वि-सृज् वि-सृप् परि-हृ प्र-द्रु उत्-पत् उत्-गम्
follow अनु-इ अनु-गम् अनु-चर् अनु-वृत् अनु-कृ

(g)

gain लभ् आप् ग्रह् उप-अर्ज् आ-सद् अश् विद् इ
gather सम्-चि सम्-आ-दा सम्-आ-हृ भृ वृ लू ऊह् पूय् सम्-गम् मिल्
get लभ् आप् ग्रह् धृ भू धा जन्विद् प्र-आप् अर्ज् आ-सद् उप-इ अभि-उप-इ उत्-पद् प्र-सू आ-सद्
give दा ऋ दद् जन् भू त्यज् दिश् नि-क्षिप् उत-सृज् वि-सृज् नि-वृत्
go इ ऋच्छ् गम् इ या व्रज् पद् सृ चल् चर् क्रम् स्यन्द् वह् सु अंह्
govern शास् पाल् ईश् गुप् तन्त्र् यम् दम् अनु-इ वि-धा नि-यन्त्र् सम्-हृ नि-यम् नि-ग्रह् सम्-यम् नि-यम्
grieve शुच् दु पीड् बाध् क्लिश् व्यथ् तप् खिद् उद्-विज्
grow स्फुद् फुल्ल् रुह् ऋध् वृध् स्फाय् प्यै एध् पुष् भू सम्-जन् वि-कस्

(h)

harm हिंस क्लिश् दु अर्द् पीड् बाध् द्रुह् क्षण् अप-कृ वि-कृ प्र-कृ उप-द्रु
have अस् भू वृत् विद् धा ग्रह् लभ् आप् धृ भुज् शील्
hear श्रु, आ-कर्ण्, सम-आ-कर्ण्
hide गुप् गुह् स्थग् लुप् नि-ली अप-वृ
hinder रुध् स्तम्भ् बाध् प्रति-बन्ध् नि-वृ वि-हन्
hold धृ धा भृ पा पाल् सेव् समृ-पद् आ-दा अव-लम्ब् रक्ष् शील् आप् नि-रुध् बन्ध्
hurt तुद् दु दूय् क्षि हिंस् अर्द् पीड् क्षण् अप-कृ रिष् द्रुह्

(i)

ignore अ-बुध् न-ज्ञा न-स्वी-कृ

imagine मन् चिन्त् बुध् तर्क् ध्यै क्लृप् अव-इ अव-गम् भू सम्-भू उत-प्रेक्ष् उप-लभ् अव-गम् उप-लभ्

imply सूच् वच् ध्वन् बुध् अभि-धा उप-लक्ष् प्रति-इ

improve सम्-कृ उत्-कृष् उप-चि अभि-वृध् सम्-वृध् वि-वृध् सम्-आ-धा बृंह् प्र-युज्

include सम्-आ-विष् परि-सम्-आप् परि-गृह् अन्तर्-भू अन्तर्-गम् अन्तर्-गम् अन्तर्-गण् अन्तर्-वृत्

increase वृध् ऋध् बृंह् स्फाय् गम् एध् आ या इ प्यै वि-स्तृ उप-चि प्र-सृ

inform ज्ञा विद् कथ् बुध् श्रु अव-गम् सम्-दिश् आ-ख्या वि-ज्ञा नि-विद् आ-ह्वे

injure हन् हिंस् दु पीड् अर्द् क्षण् क्षि व्यध् व्यथ् द्रुह् अप-राध् अप-कृ सम्-बाध्

inquire प्रच्छ् ज्ञा बुध् गवेष् चर्च् नि-रूप् वि-मृश् वि-चर् परि-ईक्ष् अव-ईक्ष् अनु-इष्

inspire चुद् प्रेर् श्वस् जन् प्र-वृत् उत्-पद् उद्-तिज् प्र-उत्-सह् नि-धा उप-नि-धा नि-विश्

instruct शास् शिक्ष् बुध् ज्ञा सूच् पठ् आ-ज्ञा अधि-आप् नि-विद् उप-दिश् अनु-शास्

insult भर्त्स् कुत्स् अव-ज्ञा अव्-क्षप् परि-भू अव-मन्

interrupt भिद् भञ्ज् प्रति-बध् वि-हन् वि-छिद् आ-क्षिप्

invade आ-क्रम् आस्कन्द् आ-सद् उप-द्रु अभि-सृ

invent रच् घट् क्लप् चिन्त् वि-धा सृज् निर्-मा

investigate चर्च् मृग् अव-ईक्ष् सम्-ईक्ष् परि-ईक्ष् अनु-युज् अनु-सम्-धा वि-चर् वि-मृश् निर्-नी निस्-चि निर्-धृ आ-लोच्

invite आ-मन्त्र् नि-मन्त्र् आ-ह्वे प्र-लुभ् केत् आ-कृ प्र-लुभ्

irritate कुप् क्रुध् सम्-तप् दह् रुष् उद्-तिज्

(j)

join मिल युज् मिल् सम्-गम् सम्-धा सम्-बन्ध् सम्-मिल्

(k)

keep स्था अनु-स्था वि-धा अव-लम्ब् आ-श्रि धृ रक्ष् पाल्

kill हन् सूद् मृ तृह् शद् नि-सूद नि-शस् उत्-जस्

know ज्ञा बुध् विद् ग्रह् अभि-ज्ञा वि-ज्ञा अनु-भू अव-इ अव-गम् मन् उप-लभ् ग्रह् भज्

(l)

lament शुच् रुद् कुश् क्रन्द् वि-सद् परि-दिव् अनु-शुच् परि-देव् वि-लप्

laugh हस् स्मि अव-मन् प्र-हस्

learn शिक्ष् पठ् लभ् बुध् विद् ज्ञा अधि-गम् अभि-अस् अधि-इ

leave मुञ्च् मोक्ष् त्यज् रह् उञ्झ् वर्ज् हा न्यस् अप-क्रम् निस्-क्रम् निर्-गम् अप-सृ

lessen अप-चि ण्यूनी-भू अल्पी-भू ह्रस् क्षि

liberate मुञ्च् मोक्ष् वि-मुच् वि-सृज् निस्-तृ उद्-धृ

lie शी मृश् अधि-शी नि-पत् नि-ली

lift उत्-धृ उत्-क्षिप् उत्-स्था उत्-श्रि उत्-तुल्

like रुच् इष् कम् वाञ्छ् अभि-लष् अनु-मन् अनु-मुद् तुष्

live वस् श्वस् विद् वृत् जीव् निर्-वह् नि-वस् अधि-स्था

love स्निह् रञ्ज् उच् नन्द् मुद् तुष् कम् अनु-रञ्ज्

(m)

make कृ घट् सृज् क्लृप् जन् सम्-पद् उत्-पद् आ-चर् अनु-स्था वि-धा रच् निर्-मा साध् कल्

manifest स्पश् दृश् स्फुद् भू काश् सृज् चर् गम्-चर् प्र-काश् आविर्-भू प्रादुर्-भू अभि-विज् परि-स्फुट् प्र-कट्

march चल् व्रज् प्र-चल् वि-प्र-चल् सम्-चल प्र-गम् प्र-स्था अभि-या प्रति-व्रज्

marry वृ वॄ लभ् वि-वह् परि-नी उप-यम् परि-ग्रह् प्रति-ग्रह् सम्-बन्ध् सम्-युज्

measure मा तुल् ज्ञा गण् परि-क्लप् परि-ईक्ष् मापनम्-कृ

meet मिल् सम्-मिल् उप-आ-गम् सम्-गम् आ-सद् या

mimic अनु-कृ, अनु-वद्

molest बल् प्र-कृ बाध् उध् तप् पीड् क्लिश् अर्द व्यथ्

mourn रुद् आ-क्रश् वि-लप् आ-क्रन्द् अनु-शुच् परि-देव् परि-दिव्

move चल् चर् सृप् गम् या इ भ्रम् सम्-चर् परि-वृत् प्र-स्था सृ प्रेर् चुद् नुद् प्र-युज् उत-सह् चेष्ट् प्र-उव्

(n)

name नाम-कृ अभि-धा आ-ख्या कृत् प्र-चक्ष् सम्-बुध्

neglect उप-ईक्ष् वि-स्मृ प्र-मद् न-अव-धा उप-ईक्ष् वि-अति-क्रम् अव-ज्ञा अव-मन् त्यज् लङ्घ् वि-स्मृ

nourish पुष् सम्-वृध् परि-पा पाल् तृष् बृंह् जीव्

(o)

obey अनु-मन् अनु-रुध् उप-सेव् उप-चर् उप-आस् पाल्

oblige उप-कृ अनु-ग्रह्

observe ईक्ष् दृश् लक्ष् लोक् वि-ज्ञा

occupy स्था अधि-वस् आ-श्रि अधि-स्था आ-विश् आ-क्रम् वि-आ-पृ

open जृम्भ् वि-तन् वि-स्तृ उद्-घट् अप्-आ-वृत् वि-वृत् प्र-बुध् उत्-मिल् प्र-काश्

order अनु-धा वि-न्यस् आ-दिश् क्लप् चुद् प्रेर् शास्

(p, q)

pass अति-क्रम् सम्-तृ अति-तृ अति-गम् वृत् वह्

perish नश् ली क्षि ध्वंस् भ्रंस् मृ प्र-वि-ली उप-गम् पत्

play क्रीड् दिव् रम् खेल् ग्लह् नद् वि-लस् वि-हृ लल्

be pleaseed तुष् हृष् रम् मुद् नन्द् ह्लाद् रञ्ज् अनु-रञ्ज् आ-ह्लाद् प्र-सद् प्र-मुद् सुख् प्री तृप् वि-नुद् रुच्

pour सिच् पत् प्र-स्रु निर्-मुच् उत्-सृज् उत्-क्षिप्

practice कृ सेव् अनु-स्था प्र-युज् आ-चर् अभि-अस्

preside अधि-स्था अधि-आस् अधि-ईश् अव-ईक्ष् प्र-भू अधि-कृ

presume तर्क् धृष् दृप् अनु-मा सम्-भू प्र-गल्भ्

produce कृ सृज् जन् साध् वि-रच् प्र-सृ उत्-पद् निर्-मा सम्-भू आ-नी प्र-सु क्लप् वि-धा प्र-दा

protect पा त्रै रक्ष् गुप् सम्-वृध् अव-ईक्ष् आ-धृ

put स्था दा कृ ऋ न्यस् त्यज् पद् अनु-स्था वि-धा अव-लम्ब् आ-श्रि

quit त्यज् हा अपास् वि-सृज् निर्-गम् नि-वृत् वि-मुच्

(r)

raise भृ पाल् उत्-स्था उत्-तुल् उत्-धृ उत्-क्षिप् उत-यम्

receive आप् ग्रह् लभ् प्र-आप् आ-दा अंगी-कृ प्रति-इष्

recognize विद् प्रति-सम्-विद् प्रति-अभि-ज्ञा अनु-स्मृ चि

refuse अप-ज्ञा तिरस्-कृ अप-वद् नि-षिध् न-स्वी-कृ

remedy प्रति-कृ सम्-आ-धा शम् कित् उपचारम्-कृ

remove विर्-अस् निर्-आ-कृ अप-क्रम् अप-नी वि-अप-नी

renounce त्यज् हा अपास् उत्-सृज् सम्-न्यस् वि-रह्

reply प्रति-वद् उत्-तृ समा-धा प्रति-वच् ब्रू पुनर्-भाष्

request याच् अर्थ् प्र-अर्थ अभि-अर्थ वि-ज्ञा नि-विद् अप-ईक्ष् अभि-लष् वृ काङ्क्ष्

resist रुध् वि-रुध् नि-वार् प्रति-कृ नि-ग्रह् प्रति-बन्ध्

respect अर्च् पूज् सेव् भज् अव-ईक्ष् अप-ईक्ष् सम्-मन् नमस-कृ आ-दृ सेव् भज् अर्ह् अर्च्

rest आ-रम् वि-श्रम् शी सम्-विश् आ-धा निद्राम्-कृ

retire त्यज् सम्-न्यस् वि-रम् नि-वृत् अप-क्रम् अप-गम् परा-वृत्

return प्रति-आ-गम् आ-वृत् परि-वृत् नि-वृत् प्रति-या पुनर्-इ पुनर्-आ-व्रज् पुनर्-आ-गम्; प्रति-दा प्रति-पद्

ride गम् चल् या वह् सम्-चर् आ-क्रम् आ-रुह्

roam अद् भ्रम् परि-भ्रम् सम्-चर् वि-चर् गाह् भ्रमणम्-कृ

run धाव् द्रु स्यन्द् वह् गम् प्र-चल् रंह् चर् सु स्पन्द् गल्

(s)

sadden सद् म्लान् शुच् विज् खिद् तप् व्यथ् क्लिश् दु

say कथ् विद् गद् वद् भण् भाष् ब्रू वच् मन्त्र् उद्-चर् आ-

लप् अभि-धा प्र-कृ उदा-हृ ईर् जल्प् आह् आ-ख्या
scare उत्-आ-कृ भी त्रस् उत्-विज्‌वि-द्रु
scoff उप-हस् अव-हस् अव-ज्ञा तिरस्-कृ धिक्-कृ अव-मन् आ-क्षिप् अव-हेल् गर्ह् भर्त्स् निन्द् परि-भू तुच्छी-कृ
scold भर्त्स् निन्द् गर्ह् परि-भाष् निर्-भर्त्स् आ-क्रुश् आ-क्षिप् अधि-क्षिप् गुप् क्षिप् तिरस्-कृ परि-भाष्
see दृश् ईश् लक्ष् लोक् ज्ञा बुध् अव-इ; अव-गम् अव-ई
serve भज् सेव् ऊप-आस् उप-कृ उप-चर् प्र-पद् परि-चर्
shine दीप् भा भास् ज्वल् चकास् प्र-भा वि-द्युत्
shorten सम्-क्षिप् ह्रस् अल्पी-भू न्यूनी-कृ सम्-कुच्
sit आस् नि-सद् नि-धा अधि-आस् उप-विश्
sleep स्वप् नि-द्रा शी नि-मील्
smell घ्रा गन्ध् अनु-भू
speak अह ब्रू वद् कथ् विद् गद् भण् भाष् वच् मन्त्र् उद्-चर् आ-लप् अभि-धा निर्-दिश्
spread तन् वृध् स्तृ स्तॄ वि-आप् वि-सृ सम्-चर् आ-यम् आ-चि
stand स्था स्तम्भ् उद्-स्था वृत् आ-स्था
stay वस् विद् वृत् स्था अधि-स्था वि-रम् अधि-वस् उप-वस् नि-वस् प्र-वस् अव-स्था वि-लम्ब् स्तम्भ् सम्-धृ
steal स्तेन् चुर् मुष् अप-हृ
stop वि-रम् उप-आ-रम् नि-वृत् सम्-हृ अव-ख्या स्तम्भ्
strike हन् तुद् तड् पीड् अर्द् आ-स्फल् प्र-हृ
study पठ् शिक्ष् ध्यै चिन्त् क्लृप् अभि-अस् अधि-इ अधि-गम् आ-वृत् नि-विश् उप-सेव्
suit अर्ह् उप-पद् युज्
suppress नि-रुध् नि-यम् नि-यन्त्र् नि-वृत् सम्-यम् अव-रोध् नि-रोध् उप-गुह् धृ जि दम्
swim तृ उत्-तृ सम्-तृरुध्
t)
take ग्रह् धृ हृ नी वह् अव-लम्ब् आ-दा स्वी-कृ अंगी-कृ
tell कथ् ब्रू वद् विद् गद् भण् भाष् वच् मन्त्र् आ-चक्ष् नि-विद् आ-ख्या उद्-चर् अभि-धा निर्-दिश्
test, try परि-ईक्ष् ज्ञा अनु-भू परिक्षां-कृ यत् चेष्ट् उद्-यम्
think चिन्त् विद् ध्यै तर्क् मन् गण् स्मृ अप-ईक्ष् वि-मृश् वि-चर् सम्-ज्ञा
throw क्षिप्, उत्-धिप् अस् मुच् त्यज् पत् सृज् प्रेष् च्यु
touch स्पृश् आ-लभ् लग्
trade पण् कृ क्री वि-क्री वाणिज्यम्-कृ क्रयविक्रयम्-कृ
trust प्रति-इ नि-धा वि-श्वस् वि-श्वस् प्रति-इ
(u)
understand ज्ञा बुध् ग्रह अव-गम् अधि-गम् उप-लभ्
unite युज् सम्-गम् सम-युज् सम-घट् सम्-धा
(v)
vanish वि-नश् प्र-वि-ली अप-इ अनत्-धा तिरो-भू
vow प्रति-ज्ञा सम्-क्लृप् आ-स्था व्रतम्-कृ संकल्पम्-कृ
(w)
wake जागृ प्र-बुध्
walk पद् चल् चर् गम् पादाभ्याम्-गम् क्रम् व्रज्
want काङ्क्ष् इष् अप-ईक्ष्
wash मार्ज् धाव् प्र-क्षल् प्र-मृज्
waste क्षि क्षै व्यय् अप-चि अव-सद्
wear परि-धा आ-वह् धृ भृ वस्
wed उद-वह् वि-वह् परि-णी पाणिग्रहणम्-कृ
win जि वि-जि प्र-आप् प्र-लुभ् आ-राध्
worship पूज् अर्च् सेव् उप-आस् उप-स्था भज् आ-राध् नमस् श्रु मह् सभाज् यज् नमस्कारम्-कृ इज्याम्-कृ
write लिख् रच् ग्रन्थ् प्र-बन्ध् नि-बन्ध् लेखनम्-कृ क्लृप्
(y)
yawn जृम्भ् हर्म्म
yell आ-क्रोश् रु नद् रस् चित्कारम्-कृ दीर्घारवम्-कृ

APPENDIX - 7

TENSES AND MOODS OF 80 COMMON VERBS

तिङन्तप्रकरणम् ।

2p√ad (√अद्) to eat

see section 24.2

1p√arć (√अर्च्) to worship

Present Tense (लट्)

अर्चामि	अर्चाव:	अर्चाम:
अर्चसि	अर्चथ:	अर्चथ
अर्चति	अर्चत:	अर्चन्ति

Past Tense (लङ्)

आर्चम्	आर्चाव	आर्चाम
आर्च:	आर्चतम्	आर्चत
आर्चत्	आर्चताम्	आर्चन्

Future Tense (लृट्)

अर्चिष्यामि	अर्चिष्याव:	अर्चिष्याम:
अर्चिष्यसि	अर्चिष्यथ:	अर्चिष्यथ
अर्चिष्यति	अर्चिष्यत:	अर्चिष्यन्ति

Imperative mood (लोट्)

अर्चानि	अर्चाव	अर्चाम
अर्च	अर्चतम्	अर्चत
अर्चतु	अर्चताम्	अर्चन्तु

Potential mood (विधिलिङ्)

अर्चेयम्	अर्चेव	अर्चेम
अर्चे:	अर्चेतम्	अर्चेत
अर्चेत्	अर्चेताम्	अर्चेयु:

2p√as (√अस्) to be

Present Tense (लट्)

अस्मि	स्व:	स्म:
असि	स्थ:	स्थ
अस्ति	स्त:	सन्ति

Past Tense (लङ्)

आसम्	आस्व	आस्म
आसी:	आस्तम्	आस्त
आसीत्	आस्ताम्	आसन्

Future Tense (लृट्)

भविष्यामि	भविष्याव:	भविष्याम:
भविष्यसि	भविष्यथ:	भविष्यथ
भविष्यति	भविष्यत:	भविष्यन्ति

Imperative mood (लोट्)

असानि	असाव	असाम
एधि	स्तम्	स्त
अस्तु	स्ताम्	सन्तु

Potential mood (विधिलिङ्)

स्याम्	स्याव	स्याम
स्या:	स्यातम्	स्यात
स्यात्	स्याताम्	स्यु:

2a√ās (√आस्) to sit

Present Tense (लट्)

आसे	आस्वहे	आस्महे
आस्से	आसाथे	आद्ध्वे
आस्ते	आसाते	आसते

Past Tense (लङ्)

आसि	आस्वहि	आस्महि
आस्था:	आसाथाम्	आद्ध्वम्
आस्त	आस्याताम्	आसत

Future Tense (लृट्)

आसिष्ये	आसिष्यावहे	आसिष्यामहे
आसिष्यसे	आसिष्येथे	आसिष्यध्वे
आसिष्यते	आसिष्येते	आसिष्यन्ते

Imperative mood (लोट्)

आसै	आसावहै	आसामहै
आस्स्व	आसाथाम्	आद्ध्वम्
आस्ताम्	आसाताम्	आसताम्

Potential mood (विधिलिङ्)

आसीय	आसीवहि	आसीमहि
आसीथा:	आसीयाथाम्	आसीध्वम्
आसीत	आसीयाताम्	आसीरन्

2p√iṇ (√इ) to go

Present Tense (लट्)

एमि	इव:	इम:
एषि	इथ:	इथ
एति	इत:	यन्ति

Past Tense (लङ्)

आयम्	ऐव	ऐम
ऐ:	ऐतम्	ऐत
ऐत्	ऐताम्	आयन्

Future Tense (लृट्)

एष्यामि	एष्याव:	एष्याम:
एष्यसि	एष्यथ:	एष्यथ
एष्यति	एष्यत:	एष्यन्ति

Imperative mood (लोट्)

अयानि	अयाव	अयाम
इहि	इतम्	इत
इतु	इताम्	यन्तु

Potential mood (विधिलिङ्)

इयाम्	इयाव	इयाम
इया:	इयातम्	इयात
इयात्	इयाताम्	इयु:

2a√iṅ (√इ) to learn

Present Tense (लट्)

अधीये	अधीवहे	अधीमहे
अधीषे	अधीयाथे	अधीध्वे
अधीते	अधीयाते	अधीयते

Past Tense (लङ्)

अध्यैयि	अध्यैवहि	अध्यैमहि
अध्यैथा:	अध्यैयाथाम्	अध्यैध्वम्
अध्यैत	अध्यैयाताम्	अध्यैयत

Future Tense (लृट्)

अध्येष्ये	अध्येष्यावहे	अध्येष्यामहे
अध्येष्यसे	अध्येष्येथे	अध्येष्यध्वे

अध्येष्यते	अध्येष्येते	अध्येष्यन्ते

Imperative mood (लोट्)

अध्ययै	अध्ययावहै	अध्ययामहै
अधीष्व	अधीयाथाम्	अधीध्वम्
अधीताम्	अधीयाताम्	अधीयताम्

Potential mood (विधिलिङ्)

अधीयीय	अधीयीवहि	अधीयीमहि
अधीयीथा:	अधीयीयाथाम्	अधीयीध्वम्
अधीयीत	अधीयीयाताम्	अधीयीरन्

6p√iṣ (√इष्) to desire

Present Tense (लट्)

इच्छामि	इच्छाव:	इच्छाम:
इच्छसि	इच्छथ:	इच्छथ
इच्छति	इच्छत:	इच्छन्ति

Past Tense (लङ्)

ऐच्छम्	ऐच्छाव	ऐच्छाम
ऐच्छ:	ऐच्छतम्	ऐच्छत
ऐच्छत्	ऐच्छताम्	ऐच्छन्

Future Tense (लृट्)

एषिष्यामि	एषिष्याव:	एषिष्याम:
एषिष्यसि	एषिष्यथ:	एषिष्यथ
एषिष्यति	एषिष्यत:	एषिष्यन्ति

Imperative mood (लोट्)

इच्छानि	इच्छाव	इच्छाम
इच्छ	इच्छतम्	इच्छत
इच्छतु	इच्छताम्	इच्छन्तु

Potential mood (विधिलिङ्)

इच्छेयम्	इच्छेव	इच्छेम
इच्छे:	इच्छेतम्	इच्छेत
इच्छेत्	इच्छेताम्	इच्छेयु:

6p√ṛććh (√ऋच्छ्) to go

Present Tense (लट्)

ऋच्छामि	ऋच्छाव:	ऋच्छाम:
ऋच्छसि	ऋच्छथ:	ऋच्छथ
ऋच्छति	ऋच्छत:	ऋच्छन्ति

Past Tense (लङ्)

आर्च्छम्	आर्च्छाव	आर्च्छाम
आर्च्छ:	आर्च्छतम्	आर्च्छत
आर्च्छत्	आर्च्छताम्	आर्च्छन्

Future Tense (लृट्)

ऋच्छिष्यामि	ऋच्छिष्याव:	ऋच्छिष्याम:
ऋच्छिष्यसि	ऋच्छिष्यथ:	ऋच्छिष्यथ
ऋच्छिष्यति	ऋच्छिष्यत:	ऋच्छिष्यन्ति

Imperative mood (लोट्)

ऋच्छानि	ऋच्छाव	ऋच्छाम
ऋच्छ	ऋच्छतम्	ऋच्छत
ऋच्छतु	ऋच्छताम्	ऋच्छन्तु

Potential mood (विधिलिङ्)

ऋच्छेयम्	ऋच्छेव	ऋच्छेम
ऋच्छे:	ऋच्छेतम्	ऋच्छेत
ऋच्छेत्	ऋच्छेताम्	ऋच्छेयु:

1p√edh (√एध्) to grow

Present Tense (लट्)

एधे	एधावहे	एधामहे

एधसे	एधेथे	एधध्वे
एधते	एधेते	एधन्ते

Past Tense (लङ्)

ऐधे	ऐधावहि	ऐधामहि
ऐधथा:	ऐधेथाम्	ऐधध्वम्
ऐधत	ऐधेताम्	ऐधन्त

Future Tense (लृट्)

एधिष्ये	एधिष्यावहे	एधिष्यामहे
एधिष्यसे	एधिष्येथे	एधिष्यध्वे
एधिष्यते	एधिष्येते	एधिष्यन्ते

Imperative mood (लोट्)

एधै	एधावहै	एधामहै
एधस्व	एधेथाम्	एधध्वम्
एधताम्	एधेताम्	एधन्ताम्

Potential mood (विधिलिङ्)

एधेय	एधेवहि	एधेमहि
एधेथा:	एधेयाथाम्	एधेध्वम्
एधेत	एधेयाताम्	एधेरन्

10p√kath (√कथ्) to tell

Present Tense (लट्)

कथयामि	कथयाव:	कथयाम:
कथयसि	कथयथ:	कथयथ
कथयति	कथयत:	कथयन्ति

Past Tense (लङ्)

अकथयम्	अकथयाव	अकथयाम
अकथय:	अकथयतम्	अकथयत
अकथयत्	अकथयताम्	अकथयन्

Future Tense (लृट्)

कथयिष्यामि	कथयिष्याव:	कथयिष्याम:
कथयिष्यसि	कथयिष्यथ:	कथयिष्यथ
कथयिष्यति	कथयिष्यत:	कथयिष्यन्ति

Imperative mood (लोट्)

कथयानि	कथयाव	कथयाम
कथय	कथयतम्	कथयत
कथयतु	कथयताम्	कथयन्तु

Potential mood (विधिलिङ्)

कथयेयम्	कथयेव	कथयेम
कथये:	कथयेतम्	कथयेत
कथयेत्	कथयेताम्	कथयेयु:

1a√kam (√कम्) to desire

Present Tense (लट्)

कामये	कामयावहे	कामयामहे
कामयसे	कामयेथे	कामयध्वे
कामयते	कामयेते	कामयन्ते

Past Tense (लङ्)

अकामये	अकामयावहि	अकामयामहि
अकामयथा:	अकामयेथाम्	अकामयध्वम्
अकामयत	अकामयेताम्	अकामयन्त

Future Tense (लृट्)

कमिष्ये	कमिष्यावहे	कमिष्यामहे
कमिष्यसे	कमिष्येथे	कमिष्यध्वे
कमिष्यते	कमिष्येते	कमिष्यन्ते

Imperative mood (लोट्)

कामयै	कामयावहै	कामयामहै

कामयस्व	कामयेथाम्	कामयध्वम्
कामयताम्	कामयेताम्	कामयन्ताम्

Potential mood (विधिलिङ्)

कामयेय	कामयेवहि	कामयेमहि
कामयेथा:	कामयेयाथाम्	कामयेध्वम्
कामयेत	कामयेयाताम्	कामयेरन्

8p√kṛ (√कृ) to do

see section 24.8

8a√kṛ (√कृ) to do

see section 24.8

8a√kray (√क्रय्) to trade

see section 24.9

1p√krīḍ (√क्रीड्) to play

Present Tense (लट्)

क्रीडामि	क्रीडाव:	क्रीडाम:
क्रीडसि	क्रीडथ:	क्रीडथ
क्रीडति	क्रीडत:	क्रीडन्ति

Past Tense (लङ्)

अक्रीडम्	अक्रीडाव	अक्रीडाम
अक्रीड:	अक्रीडतम्	अक्रीडत
अक्रीडत्	अक्रीडताम्	अक्रीडन्

Future Tense (लृट्)

क्रीडिष्यामि	क्रीडिष्याव:	क्रीडिष्याम:
क्रीडिष्यसि	क्रीडिष्यथ:	क्रीडिष्यथ
क्रीडिष्यति	क्रीडिष्यत:	क्रीडिष्यन्ति

Imperative mood (लोट्)

क्रीडानि	क्रीडाव	क्रीडाम
क्रीड	क्रीडतम्	क्रीडत
क्रीडतु	क्रीडताम्	क्रीडन्तु

Potential mood (विधिलिङ्)

क्रीडेयम्	क्रीडेव	क्रीडेम
क्रीडे:	क्रीडेतम्	क्रीडेत
क्रीडेत्	क्रीडेताम्	क्रीडेयु:

1p√kṣi (√क्षि) to perish

Present Tense (लट्)

क्षयामि	क्षयाव:	क्षयाम:
क्षयसि	क्षयथ:	क्षयथ
क्षयति	क्षयत:	क्षयन्ति

Past Tense (लङ्)

अक्षयम्	अक्षयाव	अक्षयाम
अक्षय:	अक्षयतम्	अक्षयत
अक्षयत्	अक्षयताम्	अक्षयन्

Future Tense (लृट्)

क्षेष्यामि	क्षेष्याव:	क्षेष्याम:
क्षेष्यसि	क्षेष्यथ:	क्षेष्यथ
क्षेष्यति	क्षेष्यत:	क्षेष्यन्ति

Imperative mood (लोट्)

क्षयाणि	क्षयाव	क्षयाम
क्षय	क्षयतम्	क्षयत
क्षयतु	क्षयताम्	क्षयन्तु

Potential mood (विधिलिङ्)

क्षयेयम्	क्षयेव	क्षयेम

क्षये: क्षयेतम् क्षयेत
क्षयेत् क्षयेताम् क्षयेयु:

1a√kṣubh (√क्षुभ्) to agitate

Present Tense (लट्)

क्षोभे क्षोभावहे क्षोभामहे
क्षोभसे क्षोभेथे क्षोभध्वे
क्षोभते क्षोभेते क्षोभन्ते

Past Tense (लङ्)

अक्षोभे अक्षोभावहि अक्षोभामहि
अक्षोभथा: अक्षोभेथाम् अक्षोभध्वम्
अक्षोभत अक्षोभेताम् अक्षोभन्त

Future Tense (लृट्)

क्षोभिष्ये क्षोभिष्यावहे क्षोभिष्यामहे
क्षोभिष्यसे क्षोभिष्येथे क्षोभिष्यध्वे
क्षोभिष्यते क्षोभिष्येते क्षोभिष्यन्ते

Imperative mood (लोट्)

क्षोभै क्षोभावहै क्षोभामहै
क्षोभस्व क्षोभेथाम् क्षोभध्वम्
क्षोभताम् क्षोभेताम् क्षोभन्ताम्

Potential mood (विधिलिङ्)

क्षोभेय क्षोभेवहि क्षोभेमहि
क्षोभेथा: क्षोभेयाथाम् क्षोभेध्वम्
क्षोभेत क्षोभेयाताम् क्षोभेरन्

10p√gaṇ (√गण्) to count

Present Tense (लट्)

गणयामि गणयाव: गणयाम:
गणयसि गणयथ: गणयथ
गणयति गणयत: गणयन्ति

Past Tense (लङ्)

अगणयम् अगणयाव अगणयाम
अगणय: अगणयतम् अगणयत
अगणयत् अगणयताम् अगणयन्

Future Tense (लृट्)

गणयिष्यामि गणयिष्याव: गणयिष्याम:
गणयिष्यसि गणयिष्यथ: गणयिष्यथ
गणयिष्यति गणयिष्यत: गणयिष्यन्ति

Imperative mood (लोट्)

गणयानि गणयाव गणयाम
गणय गणयतम् गणयत
गणयतु गणयताम् गणयन्तु

Potential mood (विधिलिङ्)

गणयेयम् गणयेव गणयेम
गणये: गणयेतम् गणयेत
गणयेत् गणयेताम् गणयेयु:

1p√gad (√गद्) to speak

Present Tense (लट्)

गदामि गदाव: गदाम:
गदसि गदथ: गदथ
गदति गदत: गदन्ति

Past Tense (लङ्)

अगदम् अगदाव अगदाम
अगद: अगदतम् अगदत
अगदत् अगदताम् अगदन्

Future Tense (लृट्)

गदिष्यामि	गदिष्याव:	गदिष्याम:
गदिष्यसि	गदिष्यथ:	गदिष्यथ
गदिष्यति	गदिष्यत:	गदिष्यन्ति

Imperative mood (लोट्)

गदानि	गदाव	गदाम
गद	गदतम्	गदत
गदतु	गदताम्	गदन्तु

Potential mood (विधिलिङ्)

गदेयम्	गदेव	गदेम
गदे:	गदेतम्	गदेत
गदेत्	गदेताम्	गदेयु:

1p√gam (√गम्) to go

Present Tense (लट्)

गच्छामि	गच्छाव:	गच्छाम:
गच्छसि	गच्छथ:	गच्छथ
गच्छति	गच्छत:	गच्छन्ति

Past Tense (लङ्)

अगच्छम्	अगच्छाव	अगच्छाम
अगच्छ:	अगच्छतम्	अगच्छत
अगच्छत्	अगच्छताम्	अगच्छन्

Future Tense (लृट्)

गमिष्यामि	गमिष्याव:	गमिष्याम:
गमिष्यसि	गमिष्यथ:	गमिष्यथ
गमिष्यति	गमिष्यत:	गमिष्यन्ति

Imperative mood (लोट्)

गच्छानि	गच्छाव	गच्छाम
गच्छ	गच्छतम्	गच्छत
गच्छतु	गच्छताम्	गच्छन्तु

Potential mood (विधिलिङ्)

गच्छेयम्	गच्छेव	गच्छेम
गच्छे:	गच्छेतम्	गच्छेत
गच्छेत्	गच्छेताम्	गच्छेयु:

9p√grah (√ग्रह्) to accept

Present Tense (लट्)

गृह्णामि	गृह्णीव:	गृह्णीम:
गृह्णासि	गृह्णीथ:	गृह्णीथ
गृह्णाति	गृह्णीत:	गृह्णन्ति

Past Tense (लङ्)

अगृह्णाम्	अगृह्णीव	अगृह्णीम
अगृह्णा:	अगृह्णीतम्	अगृह्णीत
अगृह्णात्	अगृह्णीताम्	अगृह्णन्

Future Tense (लृट्)

ग्रहिष्यामि	ग्रहिष्याव:	ग्रहिष्याम:
ग्रहिष्यसि	ग्रहिष्यथ:	ग्रहिष्यथ
ग्रहिष्यति	ग्रहिष्यत:	ग्रहिष्यन्ति

Imperative mood (लोट्)

गृह्णानि	गृह्णाव	गृह्णाम
गृह्ण	गृह्णीतम्	गृह्णीत
गृह्णातु	गृह्णीताम्	गृह्णन्तु

Potential mood (विधिलिङ्)

गृह्णीयाम्	गृह्णीयाव	गृह्णीयाम
गृह्णीया:	गृह्णीयाताम्	गृह्णीयात
गृह्णीयात्	गृह्णीयाताम्	गृह्णीयु:

9a√grah (√ग्रह्) to accept

Present Tense (लट्)

गृह्णे	गृह्णीवहे	गृह्णीमहे
गृह्णीषे	गृह्णाथे	गृह्णीध्वे
गृह्णीते	गृह्णाते	गृह्णते

Past Tense (लङ्)

अगृह्णि	अगृह्णीवहि	अगृह्णीमहि
अगृह्णीथा:	अगृह्णाथाम्	अगृह्णीध्वम्
अगृह्णीत	अगृह्णाताम्	अगृह्णत

Future Tense (लृट्)

ग्रहिष्ये	ग्रहिष्यावहे	ग्रहिष्यामहे
ग्रहिष्यसे	ग्रहिष्येथे	ग्रहिष्यध्वे
ग्रहिष्यते	ग्रहिष्येते	ग्रहिष्यन्ते

Imperative mood (लोट्)

गृह्णै	गृह्णावहै	गृह्णामहै
गृह्णीष्व	गृह्णाथाम्	गृह्णीध्वम्
गृह्णीताम्	गृह्णाताम्	गृह्णताम्

Potential mood (विधिलिङ्)

गृह्णीय	गृह्णीवहि	गृह्णीमहि
गृह्णीथा:	गृह्णीयाथाम्	गृह्णीध्वम्
गृह्णीत	गृह्णीयाताम्	गृह्णीरन्

1p√ghrā (√घ्रा) to smell

Present Tense (लट्)

जिघ्रामि	जिघ्राव:	जिघ्राम:
जिघ्रसि	जिघ्रथ:	जिघ्रथ
जिघ्रति	जिघ्रत:	जिघ्रन्ति

Past Tense (लङ्)

अजिघ्राम्	अजिघ्राव	अजिघ्राम
अजिघ्र:	अजिघ्रतम्	अजिघ्रत
अजिघ्रत्	अजिघ्रताम्	अजिघ्रन्

Future Tense (लृट्)

घ्रास्यामि	घ्रास्याव:	घ्रास्याम:
घ्रास्यसि	घ्रास्यथ:	घ्रास्यथ
घ्रास्यति	घ्रास्यत:	घ्रास्यन्ति

Imperative mood (लोट्)

जिघ्राणि	जिघ्राव	जिघ्राम
जिघ्र	जिघ्रतम्	जिघ्रत
जिघ्रतु	जिघ्रताम्	जिघ्रन्तु

Potential mood (विधिलिङ्)

जिघ्रेयम्	जिघ्रेव	जिघ्रेम
जिघ्रे:	जिघ्रेतम्	जिघ्रेत
जिघ्रेत्	जिघ्रेताम्	जिघ्रेयु:

1p√ćal (√चल्) to move

Present Tense (लट्)

चलामि	चलाव:	चलाम:
चलसि	चलथ:	चलथ
चलति	चलत:	चलन्ति

Past Tense (लङ्)

अचलम्	अचलव	अचलाम
अचल:	अचलतम्	अचलत
अचलत्	अचलताम्	अचलन्

Future Tense (लृट्)

चलिष्यामि	चलिष्याव:	चलिष्याम:
चलिष्यसि	चलिष्यथ:	चलिष्यथ

चलिष्यति	चलिष्यत:	चलिष्यन्ति

Imperative mood (लोट्)

चलानि	चलाव	चलाम
चल	चलतम्	चलत
चलतु	चलताम्	चलन्तु

Potential mood (विधिलिङ्)

चलेयम्	चलेव	चलेम
चले:	चलेतम्	चलेत
चलेत्	चलेताम्	चलेयु:

10p√ćint (√चिन्त्) to think

Present Tense (लट्)

चिन्तयामि	चिन्तयाव:	चिन्तयाम:
चिन्तयसि	चिन्तयथ:	चिन्तयथ
चिन्तयति	चिन्तयत:	चिन्तयन्ति

Past Tense (लङ्)

अचिन्तयम्	अचिन्तयाव	अचिन्तयाम
अचिन्तय:	अचिन्तयतम्	अचिन्तयत
अचिन्तयत्	अचिन्तयताम्	अचिन्तयन्

Future Tense (लृट्)

चिन्तयिष्यामि	चिन्तयिष्याव:	चिन्तयिष्याम:
चिन्तयिष्यसि	चिन्तयिष्यथ:	चिन्तयिष्यथ
चिन्तयिष्यति	चिन्तयिष्यत:	चिन्तयिष्यन्ति

Imperative mood (लोट्)

चिन्तयानि	चिन्तयाव	चिन्तयाम
चिन्तय	चिन्तयतम्	चिन्तयत
चिन्तयतु	चिन्तयताम्	चिन्तयन्तु

Potential mood (विधिलिङ्)

चिन्तयेयम्	चिन्तयेव	चिन्तयेम
चिन्तये:	चिन्तयेतम्	चिन्तयेत
चिन्तयेत्	चिन्तयेताम्	चिन्तयेयु:

10p√ćur (√चुर्) to steal

see section 24.10

4a√jan (√जन्) to be born

Present Tense (लट्)

जाये	जायावहे	जायामहे
जायसे	जायेथे	जायध्वे
जायते	जायेते	जायन्ते

Past Tense (लङ्)

अजाये	अजायावहि	अजायामहि
अजायथा:	अजायेथाम्	अजायध्वम्
अजायत	अजायेताम्	अजायन्त

Future Tense (लृट्)

जनिष्ये	जनिष्यावहे	जनिष्यामहे
जनिष्यसे	जनिष्येथे	जनिष्यध्वे
जनिष्यते	जनिष्येते	जनिष्यन्ते

Imperative mood (लोट्)

जायै	जायावहै	जायामहै
जायस्व	जायेथाम्	जायध्वम्
जायताम्	जायेताम्	जायन्ताम्

Potential mood (विधिलिङ्)

जायेय	जायेवहि	जायेमहि
जायेथा:	जायेयाथाम्	जायेध्वम्
जायेत	जायेयाताम्	जायेरन्

1p√ji (√जि) to win

Present Tense (लट्)

जयामि	जयाव:	जयाम:
जयसि	जयथ:	जयथ
जयति	जयत:	जयन्ति

Past Tense (लङ्)

अजयम्	अजयाव	अजयाम
अजय:	अजयतम्	अजयत
अजयत्	अजयताम्	अजयन्

Future Tense (लृट्)

जयिष्यामि	जयिष्याव:	जयिष्याम:
जयिष्यसि	जयिष्यथ:	जयिष्यथ
जयिष्यति	जयिष्यत:	जयिष्यन्ति

Imperative mood (लोट्)

जयानि	जयाव	जयाम
जय	जयतम्	जयत
जयतु	जयताम्	जयन्तु

Potential mood (विधिलिङ्)

जयेयम्	जयेव	जयेम
जये:	जयेतम्	जयेत
जयेत्	जयेताम्	जयेयु:

9p√jñā (√ज्ञा) to know

Present Tense (लट्)

जानामि	जानीव:	जानीम:
जानासि	जानीथ:	जानीथ
जानाति	जानीत:	जानन्ति

Past Tense (लङ्)

अजानाम्	अजानीव	अजानीम
अजाना:	अजानीतम्	अजानीत
अजानात्	अजानीताम्	अजानन्

Future Tense (लृट्)

ज्ञास्यामि	ज्ञास्याव:	ज्ञास्याम:
ज्ञास्यसि	ज्ञास्यथ:	ज्ञास्यथ
ज्ञास्यति	ज्ञास्यत:	ज्ञास्यन्ति

Imperative mood (लोट्)

जानानि	जानाव	जानाम
जानीहि	जानीतम्	जानीत
जानातु	जानीताम्	जानन्तु

Potential mood (विधिलिङ्)

जानीयाम्	जानीयाव	जानीयाम
जानीया:	जानीयातम्	जानीयात
जानीयात्	जानीयाताम्	जानीयु:

4a√ḍī (√डी) to fly

Present Tense (लट्)

डीये	डीयावहे	डीयामहे
डीयसे	डीयेथे	डीयध्वे
डीयते	डीयेते	डीयन्ते

Past Tense (लङ्)

अडीये	अडीयावहि	अडीयामहि
अडीयथा:	अडीयेथाम्	अडीयध्वम्
अडीयत	अडीयेताम्	अडीयन्त

Future Tense (लृट्)

डयिष्ये	डयिष्यावहे	डयिष्यामहे

डयिष्यसे	डयिष्येथे	डयिष्यध्वे
डयिष्यते	डयिष्येते	डयिष्यन्ते

Imperative mood (लोट्)

डीयै	डीयावहै	डीयामहै
डीयस्व	डीयेथाम्	डीयध्वम्
डीयताम्	डीयेताम्	डीयन्ताम्

Potential mood (विधिलिङ्)

डीयेय	डीयेवहि	डीयेमहि
डीयेथा:	डीयेयाथाम्	डीयेध्वम्
डीयेत	डीयेयाताम्	डीयेरन्

8p√tan (√तन्) to spread

see section 24.8

1p√tap (√तप्) to be angry

Present Tense (लट्)

तपामि	तपाव:	तपाम:
तपसि	तपथ:	तपथ
तपति	तपत:	तपन्ति

Past Tense (लङ्)

अतपम्	अतपाव	अतपाम
अतप:	अतपतम्	अतपत
अतपत्	अतपताम्	अतपन्

Future Tense (लृट्)

तप्स्यामि	तप्स्याव:	तप्स्याम:
तप्स्यसि	तप्स्यथ:	तप्स्यथ
तप्स्यति	तप्स्यत:	तप्स्यन्ति

Imperative mood (लोट्)

तपानि	तपाव	तपाम
तप	तपतम्	तपत
तपतु	तपताम्	तपन्तु

Potential mood (विधिलिङ्)

तपेयम्	तपेव	तपेम
तपे:	तपेतम्	तपेत
तपेत्	तपेताम्	तपेयु:

1p√tud (√तुद्) to hurt

see section 24.6

4p√tuṣ (√तुष्) to be pleased

Present Tense (लट्)

तुष्यामि	तुष्याव:	तुष्याम:
तुष्यसि	तुष्यथ:	तुष्यथ
तुष्यति	तुष्यत:	तुष्यन्ति

Past Tense (लङ्)

अतुष्यम्	अतुष्याव	अतुष्याम
अतुष्य:	अतुष्यतम्	अतुष्यत
अतुष्यत्	अतुष्यताम्	अतुष्यन्

Future Tense (लृट्)

तोक्ष्यामि	तोक्ष्याव:	तोक्ष्याम:
तोक्ष्यसि	तोक्ष्यथ:	तोक्ष्यथ
तोक्ष्यति	तोक्ष्यत:	तोक्ष्यन्ति

Imperative mood (लोट्)

तुष्याणि	तुष्याव	तुष्याम

तुष्य	तुष्यतम्	पुष्यत
तुष्यतु	तुष्यताम्	तुष्यन्तु

Potential mood (विधिलिङ्)

तुष्येयम्	तुष्येव	तुष्येम
तुष्ये:	तुष्येतम्	तुष्येत
तुष्येत्	तुष्येताम्	तुष्येयु:

1p√tyaj (√त्यज्) to renounce

Present Tense (लट्)

त्यजामि	त्यजाव:	त्यजाम:
त्यजसि	त्यजथ:	त्यजथ
त्यजति	त्यजत:	त्यजन्ति

Past Tense (लङ्)

अत्यजम्	अत्यजाव	अत्यजाम
अत्यज:	अत्यजतम्	अत्यजत
अत्यजत्	अत्यजताम्	अत्यजन्

Future Tense (लृट्)

त्यक्ष्यामि	त्यक्ष्याव:	त्यक्ष्याम:
त्यक्ष्यसि	त्यक्ष्यथ:	त्यक्ष्यथ
त्यक्ष्यति	त्यक्ष्यत:	त्यक्ष्यन्ति

Imperative mood (लोट्)

त्यजानि	त्यजाव	त्यजाम
त्यज	त्यजतम्	त्यजत
त्यजतु	त्यजताम्	त्यजन्तु

Potential mood (विधिलिङ्)

त्यजेयम्	त्यजेव	त्यजेम
त्यजे:	त्यजेतम्	त्यजेत
त्यजेत्	त्यजेताम्	त्यजेयु:

1a√trai (√त्रै) to protect

Present Tense (लट्)

त्राये	त्रायावहे	त्रायामहे
त्रायसे	त्रायेथे	त्रायध्वे
त्रायते	त्रायेते	त्रायन्ते

Past Tense (लङ्)

अत्राये	अत्रायावहि	अत्रायामहि
अत्रायथा:	अत्रायेथाम्	अत्रायध्वम्
अत्रायत	अत्रायेताम्	अत्रायन्त

Future Tense (लृट्)

त्रास्ये	त्रास्यावहे	त्रास्यामहे
त्रास्यसे	त्रास्येथे	त्रास्यध्वे
त्रास्यते	त्रास्येते	त्रास्यन्ते

Imperative mood (लोट्)

त्रायै	त्रायावहै	त्रायामहै
त्रायस्व	त्रायेथाम्	त्रायध्वम्
त्रायताम्	त्रायेताम्	त्रायन्ताम्

Potential mood (विधिलिङ्)

त्रायेय	त्रायेवहि	त्रायेमहि
त्रायेथा:	त्रायेयाथाम्	त्रायेध्वम्
त्रायेत	त्रायेयाताम्	त्रायेरन्

1a√dad (√दद्) to give

Present Tense (लट्)

ददे	ददावहे	ददामहे
ददसे	ददेथे	ददध्वे
ददते	ददेते	ददन्ते

Past Tense (लङ्)

अददे	अददावहि	अददामहि
अददथा:	अददेथाम्	अददध्वम्
अददत	अददेताम्	अददन्त

Future Tense (लृट्)

ददिष्ये	ददिष्यावहे	ददिष्यामहे
ददिष्यसे	ददिष्येथे	ददिष्यध्वे
ददिष्यते	ददिष्येते	ददिष्यन्ते

Imperative mood (लोट्)

ददै	ददावहै	ददामहै
ददस्व	ददेथाम्	ददध्वम्
ददताम्	ददेताम्	ददन्ताम्

Potential mood (विधिलिङ्)

ददेय	ददेवहि	ददेमहि
ददेथा:	ददेयाथाम्	ददेध्वम्
ददेत	ददेयाताम्	ददेरन्

1p√dah (√दह्) to burn

Present Tense (लट्)

दहामि	दहाव:	दहाम:
दहसि	दहथ:	दहथ
दहति	दहत:	दहन्ति

Past Tense (लङ्)

अदहम्	अदहाव	अदहाम
अदह:	अदहतम्	अदहत
अदहत्	अदहताम्	अदहन्

Future Tense (लृट्)

धक्ष्यामि	धक्ष्याव:	धक्ष्याम:
धक्ष्यसि	धक्ष्यथ:	धक्ष्यथ
धक्ष्यति	धक्ष्यत:	धक्ष्यन्ति

Imperative mood (लोट्)

दहानि	दहाव	दहाम
दह	दहतम्	दहत
दहतु	दहताम्	दहन्तु

Potential mood (विधिलिङ्)

दहेयम्	दहेव	दहेम
दहे:	दहेतम्	दहेत
दहेत्	दहेताम्	दहेयु:

3p√dā (√दा) to give

Present Tense (लट्)

ददामि	दद्व:	दद्म:
ददासि	दत्थ:	दत्थ
ददाति	दत्त:	ददति

Past Tense (लङ्)

अददाम्	अदद्व	अदद्म
अददा:	अदत्तम्	अदत्त
अददात्	अदत्ताम्	अददु:

Future Tense (लृट्)

दास्यामि	दास्याव:	दास्याम:
दास्यसि	दास्यथ:	दास्यथ
दास्यति	दास्यत:	दास्यन्ति

Imperative mood (लोट्)

ददानि	ददाव	ददाम
देहि	दत्तम्	दत्त
ददातु	दत्ताम्	ददतु

Potential mood (विधिलिङ्)

दद्याम्	दद्याव	दद्याम
दद्याः	दद्यातम्	दद्यात
दद्यात्	दद्याताम्	दद्युः

3a√dā (√दा) to give

Present Tense (लट्)

ददे	दद्वहे	दद्महे
दत्से	ददाथे	दद्ध्वे
दत्ते	ददाते	ददते

Past Tense (लङ्)

अददि	अदद्वहि	अदद्महि
अदत्थाः	अददाथाम्	अदद्ध्वम्
अदत्त	अददाताम्	अददत

Future Tense (लृट्)

दास्ये	दास्यावहे	दास्यामहे
दास्यसे	दास्येथे	दास्यध्वे
दास्यते	दास्येते	दास्यन्ते

Imperative mood (लोट्)

ददै	ददावहै	ददामहै
दत्स्व	ददाथाम्	दद्ध्वम्
दत्ताम्	ददाताम्	ददताम्

Potential mood (विधिलिङ्)

ददीय	ददीवहि	ददीमहि
ददीथाः	ददीयाथाम्	ददीध्वम्
ददीत	ददीयाताम्	ददीरन्

4p√div (√दिव्) to play

see section 24.4

4a√dīp (√दीप्) to shine

Present Tense (लट्)

दीप्ये	दीप्यावहे	दीप्यामहे
दीप्यसे	दीप्येथे	दीप्यध्वे
दीप्यते	दीप्येते	दीप्यन्ते

Past Tense (लङ्)

अदीप्ये	अदीप्यावहि	अदीप्यामहि
अदीप्यथाः	अदीप्येथाम्	अदीप्यध्वम्
अदीप्यत	अदीप्येताम्	अदीप्यन्त

Future Tense (लृट्)

दीपिष्ये	दीपिष्यावहे	दीपिष्यामहे
दीपिष्यसे	दीपिष्येथे	दीपिष्यध्वे
दीपिष्यते	दीपिष्येते	दीपिष्यन्ते

Imperative mood (लोट्)

दीप्यै	दीप्यावहै	दीप्यामहै
दीप्यस्व	दीप्येथाम्	दीप्यध्वम्
दीप्यताम्	दीप्येताम्	दीप्यन्ताम्

Potential mood (विधिलिङ्)

दीप्येय	दीप्येवहि	दीप्येमहि
दीप्येथाः	दीप्येयाथाम्	दीप्येध्वम्
दीप्येत	दीप्येयाताम्	दीप्येरन्

4a√dū (√दू) to hurt

Present Tense (लट्)

दूये	दूयावहे	दूयामहे
दूयसे	दूयेथे	दूयध्वे
दूयते	दूयेते	दूयन्ते

Past Tense (लङ्)

अदूये	अदूयावहि	अदूयामहि
अदूयथा:	अदूयेथाम्	अदूयध्वम्
अदूयत	अदूयेताम्	अदूयन्त

Future Tense (लृट्)

दविष्ये	दविष्यावहे	दविष्यामहे
दविष्यसे	दविष्येथे	दविष्यध्वे
दविष्यते	दविष्येते	दविष्यन्ते

Imperative mood (लोट्)

दूयै	दूयावहै	दूयामहै
दूयस्व	दूयेथाम्	दूयध्वम्
दूयताम्	दूयेताम्	दूयन्ताम्

Potential mood (विधिलिङ्)

दूयेय	दूयेवहि	दूयेमहि
दूयेथा:	दूयेयाथाम्	दूयेध्वम्
दूयेत	दूयेयाताम्	दूयेरन्

1p√dṛś (√दृश्) to see

Present Tense (लट्)

पश्यामि	पश्याव:	पश्याम:
पश्यासि	पश्यथ:	पश्यथ
पश्यति	पश्यत:	पश्यन्ति

Past Tense (लङ्)

अपश्यम्	अपश्याव	अपश्याम
अपश्य:	अपश्यतम्	अपश्यत
अपश्यत्	अपश्यताम्	अपश्यन्

Future Tense (लृट्)

द्रक्ष्यामि	द्रक्ष्याव:	द्रक्ष्याम:
द्रक्ष्यसि	द्रक्ष्यथ:	द्रक्ष्यथ
द्रक्ष्यति	द्रक्ष्यत:	द्रक्ष्यन्ति

Imperative mood (लोट्)

पश्यानि	पश्याव	पश्याम
पश्य	पश्यतम्	पश्यत
पश्यतु	पश्यताम्	पश्यन्तु

Potential mood (विधिलिङ्)

पश्येयम्	पश्येव	पश्येम
पश्ये:	पश्येतम्	पश्येत
पश्येत्	पश्येताम्	पश्येयु:

3p√dhā (√धा) to bear

Present Tense (लट्)

दधामि	दध्व:	दध्म:
दधासि	धत्थ:	धत्थ
दधाति	धत्त:	दधति

Past Tense (लङ्)

अदधाम्	अदध्व	अदध्म
अदधा:	अधत्तम्	अधत्त
अदधात्	अधत्ताम्	अदधु:

Future Tense (लृट्)

धास्यामि	धास्याव:	धास्याम:
धास्यसि	धास्यथ:	धास्यथ
धास्यति	धास्यत:	धास्यन्ति

Imperative mood (लोट्)

दधानि	दधाव	दधाम
धेहि	धत्तम्	धत्त
दधातु	धत्ताम्	दधतु

Potential mood (विधिलिङ्)

दध्याम्	दध्याव	दध्याम
दध्या:	दध्यातम्	दध्यात
दध्यात्	दध्याताम्	दध्यु:

3a√dhā (√धा) to bear

Present Tense (लट्)

दधे	दध्वहे	दध्महे
धत्से	दधाथे	धद्ध्वे
धत्ते	दधाते	दधते

Past Tense (लङ्)

अदधि	अदध्वहि	अदध्महि
अधत्था:	अधाथाम्	अधद्ध्वम्
अधत्त	अदधाताम्	अदधत

Future Tense (लृट्)

धास्ये	धास्यावहे	धास्यामहे
धास्यसे	धास्येथे	धास्यध्वे
धास्यते	धास्येते	धास्यन्ते

Imperative mood (लोट्)

दधै	दधावहै	दधामहै
धत्स्व	दधाथाम्	धद्ध्वम्
धत्ताम्	दधाताम्	दधताम्

Potential mood (विधिलिङ्)

दधीय	दधीवहि	दधीमहि
दधीथा:	दधीयाथाम्	दधीध्वम्
दधीत	दधीयाताम्	दधीरन्

1p√dhṛ (√धृ) to hold

Present Tense (लट्)

धरामि	धराव:	धराम:
धरसि	धरथ:	धरथ
धरति	धरत:	धरन्ति

Past Tense (लङ्)

अधरम्	अधराव	अधराम
अधर:	अधरतम्	अधरत
अधरत्	अधरताम्	अधरन्

Future Tense (लृट्)

धरिष्यामि	धरिष्याव:	धरिष्याम:
धरिष्यसि	धरिष्यथ:	धरिष्यथ
धरिष्यति	धरिष्यत:	धरिष्यन्ति

Imperative mood (लोट्)

धरानि	धराव	धराम
धर	धरतम्	धरत
धरतु	धरताम्	धरन्तु

Potential mood (विधिलिङ्)

धरेयम्	धरेव	धरेम
धरे:	धरेतम्	धरेत
धरेत्	धरेताम्	धरेयु:

1a√dhṛ (√धृ) to hold

Present Tense (लट्)

धरे	धरावहे	धरामहे
धरसे	धरेथे	धरध्वे
धरते	धरेते	धरन्ते

Past Tense (लङ्)

अधरे	अधरावहि	अधरामहि
अधरथा:	अधरेथाम्	अधरध्वम्

अधरत	अधरेताम्	अधरन्त

Future Tense (लृट्)

धरिष्ये	धरिष्यावहे	धरिष्यामहे
धरिष्यसे	धरिष्येथे	धरिष्यध्वे
धरिष्यते	धरिष्येते	धरिष्यन्ते

Imperative mood (लोट्)

धरै	धरावहै	धरामहै
धरस्व	धरेथाम्	धरध्वम्
धरताम्	धरेताम्	धरन्ताम्

Potential mood (विधिलिङ्)

धरेय	धरेवहि	धरेमहि
धरेथा:	धरेयाथाम्	धरेध्वम्
धरेत	धरेयाताम्	धरेरन्

1p√dhāv (√धाव्) to run

Present Tense (लट्)

धावामि	धावाव:	धावाम:
धावसि	धावथ:	धावथ
धावति	धावत:	धावन्ति

Past Tense (लङ्)

अधावम्	अधावाव	अधावाम
अधाव:	अधावतम्	अधावत
अधावत्	अधावताम्	अधावन्

Future Tense (लृट्)

धाविष्यामि	धाविष्याव:	धाविष्याम:
धाविष्यसि	धाविष्यथ:	धाविष्यथ
धाविष्यति	धाविष्यत:	धाविष्यन्ति

Imperative mood (लोट्)

धावानि	धावाव	धावाम
धाव	धावतम्	धावत
धावतु	धावताम्	धावन्तु

Potential mood (विधिलिङ्)

धावेयम्	धावेव	धावेम
धावे:	धावेतम्	धावेत
धावेत्	धावेताम्	धावेयु:

1a√dhāv (√धाव्) to run

Present Tense (लट्)

धावे	धावावहे	धावामहे
धावसे	धावेथे	धावध्वे
धावते	धावेते	धावन्ते

Past Tense (लङ्)

अधावे	अधावावहि	अधावामहि
अधावथा:	अधावेथाम्	अधावध्वम्
अधावत	अधावेताम्	अधावन्त

Future Tense (लृट्)

धाविष्ये	धाविष्यावहे	धाविष्यामहे
धाविष्यसे	धाविष्येथे	धाविष्यध्वे
धाविष्यते	धाविष्येते	धाविष्यन्ते

Imperative mood (लोट्)

धावै	धावावहै	धावामहै
धावस्व	धावेथाम्	धावध्वम्
धावताम्	धावेताम्	धावन्ताम्

Potential mood (विधिलिङ्)

धावेय	धावेवहि	धावेमहि
धावेथा:	धावेयाथाम्	धावेध्वम्

धावेत धावेयाताम् धावेरन्

1a√dhvaṁs (√ध्वंस्) to perish

Present Tense (लट्)

ध्वंसे	ध्वंसावहे	ध्वंसामहे
ध्वंससे	ध्वंसेथे	ध्वंसध्वे
ध्वंसते	ध्वंसेते	ध्वंसन्ते

Past Tense (लङ्)

अध्वंसे	अध्वंसावहि	अध्वंसामहि
अध्वंसथा:	अध्वंसेथाम्	अध्वंसध्वम्
अध्वंसत	अध्वंसेताम्	अध्वंसन्त

Future Tense (लृट्)

ध्वंसिष्ये	ध्वंसिष्यावहे	ध्वंसिष्यामहे
ध्वंसिष्यसे	ध्वंसिष्येथे	ध्वंसिष्यध्वे
ध्वंसिष्यते	ध्वंसिष्येते	ध्वंसिष्यन्ते

Imperative mood (लोट्)

ध्वंसै	ध्वंसावहै	ध्वंसामहै
ध्वंसस्व	ध्वंसेथाम्	ध्वंसध्वम्
ध्वंसताम्	ध्वंसेताम्	ध्वंसन्ताम्

Potential mood (विधिलिङ्)

ध्वंसेय	ध्वंसेवहि	ध्वंसेमहि
ध्वंसेथा:	ध्वंसेयाथाम्	ध्वंसेध्वं
ध्वंसेत	ध्वंसेयाताम्	ध्वंसेरन्

1p√nand (√नन्द्) to enjoy

Present Tense (लट्)

नन्दामि	नन्दाव:	नन्दाम:
नन्दसि	नन्दथ:	नन्दथ
नन्दति	नन्दत:	नन्दन्ति

Past Tense (लङ्)

अनन्दम्	अनन्दाव	अनन्दाम
अनन्द:	अनन्दतम्	अनन्दत
अनन्दत्	अनन्दताम्	अनन्दन्

Future Tense (लृट्)

नन्दिष्यामि	नन्दिष्याव:	नन्दिष्याम:
नन्दिष्यसि	नन्दिष्यथ:	नन्दिष्यथ
नन्दिष्यति	नन्दिष्यत:	नन्दिष्यन्ति

Imperative mood (लोट्)

नन्दानि	नन्दाव	नन्दाम
नन्द	नन्दतम्	नन्दत
नन्दतु	नन्दताम्	नन्दन्तु

Potential mood (विधिलिङ्)

नन्देयम्	नन्देव	नन्देम
नन्दे:	नन्देतम्	नन्देत
नन्देत्	नन्देताम्	नन्देयु:

4p√naś (√नश्) to vanish

Present Tense (लट्)

नश्यामि	नश्याव:	नश्याम:
नश्यसि	नश्यथ:	नश्यथ
नश्यति	नश्यत:	नश्यन्ति

Past Tense (लङ्)

अनश्यम्	अनश्याव	अनश्याम
अनश्य:	अनश्यतम्	अनश्यत
अनश्यत्	अनश्यताम्	अनश्यन्

Future Tense (लृट्)

नंक्ष्यामि	नंक्ष्याव:	नंक्ष्याम:
नंक्ष्यसि	नंक्ष्यथ:	नंक्ष्यथ
नंक्ष्यति	नंक्ष्यत:	नंक्ष्यन्ति

Imperative mood (लोट्)

नश्यानि	नश्याव	नश्याम
नश्य	नश्यतम्	नश्यत
नश्यतु	नश्यताम्	नश्यन्तु

Potential mood (विधिलिङ्)

नश्येयम्	नश्येव	नश्येम
नश्ये:	नश्येतम्	नश्येत
नश्येत्	नश्येताम्	नश्येयु:

1p√nī (√नी) to carry

Present Tense (लट्)

नयामि	नयाव:	नयाम:
नयसि	नयथ:	नयथ
नयति	नयत:	नयन्ति

Past Tense (लङ्)

अनयम्	अनयाव	अनयाम
अनय:	अनयतम्	अनयत
अनयत्	अनयताम्	अनयन्

Future Tense (लृट्)

नेष्यामि	नेष्याव:	नेष्याम:
नेष्यसि	नेष्यथ:	नेष्यथ
नेष्यति	नेष्यत:	नेष्यन्ति

Imperative mood (लोट्)

नयानि	नयाव	नयाम
नय	नयतम्	नयत
नयतु	नयताम्	नयन्तु

Potential mood (विधिलिङ्)

नयेयम्	नयेव	नयेम
नये:	नयेतम्	नयेत
नयेत्	नयेताम्	नयेयु:

1a√nī (√नी) to carry

Present Tense (लट्)

नये	नयावहे	नयामहे
नयसे	नयेथे	नयध्वे
नयते	नयेते	नयन्ते

Past Tense (लङ्)

अनये	अनयावहि	अनयामहि
अनयथा:	अनयेथाम्	अनयध्वं
अनयत	अनयेताम्	अनयन्त

Future Tense (लृट्)

नेष्ये	नेष्यावहे	नेष्यामहे
नेष्यसे	नेष्येथे	नेष्यध्वे
नेष्यते	नेष्येते	नेष्यन्ते

Imperative mood (लोट्)

नयै	नयावहै	नयामहै
नयस्व	नयेथाम्	नयध्वम्
नयताम्	नयेताम्	नयन्ताम्

Potential mood (विधिलिङ्)

नयेय	नयेवहि	नयेमहि
नयेथा:	नयेयाथाम्	नयेध्वम्
नयेत	नयेयाताम्	नयेरन्

1p√pać (√पच्) to cook

Present Tense (लट्)

पचामि	पचाव:	पचाम:
पचसि	पचथ:	पचथ
पचति	पचत:	पचन्ति

Past Tense (लङ्)

अपचम्	अपचाव	अपचाम
अपच:	अपचतम्	अपचत
अपचत्	अपचताम्	अपचन्

Future Tense (लृट्)

पक्ष्यामि	पक्ष्याव:	पक्ष्याम:
पक्ष्यसि	पक्ष्यथ:	पक्ष्यथ
पक्ष्यति	पक्ष्यत:	पक्ष्यन्ति

Imperative mood (लोट्)

पचानि	पचाव	पचाम
पच	पचतम्	पचत
पचतु	पचताम्	पचन्तु

Potential mood (विधिलिङ्)

पचेयम्	पचेव	पचेम
पचे:	पचेतम्	पचेत
पचेत्	पचेताम्	पचेयु:

1a√pać (√पच्) to cook

Present Tense (लट्)

पचे	पचावहे	पचामहे
पचसे	पचेथे	पचध्वे
पचते	पचेते	पचन्ते

Past Tense (लङ्)

अपचे	अपचावहि	अपचामहि
अपचथा:	अपचेथाम्	अपचध्वम्
अपचत	अपचेताम्	अपचन्त

Future Tense (लृट्)

पक्ष्ये	पक्ष्यावहे	पक्ष्यामहे
पक्ष्यसे	पक्ष्येथे	पक्ष्यध्वे
पक्ष्यते	पक्ष्येते	पक्ष्यन्ते

Imperative mood (लोट्)

पचै	पचावहै	पचामहै
पचस्व	पचेथाम्	पचध्वम्
पचताम्	पचेताम्	पचन्ताम्

Potential mood (विधिलिङ्)

पचेय	पचेवहि	पचेमहि
पचेथा:	पचेयाथाम्	पचेध्वम्
पचेत	पचेयाताम्	पचेरन्

4a√pad (√पद्) to walk

Present Tense (लट्)

पद्ये	पद्यावहे	पद्यामहे
पद्यसे	पद्येथे	पद्यध्वे
पद्यते	पद्येते	पद्यन्ते

Past Tense (लङ्)

अपद्ये	अपद्यावहि	अपद्यामहि
अपद्यथा:	अपद्येथाम्	अपद्यध्वम्
अपद्यत	अपद्येताम्	अपद्यन्त

Future Tense (लृट्)

पत्स्ये	पत्स्यावहे	पत्स्यामहे
पत्स्यसे	पत्स्येथे	पत्स्यध्वे

पत्स्यते	पत्स्येते	पत्स्यन्ते

Imperative mood (लोट्)

पद्यै	पद्यावहै	पद्यामहै
पद्यस्व	पद्येथाम्	पद्यध्वम्
पद्यताम्	पद्येताम्	पद्यन्ताम्

Potential mood (विधिलिङ्)

पद्येय	पद्येवहि	पद्येमहि
पद्येथा:	पद्येयाथाम्	पद्येध्वम्
पद्येत	पद्येयाताम्	पद्येरन्

1√pā (√पा) to drink

Present Tense (लट्)

पिबामि	पिबाव:	पिबाम:
पिबसि	पिबथ:	पिबथ
पिबति	पिबत:	पिबन्ति

Past Tense (लङ्)

अपिबम्	अपिबाव	अपिबाम
अपिब:	अपिबतम्	अपिबत
अपिबत्	अपिबताम्	अपिबन्

Future Tense (लृट्)

पास्यामि	पास्याव:	पास्याम:
पास्यसि	पास्यथ:	पास्यथ
पास्यति	पास्यत:	पास्यन्ति

Imperative mood (लोट्)

पिबानि	पिबाव	पिबाम
पिब	पिबतम्	पिबत
पिबतु	पिबताम्	पिबन्तु

Potential mood (विधिलिङ्)

पिबेयम्	पिबेव	पिबेम
पिबे:	पिबेतम्	पिबेत
पिबेत्	पिबेताम्	पिबेयु:

2p√pā (√पा) to protect

Present Tense (लट्)

पामि	पाव:	पाम:
पासि	पाथ:	पाथ
पाति	पात:	पान्ति

Past Tense (लङ्)

अपाम्	अपाव	अपाम
अपा:	अपातम्	अपात
अपात्	अपाताम्	अपु:

Future Tense (लृट्)

पास्यामि	पास्याव:	पास्याम:
पास्यसि	पास्यथ:	पास्यथ
पास्यति	पास्यत:	पास्यन्ति

Imperative mood (लोट्)

पानि	पाव	पाम
पाहि	पातम्	पात
पातु	पाताम्	पान्तु

Potential mood (विधिलिङ्)

पायाम्	पायाव	पायाम
पाया:	पायातम्	पायात
पायात्	पायाताम्	पायु:

4p√puṣ (√पुष्) to nourish

Present Tense (लट्)

पुष्यामि	पुष्याव:	पुष्याम:

पुष्यसि	पुष्यथ:	पुष्यथ
पुष्यति	पुष्यत:	पुष्यन्ति

Past Tense (लङ्)

अपुष्यम्	अपुष्याव	अपुष्याम
अपुष्य:	अपुष्यतम्	अपुष्यत
अपुष्यत्	अपुष्यताम्	अपुष्यन्

Future Tense (लृट्)

पोक्ष्यामि	पोक्ष्याव:	पोक्ष्याम:
पोक्ष्यसि	पोक्ष्यथ:	पोक्ष्यथ
पोक्ष्यति	पोक्ष्यत:	पोक्ष्यन्ति

Imperative mood (लोट्)

पुष्याणि	पुष्याव	पुष्याम
पुष्य	पुष्यतम्	पुष्यत
पुष्यतु	पुष्यताम्	पुष्यन्तु

Potential mood (विधिलिङ्)

पुष्येयम्	पुष्येव	पुष्येम
पुष्ये:	पुष्येतम्	पुष्येत
पुष्येत्	पुष्येताम्	पुष्येयु:

10p√pūj (√पूज्) to worship

Present Tense (लट्)

पूजयामि	पूजयाव:	पूजयाम:
पूजयसि	पूजयथ:	पूजयथ
पूजयति	पूजयत:	पूजयन्ति

Past Tense (लङ्)

अपूजयम्	अपूजयाव	अपूजयाम
अपूजय:	अपूजयतम्	अपूजयत
अपूजयत्	अपूजयताम्	अपूजयन्

Future Tense (लृट्)

पूजयिष्यामि	पूजयिष्याव:	पूजयिष्याम:
पूजयिष्यसि	पूजयिष्यथ:	पूजयिष्यथ
पूजयिष्यति	पूजयिष्यत:	पूजयिष्यन्ति

Imperative mood (लोट्)

पूजयानि	पूजयाव	पूजयाम
पूजय	पूजयतम्	पूजयत
पूजयतु	पूजयताम्	पूजयन्तु

Potential mood (विधिलिङ्)

पूजयेयम्	पूजयेव	पूजयेम
पूजये:	पूजयेतम्	पूजयेत
पूजयेत्	पूजयेताम्	पूजयेयु:

4a√budh (√बुध्) to know

Present Tense (लट्)

बुध्ये	बुध्यावहे	बुध्यामहे
बुध्यसे	बुध्येथे	बुध्यध्वे
बुध्यते	बुध्येते	बुध्यन्ते

Past Tense (लङ्)

अबुध्ये	अबुध्यावहि	अबुध्यामहि
अबुध्यथा:	अबुध्येथाम्	अबुध्यध्वम्
अबुध्यत	अबुध्येताम्	अबुध्यन्त

Future Tense (लृट्)

भोत्स्ये	भोत्स्यावहे	भोत्स्यामहे
भोत्स्यसे	भोत्स्येथे	भोत्स्यध्वे
भोत्स्यते	भोत्स्येते	भोत्स्यन्ते

Imperative mood (लोट्)

बुध्यै	बुध्यावहै	बुध्यामहै

बुध्यस्व	बुध्येथाम्	बुध्यध्वम्
बुध्यताम्	बुध्येताम्	बुध्यन्ताम्

Potential mood (विधिलिङ्)

बुध्येय	बुध्येवहि	बुध्येमहि
बुध्येथा:	बुध्येयाथाम्	बुध्येध्वम्
बुध्येत	बुध्येयाताम्	बुध्येरन्

6p√pracch (√प्रच्छ्) to ask

Present Tense (लट्)

पृच्छामि	पृच्छाव:	पृच्छाम:
पृच्छसि	पृच्छथ:	पृच्छथ
पृच्छति	पृच्छत:	पृच्छन्ति

Past Tense (लङ्)

अपृच्छम्	अपृच्छाव	अपृच्छाम
अपृच्छ:	अपृच्छतम्	अपृच्छत
अपृच्छत्	अपृच्छताम्	अपृच्छन्

Future Tense (लृट्)

प्रक्ष्यामि	प्रक्ष्याव:	प्रक्ष्याम:
प्रक्ष्यसि	प्रक्ष्यथ:	प्रक्ष्यथ
प्रक्ष्यति	प्रक्ष्यत:	प्रक्ष्यन्ति

Imperative mood (लोट्)

पृच्छानि	पृच्छाव	पृच्छाम
पृच्छ	पृच्छतम्	पृच्छत
पृच्छतु	पृच्छताम्	पृच्छन्तु

Potential mood (विधिलिङ्)

पृच्छेयम्	पृच्छेव	पृच्छेम
पृच्छे:	पृच्छेतम्	पृच्छेत
पृच्छेत्	पृच्छेताम्	पृच्छेयु:

2p√brū (√ब्रू) to speak

Present Tense (लट्)

ब्रवीमि ब्रूव: ब्रूम: ।
ब्रवीषि ब्रूथ: ब्रूथ । आत्थ आहथु:ब्रूथ
ब्रवीति ब्रूत: ब्रुवन्ति । आह आहतु: आहु:

Past Tense (लङ्)

अब्रवम्	अब्रूव	अब्रूम
अब्रवी:	अब्रूतम्	अब्रूत
अब्रवीत्	अब्रूताम्	अब्रुवन्

Future Tense (लृट्)

वक्ष्यामि	वक्ष्याव:	वक्ष्याम:
वक्ष्यसि	वक्ष्यथ:	वक्ष्यथ
वक्ष्यति	वक्ष्यत:	वक्ष्यन्ति

Imperative mood (लोट्)

ब्रवाणि	ब्रवाव	ब्रवाम
ब्रूहि	ब्रूताम्	ब्रूत
ब्रवीतु	ब्रूताम्	ब्रुवन्तु

Potential mood (विधिलिङ्)

ब्रूयाम्	ब्रूयाव	ब्रूयाम
ब्रूया:	ब्रूयातम्	ब्रूयात
ब्रूयात्	ब्रूयाताम्	ब्रूयु:

2a√brū (√ब्रू) to speak

Present Tense (लट्)

ब्रुवे	ब्रूवहे	ब्रूमहे
ब्रूषे	ब्रुवाथे	ब्रूध्वे
ब्रूते	ब्रुवाते	ब्रुवते

Past Tense (लङ्)

अब्रुवि	अब्रूवहि	अब्रूमहि
अब्रूथा:	अब्रुवाथाम्	अब्रूध्वम्
अब्रूत	अब्रुवाताम्	अब्रुवत्

Future Tense (लृट्)

वक्ष्ये	वक्ष्यावहे	वक्ष्यामहे
वक्ष्यसे	वक्ष्येथे	वक्ष्यध्वे
वक्ष्यते	वक्ष्येते	वक्ष्यन्ते

Imperative mood (लोट्)

ब्रवम्	ब्रवावहै	ब्रवामहै
ब्रूष्व	ब्रुवाथाम्	ब्रूध्वम्
ब्रूताम्	ब्रूवाताम्	ब्रुवताम्

Potential mood (विधिलिङ्)

ब्रूवीय	ब्रूवीवहि	ब्रूवीमहि
ब्रुवीथा:	ब्रवीयाथाम्	ब्रवीध्वम्
ब्रुवीत	ब्रुवीयाताम्	ब्रुवीरन्

10p√bhakṣ (√भक्ष्) to eat

Present Tense (लट्)

भक्षयामि	भक्षयाव:	भक्षयाम:
भक्षयसि	भक्षयथ:	भक्षयथ
भक्षयति	भक्षयत:	भक्षयन्ति

Past Tense (लङ्)

अभक्षयम्	अभक्षयाव	अभक्षयाम
अभक्षय:	अभक्षयतम्	अभक्षयत
अभक्षयत्	अभक्षयताम्	अभक्षयन्

Future Tense (लृट्)

भक्षयिष्यामि	भक्षयिष्याव:	भक्षयिष्याम:
भक्षयिष्यसि	भक्षयिष्यथ:	भक्षयिष्यथ
भक्षयिष्यति	भक्षयिष्यत:	भक्षयिष्यन्ति

Imperative mood (लोट्)

भक्षयाणि	भक्षयाव	भक्षयाम
भक्षय	भक्षयतम्	भक्षयत
भक्षयतु	भक्षयताम्	भक्षयन्तु

Potential mood (विधिलिङ्)

भक्षयेयम्	भक्षयेव	भक्षयेम
भक्षये:	भक्षयेतम्	भक्षयेत
भक्षयेत्	भक्षयेताम्	भक्षयेयु:

1p√bhaj (√भज्) to serve

Present Tense (लट्)

भजामि	भजाव:	भजाम:
भजसि	भजथ:	भजथ
भजति	भजत:	भजन्ति

Past Tense (लङ्)

अभजम्	अभजाव	अभजाम
अभज:	अभजतम्	अभजत
अभजत्	अभजताम्	अभजन्

Future Tense (लृट्)

भक्ष्यामि	भक्ष्याव:	भक्ष्याम:
भक्ष्यसि	भक्ष्यथ:	भक्ष्यथ
भक्ष्यति	भक्ष्यत:	भक्ष्यन्ति

Imperative mood (लोट्)

भजानि	भजाव	भजाम
भज	भजतम्	भजत
भजतु	भजताम्	भजन्तु

Potential mood (विधिलिङ्)

भजेयम्	भजेव	भजेम
भजे:	भजेतम्	भजेत
भजेत्	भजेताम्	भजेयु:

1a√bhaj (√भज्) to serve

Present Tense (लट्)

भजे	भजावहे	भजामहे
भजसे	भजेथे	भजध्वे
भजते	भजेते	भजन्ते

Past Tense (लङ्)

अभजे	अभजावहि	अभजामहि
अभजथा:	अभजेथाम्	अभजध्वम्
अभजत	अभजेताम्	अभजन्त

Future Tense (लृट्)

भक्ष्ये	भक्ष्यावहे	भक्ष्यामहे
भक्ष्यसे	भक्ष्येथे	भक्ष्यध्वे
भक्ष्यते	भक्ष्येते	भक्ष्यन्ते

Imperative mood (लोट्)

भजै	भजावहै	भजामहै
भजस्व	भजेथाम्	भजध्वम्
भजताम्	भजेताम्	भजन्ताम्

Potential mood (विधिलिङ्)

भजेय	भजेवहि	भजेमहि
भजेथा:	भजेयाथाम्	भजेध्वम्
भजेत	भजेयाताम्	भजेरन्

2p√bhā (√भा) to shine

Present Tense (लट्)

भामि	भाव:	भाम:
भासि	भाथ:	भाथ
भाति	भात:	भान्ति

Past Tense (लङ्)

अभाम्	अभाव	अभाम
अभा:	अभातम्	अभात
अभात्	अभाताम्	अभु:

Future Tense (लृट्)

भास्यामि	भास्याव:	भास्याम:
भास्यसि	भास्यथ:	भास्यथ
भास्यति	भास्यत:	भास्यन्ति

Imperative mood (लोट्)

भानि	भाव	भाम
भाहि	भातम्	भात
भातु	भाताम्	भान्तु

Potential mood (विधिलिङ्)

भायाम्	भायाव	भायाम
भाया:	भायातम्	भायात
भायात्	भायाताम्	भायु:

3p√bhī (√भी) to fear

Present Tense (लट्)

बिभेमि	बिभीव:	बिभीम:
बिभेषि	बिभीथ:	बिभीथ
बिभेति	बिभीत:	बिभ्यति

Past Tense (लङ्)

अबिभयम्	अबिभीव	अबिभीम

अबिभे:	अबिभीतम्	अबिभीत
अबिभेत्	अबिभीताम्	अबिभयु:

Future Tense (लृट्)

भेष्यामि	भेष्याव:	भेष्याम:
भेष्यसि	भेष्यथ:	भेष्यथ
भेष्यति	भेष्यत:	भेष्यन्ति

Imperative mood (लोट्)

बिभयानि	बिभयाव	बिभयाम
बिभिहि	बिभीतम्	बिभीत
बिभेतु	बिभिताम्	बिभ्यतु

Potential mood (विधिलिङ्)

बिभियाम्	बिभियाव	बिभियाम
बिभिया:	बिभियातम्	बिभियात
बिभियात्	बिभियाताम्	बिभियु:

7p√bhuj (√भुज्) to enjoy

Present Tense (लट्)

भुनज्मि	भुञ्व:	भुञ्ज्म:
भुनक्षि	भुङ्क्थ:	भुङ्क्थ
भुनक्ति	भुङ्क्त:	भुञ्जन्ति

Past Tense (लङ्)

अभुनजम्	अभुञ्ज्व	अभुञ्ज्म
अभुनक्	अभुङ्क्तम्	अभुङ्क्त
अभुनक्	अभुङ्क्ताम्	अभुञ्जन्

Future Tense (लृट्)

भोक्ष्यामि	भोक्ष्याव:	योक्ष्याम:
भोक्ष्यसि	भोक्ष्यथ:	भोक्ष्यथ
भोक्ष्यति	भोक्ष्यत:	भोक्ष्यन्ति

Imperative mood (लोट्)

भुनजानि	भुनजाव	भुनजाम
भुङ्ग्धि	भुङ्क्तम्	भुङ्क्त
भुनक्तु	भुङ्क्ताम्	भुञ्जन्तु

Potential mood (विधिलिङ्)

भुञ्ज्याम्	भुञ्ज्याव	भुञ्ज्याम
भुञ्ज्या:	भुञ्ज्यातम्	भुञ्ज्यात
भुञ्ज्यात्	भुञ्ज्याताम्	भुञ्ज्यु:

7a√bhuj (√भुज्) to enjoy

Present Tense (लट्)

भुञ्जे	भुञ्ज्वहे	भुञ्ज्महे
भुङ्क्षे	भुञ्जाथे	भुङ्ग्ध्वे
भुङ्क्ते	भुञ्जाते	भुञ्जते

Past Tense (लङ्)

अभुञ्जि	अभुञ्ज्वहि	अभुञ्ज्महि
अभुङ्क्था:	अभुञ्जाथाम्	अभुङ्ग्ध्वम्
अभुङ्क्त	अभुञ्जाताम्	अभुञ्जत

Future Tense (लृट्)

भोक्ष्ये	भोक्ष्यावहे	भोक्ष्यामहे
भोक्ष्यसे	भोक्ष्येथे	भोक्ष्यध्वे
भोक्ष्यते	भोक्ष्येते	भोक्ष्यन्ते

Imperative mood (लोट्)

भुनजै	भुनजावहै	भुनजामहै
भुङ्क्ष्व	भुञ्जाथाम्	भुङ्ग्ध्वम्
भुङ्क्ताम्	भुञ्जाताम्	भुञ्जन्ताम्

1p,ā√bhū (√भू) to become

see Appendix 1

3p√bhṛ (√भृ) to raise

Present Tense (लट्)

बिभर्मि	बिभृव:	बिभृम:
बिभर्षि	बिभृथ:	बिभृथ
बिभर्ति	बिभृत:	बिभ्रति

Past Tense (लङ्)

अबिभ्रम्	अबिभृव	अबिभृम
अबिभ:	अबिभृतम्	अबिभृत
अबिभ:	अबिभृताम्	अबिभरु:

Future Tense (लृट्)

भरिष्यामि	भरिष्याव:	भरिष्याम:
भरिष्यसि	भरिष्यथ:	भरिष्यथ
भरिष्यति	भरिष्यत:	भरिष्यन्ति

Imperative mood (लोट्)

बिभराणि	बिभराव	बिभराम
बिभृहि	बिभृतम्	बिभृत
बिभर्तु	बिभृताम्	बिभ्रतु

Potential mood (विधिलिङ्)

बिभृयाम्	बिभृयाव	बिभृयाम
बिभृया:	बिभृयातम्	बिभृयात
बिभृयात्	बिभृयाताम्	बिभृयु:

3a√bhṛ (√भृ) to raise

Present Tense (लट्)

बिभ्रे	बिभृवहे	बिभृमहे
बिभृषे	बिभ्राथे	बिभृध्वे
बिभृते	बिभ्राते	बिभ्रते

Past Tense (लङ्)

अबिभ्रि	अबिभृवहि	अबिभृमहि
अबिभृथा:	अबिभ्राथाम्	अबिभृध्वम्
अबिभृत	अबिभ्राताम्	अबिभ्रत

Future Tense (लृट्)

भरिष्ये	भरिष्यावहे	भरिष्यामहे
भरिष्यसे	भरिष्येथे	भरिष्यध्वे
भरिष्यते	भरिष्येते	भरिष्यन्ते

Imperative mood (लोट्)

बिभरै	बिभरावहै	बिभरामहै
बिभृष्व	बिभ्राथाम्	बिभृध्वम्
बिभृताम्	बिभ्राताम्	बिभ्रताम्

Potential mood (विधिलिङ्)

बिभ्रीय	बिभ्रीवहि	बिभ्रीमहि
बिभ्रीथा:	बिभ्रीयाथाम्	बिभ्रीध्वम्
बिभ्रीत	बिभ्रीयाताम्	बिभ्रीरन्

1p√bhram (√भ्रम्) to roam

Present Tense (लट्)

भ्रमामि	भ्रमाव:	भ्रमाम:
भ्रमसि	भ्रमथ:	भ्रमथ
भ्रमति	भ्रमत:	भ्रमन्ति

Present Tense (लट्)

भ्रम्यामि	भ्रम्याव:	भ्रम्याम:
भ्रम्यसि	भ्रम्यथ:	भ्रम्यथ

भ्रम्यति	भ्रम्यत:	भ्रम्यन्ति

Past Tense (लङ्)

अभ्रमम्	अभ्रमाव	अभ्रमाम
अभ्रम:	अभ्रमतम्	अभ्रमत
अभ्रमत्	अभ्रमताम्	अभ्रमन्

Past Tense (लङ्)

अभ्रम्यम्	अभ्रम्याव	अभ्रम्याम
अभ्रम्य:	अभ्रम्यतम्	अभ्रम्यत
अभ्रम्यत्	अभ्रम्यताम्	अभ्रम्यन्

Future Tense (लृट्)

भ्रमिष्यामि	भ्रमिष्याव:	भ्रमिष्याम:
भ्रमिष्यसि	भ्रमिष्यथ:	भ्रमिष्यथ
भ्रमिष्यति	भ्रमिष्यत:	भ्रमिष्यन्ति

Imperative mood (लोट्)

भ्रमाणि	भ्रमाव	भ्रमाम
भ्रम	भ्रमतम्	भ्रमत
भ्रमतु	भ्रमताम्	भ्रमन्तु

Imperative mood (लोट्)

भ्रम्याणि	भ्रम्याव	भ्रम्याम
भ्रम्य	भ्रम्यतम्	भ्रम्यत
भ्रम्यतु	भ्रम्यताम्	भ्रम्यन्तु

Potential mood (विधिलिङ्)

भ्रमेयम्	भ्रमेव	भ्रमेम
भ्रमे:	भ्रमेतम्	भ्रमेत
भ्रमेत्	भ्रमेताम्	भ्रमेयु:

Potential mood (विधिलिङ्)

भ्रम्येयम्	भ्रम्येव	भ्रम्येम
भ्रम्ये:	भ्रम्येतम्	भ्रम्येत
भ्रम्येत्	भ्रम्येताम्	भ्रम्येयु:

1√bhraṁs (√भ्रंस्) to perish

Present Tense (लट्)

भ्रंसे	भ्रंसावहे	भ्रंसामहे
भ्रंससे	भ्रंसेथे	भ्रंसध्वे
भ्रंसते	भ्रंसेते	भ्रंसन्ते

Past Tense (लङ्)

अभ्रंसे	अभ्रंसावहि	अभ्रंसामहि
अभ्रंसथा:	अभ्रंसेथाम्	अभ्रंसध्वम्
अभ्रंसत	अभ्रंसेताम्	अभ्रंसन्त

Future Tense (लृट्)

भ्रंसिष्ये	भ्रंसिष्यावहे	भ्रंसिष्यामहे
भ्रंसिष्यसे	भ्रंसिष्येथे	भ्रंसिष्यध्वे
भ्रंसिष्यते	भ्रंसिष्येते	भ्रंसिष्यन्ते

Imperative mood (लोट्)

भ्रंसै	भ्रंसावहै	भ्रंसामहै
भ्रंसस्व	भ्रंसेथाम्	भ्रंसध्वम्
भ्रंसताम्	भ्रंसेताम्	भ्रंसन्ताम्

Potential mood (विधिलिङ्)

भ्रंसेय	भ्रंसेवहि	भ्रंसेमहि
भ्रंसेथा:	भ्रंसेयाथाम्	भ्रंसेध्वम्
भ्रंसेत	भ्रंसेयाताम्	भ्रंसेरन्

8a√man (√मन्) to agree

Present Tense (लट्)

मन्वे	मन्वहे	मन्महे
मनुषे	मन्वाथे	मनुध्वे

मनुते	मन्वाते	मन्वते

Past Tense (लङ्)

अमन्वि	अमन्वहि	अमन्महि
अमनुथा:	अमन्वाथाम्	अमनुध्वम्
अमनुत	अमन्वाताम्	अमन्वत

Future Tense (लृट्)

मनिष्ये	मनिष्यावहे	मनिष्यामहे
मनिष्यसे	मनिष्येथे	मनिष्यध्वे
मनिष्यते	मनिष्येते	मनिष्यन्ते

Imperative mood (लोट्)

मनवै	मनवावहै	मनवामहै
मनुष्व	मन्वाथाम्	मनुध्वम्
मनुताम्	मन्वाताम्	मन्वताम्

Potential mood (विधिलिङ्)

मन्वीय	मन्वीवहि	मन्वीमहि
मन्वीथा:	मन्वीयाथाम्	मन्वीध्वम्
मन्वीत	मन्वीयाताम्	मन्वीरन्

6p√mil (√मिल्) to meet

Present Tense (लट्)

मिलामि	मिलाव:	मिलाम:
मिलसि	मिलथ:	मिलथ
मिलति	मिलत:	मिलन्ति

Past Tense (लङ्)

अमिलम्	अमिलाव	अमिलाम
अमिल:	अमिलतम्	अमिलत
अमिलत्	अमिलताम्	अमिलन्

Future Tense (लृट्)

मेलिष्यामि	मेलिष्याव:	मेलिष्याम:
मेलिष्यसि	मेलिष्यथ:	मेलिष्यथ
मेलिष्यति	मेलिष्यत:	मेलिष्यन्ति

Imperative mood (लोट्)

मिलानि	मिलाव	मिलाम
मिल	मिलतम्	मिलत
मिलतु	मिलताम्	मिलन्तु

Potential mood (विधिलिङ्)

मिलेयम्	मिलेव	मिलेम
मिले:	मिलेतम्	मिलेत
मिलेत्	मिलेताम्	मिलेयु:

6a√mil (√मिल्) to join

Present Tense (लट्)

मिले	मिलावहे	मिलामहे
मिलसे	मिलेथे	मिलध्वे
मिलते	मिलेते	मिलन्ते

Past Tense (लङ्)

अमिले	अमिलावहि	अमिलामहि
अमिलथा:	अमिलेथाम्	अमिलध्वम्
अमिलत	अमिलेताम्	अमिलन्त

Future Tense (लृट्)

मेलिष्ये	मेलिष्यावहे	मेलिष्यामहे
मेलिष्यसे	मेलिष्येथे	मेलिष्यध्वे
मेलिष्यते	मेलिष्येते	मेलिष्यन्ते

Imperative mood (लोट्)

मिलै	मिलावहै	मिलामहै
मिलस्व	मिलेथाम्	मिलध्वम्

मिलताम्	मिलेताम्	मिलन्ताम्

Potential mood (विधिलिङ्)

मिलेय	मिलेवहि	मिलेमहि
मिलेथा:	मिलेयाथाम्	मिलेध्वम्
मिलेत	मिलेयाताम्	मिलेरन्

6p√muñć (√मुञ्च्) to leave

Present Tense (लट्)

मुञ्चामि	मुञ्चाव:	मुञ्चाम:
मुञ्चसि	मुञ्चथ:	मुञ्चथ
मुञ्चति	मुञ्चत:	मुञ्चन्ति

Past Tense (लङ्)

अमुञ्चम्	अमुञ्चाव	अमुञ्चाम
अमुञ्च:	अमुञ्चतम्	अमुञ्चत
अमुञ्चत्	अमुञ्चताम्	अमुञ्चन्

Future Tense (लृट्)

मोक्ष्यामि	मोक्ष्याव:	मोक्ष्याम:
मोक्ष्यसि	मोक्ष्यथ:	मोक्ष्यथ
मोक्ष्यति	मोक्ष्यत:	मोक्ष्यन्ति

Imperative mood (लोट्)

मुञ्चानि	मुञ्चाव	मुञ्चाम
मुञ्च	मुञ्चतम्	मुञ्चत
मुञ्चतु	मुञ्चताम्	मुञ्चन्तु

Potential mood (विधिलिङ्)

मुञ्चेयम्	मुञ्चेव	मुञ्चेम
मुञ्चे:	मुञ्चेतम्	मुञ्चेत
मुञ्चेत्	मुञ्चेताम्	मुञ्चेयु:

6a√muñć (√मुञ्च्) to leave

Present Tense (लट्)

मुञ्चे	मुञ्चावहे	मुञ्चामहे
मुञ्चसे	मुञ्चेथे	मुञ्चध्वे
मुञ्चते	मुञ्चेते	मुञ्चन्ते

Past Tense (लङ्)

अमुञ्चे	अमुञ्चावहि	अमुञ्चामहि
अमुञ्चथा:	अमुञ्चेथाम्	अमुञ्चध्वम्
अमुञ्चत	अमुञ्चेताम्	अमुञ्चन्त

Future Tense (लृट्)

मोक्ष्ये	मोक्ष्यावहे	मोक्ष्यामहे
मोक्ष्यसे	मोक्ष्येथे	मोक्ष्यध्वे
मोक्ष्यते	मोक्ष्येते	मोक्ष्यन्ते

Imperative mood (लोट्)

मुञ्चै	मुञ्चावहै	मुञ्चामहै
मुञ्चस्व	मुञ्चेथाम्	मुञ्चध्वम्
मुञ्चताम्	मुञ्चेताम्	मुञ्चन्ताम्

Potential mood (विधिलिङ्)

मुञ्चेय	मुञ्चेवहि	मुञ्चेमहि
मुञ्चेथा:	मुञ्चेयाथाम्	मुञ्चेध्वम्
मुञ्चेत	मुञ्चेयाताम्	मुञ्चेरन्

6a√mṛ (√मृ) to die

(see section 24.6)

6a√mṛś (√मृश्) to touch

Present Tense (लट्)

मृशामि	मृशाव:	मृशाम:
मृशसि	मृशथ:	मृशथ
मृशति	मृशत:	मृशन्ति

Past Tense (लङ्)

अमृशम्	अमृशाव	अमृशाम
अमृश:	अमृशतम्	अमृशत
अमृशत्	अमृशताम्	अमृशन्

Future Tense (लृट्)

म्रक्ष्यामि	म्रक्ष्याव:	म्रक्ष्याम:
म्रक्ष्यसि	म्रक्ष्यथ:	म्रक्ष्यथ
म्रक्ष्यति	म्रक्ष्यत:	म्रक्ष्यन्ति

Imperative mood (लोट्)

मृशानि	मृशाव	मृशाम
मृश	मृशतम्	मृशत
मृशतु	मृशताम्	मृशन्तु

Potential mood (विधिलिङ्)

मृशेयम्	मृशेव	मृशेम
मृशे:	मृशेतम्	मृशेत
मृशेत्	मृशेताम्	मृशेयु:

1p√mlai (√म्लै) to fade

Present Tense (लट्)

म्लायामि	म्लायाव:	म्लायाम:
म्लायसि	म्लायथ:	म्लायथ
म्लायति	म्लायत:	म्लायन्ति

Past Tense (लङ्)

अम्लायम्	अम्लायाव	अम्लायाम
अम्लाय:	अम्लायतम्	अम्लायत
अम्लायत्	अम्लायताम्	अम्लायन्

Future Tense (लृट्)

म्लास्यामि	म्लास्याव:	म्लास्याम:
म्लास्यसि	म्लास्यथ:	म्लास्यथ
म्लास्यति	म्लास्यत:	म्लास्यन्ति

Imperative mood (लोट्)

म्लायानि	म्लायाव	म्लायाम
म्लाय	म्लायतम्	म्लायत
म्लायतु	म्लायताम्	म्लायन्तु

Potential mood (विधिलिङ्)

म्लायेयम्	म्लायेव	म्लायेम
म्लाये:	म्लायेतम्	म्लायेत
म्लायेत्	म्लायेताम्	म्लायेयु:

1p√yaj (√यज्) to worship

Present Tense (लट्)

यजामि	यजाव:	यजाम:
यजसि	यजथ:	यजथ
यजति	यजत:	यजन्ति

Past Tense (लङ्)

अयजम्	अयजाव	अयजाम
अयज:	अयजतम्	अयजत
अयजत्	अयजताम्	अयजन्

Future Tense (लृट्)

यक्ष्यामि	यक्ष्याव:	यक्ष्याम:
यक्ष्यसि	यक्ष्यथ:	यक्ष्यथ
यक्ष्यति	यक्ष्यत:	यक्ष्यन्ति

Imperative mood (लोट्)

यजानि	यजाव	यजाम
यज	यजतम्	यजत
यजतु	यजताम्	यजन्तु

Potential mood (विधिलिङ्)

यजेयम्	यजेव	यजेम
यजे:	यजेतम्	यजेत
यजेत्	यजेताम्	यजेयु:

1a√yaj (√यज्) to worship

Present Tense (लट्)

यजे	यजावहे	यजामहे
यजसे	यजेथे	यजध्वे
यजते	यजेते	यजन्ते

Past Tense (लङ्)

अयजे	अयजावहि	अयजामहि
अयजथा:	अयजेथाम्	वम्
अयजत	अयजेताम्	अयजन्त

Future Tense (लृट्)

यक्ष्ये	यक्ष्यावहे	यक्ष्यामहे
यक्ष्यसे	यक्ष्येथे	यक्ष्यध्वे
यक्ष्यते	यक्ष्येते	यक्ष्यन्ते

Imperative mood (लोट्)

यजै	यजावहै	यजामहै
यजस्व	यजेथाम्	यजध्वम्
यजताम्	यजेताम्	यजन्ताम्

Potential mood (विधिलिङ्)

यजेय	यजेवहि	यजेमहि
यजेथा:	यजेयाथाम्	यजेध्वम्
यजेत	यजेयाताम्	यजेरन्

2p√yā (√या) to attain

Present Tense (लट्)

यामि	याव:	याम:
यासि	याथ:	याथ
याति	यात:	यान्ति

Past Tense (लङ्)

अयाम्	अयाव	अयाम
अया:	अयातम्	अयात
अयात्	अयाताम्	अयु:

Future Tense (लृट्)

यास्यामि	यास्याव:	यास्याम:
यास्यसि	यास्यथ:	यास्यथ
यास्यति	यास्यत:	यास्यन्ति

Imperative mood (लोट्)

यानि	याव	याम
याहि	यातम्	यात
यातु	याताम्	यान्तु

Potential mood (विधिलिङ्)

ययाम्	ययाव	ययाम
याया:	यायातम्	यायात
यायात्	यायाताम्	यायु:

7p√yuj (√युज्) to join

Present Tense (लट्)

युनज्मि	यञ्व:	युञ्ज्म:
युनक्षि	युङ्क्थ:	युङ्क्थ

युनक्ति	युङ्क्तः	युञ्जन्ति

Past Tense (लङ्)

अयुनजम्	अयुञ्ज्व	अयुञ्ज्म
अयुनक्	अयुङ्क्तम्	अयुङ्क्त
अयुनक्	अयुङ्क्ताम्	अयुञ्जन्

Future Tense (लृट्)

योक्ष्यामि	योक्ष्यावः	योक्ष्यामः
योक्ष्यसि	योक्ष्यथः	योक्ष्यथ
योक्ष्यति	योक्ष्यतः	योक्ष्यन्ति

Imperative mood (लोट्)

युनजानि	युनजाव	युनजाम
युङ्ग्धि	युङ्क्तम्	युङ्क्त
युनक्तु	युङ्क्ताम्	युञ्जन्तु

Potential mood (विधिलिङ्)

युञ्ज्याम्	युञ्ज्याव	युञ्ज्याम
युञ्ज्याः	युञ्ज्यातम्	युञ्ज्यात
युञ्ज्यात्	युञ्ज्याताम्	युञ्ज्युः

7a√yuj (√युज्) to join

Present Tense (लट्)

युञ्जे	युञ्ज्वहे	युञ्ज्महे
युङ्क्षे	युञ्जाथे	युङ्गध्वे
युङ्क्ते	युञ्जाते	युञ्जते

Past Tense (लङ्)

अयुञ्जि	अयुञ्ज्वहि	अयुञ्ज्महि
अयुङ्क्थाः	अयुञ्जाथाम्	अयुङ्ग्ध्वम्
अयुङ्क्त	अयुञ्जाताम्	अयुञ्जत

Future Tense (लृट्)

योक्ष्ये	योक्ष्यावहे	योक्ष्यामहे
योक्ष्यसे	योक्ष्येथे	योक्ष्यध्वे
योक्ष्यते	योक्ष्येते	योक्ष्यन्ते

Imperative mood (लोट्)

युनजै	युनजावहै	युनजामहै
युङ्क्ष्व	युञ्जाथाम्	युङ्ग्ध्वम्
युङ्क्ताम्	युञ्जाताम्	युञ्जन्ताम्

Potential mood (विधिलिङ्)

युञ्जीय	युञ्जीवहि	युञ्जीमहि
युञ्जीथाः	युञ्जीयाथाम्	युञ्जीध्वम्
युञ्जीत	युञ्जीयाताम्	युञ्जीरन्

1p√raks̩ (√रक्ष्) to protect

Present Tense (लट्)

रक्षामि	रक्षावः	रक्षामः
रक्षसि	रक्षथः	रक्षथ
रक्षति	रक्षतः	रक्षन्ति

Past Tense (लङ्)

अरक्षम्	अरक्षाव	अरक्षाम
अरक्षः	अरक्षतम्	अरक्षत
अरक्षत्	अरक्षताम्	अरक्षन्

Future Tense (लृट्)

रक्षिष्यामि	रक्षिष्यावः	रक्षिष्यामः
रक्षिष्यसि	रक्षिष्यथः	रक्षिष्यथ
रक्षिष्यति	रक्षिष्यतः	रक्षिष्यन्ति

Imperative mood (लोट्)

रक्षाणि	रक्षाव	रक्षाम
रक्ष	रक्षतम्	रक्षत

रक्षतु	रक्षताम्	रक्षन्तु

Potential mood (विधिलिङ्)

रक्षेयम्	रक्षेव	रक्षेम
रक्षेः	रक्षेतम्	रक्षेत
रक्षेत्	रक्षेताम्	रक्षेयुः

1a√ram (√रम्) to entertain

Present Tense (लट्)

रमे	रमावहे	रमामहे
रमसे	रमेथे	रमध्वे
रमते	रमेते	रमन्ते

Past Tense (लङ्)

अरमे	अरमावहि	अरमामहि
अरमथाः	अरमेथाम्	अरमध्वम्
अरमत	अरमेताम्	अरमन्त

Future Tense (लृट्)

रमिष्ये	रमिष्यावहे	रमिष्यामहे
रमिष्यसे	रमिष्येथे	रमिष्यध्वे
रमिष्यते	रमिष्येते	रमिष्यन्ते

Imperative mood (लोट्)

रमै	रमावहै	रमामहै
रमस्व	रमेथाम्	रमध्वम्
रमताम्	रमेताम्	रमन्ताम्

Potential mood (विधिलिङ्)

रमेय	रमेवहि	रमेमहि
रमेथाः	रमेयाथाम्	रमेध्वम्
रमेत	रमेयाताम्	रमेरन्

1p√ram (वि√रम्) to retire

NOTE : when a prefix is attached, the *√ram* verb becomes *parasmaipadī*

Present Tense (लट्)

विरमामि	विरमावः	विरमामः
विरमसि	विरमथः	विरमथ
विरमति	विरमतः	विरमन्ति

Past Tense (लङ्)

अविरमम्	अविरमाव	अविरमाम
अविरमः	अविरमतम्	अविरमत
अविरमत्	अविरमताम्	अविरमन्

Future Tense (लृट्)

विरंस्यामि	विरंस्यावः	विरंस्यामः
विरंस्यसि	विरंस्यथः	विरंस्यथ
विरंस्यति	विरंस्यतः	विरंस्यन्ति

Imperative mood (लोट्)

विरमाणि	विरमाव	विरमाम
विरम	विरमतम्	विरमत
विरमतु	विरमताम्	विरमन्तु

Potential mood (विधिलिङ्)

विरमेयम्	विरमेव	विरमेम
विरमेः	विरमेतम्	विरमेत
विरमेत्	विरमेताम्	विरमेयुः

1a√ruć (√रुच्) to like

Present Tense (लट्)

रोचे	रोचावहे	रोचामहे
रोचसे	रोचेथे	रोचध्वे

रोचते	रोचेते	रोचन्ते

Past Tense (लङ्)

अरोचे	अरोचावहि	अरोचामहि
अरोचथा:	अरोचेथाम्	अरोचध्वम्
अरोचत	अरोचेताम्	अरोचन्त

Future Tense (लृट्)

रोचिष्ये	रोचिष्यावहे	रोचिष्यामहे
रोचिष्यसे	रोचिष्येथे	रोचिष्यध्वे
रोचिष्यते	रोचिष्येते	रोचिष्यन्ते

Imperative mood (लोट्)

रोचै	रोचावहै	रोचामहै
रोचस्व	रोचेथाम्	रोचध्वम्
रोचताम्	रोचेताम्	रोचन्ताम्

Potential mood (विधिलिङ्)

रोचेय	रोचेवहि	रोचेमहि
रोचेथा:	रोचेयाथाम्	रोचेध्वम्
रोचेत	रोचेयाताम्	रोचेरन्

2p√rud (√रुद्) to cry

Present Tense (लट्)

रोदिमि	रुदिव:	रुदिम:
रोदिषि	रुदिथ:	रुदिथ
रोदिति	रुदित:	रुदन्ति

Past Tense (लङ्)

अरोदिम्	अरुदिव	अरुदिम
अरोदि:	अरुदितम्	अरुदित
अरोदीत्	अरुदिताम्	अरुदन्

Future Tense (लृट्)

रोदिष्यामि	रोदिष्याव:	रोदिष्याम:
रोदिष्यसि	रोदिष्यथ:	रोदिष्यथ
रोदिष्यति	रोदिष्यत:	रोदिष्यन्ति

Imperative mood (लोट्)

रोदानि	रोदाव	रोदाम
रुदिहि	रुदितम्	रुदित
रोदितु	रुदिताम्	रुदन्तु

Potential mood (विधिलिङ्)

रुद्याम्	रुद्याव	रुद्याम
रुद्या:	रुद्याम्	रुद्यात
रुद्यात्	रुद्याताम्	रुद्यु:

7p√rudh (√रुध्) to resist

see section 24.7

1a√labh (√लभ्) to get

Present Tense (लट्)

लभे	लभावहे	लभामहे
लभसे	लभेथे	लभध्वे
लभते	लभेते	लभन्ते

Past Tense (लङ्)

अलभे	अलभावहि	अलभामहि
अलभथा:	अलभेथाम्	अलभध्वम्
अलभत	अलभेताम्	अलभन्त

Future Tense (लृट्)

लप्स्ये	लप्स्यावहे	लप्स्यामहे
लप्स्यसे	लप्स्येथे	लप्स्यध्वे
लप्स्यते	लप्स्येते	लप्स्यन्ते

Imperative mood (लोट्)

लभै	लभावहै	लभामहै
लभस्व	लभेथाम्	लभध्वम्
लभताम्	लभेताम्	लभन्ताम्

Potential mood (विधिलिङ्)

लभेय	लभेवहि	लभेमहि
लभेथा:	लभेयाथाम्	लभेध्वम्
लभेत	लभेयाताम्	लभेरन्

2p√lā (√ला) to bring

Present Tense (लट्)

लामि	लाव:	लाम:
लासि	लाथ:	लाथ
लाति	लात:	लान्ति

Past Tense (लङ्)

अलाम्	अलाव	अलाम
अला:	अलातम्	अलात
अलात्	अलाताम्	अलु:

Future Tense (लृट्)

लास्यामि	लास्याव:	लास्याम:
लास्यसि	लास्यथ:	लास्यथ
लास्यति	लास्यत:	लास्यन्ति

Imperative mood (लोट्)

लानि	लाव	लाम
लाहि	लातम्	लात
लातु	लाताम्	लान्तु

Potential mood (विधिलिङ्)

लायाम्	लायाव	लायाम
लाया:	लायातम्	लायात
लायात्	लायाताम्	लायु:

6p√likh (√लिख्) to write

Present Tense (लट्)

लिखामि	लिखाव:	लिखाम:
लिखसि	लिखथ:	लिखथ
लिखति	लिखत:	लिखन्ति

Past Tense (लङ्)

अलिखम्	अलिखाव	अलिखाम
अलिख:	अलिखतम्	अलिखत
अलिखत्	अलिखताम्	अलिखन्

Future Tense (लृट्)

लेखिष्यामि	लेखिष्याव:	लेखिष्याम:
लेखिष्यसि	लेखिष्यथ:	लेखिष्यथ
लेखिष्यति	लेखिष्यत:	लेखिष्यन्ति

Imperative mood (लोट्)

लिखानि	लिखाव	लिखाम
लिख	लिखतम्	लिखत
लिखतु	लिखताम्	लिखन्तु

Potential mood (विधिलिङ्)

लिखेयम्	लिखेव	लिखेम
लिखे:	लिखेतम्	लिखेत
लिखेत्	लिखेताम्	लिखेयु:

1p√vad (√वद्) to speak

Present Tense (लट्)

वदामि	वदाव:	वदाम:

वदसि	वदथ:	वदथ
वदति	वदत:	वदन्ति

Past Tense (लङ्)

अवदम्	अवदाव	अवदाम
अवद:	अवदतम्	अवदत
अवदत्	अवदताम्	अवदन्

Future Tense (लृट्)

वदिष्यामि	वदिष्याव:	वदिष्याम:
वदिष्यसि	वदिष्यथ:	वदिष्यथ
वदिष्यति	वदिष्यत:	वदिष्यन्ति

Imperative mood (लोट्)

वदानि	वदाव	वदाम
वद	वदतम्	वदत
वदतु	वदताम्	वदन्तु

Potential mood (विधिलिङ्)

वदेयम्	वदेव	वदेम
वदे:	वदेतम्	वदेत
वदेत्	वदेताम्	वदेयु:

6a ud√vij (उद्√विज्) to bother

Present Tense (लट्)

उद्विजे	उद्विजावहे	उद्विजामहे
उद्विजसे	उद्विजेथे	उद्विजध्वे
उद्विजते	उद्विजेते	उद्विजन्ते

Past Tense (लङ्)

उदविजे	उदविजावहि	उदविजामहि
उदविजथा:	उदविजेथाम्	उदविजध्वम्
उदविजत	उदविजेताम्	उदविजन्त

Future Tense (लृट्)

उद्विजिष्ये	उद्विजिष्यावहे	उद्विजिष्यामहे
उद्विजिष्यसे	उद्विजिष्येथे	उद्विजिष्यध्वे
उद्विजिष्यते	उद्विजिष्येते	उद्विजिष्यन्ते

Imperative mood (लोट्)

उद्विजै	उद्विजावहै	उद्विजामहै
उद्विजस्व	उद्विजेथाम्	उद्विजध्वम्
उद्विजताम्	उद्विजेताम्	उद्विजन्ताम्

Potential mood (विधिलिङ्)

उद्विजेय	उद्विजावहि	उद्विजामहि
उद्विजेथा:	उद्विजेयाथाम्	उद्विजेध्वम्
उद्विजेत	उद्विजेयाताम्	उद्विजेरन्

2p√vid (√विद्) to know

Present Tense (लट्)

वेद	विद्व	विद्म ।	वेद्मि	विद्व:	विद्म:
वेत्थ	विदथु:	विद ।	वेत्सि	वित्थ:	वित्थ
वेद	विदतु:	विदु: ।	वेत्ति	वित्त:	विदन्ति

Past Tense (लङ्)

अवेदम्	अविद्व	अविद्म
अवे:	अवित्तम्	अवित्त
अवेत्	अवित्ताम्	अविदु:

Future Tense (लृट्)

वेदिष्यामि	वेदिष्याव:	वेदिष्याम:
वेदिष्यसि	वेदिष्यथ:	वेदिष्यथ
वेदिष्यति	वेदिष्यत	वेदिष्यन्ति

Imperative mood (लोट्)

विदाङ्करवाणि	विदाङ्करवाव	विदाङ्करवाम

विदाङ्कुरु विदाङ्कुरुतम् विदाङ्कुरुत

विदाङ्करोतु विदाङ्कुरुताम् विदाङ्कुर्वन्तु

Potential mood (विधिलिङ्)

विद्याम्	विद्याव	विद्याम
विद्याः	विद्यातम्	विद्यात
विद्यात्	विद्याताम्	विद्युः

4a√vid (√विद्) to stay

Present Tense (लट्)

विद्ये	विद्यावहे	विद्यामहे
विद्यसे	विद्येथे	विद्यध्वे
विद्यते	विद्येते	विद्यन्ते

Past Tense (लङ्)

अविद्ये	अविद्यावहि	अविद्यामहि
अविद्यथाः	अविद्येथाम्	अविद्यध्वम्
अविद्यत	अविद्येताम्	अविद्यन्त

Future Tense (लृट्)

वेत्स्ये	वेत्स्यावहे	वेत्स्यामहे
वेत्स्यसे	वेत्स्येथे	वेत्स्यध्वे
वेत्स्यते	वेत्स्येते	वेत्स्यन्ते

Imperative mood (लोट्)

विद्यै	विद्यावहै	विद्यामहै
विद्यस्व	विद्येथाम्	विद्यध्वम्
विद्यताम्	विद्येताम्	विद्यन्ताम्

Potential mood (विधिलिङ्)

विद्येय	विद्येवहि	विद्येमहि
विद्येथाः	विद्येयाथाम्	विद्येध्वम्
विद्येत	विद्येयाताम्	विद्येरन्

6p√vid (√विद्) to attain

Present Tense (लट्)

विन्दामि	विन्दावः	विन्दामः
विन्दसि	विन्दथः	विन्दथ
विन्दति	विन्दतः	विन्दन्ति

Past Tense (लङ्)

अविन्दम्	अविन्दाव	अविन्दाम
अविन्दः	अविन्दतम्	अविन्दत
अविन्दत्	अविन्दताम्	अविन्दन्

Future Tense (लृट्)

वेत्स्यामि	वेत्स्यावः	वेत्स्यामः
वेत्स्यसि	वेत्स्यथः	वेत्स्यथ
वेत्स्यति	वेत्स्यतः	वेत्स्यन्ति

Imperative mood (लोट्)

विन्दानि	विन्दाव	विन्दाम
विन्द	विन्दतम्	विन्दत
विन्दतु	विन्दताम्	विन्दन्तु

Potential mood (विधिलिङ्)

विन्देयम्	विन्देव	विन्देम
विन्देः	विन्देतम्	विन्देत
विन्देत्	विन्देताम्	विन्देयुः

6a√vid (√विद्) to attain

Present Tense (लट्)

विन्दे	विन्दावहे	विन्दामहे
विन्दसे	विन्देथे	विन्दध्वे
विन्दते	विन्देते	विन्दन्ते

Past Tense (लङ्)

अविन्दे	अविन्दावहि	अविन्दामहि

अविन्दथा:	अविन्देथाम्	अविन्दध्वम्
अविन्दत	अविन्देताम्	अविन्दन्त

Future Tense (लृट्)

वेत्स्ये	वेत्स्यावहे	वेत्स्यामहे
वेत्स्यसे	वेत्स्येथे	वेत्स्यध्वे
वेत्स्यते	वेत्स्येते	वेत्स्यन्ते

Imperative mood (लोट्)

विन्दै	विन्दावहै	विन्दामहै
विन्दस्व	विन्देथाम्	विन्दध्वम्
विन्दताम्	विन्देताम्	विन्दन्ताम्

Potential mood (विधिलिङ्)

विन्देय	विन्देवहि	विन्देमहि
विन्देथा:	विन्देयाथाम्	विन्देध्वम्
विन्देत	विन्देयाताम्	विन्देरन्

7a√vid (√विद्) to think

Present Tense (लट्)

विन्दे	विन्द्वहे	विन्द्महे
विन्त्से	विन्दाथे	विन्दध्वे
विन्ते	विन्दाते	विन्दते

Past Tense (लङ्)

अविन्दि	अविन्द्वहि	अविन्द्महि
अविन्त्था:	अविन्दाथाम्	अविन्द्ध्वम्
अविन्त	अविन्दाताम्	अविन्दन्त

Future Tense (लृट्)

वेत्स्ये	वेत्स्यावहे	वेत्स्यामहे
वेत्स्यसे	वेत्स्येथे	वेत्स्यध्वे
वेत्स्यते	वेत्स्येते	वेत्स्यन्ते

Imperative mood (लोट्)

विनदै	विनदावहै	विनदामहै
विन्त्स्व	विन्दाथाम्	विन्द्ध्वम्
विन्ताम्	विन्दाताम्	विन्दताम्

Potential mood (विधिलिङ्)

विन्दीय	विन्दीवहि	विन्दीमहि
विन्दीथा:	विन्दीयाथाम्	विन्दीध्वम्
विन्दीत	विन्दीयाताम्	विन्दीरन्

10a√vid (√विद्) to say

Present Tense (लट्)

वेदये	वेदयावहे	वेदयामहे
वेदयसे	वेदयेथे	वेदयध्वे
वेदयते	वेदयेते	वेदयन्ते

Past Tense (लङ्)

अवेदये	अवेदयावहि	अवेदयामहि
अवेदयथा:	अवेदयेथाम्	अवेदयध्वम्
अवेदयत	अवेदयेताम्	अवेदयन्त

Future Tense (लृट्)

वेदयिष्ये	वेदयिष्यावहे	वेदयिष्यामहे
वेदयिष्यसे	वेदयिष्येथे	वेदयिष्यध्वे
वेदयिष्यते	वेदयिष्येते	वेदयिष्यन्ते

Imperative mood (लोट्)

वेदयै	वेदयावहै	वेदयामहै
वेदयस्व	वेदयेथाम्	वेदयध्वम्
वेदयताम्	वेदयताम्	वेदयन्ताम्

Potential mood (विधिलिङ्)

वेदयेय	वेदयेवहि	वेदयेमहि
वेदयेथा:	वेदयेयाथाम्	वेदयेध्वम्
वेदयेत	वेदयेयाताम्	वेदयेरन्

6p√viś (√विश्) to enter

Present Tense (लट्)

विशामि	विशाव:	विशाम:
विशसि	विशथ:	विशथ
विशति	विशत:	विशन्ति

Past Tense (लङ्)

अविशम्	अविशाव	अविशाम
अविश:	अविशतम्	अविशत
अविशत्	अविशताम्	अविशन्

Future Tense (लृट्)

वेक्ष्यामि	वेक्ष्याव:	वेक्ष्याम:
वेक्ष्यसि	वेक्ष्यथ:	वेक्ष्यथ
वेक्ष्यति	वेक्ष्यत:	वेक्ष्यन्ति

Imperative mood (लोट्)

विशानि	विशाव	विशाम
विश	विशतम्	विशत
विशतु	विशताम्	विशन्तु

Potential mood (विधिलिङ्)

विशेयम्	विशेव	विशेम
विशे:	विशेतम्	विशेत
विशेत्	विशेताम्	विशेयु:

9p√vṛ (√वृ) to accept

Present Tense (लट्)

वृणामि	वृणीव:	वृणीम:
वृणासि	वृणीथ:	वृणीथ
वृणाति	वृणीत:	वृणन्ति

Past Tense (लङ्)

अवृणाम्	अवृणीव	अवृणीम
अवृणा:	अवृणीतम्	अवृणीत
अवृणात्	अवृणीताम्	अवृणन्

Future Tense (लृट्)

वरिष्यामि	वरिष्याव:	वरिष्याम:
वरिष्यसि	वरिष्यथ:	वरिष्यथ
वरिष्यति	वरिष्यत:	वरिष्यन्ति

Imperative mood (लोट्)

वृणानि	वृणाव	वृणाम
वृणीहि	वृणीतम्	वृणीत
वृणातु	वृणीताम्	वृणन्तु

Potential mood (विधिलिङ्)

वृणीयाम्	वृणीयाव	वृणीयाम
वृणीया:	वृणीयाताम्	वृणीयात
वृणीयात्	वृणीयाताम्	वृणीयु:

9a√vṛ (√वृ) to accept

Present Tense (लट्)

वृणे	वृणीवहे	वृणीमहे
वृणीषे	वृणीथे	वृणीध्वे
वृणीते	वृणाते	वृणते

Past Tense (लङ्)

अवृणि	अवृणीवहि	अवृणीमहि
अवृणीथा:	अवृणाथाम्	अवृणीध्वम्
अवृणीत	अवृणाताम्	अवृणत

Future Tense (लृट्)

वरिष्ये	वरिष्यावहे	वरिष्यामहे

वरिष्यसे	वरिष्येथे	वरिष्यध्वे
वरिष्यते	वरिष्येते	वरिष्यन्ते

Imperative mood (लोट्)

वृणै	वृणावहै	वृणामहै
वृणीष्व	वृणाथाम्	वृणीध्वम्
वृणीताम्	वृणाताम्	वृणताम्

Potential mood (विधिलिङ्)

वृणीय	वृणीवहि	वृणीमहि
वृणीथाः	वृणीयाथाम्	वृणीध्वम्
वृणीत	वृणीयाताम्	वृणीरन्

1a√vṛt (√वृत्) to stay

Present Tense (लट्)

वर्ते	वर्तावहे	वर्तामहे
वर्तसे	वर्तेथे	वर्तध्वे
वर्तते	वर्तेते	वर्तन्ते

Past Tense (लङ्)

अवर्ते	अवर्तावहि	अवर्तामहि
अवर्तथाः	अवर्तेथाम्	अवर्तध्वम्
अवर्तत	अवर्तेताम्	अवर्तन्त

Future Tense (लृट्)

वर्तिष्ये	वर्तिष्यावहे	वर्तिष्यामहे
वर्तिष्यसे	वर्तिष्येथे	वर्तिष्यध्वे
वर्तिष्यते	वर्तिष्येते	वर्तिष्यन्ते

Imperative mood (लोट्)

वर्तै	वर्तावहै	वर्तामहै
वर्तस्व	वर्तेथाम्	वर्तध्वम्
वर्तताम्	वर्तेताम्	वर्तन्ताम्

Potential mood (विधिलिङ्)

वर्तेय	वर्तेवहि	वर्तेमहि
वर्तेथाः	वर्तेयाथाम्	वर्तेध्वम्
वर्तेत	वर्तेयाताम्	वर्तेरन्

1p√vraj (√व्रज्) to go

Present Tense (लट्)

व्रजामि	व्रजावः	व्रजामः
व्रजसि	व्रजथः	व्रजथ
व्रजति	व्रजतः	व्रजन्ति

Past Tense (लङ्)

अव्रजम्	अव्रजाव	अव्रजाम
अव्रजः	अव्रजतम्	अव्रजत
अव्रजत्	अव्रजताम्	अव्रजन्

Future Tense (लृट्)

व्रजिष्यामि	व्रजिष्यावः	व्रजिष्यामः
व्रजिष्यसि	व्रजिष्यथः	व्रजिष्यथ
व्रजिष्यति	व्रजिष्यतः	व्रजिष्यन्ति

Imperative mood (लोट्)

व्रजानि	व्रजाव	व्रजाम
व्रज	व्रजतम्	व्रजदत
व्रजतु	व्रजताम्	व्रजन्तु

Potential mood (विधिलिङ्)

व्रजेयम्	व्रजेव	व्रजेम
व्रजेः	व्रजेतम्	व्रजेत
व्रजेत्	व्रजेताम्	व्रजेयुः

1p√vah (√वह्) to carry

Present Tense (लट्)

वहामि	वहाव:	वहाम:
वहसि	वहथ:	वहथ
वहति	वहत:	वहन्ति

Past Tense (लङ्)

अवहम्	अवहाव	अवहाम
अवह:	अवहतम्	अवहत
अवहत्	अवहताम्	अवहन्

Future Tense (लृट्)

वक्ष्यामि	वक्ष्याव:	वक्ष्याम:
वक्ष्यसि	वक्ष्यथ:	वक्ष्यथ
वक्ष्यति	वक्ष्यत:	वक्ष्यन्ति

Imperative mood (लोट्)

वहानि	वहाव	वहाम
वह	वहतम्	वहत
वहतु	वहताम्	वहन्तु

Potential mood (विधिलिङ्)

वहेयम्	वहेव	वहेम
वहे:	वहेतम्	वहेत
वहेत्	वहेताम्	वहेयु:

1a√vah (√वह्) to carry

Present Tense (लट्)

वहे	वहावहे	वहामहे
वहसे	वहेथे	वहध्वे
वहते	वहेते	वहन्ते

Past Tense (लङ्)

अवहे	अवहावहि	अवहामहि
अवहथा:	अवहेथाम्	अवहध्वम्
अवहत	अवहेताम्	अवहन्त

Future Tense (लृट्)

वक्ष्ये	वक्ष्यावहे	वक्ष्यामहे
वक्ष्यसे	वक्ष्येथे	वक्ष्यध्वे
वक्ष्यते	वक्ष्येते	वक्ष्यन्ते

Imperative mood (लोट्)

वहै	वहावहै	वहामहै
वहस्व	वहेथाम्	वहध्वम्
वहताम्	वहेताम्	वहन्ताम्

Potential mood (विधिलिङ्)

वहेय	वहेवहि	वहेमहि
वहेथा:	वहेयाथाम्	वहेध्वम्
वहेत	वहेयाताम्	वहेरन्

1p√śuć (√शुच्) to grieve

Present Tense (लट्)

शोचामि	शोचाव:	शोचाम:
शोचसि	शोचथ:	शोचथ
शोचति	शोचत:	शोचन्ति

Past Tense (लङ्)

अशोचम्	अशोचाव	अशोचाम
अशोच:	अशोचतम्	अशोचत
अशोचत्	अशोचताम्	अशोचन्

Future Tense (लृट्)

शोचिष्यामि	शोचिष्याव:	शोचिष्याम:
शोचिष्यसि	शोचिष्यथ:	शोचिष्यथ

शोचिष्यति	शोचिष्यत:	शोचिष्यन्ति

Imperative mood (लोट्)

शोचानि	शोचाव	शोचाम
शोच	शोचतम्	शोचत
शोचतु	शोचाम्	शोचन्तु

Potential mood (विधिलिङ्)

शोचेयम्	शोचेव	शोचेम
शोचे:	शोचेतम्	शोचेत
शोचेत्	शोचेताम्	शोचेयु:

1a√śubh (√शुभ्) to look good

Present Tense (लट्)

शोभे	शोभावहे	शोभामहे
शोभसे	शोभेथे	शोभध्वे
शोभते	शोभेते	शोभन्ते

Past Tense (लङ्)

अशोभे	अशोभावहि	अशोभामहि
अशोभथा:	अशोभेथाम्	अशोभध्वम्
अशोभत	अशोभेताम्	अशोभन्त

Future Tense (लृट्)

शोभिष्ये	शोभिष्यावहे	शोभिष्यामहे
शोभिष्यसे	शोभिष्येथे	शोभिष्यध्वे
शोभिष्यते	शोभिष्येते	शोभिष्यन्ते

Imperative mood (लोट्)

शोभै	शोभावहै	शोभामहै
शोभस्व	शोभेथाम्	शोभध्वम्
शोभताम्	शोभेताम्	शोभन्ताम्

Potential mood (विधिलिङ्)

शोभेय	शोभेवहि	शोभेमहि
शोभेथा:	शोभेयाथाम्	शोभेध्वम्
शोभेत	शोभेयाताम्	शोभेरन्

4p√śuṣ (√शुष्) to dry

Present Tense (लट्)

शुष्यामि	शुष्याव:	शुष्याम:
शुष्यसि	शुष्यथ:	शुष्यथ
शुष्यति	शुष्यत:	शुष्यन्ति

Past Tense (लङ्)

अशुष्यम्	अशुष्याव	अशुष्याम
अशुष्य:	अशुष्यतम्	अशुष्यत
अशुष्यत्	अशुष्यताम्	अशुष्यन्

Future Tense (लृट्)

शोक्ष्यामि	शोक्ष्याव:	शोक्ष्याम:
शोक्ष्यसि	शोक्ष्यथ:	शोक्ष्यथ
शोक्ष्यति	शोक्ष्यत:	शोक्ष्यन्ति

Imperative mood (लोट्)

शुष्याणि	शुष्याव	शुष्याम
शुष्य	शुष्यतम्	शुष्यत
शुष्यतु	शुष्यताम्	शुष्यन्तु

Potential mood (विधिलिङ्)

शुष्येयम्	शुष्येव	शुष्येम
शुष्ये:	शुष्येतम्	शुष्येत
शुष्येत्	शुष्येताम्	शुष्येयु:

1p√śru (√श्रु) to hear

Present Tense (लट्)

शृणोमि	शृणुव:	शृणुम:
शृणोसि	शृणुथ:	शृणुथ
शृणोति	शृणुत:	शृण्वन्ति

Past Tense (लङ्)

अशृणवम्	अशृणुव	अशृणुम
अशृणो:	अशृणुतम्	अशृणुत
अशृणोत्	अशृणुताम्	अशृण्वन्

Future Tense (लृट्)

श्रोष्यामि	श्रोष्याव:	श्रोष्याम:
श्रोष्यसि	श्रोष्यथ:	श्रोष्यथ
श्रोष्यति	श्रोष्यत:	श्रोष्यन्ति

Imperative mood (लोट्)

शृणवानि	शृणवाव	शृणवाम
शृणु	शृणुतम्	शृणुत
शृणोतु	शृणुताम्	शृण्वन्तु

Potential mood (विधिलिङ्)

शृणुयाम्	शृणुयाव	शृणुयाम
शृणुया:	शृणुयातम्	शृणुयात
शृणुयात्	शृणयाताम्	शृणुयु:

6p√sad (√सद्) to sadden

Present Tense (लट्)

सीदामि	सीदाव:	सीदाम:
सीदसि	सीदथ:	सीदथ
सीदति	सीदत:	सीदन्ति

Past Tense (लङ्)

असीदम्	असीदाव	असीदाम
असीद:	असीदतम्	असीदत
असीदत्	असीदताम्	असीदन्

Future Tense (लृट्)

सत्स्यामि	सत्स्याव:	सत्स्याम:
सत्स्यसि	सत्स्यथ:	सत्स्यथ
सत्स्यति	सत्स्यत:	सत्स्यन्ति

Imperative mood (लोट्)

सीदानि	सीदाव	सीदाम
सीद	सीदतम्	सीदत
सीदतु	सीदताम्	सीदन्तु

Potential mood (विधिलिङ्)

सीदेयम्	सीदेव	सीदेम
सीदे:	सीदेतम्	सीदेत
सीदेत्	सीदेताम्	सीदेयु:

5p√su (√सु) to bathe

see section 24.5

4a√sū (√सू) to deliver

Present Tense (लट्)

सूये	सूयावहे	सूयामहे
सूयसे	सूयेथे	सूयध्वे
सूयते	सूयेते	सूयन्ते

Past Tense (लङ्)

असूये	असूयावहि	असूयामहि
असूयथा:	असूयेथाम्	असूयध्वम्
असूयत	असूयेताम्	असूयन्त

Future Tense (लृट्)

सविष्ये	सविष्यावहे	सविष्यामहे

सविष्यसे	सविष्येथे	सविष्यध्वे
सविष्यते	सविष्येते	सविष्यन्ते

Imperative mood (लोट्)

सूयै	सूयावहै	सूयामहै
सूयस्व	सूयेथाम्	सूयध्वम्
सूयताम्	सूयेताम्	सूयन्ताम्

Potential mood (विधिलिङ्)

सूयेय	सूयेवहि	सूयेमहि
सूयेथा:	सूयेयाथाम्	सूयेध्वम्
सूयेत	सूयेयाताम्	सूयेरन्

4a√sṛj (√सृज्) to produce

Present Tense (लट्)

सृज्ये	सृज्यावहे	सृज्यामहे
सृज्यसे	सृज्येथे	सृज्यध्वे
सृज्यते	सृज्येते	सृज्यन्ते

Past Tense (लङ्)

असृज्ये	असृज्यावहि	असृज्यामहि
असृज्यथा:	असृज्येथाम्	अबुध्यध्वम्
असृज्यत	असृज्येताम्	असृज्यन्त

Future Tense (लृट्)

स्रक्ष्ये	स्रक्ष्यावहे	स्रक्ष्यामहे
स्रक्ष्यसे	स्रक्ष्येथे	स्रक्ष्यध्वे
स्रक्ष्यते	स्रक्ष्येते	स्रक्ष्यन्ते

Imperative mood (लोट्)

सृज्यै	सृज्यावहै	सृज्यामहै
सृज्यस्व	सृज्येथाम्	सृज्यध्वम्
सृज्यताम्	सृज्येताम्	सृज्यन्ताम्

Potential mood (विधिलिङ्)

सृज्येय	सृज्येवहि	सृज्येमहि
सृज्येथा:	सृज्येयाथाम्	सृज्येध्वम्
सृज्येत	सृज्येयाताम्	सृज्येरन्

1p√sthā (√स्था) to stay

Present Tense (लट्)

तिष्ठामि	तिष्ठाव:	तिष्ठाम:
तिष्ठसि	तिष्ठथ:	तिष्ठथ
तिष्ठति	तिष्ठत:	तिष्ठन्ति

Past Tense (लङ्)

अतिष्ठम्	अतिष्ठाव	अतिष्ठाम
अतिष्ठ:	अतिष्ठतम्	अतिष्ठत
अतिष्ठत्	अतिष्ठताम्	अतिष्ठन्

Future Tense (लृट्)

स्थास्यामि	स्थास्याव:	स्थास्याम:
स्थास्यसि	स्थास्यथ:	स्थास्यथ
स्थास्यति	स्थास्यत:	स्थास्यन्ति

Imperative mood (लोट्)

तिष्ठानि	तिष्ठाव	तिष्ठाम
तिष्ठ	तिष्ठतम्	तिष्ठत
तिष्ठतु	तिष्ठताम्	तिष्ठन्तु

Potential mood (विधिलिङ्)

तिष्ठेयम्	तिष्ठेव	तिष्ठेम
तिष्ठे:	तिष्ठेतम्	तिष्ठेत
तिष्ठेत्	तिष्ठेताम्	तिष्ठेयु:

1a√sthā (√स्था) to stay

Present Tense (लट्)

तिष्ठे	तिष्ठावहे	तिष्ठामहे
तिष्ठसे	तिष्ठेथे	तिष्ठध्वे
तिष्ठते	तिष्ठेते	तिष्ठन्ते

Past Tense (लङ्)

अतिष्ठे	अतिष्ठावहि	अतिष्ठामहि
अतिष्ठथा:	अतिष्ठेथाम्	अतिष्ठध्वम्
अतिष्ठत	अतिष्ठेताम्	अतिष्ठन्त

Future Tense (लृट्)

स्थास्ये	स्थास्यावहे	स्थास्यामहे
स्थास्यसे	स्थास्येथे	स्थास्यध्वे
स्थास्यते	स्थास्येते	स्थास्यन्ते

Imperative mood (लोट्)

तिष्ठै	तिष्ठावहै	तिष्ठामहै
तिष्ठस्व	तिष्ठेथाम्	तिष्ठध्वम्
तिष्ठताम्	तिष्ठेताम्	तिष्ठन्ताम्

Potential mood (विधिलिङ्)

तिष्ठेय	तिष्ठेवहि	तिष्ठेमहि
तिष्ठेथा:	तिष्ठेयाथाम्	तिष्ठेध्वम्
तिष्ठेत	तिष्ठेयाताम्	तिष्ठेरन्

1p√snā (√स्ना) to bathe

Present Tense (लट्)

स्नामि	स्नाव:	स्नाम:
स्नासि	स्नाथ:	स्नाथ
स्नाति	स्नात:	स्नान्ति

Past Tense (लङ्)

अस्नाम्	अस्नाव	अस्नाम
अस्ना:	अस्नातम्	अस्नात
अस्नात्	अस्नाताम्	अस्नान्

Future Tense (लृट्)

स्नास्यामि	स्नास्याव:	स्नास्याम:
स्नास्यसि	स्नास्यथ:	स्नास्यथ
स्नास्यति	स्नास्यत:	स्नास्यन्ति

Imperative mood (लोट्)

स्नानि	स्नाव	स्नाम
स्नहि	स्नातम्	स्नात
स्नातु	स्नाताम्	स्नान्तु

Potential mood (विधिलिङ्)

स्नायाम्	स्नायाव	स्नायाम
स्नाया:	स्नायातम्	स्नायात
स्नायात्	स्नायाताम्	स्नायु:

1a√sraṁs (√स्रंस्) to fall

Present Tense (लट्)

स्रंसे	स्रंसावहे	स्रंसामहे
स्रंससे	स्रंसेथे	स्रंसध्वे
स्रंसते	स्रंसेते	स्रंसन्ते

Past Tense (लङ्)

अस्रंसे	अस्रंसावहि	अस्रंसामहि
अस्रंसथा:	अस्रंसेथाम्	अस्रंसध्वम्
अस्रंसत	अस्रंसेताम्	अस्रंसन्त

Future Tense (लृट्)

स्रंसिष्ये	स्रंसिष्यावहे	स्रंसिष्यामहे
स्रंसिष्यसे	स्रंसिष्येथे	स्रंसिष्यध्वे
स्रंसिष्यते	स्रंसिष्येते	स्रंसिष्यन्ते

Imperative mood (लोट्)

स्रंसै	स्रंसावहै	स्रंसामहै
स्रंसस्व	स्रंसेथाम्	स्रंसध्वम्
स्रंसताम्	स्रंसेताम्	स्रंसन्ताम्

Potential mood (विधिलिङ्)

स्रंसेय	स्रंसेवहि	स्रंसेमहि
स्रंसेथा:	स्रंसेयाथाम्	स्रंसेध्वम्
स्रंसेत	स्रंसेयाताम्	स्रंसेरन्

2p√han (√हन्) to kill

Present Tense (लट्)

हन्मि	हन्व:	हन्म:
हंसि	हथ:	हथ
हन्ति	हत:	घ्नन्ति

Past Tense (लङ्)

अहनम्	अहन्व	अहन्म
अहन्	अहतम्	अहत
अहन्	अहताम्	अघ्नन्

Future Tense (लृट्)

हनिष्यामि	हनिष्याव:	हनिष्याम:
हनिष्यसि	हनिष्यथ:	हनिष्यथ
हनिष्यति	हनिष्यत:	हनिष्यन्ति

Imperative mood (लोट्)

हनानि	हनाव	हनाम
जहि	हतम्	हत
हन्तु	हताम्	घ्नन्तु

Potential mood (विधिलिङ्)

हन्याम्	हन्याव	हन्याम

हन्या:	हन्यातम्	हन्यात
हन्यात्	हन्याताम्	हन्यु:

1p√has (√हस्) to laugh

Present Tense (लट्)

हसामि	हसाव:	हसाम:
हससि	हसथ:	हसथ
हसति	हसत:	हसन्ति

Past Tense (लङ्)

अहसम्	अहसाव	अहसाम
अहस:	अहसतम्	अहसत
अहसत्	अहसताम्	अहसन्

Future Tense (लृट्)

हसिष्यामि	हसिष्याव:	हसिष्याम:
हसिष्यसि	हसिष्यथ:	हसिष्यथ
हसिष्यति	हसिष्यत:	हसिष्यन्ति

Imperative mood (लोट्)

हसानि	हसाव	हसाम
हस	हसतम्	हसत
हसतु	हसताम्	हसन्तु

Potential mood (विधिलिङ्)

हसेयम्	हसेव	हसेम
हसे:	हसेतम्	हसेत
हसेत्	हसेताम्	हसेयु:

3p√hā (√हा) to renounce

Present Tense (लट्)

जहामि	जहिव:	जहिम:

जहासि	जहिथ:	जहिथ
जहाति	जहित:	जहति

Past Tense (लङ्)

अजहाम्	अजहीव	अजहीम
अजहा:	अजहीतम्	अजहीत
अजहात्	अजहीताम्	अजहु:

Future Tense (लृट्)

हास्यामि	हास्याव:	हास्याम:
हास्यसि	हास्यथ:	हास्यथ
हास्यति	हास्यत:	हास्यन्ति

Imperative mood (लोट्)

जहानि	जहाव	जहाम
जहीहि	जहीतम्	जहीत
जहातु	जहिताम्	जहतु

Potential mood (विधिलिङ्)

जह्याम्	जह्याव	जह्याम
जह्या:	जह्यातम्	जह्यात
जह्यात्	जह्याताम्	जह्यु:

7p√hiṁs (√हिंस्) to injure

Present Tense (लट्)

हिनस्मि	हिंस्व:	हिंस्म:
हिनस्सि	हिंस्थ:	हिंस्थ
हिनस्ति	हिंस्त:	हिंसन्ति

Past Tense (लङ्)

अहिनसम्	अहिंस्व	अहिंस्म
अहिन:	अहिंस्तम्	अहिंस्त
अहिनत्	अहिंस्ताम्	अहिंसन्

Future Tense (लृट्)

हिंसिष्यामि	हिंसिष्याव:	हिंसिष्याम:
हिंसिष्यसि	हिंसिष्यथ:	हिंसिष्यथ
हिंसिष्यति	हिंसिष्यत:	हिंसिष्यन्ति

Imperative mood (लोट्)

हिनसानि	हिनसाव	हिनसाम
हिंसि	हिंस्तम्	हिंस्त
हिनस्तु	हिंस्ताम्	हिंसन्तु

Potential mood (विधिलिङ्)

हिंस्याम्	हिंस्याव	हिंस्याम
हिंस्या:	हिंस्यातम्	हिंस्यात
हिंस्यात्	हिंस्याताम्	हिंस्यु:

3p√hu (√हु) to perform yajña

see section 24.3

1p√hṛ (√हृ) to take away

Present Tense (लट्)

हरामि	हराव:	हराम:
हरसि	हरथ:	हरथ
हरति	हरत:	हरन्ति

Past Tense (लङ्)

अहरम्	अहराव	अहराम
अहर:	अहरतम्	अहरत
अहरत्	अहरताम्	अहरन्

Future Tense (लृट्)

हरिष्यामि	हरिष्याव:	हरिष्याम:
हरिष्यसि	हरिष्यथ:	हरिष्यथ

हरिष्यति	हरिष्यत:	हरिष्यन्ति

Imperative mood (लोट्)

हराणि	हराव	हराम
हर	हरतम्	हरत
हरतु	हरताम्	हरन्तु

Potential mood (विधिलिङ्)

हरेयम्	हरेव	हरेम
हरे:	हरेतम्	हरेत
हरेत्	हरेताम्	हरेयु:

1a√hṛ (√हृ) to take away

Present Tense (लट्)

हरे	हरावहे	हरामहे
हरसे	हरेथे	हरध्वे
हरते	हरेते	हरन्ते

Past Tense (लङ्)

अहरे	अहरावहि	अहरामहि
अहरथा:	अहरेथाम्	अहरध्वम्
अहरत	अहरेताम्	अहरन्त

Future Tense (लृट्)

हरिष्ये	हरिष्यावहे	हरिष्यामहे
हरिष्यसे	हरिष्येथे	हरिष्यध्वे
हरिष्यते	हरिष्येते	हरिष्यन्ते

Imperative mood (लोट्)

हरै	हरावहै	हरामहै
हरस्व	हरेथाम्	हरध्वम्
हरताम्	हरेताम्	हरन्ताम्

Potential mood (विधिलिङ्)

हरेय	हरेवहि	हरेमहि
हरेथा:	हरेयाथाम्	हरेध्वम्
हरेत	हरेयाताम्	हरेरन्

4p√hṛṣ (√हृष्) to be pleased

Present Tense (लट्)

हृष्यामि	हृष्याव:	हृष्याम:
हृष्यसि	हृष्यथ:	हृष्यथ
हृष्यति	हृष्यत:	हृष्यन्ति

Past Tense (लङ्)

अहृष्यम्	अहृष्याव	अहृष्याम
अहृष्य:	अहृष्यतम्	अहृष्यत
अहृष्यत्	अहृष्यताम्	अहृष्यन्

Future Tense (लृट्)

हर्षिष्यामि	हर्षिष्याव:	हर्षिष्याम:
हर्षिष्यसि	हर्षिष्यथ:	हर्षिष्यथ
हर्षिष्यति	हर्षिष्यत:	हर्षिष्यन्ति

Imperative mood (लोट्)

हृष्याणि	हृष्याव	हृष्याम
हृष्य	हृष्यतम्	हृष्यत
हृष्यतु	हृष्यताम्	हृष्यन्तु

Potential mood (विधिलिङ्)

हृष्येयम्	हृष्येव	हृष्येम
हृष्ये:	हृष्येतम्	हृष्येत
हृष्येत्	हृष्येताम्	हृष्येयु:

3p√hrī (√ह्री) to be shy

Present Tense (लट्)

जिह्रेमि	जिह्रीव:	जिह्रीम:

जिहेषि	जिहीथः	जिहीथ
जिहेति	जिहीतः	जिह्रियति

Past Tense (लङ्)

अजिहयाम्	अजिहीव	अजिहीम
अजिहेः	अजिहीतम्	अजिहीत
अजिहेत्	अजिहीताम्	अजिहयुः

Future Tense (लृट्)

हेष्यामि	हेष्यावः	हेष्यामः
हेष्यसि	हेष्यथः	हेष्यथ
हेष्यति	हेष्यतः	हेष्यन्ति

Imperative mood (लोट्)

जिहयाणि	जिहयाव	जिहयाम
जिहीहि	जिहीतम्	जिहीत
जिहेतु	जिहताम्	जिह्रियतु

Potential mood (विधिलिङ्)

जिहीयाम्	जिहीयाव	जिहीयाम
जिहीयाः	जिह्वीयातम्	जिहीयात
जिहीयात्	जिहीयाताम्	जिहीयुः

1p√hve (√ह्वे) to challenge

Present Tense (लट्)

ह्वयामि	ह्वयावः	ह्वयामः
ह्वयसि	ह्वयथः	ह्वयथ
ह्वयति	ह्वयतः	ह्वयन्ति

Past Tense (लङ्)

अह्वयम्	अह्वयाव	अह्वयाम
अह्वयः	अह्वयतम्	अह्वयत
अह्वयत्	अह्वयताम्	अह्वयन्

Future Tense (लृट्)

ह्वास्यामि	ह्वास्यावः	ह्वास्यामः
ह्वास्यसि	ह्वास्यथः	ह्वास्यथ
ह्वास्यति	ह्वास्यतः	ह्वास्यन्ति

Imperative mood (लोट्)

ह्वयानि	ह्वयाव	ह्वयाम
ह्वय	ह्वयतम्	ह्वयत
ह्वयतु	ह्वयताम्	ह्वयन्तु

Potential mood (विधिलिङ्)

ह्वयेयम्	ह्वयेव	ह्वयेम
ह्वयेः	ह्वयेतम्	ह्वयेत
ह्वयेत्	ह्वयेताम्	ह्वयेयुः

APPENDIX - 8

RATNAKAR'S CHART OF PARTICIPLES

ADJECTIVES AND INDECLINABLES

(1) ADJECTIVE PARTICIPLES

Participle	Suffix		Example - root verbs √कृ √लभ्	
1.Past Passive Participle	त	(क्त)	कृत	(done, has been done)
2.Past Active Participle	तवत्	(क्तवतु)	कृतवत्	(has done)
3.Present Active Participle	अत्	(शतृ)	कुर्वत्	(doing, while doing, doer)
4.Present Active Participle	आन	(शानच्)	कुर्वाण	(doing)
5.Present Active Participle	मान	(शानच्)	लभमान	(getting)
6.Present Passive Participle	यमान	(शानच्)	क्रियमाण	(being done)
7.Potential Passive Participle	तव्य	(तव्यत्)	कर्तव्य	(ought, fit to be done)
	अनीय	(अनीयर्)	करणीय	(ought, fit to be done)
	य	(यत्)	कार्य	(ought, fit to be done)

(2) INDECLINABLE PARTICIPLES

Participle	Suffix		Example - root verbs √कृ √लभ्
8. Indeclinable Past Participle (without a prefix, Gerund)	त्वा	(क्त्वा)	कृत्वा (having done)
9. Indeclinable Past Participle (with a prefix)	य	(ल्यप्)	अनुकृत्य (having done accordingly)
10. Infinitive of Purpose	तुम्	(तुमुन्)	कर्तुम् (for doing)

APPENDIX - 9

TRANSLITERATION, SIMPLIFICATION AND MEANING

OF THE SANSKRIT VERSES GIVEN IN THIS BOOK

THE LINES MARKED TITH ** INDICATE THE THE WORDS WITHOUT SANDHI

** वीणा-वाद्य-प्रवीणाम् वाणी-विताय वाग्-अधिष्टात्रीम् । वन्दे-वारण-वक्त्रम् विकटम् विघ्नाय विघ्नानाम् ।। *viṇā-vādya-praviṇāṁ vāṇī-vitāya vāg-adhiṣṭātrīm, vande-vāraṇa-vaktraṁ vikaṭaṁ vighnāya vighnānām.* * Salute to the Goddess of music of Viṇa, the Giver of the speech, the Goddess of the language, the Savior from difficulties and destroyer of the destroyers.

** रत्नाकर-आधौत-पदाम् हिमालय-किरीटिनीम् । ब्रह्म-राजर्षि-रत्नाढ्याम् वन्दे भारत-मातरम् ।। *ratnākara-ādhaut-padāṁ himālaya-kiriṭinīm, brahma-rājarṣi-ratnāḍhyāṁ vande bhārata-mātaram.* * Salute to Mother Bhāratī, whose feet are washed around by the oceans, whose crown is adorned with the Himalayas and whose jewels are the great sages and seers.

** शारदा सदा श्रयणीया । स्वर-दा वर-दा स्मरणीया । भारत-जननी स्तवनीया । संस्कृत-वाणी श्रवणीया । अनुकंपा हृदि धरणीया । सेवा मनसा करणीया ।। *śāradā sadā śryaṇīyā, svara-dā vara-dā smaraṇīyā, bhārata-jananī stavanīyā, saṁskṛta-vāṇī śravaṇīyā. anukampā hṛdi dharaṇīyā, seva manasā karaṇīyā.* * Śaradā must always be surrendered to, the Goddess of music and the Bestower of boons must be remembered. The Mother-India must be prayed to; the Sanskrit words must be heard. I must be caring at heart; I must serve people with my haear.

** नहि सुख-शय्या शयनीया । न नीच-चिन्ता चयनीया । रजः कामना शमनीया । तमः वासना दमनीया । *nahi sukha-śaiyā śayanīyā, na nīca-ćintā ćayanīyā, rajaḥ kāmanā śamanīyā, tamaḥ vāsanā damanīyā.* * I should not sleep in leasure; I should not think of things unworthy of thinking. Rājasic desire should be suppressed; Tāmasik cravings should be subdued.

** सतत सु-बुद्धिः धरणीया । मानस-शुद्धिः वरणीया । शुभा सरणिः अनुसणीया । सत्-सङ्गतिः अभिलषणीया । *satata su-buddhiḥ dharaṇīya, mānasa-śuddhiḥ varaṇīyā, subhā-saraṇiḥ-anusaraṇīyā, sat-saṅgatiḥ abhilaṣaṇīyā.* * I must always possess good mind; I must stay clean from inside and outside. I must choose the right-path; I must desire the right company.

** जाति-कु-प्रथा त्यजनीया । बन्धु-भावना भजनीया । अखिल संघता करणीया । विश्वे समाता भरणीया । *jāti-*

ku-prathā tyajanīyā, bandhu-bhāvanā bhajanīyā, akhila saṅghatā karaṇīyā, viśve samatā bharaṇīyā * The bad system of casts should be abandoned; universal brotherhood must be honoured; everyone should be brought togrther, the world should be filled with equanimity.

** प्रमत्त-कु-मतिः दहनीया । आगता हानिः सहनीया । प्रजा-प्रतिष्ठा वहनीया । मया प्रतिज्ञा ग्रहणीया । *pramatta-ku-matiḥ dahanīyā, āgatā hāniḥ sahanīyā, prajā-pratiṣṭhā vahanīyā, mayā pratijñā grahanīyā.* * Evil thinking should be burnt down; whatever loss may come must be borne; people must be always served; it must be my oath.

** श्लोके षष्ठम् गुरु ज्ञेयम् सर्वत्र लघु पञ्चमम् । द्वि-चतुष्-पादयोः ह्रस्वम् सप्तमम् दीर्घम् अन्ययोः । *śloke ṣaṣṭham guru jñeyam sarvatra laghu pañćamam, dvi-ćatuṣ-pādayoḥ hrasvam, saptamam dīrgham anyayoḥ.* * In a śloka the sixth letter is known to be longer (in each quarter), the fifth should be short in all quarters, short in second and fourth quarter and long in other two quarters.

** धर्म-क्षेत्रे कुरु-क्षेत्रे समवेताः युयुत्सवः मामकाः पाण्डवाः च एव किम् अकुर्वत सञ्जय ।। *dharma-kṣetre kuru-kṣetre samavetāḥ yuyutsavaḥ, māmakāḥ pāṇḍvāḥ ća eva kim akurvata? sañjaya!* * O Sanjaya, mine and Pandu's sons have gathered together on the holy place of Kurukṣetra with the desire of a war, what did they do?

(1) सु-रस-सु-बोधा, विश्व-मनोज्ञा, ललिता, हृद्या, रमणीया । अमृत-वाणी संस्कृत-भाषा न-एव क्लिष्टा न च कठिना ।। *su-rasa-su-bodhā viśva-manojñā lalitā hṛdyā ramanīyā, amṛta vāṇī saṁskṛta-bhāṣā na eva kliṣṭā na ća kaṭhinā.* * Pleasing and easily understood, most beautiful in the world, gracefully elegant, hearty, enjoyable and eternal -the words of Sanskrit language- are neither strenuous nor difficult.

(2) कवि-कोकिल-वाल्मीकि-विरचिता, रामायण-रमणीय-कथा, अतीव सरला मधुरा मञ्जुला, न-एव क्लिष्टा न च कठिना ।। *kavi-kokila-vālmīki-viraćitā rāmāyaṇa-ramaṇīya-kathā, atīva saralā madhurā mañjulā, na eva kliṣṭā na ća kaṭhinā.* * The delightful story of Rāmāyaṇa, written by poet lauret Vālmīki, is very simple and melodious, it is neither strenuous nor difficult

(3) श्री-कृष्ण! गोविन्द! हरे! मुरारे! हे नाथ! नारायण! वासुदेव! । जिह्वे! पिबस्व अमृतम् एतत् एव, गोविन्द! दामोदर! माधव! इति ।। *śrī-kṛṣṇa! govinda! hare! murāre! he nātha! nārāyaṇa! vāsudeva! jihve! pibasva amṛtam etat eva, govind! dāmodara! mādhava! iti.* * O Śrī-Kṛṣṇa! O

Govinda! O Hari! O Murārī! O Lord! O Nārāyaṇa! O Vāsudeva! O My dear tongue! Please taste the necter of these names only, and utter thus O Govinda! O Dāmodara! O Mādhava!

(4) जिह्वे सदैव भज सुन्दराणि नामानि कृष्णस्य मनोहराणि । समस्त भक्तार्ति-विनाशनानि गोविन्द! दामोदर! माधव! इति ।। *jihve! sadaiva bhaja sundarāṇi nāmāni kṛṣṇasya manoharāṇi, samasta bhaktārti-vināśanāni govind! dāmodara! mādhava! iti.* * O My dear tongue! Always chant the beautiful and fascinating names of kṛṣṇa; the names that remove the pains of the devotees, by chanting, O Govinda! O Dāmodara! O Mādhava!

(5) श्री-कृष्ण! राधा-वर! गोकुलेश! गोपाल! गोवर्धन! नाथ! विष्णो! । जिह्वे पिबस्व अमृतम् एतत् एव गोविन्द दामोदर माधव इति ।। *śrī-kṛṣṇa! rādhā-vara! gokuleśa! gopāla! govardhana! nātha! viṣṇo! jihve! pibasva amṛtam etat eva, govind! dāmodara! mādhava! iti.* * O Śrī-Kṛṣṇa! O Favourite of Rādhā, O Lord of Gokula! O Govardhana! O Lord Viṣṇu! O My Dear tongue! Please taste the nectar of these names only and utter thus O Govinda! O Dāmodara! O Mādhava!

(6) व्यास-विरचिता, गणेश-लिखिता, महाभारते दिव्य-कथा । कौरव-पाण्डव-सङ्गर-मथिता, न-एव क्लिष्टा न च कठिना ।। *vyāsa-viraćitā gaṇeśa-likhitā mahābhārate divya kathā, kaurava-pāṇḍava-saṅgara-mathitā, na eva kliṣṭā na ća kaṭhinā.* * Composed by Vyāsa, written by Gaṇeśa, the divine-story is told in the Mahābhārata; by extracting the battle stories of the Kauravas and the Pāṇḍavas. The eternal words of Sankkrit language are neither strenuous nor difficult.

(7) कुरुक्षेत्र-समराङ्गण-गीता विश्व-वन्दिता भगवद्गीता । अमृत-मधुरा कर्म-दीपिका न-एव क्लिष्टा न च कठिना ।। *kuru-kṣetra-samarāṅgaṇa-gītā viśva-vanditā bhagavad-gītā, amṛta-madhurā karma-dīpikā, na eva kliṣṭā na ća kaṭhinā.* * The Song Celestial of the battlefield of the Kurukṣetra, the one respected all over the world, the Bhagavad-Gītā, is sweet like nectar, and the guiding light of karma. The eternal words of Sankkrit language are neither strenuous nor difficult.

(8) न मे द्वेष-रागौ न मे लोभ-मोहौ । मदः न-एव मे न-एव मात्सर्य-भावः न धर्मः न च अर्थः न कामः न मोक्षः चिदानन्द-रूपः शिवः अहम् शिवः अहम् ।। *na me dveṣaḥ-rāgau na me lobha-mohau, madaḥ na-eva me na mātsarya-bhāvaḥ, na dharmaḥ na ća arthaḥ na kāmaḥ na mokṣaḥ, ćidānanda-rūpaḥ śivaḥ ahaṁ śivaḥ aham.* * I have neither an attachment nor detachment nor do I have desire nor lust; neither have I insanity nor do I have jealousy; neither do I have craving for

dharma, nor wealth, nor passion, nor heaven; I am the delightful consciousness of Śiva, I am Śiva.

(9) न पुण्यम् न पापम् न सौख्यम् न दुःखम् । न मन्त्रः न तीर्थम् न वेदाः न यज्ञाः अहम् भोजनम् न-एव भोज्यम् न भोक्ता । चिदानन्द-रूपः शिवः अहम् शिवः अहम् ।। *na puṇyaṁ na pāpaṁ na saukhyaṁ na duḥkham, na mantraḥ na tīrthaṁ na vedāḥ na yajñāḥ, ahaṁ bhojanaṁ na-eva bhojyaṁ na bhoktā, ćidānanda-rūpaḥ śivaḥ ahaṁ śivaḥ aham.* * Neither I am the purity not the sin nor the happiness, nor the sorrow, nor the holy chant, nor the sacred object, nor the Vedas, nor the Yajñas, nor the feeding, nor the food, nor the eater; I am the delightful consciousness of Śiva, I am Śiva.

(10) न मे मृत्यु-शङ्का न मे जाति-भेदः । पिता न-एव मे न-एव माता न जन्म । न बन्धुः न मित्रम् गुरुः न-एव शिष्यः । चिदानन्द-रूपः शिवः अहम् शिवः अहम् ।। *na me mṛtyu-śaṅkā na me jāti-bhedaḥ, pitā na-eva mātā na janma, na bandhuḥ na mitraṁ guruḥ na-eva śiṣyaḥ, ćidānanda-rūpaḥ śivaḥ ahaṁ śivaḥ aham.* * Neither do I have doubt in the death, nor do I have discrimination of the castes, nor do I have father, nor mother, nor birth, nor relative, nor friend, nor teacher nor a pupil; I am the delightful consciousness of Śiva, I am Śiva.

(11) अहम् निर्विकल्पः निराकार-रूपः । विभुः व्याप्य-सर्वत्र सर्वेन्द्रियाणाम् । सदा मे समत्वम् न मुक्तिः न बन्धः । चिदानन्द-रूपः शिवः अहम् शिवः अहम् ।। *ahaṁ nirvikalpaḥ nirākāra-rūpaḥ, vibhuḥ-vyāpya-sarvatra sarvendriyāṇām, sadā me samatvaṁ na mukti na bandhaḥ, ćidānanda-rūpaḥ śivaḥ ahaṁ śivaḥ aham.* * I am undetermined and formless, capable of pervading everywhere and everything; everything is the same to me, neither do I have liberation nor the bondage; I am the delightful consciousness of Śiva, I am Śiva.

(12) वन्दे मातरम् । सुजलाम् सुफलाम् मलयज-शीतलाम् । शस्य-श्यामलाम् मातरम् । वन्दे मातरम् ।। I salute to the Motherland; to the one that is abundant in waters, abundant in fruits, abundant in food grains, cooled by the winds from the Malaya Mountains, to that Mother I salute.

(13) शुभ्र-ज्योत्स्नाम् पुलकित-यामिनीम् । सुहासिनीम् सुमधुर-भाषिणीम् । सुखदाम् वरदाम् मातरम् । वन्दे मातरम् ।। To that Motherland with bright moon-lit and rejoiced nights, to the one with beautiful smile, to the one with very sweet speech, to the bestower of happiness, to the bestower of boons, to that Mother I salute.

(14) विद्या-दायिनि! नमामि त्वाम् । नमामि कमलाम् अमलाम् अतुलाम् । सुजलाम् सुफलाम् मातरम् । वन्दे मातरम् ।। O Bestower of knowledge! I salute you. I salute to that excellent Motherland, to the Pure one, to the Peerless, to the Motherland plentiful of water, bountiful of fruits, to that Mother I salute.

(15) श्यामलाम् सरलाम् । सुस्मिताम् भूषिताम् । धरणीम् भरणीम् मातरम् । वन्दे मातरम् ।। To the Dark-blue, to the Simple one, to the One adored with with sweet smile, to the Motherly nourishing land, to that Mother I salute.

(16) गीता गङ्गा च गायत्री गोविन्द इति हृदि स्थिते । चतुर्-गकार-संयुक्ते पुनर्-जन्म न विद्यते ।। The Gītā, the Ganges, the Gāyatrī chant and the name of Govinda, while these four G-words staying in the heart, there is no rebirth.

(17) ॐ भूर्भुव: स्व: तत् सवितु: वरेण्यम् भर्ग: देवस्य धीमहि । धिय: य: न: प्रचोदयात् ।। Om! O Lord! You are the giver of life, heavenly and bestower of happiness. Let us meditate upon that Lord who is the Sun of knowledge, worthy of imploring, giver of life. May He inspire our intellects.

(18) ॐ एक-दन्ताय विद्महे । वक्र-तुण्डाय धीमहि । तत् न: दन्ती प्रचोदयात् ।। Om! O Lord, the one whom we know as Eka-danta (the One toothed one). Let us meditate upon the one with curved trunk. May that Gaṇeśa inspire us.

(19) ॐ तत् पुरुषाय विद्महे । महा-देवाय धीमहि । तत् न: रुद्र: प्रचोदयात् ।। Om! O' Lord, the one whom we know as Puruṣa, let us meditate on that Great Lord. May that Lord Śiva inspire us.

(20) ॐ नारायणाय विद्महे । वासुदेवाय धीमहि । तत् न: विष्णु: प्रचोदयात् ।। Om! O Lord, the one whom we know as Nārayaṇa. Let us meditate up on that Vāsudeva. May that Lord Viṣṇu inspire us.

(21) ॐ देव्यै ब्रह्माण्यै विद्महे । महा-शक्त्यै च धीमहि । तत् न: देवी प्रचोदयात् ।। Om! O Lord, to whom we know as Brahmāṇī. Let us meditate upon that Great Śakti (Pārvatī). May that Goddess inspire us.

(22) ॐ महा-लक्ष्म्यै च विद्महे । विष्णु-पत्न्यै च धीमहि । तत् न: लक्ष्मी प्रचोदयात् ।। Om! O Lord, to whom we know as the Great Goddess Lakṣmī. Let us meditate uopn that wife of Lord Viṣṇu. May Goddess Lakṣmī inspire us.

(23) ॐ भास्कराय विद्महे । महत्-द्युतिकराय धीमहि । तत् न: आदित्य: प्रचोदयात् ।। Om! O Lord, to who

we know as Lord Bhāskara (Sun). Let us meditate upon that great light producer. May that Lord Āditya (Sun) inspire us.

(24) गायत्र्याः तु परम् नास्ति शोधनम् पाप-कर्मणाम् । गायन्तम् त्रायते यस्मात् गायत्री सा ततः स्मृता ।। There is none greater purifier of sinful acts, than the Gāyatrī chant. By which while singing one achives protection, thus She is called the Gāyatrī.

(25) पश्य एताम् पाण्डु-पुत्राणाम् आचार्य महतीम् चमूम् ।। *paśya etāṁ pāṇḍu-putrāṇām āćārya mahatīṁ ćamūm.* * O Āchārya (Droṇa)! Behold, this great army of the sons of Pāṇḍu.

(26) पर्याप्तम् तु इदम् एतेषाम् बलम् भीम-अभिरक्षितम् ।। *paryāptaṁ tu idam eteṣāṁ balaṁ bhīma-abhirakṣitam* * This their army protected by Bhīma is limited.

(28) काकः कृष्णः पिकः कृष्णः कः भेदः पिक-काकयोः वसन्त-समये प्राप्ते काकः काकः पिकः पिकः । *kākaḥ kṛṣṇaḥ pikaḥ kṛṣṇaḥ kaḥ bhedaḥ pika-kākayoḥ? vasant-samaye prāpte kākaḥ kākaḥ pikaḥ pikaḥ.* * The crow is black. the cuckoo is black. What is the difference between the crow and the cockoo? When the spring season comes, the crow is (just) a crow, whie the cuckoo is (singing) cuckoo.

(29) जीर्यन्ते जीर्यतः केशाः दन्ताः जीर्यन्ति जीर्यतः । क्षीयते जीर्यते सर्वम् तृष्णा एव एका न जीर्यते ।। *jīryante jīryataḥ keśāḥ dantāḥ jīryanti jīryataḥ, kṣīyate jīryate sarvaṁ tṛṣṇā ekā na jīryate.* * The hair of the person getting older get older, the teeth of the person getting older get older, his everything else gets weaker and older, only the desire does not get weaker.

(30) भ्वादि-अदादि-जुहोत्यादिः दिवादिः स्वादिः एव च । तुदादिः च रुधादिः च तनादिः क्री-चुरादयः ।30।। *bhvādi-adādi-juhotyādiḥ divādiḥ svādiḥ eva ća, tudādiḥ ća rudhādiḥ ća tanādiḥ krī-ćurādayaḥ.* * bhvādi, adādi, hvādi, divādi, svādi, tudādi, rudhādi, tanādi, kryādi and ćurādi.

(31) रामः राज-मणिः सदा विजयते । रामम् रमेशम् भजे । रामेण अभिहिता निशा-चर-चमू । रामाय तस्मै नमः रामात् नास्ति परायणम् पर-तरम् । रामस्य दासः अस्मि अहम् । रामे चित्तलयः सदा भवतु मे । भोः राम! माम् उद्धर ।। *rāmaḥ rāja-maṇiḥ sadā vijayate, rāmaṁ rameśaṁ bhaje, rāmeṇa abhihitā niśā-ćara-ćamū, rāmāya tasmai namaḥ. rāmāt nāsti parāyaṇaṁ para-taram, rāmasya dāsaḥ asmi aham. rāme ćittalayaḥ sadā bhavatu me, bhoḥ rāma! mām uddhara.* * Lord Rāma, the jewel king is always victorious. I salute to that Lord Rāma, the husband of Ramā (Sītā). The night-dwelling demons are destroyed by Lord Rāma. Salute to that Lord Rāma. There is no better

aim than Lord Rāma. I am a servant of Lord Rāma. In Lord Rāma may my heart always stay. O Lord Rāma! Please rescue me.

(32) विद्यार्थी सेवकः पान्थः क्षुधार्थी भयकातरः । भाण्डारी प्रतिहारी च सप्त सुप्तान् प्रबोधयेत् ।। *vidyārthī sevakaḥ pānthaḥ kṣudhārthi bhayakātaraḥ, bhāṇḍārī pratihārī ća sapta sauptān prabodhayet.* * One should awake any of these seven persons if they are sleeping: a student, servant, traveller, hungry person, scared person, storekeeper or a watchman.

(33) शोकः नाशयते धैर्यम् शोकः नाशयते श्रुतम् । शोकः नाशयते सर्वम् न-अस्ति शोक-समः रिपुः । *śokaḥ nāśayate dhairyaṁ śokaḥ nāśayate śrutam, śokaḥ nāśayate sarvaṁ na-asti śoka-sama ripuḥ.* * The grief destroys courage, the grief destroys the knowledge earned by hearing. The grief destroys everything. There is no greater enemy than the grief.

(34) वृक्षाग्र-वासी न च पक्षि-राजः त्रि-नेत्र-धारी न च शूल-पाणिः जटाभिः युक्तः न च सिद्ध-योगी जलम् च बिभ्रत् न घटः न मेघः । *vṛkṣāgra-vāsī na ća pakṣi-rājaḥ, tri-netra-dhārī na ća śula-pāṇiḥ, jaṭābhiḥ yuktaḥ na ća siddha-yogī jalaṁ ća vibhrat na ghaṭaḥ na meghaḥ.* It dwells at the top of a tree, but is not an eagle. It has three eyes, but is not Lord Śiva. It bears long hair, but is not an ascetic. It fills with water, but is neither a jug nor a cloud (then what is it?)

(35) अहिम् नृपम् च शार्दूलम् कीटिम् च बालकम् तथा । पर-श्वानम् च मूर्खम् च सप्त सुप्तान् न बोधयेत् ।। *ahiṁ nṛpaṁ ća śārdūlaṁ kīṭiṁ ća bālakaṁ tathā, para-śvānaṁ ća mūrkhaṁ ća sapta suptān na bodhayet.* * One should not awake any of these seven while they are sleeping: a snake, king, lion, insect, child, someone else's dog or a fool.

(36) न चौर-हार्यम् न च राज-हार्यम् न भ्रातृ-भाज्यम् न च भार-कारी । व्यये कृते वर्धते एव नित्यम् विद्या-धनम् सर्व-धन-प्रधानम् ।। *na chaurya hāryaṁ na ća rāja-hāryam, na bhrātṛ-bhājyaṁ na ća bhāra-kārī, vyaye kṛte vardhate eva nityam, vidyā-dhanaṁ sarva-dhana-pradhānam.* Neither can be confiscated by the king, nor can be stolen by a thief, nor can be divided and shared by a brother, nor it is burdensome. More you spend, more it ever grows, such wealth of knowledge is the most superior in all the wealths.

(37) परोक्षे कार्य-हन्तारम् प्रत्यक्षे प्रिय-वादिनम् । वर्जयेत् तादृशम् मित्रम् विष-कुम्भम् पयः मुखम् ।। *parokṣe kārya-hantāraṁ pratyakṣe priya-vādinam, varjayet tādṛśaṁ mitraṁ viṣa-kumbhaṁ payaḥ-mukham.* * Avoide such friend who acts against you behind your back, while he is a sweet

talker in front of you. He is a poison filled jar with a sweet looking spout.

(38) पयसा कमलम्, कमलेन पयः । पयसा कमलेन विभाति सरः । *payasā kamalaṁ kamalena payaḥ, payasā kamalena vibhāti saraḥ.* * With water the lotus, with lotus the water and with water and lotus the lake looks beautiful.

(39) शशिना च निशा, निशया च शशी । शशिना निशया च विभाति नभः । *śaśinā ća niśā niśayā ća śaśī, śasinā niśayā ća vibhāti nabhaḥ.* * With the moon the night, with the night the moon and with the moon and the night the sky looks beautiful.

(40) मणिना वलयम्, वलयेन मणिः । मणिना वलयेन विभाति करः । *maṇinā valayaṁ valayena maṇiḥ, maṇinā valayena vibhāti karaḥ.* * With the pearl the bracelet, with the bracelet the pearl and with the pearl and the bracelet the hand looks beautiful.

(41) सभया च भवान्, भवता च सभा । सभया भवता च विभाति जगत् ।। *sabhayā ća bhavān bhavatā ća sabhā, sabhayā bhavatā ća vibhāti jagat.* * With assembly you, with you the assembly and with the assembly and you the world looks beautiful.

(42) सद्भिः तु लीलया प्रोक्तम् शिला-लिखितम् अक्षरम् । असद्भिः शपथेन अपि जले लिखितम् अक्षरम् ।। *sadbhiḥ tu līlayā proktaṁ śilā-likhitam akṣaram, asadbhiḥ śapathena api jale likhitam akṣaram.* * A word spoken even casually by the wise is like a letter carved in a stone. A word spoken by unwise people, even on oath, is like a letter written on the surface of water.

(43) एकेन अपि सु-पुत्रेण, विद्या-युक्तेन भासते । कुलम् पुरुष-सिंहेन चन्द्रेण इव हि शर्वरी ।। *ekena api su-putreṇa vidyā yuktena bhāsate, kulaṁ puruṣa-siṁhena ćandreṇa iva hi śarvarī.* * With even one good, learned and brave son the family looks glorious just as the night with moon.

(44) यथा हि एकेन चक्रेण न रथस्य गतिः भवेत् । एवम् पुरुष-कारेण विना दैवम् न सिद्ध्यति ।। *yathā hi ekena ćakreṇa na rathasya gatiḥ bhavet, evaṁ puruṣa-kāreṇa vinā daivaṁ na sidhyati.* * Just as a chariot does not run with only one wheel, similarly things can not be accomplished by man only with action without the help of luck.

(45) चक्षुषा मनसा वाचा कर्मणा च चतुर्-विधम् । प्रसादयति यः लोकम् तम् लोकः अनुप्रसीदति ।। *ćakṣuṣā manasā vāćā karmaṇā ća ćatur-vidham, prasādayati yaḥ lokaṁ taṁ lokaḥ anuprasīdati.* * He who pleases plople with his vision, mind, speech and work, to him people also please in return.

(46) विद्या विवादाय धनम् मदाय । शक्तिः परेषाम् परिपीडनाय । खलस्य साधोः विपरीतम् एतत् । ज्ञानाय दानाय च रक्षणाय ।। *vidyā vivādāya dhanaṁ madāya, śakti pareṣāṁ paripīḍanāya, khalasya sādhoḥ viparītam etat, jñānāya dānāya ća rakṣaṇāya.* * Of the unwise person, the knowledge is for arguing, wealth for intoxication and power for hurting others. Of wise person it is opposite - (their knowledge is) for erudition, (wealth) for charity and (power) for protection of others.

(47) रामाय राम-भद्राय राम-चन्द्राय वेधसे । रघु-नाथाय नाथाय सीतायाः पतये नमः । *rāmāya rāma-bhadrāya rāma-ćandrāya vedhase, raghu-nāthāya nāthāy sītāyāḥ pataye namaḥ.* Salutation to Lord Rāma, Rāmabhadra, Rāmaćandra, the Creator, the Raghunātha, The Master, the Husband of Sītā.

(48) विद्या ददाति विनयम् विनयात् याति पात्रताम् । पात्रत्वात् धनम् आप्नोति धनात् धर्मः ततः सुखम् ।। *vidyā dadāti vinayam, vinayāt yāti pātratām, pātratvāt dhanam āpnoti, dhanāt dharmaḥ tataḥ sukham.* * Learning gives humility; from humility one attains competence; from competence one attains wealth; and from wealth, the Dharma; and from there, the happiness.

(49) आदित्यानाम् अहम् विष्णुः ज्योतिषाम् रविः अंशुमान् । मरीचिः मरुताम् अस्मि नक्षत्राणाम् अहम् शशी ।। *ādityānām ahaṁ viṣṇuḥ jyotiṣāṁ raviḥ aṁśumān, marīćiḥ marutām asmi nakṣatrāṇām ahaṁ śaśī.* * Among the sons of Aditi, I am Viṣṇu; among the luminaries, I am the radiant Sun; among the planets I am the Moon.

(50) वेदानाम् साम-वेदः अस्मि देवानाम् अस्मि वासवः इन्द्रियाणाम् मनः च अस्मि भूतानाम् अस्मि चेतना ।। *vedānaṁ sāma-vedaḥ asmi, devānām asmi vāsavaḥ, indriyāṇāṁ manaḥ ća asmi, bhūtānām asmi ćetanā.* * Among the Vedas I am the Sāma; among the Gods I am the Indra; Among the sense organs I am the mind and; in the beings I am the consciousness.

(51) नरस्य आभरणम् रूपम् रूपस्य आभरणम् गुणः गुणस्य आभरणम् ज्ञानम् ज्ञानस्य आभरणम् क्षमा ।। *narasya ābharaṇaṁ rūpam, rūpasya ābharaṇaṁ guṇaḥ, guṇasya ābharaṇaṁ jñānam, jñānasya ābharaṇaṁ kṣamā.* * Beauty is the adornment of the mankind, virtue is the ornament of the beauty, knowledge is the beauty of the virtue and forgiveness is the beauty of the virtue.

(52) यस्य नास्ति स्वये प्रज्ञा शास्त्रम् तस्य करोति किम् । नेत्राभ्याम् तु विहीनस्य दर्पणः किम् करिष्यति ।। *yasya nāsti svaye prajñā, śāstraṁ tasya karoti kim? netrābhyāṁ tu vihīnasya, darpaṇaḥ kiṁ kariṣyati?* * One who does not have his own intelligence, what good are the scriptures for

him? One who does not have vision, what will a mirror do?

(53) आदानस्य प्रदानस्य कर्त्तव्यस्य च कर्मणः क्षिप्रम् अ-क्रियमाणस्य कालः पिबति तत् रसम् ।। *ādānasya pradānasya karttavyasya ća karmaṇaḥ, kṣipram-a-kriyamāṇasya kālaḥ pibati tat rasam.* * The act of receiving, the act of giving and the act that ought to be done (must be done as early as possible); the time takes away the sweetness from the things put off.

(54) अयम् निजः परः वा इति गणना लघु-चेतसाम् । उदार-चरितानाम् तु वसुधा एव कुटुम्बकम् ।। *ayaṁ nijaḥ paraḥ vā iti gaṇanā laghu-ćetasām, udāra-ćaritānāṁ tu vasudhā eva kuṭumbakam.* * 'This person belongs to us and this one does not,' is the outlook of those with a small heart; for the whole hearted ones, the whole world is one family.

(55) दक्षिणे लक्ष्मणः यस्य वामे तु जनक-आत्मजा । पुरतः मारुतिः यस्य तम् वन्दे रघु-नन्दनम् ।। *dakṣiṇe lakṣmaṇaḥ yasya vāme tu janaka-ātmajā, purataḥ mārutiḥ yasya taṁ vande raghu-nandanam.* * On whose right side is Lakṣamaṇa, on the left side is King Janaka's daughter (Sītā) and in front is Māruti, to that Son-of-Raghu (Lord Rāma) I salute.

(56) मातृ-वत् पर-दारेषु पर-द्रव्येषु लोष्ट-वत् । आत्म-वत् सर्व-भूतेषु यः पश्यति सः पण्डितः । *mātṛ-vat para-dāreṣu para-dravyeṣu loṣṭa-vat, ātma-vat sarva-bhūteṣu yaḥ paśyati saḥ paṇḍitaḥ.* * He who looks upon others' women as his mothers, others' wealth equal to a piece of stone and other beings as his own self, is a wise person.

(57) कर्मणि एव अधिकारः ते मा फलेषु कदाचन ।। *karmaṇi eva adhikāraḥ te, mā phaleṣu kadāćana.* * Your duty is only to do what ought to be done, and not to desire the fruit there of.

(58) दुःखेषु अनुद्विग्न-मनाः सुखेषु विगत-स्पृहः वीत-राग-भय-क्रोधः स्थितधीः मुनिः उच्यते ।। *duḥkheṣu anudvigna-manāḥ, sukheṣu vigata-spṛhaḥ, vīta-rāga-bhaya-krodhaḥ sthitadhīḥ muniḥ ućyate.* * One who is neither sad in suffering nor has desire for pleasures, and who is away from attachment, fear and anger, that person of steady wisdom, is called a Muni.

(59) रसः अहम् अप्सु कौन्तेय प्रभा अस्मि शशि-सूर्ययोः । प्रणवः सर्व-वेदेषु शब्दः खे पौरुषम् नृषु ।। *rasaḥ aham apsu kaunteya! prabhā asmi śasi-sūryayoḥ, praṇavaḥ sarva-vedeṣu śabdaḥ khe pauruṣaṁ nṛṣu.* * O Arjuna! I am the sapidity of the waters, I am the rediance of the moon and the sun, I am the Om mentioned in all the Vedas, I am the sound in the space and I am the manhood of the men.

(60) पुण्य: गन्ध: पृथिव्याम् च तेज: च अस्मि विभावसौ । जीवनम् सर्व-भूतेषु तप: च अस्मि तपस्विषु ।। *puṇyaḥ gandhaḥ pṛthivyāṁ ća, tejaḥ ća asmi vibhāvasau, jīvanaṁ sarva-bhūteṣu tapaḥ ća asmi tapasviṣu.* * O Arjuna! I am the pure aroma in the earth, I am the heat in the fire, I am the life in all living beings and I am the austerity in the ascetics.

(61) तस्मात् सर्वेषु कालेषु योग-युक्त: भव अर्जुन ।। *tasmāt sarveṣu kāleṣu, yoga-yuktaḥ bhava arjuna!* * Therefore, O Arjuna, at all times be steadfast in Yoga.

(62) सम: शत्रौ च मित्रे च तथा मान-अपमानयो: । शीत-उष्ण-सुख-दु:खेषु सम: सङ्ग-विवर्जित: । *samaḥ śatrau ća mitre ća tathā māna-apamānayoḥ, śīta-uṣṇa-sukha-duḥkheṣu samaḥ saṅga-vivarjitaḥ.* * One who is indifferent to a foe and friend, honour and dishonour, cold and warmth, pleasure and pain;

(63) समम् सर्वेषु भूतेषु तिष्ठन्तम् परमेश्वरम् ।। *samaṁ sarveṣu bhūteṣu, tiṣṭhantaṁ parameśvaram.* * The Lord, dwelling alike in everything,

(64) धर्म: जयति न अधर्म: सत्यम् जयति न अनृतम् । क्षमा जयति न क्रोध: देव: जयति न असुर: । *dharmaḥ jayati na adharmaḥ, satyaṁ jayati na anṛtam, kṣamā jayati na krodhaḥ, devaḥ jayati na asuraḥ.* * The right always wins, not the unrighteousness, The truth always wins, not the false, forgiveness always wins not the anger, God always wins not a demon.

(65) कुर्यात्, क्रियेत, कर्तव्यम्, भवेत्, स्यात् इति पञ्चमम् । एतत् स्यात् सर्व-वेदेषु नियतम् विधि-लक्षणम् ।। *kuryāt kriyet kartavyam, bhavet syāt iti pañćamam, etat syāt sarva-vedeṣu niyataṁ vidhi-lakṣaṇam.* * Should do, Should be done, ought to be done, should become and the fifth, may be - this is fixed in all Vedas as the sign of the Potential Mood.

(66) गते शोक: न कर्तव्य: भविष्यम् न चिन्तयेत् । वर्तमानेन कालेन प्रवर्तन्ते विचक्षणा: । *gate śokaḥ na kartavyaḥ, bhaviṣyaṁ na ćintayet, vartamānena kālena, pravartante vićakṣaṇāḥ.* * The thing that has passed ought not to be grieved upon, the wise people act with the present time.

(67) लालयेत् पञ्च-वर्षाणि दश-वर्षाणि ताडयेत् । प्राप्ते तु षोडशे वर्षे पुत्रम् मित्र-वत् आचरेत् ।। *lālayet pañća-varṣāṇi, daśa-varṣāṇi tāḍayet, prāpte tu ṣoḍaśe varṣe putraṁ mitra-vat āćaret.* * Up to five years a son may be cuddled, up to ten he may be punished, at sixteen he should be treated like a friend.

(68) दृष्टि-पूतम् न्यसेत् पादम् वस्त्र-पूतम् पिबेत् जलम् । सत्य-पूताम् वदेत् वाचम् मन: पूतम् समाचरेत् ।। *dṛṣṭi-*

pūtaṁ nyaset pādam, vastra-pūtaṁ pibet jalam, satya-pūtāṁ vadet vāćam, manaḥ-pūtaṁ samāćaret. * One should set foot where eyes can see clearly, one should drink water that is filtered (with cloth), one should speak that which is purified with truth and one should act with a clean mind.

(69) सर्वे भवन्तु सुखिनः सर्वे सन्तु निरामयाः सर्वे भद्राणि पश्यन्तु मा कश्चित् दुःख-भाग् भवेत् ।। *sarve bhavantu sukhinaḥ, sarve santu nirāmayaḥ, sarve bhadrāṇi paśyantu, mā kaśćit duḥkha-bhāg bhavet.* * May all be happy; may all be healthy; may all see well; no one may face sorrow.

(70) सद्भिः एव सहासीत सद्भिः कुर्वीत सङ्गतीम् । सद्भिः विवादम् मैत्रीम् च न असद्भिः किंचित् आचरेत् ।। *sadbhiḥ eva sahāsīta, sadbhiḥ kurvīta saṅgatīm, sadbhiḥ vivādaṁ maitrīṁ ća, na a-sadbhiḥ kiñćit āćaret.* * One should stay with good people, with good people one should keep compaany, with good people one should argue and do friendship, one should not associate even briefly with bad people.

(71) यदि माम् अ-प्रतीकारम् अ-शस्त्रम् शस्त्र-पाणयः । धार्तराष्ट्राः रणे हन्युः तत् मे क्षेम-तरम् भवेत् ।। *yadi mām a-pratikāram, a-śastraṁ śastra-pāṇayaḥ, dhārtarāṣṭrāḥ raṇe hanyuḥ, tat me kṣema-taraṁ bhavet.* * Even if the weapon bearing sons of Dhṛtarāṣṭra were to kill me, unresisting and unarmed in the battle, it would be better for me.

(72) सुखार्थी वा त्यजेत् विद्याम् विद्यार्थी वा त्यजेत् सुखम् । सुखार्थिनः कुतः विद्या विद्यार्थिनः कुतः सुखम् ।। *sukhārthī vā tyajet vidyāṁ vidyārthī vā tyajet sukham, sukhārthinaḥ kutaḥ vidyā vidyārthinaḥ kutaḥ sukham?* * The pleasure loving people should give up learning, the learner should give up the pleasures; Where will merry makers earn knowledge? Where is the merry making for the learners?

(73) प्रथमे न अर्जिता विद्या द्वितीये न अर्जितः अर्थः (अर्जितम् धनम्) । तृतीये न अर्जितम् पुण्यम् चतुर्थे किम् करिष्यति ।। *prathame na arjitā vidyā, dvitīye na (arjitaḥ arthaḥ arjitaṁ dhanam), tṛtīye na arjitaṁ puṇyam, ćaturthe kiṁ kariṣyati?* * If one has not earned education in the first (quarter of life), wealth in the second quarter, goodness in the third quarter, what will he do in the fourth quarter?

(74) लोक हितम् मम करणीयम् । मनसा सततम् स्मरणीयम् । वचसा सततम् वदनीयम् । न भोग-भवने रमणीयम्

। न च सुख-शयने शयनीयम् । अहर्निशम् जागरणीयम् । न जातु दुःखम् गणनीयम् । न च निज-सौख्यम् मननीयम् । कार्य-क्षेत्रे त्वरणीयम् । दुःख-सागरे तरणीयम् । विपत्ति-विपिने भ्रमणीयम् । लोक-हितम् मम करणीयम् ।। *loka hitaṁ mama karaṇīyaṁ manasā satataṁ smaraṇīyam; vaćasā satataṁ vadanīyaṁ na bhoga-bhavane ramaṇīyam; na ća sukha-śayane śayanīyam aharniśaṁ jāgaraṇīyam; na jātu duḥkhaṁ gaṇanīyaṁ na ća nija-saukhyaṁ mananīyam; kārya-kṣetre tvaraṇīyaṁ duḥkha-sāgare taranīyam; vipatti-vipine bhramaṇīyaṁ loka-hitaṁ mama karaṇīyam.* * I must do good for people; I must memember not to relax in the pleasures, not to indulde in enjoyments, not to think of my own good, to be quick in my duty, to cross over the ocean of pains, to pass through the jungle of challenges, I must do good for people.

(75) सदृशम् त्रिषु लिङ्गेषु सर्वासु च विभक्तिषु । वचनेषु च सर्वेषु यत् न व्येति तत् अव्ययम् ।। *sadṛśaṁ triṣu liṅgeṣu sarvāsu ća vibhaktiṣu, vaćaneṣu ća sarveṣu yat na vyeti tat avyayam.* * That, which is same in three genders and same all cases and that which dees not change in all three numbers, is an 'indeclinable' word.

(76) एवम् उक्त्वा अर्जुनः संख्ये रथ-उपस्थे उपाविशत् । विसृज्य स-शरम् चापम् शोक-संविग्न-मानसः । *evam uktvā arjunaḥ saṅkhye ratha-upasthe upāviśat, visṛjya sa-śaraṁ ćāpaṁ śoka-saṁvigna-mānasaḥ.* * Having spoken thus on the battlefield and having kept away his bow and arrow, Arjuna, distressed with sorrow, sat in the middle part of the chariot.

(77) सिद्धि-असिद्ध्योः समः भूत्वा समत्वम् योग उच्यते ।। *siddhi-asiddhyoḥ samaḥ bhūtvā samatvaṁ yoga ućyate.* * Being even, the evenness of mind in the success and failure, is known as Yoga.

(78) योगिनः कर्म कुर्वन्ति सङ्गम् त्यक्त्वा आत्म-शुद्धये ।। *yoginaḥ karma kurvanti saṅgaṁ tyaktvā ātma-viśuddaye.* * The devotees of Karmayoga perform action, having renounced attachment, for the purification of the heart.

(79) श्रोतुम् कर्णौ वक्तुम् अस्यम् सु-हास्यम् घ्रातुम् घ्राणम् पाद-युग्मम् विहर्तुम् । द्रष्टुम् नेत्रे हस्त-युग्मम् च दातुम् ध्यातुम् चित्तम् येन सृष्टम् सः पातु ।। *śrotuṁ karṇau vaktum asyaṁ su-hāsyaṁ ghrātuṁ ghrāṇaṁ pāda-yugmaṁ vihartum, draṣṭuṁ netre hasta-yugmaṁ ća dātuṁ dhyātuṁ ćittaṁ yena sṛṣṭaṁ sa pātu.* * He who has given two ears for hearing, mouth for speaking and smiling, nose for smelling, two feet for walking, two eyes for seeing, two hands for giving and mind for

meditation, may he protect us.

(80) न कश्चित् अपि जानाति, किम् कस्य श्वः भविष्यति । अतः श्वः करणीयानि कुर्यात् अद्य एव बुद्धिमान् ।। *na kaśćit api jānāti kiṁ kasya śvaḥ bhavati, ataḥ śvaḥ karaṇīyāni kuryāt adya eva buddhimān.* * Nobody knows what will happen to who tomorrow, therefore, a wise person should do it today what is to be done tomorrow.

(81) दिवा पश्यति न उलुकः काकः नक्तम् न पश्यति । विद्या-विहीनः मूढः तु, दिवा नक्तम् न पश्यति ।। *divā paśyati na ulukaḥ, kākaḥ naktaṁ na paśyati, vidyā-vihīnaḥ mūdhaḥ tu, divā naktaṁ na paśyati.* * The bat can not see in the day time, a crow can not see in the night time, but the uneducated fool does not see in the day as well as in the night.

(82) यथा पर-उपकारेषु नित्यम् जागर्ति सज्जनः । तथा पर-अपकारेषु नित्यम् जागर्ति दुर्जनः ।। *yathā para-upakāreṣu nityaṁ jāgarti sajjanaḥ, tathā para-apakāreṣu nityaṁ jāgarti durjanaḥ.* * As a virtuous person is alert all the time to help others, so is a bad person busy all the time to cause harm to others.

(83) यथा देशः तथा भाषा यथा राजा तथा प्रजा । यथा भूमिः तथा तोयम्, यथा बीजम् तथा अंकुरः ।। *yathā deśaḥ tathā bhāṣā, yathā rājā tathā prajā, yathā bhūmiḥ tathā toyam, yathā bījaṁ tathā aṅkuraḥ.* * As is a country so is its language, as is the king so are his subjects, as is the land so is its water, as is the seed so is its seedling.

(84) स्वभावः न उपदेशेन शक्यते कर्तुम् अन्यथा । सु-तप्तम् अपि पानीयम् पुनर् गच्छति शीतताम् ।। *sva-bhāvaḥ na upadeśena śakyate kartum anyathā, su-taptam api pānīyaṁ punar-gaććhati śītatām.* * It is not possible to alter somebody's nature by advice, as a drink even boiled long enough, cooles off again.

(85) क्षणशः कणशः च एव, विद्याम् अर्थम् च साधयेत् । क्षण-त्यागे कुतः विद्या, कण-त्यागे कुतः धनम्? ।। *kṣaṇaśaḥ kaṇaśaḥ ća eva, vidyām arthaṁ ća sādhayet, kṣaṇa-tyage kutaḥ vidyā, kaṇa-tyāge kutaḥ dhanam?* * Education and wealth are to be earned little by little, how can education be earned by wasting moments and how can wealth be gained by wasting money little by little?

(86) पूर्व-पदार्थ-प्रधानः अव्ययीभावः उत्तर-पदार्थ-प्रधानः तत्पुरुषः । अन्य-पदार्थ-प्रधानः बहुव्रीहिः उभय-पदार्थ-प्रधानः द्वंद्वः । *pūrva-padārtha-pradhānaḥ avyayībhāvaḥ, uttara-padārtha-pradhānaḥ tatpuruṣaḥ, anya-padārthaḥ-pradhānaḥ bahuvrīhiḥ, ubhaya-padārtha-ptadhānaḥ dvandvaḥ.* *

Where the first word is dominant, it is avyayī-bhāva samāsa; when the last word is dominant, it is Tatpuruṣa samāsa; when an outside word is dominant, it is Bahuvrīhi samāsa; when both (all) words are dominant, it is Dvandva samāsa.

(101) अ-विचार्य न वक्तव्यम् वक्तव्यम् सु-विचारितम् । किम्-च तत्र-एव वक्तव्यम् यत्र उक्तम् सफलम् भवेत् ।। *a-vićārya na vaktavyam, vaktavyaṁ su-vićāritam, kiṁ-ća tatra-eva vaktavyam, yatra uktaṁ saphalaṁ bhavet.* * One should not speak without thinking, one should speak what is properly thought, one should speak only there where the spoken word may accomplish something.

(102) उपकार: अपि नीचानाम् अपकार: हि जायते । पय: पानम् भुजङ्गानाम् केवलम् विष-वर्धनम् ।। *upakāraḥ api nīćānām apakāraḥ hi jāyate, payaḥ-pānaṁ bhujaṅgānāṁ kevalaṁ viṣa-vardhanam.* * A favour done to bad people turns into a loss to yourself, as the milk fed to the snakes only turns into poison.

(103) क्षमा-शस्त्रम् करे यस्य दुर्जन: किम् करिष्यति । अ-तृणे पतित: वह्नि: स्वयम् एव उपशाम्यति ।। *kśamā-śastraṁ kare yasya, durjanaḥ kiṁ kariṣyati? a-tṛṇe patitaḥ vahniḥ svayam eva upaśāmyati.* * What a bad person can do to him who holds the weapon of forgiveness? The fire fell on a grassless bare ground extinguishes by itself.

(104) यत् अ-शक्यम् न तत् शक्यम् तत् शक्यम् शक्यम् एव यत् । न जले शकटम् याति न च नौ: गच्छति स्थले ।। *yat a-śakyaṁ na tat śakyam, tata śakyaṁ śakyam eva yat, na jale śakaṭaṁ yāti, na ća nauḥ gaććhati sthale.* * What is impossible is not possible, what is possible that only is possible; neither a cart runs on water nor a boat goes on the ground.

(105) अ-कृत्वा पर-सन्तापम् अ-गत्वा खल-मन्दिरम् । अनुत्सृज्य सताम् वर्त्म यत् स्वल्पम् अपि तत् बहुम् ।। *a-kṛtvā para-santāpam, a-gatvā khala-mandiram, anusṛjya satāṁ vartma yat svalpam api tat bahum.* * Not doing that which will hurt others, not visiting the place of a bad person and not leaving the path of righteousness, whatever little is obtained is plenty.

(106) कुसुमम् वर्ण-सम्पन्नम् गन्ध-हीनम् न शोभते । न शोभते क्रिया-हीनम् मधुरम् वचनम् तथा ।। *kusumaṁ varṇa-sampannam, gandha hīnaṁ na śobhate, na śobhate kriyā-hīnam, madhuraṁ vaćanaṁ tathā.* * A colourful flower without fragrance has no beauty. Similarly, an actionless sweet, is no good.

(107) उद्यमेन हि सिध्यन्ति कार्याणि न मनोरथैः । न हि सुप्तस्य सिंहस्य प्रविशन्ति मुखे मृगाः । *udyamena hi sidhyanti, kāryāṇi, na manorathaiḥ, na hi suptasya siṁhasya, praviśanti mukhe mṛgāḥ.* * The things are accomplished by action, not with imagination, because, the animals do not enter in the mouth of the lion that is sleeping.

(108) उद्यमः साहसम् धैर्यम् बुद्धिः शक्तिः पराक्रमः । षड् एते यत्र वर्तन्ते तत्र दैवम् प्रसीदति ।। *udyamaḥ sāhasaṁ dhairyam, buddhiḥ śaktiḥ parākramaḥ, ṣad ete yatra vartante, tatra daivaṁ prasīdati.* * Where industriousness, boldness, courage, intelligence, strength and bravery these six exist, there luck stays.

(109) गच्छन् पिपीलिका याति योजनानाम् शतानि अपि । अ-गच्छन् वैनतेयः अपि पदम् एकम् न गच्छति ।। *gaććhan pipīlikā yāti, yojanānāṁ śatān api, a-gaććhan vainateyaḥ api, padam ekaṁ na gaććhati.* * A moving ant goes hundreds of miles, non-moving eagle does not advance a foot.

(110) स्व-गृहे पूज्यते मूर्खः स्व-ग्रामे पूज्यते प्रभुः । स्व-देशे पूज्यते राजा विद्वान् सर्वत्र पूज्यते ।। *sva-gṛhe pūjyate mūrkhaḥ, sva-grāme pūjyate prabhuḥ, sva-deśe pūjyate rājā, vidvān sarvatra pūjyate.* * A fool is respected in his house, a chief is respected in his town, a king is respected in his country, but the wise is respected everywhere.

(111) सर्प-दुर्जनयोः मध्ये वरम् सर्पः न दुर्जनः । सर्पः दंशति कालेन दुर्जनः तु पदे पदे ।। *sarpa-durjanayoḥ madhye, varaṁ sarpaḥ na durjanaḥ, sarpaḥ daṁśati kālena, durjanaḥ tu pade pade.* * Between a snake and a bad person, the snake is better. The snake bites only at times, but the bad person stabs all the time.

(112) रविः चन्द्रः घनाः वृक्षाः नदी गौ च सज्जनाः । एते परोपकाराय भुवि दैवेन निर्मिताः ।। *raviḥ ćandraḥ ghanāḥ-vṛkṣāḥ, nadī gau ća sajjanāḥ, ete paropakārāya bhuvi daivena nirmitāḥ.* * Sun, moon, dense trees, river, cow and good men are created on the earth by God for the benefit of others.

(113) छायाम् अन्यस्य कुर्वन्ति तिष्ठन्ति स्वयम् आतपे । फलानि अपि पर-अर्थाय वृक्षाः सत्-पुरुषाः इव ।। *ćhāyām anyasya kurvanti, tiṣṭhanti svayam ātape, phalāni api para-arthāya, vṛkṣāḥ sat-puruṣāḥ ive.* * Trees give shadow to others, while they remain themselves in the heat. Like good men (who themselves remain in distress while helping others), they also give fruits to others.

(114) यः ध्रुवाणि परित्यज्य अ-ध्रुवम् परिसेवते । ध्रुवाणि तस्य नश्यन्ति अ-ध्रुवम् नष्टम् एव च ।। *yaḥ dhruvāṇi parityajya, a-dhruvaṁ parisevate, dhruvāṇi tasya naśyanti, a-dhruvaṁ naṣṭam eva ća.* * He who runs after temporary things, leaving aside the lasting one, his lasting as well as temporary things vanish.

(115) यस्मिन् देशे न सन्मानः न वृत्तिः न च बान्धवाः । न च विद्यागमः अपि अस्ति वासम् तत्र न कारयेत् ।। *yasmin deśe na sanmānaḥ, na vṛttiḥ na ća bāndhavāḥ, na ća vidyāgamaḥ api asti, vāsaṁ tatra na kārayet.* * Where there is no respect, no business, no brotherly people and no learning, one should not live there.

(116) न देवः विद्यते काष्ठे न पाषाणे न मृन्मये । भावे हि विद्यते देवः तस्मात् भावाः हि कारणम् ।। *na devaḥ vidyate kāṣṭhe, na pāṣāṇe na mṛnmaye, bhāve hi vidyate devaḥ, tasmāt bhāvāḥ hi kāraṇam.* * God does not exist in wooden, stone or in the earthern idole. God exists in the faith only. Therefore, the faith therein is the reason (of idole worship).

PRONOUN DERIVATIVES

Pron∘	→ Derivatives
अस्मद्	मदीय, मामक, मामकीन (my, m∘ n∘)
अस्मद्	अमदीय, अस्माक, आस्मामकीन (our, m∘ n∘)
अस्मद्	मदीया, मामिका, मामकीना (my, f∘)
अस्मद्	अमदीया, आस्माकी, आस्मामकीना (our, f∘)
युष्मद्	त्वदीय, तावक, तावकीन (my, m∘ n∘)
युष्मद्	युष्मदीय, यौष्माक, यौष्माकीण (our, m∘ n∘)
युष्मद्	त्वदीया, तावकी, तावकीना (my, fn∘)
युष्मद्	युष्मदीया, यौष्माकी, यौष्माकीणा (our, f∘)
अस्मद्	मादृश्, मादृश, मादृशी (like me, m∘ n∘ f∘)
अस्मद्	अस्मादृश् अस्मादृश, अस्मादृशी (like us, m∘ n∘ f∘)
युष्मद्	त्वादृश्, त्वादृश, त्वादृशी (like you, m∘ n∘ f∘)
युष्मद्	युष्मादृश्, युष्मादृश, युष्मादृशी (like you, m∘ n∘ f∘)

Pron∘	→ Derivatives
तद्	तदीय (His, its, m∘ n∘)
तद्	तदीया (her, f∘)
तद्	तादृश् तादृश तादृशी like it, m∘ n∘ f∘
इदम्	ईदृश् ईदृश ईदृशी like this, m∘ n∘ f∘
एतद्	एतादृश् एतादृश एतादृशी like it m∘ n∘ f∘
यत्	यादृश् यादृश यादृशी like which, m∘ n∘ f∘
किम्	कीदृश् कीदृश कीदृशी like what, mnf∘
भवत्	भवादृश् भवादृश भवादृशी like you mnf∘

APPENDIX - 10

ANSWERS TO THE EXERCISES

Uttarāṇi उत्तराणि ।

EXERCISE 1 : (1) आ (2) ओ (3) ए

EX◦ 2: (1) र् + आ + म् + अ (2) स् + ई + त् + आ (3) प् + उ + ष्+ प् + अ (4) क् + ऋ + ष् + ण् + अ (5) स् + अं + स् + क् + ऋ + त् + अ (6) म् + अ + न् + अ + स् + अ (7) भ् + आ + न् + उ (8) व् + अ + ध् + ऊ (9) व् + ए + द् + अ (10) व् + ऐ + द् + य् + अ (11) ब् + र् + अ + ह् + म् + आ

EX◦ 3 : 1. क, ब, क 2. ब, व, ब 3. व, क, ब 4. ब, व, क5. क, व, ब 6. व, ब, क

EX◦ 4 : 1. प, फ 2. फ, ब 3. व, प, क 4. प, ष, ण 5. फ, ष, प 6. ष, प, फ ।

EX◦ 5 : 1. म, भ 2. भ, ग 3. म, न 4. क, त, ग 5. व, ष 6. प न

EX◦ 6 : 1. क, च, ण, प 2. ल, म, ज, त 3. भ, फ, ष 4. मन, मनन 5. कण, वन 6. लभ, चल

EX◦ 7: 1 च, ज, ल 2 ञ, ज, च 3 ल, च, ज 4 स, ख, र 5. स, श, ख 6. र, स, श 7. ća, ja, ña, la 8. ra, sa, kha, śa. 9. *ćala* (moving), *jala* (water), *jana* (person) 10. *kalaśa* (pot), *ćaraṇa* (foot), *rasa* (juice), *śara* (summary), *sama* (equal), *phala* (fruit), *kamala* (lotus), *sarala* (straight), *bharata* (Bharat) 11. *ćaṇaka* (chikc pea), *ćarama* (extreme), *samara* (battle), *tana* (body), *mana* (mind), *kaṇa* (particle), *parama* (supreme), *ćapala* (quick), *pata* (fall), *nara* (man) 12. *nabha* (sky), *naraka* (hell), *jala* (water), *khala* (enemy), *śara* (summary), *para* (other), *sama* (equal), *ćala* (moving), *śaraṇa* (surrender), *sabala* (powerful).

EX◦ 8 : 1. च, ग, छ 2. न, च, म, छ 3. भ, च, घ 4. gha, dha, na, ga 5. ćha, ća, bha, ta 6. ma, ćha, bha, ća

7. *naga* (mountain), *ghana* (dense), *dhana* (wealth) 8. *tana* (body), *manana* (contemplation), *gata* (gone) 9. *mama* (my), *vaćana* (speech), *kanaka* (gold) 10. *ćhala* (cunning), *vadha* (murder), *dhavala* (white), *maraṇa* (death), *vamana* (vomit), *khara* (donkey), *bala* (strength), *pala* (moment), *phala* (fruit), *mala* (dirt)

EX◦ 9 : (A) 1. छ, घ, ध 2. ध, घ 4. कष, ज्ञ 5. घ, ज्ञ, य, थ 6. ज्ञ, ध, थ, घ

(B) 4. क्षय (decline), शर (arrow), यक्ष (a demon) 5. यज्ञ (a sacrifice), रथ (chariot), धन (wealth) 6. घन (dense), यम (control), क्षर (perishable) 7. तन (body) मय (full of) धन (wealth), वध (slaughter), जय (victory), लय (decline), यजन (performing yajña), छल (cheating), सधन (wealthy), घन (thick), सम (equal), शरण (surrendered); 8. भय (fear), शयन (sleep), रण (war), रक्षण (protection), कक्ष (room), क्षण (moment), पक्ष (wing), लभ (obtaining), तरल (liquid), सरल (simple), गरल (poison) 9. चल (movable), मत (opinion), यज्ञ (a sacrifice), भक्षण (eating), कर (hand), वर (better), धर (holding), भर (filling), खर (donkey), चर (moving), नर (man), हर (Shiva), शर (arrow) 10. भक्ष (food), यक्ष (a demon), रक्ष (protect), तक्षक (snake), तज्ञ (expert), कक्ष (room), यम (lord of death), शम (control), क्षण (moment), रक्षण (protection), सज्ञ (educated), यज्ञ (sacrifice), कक्ष (room), पक्ष (wing), भक्ष (food), लक्ष (aim), वक्ष (bosom), रक्षक (protector), भक्षक (eater), सयज्ञ (yajña performer) ।

EX॰ 10 : 1. ठ, ट, ड, ह 2. ड, ट, ठ 3. ङ, ड, ठ 4. ढ, ड, झ 5. द, ढ, झ 6. ट, ठ, ड, ढ 7. दल (army), दम (conrol), लभ (attainment), जनन (reproduction) 8. डयन (flying), रम (entertain), बक (stork), झष (fish), हत (defeated), कर (hand), तमस (darkness), तल (bottom), दम (control), शम (quietning), पवन (wind), हर (Shiva) 9. झष (fish), वर (better), नर (man), मद (intoxication), पट (cloth), पटल (layer), पद (foot), बल (power), वन (jungle), सतत (always), खग (bird), चल (moving) 10. भव (earthy), मन (mind), बक (stork), भज (worship), वश (win), लक्ष (aim), लक्षण (sign), घन (thick), धन (wealth), वरण (choosing), हय (horse) ।

EX॰ 11 : (4) अक्ष (eye) आगम (scripture) आगार (storehouse) (5) ओघ (flow) ओज (power) (6) औदक (watery) औक्ष (ox)

EX॰ 12 : 1. अ, आ 2. इ, ई 3. आ, आ. 4. अ, ई 5. आ, ई 7. i, ī, *īraṇa* (going), *iha* (here), *īḍa* (praise), *īśaḥ* (god), *īkṣaka* (exhibitor), *itara* (other), *ikṣava* (sugarcane), *īkṣaṇa* (eye), *iva* (as if, like).

EX ॰13 : (2). उक्षण (spraying), उदर (stomach) 3. उप (subordinate), उपग (follower) कृपा (mercy) 4. उपपद (subordinate term), अवकर (garbage, dirt) 5. उपमान (similar), उपल (stone) 6. ऊत (stiched), ऊषक (morning)

EX॰ 14 : 1. एक (one) एकतर (one in two) एषण (desire) ऐक्षव (sugar) ऐरावत (Indra's elephant)

ऐल (Iḍā's son) एतद् (this) एकादश (elevan) ऐरावण (Indra's elephent) ऐश (godly)

EX◦ 15 : 1. जयी (victor), जयति (he wins), जिगीषा (enquiry) 2. जिगीषु (desirous), कति (how many) 3. शृणु (please listen), कृपा (mercy) 4. दीप (lamp) हृदयं (heart), पूत (purified) पूति (rotten) 5. पूजक (worshipper), पूजन (worship) 6. दृति (rush), दृढ (firm) 7. ज्ञानी (wise), महा (great), अहङ्कार (ego) सुख (pleasure), दुःख (pain), दृश् (to see), दूषण (polution), वृथा (false), पृथा (Kuntī), पृथिवी (earth) 8. ज्ञानयोग (yoga of knowledge) महाभारतीय (of mahabharata) संशय (doubt) नील (blue) पौराणिक (of Puranas), भिक्षु (begger) पितृणाम (of forefathers), गुरु (teacher), रूप (form), तरु (tree), तरुण (youth), करुण (kind)

EX◦ 23 : 1. युक्तम् 2. दशरथ 3. रामः 4. नियोजयामि 5. वयम्

EX◦ 25 : 1. भज 2. नामानि 3. समस्त 4. गोकुलेश 5. नाथ 6. गोविन्द ।

EX◦ 27 : (1) पाण्डवाः (2) दक्षिणम् (3) दूरे ।

EX◦ 29 : (1) मधुसूदनः (2) विषमे (3) त्यक्त्वा ।

EX◦ 37 : (A) 1. We are 2. She is 3. They are 4. You are 5. You are 6. They are. (B) 1. आवाम् स्वः 2. ताः सन्ति 3. एतत् अस्ति 4. ते स्तः 5. सा अस्ति 6. तानि सन्ति 7. रामः अस्ति 8. सीता अस्ति 9. बालकाः सन्ति 10. बालिकाः सन्ति ।

EX◦ 38 : A - (1) एकः बालकः । एका बालिका । एकं गृहम् । (2) चत्वारः बालकाः । चतस्रः बालिकाः । चत्वारि गृहाणि । (3) सः एकः नरः अस्ति । सा एका स्त्री अस्ति । तद् एकं गृहम् अस्ति । (4) तानि पुस्तकानि सन्ति । ताः बालिकाः सन्ति । ते बालकाः सन्ति ।

B - (1) I am a man. (2) We are ladies. (3) We are four ladies. (4) Four houses. (5) There are four poems. (6) One boy. One girl. One book. (7) Four boys. Four girls. Four books. (8) He is a man. She isa woman. That is a house. (9) Those are books. They are ladies. They are boys.

EX◦ 40 : (A) (1) बालकः । बालिका । नरः । स्त्री (2) पुस्तकम् । गृहम् । गीतम् । (3) लता । नदी । भा ।

B - (1) एकः बालकः द्वे बाले त्रीणि च गृहाणि । (2) नव नद्यः । नव सरिताः । एका नदी । द्वे नद्यौ । (3) पञ्च पुष्पाणि षट् शिलाः सप्त च पर्वताः ।

EX◦ 41 : (1) तद् पुस्तकम् । का बाला । (2) कस्य (कस्याः) गृहम्? (3) किं कारणं (4) सः अस्ति । सा अस्ति। तत् (तद्) अस्ति । (5) भवान् अस्ति or भवती अस्ति । (6) ते (ताः) के (काः) सन्ति?

EX◦ 42 : (1) अहम आगच्छामि । सः आगच्छति । (2) सा पठति । (3) ते वदन्ति । ताः वदन्ति । (4) सा लिखति । (5) त्वं पिबसि भवान् पिबति । यूयम् पिबथ भवन्तः पिनन्ति । (6) वयं खादामः ।

EX॰ 43 : (1) चेतन:-जन्तु:-जीव: प्राणी-पशु: धेनु:-गौ: कुक्कुर:-भषक:-शुनक:-श्वान: (2) बिडाल:-मार्जार: उन्दरु:-मूषक: अश्व:-तुरङ्ग:-हय: (3) कुञ्जर:-गज:-सिंह:-केसरी; कपि:-मर्कट:-वानर: (4) वराह:-शूकर: मृग:- हरिण: झष:-मत्स्य-मीन:

EX॰ 45 : A - (1) √क्षिप्, √स्था, √धाव् (2) √रुद्, उप√विश्, √क्षल्

B - (1) Sītā read; Rāma was; Bharata saw; (2) Rāma, Bharata and Sītā saw (3) We are throwing stones, we throw stones; He is threw a stone (4) I salute Kṛṣṇa, I salute Rāma, I salute Sītā (5) The dog, cat and mouse stood; They (f॰) stand up, they are standing up. (6) The cow, goat and horse ran (7) Men and ladies laughed. The child cried, the boy cried.

EX॰ 47 : (A) (1) हंस: मत्सं खादिष्यति । (2) क्रौञ्च: बक:-सारस: जलं पास्यति । (3) कुक्कुट्य: च कुकुटा: च बीजानि खादन्ति । (4) भूजन्तव: भूमिम् खनिष्यन्ति ।

EX॰ 48 : (1) Tomorrow (3) श्व: । (2) Day before yesterday (7) परह्य: । (3) When (8) यदा । (4) Today (1) अद्य । (5) Dayafter tomorrow (6) परश्व: । (6) Yesterday (2) ह्य: । (7) Then (4) तदा । (8) When? (5) कदा?

EX॰ 49 : (1) अहं फलं खादामि । (2) त्वं मयूरं पश्यसि । (3) स: पत्रम् अलिखत् । (4) सा भविष्यति । भवती भविष्यति । (5) ते-ता: दूग्धम् आनिष्यन्ति । (6) अहं संस्कृतं पठामि । (7) राम: पुस्तकं पठति । (8) व्याघ्र: अजं खादिष्यति । (9) खगा: नीडं रचियिष्यन्ति । (10) अश्व: अधावत् । (11) वयम् अधावाम । (12) अहं संस्कृतं जानामि । (13) ते-ता: अखादन् । (14) कपय: फलानि खादन्ति । (15) फलं वृक्षात् पतति । (16) पर्णं लताया:पतति । (17) स: बालक: अस्ति । (18) सा गृहं गमिष्यति ।

EX॰ 50 : (1) It happens. एतत् घटते । (2) It looks good. एतत् शोभते । (3) She attains. सा लभते । (4) He jumps स: कूर्दते । (5) I desire अहं कामये । (6) He bargains. स: पणते ।

EX॰ 51 : (1) Intr. (2) Tr. (3) Intr. (4) Intr. (5) Tr. (6) Tr. (7) Intr. (8) Tr. (9) Intr.

EX॰ 52 : (1) I अहम् (2) She सा (3) Cow गौ: (4) Dog कुकुर: (5) One parrot एक: शुक: (6) शोक: शोक: शोक: शोकसम: रिपु: (7) वृक्षाग्रवासी, पक्षिराज: त्रिनेत्रधारी, शूलपाणि: जटाभिर्युक्त: सिद्धयोगी, बिभ्रत्, घट: मेघ:

EX॰ 53 : A - (1) पाकशालाम्; ओदनम्-भक्तम्-तण्डुलम् । रोटिकाम्-रोटीम्-पूपिकाम्-पोलिकाम्-अभ्यूषम् (2) तैलम्, नवनीतम्, लवणम् (3) लवङ्गम्, जीरकम्, कफघ्नीम् ।

B. (1) Rice; Wheat; Chick-peas (2) Corn, Oil, Clarified Butter (3) Buttermilk, Yogrut, salt (4) Cumin seeds, Cardamon, Cloves.

EX॰ 54 : (1) राम: - सिंहम् (2) सा - शुकम् (3) गौ: - दुग्धम् (4) अश्व: - घासम् (5) सर्प: - मूषकम् (6)

n◦ शीलम् - परम् भूषणम् (7) अहिम् नृपम् शार्दूलम् किटिम् बालकम् परश्वानम् मूर्खम् सप्त सुप्तान् (8) चौरहार्यम् राजहार्यम् भ्रातृभाज्यम् भारकारि विद्याधनम् सर्वधनप्रधानम् (9) कार्यहन्तारम् प्रियवादिनम् तादृशम् मित्रम् विषकुम्भम् पयोमुखम्

EX◦ 55 : (1) शाकः-शाकम्; आलुः-गोलालुः; पलाण्डुः-सुकन्दकः (2) आर्द्रकम्; लशुनम्; रक्ताङ्गः (3) उर्वारु-कर्कटी-चर्मटिका; पालकी; मरीचम् ।

EX◦ 56 : (1) अहं हस्तेन कन्दुकम् (2) सः तेन-सह क्रीडनकम् (3) सा कारयानेन (4) वयं त्वया-सह (5) ते दुग्धेन-सह ओदनम् (6) चक्षुषा मनसा वाचा कर्मणा । यः, लोकम्, तम्, लोकः ।

EX◦ 57 : (1) सूचिकया (2) कर्तरीकया (3) कुकुरेण सह (4) विद्यया (5) अक्ष्णा पादेन (6) धर्मेण-हीनः पशुना

EX◦ 58 : (1) चमसः नौः कासारः (2) रात्रिः कलपः-घटः-कुम्भः छुरिका (3) कर्तरिका-कर्तरी; सूचिः-सूचिका-सेवनी; आदर्शः-दर्पणः-मुकुरः (4) फेनिलः मार्जनवस्त्रं; पर्यङ्कम्-शय्या (5) मञ्चः-फलकः पत्रकम्; विद्या ।

EX◦ 59 : (1) तस्मै (2) मे (3) अर्जुनाय (4) बालाय (5) अग्नये (6) विवादाय मदाय परिपीडनाय ज्ञानाय दानाय रक्षणाय (7) रामाय रामभद्राय रामचन्द्राय वेधसे रघुनाथाय नाथाय सीतायाः पतये ।

EX◦ 60 : (1) पेटिकायाः । (2) गृहात् (3) कस्मात्-कुतः । (4) इतः-अत्रतः । (5) प्रजाभ्यः (6) पुष्पेभ्यः । (7) हिमालयात् (8) ज्ञानात्- विना । (9) विनयात् पात्रत्वात् धनात् ततः ।

EX◦ 62 : (1) स्वस्य (2) सीतायाः (3) माम् (4) भारतस्य (5) भारतस्य (6) श्रीलङ्कायाः (7) नरस्य रूपस्य गुणस्य ज्ञानस्य (8) यस्य नेत्राभ्यां विहीनस्य (9) आदानस्य प्रदानस्य कर्तव्यस्य कर्मणः क्षिप्रक्रियमाणस्य (10) लघुचेतसाम् उदारचरितानाम्

EX◦ 63 : (1) कुलं-वंश-परिवारः मित्रं-बन्धुः-सुहृद्-सखा-सखी; पिता-जनकः तातः (2) माता-जननी-अम्बा; पुत्री-कन्या-सुता-तनया-आत्मजा; भ्राता-सहोदरः सोदरः (3) भगिनी-स्वसा; पत्नी-भार्या-जाया-वधूः-दारा-स्त्री; पुत्रः ।

EX◦ 64 : (1) पुस्तके, पुस्तकेषु (2) मालायाम्, मालासु (3) नदीषु (4) कर्मणि, कर्मसु (5) भर्तृषु (6) परदारेषु परद्रव्येषु सर्वभूतेषु (7) कर्मणि फलेषु (8) दुःखेषु सुखेषु (9) अप्सु (शशिसूर्ययोः - षष्ठी) सर्ववेदेषु खे नृषु (10) पृथिव्याम् विभावसौ सर्वभूतेषु तपस्विषु (11) सर्वेषु कालेषु (12) शत्रौ मित्रे मानापमानयोः शीतोष्णसुखदुःखेषु (13) सर्वेषु भूतेषु ।

EX◦ 65 : (1) चिरं-वसनम्-वस्त्रम्-वासः चोलः निचुलः युतकम्; (2) उपानह्-पादत्राणं-पादुका; शाटी-शाटिका (3) स्तरणम्, प्रस्तारणं; आस्तारणम् ।

EX◦ 66 : (1) खादामि । (2) पठन्ति (3) गायामः (4) अभिलिख्यते (5) खाद्यते (6) गीयते (7) दृश्यते (8) दृश्यते।

EX◦ 67 : (1) द्वारम् अपावृतं नास्ति । (2) अहं तेन सह कर्म न करिष्यामि । (3) कृपया तस्मिन् कक्षे मा उपविशतु। (4) एष तव व्यापारः नास्ति । (5) तव उपदेशः अधिकः अवश्यकः नास्ति ।

EX॰ 68 : (1) क:? का? (2) किं कारणम्? (3) किम्? (4) कदा? (5) कथम्? (6) कुत्र? (7) कम्? काम्? (8) कियतं कालम्? (9) कियत्? (10) कति?

EX॰ 69: (1) आगच्छ, आगच्छतु (2) लिख, लिखतु (3) उपविशतु (4) कुरु, करोतु (5) गृह्णस्व (6) भव, भवतु (7) खादानि? (8) पृच्छानि? (9) गच्छाम?

EX॰ 70 : (1) कुरुत (2) कुरुत (3) आगच्छेयु: (4) गच्छेम

EX॰ 72 : A-1 द्वौ 2 पीतानि 3 उष्णं 4 नूतनं 5 सुन्दराणि B- 1. रक्तं 2. नूतनानि 3. चतुर: 4. सत्यं 5. विशाला

EX॰ 73 : (A) 1. क्षुद्रतर 2. दृढतर, ह्रस्वतर 3. स्थिरतर (B) 1. क्षुद्रतम 2. दूरतम 3. दीर्घतम, महत्तम, विद्वत्तम ।

EX॰ 74 : 1 खादितम् भूतम् भक्षितम् 2. पठित: रक्षित: श्रुतम् पतिता: 3. दृष्टा कृतम् कृतानि 4. पृष्ट: नीता नीत:

EX॰ 75 : (1) गच्छत्, भवत्, भक्षितवन्त: (2) पठत्, श्रुण्वत्, (3) पश्यत्, कृर्वत् (4) पृष्टत्, नयत्, नीतवन्त: ।

EX॰ 76: 1. खादित्वा 2. उक्त्वा 3. विक्रीय, क्रित्वा 4. प्रष्टुम् 5. स्मृत्वा 6. प्राप्य 7. छेत्तुम् 8. स्मर्तुम् 9. ज्ञातुम्

EX॰ 77 : (1) किं कारणम् (2) कथम् (3) स्पष्टम् (4) अतीव (5) अलम्

EX॰ 78 : (1) यथा तथा यथा तथा यथा तथा यथा तथा (2) अन्यथा अपि (3) क्षणश: कणश: एव कुत: कुत: ।

EX॰ 79 : (1) आम्राणि एवं (2) पत्रं वर्तिकां च । (3) क्रीणाति च विक्रीणाति च । (4) लेखनीं तथैव पत्रकम् (5) अथवा (6) बसयानेन कारयानेन वा । (7) न च अभद्रं न वा भद्रम् । (8) यत् (9) अन्यथा क्षुधित: तिष्ठतु । (10) अन्यथा । (11) परन्तु (12) परम् (13) तथापि । (14) यद्यपि स: याचितवान् । (15) यद्यपि स: (16) येन (17) यावत् – तावत् (18) कूर्म: इव (19) यत: (20) यत: अहं (21) यदा (22) तत्र – यत्र (23) यावत् – तावत्, तत्र एव (24) यदा यदा (25) यत्र यत्र (26) तस्मात् ।

EX॰ 80 : (1) अति, अधि, अनु, अनु । (2) अन्तर्, अप, उप, अप, उप । (3) अपि, अभि, अभि, अव । (4) अव, अव, आ, आ, उद्, उत् । (5) उद्, उप, उप, दुर्. दुस् । (6) नि, निस्, निर् । (7) परा, प्रति, प्रति । (8) वि, वि, वि । (9) सम्, सम्, सु, सु ।

EX॰ 81: सु, प्र, सम्, वि, आ, उद्, आ, अप, सम्, प्र, अनु, परा, प्र, प्र, दुस्, वि, उत्, अभि, उत्, उत्, अ, अ, वि, अ, प्रति, उप, अति, अति, आ, दुर्, दुर्, दुर्, दुस्, परि, परि, वि, वि, वि, वि, आ, अ, आ, अ, सम्, अनु, प्रति, प्रति, उप, प्र, अव, वि, वि, परि, अनु, उप, वि ।

EX॰ 83: 1. अधुना सा कथम् अस्ति 2. तस्य नामधेयं किम् 3. कृपया आस्यताम् 4. अहं कृतज्ञ: उपकृत: अस्मि 5. साफल्याय हार्दिका: शुभेच्छा: 6. आरोग्यं शीघ्रं भूयात् 7. कोलाहलं मा कुरु 8. तूष्णीं तिष्ठ 9. धैर्यं धारयतु 10. सम्यक् चल-चलतु 11. इत: आगच्छतु 12. मां मार्गं दर्शयतु 13. उच्चै: (मन्दम्) मा वदतु 14. कृपया मम हस्तं धरतु 15. त्वं पाठशालां गच्छसि-गच्छति वा 16. कोपं मा कुरु-करोतु 17. मम व्यापारे हस्तक्षेपं मा कुरु-करोतु 18. इदं दुग्धं मा पिबतु 19. तं मा बाधस्व-बाधयताम् 20. विलम्बं मा कुरु-करोतु ।

REFERENCES

Apte, Vaman Shivram; *The Practical Sanskrit English Dictionary*; MLBD Pubulishers. Pvt. Ltd, Dehli, 1998.

Kale, M.R.; *A Higher Sanskrit Grammar*; Motilal Banarasidas, Delhi, 1995

Katre, Sumitra M; *Astadhyayi of Panini*; MLBD Pubulishers. Pvt. Ltd, Dehli, 1989.

Monir-Williams, Sir Monir; *A Sanskrit-English Dictionary*; Motilal Banarasidass Pvt. Ltd, Dehli, 1993.

Monir-Williams, Sir Monir; *A Practical Grammar of Sanskrit Language*; Oriental Books Reprint Co., New Dehli, 1978

Narale, Ratnakar; *Sanskrit for English Speaking People*; Prabhat Prakashan, New Delhi, 2003

Whitney, William Dwight; *The Roots Verb-forms And Primary Derivatives of the Sanskrit Language*; MLBD, Delhi 1997

Wilson, Prof. H.H.; *An Introduction to the Grammar of Sanskrit Language*; Choukhamba Sanskrit Series XI., Varanasi, 1979

गोयल, डा. प्रीतिप्रभा; संस्कृत व्याकरण, राजस्थानी ग्रन्थागार, जोधपुर, 2000

झा, पं. रामचन्द्र व्याकरणाचार्य; रूपचन्द्रिका; हरिदास संस्कृत ग्रन्थमाला 156; चौखम्बा संस्कृत सीरीज, वाराणसी, सं 2051.

द्विवेदी, पद्मश्री डॉ. आचार्य कपिलदेव; संस्कृत-व्याकरण एवं लघुसिद्धान्तकौमुदी; विश्वविद्यालय प्रकाशन, वाराणसी, 1996.

मिश्र, पं. गोमतीप्रसादशास्त्री; श्री वरदाचार्यकृत लघुसिद्धान्तकौमुदी, चौखम्बा सुरभारती प्रकाशन, वाराणसी, 1999

मिश्र, पं. हरेकान्त; बृहद्धातुकुसुमाकरः; चौखम्बा संस्कृत प्रतिष्टान, दिल्ली, 2003

वैद्य, आचार्य रामशास्त्री; संस्कृत-शिक्षण-सरणी, आर्यसमाज कार्यालय, दिल्ली, 1960

शर्मा, चतुर्वेदी द्वारकाप्रसाद; **झा,** पण्डित तारिणीश; संस्कृत-शब्दार्थ-कौस्तुभ; रामनारायणलाल बेनीप्रसाद; इलाहाबाद 1928

शास्त्री, चक्रधर नौटियाल हंस; बृहद्-अनुवाद-चन्द्रिका; मोतीलाल बनारसीदास; दिल्ली 1999

सातवलेकर, पं. श्रीपाद दामोदर; संस्कृत-पाठ-माला, स्वाध्याय मंडल, पारडी, 1988

सोमयाजी, पं. धन्वाडगोपलकृष्णाचार्य; तिङन्तार्णवतरणि; कृष्णदास संस्कृत सी. 31; कृष्णदास अकादमी, वाराणसी, 1980

Lightning Source UK Ltd.
Milton Keynes UK
UKHW031809310120
357971UK00009B/156

9 781897 416549